CORPORATE SCANDALS AND THEIR IMPLICATIONS

Third Edition

NANCY B. RAPOPORT
GARMAN TURNER GORDON PROFESSOR OF LAW
WILLIAM S. BOYD SCHOOL OF LAW

JEFFREY D. VAN NIEL

WEST ACADEMIC PUBLISHING

444 Cedar Street, Suite 700
St. Paul, MN 55101
1-877-888-1330

Printed in the United States of America

ISBN: 978-1-63460-489-5

Introduction to the Third Edition

We've written two earlier editions of this book. The first one, NANCY B. RAPOPORT & BALA G. DHARAN, ENRON: CORPORATE FIASCOS AND THEIR IMPLICATIONS (Foundation Press 2004), represented our attempt to examine the Enron scandal from as many angles as humanly possible. Our goal was to learn from Enron's mistakes so that no one would repeat them. A few years later, the wonderful Foundation Press folks published our second edition, NANCY B. RAPOPORT, JEFFREY D. VAN NIEL & BALA G. DHARAN, ENRON AND OTHER CORPORATE FIASCOS: THE CORPORATE SCANDAL READER (Foundation Press 2d ed. 2009), after we'd realized that no one actually *had* learned anything from dissecting the Enron scandal. Corporate scandals kept churning themselves out, roughly every ten years, though recently that cycle has shortened considerably. The goal of our second edition was to use what we know about social science to try to figure out why it is that the cycle of corporate scandals keeps recurring, no matter how smart the people are who run the businesses.

So why a third edition of this book? We did it in part because West Academic asked us to update the book (surprise!) and in part, because—though it saddens us—Enron is now "history." It's just not current, though the two of us will always remember exactly where we were when Enron filed what was then the country's largest Chapter 11 bankruptcy case. It's time to take a look at more recent scandals and give you a chance to apply what we know about social science to failures in business, government agencies, and law firms.

What do we want you to learn from this book? You already probably know lesson #1: corporate scandals are here to stay because humans are hardwired to make certain types of cognitive errors. But lesson #2 is equally important: when you're in charge of running something, you need to figure out how to build internal structures and incentives to minimize the odds of having your organization implode before your eyes.

One more thing before you start reading: for some of these chapters, we've edited out sections of the original material, which changed the numbering of the footnotes and thus made the *supra* and *infra* cross-referencing (reflecting the original numbering) a bit hinky. We mention this issue because we don't want you to worry that you've been studying so hard that you're hallucinating.

Now, let's roll up our collective sleeves and figure out the all-encompassing question of what *not* to do. As you make your way through our book, keep asking yourself this one question: when I'm in charge (of a business/of a division/of any group), how can I check to see if what my colleagues are doing is what they're *supposed* to be doing?

Nancy B. Rapoport
Jeffrey D. Van Niel

March 27, 2018

Acknowledgments

Nancy B. Rapoport

I want to thank the exceptionally patient team at West Academic, which has suffered without complaint through the fact that my changing jobs within UNLV roughly every 10–12 months has caused this edition to be egregiously late in going to print. I also thank the world's most patient human, Jeff Van Niel, who lets me tackle crazy new things in rapid succession and is still my best editor; my father, Morris Rapoport, who raised me to take reasonable (and some unreasonable) risks and who also has a keen editing eye; Jamilah Brewington and Nettie Mann, my partners-in-crime at UNLV; Jennifer Gross, my phenomenal law librarian colleague; Mridul Gautam, the Vice President for Research and Innovation and a Professor of Mechanical Engineering at the University of Nevada, Reno, for talking me through the engineering side of the VW issue; our long-time friends Rob Foehl and George Kuney, who reviewed earlier drafts of this book; Francisco Reyes, the Superintendencia de Sociedades of Colombia, who has been so kind as to share his knowledge of corporations with me over the years; Walter Effross, who always has great ideas for topics and books; Randy Barnes, who gave me a phenomenal view of what great leadership looks like; and my seminar students in the Spring 2016 Business Law and Ethics course, including but not limited to those who had specific suggestions for the 3d edition of this book: Claudia Andracki, Shani Coleman, Christina Kim, Teddy Medlyn, and E.A. Reed. And, of course, special thanks go to Steve Errick, whose idea for the original edition of this book got the whole project started; Jim Cahoy, who successfully talked us into updating it; and Elizabeth Eisenhart, who has never once indicated that, in taking over as editor, she drew the short straw.

Jeffrey D. Van Niel

I want to thank my loving wife, Nancy Rapoport, who invited me to participate in this effort from the beginning. She has been patient and understanding about my hectic schedule and has encouraged me to use what is left of my artistic skills to craft the cover art on every edition of this book. Surprisingly, Nancy also appreciates my editing skills and has made use of them since the beginning of our relationship. I have mastered the short sentence. I would also like to thank my exceedingly sweet cat Shadow for her tenacity and perseverance in following her never-ending quest of walking on my keyboard and adding her own edits to our work. Finally, I must thank Grace, the alpha female in our household; without her, ours would be a squeakless habitat.

Editors' Biographies

Nancy B. Rapoport is the Special Counsel to the President of the University of Nevada, Las Vegas. She is also the Garman Turner Gordon Professor of Law at the William S. Boyd School of Law, University of Nevada, Las Vegas, and is an Affiliate Professor of Business Law and Ethics in the Lee Business School at UNLV. After receiving her B.A., *summa cum laude,* from Rice University in 1982 and her J.D. from Stanford Law School in 1985, she clerked for the Honorable Joseph T. Sneed III on the United States Court of Appeals for the Ninth Circuit and then practiced law (primarily bankruptcy law) with Morrison & Foerster in San Francisco from 1986–1991. She started her academic career at The[1] Ohio State University College of Law in 1991, and she moved from Assistant Professor to Associate Professor with tenure in 1995 to Associate Dean for Student Affairs (1996) and Professor (1998) (just as she left Ohio State to become Dean and Professor of Law at the University of Nebraska College of Law). She served as Dean of the University of Nebraska College of Law from 1998–2000. She then served as Dean and Professor of Law at the University of Houston Law Center from July 2000–May 2006 and as Professor of Law from June 2006–June 2007, when she left to join the faculty at Boyd. She served as Interim Dean of Boyd from 2012–2013, as Senior Advisor to the President of UNLV from 2014–2015, and as Acting Executive Vice President & Provost from 2015–2016. Her specialties are bankruptcy ethics, ethics in governance, law firm behavior, and the depiction of lawyers in popular culture. She is admitted to the bars of the states of California, Ohio, Nebraska, Texas, and Nevada and of the United States Supreme Court. In 2001, she was elected to membership in the American Law Institute, and in 2002, she received a Distinguished Alumna Award from Rice University. In 2017, she was inducted into Phi Kappa Phi (Chapter 100). In October 2017, she received the Commercial Law League of America's Lawrence P. King Award for Excellence in Bankruptcy. She is the Secretary of the Board of Directors of the National Museum of Organized Crime and Law Enforcement (the Mob Museum). She is also a Fellow of the American Bar Foundation and a Fellow of the American College of Bankruptcy. In 2009, the Association of Media and Entertainment Counsel presented her with the Public Service Counsel Award at the 4th Annual Counsel of the Year Awards. She has also appeared in the Academy Award®-nominated movie, *Enron: The Smartest Guys in the Room* (Magnolia Pictures 2005) (as herself). Although the movie garnered her a listing in

1 "The" really is capitalized as part of The Ohio State University's official name.

www.imdb.com, she still hasn't been able to join the Screen Actors Guild. In her spare time, she competes, pro-am, in American Rhythm and American Smooth ballroom dancing with her teacher, Sergei Shapoval. In 2014, she won the national U.S. Open Pro/Am Rising Star American Smooth Competition B Division, and in 2017, she came in 2nd in the Open to the World Pro/Am American Style 9-Dance Championship. The most interesting thing about her is that she is married to a former Marine scout sniper, who is also the world's best co-author.

Jeffrey D. Van Niel is a native of Columbus, Ohio. He enlisted in the United States Marine Corps immediately after graduating from high school in 1976. After four years of service in the Marines as a scout sniper, he received an Honorable Discharge and joined the Ohio State Highway Patrol. He left the Highway Patrol in 1981 to get a Bachelor's Degree in Criminal Justice at Ohio University in 1983. He started law school in 1984 in lieu of joining the Secret Service (and never looked back). Mr. Van Niel served as Executive Notes Editor for the CAPITAL UNIVERSITY LAW REVIEW, and he was graduated from Capital University Law School in 1987, *cum laude,* having received the honors of the Order of the Curia and the Order of the Barristers. He clerked for Ohio Supreme Court Justice Andrew Douglas after graduation, and then he joined the Cleveland, Ohio law firm of Hahn Loeser Δ Parks in 1988. When one of the firm's partners became the Ohio Attorney General, Mr. Van Niel followed him to serve in the Ohio Attorney General's Public Utilities Commission Practice Group. He volunteered for a second tour of duty with the Supreme Court of Ohio in 1993 as the Court's Utilities Law Master Commissioner. Moving from Ohio to Nebraska to Houston (to join his wife at each of her academic positions), Mr. Van Niel worked as a consultant until 2004, when he joined the Harris County Community Service and Corrections Department as Staff Counsel. In yet another move to satisfy his wife's wanderlust, this time to Las Vegas, Mr. Van Niel became a consultant in regulatory and governmental affairs to Nye County in the Yucca Mountain licensing proceeding in October 2007. After Congress zeroed out the Yucca Mountain project's budget, Mr. Van Niel became a law clerk for the United States Bankruptcy Court for the District of Nevada. He is currently the career law clerk for the Hon. August B. Landis, United States Bankruptcy Judge, District of Nevada, while awaiting the restart of the Yucca Mountain licensing proceeding.

Contributing Authors

Harvey Gilmore has been a faculty member in the School of Business & Accounting at Monroe College for the past twenty years. He teaches courses in Personal Taxation, Corporate Taxation, Estate & Gift Taxation, and Commercial Law. His personal and professional credo is: "When you enjoy what you do for a living, it's NOT work." He holds a Bachelor's Degree in Accounting from Hunter College, a Master's Degree in Taxation from Long Island University, a Juris Doctor from the University of Massachusetts-Dartmouth School of Law, and a Masters of Law from Touro Law School. Among his published articles are *Standardized Testing, Race, & Meritocracy: A Reply to Professor Dan Subotnik*, 32 TOURO LAW REVIEW 387 (2016), *The SAT, LSAT, & Discrimination: Professor Gilmore Again Responds to Professor Subotnik*, 34 MINNESOTA J. L. & INEQUALITY 153 (2016), and *The Chicago Cubs from 1945—History's Automatic Out,* 6 PACE INTELL. PROP. SPORTS & ENT. L.F. 225 (2016) (right in time for the Cubs' historic run to the World Series title). Finally, in November 2015, Professor Gilmore had the opportunity to present his University of Minnesota article on standardized testing at the Duke University Law School Symposium, *The Present and Future of Civil Rights Movements: Race and Reform in 21st Century America.*

Michelle M. Harner is a U.S. Bankruptcy Judge for the District of Maryland. She graduated from The Ohio State University College of Law, *summa cum laude,* in 1995, and from Boston College, *cum laude,* in 1992. Prior to her appointment to the bench, Judge Harner served as the Francis King Carey Professor of Law and the Director of the Business Law Program at the University of Maryland Francis King Carey School of Law. At UM Carey Law School, Judge Harner taught courses in Bankruptcy and Creditors Rights, Business Associations, Business Planning, Corporate Finance, and Legal Profession. She lectured frequently during her academic career on various topics involving corporate governance, financially distressed entities, risk management, and related legal issues. Her academic scholarship is widely published, with her publications appearing in, among others, the *Vanderbilt Law Review, Notre Dame Law Review, Washington University Law Review, Minnesota Law Review, Indiana Law Journal, Fordham Law Review* (reprinted in *Corporate Practice Commentator*), *Washington & Lee Law Review, William & Mary Law Review, University of Illinois Law Review, Arizona Law Review* (reprinted in *Corporate Practice Commentator*), and *Florida Law Review.* Judge Harner has served as the Associate Reporter to the Advisory Committee on the Federal Rules of Bankruptcy Procedure, the Reporter to the ABI Commission to Study the Reform of Chapter 11, and a member of the Dodd-Frank Study Working Group for the Administrative Office of the United States Courts. She also served as the Robert M. Zinman ABI Resident Scholar for the fall of 2015. She is an elected member of the American Law Institute and fellow of the American College of Bankruptcy. Judge Harner previously was in private practice in the business restructuring, insolvency, bankruptcy, and related transactional fields, most recently as a partner at the Chicago office of the international law firm Jones Day.

Scott Killingsworth is a lawyer focused on organizational compliance and ethics and business transactions. He is one of seven private-practice attorneys named to Ethisphere's list of "Attorneys Who Matter" in ethics and compliance from 2013 through 2016 and was one of only 17 U.S. lawyers designated as BTI "Client Service All-Stars" in both 2007 and 2008. He has served on the Board of Governors of the Center for Ethics and Corporate Responsibility, the Editorial Board of the *Journal of Business Compliance,* the Executive Committee of the Board of the Georgetown Corporate Counsel Institute, the Yale Law School Executive Committee, and the Board of Governors of the Yale Alumni Association. His "Modeling the Message" paper on ethical leadership, organizational culture, and compliance earned a Burton Award for Distinguished Legal Writing in 2013. He grew up in the South Georgia farming community of Edison and now lives in Atlanta.

David Luban is University Professor in Law and Philosophy at Georgetown University Law Center, and Distinguished Visitor in Ethics at the Stockdale Center for Ethical Leadership, U.S. Naval Academy. His books include LAWYERS AND JUSTICE: AN ETHICAL STUDY, LEGAL MODERNISM, LEGAL ETHICS AND HUMAN DIGNITY, and most recently TORTURE, POWER, AND LAW (Cambridge University Press, 2014). He is a member of the American Academy of Arts and Sciences and has been a Guggenheim Fellow and a Woodrow Wilson Fellow. Currently, he is on the editorial boards of *Ethics & International Affairs* and *Legal Ethics* and is a founding editor of the weblog *Just Security*. He has held visiting chairs at the Fordham, Harvard, Stanford, and Yale Law Schools, and also taught at the University of Melbourne and the Interdisciplinary Center (Israel). His research centers on international criminal law, legal ethics, just war theory, national security, and legal theory. His particular interest is the erosion of moral responsibility in organizational settings. At the moment, he is writing a book on the legal and moral philosophy of Hannah Arendt.

Amee R. McKim is an experienced recruiter, a certified coach, and a talent management professional. Currently the Director of Legal Recruitment for Duane Morris LLP, an international law firm based in Philadelphia, PA, she oversees the firm's national and international lawyer recruiting efforts, lawyer training and development, and assists with the firm's diversity and inclusion initiatives. She has spent her entire career working with, around, and among lawyers from multiple vantage points on the legal career spectrum. She has worked as a practicing lawyer, an Assistant Dean at a law school, as a director in two different global law firms, and as a coach for high performing lawyers. She is also a frequent speaker on legal career topics and a published author. Her non-fiction book, *Maximize Your Lawyer*

Potential, is in addition to many other published articles about careers and the legal profession. She received her J.D. with honors from The[2] Ohio State University and her B.A *summa cum laude* from Otterbein College. She also completed all of the coursework and general exams for a Ph.D. in Higher Education but is currently, and forever shall be, the clichéd A.B.D (All But Dissertation). In her copious spare time, she (usually willingly) participates in home renovation with her contractor husband and often finds herself living without taken-for-granted luxuries like a kitchen or bathroom for weeks or months at a time. She's a competent stripper and hooker—old furniture and traditional wool rugs—and her repair medium of choice is caulk, not duct tape. She also enjoys drinking wine, stand-up paddle boarding, and practicing yoga, in addition to possessing the requisite passion for reading and writing.

Catherine Gage O'Grady is Professor of Law and Associate Dean of Academic Affairs at the James E. Rogers College of Law, The University of Arizona. She teaches Federal Civil Procedure, Professional Responsibility, and a seminar on Judgment, Problem Solving, and Decision Making. Her research focuses on behavioral legal ethics, an area of study that draws on empirical research in cognitive and social psychology to explore the many subtle and often unconscious influences on ethical decision making. Her work usually includes a specific focus on the new attorney's unique professional perspective in making ethical decisions. Representative work includes Catherine Gage O'Grady, *Behavioral Legal Ethics, Decision Making, and The New Attorney's Unique Professional Perspective,* 15 NEV. L.J. 671 (2015) (symposium) and Catherine Gage O'Grady, *A Behavioral Approach to Lawyer Mistake and Apology,* 51 NEW ENGL. L. REV. (2016) (symposium keynote paper). She is an elected member of the American Law Institute.

Andrew M. Perlman is the Dean and a Professor of Law at Suffolk University Law School. Dean Perlman was the chief reporter of the American Bar Association's Commission on Ethics 20/20, which was responsible for updating the ABA Model Rules of Professional Conduct to reflect changes in technology and increased globalization. He also served as the vice chair of the ABA Commission on the Future of Legal Services, which produced projects and recommendations designed to improve how legal services are delivered and accessed. Most recently, he was appointed by the president of the American Bar Association to serve as the chair of the governing council of the ABA's new Center for Innovation. Dean Perlman was the founding director of Suffolk's Institute on Law Practice Technology and Innovation as well as the related Legal

2 *See* n.1 *supra.*

Technology and Innovation Concentration. He has written numerous articles on professional responsibility that have appeared in some of the nation's leading law reviews. He is a co-author of a civil procedure casebook, CIVIL PROCEDURE: A COURSEBOOK (with Professors Joseph W. Glannon and Peter Raven-Hansen) that has been adopted at more than 80 law schools. He is an honors graduate of Yale College and Harvard Law School, and he received his LL.M from Columbia Law School.

Eugene Ressler retired from the U.S. Army as a Brigadier General in 2014 after 36 years of service. During his Army career, he served as Professor of Computer Science and Head of the Department of Electrical Engineering and Computer Science at the U.S. Military Academy at West Point (USMA). He graduated from USMA in 1978. He earned a Ph.D. in Computer Science at Cornell University (1992), and an MS in Computer Science at the University of California, Berkeley (1985).

Jennifer K. Robbennolt, J.D., Ph.D., is the Associate Dean for Research, the Alice Curtis Campbell Professor of Law, Professor of Psychology, and the Co-Director of the Illinois Program on Law, Behavior and Social Science at the University of Illinois College of Law. Her research integrates psychological theory and methods into the study of law and legal institutions, particularly in the areas of torts and dispute resolution. She is co-author of several books, including THE PSYCHOLOGY OF TORT LAW (with Valerie Hans) and PSYCHOLOGY FOR LAWYERS: UNDERSTANDING THE HUMAN FACTORS IN NEGOTIATION, LITIGATION, AND DECISION MAKING (with Jean Sternlight).

Jean R. Sternlight is the Michael and Sonja Saltman Professor of Law and also Director of the Saltman Center for Conflict Resolution at the University of Nevada-Las Vegas Boyd School of Law. Frequently cited by courts and the media, Sternlight is co-author (with Jennifer Robbennolt) of PSYCHOLOGY FOR LAWYERS: UNDERSTANDING THE HUMAN FACTORS IN NEGOTIATION, LITIGATION, AND DECISION (ABA 2012), and numerous other books. She has published articles in numerous well-respected journals, including *Stanford Law Review, University of Pennsylvania Law Review, Journal of Law & Contemporary Problems, William & Mary Law Review,* and *The Ohio State Journal of Dispute Resolution.* She received her B.A. from Swarthmore College and her J.D. from Harvard Law School.

Cass R. Sunstein is the Robert Walmsley University Professor at Harvard Law School. He clerked for Justice Benjamin Kaplan of Massachusetts Supreme Judicial Court and Justice Thurgood Marshall of the U.S. Supreme Court. He worked as an attorney-advisor in the Office of the Legal Counsel of the U.S. Department of Justice and was a faculty member at the University of Chicago Law School from 1981 to 2008. From 2009 to 2012, he served as Administrator of the White House Office of Information and Regulatory Affairs. From 2013 to 2014, he served on the President's Review Group on Intelligence and Communications Technologies. He is the author of hundreds of articles and dozens of books, including Republic.com (2001), *Nudge: Improving Decisions About Health, Wealth, and Happiness* (with Richard H. Thaler 2008), and *Simpler* (2013). His latest books are *The World According to Star Wars* (2016) and *The Ethics of Influence* (2016). He received his bachelor of arts from Harvard College in 1975 and his doctorate in law from Harvard Law School in 1978.

Roland L. Trope is a partner at *Trope and Schramm LLP*, New York City, and an Adjunct Professor in the Departments of Law and of Electrical Engineering and Computer Science at the U.S. Military Academy at West Point. He has a national security practice that includes advising on intellectual property under government contracts, reviews by the Committee on Foreign Investment in the United States (CFIUS), trade regulations (*e.g.,* export controls, trade sanctions), cybersecurity, and ethics. He was a Marshall Scholar at Oxford University where he earned a B.A. and M.A.; a J.D. at Yale Law School, and a B.A. at the University of Southern California. He was co-editor and a contributing author for GUIDE TO CYBERSECURITY DUE DILIGENCE IN M&A TRANSACTIONS, ABA, 2017.

Table of Contents

PART IV. EXAMPLE FROM THE GOVERNMENT— NASA AND THE SPACE SHUTTLE DISASTERS

PART V. EXAMPLES FROM THE LEGAL WORLD

PART VI. SOME LAST THOUGHTS

CORPORATE SCANDALS AND THEIR IMPLICATIONS

Third Edition

PART I

A Little Bit of Nostalgia: Why Enron Fascinates Us

We admit it: we can't let the Enron saga go, at least not entirely. Part of why we're reprinting these two articles is that we want to give you a flavor of some of the driving forces behind that scandal. (Another reason is that talking about Enron will give you something in common with Baby Boomers like us.)

The Enron collapse is one of the great tragedies of the 20th century. Sure, you could learn much of the Enron story by watching director Alex Gibney's movie, *Enron: The Smartest Guys in the Room* (2005).* But whether you watch the movie or read these articles, it's important to keep this phrase in mind: "Those who do not learn history are doomed to repeat it."** Our new and improved version is: "Even those who know history are doomed to repeat it because they almost always think that they're smarter than the other guys."

For the world's shortest primer on Enron, these next paragraphs should get you up to speed. Enron, with corporate headquarters based in Houston, started out as an energy company. It did well as an energy company, so it decided to branch out into other industries. Lots of companies branch out, and they do so successfully. Enron failed spectacularly. In part, Enron failed because it branched out into a lot of speculative ventures. (One thing to keep in mind is that all businesses take a certain amount of risk because that's how they make money. There's nothing wrong with taking calculated risks. But dumb risks are a different story.) Enron also failed because its internal incentives caused people to behave in ways that benefitted the individuals to the detriment of the company as a whole. Two incentives in particular come to mind.

The first involves a tool called "mark to market" accounting. The basic idea behind mark to market accounting is that a company can record the fair value of

* Inside joke.

** Most authorities attribute this quote to George Santayana.

an asset based on its market value. Companies could then estimate the profit of a contract using that fair market value and book (record) the profit at the beginning of a contract's term. Mark to market works well when there actually is a market value, when the expected profit is recorded correctly on the company's books, and when—if the company guessed wrong about the expected profit—the company reverses any profit miscalculation. So what did Enron do wrong? It made up market values for contracts that involved concepts so new and innovative that no actual market value existed, and it recorded profits based on that made-up value. You might ask yourself why Enron would do that. In part, we think the answer has to do with Enron's internal incentive that gave people bonuses based on the profits that they made for Enron. Think about this: if you wanted a bonus worth several hundred thousand dollars, and you didn't care about right and wrong, what would stop you from creating a new type of industry (say, selling empty bandwidth not being used on the internet), guessing at how many millions such an industry might make over time, accelerating that guess to record all of the profit in year one, and telling your boss that you made a "kazillion" dollars for the company—all done so that you could set your bonus for the year. If you'd like to see Enron executives joking about this approach to mark to market accounting, take a look at the movie *Enron: The Smartest Guys in the Room* (2005), starting at around minute 19:20. Mark to market works well when there's an actual market. It doesn't work so well when people are both creating the market from whole cloth and making up the projected profit based on the made-up market, too.

If you think of mark to market accounting as creating a positive incentive to, well, fib,* the second internal incentive that Enron used created a risky way of keeping its employees in line. During the time that CEO Jeffrey Skilling was in charge at Enron, he used an employee rating system jokingly referred to as "rank and yank." Here's how that system worked, and we're hoping that you understand basic statistics, because understanding bell curves will help you understand why this rating system was such a bad idea for the folks at Enron.

---

* And by "fib," we mean "lie." We also think it's possible that the bosses of the people who were making up market values for markets that didn't exist knew what was going on. We think that Enron used all sorts of accounting tricks to manipulate various documents that might otherwise have revealed its precarious financial situation. For a recap of how some people at Enron tried to bamboozle investors, take a look at Bethany McLean's article, *Is Enron Overpriced?* That article, published in *Fortune* magazine in March 2001, points out the ways in which Enron tried to hide its financial prestidigitation. And, of course, we like the article because that very same writer eventually co-authored a book with Peter Elkind called *The Smartest Guys in the Room: The Amazing Rise and Scandalous Fall of Enron* (2004)—and that book eventually became a movie. *See* n. * on page 1, *supra*.

Let's start with what's called a normal curve.

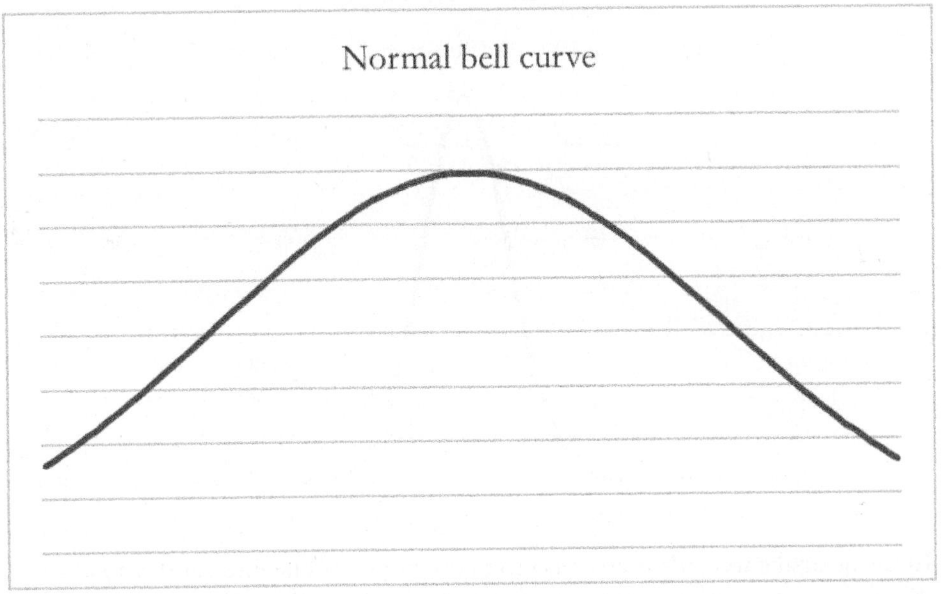

You'll notice that it's big in the middle and smaller on either end. If this were a bell curve representing the level of talent (however you measure talent) in a given workforce, we could say that the folks closer to the right-hand side are more talented, the ones on the left-hand side are less talented, and the ones in the middle are average, among this particular pool of talent.

Now let's assume that the people in a given workforce are roughly the same in terms of talent—that there are a lot of high-performing people and very few low-performing or super-high-performing ones. The curve might look something like the diagram on the next page:

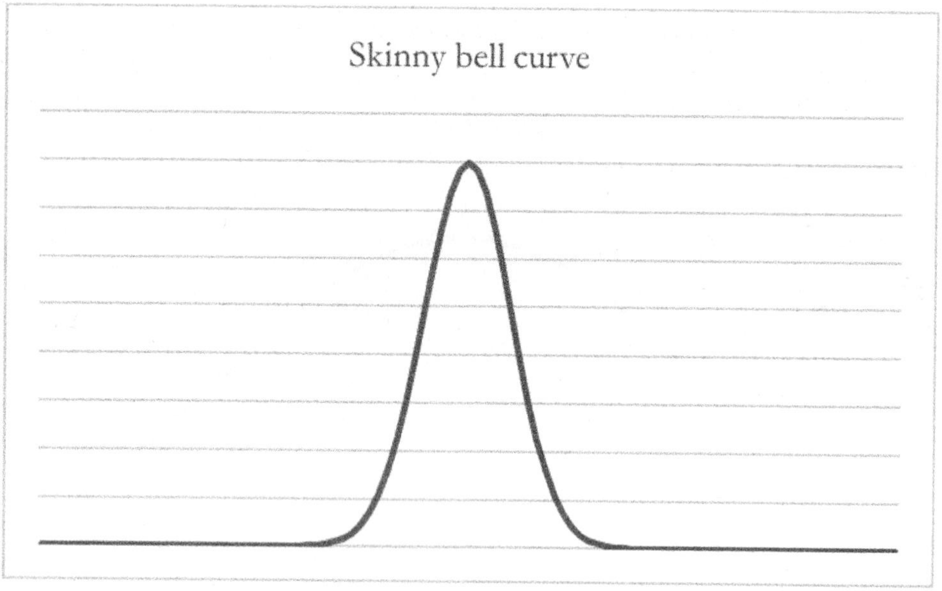

In the normal curve, it's pretty easy to figure out who's talented and who's not. In the skinny curve, most people are clustered very closely together in the middle.

Now assume that you're a manager, and you're told, once every six months, to fire the people in your company who are in the bottom 10% of talent. If you're working for a company with a wide range of talented people, you'd fire the people on the extreme left side of the curve. Then, six months later, you'd fire the people who are now the ones on the extreme left side. Six months later, you'd do the same thing. At some point, assuming no fluctuations in the level of talent at your company, you'd have to start firing the people who used to represent the fat middle of the curve when this whole "lop off the bottom 10% of performers" edict came down. That's a gut-wrenching thing to have to do.

But if you worked with a team of all-stars (see the skinny curve), who exactly would be on the left-hand side of the curve when it's time to fire a group of people? Not so easy to figure out, is it? If you can't distinguish the employees on the basis of talent, and you still have to fire 10% of your team, maybe you'd begin look at other factors: Who's the most fun to be around? Who kisses up the most? Who's the least threatening to you? Who generated the most profit (real or imaginary) for the company?

Enron's "rank and yank" process ended up distinguishing people not based on talent (because most of them were very, very smart and very, very good at their jobs) but on other factors. With a group of roughly equally talented people, when you cut your workforce, you're not cutting into the "fat" of the organization.

You're cutting into the bone. Want to know more about rank and yank? Check out that Enron movie again, at around minute 22:20.

These two incentives—the fallacious recording of profit based on made-up values and the need to kiss up to the decision-makers who were judging employees based on rank and yank—caused some very bright people at Enron to make exceptionally bad decisions at work in order to survive. Enron bet big because its employees needed to prove themselves, in big, splashy ways, to the powers-that-be in order to stay employed.

There are two articles in this chapter. The first one (*Dr. Jekyll & Mr. Skilling: How Enron's Public Image Morphed From the Most Innovative Company in the Fortune 500 to the Most Notorious Company Ever*) is one that we wrote for the first edition of this book. In addition to liking it because we wrote it, we like it because it gives you a feel for the way that Enron evolved (devolved?) and eventually imploded. The second one (*Enron,* Titanic, *and* The Perfect Storm, originally published at 71 FORDHAM L. REV. 1373 (2003)) introduces you to a theme of this book—the human factor. Years of study have convinced us that most people don't make bad decisions because they're evil people. Most of us make bad decisions because we humans have a way of talking ourselves into them. As you read both of these articles, start thinking about whether, if you worked at Enron, you would have made some of the same decisions that people there did.

CHAPTER 1

Dr. Jekyll & Mr. Skilling: How Enron's Public Image Morphed from the Most Innovative Company in the Fortune 500 to the Most Notorious Company Ever*

*Jeffrey D. Van Niel*** *& Nancy B. Rapoport****

Prior to its collapse into bankruptcy, only a few people knew Enron Corp, or any of its various subsidiaries ("Enron"), from direct dealings with the company. Most people, however, were familiar with Enron from what they had read or heard.[1] Following disclosure of the company's accounting problems and of the California electric market manipulation in 2001, the company's public image—as well as its stock price—plummeted. It is the ebb and flow of Enron's public perception that we scrutinize in this essay.

After reading about the various corporate and accounting scandals and watching former managers do their "perp walks" on television, we have had an opportunity to consider how a company that was once placed on a pedestal and

---

 This piece was originally published as Nancy B. Rapoport & Jeffrey D. Van Niel, *Dr. Jekyll & Mr. Skilling: How Enron's Public Image Morphed from the Most Innovative Company in the* Fortune 500 *to the Most Notorious Company Ever, in* ENRON: CORPORATE FIASCOS AND THEIR IMPLICATIONS 77 (Nancy B. Rapoport & Bala G. Dharan, eds.) (Foundation Press 2004).

** Jeffrey D. Van Niel is currently licensed to practice law in Nebraska and Ohio and is actively pursuing licensure in Texas. He practiced utilities regulation and utilities law in Ohio for 10 years as an Assistant Ohio Attorney General representing the Public Utilities Commission of Ohio, as a Master Commissioner on behalf of the Supreme Court of Ohio, and in private practice with Kegler, Brown, Hill & Ritter and McNees, Wallace & Nurick. Mr. Van Niel also practiced utilities law for two years in Nebraska with Woods & Aitken.

*** Nancy Rapoport is Dean and Professor of Law at the University of Houston Law Center.

1 For example, during his 12 years practicing in the utility law arena, Mr. Van Niel had many opportunities to interact with Enron personnel (including its lawyers) on numerous issues, including retail competition and the deregulation of the natural gas and electric industries.

touted as the most innovative company in the United States for six years in a row[2] could deteriorate into a seething mass of accounting scandals, civil litigation, and criminal indictments. What struck us most was the apparent dramatic shift in the public perception of Enron—at least that was the premise when we started writing this essay. As with most academic pieces, we thought we knew what we wanted to say. Unfortunately, our research provided a different conclusion from the one that we had expected.

What do we mean? Simply put, everything that happened to Enron in 2001 was predicted—and used as a reason to avoid the company—as early as 1996.[3] A careful reader of Enron-related articles in the press might have seen this coming and avoided Enron like the plague.[4]

So what happened between 1985 and 2001 that launched Enron on the road to becoming the fifth largest company in the FORTUNE 500?[5] Why, that meta-

---

2 *See, e.g.*, Harry Hurt III et al., *Power Players Enron Has Shaken Up the Sleepy Gas Pipeline and Power Businesses by Aggressively Embracing Risk and Continually Remaking Itself. So What's Not to Like?*, FORTUNE, Aug, 5, 1996, at 94 [hereinafter *What's Not to Like*] ("Competitors voted Enron the most innovative company in the U.S. in FORTUNE's poll of "Americas Most Admired Corporations" this year, ahead of high-tech highfliers like Intel and Microsoft."); *America's Most Admired Companies*, FORTUNE, Mar. 3, 1997, at F1; *America's Most Admired Companies*, FORTUNE, Mar. *2*, 1998, at F1; *Americas Most Admired Companies*, FORTUNE, Mar. 1, 1999, at 68; *Americas Most Admired Companies*, FORTUNE, Feb. 21, 2000, at F1; *America's Most Admired Companies*, FORTUNE, Feb. 19, 2001, at F1.

3 So aside from envy, what's not to like about Enron? According to some critics, the very things that have made the company a success: management's penchant for risk taking and innovation; the parent corporation's aggressive accounting practices and allegedly Byzantine methods of "managing earnings" via no fewer than six separately traded subsidiaries; an alleged overemphasis on short-term performance, symbolized by the daily posting of stock prices in the headquarters building; and the unusually complex intracompany transactions needed to drive profit growth. "Enron's just got too much hype in it for us," says a member of a multibillion-dollar Houston- based investment firm that specializes in blue-chip stocks. "A few years ago, they were promoting natural gas-powered automobiles. Then they dropped that idea like a hot potato, and started building power plants and spinning them off. It's hard to figure out what the fresh feed for this month is going to be."

What's Not to Like, *supra* note 2, at 94.

4 In feet, some very high-profile investors stayed away from Enron stock because Enron's financial statements were simply not making sense. *See, e.g.*, MIMI SWARTZ WITH SHERRON WATKINS, POWER FAILURE: THE INSIDE STORY OF THE COLLAPSE OF ENRON xi–xiii (2003) [hereinafter POWER FAILURE]; LYN M. FRASER & AILEEN ORMISTON, UNDERSTANDING THE CORPORATE ANNUAL REPORT: NUTS, BOLTS, AND A FEW LOOSE SCREWS 17–21 (2003).

5 *Fortune 500 Largest U.S. Corporations*, FORTUNE, Apr. 15, 2002, at F1 (listing Enron fifth, even though by then it was in Chapter 11). For an explanation of why it still made the list, *see* Carol J. Loomis, *And the Revenue Games People (like Enron) Play; Got energy trading contracts?*, FORTUNE, Apr. 15, 2002, at 190 ("We will explain these wacky revenue leaps. But first, an explanation as to why the Greatest Leaper of them all, Enron, is fifth on our 2001 list. . . .[W]e decided to rank Enron based on its nine-months['] revenues [because Enron had yet to release fourth quarter results]."). However, the irony of Enron's high ranking was not lost on the editors of FORTUNE who, in the same issue, published a poem with the concluding stanza:

Oh, somewhere the sun is shining, somewhere the stars are bright;
Somewhere there are investors who sleep like logs at night;
Consider these 500—how they grow! They burn! They strive!

mantra of the late 1990s and early 2000s: "thinking outside the box." Enron was considered the best company at identifying talented employees who were willing to be innovative.[6] By 1996, Enron was creating a new business every other year.[7] Ken Lay, Enron's CEO both before and after Jeffrey Skilling, explained the company's changed focus (from a stodgy natural gas pipeline company to a cutting-edge entrepreneur and moving force in electric deregulation) in an August 5, 1996 FORTUNE magazine interview by pointing out that 40% of the company's earnings in 1995 came from businesses that did not exist in 1985.[8] Lay was confident that the trend would continue: "We expect that 5 years from now, over 40% of our earnings will come from businesses that did not exist 5 years ago. It's a matter of re-creating the company and the businesses we're in."[9] Enron re-created its businesses right into the ground.

1. Enron Before the Fall—The Public Perception

Enron started out as a somewhat sleepy natural gas utility in 1985, when Houston Natural Gas Corp. and InterNorth Inc. merged. It is safe to assume that, other than the people being directly served by that utility in 1985, most people still had never heard of Enron. Seven years later, virtually everyone had heard of Enron.[10] By 1992, Enron owned the largest natural gas pipeline network in the country and had already begun its efforts to revolutionize the natural gas industry. Finally, Enron stepped out of the shadows and into the spotlight with its revolutionary concept for the "Gas Bank."[11] With the Gas Bank, Enron forever altered not only the gas industry, but also the company itself.

And could someone please explain here—Exercise your brain here!

Can someone please explain here—Why is Enron still No. 5?

Stanley Bing, *The Auditor,* FORTUNE, Apr, 15, 2002, at 402.

6 Some of Enron's mechanisms to obtain innovative thinking were draconian in nature. Every employee was ranked within his or her group each year, and the bottom 20% were let go. The pressure to produce was intense, and the internal competitions were brutal and cutthroat. *See infra* note 47 and accompanying text. Notwithstanding these factors, potential employees beat down the doors to get placed with Enron, including the "best and brightest," 20% of which would be ground into next year's compost.

7 *What's Not to Like, supra* note 2.

8 *Id.*

9 *Id.*

10 Early in 2003, NBR taught a group of 10th graders at the Schlenker School in Houston. Almost all of the students had heard of Enron and could describe in some detail what had happened to the company.

11 [I]n 1989, Skilling, who was still working at McKinsey as an Enron consultant, realized that there was plenty of gas available—from producers who were being freed from federal price controls—and there was plenty of demand, from new utilities that wanted to burn gas to make electricity. But there was no intermediary that could aggregate—and more important, *balance*—the gas supplies coming from the producers with the demand coming from consumers. Why not create a mechanism that would allow them to hook up? Skilling called his idea the Gas Bank.

A. The Puff Pieces

To the casual reader of business weeklies, Enron was riding high at the turn of the 21st century. In 1996, the WASHINGTON POST referred to Enron as a "titan in the natural gas industry."[12] In 1998, FORTUNE called Enron "the world's leading integrated natural- gas and electricity giant."[13] In 2000, FORTUNE again fawned over Enron, ranking it 25th among "the world's most admired companies."[14] In early 2001, THE ECONOMIST still referred to Enron as "a highly successful energy brokerage."[15] Enron symbolized everything that was glitzy and go-go-go—the perfect morphing of a staid energy company into an *uber*-dot.com business.

The early 1990s were times of explosive change in many areas, including the development and use of personal technology and computerization, communications and mobile phones, and most important, the perceptions of workers and their intellectual capacity (and capabilities as company assets). These changes accelerated in the mid- and late 1990s, with the advent of the dot.com bubble. Simultaneously, Enron was evolving as well—creating new businesses, pushing the envelope and morphing itself from an energy utility to a growth company.[16] Here's the question—how do you make your energy utility look as good as a dot.com growth stock? Hindsight helps us respond with the obvious answer: you cook the books. Some people knew that Enron's accounting was

---

ROBERT BRYCE & MOLLY IVINS, PIPE DREAMS: GREED, EGO, AND THE DEATH OF ENRON 54 (2002) [hereinafter PIPE DREAMS].

12 Daniel Southerland, *You've Heard of Big Oil. This is the Story of Big Gas. . . and It Begins with Enron Corp., Which Wants to Be No. 1 in World,* WASH. POST, Feb. 4, 1996, at H1.

13 Erin Davies, *Enron: The Power's Back On,* FORTUNE, Apr. 13, 1998, at 24.

14 Nicholas Srein, *The World's Most Admired Companies,* FORTUNE, Oct. 2, 2000, at 182.

15 *The Slumbering Giants Awake,* ECONOMIST, Feb. 10, 2001, at 6.

16 Enron originally wanted to become "The World's Leading Energy Company," *see* POWER FAILURE, *supra* note 4, at 112, but eventually, even that sobriquet was too limiting. According to Cokie Roberts at ABC, "You start back in January of 2001. There was a big party, lavish party in San Antonio where Kenneth Lay declared Enron the 'world's greatest company.' " *ABC News: This Wk.* (ABC television broadcast, Feb. 10, 2002). It's not far to go from calling yourself "The World's Greatest Company" to being the butt of jokes like this one:

> Making the rounds of Wall Streeters while markets were in the dumps this week was a recording from the following number: 510-809-4466: "Thank you for calling Enron, please listen closely to the following options as our menu has changed.
>
> If you wish to serve a subpoena on a current or former Enron executive, press 1; If you are an Enron shareholder, and would like to learn how to turn your Enron stock certificates into decorative origami, press 2; If your Enron 401(k) plan is worthless and you'd like some tips on how to survive your retirement eating nothing but mac and cheese, press 3; If you are an Enron executive and would like to find out which prison inmate will be making you his b***h, press 4; If you would like to invoke your constitutional right against self[-]incrimination, press 5. If you are Dick Cheney, press 6 and thanks for nothing[,] Dick.
>
> Thank you for calling Enron, the World's greatest company."

Beth Piskora et al., *Bull's Eye,* N.Y. POST, Feb. 24, 2002, at 31.

questionable long before Skilling abruptly retired as CEO and Enron's world came tumbling town.

B. The Early Critiques

Remember the old adage, "if it looks too good to be true, it usually is"? Enron illustrated that adage perfectly, and some very smart people figured out that Enron's financials were a sham. Others might not have known that Enron was cooking the books, but they looked askance at those books anyway. Even the normally effusive FORTUNE ran a story describing the impenetrability of Enron's financial information.[17] And the publication INSIDE F.E.R.C.'S GAS MARKET REPORT noted that, on December 21, 1995, Robert Christensen Jr. had downgraded Enron from a "buy" to a "hold," warning that "[t]he thin trading liquidity of these [gas derivatives] products can cause financial windfalls as well as huge potential losses. From the outside looking in, we cannot tell which way it will go for [Enron]."[18] A few outsiders looked at Enron and did not like what they saw.

There were clues as early as 1995, when FORTUNE reported Enron's losses on the power plant in Dabhol, India.[19] Also in 1995, there were rumors that Enron was "facing margin calls of hundreds of millions of dollars because it had a 'short' position on contracts to deliver natural gas in January."[20] Mind you, these problems only involved Enron's hard assets, rather than its later, "asset-lite"

---

17 To skeptics, the lack of clarity [in Enron's financials] raises a red flag about Enron's pricey stock. Even owners of the stock aren't universally sanguine. "I'm somewhat afraid of it," admits one portfolio manager. And the inability to get behind the numbers combined with ever higher expectations for the company may increase the chance of a nasty surprise. "Enron is an earnings- at-risk story," says Chris Wolfe, the equity market strategist at J.P. Morgan's private bank, who despite his remark is an Enron fan. "If it doesn't meet earnings, [the stock] could implode."

Bethany McLean, *Is Enron Overpriced?,* FORTUNE, Mar. 5, 2001, at 122.

18 *Huge Spread in Basis Differentials Complicates Hedging, Say Analysts,* INSIDE F.E.R.C.'S GAS MARKET REP., Dec. 29, 1995, at 9.

19 Rajiv M, Rao, *Enron's power outage in India*, FORTUNE, Oct. 2, 1995, at 34.

20 Bill Mintz, *Enron shares recover as buyback announced,* HOUS. CHRON., Dec. 23, 1995, at B1.

businesses.[21] And don't get us started on Enron's political maneuverings, both in the U.S. and abroad,[22] or its manipulation of the California energy markets.[23]

Why didn't more people question Enron's financial statements and business plans? Enron was well-known for bullying analysts who disagreed with Enron's

---

[21] Skilling often touted his "asset-lite" philosophy. A mere two months before his sudden resignation, Skilling argued, " 'Today the key to success is we don't need to own assets, as long as we can use [them] to acquire information such as knowledge about gas pipelines and natural gas. Once we have the information and knowledge, we no longer need to own the assets." Dr. Nikolai Dobberstein, *Creating Global Winners*, MALAYSIAN BUS., June 1, 2001 (quoting Jeffrey Skilling and encouraging Malaysian companies to follow similar business models). Skilling was a master at convincing people of this doubtful logic. For example, this interview on CNBC:

> HAINES [Newscaster]: . . . Joining us now is Enron's CEO, Jeffrey Skilling. And in spirit of full disclosure, I have some shares of Enron in my IRA. Mr. Skilling, how does revenue go up so much and the bottom line doesn't benefit more?
>
> MR. JEFFREY SKILLING (Enron CEO): Well, we had a net income increase, Mark, of over 40 percent and earnings per share up 32 percent, so I—I think it was a—a real good quarter.
>
> HAINES: Yeah, but that doesn't answer the question: Well, how can revenue go up, like 150 and—and—and the bottom line only benefit 40—40 percent?
>
> MR SKILLING: What—what drives our net income, Mark, is the increase in physical volumes delivered. Revenues are impacted by price levels and price revel—levels really don't impact us because we don't own the generation facilities, we don't own gas production assets. So prices move up and down. That impacts our revenue. But ...—what really matters to us is, how much volume are we delivering to customers? And our volumes this quarter are up 58 percent, which drove that increase in our wholesale income.

CNBC: Squawk Bax (CNBC television broadcast, July 12, 2001).

[22] For a discussion of Enron's political influence in the U.S., *see* Kevin Phillips, *The Company Presidency; Enron and the Bush family have boosted each other up the ladder of success. But have their ties created a Teapot Dome?*, L.A. TIMES, Feb. 10, 2002 at M1 (detailing the exchange of money and favors between various political figures and Enron); Eliane S. Povich, *Gramms and Enron: A Mutual Aid Society; Rules backed by senator, wife helped company*, NEWSDAY, Feb. 10, 2002, at A6 (explaining that as chief of the Commodities Futures Trading Commission, Wendy Gramm drafted rules exempting energy trades from government regulation, then shortly afterwards accepted a lucrative position on Enron's board of directors; and noting Enron "donated almost $100,000 to Sen. [Phil] Gramm [(R-Texas), and Wendy's husband] over the past decade."). Apparently, Enron attempted similar tactics abroad. However, Enron wasn't always popular overseas, and not just because of its failed businesses worldwide. A particularly colorful example of nasty press overseas occurred in 1998:

> In the hurt tone of a nun rejecting accusations of Satanism, executives and Government propagandists denounced our revelation last week that Enron, a US energy company which has bought American politicians wholesale, was sponsoring the Labour Party conference. Their protestations of injured innocence grew louder on Thursday when, as we predicted, Peter Mandelson allowed the multi-national accused of complicity with the beating and false imprisonment of Indian peasants to take over the Wessex Water monopoly in southern England.

Nick Cohen, *Hold on a minute. . . .* OBSERVER, Sept. 13, 1998, at 32.

[23] *See, e.g.*, Rebecca Smith & John R. Wilke, *Leading the News: Enron Ex-Trader Admits to Fraud In California Crisis*, WALL ST. J., Oct, 18, 2002, at A3 ("The former head of Enron Corp.'s Western energy trading desk admitted he conspired to manipulate California's electricity market and extract illegal profits for his employer, giving federal prosecutors a valuable witness who will help them develop cases against executives at Enron and ocher big energy-trading companies."); Robert Gavin, *Did Utilities Aid 'Ricochet' Trades?*, WALL ST. J., May 24, 2002, at B4 (explaining "the so-called Death Star strategy in which Enron scheduled fictitious electricity deliveries on overburdened transmission lines, in order to receive congestion relief payments . . .").

own rosy pictures of its financial health.[24] Still, a smattering of analysts and reporters stood firm in their criticism of Enron's murky financial statements—enough to convince us that our original theory (that no one knew about Enron's risky business model until after Skilling resigned as CEO) was wrong.[25] After Skilling resigned, of course, everyone began to understand what these few analysts had been saying all along.

2. Enron After the Fall—The Public Perception

Enron seemed to go from "most admired" status to "most despised" status in record time, once the revelations about the company's behavior became public. Nightly news broadcasts depicted the very real tragedy of retirees (and those close to retirement age) whose lives were forever changed by Enron's plummeting stock price.

Even in the midst of tragedy and anger, some were able to find humor in the situation:

> *Enron Business Haikus*
>
> Business model
> Too complex to understand
> It's a house of cards.
>
> Buy low and sell high.
> Our intermediations
> Raise energy costs.
>
> Our profits are made
> At the consumer's expense
> Pass the caviar.
>
> Stock price fell today.
> Management says, "Don't fear."
> I am still afraid.

---

24 PIPE DREAMS, *supra* note 11, at 249–56.

25 *See, e.g.*, Todd Mason, *Houston Oil Analyst Wouldn't Buy Enron's Story*, FORT WORTH STAR-TELEGRAM, Apr. 11, 2002, at A1 (describing John Olson's negative views of Enron and Enron's use of pressure to get him to retract his views); Jeff Donn, *Rise and Fall of Enron; Energy Giant Fed on Chaos and Change; Did Arrogance Boomerang?*, COM. APPEAL, Jan. 22, 2002, at B7 (same); Tom Fowler, *The Fall of Enron; A Year Ago, Enron's Crumbling Foundation was Revealed to All When the Company Reported Its Disastrous Third-Quarter Numbers. It's Growth-At-Any-Cost Culture Led It to Bankruptcy—and Ignominy*, HOUS. CHRON., Oct. 20, 2002, at A1 (John Olson fired by Merrill Lynch for refusing to change his views on Enron); *Courageous Warnings on Enron*, ST. PETERSBURG TIMES, Jan. 27, 2002, at 2D (Bethany McLean, a reporter for FORTUNE, wrote an article critical of Enron despite Enron's attempts to get the magazine to quash the story).

Chaos reigns within.
Reflect, repent and sell short.
Even down can be up.[26]

These jokes, and others like them, indicate how much Enron's demise—as well as the demise of other companies after Enron—has entered the public consciousness.[27] We can trace Enron's entry into the world of late-night TV jokes[28] starting roughly after Jeffrey Skilling, Enron's CEO, resigned on August 14, 2001.

What may have triggered the media's focus, in part, was the unlikely proposition that Skilling would have resigned "for personal reasons" and to spend

---

[26] TIM BARRY, THE TOTALLY UNAUTHORIZED ENRON JOKE BOOK 18 (2002) [hereinafter JOKE BOOK]. Another part of the book describes:

> **Shareholder Haikus From Enron's Last Days**
>
> CNN today
> Says Enron distress increased.
> This is not good news.
>
> Dynegy retreat
> Leaves few options available.
> My foreboding grows.
>
> The merger now dead.
> Hope fades to a mere glimmer.
> Chapter 11 looms.
>
> The official news
> Now has tolled. Enron is gone.
> So is my money.

Id. at 29.

[27] We can't resist this one, describing "Enronism" as different from capitalism and communism:

> You have two cows. You write down and set aside the debt incurred by one of the cows to an off-sheet entity. You sell all three of them to another publicly listed joint trading venture company, using equity derivative transactions created by your brother-in-law at the bank. The trading company sells to a vehicle that is capitalized with a promise of Enron stock based on the increased valuation of the third cow, with the understanding that the first 33% of the future profit is returned to the partners of the venture in the form of more cows. Then execute a debt/equity swap with an associated general offer so you get all four cows back, with a tax exemption for five cows (debt depreciation of the first [cow]). The recognized future milk funds flow of the six cows are brought forward and transferred via an intermediary to a Cayman Island company secretly owned by the majority shareholder, who "enhanced" the capital structure by selling the rights to all seven cows back to your listed company. You hire Arthur Andersen to audit your books. The annual report says the company owns eight cows, with an option on one more.

Iconoclast website, http://www.iconoclast.ca/issue/9001,3,0402,17,l.html (last visited Jan. 12, 2003).

[28] For a sampling of these jokes, *see* http://politicalhumor.about.com/library/blenronscandal.htm (last visited July 22, 2003). *See also* JOKE BOOK, *supra* note 26, at 87 (listing Enron jokes by late-night comedians). Other corporate scandals have also gotten late-night notice. *See, e.g.,* http://members.aol.com/mrdejim/oct02.html (quoting Jay Leno: "Martha Stewart's stockbroker's assistant is going to testify against her. She may have sent a coded message to him on her show today when she demonstrated how a canary with a broken neck can't sing.") (aired on *The Tonight Show with Jay* Leno (NBC television broadcast, Oct, 2, 2002)) (last visited July 22, 2003).

more time with his family.[29] Did anyone really believe that such a hard-driving, aggressive CEO was leaving in order to stop and smell the roses?[30]

The news stories kept coming fast and furious (both literally and figuratively furious), and our morning ritual of reading the newspapers while eating breakfast expanded from 15 minutes to 30 minutes to sometimes over an hour, just to keep up. Politicians started incorporating Enron references into their speeches.[31] Late-night comedians continued their assault on Enron's executives, many of whom (Skilling, Fastow, Lay) were now household words.[32] And, appropriately enough,

---

29 Skilling's resignation was the triggering event that caused Sherron Watkins to write her now-famous one-page anonymous memo to returning CEO Ken Lay. *See* POWER FAILURE, *supra* note 4, at 275–89.

30

> There were problems with Skilling's story. To begin with, Skilling was never considered much of a family man. He was divorced. He and his ex-wife had three children. Skilling loved his kids, but few saw him as a fanatical family man. Second, by quitting, Skilling left lots of money on the table. In 2000, Skilling's pay package had totaled some $10.1 million, more than double the amount he'd been paid in 1999. By leaving early, he was forgoing millions of dollars—perhaps tens of millions. Finally, it just didn't fit. Skilling had always been in it for the power, for the glory, for the thrill of having people think he was important. And *now,* now that he was finally in charge of the whole enchilada, he was throwing in the towel? No way.

PIPE DREAMS, *supra* note 11, at 293. *Compare* Dan Balz & Mike Allen, *Hughes to Leave White Home; Key Bush Aide Wants to Return to Texas with Family,* WASH. POST, Apr. 24, 2002, at A1 (reporting that Presidential Counselor Karen Hughes is resigning to focus on her family and rediscover her Texas roots); Bill Sammon, *Hughes to Leave Bush White House; Key Advisor Will Give Up Position in Summer, Focus on Her Family,* WASH. TIMES, Apr. 24, 2002, at A4 (describing Hughes's devotion to her family and her resolve to put their happiness ahead of her service to the government); Jim Vanderlei & Jeanne Cummings, *Bush Counselor Karen Hughes Will Step Down,* WALL ST. J., Apr. 24, 2002, at A5 (noting that while Hughes will officially resign, Bush asserts that she will remain in his "Inner circle").

31

> As all of you know, life is about more than the 30-second soundbites on television or slogans in campaigns. Life is about choices, and so is politics when practiced properly. And one of the first things worth fighting for is fairness, fundamental fairness. And Enron, Enron makes it crystal clear: No worker in America should be robbed of years of labor by unconscionable personal greed. No employee, no employee should see retirement savings wiped away by arrogant executives who live by special privilege. One of my colleagues compared the executives of Enron to the Corleone family. I think that's an insult . . . to the Corleones.

Senator John F. Kerry, Remarks at the California Democratic Party State Democratic Convention (Feb. 16, 2002), *available at* http://www.gwu.edu/-action/2004/kerry/kerry021602sp.html (last visited July 23, 2003). Even a local Democratic Committee inserted Enron jokes into its meeting minutes:

> Attorney General Bill Lockyer and his top 10 elements of the new periodic table:
>
> . . . .
>
> 7. Fundraisium: combines with Graydium to make governium.
>
> 6. Enronium: unstable, only attracts subpoenas.
>
> . . . .
>
> 1. DickCheneyum: Must be stored in a remote location; used to extract fundraisium from petroleum.

Minutes of the Santa Clara County Democratic Central Committee Meeting (Mar. 7, 2002), *available at* http://www.scc-democrats.org/minutes/020307.html (last visited July 23, 2003).

32 JOKE BOOK, *supra* note 26, at 87.

editorials[33] and political cartoons made short shrift of Enron's willingness to sacrifice employees at the altar of executive greed. We've kept several of these cartoons, and one of them nicely expresses the public's denunciation of Enron.[34]

Even before Enron Filed for bankruptcy, books on Enron began to crop up everywhere.[35] Since the bankruptcy filing, of course, Enron books (yes, we're counting this one, too) have become their own cottage industry.[36] Of all of the

---

[33] One of our favorite articles begins this way:

> There's a great and honorable tradition about disaster at sea: Women and children first, and the captain goes down with the ship. For Enron, it's been just the opposite. Kenneth Lay and the rest of the top executives paid themselves an average of $5 million apiece as the huge corporation staggered toward bankruptcy. And ordinary employees lost their jobs and most of their savings. The best they have been able to negotiate so far is severance pay capped at $13,500 apiece.

Enron's Disaster, BANGOR DAILY NEWS, June 22, 2002, at 8.

[34] Cartoon reprinted with permission of the Houston Chronicle. HOUS. CHRON., June 21, 2002, at 32A.

[35] HUMAN RIGHTS WATCH STAFF, THE ENRON CORPORATION: CORPORATE COMPLICITY IN HUMAN RIGHTS VIOLATIONS (1999); ICON GROUP LTD., ENRON CORP.: LABOR PRODUCTIVITY BENCHMARKS AND INTERNATIONAL GAP ANALYSIS (2000); ICON GROUP, ENRON OIL & GAS COMPANY: INTERNATIONAL COMPETITIVE BENCHMARKS AND FINANCIAL GAP ANALYSIS FINANCIAL PERFORMANCE SERIES (2000); ICON GROUP, ENRON OIL & GAS COMPANY: LABOR PRODUCTIVITY BENCHMARKS AND INTERNATIONAL GAP ANALYSIS LABOR PRODUCTIVITY SERIES (2000); JOEL KURTZMAN & GLENN RIFKIN, RADICAL E: FROM GE TO ENRON—LESSONS ON HOW TO RULE THE WEB (2001); ABHAY MEHTA, POWER PLAY: A STUDY OF THE ENRON PROJECT (2000); VAULT REPORTS, ENRON: THE VAULTREPORTS.COM EMPLOYER PROFILE FOR JOB SEEKERS (1998).

[36] The books vary in terms of audience (popular culture genre versus business analysis genre), quality (some are self-published—need we say more?), and viewpoint. As of May 27, 2003, we found these books listed at Amazon.com via an "Enron" search: *See, e.g.,* ALVIN A. ARENS ET AL., AUDITING AND ASSURANCE SERVICES AND ENRON CASE PACKAGE (9th ed. 2002); RICHARD E. BAKER ET AL., ADVANCED FINANCIAL

ACCOUNTING (5th ed. 2002); DIRK J. BARREVELD, THE ENRON COLLAPSE: CREATIVE ACCOUNTING, WRONG ECONOMICS OR CRIMINAL ACTS? A LOOK INTO THE ROOT CAUSES OF THE LARGEST BANKRUPTCY IN U.S. HISTORY (2002); JOKE BOOK, *supra* note 26; GEORGE J. BENSTON ET AL., FOLLOWING THE MONEY: CORPORATE DISCLOSURE IN AN AGE OF GLOBALIZATION (2003); DANIEL L. BERGER, ACCOUNTANTS' LIABILITY AFTER ENRON (2002); ARTHUR L. BERKOWITZ, ENRON: A PROFESSIONAL'S GUIDE TO THE EVENTS, ETHICAL ISSUES, AND PROPOSED REFORMS (2002); CRISTA BOYLES, ENRON PROOF YOUR 401(K): STEPS TO KEEP YOUR MONEY SAFE (2002); JULIA K. BRAZELTON & JANICE L. AMMONS, ENRON AND BEYOND: TECHNICAL ANALYSIS OF ACCOUNTING, CORPORATE GOVERNANCE, AND SECURITIES ISSUES (2002); LYNN BREWER & MATTHEW SCOTT HANSEN, HOUSE OF CARDS: CONFESSIONS OF AN ENRON EXECUTIVE (2002); PIPE DREAMS, *supra* note 11; HENRY R. CHEESEMAN & MICHAEL BIXBY, BUSINESS LAW—ENRON CASE STUDY (2003); CHARLES J. CICCHETTI ET AL., RESTRUCTURING ELECTRICITY MARKETS: A WORLD PERSPECTIVE POST-CALIFORNIA AND ENRON (2003); CORPORATE AFTERSHOCK: THE PUBLIC POLICY LESSONS FROM THE COLLAPSE OF ENRON AND OTHER MAJOR CORPORATIONS (Christopher L. Culp & William A. Niskanen eds., 2003); BRIAN CRUVER, ANATOMY OF GREED: THE UNSHREDDED TRUTH FROM AN ENRON INSIDER (2002) [hereinafter ANATOMY OF GREED]; LOREN FOX, ENRON: THE RISE AND FALL (2002) [hereinafter RISE AND FALL]; PETER C. FUSARO & ROSS M. MILLER, WHAT WENT WRONG AT ENRON: EVERYONE'S GUIDE TO THE LARGEST BANKRUPTCY IN U.S. HISTORY (2002) [hereinafter WHAT WENT WRONG]; CHERYL DE MESA GRAZIANO, ENRON AND THE POWERS REPORT; AN EXAMINATION OF BUSINESS AND ACCOUNTING FAILURES (2002); JOE BEN HOYLE, ADVANCED ACCOUNTING, UPDATE EDITION WITH ENRON POWERWEB (2002); ARIANNA HUFFINGTON, PIGS AT THE TROUGH; HOW CORPORATE GREED AND POLITICAL CORRUPTION ARE UNDERMINING AMERICA (2003); IDC, ENRON: A REMINDER OF FREE MARKET FUNDAMENTALS (2001), *available to download* at http://www.amazon.com; GREG JENKINS, ENRON COLLAPSE (2002); PAUL JORION, INVESTING IN A POST-ENRON WORLD (2003); STANLEY KELLER, DISCLOSURE AND OTHER LESSONS LEARNED AFTER ENRON: WHAT YOU NEED TO KNOW NOW TO FILE 10-K AND OTHER FORMS (2002); E. JOHN LARSEN, MODERN ADVANCED ACCOUNTING WITH POWERWEB: ENRON (9th ed. 2002); BETHANY MCLEAN & PETER ELKIND, SMARTEST GUYS IN THE ROOM: THE RISE AND FALL OF ENRON (2003); WILLIAM F. MESSIER, JR., AUDITING & ASSURANCE SERVICES: A SYSTEMATIC APPROACH WITH ENRON POWERWEB (2002); DANIEL QUINN MILLS, BUY, LIE, AND SELL HIGH; HOW INVESTORS LOST OUT ON ENRON AND THE INTERNET BUBBLE (2002); CATHY PETERSON, FLASHLIGHT WALKING: THE INSPIRING STORY OF ONE FAMILY'S STRUGGLE THROUGH CANCER AND THE ENRON LAYOFF (2003); JAMES POST ET AL., BUSINESS AND SOCIETY: CORPORATE STRATEGY, PUBLIC POLICY, AND ETHICS (10th ed. 2003): VIJAY PRASHAD, FAT CATS AND RUNNING DOGS: THE ENRON STAGE OF CAPITALISM (2002): PRABIR PURKAYASTHA & VIJAY PRASHAD, ENRON BLOWOUT: CORPORATE CAPITALISM AND THEFT OF THE GLOBAL COMMONS (Signpost 6) (2002); JACK C. ROBERTSON ET AL., MP AUDITING AND ASSURANCE SERVICES W/APOLLO SHOES CASEBOOKAND POWERWEB: ENRON (10th ed. 2002); PETER S. ROSE, MONEY AND CAPITAL MARKETS (8th ed. 2002); ANTHONY SAUNDERS & MARCIA MILLON CORNETT, FINANCIAL INSTITUTIONS MANAGEMENT: A RISK MANAGEMENT APPROACH (4th ed. 2002); ANTHONY SAUNDERS ET AL., FINANCIAL MARKETS AND INSTITUTIONS: A MODERN PERSPECTIVE (2d ed. 2003); RICHARD J. SCHROTH & A. LARRY ELLIOTT, HOW COMPANIES LIE: WHY ENRON IS JUST THE TIP OF THE ICEBERG (2002); CHRIS SEAY & CHRISTOPHER BRYAN, THE TAO OF ENRON: SPIRITUAL LESSONS FROM A FORTUNE 500 FALLOUT (2002); REBECCA SMITH & JOHN R. EMSHWILLER, UNCOVERING ENRON (2003); THEODORE F. STERLING, THE ENRON SCANDAL (2002); J. DAVID SPICELAND ET AL., INTERMEDIATE ACCOUNTING (UPDATE EDITION) WITH COACH, ESSENTIALS OF ACCOUNTING, ALTERNATE PROBLEMS AND S&P PACKAGE W/POWERWEB (2d ed, 2002); J. DAVID SPICELAND ET AL., INTERMEDIATE ACCOUNTING VOLUME 1 WITH COACH CD-ROM AND POWERWEB: FOCUS ON ENRON, ALTERNATE EXERCISES, PROBLEMS AND NET TUTOR (3d ed. 2002); J. DAVID SPICELAND ET AL., INTERMEDIATE ACCOUNTING VOLUME 2 WITH COACH CD-ROM AND POWERWEB: FOCUS ON ENRON AND NET TUTOR (3d ed. 2002); IRIS STUART & BRUCE STUART, ETHICS IN THE POST-ENRON AGE (2003); POWER FAILURE, *supra* note 4; U.S. GOVERNMENT, 2002 COMPENDIUM OF MAJOR FINANCIAL REPORTS TO THE SEC BY TWELVE COMPANIES UNDER SCRUTINY OR IN THE NEWS: ADELPHIA COMMUNICATIONS, AOL TIME WARNER, ENRON, GLOBAL CROSSING, HALLIBURTON, IMCLONE SYSTEMS, MARTHA STEWART LIVING OMNIMEDIA, MERRILL LYNCH, POLAROID, QWEST, WORLDCOM, AND XEROX (PROGRESSIVE MANAGEMENT (CD-ROM 2002); U.S. GOVERNMENT, 21ST CENTURY COMPLETE GUIDE TO ENRON: SECURITIES AND EXCHANGE COMMISSION [SEC] FORMS AND FILINGS FROM 1994 PLUS HOUSE AND SENATE HEARING ON THE

books listed in footnote 36, a few have emerged as useful, mass-market studies of Enron's culture as well as its downfall.[37]

One such book, PIPE DREAMS, helps to put the Enron scandal in perspective, albeit in an admittedly liberal perspective:

> The Enron failure is the biggest political scandal in American history. Teapot Dome—a scandal about payoffs to Secretary of the Interior Albert Fall by a couple of greedy oilmen—was memorable, but involved very few people. The Watergate scandal was bigger and more pernicious than Teapot Dome, but it, too, involved relatively few people: Tricky Dick Nixon, a dozen or two of his henchmen, and a few inept plumbers. Enron was different. By the time of its bankruptcy, Enron owned—or perhaps was just renting—politicians in the White House, Congress, state courts, state legislatures, and bureaucrats at every level.
>
> It's the biggest scandal ever to hit Wall Street. The problems at junk-bond trading house Drexel Burnham Lambert in the 1980s were tiny in comparison to Enron. That scandal involved Michael Milken (who went to jail for securities fraud) and a handful of others. The Enron debacle has ensnared every major investment bank in New York, including Merrill Lynch, Citigroup, J.P. Morgan Chase, UBS, and dozens of others. . . .
>
> Enron is the biggest derivatives-trading firm to go bust since the failure of the hedge fund Long-Term Capital Management in 1998. . . . [Long

---

COLLAPSE OF ENRON AND ITS IMPACT ON PENSIONS AND AUDITING, WITH REPRODUCTIONS OF INTERNAL DOCUMENTS (Progressive Management CD-ROM, 2002); U.S. GOVERNMENT, 21ST CENTURY GUIDE TO ENERGY AND COMMERCE POLICY AND OVERSIGHT; LAWS, LEGISLATION, HEARINGS, HOUSE ENERGY AND COMMERCE COMMITTEE—ENRON, HEALTH CARE, HDTV, TELECOMMUNICATIONS, ENVIRONMENT, HAZARDOUS MATERIALS, TOBACCO INDUSTRY (Core Federal Information Series Progressive Management CD-ROM, 2003); U.S. GOVERNMENT, ENRON'S CREDIT RATING: ENRON'S BANKERS' CONTACTS WITH MOODY'S AND GOVERNMENT OFFICIALS: REPORT (2003); U.S. GOVERNMENT, THE ENRON COLLAPSE AND ITS IMPLICATIONS FOR WORKER RETIREMENT SECURITY: HEARINGS BEFORE THE COMMITTEE ON EDUCATION AND THE WORKFORCE, HOUSE OF REPRESENTATIVES (2002); U.S. GOVERNMENT, THE FINANCIAL COLLAPSE OF ENRON: HEARING BEFORE THE SUBCOMMITTEE ON OVERSIGHT AND INVESTIGATIONS OF THE COMMITTEE ON ENERGY AND COMMERCE, HOUSE OF REPRESENTATIVES (2002); GORDON YALE, ENRON: AN ACCOUNTING ANALYSIS OF HOW SPES WERE USED TO CONCEAL DEBT AND AVOID LOSSES (2002); YANKEE GROUP, BANDWIDTH TRADING AFTER ENRON (2002), *available to download at* http://www.amazon.com; *see also* Frank Partnoy, F.I.A.S.C.O.: Blood in the water on Wall Street (1997); FRANK PARTNOY, F.I.A.S.C.O.: THE INSIDER STORY OF A WALL STREET TRADER (1999); FRANK PARTNOY, GUNS, BOOZE AND BLOODLUST: THE TRUTH ABOUT HIGH FINANCE (1998); FRANK PARTNOY, INFECTIOUS GREED: HOW DECEIT AND RISK CORRUPTED THE FINANCIAL MARKETS (2003).

[37] These books include PIPE DREAMS, *supra* note 11; POWER FAILURE, *supra* note 4; WHAT WENT WRONG, *supra* note 36; RISE AND FALL, *supra* note 36; ANATOMY OF GREED, *supra* note 36; *see also* BARBARA LEYTOFFLER, FINAL ACCOUNTING: AMBITION, GREED, AND THE FALL OF ARTHUR ANDERSEN (2003).

> Term's] positions involved so many banks that the New York Federal Reserve organized a multi-bank, $3.6 billion bailout, lest Long-Term's failure cause a global financial meltdown. And though Long-Term was big, Frank Partnoy, a law professor at the University of San Diego, told Congress in January 2002, that Enron's derivatives business made Long-Term "look like a lemonade stand."[38]

Bryce goes on to note that Enron's collapse also was "the biggest scandal ever to hit accounting,"[39] as well as "the most egregious example of executive piracy in American corporate history."[40]

Ultimately, corporations don't make mistakes—their leaders do. And Enron is more a tale of greed and ego run amuck than it is a tale of why certain business models fail. When the people at the top lose their moral grounding (or, worse yet, if they never had any moral grounding), that's when Enron-sized scandals are likely to occur. Someone at the top has to provide a moral compass for the organization.

Character shapes an organization's culture. It always has, and it always will. For every executive willing to take responsibility for bad decisions[41] or willing to go above and beyond for his employees,[42] there's one who is willing to sacrifice his employees or customers. Take a look at one glimpse into Skilling's character in WHAT WENT WRONG:

> A story from Jeffrey Skilling's HBS [Harvard Business School] student days may provide a telling glimpse into his character. HBS classes are typically conducted using the case method. Most cases are based on real business incidents, and students are presented with the problems that a

---

38 PIPE DREAMS, *supra* note 11, at 5–6 (footnotes omitted).

39 *Id* at 6.

40 *Id* at 7.

41

> "Overall," he tells holders, "you would have been better off last year if I had regularly snuck off to the movies during market hours."... Mr. Buffett says, "Here, I need to make a confession (ugh): The portfolio actions I took in 1998 actually decreased our gain for the year." In particular, he says his decision to sell McDonald's Corp. shares, a process Berkshire began in 1997, has proven to be "a very big mistake." McDonald's shares have risen 82.7% since January 1998.

James P. Miller & Joseph B. Cahill, *Buffett Says Berkshire Would Have Benefited If He Hadn't Made Any Stock Actions in 1998*, WALL ST. J., Mar. 15, 1999, at C2; James P. Miller, *Buffett Offers A Mea Culpa For Bad Year,* WALL ST. J., Mar. 13, 2000, at C1 (" 'Even Inspector Clouseau could find last year's guilty party: your Chairman,' Mr. Buffett told investors in the letter.")

42 *See, e.g.*, Mitchell Pacelle, *Through the Mill: Can Mr Feuerstein Save His Business One Last Time?—Textile Owner Overcame Fire and Changes in Fashion; Creditors May Be Tougher—Needed: $92 Million by July 31st*, WALL ST. J., May 9, 2003, at A1; Carey Goldberg, *A Promise Is Kept: Mill Reopens,* N.Y. TIMES, Sept. 16, 1997, at A14 (congratulating Aaron Feuerstein for keeping his employees on payroll while he rebuilt his burnt-down factory).

> business faced and must come up with solutions for themselves. Discussion of the cases, which helps determine a student's grade, is led by the professor in a pitlike classroom. A forceful student unsure of the facts is quick to be ripped to shreds by other students looking to make their mark. In one such class, Jeffrey Skilling was asked what he would do if his company were producing a product that might cause harm—or even death—to the customers that used it. According to his professor at the time, former Congressman John LeBoutillier, Jeffrey Skilling replied: "I'd keep making and selling the product. My job as a businessman is to be a profit center and to maximize return to the shareholders. It's the government's job to step in if a product is dangerous." In an Enron culture seemingly obsessed with *Star Wars,* Skilling's bloodless demeanor led his colleagues to refer to him as "Darth Vader" behind his back.[43]

Keep in mind that, after Skilling joined Enron, Enron focused on hiring relatively young[44] people who were considered to be the "best and brightest," both in Enron's estimation and in their own.[45] Young people have the relative advantage of cutting- edge training, but they have the relative disadvantage of less experience in a variety of situations. Imagine the pressure on brand-new, inexperienced Enron employees to behave like their leaders:[46] to act like them, to dress like them, to drive the same cars that they do, and to disregard the same social mores that they did.[47] (The pressure to conform to expected "Enron" codes of behavior was

---

43 WHAT WENT WRONG, *supra* note 36, at 28. Skilling was tone-deaf when it came to insensitive comments. One of his legendary comments during the California energy crisis was " 'You know what the difference is between the state of California and the *Titanic*? At least when the *Titanic* went down, the lights were on.' " *Id.* at 112.

44 *See id.* at 50.

45 *See id.* at 43. Contrast Skilling's focus with that of Enron's old guard, represented by Richard Kinder. Kinder's group represented the "old Enron": pipelines that were real assets that made real cash profits. *See* PIPE DREAMS, *supra* note 11, at 123.

46 " 'It *is* just a small group of people . . . but those people were created by the Enron System—a system that also creates hundreds of other sheep who are easily led by others.' " *See* ANATOMY OF GREED, *supra* note 11, at 180.

47 One of Enron's most well-known secrets was its tolerance of sexual escapades, whether adultery, sexual harassment, or just plain poor caste. *See* PIPE DREAMS, *supra* note 11, at 144–48. As Robert Bryce puts it so succinctly, "[f]ish rot at the head. . . . Enron failed because its leadership was morally, ethically, and financially corrupt." *Id.* at 12.

reinforced by Enron's "rank and yank" system of evaluating employees.[48]) The profligate spending at Enron,[49] the self-dealing and selfishness,[50] and the

---

48 "Enron employees were ranked every six months on the same 1-to-5 scale as new recruits; however, 15 percent of all employees were required to be in the lowest category (1), and they were yanked from Enron." WHAT WENT WRONG, *supra* note 36, at 51. For those of you more statistically inclined, imagine that you are selecting your employees from the right-most hand of a bell-shaped curve (the best and the brightest); now take that small group of employees and spread them out over a 1-to-5 scale. What you've done is take people who are roughly the same and use meaningless distinctions to separate them, yanking those on the left-hand side of this second curve out of the organization. Moreover, you're taking the glue of the organization—not the flashy superstars but the reliable team-players—and throwing them out. *See* PIPE DREAMS, *supra* note 11, at 129. Robert Bryce explains it well:

> Although the process was designed to advance the careers of top performers and punish the low performers, it quickly mutated into a numbers game. . . . The people who were rated 1's and 2's were golden. "It was all based on how much money you were able to make," said one source. With millions of dollars at stake in each annual rating, the fights over individual rankings became intense. "It was a pit of vipers. You can't believe how brutal that process could be. You had people attacking other people's integrity, morality, and values. It wasn't about supporting up, it was about tearing down."
>
> . . . .[Most of the benefits of the ranking system went to the deal-makers, not to the administrative staff. And most of the deals were ranked on profits.]
>
> Perhaps most insidious, the [rank and yank] committee gave Enron's Masters of the Universe a baseball bat they could use to intimidate the people who might stop one of their bad deals—and therefore limit their bonuses.

Id at 129–30.

49 Bill Murphy, *The Fall Of Enron; Enron's art hopes just a pipe dream; Buying spree now drawing fire,* HOUS. CHRON., July 29, 2002, at A1 (art committee at Enron Corp. given $20 million budget); Carol Vogel, *Enron's Art to Be Auctioned Off,* N.Y. TIMES, Apr. 16, 2003, at C6; Paula Span, *The Gavel Falls on Enron Artworks; Auction Puts Tiny Dent in Company Debt,* WASH. POST, May 16, 2003, at C1.

50

> [T]he independence and objectivity of the Enron Board had been weakened by financial ties between Enron and certain directors. These financial ties, which affected a majority of the outside Board members, included the following.
>
> —Since 1996, Enron paid a monthly retainer of $6,000 to Lord John Wakeham for consulting services, in addition to his Board compensation. In 2000, Enron paid him $72,000 for his consulting work alone.
>
> —Since 1991, Enron paid Board member John A. Urquhart for consulting services, in addition to his Board compensation. In 2000, Enron paid Mr. Urquhart $493,914 for his consulting work alone.
>
> —Enron Board member Herbert Winokur also served on the Board of the National Tank Company. In 1997, 1998, 1999, and 2000, the National Tank Company recorded revenues of $1,035,000, $643,793, $535,682 and $370,294 from sales to Enron subsidiaries of oilfield equipment and services.
>
> —In the past 5 years Enron and Kenneth Lay donated nearly $600,000 to the M.D. Anderson Cancer Center in Texas. In 1993, the Enron Foundation pledged $1.5 million to the Cancer Center. Two Enron Board members, Dr. LeMaistre and Dr. Mendelsohn, have served as president of the Cancer Center.
>
> —Since 1996, Enron and the Lay Foundation have donated more than $50,000 to the George Mason University and its Mercatus Center in Virginia. Enron Board member Dr. Wendy Gramm is employed by the Mercatus Center.

rudeness[51] all signaled to Enron's employees what sorts of behavior were rewarded. Is it really so hard to figure out why Enron, as an organization, was willing to lie and cheat?

When Enron was flying high, there were some who remained skeptical about all of its claims of greatness and brilliance,[52] During Enron's prominence as one of FORTUNE magazine's "most innovative" companies,[53] it bought, cajoled, and bullied to get what it wanted, from favorable deals to exemptions from rules. Once Enron began its downward slide, all of those over whom Enron had run roughshod enjoyed Enron's comeuppance. The gloves came off: aggrieved employees, customers, and competitors were happy to talk to any and all who asked about how Enron had behaved. Even those who had never spent a millisecond of their time thinking about Enron before the scandal broke came away from all of the stories with a horrible impression of a company that had also, in fact, had some very good business ideas, hired some wonderful people, and given widely to the Houston community.

> —Since 1996, Enron and Belco Oil and Gas have engaged in hedging arrangements worth tens of millions of dollars. In 1997, Belco bought Enron affiliate Coda Energy. Enron Board member Robert Belfer is former Chairman of the Board and CEO of Belco.
>
> —Charles Walker, a noted tax lobbyist, was an Enron Board member from 1985 until 1999. In 1993–1994, Enron paid more than $70,000 to two firms, Walker/Free and Wallter/Potter, that were partly owned by Mr. Walker, for governmental relations and tax consulting services. This sum was in addition to Mr. Walker's Board compensation. Enron was also, for more than 10 years ending in 2001, a major contributor of up to $50,000 annually to the American Council for Capital Formation, a non-profit corporation that lobbies on tax issues and is chaired by Mr. Walker.

PERMANENT SUBCOMMITTEE ON INVESTIGATIONS OF THE COMMITTEE OF GOVERNMENTAL AFFAIRS, THE ROLE OF THE BOARD OF DIRECTORS IN ENRON'S COLLAPSE, S. Rep. No. 107–70, at 51–52 (2002); *see also* PIPE DREAMS, *supra* note 11, at 256–66 (use of corporate jets for private business).

51 On April 17, 2001, analyst Richard Grubman (of Highfields Capital Management) participated on a conference call run by Jeffrey Skilling to discuss Enron's first-quarter results. Grubman pointed out that Enron hadn't

> provide[d] the analysts with more information prior to the conference call . . . [including cash flow statements and balance sheets]. Skilling responded that Enron had never provided those reports before analyst calls. Grubman wasn't satisfied. "You're the only financial institution that can't produce a balance sheet or a cash flow statement with their earnings" prior to conference calls, he said.
>
> "Well, thank you very much," replied Skilling. "We appreciate that. Asshole,"

PIPE DREAMS, *supra* note 11, at 268–69.

52 *See supra* notes 17–45 and accompanying text; *see also* ANATOMY OF GREED, *supra* note 36, at 19 (quoting a research analyst explaining to a friend, and recent Enron hire, that the company had serious financial problems based on a close examination of the company's 2001 Annual Report).

53 "At its zenith, Enron was named the 'most innovative' company in the United States by FORTUNE magazine *every year* between 1996 and 2001." Jeffrey D. Van Niel, *Enron—The Primer,* in NANCY B. RAPOPORT & BALA G. DHARAN, ENRON: CORPORATE FIASCOS & THEIR IMPLICATIONS 11 (2004) (citing WHAT WENT WRONG, *supra* note 36, at 172; Daniel Altman, *Finding Gems of Genius Among Enron's Crumbs,* N.Y. TIMES, Feb. 3, 2002, at D6).

The lesson? Remember that phrase that you learned when you were a kid: the bigger they are, the harder they fall.

NOTES

1. When you add up all of the essays in Chapter 1, you can see how hard it is for companies to innovate while still "coloring inside the lines" of regulation. Is it always the case that true innovation *has* to be linked with a disregard for the letter of the law (or at least the spirit of the law)? What kind of regulatory scheme could you envision that would encourage true innovation while discouraging the type of regulatory game-playing that has, historically, accompanied that innovation?

2. Assume that you are the chair of a board of directors and you are looking for a new CEO. What characteristics would you like that CEO to have? Would you want different characteristics for your CEO depending on the nature of the company's business, or maybe its place in the market? During your interview with aspiring CEO candidates, how would you go about ascertaining that your CEO has the characteristics that you want? Would you ask for a personality test? A psychological profile? Testimonials from business partners or from other companies in the same market?

CHAPTER 2

Enron, Titanic, and The Perfect Storm*

*Nancy B. Rapoport***

> [Former Enron CEO Jeffrey] Skilling offered a hypothesis for what brought Enron down, calling it a "perfect storm" of events.
>
> He speculated that questions raised about the quality of Enron's accounting and about self-dealing caused a loss of confidence in the financial community. That led to Enron's debt being downgraded.
>
> That downgrade, he said he was told by an Enron executive after he left, meant Enron couldn't access several billion dollars of back-up credit lines. A liquidity crunch followed, he said, even though Enron was solvent and highly profitable.
>
> —Laura Goldberg, *Houston Chronicle*[1]

* This piece was originally published at 71 FORDHAM L. REV. 1373 (2003). Reprinted by permission. *Editors' note:* This essay was also included in the first edition of this book, at ENRON: CORPORATE FIASCOS AND THEIR IMPLICATIONS 927 (Nancy B. Rapoport & Bala G. Dharan, eds.) (Foundation Press 2004).

** Dean and Professor of Law at the University of Houston Law Center. All views expressed in this essay are mine alone, and not those of the University of Houston or its faculty, staff, or administration. I want to thank Emily Chan-Nguyen, Kelli Cline, Luddie Collins, Bala Dharan, Patrick Flanagan, Jimmy Halvatzis, Susan Hartman, Michele Hedges, Morris & Shirley Rapoport, Harriet Richman, Jeff Van Niel, and Michelle Wu. I also want to thank the students in my 2002 Seminar on *Special Issues in Ethics:* Sara Alonso Oliver, Justin Berg, Alison Chien, Doug Du Bois, Trevor Fish, Patrick Flanagan (who gets thanked twice, because he was also one of the cite-checkers for this article), Kim Havel, Cathy Helenhouse, Colin Moore, Sandy Oballe, Kevin Powers, Barry Rienstra, Ron Smeberg, and Tiffany Toups.

1 Laura Goldberg, *Did No Wrong, Skilling Says: Defends His Role in Enron Fall*, HOUS. CHRON., Jan. 17, 2002, *available at* https://www.chron.com/business/enron/article/Ex-Enron-CEO-Skilling-defends-his-role-in-fall-2075180.php *see also Good Morning America* (ABC television broadcast, Feb. 7, 2002) ("All eyes will be on former CEO Jeff Skilling. Skilling blames Enron's collapse on an unfortunate collision of events—the perfect storm. Congressional investigators point out he was at Enron's helm at the time."). Of course, now everyone—and I mean everyone—has latched onto this "perfect storm" metaphor. *See, e.g.*, FEDERAL DOCUMENT CLEARING HOUSE, WORLDCOM CEO JOHN SIDGMORE TESTIFIES BEFORE THE U.S. SENATE COMMITTEE ON COMMERCE, SCIENCE AND TRANSPORTATION, July 30, 2002, *available at* 2002 WL 1753183, at *3

> Of course, we now know the extraordinary combination of circumstances that existed at that time which you would not meet again in 100 years; that they should all have existed just on that particular night shows, of course, that everything was against us.
>
> —Second Officer Charles Lightoller, *RMS Titanic*[2]

> I had some misgivings about calling [my book] *The Perfect Storm,* but in the end I decided that the intent was sufficiently clear. I use perfect in the meteorological sense: a storm that could not possibly have been worse.
>
> —Sebastian Junger[3]

Much has been written about the Enron fiasco, from scholarly articles[4] to popular books,[5] and I'm sure that much more will be written about the deals that brought the company down, the arrogance of some of the main players, and the ethical and moral issues that seemed to come to light only after the story broke in

---

(statement of John Sidgmore, CEO, WorldCom) ("Several factors . . . converged to create, I'll use Mr. Legere's words, a kind of perfect storm—and I guarantee you we did not rehearse this—that ripped through the telecommunications industry."); FEDERAL DOCUMENT CLEARING HOUSE, HARMING PATIENT ACCESS TO CARE: THE IMPACT OF EXCESSIVE LITIGATION, July 17, 2002, *available at* 2002 WL 1584492, at *3 (statement of Richard Anderson, CEO, The Doctor's Company) ("The combination of these factors created . . . the perfect storm . . . for medical liability insurers."); FEDERAL DOCUMENT CLEARING HOUSE, HOUSE COMMITTEE ON EDUCATION AND THE WORKFORCE HOLDS A HEARING ON ENRON'S BENEFITS PLAN AND ITS COMPLIANCE WITH LAWS ON EMPLOYER-SPONSORED PENSION PLANS, Feb. 7, 2002, *available at* 2002 WL 203240, at *12 (statement of Teresa Ghilarducci, Associate Professor of Economics, University of Notre Dame) ("The 1990s was the perfect storm for pensions to increase."); FEDERAL DOCUMENT CLEARING HOUSE, U.S. SENATE JUDICIARY COMMITTEE HOLDS HEARING ON ACCOUNTABILITY ISSUES: LESSONS LEARNED FROM ENRON'S FALL, Feb. 6, 2002, *available at* 2002 WL 188865, at *11–12 (statement of Christine Gregoire, Attorney General, Washington State) ("In Washington [State,] we feel like Enron has been the gathering of the perfect storm. First, they gouged our consumers and rate payers with highly questionable power prices last year. And now, sadly, they have defrauded our investors and others across the nation.").

One of the coolest things that can happen to a law professor happened to me after I first published this article in the FORDHAM LAW REVIEW. I sent a copy to Sebastian Junger, author of THE PERFECT STORM. He read it and said that I was correct in my understanding of the "perfect storm" concept. Thank you, Mr. Junger!

2 WALTER LORD, THE NIGHT LIVES ON 47 (1987) [hereinafter THE NIGHT LIVES ON].

3 SEBASTIAN JUNGER, THE PERFECT STORM: A TRUE STORY OF MEN AGAINST THE SEA xiv (1997).

4 *See, e.g.*, Michelle Chan-Fishel, *After Enron: How Accounting and SEC Reform Can Promote Corporate Accountability While Restoring Public Confidence*, 32 ENVTL. L. REP. 10965 (2002); Timothy P. Duane, *Regulation's Rationale: Learning from the California Energy Crisis*, 19 YALE J. ON REG. 471 (2002); Marisa Rogoway, *Recent Developments, Proposed Reforms to the Regulation of 401(k) Plans in the Wake of the Enron Disaster*, 6 J. SMALL & EMERGING BUS. L. 423 (2002); Marissa P. Viccaro, *Can Regulation Fair Disclosure Survive the Aftermath of Enron?*, 40 DUQ. L. REV. 695 (2002).

5 *See, e.g.*, DIRK J. BARREVELD, THE ENRON COLLAPSE: CREATIVE ACCOUNTING, WRONG ECONOMICS OR CRIMINAL ACTS? A LOOK INTO THE ROOT CAUSES OF THE LARGEST BANKRUPTCY IN U.S. HISTORY (2002); ROBERT BRYCE, PIPE DREAMS: GREED, EGO, AND THE DEATH OF ENRON (2002); Loren Fox, Enron: The Rise and Fall (2002); PETER C. FUSARO & ROSS M. MILLER, WHAT WENT WRONG AT ENRON: EVERYONE'S GUIDE TO THE LARGEST BANKRUPTCY IN U.S. HISTORY (2002).

the media.[6] Enron's collapse, along with the failures of such other mega-businesses as WorldCom and Global Crossing,[7] triggered new legislation[8] and introduced such heretofore arcane acronyms as "SPEs" into the general lexicon.[9] The metaphor most used to describe Enron's quick descent into chapter 11 has been the "perfect storm."

That "perfect storm" metaphor irks me no end. I maintain, and this essay is designed to illustrate, that what brought Enron down—at least as far as we know—wasn't a once-in-a-lifetime alignment of elements beyond its control.

---

6 One of the reasons that I'm sure more will be written is that I'm working on such a project: ENRON: CORPORATE FIASCOS & THEIR IMPLICATIONS (with Bala G. Dharan).

7 Take a look at the largest bankruptcies, in terms of approximate stated liabilities, in the past twelve months [2001–02]: WorldCom (7/02 bankruptcy filing) ($43 billion, including $2 billion more in liabilities discovered after the bankruptcy filing); Enron (12/01) ($32 billion); NTL, Inc. (5/02) ($23.4 billion); Adelphia (6/02) ($18.6 billion); Global Crossing (1/02) ($12.4 billion); KMart (1/02) ($10.2 billion). *See* American Bankruptcy Institute, *A Look Inside the Mega-Case,* 10th Annual Southwest Bankruptcy Conference, Sept. 12–15, 2002; Bill Atkinson, *Kmart Files Chapter 11 Bankruptcy; No. 3 Discounter Cites Weak Economy, Tough Competition; 'Couldn't Pay the Bills'; Swift Move Surprises; $2 Billion Loan to Aid Firm's Reorganization*, BALT. SUN, Jan. 23, 2002, at 1A ("The Troy, Mich.-based firm listed $17 billion in assets and $11.3 billion in liabilities. . . . [A]lthough Kmart's bankruptcy is large, it pales in comparison to the largest bankruptcy in history, filed last month by Enron Corp . . . [which] listed $49 billion in assets and $31.2 billion in debts."); Julie Creswell, *Going For Broke; Crash! There Goes Another Company into Bankruptcy. How Did We Get Here? (Long Story.) Are We on the Mend? (Don't Bet on It.),* FORTUNE, Feb. 18, 2002, *available at* 2002 WL 2190302; Lorrie Grant, *Discounter Hopes for Fast Reorganization*, USA TODAY, Jan. 23, 2002, at B02 ("Kmart listed $16.28 billion in assets and $10.34 billion in debts."); Andrew Leckey, *Bankruptcies Leave Investors in the Lurch*, CHI. TRIB., Aug. 27, 2002, *available at* 2002 WL 2689322; Alexandra R. Moses, Chern Yeh Kwok, & Thomas Lee et al., *Retailer Kmart Files for Bankruptcy; Officials Plan to Close Some Stores, Reorganize*, ST. LOUIS POST-DISPATCH, Jan. 23, 2002, at A1 ("[Kmart] has $10.25 billion in debt."); Chris Reidy, *Kmart Tumbles Discount Retail Chain in Record Chap. 11 Filing*, BOSTON GLOBE, Jan. 23, 2002, at C1 ("In its bankruptcy filing, Kmart and its US subsidiaries listed $17 billion in total assets at book value and total liabilities of $11.3 billion as of the quarter ended Oct. 31."); Gary Young, *Major Bankruptcies Filed in New York City*, 228 N.Y. L.J. 5 (Aug. 1, 2002).

8 *See, e.g.*, Sarbanes-Oxley Act of 2002, Pub. L. No. 107–204, 116 Stat. 745, Corporate and Criminal Fraud Accountability Act of 2002, Pub. L. No. 107–204, 116 Stat. 800 (codified at 18 U.S.C. § 1348, 1514A, 1519–20) [hereinafter Sarbanes-Oxley]; *Framework for Enhancing the Quality of Financial Information Through Improvement of Oversight of the Auditing Process,* 67 Fed. Reg. 44964–01 (proposed July 5, 2002) (to be codified at 17 C.F.R. pt. 210, 229).

9 If you don't believe me, just do a search in WESTLAW or LEXIS on "SPEs" and see how many documents you get, especially documents dated after October 2001, when the Enron disaster began to break. A search of major newspaper articles (Westlaw database NPMJ) for the terms "special purpose entity" or "special purpose entities" during the year 1999 yielded zero results. The first article in this database appeared in October 2001 and a search of 2002 now yields over 328 results (as of the second week in October 2002, with more being added daily).

Rather, Enron's demise was a synergistic combination of human errors and hubris: a "*Titanic*"[10] miscalculation, rather than a "perfect storm."[11]

I. Why *Titanic* Is a Better Metaphor for Enron's Eventual Downfall Than Is *The Perfect Storm*

The story of the *Titanic* is well-known. The ship was, at the time of its maiden (and only) transatlantic voyage, the largest in the world, carrying a microcosm of society.[12] The glitterati of the United States and Europe were on board, as were hundreds of immigrants trying to make their way to a new land. The ship was built with watertight compartments that extended from the keel up several decks (some to D Deck and some to E deck); she also had a double bottom for extra protection.[13] She was designed to float with any two consecutive compartments flooded and even with three of the first five compartments (out of sixteen) flooded,[14] thanks to electronic doors that could be closed by a single command.[15] And she was touted as "unsinkable," at least in some press reports.[16]

But sink she did, based upon a series of miscalculations, no single one of which might have proved fatal, but all of which, taken together, doomed the ship. In a chapter of his follow-up book to A NIGHT TO REMEMBER, called THE NIGHT LIVES ON,[17] Walter Lord enumerates the many individual mistakes made that night:

---

10 And, no, it wasn't the Leonardo DiCaprio movie (TITANIC (20th Century Fox 1997)) that first piqued my interest in the ship's history. I've been fascinated by it for probably thirty or so years. Among other things, I'm a member of the Titanic Historical Society, and I probably own virtually every book and movie about the ship. If you're wondering if I'm a bit obsessed with the ship and its tale, you're right. But everyone needs a hobby.

11 I've used the *Titanic* comparison once before. *See, e.g.*, Mike Tolson, *The Fall of Enron/ 'Convenient whipping boy'/Enron Scandal Offers Fodder for Wide Range of Groups Seeking a Symbol for Their Cause*, HOUS. CHRON., Mar. 3, 2002, at 26, *available at* 2002 WL 3245488. Others have also made the comparison between Enron and the *Titanic*. *See* Edward J. Cleary, *Lessons For Lawyers From The Enron Debacle*, BENCH & B. MINN., Apr. 2002, at 16 (footnotes omitted) (quoting George F. Will, *Indignation Over Enron is Just the Beginning*, WASH. POST, Jan. 16, 2002) ("Given that Enron employee pensions were decimated with, as one commentator noted, the employees "locked in steerage like the lower orders on the *Titanic*, and given that many state pension funds were among the casualties, both state and national public officials will be forced to act."); Martha Neil, *Partners at Risk*, 88 A.B.A. J. 44 (Aug. 2002) ("The collapse of Enron might give partners at law firms reason to ponder another epic disaster: the sinking of the *Titanic*.").

12 WALTER LORD, A NIGHT TO REMEMBER 1 (1997) [hereinafter A NIGHT TO REMEMBER].

13 *Id.* at 174–75. She did not, however, have a double hull. *Id.*

14 *Id.* at 26.

15 *Id.* at 8.

16 *Id.* at 175.

17 THE NIGHT LIVES ON, *supra* note 2.

- the calm sea, which meant that the lookouts couldn't see any waves breaking against the bergs;[18]
- the numerous, apparently ignored ice warnings from ships already crossing the Atlantic Ocean that were using the same route as the *Titanic*;[19]
- the lack of any systematic procedure to deliver ice and weather warnings from the Marconi telegraph room to the bridge;[20]
- the fact that the lookouts' binoculars had been lost earlier in the trip;[21]
- the failure of the *Titanic's* officers to urge Captain Smith (or each other) to take a more cautious approach to travel, based on the calm sea and rapidly dropping temperature;[22]
- not enough lifeboats for the number of souls aboard;[23]
- Captain Smith's failure to hold lifeboat drills[24] or to do more than a perfunctory test of the ship's braking speed and maneuverability;[25]
- First Wireless Operator Phillips's famous response to an ice warning from the *Californian* (the ship that, according to some accounts, was closest to the *Titanic* when it sunk), "Shut up, shut up . . . I am working Cape Race";[26]
- the fact that lookout Frederic Fleet spotted the berg too late to stop the ship or otherwise to avoid the berg;[27]
- First Officer Murdoch's decision to port around the berg rather than ramming it head-on, a counterintuitive action that might have saved the ship;[28] and

---

18 *Id.* at 47.

19 *Id.* at 48–53.

20 *Id.* at 53.

21 *Id.* at 60.

22 *Id.* at 53–54.

23 *Id.* at 72–80.

24 A NIGHT TO REMEMBER, *supra* note 12, at 42.

25 THE NIGHT LIVES ON, *supra* note 2, at 56.

26 *Id.* at 58.

27 *Id.* at 59–60.

28 *Id.* at 59.

- the *Californian's* decision not to come to the aid of a vessel in enough obvious distress to fire white distress rockets (apparently visible to the *Californian's* crew) at several intervals.[29]

The list of miscalculations goes on and on.[30] But Walter Lord tells it best:

> Given the competitive pressures of the North Atlantic run, the chances taken, the lack of experience with ships of such immense size, the haphazard procedures of the wireless room, the casualness of the bridge, and the misassessment of what speed was safe, it's remarkable that the *Titanic* steamed for two hours and ten minutes through ice-infested waters without coming to grief any sooner.
>
> "Everything was against us?" The wonder is that she lasted as long as she did.[31]

THE PERFECT STORM, on the other hand, describes a combination of meteorological bad luck and human miscalculation, born less of arrogance than of desperation. Granted, Billy Tyne, captain of the *Andrea Gail,* made a fatal mistake by sailing into the storm,[32] but he did "what ninety percent of us would've done—he battened down the hatches and hung on."[33] Although the signs were clear that bad weather was coming, the sheer magnitude of the storm was far beyond the experience (or imagination) of any of the ship captains in the large area covered by the storm, and each of them had to make a quick decision:

> [The weather bulletin describing Hurricane Grace] reads like an inventory of things fishermen don't want to hear. . . . Every boat in the swordfish fleet receives this information. Albert Johnston, south of the Tail, decides to head northwest into the cold water of the Labrador Current. . . . The rest of the sword fleet stays far to the east, waiting to see what the storm does. They couldn't make it into port in time anyway. The *Contship Holland,* a hundred miles south of Billy, heads straight into the teeth of the thing. Two hundred miles east, . . . the Liberian-registered *Zarah,* also heads for New York. Ray Leonard on the sloop *Sartori* has decided not to head for port; he holds to a southerly course for Bermuda. The *Laurie Dawn 8* keeps plowing out to the fishing grounds and the *Eishin Maru 78,* 150 miles due south of Sable Island,

29 *Id.* at 134–59.

30 And so have I, at some social gatherings, as my very indulgent husband can attest.

31 THE NIGHT LIVES ON, *supra* note 2, at 61.

32 Special thanks to Boyd Henderson for reminding me, at a luncheon, that some human error contributed to the fate of the *Andrea Gail.*

33 Junger, *supra* note 3, at 124 (quoting Captain Tommie Barrie, of the ship *Allison*).

> makes for Halifax harbor to the northeast. Billy can either waste several days trying to get out of the way, or he can stay on-course for home. The fact that he has a hold full of fish, and not enough ice, must figure into his decision.[34]

Billy Tyne's decision proved wrong, and the *Andrea Gail* lost all six hands aboard.[35] *Titanic* lost over 1,500 souls, with only 705 saved.[36] Both events were tragic. But only the *Titanic* can trace the loss of life directly to human arrogance.[37] When I compare the two tragedies in light of Jeffrey Skilling's claim that the fall of Enron was based on factors outside of the company's control—an economic "perfect storm"—I find that Skilling's claim falls flat.

II. How a Failure of Character Can Turn "Perfect Storms" into *Titanic* Mistakes

I'm not going to rehash the mechanics of the various Enron deals here. Others have done a good job of describing the problems with the deals,[38] with the Board's lack of oversight of the deals,[39] and with the general culture of Enron that encouraged aggressive risk-taking and short-term profits.[40] We obviously don't know enough about the deals or the people yet to reach any final conclusions, so

---

34 *Id.*

35 *Id.* at 186.

36 A NIGHT TO REMEMBER, *supra* note 12, at 176.

37 The Golden Age's love of, and faith in, science contributed to the tragedy as well, as some of the miscalculations that Captain Smith made were based on the scientific advances in ship design.

38 *See, e.g.*, William C. Powers, Jr., et al., REPORT OF INVESTIGATION BY THE SPECIAL INVESTIGATIVE COMMITTEE OF THE BOARD OF DIRECTORS OF ENRON CORP., 2002 WL 198018 (CORPSCAN 1980818 (ENRON)) [hereinafter POWERS REPORT]. The Powers Report is also available at http://i.cnn.net/cnn/2002/LAW/02/02/enron.report/powers.report.pdf. There is also a lot of good Congressional testimony on the subject. *See, e.g.*, *FEDERAL DOCUMENT CLEARING HOUSE, STRENGTHENING ACCOUNTING OVERSIGHT: HEARING BEFORE THE SUBCOMM. ON COMMERCE, TRADE AND CONSUMER PROTECTION OF THE HOUSE COMM. ON ENERGY AND COMMERCE*, June 26, 2002, *available at* 2002 WL 1381127 (statement of Bala G. Dharan, J. Howard Creekmore Professor of Management, Rice University); FEDERAL DOCUMENT CLEARING HOUSE, U.S. SENATE GOVERNMENTAL AFFAIRS COMMITTEE HOLDS A HEARING ON THE COLLAPSE OF HOUSTON-BASED ENRON CORPORATION, Jan. 24, 2002, available at 2002 WL 93421 (statement of John Langbein, Professor of Law, Yale Law School); FEDERAL DOCUMENT CLEARING HOUSE, DEREGULATING CAPITAL MARKETS, OUTLINE OF THE TESTIMONY OF PROFESSOR JOHN C. COFFEE, JR., BEFORE THE SUBCOMMITTEE ON TELECOMMUNICATIONS AND FINANCE OF THE HOUSE COMMERCE COMMITTEE, Nov. 14, 2002, *available at* 2002 WL 1381127 (statement of John C. Coffee, Jr., Columbia University).

39 *See* SENATE PERMANENT SUBCOMMITTEE ON INVESTIGATIONS OF THE COMMITTEE ON GOVERNMENTAL AFFAIRS, 107TH CONG., THE ROLE OF THE BOARD OF DIRECTORS IN ENRON'S COLLAPSE, July 8, 2002, *available at* http://www.access.gpo.gov/congress/senate/senate12lp107.html [hereinafter SENATE PRINT].

40 *See, e.g.*, Tom Fowler, *The Pride and the Fall of Enron*, HOUS. CHRON., Oct. 20, 2002, at A25 [hereinafter *The Pride and the Fall*] ("[One manager, told that a deal would take a year, said,] 'I haven't got a year. If I can't do it in three months I won't do it because my bonus depends on it' " since "bonuses were based on the total value of the deal, not the cash it brought in."); Greg Hassell, *The Fall of Enron/The Culture/Pressure Cooker Finally Exploded*, HOUS. CHRON., Dec. 9, 2001, at 1.

my comments are going to concentrate on one theme—character. If we are to believe that there is a single root cause of the Enron mess (an arguable point at best in such a complicated situation), failure of character gets my nomination.

Character and leadership are inextricably linked.[41] When the leaders are engaging in self-dealing and side deals,[42] and the supervisors of those leaders are also engaging in side deals,[43] and the gatekeepers are approving those side deals,[44] what should the rank and file be thinking? Given the magnitude of the potentially illegal profits made by CFO Andrew Fastow and CEO Jeffrey Skilling,[45] and the sense of entitlement that Enron encouraged,[46] it must have taken significant strength of character to resist getting on that gravy train. And yet, several people did resist. Who resisted, and why?

By now, those following the Enron case know that Sherron Watkins tried to alert CEO Kenneth Lay to serious concerns that she had about Enron's deals:

> Shortly after Enron announced Skilling's unexpected resignation on August 14, 2001, Watkins sent a one-page anonymous letter to Lay. The letter stated that "Enron has been very aggressive in its accounting—most notably the Raptor transactions." The letter raised serious questions concerning the accounting treatment and economic substance of the Raptor transactions (and transactions between Enron and

---

41 Mary C. Daly, *Panel Discussion on Enron: What Went Wrong?*, 8 FORDHAM J. CORP. & FIN. L. 1, S28 (2002) ("What the literature teaches is that the ethical behavior is taught from the top down . . .. It is management's commitment to ethical standards that sets the tone.").

42 The self-dealing by former Enron CFO Andrew Fastow was, apparently, approved by Enron's Board of Directors when the Board waived its ethics rules (more than once) to allow Fastow to head two partnerships that would be negotiating with Enron. *See, e.g.*, Letter from Max Hendrick, III, Vinson & Elkins, to James V. Derrick, Jr., Enron [Re: Preliminary Investigation of Allegations of an Anonymous Employee] (Oct. 15, 2001), *available at* 2001 WL 1764266 (CORPSCAN); *see also* SENATE PRINT, *supra* note 39, at 23–24; POWERS REPORT, *supra* note 38, at *68–71.

43 The Enron Board apparently had several directors who also had consulting agreements with Enron, enabling a form of double-dipping. *See* SENATE PRINT, *supra* note 39, at 51–55.

44 *See* POWERS REPORT, *supra* note 38, at *10 ("There was an absence of forceful and effective oversight by Senior Enron Management and in-house counsel, and objective and critical professional advice by outside counsel at Vinson & Elkins, or auditors at Andersen.").

45 *Fastow Charged With Fraud, Conspiracy in Enron Case*, WASH. POST, Oct. 3, 2002, at A01; April Witt & Peter Behr, *Dream Job Turns Into a Nightmare; Skilling's Success Came at High Price*, WASH. POST, July 29, 2002, at A01; *see also* SENATE PRINT, *supra* note 39, at 24, 34–36; POWERS REPORT, *supra* note 38, at *3, 10.

46 Enron employees who mastered the art of trading and deal-making could earn fantastic sums. Annual bonuses were as high as $1 million. Shortly after each bonus time, a new crop of silver Porsches—the most favored status symbol at Enron—would appear in the company garage. "I remember one trader going crazy because his bonus was only $500,000. He was cursing and screaming and throwing things at his desk," one former Enron employee recalls. "He thought because he was so brilliant, they should be paying him a lot more."

Hassell, *supra* note 40, at 1.

> Condor Trust, a subsidiary of Whitewing Associates), identifying several of the matters discussed in this Report. It concluded that "I am incredibly nervous that we will implode in a wave of accounting scandals." Lay told us that he viewed the letter as thoughtfully written and alarming.[47]

Watkins later told Lay that she had written the letter and met with him regarding her concerns.[48] Lay referred the matter to Enron's General Counsel, James Derrick, a former Vinson & Elkins partner.[49] Derrick in turn asked Vinson & Elkins, one of Enron's key outside law firms, to conduct a preliminary review of the situation—but not to review the underlying transactions that Watkins had discussed in her letter.[50] Within the confines of Derrick's request, Vinson & Elkins conducted an investigation (interviewing Watkins, among others).

V&E concluded that "none of the individuals interviewed could identify any transaction between Enron and LJM that was not reasonable from Enron's standpoint or that was contrary to Enron's best interests." On the accounting

---

47 POWERS REPORT, *supra* note 38, at 79. Note the new standards of behavior imposed on company attorneys by Sarbanes-Oxley:

> Not later than 180 days after the date of enactment of this Act, the Commission shall issue rules, in the public interest and for the protection of investors, setting forth minimum standards of professional conduct for attorneys appearing and practicing before the Commission in any way in the representation of issuers, including a rule—
>
> (1) requiring an attorney to report evidence of a material violation of securities law or breach of fiduciary duty or similar violation by the company or any agent thereof, to the chief legal counsel or the chief executive officer of the company (or the equivalent thereof); and
>
> (2) if the counsel or officer does not appropriately respond to the evidence (adopting, as necessary, appropriate remedial measures or sanctions with respect to the violation), requiring the attorney to report the evidence to the audit committee of the board of directors of the issuer or to another committee of the board of directors comprised solely of directors not employed directly or indirectly by the issuer, or to the board of directors.

Sarbanes-Oxley Act of 2002 § 307, 15 USC § 7245 (West Supp. 2002). After a whole slew of parties filed objections to the SEC's Proposed Rule regarding attorney conduct (with many of the objections focused on the "noisy withdrawal" provisions of the Proposed Rule, *see* http://www.sec.gov/rules/proposed/s74502.shtml), the SEC apparently abandoned the "noisy withdrawal" provision in its final rule, *see* http://www.sec.gov/news/press/2003-13.htm. As of this writing, I have only seen the press release regarding the final rule, not the actual text of the rule.

The days of taking an issue only partially up the chain of command are over, at least for publicly traded companies. But haven't lawyers always had the responsibility of taking matters all the way up the chain of command? *See* MODEL RULES OF PROF'L CONDUCT R. 1.13 (2002). I wonder whether Ms. Watkins, as an accountant, had a similar duty under her profession's ethics rules. If she did have such a duty, and she didn't go all the way to the Board of Directors (and beyond) with her concerns, was she really a whistleblower? (Mind you, what she did took some guts, even though she was not a whistleblower in the true sense.)

48 POWERS REPORT, *supra* note 38, at 79.

49 *See* Ellen Joan Pollock, *Anderson: Called to Account: Enron Lawyers Face Congress Over Their Role*, WALL ST. J., Mar. 15, 2002, at C13 (noting that Derrick used to be a partner at Vinson & Elkins).

50 POWERS REPORT, *supra* note 38, at 79.

issues, V&E said that both Enron and Andersen acknowledge[d] "that the accounting treatment on the Condor/Whitewing and Raptor transactions is creative and aggressive, but no one has reason to believe that it is inappropriate from a technical standpoint." V&E concluded that the facts revealed in its preliminary investigation did not warrant a "further widespread investigation by independent counsel or auditors," although the firm did note that the "bad cosmetics" of the Raptor related-party transactions, coupled with the poor performance of the assets placed in the Raptor vehicles, created "a serious risk of adverse publicity and litigation."[51]

One observation: Vinson & Elkins's undertaking of the investigation had certain restrictions, including Enron's request not to review the bona fides of the underlying transactions.[52] We don't know what sort of give and take occurred between Enron and Vinson & Elkins about the usefulness of such a request.[53] At some point, thanks to the ability of Enron's chapter 11 management to waive the attorney-client privilege,[54] we may learn more. But I have to admit, right off the

---

51 *Id.* at *80.

52 *Id.* at *79. "The result of the V&E review was largely predetermined by the scope and nature of the investigation and the process employed . . . The scope and process of the investigation appear to have been structured with less skepticism than was needed to see through these particularly complex transactions." *Id.* at *81 (footnote omitted).

53 Jordan Mintz, Enron Global Finance's General Counsel, has stated that Vinson & Elkins "fulfilled its professional duties" in terms of the advice it gave to Enron. Laura Goldberg, *Enron's Words as Relevant as Deeds/Reports May Have Told Partial Truths*, HOUS. CHRON., Feb. 11, 2002, at 1. Because of Vinson & Elkins's ties to Enron's General Counsel James Derrick, though, Mintz hired a separate firm, Fried, Frank, Harris, Shriver & Jacobson, to review the deals of which Watkins had complained. Rone Tempest, *Enron Counsel Warned About Partnerships Probe: Company's Legal Executive Asked Opinion of Law Firm in April. Congressional Investigators Say It Was to 'Halt This Practice,'* L.A. TIMES, Jan. 31, 2002, at C1. I'm not yet ready to get on the bandwagon that denounces all of Enron's lawyers.

54 The principal case involving privilege in the bankruptcy context is, of course, Commodity Futures Trading Commission v. Weintraub, 471 U.S. 343, 358 (1985) ("[W]e hold that the trustee of a corporation in [a chapter 7] bankruptcy has the power to waive the corporation's attorney-client privilege with respect to pre-bankruptcy communications."). *Weintraub* answered the question of how much control a chapter 7 trustee had over the corporation's attorney-client privilege. *Id.* Subsequent cases have answered the question about how far the *Weintraub* holding could go in a chapter 11 context. *See, e.g.*, Am. Metrocomm Corp. v. Duane Morris & Heckscher LLP, 274 B.R. 641, 654–56 (Bankr. D. Dela. 2002) (stating that debtor-in-possession controls attorney-client privilege, and debtor-in-possession can request documents from attorneys even if attorneys raise work product privilege as a defense); *In re* Bame, 251 B.R. 367, 370, 374 (Bankr. D. Minn. 2000) (converting chapter 11 case to chapter 7 case; holding that chapter 7 trustee can access the post-petition, pre-conversion communications between the debtor-in-possession and its lawyers because the privilege is held by the estate, and not by the debtor-in-possession); Whyte v. Williams (In re Williams), 152 B.R. 123, 129 (Bankr. N.D. Tex. 1992) ("The liquidating trustee [under a confirmed chapter 11 plan] controls the power to waive or invoke the evidentiary privileges that arise in connection with the causes of action transferred to the liquidating trust under Article 25.5 of the confirmed plan."); *see also* S. Air Transp., Inc. v. SAT Group, Inc., 255 B.R. 706, 711 (Bankr. S.D. Ohio 2000) (citations omitted).

> The Court agrees that a corporate fiduciary is precluded from asserting privileges to protect his own interests that are adverse to those of the corporation. Corporate officers must "exercise the privilege

bat, that I have a hard time believing that Vinson & Elkins, or any of Enron's other law firms, knowingly advised Enron to do anything that was clearly illegal. The real issue is how Enron handled the grey areas of the law, based on the advice of all of its lawyers (both its in-house and outside counsel).

Watkins wasn't the lone voice questioning Enron's deals; others, including Enron Global Finance's General Counsel Jordan Mintz, were concerned about the structure and disclosure of the various deals.[55] Apparently, Fastow and Skilling didn't brook disagreement willingly. Those who objected often found themselves the subject of pressure, downright abuse, and exile.[56]

I'd like to put forward one striking similarity between the *Titanic* and Enron: a failure of meaningful communication stemming from a belief that someone else had "taken care of it." Here's how a recent newspaper article described the problem:

> in a manner consistent with their fiduciary capacity to act in the best interests of the corporation and not of themselves individually."

Id. The interesting part about the privilege issue in the Enron bankruptcy context is whether Steve Cooper (the restructuring expert currently running Enron) is going to waive the privilege in order to get information from the various law firms that represented Enron and then, if the information gives rise to a cause of action against any of Enron's lawyers, use that very information to pursue them in bankruptcy court. Mr. Cooper can also pursue Enron's officers and directors using that privileged information, as the privilege belongs to the client (Enron) and not to any of the client's employees. I've been following the work of the Severed Enron Employees Coalition in the pursuit of the prepetition bonuses paid to certain Enron executives on the theory that the bonuses were fraudulent conveyances. Severed Enron Employees Coalition v. N. Trust Co., No. 02-0267 (S.D. Tex. complaint, filed Jan. 24, 2002). Any privileged advice, on the order of "Should we pay this person a retention bonus? What will we get in terms of a benefit for the retention bonus?," could be helpful in this regard.

55 *See, e.g.*, SENATE PRINT, *supra* note 39, at 28 n.81 (quoting an internal memorandum from Mintz):

> [T]he Company needs to improve both the process it follows in executing such transactions and implement improved procedures regarding written substantiation supporting and memorializing the Enron/LJM transactions . . . . [F]irst is the need for the Company to implement a more active and systematic effort in pursuing non-LJM sales alternatives before approaching LJM . . .; the second is to . . . impose a more rigorous testing of the fairness and benefits realized by Enron in transacting with LJM.

Id.; *see also* Dan Feldstein, *Skilling Says He Did No Wrong/Lawyer Told Not to Stick Neck Out*, HOUS. CHRON., Feb. 8, 2002, at 1 (describing how Fastow tried to bully Mintz into blessing irregularities in certain Enron deals).

56 *See, e.g.*, *The Pride and the Fall*, *supra* note 40, at 27A (listing three people—Andersen partner Carl Bass, former Enron CFO (after Fastow) Jeff McMahon, and former Merrill Lynch analyst John Olson—who were demoted (Olson was fired) after criticizing the aggressive Enron deals and accounting methods); *see also* Editorial Desk, *Not Quite a Whistle-Blower*, N.Y. TIMES, Feb. 15, 2002, at A20; Andy Geller, *"I Believe Mr. Skilling and Mr. Fastow Duped Mr. Lay"—Enron VP Rips Duo Before Congress*, N.Y. POST, Feb. 15, 2002, at 9; Susan Schmidt, *CEO Was 'Misserved' At Enron, Hill Told; Former Executive Blames Other Top Managers*, WASH. POST, Feb. 15, 2002, at A01; Peter Spiegel, *The Architect of Enron's Downfall: Internal Probe Reveals Andy Fastow as a CFO who Bullied Staff and Even Wall Street Banks, Enriching Himself by More than Dollars 45m in the Process*, FIN. TIMES, May 21, 2002, at A20.

> [S]ince most only saw their part of the business, they assumed the problems were isolated. . . . "You understood your piece of the business and maybe what the guy next to you did, but very few understood the big picture. . . . That segmentation allowed us to get work done very quickly, but it isolated that institutional knowledge into the hands of very few people."[57]

Certainly, the Powers Report describes the failure of follow-through regarding several of the Enron deals—the failure to ascertain if the checks and balances, supposedly part of each deal's structure, were in place and working.[58] As John Coffee explains,

> Enron . . . furnish[es] ample evidence of a systematic governance failure. Although other spectacular securities frauds have been discovered from time to time over recent decades, they have not generally disturbed the overall market. In contrast, Enron has clearly roiled the market and created a new investor demand for transparency. Behind this disruption lies the market's discovery that it cannot rely upon the professional gatekeepers—auditors, analysts, and others—whom the market has long trusted to filter, verify and assess complicated financial information. Properly understood, Enron is a demonstration of gatekeeper failure, and the question it most sharply poses is how this failure should be rectified.[59]

Failures of gatekeeper professionals aren't new. The savings and loan crisis, which also represented a significant gatekeeper failure, occurred a mere twenty years ago;[60] the Salomon Brothers Treasury bonds trading scandal occurred just ten years ago.[61]

---

[57] *See, e.g.*, *The Pride and the Fall*, *supra* note 40, at 27A. Remember that those "very few people" included members of the Board of Directors, which waived Enron's ethics rules more than once to allow self-dealing by some of Enron's executives. *See supra* note 42.

[58] *See* POWERS REPORT, *supra* note 38, at *18–28.

[59] John C. Coffee, Jr., *Understanding Enron: It's About the Gatekeepers, Stupid*, 57 BUS. LAW. 1403 (2002) (footnote omitted).

[60] Now that I wear bifocals, twenty years just doesn't seem that long ago. *Editors' note:* No more bifocals, but LASIK doesn't take away years of living—just some myopia.

[61] Daly, *supra* note 41, at S25–S28; FEDERAL DOCUMENT CLEARING HOUSE, U.S. SENATE COMMITTEE ON COMMERCE, SCIENCE AND TRANSPORTATION HOLDS A HEARING ON ENRON BANKRUPTCY, Dec. 18, 2001, *available at* 2001 WL 1623334 (statement of John Coffee, Columbia University) ("Well, when a debacle like Enron occurs, the critical question for Congress and for regulators is to ask, as you've been beginning to ask, where were the gatekeepers; where were the watchdogs? . . . Here, all failed, and all failed fairly abysmally.").

> The fallout from [the savings and loan] scandal included a Justice Department action against the prestigious New York firm of Kaye, Scholer, Fierman, Hays & Handler. Kaye, Scholer and

It's certainly possible that many of the legal and accounting professionals (the in-house and the outside professionals) who advised Enron assumed that Enron's own businesspeople were doing the follow-through; moreover, many of those same professionals may well have thought that it was not the lawyers' or accountants' "place" to bill Enron for continued checks of the system. (I know nothing about the training of accountants, so I'm going to limit the rest of this discussion to the training of lawyers.) If the lawyers saw themselves as morally independent from Enron, rather than morally interdependent, then they might well have believed that it was Enron's job, not theirs, to ensure follow-through. A more complex explanation is that cognitive dissonance—well-documented in social science literature and applied to lawyers by, among others, David Luban—prevented the lawyers from seeing some of these deals more clearly. My hunch is that both concepts (a mistaken belief in moral independence, rather than interdependence, and the effects of cognitive dissonance) played a part in any failures by the gatekeepers.

A. "Moral Independence" Versus "Moral Interdependence" as an Explanation

For the longest time, lawyers have done everything they could to distinguish the client's ends from the means that the lawyers used to achieve those ends. This "moral independence" theory has been used to justify everything from lawyers who take on unpopular causes to lawyers who facilitate shady deals, even though the original theory was never intended to justify shady deals.[62]

> partner Peter Fishbein were said to have gone beyond mere aggressive lawyering, and more than one observer viewed their representation as akin to aiding and abetting, while others attributed any errors to simple inattentiveness. Ultimately, the case was settled, with the firm and its malpractice carrier paying $41 million in settlement, and the Keating lawyers paid for their alleged sins, notwithstanding their ability to spread the loss to other lawyers via malpractice insurance coverage.

Jeffrey W. Stempel, *Embracing Descent: The Bankruptcy of a Business Paradigm for Conceptualizing and Regulating the Legal Profession*, 27 FLA. ST. U. L. REV. 25, 111–12 (1999) (footnotes omitted). For a wonderful discussion of the Kaye, Scholer firm and the savings and loan crisis, see David B. Wilkins, *Making Context Count: Regulating Lawyers After Kaye, Scholer*, 66 S. CAL. L. REV. 1147 (1993). As Clarence Darrow apparently said, "History repeats itself, and that's one of the things that's wrong with history." The Quotations Home Page, *available at* http://www.geocities.com/~spanoudi/topic-h3.html#history.

62 According to a study by Erwin Smigel, lawyers'

> independence derived from two sources. First, "they . . . 'represent' the law and must therefore separate themselves from the client." Second, the commodity they sold was "[i]ndependent legal opinion." Smigel observed that "client[s] desire that a firm maintain its autonomy" so that they can obtain the best advice. Moreover, as the large firms grew older, they increased their number of clients and moved away from fundamentally relying on one or a few clients. This shift "strengthened . . . a firm's ability to retain its independence" because "no one client provid[es] enough income to materially or consciously influence the law office's legal opinion."

Russell G. Pearce, *Lawyers as America's Governing Class: The Formation and Dissolution of the Original Understanding of the American Lawyer's Role*, 8 U. CHI. L. SCH. ROUNDTABLE 381, 406 (2001) (footnotes omitted) [hereinafter

Several scholars have recognized, though, that the complexity of modern legal practice forces lawyers to take a more active role in shaping not just the clients' advice but the clients' deals and litigation as well.[63] Richard Painter's "moral interdependence" theory of the lawyer-client interaction is a more realistic view of the lawyer's modern role, especially when it comes to complex transactions or complex litigation.[64]

When you overlay the lawyer's moral interdependence on top of a cutthroat culture, you get Enron (and WorldCom, and Tyco, etc.). We still don't know a lot of the facts behind Enron's various deals, including what the various lawyers said, Enron's response to that advice, or how much the accountants' advice contradicted (or supported) the lawyers' advice. But we do know that the structure of Enron itself encouraged a constant pushing of the outside of the envelope.[65] Enron encouraged a "me, first" structure, not a cooperative one.

> "Enron sought to redefine the rules of the industry," said Robert Bruner, a professor at the University of Virginia who has made a case study of Enron's culture. "It was a culture of challenge and confrontation."
>
> . . . .

Governing Class] (quoting ERWIN O. SMIGEL, THE WALL STREET LAWYER: PROFESSIONAL ORGANIZATION MAN? (1964)).

The fun part about the history of the bar's independence theory is its link with the robber barons of yesteryear. *See, e.g.*, Thomas L. Shaffer, *The Profession as a Moral Teacher*, 18 ST. MARY'S L.J. 195, 222–23 (1986) [hereinafter *Moral Teacher*]; Thomas L. Shaffer, *The Unique, Novel, and Unsound Adversary Ethic*, 41 VAND. L. REV. 697, 703–04 (1988). As Russell Pearce points out,

> In becoming hired guns, elite lawyers abandoned the traditional governing class ideology. They were no longer acting as a disinterested political leadership capable of discerning and pursuing the common good. Instead, they were advocates of private interests. They had violated professionalism's taboo on acting as a servant of big business and could no longer claim the special tie to the public good which distinguished them from those in business.

Pearce, *Governing Class*, *supra*, at 400–10.

[63] Richard W. Painter, *The Moral Interdependence of Corporate Lawyers and Their Clients*, 67 S. CAL. L. REV. 507, 511, 544–45 (1994); *see also id.* at 526 ("Joint decisionmaking by lawyer and client has become both efficient and prudent.") (footnote omitted).

[64] For example, the Powers Report points out that, with respect to preparing the various disclosure forms that Enron filed, "[w]hile accountants took the lead in preparing the financial statement footnote disclosures, lawyers played a more central role in preparing the proxy statements, including the disclosures of the related-party transactions." POWERS REPORT, *supra* note 38, at 84. This interdependence is by no means limited to the lawyers who worked on Enron's deals. *See Governing Class*, *supra* note 62, at 408–09 (citing Robert A. Kagan and Robert Eli Rosen, *On the Social Significance of Large Law Firm Practice*, 37 STAN. L. REV. 399 (1985) and Robert L. Nelson, *Ideology, Practice, and Professional Autonomy: Social Values and Client Relationships in the Large Law Firm*, 37 STAN. L. REV. 503 (1985)). Both the Kagan & Rosen study and the Nelson study are well worth reading.

[65] I first saw this phrase in TOM WOLFE, THE RIGHT STUFF 12 (1979).

> [Former CEO Jeffrey] Skilling also is responsible, many insiders say, for creating a mercenary, cutthroat culture to stoke the fires beneath the enterprise. One of the hallmarks of the Skilling regime was a performance review process that employees called "rank and yank." The evaluations compared the performance of employees against one another, with the bottom 15 percent getting axed every year.
>
> The evaluations were done by asking employees to judge others' performance. They did so knowing their own promotions and survival hung in the balance.
>
> "Because of that, you never helped one another," said one former Enron employee. "Everyone was in it for themselves. People stabbed you in the back."
>
> Teamwork, once a source of strength, started to disappear.
>
> "It was every man for himself," a former Enron executive said.
>
> What sense of teamwork survived "rank and yank" was undermined by Enron's reward system, which seemed to place no value on group goals but lavishly rewarded individual accomplishment. An employee who could close big deals got big bonuses and promotions. Those who couldn't were shown the door.[66]

Let's take this moral interdependence theory one step further. Add to the theory (1) Enron's culture, and (2) the personality traits of a large number of lawyers (whether or not they ever had Enron as a client), and you have a disaster just waiting to happen. Susan Daicoff has summarized the literature on lawyers' personality traits quite nicely in a series of articles.[67] Lawyers tend to have certain personality characteristics that contribute to their need to "win." They "appear to be more competitive, aggressive, and achievement-oriented, and overwhelmingly Thinkers (instead of Feelers). . . . Lawyers are more often motivated by a need for achievement than are others, which includes a need to compete against an internal or external standard of intelligence."[68] No matter which way you slice it, these

66 Hassell, *supra* note 40. For a masterful compendium of the theories surrounding community norms in monitoring and shaping the roles of lawyers, see W. Bradley Wendel, *Nonlegal Regulation of the Legal Profession: Social Norms in Professional Communities*, 54 VAND. L. REV. 1955 (2001) [hereinafter *Social Norms*].

67 *See, e.g.*, Susan Daicoff, *Lawyer, Know Thyself: A Review of Empirical Research on Attorney Attributes Bearing on Professionalism*, 46 AM. U. L. REV. 1337 (1997) [hereinafter *Know Thyself*]; Susan Daicoff, *(Oxymoron?) Ethical Decisionmaking by Attorneys: An Empirical Study*, 48 FLA. L. REV. 197, 217–18 (1996).

68 *Know Thyself*, *supra* note 67, at 1408–09 (footnotes omitted). According to Daicoff, law students come into law school hard-wired with these traits. *Id.* at 1349–50. Imagine my relief at knowing that law school didn't "ruin" them.

gatekeepers were too closely involved with their client[69] to be able to stand up and say, "You shouldn't do that." At some point, we need lawyers to say, "The law lets you do it, but don't. . . . It's a rotten thing to do."[70]

B. Cognitive Dissonance as an Explanation

Even if the gatekeepers weren't so closely involved with the client, there's yet another reason for their failure to protest the deals that were on (or over) the edge: cognitive dissonance. My sociologist friends[71] tell me that moral development alone—which is an individual trait—can't explain how an individual will react to a particular situation.[72] The situation itself will interact with the traits of the individual, and both the person's individual traits and his situation will affect an outcome.[73]

Peer pressure is one such particular influence. There are some well-regarded studies showing that even relatively obvious physical conclusions, such as the distance from one point to another or the length of a line, can become subject to "groupthink," placing peer pressure on the unbelieving minority to conform to the wrong-headed thinking of the majority.[74] And if hard-wired concepts, such as size and location, are manipulable by the particulars of the situation, what about the fuzzier concept of behavior?

Stanley Milgram's studies on the willingness of experimental subjects to inflict pain (electrical shocks) on complete strangers can give us a glimpse into how powerful the effect of a particular situation can be. In Milgram's best-known

---

69 *See, e.g.*, *supra* notes 49–50 and accompanying text.

70 Sol M. Linowitz, *Moment of Truth for the Legal Profession,* Address at the University of Wisconsin Law School (Oct. 24, 1997), *in* 1997 WIS. L. REV. 1211, 1214–15 ("I believe Elihu Root once again had it exactly right when he told a client: "The law let[s] you do it, but don't . . . . It's a rotten thing to do.").

71 Special thanks go to Julia McQuillan, who guided me through the literature and theories in her field.

72 *Cf.* Julia McQuillan & Julie Pfeiffer, *Why Anne Makes us Dizzy: Reading Anne of Green Gables from a Gender Perspective*, 16 MOSAIC 34/2, June 2001, at 19 ("In an attempt to explain variation within sex categories, sociologists have argued that external social structures (our actual experiences in the world) organize our behavior more than socialization (how we've been told to behave).").

73 The thought that moral development alone can predict a person's behavior without regard to the particular situation is called the "fundamental attribution error." *See* David J. Luban, *The Ethics of Wrongful Obedience, in* ETHICS IN PRACTICE: LAWYERS' ROLES, RESPONSIBILITIES, AND REGULATION 94, 101 (Deborah L. Rhode ed., 2000) [hereinafter *Wrongful Obedience*]; *see also* Lee M. Johnson, et al., *General Versus Specific Victim Blaming,* 142 J. OF SOC. PSYCHOL. 249 (Apr. 2002) ("The fundamental attribution error occurs when individuals overemphasize personal attributes and discount environmental attributes in their judgments of others"); Lee Ross, *The Intuitive Psychologist and His Shortcomings: Distortions in the Attribution Process,* in 10 ADVANCES IN EXPERIMENTAL SOCIAL PSYCH. 173 (Leonard Berkowitz ed., 1977); *see generally* DAVID C. FUNDER, PERSONALITY JUDGMENT: A REALISTIC APPROACH TO PERSONAL PERCEPTION (1999).

74 LEE ROSS & RICHARD E. NISBETT, THE PERSON AND THE SITUATIONS: PERSPECTIVES OF SOCIAL PSYCHOLOGY 30 (1991) ("Our most basic perceptions and judgments about the world are socially conditioned and dictated.") (citing Sherif's "autokinetic effect" studies and Asch's "comparison lines" studies).

study, the actual subject was asked to give a series of progressively more severe shocks to someone who was posing as a fellow experimental subject. Although the actual subject usually agonized about administering the shocks, he went ahead and administered them nonetheless.[75]

In analyzing Milgram's experiment, Lee Ross and Richard Nisbett concluded that the powerful structure of the situation—the authority figure setup; the calm tones of the experimenter standing next to the subject who was administrating the shocks; the experimenter's repetition of the phrases, "The experiment requires that you continue; you have no choice"—served to overcome the subjects' expressed desire to stop the experiment before reaching the "severe shock" stage.[76] Most of the subjects were stymied by uncertainty and couldn't overcome the social pressure of the situation. It's not that the subjects were sadists. But the structure of the situation prevented them from acting on their own reluctance to continue the shocks.

David Luban has also described the Milgram experiment and has pointed out that almost two-thirds of the subjects in Milgram's experiments actually did go all the way to 450 volts.[77] He posits that a "corruption of judgment" stemming from cognitive dissonance caused two-thirds of the subjects of Milgram's experiments to "kill" the learner:

> [T]he key to understanding Milgram compliance lies in features of the experimental situation. . . . The teacher moves up the scale of shocks by 15-volt increments, and reaches the 450-volt level only at the thirtieth shock. Among other things, this means that the subjects never confront the question "Should I administer a 330-volt shock to the learner?" The question is "Should I administer a 330-volt shock to the learner given that I've just administered a 315-volt shock?" It seems clear that the latter question is much harder to answer. . . .
>
> Cognitive dissonance theory teaches that when our actions conflict with our self-concept, our beliefs and attitudes change until the conflict is removed. . . . Cognitive dissonance theory suggests that when I have given the learner a series of electrical shocks, I simply won't view giving

75 *Id.* at 56–57.

76 One of Milgram's later variations on the study involved changing the setting from Yale to an inner-city, run-down, suspicious-looking lab in another town. He recorded approximately the same results, no matter the setting. *See id.* at 55.

77 *Wrongful Obedience*, *supra* note 73, at 97 ("In reality, 63 percent of subjects complied all the way to 450 volts. Moreover, this is a robust result: it holds in groups of women as well as men, and experimenters obtained comparable results in Holland, Spain, Italy, Australia, South Africa, Germany, and Jordan. . . .") (footnote omitted).

the next shock as a wrongful act, because I won't admit to myself that the previous shocks were wrong.[78]

Luban's most important point is that lawyers aren't immune to the effects of cognitive dissonance. He does a masterful job of linking the *Berkey Photo-Inc. v. Eastman Kodak Co.*[79] case and Stanley Milgram's experiments on obedience to explain how very well-intentioned lawyers can find themselves slipping into serious breaches of ethics. For those who aren't familiar with this case, Brad Wendel describes it nicely:

> The lawyers representing Kodak had retained an economist as an expert witness, expecting that he would testify that Kodak's domination of the market was due to its superior technological innovations, not to anticompetitive behavior. The plaintiff's counsel requested any documents pertinent to the expert's testimony, Kodak's lawyer's resisted, and ultimately a magistrate ordered production of numerous documents including interim reports prepared by the economist. At the economist's deposition, one of Kodak's lawyers stated that he had destroyed the interim reports, which were somewhat unfavorable to Kodak's defense. The lawyer even filed an affidavit in a subsequent discovery dispute in the case, stating under oath that the documents had been destroyed. In fact, the lawyer had not destroyed the documents, but had hidden them in his office and withheld them from production. The affidavit was perjurous. The fallout was a calamity for the firm. Kodak fired it and hired one of its arch-rivals to defend the antitrust case. The firm paid its client over $600,000 to settle Kodak's claims related to its conduct of the litigation. It lost Kodak's business, which had accounted for approximately one-fourth of the firm's billings and had employed thirty lawyers full-time. The partner who had coordinated the firm's preparation of the economist's testimony was released from the firm and spent twenty-seven days in jail for contempt of court.[80]

In his discussion of the *Berkey-Kodak* case, Luban relates the following episode:

> Joseph Fortenberry, the associate working for [Mahlon Perkins, the partner representing Kodak], knew that Perkins was perjuring himself

[78] *Id.* at 102 (footnotes omitted).

[79] 74 F.R.D. 613 (S.D.N.Y. 1977).

[80] W. Bradley Wendel, *Morality, Motivation, and the Professionalism Movement*, 52 S.C. L. REV. 557, 606–07 (2001) (footnotes omitted); *see also* Walter Kiechell III, *The Strange Case of Kodak's Lawyers*, FORTUNE, May 8, 1978, at 188. If I were a superstitious sort, I'd worry about the fact that one of the two "smoking guns" in the case was Exhibit 666. *Id.* I am *not* making this up.

and whispered a warning to him; but when Perkins ignored the warning, Fortenberry did nothing further to correct his misstatements. "What happened" recalls another associate, "was that he saw Perkins lie and really couldn't believe it. And he just had no idea what to do. I mean, he . . . kept thinking there must be a reason. Besides, what do you do? The guy was his boss and a great guy!"[81]

Fortenberry's comments highlight how fledgling lawyers will take many social cues from those more experienced lawyers whom they respect.[82] Of course, the pressure that the senior lawyers have to keep their clients, maintain their billings, and compete with other elite lawyers at other firms (who are all too happy to steal clients away), is relentless pressure indeed. But if the more senior lawyers can't withstand the pressure, then who will teach the fledgling lawyers to resist?

III. Where Do We Go from Here?

If we want lawyers to spend more time understanding themselves and their relationship to their clients, then we're going to have to lead from the top, with judges, partners, bar associations, and other senior lawyers all singing the same tune. It won't be sufficient for law professors to warn students against the temptations and pressures of law practice. As a matter of fact, it's depressing how little influence law professors have on their students' understanding of legal ethics.

Larry Hellman's study on cognitive dissonance in a legal ethics class is proof of the need to have top lawyers do the preaching, not law professors.[83] Hellman

---

81 *Wrongful Obedience, supra* note 73, at 95 (footnotes omitted).

82 Cognitive dissonance isn't limited to outside counsel. In a study of inside counsel, Hugh and Sally Gunz found that the lawyers' advice was not always independent from the direction that the company itself intended to go:

> From a practitioner standpoint, the model highlights issues surrounding the nature of the advice that organizations can expect to obtain from their in-house counsel when placed in positions of ethical conflict. In our original study of OPC [organizational professional conflict], we suggested that an important implication of our findings was that in-house counsel might not necessarily always provide disinterested professional advice. In their different ways, the Technician and Organization Person might produce superficially helpful advice, which could, under certain circumstances, be dangerously misleading. The Technician, for example, may deliver clever but myopic solutions, and the Observer could well misjudge a situation and remain silent inappropriately. But the Advisor, by avoiding the "cop" aspect of the Lawyer role (in the sense that there is no implication that he or she intends to report the situation to the next level higher within the organization, or to a regulator outside the organization), stays closer to the Lawyer's advice. So the model, as revised, suggests an even greater variety of potential responses than in its initial L[awyer], T[echnician], and O[bserver] form, underlining yet more firmly the need to avoid making simplistic assumptions about the nature of the advice in-house counsel provide their employer[s].

Hugh P. Gunz & Sally P. Gunz, *The Lawyer's Response to Organizational Professional Conflict: An Empirical Study of the Ethical Decision Making of In-House Counsel*, 39 AM. BUS. L.J. 241, 279–80 (2002) (footnotes omitted).

83 Lawrence K. Hellman, *The Effects of Law Office Work on the Formation of Law Students' Professional Values: Observation, Explanation, Optimization*, 4 GEO. J. LEGAL ETHICS 537 (1991).

asked the students in his ethics course to keep diaries of possible ethics violations that they observed while working for lawyers during the semester, and those students recounted bad lawyering in an astonishing variety of forms—neglect, incompetence, conflicts of interest, and the like.[84] If we want to train newly minted lawyers to be ethical, it's just not enough for law professors to talk the talk. We must join forces with the lawyers and judges in the "real world," those who can walk the walk.

Lawyers need to behave as true counselors to their clients, rather than as hired guns who are just following orders. Society needs us to take on the role of the social conscience (or, if that sounds too darn highfallutin', the role of the grease that helps society run). As David Luban has pointed out,

> If lawyers have special responsibilities to legal justice, that is not because they are divinely elected, or better and holier that [sic] the rest of us. It is because of how their role fits into an entire division of social labor. Lawyers represent private parties before public institutions, or advise private parties about the requirements of public norms, or reduce private transactions to a publicly-prescribed form, or ratify that transactions are in compliance with public norms. To say that they have special duties of fidelity to those norms is no more ecstatic and supernatural than saying that food-preparers have heightened duties to ensure their hands are clean. It is their social role, not the brush of angels' wings on their foreheads, that requires [food service workers] to wash their hands every time they go to the bathroom.[85]

We used to be better at setting good examples, or so I've heard. In the "golden days" that Tom Shaffer recounts, some of the lawyers that he observed set wonderful examples for their newly minted lawyer colleagues. In my favorite article of his, *The Profession as a Moral Teacher,* he tells story after story of lawyers who did the right thing.[86] The constant choice of ethical over unethical behavior helped mold the lawyer that Shaffer eventually became:

> [Those two partners in my former law firm] were philosophically and temperamentally different and . . . practiced law in different ways. That they were so much alike in these moral matters said something about their personal character, of course, but, in view of their personal differences, it also said something about the way the firm practiced

84 *Id.* at 601–05.

85 David Luban, *Asking the Right Questions*, 72 TEMP. L. REV. 839, 849–50 (1999).

86 *Moral Teacher*, *supra* note 62, at 214–17.

> law—about the way the firm functioned as the profession (for me) and, as the profession, functioned (for me) as a moral teacher. It was not, that is, an apprenticeship, in which I was learning my craft, and the morals of my craft, from a master—or at least it didn't seem, then, that it was. It was the profession (the law firm) that was the moral teacher. . . . It was even more like the moral formation a person gets from family, town, and church. Which is to say that, here, code depended on character.[87]

From his experience as a young lawyer, Shaffer took the moral lesson that a lawyer should also be a gentleman.[88] Tom Shaffer's view of the "gentlemanly" lawyer, of course, has its critics,[89] including Shaffer himself.[90] And yet, we do understand the concept that he's trying to express:[91] that of a lawyer who understands her role in society as more than just a mere scrivener or functionary, and who tries always to take the moral high ground.[92]

---

87 *Id.* at 216–17.

88 Thomas L. Shaffer, *On Being a Professional Elder*, 62 NOTRE DAME L. REV. 624, 630–31 (1987) [hereinafter *Professional Elder*] ("When character is in place, fortified by 'a few rules' that have to do with professional craft, the professional person becomes dependable. Professional character is the connection between virtue and craft. The convention has been to describe that connection with the word gentleman.") (footnotes omitted). If you haven't read Tom Shaffer's work on this topic, you should. For a quick shortcut—not to be confused with reading Shaffer's work—Leslie Gerber has created a good primer. *See* Leslie E. Gerber, *Can Lawyers Be Saved? The Theological Legal Ethics of Thomas Shaffer*, 10 J.L. & RELIGION 347 (1994).

89 *See, e.g.*, Ann Bartow, *Still Not Behaving Like Gentlemen*, 49 U. KAN. L. REV. 809, 810–11 (2001); Susan Daicoff, *Asking Leopards to Change Their Spots: Should Lawyers Change? A Critique Of Solutions to Problems with Professionalism by Reference to Empirically-Derived Attorney Personality Attributes*, 11 GEO. J. LEGAL ETHICS 547, 582–83 (1998); William J. Wernz, *Does Professionalism Literature Idealize the Past and Over-Rate Civility? Is Zeal a Vice or a Cardinal Virtue?*, 13 PROF. LAW. 1 (2001) (disputing the claim that "back then"—whenever "then" was—lawyers were more professional and more civil).

90 Thomas L. Shaffer, *The Gentleman in Professional Ethics*, 10 QUEEN'S L.J. 1, 11 (1984).

> The 19th century gentleman in North America gave us slavery, Manifest Destiny, the theft of half of Mexico, the subjugation of women, the exploitation of immigrant children, Pinkerton detectives, yellow-dog contracts, and the implacable genocide of American Indians. You could make a case . . . that the gentleman's ethic is not worth taking seriously. If the gentleman has left the professions, the best thing for us would be to bar the door lest he get back in.

Id.; *see also* Thomas L. Shaffer, *Inaugural Howard Lichtenstein Lecture in Legal Ethics: Lawyer Professionalism as a Moral Argument*, 26 GONZ. L. REV. 393, 400 (1991); *Professional Elder*, *supra* note 88, at 633–34.

91 Edward McGlynn Gaffney, Jr., *In Praise of a Gentle Soul, Remarks at the Annual Banquet of the Journal of Law and Religion* (Oct. 14, 1993), *in* 10 J.L. & RELIGION 279, 284 (1993/1994).

> The acid test of [Tom Shaffer's] reliance on the ethics of gentlemen is whether it, too, is not flawed at its core. Is it not by definition limited to males, and does it have any space for minorities? Only one like Shaffer, who by decades of living like a gentleman himself and reflecting carefully on that ethic, could have come to the conclusion that the ethic of the gentleman-lawyer has greater possibilities for the subversion of patriarchy than the ABA's model of professionalism.

Id. (footnotes omitted).

92 Bill Hodes points out that "[t]he acid test of ethical lawyering is rarely what to do in the face of crisis—a client shows you the buried bodies or drops a bloody knife on your desk or commits perjury or destroys or

What happens when we don't set the right example? We can call doing the right thing "behaving like gentlemen," or we can use some other, less "loaded" phrase. If we don't exert some leadership and emphasize the role of character in the practice of law, some very smart lawyers will continue to do stupid things, and some clients will continue to do stupid (or venal) things. Some of these people will even trot out the hoary (and discredited) old saw that they were "just following orders."[93]

So how do we encourage lawyers to withstand peer pressure and client pressure, especially in those grey areas in which the lawyer gives advice akin to "it's an aggressive interpretation of the law" and the client chooses to use that aggressive interpretation, even at the risk of later litigation? Remember, we're not talking about lawyers who deliberately counsel clients to flout the law. Rather, we're talking about lawyers who say that a particular interpretation could go either in favor of the client or against it.

Personally, I like Russ Pearce's idea that we create a new Model Rule 1.0. His Model Rule 1.0 would provide that "lawyers are morally accountable for their conduct as lawyers."[94] That rule hits the question of moral interdependence head on, and it provides a powerful reminder that "just following orders" is the weakest of excuses.[95]

We can blame part of Enron's downfall on the economy. We can blame part of it on corporate misbehavior, on board malfeasance, and on pure greed. We can

---

hides material property asked for in discovery." W. William Hodes, *Accepting and Rejecting Clients—The Moral Autonomy of the Second-to-the-Last Lawyer in Town*, 48 U. KAN. L. REV. 977, 978 (2000) (citing the classic cases of People v. Belge, 372 N.Y.S. 2d 798 (N.Y. Crim. Ct. 1975) (buried bodies), State v. Olwell, 394 P.2d 681 (Wash. 1964) (bloody knife), Nix v. Whiteside, 475 U.S. 157 (1986) (perjury), and Berkey Photo, Inc. v. Eastman Kodak Co., 74 F.R.D. 613 (S.D.N.Y. 1977) (work product)). For a wonderful discussion of how social norms affect lawyering, see *Social Norms*, *supra* note 66.

[93] *See, e.g.*, Tom Fowler, *Ex-Andersen auditor defended/Aide: Boss was told to shred files*, HOUS. CHRON., Mar. 7, 2002, at 1 ("An assistant to the Arthur Andersen lead partner who handled the Enron account said she believes her boss was just following orders when he told workers to destroy Enron-related documents last fall."); Marcy Gordon, *SEC, Informal Wall Street System Failed to Detect Enron Failure, Report Finds*, Associated Press Newswires, Oct. 7, 2002, Westlaw, Allnewsplus Library (Fastow's lawyer contends that his client was just following orders).

[94] Russell G. Pearce, *Model Rule 1.0: Lawyers are Morally Accountable*, 70 FORDHAM L. REV. 1805, 1807–08 (2002). Pearce points out that Model Rule 1.0 would not take sides in current disputes regarding the lawyer's role. What it would do is move the debates regarding the lawyer's moral duties, like that between Freedman, who favors zealous representation, and Luban, Rhode, and Simon, who favor some significant limits on that representation, to the center of the bar's legal ethics conversations. While the bar currently pays some slight attention to these issues, Model Rule 1.0 would move them to a more prominent place in the bar's official deliberations and continuing legal education courses, as well as in the efforts of the conscientious lawyer to explore her own moral accountability.

[95] I'm not sure how one might enforce a Model Rule 1.0, but at least Pearce is heading in the right direction.

blame part of it on a structure that allowed gatekeepers and reputational intermediaries—the board, the accountants, and the lawyers—to rely on the other two categories to understand the overall picture of what Enron was doing. We can even blame the Enron employees who chose to place too much Enron stock in their own 401(k) plans, thereby betting twice with the same money.[96] But one thing we can't blame is fate. Enron's collapse wasn't due to a "perfect storm" of mere coincidence—the collapse was caused by humans and their hubris. We need to ensure that hubris doesn't blind us to the first rule of leadership: It's all about character.

NOTES

You're probably familiar with the story of *Titanic,* but you might be less familiar with the story of the "perfect storm," even though both stories have been told through some wonderful books and movies. For Titanic's story, we're partial to Walter Lord's A NIGHT TO REMEMBER (1955), and for the 1991 "storm of the century," we like Sebastian Junger's THE PERFECT STORM: A TRUE STORY OF MEN AGAINST THE SEA (1997). The latter book tells the story of what happens when several storm systems intersect in a specific way. The storm wasn't "perfect" because it was a good storm. It was "perfect" because of the confluence of several low-odds events happening in one location at one time. Weather.com has a very good story about this particular storm.

Now, back to Enron: No discussion about Enron is complete without at least a hat tip to the three groups with special responsibilities toward the company: its board of directors, its lawyers (both inside the firm and at various law firms), and its accountants. In the Final Report filed in the Enron bankruptcy case, Neal Batson, who was the court-appointed examiner in the case, concluded in part that there was plenty of blame to go around:

> [I]n this Report the Examiner concludes that:
>
> *Andersen*
>
> - There is sufficient evidence from which a fact-finder could conclude that Andersen: (i) committed professional negligence in the rendering of accounting services to Enron; and (ii) aided and abetted certain

---

96 *See, e.g.*, Mark Davis, *The Fallout of a Fallen Enron; Too Much Company Stock in 401(k); Plans Poses Risk*, KAN. CITY STAR, Jan. 20, 2002, at A1; Kaja Whitehouse, *401(k) Woes? Might Be Your Own Fault*, DOW JONES NEWS SERV., Jan. 18, 2002, Westlaw, Allnewsplus Library. Of course, the freeze on selling stock as the value of the stock spiraled downward also had something to do with the losses in the employees' 401(k) plans. *See, e.g.*, Davis, *supra*; Editorial, *Enron and Frontier Justice Fear of Angry Workers Sends Energy Trading Firm to New York to File for Bankruptcy*, PORTLAND OREGONIAN, Dec. 4, 2001, at D06.

Enron officers in breaching their fiduciary duties to Enron by causing Enron to enter into SPE transactions that were designed to manipulate the Debtors' financial statements and that resulted in the dissemination of financial information known by these officers to be materially misleading. Because Enron's officers participated in the wrongful conduct, however, Andersen may assert that the actions by the Enron officers should be imputed to Enron and consequently, that claims by Enron should be barred or reduced under comparative fault rules.

In-house Attorneys

- There is sufficient evidence from which a fact-finder could conclude that certain Enron in-house attorneys committed legal malpractice by: (i) failing to advise Enron adequately regarding the disclosure of its SPE transactions, including the related party transactions; (ii) failing to advise adequately Enron's Board of Directors (the "Board" or the "Enron Board") and certain of its committees with respect to legal and corporate governance issues raised by certain related party transactions; and (iii) failing to advise the Enron Board of material facts surrounding Enron's use of SPEs.* There is also sufficient evidence from which a fact-finder could conclude that certain in-house attorneys breached their fiduciary duties by assisting certain officers who breached their fiduciary duties to Enron by causing the Debtors to enter into SPE transactions that were designed to manipulate the Debtors' financial statements and that resulted in the dissemination of financial information known to be materially misleading. Because Enron's officers participated in the wrongful conduct, however, these attorneys may assert that the actions by the Enron officers should be imputed to Enron and consequently, that claims by Enron should be barred or reduced under comparative fault rules.

Outside Attorneys

- There is sufficient evidence from which a fact-finder could conclude that certain of Enron's outside attorneys: (i) committed legal malpractice in connection with their legal services provided to Enron with respect to the SPE transactions; or (ii) aided and abetted certain Enron officers in breaching their fiduciary duties. Because Enron's

* Editors' Note: An "SPE" is a special purpose entity. It is designed to segregate the risk associated with that entity's activities from a company's main balance sheet.

officers participated in the wrongful conduct, however, these attorneys may assert that the actions by the Enron officers should be imputed to Enron and consequently, that claims by Enron should be barred or reduced under comparative fault rules.

Lay and Skilling

- There is sufficient evidence from which a fact-finder could conclude that Kenneth Lay ("Lay"), Enron's Chairman and Chief Executive Officer, and Jeffrey Skilling ("Skilling"), Enron's President and Chief Operating Officer, in their capacities as officers, breached their fiduciary duties under applicable law by failing to provide adequate oversight of Enron's use of SPEs because they failed to respond appropriately to the existence of "red flags" indicating that certain senior officers were misusing SPE transactions to disseminate materially misleading financial information. If a fact-finder so concludes, the director exculpation provision in Enron's articles of incorporation would not protect Lay and Skilling from such a claim because this failure occurred in their capacity as officers.
- There is sufficient evidence from which a fact-finder could conclude that Lay and Skilling, in their capacities as members of the Enron Board, breached their fiduciary duty of good faith under applicable law in approving [certain] hedging transaction[s] . . . because there is evidence that they were in possession of facts necessary to conclude that these transactions lacked any rational business purpose. If a fact-finder so concludes, the director exculpation provision in Enron's articles of incorporation would not protect Lay and Skilling from such a claim because it involves acts or omissions not in good faith.
- There is sufficient evidence from which a fact-finder could conclude that Skilling, in his capacity as an officer, breached his fiduciary duties under applicable law by failing adequately to inquire into red flags with respect to the transactions between [CFO Andrew Fastow's separately created companies, which Fastow used to generate personal profits in negotiations against Enron itself] . . . including red flags relating to the compensation that Fastow received in connection with [those companies]. Because this failure occurred in Skilling's capacity as an officer, the director exculpation provision in Enron's articles of incorporation would not apply to such a claim.
- There is sufficient evidence from which a fact-finder could conclude that: (i) Lay's repayment to Enron of more than $94 million of loans

with Enron stock was not duly authorized or approved by the Enron Board under applicable corporate law; and (ii) the repayment is voidable by Enron, which would result in Lay being obligated to repay in excess of $94 million to Enron and Enron returning the stock to Lay.

- There is sufficient evidence from which a fact-finder could conclude that: (i) Skilling's repayment to Enron of more than $2 million of loans with Enron stock was not duly authorized or approved by the Enron Board under applicable corporate law; and (ii) the repayment is voidable by Enron, which would result in Skilling being obligated to repay in excess of $2 million to Enron and Enron returning the stock to Skilling.

Outside Directors

- Although the oversight of the SPE transactions by the Enron Board, the Audit and Compliance Committee of the Enron Board (the "Audit Committee") and the Finance Committee of the Enron Board (the "Finance Committee") may be criticized, the Examiner has not discovered sufficient evidence from which a fact-finder could conclude that members of the Enron Board who served during the period 1997 to the Petition Date [that's December 2, 2001, the date on which Enron filed for chapter 11 bankruptcy protection], other than Lay and Skilling (the "Outside Directors") and these committees either (i) abdicated or displayed sustained inattention to their monitoring responsibilities or (ii) consciously disregarded red flags indicating Enron officers were misusing the SPE transactions to disseminate materially misleading financial information. In the absence of this type of conduct, because of the director exculpation provision in Enron's articles of incorporation, the Outside Directors would not have liability to Enron arising out of their duty of oversight.
- There is sufficient evidence from which a fact-finder could conclude that certain of the Outside Directors breached their fiduciary duty of good faith under applicable law in approving [certain transactions] because there is evidence that they were in possession of facts necessary to conclude that these transactions lacked any rational business purpose. If a fact-finder so concludes, the director exculpation provision in Enron's articles of incorporation would not protect the Outside Directors from such a claim because it involves acts or omissions not in good faith.

. . . .*

Later in the same report, Batson concluded that

> Enron's professionals could have provided a check against the officers' misconduct. To varying degrees, these professionals were involved in the structuring documentation and disclosure of these transactions. It appears that they had opportunities to prevent or limit this misconduct at several points in time.
>
> *Andersen*
>
> As previously discussed, Andersen's certification of Enron's financial statements was indispensable to Enron in accessing the capital markets. Andersen's audits of Enron's financial statements should have provided a check against Enron's misuse of the SPEs. . . . Despite these fundamental precepts, on many occasions, it appears that Andersen acted in a manner inconsistent with its duties. . . .**
>
> *Attorneys*
>
> By analyzing the structure of the SPE transactions and documenting them, and by providing opinions in various transactions, Enron's attorneys also played a vital role in Enron's access to the capital markets. These attorneys could have provided a check and balance against the Enron officers' wrongdoing. Among other things, these attorneys could have apprised [General Counsel Jim] Derrick or the Enron Board when they knew of conduct that could result in Enron disseminating materially misleading financial information, or they could have refused to render legal services in connection with SPE transactions when they had concerns about their propriety.
>
> One explanation for the attorneys' failure may be that they lost sight of the fact that the corporation was their client. It appears that some of these attorneys considered the officers to be their clients when, in fact, the attorneys owed duties to Enron. Another explanation may be that some of these attorneys saw their role in very narrow terms, as an implementer, not a counselor. That is, rather than conscientiously raising known issues for further analysis by a more senior officer or the Enron Board or refusing to participate in transactions that raised such issues, these lawyers seemed to

---

* *Final Report of Neal Batson, Court-Appointed Examiner, In re* Enron Corp., Case No. Case No. 01-16034 (AJG), at 7–13 (footnotes omitted).

** *Id.* at 110–11 (footnotes omitted).

focus only on how to address a narrow question or simply to implement a decision (or document a transaction).*

. . . .

[The Board of Directors]

The Enron Board could have been the ultimate check in preventing or minimizing the impact of the officers' misconduct. The Board had the authority to stop the misconduct by, for example, terminating the employment of these officers, refusing to approve Enron's financial statements, and other disclosures in its 10-Ks and other public filings or notifying the SEC of wrongdoing. In practice, however, particularly in circumstances involving complex matters and obfuscation by officers of a company, there are limitations to a board serving as an effective check in the area of oversight. This may help to explain why director liability for breach of the duty of oversight is rare absent egregious facts.

The Enron Board did not serve as an effective check on the officers' misuse of Enron's SPE transactions. There are several factors that might explain this failure. Some of these factors were not within the control of the Enron Board. Other factors, however, were within the control of the Enron Board and, if handled differently, might have resulted in the Board limiting the harm caused to Enron.**

. . . .

Possible Explanations for the Enron Board's Failure

Many of Enron's Outside Directors had skills and talents that likely were beneficial to Enron in the operation of its business, and these contributions should not be underestimated. It appears from the evidence, however, that the Outside Directors did not understand important aspects about Enron's use of SPE transactions.

There may be several possible explanations for the Board's failure to understand these transactions. As discussed above, Enron officers often used misleading terms and confusing jargon, and they presented information to the Enron Board and its committees in a manner that obfuscated the substance of the SPE transactions. In addition, the length of Board and committee meetings, given the complexity and the number of agenda items covered, raises questions of whether sufficient time was devoted to allowing the Outside Directors to understand the transactions.

* *Id.* at 114–15 (footnotes omitted).

** *Id.* at 119–20 (footnotes omitted).

Finally, Enron's Board was unusually large, which may have increased the tendency for individual directors not to feel personally responsible for understanding complex matters. Despite the large number of directors, however, the Board did not appear to have sufficient expertise in the kinds of complicated structured financings in which Enron engaged.

Time. In addition to being large and complex, Enron changed its business strategy dramatically during the late 1990s, requiring the Outside Directors to learn and adjust to the company's transition from a "pipeline company" to a "trading company." Board meetings typically lasted a total of about four to five hours, and committee meetings were generally not more than ninety minutes each. With the large number of significant agenda topics presented at each meeting, these circumstances raise questions of whether the Outside Directors had sufficient time to discuss and understand the matters fully.

. . . .

Reliance on Other Board Members. The Enron Board was unusually large. A recent survey of public companies reported an average board size of 9.4 total directors, with an average of 6.9 "independent" or outside directors, less than Enron's 15 to 19 directors. A consequence of the large size can be a tendency for the individual directors not to feel personal responsibility for understanding complex matters. Several of the Outside Directors testified that they might not have understood an area of the company's operations or a particular matter, but they were not concerned because they expected that someone else on the Board did. For example, [one board member] who served on both the Audit and Finance Committees . . . testified that he relied on other Audit Committee members [ ] to understand whether it was appropriate for Andersen to provide both external and internal audit functions at Enron: . . . .

Lack of Structured Finance Expertise. The Board did not include a large number of Outside Directors who had hands-on experience in the types of sophisticated financings employed by Enron. In the 2001 Board Assessment, the directors acknowledged this lack of depth on the Board. A summary of the self-assessment responses quoted the directors' responses, but without attributing the quotes to individual directors.

. . . .

Conclusions

For several reasons, the Enron Board did not function as an effective check and balance. This failure may have resulted from (i) a carefully

> orchestrated strategy of Enron's senior officers, (ii) the failure of Lay and Skilling, in their capacities as executive officers, to assist the Outside Directors, (iii) inadequate assistance from Enron's professionals, (iv) inattention by the Enron Board to its oversight function or (v) insufficient understanding of how the SPE transactions were being used by Enron's officers.*

Why, might you ask, did we end the chapter with excerpts from the Examiner's Final Report? One reason concerns how much finger-pointing went on. Given how complex Enron's transactions were, you can imagine what the accountants, lawyers, and board members all could have said: "It wasn't my fault. It was theirs." We disagree. Everyone breached fiduciary responsibilities to the company. Everyone shared in the responsibility.

But there's a second reason that relates more directly to you. You're smart. The people in charge of Enron were smart. The lawyers were smart. The accountants were smart. "Smart" isn't a get-out-of-jail card** when it comes to running an organization. This book is designed to help you realize that "smart" may be necessary, but it's far from sufficient. You'll have to consider how much detail on a business deal or strategy you're going to disclose to your co-workers and to your superiors. You'll also have to think long and hard, when you're in charge, about how many things you're not being told by your colleagues. You'll have to think about whether people might be lying to you. And you'll have to ask yourself if you have the right structures—and the right people—in place to help you figure out the truth.

---

* *Id.* at 132–36 (footnotes omitted).

** Literally, in Enron's case.

PART II

The Framework: Why Do Smart People Do Dumb Things?

Now that you've seen a particular scandal (Enron) "up close and personal," it's time to branch out into a bit of social science, so that when you read the rest of the book, you can keep some lessons about human behavior in mind. This chapter is designed to give you a feel for some of the reasons that corporate scandals perpetuate themselves. We want you to learn two things: why humans (even smart, well-educated ones like you) can find themselves making what can only be called boneheaded decisions, and how some types of organizational structures are more likely to generate scandals than others.

We start the chapter with a primer on some social science concepts about how people think and how they tend to behave in groups. Andrew Perlman's *Unethical Obedience by Subordinate Attorneys: Lessons from Social Psychology,* walks you through two classic experiments in social psychology—one by Solomon Asch and one by Stanley Milgram. Our second article in this chapter, Catherine Gage O'Grady's article, *Wrongful Obedience and the Professional Practice of Law,* provides some updated studies based on Milgram's experiments and teases out whether the presumption that "forewarned is forearmed"—that if you know about these studies, you won't replicate the bad behavior. Both articles give you a feel for the hierarchical way in which law is practiced and how being at the bottom rung of such a hierarchy might make it harder for you to resist pressures to conform or obey. Both of these articles deal with cognitive errors that lawyers face, but the social science principles that the authors discuss apply to everyone, not just to lawyers. When we discuss some real-world examples in subsequent chapters, we'll be talking about car companies and banks and a government agency as well as the world of law firms.

After you understand a bit more about cognitive errors, you'll be able to consider systemic risk in light of how even smart people tend to behave. The third article in this chapter is by Harvey Gilmore. His article, *This Is Not a Symposium on How to Commit Fraud—But If It Were . . .*, gives you a primer on the conditions that make fraud more likely to occur. In particular, we'd like you to pay attention to a classic theory—the fraud triangle—that he discusses. After reading his article, you'll move to an article written by the Hon. Michelle Harner, *Barriers to Effective Risk Management.* Judge Harner's article helps to answer this question: "If we know that there are easy ways for people to commit fraud, are there some ways to build countermeasures into an organization's structure?" We included this article because knowing how people tend to think and knowing how the most common types of fraud occur should make you crave some sort of fraud safety net—some way of protecting yourself from the types of allegations that the Enron board faced in the Enron Examiner's report that we referenced at the end of our first chapter.

Let's be clear. Someday, you may be on a board (or more than one), or you'll run a company, or you'll be a key executive at a company, or you'll be a lawyer representing one. The job of anticipating risk factors will fall on your shoulders. The final article in this chapter, *Black Swans, Ostriches, and Ponzi Schemes,* gives you a heads-up on how to think about unusual risk. Sure, after the Great Recession, nearly everyone says, "Oh, I realized a long time ago that the housing bubble was going to burst." But, actually, very few of us realized that. The warning signs were all obvious—for a quick history of the housing bubble, you can watch the movie *The Big Short* (2015)—but none of us were looking for those warning signs, so it's not surprising that we didn't see them. When you're in charge of an organization, part of your job will be to ask yourself what you're *not* thinking about, and why you're not.

Here's the bottom line for this chapter. There are many reasons that could cause you to make a very bad (read: unethical) decision in the course of your career.* You might be given incorrect or incomplete information. You might not be able to root out accurate information. Your colleagues could be lying to you. You could find yourself framing the situation incorrectly (cognitive errors affecting "the person," as psychologists like to say). You could be subject to hard-to-detect peer pressure (cognitive errors resulting from "the situation," which is how sociologists think about interactions among people). But we don't think that anyone reading this book is dumb, and we think that everyone reading this book needs to know enough about the various factors affecting decision-making

* A very, very small number of people are psychopaths and sociopaths, and we hope that none of them is reading this book. It's not supposed to be a "how to" about getting away with corporate scandals.

(cognitive errors, bad incentives, failures to anticipate certain types of risk) to get a leg up on the complexities of organizational behavior.

CHAPTER 3

Unethical Obedience by Subordinate Attorneys: Lessons from Social Psychology*

*Andrew M. Perlman***

I. Introduction

Consider the plight of a lawyer—fresh out of law school with crushing loan debt and few job offers—who accepts a position at a medium-sized firm. A partner asks the young lawyer to review a client's documents to determine what needs to be produced in discovery. In the stack, the associate finds a "smoking gun" that is clearly within the scope of discovery and spells disaster for the client's case. The associate reports the document to the partner, who without explanation tells the associate not to produce it. The associate asks the partner a few questions and quickly drops the subject when the partner tells the associate to get back to work.

We would like to believe that the young lawyer has the courage to ensure that the partner ultimately produces the document. We might hope, or expect, that the lawyer will report the issue to the firm's ethics counsel, if the firm is big enough to have one, or consult with other lawyers in the firm, assuming that she has developed the necessary relationships with her colleagues despite her junior status.

---

* This piece was originally published as Andrew M. Perlman, *Unethical Obedience by Subordinate Attorneys: Lessons from Social Psychology*, 36 HOFSTRA L. REV. 451 (2007).

** Associate Professor of Law, Suffolk University Law School. B.A., Yale College; J.D., Harvard Law School; LL.M., Columbia Law School. Several friends and colleagues have given me valuable suggestions for this Article, including Lisa Aidlin, Thomas Blass, Robert Keatinge, Sung Hui Kim, Jeffrey Lipshaw, and John Steele. I also benefited enormously from the assistance of research librarian Ellen Delaney and from comments and questions during presentations at Cumberland and Suffolk Law Schools and at the Hofstra Legal Ethics Conference. I also received very useful insights from several students in my professional responsibility classes at Suffolk.

In fact, research in the area of social psychology suggests that, in some contexts, a subordinate lawyer will often comply with unethical instructions of this sort.[1] This basic, but crucial, insight into human behavior suggests that there is often a significant gap between what the legal ethics rules require and how lawyers will typically behave. Indeed, lawyers will too often obey obviously unethical or illegal instructions or fail to report the wrongdoing of other lawyers.[2]

This Article explores what lessons we can learn from social psychology regarding a lawyer's willingness to comply with authority figures, such as senior partners or deep-pocketed clients, when they make unlawful or unethical demands. Part II reviews some of the basic literature in social psychology regarding conformity and obedience, much of which emphasizes the importance of context as a primary factor in predicting people's behavior.[3]

Part III contends that lawyers frequently find themselves in the kinds of contexts that produce high levels of conformity and obedience and low levels of resistance to illegal or unethical instructions. The result is that subordinate lawyers, like the attorney in the initial example, will find it difficult to resist a superior's commands in circumstances that should produce forceful dissent.

Part IV proposes several changes to existing law in light of these insights, including giving lawyers the benefit of whistleblower protection, strengthening a lawyer's duty to report the misconduct of other lawyers,[4] and enhancing a subordinate lawyer's responsibilities upon receiving arguably unethical instructions from a superior.[5] These proposals, however, are ultimately less important than the insights that underlie them. Namely, by gaining a deeper understanding of social psychology, the legal profession can more effectively prevent and deter attorney misconduct.

---

1 *See infra* Parts II and III. Although there is limited research on whether lawyers tend to obey authority figures, there is no reason to think that attorneys are somehow immune from the pressures that lead to obedience. *See, e.g., infra* note 80.

2 *See* MODEL RULES OF PROF'L CONDUCT R. 5.2(a)–(b) (2007) (subjecting subordinates to the Rules of Professional Conduct unless the supervisory lawyer's instructions reflect a "reasonable resolution of an arguable question of professional duty"); MODEL RULES OF PROF'L CONDUCT R. 8.3(a) (2007) (requiring a lawyer to report another lawyer's misconduct if that conduct "raises a substantial question as to that lawyer's honesty, trustworthiness or fitness as a lawyer").

3 As explained in more detail in Part II, social context plays a significant role in human behavior. *See* LEE ROSS & RICHARD E. NISBETT, THE PERSON AND THE SITUATION xiv (1991) ("[W]hat has been demonstrated through a host of celebrated laboratory and field studies is that manipulations of the immediate social situation can overwhelm in importance the type of individual differences in personal traits or dispositions that people normally think of as being determinative of social behavior.").

4 MODEL RULES OF PROF'L CONDUCT R. 8.3(a) (2007).

5 MODEL RULES OF PROF'L CONDUCT R. 5.2(b) (2007).

II. Basic Lessons from Social Psychology About Conformity and Obedience

Studies on conformity and obedience suggest that professionals, whom we would ordinarily describe as "honest," will often suppress their independent judgment in favor of a group's opinion or offer little resistance in the face of illegal or unethical demands.[6] These studies demonstrate that we ascribe too much weight to personality traits like honesty,[7] and that contextual factors have far more to do with human behavior than most people recognize.[8] Social psychologists have called this tendency to overemphasize individual personality differences and underestimate the power of the situation "the fundamental attribution error."[9] Indeed, a number of experiments have amply demonstrated that situational forces are often more powerful predictors of human behavior than dispositional traits like honesty.

A. Foundational Studies on Conformity

The importance of context is apparent from a number of experiments related to conformity, the most celebrated of which is a 1955 study by Solomon Asch.

Asch wanted to determine how often a group member would express independent judgment despite the unanimous, but obviously mistaken, contrary opinions of the rest of the group.[10] To make this determination, Asch designed a study involving two cards similar to those shown on the next page.[11]

---

6 Although there is a growing legal ethics literature that draws on social psychology, there is surprisingly little scholarship that draws on social psychology to explain the particular problem of wrongful obedience among lawyers. For a few notable exceptions, see MILTON C. REGAN, JR., EAT WHAT YOU KILL: THE FALL OF A WALL STREET LAWYER 307, 323–24 (2004); David J. Luban, *The Ethics of Wrongful Obedience,* in ETHICS IN PRACTICE: LAWYERS' ROLES, RESPONSIBILITIES, AND REGULATION 94, 95 (Deborah L. Rhode ed., 2000); Sung Hui Kim, *The Banality of Fraud: Re-Situating the Inside Counsel As Gatekeeper,* 74 FORDHAM L. REV. 983, 1001–26 (2005).

7 *See generally* JOHN M. DORIS, LACK OF CHARACTER: PERSONALITY AND MORAL BEHAVIOR (2002) (arguing that context explains far more about human behavior than individual differences in character traits). For a detailed examination of the importance of context in determining lawyer behavior, *see* REGAN, *supra* note 6, at 4–6, 10, 294–95, 302–04.

8 ROSS & NISBETT, supra note 3, at 4.

9 *Id.* (citation omitted); *see also* DORIS, *supra* note 7, at 93.

10 Solomon E. Asch, *Opinions and Social Pressure,* SCI. AM., Nov. 1955, at 31, 32.

11 *Id.* This image appears at http://en.wikipedia.org/wiki/Image:Asch_experiment.png (last visited Jan. 20, 2008).

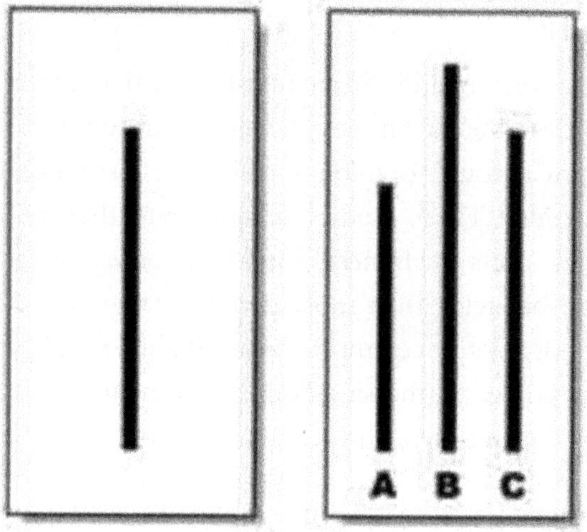

In one version of the study, the experimenter told the subject that he was about to participate in a vision test and asked the subject to sit at a table with four other individuals who were secretly working with the experimenter.[12]

All five people were shown the two cards and asked to identify which line in the card on the right (A, B, or C) was the same length as the line shown in the card on the left.[13] Each person was asked his opinion individually and answered out loud,[14] with the subject of the experiment going near the end.[15] After each person had answered, a new set of cards was produced, and the participants were once again asked their opinions.[16]

During the initial rounds, all of the confederates chose the obviously right answer.[17] Not surprisingly, under this condition, the subject also chose the right answer.[18]

In some subsequent rounds, however, Asch tested the subject's willingness to conform by prearranging for the confederates to choose the same wrong

---

12 Asch, *supra* note 10, at 32.

13 *Id.*

14 *Id.* All of the subjects were male college students. Subsequent work has revealed that women are, under certain circumstances, even more susceptible to conformity than men. *See, e.g.,* Alice H. Eagly & Carole Chrvala, *Sex Differences in Conformity: Status and Gender Role Interpretations,* 10 PSYCHOL. OF WOMEN Q. 203, 217 (1986).

15 Asch, *supra* note 10, at 32.

16 *Id.*

17 *Id.*

18 *Id.*

answer.[19] Even though the four confederates were obviously mistaken, subjects of the experiment nevertheless provided the same wrong answer as the confederates 35.1% of the time,[20] with 70% of subjects providing the wrong answer at least once during the experiment.[21]

Most importantly, Asch found that the introduction of certain variables dramatically affected conformity levels. For example, Asch found that conformity fell quickly as the confederate group size dropped from three (31.8% of the answers were wrong) to two (13.6% were wrong) to one (3.6% were wrong), but did not increase much in groups larger than seven (maxing out at about 37%).[22] Moreover, conformity fell by more than 50% in most variations of the experiment when one of the confederates dissented from the group opinion.[23]

Not surprisingly, other studies have shown that conformity levels increase when (as is true in the law) the answer is more ambiguous. For example, in studies pre-dating Asch's, Muzafer Sherif placed a subject in a dark room and asked the person to look at a projected spot of light and guess how far it moved.[24] Notably, the light did not move at all, but only appeared to move due to an optical illusion called the autokinetic effect.[25] The precise extent of the perceived movement was thus impossible for subjects to determine objectively.[26]

In one variation of the experiment, a subject gave individual assessments and was subsequently put in a room with a confederate, whose opinion intentionally varied from the subject's.[27] As expected, the subject's assessments quickly came into line with the confederate's or (when the subject was placed in a group) with the group's.[28] Thus, Sherif found that questions with ambiguous answers tended to produce more conformity, because people were understandably less certain of their original assessments.

---

19 *Id.*

20 *Id.* at 35.

21 PHILIP ZIMBARDO, THE LUCIFER EFFECT: UNDERSTANDING HOW GOOD PEOPLE TURN EVIL 263 (2007). Some subjects always went along with the wrong answer, while other subjects never chose the wrong answer. Still others chose the wrong answer occasionally. Overall, though, the "wrong" answer was given thirty-five percent of the time. Asch, *supra* note 10, at 33, 35.

22 Asch, *supra* note 10, at 35.

23 *Id.* at 34–35.

24 MUZAFER SHERIF, THE PSYCHOLOGY OF SOCIAL NORMS 95–96 (1973).

25 *Id.* at 91–92.

26 *Id.* at 92.

27 *Id.* at 93.

28 *Id.* at 100–08; *see also* Muzafer Sherif, *A Study of Some Social Factors in Perception*, in 27 ARCHIVES OF PSYCHOLOGY 5, 32–41 (R.S. Woodworth ed., 1935).

The Asch and Sherif studies offer compelling evidence—also supported by more recent experiments—that a group member's opinion is easily affected by the group's overall judgment.[29] Critically, the studies also reveal that this effect varies considerably, depending on situational variables, such as the level of ambiguity in the assigned task, the number of people in the group, the status of the person in the group (e.g., high status people feel more comfortable offering a contrasting view), and the existence of dissenters.[30] The situation, in short, has a powerful effect on human behavior.

B. Foundational Studies on Obedience

Not long after Asch's provocative study, Stanley Milgram focused on a different but related question: When will people follow the unethical or immoral orders of an authority figure?[31]

The answer turned out to be both surprising and alarming. Milgram found that, under the right conditions, an experimenter could successfully order more than sixty percent of people to administer painful and dangerous electric shocks to an innocent, bound older man with a heart condition, despite the man's repeated pleas to be let go.[32]

These results came out of Milgram's brilliantly staged and oft-cited experiment. It typically[33] began with a subject and a secret accomplice of the experimenter drawing lots to determine who would be a "teacher" and who would be a "learner" in a study that the subject believed to be about the learning process.[34] In fact, the experiment had nothing to do with learning theory, and the drawing was "rigged so that the subject was always the teacher and the accomplice always the learner."[35]

The teacher (the subject) and the learner (the accomplice) were then taken to another room where the teacher watched the experimenter connect electrical

---

29 ROSS & NISBETT, *supra* note 3, at 33 (explaining that "studies [have] demonstrated again and again that arbitrarily constructed groups, even ones that hold no long-term power to reward conformity or punish dissent, can exert potent conformity pressures").

30 *Id.* at xiv (noting that "what has been demonstrated through a host of celebrated laboratory and field studies is that manipulations of the immediate social situation can overwhelm in importance the type of individual differences in personal traits or dispositions that people normally think of as being determinative of social behavior").

31 For a discussion of the differences between conformity and obedience, *see infra* Part III.

32 STANLEY MILGRAM, OBEDIENCE TO AUTHORITY: AN EXPERIMENTAL VIEW 55–57, 60 (1974).

33 Milgram conducted many versions of this experiment, but the variation described here is among the most commonly described.

34 MILGRAM, *supra* note 32, at 18–19.

35 *Id.* at 19.

wires to the learner.[36] The experimenter explained that the teacher was soon going to have to ask the learner a series of questions and that, after each wrong answer, the teacher was going to have to administer an electric shock through the attached wires using a generator in another room.[37]

After the experimenter applied a gel that was supposed to help the electrical current flow to the learner without causing blistering or burning,[38] the learner (in one version of the study) informed the experimenter and the teacher that he had a heart condition.[39] The experimenter explained that, although the shocks might be painful, they would not be dangerous.[40] While in the teacher's presence, the experimenter then strapped the learner to a chair to ensure that he could not break free.[41] The teacher/subject was subsequently brought back to the original room and placed in front of the electric shock generator.[42]

The experimenter instructed the teacher to ask the learner questions through an intercom (the subject could not see the learner in this variation of the experiment) and to shock the learner for each wrong answer, starting with 15 volts.[43] With every additional wrong answer, the experimenter explained that the teacher had to increase the shock by one increment on the generator, with each increment producing an extra 15 volts of electricity.[44] The generator, which was clearly marked, went as high as 450 volts.[45] At 375 volts, the generator read: "Danger: Severe Shock," and between 435 and 450 volts, the generator's label simply indicated "XXX."[46]

Unbeknownst to the teacher, the learner was not actually attached to the generator and was instructed to provide numerous wrong answers through a nearby key pad.[47] Milgram's objective was to measure how long the teachers would continue to follow the experimenter's orders to apply the shocks.[48]

---

36 *Id.*

37 *Id.* at 19–21.

38 *Id.* at 19.

39 *Id.* at 55–57.

40 *Id.* at 56.

41 *Id.* at 19.

42 *Id.* at 3.

43 *Id.* at 20–21, 28.

44 *Id.* at 20–21.

45 *Id.* at 28.

46 *Id.*

47 *Id.* at 19–20, 22.

48 *Id.* at 23–24, 26.

In the initial stages, nearly all of the subjects/teachers willingly applied the lowest level of shocks on the generator. But as the experiment continued, the learner/confederate produced increasingly loud and forceful objections to the experiment, including (as time went on) requests to be let out of the experiment and complaints about heart pain.[49] Eventually, the learner refused to answer and became ominously silent.[50] The subject, of course, had no idea that these objections and protests were pre-recorded and played at precise points during the experiment.

Despite the learner's pleas to be released, his complaints about heart pain, his refusals to answer, and his eventual silence, Milgram found that the majority of subjects complied with the experimenter's instructions fully, including repeated applications of the 450 volt shock lever. A startling sixty-five percent of subjects obeyed the instructions to the bitter end in this scenario.[51]

Critically, Milgram, like Asch and Sherif before him, found that context was essential. Obedience varied a great deal depending on a number of situational factors, such as whether the learner was in the same room as the teacher,[52] whether the person issuing the orders was in the same room as the teacher,[53] whether subjects assisted a confederate with the shocks instead of administering the shocks themselves,[54] and whether someone dissented (such as when the experiment occurred in a group setting).[55]

Milgram's findings have been replicated throughout the world, with similar results in both genders, different socioeconomic groups, and different countries.[56] Moreover, because of new ethics guidelines that make Milgram's work difficult to reproduce today,[57] his work still stands as one of the most significant contributions to our understanding of human obedience to authority. We know

---

49 *Id.* at 22–23, 56–57.

50 *Id.* at 23.

51 *Id.* at 60. In fact, compliance levels varied and were even higher in other versions of the experiment. *Id.* at 35, 60–61, 119.

52 *Id.* at 34–36.

53 *Id.* at 59–60, 62.

54 *Id.* at 119, 121–22.

55 *Id.* at 118–21.

56 *Id.* at 5, 170 (socioeconomic groups), 62–63 (gender), 170–71 (international replications).

57 SHELLEY E. TAYLOR ET AL., SOCIAL PSYCHOLOGY 228 (11th ed. 2003). There are also other reasons to expect that a similar experiment could not be fully replicated today, including the increasing sophistication of subjects and the expense of such work. *See* David J. Luban, *Milgram Revisited,* 9 RESEARCHING L. (Am. B. Found., Chi., Ill.), Spring 1998, at 1, 6. Nevertheless, a partial replication was recently conducted and produced results very similar to Milgram's. Jerry Burger, *Replicating Milgram,* APS OBSERVER, Dec. 2007, available at http://www.psychologicalscience.org/observer/getArticle.cfm?id=2264.

from his work that, given the right situation, most people will follow orders that they would ordinarily consider blatantly immoral.

C. The Power of the Situation

The basic point of these studies is not that people are social conformists, mindless followers of authority, or latent sadists. Indeed, the studies do not suggest that "people are disposed to obey authority figures unquestioningly."[58] Rather, the point is that "manipulations of the immediate social situation can overwhelm in importance the type of individual differences in personal traits or dispositions that people normally think of as being determinative of social behavior."[59] As a result, "subtle features of . . . [the] situation . . . prompt[ ] ordinary members of our society to behave . . . extraordinarily."[60]

The importance of context is clear. Asch's studies showed that a single variable, such as reducing the number of people in the group or introducing a dissenting group member, could dramatically reduce conformity levels.[61] Milgram also found that the existence of a dissenter could reduce obedience and that other factors, such as placing the experimenter outside of the room or moving the "learner" into the same room as the subject, produced a similar effect.[62] Social psychologists, in short, have found that conformity and obedience are heavily context-dependent and that social forces play a much greater role—and dispositional traits a much weaker role—in determining human behavior than most people assume.

III. Situational Conformity and Obedience: Implications for Lawyer Behavior

Conformity and obedience are different in subtle but important ways. According to Milgram, "[o]bedience to authority occurs within a hierarchical structure in which the actor feels that the person above has the right to prescribe behavior. Conformity regulates the behavior among those of equal status . . . ."[63] So, for example, the discovery hypothetical primarily implicates issues of obedience, because a superior is issuing an order to a subordinate. The hypothetical would implicate conformity if the young lawyer saw her colleagues at the firm concealing "smoking guns" and consequently followed their lead without

58 ROSS & NISBETT, *supra* note 3, at 58.

59 *Id.* at xiv.

60 *Id.* at 56.

61 *See supra* notes 10–30 and accompanying text.

62 MILGRAM, *supra* note 32, at 34–36, 59–60, 62.

63 *Id.* at 114.

being instructed to do so. Despite the differences in the two concepts, both of them can exist in many law practice settings.

A. Situational Factors that Produce Conformity in Law Practice

Recall that numerous factors contribute to conformity, including the size of the group, the level of unanimity, the ambiguity of the issues involved, group cohesiveness, the strength of an individual's commitment to the group, the person's status in the group, and basic individual tendencies, such as the desire to be right and to be liked.[64]

Many of these factors frequently exist in law practice.[65] For instance, lawyers often have to tackle problems that contain many ambiguities of law and fact. Even questions that, at first, seem to have well-settled answers are often susceptible to an analysis that can make the answers seem unclear. Indeed, law students are trained to perform this particular art of legal jiu jitsu.[66]

Given the uncertainty of many legal answers and lawyers' expertise in identifying (or manufacturing) those uncertainties, lawyers are especially susceptible to the forces of conformity. For example, the subordinate in the initial discovery hypothetical may review the discovery rules and find language that could theoretically (though implausibly) support the partner's position, particularly if she perceives that other lawyers at the firm are engaging in similar behavior.[67] Thus, despite her initial belief about the document's discoverability, she might begin to believe that her original view was either a product of inexperience or a failure to appreciate fully all of the nuances about how discovery works in practice.[68] She might consequently come to think that her initial view was wrong, even though it was quite clearly right. And if the document's discoverability fell into an area that

---

[64] *See supra* notes 22–30 and accompanying text.

[65] Obviously, law practice occurs in a wide range of environments, and each setting produces its own constraints and social forces that profoundly influence attorney behavior. *See generally* Andrew M. Perlman, *A Career Choice Critique of Legal Ethics Theory,* 31 SETON HALL L. REV. 829 (2001). Thus, the analysis offered here is not universally applicable.

[66] *See, e.g.,* Duncan Kennedy, *Legal Education and the Reproduction of Hierarchy,* 32 J. LEGAL EDUC. 591, 595–96 (1982).

[67] Again, obedience and conformity are related, but distinct, forces. Technically, conformity is an effect that occurs in groups, whereas the original hypothetical primarily concerns obedience. *See supra* note 63 and accompanying text.

[68] One recent study suggests that the social forces that produce conformity actually affect one's subjective perception of a situation and do not simply push someone to conform for the sake of fitting in with the group. Gregory S. Berns et al., *Neurobiological Correlates of Social Conformity and Independence During Mental Rotation,* 58 BIOLOGICAL PSYCHIATRY 245, 251 (2005). For a useful summary of the experiment, see Zimbardo, *supra* note 21, at 264–65. The study implies that the associate may truly believe that the partner is right and will not consciously recognize that she is engaging in an act of conformity.

was even slightly grey instead of black and white, the tendency to conform would be even greater.[69]

The hierarchical structure of lawyering also makes conformity more likely. Studies suggest that strong conformity forces exist even in "arbitrarily constructed groups . . . that hold no long-term power to reward conformity or punish dissent."[70] Lawyers, however, work in groups that are not arbitrarily constructed and actually do hold long-term power to reward conformity or punish dissent. Attorneys typically work in settings where other group members, such as senior partners or corporate executives (e.g., in-house counsel jobs), control the professional fates of subordinates, a condition that increases the likelihood of conformity.[71] So, for example, the young lawyer in the initial hypothetical would feel a powerful, though perhaps unconscious, urge to conform, especially given that she had trouble finding a job and faced significant financial burdens.

Social status also affects conformity. There is evidence that people with more social prestige feel more comfortable deviating from the prevailing opinion.[72] By contrast, a person with a lower status, such as the junior law firm associate in the hypothetical, will be more likely to conform to protect her more vulnerable position.

Unanimity also encourages conformity, and unanimity is common among lawyers who are working together on the same legal matter. Studies have shown that zealous advocacy tends to make lawyers believe that the objectively "correct" answer to a legal problem is the one that just so happens to benefit the client.[73] This tendency causes teams of lawyers to agree on many issues, making it even more difficult for dissenting voices to be heard. So in the discovery example, the absence of a dissenting voice would make the subordinate more likely to assume that her initial position was incorrect or, at the very least, not worth pursuing.

The point here is not that lawyers will always conform to the views of superiors or colleagues. Plenty of lawyers express their own beliefs, even under

---

69 *See, e.g.*, Wash. State Physicians Ins. Exch. & Ass'n v. Fisons Corp., 858 P.2d 1054 (Wash. 1993).

70 ROSS & NISBETT, *supra* note 3, at 33.

71 *See* Perlman, *supra* note 65, at 834–39; *see also* Kim, *supra* note 6, at 1005–06, 1008 (describing the particularly strong social forces that act on in-house counsel).

72 *See, e.g.*, CASS R. SUNSTEIN, CONFORMITY AND DISSENT 12 (Univ. of Chi. Law Sch. Pub. Law & Legal Theory Working Paper Series, Paper No. 34, 2002), available at http://www.law.uchicago.edu/academics/publiclaw/resources/34.crs.conformity.pdf; *see also* Sherif, *supra* note 28, at 42.

73 *See, e.g.*, Donald C. Langevoort, *Where Were the Lawyers? A Behavioral Inquiry Into Lawyers' Responsibility for Clients' Fraud,* 46 VAND. L. REV. 75, 95–111 (1993).

very difficult circumstances.[74] The claim is that powerful social forces exist in many law practice settings that make conformity more likely than most people would expect.

B. Situational Factors that Produce Obedience in Law Practice

Law practice also tends to produce excessive obedience. To understand why this happens, consider just a few of the key variables that affected obedience in Milgram's experiments: (1) the existence of a plausible legitimate reason for the wrongful conduct (in Milgram's experiment, it was to study the learning process); (2) the use of positive language to describe the negative behavior (e.g., the shocks help the person to learn); (3) the presentation of rules that, on their face, seem benign (e.g., hit the lever when the learner gives a wrong answer); (4) the creation of some kind of verbal or contractual obligation to help (e.g., the experimenter asked participants to agree to follow certain procedures before starting the experiment); (5) the assignment of specific roles (e.g., teacher/learner); (6) the physical separation of the person carrying out the orders and the victim (e.g., the learner being in an adjoining room); (7) the close proximity of the person issuing the orders and the person following them (e.g., the experimenter being in the same room as the subject); (8) the blurring of responsibility or the assignment of responsibility to someone else (e.g., when a subject asked the experimenter who was responsible for the fate of the bound man, the experimenter told the subject that the experimenter, not the subject, was responsible); (9) the incremental nature of the experiment (e.g., starting with only fifteen volts and increasing the shocks by small increments); (10) the social prestige of the setting (e.g., Milgram's initial experiment occurred in a laboratory at Yale University);[75] and (11) the elimination of dissent (e.g., Milgram found that, when the experiment was done in groups, the presence of a dissenter dramatically reduced obedience).[76]

---

74 *See, e.g.*, Meyerhofer v. Empire Fire & Marine Ins. Co., 497 F.2d 1190, 1192–93 (2d Cir. 1974) (describing a junior associate who resigned from his job and reported his firm's misconduct to the Securities and Exchange Commission); Jane Mayer, *The Memo: How an Internal Effort to Ban the Abuse and Torture of Detainees Was Thwarted*, NEW YORKER, Feb. 27, 2006, at 32, 32 (describing Alberto Mora's defiance of his superiors in an attempt to stop the torture of detainees at the Guantanamo Bay prison); Douglas McCollam, *The Trials of Jesselyn Radack*, AM. LAW., July 1, 2003, at 19–21 (describing Jesselyn Radack's defiance of superiors in the Justice Department regarding the Department's tactics in questioning John Walker Lindh, the so-called American Taliban).

75 Obedience levels dropped when Milgram moved the experiment to a rundown office building unaffiliated with Yale. MILGRAM, *supra* note 32, at 66–70 (noting a reduction in obedience from sixty-five percent to forty-eight percent when the study was moved from Yale to a rundown office building that had no apparent ties to the University). Although Milgram's particular results were not statistically significant, subsequent studies reveal that the status of the authority figure is a factor that influences obedience. ZIMBARDO, *supra* note 21, at 275–76.

76 Social psychologists have offered many explanations for Milgram's results, but the explanations described here are some of the most common. *See* ZIMBARDO, *supra* note 21, at 273–75. For a slightly different

Many of these factors exist in law practice. First, lawyers can usually frame unethical or illegal requests in ways that fit the first and second factors. For example, the partner who requested the withholding of the smoking gun document could articulate a legitimate reason for the request, such as "it's not within the scope of discovery" or "it's arguably privileged," even though neither statement is objectively accurate. The partner could also explain that withholding the document will produce the salutary effect of promoting zealous advocacy and advancing the client's cause. In these ways, the authority figure—in this case, a partner—could give the subordinate a seemingly plausible explanation for refusing to disclose the document and argue that it promotes a positive outcome (factors one and two respectively).

The partner could also frame the instruction as part of litigation's unwritten "rules of the game" (factor three).[77] In this way, the demand appears entirely benign. Moreover, the consequences may also appear inconsequential. Unlike Milgram's experiments, where obedience resulted in painful electric shocks to a man with a heart condition, compliance in many (but not all)[78] lawyering contexts produces far less dire consequences. For instance, in the discovery example, the lawyer is "merely" withholding a document as part of the discovery "game" that all lawyers play,[79] not causing somebody physical pain or risking someone's life. The seemingly benign nature of the request can enhance the subordinate's willingness to obey.

This factor is likely to have more weight if the subordinate has little litigation experience and does not have the necessary expertise to question the partner's

---

list, *see* Philip G. Zimbardo, *A Situationist Perspective on the Psychology of Evil: Understanding How Good People Are Transformed into Perpetrators*, in THE SOCIAL PSYCHOLOGY OF GOOD AND EVIL 21, 27–28 (Arthur G. Miller ed., 2004).

77 *See, e.g.,* Wash. State Physicians Ins. Exch. & Assoc. v. Fisons Corp., 858 P.2d 1054, 1074–85 (Wash. 1993) (remanding the case for the imposition of sanctions on attorneys who had abused the judicial process by failing to disclose a smoking gun document in discovery); *see also* Kimberly Kirkland, *Ethics in Large Law Firms: The Principle of Pragmatism,* 35 U. MEM. L. REV. 631, 718–19, 724 (2005) (concluding from her study of large law firm litigators that they frequently "view zealous advocacy as an affirmative moral obligation" and view the ideal of litigation as "a game well-played").

78 *See, e.g.,* Balla v. Gambro, 584 N.E.2d 104, 107 (Ill. 1991) (describing the firing of an in-house counsel after he warned the company's president that one of the company's products could cause "death or serious bodily harm to patients").

79 Discovery is a "game" in both an academic and layman's sense. From an academic perspective, discovery has an interesting game theory dimension. For a very nice discussion of game theory's implications for discovery in the context of a subordinate lawyer, see David McGowan, *Politics, Office Politics, and Legal Ethics: A Case Study in the Strategy of Judgment,* 20 GEO. J. LEGAL ETHICS 1057, 1071–75 (2007). But discovery is also a game in the more ordinary sense of the word. Namely, lawyers frequently think of the process not so much as a method for discovering the truth, but as a game that needs to be won. *See generally* Robert L. Nelson, Essay, *The Discovery Process as a Circle of Blame: Institutional, Professional, and Socio-Economic Factors that Contribute to Unreasonable, Inefficient, and Amoral Behavior in Corporate Litigation,* 67 FORDHAM L. REV. 773, 794–95 (1998).

authority. In contrast, if the subordinate has handled numerous document productions and has a strong experiential basis to know that the partner's request is impermissible, the subordinate is less likely to give the partner's demand a benign gloss. Of course, even when it is absolutely clear that the partner's behavior is unethical or illegal, the subordinate may still comply if some of the other factors favoring obedience are present.[80]

Factors four (an agreement to help the authority figure) and five (the presence of assigned roles) also frequently exist in law practice. The lawyer-client relationship itself is essentially an agreement to help clients achieve their goals (factor four). When combined with the common perception that a lawyer's morality is distinct from individual morality (i.e., role differentiation),[81] lawyers are more apt to view arguably legal conduct as part of their job as an advocate (factor five). Thus, subordinates, such as the associate in the discovery example, will view the authority's instructions as part of the agreement to help the client, with the mindset of role-differentiation only adding to the belief that any moral consequences are not the subordinate's primary concern.[82]

The effect that role has on judgment is nicely illustrated by a study involving 139 auditors at major accounting firms. The auditors were given hypothetical accounting scenarios and asked to assess the accounting in each situation.[83] Roughly half of the accountants were asked to assume that they were retained by the firm that they were auditing, while the rest were supposed to assume that they had been hired by an outside investor who was considering making an investment in the company.[84] On average, the auditors were significantly more likely to find that the company's financial reports complied with generally accepted accounting standards when they played the role of the company's accountant than when they

80 For a recent real world illustration of this effect, see Qualcomm Inc. v. Broadcom Corp., No. 05cv1958-B, 2008 WL 66932, at *13 n.10 (S.D. Cal. Jan. 7, 2008); *see also* REGAN, supra note 6, at 4–6, 294, 323–24 (emphasizing the role that social context played in a lawyer's failure to disclose pertinent information); Lawrence J. Fox, *I'm Just an Associate. . At a New York Firm,* 69 FORDHAM L. REV. 939 (2000) (offering a realistic account of a subordinate who is asked to bury discovery documents); Luban, *supra* note 6, at 95–96 (describing a subordinate's complicity with a partner's obvious perjury to a federal judge).

81 DAVID LUBAN, LAWYERS AND JUSTICE: AN ETHICAL STUDY 104–47 (1988) (describing and criticizing this view); Richard Wasserstrom, *Lawyers as Professionals: Some Moral Issues,* 5 HUM. RTS. 1, 3–4 (1975) (same).

82 *See generally* ZIMBARDO, *supra* note 21 (describing his well-known Stanford Prison Experiments, in which he demonstrated the substantial impact that social role has on behavior); *see also* Kim, *supra* note 6, at 1012 (making a similar point); David Luban, *Integrity: Its Causes and Cures,* 72 FORDHAM L. REV. 279, 292–93 (2003) (reviewing the social psychology literature, including Professor Zimbardo's work, that highlights the extent to which role influences behavior).

83 *Id.* at 1009–10 (citing DON A. MOORE ET AL., CONFLICT OF INTEREST AND THE UNCONSCIOUS INTRUSION OF BIAS (Harv. Bus. Sch. Negotiations, Orgs. & Mkts. Unit, Working Paper No. 02–40, 2002)).

84 *Id.* at 1009.

played the role of the investor's accountant.[85] Their assigned roles, in other words, heavily influenced their perspectives.

Another factor that contributes to obedience is that attorney misbehavior will typically affect victims who are more remote in time and place than the victims in Milgram's experiments (factor six). For example, the failure to produce a smoking gun document will affect an adverse party, but in a much more indirect way than the application of an electric shock. Similarly, assisting a company's financial fraud (e.g., the Enron scandal) will primarily harm shareholders and lower-level employees, people with whom lawyers have little contact.[86] Because a lawyer will perceive these harms to be less immediate and proximate than someone suffering painful electric shocks in an adjoining room, this factor favors obedience in the lawyering context even more strongly than what Milgram found in many of his experiments.

Not only will the victims of legal misconduct be relatively remote, but the person issuing the orders will be nearby. Milgram found that obedience increased when the authority figure and the subordinate were in the same room and decreased when the experimenter issued orders using a tape recorder or from another location.[87] For lawyers, the authority figure who issues the instruction will typically be a colleague or a client with whom the subordinate has a great deal of contact and who may exercise considerable power regarding the subordinate's future at the firm, thus further adding to the likelihood of obedience (factor seven).[88]

Subordinates may also discount their responsibility for their conduct (factor eight) by shifting moral responsibility to the person issuing the orders. Indeed, when Milgram's subjects asked who was responsible for what happened in the laboratory, the experimenter said that he (the experimenter) was ultimately responsible for any harm to the learner.[89] This shifting of responsibility is especially likely in the legal ethics context, where Model Rule 5.2(b) states that "[a] subordinate lawyer does not violate the Rules of Professional Conduct if that lawyer acts in accordance with a supervisory lawyer's reasonable resolution of an

---

85 *Id.* at 1009–10; *see also* ROSS & NISBETT, *supra* note 3, at 72–75 (describing partisans' inability to view a given situation objectively); Linda Babcock et al., *Biased Judgments of Fairness in Bargaining*, 85 AM. ECON. REV. 1337, 1339–42 (1995) (finding that lawyers' assessment of the value of a case varies dramatically depending on which side they are assigned to represent); Langevoort, *supra* note 73, at 95–111.

86 Kim, *supra* note 6, at 1033 (making this point in the context of securities fraud).

87 MILGRAM, *supra* note 32, at 59–62.

88 Kim, *supra* note 6, at 1003–04, 1011 (making a similar observation).

89 MILGRAM, *supra* note 32, at 7–8.

arguable question of professional duty."[90] Given the ambiguity of so many legal and ethical duties, subordinates will frequently find that a supervisory lawyer's instructions reflect a "reasonable resolution of an arguable question of professional duty."[91] Thus, subordinate lawyers are likely to believe that responsibility for their actions ultimately lies with superiors.

Another significant factor that contributed to obedience in Milgram's subjects was the incremental nature of the experiment (factor nine).[92] Each new shock was only modestly larger than the last, making it difficult for subjects to distinguish morally what they were about to do from what they had already done.[93] This phenomenon of justifying past actions in a way that makes conduct of a similar type in the future seem ethical is known as cognitive dissonance.[94] In Milgram's experiment, it meant that obedience was more likely at higher voltages because subjects had already complied with shocks at lower voltages.[95]

In one of the few articles to describe in detail the implications of Milgram's work for legal ethics, Professor David Luban contends that the incremental nature of the experiment offers the best explanation for the obedience that Milgram observed.[96] Luban explains that "[b]y luring us into higher and higher level shocks, one micro-step at a time, the Milgram experiments gradually and subtly disarm our ability to distinguish right from wrong."[97]

Professor Luban is clearly right that obedience in Milgram's experiments occurred, in part, because the experimenter made seemingly benign initial requests followed by gradually larger requests for punishment.[98] Nevertheless, the incremental nature of the experiment probably did not play the decisive role that Luban suggests. Although each step up on the shock generator was only fifteen volts, subjects did not experience each step in precisely the same way. In fact, some of the shocks were meaningfully different from the shocks that had come before. For example, the learner eventually requested to be let go at 150 volts,

---

[90] MODEL RULES OF PROF'L CONDUCT R. 5.2(b) (2007).

[91] *See* Luban, *supra* note 57, at 5 (making a similar point).

[92] MILGRAM, *supra* note 32, at 20–21.

[93] *Id.* at 149; *see also* Luban, *supra* note 57, at 8.

[94] Luban, *supra* note 57, at 8.

[95] MILGRAM, *supra* note 32, at 149.

[96] Luban, *supra* note 6, at 103.

[97] *Id.* Professor Luban also pointed out how this force can affect law practice, such as in the discovery context. He explained that an initial attempt to avoid producing a document can lead to more and increasingly problematic attempts to resist the production of relevant information, leading ultimately to the type of situation described in the initial hypothetical. *Id.* at 106.

[98] MILGRAM, *supra* note 32, at 20–21.

making any additional shocks quite different in effect. Indeed, when subjects resisted Milgram's commands, more did so at this point in the experiment than at any other time.[99] Moreover, the learner's complaints about heart pain and his subsequent ominous silence made additional shocks clearly distinguishable from the shocks that the subjects had already administered. Thus, cognitive dissonance and the incremental nature of the experiment were important, but clearly not the only—or even the primary—factors.

In fact, Professor Luban offers an example that illustrates the limited explanatory force of increments. In the famous Berkey-Kodak case, an associate failed to report the blatant lying of a respected senior colleague.[100] Luban contends that the associate's obedience reflected the kind of incremental "corruption-of-judgment" that produced obedience in Milgram's experiments.[101] Namely, the associate's loyalty to his lying superior was the "end of a slippery slope, beginning with lawful adversarial deception and culminating with lies, perjury, and wrongful obedience."[102]

The problem is that, even if a contentious discovery process had preceded the lying, there is quite a leap from engaging in contentious discovery to helping a partner lie to a federal judge. The Berkey-Kodak case, according to Professor Luban's own account, involves a large jump on the legal ethics equivalent of the shock generator from a small shock to a potentially lethal one. Such a jump is not consistent with Luban's contention that subordinates follow orders as a result of a gradual corruption of judgment. Of course, increments play a role in excessive obedience, but such obedience can readily occur in cases like Berkey-Kodak without increments, assuming other forces are present.[103]

---

99 *Id.* at 35–37 (noting that in this version of the experiment, five of the fifteen people who disobeyed the experimenter did so at 150 volts, the point at which the "learner" demanded to be let go); *see also* Doris, supra note 7, at 50 (making a similar observation).

100 Luban, *supra* note 57, at 4.

101 *Id.* at 9.

102 *Id.*

103 Professor Luban also argues that "[t]he Achilles' heel of situationism is explaining why anyone deviates from the majority behavior." Luban, *supra* note 6, at 101; Luban, *supra* note 82, at 295–96 (making a similar point). In fact, this Achilles' heel can only be found on a straw man version of situationism. Situationists do not claim that context fully explains all human behavior or that everyone will act the same way in the same situation. Doris, *supra* note 7, at 25 (asserting that neither he nor any situationist he knows of maintains that "correlations between measurable dimensions of situations and single behaviors typically approach 1.0"); *id.* at 46 (acknowledging that dispositional differences provide a partial explanation for why some people did not comply with the experimenter's commands in Milgram's experiments). Rather, situationists make more modest claims, such as that dispositional traits are far less important than most people realize and that context is a much more significant determinant of human behavior than people typically believe. *Id.* at 24–25.

Social prestige (factor ten) is another of those forces.[104] Many law firms, especially larger firms, are held in high esteem among lawyers. These firms are thus likely to produce the same social forces that Yale University produced in Milgram's subjects.[105] Moreover, smaller firms can also produce the same effect, especially if the superior is an experienced and respected partner.[106]

Finally, the partner in the example is the only person to offer an opinion, so the subordinate has not heard any dissent regarding the partner's interpretation. The absence of dissent (factor eleven) is yet another force that favors obedience.[107]

In addition to the factors that contributed to obedience in Milgram's experiment, there is one factor that favors obedience in the lawyer situation that did not exist for Milgram: professional and financial self-interest.[108] In Milgram's experiments, subjects were told that they could keep the modest amount of money that they had been given, even if they refused to continue with the experiment.[109] Moreover, their professional fortunes were in no way affected by whether they complied. In contrast, a subordinate lawyer has a lot to lose by refusing to obey: a job. The subordinate's concern for her job, particularly a junior lawyer who may have had few other professional opportunities, is likely to be substantial. Thus, this factor also weighs heavily in favor of compliance and suggests that lawyers might be even more likely to comply than the subjects of Milgram's experiments.

There is, however, one factor that weighs against the hypothetical lawyer's compliance: obedience could lead to monetary sanctions or disbarment. If the lawyer believes that she faces a real chance of discipline, she arguably would be more likely to resist the partner's demands. The powerful concern for professional survival might trump the other social forces that favor obedience and conformity

---

[104] MILGRAM, *supra* note 32, at 66–70 (noting a reduction in obedience from sixty-five percent to forty-eight percent when the study was moved from Yale to a rundown office building that had no apparent ties to the University). *But see supra* note 75.

[105] MILGRAM, *supra* note 32, at 66–70.

[106] Luban himself offers a nice description of this phenomenon in the context of the Berkey-Kodak case, *see* Luban, *supra* note 6, at 95–96, though he does not ultimately identify it as a force that could impact the associate's behavior independently of his corruption of judgment theory.

[107] *See, e.g.*, Kim, *supra* note 6, at 1021 (making this point in the in-house counsel context); *see also* ROSS & NISBETT, *supra* note 3, at 41 (explaining why people who witness, or find themselves in, a potentially dangerous situation will fail to act if other people also fail to do so). There are, of course, many other forces that contribute to obedience that were not part of Milgram's experiment. For example, a superior can increase obedience by demeaning the intended victim. MILGRAM, *supra* note 32, at 9. Thus, the common tendency among lawyers to demonize an opponent or the opponent's lawyers makes it more likely that a subordinate will carry out an unethical command that adversely affects that opponent.

[108] Kim, *supra* note 6, at 1027 (describing this self-serving bias).

[109] *See* MILGRAM, *supra* note 32, at 14–15 (showing the newspaper announcement that was used to recruit subjects).

and make compliance less likely than in Milgram's experiments, where subjects had no equivalent incentive to dissent.

There are three problems with this view. First, it assumes that the subordinate will recognize that the partner's demands implicate her ethical duties. The reality is that, given the forces at work, she may easily begin to question her initial opinion and view the partner's opinion as, at the very least, justifiable.[110] This tendency to interpret the situation so that it does not implicate one's ethical or moral responsibility is sometimes called ethical fading.[111] Specifically, the actor reinterprets the situation in such a way that the ethical nature of the situation fades from view. If the subordinate does not even identify the ethics issue, the concern for professional survival cannot override the social forces favoring conformity and obedience.

Second, even if the subordinate recognizes the ethical dilemma, she is not likely to be terribly concerned about discipline. Rule 5.2 only imposes discipline if the superior's instructions were clearly unethical. So unless the instruction is blatantly impermissible, the subordinate is not likely to fear any disciplinary consequences.

Third, even if the instruction is blatantly unethical or illegal, a lawyer may still not fear discipline, at least in the discovery context. Bar discipline for this sort of misconduct occurs rarely, and sanctions are usually far below what would be necessary to discourage this sort of behavior.[112]

The case of *Washington State Physician Insurance Exchange & Associates v. Fisons Corp.* is illustrative.[113] The original plaintiff in that case was a child who had suffered seizures and permanent brain damage after taking medicine that Fisons manufactured.[114] The plaintiff's discovery requests called for all documents related to a particular ingredient in the medicine and any information that Fisons had

---

110 Luban, *supra* note 6, at 95–96 (describing this phenomenon in the context of the Berkey-Kodak case).

111 Ann E. Tenbrunsel & David M. Messick, *Ethical Fading: The Role of Self-Deception in Unethical Behavior*, 17 SOC. JUST. RES. 223, 224–25 (2004); *see also* Kim, *supra* note 6, at 1026–29 (citing additional studies that have reached a similar conclusion); Luban, *supra* note 82, at 280 (observing that "hundreds of experiments reveal that when our conduct clashes with our prior beliefs . . . our beliefs swing into conformity with our conduct, without our ever noticing").

112 *See* John S. Beckerman, *Confronting Civil Discovery's Fatal Flaws*, 84 MINN. L. REV. 505, 572–73 (2000) (noting the general reluctance of courts to refer discovery violations to disciplinary authorities); Bruce A. Green, *Policing Federal Prosecutors: Do Too Many Regulators Produce Too Little Enforcement?*, 8 ST. THOMAS L. REV. 69, 90 (1995) (citing Commission on Evaluation of Disciplinary Enforcement, Am. Bar Ass'n, Report to the House of Delegates 36 (1991)). It is too early to tell whether the recent sanctions for discovery abuses in the recent high profile case of Qualcomm Inc. v. Broadcom Corp., No. 05cv1958-B, 2008 WL 66932, at *13 n.10 (S.D. Cal. Jan. 7, 2008), will have any impact on lawyers' behavior.

113 858 P.2d 1054 (Wash. 1993).

114 *Id.* at 1058.

about that ingredient's dangerousness in children.[115] Despite these requests, the defense lawyers relied on a contorted and frivolous rationale for not turning over documents that proved that Fisons knew about the ingredient's toxicity in children.[116]

After an anonymous copy of the smoking gun emerged, the trial court considered and rejected any sanctions against the company or its lawyers.[117] The trial court relied heavily on the notion that "the conduct of the drug company and its counsel was consistent with the customary and accepted litigation practices of the bar of [the county] and of [Washington] state."[118] The Washington Supreme Court reversed that determination,[119] but the ultimate sanction for the lawyers was an out-of-court settlement of a mere $325,000,[120] a small fraction of the fees that the firm had generated from the case. Put simply, the defense lawyers received a slap on the wrist for a rather blatant discovery violation that was similar to the one in the initial hypothetical.

Finally, the risks of sanctions and discipline are no higher (and may be lower) than the risks associated with making the report. Many lawyers in this circumstance would be concerned not only about losing their current jobs, but about whether a report of this sort might make it difficult to get jobs in the future once they were labeled as whistleblowers.

To summarize, the hypothetical associate faces considerable pressures to conform and obey and few risks from compliance and obedience. Even if the misconduct is uncovered, a risk that may be rather small, she is unlikely to face any punishment that will adversely affect her career. The ultimate and disturbing result is that she is prone to obey the partner who has issued the unethical and illegal command.

IV. Implications for the Law of Lawyering

The challenge for legal ethicists is to counter the social forces that contribute to excessive conformity and obedience. In one of the few efforts to address that challenge, Professor Luban has suggested that, by educating lawyers about their own tendencies to obey authorities, they might be better able to resist an order to

---

[115] *Id.* at 1080–83.

[116] *Id.* at 1079–84.

[117] *Id.* at 1074–75.

[118] *Id.* at 1078.

[119] *Id.* at 1085.

[120] Stuart Taylor, Jr., *Sleazy in Seattle,* AM. LAW., Apr. 1994, at 5, 5.

commit illegal or unethical conduct.[121] Unfortunately, there is little evidence that this so-called "enlightenment effect" holds much promise, at least in this particular context.[122]

There are some steps, however, that might make a difference in some cases. Rather than offering an exhaustive list of potential remedies, the following proposals are illustrations of how social psychology could play a more active role in debates about professional regulation.[123]

A. Providing Whistleblower Protections for Attorneys

Currently, some states do not offer whistleblower protections for lawyers.[124] In those jurisdictions, lawyers who are fired after disclosing illegal conduct have no legal recourse against their employers. This lack of whistleblower protection is unwise, given that it reinforces the already strong social forces that weigh against defiance in such circumstances.[125]

The problem is amply illustrated by the well-known Illinois case, *Balla v. Gambro, Inc.*,[126] in which Gambro's general counsel, Mr. Balla, learned that his company was selling dialyzers for dialysis machines that were not within federal specifications and that could cause potentially serious medical complications.[127] After Balla unsuccessfully urged Gambro not to put the dialyzers on the market, Gambro fired Balla.[128] Balla subsequently revealed the defects to the Federal Food

---

121 Luban, *supra* note 6, at 116 ("Perhaps the best protection [for lawyers against the forces described in Milgram's experiments] is understanding the . . . insidious way [those forces] work on us."); *see also* Deborah L. Rhode, *Ethics by the Pervasive Method*, 42 J. LEGAL EDUC. 31, 47 (1992) (suggesting that exposure to Milgram's work might help law students avoid unethical behavior).

122 Thomas Blass, *The Milgram Paradigm After 35 Years: Some Things We Now Know About Obedience to Authority*, in OBEDIENCE TO AUTHORITY: CURRENT PERSPECTIVES ON THE MILGRAM PARADIGM 35, 50–53 (Thomas Blass ed., 2000) (drawing on several studies and concluding that "[b]eing enlightened about the unexpected power of authority may help a person stay away from an authority-dominated situation, but once he or she is already in such a situation, knowledge of the drastic degree of obedience authorities are capable of eliciting does not necessarily help free the individual from the grip of the forces operating in that concrete situation"). Despite this lack of evidence, I share Professor Luban's intuition that enlightening lawyers about this tendency is worthwhile. I show my students a video of the Milgram experiments on the last day of class in the hope that it might make some difference at some point in their professional lives.

123 For an excellent analysis of social psychology's implications for the regulation of lawyers who represent publicly traded companies, see Kim, *supra* note 6, at 1034–75.

124 *See, e.g.*, Balla v. Gambro, Inc., 584 N.E.2d 104, 107 (Ill. 1991).

125 Kim, *supra* note 6, at 1042–44, 1064–71 (arguing that securities lawyers should receive whistleblower protection under the Sarbanes-Oxley Act for reasons similar to those described here); Douglas R. Richmond, *Professional Responsibilities of Law Firm Associates*, 45 BRANDEIS L.J. 199, 257 (2007) (arguing in favor of whistleblower protection for lawyers).

126 *Balla*, 584 N.E.2d at 104.

127 *Id.* at 106.

128 *Id.*

and Drug Administration and sued for retaliatory discharge under the state's whistleblower statute.[129]

The Illinois Supreme Court rejected Balla's claim, explaining that whistleblower statutes exist to protect employees who might otherwise be reluctant to report corporate malfeasance.[130] The court's primary rationale was that, since lawyers in Illinois already had an ethical obligation to report misconduct like the selling of the defective dialyzers, Mr. Balla did not need whistleblower protection.[131]

On its face, the Illinois Supreme Court's logic is sound. If the whistleblower statute is unclear regarding its application to lawyers and if the purpose of the statute would not be furthered by applying it to attorneys, Balla should not receive protection.

The problem is that the court's opinion rested on a flawed assumption about human behavior. Social psychology suggests that lawyers in Balla's situation would find it difficult to disclose information of the sort described in the opinion, especially without whistleblower protection. First, lawyers like Balla are unlikely to put much stock in the ethical obligation that the court referenced. The rule is ambiguous, and the various forces described earlier can lead a lawyer to interpret the rule as not requiring disclosure. Moreover, there are very few instances where lawyers have been disciplined for failing to disclose information under similar circumstances. Thus, any fear of discipline would be overshadowed by what the lawyer had to lose (i.e., a job) by reporting the misconduct and by other situational forces, such as Balla's distance from the prospective victims, his proximity to his bosses, the hierarchical structure of a corporation, and the presumptive absence of dissent.

Balla's refusal to comply given these variables was notable (and one of the reasons the case is so widely reported), but there is no reason to think that his response was typical. Given similar circumstances, lawyers will face considerable pressure to conceal a client's harmful conduct and to develop legal justifications for that concealment. The reality, in other words, is that lawyers—like most people—face significant social pressures that make it difficult to resist a client's insistence on harmful and potentially illicit courses of conduct, even if a duty to report exists. Justice Freeman, in his dissent, stated this point convincingly:

---

129 *Id.*

130 *Id.* at 108.

131 *Id.* at 108–09.

> [T]o say that the categorical nature of ethical obligations is sufficient to ensure that the ethical obligations will be satisfied simply ignores reality. Specifically, it ignores that, as unfortunate for society as it may be, attorneys are no less human than nonattorneys and, thus, no less given to the temptation to either ignore or rationalize away their ethical obligations when complying therewith may render them unable to feed and support their families.

I would like to believe, as my colleagues apparently conclude, that attorneys will always "do the right thing" because the law says that they must. However, my knowledge of human nature, which is not much greater than the average layman's, and, sadly, the recent scandals involving the bench and bar of Illinois are more than sufficient to dispel such a belief. Just as the ethical obligations of the lawyers and judges involved in those scandals were inadequate to ensure that they would not break the law, I am afraid that the lawyer's ethical obligation to "blow the whistle" is likewise an inadequate safeguard for the public policy of protecting lives and property of Illinois citizens.

As reluctant as I am to concede it, the fact is that this court must take whatever steps it can, within the bounds of the law, to give lawyers incentives to abide by their ethical obligations, beyond the satisfaction inherent in their doing so. We cannot continue to delude ourselves and the people of the State of Illinois that attorneys' ethical duties, alone, are always sufficient to guarantee that lawyers will "do the right thing." In the context of this case, where doing "the right thing" will often result in termination by an employer bent on doing the "wrong thing," I believe that the incentive needed is recognition of a cause of action for retaliatory discharge, in the appropriate case.[132]

Justice Freeman got it exactly right. The court should have acknowledged how human beings are likely to behave, discounted the ethical obligation to disclose, and affirmed the value of whistleblower protection. Of course, the existence of whistleblower protection will not ensure that all lawyers reveal information about a client's illicit actions, but such protection could make a difference in some cases by weakening the significant psychological forces that weigh against such disclosures.

---

132 *Id.* at 113 (Freeman, J., dissenting).

B. Enforcing the Duty to Report Misconduct

Most states impose on attorneys a duty to report another lawyer's misconduct if the misconduct implicates the lawyer's trustworthiness, honesty, or fitness to practice law.[133]

The problem with the rule is that most lawyers, especially subordinates, are not eager to report the misconduct of other attorneys. For instance, the associate in the discovery example may find it difficult to report the partner, even if she were convinced that the partner had engaged in an intentional and egregious discovery violation that reflected on the partner's trustworthiness or honesty.[134] As Part III explained, the subordinate is likely to feel considerable pressure to obey the authority figure and to be complicit in the authority's misconduct. It would take an unusual subordinate to not only resist that temptation, but to take the next step of reporting the superior to the bar.[135]

Part of the problem is that Rule 8.3, like the disclosure duty in Illinois, is rarely enforced. The vast majority of states do not have a single reported case where a lawyer was disciplined under this rule.[136] As a result, lawyers are willing to run the very negligible risk of discipline in order to avoid having to report another attorney to the bar.

One potential solution is to increase enforcement of the rule so that lawyers perceive a greater threat to their own professional well-being if they fail to report the misconduct of other attorneys under Model Rule 8.3. Indeed, Illinois's experience with this rule suggests that modest increases in enforcement can have a discernable effect on reporting. After the Illinois Supreme Court issued an opinion that disciplined a lawyer under Rule 8.3,[137] Illinois's bar disciplinary authorities observed a substantial increase in Rule 8.3 reports.[138]

---

133 MODEL RULES OF PROF'L CONDUCT R. 8.3(a) (2007).

134 *See, e.g.*, Luban, *supra* note 6, at 95 (describing an associate's failure to report a partner's obvious perjury in a well-known case).

135 *See* Meyerhofer v. Empire Fire & Marine Ins. Co., 497 F.2d 1190, 1192–93 (2d Cir. 1974) (describing the actions of a junior associate who resigned from his firm and reported the firm's misconduct to the Securities and Exchange Commission).

136 *See* Fred C. Zacharias, *What Lawyers Do When Nobody's Watching: Legal Advertising as a Case Study of the Impact of Underenforced Professional Rules*, 87 IOWA L. REV. 971, 999 & n.134 (2002) (noting the lack of enforcement of this rule).

137 *In re* Himmel, 533 N.E.2d 790, 794–95 (Ill. 1988).

138 Leonard E. Gross, *Legal Ethics for the Future: Time to Clean Up Our Act?*, 77 ILL. B.J. 196, 198 n.26 (1988).

The increase in Illinois implies that the fear of discipline can prompt lawyers to report misconduct that they otherwise would have swept under the rug.[139] Thus, increased enforcement of Rule 8.3 can also help to weaken the social forces that would ordinarily encourage lawyers, especially subordinate lawyers, to ignore perceived misconduct.

C. Strengthening the Responsibilities of Subordinate Lawyers

Another Model Rule that impacts the conduct of subordinate lawyers is, unsurprisingly, the rule written specifically for subordinate lawyers—Rule 5.2. That rule states that "[a] subordinate lawyer does not violate the Rules of Professional Conduct if that lawyer acts in accordance with a supervisory lawyer's reasonable resolution of an arguable question of professional duty."[140] The rule essentially permits a lawyer to carry out a superior's orders as long as those orders constitute a reasonable interpretation of the relevant ethical obligation.

On its face, the rule makes sense. After all, why should a lawyer face discipline for following the arguably ethical and legal orders of a superior?

But as with the *Balla* decision, the rule rests on a questionable assumption about human behavior. By allowing a lawyer to avoid responsibility for "reasonable resolutions of an arguable question of professional duty," the rule opens the door to interpreting a wide range of instructions as "arguably" ethical. For example, the subordinate in the discovery example is likely to understand her ethical obligations through the distorted prism of what the partner wants, leading her to construe the discovery issue as "arguable" and the partner's resolution of it as "reasonable." This tendency, referred to earlier as ethical fading,[141] suggests that the typical subordinate attorney will conclude that Rule 5.2 applies and that she can carry out the partner's commands without fear of professional discipline.[142]

One possible solution is to repeal Rule 5.2(b) to make it clear that subordinates have an independent duty to assess whether a particular course of action is ethical and legal.[143] Of course, the "just following orders" defense could still be raised as a mitigating factor when determining the appropriate

---

139 Mary T. Robinson, *A Lawyer's Duty to Report Another Lawyer's Misconduct: The Illinois Experience*, 2007 SYMP. ISSUE PROF. LAW. 47, 49–50 (observing an increase in reporting after Himmel); Patricia A. Sallen, *Combating Himmel Angst*, 2007 SYMP. ISSUE PROF. LAW. 47, 49–50 (describing a similar phenomenon in Arizona).

140 MODEL RULES OF PROF'L CONDUCT R. 5.2(b) (2007).

141 *See supra* note 111 and accompanying text.

142 *See* Luban, *supra* note 57, at 5 (making a similar point).

143 *See* Carol M. Rice, *The Superior Orders Defense in Legal Ethics: Sending the Wrong Message to Young Lawyers*, 32 WAKE FOREST L. REV. 887, 931–34 (1997) (making a similar proposal). *But see* Richmond, *supra* note 125, at 213 (endorsing Rule 5.2(b)).

punishment.[144] But it should not allow a lawyer to avoid discipline entirely. Indeed, such a defense is generally rejected in most other contexts.[145] Moreover, by putting subordinates on notice that they have an independent duty to question a superior's orders, subordinates would be less likely to assume that a superior's actions are permissible and more likely to offer resistance to unethical or illegal commands.[146]

V. Conclusion

More than forty years of research into social psychology has revealed that, under certain conditions, we will conform to group opinions and obey authorities who issue illegal instructions. If a majority of people are willing to apply dangerous electric shocks to a bound older man with a heart condition just because someone with a lab coat says so, there is every reason to believe that lawyers will frequently obey their superiors when instructed to perform unethical or illegal tasks.

By drawing on a tiny fraction of social psychology research, this Article suggests some steps that the profession can take to weaken the social forces that produce excessive obedience and conformity. These suggestions, however, have important limitations, such as the problem of ethical fading.[147] Nevertheless, they hint at a much broader project, one that draws on the very rich literature in social psychology to address various causes of attorney misconduct.

NOTES

1. Professor Perlman argues that lawyers are "especially susceptible to the forces of conformity. . . ." Part of his argument involves the interaction of law's many ambiguities ("the answer could be this, or it could be that—it depends") with the pressure of practice. When you're working for someone who has several more years of experience than you do, how confident will you be that your assessment of a situation is right and the more senior person's assessment is wrong? And how hard will you push to persuade the more senior person that your assessment is the right one?

2. Are the protections (like whistleblower protections) or sanctions (duty to report misconduct) that Professor Perlman emphasizes likely to change a subordinate's behavior? Does it matter to you that the protections or sanctions might

---

[144] *See* Rice, *supra* note 143, at 889 n.5, 912–14; *see also* Richmond, *supra* note 125, at 212.

[145] *See* Rice, *supra* note 143, at 904–14.

[146] Of course, this approach cannot counter the ethical fading phenomenon. A lawyer will only consider reporting another lawyer if she recognizes the ethical issue.

[147] *See supra* note 111 and accompanying text.

come months or years after you make a decision about whether or not to speak out when you think someone more senior to you is doing something wrong?

3. We will be discussing the behavior of Mahlon Perkins in the Berkey-Kodak case in more detail in Chapter V. We could have put that article in this chapter, but we believe that grouping it with a discussion of Dewey & LeBeouf's failures is a good bookend to the choices that the leaders of the Dewey & LeBeouf firm made.

CHAPTER 4

Wrongful Obedience and the Professional Practice of Law[*]

Catherine Gage O'Grady[**]

Abstract

Occasionally, brand new attorneys engage in unprofessional or unethical conduct. This article explores the probable impact of one theory, grounded in social psychology, that may help explain egregious conduct in a new lawyer—wrongful obedience. The article begins by discussing the seminal studies on obedience conducted by Stanley Milgram in the 1960s, which were recently partially replicated. Applying what we know about obedience to the professional practice of law presents an interesting dichotomy: every lawyer, even a brand new lawyer, has, at a minimum, an individual, autonomous professional obligation to practice law ethically and professionally. Yet, attorneys work in groups, often in hierarchies that exist within established office cultures, and new attorneys face overwhelming pressures to conform to the perceived group ethic. The fact that every new lawyer knows about her independent professional obligations does not appear to weaken an attorney's desire to obey a supervising authority.

While rule changes may help facilitate defiance against wrongful directives and encourage attorney whistleblowing, this article argues that revising statutes and rules of professional conduct will not go far enough to ward off a new attorney's tendency to obey—attorneys simply will not actively resist their own wrongful obedience, and indeed may not even recognize it as such, unless the culture of their immediate work environment encourages them to exercise autonomous independent judgment in the face of conformance pressures. This conclusion finds recent support within the tragic

---

* This piece was originally published as Catherine Gage O'Grady, *Wrongful Obedience and the Professional Practice of Law*, 19 J.L. BUS. & ETH. 9 (2013).

** Professor of Law, Sandra Day O'Connor College of Law at Arizona State University. My thanks to Michael Saks and Ted Schneyer for helpful comments on this article and to Ashley Votruba for skilled research assistance.

circumstances of the long time child sexual abuse committed by Pennsylvania State University football coach Gerald Sandusky and the conclusions of the Special Investigative Counsel, as found in the recent report known as the "Freeh Report." In the last section of this paper, I draw parallels to Milgram's conclusions as well as to recent efforts within and outside of law, including the Freeh Report's recommendations to universities, to offer suggestions for managing and supervising lawyers within legal organizations to guard against wrongful obedience and ensure that conformance pressures do not override autonomous professional judgment in the legal workplace.

I. Introduction

> "[O]ften, it is not so much the kind of person a man is as the kind of situation in which he finds himself that determines how he will act."
>
> —Stanley Milgram[1]

Gerry Deegan was fresh out of law school and had been a prosecutor for the Orleans Parish District Attorney's Office for less than one year when he hid exculpatory blood evidence.[2] As a direct result of Deegan's conduct, an innocent man, John Thompson, served 18 years in prison, with 14 years in isolation on death row.[3] Although Deegan was inexperienced and had not been long out of law school, we can surmise that he was not completely naïve about what he had done because many years later, by way of an apparent death bed confession, he confided in a friend, another lawyer, that he hid blood evidence in the Thompson case and the defendant remained on death row.[4] Joseph Fortenberry was an

---

1 STANLEY MILGRAM, OBEDIENCE TO AUTHORITY: AN EXPERIMENTAL VIEW 205 (1974).

2 *See generally* Connick v. Thompson, 131 S. Ct. 1350 (2011).

3 *See id.* at 1355. The evidence Deegan hid was a fabric swatch a police technician took from a robbery victim's pants that was stained with the perpetrator's blood. Shortly before Thompson's trial for armed robbery, the prosecutor's office sent the fabric to the crime laboratory for testing. After the blood was tested, a report was delivered to the district attorney's office indicating that the blood on the swatch was type B. Although there is no evidence that at the time the report was received that anyone in the District Attorney's office knew Thompson's blood type, Thompson's blood was later determined to be type O. *Id.* at 1356. Neither the swatch nor the crime lab's report was ever turned over to the defense. Instead, on the first day of trial, Gerry Deegan checked all of the physical evidence out of the police property room, including the blood stained fabric swatch. Later, Deegan checked all of this physical evidence except the fabric swatch into the courthouse property room. The swatch was never seen again. *Id.* Thompson was convicted of armed robbery and then later convicted and sentenced to death for murder in a crime unrelated to the armed robbery. Just weeks before Thompson's execution date, an investigator hired by the post-conviction defense attorneys discovered micro-fiche records of the crime lab report that had been delivered to the prosecutors in Thompson's armed robbery case indicating that a blood stained swatch had been tested and that the test demonstrated that the perpetrator's blood type was B. After confirming that Thompson's blood type was O, the case against Thompson unraveled, a new jury on re-trial found him not guilty, and Thompson was released from prison. *Id.* at 1356–57.

4 Several years after the conclusion of Thompson's armed robbery trial, Deegan learned that he was terminally ill with colon cancer, and he knew he did not have long to live. He asked a friend, lawyer Michael Riehlmann, to meet him at a bar after work and at that meeting told him that he had hidden blood evidence in Thompson's armed robbery trial that might have been exculpatory to Thompson, who was currently on death

associate at a large New York law firm when he heard his supervising partner perjure himself before a federal judge, did nothing to correct the misstatements, and later took steps to support the partner's lie by hiding documents that should have been disclosed in a large antitrust suit.[5] The lawyers' fraud on the court was dramatically revealed during cross-examination of a key witness, after which the judge expressed outrage. The jury—left with the impression that the defense hid evidence—returned a plaintiff's verdict, and Fortenberry's budding career at the law firm was cut short.[6]

Finally, consider the recent stark example of David L. Helmers, a new attorney recognized by the Kentucky Supreme Court as "inexperienced, impressionable, and [who] may have been influenced, and perhaps even led astray, by [] more seasoned lawyers."[7] The Kentucky Supreme Court permanently disbarred Helmers for "personally and directly deceiving" his clients notwithstanding that he may have acted at the direction of his supervising attorney, who was then a "well-regarded and reputable attorney."[8]

---

row. Riehlmann urged Deegan to rectify the ethical wrongdoing by confessing it, but Deegan did not. A short time later, Deegan died. For five years, Riehlmann kept Deegan's confession to himself—he did not report Deegan's conduct to any authority until the investigator uncovered the lab report shortly before Thompson's execution date. *Id.* at 1374–75 (Ginsburg, J., dissenting). The Supreme Court of Louisiana sanctioned Riehlmann with a public reprimand for failure to report the wrongdoing once Deegan told him about it. *In re* Riehlmann, 891 So. 2d 1239, 1249–1250 (La. 2005). Although the Disciplinary Board had recommended a six-month suspension, on appeal the Supreme Court determined that Riehlmann's conduct was "merely negligent" and it imposed a reprimand instead, the ABA baseline sanction. *Id.* at 1242–49 (accepting Riehlmann's contention that his 5 year reporting delay was due to personal issues and the shock of hearing that his friend, Deegan, was dying of cancer).

5 *See* David J. Luban, *The Ethics of Wrongful Obedience,* in ETHICS IN PRACTICE: LAWYERS' ROLES, RESPONSIBILITIES, AND REGULATION 94, 95 (Deborah L. Rhode ed., 2000) (discussing the painfully infamous *Berkey v. Kodak* case); JAMES B. STEWART, THE PARTNERS 327–65 (1983) (During a judicially overseen deposition, the senior partner told a federal judge that documents requested by the other side had been inadvertently destroyed. *Id.* at 341. Fortenberry reacted to this misstatement during the deposition by whispering to the partner that the documents were back at the office, but the partner ignored Fortenberry and continued to assert that he had in fact been responsible for overseeing the documents' destruction. *Id.* at 341, 356. During a break, Fortenberry tried again to explain to the partner that the documents he told the judge were destroyed were in fact back at the office and he was again ignored. *Id.* At that point, Fortenberry returned to the office, found the documents, and took them to the Rockefeller Center offices where he hid them by storing them in a locked closet. *Id.* at 356. At this point, the senior partner treated the documents as though they had been destroyed and signed an affidavit attesting to their destruction. *Id.* at 344); *see also* Catherine Gage O'Grady, *Preparing Students for the Profession: Clinical Education, Collaborative Pedagogy, and the Realities of Practice for the New Lawyer,* 4 CLINICAL L. REV. 485, 505–06 (1997); *Ted Schneyer, Professional Discipline for Law Firms?,* 77 CORNELL L. REV. 1, 2 (1991); Mary Twitchell, *The Ethical Dilemmas of Lawyers on Teams,* 72 MINN. L. REV. 697, 743–46 (1987).

6 Luban, *supra* note 5, at 95; Stewart, *supra* note 5, at 363.

7 Kentucky Bar Ass'n v. Helmers, 353 S.W.3d. 599, 603 (Ky. 2011).

8 *Id.* at 602. The Kentucky Bar Association Board of Governors found Helmers guilty of six counts of professional ethics violations for, among other things, failing to inform or explain to class action clients relevant

This article explores the professional practice dynamics that may help explain why new attorneys like Deegan and Fortenberry engage in unprofessional and unethical conduct. A number of theories might explain egregious conduct in a new lawyer, and I do not attempt to evaluate them all.[9] Instead, I explore the probable impact of one viable theory grounded in social psychology: wrongful obedience in the practice of law.[10] I begin by discussing the seminal study on obedience conducted by Stanley Milgram in the 1960s and recently partially replicated by Jerry Burger of Santa Clara University. Applying what we know about obedience to the professional practice of law presents an interesting dichotomy: every lawyer, even a brand new lawyer, has, at a minimum, an autonomous professional obligation to practice law ethically and professionally. Professional obligations attach to attorneys as individuals. Yet, attorneys work in groups, often in hierarchies that exist within established office cultures, and new attorneys face overwhelming pressures to conform to the perceived group ethic. The fact that every new lawyer knows about her independent professional obligations does not appear to weaken an attorney's desire to obey a supervising authority. After exploring the studies on obedience, I discuss the profession of

---

settlement information, failing to exercise independent professional judgment, and violating the Rules of Professional Conduct at the direction of other lawyers. *Id.* at 601–01

[9] For example, in the Thompson case, a number of theories were advanced to account for Deegan's conduct. Given Deegan's death-bed confession, it is likely that he at least knew about a prosecutor's duty under Brady v. Maryland to turn exculpatory evidence over to the defense. *Connick,* 131 S. Ct. at 1370 (Ginsberg, J., dissenting); *see* Brady v. Maryland, 373 U.S. 83, 87 (1963) (holding that due process requires the prosecution to turn over to the defense any evidence that is favorable to the accused and material to guilt or punishment). Perhaps Thompson wrongly concluded that the evidence at issue did not fall within *Brady* as "exculpatory" because the prosecutors did not know Thompson's blood type at that time. *See Connick,* 131 S. Ct. at 1357 (noting that Connick conceded that the failure to produce the crime lab report constituted a Brady violation). Alternatively, perhaps, as Thompson suggested recently in the United States Supreme Court, the Parish District Attorney's Office needed to do a better job training its prosecutors on the scope of Brady v. Maryland and general prosecutorial responsibilities and ethics. *Id.* Or finally, perhaps Deegan was just an irrepressible rogue. *See id.* at 1368 (Scalia, J., concurring) (concluding that the misconduct in the case was likely the work of a single "miscreant prosecutor" who was willfully making an effort to "railroad Thompson"). In this article, I propose another theory: perhaps Deegan was not an uneducated, unreflective practitioner or an unethical rogue—perhaps instead he was responding to a desire to obey the perceived wishes of his supervisors and conform, not to a set of professional ethical standards, but to a perceived office culture.

[10] This article contributes to a small collection of scholarship on wrongful obedience among lawyers. *See, e.g.,* Luban, *supra* note 5 (describing Milgram's work and relating it to the *Berkey v. Kodak* example of wrongful obedience); Andrew M. Perlman, *Unethical Obedience by Subordinate Attorneys: Lessons From Social Psychology,* 36 HOFSTRA L. REV. 451 (2008) (describing Milgram's work and relating it to the legal profession); *Sung Hui Kim, The Banality of Fraud: Resituating the Inside Counsel as Gatekeeper,* 74 FORDHAM L. REV. 983, 992–97, 1001–26 (2005) (describing Milgram's work and relating it to the obedience pressures on corporate in-house counsel); *see also* Nancy M. Maurer & Robert F. Seibel, *Addressing Problems of Power and Supervision in Field Placements,* 17 CLINICAL L. REV. 145 (2010) (addressing problems of power imbalances in law student field placements); O'Grady, *supra* note 5, at 513–14 (1998) (addressing power imbalances in work collaborations, distinguishing clinical collaborations from law practice collaborations, and suggesting ways clinics can foster independent judgment to better prepare students for the realities of law practice).

law including Model Rules of Professional Responsibility 5.1 and 5.2, which pertain to associates and partners working in groups, as well as the Supreme Court's recent musings on a new attorney's competencies.

I conclude by extending Milgram's findings to the legal practice environment. While other scholars have offered rule changes that might help facilitate defiance against wrongful directives and encourage attorney whistleblowing,[11] my thesis is that revising statutes and rules of professional conduct will not go far enough to ward off a new attorney's tendency to obey—attorneys simply will not actively resist their own wrongful obedience, and indeed may not even recognize it as such, unless the culture of their immediate work environment encourages them to exercise autonomous independent judgment in the face of conformance pressures. This conclusion finds recent support within the tragic circumstances of the long time child sexual abuse committed by Pennsylvania State University ("Penn State") football coach Gerald Sandusky and the conclusions of the Special Investigative Counsel, as found in the June 12, 2012 report known as the "Freeh Report." The Freeh Report places blame squarely on the leaders of Penn State and the university's entrenched culture, which allowed Sandusky to continue sexually abusing children over a long period of time, despite the fact that Penn State employees had witnessed abuses and Penn State leaders knew about them.[12] In the last section of this paper, I draw significantly on the Freeh Report's final recommendations to university leaders in offering my own suggestions to the managing and supervising lawyers of legal organizations, law firms, and agencies to guard against wrongful obedience or complicity with improper practices and to ensure that conformance pressures do not override autonomous professional judgment in the legal workplace.[13]

---

[11] *See* Perlman, *supra* note 10, at 472–77 (suggesting changes to existing laws and rules of professional conduct to give lawyers whistleblower protection, strengthen a lawyer's duty to report the misconduct of other lawyers, and enhance a junior lawyer's responsibilities when receiving arguably unethical instructions from a superior); Luban, *supra* note 5, at 116 (suggesting that "[p]erhaps the best protection is understanding the illusions" of the "spirit of authority" because "forewarned truly is forearmed, at least to some extent"); Alex B. Long, *Whistleblowing Attorneys and Ethical Infrastructures,* 68 MD. L. REV. 786 (2009); Kenneth J. Wilbur, *Wrongful Discharge of Attorneys: A Cause of Action to Further Professional Responsibility*, 92 DICK. L. REV. 77 (1988).

[12] *See* FREEH SPORKIN & SULLIVAN, LLP, REPORT OF THE SPECIAL INVESTIGATIVE COUNSEL REGARDING THE ACTIONS OF THE PENNSYLVANIA STATE UNIVERSITY RELATED TO THE CHILD SEXUAL ABUSE COMMITTED BY GERALD A. SANDUSKY 16–17 (2012) [Hereinafter FREEH REPORT]; *see also* Ken Belson, Abuse Scandal Inquiry Damns Paterno and Penn State, N.Y. TIMES, July 12, 2012, available at http://www.nytimes.com/2012/07/13/sports/ncaafootball/13pennstate.html?pagewanted=all (quoting Russell Frank's description of the Freeh Report as offering conclusions that "could not be any more harsh" and which are "a very powerful indictment of the people in charge").

[13] In focusing my recommendations on the internal policies and procedures of a legal workplace to diminish wrongful obedience, rather than external regulatory reforms, this article joins other current theories of regulation that recognize the importance of evaluating the internal management structure and culture of the legal workplace to accomplish professional and ethical goals. *See* Ted Schneyer, *On Further Reflection: How*

II. Milgram and Burger: Obedience to Authority and Conformity to Perceived Norms

Much of what we understand today about obedience derives from Stanley Milgram's groundbreaking studies conducted in the early 1960s while he was in the Psychology Department at Yale University.[14] Milgram found that approximately two-thirds of the participants in his experiments would obey the commands of an authoritative experimenter who ordered them to inflict what the participant believed were painful shocks on an innocent victim.[15] In most cases, obeying the experimenter and causing another person to endure pain created enormous visible strain on the participants, but in significant numbers they nonetheless obeyed orders to shock people to such an extent that even Milgram was surprised by his results.[16]

Milgram designed a basic scenario and several variations on the basic scenario that were intended to test numerous theories on obedience and conformity. Forty-five years later, Jerry Burger, of Santa Clara University partially replicated Milgram's basic scenario.[17] In this section, I describe the general parameters of the Milgram and Burger basic scenarios and discuss the separate implications of conformity and enlightenment.[18] Later in the paper, I explore some of the findings of the experiments as well as some of Milgram's variations on the basic scenario and apply the findings to an understanding of obedience and conformity in the professional practice of law.

"Professional Self-Regulation" Should Promote Compliance With Broad Ethical Duties of Law Firm Management, 53 ARIZ. L. REV. 577, 578, 585 (2011) (suggesting state supreme courts adopt a meaningful program of "proactive, management-based regulation," which would require law firms to designate one or more lawyer-managers to be responsible for the firm's "ethical infrastructure"); Orly Lobel, *Lawyering Loyalties: Speech Rights and Duties Within 21st Century New Governance,* 77 FORDHAM L. REV. 1245 (2008) (discussing evidence that suggests that institutional culture has a significant impact on individual behavior in the organization); Marc L. Miller & Ronald F. Wright, *The Black Box,* 94 IOWA L. REV. 125 (2008) (evaluating the effectiveness in prosecutors' offices of focusing on internal regulation instead of external regulation).

14 MILGRAM, *supra* note 1, at 2–3.

15 *See generally* MILGRAM, *supra* note 1 (describing experiments where approximately two-thirds of the participants in the role of "teacher" obeyed the requests of an experimenter to shock a "learner" in 15-volt increments up to the end of the shock machine at 450 volts even though the learner was apparently in pain and wished to discontinue the experiment).

16 *Id.* at 33.

17 Jerry M. Burger, *Replicating Milgram: Would People Still Obey Today?,* 64 AM. PSYCHOLOGY 1, 1 (2009).

18 The description of Milgram's basic scenario is derived primarily from Milgram's 1974 book OBEDIENCE TO AUTHORITY: AN EXPERIMENTAL VIEW. An excellent general description of the experiments can also be found in David J. Luban, *The Ethics of Wrongful Obedience,* in ETHICS IN PRACTICE: LAWYER'S ROLES, RESPONSIBILITIES, AND REGULATIONS 94, 96–97 (Deborah L. Rhode ed., 2000).

A. The General Parameters of Milgram's Obedience Experiments

To attract participants in the experiments, Milgram placed a public announcement in the local newspapers seeking "persons needed for a study of memory" and offering to pay volunteers what would amount to about twenty dollars today.[19] In addition to the announcement, Milgram used direct mail solicitation to recruit participants.[20] Ultimately, Milgram's subjects included professional and blue-collar workers, highly educated and high-school educated persons, and middle class and affluent persons.[21] His early studies involved only men, but he later replicated the basic scenario with a variation that used women.[22] The "subject" of the study would arrive at the laboratory and meet another "participant" and the experimenter, who looked official in a gray lab coat.[23] The other participant was actually a confederate of the experimenter.[24] He was a forty-seven year old mild-mannered accountant who was trained for his role in the study.[25] The experimenter told the two participants that the study was about the impact of punishment on memory and learning, and that one volunteer would be the "learner" in the experiment while the other would be the "teacher."[26] The two participants drew slips of paper to receive their role assignments, but of course the drawing was rigged—the confederate was always the learner.[27] The learner was instructed to memorize word pairs and, using an intercom and lights system, the teacher would quiz him on the words.[28] If the learner made mistakes, he would receive increasingly severe electrical shocks from the teacher as punishment.[29] The experimenter showed the participants the shock generator with thirty switches: it started at 15 volts and increased to 450 volts and contained words to describe the

---

19 *See* MILGRAM, *supra* note 1, at 15. The announcement stated: "We will pay five hundred New Haven men to help us complete a scientific study of memory and learning." *Id.* It further stated: "Each person who participates will be paid $4.00 (plus 50 cents carfare) for approximately 1 hour's time," and "You will be paid $4.00 (plus 50 cents carfare) as soon as you arrive at the laboratory." *Id.*

20 *Id.* at 16 ("Names were sampled from the New Haven telephone directory, and a letter of invitation was sent to several thousand residents.").

21 *Id.* (noting that "[t]ypical subjects were postal clerks, high school teachers, salesmen, engineers, and laborers. Subjects ranged in educational level from one who had not finished high school to those who had doctoral and other professional degrees."). In addition, the subjects fell within three age categories: those in their twenties, thirties and forties. *Id.*

22 *Id.* at 62–63; Burger, *supra* note 17, at 4 (describing that one version of Milgram's experiments used women as subjects).

23 MILGRAM, *supra* note 1, at 16.

24 *Id.*

25 *Id.*

26 *Id.* at 18.

27 *Id.* at 19.

28 *Id.* at 19–20.

29 *Id.* at 20–21.

increasing severity of the shocks such as "slight shock" and "danger—severe shock."[30] The shocks increased in 15-volt increments. The experimenter gave the teacher a sample shock at 45 volts (the third switch on the generator), which "strengthened the subject's belief in the authenticity of the generator."[31] Before getting strapped in the hot seat, which was separated from the generator by a wall, the learner would mention in front of the subject that he had a mild heart problem to which the experimenter would reply: "Although the shocks can be extremely painful, they cause no permanent tissue damage."[32]

After the study was underway for a short while, the learner began to make mistakes.[33] At the 75-volt level, the learner grunted in pain (what Milgram described as "ugh"), which the teacher and the experimenter could hear through the wall.[34] Of course, no pain was actually received. The grunts continued as the shocks escalated, and each grunt was slightly louder than the previous one.[35] At 150 volts, the learner announced in agitation that he wanted to stop the experiment.[36] At other later points, the learner screamed.[37] Ultimately, the learner shouted that he needed to stop because his heart was bothering him. While the teachers almost always became upset, concerned, or confused, the experimenter remained steadfast: if the teacher paused or expressed reluctance to continue, the experimenter repeated the same language, pursuant to planned prompts, saying things like "the experiment requires you to continue" and "the learner must learn all the word pairs."[38] Throughout the experiment, the experimenter referred to the subject as "teacher" and the victim as "learner."[39] If the teacher stopped and wanted to know who would take responsibility for inflicting pain on the learner, the experimenter would reply, "I'm responsible for anything that happens to him."[40] At 300 volts, the learner refused to answer and the experimenter instructed the subject to treat silence as a wrong answer and continue with the shocks.[41] At 330 volts, the learner stopped responding altogether and was silent.[42] The

---

30 *Id.* at 20.

31 *Id.*

32 *Id.* at 19.

33 *Id.* at 22.

34 *Id.* at 23.

35 *Id.*

36 *Id.*

37 *Id.*

38 *Id.* at 21.

39 *Id.* at 18.

40 *Id.* at 74.

41 *Id.* at 23.

42 *Id.*

ominous silence continued all the way to the end of the shock machine. A session ended only when a participant expressed resistance to four prods by the experimenter or when the participant had pressed the highest switch on the generator, 450 volts, three times.[43]

The results of the basic scenario are now well known: despite their obvious uneasiness or dismay, 63% of the subjects complied with the experimenter all the way to the end of the shock machine—450 volts.[44] The studies were replicated around the world and involved over 1,000 participants.[45] Moreover, follow up studies demonstrated a stark contrast between what people unfamiliar with Milgram's experiments predicted regarding obedience and the actual results of the experiments. For example, in a fascinating follow up study, people who were unfamiliar with the experiments were given a description of the experiment and asked to predict how many people they thought would comply up the full range of the shock machine.[46] Most people predicted that only one teacher in one thousand would comply all the way to the end of the shock generator, and no one believed that they would comply.[47] Milgram himself found that a group of Yale seniors predicted an obedience rate of 1.2%, way below the actual obedience findings, and a "group of psychiatrists predicted that only .125% of participants would be fully obedient."[48] Further studies called into question the extent of the gap between predicted and actual obedience rates, finding it to be much smaller than Milgram found, but naïve subjects consistently and uniformly continued to underestimate rates of wrongful obedience.[49]

---

43 *Id.* at 21. Teachers discovered, to their dismay, that they were not finally finished with the experiment when they reached the last switch on the shock machine—at that point, the experimenter requested that they keep shocking the learner at the 450-volt level—until the learner (who had been utterly nonresponsive since the shock at voltage level 330) learned all the word pairs.

44 *Id.* at 35.

45 *Id.* at 3.

46 Luban, *supra* note 5, at 97.

47 *Id.*

48 Thomas Blass, *The Milgram Paradigm After 35 Years: Some Things We Now Know About Obedience to Authority*, in OBEDIENCE TO AUTHORITY: CURRENT PERSPECTIVES ON THE MILGRAM PARADIGM 35, 44 (Thomas Blass ed., 2000) (noting that Milgram described the results in a letter as follows: "Recently I asked a group of 40 Yale psychiatrists to predict the behavior of experimental subjects in a novel, though significant situation. The psychiatrists—although they expressed great certainty in the accuracy of their predictions—were wrong by a factor of 500.").

49 *See id.* at 53–54 (concluding after reviewing prediction studies that although naïve subjects did underestimate actual obedience rates, "the gap between estimated and actual obedience rates is often quite a bit smaller than what Milgram found").

B. A Recent Partial Replication of Milgram's Obedience Experiments

Milgram completed his work before implementation of the federal laws that created Institutional Review Board (IRB) guidelines—indeed Milgram's obedience studies are generally cited as an impetus for the creation of IRB guidelines and approval procedures.[50] Milgram's studies ignited enormous criticism and generated a number of ethical questions primarily because many of the participants visibly suffered significant short-term stress during the experiment. Thus, while some studies were "patterned" after Milgram's procedures, it would be several decades before an IRB approved study using procedures similar to Milgram's was conducted.[51]

In 2006, Jerry Burger from Santa Clara University received IRB approval to conduct an experiment that was a partial replication of Milgram's basic scenario.[52] To allow what he hoped would be useful comparisons to Milgram's results, Burger notes that he "did [his] best to replicate Milgram's procedures" using, for example, the same words in the memory test.[53] But Burger had to make several substantial changes to receive IRB approval, including ending the experiment at the 150-volt switch and then extrapolating on what a participant would do if allowed to continue to the end of the shock generator.[54] The 150-volt mark is the first time the learner shouts through the wall and asks to be released.[55] In reviewing Milgram's data, Burger found that 79% of the participants who went past the 150-volt mark would continue all the way to 450 volts.[56] Viewing the 150-volt mark as a "point of no return," Burger's experiment stopped immediately after the teacher either insisted on stopping despite the experimenter's series of prods or continued to the next switch on the generator.[57]

---

50 Burger, *supra* note 17, at 2. IRBs are governed by Title 45 CODE OF FEDERAL REGULATIONS Part 46. 45 C.F.R. §§ 46.101–46.505 (2012).

51 Burger, *supra* note 17, at 2.

52 *Id.*

53 *Id.* at 10.

54 *Id.* at 2, 7.

55 *Id.* at 2.

56 *Id.*

57 *Id.* at 1. In addition, Burger made the following additional refinements to Milgram's basic procedures: (1) Burger used a two-step detailed screening process to weed out participants who might have a negative reaction to the stress of the experience; (2) Burger's participants were told at least three times (twice in writing) that they could withdraw from the study at any time and keep the money they were paid (Milgram's participants were also told this but not as frequently); (3) Burger's participants received a 15-volt sample shock rather than the 45-volt sample shock Milgram gave his participants; (4) Burger allowed only a few seconds to elapse at the end of the experiment before the learner came into the room to reassure the participant that he was unharmed; and (5) the experimenter who ran the study was a clinical psychologist instructed to stop the experiment immediately if he saw any signs of excessive stress. *Id.* at 2.

After careful screening, Burger ended up with seventy participants (both men and women) whom he assigned to one of two conditions: a base condition and a modeled refusal condition.[58] The base condition operated like Milgram's basic scenario. The model refusal condition used two confederates, one posing as the learner and the other as a second teacher. At the 90-volt mark the confederate teacher refused to continue, despite the experimenters prods and the subject was then asked to proceed with the experiment.[59] In Burger's experiments, 70% of the participants in the base condition continued the procedure after pressing the 150-volt switch and 63.3% continued in the modeled refusal condition.[60] The 70% number is slightly lower than Milgram's comparable condition, but not statistically significant, and the 63.3% result from the modeled refusal condition was not statistically different from the percentage obtained in the base condition.[61] Thus, on the basis of this result, Burger concluded that "average Americans react to this laboratory situation today much the way they did 45 years ago."[62]

C. Conformance

Obedience is closely related to another powerful force in team dynamics: conformance pressures. While obedience refers to the action of a subject who complies with an explicit authority, conformance refers more generally to "the action of a subject when he goes along with his peers," who have "no special right to direct his behavior."[63] A number of well-known studies have established the

---

58 *Id.* at 3.

59 *Id.* at 8.

60 *Id.*

61 *Id.* Burger notes on his home page that "[c]ontrary to expectations, participants who saw a confederate refuse the experimenter's instructions obeyed as often as those who saw no model." Jerry Burger, Santa Clara University College of Arts & Sciences, http://www.scu.edu/cas/psychology/faculty/burger.cfm (last visited Aug. 1, 2012). This finding is in contrast to Milgram's findings, as described infra at notes 213–15 and accompanying text (describing Milgram's "two peers rebel" experimental condition that resulted in a drop in obedience when the subject witnessed confederate teachers disobeying the experimenter's instructions).

62 Burger, *supra* note 17, at 9. Like Milgram, Burger found no difference in obedience between men and women. *Id.* at 8. Social psychologists have suggested that there are too many differences between Milgram's experiments and Burger's to make any direct comparisons of absolute obedience levels, but that Burger's procedures might be useful to explore situational variables. *See* Kendra Cherry, *Researchers Replicate Milgram's Famous Obedience Experiment*, About.com: Psychology (Jan. 14, 2009), http://psychology.about.com/b/2009/01/14/researchers-replicate-milgrams-famous-obedience-experiment.htm (noting the following critiques of Burger's study: first, that " 'there are simply too many differences between this study and the earlier obedience research to permit conceptually precise and useful comparisons' " (quoting Arthur D. Miller) and, second, that "while 'direct comparisons of absolute levels of obedience cannot be made between the 150-volt maximum of Burger's research design and Milgram's 450-volt maximum, Burger's "obedience lite" procedures can be used to explore further some of the situational variables studied by Milgram as well as to look at additional variables,' such as situational and personality differences" (quoting Alan C. Elms)).

63 MILGRAM, *supra* note 1, at 113; *see also* PHILIP G. ZIMBARDO & MICHAEL R. LEIPPE, THE PSYCHOLOGY OF ATTITUDE CHANGE AND SOCIAL INFLUENCE 55 (1991) (defining conformity as "a change

power of conformity. Milgram's mentor, for example, Solomon Asch, conducted experiments in 1955 that placed a group of people in a room together, all confederates but for one subject, and asked everyone to match line lengths.[64] Despite the clear evidence of line length as seen with their own eyes, subjects overall went along with the plainly wrong answer from the group 36.8% of the time.[65] Moreover, Asch found that conformity rates dropped in smaller groups, where fewer people would be agreeing on the wrong answer, but rates did not increase when groups were larger than seven.[66] Follow up studies have shown that conformity rates increased when the answer is more ambiguous than Asch's plain line length question because people were naturally less certain of their own responses.[67] Such conformity experiments demonstrate the power that peer group dynamics and group norms can have over individual autonomous judgment, even when individuals have no long term stake in the group and even when correct solutions are clear rather than ambiguous.[68]

While the conformity experiments analyzed the influence of the group norm resulting in participants behaving in ways that led to group acceptance, Milgram specifically wanted to analyze the impact of direct commands to a person "to behave in ways that challenged his or her conscience and morality."[69] Milgram distinguished obedience from conformity, concluding that the most important difference between conformity and obedience is an individual's own sense of voluntarism.[70] Because the pressures to conform are implicit, subjects interpret their own conforming behavior as voluntary and maintain a sense of responsibility for their actions. Subjects tend to deny conformity: they do not recognize or

---

in belief or behavior in response to real or imagined group pressure when there is no direct request to comply with the group nor any reasons given to justify the behavior change").

64 *See* Solomon E. Asch, *Opinions and Social Pressure,* 193 SCI. AM. 31, 32 (1955).

65 PHILIP ZIMBARDO, THE LUCIFER EFFECT: UNDERSTANDING HOW GOOD PEOPLE TURN EVIL 263 (2007); MILGRAM, *supra* note 1, at 114. Some people chose the wrong answer occasionally. Over seventy percent of subjects provided the wrong answer at least once and only one-quarter of subjects never conformed at all. Asch, *supra* note 64, at 33, 35; *see also* Kim, *supra* note 10, at 1020 (describing Asch's experiments and findings).

66 Asch, *supra* note 64, at 35 (finding that conformity rates dropped to 31.8% in groups that included three others, to 13.6% in groups of two others, and to 3.6% in a group with one other person, and finding that conformity did not exceed a maximum rate of 37% in groups larger than seven).

67 Perlman, *supra* note 10, at 455 (describing experiments in MUZAFAR SHERIF, THE PSYCHOLOGY OF SOCIAL NORMS (1973)).

68 SOLOMON E. ASCH, SOCIAL PSYCHOLOGY 483–84 (1952) (noting that the tendency to reach agreement within a group is a "dynamic requirement of the situation").

69 Philip Zimbardo, *Zimbardo on Milgram and Obedience—Part I,* THE SITUATIONIST (April 14, 2009, 12:01 AM), http://thesituationist.wordpress.com/2009/04/14/zimbardo-milgram-and-obedience-part-i/.

70 MILGRAM, *supra* note 1, at 114–115 (identifying hierarchy, imitation, explicitness, and voluntarism as the key difference between obedience and conformity).

acknowledge that their actions were conforming to group norms. On the other hand, obedience to explicit authority is embraced: subjects deny personal involvement and attribute their behavior "exclusively to an external requirement imposed by authority."[71]

Thus, obedience and conformity are distinguishable forms of social influence; yet, in hierarchical, competitive workplaces, it may be difficult or impossible to separate the two pressures on individual workers—they work together in the workplace. A senior partner's vague facial expression or impatient wave of a hand, for example, might be interpreted by a newcomer in the work environment as an explicit directive, especially if the result of such an interpretation is consistent with the peer group norms or the established culture of that workplace.[72] Thus, in hierarchies, newer employees may be responding to numerous overlapping pressures including the pressure to obey a perceived wish from an authority in the workplace and the pressure to conform to a perceived entrenched workplace culture.

D. Enlightenment Effects: Knowledge and Resistance

Applying psychology's "enlightenment effect," constructed primarily by Kenneth J. Gergen, to obedience dynamics suggests that participants who know about Milgram's work and are "enlightened" on the underlying psychological principles of obedience will be liberated from the unwanted demands of authority.[73] Similarly, in discussing the optical illusions of the spirit engendered by authority and cognitive dissonance, David Luban concludes that "[p]erhaps the best protection is understanding the illusions themselves, their pervasiveness, the insidious way they work on us. Understanding these illusions warns us against them, and forewarned truly is forearmed, at least to some extent."[74] Milgram himself presented letters and testimonials from his participants suggesting that they learned something important through the studies that helped them resist future unwanted demands of authority.[75]

---

71 *Id.* at 115.

72 *See, e.g.,* MILTON C. REGAN, JR., EAT WHAT YOU KILL: THE FALL OF A WALL STREET LAWYER 323–24 (2004) (noting that for a subordinate lawyer (John Gellene) to conclude that a more senior lawyer wanted him to withhold information, "the older lawyer need not have explicitly advised Gellene to that effect" and that Gellene could have "acquiesced in [a] tacit message rather than press for a more sharply focused discussion of the issue"); *cf.* Harvey S. James, Jr., *Reinforcing Ethical Decision Making Through Organizational Structure,* 28 J. BUS. ETHICS 43, 49 (2000) (concluding that "employees may do 'bad things' because they believe that their superiors and the organization expect such behavior of them").

73 Kenneth J. Gergen, *Social Psychology as History,* 26 J. PERSONALITY & SOC. PSYCHOL. 309, 314 (1973); Blass, *supra* note 48, at 52.

74 Luban, *supra* note 5, at 116.

75 *See* MILGRAM, *supra* note 1, at app. 1; Blass, *supra* note 48, at 53; Luban, *supra* note 5, at 116.

No study, however, proves the enlightenment effect in obedience.[76] Indeed, one creative and interesting (but unpublished) obedience study suggests that the instinct to obey is so strong that even informed subjects will succumb to it almost unwittingly.[77] In 1982, a doctoral student named G.A. Shelton demonstrated that people have difficulty drawing parallels between their own obedient behavior and the behavior of others. Shelton first had all her participants read a detailed synopsis of Milgram's obedience experiments and she then asked them a set of questions about what they had read to ensure that they fully understood the underlying psychological principles regarding obedience to authority.[78] Thus, Shelton's subjects were fully aware of Milgram's work and appreciated the underlying psychological principles pertaining to obedience. Shelton then asked them to serve in the role of experimenters in what she explained would be an experiment similar to Milgram's: they were to be the experimenter overseeing a "teacher" who was to administer increasing shocks to a learner.[79] The experimenters were told that the learner was a confederate, but unbeknownst to the experimenters, the teacher was also a confederate.[80] As the experiment proceeded and the shock levels increased, the confederate teacher became increasingly upset at having to continue to issue shocks—expressing uneasiness, anxiety, anger, and pain.[81] At various points, the teacher was on the verge of tears, asked for a glass of water, complained of stomach pains, and ultimately pleaded with the experimenter to stop the session.[82] In spite of this and notwithstanding the experimenters' enlightened knowledge of obedience, 22 out of 24 experimenters continued to insist that the experiment continue, commanding distraught teachers to keep increasing the shocks until the maximum voltage level.[83] Apparently, despite their knowledge on obedience, their loyalty to the experiment and instinct to obey Shelton, their teacher, overrode their own desire not to cause another person, this time the "teacher" in the experiment, increased anxiety or pain.[84]

---

76 Blass, *supra* note 48, at 50–53; Perlman, *supra* note 10, at 472.

77 This study is described in Blass, *supra* note 48, at 52–53.

78 *Id.* at 52.

79 *Id.*

80 *Id.*

81 *Id.*

82 *Id.*

83 *Id.*

84 *See id.* at 52–53; *see also* Jan De Vos, *Now That You Know, How Do You Feel? The Milgram Experiment and Psychologization,* 7 ANN. REV. CRITICAL PSYCHOL. 223, 233 n.10 (2009). Blass attempts to reconcile Shelton's finding with the "life-changing testimonials" of Milgram's participants, concluding that "[b]eing enlightened about the unexpected power of authority may help a person stay away from an authority-dominated situation, but once he or she is already in such a situation, knowledge of the drastic degree of obedience authorities are

III. The Legal Profession: Law's Hierarchies and the New Lawyer

The practice of law is collaborative—many attorneys practice law in law firms, governmental agencies, or some form of legal organization, and even sole practitioners often work with other attorneys on work teams.[85] It is also frequently overtly hierarchical. As Andrew Perlman notes, a number of situational variables exist that make the legal practice market particularly fertile ground for obedience.[86] Moreover, recent market downturn and high student loans for law school have put particular stress on recent law graduates who need to find jobs and keep them.[87] In this section, I explore the general practice environment for new attorneys, beginning with the presumptions the United States Supreme Court is willing to make on their competencies. In addition, I explore the rules of professional conduct that guide junior/senior attorney work collaborations. This section demonstrates that although the Court's view of new attorneys, and the States' view of new attorneys as reflected in the rules of professional responsibility, are grounded on individual professional judgment and autonomy; the hierarchies present in the legal profession and the realities of practice for the new attorney create an environment that is highly conducive to wrongful obedience.

A. Presumed Competent

Inexperienced lawyers, including those who are fresh out of law school, are presumed to be independently competent in representing clients.[88] Recently, in Connick v. Thompson, the Court surmised that new attorneys who have graduated from law school and passed a substantive bar examination presumably

capable of eliciting does not necessarily help free the individual from the grip of the forces operating in that concrete situation (i.e., to defy the authority in charge)." Blass, *supra* note 48, at 53.

85 The percentage of lawyers working in some form of legal organization has steadily increased since 1980. *See* Carrie Menkel-Meadow, *Culture Clash in the Quality of Life in the Law: Changes in the Economics, Diversification and Organization of Lawyering*, 44 CASE W. RES. L. REV. 621, 628–29 (1994); Mark V. Tushnet, *Evaluating Students as Preparation for the Practice of Law*, 8 GEO. J. LEGAL ETHICS 313, 313 n.1 (1995) (noting that "for most lawyers, the practice of law is a collaborative enterprise").

86 *See* Perlman, *supra* note 10, at 460–71 (identifying ambiguity of issues as contributing to conformity in law practice and identifying numerous factors as contributing to obedience in law practice including a senior lawyer's ability to frame an instruction with positive language and as based on a plausible reason and benign "rules of the game"; and the presence in law of role differentiation; agreements to help clients; remote victims; and the social prestige of law firms and senior partners). As Perlman points out, "there is no reason to think that attorneys are somehow immune from the pressures that lead to obedience." *Id.* at 452 n.1. He identifies a variety of situational forces in law that would make such pressures even stronger than they would be in other work environments. *Id.* at 460–71.

87 *See* Jennifer Smith, *Law Firms Keep Squeezing Associates*, WALL ST. J. (Jan. 30, 2012), http://online.wsj.com/article/SB10001424052970203363504577186913589594.

88 *See* United States v. Cronic, 466 U.S. 648, 658 (1984); *see also* Connick v. Thompson, 131 S. Ct. 1350, 1361–62 (2011) (noting that "the presumption 'that the lawyer is competent to provide the guiding hand that the defendant needs' applies even to young and inexperienced lawyers in their first jury trial and even when the case is complex").

know how to "find, understand, and apply legal rules," and that the legal training provided by law school and the bar examination ensures that new attorneys are "equipped with the tools to . . . understand constitutional limits, and exercise legal judgment."[89] The Court concluded that this foundational legal training importantly differentiates attorneys from police officers and other public employees, and the Court relied on this difference to support its conclusion that a single-incident of a prosecuting attorney's unprofessional conduct cannot be used to trigger municipal liability based on an obvious need for specific legal training.[90] Thus, the Court suggests that the fact that new attorneys enter the profession with some substantive legal knowledge and some legal training in necessary legal "tools," presumably legal research and analysis, supports a presumption of competency for the new attorney.[91]

In addition to being presumed competent by training, the new attorney enters the profession of law with ethical responsibilities and obligations that attach to every attorney who has been sworn into their state bar as an independent professional. In the legal profession, ethical rules are premised on individual responsibility for conduct.[92] The Model Rules of Professional Conduct, for example, do not provide for professional discipline of a law firm when a firm's lawyer engages in ethical misconduct.[93] The rules apply to all attorneys, including the newest associates in a firm—among other things, state professional rules

---

[89] *Connick*, 131 S. Ct. at 1361.

[90] *Id.* at 1363.

[91] *See id.*

[92] Professional conduct rules adopted by each state are the primary source of lawyer regulation, and the American Bar Association's Model Rules of Professional Conduct are the rules states either rely on or start with in crafting their own rules. In recent years, state courts have deferred less to the ABA's Model Rules of Professional Conduct and exercised greater oversight over their own rules, but the dominant influence of the Model Rules remains tremendous. *See* STEPHEN GILLERS, REGULATIONS OF LAWYERS—PROBLEMS OF LAW AND ETHICS 10–11 (9th ed. 2012).

[93] *Cf.* Schneyer, *supra* note 5, at 11 (1991) (calling for the imposition of an entity duty of supervision with the possibility of sanctions against firms to promote firm-wide compliance with the professional rules). Only New York and New Jersey have ethical codes that provide for law firm discipline. *See* Schneyer, *supra* note 11, at 591; Arthur J. Lachman, *What You Should Know Can Hurt You: Management and Supervisory Responsibility for the Misconduct of Others Under Model Rules 5.1 and 5.3,* 18 PROF'L. LAW. 1 (2007). British Columbia has adopted law firm discipline provisions and Nova Scotia, Australia, and the United Kingdom are actively evaluating law firm culture, ethics, and responsibility issues.

generally require that an attorney is competent,[94] diligent,[95] organized,[96] and discreet.[97] Furthermore, as discussed in more detail below, the professional rules generally apply to inexperienced attorneys even when they act at the direction of another person.[98]

B. Law's Hierarchies

The following picture thus emerges: recently educated in law school, presumed to be trained, competent, and professionally responsible as an independent professional, a new lawyer begins to work in a legal environment that is loosely hierarchical, bureaucratic, stressful, competitive, and often shrouded in an entrenched culture. Lawyers increasingly work in law firms that are "large enough to qualify as bureaucracies."[99] Ted Schneyer has dubbed the trappings of a law firm bureaucracy the "ethical infrastructure" of a lawyer's workplace.[100] Law firms now are thought to be more loosely organized than they were a quarter century ago, with some partners "more akin to individual entrepreneurs,"[101] but a typical firm hierarchy nonetheless differentiates among partners, experienced senior associates, less-experienced junior associates, and non-legal staff. Managing partners or senior partners on an executive management committee have the power to make important decisions on behalf of the firm. Frequently, a non-lawyer CEO oversees the firm's financial management. Increasingly, a firm may

---

94 *See* MODEL RULES OF PROF'L CONDUCT R. 1.1 (2011) (requiring that a lawyer provide clients with "competent" representation, defined to require "the legal knowledge, skill, thoroughness and preparation reasonably necessary for the representation").

95 *See* MODEL RULES OF PROF'L CONDUCT R. 1.3 (requiring that a lawyer act with "reasonable diligence and promptness in representing a client").

96 Among other things, a lawyer must be sufficiently organized to avoid conflicts of interest, *see* MODEL RULES OF PROF'L CONDUCT R. 1.7, 1.9–1.12, and to keep and use client trust funds properly, *see* MODEL RULES OF PROF'L CONDUCT R. 1.15.

97 *See generally* MODEL RULES OF PROF'L CONDUCT R. 1.6 (defining a category of "information relating to the representation of a client" that a lawyer may not reveal unless there is an exception).

98 *See* MODEL RULES OF PROF'L CONDUCT R. 5.2 (a) (providing that "[a] lawyer is bound by the Rules of Professional Conduct notwithstanding that the lawyer acted at the direction of another person"); *see also infra* notes 127–28 and accompanying text.

99 Ted Schneyer, *An Interpretation of Recent Developments in the Regulation of Law Practice,* 30 OKLA. CITY U. L. REV. 559, 603 (2005) (noting data that indicates growth of the large firm practice); *see also* ROBERT L. NELSON, PARTNERS WITH POWER: THE SOCIAL TRANSFORMATION OF THE LARGE LAW FIRM 225 (1988) (noting the trend toward bureaucracy in law firms and predicting it will continue and accelerate).

100 Ted Schneyer, *A Tale of Four Systems: Reflections on How Law Influences the "Ethical Infrastructure" of Law Firms,* 39 S. TEX. L. REV. 245, 246 (1998).

101 REGAN, *supra* note 72, at 42 (noting that as large law firms become more decentralized, lawyers may find themselves responding to the culture of their practice group rather than to the broader firm's general culture).

have a formal ethics committee or designate an in-house compliance specialist for consultation with firm lawyers when ethical issues arise.[102]

In modern law firms, lawyers often work on client matters in hierarchical work teams assembled for specific projects—a large case, for example, might be staffed by a senior partner, a junior partner, an associate, and a paralegal.[103] Ideally, newer associates are closely supervised by more experienced lawyers; however, a senior partner may assume that the new associate on a team is receiving adequate supervision from a mid-level lawyer, who may not have much more experience than the new associate.[104] Lawyers often work on complex projects that are fast paced and time-sensitive. Competition for clients, identification with the client, the desire to receive future business, and the intense interdependence of the team experience typically all combine to create a distinct "cognitive and moral universe" that shapes lawyers' ethical decision making and makes "winning" the central mission of the team.[105] In addition, a team's decisions can be impacted by "groupthink," a dynamic of group influence that "deteriorate[s] mental efficiency, reality testing, and moral judgment that results from in-group pressures."[106] In particular, lawyers working in teams "may take ethical risks they would not take individually" because accountability is diffused and responsibility for the decision is diluted.[107] Moreover, studies suggest that ethically ambiguous tasks are likely to

---

[102] *See* Elizabeth Chambliss and David B. Wilkins, *The Emerging Role of Ethics Advisors, General Counsel, and Other Compliance Specialists in Large Law Firms,* 44 ARIZ. L. REV. 559, 559 (2002) (noting that "[a]necdotal evidence suggests that large law firms increasingly are turning to in-house ethics advisors, firm general counsel, and other specialists to manage the firm's compliance with professional regulation"); Elizabeth Chambliss & David B. Wilkins, *A New Framework for Law Firm Discipline,* 16 GEO. J. LEGAL ETHICS 335, 336 (2003) (proposing that Model Rules require all firms to designate at least one partner as the firm's compliance specialist to avoid the law-firm discipline problems that arise under Rule 5.1(a)); see also infra notes 169–69 and accompanying text (analyzing the importance within the obedience dynamic of a senior ethics partner or officer).

[103] REGAN, *supra* note 72, at 40–41.

[104] In Connick v. Thompson, 131 S. Ct. 1350 (2011), for example, District Attorney Connick testified at trial that he relied on lawyers with less than five years of experience to supervise new prosecutors fresh out of law school and ensure that they were familiar with their Brady obligations, yet Connick "did not inquire whether the supervisors themselves understood the importance of teaching newer prosecutors about Brady." *Id.* at 1379 (noting that neither of Deegan's supervisors in the *Thompson* case had even five years of experience as a prosecutor, but "huge turnover" in the Orleans Parish District Attorney's Office allowed attorneys with little experience to obtain the highest ranking in the office). Another witness at trial, a lawyer in the office, agreed that "it was possible for 'inexperienced lawyers, just a few weeks out of law school with no training,' to bear responsibility for 'decisions on . . . whether material was Brady material and had to be produced.' " *Id.* at 1380.

[105] Regan, supra note 72, at 41 (noting that it is "probably fairly common for lawyers to construct a moral universe that's particular to the matter on which they're working").

[106] IRVING L. JANIS, GROUPTHINK: PSYCHOLOGICAL STUDIES OF POLICY DECISIONS AND FIASCOES 9 (1982); *see also* Mary Twitchell, *The Ethical Dilemmas of Lawyers on Teams,* 72 MINN. L. REV. 697, 753 n.230 (1988) (describing problems of "groupthink" within lawyer work teams).

[107] Schneyer, *supra* note 5, at 8.

be assigned to the lawyer on the work team who is at the bottom of the hierarchy, where ethical conflicts are felt the strongest.[108] In hierarchical organizations, middle managers have been found to be more likely to take unethical actions than top management.[109]

The work team's dynamic plays a critical role in shaping the perceptions and decision making of the new attorney. Work allocation and responsibility is often assigned on hierarchical grounds. For example, associates typically receive work assignments from senior lawyers—not from clients—so associates may feel, quite naturally, more responsible to the senior lawyers they report to regularly than they do to clients. Associates on the work team are frequently assigned discrete tasks, such as overseeing document disclosure and discovery. Moreover, the increasingly competitive environment of legal practice coupled with a decreasing demand for new attorneys who are entering a difficult job market all place additional burdens on the associate to impress senior lawyers and succeed at the job. Associates are generally reviewed annually by a senior partner who considers input from the senior lawyers the associate worked with and the job evaluation may concentrate on short term, bottom-line results such as the number of hours billed to a client, new client originations, and new matter originations.

To new lawyers, these economic and organizational dynamics may reinforce a view of themselves as "employees" in a firm, with little autonomy.[110] Of course, law firm associates are employees of the firm, "generally subject to the partner's control, or at least to the partner's right to control" and owing a "duty of obedience" to the firm.[111] Yet, they are also independent professionals; thus, they are expected to comply with applicable ethical standards notwithstanding the fact that other lawyers supervise them and they should obey firm instructions only if such instructions are reasonable.[112] In other words, a new lawyer is expected to

---

108 *See* JEROME E.J. CARLIN, LAWYERS' ETHICS: A SURVEY OF THE NEW YORK CITY BAR 96–117 (1966) (describing a study of professional ethics suggesting that unpleasant tasks which require arguably questionable behavior for successful completion are delegated to the subordinate associates on a hierarchically structured work team); James, *supra* note 72, at 51 (noting that "research indicates that ethical conflicts are felt the strongest at the bottom rather than at the top of the corporate ladder").

109 *Id.*

110 O'Grady, *supra* note 5, at 503, 506–07 (suggesting that law school graduates may be more willing to adopt an "employee" role in an economically competitive market to secure employment and preserve job security, and suggesting that hierarchical structure and power differentials reinforce a new lawyer's tendency to view herself as an "employee" in the firm).

111 Leonard Gross, *Ethical Problems of Law Firm Associates*, 26 WM. & MARY L. REV. 259, 260–61, 266 (1984) (recognizing the "customary" definition of the term "law firm associate" as "any attorney who is a regular employee of a law firm" and who, as an employee of the law firm, owes a duty of obedience to the firm and each partner).

112 MODEL RULES OF PROF'L CONDUCT R. 5.2(a) (a supervised lawyer is bound by applicable ethics rules notwithstanding the fact that the lawyer is supervised by another lawyer); MODEL RULES OF PROF'L CONDUCT

disobey an instruction from a supervising attorney if it requires the new lawyer to do something unethical. The conflict of bureaucratic norms and professional norms creates stress on associates, but not partners, that one scholar described as "typical."[113] Ultimately, any workplace dynamic that reinforces the "employee" role for new lawyers is conducive to increased wrongful obedience and decreased autonomous judgment.[114]

Traditionally, success in a law firm has been achieved by advancing up the hierarchy to partnership in the firm. Under this classic model of law firm structure, all firm lawyers are either actual or aspiring partners working within an "up or out" policy that does not recognize a place for permanent associates and rewards partnership status to only a select few.[115] Recent economic and market downturns in the legal profession have changed the way many law firms are organized; thus, more firms are now employing lawyers that fall into numerous categories including non-equity partners and permanent associates.[116] While casting all associates as aspiring partners, rather than aspiring permanent associates, has been viewed as ostensibly preserving "the ideal of the lawyer as an independent professional rather than an organizational employee,"[117] the "promotion to partner tournament" actually reinforces the law firm's hierarchy—a special feature of a hierarchy is that it rewards those who comply by promoting them within the established hierarchy, thus providing emotional gratification to the individual and ensuring continuity of the hierarchical form.[118] Milgram posited that individual conscience is "perforce diminished at the point of entering a hierarchical structure."[119] Thus, it may be that any shift away from the entrenched, hierarchical

---

R. 5.2 (b) (allows associates to follow instructions given by supervisor if question is arguable and the proposed course is reasonable).

113 ERWIN O. SMIGEL, THE WALL STREET LAWYER: PROFESSIONAL ORGANIZATION MAN? 292, 302 (1964) (noting that the professional strain caused by the conflict of professional norms against business norms affects primarily associates, and not partners, because partners are not employees and are closer to the traditional "free" professional).

114 *See* Kim, *supra* note 10, at 1001 (identifying the role of "mere employee" as one assumed by in-house counsel and viewing that role as conducive to obedience).

115 REGAN, *supra* note 72, at 21. Professors Marc Galanter and Thomas Palay applied "tournament" theory to describe this model of law-firm operation and organization. *See generally* MARC GALANTER & THOMAS PALAY, TOURNAMENT OF LAWYERS: THE TRANSFORMATION OF THE BIG LAW FIRM (1991).

116 *See* Susan Saab Fortney, *Leaks, Lies, and the Moonlight: Fiduciary Duties of Associates to Their Law Firms,* 41 ST. MARY'S L.J. 595, 599 (2009) (noting that economic and organizational changes have resulted in law firms employing lawyers in "an array of categories including non-equity partners, permanent (staff) associates, and 'of counsel' lawyers").

117 REGAN, *supra* note 72, at 21.

118 *See* MILGRAM, *supra* note 1, at 138; CAMERON STRACHER, DOUBLE BILLING: A YOUNG LAWYER'S TALE OF GREED, SEX, LIES, AND THE PURSUIT OF A SWIVEL CHAIR 19–20 (1998).

119 *See* MILGRAM, *supra* note 1, at 132 (asking "[h]ow is it that a person who is usually decent and courteous acts with severity against another person within the experiment? He does so because conscience,

aspiring partner "tournament model" to a model that has a place for permanent associates may moderate the impact of associates as "employees" and affect the work environment in ways that facilitate defiance and diminish wrongful obedience.

Finally, as discussed in more detail in Section IV below, a firm's "culture," which reflects the firm's "stated values, its perceived values, and the values it actually rewards," is a singularly important dynamic in the new attorney's work environment. Professor Ted Schneyer notes that the components that constitute a law firm's culture may be "as much a determinant of lawyers' behavior as their individual skills, values, and dispositions are."[120] All lawyers in the firm, even senior lawyers who have enjoyed enormous success, are impacted by "the subtle but powerful forces that shape behavior" in the law firm.[121] For new attorneys, the experience is likely confusing and stressful. Time shortages and other competitive stresses often result in new attorneys attempting to understand quickly their unfamiliar work environment and conforming to the firm's culture as a shortcut in decision making.[122] When confronted with ambiguity, for example, a new associate may understandably decide not to bother a senior lawyer by seeking clarification, but rather to proceed quickly in a manner perceived by the associate as supporting the firm's culture.[123]

C. The Ethical Responsibilities of Partners and Associates

Professional supervisory responsibility on attorney work teams is delineated in Model Rule 5.1, which purports to reflect an understanding that "the ethical atmosphere of a firm can influence the conduct of all its members and the partners

---

which regulates impulsive aggressive action, is per force diminished at the point of entering a hierarchical structure").

[120] Schneyer, *supra* note 99, at 603.

[121] REGAN, *supra* note 72, at 10.

[122] *Cf.* Geoffrey C. Hazard, Jr., *Personal Values and Professional Ethics,* 40 CLEV. ST. L. REV. 133, 138–39 (1992) (noting that "shortage of time and urgency of circumstances" may prevent lawyers from consulting with colleagues or with ethics committees).

[123] REGAN, *supra* note 72, at 323–24 (noting that ambitious associates will try to anticipate what superiors want them to do and "intuit what orders they would be given" because waiting for explicit instructions can be seen as a lack of initiative). In his fictional account of life in a large law firm, described as "composites" based on his experience as an associate at a large law firm, Cameron Stracher describes the difficulties faced by junior associates who receive assignments with very little information and feel pressured to understand their role without asking questions. In one example, Stracher describes the mounting panic of a junior associate who realizes he knows virtually nothing about the facts of a case he is working on: "This is the first moment of panic. You think you should know. Maybe you missed something when you were given the assignment. Did you listen closely enough? . . . Finally, you straighten your backbone and return to the office of the senior associate who gave you the assignment. He's very busy, but he takes two seconds to explain the facts of an extremely complicated matter to you. You nod, but now you're really in a panic . . . the more you learn about a case, the more you need to know." STRACHER, *supra* note 118, at 50.

may not assume that all lawyers associated with the firm will inevitably conform to the Rules."[124] Rule 5.1 describes the responsibilities of law firm partners, managers, and those who supervise other lawyers, imposing certain duties on managing and supervising lawyers without altering the "personal duty of each lawyer in a firm to abide by the Rules of Professional Conduct."[125] Under Rule 5.1 (a), law firm partners and lawyers with managerial authority must make "reasonable efforts to ensure that the firm has in effect measures giving reasonable assurance that all lawyers in the firm conform to the Rules of Professional Conduct." Such policies include client conflict of interest checks, master calendars, client funds management systems, and policies that "ensure that inexperienced lawyers are properly supervised."[126] Moreover, the comments encourage large firms to adopt procedures for junior lawyers to make confidential referrals of ethical problems directly to a firm partner or committee.[127] Rule 5.1(b) requires that any lawyer with direct supervisory authority over another lawyer must make "reasonable efforts to ensure that the other lawyer conforms to the Rules of Professional Conduct." Finally, Rule 5.1(c) makes a lawyer directly responsible for another lawyer's conduct if the lawyer either (1) ordered or knowingly ratified the conduct, or (2) is a partner, manager, or supervisor and "knows of the conduct at a time when its consequences can be avoided or mitigated but fails to take reasonable remedial action."[128]

Model Rule 5.2 notes that all lawyers are bound by the Rules of Professional Conduct, even if acting at the direction of another, but it further provides that "[a] subordinate lawyer does not violate the Rules of Professional Conduct if that lawyer acts in accordance with a supervisory lawyer's reasonable resolution of an arguable question of professional duty."[129] This rule is generally viewed as intended not for use in disciplinary proceedings, but rather to facilitate law firm management and influence associate behavior by "encouraging law firm associates to follow the directions of the senior lawyer without fear of the consequences."[130] The comments to the rule provide as much, noting that "if the question is reasonably arguable, someone has to decide upon the course of action" and that

---

[124] MODEL RULES OF PROF'L CONDUCT R. 5.1 cmt. 3 (2000).

[125] *Id.* at cmt. 8.

[126] *Id.* at cmt. 2.

[127] *Id.* at cmt. 3.

[128] *Id.* at 5.1(c).

[129] *Id.* at 5.2(b).

[130] Carol M. Rice, *The Superior Orders Defense in Legal Ethics: Sending the Wrong Message to Young Lawyers*, 32 WAKE FOREST L. REV. 887, 904 (1997).

authority should be in the supervisor.[131] Because the ethical question, however, must be "arguable" and the supervisory lawyer's resolution "reasonable," it is generally agreed that law firm "associates should take little comfort in Rule 5.2(b)."[132]

A number of scholars have criticized Rule 5.2 and advocated, quite reasonably, that states should not adopt the rule, arguing that it is at best meaningless and at worst harmful.[133] I agree that Rule 5.2(b) sends the wrong message, and is both meaningless and even potentially harmful, but I contend that the existence or non-existence of the Rule is unlikely to make much difference to a junior attorney's tendency to obey when working within the realities of the legal workplace. Indeed, the rules of professional responsibility create essentially an independent voice of authority for new attorneys, and the rules will presumably conflict with a wrongful order from a supervising attorney; yet, the rules cannot compete with the proximate and clear assertions of authority in work dynamics or with an existing workplace culture if the culture promotes winning at all costs or deference to authority. To attorneys working within law's hierarchies, the rules are a distant voice—not a clear directive.[134] Thus, as discussed in the final section below, I argue that the strong obedience factors found in legal work groups should first be understood by leaders in a legal institution and then confronted directly by implementing management and supervisory procedures geared toward diminishing wrongful obedience and supporting an ethics based work culture.[135]

---

131 *Supra,* note 124 at cmt. 2.

132 Douglas R. Richmond, *Professional Responsibilities of Law Firm Associates,* 45 BRANDEIS L.J. 199, 208 (2007).

133 Rice, *supra* note 130, at 893 (describing Rule 5.2(b) as meaningless because a "reasonable resolution of an arguable question" would never violate the Rules of Professional Conduct regardless of the actor); *see also* Andrew M. Perlman, *The Silliest Rule of Professional Conduct: Model Rule 5.2(b),* 19 PROF. LAW. 14, 14–17 (2009) (arguing among other things that Rule 5.2(b) is harmful because it gives "subordinate attorneys a justification to defer to authority figures in situations that warrant forceful dissent").

134 *See, e.g.,* Ted Schneyer, *Professionalism as Bar Politics: The Making of the Model Rules of Professional Conduct,* 14 L. & SOC. INQUIRY 677 (1989) (citing early studies demonstrating that ethical rules do not provide clear or immediate guidance). Moreover, an individual attorney's own moral code is taken out of the wrongful obedience analysis. Wrongful obedience occurs in spite of moral concerns to the contrary—individual moral conflicts were, of course, present in Milgram's experiments as individuals struggled with their moral concerns about harming another. *See, e.g.,* MILGRAM, *supra* note 1, at 41–42 (Milgram noted that it was "clear from the remarks and behavior of many participants that in punishing the victim they were often acting against their own values. Such a tension presents conflict because one psychological force (a tendency to comply with authority) operates against another psychological force (moral pull/sympathy for the victim)."). Reliance on an individual's set of values to defeat the power of obedience is not sufficient.

135 A number of motivators exist to encourage leaders in law firms and other organizations to understand the dynamics of wrongful obedience and institute procedures to guard against such obedience including (1) a focus on requiring that young attorneys express their own judgment will contribute significantly to the attorneys' professional growth; thus, it is a good investment in the newest members of the work group; (2) a focus on ethics generally strengthens the organization and is ultimately good for business, *see* Lynn Sharp Paine,

To that end, I offer some suggestions, drawing parallels to Milgram's conclusions as well as to recent efforts outside of law, such as the Freeh Report recommendations to universities, to guard against wrongful obedience and complicity in the legal workplace.

IV. Applying Obedience Findings to the Professional Practice of Law

Milgram drew a number of conclusions from his studies that are applicable to law's professional work hierarchies and cultures.[136] As noted above, no study proves that simply understanding the powerful human tendencies to obey helps arm one against wrongful obedience. Because it is difficult to perceive our own wrongful obedience, as opposed to recognizing it in others, it seems likely that we need to instill more safeguards than knowledge of the psychology underlying wrongful obedience.[137] Thus, recognizing the situational factors that make wrongful obedience the easier choice—those situational factors that facilitate wrongful obedience—is an important step toward diminishing its impact.

Milgram conducted 18 variations on the basic scenario described above to test numerous situational variables and their impact on obedience. In this section, I will categorize the findings Milgram drew from both his basic obedience experiment and the variation experiments. I group the findings into four situational categories: (1) authority variables, (2) victim variables, (3) responsibility variables, and (4) group dynamic variables.[138] After describing these findings, I will

---

Moral Thinking in Management: An Essential Capability, in ETHICS IN PRACTICE: LAWYERS' ROLES, RESPONSIBILITIES, AND REGULATION 59, 59 (Deborah L. Rhode ed. 2000) (positing that many corporate leaders have recently begun to pay serious attention to ethics because they believe such attention will "strengthen the organization and contribute to its performance in the marketplace"); and (3) a focus on guarding against wrongful obedience and complicity is an organization's best insurance against suffering what may be extremely difficult consequences of such behavior; *see, e.g.,* Pete Themel, *Sanctions Decimate the Nittany Lions Now and for Years to Come,* N.Y. TIMES, July 23, 2012, at B15, available at http://www.nytimes.com/2012/07/24/sports/ncaafootball/penn-state-penalties-include-60-million-fine-and-bowl-ban.html (describing some of the consequences of the Penn State long-time child sexual abuse tragedy).

136 Burger's findings are generally consistent with Milgram's; for example, Burger found obedience rates in 2006 to be only slightly lower than what Milgram found 45 years earlier, and he found no difference between men and women. *See supra* notes 60–12 and accompanying text.

137 *See* Blass, *supra* note 48 and accompanying text (describing follow-up studies to Milgram's experiments demonstrating under-prediction of obedience rates coupled with virtually no one thinking they would obey, suggesting difficulty in recognizing tendencies to obey in ourselves, as opposed to in others). *Cf.* D.L. Rosenhan, *Moral Character,* 27 STAN. L. REV. 925, 925 (1975) (suggesting that people are not always aware of what makes them do what they do). *But cf.* Luban, *supra* note 5, at 116 (suggesting that while there is "no fail-safe remedy to protect lawyers or anyone else from the optical illusions of the spirit that authority and cognitive dissonance engender," the best protection might be "understanding the illusions themselves, their pervasiveness, [and] the insidious way they work on us").

138 *Cf.* Perlman, *supra* note 10, at 462–63 (identifying eleven key variables that impacted obedience in Milgram's experiments). All the key variables are incorporated within the situational categories I use to organize Milgram's findings.

apply them to the professional practice of law, offering suggestions to facilitate individual autonomy even among the newest attorneys and guard against wrongful obedience while working within professional practice groups and hierarchies. My suggestions are geared not toward rule changes, but rather toward changes in the real world work environment itself.[139]

One theme resonates across all the situational categories identified below: the importance of creating and maintaining what Milgram called "strain" on the new attorney. In general, Milgram defined the state of "mental organization" that facilitated wrongful obedience as a person's "agentic state" and found that any increased "strain" on the actor interfered with the agentic state thus promoting independent thinking and defiance.[140] Mechanisms that diminish strain and protect self-image make it easy for the actor to obey and thereby maintain his relationship with the person of authority.[141] Strain is uncertainty and conflict—even chaos. Strain is unpleasant for the actor, making it harder for the actor to know what to do. Strain can be caused by any number of factors; for example, strain on the actor exists when a clear line of authority is not present or when the harm caused to a victim is undeniable and occurring uncomfortably right before the actor, as a direct result of action taken.[142] Milgram demonstrated that independent disobedience is in fact a difficult, deliberate act while obedience, even wrongful obedience, is frequently seen as the clearest and easiest choice for

139 The obedience dynamic has been applied to a variety of real-life situations including an analysis of a Swiss Police Captain who defied government authority to protect refugees from Nazi persecution, *see* Francois Rochat and Andre Modigliani, *Captain Paul Grueninger: The Chief of Police Who Saved Jewish Refugees by Refusing To Do His Duty,* in OBEDIENCE TO AUTHORITY: CURRENT PERSPECTIVES ON THE MILGRAM PARADIGM 91 (Thomas Blass ed., 2000), and an analysis of the dynamics in an airplane cockpit where the National Transportation Safety Board noted high levels of wrongful obedience to erring captains with disastrous consequences, *see* Eugen Tarnow, *Self-Destructive Obedience in the Airplane Cockpit and the Concept of Obedience Optimization,* in OBEDIENCE TO AUTHORITY: CURRENT PERSPECTIVES ON THE MILGRAM PARADIGM 111 (Thomas Blass ed., 2000); *see also* MALCOLM GLADWELL, OUTLIERS—THE STORY OF SUCCESS 177–223 (2008) (exploring the theory that a cultural legacy grounded in respect for authority underlies a series of plane crashes). In addition, a 1966 field experiment provides an example of an obedience experiment conducted in a real work setting—a hospital—which demonstrated that nurses will frequently obey a perceived doctor's telephonic orders to give a patient an excessive dose of medication, even when the order clearly violates hospital policy, and further demonstrated that when told about the hypothetical situation, graduate and student nurses unfamiliar with the experiment overwhelmingly predicted that they would not have followed the doctor's orders and a majority under-predicted the obedience rate of the subjects in the experiment. *See* Charles K. Hofling, Eveline Brotzman, Sarah Dalrymple, Nancy Graves, and Chester M. Pierce, *An Experimental Study in Nurse-Physician Relationships,* 143 J. NERVOUS & MENTAL DISEASE 171, 174–76 (1966).

140 MILGRAM, *supra* note 1, at 148, 154–55 (further explaining the agentic state).

141 *Id.* at 162 (identifying mechanisms that diminish strain as including avoidance to visceral reactions, denial, physical conversion, minimal compliance, subterfuge, the search for social reassurance, blaming the victim, and noninstrumental dissent).

142 *Id.* at 155–56.

someone who is asked to exercise their own judgment.[143] Milgram concluded that strain reduces the clarity and ease of the obedient choice and shows that the subject has "transformed to the agentic state only partially."[144] Thus, introducing strain is essential across all situational variable categories identified below in any effort to reduce wrongful obedience.

A. Authority Variables

Milgram concluded from his experiments that when people are placed in situations where they must exercise judgment, they will immediately attempt to identify an authority figure and look for a clear hierarchy or a "coherent line of action."[145] Once the authority is identified, the tendency to obey found in the basic scenario will adhere to orders from that person. Proximity of the authority figure to the subject is an important factor. In a number of variations on the basic experiment, for example, Milgram found that "the physical presence of an authority was an important force contributing to the subject's obedience or defiance."[146] Moreover, when confronted with competing orders, the actor will be forced to choose among incompatible demands—a dynamic Milgram labeled "recapitulation."[147] Milgram described the experimenter's authority over the subject, for example, as operating "not in a free field but against ever-mounting countervailing pressures from the person being punished."[148] The subject is hearing two demands: one from the experimenter (demanding he continue) and one from the learner (begging him to stop). The subject will strive to identify the authority figure among the competing voices.

When the hierarchy is not clear because competing authorities exist, the subject will make every effort to clarify the line of authority and find, for themselves, a hierarchy that lacks contradictions.[149] Milgram tested this thesis with a variation on the basic scenario that required the teacher to confront two

---

143 *Id.* at 163–64 (noting that "[t]he price of disobedience is a gnawing sense that one has been faithless. Even though he has chosen the morally correct action, the subject remains troubled by the disruption of the social order he brought about, and cannot fully dispel the feeling that he deserted a cause to which he had pledged support. It is he, and not the obedient subject, who experiences the burden of his action").

144 *Id.* at 154–55.

145 *Id.* at 110–111 (noting that "[s]ubjects are predisposed to perceive clear hierarchies lacking contradictions and incompatible elements. They will, therefore, use whatever bases are possible to ascertain and respond to the higher authority").

146 *Id.* at 62. In experimental variations, the experimenter issued his orders from another room or, in one variation, over the telephone. Obedience dropped as the experimenter got further away from the teacher.

147 *Id.* at 24.

148 *Id.*

149 *Id.* at 111 (Milgram noted that "subjects are predisposed to perceive clear hierarchies lacking contradictions and incompatible elements. They will, therefore, use whatever bases are possible to ascertain and respond to the higher authority.")

experimenters—two authorities—who disagreed with each other. When one experimenter called for the experiment to end, but another required it continue, every teacher stopped the experiment. Not a single subject continued to follow the instructions of the experimenter who ordered that the shocks continue. Milgram noted that "nothing the victim did—no pleas, screams, or any other response to the shocks—produced an effect as abrupt and unequivocal."[150] Thus, if the coherence of the hierarchy is destroyed at the highest level, the subject will disobey a secondary authority figure. In another variation, when an experimenter commanded that the subject shock his colleague—a second experimenter—and the second experimenter took the learner's position, the second experimenter's screams and protests had no more effect on the teacher than an ordinary person's protests.[151] Thus, once in the victim seat, the experimenter loses all his authority, and the commands of the first experimenter become the "coherent line of action" to which the subject will respond.

Social psychologists and scholars have attempted to characterize more precisely the kind of authority that evokes the obedience Milgram found in his experiments. Mario F. Morelli, a critic of Milgram, accused Milgram of failing adequately to distinguish between a legitimate authority—someone who is simply in a position of authority—and an expert authority—someone with expertise on a topic who thus is an authority.[152] Thomas Blass suggests that Milgram saw his experimenter primarily as a "legitimate authority," which Milgram defined as one who is "perceived to be in a position of social control within a given situation" with authoritative power that stems not from any personal characteristics or knowledge but rather from a "perceived position in a social structure."[153] In an effort to identify the key characteristics of Milgram's authority figure, Blass conducted an experiment with naïve external perceivers in which he used a conceptual framework developed by French and Raven on the bases of power: the classic formulation identified six different power types (reward power, coercive power, legitimate power, referent power, expert power, and

---

150 *Id.* at 107.

151 *Id.* at 110.

152 M.F. Morelli, *Milgram's Dilemma of Obedience,* 14 METAPHILOSOPHY 183 (1983); Blass, supra note 48, at 39.

153 Blass, *supra* note 48, at 39. Blass notes, however, that in one of the last things Milgram wrote about obedience before his death, he replied to Morelli by stating that with regard to the distinction between legitimate and expert authority, his experimenter was both the person "in charge" and the one "presumed by the subjects to have expert knowledge." *Id.* at 41 (noting Milgram's remarks that "[a]s frequently happens, real life is more complex than textbooks: both components co-exist in one person").

informational power).[154] In his experiment, Blass asked subjects (college students) to view a 12-minute video of Milgram's experiments from the documentary film Obedience and rank the six categories to explain why they thought the subject obeyed the experimenter. Blass found that the two attributes seen as the most salient by the naïve perceivers were the ones that have been focused on in years of scholarly analysis of Milgram's work: legitimate and expert authority. Blass further noted that the results suggest that both factors likely combined in Milgram's experimenter to provide him with the "tremendous" power he had over the subjects.[155]

Milgram conducted an experimental variation specifically to test the importance of the perceived social prestige or status of the authority figure. When experimental sessions were held in a rundown office building that had no connection with prestigious Yale University, Milgram did note a reduction in obedience from sixty-five percent to forty-eight percent, but that drop was not statistically significant.[156] Other studies suggest that the perceived status of the authority figure is a factor in an obedience analysis.[157] A field experiment, for example, examined the relationship between perceived authority and its influence on compliance, finding that attire influenced how likely people were to comply with a request for money and that compliance increased when dress created a perception of authority.[158] Moreover, language used for issuing direct orders is thought to be important in the obedience analysis—wrongful directives issued in firm, positively framed language that can be interpreted as simple benign requests are more likely to result in obedience.[159]

---

[154] *Id.* at 41–42. Reward power posits that the experimenter is a figure of authority whose positive evaluations and approval are important to the participant; coercive power posits that many of the experimenter's statements, such as "the experiment requires you to continue," suggest to the subjects that negative consequences will result if they disobey; legitimate power posits that the experimenter represents the authority of science, with the right to control the participants' actions; referent power posits that the participant has respect and admiration for the experimenter and wants to be like him; expert power posits that the experimenter is a scientific expert whom the participant trusts will not harm the learner; and informational power posits that the study which the participant believes is on the effect of punishment on memory has value and must be continued. *Id.* at 42 tbl. 4.1. The participants in Blass's experiment ranked expert power as the most likely source of the experimenter's power, legitimate power a close second, and coercive power third. *Id.* at 43.

[155] *Id.* at 43–44.

[156] MILGRAM, *supra* note 1, at 66–70.

[157] *See* Perlman, *supra* note 10, at 463 (citing Zimbardo's studies).

[158] *See* Brad J. Bushman, *Perceived Symbols of Authority and Their Influence on Compliance,* 14 J. APPLIED SOC. PSYCHOL. 501, 507 (1984) (finding that attire—business suit, firefighter uniform, or bum clothing—influenced how likely people were to comply with a request for a dime for a parking meter).

[159] Perlman, *supra* note 10, at 462 (identifying key variables from Milgram's experiments).

Finally, Milgram conducted other variations on the basic scenario specifically to gauge the importance of the authority figure against other voices and pressures on the teacher. In one variation, the learner (supposedly to demonstrate his toughness or manliness) demanded that he be shocked, while the experimenter, in contrast, called for the session to end. Not a single teacher followed the orders of the learner—everyone stopped the session.[160] In another variation, a confederate observer (called the "common man") was given the role of recorder and placed in the room with the teacher and the experimenter. At some point in the experiment, the experimenter announced that he needed to leave the room but he gave his blessing to the common man to step into his shoes. Compliance dropped way down: "only a third as many subjects followed the common man as followed the experimenter."[161] In another variation, the common man became frustrated when the teacher did not comply with his orders and attempted to take over the position of teacher, saying, "I'll do the shocks myself and you can be the recorder." Despite the fact that the subject would then be relieved of personally administering the shocks, all the subjects protested this action and some physically restrained the aggressive common man to prevent him from sitting at the shock machine.[162]

The follow up studies and Milgram's numerous variation studies demonstrate the importance in an obedience analysis of a perceived authority figure—applying these findings to the professional dynamics in the legal profession underscores the need to understand a new attorney's perception of their supervising attorney's legitimate and expert authority. If the authority figure in a legal work group is unclear, a new attorney will unconsciously strive to name one. In the legal work setting, the characteristics of both expert and legitimate authority have import—like Milgram's study—because a senior lawyer is likely easily perceived by junior lawyers to be endowed with both expert and legitimate authority.[163]

With respect to expert authority, typically a junior lawyer will quickly and quite accurately perceive that a senior lawyer is an expert in the field—at least more of an expert than the junior lawyer. Even if a junior lawyer recognizes that a senior lawyer does not have expertise in an area, an entrenched work hierarchy and steep learning curve ensure that it will be difficult for a junior lawyer to trust his own observations and conclude that his perceptions of weakness in the senior lawyer's abilities are accurate. Thus, by endowing his supervising attorney as an

---

160 MILGRAM, *supra* note 1, at 90, 104.

161 *Id.* at 97.

162 *Id.*

163 Blass, *supra* note 48, at 41.

expert authority, the junior lawyer will be free of strain and vulnerable to wrongful obedience.

Supervising attorneys can take steps to encourage junior attorneys to exercise and express independent judgment, and help ward off undue obedience, by pointedly diminishing their own expertise and their own authority in the team. The notion that an experienced attorney should expressly diminish her authority will seem like a bold suggestion to many veteran attorneys. It is, however, a technique increasingly used in hierarchical teams—especially where obedience can have disastrous consequences. For example, in an analysis of airplane crashes, Malcolm Gladwell highlights the success of veteran airplane pilot Suren Ratwatte who consciously made efforts to guard against the reflexive obedience that others in the cockpit would be inclined to give to him in a crisis by, among other things, undermining his own authority with his copilots: "[o]ne thing I personally try to do is, I try to put myself a little down. I say to my copilots, 'I don't fly very often. Three or four times a month. You fly a lot more. If you see me doing something stupid, it's because I don't fly very often. So tell me. Help me out.' "[164] This strategy helped ensure an openly communicative, and thus safer, environment in the cockpit. Similarly, in law's hierarchies, the pull toward obedience is likely to be so strong that an experienced supervising attorney concerned about wrongful obedience should consciously give junior attorneys the express permission to speak out and participate as independent valued members of the team.[165] While it sounds like a humble and accommodating approach to working with others on a team, this conscious effort to level the playing field will actually create strain for

---

[164] GLADWELL, *supra* note 139, at 191–92, 197–98. This strategy is reflected in the aviation industry's "Threat and Error Management in Aviation" model, widely used in pilot training, which identifies one of five latent threats to aviation safety as a "national culture" which dictates that a person in authority is not questioned, so that "the captain is always right, even when he is wrong." *See Threat and Error Management Model, Wikidot: Aviation Knowledge,* http://aviationknowledge.wikidot.com/aviation:tem-model (last visited Oct. 20, 2012).

[165] In addition, a situational social etiquette may have played an important role to facilitate wrongful obedience in Milgram's experiments, which can be addressed by a more level playing field on work teams. Milgram found that a teacher who defiantly renounced his obligation to the experimenter breached an "implicit set of understandings" that were part of the social occasion, and Milgram concluded that most subjects did not undertake this lightly. MILGRAM, *supra* note 1, at 149–50. Many subjects, Milgram concluded, found it less painful to shock the victim than to "hurt" the experimenter's feelings or face the awkwardness of defiance. *Id.* at 151. Videos of the experiment illustrate many examples of a polite etiquette on the part of the teachers that seems out of place under the circumstances of the experiment. One subject, for example, thinking the learner might be dead said: "I don't mean to be rude, but I think you should look in on him." THE STANLEY MILGRAM FILMS ON SOCIAL PSYCHOLOGY: OBEDIENCE (STANLEY MILGRAM, Penn State Media Sales 1962) [hereinafter Obedience]. In addition, depersonalized labels used in the experiment, such as calling the subject "teacher" and the victim "learner," likely created an altered reality that diffused personal responsibility for the harm caused the victim.

the newest attorneys on the team, who, as Milgram suggests, may be unconsciously making every effort to identify and obey an authority.

With respect to legitimate authority, the power of the supervisor to issue commands to which junior lawyers feel an obligation to obey is importantly defined by both the formal organizational structure and the culture of the particular work environment. If a legal organization's formal structure or culture promotes winning at all cost or deference to authority, the organization is essentially issuing a powerful command to its attorneys that can override competing voices in the work place, rules of professional responsibility, and an attorney's individual moral code.[166] In the business environment, for example, Harvey James concluded, "an examination of the ethical impact of the formal structure of organizations is necessary and, when combined with an appropriate corporate culture, will generally be sufficient in promoting the ethical behavior of workers."[167] In another example outside of the legal workplace, the Freeh Report's analysis of the Penn State child sex abuse crisis focused on the importance of the university's "culture" as it contributed to an environment that allowed for on-going wrongful abuse, noting that as a first step, the university must conduct an honest, open, and thorough examination of its existing culture and confront "[o]ne of the most challenging of the tasks [before it] . . . transforming the culture that permitted Sandusky's behavior."[168] Ultimately, identifying Penn State's singular focus on athletics, especially its football program, as a key component of the university's culture helps explain why a janitor who witnessed Sandusky engaged in child sexual abuse in November of 2000 did not report the abuse for fear that "they'll get rid of all of us" and the "University will close ranks to protect the football program."[169]

Legal organizations would similarly benefit from such an examination and articulation of their formal organizational structure and their existing culture. James defined an organization's "formal structure" as having three "distinct, but

---

166 *See supra* notes 118–19 and accompanying text (defining a law firm's "culture"). In many legal organizations, the power of the legal workplace's culture is reinforced by the characterization of associates as "employees" of the firm who are "generally subject to the partner's control, or at least to the partner's right to control." *See supra* note 110 and accompanying text.

167 James, *supra* note 72, at 44.

168 FREEH REPORT, *supra* note 12, at 18, 128–29. In its own effort to articulate what it saw as the existing culture at Penn State, the Freeh Report first noted a number of laudable components including "collegiality, high standards of educational excellence and research, and respect for the environment." *Id.* at 129. But the Report was highly critical of other aspects of the university's culture, noting an "over-emphasis on 'The Penn State Way' as an approach to decision-making, a resistance to seeking outside perspectives, and an excessive focus on athletics." *Id.*

169 *Id.* at 22.

related" components: "(1) the structure of monetary and non-monetary rewards; (2) the performance-evaluation, monitoring, and control processes for individuals and business units; and (3) the systems of partitioning and assigning decision-making rights and responsibilities to workers, including job design and the level of empowerment.[170] A law firm's culture reflects the firm's "stated values, its perceived values, and the values it actually rewards."[171] Associates find evidence of the firm's express and implied values in the firm's compensation systems, policies, procedures, management systems, problem solving systems, committees, departmental lines, methods of supervision, methods of communication, methods of adopting changes to the culture, and methods of assuring that new members know the organization's culture.[172] Thus, a thorough examination of a firm's existing formal structure and culture would require an honest look into all these facets of the work environment, with an eye toward whether independent judgment and autonomy from junior lawyers is rewarded or stifled.

The elements that comprise a firm's formal structure and culture all work together to impact ethical decision making of the firm's lawyers.[173] In particular, a firm's compensation and incentive system is critically important to promoting ethical decision making and warding off wrongful obedience.[174] Because ethical decision making is not often observed, the best firm managers may be able to strive for is to "ensure that their company compensation practices do not reward, but rather punish, unethical employee conduct" such as, for example, overlooking conflicts of interest to bring new business to the firm.[175] In evaluating law firm's compensation systems, attorney Peter J. Winders concluded that the worst system is "the formula system that allocates incoming dollars based on client originations,

---

170 James, *supra* note 72, at 45.

171 Peter J. Winders, *Law Firm Culture—Its Importance and How to Overcome It,* PROF. LAW. 11, 11 (2004).

172 *Id.;* Schneyer, *supra* note 99, at 603. A firm's new associate training, for example, serves "not only to impart legal skills, but also to socialize lawyers in the culture of the organization." REGAN, *supra* note 72, at 25. In addition to organizational culture, practice specialties generate "distinct practice cultures with their own norms and understandings of ethical obligations." *Id.* at 4 (concluding that "[a]ppreciating how lawyers identify, frame, and resolve ethical questions . . . requires sensitivity to both the types of organizations in which they work and the particular fields in which they practice").

173 James, *supra* note 72, at 46 (noting the importance of examining each structural element of the organization separately and together and finding that an "ethically balanced company is one in which the three elements of the formal organizational structure neither intentionally nor unintentionally discourage ethical behavior of workers but rather complement an ethical corporate culture, ethics codes, and ethics training programs").

174 *Id.* at 47 (noting that workers can be quite resourceful in responding to incentive programs and describing an "extensive theoretical and empirical literature showing that a firm's reward system affects the propensity of workers to engage in unethical behavior).

175 *See id.; see also* REGAN, *supra* note 72 (describing fallout that occurred when firm lawyer ignored conflicts of interest to bring new clients to the firm).

matter originations, and billed hours" because this formula, which is made up of the elements of a firm's long-term success, allows "the impression that decisions are based on greed" and encourages decision making that favors an individual attorney's immediate income at the expense of the mid-term or long-term welfare of the firm.[176] Moreover, the firm's stated policies and procedures for monitoring and evaluating lawyers must avoid creating pressures for lawyers to comply with decisions they believe are ethically questionable.[177] In short, attention to wrongful obedience should be carefully and consciously incorporated in the firm's compensation and reward programs as well as in the new attorney's evaluation.

Finally, Milgram found that the existence of competing authorities creates strain, making it more difficult for a decision maker to identify a clear line of authority and simply to defer to one particular authority.[178] Thus, ensuring that authoritative checks exist outside a structured work team or department can help guard against wrongful obedience, both by providing an ethical check and by creating the type of strain on the decision maker that diminishes the likelihood of wrongful obedience in the first place. The Freeh Report, for example, recommends that universities appoint an ethics officer to provide ethics training and report to the university president and board of trustees, and an ethics council to assist the ethics officer.[179] This is not a new idea in law's work settings, especially within larger firms and agencies, but it assumes a renewed importance in a wrongful obedience analysis.[180] In a legal environment, a high-level senior lawyer serving as the ethics officer provides both an alternative authoritative voice for newer attorneys, creating strain by making the line of authority less clear, and it provides a safe method for the junior attorney to check on ethics questions without the need to question their supervising attorney directly.[181] A work environment without organizational checks, that provides boundless discretion to single departments or partners, is fertile ground for wrongful obedience.[182]

---

176 Peter J. Winders, *The Ideal Law Firm Compensation System,* 16 PROF. LAW. 1 (2005) (providing as an example a hypothetical of a lawyer who pushes to keep a client that the firm would actually be three times better off not having due to the client's restrictive conflict waiver policy).

177 James, *supra* note 72, at 49.

178 *See supra* notes 140–40 and accompanying text.

179 *See* FREEH REPORT, *supra* note 12, at 130.

180 *See* Ted Schneyer, *supra* note 99, at 607 (noting that "many large firms now designate a partner to serve as their ethics advisor or general counsel"); *see also supra* note 102 (citing authorities analyzing the existence of a firm designated ethics advisor, compliance specialist, or loss prevention partner).

181 *Cf.* Schneyer, *supra* note 5, at 2 n.11 (suggesting that a firm's ethics committee can proactively help an associate by stepping in to clarify the associate's duties with the firm partners).

182 *See* FREEH REPORT, supra note 12, at 139 (describing the athletic department as "an island" because it was given too much independence from the university); see also Freeh Report, supra note 12, at 15 (finding

Moreover, an ethics partner can also be responsible for periodically benchmarking the legal organization's practices and policies with peer institutions to facilitate a focus on improvement.[183] Finally, it is not enough for a firm merely to designate an "ethics partner"; managing lawyers must encourage the firm's junior lawyers to make use of the partner's guidance and expertise in resolving ethical questions and make sure the firm's lawyers understand the process for working with the ethics partner.

B. Victim Variables

Milgram's experiments demonstrated that when the victim of wrongful obedience is close in proximity to the actor, wrongful obedience drops and defiance increases. In two variations on the basic scenario, Milgram situated the learner closer to the teacher to assess the impact of victim proximity. When the victim was moved into the same room as the teacher, 60% of the teachers refused to obey. When the teacher was required to place the victim's hand on the shock device, 70% of the teachers refused to obey.[184] Milgram posited several theories to explain the importance of victim proximity. Of course, empathy for the victim—gaining a more complete grasp of the victim's experience—may be a trigger for disobedience.[185] In addition, proximity narrows the visual field and prohibits denial. When a victim is close, it becomes impossible for the actor to forget or deny that there is a real person on the receiving end of their wrongful obedience.[186] In addition, proximity creates reciprocal fields: a close victim can observe the subject who is harming him, and it is quite simply easier to harm someone when he is unable to watch you do it.[187] Moreover, proximity responds to learned behavior—we have learned not to harm someone who is close to us because they may retaliate, but "this learning occurs in a context of proximity to others and may not be generalized to situations in which others are physically remote from us."[188] In addition, in proximity there is unity of the act. It is easier

---

a failure of governance on behalf of the university officials and the board of trustees and a failure to create an environment in which top officials "felt accountable").

183 *See, e.g.*, FREEH REPORT, supra note 12, at 130 (recommending benchmarking practices with peer institutions to focus on continuous improvement).

184 MILGRAM, *supra* note 1, at 36. These findings are in stark contrast to the base experiment where approximately 33% of the teachers refused to obey.

185 *Id.* at 36, 38 (noting that "[i]t is probable that the visual cues associated with the victim's suffering trigger empathic responses in the [participant] and give him a more complete grasp of the victim's experience").

186 *Id.* at 36.

187 *Id.* at 39 (noting that "[t]he manifest function of allowing the victim of a firing squad to be blindfolded is to make the occasion less stressful for him, but it may also serve a latent function of reducing the stress of the executioner").

188 *Id.* at 40.

to see the connection between the action and the consequences, which decreases the likelihood of wrongful obedience.[189] Finally, proximity of the victim prevents an incipient group to form between the experimenter and the teacher, from which the victim is excluded. If an alliance is formed between actors and the victim is out of sight, it is easier to inflict pain.[190] In general, Milgram found that "[a]ny feature that reduces the psychological closeness between the subject's actions and the consequences of the action also reduces the level of strain" on the subject, which increases obedience.[191]

In addition to victim proximity as a critical variable, Milgram found that if a subject can convince himself that a victim is an "unworthy person," he will "not be concerned about inflicting pain on him."[192] For example, a teacher might "blame" the victim for volunteering for the experiment in the first place, thus attempting to justify any pain inflicted on him. Moreover, if the harm inflicted on the victim starts as seemingly inconsequential and builds in incremental steps, obedience is facilitated. Scholars have viewed the sequential, small-step, 15-volt increase of the shocks given in Milgram's experiment as facilitating wrongful obedience because in order to break the pattern and defy the experimenters orders, the subject first needs to acknowledge to himself that what he just did was probably wrong—going on is the subject's only way to justify the correctness of his past performances.[193] David Luban has described this as an incremental "corruption of judgment" and "slippery slope" that leads, step by small step, to wrongful conduct.[194]

The ramifications of victim considerations applied to real-life obedience situations are significant. For example, in an analysis of Swiss Police Captain Paul Grueninger, who defied the authority of the federal government to protect refugees from Nazi persecution, Francois Rochat and Andre Modigliani suggest that "Grueninger's conscientious habit of regularly visiting the border and meeting face-to-face with refugees may well have had two important effects: (a) it increased his sympathetic response by allowing him actually to observe their fear, exhaustion, and suffering; (b) it made it more difficult for him to turn down their

---

189 *Id.* at 39.

190 *Id.* at 33, 39–40.

191 *Id.* at 156–58.

192 *Id.* at 160–61.

193 MILGRAM, *supra* note 1, at 149.

194 *See* Luban, *supra* note 5, at 9, 103 (further arguing that the incremental nature of the action is a critical factor in explaining Milgram's results); *see also* Perlman, *supra* note 10, at 467 (describing "cognitive dissonance" and debating the importance of this particular factor in the wrongful obedience analysis).

requests, because they could watch him as he pondered whether to allow them to remain in Switzerland."[195]

In the legal profession, attorney actions are frequently completed out of sight of either a beneficiary or a potential victim. To new attorneys, their actions may not seem particularly concrete or immediately impactful. Because new lawyers have little conception of the real world impact of their actions, one of the most important things supervising attorneys can do is look for ways to introduce the newer lawyer to context. If possible, for example, supervising attorneys should ensure that all members of the work team have an opportunity to meet and interact with the client, who is the direct recipient and beneficiary of the team's efforts. Because junior attorneys generally receive their work assignments—and work evaluations—from senior attorneys, they may not have sufficient insight into the client's perspective to appropriately factor it into decision-making. Moreover, understanding the client's input will provide the new lawyer with one more "voice" and introduce one more perspective, all of which may diminish the strength of the new lawyer's chosen authority figure.

A victim of wrongful obedience, however, is frequently not a client and it may not be obvious to the lawyer who would suffer the impact of an ethical breach. For example, assume a senior lawyer instructs a new lawyer to pretend they are someone else to obtain information under pretext or instructs the new lawyer to shred documents that the new lawyer thinks must be disclosed under the relevant disclosure rules.[196] It may not be immediately clear to a young lawyer who the victim would be if the lawyer simply followed a senior lawyer's request and the potential harm that might be caused may seem slight. As Andrew Perlman noted, "[u]nlike Milgram's experiments, where obedience resulted in painful electric shocks to a man with a heart condition, compliance in many (but not all) lawyering contexts produces far less dire consequences."[197]

---

195 Rochat & Modigliani, *supra* note 139, at 104.

196 *See, e.g.*, Lawrence K. Hellman, *The Effects of Law Office Work on the Formation of Law Students' Professional Values: Observation, Explanation, Optimization*, 4 GEO J. LEGAL ETHICS 537 (1991). Professor Lawrence Hellman conducted a study with 81 externship students over a period of seven law school semesters who were placed as legal interns in positions working with attorney supervisors and instructed by Professor Hellman to maintain journals identifying and discussing "issues of professional responsibility that arose in their work environments." As I noted in an earlier article, the character and range of examples of misconduct observed by students was startling and included instances of the student being instructed to engage in unethical conduct including "instructing the intern on how to lie to the court clerk to obtain a case file under pretext" and "instructing the intern to misrepresent his or her identity to a third person." *See also* O'Grady, *supra* note 5, at 499–500 (discussing Hellman's study).

197 Perlman, *supra* note 10, at 463–64.

Milgram's work demonstrates that placing potential victims "in sight"—making them real—can make a meaningful difference in the obedience analysis. Thus, for example, document destruction can potentially result in an innocent person's conviction, but new lawyers working at an early stage in the process of a case may have no understanding of that potentiality. A prosecutor's office can attend directly to that gap by requiring that all prosecutors in the office attend lectures that introduce them to wrongly convicted defendants and their families. In-house continuing legal education programs that highlight victims of unprofessional or unethical attorney conduct can help introduce new attorneys to real world context. In addition, Milgram's work suggests that law offices should strive to ensure that a professional work culture does not unwittingly label potential victims of wrongful obedience as "unworthy"—a lesson that might be particularly relevant to prosecutors if they face pressures to conclude that defendants are not generally good guys and are not worthy of concern if victimized by wrongful obedience. Finally, the seemingly inconsequential impact of harm to victims of a lawyer's wrongful obedience, which may build incrementally, can be addressed through managing lawyer's careful attention, when revamping the work culture, communicating with firm lawyers, and supervising junior lawyers, to all ethical or professional breaches, even those that may seem relatively "minor" or inconsequential.

C. Responsibility Variables

Milgram concluded from his studies that a person who assumes responsibility for his actions will be inclined to exercise the independent judgment and personal courage needed to disobey a supervisor while one who places responsibility for an action on another is more likely to obey that person. In Milgram's studies, teachers uncomfortable with continuing the shocks would frequently ask the experimenter to tell them who was going to be "responsible" for any harm caused to the learner, a question which the experimenter always answered by taking full responsibility himself for the action and any resulting harm.[198] Milgram noted that "[o]nce the experimenter has reassured the subject that he is not responsible for his actions, there is a perceptible reduction in strain."[199] The obedient subjects essentially reduced strain for themselves by denying responsibility for their actions.[200] Ultimately, although the subject was the actual actor—the one pushing the switch on the shock machine—subjects who obeyed to the end of the shock machine

---

198 MILGRAM, *supra* note 1, at 77. *See also* OBEDIENCE, *supra* note 165 (subject teacher asks, "do you accept all responsibility?" to which the experimenter replies, "the responsibility is mine").

199 MILGRAM, *supra* note 1, at 160.

200 *Id.* at 159.

often did not see themselves as primarily responsible for causing pain; instead, they viewed the experimenter as equally or more responsible than they were.[201] Thus, Milgram concluded that defiant subjects generally saw themselves as principally responsible for the suffering of the learner, while obedient subjects were willing to accept less responsibility and did not generally see themselves as any more responsible than the experimenter.[202]

The assumption of responsibility is closely related to the concept of voluntariness in the experiments. Many subjects in Milgram's studies did not see their actions as voluntary; rather, they felt compelled to act by the orders of the experimenter. Indeed, a number of the experimenter's scripted prods, recited by the experimenter when the teacher expressed reluctance to continue the shocks, suggested to the teacher an absence of voluntariness: "the experiment requires that you continue" (prod #2), "it is absolutely essential that you continue" (prod #3), and "you have no other choice, Teacher" (prod #4). As noted above, voluntariness is the key factor distinguishing obedience from conformity.[203] Moreover, some subjects relied importantly on a contract theory to explain their sense that they were under a duty to obey—"[t]hey had contracted with the experimenter to relinquish some of their freedom in the pursuit of a commonly held value [the advancement of knowledge]."[204] This "contract" reinforced for the participant the "existence of a plausible legitimate reason for the wrongful conduct," for example, studying the learning process, and it included an agreement from the participant to "follow certain procedures before starting the experiment."[205]

Applying these variables to the practice of law, results in the sensible conclusion that new attorneys who understand their own individual responsibility for professional conduct will be more inclined to speak up when called up to exercise professional judgment. As noted above, the Rules of Professional Conduct impose codes of responsibility on all attorneys as individuals, rather than

---

201 *See also* OBEDIENCE, *supra* note 165 (As one subject in the experiment put it: "I wanted to stop but he wouldn't let me.").

202 MILGRAM, *supra* note 1, at 203–04, app. B (the Responsibility Clock) (noting that "[t]he major finding is that the defiant subjects see themselves as principally responsible for the suffering of the learner assigning 48 percent of the total responsibility to themselves and 39 percent to the experimenter. The balance tips slightly for the obedient subjects, who do not see themselves as any more responsible than the experimenter, and indeed, are willing to accept slightly less of the responsibility").

203 *See supra* note 71 and accompanying text (noting that when an actor conforms to a perceived state he admits to acting voluntarily; however, when an actor obeys the order of a person with authority he contends he was not acting voluntarily).

204 MILGRAM, *supra* note 1, at 63–65.

205 *See, e.g.*, Perlman, *supra* note 10, at 462 (identifying situational factors).

imposing rules on groups or law firms, and even the newest attorneys can be disciplined for failure to abide by the rules.[206] But in the dynamics and pressures of day to day work, the rules are likely insufficiently concrete to influence a new attorney's assumption of personal responsibility, especially in the face of pressures to conform or obey. Moreover, obedience instincts and pressures to conform are likely at their highest influential peak early in an attorney's career, when work with senior lawyers is powerful professional training ground.[207] Finally, as noted above, one rule—Model Rule 5.2(b)—is intended essentially to encourage obedience for "reasonable resolutions" of "arguable questions," effectively giving permission to junior lawyers to relax into their natural tendencies to obey.[208]

A legal organization's management and supervising attorneys must understand that all these forces effectively work against the likelihood that even the most confident and conscientious of new attorneys will assume individual responsibility for their professional conduct and senior lawyers cannot assume that new attorneys will understand that they are supposed to accept responsibility for their actions. Instead, senior lawyers in the workplace must be proactive. They can do so in two important ways: (1) managing lawyers should use various media and methods, including written contracts, to consistently communicate the value the firm places on independent thinking and the importance the firm places on lawyers assuming individual professional responsibility in their work and the firm should ensure that new lawyers, in turn, have the opportunity to communicate with them; and (2) supervising lawyers should use "non-directive" supervisory techniques to help guide new lawyers toward their own individual acceptance of responsibility.

With respect to consistent communication, insisting on two-way, transparent communication among the various participants of an organization or work team,

---

206 *Supra* notes 92–96 and accompanying text.

207 O'Grady, *supra* note 5, at 497; *see also* TASK FORCE ON LAW SCHOOLS AND THE PROFESSION: NARROWING THE GAP, AMERICAN BAR ASSOCIATION SECTION OF LEGAL EDUCATION AND ADMISSIONS TO THE BAR, LEGAL EDUCATION AND PROFESSIONAL DEVELOPMENT—AN EDUCATIONAL CONTINUUM 235 (1992) (known as the "MacCrate Report") (concluding that "a new lawyer's ethical standards are likely to be shaped far more by his or her mentors in the early years of practice than by the experiences one acquires in the limited practice setting available in law school"); Hellman, *supra* note 194, at 611 (workplace experiences, especially those that occur early in a career, strongly influence professional behavior and supersede law school lessons). *Cf.* SOL M. LINOWITZ WITH MARTIN MAYER, THE BETRAYED PROFESSION: LAWYERING AT THE END OF THE TWENTIETH CENTURY 131 (1994) (quoting Professor Stephen Gillers as saying that perhaps "young lawyers lack ethical standards not because they've been poorly taught in law school but because their experience on their first job tells them nobody cares").

208 *See* Perlman, *supra* note 133, at 14. As previously noted, I agree with Professor Perlman and others that Rule 5.2(b) is harmful because it further encourages what Milgram found was already an overriding human tendency—the instinct to obey needs to be countered by pause and reflection—rather than encouragement.

and at all levels of a hierarchy, is a critical component of guarding against wrongful obedience. The Freeh Report, for example, focuses on enhancing communication and transparency by recommending that the university "[c]ommunicate regularly with University students, faculty, staff, alumni, and the community regarding significant University policies and issues through a variety of methods and media" and "[e]mphasize and practice openness and transparency at all levels and within all areas of the University."[209] In the legal workplace, a firm's expectations should be communicated to new attorneys in numerous ways including through firm seminars; small supervisory meetings; written firm mission statements; written employment contracts with firm lawyers; firm policies, resolutions, and procedures; social media; and compensation and promotion programs. A legal organization should stress, for example, that attorney's sanctioned within the state's disciplinary regime or determined by the firm's ethics partner to have engaged in unprofessional conduct, will assume full responsibility for those decisions and may suffer appropriate consequences within the firm's compensation and track to promotion programs. Milgram's findings regarding reliance on contracts suggest that people generally take their contractual commitments seriously; in a legal organization, attorney employment contracts can effectively contain specific resolutions to acknowledge the importance of an attorney's independent attendance to the rules of professional responsibility and a written commitment to follow the firm's process for clarifying questionable directives.[210] Finally, the firm should ensure that newer lawyers understand the avenues available to them to communicate with managing lawyers and the firm should encourage them to do so. The power of multi-faceted, two-way, consistent communication of the firm values for the firm's newest attorneys is significant—it reflects a work place culture that encourages communication of ideas, respects a variety of judgments, and encourages the new attorney to assume individual responsibility thus guarding against wrongful obedience.

With respect to supervisory techniques, senior lawyers can help newer lawyers exercise judgment and assume responsibility by understanding and employing "non-directive" supervision techniques, which are widely embraced in

---

[209] FREEH REPORT, *supra* note 12, at 130; *see also* GLADWELL, *supra* note 139, at 191–98 (2008) (attributing full communication as a key component of an airplane pilot's success in an emergency landing situation where the pilot talked and listened in the most transparent manner possible "to the passengers, to the doctors, to his copilot, to the second crew he woke up from their nap, to his superiors back home in Dubai, [and] to ATC at Helsinki").

[210] *See, e.g.,* Menkel-Meadow, *supra* note 85, at 656 (suggesting that law firms adopt "resolutions" to encourage a better quality of life in the practice of law).

clinical legal education.[211] Clinical law professors working with students on cases ensure that students "learn by doing" by insisting that students perform key work, think through all decisions, and provide active input in decision making. One key method for achieving these pedagogic goals is "non-directive" supervision—which is basically a conscious effort by the senior supervising lawyer to avoid simply telling the junior lawyer what to do on a case. When a newer lawyer asks for input on a case matter, for example, the non-directive supervisor will respond to the request not with "an answer" or some "direction," but rather with "careful questions specifically designed to shape the discussion and help the student [or junior lawyer] understand the process of thinking through solutions and arriving at answers."[212] While this process takes longer and is thus not always practical in a busy law office, a supervising attorney can use it as time permits to the great benefit of the newer lawyer.

An example may highlight the usefulness of non-directive supervision for the new lawyer's emerging professional judgment and sense of independent responsibility. Suppose a new lawyer on a work team representing an employee in a wrongful discharge case asks the senior lawyer on the team: "How much detail should I include in the complaint against ABC, Inc. with regard to the circumstances of our client's firing?" After getting an update on the facts learned in the client interview, a busy lawyer would likely be inclined to answer the question directly; for example, "that's great stuff—I think it will tell a compelling story, it's relevant, and it sets up the theory underlying our wrongful discharge claim. Do we have more than just our client's version of this event? If not, you should probably see if there is anyone at the office who witnessed or overheard what happened and interview them, unless we need to go through ABC's counsel first. Will you look into all of that?" This encounter leaves the young lawyer with a lot of legal research and fact investigation work to do and certainly advances the client's case forward in an effective way. But the junior lawyer has had no input into the decisions that followed her instinct that detail in the complaint would be helpful; thus, she likely does not feel any sense of responsibility for the lawyering actions that will follow. Contrast the "directive" scenario with the approach of the non-directive supervisor. He will respond to the junior lawyer's initial question with his own questions: "Why do you think factual detail with regard to the firing is important? How is it helpful to our theory of the case? How do you know this

[211] *See, e.g.,* Margaret Martin Barry, *Clinical Supervision: Walking That Fine Line,* 2 CLINICAL. L. REV. 137 (1995); Ann Shalleck, *Clinical Contexts: Theory and Practice in Law and Supervision,* 21 N.Y.U. REV. L. & SOC. CHANGE 109 (1994); Peter Toll Hoffman, *The Stages of the Clinical Supervisory Relationship,* 4 ANTIOCH L.J. 301 (1986); Frank S. Bloch, *The Andragogical Basis of Clinical Legal Education,* 35 VAND. L. REV. 321 (1982).

[212] O'Grady, *supra* note 5, at 517 (describing hypothetical non-directive supervisory sessions).

story is accurate? Do we need more than just our client telling us that version? What do the rules require we get for factual support? How can we confirm the facts and flesh them out more? Are we permitted to talk to other employees at ABC, Inc. without going through ABC's counsel? What do you think you should do next?"

As the junior lawyer reflects on and responds to the senior lawyer's questions, and is thus guided through the decision-making process, she both practices the skills that lead to good judgment and assumes independent responsibility for decisions made because she has been integral to the process of making them. While it is time-consuming, even an occasional use of non-directive supervision techniques can instill in a new lawyer the realization that she is expected to assume responsibility for her actions rather than seeing them as derivative of her supervising lawyer's input. Milgram's work suggests this assumption of responsibility will go a long way toward preventing wrongful obedience.

D. Peer Group Dynamic Variables

One of Milgram's variations on the basic scenario demonstrated that when one person in a group of peers refuses to wrongfully obey the orders of a superior, the wrongful obedience of all members of the group is significantly diminished. In this variation, which he called the "two peers rebel" experiment, the teacher was paired with two other confederate teachers. When both of the other teachers in the group refused to continue the experiment, 36 out of 40 subjects defied the experimenter's orders to continue, instead joining their rebelling peers. Milgram noted that "[t]he effects of peer rebellion are very impressive in undercutting the experimenter's authority."[213]

Milgram noted numerous reasons why group dynamics are so effective in overcoming authority. Rebelling peers, for example, may introduce to the subject the very idea of defiance, a notion that may not have occurred to the subject as a possibility.[214] In addition, the rebelling peers introduce defiance as a natural reaction to the situation and provide confirmation for the subject's suspicion that shocking the victim is wrong.[215] Moreover, when a peer withdraws, the responsibility for the action is less diffused and the subject not only shoulders more of that burden but feels judged by those who have pronounced it unacceptable.[216] Finally, subjects see that the consequences for defiance are

---

213 MILGRAM, *supra* note 1, at 118 (further noting that "of the score of experimental variations completed in this study, none was so effective in undercutting the experimenter's authority as [this] manipulation").

214 *Id.* at 120.

215 *Id.*

216 *Id.*

minimal and begin to understand that they have power while the experimenter's power is diminished.[217]

Applying peer group dynamics to law suggests that newer attorneys working within a hierarchy have power against wrongful obedience when they come together as a group. Rather than fearing that power, legal organization managers should work with it, recognizing its value. Associates working for the same firm, for example, should be encouraged to gather routinely to discuss work and office environment issues.[218] In his assessment of the professional responsibility of law firm associates, for example, Douglas Richmond suggests that when a partner instructs an associate to do something unethical, the associate should "first consult another associate whose judgment she trusts to see whether she perceives the issue correctly."[219] People naturally feel more comfortable discussing sensitive issues with their peers, and Milgram's work suggests that defiance against wrongful obedience would increase if even one peer suggests taking a questionable or troubling circumstance outside of the work team hierarchy, rather than going along with it.[220]

V. Conclusion

Lawyers, both experienced and inexperienced, too often fail to recognize the lessons from Milgram's seminal experiments on obedience and the need to think and behave independently in the face of pressures to obey or conform to an entrenched workplace culture. Lawyers, despite presumptions of competence and faithful adherence to rules of professional conduct, are not immune from pressures to obey. Indeed, such pressures are acute within the realities of the practice of law. While changes to professional rules could theoretically facilitate appropriate defiance in the face of wrongful directives, rule changes will not go

---

217 After a confederate teacher refused to continue, he would get up from his chair in front of the shock machine, move to another part of the room, and the experimenter would simply instruct the other teachers to continue with the experiment without punishing the rebel. *Id.* at 117. Studies on conformity also show the importance of peer group influence. *See supra* notes 64–66 and accompanying text.

218 Of course, associates working for the same firm can often, but not always, speak freely about cases without jeopardizing client confidentiality protections; thus, confidentiality concerns must be considered. *See* MODEL RULES OF PROF'L CONDUCT R. 1.6. With careful attention to protecting client confidentiality, associates working for different firms have been known to gather at bar groups and professional meetings and to "gather" virtually on Internet and blog sites such as Anonymous Lawyer, www.anonymouslawyer.blogspot.com, and Above the Law, www.abovethelaw.com.

219 Richmond, *supra* note 132, at 208.

220 For example, when a janitor at Penn State University witnessed Sandusky engaged in child sexual abuse, he told his peers—other janitors—what he saw and they discussed it as a group. Unfortunately, the university's entrenched culture made them fear for their jobs as they concluded that the university would "close ranks to protect the football program" and "get rid of all of us" if the abuse were reported. FREEH REPORT, *supra* note 12, at 22.

far enough to guard against the power of obedience for newer attorneys. Law firms and legal workplaces can and should take steps to understand the underpinnings of wrongful obedience and actively counterbalance the powerful tendencies of junior lawyers to wrongfully obey supervising attorneys or wrongfully conform to an entrenched workplace culture.

NOTES

1. Now that you know more about obedience and conformity, thanks to the studies discussed in this article, think about yourself in your current role as a student. Have there been times when you did things that you later regretted, either because you started down a path that you later realized was a bad idea or because your fellow students were all behaving in a certain way, so that you felt like the odd person out if you didn't follow their lead? What lessons can you take from your own behavior before you rejoin the work force?

2. One of us has a best friend, Randy Morgan, who works on projects for the International Space Station.* Randy has a habit of taking a look at a picture of who's up there on the International Space Station before he starts work each morning, just to remind himself of the high stakes of his job. Are there similar reminders that you might want to give yourself before you start work each day? And might those reminders "wear off" over time?

---

* Randy is a friend to both of us, but he's Jeff's best friend.

CHAPTER 5

This Is Not a Symposium on How to Commit Fraud—But If It Were . . .*

*Harvey Gilmore***

Introduction

"A lawyer with his briefcase can steal more than 100 men with guns."[1]

Don Vito Corleone

We know the names: Bernard Madoff, Kenneth Lay, Jeffrey Skilling, Andrew Fastow, Dennis Kozlowski, Phillip R. Bennett, and Bernard Ebbers. These are but a few of the biggest corporate thieves in recent memory. Similarly, the names of certain corporations will also conjure up lasting images of massive corporate frauds: Enron, World-Com, Tyco, Adelphia, Refco, Global Crossing, and Sunbeam, again, to name just a few.

The most disquieting aspect of all these financial frauds really isn't the massive amounts of money that was looted from the victimized companies. Instead, the truly unnerving fact regarding most financial frauds is that they are deceptively easy to formulate and sometimes even easier to implement.

In this piece, I will first give several definitions as to what constitutes fraud. I will next argue how and why committing certain types of financial fraud is in fact fairly simple. In doing so, I must point out that I am not deliberately giving a clinic on how to commit fraud (title notwithstanding) and live happily ever after

* This piece was originally published in the MICHIGAN STATE JOURNAL OF BUSINESS AND SECURITIES LAW, 11 J. BUS. & SEC. L. 199 (2011).

** Professor of Taxation and Business Law at Monroe College, The Bronx, New York; B.S., Hunter College of the City University of New York (1987), M.S., Long Island University (1990), J.D., Southern New England School of Law (1998), LL.M., Touro College Jacob D. Fuchsberg Law Center (2005). My thanks to Todd Jennings, Adam Kocaj, Ellen Durkee, and Sarah Lierman for their generous help and guidance with this article. This article was originally published in the MICHIGAN STATE JOURNAL OF BUSINESS AND SECURITIES LAW, 11 J. BUS. & SEC. L. 199 (2011).

1 MARIO PUZO, THE GODFATHER 52 (Putnam, 1969).

in a nice offshore tax shelter. That said, keep in mind that in order for forensic accountants and fraud investigators to successfully detect and prevent fraud, they necessarily need to have some idea of how a financial crime might be perpetrated. This knowledge is essential in order to beat the bad guys at their own game. Or, to put it another way, in order to catch a criminal, one has to think like a criminal.

Finally, I will give my take on several factors that enable people to commit financial fraud, including weak internal controls, corporate cronyism, and negligent audits, to name a few.

I. What Exactly Is Fraud?

In its most generic form, fraud means that one party induces another party to enter into a transaction under false pretenses. Or, in the opinion of Susan P. Koniak, fraud is "in plain English, lying to someone to get them to give you their stuff."[2] My own definition of fraud is that of separating some sucker from his money by getting him to agree to it first.

Of course, there are more technical definitions as to what constitutes fraud. For example, the United States Supreme Court in Southern Development Company v. Silva[3] defined civil fraud as follows:

> First. That the defendant has made a representation in regard to a material fact;
>
> Secondly. That such representation is false;
>
> Thirdly. That such representation was not actually believed by the defendant, on reasonable grounds, to be true;
>
> Fourthly. That it was made with intent that it should be acted on,
>
> Fifthly. That it was acted on by complainant to his damage; and,
>
> Sixthly. That in so acting on it the complainant was ignorant of its falsity, and reasonably believed it to be true.[4]

Next, the Securities and Exchange Commission's (SEC) famous Rule 10b–5[5] describes fraud this way:

---

[2] Susan P. Koniak, *Law and Truth Roundtable: The Lawyer's Responsibility to the Truth,* 26 HARV. J.L. & PUB. POL'Y 195, 197 (2003).

[3] 125 U.S. 247 (1888).

[4] *Id.* at 250.

[5] 17 C.F.R. 240.10b–5 (2011).

> It shall be unlawful for any person, directly or indirectly, by the use of any means or instrumentality of interstate commerce, or of the mails or of any facility of any national securities exchange,
>
> (a) To employ any device, scheme, or artifice to defraud,
>
> (b) To make any untrue statement of a material fact or to omit to state a material fact necessary in order to make the statements made, in the light of the circumstances under which they were made, not misleading, or
>
> (c) To engage in any act, practice, or course of business which operates or would operate as a fraud or deceit upon any person, in connection with the purchase or sale of any security.[6]

Finally, the Federal Bureau of Investigation (FBI) characterizes fraud this way:

> White-collar crimes are categorized by deceit, concealment, or violation of trust and are not dependent on the application or threat of physical force or violence. Such acts are committed by individuals and organizations to obtain money, property, or services, to avoid the payment or loss of money or services, or to secure a personal or business advantage.[7]

Thus, while there is no one dominant definition as to what constitutes fraud, the SEC, FBI, and Supreme Court definitions do agree on the common elements of fraud (misrepresentation, intent, and reliance).

II. A Few Simple Schemes

In keeping with the general premise that one has to think like a criminal in order to catch a criminal (without becoming one[,] of course), one has to always remember that the key to committing a successful financial fraud always lies in the details. Thus, in any financial fraud one has to start small—that is, the amount that the fraudster misappropriates in the beginning should not be a material amount.[8]

It will be necessary to plan ahead first, and account for every possible contingency in staying one step ahead. Otherwise, a potential fraudster is just

---

6 *Id.*

7 Facts and Figures 2003, Federal Bureau of Investigation (2003), http://www.fbi.gov/stats-services/publications/fcs_report2005.

8 D. LARRY CRUMBLEY ET AL., FORENSIC AND INVESTIGATIVE ACCOUNTING 4–4 (Kurt Diefenbach et al. eds., 3d ed. 2007) ("[T]he measure of whether something is significant enough to change an investor's investment decision . . . .").

inviting law enforcement into his living room if he comes up with an idea on Tuesday and tries to put it into practice on Friday.

A. Check Misappropriation

Let us assume that I work for XYZ Corporation as the accounts receivable manager. In my position, I process the payments received from vendors, record the payments in the company books, and also put together the monthly bank reconciliations. One day, the corporation receives a check from Acme Company for $800, and, while no one is watching me, I put Acme's check in my pocket.

Now that I have the check, my immediate problem is how can I possibly cash a check payable to XYZ Corporation without anyone asking questions? Unless I somehow had signature authority with XYZ's bank, I would not otherwise be able to indorse that check under my own name. Next, the check would most likely be payable "to the order of XYZ Corporation," and the Uniform Commercial Code requires both an indorsement[9] and delivery[10] of the instrument before I could successfully negotiate an order instrument and receive payment.

Here's how I solve the problem (again, the successful fraudster would have planned this long before the actual theft): first, I will set up a shell company[11] in the name of "XYZ Company." My second step is to go to Staples and simply order an indorsement stamp. The stamp would read as follows:

PAY TO XYZ COMPANY
ACCOUNT #544460
FOR DEPOSIT ONLY

Thirdly, I will then set up a bank account in the name of the fictitious XYZ Company. Why is this necessary? First, I am relying on the fact that the bank's personnel will not pay attention to the fact that I am depositing a check payable to "XYZ Corporation" into "XYZ Company's" account, and that the bank's less than diligent personnel would most likely assume that "XYZ Corporation" and "XYZ Company" are, in fact, the same business.

Then, when I am required to indorse the check, all I have to do is stamp the back of it. This serves two very important purposes. First, when Acme Company (our vendor) receives its cancelled checks with its bank statement, it will see that

---

9 U.C.C. § 3–201(b) (2010).

10 *Id.*

11 W. STEVE ALBRECHT ET AL., FRAUD EXAMINATION 510 (Rob Dewey et al. eds., 3d ed. 2009) ("Dummy or shell companies are fictitious entities created for the sole purpose of committing fraud. Many times, they are nothing more than a fabricated name and a post office box that an employee uses to collect disbursements from false billings.").

the $800 liability was in fact paid (unknowingly to a different payee) and indorsed. Secondly, using an indorsement stamp will save me from writing anything on the back of any check and there would not be any handwriting samples that could be traced back to me. When the funds become available, I can withdraw the money as I see fit by going to any supermarket or gas station that has an ATM (and preferably no cameras) to make my withdrawals.

The end result, if I'm both discreet and successful, is the acquisition of several hundred thousand (or even million) dollars of the company's money before anyone realizes that anything is missing.

B. Some Real Life & Simple (Yet Creative) Accounting

It's never a good thing when someone owes you money and then stiffs you by not paying; yet, this is something that most people can relate to. Sometimes, a corporation can have a similar experience on a much bigger scale. Imagine being the Chief Executive Officer (CEO) of a corporation where the clients owe $430 million that the company might not be able to collect. This was what Refco, and its CEO, Phillip R. Bennett, faced in late 2005, when its books showed $430 million in bad debts.

The solution that Bennett came up with to solve the bad debt problem was astounding for its simplicity. It was nothing more than a series of welltimed, yet simple, accounting entries on Refco's books that enabled Bennett to take $430 million of bad debts off the company's books.[12]

Every quarter, Bennett would have Refco Capital, a Refco subsidiary, lend money to a third party.[13] The third party would then lend that money to another corporation (Refco Group Holdings, Inc., "RGHI")[14] in which Bennett himself was the sole shareholder.[15] Then, RGHI would give the cash to Refco in payment of the bad debts.[16] This sleight of hand gave Refco's auditors the belief that 1) Refco's receivables had been paid by its customers, and 2) Refco had another legitimate outstanding receivable due to its subsidiary from a third party. After Refco's external auditing firm completed its quarterly examination of Refco's

---

12 *In re* Refco, Inc. Sec. Litig., 503 F. Supp. 2d 611 (S.D.N.Y. 2007). *See also* Allan Dodds Frank, *The Refco Debacle: Reporter on the Hunt,* http://www.evesmag.com/refco.htm (last visited Oct. 1, 2010); Paritosh Bansal, *Ex-Refco Executive Pleads Guilty,* REUTERS, Dec. 19, 2007, http://www.reuters.com/article/2007/12/19/us-refco-plea-idUSN1960240320071219.

13 *In re* Refco, *supra* note 12 at 619.

14 *In re* Refco, *supra* note 12 at 619.

15 Adam J. Levitin, *Finding Nemo: Rediscovering the Virtues of Negotiability in the Wake of Enron,* 2007 COLUM. BUS. L. REV. 83, 161 (2007).

16 *In re* Refco, *supra* note 12 at 619.

books, Bennett would quietly reverse the transaction between RGHI and Refco and, in effect, put everything back where it was. . .that is, until the next quarterly audit.[17]

Although Bennett's fraud resulted in $2.4 billion in losses to shareholders and creditors,[18] the real genius of the scheme was in the simple recording in the accounting records. First, by directing Refco Capital to make the loan to the third party, Bennett created an asset on Refco Capital's books in the form of a receivable. Next, when the third party makes the same loan to RGHI, RGHI pays the money back to Refco. Now, Refco has what appears to be an additional infusion of cash as it looks like the previously uncollectible debts have been paid in full. The end result is an isosceles triangle in which money owed to Refco was in fact paid by Refco!

C. A Ponzi Scheme Du Jour

What fraud investigators commonly refer to as a "Ponzi scheme" is (dis)credited to Charles Ponzi,[19] who originated the idea of creating a "pyramid scheme where investors are encouraged to invest in a 'Great Idea' of one sort or another."[20]

For example, I hold myself out as an investment broker. I send a prospectus to potential suckers, I mean . . . investors, in which I promise a 20 percent return to every client who invests $1000 with my company within sixty days. On April 1, I get 100 investors who are willing to give me $1000 apiece, and I have an initial investment of $100,000. On June 1, sixty days later, as promised I send each investor a certified check for $200. As one of the elements of fraud is reliance, I have to make my story look good enough and sound convincing enough so that I can get my potential victims to create the contract with me based on the story I am telling them. Right now, two things happened that have convinced my initial group of investors that I am in fact the real deal.

First, since I sent each client a $200 check, this will confirm in his mind that I am someone who is able to deliver the goods. Second, the fact that I took the time and effort (and expense) to send each client a certified check would most likely also convince each client that I am legitimate. After all, anyone who would

---

17 *Id.*

18 U.S. v. Bennett, S3 05 Cr. 1192 (NRB), Government's Sentencing Memorandum.

19 Cunningham v. Brown, 265 U.S. 1 (1924).

20 Cabot Christianson, *You can't cheat an honest man: Everything you want to know about Ponzi schemes,* 23 ALASKA B. RAG 23, 23 (1999).

pay good money to have that many checks certified certainly cannot be committing any fraud. . .can he?

Once I have delivered the "goods" to my first group of investors, two things are likely to happen next. First, my initial group of investors would likely invest even more money into my company, which I am all too happy to take. Secondly, my initial investor group will likely tell their friends about their successful venture with my firm, and this second group would also be willing to invest their money with my firm, which again, I will be very happy to take. The same thing happens with the next round of investments with my firm: I am again able to send each of my clients a certified check representing what they believe is a 20 percent return on their investment.

What really happened here? Each client gave me $1000 as an investment, and I gave each client $200, representing 20 percent. However, the $200 that I gave each client is not a 20 percent profit on the investment. All I did was take $200 off the top, and give that money back to the client. So, that $200 is nothing but a refund, and I pocket the rest.

There's more. How can I keep doing this? According to this hypothetical, I have two groups of investors. Thus it will be necessary for me to segregate which investor belongs to which group. So when the money comes in, I will skim some of the money from Investor Group #2 in order to pay Investor Group #1. Then, with Investor Group #2, I will pay their $200 out of whatever is left of their $1000 investment. So, Investor Group #2 really got skimmed twice.

The more levels of investors I can get for my business, the longer I can carry out this scam. This results in the more money I can steal as I skim from Investor Group #5 to pay Investor Group #4, Investor Group #4 to pay Investor Group #3, and so on as I go further up the food chain. Unfortunately for the investors, the money that I'm using to pay the 20 percent return has never come from any profits from my business idea; I'm just taking money from one gullible chump to pay off another gullible chump and pocketing the difference. By the time the scheme ultimately breaks down, the last group of investors that I can bring into the fold will be the group left holding the bag and having nothing left to show for it.[21] Charles Ponzi's original scheme on which I based the above hypothetical is discussed at length in the Supreme Court case Cunningham v. Brown.[22]

---

[21] *Id.* ("Early investors invest, and are rewarded with huge profits. More investors invest, and then still more. After the bubble bursts, it turns out that investor #1was paid off, not by the proceeds of the great idea, but by investor #2's investment. Investor #2 was actually paid off by investor #3. And so on. The early investors win big, and the later investors lose big.").

[22] *Cunningham,* 265 U.S. at 34.

D. Fictitious Payee Scams

1. Ghost Employees

An unscrupulous payroll manager could steal a sizeable amount of money by having payroll checks issued to former employees who no longer work for the company.[23] How could this happen? Just do not remove the former employee from the payroll records. And, as an additional measure of the fraudster's covering his tracks, the fraudster could make sure that the ghost employee check has the correct amount of deductions for federal income taxes, state & local income taxes, Social Security Taxes and Medicare Taxes. And, similar to my earlier discussion of check misappropriation, I can easily have a deposit stamp created that reads "pay to (insert name), for deposit only."

2. Fictitious Payees

Believe it or not, under the Uniform Commercial Code, any instrument that is payable to a fictitious payee can be enforced by an innocent holder against the maker of a note or the drawer of a draft.[24]

For example, the Jimmy Fund[25] is a charitable organization that supports the Dana-Farber Cancer Institute, a well-known hospital in the Boston area. If I wanted to take grievous advantage of people's altruism, I could set up a scheme where I solicit donations for the Jimmy Fund. For those people who are willing to pay by check, I would have them make their checks payable to Jimmy Fund. In the meantime, I will have a bank account made up in the name of "Jimmy Fund," or even "James Fund," if I wanted to be more formal. Since "Jimmy" is generally accepted as the common nickname for "James," no one would think anything suspicious about it. And, again, I can have a deposit stamp created that reads "pay to Jimmy Fund, for deposit only." This again saves me from giving any handwriting samples on any checks that I would deposit into Jimmy Fund's account.

3. Fictitious Vendors

Similar to the scams involving shell companies, ghost employees and fictitious payees, setting up phony vendors is also a relatively simple way of committing occupational fraud, the object of which is to separate an innocent person from his money and putting the money in the fraudster's guilty pocket. In this kind of scheme, the business "makes payments for fictitious invoices to a

---

23 CRUMBLEY ET AL., *supra* note 8, at 5–18.

24 *See* UCC § 3–404(b) (2010); *see also* UCC § 3–405 (2010); Gregory C. Cook & John D. Pickering, *A Primer on Applying Articles 3 and 4 to the Ten Most Common Check Disputes,* 70 ALA. L. REV. 278, 283 (2009).

25 The Jimmy Fund, http://www.jimmyfund.org/abo/default.html (last visited Oct. 5, 2010).

company owned by a corrupt employee, his or her relatives, or other accomplices."[26] A real-life incident involving an oncology practice in Florida resulted in the office bookkeeper embezzling millions of dollars over an eight-year period.[27]

"A few months after she began working for the practice, she started opening up fictitious companies with names similar to the practice's legitimate vendors. For example, instead of 'Cardinal Health,' her shell company was 'Cardinal.' In place of 'McKesson Drug Company' her fake company was 'McKesson." '[28]

Unfortunately for the doctor who owned the practice, the bookkeeper's fraud resulted in the doctor's filing for personal bankruptcy as well as getting a divorce.[29]

E. Let's Play Make Believe . . . Aka Padding One's Credentials

As a college professor (see note 1), my tuition-paying students would have an expectation (and more important, a contract right) that when I walk into the classroom, I would have the practical experience and academic training necessary to deliver the subject matter that shows my students that I actually knew what I was talking about. Instead of actually having those academic credentials, let us assume that I was someone who dropped out of grade school after the fourth grade. On top of that, my only steady job is that I dig graves. But, my dream in life was to actually teach college level taxation and business law courses, and come hell or high water, I'm going to find a way to do just that. I am not at all worried about not having graduated from either college or law school; those are minor details—after all, I'm not actually going to spend 7–10 years actually going to college, graduate school and law school. If I can successfully pull off this charade, well, why would I go to the trouble of actually taking classes?

How could I pull this off? Part of my job is to be a good actor. I can go to websites like www.higheredjobs.com, www.chronicle.com/jobs, or any college's website and look at the job postings for open faculty positions. I can also go online and gather information on how to conduct myself at an academic interview. Once I get that information, I can certainly rehearse and practice to the point where I might actually sound like a legitimate polished applicant for a professorship.

Next, what do I do about transcripts? If I show on my resume that I've graduated from the institutions shown on my resume, common sense would

---

26 Lee Ann H. Webster, *Detecting Office Fraud in Your Practice,* 6 COMMUNITY ONCOLOGY 412, 413 (2009), available at http://www.communityoncology.net/journal/articles/0609412.pdf.

27 *Id.*

28 *Id.*

29 *Id.*

suggest that any potential employer would want me to furnish them with official copies of my transcripts. Since part of my fraud is misrepresenting my education, it would also be easy for me to manufacture fictitious transcripts. First, I could go to Staples or Office Max and purchase a more expensive, fancier type of paper. Next, while I'm there, I can order a special stamp that approximates the official seal of each school that I allegedly graduated from. After that, I put the special paper into my printer and I can make up a transcript showing what courses I've taken in which semesters, as well as the grades that I received in each course. Last, I visit the schools I "graduated" from, procure some letterhead envelopes, and I mail my transcripts from the nearest post office which will have the postmark from my school's nearby location.

If I say that I have a Bachelor's degree in accounting from Hunter College, I could go to the department's website and carefully copy the sequence of courses. Again, planning ahead is a key component in committing a successful fraud. My plan would severely go up in smoke if my transcript showed that I took Principles of Accounting 1 and Advanced Accounting in the same semester. How careless is that? Finally, what were my grades in my accounting classes? Whatever I wanted them to be! Then, if I actually get hired by a college that I've interviewed with, I'll be stealing the college's money as a salaried employee.

Obviously, I'm being a little facetious with the above hypothetical. Unfortunately, however, not only are scams like this not at all that farfetched, but they have actually happened. A well-publicized incident involved Ms. Marilee Jones, who was the dean of admissions at the Massachusetts Institute of Technology (MIT).[30] She began working for the school back in 1979 and over the next twenty-eight years made her way up the ranks and eventually became a dean.[31] Ms. Jones had proven herself to be very good at the jobs she had prior to her becoming a dean[32] and was beloved by her students.[33] Ms. Jones had claimed that she received degrees from Albany Medical College, Union College, and Rensselaer Polytechnic Institute.[34] As it eventually turned out, Ms. Jones never graduated from any of the schools that she mentioned.[35] In a bizarre twist to the story, Ms.

30 Tamar Lewin, *Dean at M.I.T. Resigns, Ending a 28-Year Lie,* N.Y. TIMES, Apr. 27, 2007, http://www.nytimes.com/2007/04/27/us/27mit.html.

31 *Id.*

32 *Id.*

33 *Id.*

34 *Id.*

35 *Id.*

Jones did receive a bachelor's degree from the College of Saint Rose, but she never listed it anywhere on her resume.[36]

Unfortunately, this is not the only incident where someone falsified their academic credentials. A New Jersey attorney (Daniel J. Scavone) had his law license revoked after the state's disciplinary review board found that he, among other things, altered his law school transcript and failed to disclose on his bar application that he was kicked out of one law school for altering his transcript.[37] Scavone's first misdeed was that he applied to the University of Pennsylvania Law School as a minority student, which he was not.[38] In his second year, Scavone altered his first-year law grades on his transcript.

"Respondent altered his transcript to show that in his first year he received three 'Excellents' and five 'Goods' whereas his true grades were two 'Goods' and six 'Qualifieds.' He submitted the altered transcript to two New York law firms which were engaged in on-campus recruiting. Respondent also falsified his resume by indicating that he received a score of 705 on the LSAT whereas he had received only 564 and 539. He submitted the altered resume during the on-campus recruiting to a New York law firm."[39]

The law school administration, after discovering Scavone's chicanery, gave him the option to either withdraw or face a disciplinary hearing likely to result in expulsion.[40] Scavone agreed to withdraw.[41] After Scavone graduated from the St. Louis University School of Law,[42] he applied for admission to the New Jersey bar.[43] A key question that Scavone had to answer truthfully asked the following: "Have you ever been disciplined, reprimanded, suspended, expelled or asked to resign from any educational institution?"[44] Scavone answered no: "Respondent answered that question in the negative. He certified his answers were true and accurate to the best of his knowledge and belief, further stating he was aware that any willful misstatement could prejudice his admission to the bar and subject him to such penalties as provided by law."[45] The court agreed with the review board's

---

36 Marcella Bombardieri, *Marilee Jones Did Receive Degree*, THE TECH, May 4, 2007, http://tech.mit.edu/V127/N23/marileeupdate.html.

37 *In re* Scavone, 106 N.J. 542 (1987).

38 *See id.* at 544.

39 *Id.* at 545.

40 *Id.*

41 *Id.*

42 *Id.*

43 *Id.*

44 *Id.* at 546.

45 *Id.*

findings that Scavone was not truthful in answering that specific question.[46] Consequently, the court revoked Scavone's license to practice law.[47]

These are but a few of the various ways that anyone could commit a massive fraud with a little ingenuity. Now that we have explored some of the how, the next question to tackle is . . .

III. Why Does Such Fraud Take Place?

The answers to this question could be as numerous as the fraud schemes themselves. They could range from company culture,[48] lax internal controls,[49] personal pressure situations,[50] rationalizations,[51] and audits generally not designed to specifically find fraud other than financial statement fraud,[52] to name but a few.

A. The Fraud Triangle

Any discussion as to why individuals commit occupational fraud must include the "fraud triangle." Criminologist Donald Cressey (1919–1987)[53] developed a theory that explains certain elements that are necessary for a fraud to take place.[54] Dr. Cressey's theory became the well-known "Fraud Triangle."

---

[46] *Id.* at 550–554.

[47] *Id.* at 554.

[48] Pamela H. Bucy et al., *Why do they do it?: The Motives, Mores, and Character of White Collar Criminals,* 28 ST. JOHN'S L. REV. 401, 401 (2008) ("Why do talented, bright, highly educated, successful people, who have 'made it,' risk it all by lying, stealing, and cheating, especially when what they're stealing is not much compared to what they have? The simple answer is, 'because they can." '). *See also* Daniel J. H. Greenwood, *Enronitis: Why Good Corporations Go Bad,* 2004 COLUM. BUS. L. REV. 773 (2004).

[49] *See, e.g.,* Lawrence A. Cunningham, *A New Product for the State Corporation Law Market: Audit Committee Certifications,* 1 BERKELEY BUS. L.J. 327, 335 (2004) ("Many financial calamities that brewed during the late 1990s are attributed to internal control failure, however, including within audit committees.").

[50] *See* Bucy et al., *supra* note 48, at 408. ("For example, Walt Pavlo, Credit Collections Manager at MCI Telecommunications, Inc., who falsified MCI accounts receivables and stole $6 million from MCI, spoke of greed, opportunity, and culture . . . . But, he also felt a lot of pressure from within MCI and did not know how to meet MCI's mandates without cheating. His performance reviews were based entirely on how much MCI's bad debt he collected.").

[51] *See, e.g.,* TOMMIE SINGLETON ET AL., FRAUD AUDITING AND FORENSIC ACCOUNTING 10 (3d ed. 2006).

[52] CRUMBLEY ET AL., *supra* note 8, at 4–5.

[53] Megan Cook, *Financial Fraud 101: Understanding the Fraud Triangle,* EXAMINER.COM, June 17, 2009, http://www.examiner.com/financial-fraud-innational/financial-fraud-101-understanding-the-fraud-triangle.

[54] *Id.*

Dr. Cressey's theory establishes that there are three specific elements (like points in a triangle) that would lead a person to commit occupational fraud. The elements are (a) pressure,[55] (b) opportunity,[56] and (c) rationalization.[57]

What is pressure? One might describe pressure as a deep-seated need to come up with money right away as a result of gambling, alcoholism, divorce, or a high-maintenance lifestyle, to name just a few.[58]

Next, what is opportunity? Opportunity is the occupational fraudster's sensing that he has a chance to steal company funds while no one is looking and the getting is good.[59]

Finally, what is rationalization? Rationalization is when the fraudster comes up with excuses as to why his bad act really isn't so bad.[60] Some rationalizations include the following: I'm overworked, underpaid, and unappreciated; my 99-year-old aunt needs hip replacement surgery; my bosses treat me like crap; I was only borrowing the money; this is a billion-dollar company—they won't miss $250,000; I had to pay my bills; I had to save my family from eviction. The list goes on and on.

B. Permissive Corporate Culture

At the corporate level, the general premise is that management's primary objective is to maximize the value of the corporation, and by extension, shareholder wealth.[61] Since a corporation is owned by its shareholders,[62] the corporation's management team is working on behalf of the shareholders, and is thus charged with the responsibility of taking a course of action that would

---

55 *Id.*

56 *Id.*

57 *Id.*

58 *See, e.g.*, Kathleen Barney, *This Thing Called Forensic Accounting*, 43 ARIZ. ATT'Y 34, 38 (2007) ("First, an employee feels the pressure of a financial burden such as a divorce, a gambling problem, alcoholism or an excessive lifestyle. This becomes his or her motivation to steal.").

59 *Id.* ("Second, opportunity exists in the loopholes of the internal controls, which allow the employee to exploit his or her position for personal gain.").

60 *Id.* ("Finally, the fraudster must be able to rationalize the behavior. I have never met a perpetrator of fraud who considered himself a crook. The most common rationalizations are 'I will pay it back,' 'The firm can afford it' and 'I'm not hurting anyone." ').

61 *See, e.g.*, MICHAEL C. EHRHARDT & EUGINE F. BRIGHAM, CORPORATE FINANCE: A FOCUSED APPROACH 7 (3d ed. 2008); *see also* Edward B. Rock, *Commentary, The General Counsel of a Nonprofit Enterprise: Some Questions*, 46 HOUS. L. REV. 17, 19 (2009) ("In the for-profit corporation, the roles played by shareholders mean that, as a theoretical and practical matter, the corporation will ultimately be managed for the shareholders. Great discretion is given to the managers in how they maximize shareholder value and even, in the short term, whether they maximize shareholder value.").

62 *See, e.g.*, ROGER LEROY MILLER & GAYLORD A. JENTZ, FUNDAMENTALS OF BUSINESS LAW 520–21 (8th ed. 2010).

maximize shareholder wealth.[63] So, if it happens that some questionable corporate ethics were instrumental in maximizing shareholder wealth with shareholders and managers making money hand over fist,[64] should one be really surprised to find after the fact that people might have been asleep at the wheel (or may have looked the other way) as to not stop the gravy train?

. . . [D]uring Enron's peak years, money was pouring in by the boatload. "Enron exemplified an era. At its peak, it was celebrated as a new and better way of doing business, making shareholders and employees money by the bushel while increasing the efficiency of our energy markets to everyone's benefit."[65]

1. Dennis Kozlowski and Tyco*

That said, in keeping with the premise of maximizing shareholder wealth, we have seen a number of lurid cases in the very recent past where managers have taken advantage of their positions to maximize their own personal wealth, at the expense of the very shareholders they were supposed to serve,[66] sometimes to the point of committing fraud.[67] Consider the now classic case of former Tyco International Inc. Chief Executive Officer Dennis Kozlowski, who is currently serving a 25-year prison sentence for looting $600 million from the corporation.[68] Not only that, Kozlowski's larceny was taken on top of his having earned $332 million in salary between 1999 and 2002.[69] Kozlowski's fraud is well known for having included a $2 million birthday toga party for his wife, for which Tyco paid half of the cost,[70] having a $6,000 shower curtain in his Manhattan apartment,[71] as well as his forgetting to report a $25 million loan forgiveness from the corporation on his income tax return.[72]

---

63 Ehrhardt & Brigham, *supra* note 61, at 7.

64 Greenwood, *supra* note 48, at 777.

65 Greenwood, *supra* note 48, at 790.

* [Editors' note: According to the reported criminal allegations, Koslowski used Tyco as a sort of personal piggy-bank, using company funds to pay for personal extravagances and hiding their fraud in a variety of ways.]

66 Stephen V. Arbogast, *Commentary on Legal and Managerial "Cultures" in Corporate Representation,* 46 HOUS. L. REV. 33, 36 (2009) ("In essence, it concerns firm managers, who are hired to work for shareholders, using their corporate positions to pursue personal financial agendas.").

67 *Id.*

68 *See, e.g.,* Susan Lorde Martin, *Executive Compensation: Reining in Runaway Abuses—Again,* 41 U.S.F. L. REV. 147, 161 (2006).

69 *Id.*

70 *Ex-Tyco CEO Dennis Kozlowski Found Guilty,* MSNBC, June 17, 2005, http://www.msnbc.msn.com/id/8258729.

71 *Id.*

72 *Id.*

2. Enron and Its Ballooning Revenues

In the last ten years, Enron has emerged as perhaps the poster child for corporate fraud.[73] In a nutshell, Enron's creative accounting practices resulted in untold millions of dollars of income that accrued on the books, but the resulting cash inflows never existed in fact.[74] How could this happen? It started with an accounting treatment that Enron utilized in preparing its financial statements called "mark to market accounting."[75] Mark to market accounting allows a company to record expected future earnings on its books in the current period as revenue. For example, in 2010 my law practice enters into a long-term retainer agreement with a client and the client will pay me $10 million over the ten-year life of the contract. Instead of my recording a prorated amount of the contract price as revenue every year, mark to market accounting allows me to hit a home run and report the entire $10 million on my books as revenue this year. In essence, mark to market accounting allows me to record non-cash earnings now with the expectation that I would realize the cash receipts in the future.[76]

The catalyst that projected Enron to use mark to market accounting was that in 1991 President Jeffrey Skilling was able to convince CEO Kenneth Lay and the rest of the top management that mark to market accounting was the way for the company to go.[77] All the more amazing (in light of what eventually happened) was that Skilling was able to convince Enron's auditing firm, Arthur Andersen, as well as the Securities and Exchange Commission (SEC) that the change in Enron's accounting method was necessary and appropriate.[78]

3. The In Crowd

A common denominator that might have been a factor with the big name corporate accounting scandals seems to be that the perpetrators were part of a powerful clique that ran the day to day operation. For example, several of Enron's key players all had MBA degrees.

The credentials for the Enron executive team were as follows:

> Jeffrey K. Skilling, the former CEO of Enron, held an MBA from Harvard; Andrew Fastow, the former CFO, held a Northwestern MBA;

---

73 Greenwood, *supra* note 48, at 783–84.

74 Greenwood, *supra* note 48, at 784.

75 *See, e.g.*, John R. Kroeger, *Enron, Fraud, and Securities Reform: An Enron Prosecutor's Perspective*, 76 U. COLO. L. REV. 57, 75 (2005).

76 *Id.* at 75.

77 HAROLD BIERMAN, JR., ACCOUNTING/FINANCE LESSONS OF ENRON: A CASE STUDY 156 (2008).

78 *Id.*

> Clifford Baxter, a former vice chairman, who killed himself shortly after the Enron revelations became a daily media event, was a Columbia MBA.[79]

And Kenneth Lay, as Enron's leader, pointed the way to corporate success that his underlings were only too happy to follow.

> Mr. Skilling and Mr. Fastow were so well regarded in the business community that none dared raise a question about them or their methodologies. And Mr. Lay had planted in them the goal of Enron's continuing achievement above and beyond the crowd. As a CEO a full generation older and chairman of the Enron board, Fastow and Skilling continued to perform in the manner that Mr. Lay had come to expect.[80] By the way, Kenneth Lay himself had a Ph.D. in Economics from the University of Houston.[81]

Similarly, in the situation regarding Tyco, Dennis Kozlowski found an interesting method to bind his underlings to the corporation and to himself personally. Kozlowski orchestrated two employee loan programs which effectively ensured employee silence at best, or employee complicity, at worst.[82] The first was a loan available to Tyco employees to cover the income tax liability that triggered when their stock options vested.[83]

The second loan helped Tyco employees cover their moving expenses when they relocated from Tyco's headquarters in New Hampshire to its corporate offices in New York.[84] Kozlowski had declared in no uncertain terms that these loans were available for his new hires, including Chief Financial Officer Mark Schwartz and General Counsel Mark Belnick.[85] Over time, both Schwartz and Belnick found themselves increasingly beholden to Kozlowski as they both received additional loans as well as salary increases.[86]

---

79 Marianne M. Jennings, *A Primer on Enron: Lessons From A Perfect Storm of Financial Reporting, Corporate Governance and Ethical Culture Failures,* 39 CAL. W. L. REV. 163, 226 (2003) (citation omitted).

80 Marianne M. Jennings, *Restoring Ethical Gumption in the Corporation: A Federalist Paper on Corporate Governance—Restoration of Active Virtue in the Corporate Structure to Curb the 'YeeHaw Culture' in Organizations,* 3 WYO. L. REV. 387, 401–02 (2003) (citation omitted).

81 WILLIAM G. FLANAGAN, DIRTY ROTTEN CEOS: HOW BUSINESS LEADERS ARE FLEECING AMERICA 57 (2004).

82 Jennings, *supra* note 80, at 467–74.

83 Jennings, *supra* note 80, at 474.

84 Jennings, *supra* note 80, at 474.

85 Jennings, *supra* note 80, at 474.

86 Jennings, *supra* note 80, at 467–68.

C. Audit Failures

We all know the story of how the complicity of Enron's not-so-independent auditing firm Arthur Andersen ("Andersen") played a huge role in not only Enron's demise, but also the deterioration of Andersen's own reputation to that of a national punch line before going out of business. I'll discuss the details of Andersen's independence follies a little later. However, Andersen's role in the Enron mess does shine a bright light on the fact that it does not take much to compromise audit firm independence.

Federal law requires that a publicly traded corporation have its financial statements audited every year.[87] An auditing firm is required to be independent from the client whose financial records it is examining.[88] A corporate client hires a CPA firm to [go to] its headquarters to test samples of the company's records . . . things like bank reconciliations, journal entries, general ledgers, payroll records, and tax records, to name a few. The firm will conduct the audit in accordance with the professional auditing rules called Generally Accepted Auditing Standards.[89] Generally Accepted Auditing Standards are the rules of the accounting profession that control how accountants perform audits. At the end of the audit, the audit partner will sign a letter in which the firm gives its opinion whether the client's accounting practices give a fair representation of its financial condition.[90]

The requirement of auditor independence is thus the key in the auditor being able to do his job in a dispassionate manner. "An auditor cannot be the client's advocate. The Court in the *Arthur Young* case concluded by saying that 'the public watchdog' function demands that the accountant maintain total independence from the client at all times and requires complete fidelity to the public trust."[91]

Next, the auditor and client agree ahead of time how much the client will pay for the audit engagement. So, right out of the gate, an auditing firm gets paid by the very company whose financial practices the auditor is investigating. This arrangement now opens the door to the possibility that the auditor's independence might be compromised on that very basis alone. "[T]hose who defend the propriety of consulting services by auditors respond that the growth of consulting

---

87 15 U.S.C. § 77aa (25)–(27) (2000); 15 U.S.C.S. § 78q (e) (LexisNexis 2006).

88 Arthur B. Laby, *Differentiating Gatekeepers,* 1 BROOK. J. CORP. FIN. & COM. L. 119, 125 (2006).

89 *See, e.g.,* United States v. Arthur Young & Co., 465 U.S. 805, 811 (1984).

90 *Id.*

91 Laby, *supra* note 88, at 124.

services made little real difference because the audit firm was already conflicted by the fact that the client paid its fees."[92]

Of course, this does not necessarily mean that the auditor is automatically subject to the client's influence and power of suggestion to push the envelope, stretch the rules, or even help the client commit fraud, but this raises the specter that a client could prevail on the auditor's potential fear of losing the client to a competitor. If I'm the CEO of a publicly traded corporation and KPMG is auditing my company's books, I could conceivably suggest to the audit partner that if things are not "just so" at the end of this year's engagement, I may take my business to Price Waterhouse Coopers next year. So, I could subtly (or not so subtly) maneuver the auditing firm into doing my bidding simply by using their competition as my leverage.

> Put as bluntly as possible, the audit partner of a major client (such as Enron) is always conflicted by the fact that such a partner has a 'one client' practice. Whoever is the gatekeeper—attorney, auditor, or analyst—a 'one client' practice compromises the agent. Should the partner lose that client for any reason, the partner will not easily find a replacement client and may need to find employment elsewhere.[93]

1. Arthur Andersen's Conflict of Interest Problem

Let us go back to the Enron debacle and how Andersen's chummy relationship with its favorite client ultimately led to the spectacular failure of both firms. If we accept the proposition that the auditing firm is to be independent from its client, then common sense might suggest that the auditor should not do any non-audit (tax, consultation, financial statement preparation, etc.) work for the client.

a) Who did what? In addition to being Enron's external auditor, Andersen also did management consulting and tax work for Enron, for which Enron paid $25 million for the auditing work and another $27 million for the non-audit work.[94]

b) Who worked where? Quite a few members of Andersen's staff had permanent offices in the Enron headquarters and were eventually hired to work

---

[92] John C. Coffee, Jr., *Gatekeeper Failure and Reform: The Challenge of Fashioning Relevant Reforms*, 84. B.U. L. REV. 301, 322 (2004).

[93] *Id.* at 322.

[94] Jennings, *supra* note 80, at 214. *See also* Deborah Solomon, *After Enron, a Push to Limit Accountants to . . . Accounting*, WALL ST. J., Jan. 25, 2002, at C1.

for Enron.[95] In addition to that, "Andersen performed and reviewed both the internal and external audit functions."[96]

c) Who was close with whom? David Duncan, who was Andersen's audit partner in the Houston office (where Enron was located), was a golfing buddy of Rick Causey, who was Enron's Chief Accounting Officer and himself a former Andersen partner.[97] Thus, it became easier over time for Andersen to acquiesce to Enron's additional demands over time.[98]

While Andersen's "misadventures" with Enron have now become legendary, it is worth noting here that several of the biggest corporate accounting frauds in recent history have the same common denominator: Arthur Andersen was the auditor.[99]

The investor losses tied to fraud by Arthur Andersen's clients are enormous. Three hundred billion dollars is the total loss in market capitalization, i.e., stockholder value, for only the following six fraud-tainted firms: Sunbeam, Waste Management, WorldCom, Qwest, Global Crossing and Enron. These wayward firms have more in common than staggering losses due to financial fraud: They all shared Arthur Andersen as their auditor.[100]

That said, I do not mean to suggest that Arthur Andersen is the only big accounting firm that was ever in bed with a client to the point of committing massive fraud. As of this writing, Big Four accounting firm Ernst and Young is currently under investigation for its work with the now bankrupt investment firm Lehman Brothers.[101] Similarly, PricewaterhouseCoopers, another Big Four accounting firm, is under scrutiny for giving American International Group (AIG) a clean bill of health before AIG nearly collapsed.[102]

---

95 Jennings, *supra* note 80, at 214. *See also* Charles M. Elson & Christopher J. Gyves, *The Enron Failure and Corporate Governance Reform,* 38 WAKE FOREST L. REV. 855, 868 (2003).

96 Jennings, *supra* note 80, at 214.

97 Flynn McRoberts, *Ties to Enron Blinded Anderson,* CHI. TRIB., Sept. 2, 2010, http://www.chicagotribune.com/news/chi-0209030210sep03,0,7490166.story?page=2. *See also* Jennings, *supra* note 80, at 214.

98 McRoberts, *supra* note 97.

99 John Freeman, *Ethics Watch: Lawyers and Corporate Disgrace,* 14 S.C. LAW. 9, 9 (2003).

100 *Id.*

101 *See, e.g.,* Kevin Reed, *E & Y Investigated over Lehman Brothers,* THE ACCOUNTANCY AGE (Oct. 4, 2010), http://www.accountancyage.com/accountancyage/news/2270880/y-auditors-investgiated-lehman; Emily Chasan, *Could Lehman Be Ernst & Young's Enron?,* REUTERS, Mar. 12, 2010, available at Factiva, Doc No. LBA0000020100313e63d0000r; John Carney, *Will Ernst and Young Survive the Lehman Fiasco?,* BUS. INSIDER, Mar. 12, 2010, http://www.businessinsider.com/will-ernst-andyoungsurvive-the-lehman-fiasco-2010-3.

102 Joseph Weber et al., *Tough Questions for AIG's Auditors,* BUS. WK., Apr. 11, 2005, http://www.businessweek.com/magazine/content/05_15/b3928047_mz011.htm.

D. Internal Controls, Anyone?

The ease with which one can perpetrate a financial fraud also depends on the quality of the company's internal controls (or lack thereof). What exactly are internal controls? Generically speaking, internal controls are defensive mechanisms a business puts in place to maintain the integrity of its financial reporting, as well as protecting itself from financial fraud. "Internal control consists of all of the related methods and measures adopted within an organization to safeguard its assets, enhance the reliability of its accounting records, increase efficiency of operations, and ensure compliance with laws and regulations."[103]

Typically, a company's internal control policies will have specific principles that the responsible employees must adhere to in order to conduct its operations (financial and otherwise with reliability and integrity). "The six principles of control activities are as follows: establishment of responsibility; separation of duties; documentation procedures; physical controls; independent internal verification; and human resource controls."[104]

How can an unscrupulous, enterprising individual circumvent his company's control devices? Similar to my hypothetical regarding check misappropriations, a common possibility can arise from the fact that if an individual does all of the accounting functions from start to finish, the temptation to take advantage of the situation can be more than the individual can withstand. For example:

1. Failing to Separate the Duties

> Angela Bauer was an accounts payable clerk for Aggasiz Corporation. She prepared and issued checks to vendors and reconciled bank statements. She perpetrated a fraud this way: She wrote checks for costs that the company had not actually incurred (e.g., fake taxes). A supervisor then approved and signed the checks. Before issuing the check, though, she would 'white-out' the payee line on the check and change it to personal accounts that she controlled. She was able to conceal the theft because she also reconciled the bank account. That is, nobody else ever saw that the checks had been altered. Total take: $570,000.[105]

---

[103] JERRY J. WEYGANDT ET AL., ACCOUNTING PRINCIPLES 348 (9th ed. 2009).

[104] *Id.* at 349.

[105] *Id.* at 351.

2. Fictitious Vendor Payments

As discussed previously, in a fictitious vendor situation, I could create a shell company, have its address as a post office box, and have my employer mail checks to the phony address, and I'm off and running.

> Lawrence Fairbanks, the assistant vice chancellor of communications at Aesop University, was allowed to make purchases for his department of under $2,500 without external approval. Unfortunately, he also sometimes bought items for himself, such as expensive antiques and other collectibles. How did he do it? He replaced the vendor invoices he received with fake vendor invoices that he created. The fake invoices had descriptions that were more consistent with the communication department's operations. He submitted these fake invoices to the accounting department as the basis for their journal entries and to accounts payable as the basis for payment. Total take: $475,000.[106]

3. Fictitious Receivable

If I run a legitimate business, I provide goods or services for my clients, and they pay me. For example, I prepare a client's tax return and charge him $200. If the client pays me up front, I will prepare a journal entry in my books showing two things. First, my accounting records will show that my cash account balance increased by $200. Second, my accounting records will show that my revenue account balance also increased by $200 because I did the actual work, and thus earned the money. Or, if my client is to pay me at the end of the month, instead of my cash balance increasing by $200, my receivables balance will instead increase by $200 because my client owes me the money and will pay me later. My revenue balance will also go up by $200 because, again, I did the work. My having done the work now fixes my right to receive payment as well as the client's contract obligation to pay me. Either way, this transaction increases both my assets and more importantly, my earnings.

On the flip side, if I am not legitimate and I wanted to inflate both my assets and my revenues simultaneously, I could make simple accounting entries on my books (using the methodology explained above) to show that I provided tax preparation services for 100 additional clients at $200 per return, on credit. This results in an additional $20,000 in both revenues and receivables. In actuality, I never did any work, and my 100 additional "clients" are nothing more than 100 made-up names.

---

106 *Id.*

Now that I have misrepresented $20,000 in both assets and earnings, how can I use this to my additional advantage? If I wanted to borrow $15,000 from a bank, I could show the loan officer my (albeit inflated) financial statements that my business is both solvent and profitable (irrespective of the true financial condition of my business). Thanks to my inflated receivables, I have an asset on my books that I can give the bank as collateral to secure the loan. If I default on the loan, the bank will simply notify my "customers" to pay the bank instead of paying me, pursuant to the terms of the loan contract between myself and my bank.

And, if I need to carry the charade one step further, I can show the loan officer my ledger showing my legitimate customers who have previously paid me on a timely basis. Assuming that the loan officer does not find anything out of the ordinary, and therefore approves my $15,000 loan, I am now off and running, as I can pull off this same scam at more than one bank.

A well-known incident involving a fictitious revenue scam was perpetrated by an entity called Equity Funding.

> Equity Funding was an insurance company, to be specific, a reinsurer. To create fictitious revenues, the CEO simply created phony insurance policies. After seven years, the fraud was finally exposed in 1973 by a recently fired and disgruntled employee. At that time, $2 billion of the $3 billion in Receivables was phony.[107]

E. How Far Do Auditors Really Go to Detect Fraud?

Unfortunately, not all that far. After the recent creative accounting scandals involving Enron, Tyco, et. al., the most popular question was: where were the auditors? As we know with Arthur Andersen, as discussed above, the auditors were in bed with at least one client (Enron). As I've mentioned elsewhere, Andersen was not the only CPA firm that was ever in bed with one or more of its clients.[108]

Unfortunately, the single biggest problem with an external audit is this: an external audit is not generally designed to be a forensic fraud investigation. The typical external audit is conducted by an outside certified public accounting (CPA)

---

[107] SINGLETON ET AL., *supra* note 51, at 109.

[108] Greg Burns, *Accounting's Power Slips Into Loss Column,* CHI. TRIB., Nov. 10, 2002, http://articles.chicagotribune.com/2002-11-10/news/0211100536_1_accountingoversightboard-accounting-lecturer-accounting-industry/4.

firm "to obtain reasonable assurance as to whether the financial statements are free of any material misstatements."[109]

1. How Auditors Historically Handled the Fraud Issue

Prior to 2002, the American Institute of Certified Public Accountants (AICPA) was the professional governing body responsible for setting auditing standards. Consequently, the AICPA (through its Auditing Standards Board (ASB)) issued several Statements of Auditing Standards (SAS) that control how external accountants perform their audits.

a) SAS No. 16: "The Independent Auditor's Responsibility for the Detection of Errors or Irregularities," issued in 1977, says the following:

> The independent auditor's objective in making an examination of financial statements in accordance with (GAAS) is to form an opinion on whether the financial statements present fairly financial position, results of operations, and the changes in financial position in conformity with (GAAP). . . .). Consequently, under (GAAS), the independent auditor has the responsibility within the inherent limitations of the auditing process. . .to plan his examination to search for (material) errors and irregularities.[110]

b) SAS No. 53: In 1987, the AICPA issued SAS 53, "The Auditor's Responsibility to Detect and Report Errors and Irregularities." SAS 53 "modified the auditor's responsibility to require the auditor to 'design the audit to provide reasonable assurance of detecting errors and irregularities.' "[111]

c) SAS No. 82: Ten years later, the AICPA instituted SAS 82, "Consideration of Fraud in a Financial Statement Audit." SAS 82 gave the auditor the responsibility to detect and report any material misstatements due to fraud.[112] SAS 82 now gave auditors some guidance on how to consider the possibility of fraud[113] in terms of exercising due professional care,[114] planning the audit,[115]

---

109 Gideon Mark, *Accounting Fraud: Pleading Scienter of Auditors Under the PSLRA*, 39 CONN. L. REV. 1097, 1148 (2007).

110 ALBRECHT ET AL., *supra* note 11, at 644.

111 ALBRECHT ET AL., *supra* note 11, at 645.

112 Barbara R. Farrell & Joseph R. Franco, *The Role of the Auditor in the Prevention and Detection of Business Fraud: SAS No. 82*, W. CRIMINOLOGY REV. (1999), http://wcr.sonoma.edu/v2n1/farrell.html.

113 ALBRECHT ET AL., *supra* note 11, at 646.

114 ALBRECHT ET AL., *supra* note 11, at 646.

115 ALBRECHT ET AL., *supra* note 11, at 646.

evaluating the company's internal controls,[116] and getting supportive evidence for the audit opinion.[117]

d) SAS No. 99: Finally, the AICPA issued SAS 99, "Considerations of Fraud in a Financial Statement Audit," effective December 15, 2002. SAS 99 gave auditors additional guidance regarding the specific issue of fraud. SAS 99 now gives a description of fraud and its characteristics, requires auditors to discuss amongst themselves the risks of material misstatements due to fraud, and conferring with the client's management team and other employees about the risks of financial statement fraud among others.[118]

2. Then Came SOX

After the train wreck that was the accounting fraud scandals in the early 2000's, Congress responded by enacting the Sarbanes-Oxley Act of 2002 (SOX), which President George W. Bush signed into law in July 2002.[119] This statute was based on legislative concerns that the accounting profession, self-regulating as it was, was doing a rather poor job as a financial watchdog in auditing publicly traded companies.[120] In fact, Congress' SOX legislation kicked the AICPA out of the job of setting auditing standards. SOX created an administrative agency called the Public Corporation Accounting Oversight Board (PCAOB) and gave the PCAOB that responsibility. As such, the PCAOB is the entity now legally recognized to develop " 'Professional Auditing Standards' that must be followed by registered public accounting firms for audits of public companies."[121]

Conclusion

As shown above, in order to commit a financial fraud, the three main ingredients are a well-planned idea, some ingenuity, and good acting skills. Again, just because these pages show a kind of a blueprint as to how to commit certain fraud, that does not mean that I'm giving any future Bernie Madoff inspiration for the next great mass swindle. That is not my intention.

The focus of this note is to reinforce the understanding that in order to know how to detect and investigate fraud, one has to know what to look for in order to

---

116 ALBRECHT ET AL., *supra* note 11, at 646.

117 ALBRECHT ET AL., *supra* note 11, at 646.

118 American Institute of CPAs, AU § 316: Consideration of Fraud in a Financial Statement Audit 169, available at http://www.aicpa.org/Research/Standards/AuditAttest/DownloadableDocuments/AU00316.pdf (last updated April 2007).

119 Elisabeth Bumiller, *Bush Signs Bill Aimed at Fraud in Corporations,* N.Y. TIMES, Jul. 31, 2002, at A1, available at Factiva, Doc. No. nytf000020020731dy7v00039.

120 ALBRECHT ET AL., *supra* note 11, at 389.

121 ALBRECHT ET AL., *supra* note 11, at 1147.

prevent the fraud. Finally, I would like to pass along some professorial advice to any accounting students (including my own) and future fraud investigators who may read this piece: Knowledge is power. Therefore, take the information in these pages and be sure to use it as agents for the forces of good.

NOTES

1. In a recent Las Vegas case, probate attorney Robert Graham was sentenced to serve 16–40 years behind bars for stealing over $16 million from his clients. (Probate attorneys deal with estates—the bundle of rights after someone dies. Given that the beneficiaries of the estates probably weren't aware of how much of their money was sitting in Graham's trust account,* the massive fraud took a while to discover.) In an article describing the sentencing, reporter David Ferrara described some of Graham's justifications:

> Court records show Graham secretly funneled an average of $187,000 a month in client funds for several years to a special bank account to run his law practice and pay personal bills.
>
> He used client funds to pay $244,000 in taxes and $700,000 a year in advertising for his law firm. He also used the money to make thousands of dollars more in charitable donations to numerous organizations. . . .
>
> . . . .
>
> As Graham told [Judge] Earley he was trying to protect attorneys in his sinking firm, the judge interrupted: "How can you sleep at night? What about your clients? Oh my goodness, your clients."
>
> Wearing a lime green shirt, black pants and a beard, Graham blamed his crimes on an economic crash, expounded on his own struggles, told the judge he has no money left and asked forgiveness from those he robbed. He stopped short of apologizing directly to them.
>
> "It was total devastation, and I just didn't make the right decisions," he said. "I'm not a gambler, but I had a gambler's mentality. I thought if I put more in I'd get more out."**

* Client funds go into a trust account, segregated from the firm's operating funds. Lawyers pay their bills out of their operating funds, and they're not supposed to touch the money in the client trust account, except when they've earned a fee payable from that account. But in Graham's case, he used the client money stored in the law firm's trust account for various personal purposes. That's one of the fastest ways to trigger state bar discipline, by the way—state bars definitely want to keep client money sacrosanct.

** David Ferrara, *Las Vegas lawyer who stole millions gets 16 to 40 years behind bars,* LAS VEGAS REVIEW-JOURNAL (Dec. 8, 2017), at https://www.reviewjournal.com/crime/courts/las-vegas-lawyer-who-stole-millions-gets-16-to-40-years-behind-bars/.

You're now very, very familiar with the Milgram experiments. How might someone go from depositing client funds to embezzling millions, using what you know about cognitive dissonance?

2. Professor Gilmore discusses the three elements of the fraud triangle: pressure, opportunity, and rationalization. How might you fit attorney Robert Graham's statements into these three elements?

3. Not only does Professor Gilmore give you a good recap of some of Enron's and Arthur Andersen's behavior, but he also does a good job of showcasing the many, many ways in which small frauds can add up to large crimes. His article scared us, given how hard it can be to discover clever fraud. We hope that it scared you, too.

CHAPTER 6

Barriers to Effective Risk Management*

*Michelle M. Harner***

"[A]s long as the music is playing, you've got to get up and dance. We're still dancing."***

This now infamous quote by Charles Prince, Citigroup's former Chief Executive Officer, captures the high-risk, high-reward mentality and overconfidence that permeates much of corporate America. These attributes in turn helped to facilitate a global recession and some of the largest economic losses ever experienced in the financial sector. They also represent certain cognitive biases and cultural norms in corporate boardrooms and management suites that make implementing a meaningful risk culture and mitigating the impact of future economic downturns a challenging proposition.

The global recession highlighted significant failures in firms' risk-management practices. These failures implicated weaknesses not only in firms' financial risk modeling, but also the human or governance side of risk management. Unfortunately, fixing the former might be significantly easier than attending to the latter. Studies suggest that cognitive biases, including confirmation bias, overconfidence or optimism bias, and framing, can impair a

---

* This piece was originally published as Michelle M. Harner, *Barriers to Effective Risk Management*, 40 SETON HALL L. REV. 1323 (2010).

** Associate Professor of Law, University of Maryland School of Law. I would like to thank Jeffrey Lipshaw and Robert Rhee for their comments on earlier drafts of this Article. I also benefited from discussions with the participants in the Fourth Annual Law & Entrepreneurship Retreat hosted by Brigham Young University Law School and the Securities Regulation and the Global Economic Crisis Symposium hosted by Seton Hall University School of Law. In addition, I appreciate the assistance of Lauren Genvert and Alice Johnson. Nevertheless, all opinions, errors, and omissions in this Article are my own. Finally, I thank the University of Maryland School of Law for financial support.

*** Michiyo Nakamoto & David Wighton, *Citigroup Chief Stays Bullish on Buy-Out*, FINANCIAL TIMES, July 9, 2007, https://www.ft.com/content/80e2987a-2e50-11dc-821c-0000779fd2ac.

board's and management's ability to assess risk accurately. These problems are compounded by the typical incentive structure and the "winner-take-all" mentality adopted by many corporations in the United States.

This Article analyzes the potential benefits of improved risk-management practices, commonly called enterprise risk management (ERM), and the potential barriers to implementing meaningful ERM at U.S. firms. ERM is an integrated risk-management framework that seeks to improve knowledge of and communication about potential risks throughout the firm, starting with the board and senior management team. Indeed, the board and senior management team are vital to creating a risk culture. This Article considers the impact of boardroom dynamics and U.S. corporate culture on risk-management practices. This Article further considers whether regulation or a different approach is needed to encourage U.S. corporations to invest the necessary human capital in meaningful ERM.

I. Introduction

Risk management is not a new concept, but it typically garners renewed attention during periods of corporate scandals or market turmoil.[1] The global recession of 2008 ("2008 recession") is no exception.[2] Many commentators have highlighted significant risk-management failures as contributing factors to that recession.[3]

---

[1] For example, Barings Bank, Long-Term Capital Management, and the Asian Crisis each are often viewed as a case study in risk management failures. *See, e.g.*, JOHN MARTHINSEN, RISK TAKERS: USES AND ABUSES OF FINANCIAL DERIVATIVES (2003) (discussing risk management issues raised by derivatives trading and analyzing the Barings Bank and Long-Term Capital Management scenarios, among others); GEOFFREY POITRAS, RISK MANAGEMENT, SPECULATION, AND DERIVATIVE SECURITIES (2002) (same); Wing Thye Woo, *Lessons from the Asian Financial Crisis, and the Prospects for Resuming High Growth*, in EXCHANGE RATE REGIMES AND MACROECONOMIC STABILITY 9–31 (Lok-Sanh Ho & Chi-Wa Yuen eds., 2003); Case Studies, Int'l Fin. Risk Inst., http://riskinstitute.ch/Introduction.htm (last visited Mar. 31, 2010) (analyzing Barings Bank, Long-Term Capital Management, and the Asian Crisis in the context of risk management).

[2] This Article uses the term "2008 recession" to reference the entire period of financial turmoil, which became widely evident in late 2007 and continued into 2009.

[3] *See, e.g.*, Roger Barker, *Observations on the Current Crisis from a Corporate Governance Perspective*, INST. DIRECTORS, Feb. 20, 2009, at 2, available at https://www.iod.com/MainWebSite/Resources/Document/article_responding_crisis.pdf; Grant Kirkpatrick, *The Corporate Governance Lessons from the Financial Crisis*, FIN. MARKET TRENDS, Feb. 2009, at 4, available at http://www.oecd.org/dataoecd/32/1/42229620.pdf; Joe Nocera, *Risk Mismanagement*, N.Y. TIMES, Jan. 4, 2009, at MM24, available at http://www.nytimes.com/2009/01/04/magazine/04risk-t.html?_r=1&pagewanted=print; Ben S. Bernanke, Chairman, Fed. Reserve, *Address at the Federal Reserve Bank of Chicago's Annual Conference on Bank Structure and Competition* (May 15, 2008) (transcript available at http://www.federalreserve.gov/newsevents/speech/bernanke20080515a.htm); RISK & INS. MGMT. SOC'Y, INC., THE 2008 FINANCIAL CRISIS: A WAKE-UP CALL FOR ENTERPRISE RISK MANAGEMENT 3 (Bill Coffin ed., 2009), available at http://www.RIMS.org/ERMwhitepaper [hereinafter RIMS PAPER]. For a summary of the role of risk management in the 2008 recession, see Michelle M. Harner, *Ignoring the Writing on the Wall: The Role of Enterprise Risk Management in the Economic Crisis*, 5 J. BUS. TECH. L. 45 (2010).

The recurring nature of the risk-management problem suggests that the approach to, or the implementation of, corporate risk-management practices is lacking in some respect.[4] Prior studies show that meaningful risk-management and as evidenced by the 2008 recession, even when they do, the results are underwhelming.[5]

This Article examines two possible barriers to effective risk management: individual biases and cultural norms.[6] At its core, any risk-management technique attempts to provide corporate decision makers with better and more accurate information to identify, assess, and mitigate events that threaten firm value (i.e., risk events).[7] A firm certainly can adopt strict procedures instructing managers on how and what types of information to evaluate, detailing the timing and participants in risk assessment meetings and requiring periodic reports to the board of directors and senior executives. Those procedures alone, however, will not necessarily change a firm's decision regarding any particular risk, deter corporate fraud, or help moderate market turmoil.[8] Individuals still make those decisions, and their possible biases and surrounding environment may be more influential than any risk assessment reports.[9]

This reality raises an important question: Can the law change the way individuals receive and filter information, or is the human component of risk

---

4 *See* Lori A. Brassell-Cicchinit, *The Shareholder Value of Crisis Handling,* RISK MGMT., May 2003 (explaining 1997 study showing value in risk planning and discussing case studies); Steven M. Cassidy et al., *The Market Value of the Corporate Risk Management Function,* 57 J. RISK & INS. 664, 668 (1990) (explaining that markets react positively to risk management); Patrick J. Stroh, *Enterprise risk management at UnitedHealth Group,* 87 STRATEGIC FIN. 26 (2005); MARCEL BOYER ET AL., THE VALUE OF RISK MANAGEMENT: A FRONTIER ANALYSIS 1 (Mar. 15, 2005) (unpublished manuscript), available at http://papers.ssrn.com/sol3/papers.cfm?abstract_id=687127 (describing a study showing that the "role of financial risk management is to create flexibility to alleviate this inefficiency problem . . . [and] it does contribute indirectly to the value of the firm"); Brian W. Nocco & Rene M. Stulz, *Enterprise Risk Management: Theory and Practice* (July 2006) (unpublished manuscript), available at http://papers.ssrn.com/sol3/papers.cfm?abstract_id=921402 (discussing value of risk management in context of competitive advantage and shareholder wealth).

5 *See infra* Parts II.A, II.C.

6 *See* discussion *infra* Part V.A (explaining that many of the biases discussed in the individual context apply in the group or collective board context as well); *see also* Stephen M. Bainbridge, *Why a Board? Group Decisionmaking in Corporate Governance,* 55 VAND. L. REV. 1 (2002); Marleen A. O'Connor, *The Enron Board: The Perils of Groupthink,*71 U. CIN. L. REV. 1233 (2003); James D. Cox & Harry L. Munsinger, *Bias in the Boardroom: Psychological Foundations and Legal Implications of Corporate Cohesion,* 48 LAW & CONTEMP. PROBS. 83, 83–84, 99–108 (1985) (describing bases of ingroup bias among directors).

7 *See infra* Parts II.A, III.A.

8 *See* Jeffrey M. Lipshaw, *The Venn Diagram of Business Lawyering Judgments: Toward a Theory of Practical Metadisciplinarity,* 41 SETON HALL L. REV. (forthcoming 2011) (manuscript at 12), available at http://papers.ssrn.com/sol3/papers.cfm?abstract_id=1551243 (using boardroom conference example to illustrate uncertainty in decision-making process and noting that, despite extensive advice provided at meeting, "when the time came to make the decision, the CEO had no authority upon which to fall back except her own").

9 *See infra* Part V.A.

management an inevitable limitation on its utility? The question is difficult to answer definitively, but this Article suggests that policymakers will encourage, and corporate boards will design and implement, more effective risk-management practices if they acknowledge and attempt to address this limitation.

To assist in this endeavor, this Article analyzes three of the cognitive biases that may impede risk assessment—confirmation bias, overconfidence/optimism bias, and framing—and considers how other legal disciplines have addressed bias in decision making.[10] This Article uses Citigroup Inc. as a case study to highlight potential behavioral and cultural barriers to effective risk management.[11] This Article suggests that training and outside assessment may help corporate decision makers avoid some biases in risk assessment and response decisions.

This Article also considers corporate culture and whether the environment at entrepreneurial or risk-aggressive firms poses a barrier to effective risk-management practices.[12] Most commentators acknowledge that some risk taking is healthy and often necessary to enhancing firm performance.[13] The goal of risk management should not be the elimination of all risk, but rather the pursuit of prudent and informed risk profiling and decision making. The challenge then is to convince firms that value and reward successful high-risk endeavors that risk management can enhance their decisions without changing their profit-oriented objectives.

This Article evaluates these complex issues in the context of enterprise risk management ("ERM").[14] As explained below, ERM is a holistic approach to risk management that goes beyond financial risk modeling and seeks to integrate a

---

[10] For a general discussion of cognitive biases and decision making, see Amos Tversky & Daniel Kahneman, *Judgment Under Uncertainty: Heuristics and Biases,* 185 SCIENCE 1124 (1974). *See also infra* Part IV.A.

[11] *See infra* Parts IV, V.

[12] For a general discussion of corporate culture, see Alice Belcher, *Imagining How a Company Thinks: What is Corporate Culture?,* 11 DEAKIN L. REV. 1, 18 (2006). *See also infra* Part IV.B.

[13] *See, e.g.,* ASWATH DAMODARAN, STRATEGIC RISK TAKING: A FRAMEWORK FOR RISK MANAGEMENT 7 (2007) ("A business that decides to protect itself against all risk is unlikely to generate much upside for its owners; however, a business that exposes itself to the wrong types of risk may be even worse off, because it is more likely to be damaged than helped by the risk exposure."); Diane Brady, *Sarbanes-Oxley = a Downturn in Corporate Risk-Taking,* BUSINESSWEEK (Sept. 26, 2007), http://www.businessweek.com/careers/managementiq/archives/2007/09/sarbanes-oxley.html (discussing the need for risk taking to spur economic growth and citing two academic papers suggesting that the Sarbanes Oxley Act of 2002 reduced risk-taking); Donald L. Kohn, Fed. Reserve Bank, *Address at the Official Celebration of the 10th Anniversary of the Banque Centrale du Luxembourg* (Nov. 12, 2008) (transcript available at http://www.federalreserve.gov/newsevents/speech/kohn20081112a.htm) ("A central challenge will be to structure financial oversight to both deter unwanted and excessive risk-taking and permit the innovation that can ultimately boost economic growth.").

[14] *See infra* Part II.

firm's risk assessment and response practices.[15] It also is a form of risk management that holds value for firms outside of the financial and insurance industries. Consequently, although this Article uses financial institution examples from the 2008 recession, the analysis and suggested prescriptions apply across industries and have far broader implications than simply addressing the fallout from the recession.[16]

Part II of this Article provides an overview of the ERM movement, discussing its origins, key components, and perceived role in the 2008 recession. Part III summarizes the various regulatory and judicial responses to the 2008 recession that involve some aspect of risk management. Part IV presents a case study of Citigroup Inc. and analyzes its decision-making process during the 2008 recession in light of events and developments in its industry and the economy more generally at the time. Part V then uses the Citigroup case study to evaluate the impact of cognitive biases and corporate culture on risk-management decisions. This analysis leads to a discussion of potential regulatory and market responses to strengthen the ERM movement. This Article concludes by encouraging policymakers and corporate boards to consider cognitive biases and the importance of corporate culture as part of their risk-management dialogue.

II. Overview of ERM

Risk often is defined simply as "the possibility of loss or injury."[17] In the business context, the concept of risk includes not only the probability of loss but also the consequences of that loss or risk event.[18] Managing quantifiable risk is a much easier task than considering unquantifiable risk. Nevertheless, as suggested by the 2008 recession, prudent risk management needs to consider both.[19]

---

15 *See id.; see also* COMM. OF SPONSORING ORGS. OF THE TREADWAY COMM'N, ENTERPRISE RISK MANAGEMENT—INTEGRATED FRAMEWORK: EXECUTIVE SUMMARY (2004), available at http://www.coso.org/Publications/ERM/COSO_ERM_ExecutiveSummary.pdf [hereinafter COSO Report] (describing ERM framework).

16 *See, e.g.*, Steven J. Dreyer & Amra Balic, *Progress Report: Integrating Enterprise Risk Management Analysis into Corporate Credit Ratings*, STANDARD & POOR'S, July 22, 2009, at 2, available at http://www2.standardandpoors.com/spf/pdf/events/IntegratingERM72209.pdf ("In May 2008, Standard & Poor's Ratings Services announced its intention to include enterprise risk management ("ERM") assessments in ratings of nonfinancial companies."); Kirkpatrick, *supra* note 3, at 17–18 (discussing broad utility of ERM and emphasizing its application in the context of non-financial firms).

17 MERRIAM WEBSTER'S DICTIONARY 1018 (9th ed. 1985).

18 Damodaran, *supra* note 13, at 5–6.

19 "Everything that can be counted does not necessarily count; everything that counts cannot necessarily be counted." Albert Einstein. *See also* NASSIM NICHOLAS TALEB, THE BLACK SWAN: THE IMPACT OF THE HIGHLY IMPROBABLE (2007) (discussing challenges of identifying and addressing surprise risk events); CROWE HORWATH, AVOIDING THE BLACK SWAN: BARRIERS TO IMPROVING RISK MANAGEMENT (2009), available

Yet taking this type of broad, all-encompassing approach to managing business risk is a relatively new development.[20] Traditionally, financial institutions and insurance companies used risk-management techniques to hedge financial risk exposures.[21] Risk managers at those companies would analyze the specific type of risk assigned to them (e.g., credit, market, foreign currency, etc.) and design or purchase financial products to mitigate that risk.[22] Risk managers rarely discussed or assessed the company's overall risk profile; rather, risk management was confined to separate and individual silos.[23] Any meaningful consideration of risk management was even rarer outside of the financial and insurance industries. ERM seeks to address these limitations. This Part provides an overview of the ERM theory, its application in practice, and its perceived role in the 2008 recession.

A. Development of ERM

Although the Barings Bank and Long-Term Capital Management meltdowns highlighted risk-management flaws, it was the Enron, WorldCom, and other corporate scandals of the early 2000s that sparked a call for more comprehensive risk management.[24] For example, in describing the internal controls adopted by Enron to manage risks associated with related-party transactions, the report of the Enron Special Investigation Committee observed that the "controls as designed

---

at http://www.cfo.com/whitepapers/index.cfm/download/14467404 (describing a study showing challenges with risk management highlighted by the 2008 recession, including surprise risk events).

20 As discussed below, COSO introduced its first proposal for a comprehensive risk management or ERM framework in 2004. *See* COSO Report, supra note 15; *see also infra* Part II.A.

21 *See, e.g.,* Damodaran, *supra* note 13, at 3–5 (describing origins of risk management); DOUGLAS W. HUBBARD, THE FAILURE OF RISK MANAGEMENT: WHY IT'S BROKEN AND HOW TO FIX IT 21–35 (2009) (same); THOMAS L. BARTON ET AL., MAKING ENTERPRISE RISK MANAGEMENT PAY OFF 11 (2002) (discussing silo approach to risk management); Betty Simkins & Steven A. Ramirez, *Enterprise-Wide Risk Management and Corporate Governance,* 39 LOY. U. CHI. L.J. 571, 581 (2008) (same); *see also* CFO RESEARCH SERVS. & IBM CORP., THINKING THROUGH UNCERTAINTY: CFOS SCRUTINIZE NON-FINANCIAL RISK 4 (2007), available at https://www-935.ibm.com/services/us/gbs/bus/pdf/ibm-risk-mgmt-final-032807.pdf (exploring proposition that "[c]ompanies seek a more expansive view of the risks that place their business performance in jeopardy"). For an explanation of the financial risk modeling technique commonly used by firms, called "Value at Risk" or VaR, and viewed as flawed in the context of the 2008 recession, see Nocera, *supra* note 3.

22 *See, e.g.,* GABRIELE SABATO, FINANCIAL CRISIS: WHERE DID RISK MANAGEMENT FAIL?, at 3–4, available at http://www.fma.org/NY/Papers/Financial_crisis_RM_failure_final.pdf.

23 *See supra* note 21.

24 *See generally* Robert Prentice, *Enron: A Brief Behavioral Autopsy,* 40 AM. BUS. L.J. 417 (2008) (discussing the business practices leading to the Enron scandal and the Congressional actions that followed); Robert Rosen, *Risk Management and Corporate Governance: The Case of Enron,* 35 CONN. L. REV. 1157 (2003) (discussing the corporate governance problems of Enron as a redesigned corporation and its risk-management practices); J. Gregory Sidak, *The Failure of Good Intentions: The WorldCom Fraud and the Collapse of American Telecommunications After Deregulation,* 20 YALE J. ON REG. 207 (2003) (discussing Worldcom's fraud and bankruptcy and the implications on the telecommunications industry); *see also supra* note 1.

were not rigorous enough, and their implementation and oversight was inadequate at both the Management and Board levels."[25] The report concluded that Enron's board failed "to demand more information, and . . . to probe and understand the information that did come to it."[26] The response to Enron and similar governance failures was swift and emerged in at least two separate forms: new risk-related disclosure regulations and redefined best practices.[27]

Risk-related regulations were included in the Sarbanes-Oxley Act of 2002, the listing standards for the New York Stock Exchange ("NYSE"), and the U.S. Department of Justice Sentencing Guidelines. The most extensive of these regulations is section 404 of the Sarbanes-Oxley Act, which requires management to explain and assess the company's internal control structure and procedures for financial reporting.[28] Section 406 of the Act also requires reporting companies to adopt a code of ethics for its senior officers or explain why it does not have a code.[29] The NYSE listing standards address both internal controls and codes of ethics and specifically identifies risk assessment as an audit committee responsibility.[30] Moreover, the Sentencing Guidelines offer reduced penalties for companies that demonstrate effective compliance programs that, among other things, incorporate ongoing risk assessment practices.[31]

To assist companies in meeting these various requirements, the Committee of Sponsoring Organisations of the Treadway Commission ("COSO") developed

---

25 WILLIAM C. POWERS JR. ET AL., REPORT OF INVESTIGATION BY THE SPECIAL INVESTIGATION COMMITTEE OF THE BOARD OF DIRECTORS OF ENRON CORP. 10 (2002), available at http://news.findlaw.com/hdocs/docs/enron/sicreport/index.html.

26 *Id.* at 23. The United States Permanent Subcommittee on Investigations reached similar conclusions, faulting Enron's board for approving "new business ventures and complex transactions" with insufficient information and oversight. *See* Rosen, *supra* note 24, at 1170.

27 *See, e.g.*, Troy A. Paredes, *Foreword: After the Sarbanes-Oxley Act: The Future of the Mandatory Disclosure System*, 81 WASH. U. L. Q. 229 (2003) (explaining the events leading up to the corporate scandals of the early 2000s and the regulatory and legislative responses).

28 *See* 15 U.S.C. § 7262 (2006); *William J. Carney, The Costs of Being Public After Sarbanes-Oxley: The Irony of "Going Private,"* 55 EMORY L.J. 141, 142 (2006) (explaining the impact of the Act, including Section 404 on corporations); *see also* Larry E. Ribstein, Bubble Laws, 40 HOUS. L. REV. 77 (2003) (same).

29 *See* 15 U.S.C. § 7264 (2006); Elizabeth F. Brown, *No Good Deed Goes Unpunished: Is There a Need for a Safe Harbor for Aspirational Corporate Codes of Conduct?*, 26 YALE L. & POL'Y REV. 367, 380–81 (2008) (exploring the requirements of Section 406); *see also* Lawrence E. Mitchell, *The Sarbanes-Oxley Act and the Reinvention of Corporate Governance?*, 48 VILL. L. REV. 1189, 1202–03 (2003) (discussing various requirements of the Act, including the code of ethics).

30 *See* NYSE, Inc., Listed Company Manual; Robert B. Thompson, *Collaborative Corporate Governance: Listing Standards, State Law and Federal Regulation*, 38 WAKE FOREST L. REV. 961 (2003) (explaining and analyzing changes to listing standards).

31 *See generally* David Hess, *A Business Ethics Perspective on Sarbanes Oxley & the Organizational Sentencing Guidelines*, 105 MICH. L. REV. 1781 (2007) (explaining and analyzing changes to sentencing guidelines); David Hess et al., *The 2004 Amendments to the Federal Sentencing Guidelines and Their Implicit Call for a Symbiotic Integration of Business Ethics*, 11 FORDHAM J. CORP. & FIN. L. 725 (2006).

a more comprehensive framework for risk-management practices referred to as ERM.[32] COSO defines ERM as

> [A] process, effected by an entity's board of directors, management and other personnel, applied in strategy setting and across the enterprise, designed to identify potential events that may affect the entity, and manage risk to be within its risk appetite, to provide reasonable assurance regarding the achievement of entity objectives.[33] ERM is a holistic approach to risk management that considers strategic and operational risks in addition to financial risks and focuses on identifying, assessing, and responding to risk events.[34]

ERM takes a top-down approach to risk management.[35] COSO and other commentators stress the importance of the board's and senior management's role

---

[32] A detailed explanation of the components of ERM is beyond the scope of this Article. Nevertheless, the COSO report contains those details and additional information. *See* COSO Report, *supra* note 15. In certain respects, ERM resembles prior organizational literature by emphasizing the need to restructure how firms conceive and utilize knowledge, information, and channels of communication. *See, e.g.*, JAMES CHAMPY & MICHAEL HAMMER, REENGINEERING THE CORPORATION: A MANIFESTO FOR BUSINESS REVOLUTION (2003); PETER M. SENGE, THE FIFTH DISCIPLINE—THE ART AND PRACTICE OF THE LEARNING ORGANIZATION (1990); PETER M. SENGE ET AL., THE DANCE OF CHANGE: THE CHALLENGES OF SUSTAINING MOMENTUM IN LEARNING ORGANIZATIONS (1999). ERM tries, however, to offer a simplified process for implementing the necessary changes and improving firm culture and governance. *See infra* Part II.B. Although initial reports suggest that ERM is effective, the longevity of the movement remains to be seen. *See supra* note 4; *infra* notes 52–55.

[33] COSO Report, *supra* note 15, at 2 (emphasis in original); see Kirkpatrick, *supra* note 3, at 7. Federal Reserve Bank Governor Susan Bies defined ERM as "a process that enables management to deal effectively with uncertainty and the associated risk and opportunity, enhancing the capacity to build stakeholder value." Susan Schmidt Bies, Fed. Reserve Bank, *Address at the National Credit Union Administration 2007 Risk Mitigation Summit on Enterprise Risk Management and Mortgage Lending* (Jan. 11, 2007) (transcript available at http://www.federalreserve.gov/newsevents/speech/Bies20070111a.htm).

[34] ERM generally targets all potential risk events, including financial risks, operational risks, business risks, litigation risks, and governance and human resource risks. *See, e.g.*, CAROLYN KAY ET AL., [CONFERENCE BD.], THE ROLE OF U.S. CORPORATE BOARDS IN ENTERPRISE RISK MANAGEMENT 11 (2006) [hereinafter Conference Board Report], available at http://www.ucop.edu/riskmgt/erm/documents/role_uscorpboards.pdf; see also Simkins & Ramirez, supra note 21, at 584 ("Under ERM, risks can be viewed as falling into two broad areas: core risks (risks which a firm should have as a competitive advantage to handle in their business model) and non-core risks (risks which could be hedged by the business or transferred through risk management techniques)."). "ERM consists of eight interrelated components, which are derived from the way management runs an enterprise and integrated with the management process: (1) internal environment, (2) objective setting, (3) event identification, (4) risk assessment, (5) risk response, (6) control activities, (7) information and communication, and (8) monitoring." Bies, *supra* note 33; COSO Report, *supra* note 15, at 3–4.

[35] *See* COMM. OF SPONSORING ORGS. OF THE TREADWAY COMM'N (COSO), STRENGTHENING ENTERPRISE RISK MANAGEMENT FOR STRATEGIC ADVANTAGE 4–5, 17 (2009), available at http://www.coso.org/documents/COSO_09_board_position_final102309PRINTandWEBFINAL.pdf [hereinafter COSO Paper]; RIMS PAPER, *supra* note 3, at 9.

in ERM.[36] Under this framework, the board and senior management are critical in creating a risk culture at the firm (i.e., a culture that values and rewards meaningful assessment and communication regarding risk events).[37] The board also plays an important role in setting the firm's risk appetite and designing and monitoring the firm's ERM program.[38] Many commentators view COSO's ERM framework as best practices in business risk-management practices.

Notably, despite the regulatory and industry endorsements for enhanced risk-management practices, corporate boards voiced resistance to the concept.[39] Many directors opined that extensive risk-management procedures were unnecessary or too cumbersome; others resisted any mandated approach to risk management.[40] Studies suggest that these sentiments linger in corporate boardrooms even after the 2008 recession.[41]

---

36 CONFERENCE BD., EMERGING GOVERNANCE PRACTICES IN ENTERPRISE RISK MANAGEMENT 8–9, 13–17 (2007); CONFERENCE BOARD REPORT, *supra* note 34, at 15–18; see also infra Part III.A.

37 John Michael Farrell & Angela Hoon, *What's Your Company's Risk Culture?*, NAT'L ASS'N CORP. DIRECTORS DIRECTORSHIP, April 15, 2009, available at http://www.mgt.ncsu.edu/erm/index.php/articles/entry/risk-culture-companies ("Risk culture is the system of values and behaviors present in an organization that shapes risk decisions of management and employees."); Peter Green & Jeremy Jennings-Mares, *IIF's Final Report on Market Best Practices for Financial Institutions and Financial Products*, BANKING & FIN. SERV. POL'Y REP., Sept. 2008, at 1 ("Cultivation of a consistent 'risk culture' throughout firms is the most important element in risk management."); COSO Paper, *supra* note 35, at 4–5.

38 *See, e.g.*, Barker, *supra* note 3 (explaining that boards should "(i) evaluat[e] the risks associated with corporate strategies, (ii) defin[e] the risk appetite of the company, [and] (iii) ensur[e] that appropriate resources are devoted to risk identification, avoidance, and mitigation"); Conference Board Report, *supra* note 34, at 6–7 (recommending six primary tasks for boards considering ERM); COSO Report, *supra* note 15, at 6–7 (defining role of board in ERM).

39 *See* RIMS PAPER, *supra* note 3, at 6; Richard Clune, *ERM: A Status Report*, INTERNAL AUDITOR, Feb. 1, 2005, available at http://www.mgt.ncsu.edu/erm/documents/ERMJFAPaper21306.pdf (describing a study finding that less than half of respondents adopted ERM-like procedures); Simkins & Ramirez, *supra* note 21, at 584–85 ("Evidence from studies and surveys indicates that, to date, only about 10% of major companies claim to have implemented many aspects of ERM, while almost all the others claim that they plan to do so in the future.").

40 *See, e.g.*, Conference Board Report, *supra* note 34, at 18 (noting that "many directors interviewed resisted what they termed 'an excessively formal' way to incorporate risk management into their deliberations").

41 *See, e.g.*, Horwath, *supra* note 19, at 4 (describing a study finding that one-third of respondents view risk management "as an unnecessary interference with business activities"); PRICEWATERHOUSECOOPERS, ENTERPRISE RISK MANAGEMENT BENCHMARKING SURVEY 6 (2008), available at http://www.pwc.com/fi_FI/fi/julkaisut/tiedostot/erm_benchmarking_survey_2008.pdf (explaining that approximately 31% of respondents did not have risk management practices in place); AUDIT COMMITTEES PUT RISK MANAGEMENT AT THE TOP OF THEIR AGENDAS, KPMG (June 16, 2008), http://www.kpmg.co.uk/news/detail.cfm?pr=3120 (describing a study finding that only 46% of respondents were very satisfied with risk practices); FINANCIAL CRISIS INTENSIFIES INTEREST IN RISK MANAGEMENT AMONG CFOS, TOWERS PERRIN (Sept. 2008), http://www.towersperrin.com/tp/showdctmdoc.jsp?country=global&url=Master_Brand_2/USA/News/Spotlights/2008/Sept/2008_09_30_spotlight_cfo_survey.htm (explaining that "72% of respondents expressed concern about their own company's risk management practices and ability to meet strategic plans").

B. Implementation of ERM

The design and implementation of ERM is firm-specific but generally involves the board of directors and senior management first mapping the firm's business strategies and risks. "Developing an understanding of the linkages between top risk exposures and key strategies and objectives can help both management . . . and risk oversight by identifying where risks are overlapping within an individual strategy and where certain risks may affect multiple strategies."[42] With this information, the board and management can evaluate the firm's portfolio of key risks—assessing the impact and likelihood of each risk event—and set the firm's risk appetite.[43]

The core elements of the ERM program then revolve around efficient and effective communication channels and active monitoring of the firm's risks against its risk portfolio and risk appetite.[44] Commentators stress the need for risk managers to have direct access to the board and multiple contact points to encourage the free-flow of information and reduce the likelihood that risk reports are presented but not heard.[45] Firms also are encouraged to develop key risk indicators that facilitate more effective monitoring of potential risk events.[46]

C. ERM and the 2008 Recession

The 2008 recession revealed significant weaknesses in existing risk-management practices.[47] Risk-management failures alone did not trigger the recession, but many commentators identify such failures as contributing to the severity of the economic losses. For example, Chairman Ben Bernanke stated: "Among other things, our analysis reaffirms that capital adequacy, effective liquidity planning, and strong risk management are essential for safe and sound banking; the . . . [recession] revealed serious deficiencies on the part of some

---

42 COSO PAPER, *supra* note 35, at 13.

43 *Id.* at 14–15.

44 *Id.*

45 *See supra* Part II.A and *infra* Part III.A.

46 COSO PAPER, *supra* note 35, at 17–18 ("Key risk indicators . . . are metrics used by some organizations to provide an early signal of increasing risk exposure in various areas of organization.").

47 Kirkpatrick, *supra* note 3, at 7 ("Despite the importance given to risk management by regulators and corporate governance principles, the financial turmoil has revealed severe shortcomings in practices both in internal management and in the role of the board in overseeing risk management systems at a number of banks."); *see also supra* note 3. For example, a study revealed that risk managers at UBS AG were aware of potential losses in the firm's subprime mortgage holdings in early 2007 but did not advise senior executives of these potential losses until July 2007. Kirkpatrick, *supra* note 3, at 11. Moreover, UBS's board did not learn of the firm's financial situation until August 2007. *Id.* at 11–12. UBS subsequently acknowledged that "[a]s a result of [risk management] weaknesses, the firm failed to adequately assess correlated risks and risk concentrations." UBS AG, ANNUAL REPORT ON FORM 20-F FOR 2009, at 120 (Mar. 11, 2009), available at http://www.ubs.com/1/e/investors/sec_filings.html.

financial institutions in one or more of the areas."[48] Similarly, the Chairman of Morgan Stanley, John Mack, testified before the Financial Crisis Inquiry Commission that "[i]n retrospect, many firms were too highly leveraged, took on too much risk and did not have sufficient resources to manage those risks effectively in a rapidly changing environment."[49]

Although it is difficult to pinpoint one key deficiency in existing risk-management practices, a lack of integration and communication appears to be one of the most significant problems.[50] The traditional segregated approach to risk management prevented many firms from understanding their true exposure if various identified risks converged and from communicating those risks efficiently to senior executives and directors.[51] Consequently, firms' responses to the changing financial landscape during 2007–2008 were slow and in many cases too late.

At least one study suggests that financial institutions with more integrated risk-management programs performed better during the 2008 recession.[52] The study posits that these firms communicated information throughout the organization more efficiently and were able to implement necessary changes more effectively.[53] A nimble response to a risk event can preserve significant value.[54] More studies and data are needed to evaluate fully the impact of ERM, but initial studies and anecdotal evidence suggest that ERM provides more timely information to boards and senior management and thus may better equip them to respond both proactively and reactively to risk events.[55]

---

48 Ben S. Bernanke, Chairman, Fed. Reserve, *Address at the Federal Reserve Bank of Chicago's Annual Conference on Bank Structure and Competition* (May 7, 2009) (transcript available at http://www.federalreserve.gov/newsevents/speech/bernanke20090507a.htm).

49 *Highlights: Quotes from U.S. Financial Crisis Commission Hearing*, REUTERS, Jan. 13, 2010, available at http://www.reuters.com/article/idUSTRE60C3AI20100113.

50 *See* Kirkpatrick, *supra* note 3, at 8–12.

51 *See* Harner, *supra* note 3, at 50–51 (describing silo approach to risk management and its role in the 2008 recession).

52 SENIOR SUPERVISORS GROUP, OBSERVATIONS ON RISK MANAGEMENT PRACTICES DURING THE RECENT MARKET TURBULENCE (2008), available at http://www.newyorkfed.org/newsevents/news/banking/2008/ssg_risk_mgt_doc_final.pdf. The study concluded that "[f]irms that avoided . . . [significant] problems demonstrated a comprehensive approach to viewing firm-wide exposures and risk, sharing quantitative and qualitative information more efficiently across the firm and engaging in more effective dialogue across the management team." *Id.; see also* Kirkpatrick, *supra* note 3, at 8 (summarizing findings of the Senior Supervisors Group Study).

53 *See* SENIOR SUPERVISORS GROUP, *supra* note 52.

54 *See, e.g.*, RIMS PAPER, *supra* note 3, at 3–4 (explaining the impact of risk management failures on firms during the 2008 recession and how to address those issues).

55 *See, e.g.*, KURT A. DESENDER, THE INFLUENCE OF BOARD COMPOSITION, AUDIT FEES AND OWNERSHIP CONCENTRATION ON ENTERPRISE RISK MANAGEMENT (Oct. 2007) (unpublished manuscript),

III. Risk-Management Reponses to the 2008 Recession

By most accounts, the 2008 recession was the most significant recession since the Great Depression of the 1930s.[56] The economic losses were steep and the recovery slow. The International Monetary Fund estimates that global financial institutions lost approximately $4.05 trillion in value, with $2.7 trillion of that relating to loans originating in the United States.[57] The U.S. Bureau of Labor Statistics estimates that the United States lost approximately 8.4 million jobs during the recession, with the U.S. unemployment rate hovering between nine to ten percent since 2009.[58]

Not surprisingly, policymakers and commentators are scrutinizing the causes of the 2008 recession and searching for ways to avoid, or at least mitigate, the next economic downturn.[59] Some of this discussion has focused on risk management and improving firms' risk- management practices.[60] This Part highlights the developments regarding risk management as a result of the 2008 recession. As discussed below, industry proponents are encouraging more attention to ERM, while regulatory responses focus on enhanced disclosure regarding risk management and governing risk through executive compensation schemes. Part V then considers how neither approach fully accounts for the behavioral and cultural barriers to effective risk management.

---

available at http://papers.ssrn.com/sol3/papers.cfm?abstract_id=1025982 (exploring value components of ERM); ROBERT E. HOYT & ANDRE P. LIEBENBERG, THE VALUE OF ENTERPRISE RISK MANAGEMENT 1 (July 29, 2009) (unpublished manuscript), available at http://papers.ssrn.com/sol3/papers.cfm?abstract_id=1440947 (describing a study finding "a positive relation between firm value and the use of ERM"); *see also supra* notes 39–41.

56 "The financial market crisis that erupted in August 2007 has developed into the largest financial shock since the Great Depression, inflicting heavy damage on markets and institutions at the core of the financial system." INT'L MONETARY FUND, WORLD ECONOMIC OUTLOOK: HOUSING AND THE BUSINESS CYCLE 4 (2008), available at http://imf.org/external/pubs/ft/weo/2008/01/pdf/text.pdf.

57 Mark Landler, *I.M.F. Puts Bank Losses from Global Financial Crisis at $4.1 Trillion,* N.Y. TIMES, Apr. 22, 2009, at A6, available at http://www.nytimes.com/2009/04/22/business/global/22fund.html.

58 News Release, Bureau of Labor Statistics, The Employment Situation—February 2010, at 1–2 (Mar. 5, 2010), available at http://www.bls.gov/news.release/pdf/empsit.pdf.

59 *See, e.g.,* Patrice Hill, *CEOs Trade Blame with Congress over Financial Crisis,* WASH. TIMES, Jan. 14, 2010, at A1, available at http://www.washingtontimes.com/news/2010/jan/14/ceos-trade-blame-with-congress-over-finance-crisis/ ("Wall Street clashed with Washington on Wednesday over the causes of the biggest financial crisis since the Great Depression, with political leaders and financial chieftains trying to cast the blame on each other."); Dawn Kopecki & Matthew Leising, *Derivatives Industry Gets Second Look from Congress,* BLOOMBERG (June 22, 2009, 11:45 AM), http://www.bloomberg.com/apps/news?pid=20601087&sid=aTZhIZJYCeS8 ("Congress will take a second shot at the derivatives industry after its decision nine years ago to forgo regulations led to a $592 trillion market that brought financial firms to their knees.").

60 *See, e.g.,* Mary Schapiro, Sec. & Exch. Comm'n, *Address at the Council of Institutional Investors* (Apr. 6, 2009), available at http://www.sec.gov/news/speech/2009/spch040609mls.htm. ("The Commission will be considering whether greater disclosure is needed about how a company—and the company's board in particular—manages risks, both generally and in the context of setting compensation.").

A. ERM as a Potential Solution

In a speech in January 2007, Federal Reserve Bank Governor Susan Bies stated, "A successful enterprise risk-management process can help an organization meet many of [its] challenges by providing a framework within which managers can explicitly consider how the organization's risk exposures are changing."[61] Governor Bies discussed the importance of ERM not only in the context of large financial institutions and subprime-lending practices but also as universal principles valuable to firms of all sizes in all industries.[62] As she explained,

> [W]hether someone is designing a new branch office, shipping tapes to a backup site for storage, developing the layout for a newspaper ad, or training new employees, they [should] consciously think about risk as one of the elements of that business activity. Increased risk awareness by staff throughout the enterprise is integral to managing risk successfully.[63]

Many commentators agree with Governor Bies' focus on firm-wide risk responsibility and the creation of a risk culture within firms as a response to the 2008 recession. In 2009, COSO issued a thought paper, titled *Strengthening Enterprise Risk Management for Strategic Advantage,* to assist boards in strengthening risk-management practices and complying with anticipated regulatory mandates on risk management, such as the SEC rule on proxy disclosure enhancement.[64] Much of the thought paper discusses the importance of the board's role in ERM and provides guidance for boards in fulfilling that role.[65] COSO explains that "[b]ecause management is accountable to the board of directors, the board's focus on effective risk oversight is critical to setting the tone and culture towards effective risk management through strategy setting, formulating high-level objectives, and approving broad-based resource allocations."[66]

Specifically, COSO identifies four areas of risk-related tasks for boards: (1) "[d]iscuss risk-management philosophy and risk appetite;" (2) "[u]nderstand enterprise risk-management practices;" (3) "[r]eview portfolio of risks in relation to risk appetite;" and (4) "[b]e apprised of the most significant risks and related

61 Bies, *supra* note 33. Governor Bies identified those challenges as including "emerging technologies and business processes, new financial instruments, the growing scale and scope of financial institutions, and changing regulatory frameworks." *Id.*

62 *Id.*

63 *Id.*

64 *See* COSO PAPER, *supra* note 35. For a discussion of the SEC rule on proxy disclosure enhancement, *see infra* Part II.B.1.

65 *See* COSO PAPER, *supra* note 35.

66 *Id.* at 4.

responses."[67] This type of board involvement provides more information to directors and can help them better understand the overall business enterprise. It also signals to management and others at the firm the importance of risk responsibility and the need to align the firm's risk appetite with its business strategies.

Other commentators suggest that ERM, as opposed to more traditional financial risk management, can facilitate a more complete risk assessment that captures at some level what generally is viewed as unquantifiable risk. Speaking to this point, the Risk and Insurance Management Society, Inc. ("RIMS") observed, "A number of actuaries, financial managers and consultants regularly advocate a primarily 'scientific' and quantifiable approach for enterprise risk management. Certain financial institutions seem to have replaced sound business judgment with this 'scientific' approach."[68] RIMS perceives ERM as a means of reintroducing sound business judgment to the risk-management process, allowing firms to identify and respond more effectively and efficiently to both quantifiable and unquantifiable risks.[69]

A report prepared for the Organisation for Economic Co-operation and Development reached similar conclusions regarding the 2008 recession and the value of ERM in that context.[70] The report urges more emphasis on the corporate governance or human component of risk management and suggests ERM as a technique for achieving that objective.[71] Among other things, the report stresses the need for better understanding of and communication regarding risks, noting that "[e]ven if risk-management systems in the technical sense are functioning, it will not impact the company unless the transmission of information is through effective channels, a clear corporate governance issue."[72]

---

67 *Id.* at 5.

68 RIMS PAPER, *supra* note 3, at 5. RIMS faults over-reliance on historic controls and risk metrics for some of the losses experienced during the 2008 recession. *Id.* at 6. It posits that "[t]here was a failure to embed enterprise risk management best practices from the top all the way down to the trading floor, with the mistaken assumption that there is only one way to view a particular risk." *Id.* at 7; *see also* Nocera, *supra* note 3, at 9 (discussing flaws in relying solely on VaR and noting that, in the context of the 2008 recession, "[i]nstead of scrutinizing VaR for signs of impending trouble, they took comfort in a number and doubled down, putting more money at risk in the expectation of bigger gains").

69 RIMS PAPER, *supra* note 3.

70 *See* Kirkpatrick, *supra* note 3, at 4.

71 *Id.* at 2 ("The risk management systems have failed in many cases due to corporate governance procedures rather than the inadequacy of computer models alone: information about exposures in a number of cases did not reach the board and even senior levels of management, while risk management was often activity rather than enterprise-based.").

72 *Id.* at 11.

In addition, Standard & Poor's has integrated ERM assessment into its ratings analysis.[73] For example, Standard & Poor's is interviewing its rated, nonfinancial issuers regarding their ERM practices.[74] The questions asked during these interviews concern: (1) the company's process for identifying top risks; (2) how often that process takes place; (3) how those risks are managed; (4) who is responsible for risk management; (5) the board's role in risk management; and (6) how the company has responded to unexpected information in its industry.[75] Standard & Poor's and ERM proponents generally view the ERM framework as an important tool for mitigating future economic downturns through better information flow and core cultural changes.[76]

B. Risk-Related Policy

Even before the extent of the 2008 recession was apparent, U.S. federal financial regulatory agencies issued Interagency Guidance on Nontraditional Mortgage Product Risks ("Interagency Guidance") that emphasized the importance of risk management with respect to nontraditional mortgage products, including subprime mortgages.[77] The Interagency Guidance, dated September 29, 2006, observed that "risk layering, combined with the broader marketing of nontraditional mortgage loans, exposes financial institutions to increased risk relative to traditional mortgage loans."[78] It urged financial institutions to adopt rigorous risk-management practices that closely monitor the volume and volatility of nontraditional mortgage loan originations and investments.[79] Among other guidelines, it suggested that financial institutions "[m]aintain capital at levels that

---

73 BIG CHANGES IN STANDARD & POOR'S RATING CRITERIA, STANDARD & POOR'S, http://www.standardandpoors.com/ratings/erm/en/us (last visited Oct. 1, 2010) ("Standard & Poor's Ratings Services has expanded its review of the financial service industry's enterprise risk management (ERM) practices.").

74 *See, e.g.*, Dreyer & Balic, *supra* note 16, at 2 ("Since the third quarter of last year, our analysts have begun to incorporate specific ERM discussions into their regular meetings with the companies we rate, focusing on risk-management culture and strategic-risk management as two universally applicable aspects of ERM."); AON GLOBAL RISK CONSULTING, ENTERPRISE RISK MANAGEMENT: S&P ENHANCEMENT WHITE PAPER 3 (2009), available at http://www.aon.com/about-aon/intellectual-capital/attachments/risk-services/enterprise_risk_management_enhancement_white_paper.pdf [hereinafter Aon Paper].

75 *See, e.g.*, Dreyer & Balic, *supra* note 16, at 2–3 (identifying seven key questions for company interviews and noting that Standard & Poor's "analysts have explored managements' views of the most consequential risks that their firms face, their likelihood of occurring, how these top risks are identified, monitored, and updated, and the influence of risk sensitivity on liability management and financing decisions"); Aon Paper, *supra* note 74, at 4.

76 *See, e.g.*, Dreyer & Balic, *supra* note 16, at 2 (explaining the purpose of ERM consideration); Aon Paper, *supra* note 74, at 4.

77 Memorandum from Scott M. Albinson to Chief Executive Officers, Interagency Guidance on Nontraditional Mortgage Product Risks (Oct. 10, 2006), available at http://www.ots.treas.gov/_files/25244.pdf.

78 *Id.* at 2.

79 *Id.* at 1–2, 4.

reflect portfolio characteristics and the effect of stressed economic conditions on collectability."[80]

Nevertheless, many financial institutions failed to implement the types of controls, monitoring, and communication procedures recommended by the Interagency Guidance. For example, despite the warning that nontraditional mortgage products may not perform well in a stressed environment, and that firms should consider collectability issues, many financial institutions did not account for a decline in the housing market in their financial risk modeling.[81] Likewise, communication between risk managers and senior management was delayed, incomplete, or both.

In response, policymakers introduced several risk-related initiatives, and the courts weighed in on the issue as well. As discussed below, many of the regulatory responses focus on increased disclosure regarding risk-management practices and regulating risk through restrictions on executive compensation schemes. This Part also discusses the Delaware Court of Chancery's decision in the Citigroup litigation, which posits a low threshold for boards' risk oversight responsibilities and, consequently, may underscore the need to explore disclosure, executive compensation, and other alternative means to help regulators and markets monitor firms' risk-management practices.

1. Proposed or Adopted Regulatory Responses

In May 2009, Senator Charles Schumer introduced the Shareholder Bill of Rights Act of 2009 in the Senate ("Shareholder Bill").[82] The stated purpose of the Shareholder Bill was "[t]o provide shareholders with enhanced authority over the nomination, election, and compensation of public company executives."[83] Section 5 of the Shareholder Bill provides that reporting companies shall "establish a risk committee, comprised entirely of independent directors, which shall be

---

[80] *Id.* at 6.

[81] *See, e.g.*, Eric Dash & Julie Creswell, *Citigroup Saw No Red Flags Even as It Made Bolder Bets*, N.Y. TIMES, Nov. 23, 2008, at A1, available at http://www.nytimes.com/2008/11/23/business/23citi.html?pagewanted=1 ("Citigroup's risk models never accounted for the possibility of a national housing downturn, this person said, and the prospect that millions of homeowners could default on their mortgages."); Nocera, *supra* note 3, at 10 ("The fact that [risk models] didn't measure the possibility of an extreme event was a blessing to the executives. It made black swans all the easier to ignore."); Eric S. Rosengren, Fed. Reserve Boston, Address at The Global Interdependence Center's Conference on Financial Interdependence in the World's Post-Crisis Capital Markets (Mar. 3, 2010) (transcript available at http://www.bos.frb.org/news/speeches/rosengren/2010/030310/index.htm) ("There is evidence that financial institutions understood the risks that would arise if house prices fell, but assigned too low a probability to this potential outcome. Thus, they were woefully unprepared to weather the consequences when prices did indeed fall.").

[82] Shareholder Bill of Rights Act of 2009, S. 1074, 111th Cong. (2009).

[83] *Id.* § 5.

responsible for the establishment and evaluation of the risk management practices of the issuer."[84]

In addition, in December 2009, the Securities and Exchange Commission ("SEC") addressed risk-management practices in its final rule on proxy disclosure enhancement.[85] The rule requires reporting companies to discuss their general risk-management practices and how their compensation schemes relate to risk profiles.[86] It also mandates a disclosure regarding the board's role in and oversight of risk management.[87] The SEC posits that "disclosure about the board's involvement in the oversight of the risk management process should provide important information to investors about how a company perceives the role of its board and the relationship between the board and senior management in managing the material risks facing the company."[88]

Also in December 2009, the U.S. House of Representatives approved the Wall Street Reform Act and Consumer Protection Act of 2009 ("Wall Street Act").[89] The Wall Street Act addresses risk management in the context of executive compensation.[90] Specifically, it grants regulators extensive authority to assess whether a firm's compensation scheme "is aligned with sound risk management" and "to prescribe joint regulations prohibiting any feature of any incentive-based arrangement that encourages such inappropriate risks."[91] Other regulations relate risk to executive compensation and seek to control risk through firms' compensation schemes.[92]

---

84 *Id.*

85 Final Rule: Proxy Disclosure Enhancements, 74 Fed. Reg. 68334–01 (Dec. 16, 2009) (to be codified at 17 C.F.R. pt. 249).

86 *Id.* at 68336–7.

87 *Id.* at 68344–45.

88 *Id.* at 68345.

89 Wall Street Reform and Consumer Protection Act, H.R. 4173, 111th Cong. (2009).

90 *Id.*

91 *Id.* § 2004.

92 For example, the TARP legislation and the Federal Reserve Bank's proposed guidance on incentive compensation practices also seek to ensure that compensation incentives do not encourage inappropriate risk taking. For a thoughtful discussion of those and other regulations governing risk through compensation practices, see KARL S. OKAMOTO & DOUGLAS O. EDWARDS, RISK-TAKING 13–21 (Mar. 1, 2010) (unpublished manuscript), available at http://papers.ssrn.com/sol3/papers.cfm?abstract_id=1562018&utm_source=twitterfeed&utm_medium=twitter. Although this Article does not focus on the relation between risk and compensation structures, that factor is an important consideration in designing and evaluating any risk management program, including ERM. Several commentators have addressed this relationship. *See, e.g.,* Lucian A. Bebchuk & Holger Spamann, *Regulating Bankers' Pay,* 98 GEO. L.J. 247 (2010); Douglas O. Edwards, *Comment, An Unfortunate "Tail": Reconsidering Risk Management Incentives After the Financial Crisis of 2007–2009*, 81 U. COLO. L. REV. 247 (2010); KARL S. OKAMOTO, *AFTER THE BAILOUT: REGULATING SYSTEMIC MORAL HAZARD,* 57 UCLA L. REV. 183 (2009); FREDERICK TUNG, PAY FOR BANKER PERFORMANCE:

2. The Judicial Response

As discussed above, several proposed regulatory responses to the 2008 recession focus on executive compensation.[93] The relation between risk and executive compensation is an important component of any risk-management program, including ERM.[94] Several commentators, however, have observed significant flaws in trying to reduce risk and achieve financial stability through compensation reform.[95] In fact, such an approach appears incomplete at best.[96] Nonetheless, public outrage over executive compensation during the 2008 recession and the perceived difficulty in enhancing board oversight duties under state law likely influenced the compensation-reform approach.

Consider the views of the Delaware Chancery Court in the In re Citigroup Inc. Shareholder Derivative Litigation.[97] The court granted the defendants' motion to dismiss with respect to the plaintiffs' allegations that "director defendants breached their duty of oversight either because the oversight mechanisms were not adequate or because the director defendants did not make a good faith effort to comply with the established oversight procedures."[98] The court discussed those allegations under the standard articulated in *In re Caremark*

STRUCTURING EXECUTIVE COMPENSATION FOR RISK REGULATION (Mar. 13, 2010) (unpublished manuscript), available at http://papers.ssrn.com/sol3/papers.cfm?abstract_id=1546229.

93 *See supra* Part III.B.1.

94 *See* Daniel K. Tarullo, Fed. Reserve, Address at the University of Maryland's Robert H. Smith School of Business Roundtable on Executive Compensation: Practices and Reforms (Nov. 2, 2009) (transcript available at http://www.federalreserve.gov/newsevents/speech/tarullo20091102a.htm) (explaining that "some firms gave loan officers incentives to write a lot of loans, or traders incentives to generate high levels of trading revenues, without sufficient regard for the risks associated with those activities," and that those incentives undermine "the very foundation of sound risk management"); Kirkpatrick, *supra* note 3, at 14 (discussing components of compensation that might encourage short-termism and risk taking and noting that "the system of bonuses in investment banking provides incentives for substantial risk taking while also allowing no flexibility for banks to reduce costs when they have to: at the upper end, the size of the bonus is unlimited while at the lower end it is limited to zero"); *see also* ALIGNING RISK MANAGEMENT AND EXECUTIVE COMPENSATION, ENTERPRISE RISK MGMT. INITIATIVE, Dec. 1, 2008, available at http://www.mgt.ncsu.edu/erm/index.php/articles/entry/aligning-executive-compensation ("A 2008 study conducted by The Wall Street Journal and ERI Economic Research Institute found that the median CEO salary of a Standard and Poor's 500 company increased 20.5 percent from the previous year while corporate revenues increased only 2.8 percent."); Okamoto & Edwards, *supra* note 92, at 21–25 (discussing additional empirical studies analyzing links between executive compensation and firm performance).

95 *See* Okamoto & Edwards, *supra* note 92, at 26–44 (criticizing prevailing views that "excessive" risk can be controlled through compensation-related reform on both functional and completeness grounds and discussing the difficulty with defining excessive risk and when regulating that risk might be socially desirable).

96 *See* Kirkpatrick, *supra* note 3, at 14–15 (explaining that alignment between compensation practices and long-term interests of firm does not necessarily improve risk assessment and noting that "one study . . . reports that financial institutions that collapsed had a CEO with high stock holdings so that they should normally have been risk averse, whereas the ones that survived had strong incentives to take risks").

97 964 A.2d 106 (Del. Ch. 2009).

98 *Id.* at 127.

International Inc. Derivative Litigation,[99] *Guttman v. Huang,*[100] and *Stone v. Ritter.*[101] The court explained that "[t]he presumption of the business judgment rule, the protection of an exculpatory § 102(b)(7) provision, and the difficulty of proving a Caremark claim together function to place an extremely high burden on a plaintiff to state a claim for personal director liability for a failure to see the extent of a company's business risk."[102]

The Delaware Chancery Court's reluctance to impose liability on Citigroup's directors for allegedly failed or inadequate risk-management practices is consistent with the general notion that business decisions should be made in the boardroom and not the courtroom.[103] It also reflects the complexity of assessing business risk and the delicate balance between risk and return. As Chancellor Chandler stated, "Business decision-makers must operate in the real world, with imperfect information, limited resources, and an uncertain future. To impose liability on directors for making a 'wrong' business decision would cripple their ability to earn returns for investors by taking business risks."[104]

Although no liability resulted in the Citigroup case, the conduct of Citigroup and the individuals responsible for its risk-management activities prior to and during the 2008 recession make for a compelling case study. The information available to Citigroup's executives and how they used that information provides insight into corporate risk assessment and highlights cultural norms that may impede meaningful ERM.

IV. A Case Study: Citigroup Inc.

Citigroup Inc. is a storied financial services firm. With roots dating to 1812, Citigroup "has approximately 200 million customer accounts and does business

---

[99] 698 A.2d 959 (Del. Ch. 1996).

[100] 823 A.2d 492 (Del. Ch. 2003).

[101] 911 A.2d 362 (Del. 2006). 'Under this precedent, plaintiffs generally must show "a sustained or systematic failure of the board to exercise oversight—such as an utter failure to attempt to assure a reasonable information and reporting system exists." *In re* Caremark, 698 A.2d at 971. For an excellent discussion of these three cases and their relation to failure to monitor claims, see Stephen M. Bainbridge, *Caremark and Enterprise Risk Management,* 34 J. CORP. L. 967 (2009).

[102] *In re Citigroup,* 964 A.2d at 125.

[103] *See, e.g.,* Capital Bancshares, Inc. v. Fed. Deposit Ins. Corp., 957 F.2d 203, 207 (5th Cir. 1992) ("Under this familiar rule of American jurisprudence, the courts refrain from second guessing business decisions made by corporate directors in the absence of a showing of fraud, unfairness or overreaching."); Dodge v. Ford Motor Co., 170 N.W. 668, 684 (1919) ("The judges are not business experts."); *see also* Stephen M. Bainbridge, *The Business Judgment Rule as Abstention Doctrine,* 57 VAND. L. REV. 83, 95–100 (2004) (discussing development of business judgment rule).

[104] *In re Citigroup,* 964 A.2d at 126.

in more than 140 countries."[105] It provides a variety of financial products and services to its customers, including "consumer banking, credit cards, corporate and investment banking, securities brokerage and wealth management."[106] Citigroup carries approximately $1.857 trillion of assets and approximately $1.702 trillion of liabilities on its balance sheet.[107]

The 2008 recession hit Citigroup hard, notwithstanding, or perhaps because of, its massive scope and size. It experienced losses of approximately $10 billion by the start of the fourth quarter of 2007,[108] and the losses continued into 2009.[109] Citigroup's stock price dropped precipitously as well, falling to below $4 per share in November 2008 and below $1 per share in March 2009.[110]

As a result, Citigroup accepted assistance from the U.S. government under the Troubled Asset Relief Program ("TARP"). Specifically, Citigroup received over $45 billion in capital infusions from the government, and the government agreed to guarantee approximately $306 billion in loans and securities.[111] The government converted $25 billion of its investment into Citigroup common stock.[112] Citigroup repaid the remaining $20 billion in December 2009.[113]

Prior to its participation in TARP, Citigroup, its CEO (Charles Prince), its risk managers, and its board of directors made interesting decisions. Despite various market and industry indications that the subprime-mortgage market was deteriorating quickly in early 2007, Citigroup stayed firmly committed to its large subprime mortgage and collateralized-debt obligation ("CDO") portfolios and

---

105 Citigroup Inc., Annual Report (Form 10-K), at 4 (Feb. 26, 2010), available at http://www.citigroup.com/citi/corporategovernance/ar.htm.

106 *Id.* at 7.

107 *Id.* at 39.

108 *See* Bradley Keoun, *Citigroup Posts Record Loss on $18 Billion Writedown,* BLOOMBERG (Jan. 15, 2008, 4:25 PM) http://www.bloomberg.com/apps/news?pid=newsarchive&sid=apcQNeUgOLwA.

109 *See* Eric Dash, *After Year of Heavy Losses, Citigroup Finds a Profit,* N.Y. TIMES, Apr. 18, 2009, at A1, available at http://www.nytimes.com/2009/04/18/business/18bank.html.

110 Dash & Creswell, *supra* note 81 ("Citigroup's stock has plummeted to its lowest price in more than a decade, closing Friday [November 2008] at $3.77."); Laurie Kulikowski, *Citigroup Shares in Rally Mode,* THESTREET.COM (Mar. 9, 2010, 3:49 PM), http://www.thestreet.com/story/10698901/1/citigroup-shares-in-rally-mode.html.

111 *See, e.g.,* David Enrich et al., *U.S. Agrees to Rescue Struggling Citigroup,* WALL ST. J., Nov. 24, 2008, at A1, available at http://online.wsj.com/article/SB122747680752551447.html?mod=djemalertNEWS (explaining $45 capital infusion and structure of U.S. loan guaranty).

112 *See, e.g.,* Eric Dash, *U.S. Agrees to Raise Its Stake in Citigroup,* N.Y. TIMES, Feb. 27, 2009, at A1, available at http://www.nytimes.com/2009/02/28/business/28deal.html.

113 *See, e.g.,* Matthias Rieker, *Citigroup, Wells Repay TARP Funds—Banks' Ability to Raise Capital is Sign of Health, Though Concerns About Financial Industry Linger,* WALL ST. J., Dec. 24, 2009, at C3, available at http://online.wsj.com/article/SB10001424052748704254604574614082322331.

related investment strategies.[114] In fact, in July 2007, Mr. Prince brushed aside these warnings and stated, "as long as the music is playing, you've got to get up and dance. We're still dancing."[115]

Mr. Prince's statement is not the only evidence that Citigroup as an institution failed to appreciate or ignored the significance of the subprime-mortgage crisis. Following the Bear Stearns collapse in the summer of 2007, Citigroup assured the SEC that it anticipated no subprime-mortgage losses.[116] One report suggests that Citigroup indicated that "the probability of those mortgages defaulting was so tiny that they excluded them from their risk analysis."[117] That approach proved devastating in October 2007 when Citigroup announced that "third-quarter profit would fall 60% from the prior year after huge write-downs for unsold debt it issued to finance corporate takeovers and for big losses on the value of subprime mortgage-backed securities."[118]

Standing alone, Citigroup's position would not appear unreasonable. When placed in context with the other events of late 2006 and early 2007, however, the position becomes more troubling. Consider the following sampling of information known by or available to Citigroup executives:[119]

- February 8, 2007: HSBC Holdings plc and New Century Financial Corp. announce concerns regarding performance of their subprime-mortgage portfolios and perceived risks are reflected in ABX's credit-default swap index.[120]

---

114 *See, e.g.,* Dash & Creswell, *supra* note 81 (explaining events leading up to Citigroup's announcement of significant losses in October 2007).

115 Michiyo Nakamoto & David Wighton, *Citigroup Chief Stays Bullish on Buy-Outs,* FINANCIAL TIMES, July 9, 2007, http://www.ft.com/cms/s/0/80e2987a-2e50-11dc-821c-0000779fd2ac.html.

116 *See* Dash & Creswell, *supra* note 81.

117 *Id.*

118 Greg Morcroft, *Big Write-Downs to Slash Citi's Quarterly Net 60%,* WALL ST. J., Oct. 1, 2007, http://www.marketwatch.com/story/citigroup-says-quarterly-profit-to-drop-60-but-shares-gain.

119 In addition to the sources noted below, information regarding this sample and other events relating to the 2008 recession during this and additional periods is provided in several excellent sources. *See, e.g.,* JOINT ECON. COMM., SUBPRIME MORTGAGE MARKET CRISIS TIMELINE (July 2008), available at http://jec.senate.gov/public/?a=Files.Serve&File_id=4cdd7384-dbf6-40e6-adbc-789f69131903 [hereinafter Economic Committee Timeline]; Edward Harrison, Banking Crisis Timeline, Credit Writedowns, available at http://www.creditwritedowns.com/credit-crisis-timeline/banking-crisis-timeline (last visited Mar. 23, 2010); Timeline: Banking Crisis, CNN (Oct. 16, 2008, 11:33 AM), http://edition.cnn.com/2008/BUSINESS/09/30/us.bailout.timeline/index.html.

120 Jody Shenn & Shannon D. Harrington, *Subprime Mortgage Bond Risks Surge, Index Suggests,* BLOOMBERG (Feb. 8, 2007, 5:07 PM), http://www.bloomberg.com/apps/news?pid=20601103&sid=a3ztUp9Z6_UE&refer=us.

- February 20, 2007: Federal Reserve Board Governor Susan Bies observes that " '[o]ne segment of [the mortgage market] . . . is starting to behave in a very problematic way and that is the subprime adjustable rate mortgages.' "[121]
- February 21, 2007: NovaStar Financial Inc. loses one-third of its stock value due to subprime-mortgage issues.[122]
- March 4, 2007: HSBC Holdings plc forced to take a $11 billion write-off to cover subprime-mortgage losses.[123]
- March 12, 2007: Reports predict a significant surge in home foreclosures and that "[t]he deepest housing decline in 16 years is about to get worse."[124]
- March 2007: Fremont General and New Century Financial stop making loans, and "People's Choice files for bankruptcy."[125]
- April 6, 2007: "American Home Mortgage writes down the value of risky mortgages rated one step above subprime."[126]
- April 2007: New Century Financial files for bankruptcy, and GMAC LLC and General Electric Co. announce massive reductions in workforce relating to subprime-mortgage businesses.[127]
- May 3, 2007: UBS announces the closing of its hedge fund, Dillon Read Capital Management, due to U.S. subprime-mortgage losses.[128]

---

[121] *Bad Mortgage Debt Not Widespread Problem, Fed Official Says,* USATODAY.COM (Feb. 20, 2007, 3:33 PM), http://www.usatoday.com/money/economy/housing/2007-02-20-mortgage-debts-problems_x.htm.

[122] Jody Shenn & Elizabeth Hester, *NovaStar Sheds One-Third of Value After Posting Loss,* BLOOMBERG (Feb. 21, 2007, 4:30 PM), http://www.bloomberg.com/apps/news?pid=conewsstory&refer=conews&tkr=NFI:US&sid=aKFh3Eockz2k.

[123] John Waples & Grant Ringshaw, *US Triggers $11bn HSBC Fall-Out,* SUNDAY TIMES, Mar. 4, 2007, available at http://business.timesonline.co.uk/tol/business/industry_sectors/banking_and_ finance/article1465662.ece.

[124] Bob Ivry, *Foreclosures May Hit 1.5 Million in U.S. Housing Bust,* BLOOMBERG (Mar. 12, 2007, 4:37 PM), http://www.bloomberg.com/apps/news?pid=20601087&sid=ahwzaBwuNaI1&refer=home.

[125] Economic Committee Timeline, *supra* note 119, at 24.

[126] *Id.*

[127] Rachel Layne & Greg Bensinger, *GMAC, GE Will Cut 1,400 Job Cuts on Subprime Decline,* BLOOMBERG (Apr. 19, 2007, 7:56 PM), http://www.bloomberg.com/apps/news?pid=20601103&sid=ammC8WlswFTQ&refer=news; Top Lender in Chapter 11 Move, BBC News (Apr. 2, 2007, 4:14 PM), http://news.bbc.co.uk/2/hi/business/6519051.stm.

[128] *UBS to Close Its Hedge Fund Arm,* BBC NEWS (May 3, 2007, 11:07 AM), http://news.bbc.co.uk/2/hi/business/6619033.stm.

- May 30, 2007: Report suggests manipulation in subprime-mortgage market and notes that "[s]ince the beginning of 2006, more than 50 U.S. mortgage companies have put themselves up for sale, closed or declared bankruptcy."[129]
- June 12, 2007: Bear Stearns suspends redemptions at its hedge funds, which posted an 18.97 percent loss in April 2007, and "RealtyTrac announces U.S. foreclosure filings surged 90 percent in May from May 2006."[130]
- July 2007: Standard & Poor's, Moody's, and Fitch "downgrade bonds backed by subprime mortgages," and Bear Stearns announces that its hedge funds are essentially worthless.[131]
- July 18–19, 2007: Federal Reserve Bank Chairman Ben Bernanke acknowledges that "there will be 'significant losses' due to subprime mortgages" and that "the problems 'likely will get worse before they get better.' "[132]

Admittedly, hindsight reveals information not always visible in the moment, but Citigroup faced fairly stark evidence in early to mid-2007.[133] Citigroup's inaction is perhaps even more striking given that it held approximately $55 billion in U.S. subprime-mortgage assets at the time.[134] In addition, "Citigroup was the biggest CDO underwriter, responsible for $46.9 billion of the securities sold in the first

---

129 Seth Lubove & Daniel Taub, *Subprime Fiasco Exposes Manipulation by Mortgage Brokerages,* BLOOMBERG (May 30, 2007, 12:01 AM), http://www.bloomberg.com/apps/news?pid=20601109&refer=home&sid=a8VFwgtdQ9FM. In addition, in April and June 2007, Standard & Poor's issued warnings about the acceleration in subprime mortgage payment defaults delinquencies. *See* Insurance and Government Sponsored Enterprises: Hearing Before the H. Subcomm. on Capital Markets, 109th Cong. 22 (2006) (testimony of Vickie A. Tillman, Executive Vice President, Standard & Poor's Credit Market Services).

130 Matthew Goldstein, *Bear Stearns' Subprime Bath,* BUSINESSWEEK, June 12, 2007, available at http://www.businessweek.com/bwdaily/dnflash/content/jun2007/db20070612_748264.htm; Economic Committee Timeline, *supra* note 119, at 23.

131 Economic Committee Timeline, *supra* note 119, at 22–23.

132 *Id.* at 22. Chairman Bernanke did observe that the subprime mortgage problems "have not spilled over into the greater system" and opined that the problems were " 'bumps' in 'market innovations.' " *Id.*

133 *See* Donald C. Langevoort, *Behavioral Theories of Judgment and Decision Making in Legal Scholarship: A Literature Review,* 51 VAND. L. REV. 1499, 1504 (1998) (explaining hindsight bias as "people over estimat[ing] the extent to which they could have predicted some future event (i.e., its foreseeability) once they learn what actually happened"); *see also* Joy v. North, 692 F.2d 880, 886 (2d Cir. 1982) ("[A]fter-the-fact litigation is a most imperfect device to evaluate corporate business decisions."); Jeffrey J. Rachlinski, *A Positive Psychological Theory of Judging in Hindsight,* 65 U. CHI. L. REV. 571, 576 (1998) ("Research by cognitive psychologists has shown that the folk wisdom on hindsight is correct—past events seem more predictable than they really were.").

134 Susan Pulliam & Randall Smith, *Citi, SEC Are in Talks to Settle Asset Probe,* WALL ST. J., May 28, 2009, at C1, available at http://online.wsj.com/article/SB124347855330961363.html.

nine months" of 2007.[135] Those holdings also led to significant write-downs in 2007.[136]

The remainder of this Article considers the Citigroup scenario in the context of ERM and proposed and potential regulatory responses to the perceived risk-management failures associated with the 2008 recession.[137] It is easy to posit that better or more rigorous risk-management procedures would have prevented the losses that both Citigroup shareholders and the markets more generally suffered, but it is much harder to prove that proposition.[138] The existing law governing corporate boards' compliance obligations and the basic behavioral and cultural barriers that impede many decision-making processes only intensify that challenge[139]

V. Potential Barriers to the ERM Solution

At its core, ERM strives to change corporate culture and improve information and communication regarding risk events.[140] Those objectives alone, however, will not necessarily result in better risk management.[141] Indeed, a firm could implement a process that projects an ERM façade but does nothing substantive to change the way decision makers consider and resolve risk issues. Moreover, that process likely would satisfy existing and proposed risk regulations.[142] As discussed above, those regulations focus primarily on disclosure regarding risk-management practices and do not prescribe the content or scope of those practices.

Accordingly, before firms adopt or policymakers mandate ERM, or any other risk-management protocol, all participants need to consider whether more processes alone will improve risk management and enhance firm value or whether something else is needed. Specifically, will more reporting and information necessarily result in different or better decisions? If not, how do we improve risk management and does the law have a role to play in that process?

---

[135] Bradley Keoun, *Citigroup Fires CDO Bankers After Mortgage Losses*, BLOOMBERG (Dec. 19, 2007, 5:38 PM), http://www.bloomberg.com/apps/news?pid=20601087&sid=aQmPC4T4g8Uo&refer=home.

[136] *Id.*

[137] *See infra* Part V.

[138] *Id.*

[139] *See supra* Part III.B.2 and *infra* Part V.

[140] *See supra* Parts II.A, III.A.

[141] *See* Lipshaw, *supra* note 8, at 21 ("The problem with any reduction to rules . . . is the illusion of objectivity, something fostered by the particular construct of concepts that constitutes law generally.").

[142] *See supra* Part III.B.

A. Behavioral Barriers to Effective ERM

Why did Citigroup keep dancing well into 2007? Several key indicators in its industry and the economy more generally suggested that caution was warranted.[143] Some of its competitors observed these indicators and instituted responsive measures. For example, J.P. Morgan observed red flags in late 2006 and "exited the business of securitizing subprime mortgages when it was still booming."[144] Other investors actually grossed large profits during 2007 by shorting mortgage-backed securities.[145] But Citigroup remained committed to its investment strategy, with little meaningful hedging, until arguably it was too late.

It is difficult to discern with any precision the motivation for Citigroup's conduct. Nevertheless, analyzing its course of action through the lens of behavioral economics provides an interesting perspective on risk management.[146]

---

143 *See supra* Part IV.

144 Shawn Tully, *Jamie Dimon's Swat Team: How J.P. Morgan's CEO and His Crew Are Helping the Big Bank Beat the Credit Crunch*, CNNMONEY (Sept. 2, 2008, 4:02 PM), http://money.cnn.com/2008/08/29/news/companies/tully_dimon.fortune. J.P. Morgan reportedly embraces ERM, focusing on structure and culture. *See Enterprise Risk Management,* in THE CENTENNIAL GLOBAL BUSINESS SUMMIT REPORT 3–4 (Harvard Business School 2008), available at http://www.hbs.edu/centennial/businesssummit/global-business/enterprise-risk-management.pdf (explaining that, at J.P. Morgan, "[r]isk management starts with tone set at the very top" and includes "a culture of collaboration"); *see also Cinderella's Moment,* THE ECONOMIST, Feb. 11, 2010, available at http://www.economist.com/specialreports/displaystory.cfm?story_id=15474145 (observing that financial institutions like J.P. Morgan that survived the recession better than their peers "relied largely on giving their risk-managing roundheads equal status with the risk-taking cavaliers").

145 *See, e.g.,* RIMS PAPER, *supra* note 3, at 4 ("Goldman Sachs adjusted its positions in mortgage-backed securities beginning in 2006, differentiating itself from the rest of the market at a time when some might have criticized the move as excessively cautious."). Goldman Sachs' CFO explained: "In December [2006] our mortgage business lost money for 10 days in a row. It wasn't a lot of money, but by the 10th day we thought that we should sit down and talk about it." Nocera, *supra* note 3, at 1. This recognition reportedly led Goldman Sachs to rein in risk in its subprime mortgage portfolio. *Id.; see also* Carol Loomis, *Robert Rubin on the Job He Never Wanted,* CNNMONEY (Nov. 28, 2007, 7:13 AM), http://money.cnn.com/2007/11/09/news/newsmakers/merrill_rubin.fortune/index.htm?postversion=2007111119. Notably, Goldman Sachs has been criticized for, and is the subject of a lawsuit concerning, its products and investment decisions leading up to the 2008 recession. *See* John D. McKinnon, *Senate Probes Bank for Meltdown Fraud,* WALL ST. J., July 30, 2009, at C1, available at http://online.wsj.com/article/SB124890898142691729.html; Press Release, Securities and Exchange Commission, SEC Charges Goldman Sachs with Fraud in Structuring and Marketing of CDO Tied to Subprime Mortgages (Apr. 16, 2010), available at http://www.sec.gov/news/press/2010/2010-59.htm.

146 *See* Sendhil Mullainathan & Richard H. Thaler, *Behavioral Economics* (Nat'l Bureau of Econ. Research, Working Paper No. 7948, 2000), available at https://www.msu.edu/course/aec/810/clippings/Thaler-behavioralëconomics.pdf ("Behavioral economics is the combination of psychology and economics that investigates what happens in markets in which some of the agents display human limitations and complications."); *see also* Craig Lambert, *The Marketplace of Perceptions,* HARV. MAG., Mar.–Apr. 2006, available at http://harvardmagazine.com/2006/03/the-marketplace-of-perce.html (explaining development of behavioral economics); Langevoort, *supra* note 133 (explaining role of behavioral economics in legal profession). *But see, e.g.,* Victor Fleischer, *The Rational Exuberance of Structuring Venture Capital Start-ups,* 57 TAX L. REV. 137, 141 (2003) (suggesting that behavioral economics can help create a more complete picture of the risk management problem and in turn a more complete solution; it is just one of several analytical tools that policymakers can and should utilize in this analyze) ("The broader point is that cognitive biases, though sometimes enlightening, should be used as a last resort rather than as a primary or all-purpose explanation for

Citigroup, like most financial institutions, had risk-management procedures in place prior to the 2008 recession.[147] Its risk managers and executives had access to information that suggested significant potential risk to its major asset portfolios.[148] Yet, Citigroup consistently asserted that its risk exposure was nominal.[149]

The behavioral-economics literature documents unconscious cognitive biases that might account for the Citigroup scenario.[150] Many commentators have thoughtfully analyzed the impact of individual and group biases on decisions by and relations among boards of directors and senior management.[151] This Article considers three of those biases in the risk-management context: confirmation bias, overconfidence or optimism bias, and framing.

Confirmation bias commonly is defined as "the tendency to ascribe too much weight to evidence that confirms [individuals' or groups'] views and too little

---

seemingly irrational behavior."); Richard A. Posner, *Rational Choice, Behavioral Economics, and the Law,* 50 STAN. L. REV. 1551, 1556–57 (1998) (criticizing behavioral economics).

147 *See* Citigroup Inc., Annual Report (Form 10-K), at 39–60 (Feb. 27, 2008), available at http://www.citigroup.com/citi/corporategovernance/ar.htm (describing risk-management practices).

148 *See supra* Part IV.

149 *See, e.g.,* Joshua Gallu & Donald Griffin, *SEC Says Prince, Ruben Knew of Losses on Assets at Suit's Focus,* BLOOMBERG (Sept. 9, 2010, 11:09 AM), http://www.bloomberg.com/news/2010-09-09/prince-rubin-knew-assets-at-focus-of-sec-claim-fueled-losses-agency-says.html ("The New York-based bank's executives repeatedly stated in 2007 that it had reduced exposure to subprime mortgage securities by 45 percent to $13 billion, as investors and analysts clamored for information about the deteriorating market, according to the agency's July complaint."); Jim Zarroli, *Citigroup CEO Prince Falls to Subprime Debacle,* NPR.ORG (Nov. 5, 2007), http://www.npr.org/templates/story/story.php?storyId=15995002 ("Prince, 57, was insisting jut a few months ago that Citigroup's subprime exposure was not serious.").

150 *See, e.g.,* Inga Chira et al., *Behavioral Bias Within the Decision Making Process,* 6 J. BUS. & ECON. RESEARCH 11 (2008) ("[Behavioral finance] draws on the psychology and cognitive science literatures to examine why individual decision-making often deviates from rational choices in systematic ways."); Tversky and Kahneman, *supra* note 10, at 1124 ("[P]eople rely on a limited number of heuristic principles which reduce the complex tasks of assessing probabilities and predicting values to simpler judgmental operations. In general, these heuristics are quite useful, but sometimes they lead to severe and systematic errors.").

151 *See, e.g.,* Regina F. Burch, *The Myth of the Unbiased Director,* 41 AKRON L. REV. 509 (2008); Lawrence A. Cunningham, *Beyond Liability: Rewarding Effective Gatekeepers,* 92 MINN. L. REV. 323 (2007); Lynne L. Dallas, *A Preliminary Inquiry into the Responsibility of Corporations and Their Officers and Directors for Corporate Climate: The Psychology of Enron's Demise,* 35 RUTGERS L.J. 1 (2003) [hereinafter *Psychology of Enron's Demise*]; Lynne L. Dallas, *Two Models of Corporate Governance: Beyond Berle and Means,* 22 U. MICH. J.L. REFORM 19, 73–77 (1988); Kent Greenfield, *Using Behavioral Economics to Show the Power and Efficiency of Corporate Law as Regulatory Tool,* 35 U.C. DAVIS L. REV. 581 (2002); *Donald C. Langevoort, Resetting the Corporate Thermostat: Lessons from the Recent Financial Scandals About Self-Deception, Deceiving Others and the Design of Internal Controls,* 93 GEO. L.J. 285 (2004); Donald C. Langevoort, *The Human Nature of Corporate Boards: Law, Norms, and the Unintended Consequences of Independence and Accountability,* 89 GEO. L.J. 797, 812–13 (2001); Donald C. Langevoort, *Organized Illusions: A Behavioral Theory of Why Corporations Mislead Stock Market Investors (and Cause Other Social Harms),* 146 U. PA. L. REV. 101 (1997); Oliver Marnet, *Behavior and Rationality in Corporate Governance,* J. ECON. ISSUES, Sept. 2005, at 613; Anthony Page, *Unconscious Bias and the Limits of Director Independence,* 2009 U. ILL. L. REV. 237.

weight to evidence that invalidates their views."[152] Some commentators have identified instances of confirmation bias in corporate boardrooms, including the decision of Sun Microsystems to continue an aggressive investment strategy in the face of an economic downturn.[153] This hubris encourages individuals on an unconscious level to seek out information supporting their position and discount opposing views.

Citigroup's risk supervisors were operating in an environment that fostered confirmation bias. Reports suggest that Citigroup's trading supervisor, Thomas Maheras, relied on Citigroup's ratings from the ratings agencies to bolster his position that "the bank 'would never lose a penny.' "[154] Likewise, statements from Chairman Bernanke and others during this period provided support for his position. For example, in May 2007, Chairman Bernanke repeated his March statements that "[t]he Federal Reserve does not foresee a broader economic impact from the growing number of mortgage defaults."[155] Moreover, Mr. Prince, colleagues, and subordinates at Citigroup heavily relied on Mr. Maheras' projections to continue their public statements that the bank was financially sound.[156]

---

152 Hersh Shefrin, *Behavioral Corporate Finance,* 14 J. APPLIED CORP. FIN. 113, 118 (2001); *see also* Chira et al., *supra* note 150, at 12.

153 HERSH SHEFRIN, BEHAVIORAL CORPORATE FINANCE: DECISIONS THAT CREATE VALUE 3–10 (2007).

154 *See* Dash & Creswell, *supra* note 81. *See also* Bradley Keoun, *Maheras Says Citigroup Expanded into CDOs at Urging of Bank's Consultants,* BLOOMBERG (Apr. 7, 2010, 1:34 PM) http://www.bloomberg.com/news/2010-04-07/citigroup-consultants-urged-cdo-drive-maheras-says.html ("Even in the summer and fall of 2007, I continued to believe, based upon what I understood from the experts in the business, that the bank's super-senior CDO holdings were safe.") (quoting Mr. Maheras).

155 Jeremy W. Peters, *Fed Chief Addresses Foreclosures,* N.Y. TIMES, May. 18, 2007, at C1, available at http://www.nytimes.com/2007/05/18/business/18fed.html; *see also* Economic Committee Timeline, *supra* note 119, at 22.

156 *See* Dash & Creswell, *supra* note 81. A related, but distinct bias, is commitment bias. IRVIS L. JANIS & LEON MANN, DECISION MAKING: A PSYCHOLOGICAL ANALYSIS OF CONFLICT, CHOICE, AND COMMITMENT (1977). That hubris makes it difficult to change course or exit a failing business strategy. In Citigroup's scenario, Mr. Prince committed to aggressive growth in Citigroup's CDO products early in his tenure. Dash & Creswell, *supra* note 81; *see also* Bradley Keoun, *Citi's Prince Says No One Saw CDO Losses Coming,* BLOOMBERG (Apr. 8, 2010, 2:26 PM), http://www.bloomberg.com/news/2010-04-08/prince-rubin-say-they-didn-t-recognize-citigroup-s-cdo-risk-before-crisis.html (noting Citi's executives' CDO growth strategy); Matt Pittman, *Citigroup's 'Last Roman' CDO Shows Enron Accounting,* BLOOMBERG (May 22, 2008, 4:40 PM), http://www.bloomberg.com/apps/news?pid=newsarchive&sid=a42143EyVai8 (explaining one of Citigroup's CDOs and observing that "Citigroup Inc. created a $2.5 billion mortgage-backed security called Bonifacius Ltd. in August as capital markets seized up and panic swept Wall Street"); Zarroli, *supra* note 149 (" '[Citigroup has] been very aggressive and they've been pushing profit growth very hard in a lot of areas. And that means that you pile up risks that don't necessarily bother you—unless, all of a sudden, markets chang[ed]' ") (quoting Professor Roy Smith). "From 2003 to 2005, Citigroup more than tripled its issuing of [CDOs], to more than $20 billion from $6.28 billion, . . . meaning Citigroup made up to $500 million in fees from the business in 2005 alone." Dash & Creswell, *supra* note 81. Here, "the subsequent discovery of information that indicates harmful consequences flowing from that commitment directly threatens their self-concept as good, worthwhile

In addition, Citigroup's executives' willingness to buy into rosy projections despite the realities surrounding its industry demonstrates overconfidence and an optimism bias.[157] Several studies have identified overconfidence as a trait affecting corporate CEOs.[158] Individuals in these powerful positions tend to overestimate their own abilities; they often believe that they are the exception to the rule.[159] Other financial companies may be affected by the 2008 recession, but their company will be the lone standing survivor. As one commentator observes, "[M]any companies may unintentionally engage in excessive optimism, especially when their existence depends on favorable forecasts."[160]

Finally, framing can play a significant role in risk-management decisions.[161] "Studies on framing of legal risks find, for example, that taxpayers who owe money are more likely to cheat on their taxes than taxpayers who expect a

---

individuals. Thus, cognitive processes will work to suppress such information if at all possible." Donald C. Langevoort, *Where Were the Lawyers? A Behavioral Inquiry into Lawyers' Responsibility for Clients' Fraud,* 46 VAND. L. REV. 75, 102–03 (1993).

157 *See, e.g.,* Chira et al., *supra* note 150, at 12 (explaining the common biases); Dan Lovallo & Daniel Kahneman, *Delusions of Success: How Optimism Undermines Executives Decisions,* 81 HARV. BUS. R. 56 (2003). *See also* Bernardo P. Bressane & Marcelo Verdini Maia, *CEO Overconfidence & the Impact on M&A Activity* (Sept. 1, 2010) (unpublished manuscript), available at http://papers.ssrn.com/sol3/papers.cfm?abstract_id=1674467 (empirical study suggesting association between CEO overconfidence bias and management decisions in M&A context); Paul Hribar & Holly Yang, *Does CEO Overconfidence Affect Management Forecasting and Subsequent Earnings Management?* (Mar. 2010) (unpublished manuscript), available at http://w4.stern.nyu.edu/accounting/docs/Summer_Camp/Hribar.Yang,Does.CEO.Overconfidence.Affect.Mgmt.pdf (empirical study suggesting "that [CEO] overconfidence increases the optimistic bias in voluntary forecasts, leading to both an increased likelihood of missing management forecasts and greater earnings management").

158 Edward Teach, *Watch How You Think: Insights from Behavioral Finance Could Change the Way Companies Approach Mergers and Acquisitions,* CFO MAG., Jan. 2004, available at http://www.cfo.com/article.cfm/3011331/c_3046604 ("Every CEO who goes into [an acquisition] thinks he is different—that he will be able to pull it off."); *see also* Troy A. Parades, *Too Much Pay, Too Much Deference: Behavioral Corporate Finance, CEOs and Corporate Governance,* 32 FLA. ST. U. L. REV. 673, 676 (2005) ("A rich body of subsequent empirical research has shown that acquisitions frequently destroy firm value when a bidder's managers overvalue the deal and overestimate their ability to execute the deal successfully."); Ribstein, *supra* note 28, at 81 ("Executives also are susceptible to overconfidence, particularly those who have the highest self-esteem and who may also be the most successful.").

159 *See, e.g.,* Hribar & Yang, *supra* note 157, at 4 (explaining thesis that "[o]verconfident managers are more likely to issue optimistically biased forecasts because they overestimate their ability to affect their financial results and/or underestimate the probability of random events" and testing thesis through empirical study); *see also* PAUL C. NUTT, WHY DECISIONS FAIL: AVOIDING THE BLUNDERS AND TRAPS THAT LEAD TO DEBACLES (2002) (describing overconfidence and commitment bias present in Disney's decision to open Euro Disney); Chira et al., *supra* note 150, at 12; Prentice, *supra* note 24.

160 Chira et al., *supra* note 150, at 12.

161 Ian Weinstein, *Don't Believe Everything You Think: Cognitive Bias in Legal Decision Making,* 9 CLINICAL L. REV. 783, 797 (2003) ("[F]raming bias is the tendency to view a given problem in different terms depending on the perspective from which the problem is viewed."); *see also Jeffrey J. Rachlinski, Gains, Losses, and the Psychology of Litigation,* 70 S. CAL. L. REV. 113 (1996) (explaining framing bias); X.T. Wang, *Framing Effects: Dynamics and Task Domains,* 68 ORGANIZATIONAL BEHAV. & HUMAN DECISION PROCESSES, Nov. 1996, at 145 (same).

refund."[162] Although framing arguably infected some of Citigroup's decisions in 2007, a framing bias likely had a much larger impact in creating the situation in which Citigroup found itself at that time.

Consider the following account:

> In 2005, stung by regulatory rebukes and unable to follow Mr. Weill's penchant for expanding Citigroup's holdings through rapid-fire takeovers, Mr. Prince and his board of directors decided to push even more aggressively into trading and other businesses that would allow Citigroup to continue expanding the bank internally.[163] As Mr. Prince searched for ways to regain Citigroup's prowess, he and his colleagues likely were operating in a loss frame, making them more risk seeking.[164] "This risk taking might be conscious, but decision makers can also conceal risk-preferring behavior from themselves by adjusting their estimates of risk artificially downwards."[165]

Notably, cognitive biases can overlap and often enable each other. For example, the loss framing that might have influenced Mr. Prince's initial decision to invest aggressively in the CDO market likely made him susceptible to confirmation and commitment biases with respect to the success of that strategy (as well as his overall strategic plan for Citigroup).[166] Moreover, cognitive biases were not the

---

162 Richard W. Painter, *Convergence and Competition in Rules Governing Lawyers and Auditors,* 29 J. CORP. L. 397, 404 (2004); *see also* Robert B. Thompson, *Securities Regulation in an Electronic Age: The Impact of Cognitive Psychology,* 75 WASH. U. L.Q. 779, 784 (1997) ("But I think that there are enough examples where framing leads investors to violate simple economic principles that the SEC and the courts would want to recognize it.").

163 Dash & Creswell, *supra* note 81; *see also* Mara Der Hovanesian et al., *Can Chuck Prince Clean Up Citi?,* BUSINESSWEEK, Oct. 4, 2004, at 32, available at http://www.businessweek.com/magazine/content/04_40/b3902049_mz011.htm (describing many challenges facing Mr. Prince in turning around Citigroup). For example, one commentator observed, "[Mr. Prince] came in at a time when you know a famous leader had been yanked away and there were a lot of problems in the past. All sorts of market disruptions occurred. And he wasn't a charismatic leader who could rally the troops necessarily." Jim Zarroli, *supra* note 149 (quoting Professor Roy Smith).

164 *See, e.g.,* Painter, *supra* note 162, at 403 ("Some psychological studies suggest that decision makers are risk averse when deciding between two alternatives that they perceive to result in a gain, but risk preferring when deciding between two alternatives that they perceive to result in a loss."); Wang, *supra* note 161, at 146 (describing loss framing in context of Tversky and Kahneman's prospect theory and explaining that, under this theory). "[P]eople code the possible choice outcomes as gains and losses, and tend to be risk averse when choosing among prospects seen as gains but risk seeking when choosing among prospects seen as losses." *Id.; see also* Richard H. Thaler et al., *The Effect of Myopia and Loss Aversion on Risk Taking: An Experimental Test,* Q. J. ECON., May 1997, at 647, 648, available at http://www.econ.brown.edu/fac/Kfir_Eliaz/Thaler1.pdf (explaining myopic loss aversion and noting that "[e]mpirical estimates find that losses are weighted about twice as strongly as gains").

165 Painter, *supra* note 162, at 404.

166 Indeed, even after announcing huge losses in October 2007, Mr. Prince continued to pronounce his confidence in Citigroup and his vision for the firm, stating: "No one can be happy with the results in our fixed-income business or with the results that relate to that. But, I think if you are able to look at other parts of the

only factors contributing to Citigroup's scenario. Citigroup certainly had weak controls and risk management, and it admittedly was dealing with a very difficult economic environment.[167]

The presence of cognitive biases in the decision-making process, however, cautions against blind reliance on more internal controls and risk management as the solution. As discussed below, the designers of any ERM program should consider cognitive biases.[168] Reflecting on the Citigroup scenario, having more high-level individuals responsible for risk assessment and having direct access to individuals on the ground gathering the risk-related information might have shattered the confirmation bias sooner. Part of Citigroup's problem appears to be that most risk information and decisions funneled through Mr. Maheras.[169]

B. Cultural Barriers to Effective ERM

When Mr. Prince took over as CEO of Citigroup, the firm had a reputation for being aggressive and obsessed with maximizing short-term gains.[170] At the time, Citigroup was under intense scrutiny for its roles in Enron and WorldCom, as well as questionable trading practices in Japan and Europe. Mr. Prince vowed to change corporate culture but ultimately remained aggressive in his pursuit of profits, creating a culture where "senior managers got addicted to the revenues and arrogant about the risks they were running."[171]

Citigroup is not alone in promoting an aggressive, win-at-all-cost corporate culture. That culture arguably is the norm in the United States.[172] The 2008

---

business, if you look at the strategic plan we're executing on, I think any fair-minded person would say that strategic plan is working." Zarroli, *supra* note 149.

[167] *See, e.g.,* Citigroup Inc., Annual Report (Form 10-K), at 49 (Feb. 27, 2009), available at http://www.citigroup.com/citi/corporategovernance/ar.htm ("Recent market conditions, particularly during the latter part of 2007 and 2008, have involved unprecedented dislocations and highlight the limitations inherent in using historical data to manage risk."); Eric Dash, *Citigroup Acknowledges Poor Risk Management,* N.Y. TIMES, Oct. 16, 2007, at C9, available at http://www.nytimes.com/2007/10/16/business/16citi.html ("Citigroup acknowledged yesterday that its risk management models did not function properly during this summer's credit crisis, contributing to the company's 57 percent drop in third-quarter profit.").

[168] *See infra* Part V.C.

[169] *See* Dash & Creswell, *supra* note 81.

[170] *See, e.g.,* Louise Cooper, *Scandal-hit Citigroup Rebuilds Its Image,* BBC NEWS (Mar. 14, 2005, 3:26 PM), http://news.bbc.co.uk/2/hi/business/4318333.stm.

[171] *See* Dash & Creswell, *supra* note 81; Zarroli, *supra* note 149 (noting that Citigroup under Mr. Prince has "been very aggressive and . . . pushing profit growth very hard in a lot of areas").

[172] *See, e.g.,* Francesco Guerrera et al., *Damning Insight into Corporate Culture Sheds Light on Fall of a Wall Street Giant,* FINANCIAL TIMES, Mar. 13, 2010, http://www.ft.com/cms/s/0/d0441982-2e40-11df-85c0-00144feabdc0.html (noting that the examiner report on Lehman Brothers describes the firm as an "organisation prepared to take short cuts and huge risks to boost earnings, where control and accounting procedures were found to be sorely lacking"); *Psychology of Enron's Demise, supra* note 151, at 54 ("Enron has been described as having an arrogant climate. Such a climate is prone to greater homogeneity because differing views are not valued. This homogeneity can result in exaggerating the impact of various decision-making biases."). Cynthia

recession has called into question the utility of that culture, and many policymakers and commentators, including ERM proponents, are pushing for an overhaul of corporate culture.[173] But change is hard and slow, and memories of tragic events like the 2008 recession are short. Moreover, pressure in the boardroom to increase the bottom line remains.

Notably, studies suggest a strong link between corporate culture and risk-management practices.[174] For example, one study of firms in thirty-five different countries shows a strong, negative association between harmonious corporate cultures and risk taking and a strong, positive association between individual-centric corporate cultures and risk taking.[175] The study defines "harmony" in the context of cultures that are "more accepting of traditional ways of doing business rather than striving for innovation."[176] It defines "individualism" in the context of cultures that "focus on individual freedom and personal challenge."[177] Perhaps not surprisingly, the United States scored the highest on cultures exhibiting individual-centric characteristics.[178]

Although this study focuses on corporate culture in relation to country of origin, its data provide helpful insight into the values that enhance or detract from cultivating a risk culture.[179] As demonstrated by the Citigroup scenario, a win-at-all-costs culture may impede a firm embracing ERM beyond a pure process approach. ERM proponents recognize this limitation, which drives in part their strong emphasis on corporate culture.[180] "Enterprise risk management—to be effective—must fundamentally change the way organizations think about risk."[181]

Webster & Allyn White, *Exploring the National and Organizational Culture Mix in Service Firms*, J. ACAD. MARKETING SCI. (2009) (describing a study analyzing corporate cultures in United States and Japan and observing that the "U.S. is characterized by such values as assertiveness, decisiveness, innovativeness . . . and risk-taking, which stem from its frontier-conquering history."). Interestingly, J.P. Morgan's corporate culture has been described as " 'extremely cautious, ultra-conservative,' and bureaucratic." Liz Wolgemuth, *JPMorgan and Bear Stearns: A Culture Challenge*, U.S. NEWS & WORLD REPORT, Mar. 31, 2008, available at http://www.usnews.com/money/careers/articles/2008/03/31/jpmorgan-and-bear-stearns-a-culture-challenge.html. This difference may reflect J.P. Morgan's earlier embrace of general ERM principles. *See supra* note 144.

173 *See supra* Parts II.A, III.A.

174 *See* Dale Griffin et al., *Cultural Values and Corporate Risk Taking* 1–4 (March 17, 2009) (unpublished manuscript), available at http://papers.ssrn.com/sol3/papers.cfm?abstract_id=1362163 (describing prior studies on culture and risk taking).

175 *Id.* at 7, 28–29.

176 *Id.* at 7.

177 *Id.*

178 *Id.* at 13.

179 *Id.* at 17–23.

180 International Corporate Governance Network, ICGN Corporate Governance Principles 5–7, 8 (Apr. 27, 2010).

181 RIMS PAPER, *supra* note 3, at 9.

Accordingly, in addition to mechanisms to mitigate cognitive biases, policymakers and ERM proponents must create incentives for U.S. boards and management to buy into a risk culture.

C. Strengthening ERM Proposals

More people knowing more information and accepting responsibility for risk decisions is a good first step in addressing risk-management failures. ERM provides a useful framework to achieve those objectives. But a firm adopting ERM or even just more rigorous risk-management procedures will not necessarily improve risk-management decisions.[182] Risk-related regulations and best practices need to account for cognitive biases and the challenges in creating true risk cultures, and whether through regulation or the markets, firms need incentives to commit the time and resources necessary to develop effective ERM.

1. Breaking Down the Behavioral Barrier

Overcoming cognitive bias is a tricky endeavor. One popular approach is training to sensitize individuals to their potential biases. This technique is used in a variety of settings, including discrimination in the workplace and strategic decisions in the courtroom.[183] Studies are split regarding the utility of training, and some commentators observe the risk of the training itself being biased or creating new biases.[184] Nevertheless, as boards and management consider ERM and reflect on risk-related decisions, training regarding decision-making skills, including the impact of cognitive biases, may complement the process with nominal downside risk.[185]

---

182 *See supra* Part V.A.

183 *See, e.g.*, Susan Bisom-Rapp, *An Ounce of Prevention Is a Poor Substitute for a Pound of Cure: Confronting the Developing Jurisprudence of Education and Prevention in Employment Discrimination Law,* 22 BERKELEY J. EMP. & LAB. L. 1, 20–29 (2001); Alafair Burke, *Neutralizing Cognitive Bias: An Invitation to Prosecutors,* 2 N.Y.U. J.L. & LIBERTY 512 (2007) (discussing debiasing training in prosecutor/litigation context); Tristin K. Green, *Discrimination in Workplace Dynamics: Toward a Structural Account of Disparate Treatment Theory,* 38 HARV. C.R-C.L. L. REV. 91 (2003).

184 *See* Bisom-Rapp, *supra* note 183, at 29–30 (describing uncertainty regarding success of bias training and noting dearth of empirical support for approach); Katherine L. Milkman et al., *How Can Decision Making Be Improved?* 379–80 (Persp. on Psychol. Sci., Working Paper No. 08-102, 2008) (noting that studies show that training produces only minimal success); *see also* Christine Jolls & Cass R. Sustein, *Debiasing through Law,* 35 J. LEGAL STUD. 199, 229 (2006) ("But in some circumstances, a strategy of debiasing through law could introduce new distortions through its effect on those who did not previously exhibit bounded rationality."); Lipshaw, *supra* note 8, at 21 ("But the recursiveness of self-analysis is problematic in the internal making, as opposed to the analysis, of judgments; one may attempt to assess the extent of one's own bias, framing issues, heuristics, and so, but the analysis itself may be subject to those same influences.").

185 *See, e.g.*, Lawrence A. Cunningham, *Behavioral Finance and Investor Governance,* 59 WASH. & LEE L. REV. 767,788–92 (2002) (suggesting training to combat investor biases); Jolls & Sustein, *supra* note 184, at 234 ("[D]ebiasing through law—especially debiasing through substantive law—is a distinctive and sometimes far preferable alternative to the strategy of insulating legal outcomes from the effects of bounded rationality."); *see also* Tristin K. Green, *A Structural Approach as Antidiscrimination Mandate: Locating Employer Wrong,* 60 VAND. L.

This is not to say that boards will automatically make better or unbiased decisions; they might not. The training, however, would increase the prospect of boards and management at least hesitating and reflecting on a decision before pulling the trigger.[186] That reflection time could result in some better outcomes. Many firms have incorporated ongoing training for their boards.[187] Extending that training to management to cover cognitive biases likely can be done at little cost and with significant potential return.

In addition to training, boards and management could create objective tools to gauge biases. For example, in setting the firm's risk appetite, the board and management could breakout in detail the firm's acceptable risk exposure overall and in different segments or projects and then adopt rigorous approval procedures for changing or making exceptions to those designations.[188] By setting parameters at the outset—before any surprises or exigencies—boards and management would have an objective measure for their subsequent decisions. The change/exception approval process again would mandate a moment of hesitation and give decision makers the opportunity to recognize any bias. They may still miss the opportunity, but it gives the individuals involved in the process yet another chance to get it right.

Another technique would be employing an outside consultant to model potential risks and to role-play with the board and management.[189] Here, the consultant basically would play devil's advocate, identifying remote or seemingly inconsequential risks and countering the board's and management's responses

---

REV. 849, 860 (2007) (suggesting that training, in connection with structural changes, may address biases more effectively at least in workplace discrimination context).

186 *See, e.g.*, Green, *supra* note 184, at 858–60; Timothy D. Wilson & Nancy Brekke, *Mental Contamination and Mental Correction: Unwanted Influences on Judgments and Evaluations,* 116 PSYCHOL. BULL. 117, 130–35 (1994) (explaining ways to improve outcomes of bias training by emphasizing awareness of, motivation for and consequences/direction of bias).

187 *See, e.g.*, Enterprise Risk Management Initiative: Enterprise Risk Management Executive Education, North Carolina State University, http://www.mgt.ncsu.edu/erm/index.php/about/executive-training (explaining targeted ERM training programs for boards and board committees).

188 *See supra* Part II.B (discussing mapping and profiling aspects of ERM).

189 An outside consultant could serve in various capacities. For example, studies regarding the impact of training show a greater success rate with hands-on personal coaching for the decision maker. *See* Katherine L. Milkman et al., *supra* note 184, at 382. Alternatively, the consultant could serve as a "choice architect," who "design[s] situations in which choices are made . . . to maximize the odds that decision makers will make wise choices." *Id.* at 386–87 (citing RICHARD H. THALER & CASS R. SUSTEIN, NUDGE: IMPROVING DECISIONS ABOUT HEALTH, WEALTH, AND HAPPINESS (Yale Univ. Press) (2008)). A similar proposal is being encouraged in Australia. *See* Leon Gettler, *Reversing Risks,* IN THE BLACK, Nov. 2009, at 39, available at http://www.cpaaustralia.com.au/newsletters/36-39_Reversing_%20Risks.pdf ("A real opportunity lies in developing roles in companies with risk expertise, for experts who can go in and model scenarios for managers to get a much deeper understanding of their risk profile.").

with opposing perspectives.[190] In Citigroup's scenario, a consultant could have asked the hard questions like, why are Citigroup's holdings safe while others in the industry are exposed[?] If Citigroup had responded that it was relying on its ratings from outside agencies, the consultant could have asked why an outsider's assessment of the firm's risk should trump an internal assessment and point out that outside perspectives typically are based on information provided by the firm.

It is of course easy to script this conversation with the benefit of hindsight and much more difficult to do it in the moment.[191] The purpose of the consultant would not necessarily be to identify what the board and management missed. Rather, a primary objective would be to facilitate or teach the board and management how to facilitate conversations leading to that information.[192] In that regard, the consultant technique could be a once-a-year training program or a resource tapped into in times of uncertainty.

2. Breaking Down Cultural Barriers

As articulated in the ERM literature, the board and senior management must implement and maintain the creation of a risk culture.[193] ERM training again may help boards and management appreciate exactly what it means to have a risk culture and the value of that culture. The training, however, will not create a risk culture; a risk culture will be the product of board and management initiative.[194]

Why would a board agree to create a risk culture? The board has a duty to maximize shareholder wealth, and many firms abide by a high-risk, high-reward strategy. And is not failure just a risk of doing business?

Those are difficult questions, and the answer may not be the same for every firm. Boards, management, and stakeholders looking to avoid the extraordinary and unexpected losses experienced in recent corporate scandals and the 2008 recession might find the endeavor worthwhile. As noted above, more data

---

[190] *See, e.g.*, Burke, *supra* note 183, at 523–28 (discussing potential value of having internal and external checks on decision making, including checks that challenge thinking or assumptions of decision maker); Dan Lovallo & Olivier Sibony, *The Case for Behavioral Strategy*, MCKINSEY QUARTERLY, Mar. 22, 2010, at 8, available at https://www.mckinseyquarterly.com/PDFDownload.aspx?ar=2551&srid=7&gp=1 (urging internal and external review of risk options and noting that "[s]ometimes, simply coaxing managers to articulate the experiences influencing them is valuable"). The President & CEO of the Federal Reserve Bank of Boston has suggested an outside review by regulatory supervisors that could ask firms questions regarding risk exposures, including those viewed as nominal by the particular firm, and then "could evaluate the impact and perhaps conclude that the chance of a cascading systemic financial crisis was too big of a chance to take." Rosengren, *supra* note 81.

[191] *See supra* note 133.

[192] *See* Lovallo & Sibony, *supra* note 190.

[193] *See supra* note 38.

[194] *See supra* Parts II.A, III.A.

showing the value of ERM may help convince these firms to adopt the procedures voluntarily (or involuntarily under stakeholder pressure).[195] Alternatively, policymakers could mandate compliance.[196] In either event, training and motivation will be crucial to ERM's success.

3. Regulating ERM

As business techniques, ERM and the approaches for addressing bias and creating a risk culture sound great, but do they raise legal issues or require legal intervention? ERM directly impacts corporate governance. To the extent that the law evaluates and governs the relationship between the board, management, and shareholders, ERM invokes legal consideration. Nevertheless, this Article does not suggest that the law should mandate ERM for every corporation in every context.[197]

Rather, ERM appears better suited as a best practice for corporate governance that would offer firms legal protection against certain liabilities. The framework for this approach largely exists in the regulations adopted after the corporate scandals in the early 2000s.[198] The Sarbanes-Oxley Act and the NYSE listing requirements already require corporations to consider risk and adopt codes of ethics, and the listing requirements also require board training.[199] A firm could easily expand a code of ethics to cover its risk-management policy, and it could likewise expand training in scope and attendance.[200] Moreover, firms could opt

---

195 *See supra* notes 52–55.

196 *See, e.g.,* Okamoto & Edwards, *supra* note 92, at 47–52, 54 (proposing a thoughtful approach to mandating more thorough risk management procedures through regulation that focuses on, among other things, deliberation, contemporaneous rationale and regulator oversight).

197 Imposing a mandatory risk management scheme on all public corporations likely would increase resistance to implementing meaningful ERM programs and encourage thoughtless compliance with the stated process. *See, e.g.,* Jeffrey M. Lipshaw, *Sarbanes-Oxley, Jurisprudence, Game Theory, Insurance and Kant: Toward a Moral Theory of Good Governance*, 50 WAYNE L. REV. 1083, 1088 (2004) (examining the shortcomings of the Sarbanes-Oxley Act and similar legislation and observing that "[f]rom the positivist point of view, Sarbanes-Oxley is a rule that imposes an obligation on corporate directors not to repeat the sins of the Enron and WorldCom debacles. And public companies have duly obeyed, like drivers at stop signs in empty intersections at three a.m., often out of compliance for compliance sake, and not for salutary benefit that should result from compliance"); Roberta Romano, *The Sarbanes-Oxley Act and the Making of Quack Corporate Governance*, 114 YALE L.J. 1521 (2005) (assessing the utility of the Sarbanes-Oxley Act based on the information and process underlying the legislation). The complexity of business-risk decisions and the variance based on a number of critical factors, including industry and size counsel in favor of encouraging ERM through best practices and incentives.

198 *See supra* notes 27–31.

199 *See supra* Part III.A. As discussed above, many commentators criticize the one-size-fits-all nature of many aspects of the Sarbanes-Oxley Act, as well as certain of its other features. *Id.* The proposals discussed in this Article try to avoid many of those pitfalls.

200 *See, e.g., Psychology of Enron's Demise*, *supra* note 151, at 55–58 (suggesting use of a code of ethics and training to create a more ethical corporate culture). Notably, many firms have both a code of ethics and a code

out of these requirements by disclosing their decision to do so, recognizing that they lose any protections or defenses available to firms following the guidelines.[201]

As to those protections and defenses, the Sentencing Guidelines could provide reduced penalties for firms establishing an ERM program that complies with best practices.[202] The SEC could grant additional weight to ERM programs in considering whether to file enforcement actions, and courts could use ERM best practices as evidence refuting knowledge in securities cases and proving good faith where boards are alleged to have failed to act in the face of a known duty or risk.[203] Even in the context of duty-to-monitor claims, ERM could expedite or streamline the litigation, particularly if self-regulatory organizations or similar institutions emerge to review and certify ERM programs.[204]

In determining what constitutes best practices and whether to acknowledge a process as effective ERM, policymakers and industry players need to consider the potential barriers to effective ERM, including those discussed in this Article.[205] Accordingly, best practices should include training on cognitive biases, require objective risk setting and risk-modification standards, and recommend outside consultants. They also should emphasize the board's role in creating a risk culture and require boards to demonstrate their commitment to that culture through the firm's code of ethics, dissemination of risk information, and participation in the process. Using a best-practices approach allows firms to tailor ERM programs to their specific needs or adapt those programs to internal or external changes.

---

of conduct. A firm's code of conduct also might be an appropriate place to discuss risk policies either in addition to or in lieu of discussing it in the code of ethics.

[201] *See, e.g., supra* Part II.A (discussing the "disclose or explain" nature of the ethics code requirements under the Sarbanes Oxley Act); *see also* Luca Enriques & Paolo Volpin, *Corporate Governance Reforms in Continental Europe,* 21 J. ECON. PRINCIPLES 117, 134–36 (2007) (describing process whereby German firms may opt out of certain governance requirements upon a vote of shareholders representing at least 75% of the shares).

[202] *See supra* Parts II.A, III.A; *see also* Hess, *supra* note 31, at 1806–16 (discussing challenges and benefits of trying to encourage ethical corporate cultures under the Sarbanes Oxley Act and the Sentencing Guidelines).

[203] *See supra* Part III.B.2; *see also* Harner, *supra* note 3, at 55–56.

[204] "Self-regulation is a broad concept that includes any attempt by an industry to moderate its conduct with the intent of improving marketplace behavior for the ultimate benefit of consumers. The universe of self-regulatory organizations includes industry-wide or economy-wide private groups that provide, inter alia, certification, product information, complaint resolution, quality assurance, industrial standards, product compatibility standards, professional conduct standards, and complaint resolution." Deborah Platt Majoras, Chairman, Fed. Trade Comm'n, Address before the Council of Better Business Bureaus: Self Regulatory Organizations and the FTC (Apr. 11, 2005); *see also* Roberta S. Karmel, *Should Securities Industry Self-Regulatory Organizations Be Considered Government Agencies?,* 14 STAN. J.L. BUS. & FIN. 151 (2008) (explaining use and potential issues relating to SROs); Donna M. Nagy, *Playing Peekaboo with Constitutional Law: The PCAOB and Its Public/Private Status,* 80 NOTRE DAME L. REV. 975, 1022–26 (2005) (reviewing traditional use of SROs in securities industry).

[205] *See supra* Parts V.A, V.B.

In addition to regulatory incentives to adopt ERM, the markets could be very influential in ERM's meaningful development.[206] As stakeholders realize the value of ERM, shareholders can request that firms adopt ERM either informally or through shareholder proposals, and lenders can address ERM disclosures in their transaction documents. Likewise, as investors become more knowledgeable about ERM, they may make investment decisions based on firms with certified or well-documented ERM programs. As discussed above, Standard & Poor's is already working to provide investors with this type of information.[207]

Just as risk management did not cause the 2008 recession, improving risk-management practices through ERM or otherwise will not prevent the next one. Nevertheless, thoughtful and considered risk planning may mitigate the losses suffered by firms in the next economic downturn and generally constitutes good business. To the extent that such practices preserve firm value and thereby protect stakeholders' interests, policymakers and markets should provide appropriate incentives for firms to adopt meaningful ERM.

VI. Conclusion

As some commentators have observed, the 2008 recession was a "wake-up call" for risk management.[208] Many firms not only were surprised by developments during the recession but also had no effective means to communicate or respond to the changing financial landscape. The subprime-mortgage crisis and subsequent events paralyzed their operations. Better risk-management practices would not have averted the 2008 recession, but they might have shortened the duration and eased the severity of the financial turmoil.

As policymakers and firms reflect on the recession, they should consider how risk-management improvements can help firms operate more efficiently and be better prepared for the next round of operational or economic surprises. Here, ERM offers a technique for firm-wide risk identification, assessment, and response that involves the board of directors, senior management, and appropriate individuals throughout the firm.[209] Like any risk-management practice, however, ERM has its limitations and is not a cure for all corporate ills.

---

[206] *See* Harner, *supra* note 3, at 52–53; *see also* International Corporate Governance Network, *supra* note 180 (encouraging institutional investors to take an active role in reviewing and assessing a firm's risk management practices, explaining "[t]he objective of these principles is to help investors assess how well a portfolio company's board—either unitary or supervisory—is effectively overseeing risk management.").

[207] *See supra* Part III.A.

[208] *See id.*

[209] *See supra* Parts II.A, III.A.

Policymakers and industry organizations promulgating best practices should recognize the behavioral and cultural barriers to effective risk management and encourage processes that account for those limitations. Among other things, guidelines suggesting ERM and cognitive-bias training and the integration of risk practices into codes of ethics might assist firms in developing meaningful risk assessment and not simply more risk-related process.[210] The goal of any risk-related policy should be helping firms make better-informed decisions—both as to the substance of the problem and the means for reaching the decision itself. As Warren Buffet has observed, "Risk comes from not knowing what you're doing."[211]

NOTES

1. If Professor Gilmore's article scared you, then Judge Harner's article on enterprise risk management should at least give you some comfort, even though it continues our theme of how even the best organizational structures in the world can be outfoxed by bad people or by subconsciously bad reasoning. She highlights three cognitive errors not mentioned in the earlier parts of this chapter: confirmation bias, overconfidence bias, and framing. Not that we're entirely Enron-fixated,* but how might each of these three cognitive errors have played out in Enron? We'll get you started: Enron executives probably framed their decision to engage in the bad kind of "financial engineering" (hiding the ball about the real purpose behind certain transactions) as "we have to keep our stock price up at all costs, because our first duty is to our shareholders."** Now you try it: how might confirmation bias have played out at Enron? What about overconfidence bias? Or, if you're not that interested in Enron, try another scandal—maybe what happened at Penn State under Coach Paterno's watch, or any of the countless sexual harassment stories that hit the news in 2017.

2. 2017 also saw many tragic events stemming from bad decision at fraternity and sorority parties. How might the culture of a student group make developing a good enterprise risk management plan difficult? If you're a college president, how might you start to effect culture change in student organizations—or, for that matter, within the faculty?

---

[210] *See supra* Part V.C.

[211] Brad Tuttle, *Warren Buffet's Boring, Brilliant Wisdom,* IT'S YOUR MONEY (Mar. 1, 2010, 9:06 AM), available at http://money.blogs.time.com/2010/03/01/warren-buffetts-boring-brilliant-wisdom.

* OK, yes, we are.

** Of course, we realize that some of the Enron executives may not have framed their decision to engage in bad financial engineering as a way of putting the interests of the shareholders first.

CHAPTER 7

Black Swans, Ostriches, and Ponzi Schemes[*]

Nancy B. Rapoport[**]

What did he know, and when did he know it?[***]

—Howard Baker (referring to Richard Nixon during Watergate)[1]

A few months ago, two different federal district court judges in the Southern District of New York went two different ways on the issue of whether the Madoff investors ran the risk of having to disgorge both their "on the book" profits—much of which would be fictional profits only—and the principal that they invested with Madoff.[2] In *Picard v. Merkin (*In re *Bernard L. Madoff Investment Securities, LLC)*, the district court ruled that the complaint filed by Madoff trustee Irving Picard, which alleges fraudulent transfers based on both actual and constructive fraud, could survive a motion to dismiss.[3] Judge Wood held that, when it comes to fraudulent transfers under both the Bankruptcy Code and New York state law, it's the intent of the debtor-transferor that matters, not the intent

* This piece was originally published as Nancy B. Rapoport, *Black Swans, Ostriches, and Ponzi Schemes*, 42 GOLDEN GATE U.L. REV. 627 (2012).

*** Gordon Silver Professor of Law, William S. Boyd School of Law, University of Nevada, Las Vegas. This Article was made possible in part by the research support of the Boyd School of Law. Special thanks go to Jack Ayer, Jessica Gabel, Karen Gebbia, Jennifer Gross, Nettie Mann, Morris Rapoport, Bill Rochelle, and Jeff Van Niel for their comments on earlier drafts.

1 *See* Howard Baker, Wikipedia, http://en.wikipedia.org/wiki/Howard_Baker (last visited Dec. 18, 2011).

2 A third recent case, Picard v. JPMorgan Chase & Co., 460 B.R. 84 (S.D.N.Y. 2011), also weighed in on this issue, ultimately ruling that the trustee didn't have standing to pursue all of the claims. In the one paragraph of the opinion that I liked, the court referred to the Trustee as working "relentlessly." *Id.* at 88.

3 Picard v. Merkin (*In re* Bernard L. Madoff Inv. Sec., LLC), No. 11 MC 0012(KMW), 2011 WL 3897970 (S.D.N.Y. Aug. 31, 2011).

of the transferee.[4] She also held that the section 546(e) safe harbor defense[5] wasn't a "get out of court free" card (my words, not hers) at this stage of the proceeding, either, because the bankruptcy court had not yet determined whether the safe harbor applied.

Less than a month later, in *Picard v. Katz*,[6] the district court dismissed all of Picard's claims except the actual fraud and equitable subordination claims, in part by finding that Madoff's firm "was a registered securities brokerage firm, a fact that directly invokes certain 'safe harbor' provisions of the Bankruptcy Code . . . ."[7] Judge Rakoff decided as a matter of law that section 546(e) had kicked in, thereby eliminating Picard's preference and constructive fraud claims. He further held that the investors' principal was safe from recovery absent any actual bad faith by an investor, but that the fictional profits might be recovered:[8]

> [W]hile as to payments received by the defendants from Madoff Securities equal to a return of their principal[,] defendants can defeat the Trustee's claim of actual fraud simply by proving their good faith, as to payments received by the defendants in excess of their principal[,] defendants can defeat the Trustee's claim of actual fraud only by showing that they not only were proceeding in good faith but also that they took for value.

The court then explained that mere inquiry notice that there might have been fraud wouldn't be sufficient,[9] but willful blindness to the fraud would "constitute

---

[4] *Id.* at *8–11. She pointed out, though, that under New York law, the issue of the transferee's intent gets more complicated. The transferee's intent comes into play, but just as an affirmative defense (or if the plaintiff is seeking attorney fees). *Id.* at *12–13. The tricky thing when using state law to avoid a transfer under section 544 is that state laws (by their very nature) aren't uniform. For fraudulent transfers, those state laws may be based on the Uniform Fraudulent Transfer Act or the Uniform Fraudulent Conveyance Act, but they may not follow UFTA/UFCA exactly.

[5] Section 546(e) provides:

> Notwithstanding sections. . . 547, 548 (a)(1)(B), and 548(b) of this title, the trustee may not avoid a transfer that is a margin payment. . . or settlement payment. . . made by or to (or for the benefit of) a commodity broker, forward contract merchant, stockbroker, financial institution, financial participant, or securities clearing agency, or that is a transfer made by or to (or for the benefit of) a commodity broker, forward contract merchant, stockbroker, financial institution, financial participant, or securities clearing agency, in connection with a securities contract,. . . commodity contract,. . . or forward contract, that is made before the commencement of the case, except under section 548(a)(1)(A) of this title.

11 U.S.C.A. § 546(e) (Westlaw 2012).

[6] Picard v. Katz, 462 B.R. 447 (S.D.N.Y. 2011).

[7] *Id.* at 451.

[8] *Id.* at 454 (footnote omitted).

[9] *Id.* at 455.

a lack of good faith."[10] In essence, if reasonable people confronted with the Madoff scheme might have been inclined to say, "what the hey?," that wouldn't matter. Only the most deliberate type of ignorance—the legal equivalent of plugging one's ears while humming tunes—would demonstrate a lack of good faith.[11]

So, depending on which court is correct, the Madoff investors either have several hoops to go through to establish a defense or very few hoops. The applicability of the safe harbor defense is either a question of fact or a question of law. If Judge Wood is correct, and the safe harbor defense is a question of fact, then investing in a deal that seemed too good to be true carries significant risks. If Judge Rakoff is correct, and the safe harbor defense kicks in when a business holds[12] a broker's license to buy and sell stock,[13] then investors aren't obliged to check out the bona fides of too-good-to-be-true deals unless those deals are so obviously fraudulent that no one could ever mistake them for legitimate deals. (Under Judge Rakoff's theory, I envision the fraudulent deals as carrying legends saying, "Warning! I am not a real deal. Invest at your peril.")

To me, the issue involves that very Howard Baker-ish inquiry of what the investors knew and when they knew it. In order to resolve that issue, we have to ask ourselves what clues there were to the Ponzi scheme that Madoff ran. And to do that, we must examine what we know—or think we know—about investing, period. More importantly, we must examine when and how we should question our assumptions about investing.

> Before the discovery of Australia, people in the Old World were convinced that all swans were white, an unassailable belief as it seemed completely confirmed by empirical evidence. The sighting of the first black swan might have been an interesting surprise for a few ornithologists (and others extremely concerned with the coloring of birds), but that is not where the significance of the story lies. It illustrates a severe limitation to our learning from observations or experience and the fragility of our knowledge. One single observation can invalidate a general statement derived from millennia of confirmatory sightings of

---

10 *Id.* at 454 (footnote omitted). I have to admit that I was a bit surprised by the court's rhetorical question: "But why would defendants willfully blind themselves to the fact that they had invested in a fraudulent enterprise?" *Id.* There are a lot of reasons why the defendants might have done just that, as this essay discusses.

11 The Madoff trustee has appealed Judge Rakoff's ruling.

12 ". . . Madoff Securities was a registered securities brokerage firm, a fact that directly invokes certain 'safe harbor' provisions of the Bankruptcy Code. . . ." *Id.* at 451.

13 The fact that Madoff may not have actually been buying securities didn't seem to bother the court.

> millions of white swans. All you need is one single (and, I am told, quite ugly) black bird.
>
> —NASSIM TALEB, THE BLACK SWAN: THE IMPACT OF THE HIGHLY IMPROBABLE[14]

On long drives, I like to listen to books on CD, and I've been listening to Malcolm Gladwell's book WHAT THE DOG SAW AND OTHER ADVENTURES.[15] In the chapter *Blowing Up: How Nassim Taleb Turned the Inevitability of Disaster Into An Investment Strategy,*[16] Gladwell describes Nassim Taleb's approach to investing. The gist of the chapter is that Taleb believes that he can't figure out the market (nor can anyone else), and so, instead, he's developed a system of managing risks without buying into the fallacy that he can somehow beat the system through sheer brainpower.

> Empirica [Taleb's company] follows a very particular investment strategy. It trades options, which is to say that it deals not in stocks and bonds but with bets on stocks and bonds . . . .
>
> . . . .
>
> Taleb . . . has constructed a trading philosophy predicated entirely on the existence of black swans, on the possibility of some random, unexpected event sweeping the markets. He never sells options, then. He only buys them . . . . [H]e buys options on both sides, on the possibility of the market moving both up and down.[17]

Countless gurus (and Madoff was one of them, albeit a fake one) contend that they can beat the system—that, based on their own analysis, they can determine how to make scads of money due to their choice of which stocks to buy, sell, or hold.[18] The problem is that they confuse correlation with causation. (Or, in Madoff's case, the problem was that he was flat-out lying.) The gurus assume that their stock market profits are caused by their understanding of how a particular company runs its business. Balderdash. They buy and sell; some of their

---

14 NASSIM NICHOLAS TALEB, THE BLACK SWAN: THE IMPACT OF THE HIGHLY IMPROBABLE xvii (2007) [hereinafter TALEB].

15 MALCOLM GLADWELL, WHAT THE DOG SAW: AND OTHER ADVENTURES (2009).

16 *Id.* at 51.

17 *Id.* at 58.

18 My husband swears by Jim Cramer's approach: doing some serious homework before and after investing in a company. (When we watch Cramer's show, though, I don't swear by him; I swear at him. And what on earth does "booyah!" mean?)

investments work out and some don't. The analysis may correlate with their profits, but it doesn't cause them.

Just because a person has managed to make some money on a particular stock at a particular time doesn't mean that he has figured out a way to beat the stock market.[19] What counts is his willingness to look for counter-factual evidence as a way of cross-checking his assumptions.[20] He needs to look for "black swans." "Black swans" are events that involve three components: (1) they are wildly unusual events (2) with big ramifications (3) that we rationalize as "normal" after the fact.[21] One such black swan is the investment that never, ever shows a loss. That particular black swan is a signal to abandon ship (as Jim Cramer puts it, "sell, sell, sell") and run hard in the other direction.

That's why I have less sympathy than might be seemly for the people who invested with Bernie Madoff.[22] I feel horrible that many of them lost their life savings. I feel bad for them as fellow human beings. But I wonder why so many smart people ignored the red flags that signal a fraud. With many schemes to disguise the financial statements of underperforming (or fictional) businesses, there were red flags, but people choose not to see them. They miss the black swans. In fact, they became ostriches by burying their heads in the sand.[23]

Irving Picard sees ostriches in the Madoff story, too:

> The Sterling Partners knew or should have known that Madoff's fund was too good to be true because it consistently yielded positive gains coupled with ultra low volatility. Between 1998 and 2008—a period during which the S&P 100 produced negative returns for nearly 60

---

19 For years, we were "Baby Berkshire" shareholders because we liked Warren Buffett's investment philosophy. We still like Mr. Buffett as a person, but we sold the stock when the returns lagged the market for several quarters.

20 Of course, it makes sense to pay attention to things like how a company behaves, especially after some big-name companies like Enron, Tyco, and WorldCom have imploded in very public ways. For many of us, our confidence in companies' financial statements were shaken when we read news story after news story on the type of financial engineering that misled investors. Paying attention to obvious clues is important—who wants to invest in a company that's poorly run or downright rotten?

21 TALEB, at xvii–xviii.

22 I'm not alone. Check out Jack Ayer's analysis of whether the Madoff investors actually did lose "everything." *See* Bernie's Investors: Did They Lose "Everything?", Underbelly blog (Dec. 15, 2008, 1:06 PM), http://underbelly-buce.blogspot.com/2008/12/bernies-investors-did-they-lose.html.

23 OK, ostriches don't really bury their heads in the sand. *See* American Ostrich Association, www.ostriches.org/factor.html#head (last visited Dec. 18, 2011). But from a distance, apparently, it can look as if they do. For the best opinion using pictures of an ostrich and a human, both burying their heads in the sand, see Gonzalez-Servin v. Ford Motor Co., No. 11-1665, 2011 WL 5924441 (7th Cir. Nov. 23, 2011), available at www.abajournal.com/files/DG0R2WE8.pdf. OK, it's the only such opinion, but it's a marvelous opinion just the same.

> months—Sterling's KW BLMIS Accounts rarely reported negative monthly rates of return. During that same ten-year period, of the 483 KW BLMIS Accounts administered by Sterling, none purportedly experienced more than five down months, and many purportedly never had a single down month.
>
> . . . .
>
> The disconnect between Madoff's returns and the equity market was particularly obvious during periods of market dislocation, which should have caused the Sterling Partners to question Madoff's prophetic market timing. Remarkably, Sterling's BLMIS investments were effectively immune from any number of market catastrophes, enjoying steady rates of return at times when the rest of the market was experiencing financial crises.[24]

In the *Sterling* litigation, as in the *Katz* and *Merkin* litigation, Picard seeks to recover certain transfers under sections 544(b), 547, 548, and 550(a) of the Bankruptcy Code and under state law.[25] His attempt to get the Madoff investors to pay back into the estate any fictional profits that they earned, with some clawback periods going as far back as six years,[26] is the right approach.[27] I'm not the only one saying that: the Second Circuit did, too.[28] As between those creditors who had the tools to figure out that something fishy was going on and any other types of creditors without those tools (for example, any tort creditors), my vote goes to the creditors

---

24 Complaint at 193–95, Sec. Investor Prot. Corp. v. Bernard L. Madoff Inv. Sec. LLC (*In re* Bernard L. Madoff Inv. Sec., LLC), Adv. Pro. No. 08-01789 (Bankr. S.D.N.Y. Dec. 7, 2010), available at http://graphics8.nytimes.com/packages/pdf/0204sterlingcompaintfinal.PDF [hereinafter Sterling Complaint] (on file with the Golden Gate University Law Review).

25 *Id.* at 205–364.

26 The Sterling Complaint uses reachback periods of ninety days for some counts (the preference counts), two years for others (the federal fraudulent transfer counts), and six years for still others (the state law fraudulent transfer counts). *See id.* at iii–iv.

27 His theory is called the net-investment approach. Bob Van Voris & Linda Sandler, *Madoff Trustee Picard Wins Ruling on Calculating Losses,* BUSINESSWEEK, Aug. 16, 2011, available at www.businessweek.com/news/2011-08-16/madoff-trustee-picard-wins-ruling-on-calculating-losses.html ("The federal appeals court in New York said today that trustee Irving Picard can calculate losses by subtracting the amount withdrawn from an investor's account from the total placed with Madoff, the so-called net investment method.").

28 In satisfying customer claims in this case, Mr. Picard, as the SIPA Trustee, determined that the claimants are customers with claims for securities within the meaning of SIPA. The Trustee further concluded that each customer's "net equity" should be calculated by the "Net Investment Method," crediting the amount of cash deposited by the customer into his or her BLMIS account, less any amounts withdrawn from it.

In re Bernard L. Madoff Inv. Sec. LLC, 654 F.3d 229, 233 (2d Cir. 2011); *see also* Elizabeth Amon, *Madoff Trustee Sets $272 Million Payout, Sept. 15 Record Date,* BLOOMBERG (Sept. 12, 2011, 3:36 AM), available at www.bloomberg.com/news/2011-09-12/jpmorgan-chase-bofa-kkr-madoff-dow-ford-in-court-news.html.

who had zero chance to bail out in time. There are valid reasons to penalize investors who chose to stick with investments that were too good to be true.

I. Red Flags and Black Swans—and Ostriches

> While bad business strategy and bad investment decisions can and do contribute to a company's fall, it is a company's desperate attempt to use accounting tricks to hide bad decisions that often seals its fate.
>
> —Bala G. Dharan, *Enron's Accounting Issues: What Can We Learn to Prevent Future Enrons?*[29]

Hearken back to the first wave of accounting scandals in this century: the Enrons and WorldComs and their ilk. Although an investor would have to have been paying close attention to the financial statements that these companies produced,[30] a savvy investor might have seen some patterns. At some point after Rich Kinder left Enron, all sorts of financial indicators started to go haywire. For example, there weren't any blips in Enron's cash flow from earnings:

> One of the most common measures of earnings quality used by financial analysts, debt-rating agencies, and accounting academics is the so-called accruals, which is the difference between net income and cash flow from operations ("CFO"). Accruals are positive when net income is greater than CFO. When this happens, it usually indicates poor earnings quality issues. Interestingly, Enron was apparently very aware of the importance of CFO for analysts and bond rating agencies. In fact, Enron ensured by whatever means necessary that the annual reported CFO always exceeded the net income . . . .[31]

---

[29] Bala G. Dharan, *Enron's Accounting Issues: What Can We Learn to Prevent Future Enrons?*, in ENRON: CORPORATE FIASCOS AND THEIR IMPLICATIONS 113, 115 (Nancy B. Rapoport & Bala G. Dharan eds., 2004).

[30]

> Enron's loss of investor faith started with the company's 2001 third quarter earnings release on October 16, 2001. As earnings releases go, this one must rank as one of the most misleading. The news release said, in an underlined and capitalized headline, "Enron Reports Recurring Third Quarter Earnings of $0.43 per diluted shares." The headline went on to reaffirm "recurring earnings" for the following year, 2002, of $2.15 per share, a projected increase of 19% from 2001. But an investor had to dig deep into the news release to know that Enron actually lost $618 million that quarter, for a loss of ($0.84) per share. A net loss of $618 million loss was converted to a "recurring net income" of $393 million by conveniently labeling and excluding $1.01 billion of expenses and losses as "non-recurring."

Id.

[31] Bala G. Dharan & William R. Bufkins, *Red Flags in Enron's Reporting of Revenues and Key Financial Measures*, in ENRON: CORPORATE FIASCOS AND THEIR IMPLICATIONS 97, 109 (Nancy B. Rapoport & Bala G. Dharan eds., 2004) (emphasis added); *see also id.* at 110 ("As the data illustrate for the year 2000, Enron reserved almost all of its financial management of cash flow data to the fourth quarter. Similar troubling contrasts in the

To make matters worse, Enron omitted some important information that should have put the stock analysts (and Enron shareholders) on high alert.

> Enron's 2001 third quarter earnings press release, on October 16, 2001, contained another major shortcoming—lack of information about its balance sheet and cash flows. While the company's press release provided information on net income, the company failed to provide a balance sheet. This is inexplicable—we teach in Accounting 101 that the income statement and the balance sheet are interrelated ("articulated") statements. This essentially means that we cannot really prepare one without preparing the other. Not surprisingly, almost every major company's earnings release contains the balance sheet along with its income statement. Financially responsible companies would also provide a cash flow statement. Analysts and investors puzzled with Enron's lack of balance sheet disclosure had to wait until after the markets closed on October 16, 2001, when the senior management disclosed—in response to a question during the earnings conference call—that it had taken a $1.2 billion charge against its shareholders' equity (a balance sheet item), including what was described as a $1 billion correction of an accounting error.[32]

One billion dollars is a heck of an "oops," and investors and analysts who read about this particular "oops" should have dug deeper into how the "error"

---

behavior of Enron's cash flow from operations for Quarters 1–3 and Quarter 4 existed for previous years as well, including 1998 and 1999.").

[32] Bala G. Dharan, *Enron's Accounting Issues: What Can We Learn to Prevent Future Enrons?*, in ENRON: CORPORATE FIASCOS AND THEIR IMPLICATIONS 116.

occurred.[33] I know that accounting is an art, not a science,[34] and high-magnitude errors do occur. But when they do, it's important to make sure that the errors are, well, really errors, rather than lies.

I don't expect normal people[35] to go around scrutinizing company financial statements looking for accounting signals of possible misrepresentation. And part of Enron's collapse was due to the failure of many analysts (and rating agencies)[36]

---

33 Jim Chanos dug deeper into Enron, and he didn't like what he dug up.

> Given that Enron's net income margins had also declined from over 4% of revenue to less than 1%, the negative free cash flows should have been a major red flag for any analyst trying to value Enron's equity. It certainly caught the attention of hedge fund manager Jim Chanos of Kynikos. He was quoted as saying, "No one could explain how Enron actually made money . . . . Not only was Enron surprisingly unprofitable, but its cash flow from operations seemed to bear little resemblance to reported earnings."

Dharan & Bufkins, *Red Flags in Enron's Reporting of Revenues and Key Financial Measures,* in Enron: CORPORATE FIASCOS AND THEIR IMPLICATIONS at 111 (quoting Bethany McLean, *Why Enron Went Bust,* FORTUNE, Dec. 24, 2001, at 58) (footnotes omitted); *see also* Andrew Hill, *Enron: Virtual Company, Virtual Profits,* FT.COM (Feb. 3, 2002), available at http://specials.ft.com/enron/FT3648VA9XC.html ("Enron bolstered profits by booking income immediately on contracts that would take up to 10 years to complete. It shifted debts into partnerships it created and in effect controlled, even though defined by auditors as off balance sheet. It used such entities to manipulate its accounts at the end of each quarter and employed financial derivatives and other complex transactions aggressively to the same end. It masked poorly performing assets with rapid deal-making."). In fact, at some point, we were probably all on notice that financial statements might not be as accurate as they had seemed. *See supra* text accompanying note 20.

34 *See, e.g.,* Matthew J. Barrett, *Enron and Andersen—What Went Wrong and Why Similar Audit Failures Could Happen Again,* in ENRON: CORPORATE FIASCOS AND THEIR IMPLICATIONS at 158 ("Accounting remains an art, not a science, which requires enterprises, and their auditors, to exercise professional judgment in preparing and auditing financial statements.").

35 Not that accountants are abnormal. They're not any more abnormal than lawyers—not that that's saying much.

36

> Moreover, a thorough inquiry into these dealings also should include the major financial market "gatekeepers" involved with Enron: accounting firms, banks, law firms, and credit rating agencies. Employees of these firms are likely to have knowledge of these transactions.
>
> . . . .
>
> With respect to Enron, all of these gatekeepers have questions to answer about the money they received, the quality of their work, and the extent of their conflicts of interest. . . .
>
> . . . .
>
> Finally, and perhaps most importantly, the three major credit rating agencies—Moody's, Standard & Poor's, and Fitch/IBCA—received substantial, but as yet undisclosed, fees from Enron. Yet just weeks prior to Enron's bankruptcy filing—after most of the negative news was out and Enron's stock was trading at just $3 per share—all three agencies still gave investment grade ratings to Enron's debt. The credit rating agencies in particular have benefitted greatly from a web of legal rules that essentially requires securities issuers to obtain ratings from them (and them only), and at the same time protects those agencies from outside competition and liability under the securities law. They are at least partially to blame for the Enron mess.

Frank Partnoy, *Enron and the Derivatives World,* in ENRON: CORPORATE FIASCOS AND THEIR IMPLICATIONS at 177–78.

to question Enron and to publicize their misgivings. Most analysts didn't do enough parsing of Enron's financial statements. But some did.[37]

The key for those of us with little to no accounting background isn't to learn accounting principles. It's to read news stories and ask questions. It's to be skeptical when things look too good to be true. When a magazine like FORTUNE runs stories like *Is Enron Overpriced?*,[38] that information is available and accessible to all of us. Our choice to ignore accessible information makes us ostriches.[39] And voluntarily becoming an ostrich—a know-nothing—must have consequences.

II. "Haves" and "Have Nots" in Terms of Second Chances

In bankruptcy, we often have the "haves" (e.g., fully secured creditors with collateral that goes up in value over time)[40] and the "have nots" (e.g., unsecured creditors in a bankruptcy in which the estate runs out of money before paying anything to the unsecureds). Even among unsecured creditors, we can also have "haves" and "have nots." The classic "haves" are those unsecured creditors with priority claims that must be paid in full before claims lower down the pecking order get anything.[41]

But there's another way of thinking about this "haves"/"have nots" distinction: on the one hand, there are those unsecured creditors who saw the light at the end of the tunnel, realized that the light was actually an oncoming train,[42] and had a chance to get out of the way before the train hit them; and, on the other hand, there are those who were flattened by the train before they could even see it coming. Those Madoff investors who saw their wildly implausible positive returns were among those who "had" a chance to escape before the Ponzi scheme escalated.[43] They just didn't take it.

---

[37] Jim Chanos and Bethany McLean come to mind. And in the Madoff scandal, so does Harry Markopolos, who tried to alert the SEC to Madoff's shenanigans. *See, e.g.*, Allan Chernoff, *Madoff Whistleblower Blasts SEC,* CNN MONEY, Feb. 24, 2009, available at http://money.cnn.com/2009/02/04/news/newsmakers/madoff_whistleblower/.

[38] Bethany McLean, *Is Enron Overpriced?,* FORTUNE, Mar. 5, 2001, available at http://money.cnn.com/2006/01/13/news/companies/enronoriginal_fortune/index.htm.

[39] My dad, who is a chemist, said that the most difficult part of any experiment is to analyze the parts that go "right," and to ask yourself if they went "right" because they were right, or because of luck or another factor.

[40] Unlike our home's value. Now that was a black swan that swam over, bit us hard, hit us with its wings, and then jumped up and down on our backs before it flew off, chuckling to itself.

[41] For the distribution scheme in bankruptcy, see 11 U.S.C.A. § 507 (Westlaw 2012).

[42] "The light at the end of the tunnel is just the light of an oncoming train." Robert Lowell Quotes, goodreads, www.goodreads.com/author/quotes/36912.Robert_Lowell (last visited Dec. 18, 2011).

[43] The trick, as my buddy Jessica Gabel has pointed out, is in figuring out where to draw the line between the "had-a-chance-to-get-outs" and the "never-could-have-had-a-clue" folks. Those are subjective decisions,

Few real investments only appreciate in value.[44] My husband and I have a few. Our joint savings account, with its measly interest rate, is one. Our CDs and T-bills are others. All of these types of investments, though, are exceptionally low-risk, and their low returns reflect that low risk.

But I can't think of a single investment based on the stock market that always makes a profit. And the[45] reason that I can't think of one is that I know that, in every good investment, profits ebb and flow. I don't expect every quarterly return to show steady growth, especially not in the double-digits. I know that an all-growth, all-the-time return isn't even a black swan. It's a plaid one.[46]

So the very wealthy people[47] who begged and pleaded with Bernie Madoff to handle their investments, who gave him their money in exchange for the faux double-digit returns on their investments, and who bought into the idea that Madoff "knew" the market, should have known that something was peculiar. Those very wealthy people had access to all sorts of other advisors who could have questioned the Madoff investment strategy. Those selfsame very wealthy people could have used their leverage to ask Madoff for more information. They had a chance to get out of the train tunnel. They didn't.[48]

And because they didn't get out of the train tunnel, their faux profits shouldn't be honored. Irving Picard is correct when he insists that faux profits shouldn't be part of the investors' claims.[49] He's also correct—and fair—when he suggests that, instead, the investors' legitimate claims are limited to only the dollar

---

and based on how things are going right now in the Southern District of New York, those decisions may well depend on which judge draws the case.

44 *Cf. supra* notes 40 and 42.

45 Other reasons might include a lack of knowledge or a failure of imagination, but I'm not going to explore either of those two in this Article.

46 I'm reasonably certain that no plaid swans exist, except perhaps in law school hypotheticals.

47 During Madoff's sentencing, there were several references to middle-class investors who had been harmed by his actions. *See, e.g.*, Benjamin Weiser, *Judge Explains 150-Year Sentence for Madoff*, N.Y. TIMES, June 28, 2011, available at www.nytimes.com/2011/06/29/nyregion/judge-denny-chin-recounts-his-thoughts-in-bernard-madoff-sentencing.html?pagewanted=all; Diana B. Henriques, *Madoff is Sentenced to 150 Years for Ponzi Scheme*, N.Y. TIMES, June 29, 2009, available at www.nytimes.com/2009/06/30/business/30madoff.html?scp=1&sq=madoff%20sentencing&st=cse; Tomoeh Murakami Tse, *Madoff Sentenced to 150 Years*, WASH. POST, June 30, 2009, www.washingtonpost.com/wp-dyn/content/article/2009/06/29/AR2009062902015.html. I'm not as sure that middle-class investors had easy access to the types of advisors who could have warned their clients about Madoff's red flags, but, based on seeing the type of research that my husband does before investing, it's possible that people other than the very wealthy could have figured out the warning signs, too.

48 It breaks my heart that Elie Wiesel's foundation was one of the investors.

49 *See supra* text accompanying note 28.

amounts that they paid into Madoff's fund.[50] Any other approach would give the Madoff investors two rewards: their faux profits, and a jump over those unsecured creditors who had no way of discovering that something funny was going on.

What about those Madoff investors who invested near the beginning, before the Ponzi scheme began? Should they get their profits back on the theory that those profits actually were real? That's a tough call that, to me, hinges on whether any of their Madoff returns showed some losses. Fraud that's disguised, such as fraud that depicts realistic profits and losses (even if those figures are lies), is very different from fraud that's out in the open. If those early investors made real money, and the statements that they received from Madoff looked like real (read: normal) investments, they should be able to keep those profits. The line between investors who should keep their profits and investors who should be subject to a clawback of their "profits"[51] is necessarily fuzzy, but it lies somewhere along this continuum:

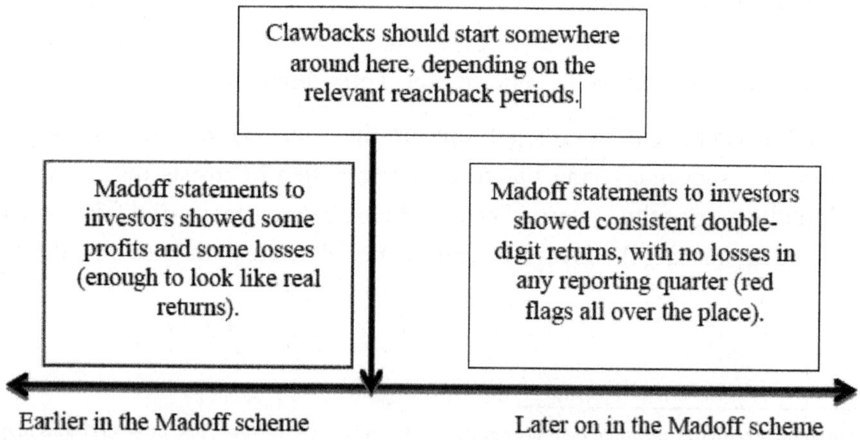

Limiting the reach of the clawbacks to some point at which the investors should have known that they should have been asking Madoff a few questions puts the dividing line between the "haves"/"have nots" near the right place.[52] There's not going to be an exact "aha" moment but, at some point, the investors

50 The trustee, Irving Picard, has argued that investor losses should be the amount deposited into the Madoff firm less any withdrawals, rather than the amount shown on their account statements.

The 2nd Circuit U.S. Court of Appeals in New York agreed.

Andrew Longstreth, *Madoff Trustee's Loss Calculation Method Upheld,* REUTERS, Aug. 16, 2011, available at http://in.reuters.com/article/2011/08/16/madoff-2ndcircuit-idINN1E77F0MU20110816.

51 I'm putting the fake "profits" in quotes to distinguish them from the real profits.

52 The exact right place is defined by the relevant statutes of limitations. There will always be some people who luck out by being on the good side of a statute of limitation.

really should have known. My conclusion puts me squarely in the *Merkin* camp[53] and not the *Katz* camp,[54] mostly because I don't believe that the safe harbor of section 546(e) is a slam-dunk—and it's definitely not a question of law, to be decided before any evidence gets introduced.[55] Without a safe harbor defense, we're back to the "what did they know and when did they know it" inquiry notice issue.

III. Can We Tell the Real Light at the End of the Tunnel From the Oncoming Train?

Madoff sure seems to have known what he was doing. He cultivated the right people (mostly rich ones), made them yearn for a scarce resource (letting him invest their money), and played into the natural human tendency to want to believe that they can beat the odds (with fake, double-digit, positive returns on phantom money). He lived the kind of lavish lifestyle that most of us will never know, but that most of us wouldn't mind having.[56] Who wouldn't want to have hung out with him in his heyday?

And it wasn't just Madoff. News of the Allan Stanford Ponzi scheme was roughly contemporaneous with the Madoff scandal's news,[57] and there are allegations that Société Générale ignored some of Stanford's red flags.[58] There are more schemes out there that we haven't yet discovered, and there will be others that will begin when the Madoff scandal dies down. There will be large-scale ones and small ones. And we'll probably keep on letting ourselves get duped.

Humans (even really, really smart ones) have an almost unlimited capacity to fool ourselves, and as Nassim Taleb has pointed out, one of the best ways to fool ourselves is to assume that what we know is all that there is to know—that because all we've seen are white swans, no other types of swans could possibly exist. Add

---

53 *See* Picard v. Merkin (*In re* Bernard L. Madoff Inv. Sec., LLC), 11 MC 0012(KMW), 2011 WL 3897970 (S.D.N.Y. Aug. 31, 2011).

54 *See* Picard v. Katz, 462 B.R. 447 (S.D.N.Y. 2011).

55 *See* 35B C.J.S. Fed. Civ. P. § 1158 ("A plaintiff's motion for summary judgment must be denied if affirmative defenses raise matters, which, if proved, may possibly preclude a judgment in favor of the plaintiff as a matter of law.").

56 Except for the go-to-prison part, and the bankruptcy part, and the being-subject-to-lawsuits part.

57 *See, e.g.*, Press Release, Sec. & Exch. Comm'n, SEC Charges R. Allen Stanford, Stanford International Bank for Multi-Billion Dollar Investment Scheme (Feb. 17, 2009), available at www.sec.gov/news/press/2009/2009-26.htm.

58 *See* Michael Rothfeld, *Bank Probe in Stanford Case: Prosecutors Are Investigating Whether Societe Generale Ignored Suspicious Transactions,* WALL ST. J., Sept. 16, 2011, available at http://online.wsj.com/article/SB10001424053111904491704576572940023060.

to human nature a modern lessening of our ability to think critically, and you get the recipe for the next round of Ponzi ripoffs.

So, critical thinking is key. At a time when we're questioning the quality of our educational system, I hear a lot about how our students can't write well and how hard it is to encourage them to go into math and science. That scares me. We need good writers, and good writing calls for clear analytical thinking. We need mathematicians, because we need people who understand how numbers relate to each other. And we need scientists, because we need people who are naturally curious about how things work and who want to find out what we don't yet know. We need people who want to ask "why."

We even need lawyers, not just to chase after Ponzi artists, but because good lawyers are always asking "what if" something might happen. Good lawyers are trained to think about black swans. Having a healthy dose of skepticism keeps us thinking about everything from "what if one of the parties wants to breach a contract this way?" to "how do we know that the other side really produced everything that we requested?"

Yet there were lawyers and business people and writers who bought into Madoff's fraud.[59] Natural curiosity, a facility with numbers, and analytical ability only work when someone with those talents uses them. Maybe the latest round of scandals will sharpen our focus, at least for a while. The clawbacks from Ponzi investors might get our attention, at least for a while. Ultimately, though, we have to keep reminding ourselves that there are black swans in the world. We've already proven that there are ostriches.

NOTES

This article focuses not just on those who perpetrated massive frauds but on those who were on the other side of those frauds: the victims. How persuasive is the argument that some of Madoff's victims should have known that they were being duped because it is impossible for stock market investments to show only positive returns over time? And if you believe that argument, where would you draw the line between the innocent investors and those who should have known better? At what point is someone who works in the investment arena obligated to speak up when the results are simply too good to be true? What effect, if any, did the sizable sales commissions that everyone was receiving for putting clients into the Madoff funds

[59] The list included a law dean, some universities, several prominent business people, and Elie Wiesel's foundation. *See* Henry Blodgett, *Bernie Madoff's Victims,* BUS. INSIDER, Dec. 8, 2008, available at www.business insider.com/2008/12/bernie-madoff-hosed-client-list.

contribute to a desire to look the other way? Should a person's education matter? A person's age? The size of a person's bank account? Should rich people get less of a "free pass" on gullibility than poor people should? What about the middle class? If someone's been burned once already by being the victim of a Ponzi scheme and he invests in a second Ponzi scheme—but early on, before anyone can realize that the investment *is* a Ponzi scheme—should he get the same percentage recovery as someone who's never been burned before?

PART III

Examples from the Business World

The last several years have provided us with what the movie *Top Gun* (1986) called a "target-rich environment." So many possible examples, so little space in the book. So we chose three different examples: General Motors's ignition switch failures, Volkswagen's emissions-rigging scandal, and Wells Fargo's decision to gin up hundreds upon hundreds of false customer accounts.

We chose the story of General Motors, as told through Anton Valukas's *Report to Board of Directors of General Motors Company Regarding Ignition Switch Recalls,* because the report gives you a feel for what happens when information is held in silos, rather than being accessible across departments. We also wanted to show you what happens when there are multiple small, bad decisions that add up to some very large mistakes. In a way, the decisions made by General Motors reminded us of some of the decisions listed in *Enron,* Titanic, *and* The Perfect Storm (Chapter 2). You never know how one misguided decision might snuggle up with countless others, leading to disaster.

We chose Volkswagen in part because it represents not a failure of omission (in GM, some of the necessary information failed to get to the right people at the right time) but a deliberate decision to create a workaround for emissions testing. We included both Trope & Ressler's *Mettle Fatigue: VW's Single-Point-of-Failure Ethics* and the VW plea bargain because we wanted to demonstrate some of the consequences when people commit deliberate fraud. Put an asterisk next to our Volkswagen segment, because we're going to do a compare-and-contrast in the next chapter.

And we chose Wells Fargo because we simply can't believe that the 5,300 employees who ended up getting fired for the fake customer accounts all woke up one day and said, "you know what I'd like to do, just for the fun of it, is to saddle real humans with fake bank accounts." The story of Wells Fargo keeps getting worse. In the fall of 2017, there were yet more news stories about Wells Fargo creating up to 3.5 million fake accounts, news stories about Wells Fargo forcing customers with car loans to buy unnecessary car insurance, and a ruling by a federal judge saying that a shareholder derivative suit against 15 officers and directors could proceed. One thing that you might want to note is how easy it is for bigwigs to want to blame lower-ranking employees. Here's a hint for you when you're in a leadership role: if you find yourself blaming someone, oh, three or four rows down in an organizational chart, spend some time considering whether you might have inadvertently triggered that employee's behavior.

Here's what you should have learned from this book, thus far: corporate scandals are going to keep occurring because some people in positions of power are going to make bad, self-dealing decisions—possibly because they're bad people, and probably because humans are hard-wired to fool themselves. One of the ways that people fool themselves is by shaping their behavior to whatever their organization rewards. (If you've ever wondered why professors spend more time researching and writing than we do teaching, it's because the reward structures—at least at research universities—favor research over teaching. Think about *that* the next time you look for a professor outside of office hours.)

Internal incentives played a role in all three of these scandals, and we'd like you to figure out for yourselves what those incentives were at GM, VW, and Wells Fargo. We're willing to bet that you're going to find a lot of similarities.

CHAPTER 8

GM—Valukas Report*

Anton R. Valukas

I. Introduction

In the fall of 2002, General Motors ("GM")[1] personnel made a decision that would lead to catastrophic results—a GM engineer chose to use an ignition switch in certain cars that was so far below GM's own specifications that it failed to keep the car powered on in circumstances that drivers could encounter, resulting in moving stalls on the highway as well as loss of power on rough terrain a driver might confront moments before a crash. Problems with the switch's ability to keep the car powered on were known within GM's engineering ranks at the earliest stages of its production, although the circumstances in which the problems would occur were perceived to be rare. From the switch's inception to approximately 2006, various engineering groups and committees considered ways to resolve the problem. However, those individuals tasked with fixing the problem—sophisticated engineers with responsibility to provide consumers with safe and reliable automobiles—did not understand one of the most fundamental consequences of the switch failing and the car stalling: the airbags would not deploy. The failure of the switch meant that drivers were without airbag protection at the time they needed it most. This failure, combined with others documented below, led to devastating consequences: GM has identified at least 54 frontal-

* Anton R. Valukas, *Report to Board of Directors of General Motors Company Regarding Ignition Switch Recalls* (May 29, 2014), available at http://www.beasleyallen.com/webfiles/valukas-report-on-gm-redacted.pdf (obviously not privileged any more).

1 Except as otherwise specifically noted, the term "GM" is used throughout this Report as follows. When reference is made to GM prior to July 10, 2009, the reference is to General Motors Corporation. On June 1, 2009, General Motors Corporation filed a Chapter 11 bankruptcy petition in the United States Bankruptcy Court for the Southern District of New York. On July 5, 2009, that court approved the sale of substantially all of the assets of General Motors Corporation lo an entity that became known as General Motors Company. That sale closed on July 10, 2009. When reference is made to GM from and after July 10, 2009, the reference is to General Motors Company, the purchaser of the assets.

impact crashes, involving the deaths of more than a dozen individuals, in which the airbags did not deploy as a possible result of the faulty ignition switch.

The below-specification switch approved in 2002 made its way into a variety of vehicles, including the Chevrolet Cobalt. Yet GM did not issue a recall for the Cobalt and other cars until 2014, and even then the initial recall was incomplete. GM personnel's inability to address the ignition switch problem for over 11 years is a history of failures.

While GM heard over and over from various quarters—including customers, dealers, the press, and their own employees—that the car's ignition switch led to moving stalls, group after group and committee after committee within GM that reviewed the issue failed to take action or acted too slowly. Although everyone had responsibility to fix the problem, nobody took responsibility. It was an example of what one top executive described as the "GM nod," when everyone nods in agreement to a proposed plan of action, but then leaves the room and does nothing.

A critical factor in GM personnel's initial delay in fixing the switch was their failure to understand, quite simply, how the car was built. GM had specifically designed the airbag system *not* to deploy, in most circumstances, in the event that the ignition switch was turned to Off or Accessory, a deliberate and sensible decision made to prevent passengers from being injured by airbags in parked cars. In 2004, however, GM engineers, faced with a multitude of reports of moving stalls caused by the ignition switch, concluded that moving stalls were not safety issues because drivers could still maneuver the cars; they completely failed to understand that the movement of the switch out of the Run position meant the driver and passengers would no longer have the protection of the airbags. As a result, GM personnel viewed the switch problem as a "customer convenience" issue—something annoying but not particularly problematic—as opposed to the safety defect it was. Once so defined, the switch problem received less attention, and efforts to fix it were impacted by cost considerations that would have been immaterial had the problem been properly categorized in the first instance. Indeed, in this same decade, GM issued hundreds of recalls at great expense (including at times when its financial condition was precarious) because in the great majority of instances, it correctly determined or agreed that the issues that came to its attention implicated safety and demanded prompt action. But in the case of the Cobalt, it did not do so.

From 2004 to 2006, not one of the committees considering a fix for the switch—filled with engineers and business people whose job was to understand how GM's cars were built and how different systems of the car interact—ever reclassified the problem from one of customer convenience to one of safety or demonstrated any sense of urgency in their efforts to fix the switch. GM's Product Investigations group, charged with identifying and remedying safety issues, made the same mistake; it opened and closed an investigation in 2005 in the span of a month, finding no safety issue to be remedied.

As the early committees failed to fix the problem, accidents and fatalities in which airbags did not deploy began coming to GM personnel's attention, including GM's in-house counsel and the engineers who worked with them. Those outside GM, including, in 2007, a trooper from the Wisconsin Safety Patrol and a research team from Indiana University, figured out the connection between the switch and the airbag non-deployment. Yet, GM personnel did not.

From 2007 on, as years passed and fatalities mounted, engineers investigating the non-deployments and attempting to understand their cause were neither diligent nor incisive. The investigators failed to search for or obtain critical documents within GM's own files, or publicly available documents that helped non-GM personnel make the connection between the switch and airbag non-deployment. Investigators, convinced that the cause of the airbag non-deployments was a complicated mystery still to be unraveled, failed to consider fully the simple, and ultimately correct, cause: the switch that caused cars to stall was turning the power off and disabling the airbags just as cars were about to crash. Along the way, the investigators were misled by the GM engineer who approved the below-specification switch in the first place; he had actually changed the ignition switch to solve the problem in later model years of the Cobalt, but failed to document it, told no one, and claimed to remember nothing about the change. While stumped by the inability to determine why different model year Cobalts performed differently, the investigating engineers nonetheless failed to take certain basic investigative steps, such as taking apart both poorly and properly functioning switches to compare the two. In 2013, an outside expert working for a plaintiff's attorney took apart two switches and quickly found the cause it took GM years to determine.

Throughout the entire 11-year odyssey, there was no demonstrated sense of urgency, right to the very end. The officials overseeing the potential fixes and investigations did not set timetables, and did not demand action. When, in December 2013, GM's recall committee initially met to discuss whether to recall Cobalts and other vehicles with the switch, members of the committee deferred the decision for another six weeks to gather yet more information, in part because the presentation provided to them failed to alert them to fatalities.

While the issue of the ignition switch passed through numerous hands at GM, from engineers to investigators to lawyers, nobody raised the problem to the highest levels of the company. As a result, those in the best position to demand quick answers did not know questions needed to be asked.

As a whole, from beginning to end, the story of the Cobalt is one of numerous failures leading to tragic results for many. As discussed below, many individuals have substantial responsibility for the delay in recalling the Cobalt. These individuals, as well as the GM committees and groups that had responsibility for the Cobalt, failed to demand action in the face of mounting injuries and fatalities, to make themselves or others accountable, and to marshal the information and expertise at their disposal to solve a problem that brought harm to GM's customers. This report traces the history of the ignition switch, from GM's design and production of the ignition switch to its belated recall in 2014, ultimately proposing recommendations to help avoid such a tragedy from ever occurring again.

II. Summary of Facts

Jenner & Block LLP ("Jenner") was directed on March 10, 2014, to determine how and why it took so long for GM to recall the Cobalt.[2] Jenner was given unfettered access to witnesses and documents, and Jenner was asked for an unvarnished account. Jenner was asked to complete this task on a very expedited timetable, recognizing, in this instance, it was critical to find the truth quickly rather than explore every possible avenue.[3] The evidence showed:

From the outset, the Cobalt ignition switch had significant problems that were known to GM personnel. Designed to be a new generation ignition switch first introduced in the Saturn Ion, the switch was so plagued with problems that the engineer who designed it labeled it then "the switch from hell." The prototype switch performed so poorly that its entire electrical concept needed to be redesigned. Upon completion, the redesigned switch failed to meet the mechanical specifications for torque—that is, it required less force to turn the key than the designers had mandated. Erroneously believing that this low torque would not affect the car's performance, an engineer—Ray DeGiorgio—approved going into production with a deviation from GM specifications. He permitted the switch to

---

2 In this report, we sometimes use "Cobalt" to refer to not just that model, but also other Delta and Kappa platform vehicles that shared the same ignition switch and that are covered by the ignition switch recall. These other models include the Chevrolet HHR, the Pontiac G5 and Solstice, and the Saturn Ion and Sky.

3 As part of this investigation, review of documents (discussed in greater detail below) continues on a daily basis. To the extent that review yields additional relevant documents that materially change the contents of this report, such information will be provided to the Board.

be produced with the low torque that would ultimately lead to accidents in which the airbags did not deploy.

As it turned out, when finally put into production, the redesigned switch initially failed for reasons entirely unrelated to the low torque. The ignition switch often would not start the car in cold weather, causing a huge volume of customer complaints and a focus on fixing the switch so that cars would start.

But starting the car was not the only issue. The low torque required to turn the ignition switch led to its own set of problems. The Cobalt (and the Saturn Ion before it) was stalling at highway speeds. From the outset, GM employees, customers, and members of the automotive press found repeatedly that they would hit the key fob or keychain with their knee, and the car would turn off. GM received some of these reports before the Cobalt's launch, and others afterwards. There were scathing reviews in the press. There were customer complaints describing the moving stalls and customers' safety concerns. The complaints were documented in GM electronic forms as a part of GM's standard vehicle improvement process, and were duly considered by multiple committees of engineers and business people, including those with oversight over entire vehicle lines.

These processes failed to resolve the issue. The teams of experienced GM engineers on the committees that considered the Cobalt ignition switch did not recognize that their colleagues had designed the car so that turning the key to Accessory or Off would disable the airbags.[4] As a result and because numerous engineers believed that consumers could still safely maneuver cars that had stalled, the engineers categorized the problem as an issue of customer satisfaction, not safety. The decision not to categorize the problem as a safety issue directly impacted the level of urgency with which the problem was addressed and the effort to resolve it.

The problem of moving stalls and the ignition switch continued throughout 2005, and was described both within GM and in the media. In May and June 2005, reviewers from two newspapers, including the *New York Times*, wrote about how they or a family member had inadvertently turned a Cobalt off with their knees. One of GM's main safety lawyers e-mailed a colleague trying to marshal evidence for the press that the risk was "remote" and "inconsequential." He wrote that he did not want to be criticized for failing to "defend a brand new launch." GM employees were upfront about the company's view about the complaints they had

[4] A single engineer involved in the review process told Jenner interviewers that he raised this issue at the time, but neither contemporaneous documents nor interviews of his colleagues corroborated his account.

heard about moving stalls; they informed the *New York Times* of their view that moving stalls in the Cobalt did not pose a safety problem.

At the same time, a different group of engineers within GM, the senior engineers charged with dealing with safety issues, attempted to determine whether the problem could be easily replicated. The Director of Product Investigations, GM's group of safety investigators, among others, succeeded in turning off the car with her knee. A more junior GM safety investigation engineer was tasked with investigating the issue, which included compiling a file of customer complaints, of which she found a number. The safety engineer presented the issue to a committee charged with reviewing such matters, and the committee closed the safety investigation with no further action, also ignorant of the fact that turning the ignition switch to Accessory disabled the airbags with potentially catastrophic results.

In 2005, various committees within GM considered proposed fixes, but those were rejected as too costly—a consideration that would not have mattered had the problem been considered a safety concern. Instead of fixing the ignition switch, in December 2005, GM sent a notice to dealers (a "Technical Service Bulletin," "bulletin," or "TSB") warning that customers might complain of ignition cut-offs caused by low ignition torque, counseling that customers remove heavy items from their key rings, and offering an insert to the key that would reduce the likelihood that the ignition switch would rotate inadvertently. That bulletin did not refer to the problem as "stalling," however, precisely because GM believed customers might associate stalling with a safety problem. Only a customer who had already experienced a stall and who came into a dealer to complain would get information about the proposed solutions. Other customers would remain unaware of the problem, as well as GM's proposed solutions.

In 2007, two years after GM closed its initial safety investigation, entities outside GM began paying attention as Cobalts crashed, airbags did not deploy, and fatalities occurred. In April 2007, a trooper of the Wisconsin Safety Patrol (Wisconsin's state police force) published an accident reconstruction report on a Cobalt fatality in which the airbags did not deploy. The trooper pointed out (a) that the ignition switch appeared to be in Accessory; (b) that GM had issued a bulletin to dealers warning that low torque could lead to inadvertent turning of the ignition switch (he found the bulletin on the NHTSA website); and (c) that airbags would not deploy when the ignition switch was turned to the Accessory position. Although an electronic copy of this report resided in GM's files as of 2007, no GM engineer investigating the ignition switch reported seeing it until 2014.

Over the years, Indiana University's Transportation Research Center and two plaintiffs' experts would also locate GM's Technical Service Bulletin and reach the same, correct conclusion regarding the connection between the ignition switch and airbag non-deployment. Within GM, however, the investigation languished. In 2007, a Field Performance Assessment ("FPA") engineer, John Sprague, whose job was to support GM's products liability defense team, was asked to track incidents of Cobalt airbag non-deployments in a spreadsheet. Sprague was given directions neither about a deliverable nor a time frame, highlighting several themes that permeated GM personnel's failed efforts to understand or solve the problem: lack of urgency, lack of ownership of the issue, lack of oversight, and lack of understanding of the consequences of the problem.

The spreadsheet simply grew. Yet Sprague was not aware of important GM records of prior problems with the ignition switch (including the bulletin sent to dealers and the prior work done to propose solutions). Over time, however, through his work on various litigation matters, Sprague and his colleagues in FPA came to recognize a pattern of non-deployment of airbags in the Cobalt and hypothesized about a cause related to the electrical connections in the ignition switch.

One of the observations Sprague made was that the non-deployments stopped in Model Year ("MY") 2008 Cobalts. Sprague wondered whether there had been some kind of part change at that time that would explain why the non-deployments had ended. He was correct. In 2006, Ray DeGiorgio, the engineer who had approved the below-specification ignition switch originally, had authorized a change in the ignition switch that increased the torque required to turn the key. But when asked in 2009 and in the years that followed whether the ignition switch had changed, DeGiorgio said that it had not. To this day, in informal interviews and under oath, DeGiorgio claims not to remember authorizing the change to the ignition switch or his decision, at the same time, not to change the switch's part number. DeGiorgio's deliberate decision not to change the part number prevented investigators for years from learning what had actually taken place.

By 2011, outside counsel, privy to the FPA engineers' data, had repeatedly warned GM in-house counsel that GM could be accused of egregious conduct due to its failure to address the problem of airbag non-deployment in the Cobalt, and that such conduct might subject GM to liability, including punitive damages. Seeing the pattern of accidents regarding non-deployments, in 2011, GM in-house lawyers called for a meeting with engineers and asked for the investigation to be taken over by GM's Product Investigations unit, which was charged with investigating potential safety issues. It was assigned to an investigator named Brian Stouffer. Once again, the investigation moved with no sense of urgency. When he began the investigation, Stouffer was handed a dossier on the matter that included information about the prior investigations into moving stalls, and he soon obtained the Technical Service Bulletin. In 2012, Stouffer was also given the 2007 Indiana University report and a report from a plaintiff's expert, both laying out the correct answer. Stouffer, however, discounted those reports, believing they did not answer the question before him, and, in doing so, ultimately prolonged the resolution of the problem. Among other things, he could not explain why MY* 2008 Cobalts did not have a problem with airbag non-deployment, having also been misled by DeGiorgio's statement that the same ignition switch was in early and later model year vehicles.

In the ensuing two years, Stouffer's investigation proceeded slowly and without significant progress, ultimately becoming "stuck" by early 2013. It was only when a plaintiff's expert in a products liability case compared switches from pre-and post-MY 2008 Cobalts by x-raying them—something GM investigators had never done—that GM engineers came to understand that the early model year Cobalts had a different ignition switch than the later model year vehicles, and that the switch used in the early model years suffered from torque well below GM's specifications.

Despite learning about what GM's outside counsel called a "bombshell" in April 2013, it was not until February 2014 that GM issued the first recall. In the interim, various additional investigative steps were taken that eventually confirmed what the plaintiff's expert had already made clear. Eventually, in December 2013, the proposed recall made its way to the Executive Field Action Decision Committee (the "EFADC"), the GM committee that considers recalls and whose members include three GM vice presidents, including its chief engineer. Still, no action was taken, because the chief engineer questioned the data demonstrating the problem and EFADC members were not presented with fatality information and therefore felt no sense of urgency to make a decision. It was not until approximately six weeks later that GM instituted its first recall of the ignition switch, and even that recall was incomplete based on the failure of GM personnel to obtain and present all relevant information to the EFADC decision-makers.

* Editors' Note: "MY" means "model year."

III. Background

A. General Motors

GM is one of the largest engineering and manufacturing enterprises in the world.[5] For 77 years until 2007, and again in 2011, GM sold more cars worldwide than any other company.[6] In 2013 alone, GM produced more than 9.7 million vehicles worldwide,[7] generating revenues of $155.4 billion and profits of S3.8 billion.[8]

GM employs more than 210,000 employees in 396 facilities located in 30 countries.[9] As a result, the most senior GM executives have literally tens of thousands of employees working under them. GM also has 21,000 dealers worldwide.[10]

Along with its strategic partners, GM produces cars and trucks through 11 brands worldwide, four in North America.[11] (Prior to its bankruptcy, GM had several other brands in North America.[12]) In 2013 alone, GM's brands sold over 9 million vehicles worldwide, in more than 120 countries.[13] Of course, older models also remain on the road, meaning that the total number of vehicles currently in production vastly understates the full number and variety of GM vehicles on the road at any given time.

Each vehicle is itself a composite of numerous subsystems and component parts. A car includes a chassis with suspension, wheels, powertrain (composed of the drivetrain, engine and transmission), a cooling system, an electrical system, a

---

5 *The 2013 Industry Week 1000,* INDUSTRY WEEK, at 1–2, *available at* www.industryweek.com/resources/iw1000/2013 (last accessed May 27, 2014) [DOC ID 000240753003].

6 Greg Gardner, *GM Is World's Largest Automaker Once More,* DETROIT FREE PRESS (Jan. 20, 2012), at 1 [DOC ID 000240753006]; Christine Tierney and Robert Snell, *Toyota Overtakes GM in Global Sales,* DETROIT NEWS (Jan. 22, 2008), at 1 [DOC ID 000240786002].

7 Press Release, GM Delivered 9.7 Million Vehicles Globally in 2013, General Motors Company (Jan. 14, 2014), *available at* http://rnedia.gm.com/rnedfa/us/en/gm/news.detail.html/content/Pages/news/us/en/2014/Jan/0114_2013gm-global-sales.html (last accessed May 29, 2014) [DOC ID 000240753002].

8 General Motors Company, 2013 Annual Report, at 14 [DOC ID 000240786006].

9 Our Company, General Motors Company, at 1, *available at* www.gm.com/company/aboutGM/our_company.hunl (last accessed May 27, 2014) [DOC ID 000240753007].

10 Our Company, General Motors Company, at 1, *available at* www.gm.com/company/aboutGM/our_company.html (last accessed May 27, 2014) [DOC ID 000240753007].

11 Our Company, General Motors Company, at 2, *available at* www.gm.com/company/abourGM/our_company.html (last accessed May 27, 2014) [DOC ID 000240753007]; General Motors Company, 2013 Annual Report, at 20 [DOC ID 000240786006].

12 *See* General Motors Corp., 2007 Annual Report, at 63 [DOC ID 000236388003].

13 General Motors Company, 2013 Annual Report, at 12 [DOC ID 000240786006]; Our Company, General Motors Company, *available at* www.gm.com/company/aboutGM/our_company.html (last accessed May 27, 2014) [DOC ID 000240753007].

fuel system, an HVAC and climate control system, steering and braking systems, and an instrument panel and controls. Vehicles have become increasingly complicated over time, and now also routinely include power systems that operate locks, windows, doors, trunks, and headlights, as well as sophisticated computerized systems controlling advanced safety features such as airbags, anti-lock brakes, electronic stability control, lane departure warnings, and parking assist, not to mention additional features like cruise control and web-based navigation and infotainment systems. Counting at the smallest possible units, a single car can have literally tens of thousands of parts—all of which must be manufactured or sourced by GM to make each of the more than 100 vehicles in its product line.[14] To fashion these parts into a car and sell it in the market, GM's employees perform a variety of functions, starting with research and development and proceeding progressively to design, manufacturing, purchasing (component parts), marketing, sales, and customer service.

B. GM's Small Car Product Line

In the early 2000s, GM looked to develop a successful small car line to supplement sagging sales of its trucks and SUVs. As late as 2004, truck and SUV sales represented 60 percent of the vehicles sold by GM in the United States and represented a substantially higher profit margin per vehicle than smaller cars.[15] As gasoline prices escalated, however, sales of trucks and SUVs suffered in the United States.[16] This decreased demand for large vehicles made the success of smaller, more efficient cars important to the Company's financial performance.[17] Sales of smaller, fuel-efficient cars were also important to GM's ability to meet federal emissions regulations.[18]

1. The "Delta Platform" of Vehicles

In developing vehicles, including its new small car product line in the 2000s, GM grouped vehicles into "platforms." Vehicles in the same platform shared certain base architectural design elements.[19] The "Delta Platform" of vehicles

---

[14] *See* John Stark, *Product Lifecycle Management: 21st Century Paradigm for Product Realization* (Springer 2006), at 23 ("There are over 20,000 parts in a car.").

[15] General Motors Corp., 2004 Annual Report, at 47 [DOC ID 000236389003]; General Motors Corp., 2005 Annual Report, at 5, 45, 48 [DOC ID 000236388002].

[16] Claudia Hirsch, *Reality Check: US Auto Brands Fizzle in June, Dealers Say,* MARKET NEWS INTERNATIONAL (June 30. 2006) at 1, 2 [DOC ID 000236387022].

[17] *See* General Motors Corp., 2005 Annual Report, at 52 [DOC ID 0002.36388002] (expressing efforts to "reallocat[e] capital and engineering to support more fuel-efficient vehicles").

[18] *See* General Motors Corp., 2005 Annual Report, at 30 [DOC ID 000236388002]; Gap Assessment to Toyota Presentation [Draft] (2005), at 19 [DOC ID 000240785002].

[19] J&B Interview of Janies Zito, May 14, 2014.

included the Saturn Ion, Chevrolet Cobalt, Chevrolet HHR, and Pontiac G5.[20] Certain model years of each of these vehicles contained the ignition switch that led to GM's recalls in 2014 (hereinafter "Ignition Switch"):[21]

1. *Saturn Ion:* The Saturn Ion was the first car in the Delta Platform to launch. It was a small sedan, first offered in MY 2003.[22] GM subsequently aimed to improve the Ion by integrating design elements from the Cobalt.[23] Production ended with MY 2007.[24]

2. *Chevrolet Cobalt:* The Chevrolet Cobalt launched in MY 2005.[25] It replaced the Cavalier, but was designed to have a higher price point than its predecessor.[26] GM ended production of the Cobalt in June 2010.[27]

3. *Chevrolet HHR:* The Chevrolet HHR was a station wagon, launched in MY 2006, and offered through MY 2011.[28]

4. *Pontiac G5:* The Pontiac G5 was first introduced in Canada for MY 2005, and was released in the U.S. in MY 2007. The 2010 model was the last sold to the public.[29]

The Ignition Switch used in the Delta Platform was also used in certain model years of Kappa Platform vehicles—the Saturn Sky and Pontiac Solstice:[30]

---

20 GM Program Architecture Brand (March 2010), at 3–4 [DOC ID 000058109415]. The Della Platform also included the Opel Astra and the Opel Zafira, *see id.* at 1. Neither car was sold in the United States.

21 EFADC Power Point Presentation (Dec. 17, 201.3), at 7 [DOC ID 000001788022: GMHEC000002 899-2947].

22 *See Ion Replaces S,* MOTOR TREND (Jan. 2002), at 1 [DOC ID 000236387010]; Tony Swan, *Preview: Saturn Ion: Coot? Yes. Electrifying? We'll See,* CAR AND DRIVER, vol. 48, no. 2 (Oct. 2002), at 2 [DOC ID 000236387030].

23 Ed Garsten. *GM Thinks Big With Small Cobalt; New Model Seeks to Turn Tide of Losses.* DETROIT NEWS (June 15, 2004), at 3 [DOC ID 000236387023].

24 GM Program Architecture Brand (March 2010), at 5 [DOC ID 000058109415].

25 GM Program Architecture Brand (March 2010), at 4 [DOC ID 000058109415].

26 Ed Garsten. *GM Thinks Big With Small Cobalt: New Model Seeks to Turn Tide of Losses.* DETROIT NEWS (June 15, 2004), at 1 [DOC ID 000236387023].

27 Mike Floyd, *Just Cruze-in': GM Drip-Feeds More Info on Baby Chevy,* MOTOR TREND, vol. 62, no. 2 (Feb. 2010), at 17 [DOC ID 000236387014].

28 GM Program Architecture Brand (March 2010) [DOC ID 000058109415].

29 GM Program Architecture Brand (March 2010) [DOC ID 000058109415].

30 J&B Interview of Raymond DeGiorgio, March 14, 2014: J&B Interview of Alberto Manzor, March 21. 2014: *see also, e.g.,* EFADC PowerPoint Presentation (Feb. 24. 2014), at 2–4 [DOC ID 000001731002; GM HEC000002735-38]; e-mail from Joint Hendler, GM, to various GM employees, including Lori Queen (Sept. 28, 2005) [DOC ID 000012168192; GMHEC000219123].

1. *Saturn Sky:* The Saturn Sky was a "roadster," initially released for MY 2007, and offered through MY 2009.[31]

2. *Pontiac Solstice:* Like the Sky, the Pontiac Solstice was a sports car. The car was introduced for MY 2006, and was offered through MY 2009.[32]

The Ignition Switch was developed as a "corporate common" part, meaning that it was designed to be used in multiple vehicle platforms.[33] This use of one common Ignition Switch across platforms was a way to reduce costs.[34]

2. GM's Marketing of the Cobalt

Lori Queen, who served as the Vehicle Line Executive for small cars beginning in 2001, explained that the Cobalt was meant to be a statement that GM was getting back into the small car game.[35] The Cobalt replaced the Chevy Cavalier in GM's product line-up and represented an effort to debunk the stereotype of GM's small cars as "cheap and cheerful.[36] The Delta Platform—and the Cobalt in particular—was designed to compete against popular mid-market, foreign compact cars like the Toyota Corolla and the Honda Civic.[37] To compete with these foreign models, GM engineers working on the Cobalt were provided additional funds to make the car quieter and smoother for passengers.[38]

GM wanted the Cobalt to be an "aspirational vehicle" to attract drivers looking for a more European touring car feel[39] and directed marketing efforts at young drivers.[40] During the launch of the Cobalt brand, GM held promotional

---

31 GM Program Architecture Brand (March 2010) [DOC ID 000058109415].

32 GM Program Architecture Brand (March 2010) [DOC ID 000058109415].

33 J&B Interview of Chris Berube, April 22, 2014; J&B Interview of Andrew Brenz, April 23, 2014; J&B Interview of Thomas Utter, April 24, 2014; *see also* e-mail from Chris Berube, GM, to Andrew Brenz, GM, and copying Ken Wasmer, GM (Nov. 21, 2004) [DOC ID 000012140259; GMHEC000330211-12].

34 J&B Interview of Thomas Utter, April 24, 2014.

35 J&B Interview of Lori Queen, Marcl1 17, 2014; *see also Review: 2005 Cobalt, GM has Finally Stepped Up to the Plate in the Small-Car Game,* MOTOR TREND (Nov. 2005).

36 J&B Interview of Lori Queen, May 12, 2014.

37 2005 Product Information, 2005 Chevrolet Cobalt (Aug. 1, 2004), at 6 [DOC ID 000233911002]; *see also, e.g.,* 2007 Cobalt Brochure, at 18 [EXPORTSM000000164] (comparing the Cobalt's audio and stereo features with those found in the Toyota Corolla, Honda Civic, and Ford Focus); Ed Garsren, *GM Thinks Big With Small Cobalt; New Model Seeks to Turn Tide of Losses,* Detroit News (June 15, 2004) [DOC ID 000236387023].

38 J&B Interview of Doug Parks, March 18, 2014.

39 J&B Interview of Lori Queen, May 12, 2014.

40 John Hendler, GM, Delta GMXOO I Electrical Content Overview v. 1.4 (April 3, 2001), at 4 [DOC ID 000136777531; GMHEC000485652-5824]; 2009 CY Aveo, Cobalt & HHR Strategic Marketing Plans: Phase I (Nov. 5, 2008), at 22, 25 [DOC ID 000233911040].

events at several popular spring break locations.[41] For the Ion, GM hosted marketing events at nightclubs.[42] GM's marketing efforts bore fruit: the Cobalt enjoyed substantial sales to younger drivers. By the end of 2008, 40 percent of Cobalt Coupe sales were to drivers under 30.[43] The Cobalt Sedan, however, was less popular with young drivers; only 18 percent of sales were to customers under 30.[44]

The release of the Cobalt was met with generally favorable reviews. *Car and Driver* reported that the Cobalt "quietly—very quietly and serenely—prove[s] that when GM decides to build an accomplished car, it can."[45] *Edmunds* complimented the Cobalt for having "materials quality, styling and comfort [that were] all light-years ahead of the Cavalier."[46] But not all reviews were so glowing. For example, *Consumer Reports* complained that although the Cobalt "is an improvement over the dated, outgoing Cavalier, . . . [i]t isn't very agile, and steering is too light at low speeds. . . . Although quick, its engine was noisy and had paltry fuel economy."[47]

In 2005, the Cobalt and other Delta Platform vehicles received substantially positive safety ratings based on crash testing prior to release.[48] Later, in 2011, data from the Insurance Institute for Highway Safety, however, suggested that the MY 2005–08 Cobalt's driver death rate was higher than any four-door vehicle in its class. Only three other vehicles across all classes had higher driver death rates during that period: the Chevy Aveo, the Nissan 350Z, and the Nissan Titan.[49]

---

41 Revolver Marketing Group, *General Motors/Chevrolet National "Cobalt" Brand Launch, available at* http://www.revolvennarketinggroup.com/project/general-motorschevrolet-national-launch-of-the-cobalt-brand/ [DOC ID 000236387003].

42 *Saturn Invites Young New Yorkers to Celebration for ION Launch,* THE AUTO CHANNEL (April 2, 2002), *available at* http://www.theautochannel.com/news/2002/04/02/038119html#.U2l-Rd-pPq8 [DOC ID 000236387008].

43 Cobalt Coupe & Sedan Compares [DOC ID 000233911053].

44 Cobalt Coupe & Sedan Compares [DOC ID 000233911053].

45 Aaron Robinson, *Road Test: Chevrolet Cobalt LS:* Plainly *Good,* CAR AND DRIVER (April 2005), at 101 [DOC ID 000236387028]; *see also id.* ("Is the Cobalt that good? For GM, it's miraculous. . . .").

46 *Full 2005 Chevrolet Cobalt Review,* Edmunds.com, *available at* http://www.edmunds.com/chevrolet/cobalt/2005/#overview-pod-anchor [DOC ID 000236387016].

47 *Chevrolet Cobalt,* CONSUMER REPORTS (May 2005), *available at* http://www.consumerreports.org/cro/cars/past-road-test/small-sedans-505/chevrolet-cob.alt/index.html [DOC ID 000236387002].

48 *See, e.g., Chevrolet Cobalt,* CONSUMER REPORTS (May 2005), *available at* http://www.consumerreports.org/cro/cars/past-road-test/small-sedans-505/chevrolet-cobalt/index.html [DOC ID 000236387002]; James R. Healey, *Cobalt's a little Bit of a Love-Hate Car,* USA Today (March 10, 2005), *available at* http://usatoday30.usatoday.com/money/autos/reviews/llealey/2005-03-10-cobalt_x.html [DOC ID 000240786004].

49 Insurance Institute For Highway Safety, Status Report, vol. 46, no. 5 (June 9, 2011), at 3, *available at* http://www.iihs.org/extemaldata/srdata/docs/sr4605.pdf [DOC ID 000236387004].

3. Cobalt and Delta Platform Sales and Profitability

A 2006 presentation for a meeting of GM's North American Strategy Board reflected that for GM to succeed, the Cobalt needed to be at least a break-even vehicle.[50] And, in fact, the Cobalt and other Delta Platform vehicles enjoyed positive sales results, particularly compared to other GM vehicles at the time. By the end of 2005, the Cobalt was GM's second-best-selling car.[51] In 2006, it was reported that sales of the Cobalt and HHR both "exceeded expectations."[52] In May 2008, while GM's overall sales declined 30 percent compared to the previous year, sales of the Cobalt were up 17.8 percent[53] But retail sales of the Cobalt also were consistently below the retail sales of its predecessor, the Cavalier.[54]

Multiple witnesses characterized the Cobalt and other Delta Platform cars as "cost conscious vehicle[s]" produced on "slim margins."[55] In an effort to boost sales, GM offered steep discounts on its cars—including the Cobalt.[56] The Cobalt was also sold in large volumes to fleet buyers, including daily rental companies, at discounted prices.[57] In both 2005 and 2006, over 60,000 Cobalts were sold to rental companies, which represented over 30 percent of GM's total sales of the Cobalt in those years.[58] By 2010—the Cobalt's last full year on the market—fleet sales reportedly accounted for approximately 60 percent of the Cobalt's sales.[59]

C. GM in the 2000s

The Cobalt was developed against the backdrop of major challenges in the American automobile industry. In the early and mid-2000s, the so-called Big Three—GM, Ford, and Chrysler—all faced financial problems. From 2001 to

---

[50] General Motors North America Strategy Board, Executive Summary, Global Delta DST Review (May 16, 2006), at 7 [GMHEC200031653-65; DOC ID H_01015014].

[51] Staff/Wire Reports, *Cobalt Ranks Second in Sales,* VINDY.COM (Jan. 5, 2006), *available at* http://www4.vindy.com/content/business_tech/372311088812641.php [DOC ID 000236387012].

[52] Daniel Howes, *Building Successes, Not Just Buyouts, Improve GM Chances,* DETROIT NEWS (June 28, 2006) [DOC ID 000236387025].

[53] *Chevy Cobalt Sales Reach Record as GM Safes Plunge,* THE BUSINESS JOURNAL (Youngstown, Ohio) (May 27. 2008), *available at* http://busincssjourualdaily.com/chevy-cobalt-saJes-reacb-record-gm-sales-phmge-2008-5-27 [DOC ID 000236387019].

[54] Seven Year History of Cavalier & Cobalt Retail Sales (July 10, 2009), at 1 [DOC ID 000233911049].

[55] J&B Interview of David Trush, March 17, 2014.

[56] Sharon Silke Carty, *GM Rolls Back Fleet's Prices: Bold Cuts Unprecedented,* USA Today (Jan. 11, 2006), at 3B [DOC ID 000240512008].

[57] Ignition Switch Recall Models—Fleet Counts (May 5, 2014) [DOC ID 000240509002].

[58] Ignition Switch Recall Models—Fleet Counts (May 5, 2014) [DOC ID 000240509002]; 2007 GM Performance Management and Feedback, Brian L. Brown, Chevrolet Cobalt Marketing Manager (July 30, 2007), at 1. [DOC ID 000233911090].

[59] Robert Schoenberger, *Strong Safes of Chevy Cruze Are Fueling Optimism at GM,* CLEVELAND PLAIN DEALER (Feb. 2, 2011), at C1 [DOC ID 000240786005].

2007, GM's global market share for automobiles declined from 15 percent to 13.3 percent.[60] Year-over-year profits for GM Automotive ("GMA") were unstable: falling in 2003, starting to recover in 2004, but then turning into large losses in 2005.[61] In 2005, GM as a whole posted a consolidated net loss of $10.6 billion.[62] By 2007, it was reported that "Ford lost an average of $1,467 on each vehicle it built in North America; GM lost $729 and Chrysler [lost] $412."[63]

In the face of these challenges, all three automakers engaged in efforts to reduce costs by cutting production, pressuring suppliers to lower costs, reducing health care and pension spending, and reducing their workforces.[64] In November 2005, GM announced a major cost-cutting effort. The plans included the shuttering of nine assembly facilities and three service and parts facilities by 2008, and a reduction of more than 30,000 manufacturing jobs.[65] Its manufacturing realignment had a goal of reducing excess assembly capacity by one million units by 2008.[66] Between 2000 and 2008, GM's salaried workforce shrunk by 33 percent, and the number of hourly workers fell by more than 50 percent.[67]

GM also pushed its suppliers to reduce costs. As part of its 2005 initiative to reduce expenses, GM announced a plan to reduce material costs by $1 billion by 2008, and set cost cutting targets for individual parts.[68] The Engineering group was included in GM's cost-cutting efforts. The U.S. engineering organization was consolidated from 11 engineering centers in the United States into one unit.[69] In its 2005 Annual Report, GM announced that Engineering would also be

---

60 General Motors Corp., 2003 Annual Report, at 44 [DOC ID 000236389002]; General Motors Corp., 2007 Annual Report, at 47 [DOC ID 000236388003].

61 General Motors Corp., 2003 Annual Report, at 44 [DOC ID 000236389002]; General Motors Corp., 2004 Annual Report, at 45 [DOC ID 000236388002]: General Motors Corp., 2005 Annual Report, at 46 [DOC ID 000236389003].

62 General Motors Corp., 2005 Annual Report, at 43 [DOC ID 000236388002].

63 Neal E. Boudette, *Detroit Levels Productivity Playing Field—Auto Makers Slash Labor-Cost Advantage of Japanese Rivals,* THE WALL STREET JOURNAL (June 6, 2008), at B3 [DOC ID 000236387017].

64 *See, e.g.,* Neal E. Boudette, *Detroit levels Productivity Playing Field—Auto Makers Slash Labor-Cost Advantage of Japanese Rivals,* THE WALL STREET JOURNAL (June 6, 2008), at B3 [DOC ID 000236387017); *DaimlerChrysler CEO: Co to Address U.S. Health-Care Costs,* DOW JONES NEWS SERVICE (Sept. 19, 2006) [DOC ID 000236387021]; Jeffrey McCracken, *DaimlerChrysler's Pain Ripples Across Industry,* DETROIT FREE PRESS (June 5, 2003) [DOC ID 000236387024].

65 General Motors Corp., 2005 Annual Report, at 50 [DOC ID 000236388002]; General Motors Corp., 2007 Annual Report, at 61 [DOC ID 000236388003].

66 General Motors Corp., 2005 Annual Report, at 6, 44 [DOC ID 000236388002].

67 *GM lost Nearly $31 Billon In 2008,* CBS News Money Watch (Feb. 26, 2009), *available at* http://www.cbsnews.com/news/gm-lost-nearly-31-billion-in-2008/ [DOC ID 000236387006].

68 General Motors Corp., 2005 Annual Report, at 6 [DOC ID 000236388002].

69 General Motors Corp., 2004 Annual Report, at 4 [DOC ID 000236389003]

"reduc[ing] development costs through the use of common vehicle architectures that can be used on a global basis."[70]

D. Preliminary Information Notices and Technical Service Bulletins

Both Preliminary Informations and Technical Service Bulletins ("TSBs") are routine ways that GM alerts dealers about service issues. Preliminary Informations alert dealers to problems by describing issues of which GM has become aware, even before engineers have devised a solution. TSBs provide more detail and instructions on how to remedy the problem.

Both are frequently used. On average, GM published more than 60 Preliminary Informations or Technical Service Bulletins every month, an average of 738 a year.

E. Recalls

From January 1, 2000, through December 31, 2013, GM issued 374 recalls—an average of 26 recalls a year—with a total of 50.1 million vehicles affected—an average of 3.6 million vehicles per year. When GM issued the Ignition Switch recall in February/March 2014, it was GM's second largest recall since 2000, and its tenth largest since 1967 (the first year for which NHTSA data are available).[71]

F. The Ignition Switch and Airbag Technology in the Vehicles at Issue

The parts at issue in this Report are the Ignition Switch (which determined whether electrical power is provided to the airbag system), and the airbag system that includes the Sensing Diagnostic Module ("SDM"). This section provides an overview of how these parts worked.

1. The Ignition Switch

The Delta and Kappa Platform vehicles described above contain the same Ignition Switch—a newly-designed discreet logic ignition switch ("DLIS") first developed in 1997.[72] The Ignition Switch is located in the vehicle's steering column.[73] In the Delta Platform vehicles, as in other cars, a driver starts the car by turning the Ignition Switch to Start (also called "Crank"), which starts the

---

[70] General Motors Corp., 2005 Annual Report. at 50 [DOC ID 000236388002]; *see also* J&B Interview of Thomas Utter, April 24, 2014; J&B Interview of Raymond DeGiorgio, May 7–8, 2014.

[71] *See* Recalls, Flat File Copies of NHTSA/ODI Databases, National Highway Traffic Safety Administration, www.odinhtsa.dot.gov/downloads/folders/Recalls/FLAT_RCL.zip (last accessed May 29, 2014) [DOC ID 000240800002]; *see also* Appendix B, Section A-6.

[72] J&B Interview of Raymond DeGiorgio, May 7–8, 2014; J&B Interview of Thomas Utter, April 24, 2014; EFADC PowerPoint Presentation (Dec. 17, 2013), at 7 [DOC ID 000001788022; GMHEC000002899-2947].

[73] J&B Interview of Raymond DeGiorgio, March 14, 2014; Engineering Drawings of Steering Column for MY 2005 GMX357, at 7, 13 [DOC ID 000103713069].

engine, then allowing the Ignition Switch to rotate back to Run.[74] When turned to the Accessory position, the Ignition Switch sends a signal to the Body Control Module ("BCM") conveying the new vehicle power mode.[75] The BCM then broadcasts a signal to the engine to turn off, causing the airbag's crash sensing system to turn off (preventing the air bag from deploying), loss of power steering, and loss of power brakes.[76] Certain limited functions in the vehicles, such as the radio, remain on in the Accessory mode.[77] When turned to the Off position—referred to in some GM Owner's Manuals as the "Lock" position—the Ignition Switch sends a signal to the BCM, which broadcasts a signal to turn power off to all systems in the vehicle, including the airbag system.[78] As discussed below, the airbag system in the Delta and Kappa Platform vehicles does, in certain circumstances, maintain an energy reserve that could be used to deploy the airbags for a very short period if the vehicle lost power during a crash.[79]

Ignition Switch

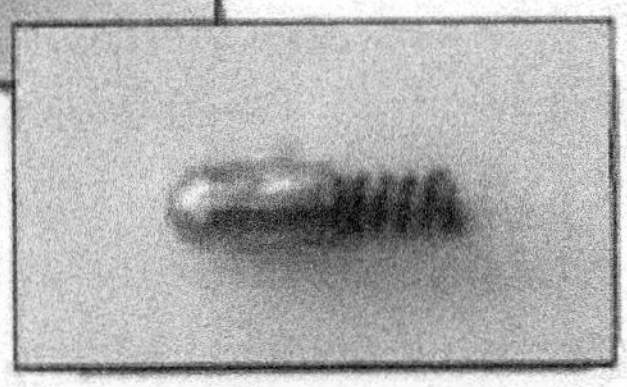

Plunger Cap and Spring

Components within the Ignition Switch control the amount of effort required to turn the switch from one position to another. A plunger cap and coiled

74 J&B Interview of James Duffy, April 24, 2014; *see also* Component Technical Specification for Column Mounted Discreet Logic Ignition Switch (Mar. 22, 2001), at 10 [DOC ID 14021301709376; GMNHTSA000441762].

75 J&B Interview of Thomas Utter, April 24, 2014; J&B Interview of James Duffy, April 24, 2014.

76 J&B Interview of Thomas Utter, April 24, 2014; J&B Interview of Thomas Mercer, May 2, 2014; J&B Interview of Vipul Modi, April 23, 2014; J&B Interview of Alan Storck, March 21, 2014.

77 J&B Interview of Thomas Mercer, May 2, 2014.

78 J&B Interview of Vipul Modi, March 20, 2014; J&B Interview of Andrew Brenz, April 23, 2014; *see also* Component Technical Specification for the Column Mounted Low Current Ignition Switch (Oct. 3, 1997), at 8 [DOC ID 000127082028; GMHEC000406323-51]; Component Technical Specification for Column Mounted Discreet Logic Ignition Switch (March 22, 2001), at 8 [DOC ID 14021301709376; GMNHTSA000441762].

79 J&B Interview of Thomas Mercer, May 2, 2014.

spring inside the Ignition Switch sit in a small groove called a "detent," which holds the switch in the position to which the driver turns the key: Off, Run, Accessory, or Crank. The driver rotates the key by applying a certain amount of torque to overcome the detent, thereby rotating the switch out of one position and into another. One method to increase the effort required to rotate the Ignition Switch from one position to another is to use a longer and more tightly coiled spring.

2. The Sensing Diagnostic Module ("SDM") and Airbag System

The 2005 Cobalt, and subsequent model years, utilized an advanced airbag system. It was designed to comply with new NHTSA requirements at the time, reflected in FMVSS (Federal Motor Vehicle Safety Standard) 208. NHTSA had issued FMVSS 208 in part to address evidence showing injuries *caused by* airbag deployment in certain circumstances.[80] The 2005 Cobalt was one of the first GM vehicles to have such advanced airbags.

A fundamental component of the airbag system in the Delta and Kappa Platform vehicles at issue is the SDM. The SDM is an onboard electronic module in airbag systems that serves two primary functions. First, the SDM tracks data in real time about the vehicle's status, including the vehicle's acceleration and speed, and whether it experiences any impacts. Second, based upon this data, the SDM determines when and whether airbags should deploy, and if so, triggers deployment. In the vehicle development process, manufacturers such as GM have SDMs programmed to deploy the airbags at the proper times and in the proper circumstances based on factors like the speed of vehicle, severity of impact, and location of impact—airbags are programmed not to deploy in non-accident circumstances such as driving over rough roads or potholes.[81] In particular, the frontal airbags are programmed to deploy only when the SDM senses a sufficient level of longitudinal deceleration.[82]

---

[80] The U.S. Intermodal Surface Transportation Efficiency Act of 1991 required for the first time that passenger cars and light trucks built after September 1, 1998, have airbags for the driver and the right front passenger. *See* National Highway Traffic Safety Administration Office of Research and Development, *Air Bag Technology in Light Passenger Vehicles* (June 27, 2001), at 1, *available at* http://www.nhtsa.gov.edgesuitcstagingnet/DOT/NRTSNNRD/Multimedia/PDFs/Crashworthiness/Airpercent20Bags/rev_report.pdf [DOC ID 000236387033].

[81] Joe T. Correia, *et al., Utilizing Data from Automotive Event Data Recorders* (June 2001), at 5–7, *available at* http://www.nhtsa.gov/DOT/NHTSA/NRD/Articles/EDR/PDF/Research/Utilizing_Data_from_Automotive_Event_Data_Recorders.pdf [DOC ID 000240512007]; PowerPoint on GMT345 SDM Issue (May 28, 2008), at 2 [DOC ID 000001615604], attached to e-mail from Harry Wiedenmeyer, GM, to Douglas Wachtel, GM (May 28, 2008) [DOC ID 000001615603].

[82] J&B Interview of Thomas Mercer, May 2, 2014; J&B Interview of Brian Everest, May 8, 2014.

By 2004, SDMs could also serve as the car's "black box" to allow forensic analysis of the causes of accidents or malfunctions of the car's components, including airbags.[83] To a certain extent, the supplier retained control over some of the forensic data gathered by the SDM by requiring that its own software analytics be used to evaluate the data. GM has relied upon the supplier to obtain analysis of certain SDM data, including information about the ignition switch position in crashes.[84]

During the 2004–2008 timeframe, the Ion and certain other Delta Platform vehicles contained an SDM manufactured by Delphi Mechatronics ("Delphi"). The Cobalt contained the SDM Epsilon, manufactured by Siemens Continental ("Continental").[85]

In all of the Delta and Kappa Platform vehicles during this period (2003–2010), if the Ignition Switch is turned to off or Accessory, then power to the SDM is lost, and the SDM powers down unless and until the ignition is returned to Run. This programming design helps to minimize the risk of unintended airbag deployments to the driver or a passenger when he or she is not sitting in the proper, restrained position, *e.g.,* a child who is in the front seat when the vehicle is stationary, or an owner who may be servicing the vehicle.[86] When the Ignition Switch is turned to Run after being in Accessory or Off, the SDM reboots, and during the few seconds of that reboot process, the airbags would not deploy.[87]

If, in a crash event, power was lost, including if the ignition moved to Accessory or Off during the crash, the SDM's crash sensing protection would continue (and airbags could still deploy) for approximately 150 milliseconds ("ms") after the power loss.[88] This feature was designed to ensure that if power was lost because of and during a crash, the airbags could still deploy.[89] As a result, the determining factor as to whether the airbags retained power to deploy was whether power was lost prior to or after the SDM started to sense the crash.

The principal functional difference between the SDMs used in the Cobalt and those used in the Ion and certain other Delta Platform vehicles lay in the

---

83 J&B Interview of Terry Woycbowski, March 21, 2014.

84 J&B Interview of William Hohnstadt, May 8, 2014.

85 SDM-Eps Usage (March 28, 2011) [DOC ID 000002153011], attached to e-mail from John Sprague, GM, to Brian Everest, Jaclyn Palmer, and Jennifer Sevigny, GM (March 3, 2011) [DOC ID 000002153010].

86 J&B Interview of Thomas Mercer, May 2, 2014.

87 J&B Interview of James Churchwell, March 21, 2014; J&B Interview of John Sprague, March 26, 2014; J&B Interview of John Dolan, May 16, 2014.

88 J&B Interview of Vipul Modi, March 20, 2014; J&B Interview of Kathy Anderson, March 19–20, 2014.

89 J&B Interview of Thomas Mercer. May 2, 2014.

SDM's recording function. In the Cobalt, the SDM retained sufficient reserve power to record data for a very brief period after losing power.[90] As a result, the Cobalt's SDM recorded whether the Ignition Switch was in the Run, Accessory, or Off position during a crash; the Ion's SDM did not.[91] This difference resulted from the fact that the SDM used in the Saturn Ion received its primary power through the ignition while the SDM in the Cobalt and the other Delta Platform vehicles received such power from the battery.[92] If the Ignition Switch were turned to Accessory or Off after a crash commenced, then the Ion's SDM would operate on a reserve power supply for a brief period sufficient to deploy the airbag but not sufficient to record data. In the same circumstance, the other Delta Platform vehicles' SDMs would both deploy the airbag and also maintain sufficient power to record deployment data.

G. The Ignition Switch and Its Impact on Airbag Deployment

Put simply, the Ignition Switch failed to stay in the Run position when it should have stayed in the Run position. The amount of effort required to rotate the Ignition Switch was too low, permitting it to move under certain circumstances from the Run position to the Accessory or Off position, when it was not the driver's intention to do so. As described above, the torque performance of the Ignition Switch was the result of the plunger and spring interacting with the detent profiles inside the switch itself. The Ignition Switch required less effort to rotate from one position to another, because the spring exerted insufficient force on the detent profiles. As a consequence, if the Ignition Switch moved out of Run to Accessory or Off when it should have stayed in Run, the airbags would not deploy in the event of a crash that would otherwise meet the criteria to trigger airbag deployment. This problem of low torque affected all cars that utilized the original Ignition Switch implemented in the Cobalt and Ion. . . .

This Report focuses on GM's delay in reporting the safety defect in the Cobalt and recalling the affected vehicles. The following sections describe the facts concerning GM's delay.

V. 1997–2006: Development, Production, and Re-Design of the Ignition Switch

Section V of this report details the development, testing, and production of the Ignition Switch, its implementation in the Delta and Kappa platforms, and

[90] J&B Interview of John Sprague. March 26, 2014.

[91] J&B Interview of Kathy Anderson, March 19–20, 2014.

[92] J&B Interview of Lisa Weber, May 22, 2014; J&B Interview of Brian Everest, May 8. 2014.

GM's initial investigations into moving stalls in the Cobalt from 2004 to 2006. As discussed in more detail below, the development of the Ignition Switch was fraught with problems from the outset, with GM personnel ultimately authorizing production of a switch that could rotate as a result of torque less than that required by GM's specifications. As GM personnel addressed multiple problems with the electrical components of the switch, they allowed this problem of low torque to persist into the production version of the Ignition Switch. As the Ignition Switch was implemented in GM vehicles, especially the Cobalt, reports of unexpected "moving stalls" (sometimes at high speed) led GM to open multiple investigations into the Ignition Switch.[93] Believing (incorrectly) that the problem of low torque that led to the stalls did not present a safety problem, the various committees or groups reviewing the issue treated it as a matter of "customer convenience" and took no action. The connection to airbag non-deployment was not made, and the issue was never elevated as a defect that might threaten the safety of GM customers and lead to a recall.

This section details the multiple failures of GM personnel and processes—among the most significant of which was the failure of many individuals involved in the investigation to understand that, if the Ignition Switch moves to Accessory or Off, the airbags will not deploy. Yet, GM personnel designed the Ignition Switch to cut electrical power to most systems when the key turned to Accessory. And GM personnel designed the airbag system to shut off when the vehicles were in the Accessory mode. Inexplicably, the engineers (and business people) interviewed who learned of moving stalls in this time period did not recognize that the loss of power from a key moving into Accessory caused the airbag system to shut off—a missed connection that led to devastating consequences. Information silos were present throughout GM and they delayed GM's response with respect to the Cobalt. Had GM personnel connected the dots and understood how their own cars were built, they might have addressed the safety defect before injuries and fatalities occurred.

As detailed below, another failure was the decision—by a single engineer who did not advise others of his decision—to accept an Ignition Switch with full knowledge that it fell well below GM's own specifications. Once moving stalls began to be reported, GM's investigations minimized the issue and failed to serve

[93] Throughout this report, there are references to moving stalls resulting from inadvertent rotation of the ignition switch attributed, by drivers of vehicles, to any number of factors. In most circumstances, we do not know all details of the incident, including whether there was additional weight on a key chain or ring, such as the key fob. GM has advised NHTSA that, based on GM's testing, the Cobalt and other vehicles are safe to drive "with only a single key on the key ring and the key fob removed," and NHTSA, in turn, has said that the safety risk has been sufficiently mitigated when the Cobalt is driven in such circumstances.

their essential purpose—to identify the Cobalt safety issue and resolve the problem expeditiously.

Finally, this section details a puzzle that stumped GM for many years to come—the fact that the Ignition Switch problem appeared in MY 2005–07 Cobalts, but not MY 2008–10 Cobalts. As discussed in more detail below, Ray DeGiorgio, the same GM engineer who originally approved the below-specification Ignition Switch, authorized a change in the Ignition Switch in 2006 that increased the torque required to turn the key. He addressed the defect, but by not changing the part number and not telling anyone that the part had been redesigned, he effectively concealed the fact that the change had been made. Even today, however, DeGiorgio claims not to remember doing so, nor does he remember authorizing the alteration without a concurrent change in the part number. As detailed in this section of the Report, DeGiorgio's failure to disclose this critical information had very significant consequences going forward. GM investigators struggled to identify the root cause of the Ignition Switch problem for years, in part because they could not explain why, if the Ignition Switch was mechanically the same in all model years, incidents ceased occurring in MY 2008. As set forth below, while the decision to change the Ignition Switch, without changing the part number, violated GM's policies, GM also failed to have in place an oversight system sufficient to ensure such decisions were reviewed and the correct decisions made. . . .

VI. 2006–2014: The Long Investigation into Root Cause

As described above, by June 2006, engineers at GM had been addressing the issue of moving stalls in the Cobalt for almost two years. Still, they did not view the problem as a safety issue and did not understand the relationship between airbag non-deployment and the ease with which the Ignition Switch could be rotated to Accessory. And, notwithstanding a decision to change the key head, no solution had, in fact, been implemented. (Although DeGiorgio had approved a redesign of the switch in 2006, it did not address the MY 2005, MY 2006, and certain MY 2007 vehicles.) By this time, GM personnel had publicly announced that there was no safety issue with Cobalt moving stalls, and GM's group of safety engineers, the Product Investigations ("PI") group, had determined no further investigation was warranted.[94]

[94] J&B Interview of Gary Altman, March 14, 2014; J&B Interview of Doug Parks, March 18, 2014; PRTS N172404 (Nov. 19, 2004) [DOC ID 000001771143; GMNHTSA0001426581]; Alan Adler, GM Statement on Chevrolet Cobalt Inadvertent Shutoffs (June 13, 2005) [DOC ID S006878_000015062; GMNHTSA30000 5313].

From 2006 to 2011, GM's PI group did not focus on issues related to the Cobalt Ignition Switch. Beginning in 2006, however, GM attorneys and a different group of engineers working in collaboration with them began to see accidents and claims in Ions and Cobalts that involved non-deployment of airbags and that, they would ultimately conclude, related to the Ignition Switch. As discussed below, the ongoing work of Field Performance Assessment ("FPA") engineers made slow progress, in no small part because they failed to search for or find information relevant to the problem of airbag non-deployment that was either public or actually in GM's own files. The FPA engineers, accustomed to focusing on individual claims or lawsuits and explanations of individual crashes, did not even consider searching for this information, which might have materially advanced their investigation.

The failure to locate and use this information, the failure to elevate issues in a timely manner, and the narrowness with which each group—lawyers and engineers alike—approached their roles, are important reasons why the investigation proceeded slowly. . . .

1. Background on the GM Legal Department

Before addressing these specific accidents, we provide some background on how the GM Legal Department (also referred to as "GM Legal Staff" or "GM Legal") dealt with product liability cases, particularly when they intersected with safety issues.

Thomas Gottschalk was General Counsel ("GC") of GM from 1994 until August 2006. He was succeeded by Robert Osborne.[95] In July 2009, Michael Millikin succeeded Osborne as GC.[96]

During the relevant period, the General Counsel of GM North America reported to the GC. That post was held by Chris Johnson until October 2008, by Michael Robinson from October 2008 to September 2009, by Fred Fromm from 2009 to 2011, and by Lucy Clark Dougherty from March 2011 to the present.

Both the lawyers in charge of safety issues and the lawyers in charge of product litigation reported to the General Counsel of GM North America. Two of Clark Dougherty's direct reports are Bill Kemp and Larry Buonomo.[97] Kemp, Counsel for Global Engineering Organization, is widely regarded as GM's most knowledgeable, experienced, and trusted safety lawyer.[98] He has been at GM for

[95] Cotsirilos, Tighe & Streicker, Poulos & Campbell, Ltd. Interview of Robert Osborne, May 12, 2014.

[96] J&B Interview of Michael Millikin, April 4, 2014.

[97] J&B Interview of Lucy Clark Dougherty, April 16, 2014.

[98] J&B Interview of Lawrence Buonomo, April 16, 2014.

decades. Buonomo's title is Practice Area Manager—Global Process & Litigation, where he oversees, among other things, product litigation cases. Before Buonomo, a GM lawyer named Michael Gruskin oversaw product litigation cases.[99]

In the area of safety, the two functions can intersect. Indeed, Kemp and his colleague Deb Nowak-Vanderhoef sit on one of the two committees that determines whether and at what price to settle product liability lawsuits.[100] A reason for that assignment is to ensure that information from lawsuits finds its way into GM's safety function, that is, to the engineers who make safety decisions.[101] Their presence is a practice specifically designed to defeat information silos, and to ensure important information makes its way to engineers.[102]

Product litigation staff attorneys have frontline responsibility for managing lawsuits and claims that are not in litigation, called not-in-suit-matters, or NISMs. When necessary to defend lawsuits or NISMs, the product litigation staff attorneys retain outside counsel. Outside counsel is required to provide a written evaluation of all lawsuits and NISMs to GM soon after receiving a matter. The purpose of these "early" evaluations is to determine whether a case is a trial candidate or a case that should be settled. Outside counsel is expected to provide updated case evaluations at key points throughout the litigation—including after the case is assigned a trial date.

Two groups of non-lawyers dedicated to assisting GM product litigators and outside counsel in defending product claims are Field Performance Assessment ("FPA") engineers and ESIS claims administrators. FPA engineers are assigned to gather information and assess technical issues in lawsuits and NISMs.[103] The FPA group is distinct from Product Investigations and the FPE [Field Performance Evaluation] process.[104] FPA engineers conduct their own technical assessments, which might include reviewing police reports and medical records, interviewing witnesses, inspecting vehicles, and analyzing SDM data.[105] FPA engineers share their technical assessments with product litigation staff attorneys and outside counsel, assist in responding to plaintiffs' discovery requests, and may testify as

99 J&B Interview of Lawrence Buonomo, April 16, 2014.

100 J&B Interview of William Kemp, April 17, 2014; J&B Interview of Deborah Nowak-Vanderhoef. May 1, 2014.

101 J&B Interview of Ronald Porter, April 30, 2014; J&B Interview of Jaclyn Palmer, April 24, 2014.

102 J&B Interview of Michael Gruskin, May 12, 2014.

103 J&B Interview of Jennifer Sevigny, March 27, 2014; J&B Interview of Douglas Brown, March 19, 2014; J&B Interview of Keith Schultz, March 18, 2014; J&B Interview of Kathy Anderson, March 19–20, 2014.

104 J&B Interview of Keith Schultz, March 18, 2014.

105 J&B Interview of Douglas Brown, March 19, 2014.

experts or 30(b)(6) witnesses. FPA engineers' technical assessments are the lawyers' primary source of technical information for the early case evaluations, and are a critical factor in the evaluation of settlement decisions.[106]

GM's claims administrators are employees of a vendor called ESIS, work solely on GM claims, and have offices at GM.[107] ESIS employees are responsible for conducting field investigations and processing NISM claims against GM.[108] ESIS field investigators photograph the vehicle, conduct interviews, and, with permission, download SDM and other diagnostic data out of a vehicle's computer.[109] ESIS forwards this information to GM legal staff. ESIS also negotiates settlements and presents claims at meetings for settlement evaluation.[110] ESIS acts at the direction of the GM product litigation staff attorneys, and the claims administrators meet with the GM attorneys on a weekly basis.

GM has a structured settlement process by which GM decides whether and for how much a case should be settled. At the lowest monetary level, product litigation staff attorneys were vested with $100,000 in settlement authority.[111] Settlements of between $100,000 and $1.5 million (a limit which was eventually increased to $2 million) required approval at a committee known as the "Roundtable." The Roundtable Committee met weekly, was led by the Litigation Practice Area Manager, and all product litigation staff attorneys were invited to attend.

Settlement offers between $2 and $5 million required approval of a group called the Settlement Review Committee ("SRC"), which met monthly, and was chaired by the head of global litigation. Members of the SRC included both the GC of GM North America and Kemp.[112] Cases over $5 million require approval by the General Counsel.

When a case was before the Roundtable or the SRC, the responsible product litigation staff attorney would present his/her case.[113] At the end of a presentation

---

106 J&B Interview of Kathy Anderson, March 19–20, 2014; J&B Interview of Douglas Brown, March 19, 2014.

107 J&B Interview of Kathy Anderson, March 19–20, 2014.

108 J&B Interview of Dan Derrick, March 31, 2014; J&B Interview of Annette Rigdon, May 14, 2014.

109 J&B Interview of Ryan Jahr, April 1, 2014; J&B Interview of Jaclyn Palmer, May 8, 2014.

110 J&B Interview of Annette Rigdon, May 14, 2014; J&B Interview of Jameia Price, May 12, 2014.

111 Michael Gruskin, GM, Legal Staff Settlement Review Processes, March 23, 2009 [DOC ID O_000 16584].

112 The current range for the SRC is $2 million to $5 million; earlier ii was $1.5 million to $5 million. If there were no matters to consider, the meetings were cancelled. Michael Gruskin, GM, Legal Staff Settlement Review Processes, March 23, 2009 [DOC ID O_00016584].

113 J&B Interview of Lawrence Buonomo, April 16, 2014.

to either group, the Roundtable and SRC committees voted.[114] The chair was the ultimate decision maker.[115] Michael Gruskin chaired both the Roundtable and SRC committees from August 2007 to March 2012. Larry Buonomo chaired both committees beginning on March 8, 2012. In terms of case volume, the SRC considered an average of 1.4 cases per meeting in 2012 and 1.3 per meeting in 2013. The Roundtables considered an average of 3.4 cases per meeting in 2012 and 3.76 per meeting in 2013.

The main function of the Roundtable was to generate better claim evaluations and settlement forecasts through a "peer review" structure.[116] But a number of GM lawyers reported that it had a second function as well: to spot trends indicating safety issues. Product litigation attorney Ron Porter stated that it was well recognized that a goal of the Roundtable and SRC process was to identify potential safety issues and refer them to engineers.[117] His product litigation colleague Jaclyn Palmer said that attorneys discussed potential product safety or accident trends at Roundtables on occasion, and the Roundtable Committee referred issues to GM engineers for a follow-up investigation.[118] Not all GM lawyers, however, agreed with this view. Buonomo, for example, said that it was not the Roundtable's function to spot trends and that if a lawyer had to flag a trend, then the system had already failed.[119]

To put this issue in a specific context, at a Roundtable discussion on the Cobalt airbag non-deployment issue in 2012, a junior lawyer recalled asking whether there should be a recall.[120] He was told that the issue had already been raised with engineering, that the engineers were working on it, and that they had not come up with a solution. This lawyer got the "vibe" that the lawyers had "done everything we can do."

We have discovered no formal written policies governing how the settlement committees should handle safety issues. Multiple witnesses, however, described how things worked in practice. In practice, the mechanism for getting safety issues from GM Legal to GM Engineering was through Bill Kemp. For example, former GC Thomas Gottschalk described how the primary responsibility for spotting

---

[114] J&B Interview of Lawrence Buonomo, April 16, 2014.

[115] J&B Interview of Lawrence Buonomo, April 16, 2014.

[116] Michael Daar, GM, *et al.,* Outside Counsel Guidelines Sub Group—Early Case Evaluation and Peer Review Process, Feb. 27, 2009 [DOC ID 000005787998].

[117] J&B Interview of Ronald Porter, April 30, 2014.

[118] J&B Interview of Jaclyn Palmer, April 24, 2014.

[119] J&B Interview of Lawrence Buonomo, April 16, 2014; J&B Interview of Lawrence Buonomo, May 13, 2014.

[120] J&B Interview of Nabeel Peracha, May 21, 2014.

trends belonged to engineering, which had access to a host of different inputs ranging from warranty claims to customer complaints. But, said Gottschalk, when lawyers did become aware of a safety issue, they were to raise the issue, and a common way of doing that was to go to Kemp or his colleague Deb Nowak-Vanderhoef—who would, in turn, raise it with engineers.[121]

GM's expectations for its lawyers—including the expectation that lawyers elevate certain issues to superiors—were reflected in a 2003 memorandum from then-GC Gottschalk to "All Attorneys."[122] Gottschalk reminded the lawyers who worked for him, "If you as an attorney are aware of any threatened, on-going, or past violation of a federal, state or local law or regulation. . . it is your responsibility to respond appropriately."[123]

Gottschalk discussed factors in determining how to respond, including the seriousness of the matter, the existence of threat of harm to others, the lawyer's degree of knowledge of the situation, and the lawyer's level of experience and position within GM. Gottschalk wrote that while some matters could be addressed directly by the attorney, in other cases "it may be more appropriate to report the situation to your supervisor . . . so that it can be handled at a higher level."

Gottschalk also discussed what to do if one's superiors had concluded that appropriate action had been taken in response to a perceived problem, but the more junior lawyer disagreed:

> If you believe . . . that the conclusion is wrong, you should continue to seek an appropriate resolution. It is your duty to bring the situation to the attention of your supervisors or their supervisors, as necessary. If you believe that they have not addressed it appropriately or if you feel that bringing it to their attention would be futile, you should pursue it higher in the organization—if necessary, to me as General Counsel.

Michael Gruskin, a long-time GM attorney who headed the product litigation team during part of the relevant period, understood Gottschalk's direction to apply to safety issues. In interviews, Osborne and Millikin, like Gottschalk, said that they expected their lawyers to elevate to them significant safety issues. . . .

---

121 Cotsirilos, Tighe & Streicker, Ltd. Interview of Thomas Gottschalk, May 12, 2014.

122 Thomas A Gottschalk, Memorandum re Standards of Professional Conduct or Attorneys (Aug. 4, 2003), at 1 [DOC ID 00136806990].

123 Thomas A Gottschalk, Memorandum re Standards of Professional Conduct of Attorneys (Aug. 4, 2003), at 1 [DOC ID 00136806990].

4. April 2007: The Indiana University Report on Accident

Also in 2007, the Indiana University ("IU") Transportation Research Center issued a report ("the Indiana University study") commissioned by NHTSA on April 25 titled "On-Site Air Bag Non-Deployment Investigation" for the crash, the same fatal accident that was the subject of the report by the Wisconsin State Patrol.[124] Although at least one person was able to find the IU study on NHTSA's website,[125] GM personnel did not. Moreover, GM personnel made no efforts to systematically monitor NHTSA's website for such information and therefore did not obtain it until years later.

More broadly, we have seen no evidence that anyone from GM asked for or sought out publicly available information that would have been relevant to the investigation of the Cobalt.[126] Indeed, many GM employees involved with the Cobalt investigation became aware of these publicly available reports only recently.[127] We are unaware of any formal system at GM for seeking out or tracking publicly available information related to crashes or investigations done by others of crashes involving GM vehicles (other than the work GM does to comply with its TREAD obligations).[128] GM did become aware of some public cases through the informal "rumor" tracking system by which ESIS investigators or other GM Legal Staff would start files on cases that were not formally involved in litigation but potentially could lead to litigation.[129] But rumor files were noted by some as being hard to track, difficult to access, and not easily searchable.[130]

---

[124] Indiana University Transportation Research Center, On-Site Air Bag Non-Deployment Investigation (April 25, 2007) [DOC ID 000001791070; GMNHTSA000223985]; Keith A. Young, Technical Reconstruction Unit, Wisconsin State Patrol Academy, Collision Analysis & Reconstruction Report, Feb. 14, 2007, attached to GM Claim form (File # 624620, et al [sic]; Feb. 28, 2007) [DOC ID 000003680368; GMNHTSA000284395].

[125] As described *infra,* in June 2012, the plaintiff's expert in an airbag non-deployment case indicated that she found the Indiana University study on the NHTSA website. We have not been able to confirm if the report was accessible on NHTSA's website in 2007.

[126] J&B Interview of Carmen Benavides, May 19, 2014; J&B Interview of Lawrence Buonomo, May 13, 2014; J&B Interview of Elizabeth Zatina, May 14, 2014.

[127] J&B Interview of Dwayue Davidson, May 6, 2014; J&B Interview of Eric Buddrius, April 29, 2014; J&B Interview of Deborah Nowak-Vanderhoef, May 1, 2014; J&B Interview of Dale Furney, May 6, 2014; J&B Interview of Mark Johnson, May 7, 2014.

[128] J&B Interview of Carmen Benavides, May 19, 2014; J&B Interview of Lawrence Buonomo, May 13, 2014; J&B Interview of Keith Schultz, March 18, 2014; J&B Interview of Mickey Sabol, April 24, 2014.

[129] J&B Interview of Ryan Jahr, April I, 2014; J&B Interview of Carmen Benavides, May 19, 2014; J&B Interview of Dwayne Davidson, May 6, 2014; J&B Interview of Lisa Stacey, May 8, 2014; J&B Interview of Ronald Porter, May 13, 2014; J&B Interview of Jameia Price, May 12, 2014; J&B interview of Annette Rigdon, May 14, 2014; J&B Interview of Gay Kent, May 16, 2014.

[130] J&B Interview of Jaclyn Palmer, May 8, 2014; J&B Interview of Ronald Porter, May 13, 2014; J&B Interview of Carmen Benavides, May 19, 2014.

The IU researchers noted that in the accident they were examining, the power mode was recorded as Accessory, and, indeed, that the deputy sheriff who responded had found the ignition switch "jammed" in the Accessory position.[131] The investigators wrote:

> It is possible the ignition switch could have been knocked to the "Accessory" position by the driver's leg or knee at the time of the vault. This investigation revealed that inadvertent contact with the ignition switch or a key chain in the 2005 Chevrolet Cobalt can in fact result in engine shut-down and loss of power.[132]

The IU researchers then described how they had examined GM's October 2006 TSB and reported: "The bulletin indicates that there is a potential for the driver to inadvertently turn off the ignition due to low ignition key cylinder torque/effort."[133] Researchers then reported that they had identified "at least" six complaints on the NHTSA website[134] relating to the engine shutting off and loss of power when the Ignition Switch or key chain was contacted by the driver. Some of the complaints reported a simple "brushing" of the key chain or touching of the ignition switch was all that was required for the engine to shut off.[135] The researchers concluded:

> It is not known what role, if any, this may have played in the non-deployment of the air bags. Such a determination would most likely require an analysis of the air bag system and ignition wiring schematic in order to determine if in fact the air bag is capable of deploying when the ignition is switched from the 'on' position to the 'accessory' position.[136]

---

[131] The physical position of the ignition switch would later become critically important. For years, GM investigators were reviewing data that reflected the ignition switch position, but because they lacked data regarding the actual key position, they were skeptical about whether the data were accurate. In particular, they state that data showing the ignition switch in "run" was a barrier for years to their understanding that this was a mechanical issue rather than all electrical issue. J&B Interview of Brian Stouffer, May 9, 2014.

[132] Indiana University Transportation Research Center, On-Site Air Bag Non-Deployment Investigation (April 25, 2007), at 7 [DOC ID 000001791070; GMNHTSA000223985].

[133] Indiana University Transportation Research Center, On-Site Air Bag Non-Deployment Investigation (April 25, 2007), at 7 [DOC ID 000001791070; GMNHTSA000223985].

[134] Indiana University Transportation Research Center, On-Site Air Bag Non-Deployment Investigation (April 25, 2007), at 7 [DOC ID 000001791070; GMNHTSA000223985].

[135] Indiana University Transportation Research Center, On-Site Air Bag Non-Deployment Investigation (April 25, 2007), at 7 [DOC ID 000001791070; GMNHTSA000223985].

[136] Indiana University Transportation Research Center, On-Site Air Bag Non-Deployment Investigation (April 25, 2007), at 7 [DOC ID 000001791070; GMNHTSA000223985].

INDIANA UNIVERSITY

TRANSPORTATION RESEARCH CENTER
School of Public and Environmental Affairs
222 West Second Street
Bloomington, Indiana 47403-1501
(812) 855-3908 Fax: (812) 855-3537

ON-SITE AIR BAG NON-DEPLOYMENT INVESTIGATION

CASE NUMBER - IN-06-033
LOCATION - WISCONSIN
VEHICLE - 2005 CHEVROLET COBALT
CRASH DATE - October 2006

way down. A search of the NHTSA, Office of Defects Investigation (ODI) web site, complaint tab, revealed at least six complaints (ODI identification numbers: 10144299, 10145959, 10129121, 10132335, 10151346, and 10197022) relating to the engine shutting off and loss of power in Chevrolet Cobalts when the ignition switch or key chain was contacted by the driver. Some of the complaints reported a simple "brushing" of the key chain or touching of the ignition switch was all that was required for the engine to shut off. It is not known what role, if any, this may have played in the non-deployment of the air bags. Such a determination would most likely require an analysis of the air bag system and ignition wiring schematic in order to determine if in fact the air bag is capable of deploying when the ignition is switched from the "on" position to the "accessory" position. Such an undertaking was beyond the scope of this investigation.

We have found no evidence that the Indiana University study was known to anyone at GM until it was referenced in the case in 2012 (discussed below). Moreover, although Indiana University investigators located the TSB on the ignition switch, inexplicably neither internal nor outside counsel working on Cobalt and Ion-related matters found the TSB (or the PRTS reports that ultimately led to the TSBs) until 2012. . . .

D. 2009: The Investigation Continues and GM Goes into Bankruptcy

In 2009, GM finally implemented the key head design change for new vehicles and continued to track and investigate Cobalt incidents.[137] There were no Roundtable or Settlement Review Committee meetings concerning Cobalt and Ion non-deployment claims.[138] Activity recommenced, however, on the product development side as engineers again began work to address the continued problems related to the Ignition Switch (discussed below).[139]

Meanwhile, at the end of 2008 and in the first half of 2009, GM received emergency funding from the federal government and, on June 1, 2009, GM filed

---

[137] GM, Complete PRTS Report (1078137) (Oct. 8, 2012) [DOC ID 140307000022778; GMNHTSA000018925]; e-mail from David Trush, GM, to Brad Cook, GM (Feb. 19, 2009) [DOC ID 000014453007; GMNHTSA000481040]; e-mail from Joe Baaki, GM, to David Trush, GM (Aug. 10, 2009) [DOC ID 000014459780]; J&B Interview of John Dobish, April 29, 2014; J&B Interview of David Trush, April 30, 2014.

[138] J&B Interview of Jaclyn Palmer, April 24, 2014.

[139] J&B Interview of David Trush, March 17, 2014; J&B Interview of John Sprague, March 26, 2014.

for bankruptcy, which stayed all litigation against the company.[140] The GM entity that filed for bankruptcy (then known as General Motors Corporation) sold substantially all of its assets to an entity sponsored by the U.S. Treasury (which became known as General Motors Company) in a transaction approved by the United States Bankruptcy Court for the Southern District of New York.[141] This sale transaction closed on July 10, 2009. . . .

F. 2006 to 2010: Failure to Take Basic Steps

In sum, 2006 to 2010 saw five years of failures, including the failure to change the part number, multiple failures to share or gather basic facts (such as materials in GM's own files and in the public record), and, at the most fundamental level, the failure by investigators to understand how GM engineers had designed their own vehicle:

- In 2006, DeGiorgio changed the part but not the part number—an act that violated GM's policies and which would throw GM investigators off the track for years. Also in 2006, airbag non-deployment cases began to come into the GM Legal Department; none of the FPA investigators, outside counsel and in-house lawyers knew of the prior investigations into the Cobalt moving stall issue or the poorly worded TSB that was their outcome.
- In 2007, two different outsiders—Trooper Young of the Wisconsin State Patrol and the Indiana University study team—both arrived at the correct answer to the non-deployment problem, the same one GM engineers would adopt six years later in 2013. But GM personnel were unaware of these reports. They would not learn about the Indiana University study until 2012 when a plaintiff's expert brought it to their attention, and would not learn of the Wisconsin State Patrol report until this internal investigation

140 GM assumed the Delphi settlement in its bankruptcy case. Order Approving (I) Master Disposition Agreement for Purchase of Certain Assets of Delphi Corporation, (II) Related Agreements, (III) Assumption and Assignment of Executory Contracts, (IV) Agreement with Pension Benefit Guaranty Corporation, and (V) Entry into Alternative Transaction in lieu thereof, Docket No. 3139, *In re* Motors Liquidation Company, No. 09-50026 (Bankr. S.D.N.Y. July 14, 2009) [DOC ID 000240790005].

141 Order (I) Authorizing Sale of Assets Pursuant to Amended and Restated Master Sale and Purchase Agreement with NGMCO, Inc., A U.S. Treasury-Sponsored Purchaser; (II) Authorizing Assumption and Assignment of Certain Executory Contracts and Unexpired Leases in Connection with the Sale; and (III) Granting Related Relief, Docket No. 2968, *In re* Motors Liquidation Company, No. 09-50026 (Bankr. S.D.N.Y. July 5, 2009) [DOC ID 24053060]; Decision on Debtors' Motion for Approval of (1) Sale of Assets to Vehicle Acquisition Holdings LLC; (2) Assumption and Assignment of Related Executory Contracts; and (3) Entry into UAW Retiree Settlement Agreement Docket No. 2967, *In re* Motors Liquidation Company, No. 09-50026 (Bankr. S.D.N.Y. July 5, 2009) [DOC ID 000240530059].

began—even though the report had been sitting in GM's own files since 2007.

- In 2008, although non-deployment lawsuits continued to come in, both outside and in-house counsel and the FPA engineers were unaware, as they assessed and investigated these cases, of the TSB, the PRTSs, the earlier Product Investigations investigation, the Wisconsin State Patrol report, and the Indiana University study.
- In 2009, the FPA engineers had what one now calls an "aha" moment, leading him to suspect that the vehicle's power mode might be causing the non-deployment of airbags in multiple cases. Yet the investigation did not pick up speed, and no safety investigation was begun by the PI group. Although they were never able to create a "bounce" in testing, engineers hung onto this incorrect theory for years. Sprague did begin to notice patterns in the data suggesting that later model years of the Cobalt did not have a problem with non-deployments. When he directly asked DeGiorgio whether there had been a change in the Ignition Switch, DeGiorgio told him there had been none that would affect the vehicle power mode shutting off—throwing Sprague and others off the track for years. Even after identifying a pattern of airbag non-deployments and learning that the ignition switch may be involved, the issue was not elevated within GM.
- In 2010, as airbag non-deployment cases mounted, GM's outside counsel warned that GM was at risk of punitive damages because the investigation into non-deployment "anomalies" had not been completed. Outside counsel issued this warning not even aware of all the facts that would later emerge, including that GM investigators had missed the main issue in 2005 when they did not grasp the fact that their colleagues had designed the airbags not to deploy when the Ignition Switch was turned to Off or Accessory. In-house and outside counsel remained unaware of the PRTSs, the TSBs, the Wisconsin State Patrol report, and the Indiana University study.

The evidence showed that obtaining the TSB, the Wisconsin State Patrol report, and the Indiana University study would have shortened the investigation. As soon as the IU report and TSBs were made known (by an outside expert) to GM, the documents began figuring prominently in evaluations by outside counsel—both in terms of causation and in terms of the possibility of punitive damages. Sprague, who had neither the TSBs nor the Indiana University study, reported that both would have assisted in his investigation.[142] Kemp similarly said that the Wisconsin Safety Patrol report would have assisted, and was concerned that Trooper Young had understood the import of the 2005 TSB when GM's engineers had failed to do so[143] Kemp said it is "always disappointing when someone outside the company knows more about your product than you do."[144] Other witnesses, however, stated that they saw less use in having them. Notably, Stouffer, the PI investigator who would take over the investigation in 2011, had the TSBs from the start of his investigation, and when he received the Indiana University study in 2012, he thought it failed to provide the correct answer.

G. 2011: Another Engineering Investigation Begins

In January 2011, after GM settled the first non-deployment case in which outside counsel had warned of the possibility of punitive damages, several GM lawyers wanted a meeting to find out more about the Cobalt Ignition Switch issue, but that meeting was not held for six months. When the meeting was finally held in July 2011, Kemp instructed Wachtel to open a PI investigation into the Ignition Switch issue. Wachtel assigned the investigation to Brian Stouffer, but conveyed no sense of urgency. As discussed below, the investigation that followed moved slowly, as engineers searched for the "root cause," and there was no timetable and no person accountable for bringing the investigation to a quick close. Stouffer's work was also made more difficult by continued misdirection from DeGiorgio's failure to remember that he had changed the Ignition Switch in 2006.

At the outset, Stouffer was given materials from the 2005 Cobalt moving stall investigation and quickly located the 2005 TSB. He thus had information that GM lawyers and FPA engineers working on airbag non-deployment cases had lacked for years. Stouffer also searched for TREAD data on airbag non-deployment incidents, but failed to include MY 2003–2004 Ions in his search, which caused him to miss numerous Ion airbag non-deployments, including fatal crashes from 2003 and 2004. His failure to collect this data meant that the Ion was left out of the FPE investigation, which would have adverse consequences in future years, including an initial recall in February 2014 that was limited to the Cobalt and the G5. . . .

142 J&B Interview of John Sprague, May 15, 2014; J&B Interview of John Sprague, April 1, 2014.

143 J&B Interview of William Kemp, May 16, 2014.

144 J&B Interview of William Kemp, May 16, 2014.

H. 2012: The Search for the "Root Cause"

In the first part of 2012, mechanical engineers and electrical engineers debated how best to proceed. In the meantime, Cobalts with a safety defect stayed on the road, while GM engineers held more meetings.

In June 2012, the plaintiff's expert in an airbag non-deployment case located the Indiana University study and cited it in her report, bringing it to the attention of GM engineers and lawyers working on the Ignition Switch issue for the first time. The expert, Erin Shipp, concluded that the airbag non-deployments were being caused by the low torque of the Ignition Switch. Stouffer discounted the Indiana University study and the Shipp report because they did not explain airbag non-deployments in cases in which the Ignition Switch was in Run, and because they did not explain why the non-deployments were limited to pre-MY 2008 vehicles. Having failed to make progress in his investigation, Stouffer enlisted the help of the Red X team, which likewise failed to make progress in the investigation. . . .

10. September 2012; The Red X Investigation

Two days later, Stouffer implemented this second action item by engaging the Red X team, who were regarded as master problem solvers and experts at determining root cause.[145]

Red X is a standard engineering diagnostic.[146] When GM has two identical products that perform differently, the engineers conduct a Red X diagnostic to determine why.[147] They take one of the BOB ("Best of the Best") and one of the WOW ("Worst of the Worst") and run tests on both vehicles to identify any differences in the two products.[148] The engineers who conduct the Red X diagnostic have to be certified in order to run the tests.

The Red X investigation began on September 6, 2012, when Stouffer e-mailed Red X North America manager Bill Merrill to request assistance "from the Red X team to examine changes on the Cobalt between 2007 and 2008 model years."[149] The Red X team was tasked with determining what changed in the Cobalt between 2007 and 2008 that put an end to the stalls.

---

[145] J&B Interview of Brian Stouffer, April 4, 2014.

[146] J&B Interview of Jim Federico, May 9, 2014.

[147] J&B Interview of Jim Federico, May 9, 2014.

[148] J&B Interview of Jim Federico (May 9, 2014).

[149] E-mail from Dan Davis, GM, to Brian Stouffer, GM (Sept. 17, 2012) [DOC ID 14030700139914; GMNHTSA000135996].

Merrill assigned Stouffer's request to Dan Davis, GM Red X Global Lead.[150] Davis measured the force necessary to turn the Ignition Switch from Run to Accessory on five Cobalts and found that his data was largely consistent with Stouffer's.[151]

After Davis observed force measurements similar to those found by Stouffer, the next step in the Red X methodology was to examine a "WOW" sample, *i.e.* a crashed Cobalt in which the airbag had failed to deploy properly. Davis planned to compare the WOW with a "COW" ("Complete Opposite of the Worst") to isolate the potential causes of the airbag non-deployment.[152] According to Davis, he requested a WOW from Stouffer, and Stouffer said he had to check with GM Legal. However, Stouffer did not recall Davis ever asking him for assistance in identifying a vehicle, and stated that since Davis worked at Milford where GM maintains many of its vehicles, it would not be logical for Davis to ask Stouffer to find him a vehicle.[153] According to Davis, he eventually followed up with Stouffer, and Stouffer said that he could not provide a WOW because crashed Cobalts, at the direction of GM Legal Staff, had been quarantined as a result of litigation. Gruskin, Buonomo, Porter, Kemp, and Palmer said that they did not tell (and were not aware of anyone else saying to) an engineer at GM that a Cobalt could not be tested, inspected, or examined because it was "quarantined."[154] Stouffer did not recall telling Davis that all of the Cobalts had been quarantined at GM Legal's direction.[155]

According to Davis, once he was told by Stouffer that a WOW could not be provided, he could not complete his work; Davis took no further action, eventually closing the Red X project in May 2013.[156] Whether Davis was following the Red X methodology or not, the failure of Davis, or anyone else, to push for a comparison of pre-and post-MY 2008 Ignition Switches at this time period was a critical error. The crux of the issue—a comparison of the switches—could have been accomplished by Davis or others, but was not. To be sure, the misinformation provided by DeGiorgio impeded the investigation, but Stouffer

---

150 E-mail from Dan Davis, GM, to Brian Stouffer, GM (Sept. 17, 2012) [DOC ID 14030700139914; GMNHTSA000135996).

151 J&B Interview of Dan Davis, May 8, 2014.

152 J&B Interview of Dan Davis, May 8, 20 14.

153 J&B Interview of Brian Stouffer, May 9, 2014.

154 J&B Interview of Michael Gruskin, May 23, 20J4; J&B Interview of Lawrence Buonomo, May 23, 2014; J&B Interview of Ronald Porter, May 24, 2014; J&B Interview of Jaclyn Palmer, May 23, 2014; J&B Interview of William Kemp, May 24, 2014.

155 J&B Interview of Brian Stouffer, May 9, 2014.

156 J&B Interview of Dan Davis, May 8, 2014.

and other engineers did not take additional steps that would have moved the investigation forward. Even accepting DeGiorgio's statements, Stouffer did not investigate whether the supplier itself had made changes to the "black box" of the Ignition Switch that might have affected the torque. Had Stouffer taken that step, which he ultimately did more than a year later, he would have discovered that the Ignition Switch had indeed changed, albeit at the direction of DeGiorgio.

As will be discussed below, the plaintiff's expert . . . did the exact comparison the Red X team was asked to undertake and uncovered the 2006 change. This was another missed opportunity for GM personnel to fully understand the issue and bring the matter to a conclusion. . . .

I. 2013: An Outsider Conclusively Demonstrates the Root Cause, But Still No Recall

In early 2013, Stouffer declared his two-year-old investigation "stuck,"[157] even though he now had the Indiana University study correctly identifying the cause of the airbag non-deployments.[158] Even when the plaintiff's expert in showed in April 2013 that the Ignition Switch had in fact been redesigned in 2006[159]—answering one of the key outstanding questions in Stouffer's search for the "root cause"—GM hired an expert to reconfirm what it had already learned in—an exercise that took another six months.[160] When Stouffer received the written report from GM's expert in late October 2013, Stouffer finally accepted the answer that Trooper Young and Indiana University had arrived at in 2007: that the Ignition Switch was inadvertently turning to Accessory, which disabled the airbags.[161] By the end of 2013, the Cobalt Ignition Switch had finally reached GM's committee that considers recalls (the EFADC), but once there, more questions were raised about root cause, and decision-makers were hamstrung by a lack of accurate data about what vehicles were affected and how many people may have been impacted by the defect. . . .

4. April 2013: Depositions in the Case Begin and There Is a "Bombshell" at DeGiorgio's Deposition

In April 2013, Philip Holladay of K&S began preparing to defend a series of GM depositions in the case. Holladay reported that in preparing for the upcoming

[157] J&B Interview of Brian Stouffer, April 4, 2014.

[158] J&B Interview of Brian Stouffer, April 4, 2014.

[159] J&B Interview of Jaclyn Palmer, May 8, 2014.

[160] J&B Interview of Gay Kent, March 18, 2014.

[161] J&B Interview of Brian Stouffer, April 4, 2014.

depositions, he reviewed the FPE investigation performed by Stouffer (and the work of Sprague before him).

On April 29, Holladay defended DeGiorgio in a deposition at the Westin Hotel at the Detroit airport. According to an e-mail that Holladay sent to Porter from the deposition, plaintiff's counsel dropped a "bombshell,"[162] namely evidence that the switch had, indeed, been changed from 2005 to 2008—evidence that had eluded GM engineers for years and that DeGiorgio testified, under oath, that he did not remember. Holladay reported that Ron Porter, the GM lawyer in charge of the litigation, drove to the Westin on his way home to pick up photographs of the different sized plungers and caps that had been provided during the deposition.[163]

Three days after the DeGiorgio deposition, Holladay participated in a telephone call with Porter and Bill Kemp. Holladay stated that GM uses Exponent and Subbaiah Malladi for its most important matters. During the call, Holladay recommended hiring Exponent and Malladi for two reasons. First, Exponent would assist with the case. Second, GM needed to bring the FPE investigation to closure without delay. Malladi became involved within days of the DeGiorgio deposition.[164]

. . .

6. May 2013: GM Lawyers and Outside Counsel Review the Matter Again

On May 15, the week after Kent's "kick-off" meeting and about two weeks after the DeGiorgio deposition, GM lawyers reviewed the matter at another Roundtable.[165] Porter's summary of the Roundtable included:

> NEW INFORMATION: Plaintiff claims the engine turned off because the Ignition switch moved from the run to the accessory position. The

---

162 J&B Interview of Philip Holladay, April 25, 2014; e-mail from Philip Holladay, K&S, to Ronald Porter, GM (Apr. 29, 2013) [DOC ID 000004640060].

163 J&B Interview of Philip Holladay, April 25, 2014. For his part, DeGiorgio said that after the deposition, he, indeed, took two switches apart and confirmed the difference. J&B Interview of Raymond DeGiorgio, March 14, 2014. He also told Brian Thompson, his supervisor, that he had been shown photographs of two different detent plungers of different lengths. DeGiorgio and Thompson then told their new group director, Craig Zinser. Zinser told DeGiorgio and Thompson to let legal handle it. J&B Interview of Raymond DeGiorgio, March 19, 2014. Zinser had no recollection of this discussion with DeGiorgio and Thompson. J&B Interview of Craig Zinser, May 27, 2014.

164 J&B Interview of Subbaiah Malladi, May 7, 2014.

165 Ronald Porter, Settlement Review Committee Case Summary (Aug. 8, 2013) [DOC ID 000002818 612]; Roundtable Agenda [DOC ID 000162270688].

> switch requires about 8 N/cm to turn from Run to Accessory. The torque curve on the drawing works out to about 20 N/cm.[166]

The Roundtable gave settlement authority, but the case did not settle and discovery continued.

K&S submitted a second case evaluation for the matter on July 22, 2013.[167] Holladay's evaluation included a conclusion that a jury would almost "certainly" find the Ignition Switch unreasonably dangerous, that low torque would lead to inadvertent shutting off of the engine:

> This case is a very poor trial candidate. A jury here will almost certainly conclude that the Cobalt's ignition switch is defective and unreasonably dangerous because the torque effort required to move the key from run to accessory is too low, which leads to inadvertent key movement and the engine shutting off with little or no warning.[168]

K&S warned that this was known virtually from the vehicle launch:

> This phenomenon was identified almost immediately after the 2005 Cobalt went into production and there were several newspaper and trade publication articles shortly after the car's launch that flagged the issue. As discussed in more detail below, the issue was assessed internally in a series of investigations conducted as part of the Product Resolution Tracking System and ultimately addressed by issuing an Information Service Bulletin in the Fall of 2005 that provided a field service fix for customers who experienced an incident involving inadvertent key movement.[169]

The evaluation then catalogued the airbag non-deployment issue, even though airbag non-deployment was not an allegation in

> More recently, this issue has surfaced again as part of an on-going FPE investigation into why frontal air bags have not deployed in certain high-speed multiple-impact frontal collisions involving 2005–2007 Chevrolet Cobalts. In more than half of those incidents, it appears the reason that the air bag did not deploy was because the car's ignition was in the

166 Ronald Porter, Settlement Review Committee Case Summary (Aug. 8, 2013), at 4–5 (emphasis omitted) [DOC ID 0000028186121].

167 Ronald Porter, Settlement Review Committee Case Summary (Aug. 8, 2013), at 11 [DOC ID 0000028 18612].

168 Ronald Porter, Settlement Review Committee Case Summary (Aug. 8, 2013), at 12–13 [DOC ID 0000 02818612].

169 Ronald Porter, Settlement Review Committee Case Summary (Aug. 8, 2013), at 12–13 [DOC ID000 0002818612].

> accessory rather than the run position. While there is no allegation here that frontal air bags should have deployed, the on-going investigation ties nicely into plaintiffs' expected theme that the original Information Service Bulletin was an inadequate "band-aid fix" for a significant safety issue that should have been addressed through a recall and design change. Given these facts, we believe that GM's defense here necessarily will have to focus almost exclusively on causation.[170]

Holladay warned of "a substantial adverse verdict."[171] Among the reasons he listed: "the ignition switch and key cylinder used on the 2005 Cobalt were problematic from the outset and plaintiffs will have little problem convincing most jurors that these components were substandard and defective."[172]

In concluding, Holladay wrote, "This case needs to be settled."[173] He warned that plaintiff would argue that GM had known of the defect from the time that Cobalts first "rolled off the assembly line" and yet it has "essentially done nothing to correct the problem for the last nine years":

> [T]here is little doubt that a jury here will find that the ignition switch used on 205 Cobalt was defective and unreasonably dangerous, and that it did not meet GM's own torque specifications. In addition, the PRTS documents referenced above and the on-going FPE investigation have enabled plaintiffs' counsel to develop a record from which he can compellingly argue that GM has known about this safety defect from the time the first 2005 Cobalts rolled off the assembly line and essentially has done nothing to correct the problem for the last nine years. He specifically will criticize GM for not doing more than implementing the field service campaign back in 2005, and point to GM's failure to take any action in the on-going FPE investigation that has now been dragging on for almost two years as proof positive of GM's conscience [sic] indifference and willful misconduct when it comes to the safety of its vehicles' occupants.[174]

---

170 Ronald Porter, Settlement Review Committee Case Summary (Aug. 8, 2013), at 13 [DOC ID00000 2818612].

171 Ronald Porter, Settlement Review Committee Case Summary (Aug. 8, 2013), at 13 [DOC ID00000 2818612].

172 Ronald Porter, Settlement Review Committee Case Summary (Aug. 8, 2013), at 13 [DOC ID00000 2818612].

173 Ronald Porter, Settlement Review Committee Case Summary (Aug. 8, 2013), at 36 [DOC ID00000 2818612].

174 Ronald Porter, Settlement Review Committee Case Summary (Aug. 8, 2013), at 36 [DOC ID 00000 2818612].

EVALUATION AND RECOMMENDATION

This case needs to be settled. As outlined above, there is little doubt that a jury here will find that the ignition switch used on [redacted] 2005 Cobalt was defective and unreasonably dangerous, and that it did not meet GM's own torque specifications. In addition, the PRTS documents referenced above and the on-going FPE investigation have enabled plaintiffs' counsel to develop a record from which he can compellingly argue that GM has known about this safety defect from the time the first 2005 Cobalts rolled off the assembly line and essentially has done nothing to correct the problem for the last nine years. He specifically will criticize GM for not doing more than implementing the field service campaign back in 2005, and point to GM's failure to take any action in the on-going FPE investigation that has now been dragging on for almost two years as proof positive of GM's conscience indifference and willful misconduct when it comes to the safety of its vehicles' occupants.

. . .

11. Conclusions: 2011 to 2013

The failures from 2011 to 2013 demonstrate a lack of urgency in the face of a pattern of airbag failures, an unwillingness by GM personnel to re-evaluate their conclusions, a lack of accountability or leadership in driving the investigations to a conclusion, and a continued reluctance to elevate issues. The 2011 failures include:

- In early January 2011, GM lawyers—including safety lawyers and product litigation lawyers—attended the Roundtable and decided that it was important to meet to "see some additional information" about the airbag "anomaly." It took until July to schedule the meeting, a delay no witness could explain.
- In July 2011, GM lawyers called a meeting to make sure that senior engineering management had "eyeballs" on the issue and "not let it flow through the normal process." Yet, Wachtel opened the investigation and did little else. The investigation would remain open and unresolved for two-and-a-half years. Neither the lawyers nor the engineers elevated the issue to the top levels of management.
- When he was assigned the investigation in the summer of 2011, Stouffer obtained an old PI file (Kiihr's) with background on the 2005 moving stall investigation, and obtained the TSBs. Stouffer did not share this information with GM product liability lawyers or with Sprague. Stouffer now knew (1) that the Cobalt had a history of the Ignition Switch being turned accidentally to Accessory because of low torque, and (2) that airbags do not deploy when the Ignition Switch is in Accessory. Regardless of whether there were

other issues affecting other model years, any driver who turned the Cobalt Ignition Switch off with a knee (a problem documented in the TSB) was disabling airbags. Instead of addressing this safety issue, he worked to find a solution that would solve the problem for all years and all positions of the Ignition Switch.

The consequence of the failures of 2011 was delay. The unexplained gap between the Roundtable and the July meeting (a meeting ostensibly to convey urgency) constituted a delay of a half a year. And the investigation that proceeded from that meeting moved forward without any sense of urgency, ultimately taking two-and-a-half years.

Failures in the Cobalt investigation continued in 2012:

- In March 2012, an electrical engineer found the TSB after a visit to a junkyard where he noticed that the keys turned extremely easily and doing his own search of GM records to see whether this was a documented problem. The TSB was forwarded to FPA engineers, in-house GM product liability lawyers and outside counsel. Based on the TSB, outside counsel reached the same conclusion that Trooper Young and Indiana University had five years earlier, and warned of the risk of punitive damages because "GM will be forced to contend with other incidents, some of which resulted in deaths, due to the non-deployment of the frontal airbags in the 2005–2007 Cobalt." No lawyer elevated the issue to the General Counsel.
- In May 2012, with the search for root cause making little progress, Kemp persuaded Terry Woychowski (a Vice President) to "champion" the issue, but Woychowski soon retired. Then Kemp recruited Federico (an Executive Director) to replace Woychowski as the second "champion," but Federico viewed himself as doing nothing but "energiz[ing] the team," not bringing the investigation to a conclusion. Neither Woychowski nor Federico elevated the issue up their chain of command.
- In June 2012, DeGiorgio once again told Stouffer, this time in writing, that there was no effect on the torque of the switch due to changes made in the Ignition Switch in 2006, again diverting investigative efforts.
- In June 2012, plaintiff's expert Erin Shipp located both the TSB and the Indiana University study and came to the same correct conclusion as the Indiana University team. Having been made

aware of the Indiana University study by the expert, Palmer transmitted it to Wachtel, Stouffer, Sprague and Kemp in July. But still GM engineers did not accept the correct theory. Rather, there were more meetings and referral to yet another group, the Red X team (which made no progress whatsoever).

Finally, in 2013, now that another plaintiff's expert had provided GM engineers with photographs of how the MY 2008 ignition switch differed from earlier Cobalts, the response was referral to an outside expert and yet more meetings:

- In February 2013, Stouffer—after almost two years—declared himself "stuck," and he and Wachtel recommended hiring an outside expert, which did not happen until the "bombshell" at DeGiorgio's deposition in April 2013.
- In April 2013, GM lawyers and engineers received photographs from an expert proving that DeGiorgio's statements had misled his colleagues for years; contrary to his repeated denials, there had been a part change years before that affected ignition switch torque. The plaintiff's expert had done what none of the GM engineers had done; he took apart two switches and compared them.
- The response to the revelation at the DeGiorgio deposition was to hire an expert. Gay Kent, who recently had become the third "champion," and who had personally replicated a moving stall eight years earlier in 2005, soon held what she called a "kick off meeting" that included the expert. It took six months after the DeGiorgio deposition for the expert to provide his written report concurring that the Ignition Switch had changed—just as the photographs had shown.
- In July 2013, outside counsel warned of a "compelling[ ]" case that GM had known about the defect since 2005 "and essentially has done nothing to correct the problem for the last nine years." Still, no GM lawyer apprised the General Counsel. The investigation under Kent awaited the completion of the outside expert's report. Delphi, GM's supplier which built the ignition switch, was not contacted until October.
- In November 2013, after receiving the written report from the outside expert verifying that the ignition switch had, indeed, changed in MY 2008 Cobalts, Stouffer finally reached the same

> conclusion that Trooper Young and Indiana University had in 2007: that the Ignition Switch was inadvertently being turned to Accessory and that, consequently, the airbags would not deploy. Stouffer's conclusion was reported to yet further committees, and it would not be until January 31, 2014 that the recall was ordered.

By this period, most of the information silos relating to the root cause had collapsed. A new set of failures became more predominant. One was the failure to revisit one's own conclusions. The GM investigator had been so focused on the SDM solution that he failed to act on what was right before his eyes—regardless of whether the Cobalt was in Run or Accessory from MY 2008, drivers were kneeing off the power in Cobalts, as they had been since 2005, and in those instances airbags did not deploy by GM's own design. Stouffer failed to revisit his first conclusions, albeit after having been misled on multiple occasions by DeGiorgio's repeated denials. After conclusion of the long investigation, the next step was referral to more committees. . . .

VII. GM's Leadership, the Tone at the Top, and GM Culture

This section addresses a number of issues that do not fit neatly into a chronology, but that broadly affected the entire company during the relevant period. Below we address the role of the current senior leadership at GM and the Board; the extent of their knowledge of the issues discussed above; the messages sent by senior leadership and the environment that they created for employees ("tone at the top"); and GM's culture and the impact that it may have had on how GM's employees responded to the Cobalt's problems.

A. Current Senior Leadership

The current CEO Mary Barra, the current Executive Vice President, Global Product Development, Purchasing & Supply Chain Mark Reuss, and the current General Counsel Michael Millikin did not learn about the Ignition Switch's safety issues and the lengthy delay in addressing them until after the EFADC decided to issue the recall on January 31, 2014. A few weeks earlier, in December 2013, Ms. Barra and Mr. Millikin had been provided limited information that data was being reviewed that could lead to a recall.

As part of Jenner's engagement, we were asked to prioritize our review of the involvement, if any, of these three current senior leaders in the events that led to the belated Ignition Switch recall. We conducted a thorough investigation that included (a) review of a large number of documents collected from numerous custodians, including potentially relevant e-mails any of the three senior leaders sent or received at pertinent times; (b) interviews of GM employees in the three leaders' respective chains of reporting who might have discussed Cobalt- related issues with them; and (c) interviews of each of Mary Barra, Mark Reuss and Michael Millikin. All of the evidence we reviewed corroborated the conclusion that none of the three current leaders had knowledge of the problems with the Cobalt's Ignition Switch or nondeployment of airbags in the Cobalt until December 2013 at the earliest.

Before becoming GM's CEO on January 15, 2014, Mary Barra had served for the preceding nearly three years as Senior Vice President and then Executive Vice President for Global Product Development, Purchasing & Supply Chain. Before becoming responsible for Global Product Development in February, 2011, Barra had served in other capacities that did not typically involve recalls or the recall decision-making process.[175] As head of the Product Development organization, Barra had responsibility for the global vehicle engineering function, headed by John Calabrese, as well as the global quality function headed by Terry Woychowski and then Alicia Boler-Davis.[176] The engineering and quality functions encompassed many of the personnel involved in the FPE process as well as the members of the EFADC. Barra became well acquainted with the recall process when the issues involving the Chevrolet Volt's lithium- ion battery arose in 2011. Based on that experience and others she believed that recall issues were addressed with appropriate urgency and that the recall decision-making process worked well.[177]

Barra first began to learn of some aspect of the Cobalt's Ignition Switch issue in December 2013, when she was told by Calabrese that the company was working on an analysis that might lead to a decision to recall the Cobalt. She did not learn more about the matter until shortly after the EFADC made the recall decision on January 31, 2014.[178]

Our review of contemporaneous e-mails and other documents corroborated these recollections. In that connection, we investigated certain e-mails that raised issues with the Cobalt or with moving stalls with Barra before year-end 2013, but those e-mails all concerned other issues, not the Ignition Switch. First, in March, 2010, Barra was among many recipients of an e-mail invitation to an FPE team meeting attaching information about a power steering problem in the Cobalt.[179]

---

175 J&B Interview of Mary Barra, April 14, 2014.

176 In mid-2013 then-CEO Daniel Akerson shifted the reporting line for Boler-Davis as Senior Vice President of Global Quality and Customer Experience directly to the CEO.

177 J&B Interview of Mary Barra, April 14, 2014.

178 J&B Interview of Mary Barra, April 14, 2014; J&B Interview of Alicia Boler-Davis, March 25, 2014.

179 J&B Interview of Mary Barra, April 14, 2014.

By that date Barra had become Vice President of Global Human Resources and had no role in such a meeting or its subject matter; she does not recall the e-mail or its attachment, which concerned a separate power steering issue, not the Ignition Switch.[180]

Second, on October 3, 2011, after Barra had become Senior Vice President for Global Product Development, the then-Vice President for Global Quality sent her a press report about a power steering problem in the Ion and questioning whether it should have been included in GM's recall of the Cobalt a year earlier for a similar issue.[181] Again, nothing in this report mentioned any problem with the Ignition Switch, moving stalls, or airbag non-deployment in either the Ion or the Cobalt.

Third, on April 22, 2012, Barra was one of two recipients of an e-mail from a former GM employee reporting a moving stall in his Buick that he described as an "isolated/freak" incident attributable to the key design and suggesting that the company investigate and perhaps issue a service bulletin. Barra forwarded the e-mail to the VP for Global Quality, Terry Woychowski, and asked him to investigate the matter.[182] Barra's e-mail was then forwarded within the company and an e-mail discussion ensued ultimately involving eight people, but no longer including Barra. In one such subsequent entry in the e-mail string, Wachtel mentioned that early Cobalts had a similar issue but a design change to the key had addressed the issue.[183] Barra was not copied on any of the subsequent e-mails and did not learn of the Cobalt issue at that time.[184]

---

180 J&B Interview of Mary Barra, April 14, 2014.

181 J&B Interview of Mary Barra, April 14, 2014.

182 J&B Interview of Mary Barra, April 14, 2014.

183 J&B Interview of Mary Barra, April 14, 2014. Barra stated that none of the subsequent e-mails in the chain, following her April 22, 2012 e-mail, had ever come to her attention. *Id.* Barra did not recall anyone communicating to her a resolution of the concern she forwarded to Woychowski on April 22, 2012. *Id.* She also stated that neither Carmen Benavides nor Maureen Foley-Gardner—both of whom are copied on Doug Wachtel's April 23, 2012 e-mail—brought the Cobalt complaints referenced in Wachtel's email to her attention, or ever spoke to be about issues with the Cobalt during the time period of this email. *Id.* We confirmed in interviews or through counsel that neither Wachtel's April 23, 2012 e-mail describing 2005 Cobalt complaints nor the historical complaints themselves were brought to Barra's attention. Wachtel confirmed that he did not speak to Barra about his email or the topic of the 2005 Cobalt complaints, of which—per his email—he heard none after 2005. Terrence Connolly also confirmed that he never discussed the email with Barra. J&B Interview of Terrence Connolly, April 28, 2014. Carmen Benavides did not recall the e-mail and did not recall having any discussions with Barra about it. Maureen Foley Gardner said she would not have paid close attention to the e-mail because she was just coming into her role, and she did not recall any follow-up to the e-mail. J&B Interview of Maureen Foley-Gardner, May 19, 2014. Jeffrey Kouchan did not recall the e-mail. J&B Interview of Jeff Konchan, May 7, 2014.

184 J&B Interview of Mary Barra, April 14, 2014; J&B Interview of Alicia Boler-Davis, March 25, 2014.

Finally, on November 19, 2013, Alicia Boler-Davis responded to an e-mail from Maureen Foley-Gardner that had alerted Boler-Davis to a likely Cobalt field action involving its Ignition Switch and airbag non-deployment, by saying that Foley-Gardner should send her a quick summary that she would then share with Barra.[185] Barra was not copied on that e-mail, and Boler-Davis reports that she did not share any information with Barra about the Cobalt issue until January 31, 2014. None of these e-mails is evidence that Barra was informed about the Cobalt Ignition Switch issues before Calabrese alerted her in December to the analysis that was being undertaken on that subject.

Mark Reuss succeeded Barra as EVP for Global Product Development, Purchasing & Supply Chain, when she became CEO. Before that he had been President of GMNA from 2009 through 2013, and before heading GMNA he had served in various engineering positions within GMNA except for brief periods when he led GM's business in Australia and New Zealand in 2008–09 and a short stint in 2009 as Global Vice President of Engineering.[186] He joined GM in 1986. He did not have engineering responsibility for the Cobalt in any of his positions.[187]

As President of GMNA, Reuss was typically informed of recalls after the EFADC had made its decisions. He learned of the Cobalt recall after the EFADC made its decision on January 31, 2014.[188] None of the documents we reviewed or interviews we conducted identified any evidence that is inconsistent with Mr. Reuss' recollection.

Michael Millikin became General Counsel in July 2009, after more than three decades in various positions in GM's Legal Department. Between 2000 and 2009 he had responsibility in various positions for coordinating GM's global legal processes and did not have any role in recalls, product liability matters or safety-related issues in the United States. Until the recall decision was made in 2014, he had not been informed of the lengthy review of the Cobalt's Ignition Switch issue in which GM lawyer Bill Kemp had participated for years. He also had been unaware of the litigation involving fatal accidents by Cobalt drivers, such as the case.[189]

Millikin's direct and indirect subordinates, who at various times before 2014 became aware of the problems with the Cobalt, confirmed in interviews that they

[185] J&B Interview of Mary Barra, April 14, 2014.

[186] J&B Interview of Mark Reuss, April 15, 2014.

[187] J&B Interview of Mark Reuss, April 15, 2014.

[188] J&B Interview of Mark Reuss, April 15, 2014.

[189] J&B Interview of Michael Millikin, April 4, 2014; J&B Interview of Lawrence Buonomo, April 16, 2014.

did not bring them to Millikin's attention.[190] The case had been settled for $5 million, the highest amount for which his subordinates had authority to resolve a litigation without obtaining his approval. In December, 2013, the General Counsel of GMNA, Lucy Clark Dougherty, mentioned to Millikin that a possible recall was under consideration.[191] Kemp and Clark Dougherty reported the recall decision to Millikin and the facts underlying it for the first time on February 6, 2014.[192] Kemp acknowledged that he could not explain why he had not raised the Cobalt safety issues with Millikin before then.[193] Our investigation did not identify any documents that were inconsistent with these recollections of Millikin or the lawyers who reported to him.

B. The Board

To investigate the Board's role in the oversight of safety issues and the information that the Board received, we interviewed several current and former outside directors and chief executive officers, as well as many of the GM executives who made pertinent reports to the Board during the 11-year period from 2003 to early 2014. We also reviewed written materials provided to the Board during that period.

The Board's oversight of vehicle safety had multiple facets; no single committee of the Board was responsible for all vehicle safety-related issues, and the Board and its committees received a wide variety of reports that related at least in part to vehicle safety. Those reports included information in an aggregate form and did not discuss individual safety issues or individual recalls except in rare circumstances. Typically, neither the Board nor any of its committees reviewed the Company's response to specific product defects, which were the subject of hundreds of product investigations globally each year, culminating in an average of approximately 30 recalls each year.[194]

As discussed in more detail below, the Board and various committees reviewed information from management on a variety of different safety-related issues:

---

190 J&B Interview of William Kemp, April 17, 2014; J&B Interview of Lawrence Buonomo, April 16, 2014; J&B Interview of Lucy Clark Dougherty, April 16, 2014; J&B Interview of Jaclyn Palmer, April 24, 2014; J&B Interview of Ronald Porter, April 30, 2014.

191 J&B Interview of Michael Millikin, April 4, 2014; J&B Interview of Lucy Clark Dougherty, April 16, 2014.

192 J&B Interview of Michael Millikin, April 4, 2014; J&B Interview of Lucy Clark Dougherty, April 16, 2014.

193 J&B Interview of William Kemp, April 17, 2014.

194 *See* Recall Data from NHTSA, ODI website, *available at* http://www-odi.uhtsa.dot.gov/downloads/flatfiles.cfm.

a) evaluations of the quality and safety of GM's vehicles by third parties such as *Consumer Reports* and *JD Power* (the full Board);

b) the Company's interactions with NHTSA (the full Board);

c) recalls and warranty costs (the full Board);

d) the annual internal audit plan, which on two occasions during the relevant period included audits that encompassed the recall decision-making process (the Audit Committee);

e) risk management matters generally, which potentially could have raised issues relating to vehicle safety (the Audit Committee); and

f) the Company's public position on potential legislation and other public policy matters, which also could have touched on vehicle safety (Public Policy Committee).

As described elsewhere in this report, the slow pace of the Cobalt investigation and the emerging pattern of accidents potentially related to the safety defect were not escalated to the Company's most senior executives who from time-to-time met with the Board. The Board of Directors was not informed of any problem posed by the Cobalt ignition switch until February 2014.

1. Board Oversight Process

a. The Full Board

During the period in question, the Board as a whole received three different types of periodic reports that related to safety issues.

i. Periodic Reports

Quality Reports. One means by which the Board exercised oversight of safety-related issues was its review of information from management concerning vehicle "quality" issues. GM had a Vice President of Quality who oversaw a group that interacted with the engineers on quality issues; worked to reduce GM's warranty costs; tracked how GM's vehicles were evaluated by publications like *Consumer Reports* and *JD Power;* identified areas for improvement, including potential solutions or best practices used by other OEMs; and participated in evaluations of potential defects and recall decisions.[195] The Company considered safety issues to be partly the responsibility of this quality function, along with the engineering and manufacturing functions, because proper design and protection against production defects should ensure safe vehicle operation, and minimize safety

---

[195] J&B Interview of Kevin Williams, May 7, 2014; J&B Interview of James Hresko. May 7. 2014.

issues resulting from product failures.[196] The Board recognized that "quality" encompassed safety.[197]

During the period 2003–2014, the Board regularly received reports from management on the quality of GM's vehicles.[198] In the earlier part of this period, the reports focused on specific regions,[199] and in the later years, after the Company had globalized its quality function, the reports were typically more detailed and often included a focus on GMNA.[200] These reports were often accompanied by an oral presentation by the Vice President of Quality or another knowledgeable executive.[201] Similar presentations were made at the regular meetings held among the CEO and his/her direct reports.[202]

These GMNA quality reports typically included information on three broad topics, all of which related in part to safety. First, these reports focused on GM's

---

196 *See, e.g.,* J&B Interview of Mary Barra, April 14, 2014; *see also* J&B Interview of Phil Laskawy, May 20, 2014; J&B Interview of Daniel Akerson, May 15, 2014; J&B Interview of Kevin Williams, May 7, 2014.

197 *See, e.g.,* J&B Interview of Phil Laskawy, May 20, 2014; J&B Interview of Erroll Davis, May 20, 2014; J&B Interview of Daniel Akerson, May 15, 2014.

198 *See, e.g.,* Quality Update Presentation to General Motors Board *of* Directors (Oct. 10, 2013) [DOC ID 000240787014]; Minutes of the Regular Meeting of the Board of Directors of General Motors Company (Oct. 9–10. 2013), at 10 [DOC ID 000240787013]; 2011 Quality Performance Summary Presentation from Boardbook for the General Motors Board of Directors Meeting (Jan. 10–11, 2012) [DOC ID 000240752013]; Consumer Reports Presentation from Boardbook for the General Motors Board of Directors Meeting (Feb. 2–3, 2009) [DOC ID 000240757047]; Minutes of the Regular Meeting of the Board of Directors of General Motors Corporation (Feb. 2–3, 2009), at 3 [DOC ID 000240787010]; GM North America Quality Review Presentation from Boardbook for the General Motors Board of Directors Meeting (June 1–2, 2004) [DOC ID 000240757010]; Minutes of the Regular Meeting of the Board of Directors of General Motors Corporation (June 1–2, 2004), at 2 [DOC ID 000240787006].

199 *See, e.g.,* GM Asia Pacific Quality Review Presentation from Boardbook for the General Motors Board of Directors Meeting (Feb. 2–3, 2004) [DOC ID 000240757007]; Minutes of the Regular Meeting of the Board of Directors of General Motors Corporation (Feb. 2–3, 2004), at 2 [DOC ID 000240787005].

200 *See, e.g.,* 2011 Quality Performance Summary Presentation from Boardbook for the General Motors Board of Directors Meeting (Jan. 10–11, 2012) [DOC ID 000240752013]; Quality Review Presentation from Boardbook for the General Motors Board of Directors Meeting (Dec. 6–7, 2010) [DOC ID 000240757074]; Minutes of the Regular Meeting of the Board of Directors of General Motors Company (Dec. 6–7, 2010), at 3–4 [DOC ID 000240787012].

201 *See. e.g.* Quality Update Presentation to General Motors Board of Directors (Oct. 10, 2013) [DOC ID 000240787014]; Minutes of the Regular Meeting of the Board of Directors of General Motors Company (Oct. 9–10, 2013), at 10 [DOC ID 000240787013]; Global Quality Process from Boardbook for the General Motors Board of Directors Meeting (April 16–17, 2012) [DOC ID 000240752012]; Minutes of the Regular Meeting of the Board of Directors of General Motors Company (April 16–17, 2012), at 2–3 [DOC ID 000238341259]; Quality Update from Boardbook for the General Motors Board of Directors Meeting (Aug. 20–21, 2012) [DOC CD 000240752011]; Minutes of the Regular Meeting of the Board of Directors of General Motors Company (Aug. 20–21. 2012), at 5 [DOC ID 000238341262]: President's Report Quality Overview Presentation from Boardbook for the General Motors Board of Directors Meeting (Oct 6, 2009) [DOC ID 000240757054]; Minutes of the Regular Meeting of the Board of Directors of General Motors Company (Oct 5–6, 2009), at 2 [DOC ID 000240787011].

202 *See, e.g.,* Global Quality Update to GM Executive Operations Committee (Dec. 18, 2012) [DOC ID 000240756004]; J&B Interview of Daniel Akerson, May 15, 2014.

rankings in buyers' guides like *Consumer Reports* and *JD Power*,[203] Because these publications are highly respected by consumers and often play a part in buying decisions, GM personnel believed it was important to compete with other manufacturers in this forum, and the Board was particularly focused on these issues.[204] *Consumer Reports* and *JD Power* both include important safety-related information. For example, *Consumer Reports* includes evaluations of each car's "accident avoidance" (based on testing of braking and steering systems) and crash test performance (based on NHTSA and Insurance Institute of Highway Safety testing).[205] *JD Power* reported on initial quality (how many defects were reported in the first three months after purchase)[206] as well as dependability over time.[207]

The reports to the Board concerning the rankings of GM's cars in *Consumer Reports* and *JD Power* made it clear that GM had ample room for improvement in those evaluations, but they did not identify that GM's vehicles were unsafe or less safe than those manufactured by GM's competitors.[208]

---

[203] *See. e.g.*, 2011 Quality Performance Summary Presentation from Board book for the General Motors Board of Directors Meeting (Jan. 10–11, 2012) [DOC ID 000240752013]; Consumer Reports Presentation from Boardbook for the General Motors Board of Directors Meeting (Feb. 2–3, 2009) [DOC ID 000240757047]; Minutes of the Regular Meeting of the Board of Directors of General Motors Corporation (Feb. 2–3, 2009), at 3 [DOC ID 000240787010]; GM North America Quality Review Presentation from Boardbook for the General Motors Board of Directors Meeting (June 1–2, 2004) [DOC ID 000240757010]; Minutes of the Regular Meeting of the Board of Directors of General Motors Corporation (June 1–2, 2004), at 2 [DOC ID 000240787006].

[204] *See, e.g.*, J&B Interview of George Fisher, May 21, 2014; J&B Interview of Daniel Akerson, May 15, 2014; J&B Interview of Thomas Stephens, May 7, 2014; J&B Interview of Erroll Davis, May 20, 2014; J&B Interview of James Hresko, May 7, 2014.

[205] *See* Consumer Reports, "Compare Safety Ratings" (last updated Feb. 2014), *available at* http://www.consumerreports.org/cro/2012/12/compare-safety-ratings/index.htm; *see also* General Motors, Consumer Reports Presentation from the GM Board of Directors Director's February 2009 Session Boardbook (Feb. 2–3 2009), at 3–5 [DOC ID 000240757047].

[206] *See, e.g.*, J.D. Power, "2013 Initial Quality Study—Car Ratings & Rankings," *available at* http://autos.jdpower.com/ratings/quality.htm; *see also* General Motors Quality Review Presentation from the GM Board of Director's June 2004 Session Boardbook (June 1–2, 2004), at 3–5 [DOC ID 000240757010].

[207] *See, e.g.*, J.D. Power, "2013 U.S. Vehicle Dependability Study" (Feb. 13, 2013). *available at* http://autos.jdpower.com/content/press-release/bTiXte5/2013-u-s-vehicle-dependability-study.htm [DOC ID 000240787039]; *see also* General Motors Quality Update Presentation to the General Motors Board of Directors (Oct. 10, 2013), at 12 [DOC ID 000240787014].

[208] *See, e.g.*, General Motors, Quality Update Presentation to General Motors Board of Directors (Oct. 10, 2013) [DOC ID 000240787014]; Minutes of the Regular Meeting of the Board of Directors of General Motors Company (Oct 9–10, 2013), at 10 [DOC ID 000240787013]; 2011 Quality Perfomance Summary Presentation from Boardbook for the General Motors Board of Directors Meeting (Jan. 10–11, 2012) [DOC ID 000240752013]; Quality Review Presentation from Boardbook for the General Motors Board of Directors Meeting (Dec. 6–7, 2010) [DOC ID 000240757074]: J.D. Power Survey Review/Quality Update Presentation from Boardbook for the General Motors Board of Directors Meeting (June 2–3, 2008) [DOC ID 000240757043]; Minutes of the Regular Meeting of the Board of Directors of General Motors Corporation (June 2–3, 2008), at 3 [DOC ID 000240787009]; Consumer Reports Review from Boardbook for the General Motors Board of Directors Meeting (Dec. 3–4, 2007) [DOC ID 000240757038]; Minutes of the Regular Meeting of the Board of Directors of General Motors Corporation (Dec. 3–4, 2007) [DOC ID 000240787008];

Second, the quality reports included information about recalls. That information typically did not reference specific vehicles or individual recall decisions, but rather represented aggregate data about GM's recalls over time. More specifically, management typically provided the Board with data concerning the costs it incurred annually for "field actions," which included recalls, as well as the actual number of recalls GM issued each year and the number of vehicles encompassed by those recalls.[209] Those numbers varied from year-to-year, sometimes significantly. For example, in December, 2010, the Board received a presentation from the Vice President for Quality showing that GM's field actions had increased that year; management committed to "turn this around while protecting the customer."[210] The Board also reviewed the same annual recall-related statistics for GM's principal competitors. Based on the recall-related information they received over the years, the Board members and executives we interviewed believed that GM's recall process was functioning appropriately.[211]

Third, the quality reports focused on GM's warranty cost experience, which was also an indicator of whether its vehicles were safe to drive.[212] Warranty claims originate with customers experiencing real-world issues with their vehicles. And while warranty claims are by no means limited to problems with safety equipment or that otherwise reflect a vehicle's safe operation, a lower warranty cost generally indicates that a vehicle is dependable and reliable, which tends to mean the vehicle is safer as well.[213] As described earlier in this report, GM's engineers also viewed warranty claims as one source of information about possible safety issues.

J.D. Power Survey Review Presentation for the General Motors Board of Directors Meeting (June 4–5, 2007) [DOC ID 000240757035]; Minutes of the Regular Meeting of the Board of Directors of General Motors Corporation (June 4–5, 2007), at 2 [DOC ID 000240787007]; GM North America Quality Review Presentation from Boardbook for the General Motors Board of Directors Meeting (June 1–2, 2004) [DOC ID 000240757010].

[209] *See, e.g.,* 2011 Quality Performance Summary Presentation from Boardbook for the General Motors Board of Directors Meeting (Jan. 10–11, 2012) [DOC ID 000240752013]; Quality Review Presentation from Boardbook for the General Motors Board of Directors Meeting (Dec. 6–7, 2010) [DOC ID 000240757074]; Minutes of the Regular Meeting of the Board of Directors of General Motors Company (Dec. 6–7, 2010), at 3–4 [DOC ID 000240787012].

[210] Quality Review Presentation from Boardbook for the General Motors Board of Directors Meeting (Dec. 6–7, 2010), at 15. [DOC ID 000240757074].

[211] *See, e.g.,* J&B Interview of George Fisher, May 21, 2014; J&B Interview of Erroll Davis, May 20, 2014; J&B Interview of Phil Laskawy, May 20, 2014; J&B Interview of George ("Rick") Wagoner, May 12, 2014; J&B Interview of Mary Barra, April 14, 2014.

[212] *See, e.g.,* President's Report Quality Overview Presentation from Boardbook for the General Motors Board of Directors Meeting (Oct. 6, 2009) [DOC ID 000240757054]; Minutes of the Regular Meeting of the Board of Directors of General Motors Company (Oct. 5–6. 2009), at 2 [DOC ID 000240787011].

[213] J&B Interview of George ("Rick") Wagoner, May 12, 2014.

Litigation Reports. In addition to the quality reports, the full Board received a second regular report concerning safety issues: The Board received, in connection with essentially every meeting, a written legal update on pending or recent legal matters, encompassing not only product liability litigation but also other types of disputes including antitrust, environmental, and employment matters.[214] Prior to GM's bankruptcy, the Board also received an Annual Report on Product Liability Litigation that described both accident cases and asbestos matters.[215] In general, these reports summarized the number, severity, complexity and subject matter of product liability claims that GM had experienced in the most recent period. Both types of reports highlighted claims that were noteworthy for some reason, for example, claims involving unusually large verdicts.[216] These reports included safety-related information to the extent that safety issues were alleged and at issue in certain litigated matters, such as rollover risks or seat belt system failures.[217] No claim, settlement, or other aspect of any litigation involving the Ignition Switch, airbags, or moving stalls in the Cobalt vehicles was specifically referenced in any of the litigation reports provided to the Board.

Regulatory Reports. The third type of safety-related report received by the full Board concerned the regulatory environment, including matters such as responses

---

214 *See, e.g.*, Legal Review and Update, from Boardbook for the General Motors Board of Directors Meeting (Feb. 3–4, 2003) [DOC ID 000240757002]; Legal Review and Update, from Boardbook for the General Motors Board of Directors Meeting (Feb. 6, 2006) [DOC ID 000240757022]; Legal Report, from Boardbook for the General Motors Board of Directors Meeting (Sept. 8–9, 2009). [DOC ID 000240757053]; Legal Report to GM Board of Directors, from Boardbook for the General Motors Board of Directors Meeting (Oct. 10–12, 2012) [DOC ID 000240787040].

215 *See, e.g.*, Legal Review and Update, from Boardbook for the General Motors Board of Directors Meeting (Feb. 3–4, 2003) [DOC ID 000240757002]; Legal Review and Update, from Boardbook for the General Motors Board of Directors Meeting (Feb. 2–3, 2004) [DOC ID 000240787047]; Legal Review and Update, from Boardbook for the General Motors Board of Directors Meeting (Jan. 31–Feb 1, 2005) [DOC ID 000240787048]; Legal Review and Update, from Boardbook for the General Motors Board of Directors Meeting (Feb. 6, 2006) [DOC ID 000240757022].

216 *See, e.g.*, Legal Review and Update from Boardbook for the General Motors Board of Directors Meeting (Feb. 2–3, 2004) [DOC ID 000240787047]; Legal Review and Update from Boardbook for the General Motors Board of Directors Meeting (Jan. 31–Feb. 1, 2005) [DOC ID 000240787048]; Legal Review and Update from Boardbook for the General Motors Board of Directors Meeting (March 1, 2005) [DOC ID 000240787048]; Legal Review and Update from Boardbook for the General Motors Board of Directors Meeting (May 9, 2005) [DOC ID 000240787045]; Legal Review and Update from Boardbook for the General Motors Board of Directors Meeting (May 2, 2006) [DOC ID 000240787046].

217 *See, e.g.*, Legal Review and Update from Boardbook for the General Motors Board of Directors Meeting (Feb. 3–4, 2003), at 13 [DOC ID 000240757002]; Legal Review and Update from Boardbook for the General Motors Board of Directors Meeting (Dec. 2, 2003) [DOC ID 000240787043]; Legal Review and Update from Boardbook For the General Motors Board of Directors Meeting (Feb. 2–3, 2004) [DOC ID 000240787047]; Legal Review and Update from Boardbook for the General Motors Board of Directors Meeting (Jan. 31–Feb 1, 2005) [DOC ID 000240787048]; Legal Review and Update from Boardbook for the General Motors Board of Directors Meeting (Feb. 6, 2006), at 8 [DOC ID 000240757022]; Legal Review and Update from Boardbook for the General Motors Board of Directors Meeting (May 2, 2006) [DOC ID 000240787046].

to the passage of the TREAD Act, GM's NHTSA obligations, and various safety-related initiatives that had been proposed. As requirements under the TREAD Act and GM's obligations to NHTSA evolved, at times the Board received additional reports about these matters,[218] including a 2004 report that the Company had agreed to pay a $1 million fine to resolve a disagreement with NHTSA.[219] This fine was reported to the Board as follows:

> Over the past two years, GM has disagreed with the federal traffic safety agency (NHTSA) over whether certain windshield wiper problems in 2002 and 2003 SUVs and certain engine stalling issues involving recent model Saabs posed an unreasonable risk to safety and should be recalled for that reason. To apply pressure on GM, the agency issued a civil penalty demand letter to GM alleging that GM had violated the Traffic Safety Act by not providing timely notification of and remedy for these alleged defects. This led to high-level discussions which toned down the rhetoric and resolved a number of other open issues on a basis satisfactory to GM. However, as part of this resolution, GM agreed to pay a one million dollar penalty relating only to the windshield wiper issues. The agency agreed to downplay the penalty and forego any press release. Through a continuation of the high-level dialogue between agency officials and GM's top engineers, GM will endeavor to minimize and avoid such situations in the future.[220]

In contrast, in 2013, the Board, including the then-CEO, was not informed that NHTSA had recently criticized GM's responsiveness regarding several specified recalls, service bulletins, and investigations.[221]

ii. Specific Reports

In unusual circumstances, management also reported about specific safety-related events. In one such case, in June, 2011 a Chevrolet Volt, GM's first production vehicle with an electric propulsion system, suffered what was

---

218 Overview of General Motors North America Legal Issues and Activity, from Boardbook for the General Motors Board of Directors Meeting (Feb. 29, 2004), at 9 [DOC ID 000240787055]; U.S. Legislative and Regulatory Issues from Boardbook for the General Motors Board of Directors Meeting (April 5–6, 2009), at 8 [DOC ID 000240787064]; Legislative and Regulatory Issues Update and Regulatory Issues Primer from Boardbook for the General Motors Board of Directors Meeting (Nov. 2–3, 2009), at 6–7 [DOC ID 000240787049].

219 Legal Review and Update from Boardbook for the General Motors Board of Directors Meeting (Aug. 3, 2004), at 10 [DOC ID 000240787042].

220 Legal Review and Update from Boardbook for the General Motors Board of Directors Meeting (Aug. 3, 2004), at 10 [DOC ID 000240787042].

221 E-mail from Michael J. Robinson, GM, to Gay Kent, GM (July 24, 2013) [DOC ID 000240755008].

described as a "thermal event" three weeks after being subjected to severe NHTSA crash testing.[222] Management reported to the Board on the status of GM's response to the Volt event,[223] and kept the Board apprised thereafter as discussions with NHTSA over the appropriate resolution proceeded.

The Board also received a report on the Toyota unintended acceleration problems in 2010.[224] GM's management had conducted a "deep dive" to determine whether any GM vehicles (other than the Pontiac Vibe, which was developed and produced with Toyota) were susceptible to a similar risk of unintended acceleration, and determined that they were not.[225] Management's report to the Board in March 2010 indicated that Toyota's problem was not shared by GM or other major manufacturers.[226]

b. Board Committees

In addition to the reports to the full Board described above, two Board committees—the Public Policy Committee and the Audit Committee—had specific responsibilities that related to some aspects of vehicle safety.

i. Public Policy Committee

The Public Policy Committee, as its name suggests, focused on the positions GM adopted on public policy issues, and on GM's activities with respect to pending legislation and regulation that affected GM. The scope of the Public Policy Committee's responsibility in the period from 2003 through mid-2013 encompassed the "social and political" issues that might affect the Company's business and reputation; the list of such issues included "automotive safety" but also encompassed other issues such as corporate social responsibility, diversity, environmental matters, education, employee health and safety, trade, and philanthropic activities.[227] In mid-2013, the Public Policy Committee revised its

[222] *See* NHTSA "Chevrolet Volt Battery Incident Overview Report" (Jan. 2012), *available at* www.nhtsa.gov/staticfiles/nvs/pdf/Final_Reports.pdf [DOC ID 000240787024].

[223] *See* Minutes of the Regular Meeting of the Board of Directors of General Motors Company (Dec. 13, 2011). [DOC ID 000240752007]; J&B Interview of Phil Laskawy, May 20, 1014; J&B Interview of Daniel Akerson, May 15, 2014.

[224] Legislative and Regulatory Issues Update from Boardbook for the General Motors Board of Directors Meeting (March 1–2, 2010), at 1 [DOC ID 000240757064]; *see also* J&B Interview of Phil Laskawy, May 20, 2014.

[225] E-mail from Michael P. Millikin, GM, to Deborah Nowak-Vanderhoef, GM (Feb. 17, 2010) [DOC ID 000006293898].

[226] *See* Legislative and Regulatory Issues Update from Boardbook for the General Motors Board of Directors Meeting (March 1–2, 2010), at 1 [DOC ID 000240757064].

[227] General Motors Company Public Policy Committee Charter (Nov. 15, 2011) [DOC ID M_00206123]; General Motors Company Public Policy Committee Charter (Oct. 6, 2009) [DOC ID 000240757055]; *see also* General Motors Corporation Proxy Statement (April 17, 2001), at 7 [DOC ID 000240787056]; General Motors Corporation Proxy Statement (April 29, 2005), at 7 [DOC ID 000240787057]; General Motors Corporation

charter to make clearer that its focus was on issues, including vehicle safety, only to the extent they affected the Company's reputation in the legislative and regulatory arenas.[228] In clarifying its charter, the Public Policy Committee noted that with respect to "Product Safety," the oversight responsibility already resided with the "Full Board."[229]

Consistent with these iterations of its charter, the Public Policy Committee did not have oversight responsibility for the recall decision-making process, nor did it undertake to review management's processes for ensuring compliance with NHTSA's regulatory requirements concerning recalls.

ii. Audit Committee

The Audit Committee, in addition to its core function overseeing GM's financial reporting process and systems of disclosure and internal controls, was also responsible for oversight of GM's external and internal auditors, and its risk management process.[230] These aspects of the Audit Committee's work provided two oversight mechanisms for the Audit Committee to receive information about processes that related to vehicle safety, among many other subjects.

First, each year the Audit Committee reviewed the annual internal audit plan that had been prepared by the internal audit function in conjunction with management.[231] Prior to that review, the chairman of the Audit Committee typically personally reviewed the proposed plan in detail at a special half-day meeting with senior internal audit staff.[232] The internal audit plan covered a broad

---

Proxy Statement (April 25, 2008), at 12 [DOC ID 000240787058]; General Motors Company Proxy Statement (April 26, 2012), at 22 [DOC ID 000240787059].

228 *See* Proposed Public Policy Committee Responsibilities, from Materials for the General Motors Company Public Policy Committee Meeting (June 5, 2013), at 1 [DOC ID 000240755006]; *see also* General Motors Company Public Policy Committee Charter (June 6, 2013) [DOC ID 000240755007]; Other GM Board Committees—Risk Management Responsibilities, from Materials for the General Motors Company Finance and Risk Policy Committee (Oct. 4, 2010), at 1–4 [DOC ID 000000018172].

229 J&B Interview of Erroll Davis, May 20, 2014; Proposed Public Policy Committee Risk Assignments, from Materials for the General Motors Company Public Policy Committee Meeting (June 5, 2013), at 2 [DOC ID 000240755006]; e-mail from Michael Millikin, GM, to Daniel Akerson, GM (Feb. 4, 2013) (noting that the quality risk received regular attention by the Board of Directors) [DOC ID 000240752014]; Minutes of the Public Policy Committee (June 12, 2012), at 2 [14051500011905]; Memorandum from Bob Ferguson to Members of the Public Policy Committee and Daniel Akerson (Oct. 11, 2011) [DOC ID 000240757081); Finance and Risk Committee Meeting Presentation (March 14, 2011), at 4–5 [DOC ID 000000018343].

230 Audit Committee Charter (Nov. 15, 2011) [DOC ID 000240752021].

231 *See, e.g.*, 2010 Global Audit Plan, from Boardbook for the General Motors Board of Directors Meeting (Nov. 30–Dec. 1, 2009) [DOC ID 000240787061]; 2009 Global Audit Plan, from Materials for the General Motors Audit Committee Meeting (Dec. 1, 2008) [DOC ID 000240787060]; Minutes of Meeting of the Audit Committee (Dec. 3, 2007), at 4 [DOC ID 000240787053].

232 *See, e.g.*, General Auditor's Report (March 3, 2008) [DOC ID 000240787027]; J&B Interview of Phil Laskawy, May 20, 2014.

array of topics affecting the global enterprise; the internal auditors have conducted on average more than 100 internal audits each year over the past decade.[233]

During that period, two internal audits included a review of GM's process concerning field actions and recalls or Field Performance Evaluations. An audit of the Global Quality organization in 2013 identified modest opportunities for process enhancement, but did not find any problem with the process by which safety issues were identified or addressed (and did not refer to any specific vehicle issue).[234] In 2006, internal auditors conducted a similar audit of GM-Europe's quality function, which it found satisfactory.[235] Thus, the internal audit function reviewed GM's process for evaluating possible defects or for making recall decisions, and that review was subject to the Audit Committee's oversight.

Second, the Audit Committee oversaw GM's risk management process, including reviewing the "risk factors" described in GM's public disclosures,[236] and meeting regularly with the Chief Risk Officer in the years his work was overseen by the Committee.[237] In recent years, the Company's internal "Enterprise Risk Management" ("ERM") process has identified "quality" as an important risk and defined it as: "[m]ajor or chronic product problems could occur, resulting in negative public image, large product recall campaigns and/or significant, unexpected increases in warranty expenses."[238] Management and the Board have

[233] *See, e.g.*, Audit Status Report—All Closed Audits 2003–2014 [DOC ID 000240794002]; Minutes of the Audit Committee (Dec. 1. 2008), at 2 [DOC ID 000240787052].

[234] Audit Report on Global Quality (Nov. 25, 2013) [DOC ID 000240755011].

[235] Report on Audit of General Motors Europe Quality (Planning and Operations) (April 12, 2006) [DOC ID 000240757023].

[236] *See, e.g.*, Enterprise Risk Management, from Boardbook for the General Motors Board of Directors Meeting (Nov. 30–Dec. 1, 2009), at 3–4 [DOC ID 000240787026]; Minutes of Meeting No. 443 of the Audit Committee (Oct 1. 2007), at 4 [DOC ID 000240787051]

[237] Agenda of the Regular Meeting of the Board of Directors of General Motors Corporation (Nov. 18, 2013), at 2 [DOC ID 000240787017]; Agenda of the Regular Meeting of the Board of Directors of General Motors Corporation (March 18, 2013), at 2 [DOC ID 000240787016]; Agenda of the Regular Meeting of the Board of Directors of General Motors Corporation (Aug. 20–21, 2012), at 2 [DOC ID 000240787015]; J&B Interview of Brian Thelen, May 2, 2014. For a two-year period between mid-2010 and mid-2012, the Board had a "Finance and Risk" committee to which oversight of general risk management was allocated. Finance and Risk Policy Committee Charter, from Materials for Meeting of the Finance and Risk Policy Committee (Oct. 1, 2010), at 14–16 [DOC ID 000000018172]; Finance and Risk Committee Meeting Presentation (May 16, 2011), at 3 [DOC ID 000000018399]. Before and after that period. the Audit Committee had general oversight responsibility for risk management. General Motors Company, 2013 Proxy Statement (April 25, 2013), at 23 [DOC ID 000240787029]; Audit Committee Charter within General Motors Corporation, 2006 Proxy Statement (April 28, 2006), at A-1–A-3 [DOC ID 000240787028].

[238] 2013 Key Risk Classification (Dec. 18, 2012), at 16 [DOC ID 000240752016]; Audit Committee Meeting Documents (Aug. 19, 2013), at 155–159 [DOC ID 000000028582]; *see also* General Motors Company, 2013 Annual Report (Form 10-K) (Feb. 6, 2014), at 23 [DOC ID 000240787033]; General Motors Company, 2012 Annual Report (Form 10-K) (Feb. 15, 2013), at 25 [DOC ID 000240787031]; General Motors Company, 2011 Annual Report (Form 10-K) (Feb. 27, 2012), at 25–26 [DOC ID 000240787032]; General Motors Company, 2010 Registration Statement (Form S-1) (Aug. 18, 2010), at 24 [DOC ID 000240787062]; General

addressed this risk through their emphasis on quality improvement,[239] and no specific vehicle safety issue was brought to the Audit Committee's attention as part of its oversight of risk management other than a risk associated with lithium ion batteries.[240]

2. The Cobalt Ignition Switch

a. The Board's Lack of Knowledge

Before 2014, none of the written reports to the Board included any information concerning the Ignition Switch. We have not identified any evidence that the Board was otherwise informed of this problem, of GM's delay in addressing it, or of the fatalities or accidents associated with it. Moreover, none of the executives we interviewed who presented on quality or recall issues at Board meetings in the pertinent period were aware of the Ignition Switch problem.

As noted above, the Board did not typically receive reports on the subject of individual defects or individual recalls; the Board also did not receive data about traffic fatalities associated with GM's vehicles, except in the context of some of the regular litigation update reports that referenced a small number of cases unrelated to the Cobalt.

b. The March 5, 2009 Body/Exterior SMT VPR Update Slide Deck

In March 2009, CEO Rick Wagoner may have viewed a slide deck that included, in a "back-up" slide, a reference to the Cobalt's inadvertent cut-off issue. That slide, in a 72-slide presentation, described the then-recent change in the Cobalt's key design from a slot to a hole.[241] The back-up slide focused solely on warranty cost reduction and did not characterize the matter as a safety issue or mention airbag non-deployment, accidents or fatalities.[242] Wagoner does not recollect reviewing any part of the slide deck.[243]

Because the slide deck was found in the data collected from Wagoner's computer, and the potential importance of Wagoner's possible review of the back-up slide, we conducted an extensive investigation of its origin and of the meetings

---

Motors Company, 2010 Annual Report (form 10-K) (March 1, 2011), at 38 [DOC ID 000160743288]; General Motors Company, 2009 Annual Report (Form 10-K) (April 7, 2010), at 31 [DOC ID 000240787031].

239 J&B Interview of Phil Laskawy, May 20, 2014; J&B Interview of George ("Rick") Wagoner, May 12, 2014.

240 Materials for the General Motors Company Audit Committee Meeting (March 18, 2013), at 117 [DOC ID 000240787039].

241 Body/Exterior SMT, VPR Update Plan/Performance (March 5, 2009), at 34 [DOC ID W_00607350].

242 Body/Exterior SMT, VPR Update Plan/Performance (March 5, 2009), at 31, 34 [DOC ID W_00607 350].

243 J&B Interview of George ("Rick") Wagoner, May 12, 2014.

in which it was discussed to determine whether Wagoner was informed of the change or of the unmentioned safety implications. The background to the slide deck follows.

As discussed above, in early 2009, GM personnel implemented a change to the design of the Cobalt's ignition key to a hole from a slot beginning with production of the Cobalt's 2010 model year in mid-2009. Wagoner did not attend the meeting in January 2009 at which the keyhole design change to save warranty cost was discussed.[244]

About six weeks later, certain slides that had been used in the January meeting were included among 57 "back-up" slides that appeared in a 72-slide deck that in turn was used for one of nine separate presentations made at a meeting on March 5, 2009, of the Vehicle Program Review ("VPR") team, which met on a close-to-weekly basis.[245] The presentation that included the back-up slides focused on both material and warranty cost reductions achieved by the "Body/Exterior SMT," one of the "system management teams" that focused on cost, quality and related issues with respect to eight separate systems across all GM vehicle platforms.[246] The presentation's primary slides addressed such actions as "supplier workshops" and a new "week of claim tool" devised to expedite issue identification; some of the many back-up slides in the presentation focused on "side closure" issues, and in turn the back-up slides to the "side closure" back-up slides included the January 2009 slides about changing the Cobalt's key head design from a slot to a hole.[247]

Wagoner did not attend the March 5, 2009 meeting or, at least typically, any other of the VPR meetings.[248] He and more than 20 other executives were routinely e-mailed summaries of the discussion after each week's VPR meeting ended, and they may have had access to the slide deck presentations on a shared internal website.[249] The engineer who believes he presented the Body/Exterior

244 J&B Interview of Gary Altman, May 20, 2014.

245 *See* Gary Altman, Program Quality Sufficiency Review (Jan. 29, 2009), at 38–40 [DOC ID 000007551904; GMNHTSA000281704]; Body/Exterior SMT, VPR Update Plan/Performance (March 5, 2009), at 30–34 [DOC ID W_00607350]; e-mail from Ran Charby, GM, to Anthony Brown, GM, et. al. (Feb. 27, 2009) [DOC ID 000106626436]; VPR Meeting Notes (March 5, 2009) [DOC ID H_00262247], attached to e-mail from Richard Ceppos, GM, to George ("Rick") Wagoner, GM, et. al. (March 5, 2009) [DOC ID H_00262244]; VPR Meeting Notes (March 5, 2009) [DOC ID H_00262247]; e-mail from Richard Ceppos, GM, to Edward Whitacre, GM (Dec. 17, 2009) [DOC ID W_00000480].

246 J&B Interview of Gary Altman, May 20, 2014; J&B Interview of James Hentschel, May 27, 2014.

247 Body/Exterior SMT, VPR Update Plan/Performance (March 5, 2009) [DOC ID W_00607350].

248 J&B Interview of George ("Rick") Wagoner, May 12, 2014; J&B Interview of Richard Ceppos, May 21, 2014; J&B Interview of James Hentschel, May 27, 2014; J&B Interview of Laurie Huizar, May 23, 2014.

249 *See e.g.*, E-mail from Ran Charby, GM, to Anthony Brown, GM, et. al. (Feb. 27, 2009) [DOC ID 000106626436]; e-mail from Richard Ceppos, GM, to George ("Rick") Wagoner, GM, et. al. (March 5, 2009)

SMT's information at the VPR meeting states that the back-up slides concerning the Cobalt key design change were not discussed at the VPR meeting, and the summary of the March 5, 2009 meeting does not mention that subject.[250]

Forensic analysis indicates that the Body/Exterior SMT presentation was opened on the evening of March 5, 2009, on Wagoner's computer, located in two files in a temporary folder bearing generic names. The presentation was not found in the data of the other custodians whose electronic files were collected in the investigation. There is no forensic evidence that Wagoner reviewed any specific slide within the presentation. As noted, Wagoner does not recollect viewing the presentation or the back-up slides; about three weeks later, on March 29, 2009, Wagoner agreed to resign as CEO at the request of the U.S. government's Auto Task Force.[251] Contemporaneous e-mails he exchanged with the person who provided the summary notes of the meeting do not mention the Cobalt issue or any other specific topic.[252]

3. Other Board Activities

One way in which the Board expressed its commitment to improving the quality of GM's vehicles was through the design of the short-term incentive compensation—bonus—plans that applied not only to corporate officers but also to employees at the executive, director, manager, and supervisor levels. With a single exception in the past decade, the annual targets GM had to achieve before any bonus would be payable included improvement of the quality of GM's vehicles. The quality component in the annual target constituted 10% of the overall calculation, and three financial and sales components accounted for the balance for each year in the past decade except 2010, when the target's components were limited to the three financial and sales metrics.[253] In about mid-2013, Alicia Boler-Davis, the head of Global Quality, became a direct report to then-CEO Dan Akerson (having previously reported to Mary Barra as EVP of Global Product Development, Purchasing & Supply Chain) and proposed an increase in the relative weighting of the "quality" factor in the incentive plan to

---

[DOC ID H_00262244]; e-mail from Richard Ceppos, GM, to Ed Whitecare, GM (Dec. 17, 2009) [DOC ID W_00000480].

250 J&B Interview of James Hentschel, May 27, 2014; VPR Meeting Notes (March 5, 2009) [DOC ID H_00262247], attached to e-mail from Richard Ceppos, GM, to George ("Rick") Wagoner, GM, et. al. (March 5, 2009) [DOC ID H_00262244].

251 J&B Interview of George ("Rick") Wagoner, May 12, 2014.

252 E-mail from George ("Rick") Wagoner, GM, to Richard Ceppos, GM (March 6, 2009) [DOC ID W_00037388]; e-mail from George ("Rick") Wagoner, GM, to Richard Ceppos, GM (March 8, 2009) [DOC ID W_00041634].

253 J&B Interview of Janice Uhlig, May 12, 2014 & May 16, 2014.

25%. The Board's Executive Compensation Committee approved the increased importance of quality improvement in determining the extent of bonuses, effective this year.[254]

Similarly, the annual performance objectives for the CEO set by the Board's Executive Compensation Committee included quality improvement as among the many factors by which the CEO's performance would be assessed by the Board.[255]

C. Tone at the Top on Safety

It is impossible to catalog all possible directives and management actions that might generally have influenced how GM employees viewed their roles and responsibilities. It is even more difficult to ascertain how the general tone set by senior leadership affected specific decisions made by individuals. Where individuals referenced specific management directives as the cause of their actions, we have identified them. In most circumstances, however, we could not ascribe a particular management action or policy directive from a senior executive as the reason for any specific action.

But the tone set at the top is relevant background for assessing GM's approach to the issues discussed in this report. Repeated throughout the interview process we heard from GM personnel two somewhat different directives—"when safety is at issue, cost is irrelevant" and "cost is everything." It is worth examining how those two messages collided.

GM personnel were quite consistent in saying that they understood that safety was a critical priority and that, if they identified a safety problem, cost should not be a factor in deciding whether and how to address the safety problem. For example, a senior manager in Accessories Engineering said that safety is the top pillar at GM.[256] Training material and directives that have been located for FPE process, the key engineering process for reviewing safety issues, make no references to cost-benefit analyses.[257] Indeed, an "FPE Sensitivity and TREAD Training" presentation from May 2004 by Kevin Williams, GM North America Vice President of Quality, notes:

> The harsh reality is—we are competing in a new world, one that demands a culture where there is no tolerance for defects at any point during in [sic] the vehicle development and manufacturing process.

---

[254] J&B Interview of Janice Uhlig, May 12, 2014 & May 16, 2014.

[255] J&B Interview of Janice Uhlig, May 12, 2014 & May 16, 2014.

[256] J&B Interview of Khris Lee, April 3, 2014.

[257] *See, e.g.*, New GMPT FPE Director's Orientation (Jan. 10, 2008) [DOC ID GMHEC000384265; GMNHTSA000383962; DOC ID 000001345940].

> Because the marketplace has zero tolerance for defects, this organization will have no tolerance for defects. If I sound alarmed, I am. . . . You must also become gatekeepers of quality. Consider every issue a potential defect and risk to the customer. I like to say 'stand in front of the train'. Stop the problems from flowing downstream! If, despite your best efforts, you cannot stop a problem, your next action is to pull your andon [sic] and escalate the issue up to someone who can. We have escalation systems in place for this very reason so don't hesitate to use them.[258]

Messages such as this are consistent with what we heard from many employees.

That said, the 2000s was a time of extraordinary cost-cutting at GM. The messages from top leadership at GM—both to employees and to the outside world—as well as their actions were focused on the need to control costs. We heard repeatedly from GM personnel about the focus on cost-cutting and the problems it caused. For example, an engineer stated that an emphasis on cost control at GM "permeates the fabric of the whole culture."[259]

Cost-cutting impacted all aspects of the business. Keeping projects on time—because of the impact on cost—became a paramount concern. One witness expressed concern that the cost and time-cutting principles known as the "Big 4" emphasized timing over quality.[260] Those principles were introduced to GM in the early 2000s.[261]

Those responsible for a vehicle were responsible for its cost, but if they wanted to make a change that incurred cost and affected other vehicles, they also became responsible for the costs incurred in the other vehicles.[262] For example, if the Cobalt team wanted an ignition switch replaced, the other vehicle lines that used the ignition switch would request that the cost for their new switches be paid for by the Cobalt team because the Cobalt team requested the change.[263]

Reductions in staff, especially in Engineering, meant that employees were forced to do more with less. In the time leading up to the bankruptcy, one cost-cutting measure was to decrease the Engineering headcount by adding to the responsibilities of the Design Release Engineer (the position held by Ray

---

258 Kevin Williams, FPE Sensitivity and TREAD Training (May 2004), at 68 [DOC ID 000087206552].

259 J&B Interview of Philip Horton, March 31, 2014.

260 J&B Interview of Mark Reuss, April 15, 2014.

261 J&B Interview of Mark Reuss, April 15, 2014.

262 J&B Intenliew of Steve Oakley, April 23, 2014.

263 J&B Interview of Steve Oakley, April 23, 2014; J&B Interview of Sarah DeVries, May 13 & May 16, 2014.

DeGiorgio).[264] Witnesses stated that the reduction in force created a difficult environment in which people were overworked and the quality of work suffered.

The cost-cutting naturally flowed through to suppliers. One cost-cutting measure in the time leading up to GM's bankruptcy was to source parts routinely to the lowest bidder, even if they were not the highest quality parts.[265]

We have uncovered no evidence that any employee made an explicit trade-off between safety and cost in the investigation of the Cobalt. To be sure, the Cobalt engineers working in the 2004–2006 timeframe rejected various fixes to the moving stall issue because there was "no acceptable business case," but those engineers' error was that they failed to understand the connection to airbags and the safety issue that they were facing. Having wrongly identified the issue as a customer convenience issue, cost considerations that would otherwise have been immaterial became part of their calculus.

That noted, we cannot conclude that the atmosphere of cost-cutting had no impact on the failure of GM to resolve these issues earlier. As discussed above, GM was under tremendous cost pressure, and it was imposing tremendous pressure on its suppliers to cut costs. Engineers did not believe that they had extra funds to spend on product improvements. Staff was cut dramatically. It is not feasible for three to do a job as effectively as eight (in the case of the team charged with pulling TREAD data), and there were specific impacts. As noted above, the responsibility of the DREs was increased. The group charged with the TREAD database "pared down" their affirmative searches to look for trends because of their reduced headcount.[266] When belts are tightened, most functions are impacted in some way, and we cannot assume that safety was immune.

D. Culture

1. Resistance to Raising Issues

Some witnesses said that there was resistance or reluctance to raise issues or concerns in the GM culture. For example, a Red X Manager said that, if an employee tried to raise a safety issue five years ago, the employee would get pushback.[267] Mary Barra explained that problems occurred during a prior vehicle

---

[264] J&B Interview of Mark Reuss, April 15, 2014.

[265] J&B Interview of Mark Reuss, April 15, 2014.

[266] J&B Interview of Dwayne Davidson, May 6, 2014. The TREAD database team was originally approximately sixteen or seventeen employees as GM worked to develop its TREAD database, but that m1mber was reduced to approximately eight after this start-up period. J&B Interview of Dwayne Davidson, May 6, 2014. The subsequent reduction to three employees was due to cost cutting. J&B Interview of Dwayne Davidson, May 6, 2014.

[267] J&B Interview of Bill Merrill, March 18, 2014.

launch as a result of engineers being unwilling to identify issues out of concern that it would delay the launch.[268] Similarly, an employee survey reflected an issue related to speaking up. In a Corporate Executive Board Company survey administered at GM in 2013, GM participants' rate of reporting misconduct they observed was below the benchmark rate developed by the Compliance and Ethics Leadership Council based on the responses and experiences of participating companies.[269] A small number of participants also suggested a fear of retaliation.

While the survey comments were unconnected to safety questions, issues of culture cannot be easily confined. Some witnesses provided examples where culture, atmosphere, and the response of supervisors may have discouraged individuals from raising safety concerns, including, in a different context than the Cobalt, supervisors warning employees to "never put anything above the company"[270] and "never put the company at risk."[271] The former Cobalt Brand Quality Manager said that he felt that GM "pushed back" on describing something as a safety issue during a relevant time period.[272]

Whether general "cultural" issues are to blame is difficult to ascertain, but the story of the Cobalt is one in which GM personnel failed to raise significant issues to key decision-makers. Senior attorneys did not elevate the issue within the Legal chain of command to the General Counsel—even after receiving the evaluation in the summer of 2013 that warned of the risk of punitive damages because of a "compelling [ ]" argument that GM had "essentially . . . done nothing to correct the problem for the last nine years."[273] Engineers, too, failed to elevate the issue. Starting in mid-2012, there were three high-level managers brought in as "champions"—Woychowski, Federico, and Kent. The very reason they were brought in was to help resolve an unexplained pattern of airbag non-deployments in an expeditious manner. But they did not elevate the issue to their superiors, and the common thread was to hold more meetings and refer the matter to additional groups or committees.

---

268 J&B Interview of Mary Barra, April 14, 2014.

269 The Corporate Executive Board Company, 2013 Risk Clarity Report—Findings and Next Steps (March 20, 2014) [DOC ID 000145003510]. In a more recent workforce survey administered by GM's Human Resources function to all salaried employees, conducted only weeks ago, there was significant improvement in the responses concerning willingness to "speak up" and trust in management over a similar survey conducted in 2012. GM "Workplace of Choice" Survey Results, May 20, 2014.

270 J&B Interview of Dan Davis, March 14, 2014.

271 J&B Interview of Christina Connor, March 19, 2014.

272 J&B Interview of Steve Oakley, May 7, 2014.

273 Settlement Review Committee Roundtable Case Summary (July 22, 2013), at 36 [DOC ID 0000028 18612]; J&B Interview of Ronald Porter, April 30, 2014; J&B Interview of William Kemp, April 17, 2014; J&B Interview of Lawrence Buonomo, April 16, 2014; *see also* J&B Interview of Michael Millikin, April 4, 2014.

Similarly on the issue of culture, GM employees received formal training as to how to write about safety issues.[274] A PowerPoint presentation from 2008 warned employees to write "smart," and not to use "judgmental adjectives and speculation."[275] Employees were given a number of words to avoid, with suggested replacements:

- "Problem = Issue, Condition, Matter"
- "Safety = Has Potential Safety Implications"
- "Defect = Does not perform to design"[276]

Employees were also given examples of sentences not to use, including "Dangerous . . . almost caused accident" and "This is a safety and security issue . . . ."[277] And they were told, in what the author described as an attempt at humor, not to use phrases such as "Kevorkianesque," "tomblike," or "maniacal," or "rolling sarcophagus."[278] The "actual examples" provided in the presentation described how a plaintiff's lawyer had used a memo from a senior manager at another automaker warning that a risk of conducting a survey about a problem was that it could provide "product liability credence to a hypothesis we have long ignored."[279]

In addition to being trained on how to write, a number of GM employees reported that they did not take notes at all at critical safety meetings because they believed GM lawyers did not want such notes taken. No witness was able to identify a lawyer who gave such an instruction, no lawyer reported having given such an instruction, and we have found no documents or e-mails reflecting such an instruction. The no-notes direction, however, reached the status of an urban myth that was followed, an instruction passed from GM employee to GM employee over the years. Thus, as we learned in our investigation, for many meetings—of GM's many committees—there are no clear records of attendance or of what was discussed or decided.

---

[274] J&B Interview of Mickey Sabol, April 24, 2014.

[275] 2008 Q1 Interior Technical Learning Symposium Soft Trim Breakout Session (2008), at 34 [GMNHT SA000258573].

[276] 2008 Q1 Interior Technical Learning Symposium Soft Trim Breakout Session (2008), at 42 [GMNHT SA000258573].

[277] 2008 Q1 Interior Technical Learning Symposium Soft Trim Breakout Session (2008), at 39 [GMNHT SA000258573].

[278] 2008 Q1 Interior Technical Learning Symposium Soft Trim Breakout Session (2008), at 42 [GMNHT SA000258573]. The employee who presented the training was later told by a lawyer who saw a version of this training to remove the slide listing words never to be used. J&B Interview of Mickey Sabol, April 24, 2014.

[279] 2008 Q1 Interior Technical Learning Symposium Soft Trim Breakout Session (2008), at 37 [GMNHT SA000258573].

Leadership at GM has tried to counter this culture with clear messages that employees should raise issues. "Winning With Integrity" (the code of conduct) instructs employees to raise problems (although it does not explicitly reference vehicle safety) and ensure they receive proper attention, and to conduct themselves with the highest ethical standards. Recommendations as to how to do this better are found below.

2. The "GM Salute" and the "GM Nod"

A cultural issue repeatedly described to us and borne out by the evidence is a proliferation of committees and a lack of accountability.

The Cobalt Ignition Switch issue passed through an astonishing number of committees. We repeatedly heard from witnesses that they flagged the issue, proposed a solution, and the solution died in a committee or with some other *ad hoc* group exploring the issue. But determining the identity of any actual decision-maker was impenetrable. No single person owned any decision. Indeed, it was often difficult to determine who sat on the committees or what they considered, as there are rarely minutes of meetings.

One witness described the GM phenomenon of avoiding responsibility as the "GM salute," a crossing of the arms and pointing outward towards others, indicating that the responsibility belongs to someone else, not me.[280] It is this same cabining of responsibility, the sense that someone else is responsible, that permeated the Cobalt investigation for years.

Similarly, Mary Barra described a phenomenon known as the "GM nod."[281] The GM nod, Barra described, is when everyone nods in agreement to a proposed plan of action, but then leaves the room with no intention to follow through, and the nod is an empty gesture.[282] It is an idiomatic recognition of a culture of that does not move issues forward quickly, as the story of the Cobalt demonstrates.

3. Failure to Share or Gather Knowledge/Information Silos

Repeatedly, over a decade, GM personnel failed to search for, share or gather knowledge, and that failure had serious consequences. There are multiple components to these failures, involving individual mistakes, organizational dysfunction, and systems inaccessible to some and impenetrable to many.

In 2004 and 2005, when complaints of moving stalls came in, the engineers who considered the issue did not know that the vehicle was designed so that the

280 J&B Interview of Andrew Brenz, April 22, 2014; J&B Interview of Alberto Manzor, May 27, 2014.

281 J&B Interview of Mary Barra, April 14, 2014.

282 J&B Interview of Mary Barra, April 14, 2014.

airbags would not deploy when the ignition switch was in Accessory. As a consequence, the engineers failed to recognize the stalls as a safety issue and resolve the problem quickly. Even the committees (VAPIR and CPIT) that were designed to have cross-disciplinary members did not connect the dots. Other examples of failure to share information and gather information include:

- In 2006, DeGiorgio did not change the part number, a system that by its very design is intended to share information with engineers—namely the critical piece of information that a part's fit, form or function had changed. DeGiorgio compounded the matter by later telling his colleagues that there was no change. As a consequence, for years engineers investigating the matter thought that the Ignition Switch was not to blame for airbag non-deployments.
- In 2007, when Sprague was directed to start tracking airbag non-deployments, no one shared with him (and he did not find) all of GM's prior work on the Cobalt moving stall issue—not the PRTSs and not the TSB. As a consequence, he did not have an opportunity to connect the non-deployments with the problem of low torque in the Ignition Switch.
- From 2007 on, GM employees failed to find publicly available materials. This included the Indiana University study, which a plaintiff's expert reportedly found on the NHTSA website.[283] It also included GM's own TSBs, which were available both internally and publicly.
- In 2011, Stouffer failed to check the TREAD database correctly, and thus did not obtain all of the information available on it. As a consequence, he missed the Ion and HHR fatalities, which were not discovered until February 2014—after the first recall.
- From 2011 on, the fact that the Cobalt accidents led to fatalities was not shared with all relevant decision-makers. These individuals say that, as a consequence, they lacked a sense of urgency.

In contrast, some of the mechanisms to share information did work, but still did not yield results. One reason for this was the use of "root cause" as a trigger for action.

---

[283] Erin M. Shipp, P.E., *Engineer's Report of the Crash,* ROBSON FORENSIC (June 12, 2012), at 5 [DOC ID 000001662122]. We have been unable to determine whether the Indiana University study was available on the NHTSA website in 2007.

4. "Root Cause"

There are two dates at which critical information resided in a single place, and yet action was not taken. Witnesses state that the reason for this lack of action at either time was that the "root cause" was not known with certainty or that a full solution had not been devised.

- In 2011, shortly after Stouffer was assigned the investigation, he knew: (1) that the MY 2005 and 2006 Cobalts had a history of the Ignition Switch being turned accidentally to Accessory because of low ignition torque (he had the TSBs); and (2) that airbags do not deploy when the Ignition Switch is in Accessory. In other words, regardless of whether other later model year Cobalts performed better, any time a MY 2005 or 2006 Cobalt Ignition Switch was inadvertently turned to Accessory, the airbags were turned off. Instead of addressing this repeating problem, the investigators worked to find an ultimate solution that would solve the problem for all years and for every permutation of the Ignition Switch. The consequence was a two-and-a-half year delay.
- In late April 2013, after the DeGiorgio deposition, engineers and GM Legal Staff knew: (1) that the Cobalt had a history of the Ignition Switch being turned accidentally to Accessory because of low torque (they had the TSB, the Indiana University study, and two reports from plaintiffs' experts); (2) that airbags do not deploy when the Ignition Switch is in Accessory; and (3) that the Ignition Switch had changed for MY 2008 Cobalts (they had seen photographs during DeGiorgio's deposition). In other words, even the difference between early Cobalts and MY 2008 Cobalts was now explained. The recall did not occur until February 2014, approximately nine months later. In the interim, GM employees confirmed what plaintiff's expert had told them, researched additional issues, and worked on a field solution.

At both of the times described above, there was a view that no action should be taken until the "root cause" of the problem was fully understood and a solution developed. To be sure, GM needed to investigate to understand the problem in the Cobalt. But the search for root cause became a basis for doing nothing to resolve the problem for years. The lengthy search for root cause thus diverted GM from its obligations and failed to produce the required urgency to bring the matter to fast closure. Indeed, it still took nine months after DeGiorgio's deposition for GM to order a recall and, even then, not all affected model years were included.

VIII. Recommendations

As described throughout this report, there were multiple, interrelated factors that led to GM's decade-long failure to recognize the safety defect in the Cobalt and initiate a recall. It is critical that GM minimize the risk of this happening again. Because of the multiplicity of causal factors, there is no simple solution, but the lessons learned from this failure can lead to a reexamination of the Company's policies, procedures, and culture, and provide the Company with an opportunity not only to improve but to innovate and become an industry leader in the processes used to ensure consumer safety.

We made preliminary recommendations to GM as the investigation was proceeding. With the benefit of further investigation and analysis, this section elaborates on and revises those recommendations. It describes a variety of measures that, working together, can improve the speed and manner in which GM addresses safety issues and help bring GM to the forefront of the industry in its approach to safety.

A. Organizational Structure

A successful overhaul of processes begins with examination of the organizational structure, which influences the degree of coordination between groups with interrelated responsibilities and the extent of emphasis the Company places on key priorities, including safety. Recommendations as to organizational structure include:

1. Ensure that the responsibilities of the Vice President of Global Vehicle Safety[284] are appropriately defined to comprehensively cover safety and compliance issues, and ensure that sufficient resources are made available to allow this executive to comprehensively address safety and compliance issues. Ensure that this executive has direct access to the CEO and the Board and is required to make reports to the Board at least quarterly.
2. Ensure that all departments, divisions, or groups that have substantial responsibilities concerning the identification, investigation, or remediation of safety issues have a direct or indirect reporting line that leads up to the Vice President of Global

---

284 The Vice President of Global Vehicle Safety is a new position created in the wake of the Ignition Switch recall. Jeff Boyer has been appointed to this position.

Vehicle Safety. These groups include, for example, FPA, Quality, the CPUs and the VAPIRs. Ensure that Global Vehicle Safety also coordinates with the Legal Staff and is aware of safety issues arising through matters handled by the Legal Staff.

3. Review the activities of all organizational departments, divisions or groups that have safety-related responsibilities (such as FPA, PI, and Quality) for the purpose of identifying any areas where multiple groups have similar or overlapping functions such as investigating or resolving safety issues. Where overlap is identified, consolidate or coordinate those functions to ensure, for example, that Quality and PI do not have independent and parallel responsibility for identifying and resolving a safety defect but rather that each group is aware of, and not duplicating, the other's activities. To the extent that areas of overlap remain, ensure that a clear owner is identified.

B. Cultural Emphasis on Safety

An organizational emphasis on, and commitment to, safety is a critical component to mitigating the risk of a situation like this recurring. To ensure that a commitment to consumer safety is a prominent part of the Company's culture and is embedded in the fabric of the organization, we recommend the following:

1. Implement regular communications with employees about safety to raise awareness and reinforce the tone at the top, for example by issuing periodic bulletins from the Vice President of Global Vehicle Safety and/or the CEO that include updates or reminders on safety issues, or including a column on safety in an employee newsletter. Ensure that employees understand that they have an obligation to raise any concerns they have about safety or compliance, and to continue to raise those concerns if they do not believe those concerns have been resolved.

2. We understand that GM has created a new "Speak Up For Safety" program to encourage employees to raise safety issues, and we recommend that GM promote that program through visible communications, such as posters on employee bulletin boards. Bulletins or newsletters could include features recognizing employees who have raised safety issues and highlight the

significance of the potential safety problem averted by the escalation of the issue.[285]

3. Consistent with ¶ 19 of the May 16, 2014 NHTSA Consent Order, visibly promote and rigorously enforce the non-retaliation policy, including for employees who report concerns regarding actual or potential safety-related defects or potential non-compliance with the Federal Motor Vehicle Safety Standards.

4. Regularly communicate to suppliers the importance of safety and GM's expectation that suppliers will promptly and accurately identify any potential safety issues. Provide suppliers with access to the Speak Up for Safety hotline or a similar mechanism for raising such safety issues.

5. Consistent with ¶ 20 of the May 16, 2014 NHTSA Consent Order, explicitly communicate to employees that they should not be reluctant to classify issues as safety issues or potential safety issues, including in written work, and eliminate any language in any guidelines, training decks, or policies that suggest otherwise or that caution against using specific words or phrases that might be deemed too sensitive or inflammatory. Communications to employees on safety policy issues like this should come from the level of the Vice President of Global Vehicle Safety or higher.

6. Develop protocols for escalating potential safety issues to appropriate levels of management. Such protocols should include identification of the types of issues to be escalated (based for example on their severity, frequency, or the amount of time they have been open) and the level to which they should be escalated. The protocols should make clear that employees who are aware of unresolved safety issues should escalate them, and should define circumstances in which the concerns should be raised to the level of the Vice President of Global Vehicle Safety and, ultimately, the CEO. The protocols should also define other circumstances in which the CEO should be made aware of safety issues, including instances in which safety issues rise to a certain level of severity or in which an investigation has not been resolved within a defined period of time.

---

[285] We understand that this is in progress with feature stories on GM's internal website.

7. As agreed to in ¶ 19 of the May 16, 2014 NHTSA Consent Order, continue to review and strengthen the process for expeditious reporting by employees of potential or actual safety issues and non-compliance. This includes the development and roll-out of training programs instructing employees on how to identify safety issues and how to raise them with supervisors and executives (see more discussion on training below).
8. Ensure that supplier quality issues that may raise safety concerns for vehicles in production are reported as safety issues and are not addressed solely as supplier quality issues. Implement specific procedures for personnel dealing with quality issues to track and report to the safety organization those quality issues that raise safety concerns, and train quality personnel on those procedures.

C. Individual Accountability

All employees have responsibility for raising safety issues, and many employees have responsibility for addressing safety issues once they have been identified. The Company should take steps to ensure that employees are aware of their safety-related responsibilities and that individuals are accountable for addressing the safety issues for which they are given responsibility. Specific recommendations are as follows:

1. Identify clear owners of safety and compliance issues to increase accountability. Clarify internal roles by defining responsibilities and accountability for those involved in processes relating to the evaluation and resolution of safety issues, including responsibilities for feeding items into the FPE process, such as from VAPIR and CPIT meetings. Clarify the role of committees such as CPITs and VAPIRs in identifying safety issues and referring them to the FPE process. Designate one person on each such committee as a safety liaison with specific responsibility for elevating safety issues.
2. Include appropriate identification, elevation, and resolution of safety and compliance issues as a factor in employee performance evaluations.
3. Require employees to certify annually that they have reported any safety issues of which they are aware and to identify, as part of that certification, any safety issues they are aware of that have not been resolved.

D. Communications Between and Within Groups

Breakdowns in communication between and within groups were a critical part of the failures described in this report. Consistent with GM's commitment in ¶ 21 of the May 16, 2014 NHTSA Consent Order to improve processes for the purpose of encouraging and improving information-sharing across functional areas and disciplines, many of the recommendations throughout this section are intended to address inadequate communication. Specific additional recommendations are:

1. Provide regular written or oral updates by the Legal Staff for relevant engineering groups on alleged or potential defects.
2. Formalize coordination between and among PI, Legal Staff, FPA, FPE, the new "emerging issues" group, and relevant engineering teams with accountability for safety and compliance issues, for example by implementing a cross-functional committee to track and review potential safety issues and set clear action items. This coordination should include the sharing across groups of information concerning significant FPA matters, FPE investigations, serious or high-volume warranty claims, trends or patterns identified, and NHTSA interactions.
3. Conduct an assessment of the adequacy of mechanisms for ensuring coordination between groups handling different subsystems of the same vehicle regarding safety-related information and items that may affect safety performance, and implement improvements as necessary. For example, ensure those working on the ignition switch understand how it interacts with airbag deployment. Similarly, ensure that committees such as the VAPIR and CPIT are structured with sufficient cross-functional expertise to ensure that safety issues are properly identified and addressed.
4. Assign the Global Ethics and Compliance Center ("GECC") to oversee the review of issues raised through the new Speak Up For Safety program. This will have the benefit of ensuring that review of issues raised through the Speak Up For Safety program is coordinated with review of issues raised to the compliance organization, and to ensure that internal inquiries and investigations prompted by the Speak Up For Safety program are

appropriately tracked and handled consistent with GECC procedures.

E. Communications with NHTSA

NHTSA should be viewed not only as a regulator but also an ally in the effort to ensure that the Company's vehicles are as safe as they can be. Interactions with NHTSA should be consistent with that type of relationship. Specific recommendations for maintaining an appropriate relationship are:

1. As required by ¶ 21 of the May 16, 2014 NHTSA Consent Order, improve communication with NHTSA regarding safety-related defects. Consent Order ¶¶ 25–28 require the Company to have monthly and quarterly meetings with NHTSA and to be prepared to address various issues at those meetings. As part of this effort, the Company should ensure that both the quality and the frequency of NHTSA communications are sufficient to keep NHTSA frilly informed of safety-related issues. The individual responsible for implementing this item should report directly or indirectly to the Vice President of Global Vehicle Safety.
2. Create a centralized database for all communications with NHTSA and train individuals who communicate with NHTSA to file their communications in this database.
3. Ensure timely notification to NHTSA of safety-related defects. Evaluate and clearly define, consistent with federal law, the trigger for the NHTSA five-day reporting requirement.

F. Role of Lawyers

The Legal Staff can and should play a critical and unique role in assisting with the identification, analysis, and resolution of safety issues that have given rise to customer claims. To ensure that Legal Staff play this critical role effectively, we recommend the following steps:

1. Hold regular discussions between each product litigation attorney and the Practice Area Manager and Global Process Leader for Litigation regarding whether the attorney has observed trends or potential safety issues in lawsuits or not-in-suit matters ("NISMs").
2. Designate a member of the Legal Staff as a liaison to provide regular reports (and real-time reports where matters are particularly significant or urgent) to the Global Vehicle Safety organization on safety-related issues identified in matters handled by Legal Staff.

Hold regular meetings between the Global Vehicle Safety group and the Legal Staff liaison. During these meetings, the Global Vehicle Safety organization will present to the Legal Staff significant or unresolved safety issues, and the Legal Staff liaison will report on any issues identified in matters handled by Legal Staff that the liaison has not already communicated.

3. Hold monthly meetings between the GM Legal Staff and FPA engineers responsible for each specialty (*e.g.,* non-deployment litigation, rollover/roof crush, power steering, etc.) to discuss observed trends and potential safety issues in that specialty area. Include in these meetings the ESIS claim administrator with the most experience in that specialty area. If any trends or safety issues are identified, ensure that the Global Process Leader for Litigation is informed, and that the trends or safety issues are discussed at the next scheduled Roundtable meeting and elevated as appropriate.

4. Ensure that at the onset of litigation, the Legal Staff and FPA generate a list of all PRTSs, FPRs, TSBs, recalls, product investigations, and issues in the FPE process for the subject vehicle make and model. Include this information in the new suit package provided to outside counsel at the onset of litigation. Ensure that the early technical assessment ("ETA") reflects consideration of whether there are relevant PRTSs, FPRs, TSBs, recalls, product investigations, and issues in the FPE process that affect the integrity of the make and model involved.

5. Include in the Roundtable case summary form a category for any safety issues, trends, lawsuits and NISMs similar to the case discussed at the Roundtable.

6. Institute a process to elevate unresolved technical issues expeditiously. If an FPA engineer is unable to determine any reason for a component failure following a vehicle inspection and technical analysis, require the FPA engineer to initiate a conference call with in-house and outside counsel within a defined period to discuss the issue and appropriate follow-up. Depending on the circumstances, appropriate follow-up might include referring the issue to the PI or FPE processes.

7. Provide specific guidance concerning the types of issues that should be elevated to the General Counsel. Those issues should

include serious safety issues and safety issues that are not being resolved expeditiously, and more broadly, any concerns that could have a significant impact on the Company, its customers, or its shareholders. Explain in this guidance that lawyers should request the General Counsel's assistance when important processes are not progressing with appropriate speed. Include such guidance in the orientation program for all new hires to the Legal Staff.

8. Consistent with "Winning with Integrity" and other prior internal guidance, ensure that in-house counsel are aware of the expectation that they will respond appropriately if they become aware of any threatened, on-going, or past violation of a federal, state or local law or regulation, a breach of fiduciary duty, or violation of GM policy, including the expectation that if they raise such an issue and believe it has not been addressed appropriately, they will bring the situation to the attention of their supervisors, and if they believe their supervisors have not addressed it appropriately, to higher levels including the General Counsel if necessary. Ensure that this expectation extends to issues of safety. Communicate similar expectations to outside counsel in written guidelines.

9. Consistent with the "Winning with Integrity" guidelines for employee conduct, specifically memorialize in writing for in-house and outside counsel the expectation that they will report to appropriate Legal Staff any observed violation of law or GM policy, including possible violations of policies pertaining to the recall decision-making process. Circulate this policy to Legal Staff on a regular basis, and circulate the policy to any outside attorneys to whom the policy applies. Include this policy in orientation programs provided to in-house lawyers when they join the Company.

10. Provide guidance for product liability attorneys on how to recognize and communicate safety issues to ensure that they are properly addressed notwithstanding ongoing litigation or claims activity, while fulfilling their obligations to defend the Company in litigation and appropriately protect attorney-client privilege.

G. Interactions with Suppliers

The Company's interactions with suppliers should reflect the significance that supplier quality control has on vehicle safety. Specific recommendations for enhancing supplier relationships are as follows:

1. Ensure that procedures are in place so that supplier quality issues that may impact safety in production vehicles are communicated to appropriate personnel with vehicle safety responsibility.
2. Identify all responsible units and personnel who are accountable for monitoring and resolving concerns with supplier quality, and ensure that they have a direct or indirect reporting line up to the Vice President for Global Vehicle Safety.
3. Conduct an assessment of the adequacy of measures taken to ensure identification of any supplier parts that do not meet GM specifications, both by the time of launch and periodically during production, including independent testing in appropriate circumstances.
4. Ensure that appropriate procedures are in place for addressing parts, including parts provided by suppliers, that do not satisfy GM specifications. These procedures should include a specific protocol for reviewing authorizations of out-of-specification parts, tracking out-of-specification parts, identifying who should be notified of them, and identifying and elevating any potential safety issues that might be associated with the use of out-of-specification parts. Require high-level review for approval to use the part.
5. Ensure that the Company receives and maintains, as part of its own files, all supplier design change and work order documents relating to supplier parts.
6. Work with suppliers to increase GM's access to stored and recorded data on SDMs, CDRs, and EDRs used in GM products.

H. Data Storage, Retrieval, and Analysis

Several of the problems discussed in this report could have been avoided or resolved much more quickly if the individuals involved had timely searched for or received accurate and complete data that in many cases was already in GM's possession. Accordingly, the Company has committed, in ¶ 22 of the May 16, 2014 NHTSA Consent Order, to revise its product quality analytics to improve its ability to identify safety consequences and the severity of those consequences, as well as to assess the number or rate of allegations, complaints, incidents, reports and/or warranty claims relating to potential safety-related defects. Specific recommendations to fulfill these commitments and to improve the Company's ability to store, retrieve, and analyze data in a way that promotes identification of safety issues are as follows:

1. Ensure that the Global Vehicle Safety organization monitors all safety-related databases (including TREAD, CVEP,[286] GART, PRTS, ESIS, CTF, etc.) as well as public sources, such as NHTSA and other crash investigation reports, for trends or patterns of issues that may raise safety concerns. This entails two sub-issues. First, monitor the databases actively so that there is a mechanism for identifying patterns of defects or incidents that raise potential safety concerns, as opposed to searching the databases only when a perceived need arises. Second, establish mechanisms for coordinating the monitoring of these databases to ensure that patterns of similar defects and incidents across different databases will be visible and receive attention.

2. Establish a standardized process for the regular monitoring of safety recalls by other manufacturers, and for the mapping of these recalls to existing internal and external investigations by PI.

3. Ensure that staffing levels in the TREAD group and elsewhere are sufficient to allow proactive monitoring of data for safety issues. Similarly, ensure that staffing levels of personnel responsible for other company databases, for information technology, and elsewhere are sufficient to ensure accuracy and completeness of the information in Company databases.

4. Improve the search functions in the databases to make it easier to locate and review data. Determine whether improvements can also be made to increase the accuracy of searches, by minimizing irrelevant data captured by searches while maximizing the ability of searches to retrieve data that is relevant even though it may have been captured from different sources using different language and different fields. In addition, address difficulties in searching across several databases, for example by consolidating the databases or

[286] The Company Vehicle Evaluation Program ("CVEP") database collects information provided by employees who drive company-owned vehicles.

improving the search mechanism, and ensure that relevant personnel are trained on search methods.

5. Work with data analytics suppliers to identify and implement available automated tools, or commission new ones if appropriate, that will enhance the Company's ability to monitor, retrieve and analyze safety-related data.
6. Provide product investigators and related personnel direct access to relevant databases where appropriate, and provide indirect access to any databases that require special expertise, such as TREAD.
7. Ensure that relevant analytics, procedures, and policies focus on severity and identification of potential safety-related consequences of a defect, even where the defect is infrequent.
8. Conduct an assessment of the adequacy of processes for dealers to identify and report safety-related issues that do not otherwise get reported through the warranty data collection process. Ensure that GM's expectations for dealers to report safety issues are clearly defined.
9. Accept NHTSA's offer to consult with GM about industry best practices for identifying safety-related defects through the screening of data.
10. Require that ESIS monitor its data concerning alleged safety defects for patterns and trends and bring such patterns and trends to the Company's attention.

I. Engineering Processes and Databases

Functions such as the PRTS and EWO processes are critical to execution of GM's engineering functions, and also to tracing prior engineering decisions when product investigations are conducted. Recommendations to improve these processes are as follows:

1. Ensure adequacy of current processes for transparency, tracking, and, where appropriate, elevation of issues being dealt with in the PRTS system. Ensure that the processes focus on quality and safety.
2. Ensure adequacy of process for determining the correct severity classification, including review by supervisory personnel of initial

severity determinations. In addition, when a PRTS has been open for a set amount of time (such as 60 days), implement a review of its severity level based on any newly available information or analysis. Establish a process through which PRTSs categorized as level 1 (safety issues) are automatically elevated for additional review, in coordination with a member of the Global Vehicle Safety organization.

3. Ensure that the standard for closing PRTSs without action is clearly defined and sufficiently rigorous. Ensure that a PRTS cannot be closed without action absent clear sign-off by named individuals and appropriate levels of review. Re-affirm that the lack of an " 'acceptable business case' " is not an acceptable reason for closing out a PRTS if the PRTS involves a safety issue.

4. Require sign-off by a validation engineer on all EWOs, with the validation engineer to consider any impact on safety and compliance as to both the design change itself and other affected subsystems in the vehicle.

5. In any processes and databases (such as PRTS and GART) where severity levels are assigned, review the criteria used to determine whether problems are identified as safety issues to ensure that those criteria adequately encompass all defects that have the potential to adversely affect consumer safety. In addition, GM should ensure that individual decisions about severity levels are reviewed, so that a single engineer does not make the decision.

J. Product Investigation Process

The product investigation of the Cobalt Ignition Switch began nearly a decade before any recall was initiated. Multiple failures contributed to that extraordinary delay. We recommend the following specific steps to improve the Product Investigations process:

1. Standardize the process for collecting and reviewing information that gives rise to product investigations. As part of this standardization, identify the categories of source information that should be reviewed during any investigation. Train investigators on the revised process.

2. Establish clear criteria for the process for assigning PIs and for documenting those assignments (or the reasons for not making an

assignment) to ensure that PIs are assigned in a manner that ensures that the requisite expertise and resources are applied to each matter.

3. Formalize other procedures governing the PI process, including how issues are escalated within the process and who is responsible and accountable for monitoring the progress and bringing the investigation to a conclusion. Ensure expedited review and escalation of investigations involving injuries and fatalities, and any other investigations where at any point a safety or compliance issue is implicated.

4. Ensure that there are adequate mechanisms to enable product investigators to identify and review any prior Company investigations regarding the same condition, in the same or other models.

5. Establish clear deadlines for each element of the PI process such that any missed deadline results in increased attention. For example, for any investigation that is not resolved within a defined time period, such as 60 days, ensure that the progress of the investigation is monitored and documented, and in appropriate circumstances, escalated.

6. Standardize the processes for creating documentation reflecting the progress and results of investigations. Documentation might be on a tracking form and/or on a separate progress reporting form, and it should include such information as major investigative activities conducted since the last report, current conclusions or hypotheses, open issues, and next steps.

7. Ensure that the PI group is staffed sufficiently to address these recommendations.

K. FPE Process

GM has agreed in ¶ 21 of the May 16, 2014 NHTSA Consent Order to increase the speed with which recall decisions are made, including by clarifying the recall decision-making process to decrease the number of steps prior to making the final decision of whether to conduct a recall. We recommend that GM review its processes and implement changes consistent with that agreement. Specific recommendations are as follows:

1. Create a specific form for initiating the FPE process that clearly identifies the issue(s) to be investigated, lists the parts that could be

implicated, identifies the suppliers of those parts, lists the potentially impacted vehicle models and years, identifies the source of the information that triggered the investigation, identifies the investigator who will have responsibility for the investigation, and identifies the individual who will be responsible for monitoring the matter and bringing it to conclusion.

2. The Company has committed, in ¶ 24 of the May 16, 2014 NHTSA Consent Order, that it shall not delay holding any meeting to decide whether or not to recommend or conduct a safety recall because the Company has not yet identified the precise cause of a defect, determined a remedy for the defect, or prepared a plan for remedying the defect. In order to comply with that commitment, develop and adopt policies and procedures that implement this commitment and train relevant employees on those policies and procedures.

3. The Company has committed, in ¶ 24 of the May 16, 2014 NHTSA Consent Order, that it shall ensure that the decision-makers for recalls are informed of safety-related concerns in a reasonably expeditious manner, including by ensuring that GM's corporate structure enables its safety organization to promptly bring safety-related issues to the attention of committees and individuals with authority to make safety recall decisions. Accordingly, in conjunction with its review of the FPE process, the Company should assess whether the current organizational structure—including the appointment of the Vice President for Global Vehicle Safety and the restructuring of the groups that report to him—fulfills this commitment.

4. In ¶ 21 of the May 16, 2014 NHTSA Consent Order, GM agreed to increase the speed with which recall decisions are made, including by clarifying the recall decision-making process to decrease the number of steps prior to making the final decision of whether to conduct a recall.[287] As GM revises this process, formalize other procedures governing the process, including how the process is initiated, who may initiate the process, how issues are escalated within the process, who is responsible and accountable for monitoring the progress and bringing the matter to a

[287] We understand that this is in progress.

conclusion, and the chain of command throughout the process. Maintain a written policy governing this process that clearly defines the procedural steps in the process and the role of each participant. Ensure that part of the FPE process includes identification and review of any prior FPE processes regarding the same condition in the same or other models.

5. Establish clear deadlines for each element of the FPE process such that any missed deadline results in increased attention. For example, for any issue that is not resolved within a short, defined time period, such as 60 days, ensure that the progress of the issue is monitored and, in appropriate circumstances, escalated.

6. Standardize and improve documentation of decision points during the FPE process, including documentation of decisions made and attendees present at those decision points. In particular, require that FPE participants document potential defects and remedies that are rejected during or as the result of the FPE process, such as root causes that are considered and rejected and model years that are examined but not included in a final recall.

7. For any investigation that is not resolved within a defined time period, such as 60 days, ensure that the progress of the investigation is documented. Documentation might be on a tracking form and/or on a separate progress reporting form, and it should include such information as major investigative activities conducted since the last report, current conclusions or hypotheses, open issues, and next steps. Document the conclusion of an investigation on a form that records the conclusions reached, the action recommended, and the reasons supporting the conclusions and recommended action.

8. Ensure that systems are in place for maintaining and organizing documentation of agendas, presentations, summaries, decision memoranda, and other documents reflecting the steps in the FPE process, and implement improvements as necessary to ensure that those materials are organized, maintained, and accessible.

9. Establish guidelines governing the ability of an investigator to remove an issue from the FPE process because PI determines it is unrelated to safety.

L. Policies and Training

In many instances in this Report, personnel were not aware of a relevant policy to govern their decisions or did not sufficiently understand an existing policy, and many employees reported receiving little to no training on policies and substantive issues relevant to their roles. As GM fulfills its training-related obligations in the May 16, 2014 NHTSA Consent Order, we recommend that it undertake the following specific steps to ensure that appropriate policies are in place and that sufficient training is provided:

1. Review policies and procedures that bear on safety issues to ensure that they are easily understood and readily accessible. In particular, revise the GRC 3.1.1 policy on determining when a new part number must be assigned. Clarify the policy to require assignment of a new part number whenever a design change alters the expected performance of a supplied part, and remove the "legitimate business case" language.

2. Review GM's compliance policies and procedures to identify revisions to ensure adequate, appropriate, and consistent treatment of safety issues. For example, make clear that Winning With Integrity covers the identification and raising of safety issues, or issue a companion policy covering those issues.

3. Improve or create standards for elevating safety issues and ensure that training covers these standards. The standards should cover, for example, situations where GM engineers are unable to determine why a product failed to perform appropriately.

4. Ensure that personnel, including legal personnel, personnel responsible for IT systems and databases, and personnel who are assigned to monitor data streams or identify emerging issues and trends, have appropriate backgrounds and training. For example, high-level legal personnel may benefit from background or training in product litigation issues and recalls. Similarly, employees with responsibility for IT systems and databases would benefit from background or training in the relevant systems or databases, and employees who monitor and digest warranty data may benefit from engineering backgrounds.

5. Train employees to recognize and elevate safety issues. Emphasize that safety issues should be actively identified and addressed

regardless of whether vehicles are in the design phase or the production phase.

6. Provide employees with appropriate function-specific training to recognize safety issues and respond appropriately. This training should include, among other things, what constitutes a safety issue and the role of various organizational units and processes in handling safety issues. For engineers, training should include the safety and compliance ramifications of design changes.
7. Train PIs and FPA engineers, and related personnel, on sources of data that are publicly available and may have information relevant to particular investigations and possible safety issues.
8. Train Legal Staff who deal with safety issues on the NHTSA recall process.
9. Extend training on safety issues to supplier employees embedded within GM where appropriate.
10. Train engineers on policies that explain the circumstances under which an engineer may deviate from a Component Technical Specification when approving a part for production, and how such a deviation must be documented.
11. Train employees on lessons learned from the Cobalt investigation.
12. Communicate to employees that a low frequency of occurrence should not prevent an issue from being escalated for appropriate investigation and review if it otherwise presents a potential safety issue.
13. Educate employees that shielding senior executives or other employees from information in order to allow them to deny knowledge is not acceptable; on the contrary, employees should err on the side of elevating potential safety issues.

M. Compliance, Auditing, and Oversight

To ensure proper implementation of remedial measures discussed above, we recommend the following:

1. After Speak Up For Safety has been in place for a year, survey employees to assess their attitudes toward safety and their willingness to raise safety concerns. In addition, within a reasonable time (perhaps one year) after the date of this Report, have a source

outside of the safety organization (such as GM Audit Services) conduct an audit to assess the progress and effectiveness of the remedial measures implemented. Also, implement regular audits of the recall decision-making process to ensure that it is functioning as intended and identify improvements. For example, audits should address whether issues that are safety- related are being appropriately designated as such.

2. Ensure that the Global Ethics and Compliance Center monitors relevant aspects of the safety program, including investigation of Speak Up For Safety complaints, the recall decision-making process, training on safety and recall issues, and periodic evaluation of safety procedures and metrics, in conjunction with the regular audits described in item 1 above.

3. Require the Global Vehicle Safety organization to document the improvements it is making related to safety, and its implementation of these recommendations, to facilitate review of those improvements.

4. Ensure that the Board receives regular reports from the Vice President of Global Vehicle Safety on at least a quarterly basis and, after one year, evaluates the Company's progress in implementing the commitments made in the May 16, 2014 NHTSA Consent Order and any recommendations in this Report the Company decides to implement; and take such other steps as the Board may find useful to monitor management's compliance with global vehicle safety-related obligations and Company vehicle safety-related policies.

N. Recordkeeping

Adequate recordkeeping will enhance the ability of product investigators and others with safety responsibilities to review past engineering and investigative measures that may impact current investigations, and will also facilitate subsequent reconstruction of investigative steps when necessary. In addition to the recommendations identified in connection with specific processes, as discussed above, recommendations to improve the Company's record-keeping relating to safety issues are the following:

1. Document the discussions during Settlement Roundtables and Settlement Review Committee meetings, including follow-up from those meetings, and not just the final decisions.

2. Maintain all significant engineering records documenting design decisions, including documentation of all design changes within a model year on a particular platform.
3. Document FPE decision points, as well as decisions made at CPUs and VAPIRs, specifically including decisions not to take suggested field actions or to downgrade the type of action taken.
4. Document, on the EWO form, whether a proposed EWO involves a change to fit, form, or function.
5. Ensure that all results of safety and compliance testing are adequately documented.
6. Ensure that all electronic documents relating to safety issues that are maintained in GM's records (including records maintained by Global Vehicle Safety and the Legal Staff) are kept in a searchable format to the extent technologically possible. For example, perform optical character recognition ("OCR") on PDF documents before storing them.

O. Conclusion

GM has begun undertaking some of the measures discussed above. Under the direction of Jeff Boyer, who has assumed the recently created role of Vice President for Global Vehicle Safety, the Company has instituted a Speak Up For Safety program designed to encourage employees to identify, report, and elevate safety issues, and train them how to do so. Staffing has been increased substantially to allow more issues to be investigated and expedite the investigation process. A new emerging issues group has been created to monitor and analyze data streams, and that group is working with data analytics suppliers to assess the suppliers' capabilities and develop recommendations for appropriate systems to employ. We recommend that GM continue to implement these measures, implement the additional steps identified above, and use the self-examination prompted by the Ignition Switch failures, so that the Company is an industry leader in the way it handles consumer safety issues.

NOTES

1. Let's assume that you work at a company (or, if you're a lawyer, that you advise a company) that makes a product where the risk of a failure is small, but the consequences of a failure are severe. The company could make cars, or it could make medical devices, or it could make any number of other things that often don't fail, but

when they do, they kill or maim people. Knowing what you know now about cognitive errors, what are some classic mistakes that you might make when analyzing a potential failure in your product?

2. In the now-infamous Ford Pinto memo (https://www.autosafety.org/wp-content/uploads/import/phpq3mJ7F_FordMemo.pdf), a table showed the likelihood of injury when there was "impact-induced fuel spillage for passenger cards in rural injury-producing accidents":

Table 2

DISTRIBUTION AND LIKELIHOOD BY IMPACT TYPE OF IMPACT-INDUCED FUEL SPILLAGE FOR PASSENGER CARS IN RURAL INJURY-PRODUCING ACCIDENTS

IMPACT DIRECTION	NUMBER OF FUEL LEAKS	PERCENT OF FUEL LEAKS	LIKELIHOOD OF FUEL LEAK
FRONT	33	25.8	33/933 = 3.5%
SIDE, FRONT HALF OF CAR	8	6.2	8/169 = 4.7%
SIDE, REAR HALF OF CAR	23	18.0	23/160 = 14.8%
REAR	37	28.9	37/140 = 26.4%
ROLLOVER	27	21.1	27/333 = 8.1%
TOTAL	128	100.0	127/1735 = 7.3%

Now take a look at how Ford looked at the cost-benefit analysis in Table 3 of that memo:

Table 3

BENEFITS AND COSTS RELATING TO FUEL LEAKAGE ASSOCIATED WITH THE STATIC ROLLOVER TEST PORTION OF [THE VEHICLES]

BENEFITS:

Savings – 180 burn deaths, 180 serious burn injuries, 2100 burned vehicles.

Unit Cost – \$200,000 per death, \$67,000 per injury, \$700 per vehicle

Total Benefit – 180 × (\$200,000) + 180 × (\$67,000) + 2100 × (\$700) = \$49.5 million.

COSTS:

Sales – 11 million cars, 1.5 million light trucks.

Unit Cost – $11 per car, $11 per light truck.

Total Cost = 11,000,000 x ($11) + 1,500,000 x ($11) = $137 million.

The paragraph in the memo that indicates how Ford analyzed the cost-benefit factors is on page 7:

> Benefit and Cost Comparison
>
> The total benefit is shown in Table 3 to be just under $50 million, while the associated cost is $137 million. Thus the cost is almost three times the benefits, even using a number of highly favorable benefit assumptions. As better estimates of the parameters used in the benefit analysis become available, they could be inserted into the general analysis framework. It does not appear likely, however, that such alternate estimates could lead to the substantial benefit estimate increase which would be required to make compliance with the rollover requirement cost effective.

So that's how Ford answered our Question #1, back when it wrote the memo.

3. Recapping the multiple failures at GM, the Valukas Report includes these:

> This section details the multiple failures of GM personnel and processes—among the most significant of which was the failure of many individuals involved in the investigation to understand that, if the Ignition Switch moves to Accessory or Off, the airbags will not deploy. Yet, GM personnel designed the Ignition Switch to cut electrical power to most systems when the key turned to Accessory. And GM personnel designed the airbag system to shut [] off when the vehicles were in the Accessory mode. Inexplicably, the engineers (and business people) interviewed who learned of moving stalls in this time period did not recognize that the loss of power from a key moving into Accessory caused the airbag system to shut off—a missed connection that led to devastating consequences. Information silos were present throughout GM and they delayed GM's response with respect to the Cobalt. Had GM personnel connected the dots and understood how their own cars were built, they might have addressed the safety defect before injuries and fatalities occurred.
>
> As detailed below, another failure was the decision—by a single engineer who did not advise others of his decision—to accept an Ignition Switch with full knowledge that it fell well below GM's own specifications.

Valukas Report at 33. Part of the reasons that organizations have silos is that it is incredibly inefficient to require "all hands on deck" decision-making for every issue. Among other benefits that silos give organizations is the expertise within a silo. People working in a single department probably have the best knowledge as to the products made within the department. The problem with silos, though, is that—by definition—there's no easy way to provide information gleaned from other silos. Unless someone above the department level makes an effort to provide a department with information from other silos, there will always be an information gap.

4. The Valukas Report also talks about the "tone at the top" at GM. GM told its employees that safety was a top priority and that GM was also very concerned about costs:

> But the tone set at the top is relevant background for assessing GM's approach to the issues discussed in this report. Repeated throughout the interview process we heard from GM personnel two somewhat different directives—"when safety is at issue, cost is irrelevant" and "cost is everything." It is worth examining how those two messages collided.
>
> GM personnel were quite consistent in saying that they understood that safety was a critical priority and that, if they identified a safety problem, cost should not be a factor in deciding whether and how to address the safety problem. . . .
>
> That said, the 2000s was a time of extraordinary cost-cutting at GM. The messages from top leadership at GM—both to employees and to the outside world—as well as their actions were focused on the need to control costs. We heard repeatedly from GM personnel about the focus on cost-cutting and the problems it caused. For example, an engineer stated that an emphasis on cost control at GM "permeates the fabric of the whole culture."

Valukas Report at 249–50 (footnote omitted). Unlike the conclusions in the Ford Pinto memo, the Valukas Report found:

> We have uncovered no evidence that any employee made an explicit trade-off between safety and cost in the investigation of the Cobalt. To be sure, the Cobalt engineers working in the 2004–2006 timeframe rejected various fixes to the moving stall issue because there was "no acceptable business case," but those engineers' error was that they failed to understand the connection to airbags and the safety issue that they were facing. Having wrongly identified the issue as a customer convenience issue, cost considerations that would otherwise have been immaterial became part of their calculus.
>
> That noted, we cannot conclude that the atmosphere of cost-cutting had no impact on the failure of GM to resolve these issues earlier. As discussed above, GM was under tremendous cost pressure, and it was imposing tremendous pressure on its suppliers to cut costs. Engineers did

> not believe that they had extra funds to spend on product improvements. Staff was cut dramatically. It is not feasible for three to do a job as effectively as eight (in the case of the team charged with pulling TREAD data), and there were specific impacts. . . .

Valukas Report at 251. The mixed message wasn't the only problem, of course. Some employees felt that raising safety concerns was a bad career move. *Id.* at 252. Ultimately, though, a lack of accountability ("this is my problem, and I'll figure out how to fix it") was a key component of the systemic failure. *Id.* at 255–58.

We're going to be comparing the decisions at GM to those at VW, Wells Fargo, and NASA. As you continue reading this chapter and the next one, ask yourself whether the systemic failures in those cases resulted from bad people, bad incentives, or a bad organizational structure—or a combination of those potential causes.

CHAPTER 9

VW, Part 1: *Mettle Fatigue: VW's Single-Point-of-Failure Ethics*[*]

Roland L. Trope | Trope and Schramm LLP
Eugene K. Ressler | US Military Academy Emeritus Faculty

After a year of denials, Volkswagen admitted in September 2015 that multiple makes and models of its diesel vehicles contained defeat device software. The decisions leading to "Dieselgate" involved a corruption of engineering ethics that the profession ought to address.

> Eleven million diesel-powered vehicles Volkswagen sold as high-performing, fuel-sipping, planet-coddling cars have turned out to be gross polluters masked by corporate fraud.—*Wired*[1]

In September 2015, after issuing denials for more than a year, Volkswagen (VW) officials admitted that multiple makes and models of its diesel vehicles contained *defeat device* software. Defeat device is a US Environmental Protection Agency (EPA) term of art for any technology that causes a vehicle to behave differently in the lab than on the road.

On 18 September 2015, the EPA and the California Air Resources Board (CARB) issued notices of violation (NoVs) to VW. The NoVs reveal a succession of dishonest actions. For seven years, from 2009 through 2015, VW personnel installed defeat devices, despite apparently knowing that doing so violated the federal Clean Air Act. And it appears that supervisors knew about and condoned these actions. As VW Chairman Dieter Hans Pötsch recently observed, there was "an attitude in some areas of our company that tolerated breaches of rules ... and I freely admit that is the factor that we all find the most difficult to accept."[2]

VW's installation of the defeat device software and VW's failure to disclose it when applying for the Certificates of Conformity (CoCs) required to import vehicles appear to violate federal and state laws. At least some VW employees knew that these CoC applications falsely represented that VW's diesel vehicles had passed emissions control tests and did not contain defeat devices. Dishonesty on this scale by engineers, supervisors, and possibly higher officials at a major engineering enterprise has struck many as incomprehensible, a senseless waste of VW's hard-earned reputation and credibility.

In December 2015, VW released an interim report of findings from a two-track investigation—by internal auditors and an outside law firm—into the use, on VW's behalf, of defeat device software. In his extended statement, Pötsch observed, "The key finding is that we are not talking of a one-off error, but a whole chain of errors that was not interrupted at any point along the timeline."[2]

This characterization seems designed to protect the company. Yet it might have unintended and undesired

---

* This piece was originally published as Roland L. Trope & Eugene K. Ressler, *Mettle Fatigue: VW's Single-Point-of-Failure Ethics*, IEEE COMPUTER AND RELIABILITY SOCIETIES (January/February 2016), available at https://www.computer.org/cms/Computer.org/ComputingNow/docs/mettle-fatigue-security-and-privacy-january-february-2016.pdf.

consequences because it blurs or obliterates some bright lines on the moral spectrum: first, between right and not right—that is, between accurate and inadvertently inaccurate—and second, between not right and wrong—that is, between inadvertently inaccurate and deliberately false. Participants in any enterprise know that moral spectrum. Mistakes happen, which is lamentable. But falsehoods don't "just happen." They require intent. One decides to do wrong.

We usually think of engineering errors as inadvertent, well-intended acts performed incorrectly or as oversights leaving undone what one knew how to do and had planned to do—for example, incorrect computations or not performing a planned computation.

What happened inside VW appears to have involved deliberate misdeeds, not mistakes: supervisors, and possibly higher officials, apparently condoned their commission. For seven consecutive years, they let the company release vehicles embodying the product of their misdeeds. When challenged by federal and state regulators, they made untrue representations on VW's behalf.

> **"What happened inside VW appears to have involved deliberate misdeeds, not mistakes: supervisors, and possibly higher officials, apparently condoned their commission."**

We're disappointed that VW Group's highest officials would use a word from one end of the moral spectrum—*errors*—to characterize conduct that trespassed far into the spectrum's opposite end. The company admits that its employees used corrupt software to cheat on emissions control tests, sold the vehicles as "clean" machines, and made disingenuous denials when challenged by regulators. Because the participants, regardless of their rank in the VW organization, were with few exceptions trained engineers, their decisions involved a corruption of engineering ethics that the profession ought to address.

We understand that VW asks for patience so that it can complete its investigations, but VW adds that completion might be months away. And it could be years before the courts decide whom to hold responsible. Yet the engineering profession shouldn't wait years before examining what has come to light. The stakes are too high, the consequences too fraught, and the need to avert repetitions of what went awry too important for delay.

Our intent here is to comprehend how engineers could abandon their mettle and to help other engineers see the perils of doing so, even when company pressure makes dishonest practices seem like part of the job—which appears to have been the case at VW.

In this article, we develop a plausible explanation for how trained VW engineers could have decided to devise corrupt software to cheat emissions control tests rather than design an engine that could pass them. We construct two chronologies: one details the decisions that brought the defeat device software into production, and the other traces VW's denials to regulators. We draw on facts the chronologies illuminate to explain the dysfunctional practices that appear to account for what happened inside VW. We then discuss serious challenges posed by the use of defeat device software. The first is that VW's development of defeat devices constitutes a new form of insider cyberthreat: the use of corrupt software for dishonest purposes. The second is the ethical breakdown that occurred and how to prevent its recurrence.

At its apex, VW's organizational structure is complex. It is our understanding that Volkswagen Aktiengesellschaft (AG) is the parent company of the VW Group. A Board of Management manages both VW AG and the VW Group, and is headed by a chairman who functions as CEO and is thus also often referred to as VW's CEO. A Supervisory Board "appoints, monitors and advises the Board of Management," is "consulted directly on decisions ... of fundamental significance," and is headed by a chairman (http://annualreport2014.volkswagenag.com/group-management-report/structure-and-business-activities.html). For clarity, we refer in this article to the head of VW's Board of Management as the "CEO" and the head of VW's Supervisory Board as the "chairman." For convenience, we refer to VW AG and VW Group as "VW."

Dysfunctional Practices

We focus on four dysfunctional practices that took root at VW and provide the most plausible explanation for how VW engineers and officers could decide to engage in widespread, repeated dishonesty. We use the term "dysfunctional practices" to denote a significant departure from good engineering, whether by engineers, their superiors up the chain of command, or their bosses at the company's apex who started out as engineers. The common ingredient in each case is dishonesty. We derive four dysfunctional practices from an analysis of facts published in open sources. When set forth in a chronology, the causal relationships become discernible. The dysfunctional practices were:

- senior officers' insistence on the pursuit of infeasible objectives with no tolerance for failure;
- suppression of open communication, enforced by an intolerance for bad news and dissenting views;
- creation of software to cheat, rather than solve, engineering problems and protection of that software from disclosure as if it were a trade secret; and
- departure from honesty in the chain of command and reckless disregard for the consequences.

The authors are not VW customers. Neither owns a car, though each used to. One of us is a software engineer; the other is legal counsel to several engineering firms. We share an admiration for German engineering. Practiced well, it's exemplary in skill, thoroughness, and reliability. German-designed machines perform to specifications. German engineers know with precision their products' capabilities and limits. Ask German naval engineers how many deep dives their design of the boat can withstand, and you'll get an answer supported by analysis and accurate test results. Their drive for boat performance is tempered by an overriding concern for crew safety, because when designing a submarine and its software, every feature is a safety feature. We thought VW had long exemplified engineering excellence and demanded the best from its engineers. Instead, it appears VW let pursuit of growth corrupt its actions. Dysfunctional practices altered the mettle of VW's chain of command. By adopting these practices, VW officers and engineers made a Faustian bargain. As each practice became further embedded, it threatened greater harm to the company. And as each practice spread through the engineering teams and product lines, those responsible took graver risks with VW's reputation to keep the deception hidden. The scale of what happened and the denials designed to cover it up make each version of the company's postadmission account a tough sell—one that pits the company's credibility against its efforts to regain public trust.

We've watched VW's unmasking with mixed emotions: sadness at how far company personnel sank before admitting engineering malpractice, frustration as VW scrambled to conduct damage control that further undermined its reputation, and ire at the hubris that seems to have characterized the company's culture as far back as 2004. Even VW's renewed focus on regaining customer trust seems off target because it emphasizes what VW wants from its customers rather than what it owes them, which is honest engineering or, as it proclaimed in the motto adopted in 2007 for its US business, "Truth in Engineering."

Chronology 1: Decisions Leading to the Defeat Device

The "Origins of the Defeat Device Software" sidebar chronicles the events and decisions that brought the defeat device to market.

This chronicle has moments of certitude—decisive actions that clearly happened—separated by interludes of shadowy human interaction, where it's unclear which of several possible actions occurred. Yet the range of possible actions, along with who performed them, is often severely limited by certitudes in the aftermath, in which public revelation shined a light on failed nitrogen oxide (NOx) emissions tests, deceived regulators, falsified CoCs, blatantly untrue ads, customers sold substandard vehicles, and other undeniable acts. Thus, the sidebar's timeline is our best estimate. Although it's only an approximation, it's close enough to let an observer discern the four dysfunctional practices that appear to have become the standard for certain engineers and supervisors at VW. Let's consider in detail what the chronology reveals about each of those practices.

Insistence on Infeasible Objectives

This practice involved insistence on objectives in the face of evidence that they were unrealistic, leaving dishonest means as the only way forward.

Ordering the pursuit of infeasible objectives is evident in the 2007 release of CEO Martin Winterkorn's ambitious "Strategy 2018" and subsequent events, which set the goal for VW to become "not only as large, but as profitable as its Japanese competitor Toyota Motor Corporation."[3] As *The Economist* observed, "The company has been obsessed with surpassing Toyota and becoming the world's biggest car company."[4] Under Strategy 2018, VW would, by that year, "increase unit sales to more than 10 million vehicles a year"[5] and become "the world's most profitable ... automobile manufacturer," in part by tripling its 2008 US sales to reach Winterkorn's US "target of one million cars a year."[6] Thus, the VW leaders set the objective in an autocratic manner, for which the CEO was known.[7] VW's interim report takes a similar view, although it traces the practice back to an earlier date: "The starting point [for the 'NOx issue'] was a strategic decision to launch a large-scale promotion of diesel vehicles in the United States in 2005."[7]

At roughly the same time as Strategy 2018's announcement, top executive decisions removed from consideration a reliable way to achieve a clean diesel engine; VW canceled its license of Daimler's AdBlue technology. AdBlue is a urea-based treatment for engine exhaust that removes NOx pollutants. If VW hadn't scrapped the license, its engineers would have had a solution to meet the new, reduced limits on NOx imposed by California. Instead, its engineers were left with no feasible alternatives, or at least no honest ones.

Origins of the Defeat Device Software

Here we present a chronicle of events and decisions—some documented facts and others inferred as probable—that brought the Volkswagen (VW) defeat device to market.

2005

VW makes "a strategic decision to launch a large-scale promotion of diesel vehicles in the United States."[1]

February 2005 Wolfgang Bernhard is appointed CEO of VW core brand (owned by VW). VW Brand begins planning a new 2-liter EA189 diesel engine chiefly for the US market.[2] CEO Bernhard "entrusts the new project to Rudolf Krebs, a developer at VW's Audi brand."[3]

May 2005 VW engineers report to senior VW officers that "it will be impossible [for the EA189 engine] to comply with US [NOx] emissions standards using [VW's] current technology." They recommend using competitor Daimler's BlueTECH with AdBlue technology.[3]

Bernhard faces a choice: license BlueTECH from Daimler, his former employer, or risk that VW's technology can be improved to meet NOx emissions limits. A group of top decision makers at Audi—CEO Martin Winterkorn, chief engineer Ulrich Hackenberg, and another senior engineer Wolfgang Hatz—favor the latter course.[3]

An unidentified executive reports that "many VW engineers felt that the company's native technology was not good enough to return sufficiently low emissions." Over opposition by Winterkorn, Bernhard licenses BlueTECH with AdBlue from Daimler.[4]

2006

5 June *Automotive News* reports, "Next year, Volkswagen AG will change its diesel systems from an old-style mechanical fuel injection system to a new high-pressure electronic version. ... Most other automakers switched years ago to computer-controlled ... systems. ... The switchover will take almost a year because VW says it needs the time to ensure that its new system will meet stringent US emission regulations."[5]

Fall First prototypes of EA189 are tested in South Africa.[3]

7 November VW's CEO Bernd Pischetsrieder resigns effective 31 December 2006;[6] Winterkorn emerges as a possible successor.

15 November Reports circulate that Bernhard might resign as threatened in May 2006 if Winterkorn is appointed CEO of VW.[7]

17 November VW states it will market diesel vehicles in the US using BlueTECH,[8] but VW will call it "Clean TDI."[9] TDI is the basic VW engine technology used in EA189. VW's Supervisory Board appoints Winterkorn as VW Group CEO.

29 November VW announces that its Clean TDI engine with BlueTECH will be used in the future Tiguan model.[9]

1 December VW posts to its website that "[n]ew powertrains, including the engine concept developed by Volkswagen under the working title 'Clean TDI' for use in the USA, are already in the prototype stage. These engines will satisfy the strictest emissions laws in the world—even the so-called Tier2Bin5 in California. The 'Clean TDI' engines are an important component of the BlueTECH."[10] The inference is that VW was on track to market emissions-compliant engines using BlueTECH.

26 December VW, with Winterkorn in charge, decides not to sell TDI-equipped Jettas until 2008.[11]

2007

January Bernhard leaves VW Brand before EA189 goes into production.[12]

23 January VW unveils Clean TDI Jetta at the Washington, DC, Auto Show, declaring that it will soon be approved in all 50 states, "satisfying the stringent 'Tier 2/Bin 5' emission requirements."[13,14]

January–February VW approves the appointment of Winterkorn's key engineers from Audi—Hackenberg[15] and Hatz—to senior VW positions, probably responsible for EA189 development, certainly with strong influence over it. Hackenberg becomes a member of VW's Brand Board for Technical Development.[16] Hatz moves from Audi head of engine and transmission development to the same job at VW.[17]

VW 2006 Annual Report (issued February 2007) states, "An innovative and advanced system that keeps CO_2 emissions particularly low while at the same time avoiding 90% of NOx emissions will soon be introduced to the market: the 'Clean TDI.' ... 'Clean TDI' is an especially clean, low-consumption diesel engine by Volkswagen that meets the toughest emissions standards—even in the US."[18] The inference is that VW's marketing group has identified features that VW cars need in the US to achieve Winterkorn's strategic sales objective: low emissions, power, and good fuel economy. Winterkorn approves.

4 April Jetta SportWagen debuts at the New York Auto Show,

Continued on page 16

(After VW admitted its use of defeat device software, it announced it would once again use AdBlue.[8])

There's convincing evidence that engineers understood the emissions control design tradeoffs very well. Yet officers at the highest levels of VW, experienced engineers themselves—placed price, performance, time-frame, and technological bounds on acceptable solutions that were infeasible.[9] They appear to have required their subordinates to achieve success without fail. Thus, managers and engineers apparently had to choose between loyalty to the company—including continued employment—and fidelity to their

continued from page 15

including a 2-liter diesel model to be available in early 2008, probably the "new BlueTECH diesels."[19]

May Winterkorn completes the February board-approved installation of Hatz as VW's engines chief and Hackenberg as leader "in charge of development."[3] The team of three that opposed use of BlueTECH while at Audi is now in charge at VW. Presumably, VW's engineering group attempts to design EA189-powered vehicles that achieve all objectives, but eventually concludes that the desired power and economy can't be obtained along with acceptable emissions using TDI alone.[20] (For convenience, we call this "the problem" in this chronology.)

As VW later admits, "Initially, it proved impossible to have the EA189 engine meet by legal means the stricter nitrogen oxide requirements in the United States within the required timeframe and budget."[1] Seeking relief from infeasible specifications is standard engineering practice—as is alerting superiors when specs cannot be met. The inference is that VW's engineering group faced decisions, including

- whether to report up the VW chain of command that the problem is intractable;
- whether to propose alternatives such as new performance objectives, reduced sufficiently to allow legal emissions; and
- what to do if no alternative is accepted.

Reporting up the chain is the most plausible course of action. It's what any responsible engineer would do.

As later reported by *Handelsblatt*, "VW uses software in its EA189 engine that allows vehicles to be switched into test mode. This is intended to make work easier for technicians. ... The software was developed by automotive supplier Bosch."[3] In a letter, "Bosch warned" VW that "it would be illegal to use engine management software ... in production cars."[21] The inference is that someone at Bosch determined that the company's software was intended for use in a defeat device.

Industry norms and CEO Winterkorn's leadership style aren't tolerant of bad news. When Ferdinand Piech, Chairman of VW's Supervisory Board until 2015, was asked what would happen if an engineering team reported they couldn't deliver, he replied: "Then I will tell them they are all fired and I will bring in a new team. ... And if they tell me they can't do it, I will fire them, too."[22] Winterkorn's reputation is such that "[b]efore anyone reports to him, they make sure they have good news."[23] The inference is that with line engineer reports in hand, VW's officers Hackenberg and Hatz face difficult decisions:

- whether and how to report to their CEO that the problem is, indeed, intractable;
- whether to request additional time and funds to attempt a redesign; and
- whether to propose alternatives—perhaps involving the Bosch software.

For Hackenberg and Hatz, the stakes were enormous: US legal compliance of several VW models. Corporate officers understand legal obligation and liability. Remaining silent would risk termination without severance pay and criminal liability. An informal report of the problem would've maximized the opportunity for the team of three to debate and devise the best possible way forward, but also would've exposed engineers to termination and liability. A formal written report directly to the CEO probably offered the best risk balance. The inference is that, despite the adverse climate for bad news, Hackenberg and Hatz might have decided to report the problem informally to their CEO along with some alternative ways forward. But it's more plausible that they put their report in a written memorandum.

VW pulls "its small diesel cars from many US markets after the 2007 model year because the old engines didn't meet new emissions standards"[24] and plans to replace them with the EA189 engine models like the Jetta SportWagen.

6 July In an email, VW informs its US dealer network of a delay in the Jetta SportWagen's launch from August 2007 to March 2008[25] (but later delays it again to August 2008).[3]

August "The diesel EA189 engine is used for the first time in the new Tiguan model. It contains the software that will later be used to cheat in emissions tests, although it is not yet being used [for that purpose]."[3]

6 August Winterkorn terminates VW participation in the BlueTECH Alliance along with its license, sealing its reliance on VW-designed emissions controls for the EA189.[28]

24 September VW announces that it plans "on toppling Toyota as world's largest car manufacturer by 2015" and "will begin by launching 12 new vehicles in the next three years."[29]

19 October Winterkorn announces VW "will be dropping prices in the US to be more in line with Toyota."[30] The inference is that VW has a new competitive advantage in production costs.

12 November *Automotive News* reports, "A problem with the

professional ethics. If they couldn't engineer a product that would meet objectives by honest means, it seems they understood implicitly that illicit means might be tolerated, even expected. They knew they had to report upward what they'd accomplished and how. Let's examine why.

Given VW's autocratic control, we can reasonably infer that its engineers were accountable to report both serious design problems and the solutions found to overcome them. Indeed, engineers are usually keen to report "we found a way!" Similarly, colleagues and bosses can't resist asking "how did you do it?" When

emissions system in Volkswagen's new Jetta TDI will delay the launch of the diesel sedan for about six months. ... VW spokesman Keith Price confirmed ... that the delay will be announced this week at the Los Angeles Auto Show. He would not give specifics about the technical problem, but he said it has been fixed. The car, though, must go through emissions testing and validation again."[26]

The time remaining until the 2008 Jetta Clean Diesel launch is insufficient for a major new emissions development effort, but the defeat device is feasible. Its near-zero cost and avoidance of delays to redesign emissions controls of the EA189 might have appealed to Winterkorn.[27] The inference is that the last remaining path was the defeat device. As long as VW could conceal the hack, it could control the risks of using a defeat device and gain all the competitive benefits, such as cost reduction, performance enhancements, and accelerated reentry to the US market. Consequently, Hackenberg and Hatz's report and discussion must have resulted in a decision—tacit or explicit—to use the defeat device.

July 2007–August 2008 By the time Jetta is released, it contains the defeat device. The inference is that with commitment to the defeat device sealed, decisions by subordinate engineers and officers probably included

- deciding to use Bosch software, despite Bosch's letter of warning;
- analyzing US Environmental Protection Agency (EPA) tests to determine how vehicle operation in tests differ from highway operation;
- determining what sensors are needed to detect emissions test conditions for the switch;
- writing and verifying the software;
- testing the defeat device to ensure it would reduce NOx emissions below the test limits;
- reporting progress up the VW chain of command; and
- planning repeat installation and verification in many more VW models.

16–25 November California Air Resources Board (CARB) Chair Mary Nichols meets with VW officers at the Los Angeles Auto Show to talk about emissions in forthcoming diesel vehicles and later recalls, "they were the only company that did not want to talk about emissions or the environment at all. They just made it pretty clear that they believed that the superior efficiency of the diesel engine was sufficient reason why we should basically leave them alone."[31]

December Winterkorn announces "Strategy 2018" at the Dresden Trade Fair,[32] with a 10-year objective for VW to become the world's largest and most profitable seller of automobiles.[33]

2008

This year, "all diesel-powered cars sold in the US had to meet significantly stricter emissions standards ... part of so-called 'Tier 2 regulations."[24]

23 June VW Group of America submits to the EPA a "Volkswagen Part 1 Application for Emissions Certification" covering model year 2009. The application provides the EPA with 10 pages of VW test results for the diesel 2-liter engine Jetta and Jetta SportWagen.[34]

VW's application expressly represents that the "test vehicles with respect to which data are submitted are in all material respects as described in the application for certification, have been tested in accordance with the applicable test procedures ... meet the requirement of such tests, and on the basis of such tests, they conform to the requirements of the regulations in 40 CFR, Part 86, Subpart S"—a section that includes this prohibition: "No new light-duty vehicle ... shall be equipped with a defeat device."[34]

VW's application is accompanied by a letter, signed by Leonard W. Kata, Manager–Emission Certification, VW Engineering and Environmental Office, representing that "[a]ll vehicles within this test group comply with all applicable regulations contained in 40 CFR Part 86."[34] Note: When VW admits in 2015 that the test vehicles included a "defeat device," VW confirms that in 2008 and in each subsequent year's applications for emissions certification that VW knowingly made untrue representations.

23 June Based on VW's application, test data, and representations, the EPA issues a Certificate of Conformity covering the VW Jetta and Jetta SportWagen.[35]

29 October VW press release cites the EPA Fuel Economy Guide 2009 as putting Jetta TDI "in the top ten low consumption and low emissions vehicles," noting it fulfills stringent California emission standards. VW explains, "This was achieved through modifications within the engine and by implementing an exhaust treatment system developed especially by Volkswagen and which reduces the nitrogen oxide emissions (NOx) by up to 90 percent. The 'Fuel Economy Guide' is published annually to help consumers make informed choices as regards consumption and environmental friendliness when purchasing new vehicles."[36] VW officers and engineers don't disclose that the press release statements are untrue, and that the EPA rating was fraudulently obtained.

20 November The *Green Car Journal* gives the Jetta TDI its 2009 Green Car of the Year award, noting its clean diesel technology "makes the car legal in all 50 states, meeting California's stringent

Continued on page 18

the stakes riding on the solution are high, the probability of this question is commensurately so, and for a simple reason: the report will draw the same question at each step in the chain of command. No one wants to be caught out, especially on news everyone wants to hear. Honest and dishonest engineering solutions are the same in this regard—good news travels fast, and with all the details intact.

How far up would the good news have reached? Because any corporate strategy would include a monitoring and progress evaluation plan, Strategy 2018 almost certainly did as well. After all, Winterkorn had "worked

continued from page 17

Air Resources Board requirements, under which is [sic] qualifies as a SULEV, or Super Low Emission Vehicle."[37] Jetta is the first diesel to win the award. A key factor: its price is less than hybrid cars.[38] No VW engineer or officer steps forward to say that the award is undeserved.

2009–2010

VW engineering groups install "defeat devices" in multiple models of VW vehicles for the US market.[39]

VW submits annual applications for CoCs, each with "a list of all auxiliary emission control devices ('AECDs') installed on the vehicles," a "justification for each AECD ... and a rationale for why it is not a defeat device,"[40] as required by EPA regulation. (An AECD is "any element of design which senses temperature, vehicle speed, engine RPM, transmission gear, manifold vacuum, or any other parameter for the purpose of activating, modulating, delaying, or deactivating the operation of any part of the emission control system."[40]) Nothing resembling the defeat device is listed. Had it been listed, the corresponding vehicles wouldn't have been certified for US sale.[40]

26 February 2010 VW issues the 2009 Annual Report that details Strategy 2018, including "Volkswagen intends to become a world leader by using intelligent innovations and technologies, while at the same time delivering customer satisfaction and quality."[41]

2010 VW introduces its code of conduct. "In the first step, the Chairman of the Board of Management [CEO] informed all the Company's managers of the importance of the Code of Conduct and called on them to lead by good example.... Each employee received a copy.... [T]he message was driven home in on-site seminars."[42]

References

1. "Volkswagen Making Good Progress with Its Investigation, Technical Solutions, and Group Realignment," Volkswagen Aktiengesellschaft (VW AG), 10 Dec. 2015; www.volkswagenag.com/content/vwcorp/info_center/en/news/2015/12/VW_PK.html.
2. J. Ewing, "Volkswagen Engine-Rigging Scheme Said to Have Begun in 2008," *New York Times*, 4 Oct. 2015; www.nytimes.com/2015/10/05/business/engine-shortfall-pushed-volkswagen-to-evade-emissions-testing.html?_r=0.
3. "Volkswagen Scandal—The Scene of the Crime," *Handelsblatt Global Ed.*, 2 Oct. 2015; https://global.handelsblatt.com/edition/276/ressort/companies-markets/article/investigating-the-scene-of-the-crime.
4. B. Zhang, "This Is the Real Cause of the Volkswagen Cheating Scandal," *Business Insider*, 7 Oct. 2015; www.businessinsider.com/this-is-the-real-cause-of-the-vw-cheating-scandal-2015-10.
5. R. Truett, "The VW Jetta TDI Will Have Limited Availability during the Changeover Scheduled for the Automaker's 2007 Model Year," *Automotive News*, 5 June 2006; www.cleanmpg.com/forums/archive/index.php/t-1051.html.
6. "Pischetsrieder Tenders Resignation," *VW Gazette*, 7 Nov. 2006; http://vwgazette.blogspot.com/2006/11/pischetsrieder-tenders-resignation.html.
7. "Bernhard May Be the Next to Go," *VW Gazette*, 15 Nov. 2006; http://vwgazette.blogspot.cz/2006/11/bernhard-may-be-next-to-go.html.
8. "Volkswagen to Go BlueTECH in the US," *VW Gazette*, 17 Nov. 2011; http://vwgazette.blogspot.com/2006/11/volkswagen-to-go-BlueTECH-in-us.html.
9. "'Concept' Tiguan Breaks Cover at LA Auto Show," *VW Gazette*, 29 Nov. 2006; http://vwgazette.blogspot.com/2006_11_01_archive.html.
10. "Driving the Future Volkswagen Engines—Today, Tomorrow and Beyond," VW AG, 1 Dec. 2006; www.volkswagenag.com/content/vwcorp/info_center/en/themes/2006/12/volkswagen_engines_today_tomorrow_and_beyond.html.
11. "TDI on Hiatus until 2008," *VW Gazette*, 26 Dec. 2006; http://vwgazette.blogspot.com/2006/12/tdi-on-hiatus-until-2008.html.
12. "Class Action Complaint," *Bourne v. Volkswagen AG*, 6 Oct. 2015; www.truthinadvertising.org/wp-content/uploads/2015/10/Bourn-v-Volkswagen-complaint.pdf.
13. "Volkswagen Unveils Clean TDI in DC," *VW Gazette*, 23 Jan. 2007; http://vwgazette.blogspot.com/2007_01_01_archive.html.
14. "Emission Standards Reference Guide: Light-Duty Vehicle, Light-Duty Truck, and Medium-Duty Passenger Vehicle—Tier 2 Exhaust Emission Standards," US Environmental Protection Agency, 15 Oct. 2015; www3.epa.gov/otaq/standards/light-duty/tier2stds.htm.
15. "Prof. Dr.-Ing. Ulrich Hackenberg: Member of the Board of Management at AUDI AG for Technical Development," Audi USA, 2015; www.audiusa.com/newsroom/corporate/audi-ag-board-of-management/ulrich-hackenberg.
16. "Ulrich Hackenberg Appointed New Board Member for Technical Development at Audi AG as of July 1, 2013," Audi MediaCenter, 21 June 2013; www.audi-mediacenter.com/en/press-releases/ulrich-hackenberg-appointed-new-board-member-for

in ... quality and production roles at VW and Audi, earning a reputation as a boss who obsesses about the tiniest product details. ..."[7] He was known for being hands-on, "insisting on having his way even over tiny details,"[10] and he was "always the one who wanted to know everything."[11] In his own words, he emphasized achieving, without fail, his objectives: "I have always been driven by the ambition to solve every problem I face, whether as a scientist, engineer or entrepreneur."[11] He also made clear that he expected to be told when a

-technical-development-at-audi-ag-as-of-july-1-2013-1396.

17. "Reports: VW Investigation Focusing on Development Managers," *Associated Press*, 5 Oct. 2015; www.winknews.com/2015/10/05/reports-vw-investigation-focusing-on-development-managers.

18. "Annual Report 2006," VW AG, Feb. 2007, p. 29; www.volkswagenag.com/content/vwcorp/info_center/en/publications/2007/03/Geschaeftsbericht_2006.bin.html/binarystorageitem/file/Annual_Report_2006_e.pdf.

19. "Jetta SportWagen Makes Debut in New York Auto Show," *VW Gazette*, 4 Apr. 2007; http://vwgazette.blogspot.com/2007_04_01_archive.html.

20. "A Mucky Business," *Economist*, 26 Sept. 2015; www.economist.com/news/briefing/21667918-systematic-fraud-worlds-biggest-carmaker-threatens-engulf-entire-industry-and.

21. "Bosch Warned VW about Illegal Software Use in Diesel Cars, Report Says," *Automotive News*, 27 Sept. 2015; www.autonews.com/article/20150927/COPY01/309279989/bosch-warned-vw-about-illegal-software-use-in-diesel-cars-report-says.

22. P.A. Eisenstein, "Just Following Orders? Who Was Really Responsible for VW's Emissions Cheating?," *Detroit Bureau*, 8 Oct. 2015; www.thedetroitbureau.com/2015/10/just-following-orders-who-was-really-responsible-for-vws-emissions-cheating.

23. J. Muller, "How Volkswagen Will Rule the World," *Forbes*, 7 Apr. 2013; www.forbes.com/sites/joannmuller/2013/04/17/volkswagens-mission-to-dominate-global-auto-industry-gets-noticeably-harder/3.

24. T. De Chant, "Volkswagen's Little Engine that Couldn't," *NOVA Next*, 22 Sept. 2015; www.pbs.org/wgbh/nova/next/tech/volkswagen-diesel-emissions.

25. "Jetta SportWagen Delayed till Next Year," *VW Gazette*, 6 July 2007; http://vwgazette.blogspot.com/2007_07_01_archive.html.

26. R. Truett, "Emissions Problem Delays VW Jetta TDI Diesel in US," *Automotive News*, 12 Nov. 2007; www.autonews.com/article/20071112/ANA03/71109022/emissions-problem-delays-vw-jetta-tdi-diesel-in-u.s.

27. A. Robinson, "VW's Winterkorn to Greens: So Get off Our Backs, Already!" 2 Oct. 2014; http://blog.caranddriver.com/vws-winterkorn-to-greens-so-get-off-our-backs-already.

28. "Volkswagen Cuts Ties with BlueTECH," *VW Gazette*, 6 Aug. 2007; http://vwgazette.blogspot.com/2007_08_01_archive.html.

29. "Volkswagen Wants to Be the World's Largest by 2015," *VW Gazette*, 24 Sept. 2015; http://vwgazette.blogspot.com/2007_09_01_archive.html.

30. "Volkswagen to Drop US Prices in Line with Toyota," *VW Gazette*, 19 Oct. 2007; http://vwgazette.blogspot.com/2007_10_01_archive.html

31. A. Dörner, "CARB Chief: Repair, Replace, Redress," *Handelsblatt Global Ed.*, 20 Nov. 2015; https://global.handelsblatt.com/edition/311/ressort/companies-markets/article/carb-chief-repair-replace-redress?ref=MTI5ODU1.

32. "VW Group Annual Report for 2008," VW AG, 12 Mar. 2009; www.volkswagenag.com/content/vwcorp/info_center/en/publications/2009/03/GB_2008.bin.html/binarystorageitem/file/Y_2008_e.pdf.

33. J. Schultz, "Volkswagen Extends C.E.E. Martin Winterkorn's Contract," *New York Times*, 4 Jan. 2011; http://wheels.blogs.nytimes.com/2011/01/04/volkswagen-extends-c-e-o-martin-winterkorns-contract.

34. "Application for Emissions Certification Part 1 2009 Model Year," VW AG, 23 June 2008; http://iaspub.epa.gov/otaqpub/display_file.jsp?docid=20177&flag=1.

35. "Certificate of Conformity Issued to VW, Cert. No. 590T2-11," US EPA, 23 June 2008; http://iaspub.epa.gov/otaqpub/display_file.jsp?docid=18976&flag=1.

36. "Volkswagen in Fuel Economy Guide 2009," VW AG, 29 Oct. 2008; www.volkswagenag.com/content/vwcorp/info_center/en/news/2008/10/vw_in_fuel_economy_guide.html.

37. W. Cunningham, "'Green Car Journal' Announces 2009 Green Car of the Year," *CNET*, 20 Nov. 2008; www.cnet.com/news/green-car-journal-announces-2009-green-car-of-the-year.

38. "VW Jetta TDI Named 'Green Car of the Year,'" *Associated Press*, 20 Nov. 2008; www.nbcnews.com/id/27825003/ns/business-autos/t/vw-jetta-tdi-named-green-car-year/#.VkzVamAlI7Q.

39. "Class Action Complaint," *Iris Stricklin v. Volkswagen Group of America, Inc.*, Central District of California, 22 Sept. 2015; www.blbglaw.com/cases/00275_data/Volkswagen%20Class%20Action%20Complaint.

40. "Notice of Violation to Volkswagen AG, Audi AG, Volkswagen Group of America, Inc.," US Environmental Protection Agency, 18 Sept. 2015; www.eenews.net/assets/2015/09/21/document_cw_01.pdf.

41. "VW AG Annual Report for 2009," VW AG, 26 Feb. 2010; www.volkswagenag.com/content/vwcorp/info_center/en/publications/2010/03/Annual_Report_2009.bin.html/binarystorageitem/file/Y_2009_e.pdf.

42. "Annual Report 2010," VW AG, 10 Mar. 2011, p. 131; www.volkswagenag.com/content/vwcorp/content/en/misc/pdf-dummies.bin.html/downloadfilelist/downloadfile/downloadfile_14/file/Y_2010_e.pdf.

solution wasn't possible. As VW's 2010 Annual Report quotes him, "If developers say that a solution is not possible from a technical, timing, or financial point of view, I am able to challenge them. And everyone knows that."[12] Withal, there's convincing evidence that, in the normal course of Strategy 2018's progress, the NOx emissions design impasse would have been reported high in the VW chain of command, if not to the top.

VW's interim report supports this analysis, acknowledging that "it proved impossible to have the EA189 engine meet by legal means" the US NOx emission requirements.[9] How else was this learned other than from an internal report? The interim report continues, "This led to the incorporation of software that adjusted nitrogen oxide emission levels according to whether vehicles were on the road or being tested."[9] Is this the "we found a way" report from internal files? It seems likely. VW installed the EA189 engine, equipped with defeat device software, for seven years in 11 million vehicles worldwide.

Thus, it's surprising that VW America's CEO Michael Horn gave the following account in his October 2015 testimony to Congress: "This was a couple of software engineers who put this in for whatever reason."[13]

For the same reasons, we think that VW's account of its R&D risk (which appeared in its 2011 Annual Report and has reappeared in substance as late as its 2014 Annual Report) is obsolete and that VW's announced commitment to revise its internal processes confirms it. An interesting window into VW's evolving culture will be to compare its descriptions of R&D risk in future annual reports to this one from 2011:[14]

> There is also a risk that it may not be possible to develop products or modules within the specified time-frame, to the required quality standards, or in line with cost specifications. To avoid this risk, we continuously and systematically monitor the progress of all projects and regularly compare this progress with the original targets. In the event of deviations, appropriate control measures are initiated in good time.

Suppression of Open Communication

This practice involved the creation of a work environment in which engineers couldn't communicate freely when attempting to solve tough design problems.

Engineering is an increasingly collaborative activity because the task of designing a cutting-edge technology is too complex for one person. Collaborative engineering thrives on open communication. The tougher the problem, the greater the need. Conversely, any factor that causes friction or discomfort in free expression impedes engineering accomplishment. Indeed, credible descriptions of VW's work environment by former personnel suggest that open communication was lacking and that what the German newspaper *Handelsblatt* aptly terms "culture of fear and hubris" more commonly characterized the workplace:[15]

> Current and former Volkswagen executives say that Mr. Piëch [supervisory board chairman from 2002 until April 2015] and his protégé Martin Winterkorn, CEO from 2007 until his resignation [in September 2015] ... created an autocratic, corrosive culture in which dissent and criticism weren't tolerated. [According to a former VW executive] "Workers and managers are afraid to speak the truth. ... Dissenting opinions are at best ignored and at worst suppressed."

German auto executives are reportedly "used to getting what they want."[16] Winterkorn's management style was reportedly one of intolerance for bad news: "He doesn't like bad news. Before anyone reports to him, they make sure they have good news."[6] He reported to a chairman who boasted publicly that he would fire any engineering team that failed to achieve an objective. The 10 December 2015 interim report confirms this by acknowledging that change was necessary. According to VW's new CEO Matthias Müller, "the future will be about more open discussions ... and a willingness to allow mistakes if they are understood as an opportunity to learn."[9]

The final caveat is a chilling hint that low tolerance for failure might remain at VW, notwithstanding the trouble it's already caused.

Use of Corrupt Software

This practice involved VW's systematic use of software for corrupt purposes. VW wrote code that gives vehicles two operating modes, but keeps their existence secret. The software implements a "switch" that detects whether the machine is operating in test or highway conditions. If the machine is undergoing tests, the switch engages features to produce good test results. If testing isn't detected, the switch disengages these features and boosts other elements of the machine's performance to levels the company can tout to market the product.

The 18 September 2015 EPA NoV regarding the VW 2-liter EA189 engine describes the switch algorithm. It's clever and sophisticated, co-opting several sensors with legitimate vehicle operation purposes:[17]

> VW manufactured and installed software in the electronic control module (ECM) of these vehicles that sensed when the vehicle was being tested for compliance with EPA emissions standards. ... [T]he EPA is calling this the "switch." The "switch" senses whether the vehicle is being tested or not based on various inputs including the position of the steering wheel, vehicle speed, the duration of the engine's operation, and barometric pressure. These inputs precisely track the parameters of the federal test procedure used for emission testing for EPA certification purposes. ... At all other times during normal vehicle operation, the "switch" was activated and the vehicle ECM software ran a separate "road calibration" which reduced the effectiveness of the emission control system. ... As a

> result, emissions of NOx increased by a factor of 10 to 40 times above the EPA compliant levels.

How did such an algorithm come to be? Engineers would have to conceive it, verify that it would work, implement it in computer code, and then test it in simulated and real operating conditions. After all, the stakes for algorithm failure were high. An erroneous "normal driving" output when a vehicle was being tested would've caused failure and a certification problem. A "test" output under normal use would've robbed vehicle performance and economy. Engineers must have repeated design, verification, and testing for every VW model in which the defeat device needed to work: some 30 models and 11 million cars over seven years.[18] As described by a mechanical engineer:[19]

Writing software code to create a cheat disguised as a solution represents the advent of a new insider cyberthreat. Such software isn't typical malware.

> [C]omputer sensors monitored the steering column. Under normal driving conditions, the column oscillates as the driver negotiates turns. But during emissions testing, the wheels of the car move, but the steering wheel doesn't. That seems to have been the signal for the "defeat device" to turn the catalytic scrubber up to full power, allowing the car to pass the test.

Engineers would also have needed to ensure that with the switch (and emissions controls) off, the engine would achieve a desired tradeoff. For VW, the gain appears to have been "better fuel economy."[20]

With the switch in place, engineers determined how to make it affect emission controls. They obtained software capable of putting the system in a low emissions mode, ostensibly for developmental testing. In 2007, when Bosch—the fuel injection and emissions controls vendor who also provided the software—discovered VW's intent to use it in production cars, it sent a letter to VW warning of its illegality.[21] It would appear that VW engaged Bosch to provide the software, sharing enough information for Bosch to infer VW's intentions. If so, a significant group of managers and engineers probably read the letter and ignored it.

Finally, VW's engine controls include—as most modern automobiles do—sophisticated onboard diagnostics that continuously assess emission controls. These diagnostics are responsible for the "check emissions" warning light you might have seen in your own car. VW engineers arranged for the onboard diagnostics to allow noncompliant operation and somehow verified by testing that no warning occurred. By keeping the warning light off when the switch engaged, VW concealed the switch from customers and regulators.

Compounding the scope of VW's misconduct is the revelation in EPA's 2 November 2015 NoV on 3-liter engines. This NoV details a substantially different technical mechanism to achieve the same result—dialing down emissions in conditions exactly corresponding to static tests, but releasing NOx emissions up to nine times the allowed amount in normal mode operation:[22]

> When this software determines the vehicle has begun the ... emission test procedure, it directs the vehicle to employ a low NOx temperature conditioning mode. ... In this ... mode, the vehicle operates ... in such a way that the parameters yield low engine-out NOx emissions ... below the applicable emissions standard.
>
> However, the software employs a "timer" that coincides with the low NOx temperature conditioning mode. At exactly one second after the completion of the initial phases of the FTP 75 Federal emissions test procedures (1,370 seconds, which is when the vehicle would normally be turned off), this software directs the vehicle to cease low NOx temperature conditioning mode. ... [T]he emission control system is immediately less effective ... [and] yields higher levels of NOx from the engine. ... In sum, as soon as the vehicle senses it is not being tested, it uses "normal mode." ... [And] tailpipe emissions of NOx are up to 9 times the applicable NOx standard levels.

Writing software code to create a cheat disguised as a solution represents the advent of a new insider cyberthreat. Such software isn't typical malware; it's not causing the machine to do anything that its designers didn't intend. What makes it unique—and a serious threat—is that it's written to satisfy an engineering objective. Yet it subverts tests. It helps bring substandard products to market. It confers a tremendous competitive advantage as long as the company can keep it hidden. Such software is effectively a trade secret—important for its value and for the peril it poses to the company if its existence ever comes to light. We call this *corrupt code*. Unlike some other cyberthreats, technical means to mitigate the effects of corrupt code are unlikely to appear. The only real counter to corrupt code is engineers with the mettle to challenge its use.

The Bosch company's role in authorship of the defeat device remains murky. We know the company furnished the control software that puts the EA189 engine in a low NOx emissions mode.[8] We don't know whether VW ordered the software specifically for the cheat or for some legitimate purpose and then diverted it to the illegitimate aim. In either case, at some point Bosch engineers perceived VW's intent, realized its illegality, and issued an official caveat—a letter. Whether this absolves Bosch of further responsibility is an interesting question that's being investigated. Nonetheless, with Bosch's software, the rest of the defeat device constituted a few tens or at most hundreds of lines of specialized code to co-opt sensor inputs meant for other purposes and to cleverly combine them to produce the fateful binary bit signifying whether the car was being tested or driven by an end user. In the "haystack" of 10^8 lines of code of typical vehicle control systems, 10^2 is indeed the proverbial needle. Corrupt code is a tough problem to solve.

Departure from Honesty

The fourth practice was the VW chain of command's departure from honesty and reckless disregard for the consequences.

Honesty as a checkpoint for quality control of engineering and corporate decisions must operate consistently. In VW's design process, it appears to have ceased performing that role, or performed it only selectively. There've been no reports of anyone in VW's senior chain of command recognizing or protesting such practices, or considering the risks that engineers and officers were taking with the company's hard-earned, intangible assets: its reputation and the trust customers and investors placed in it. There also seems to have been little or no recognition that the participants were committing a blunder. Instead, those involved were impelled to draw more participants into dishonest practices due to the expanding number of affected models over the seven years. They didn't prepare one year's application for a CoC to the EPA, but rather seven years of annual applications for each of the defeat device makes and models.

Trial lawyers often caution their witnesses that lying is a blunder, because you can never tell just one. And, the more you tell, the greater the risk you will be impeached. VW personnel seemingly discovered that each lie told required telling more to cover up what they'd done. This might help explain VW's decision to deny for more than a year that its vehicles contained defeat devices, despite EPA and CARB claims.

Chronology 2: Aftermath and Cover Up

Our second chronology details the extent to which the fourth dysfunctional practice—the departure from honesty—went from helping engender the decision to use a defeat device to covering up the software's existence when regulators confronted VW with test results of excessive NOx emissions in highway driving.

Disingenuous Denials

When regulators asked VW whether its vehicles contained an undisclosed defeat device, VW launched a campaign of denials. The "Disingenuous Denials to Regulators" sidebar documents this campaign.

No report to date has shown that VW considered admitting the defeat device deception until it faced unbearable commercial consequences. Only when the EPA threatened to prevent imports for model year 2016 by withholding necessary certification did VW revelations begin.

At some early point, the deception appeared to turn inward, with engineers, supervisors, and bosses deceiving themselves that—having succeeded in 2009—they could cheat again with more models in succeeding years. Perhaps hubris helped, along with another self-deception: that if the truth ever did come to light, the enterprise was too big to fail and that the top echelons of VW could manage the consequences with adroit damage control.

In fact, VW's postdisclosure communications have continued to disappoint. The dribble of admissions, often corrected and reversed, seems disingenuous, with both content and tone reflecting the secretive, authoritarian culture that apparently made them necessary. Euphemistic word craft abounds: "irregularities" rather than failures, "chain of errors" rather than deception, and agentless passive voice as in, "This led to the incorporation of software," so that amorphous causality seems to have controlled events rather than people. It's hard to place credence in such conspicuous efforts at managing appearances.

Moreover, the company inexplicably took postdisclosure positions that it later had to abandon. On 2 November 2015, VW's supervisory board stated, "Volkswagen AG wishes to emphasize that no software has been installed in the 3-liter V6 diesel power units to alter emissions characteristics in a forbidden manner."[23] Three weeks later, Audi's CEO met with EPA officials to admit that all 3-liter diesel engines "sold from 2009 to this year—including Audi, VW and Porsche sports utility vehicles" contained auxiliary emissions control device software in violation of the US Clean Air Act (though Audi continues to deny the software is a defeat device under the EPA definition).[24,25]

VW's Interim Report and Code of Conduct

VW's dysfunctional practices pose disquieting

challenges to the engineering profession. Perhaps the greatest is still developing. In its interim report, VW appears intent on putting what the German media designated as "Dieselgate" behind it by assigning responsibility below C-level officers:[9]

> Group Audit's examination of the relevant processes indicates that the software-influenced NOx emissions behavior was due to interaction of three factors:
>
> - The misconduct and shortcomings of individual employees,
> - Weaknesses in some processes,
> - A mindset in some areas of the Company that tolerated breaches of the rules.

"A corporate culture consistent with VW's code would probably not prevent dysfunctional practices. The code doesn't demand that engineers and officers honor a guiding set of ethical principles."

The focus on "individual employees" is worrisome. There's no assumption by top-level officers of responsibility for creating the work environment in which enormous failures occurred. Also worrisome is the chairman's drawing a distinction between being honest and more honest: "[W]hen it comes to thresholds we need the courage to be more honest. The growing industry-wide discrepancies between official emissions data and real-life levels are no longer acceptable. We need to break new ground here."[2]

VW's interim report also suggests that VW had rules that would have been sufficient if only "some areas of the Company" hadn't developed a "mindset that tolerated breaches of the rules." It's not clear which rules are being referred to, but it's reasonable to infer that some appeared in VW's code of conduct, available on its website since the code's adoption in 2010.[26]

The relationship between organizations and their written codes is complex. Leaders strive to create an environment in which individuals both accept and are motivated to achieve the company's goals. Codes are merely a leader's communication tool for this purpose—one cog in a much larger effort to make the organization an extension of the leader's will. Thus, the importance of VW's code of conduct lies not in what it caused individuals to do or not do. Rather, it's a window into the ways of thinking that VW leaders sought to promulgate and, by inference, into their own thought processes.

At first glance, the code of conduct lists standards that might have prevented Dieselgate. Yet on closer examination, there are obvious consistencies with the four dysfunctional practices. The code puts highest emphasis on VW's reputation as a means to promote its strategy. Indeed, the word "reputation" appears four times, including in the first sentence of the code: "The reputation of the Volkswagen Group is determined in large part by the demeanor, actions, and behavior of each individual employee."[26]

The aggressive company business objective is in the code's foreword: "Our common goal is to be number one among the world's automobile manufacturers … based on superior quality."[26]

The code reads as a book of rules in the same autocratic tone of recent announcements: "Each of our employees shall make sure that his or her demeanor in public does not damage the reputation of the Volkswagen Group. The fulfillment of his or her duties must always be directed hereto in all respects."[26]

By contrast, we have seen other companies' codes that speak in the first person, addressing all in the enterprise as "we," evoking equal applicability to officers and employees, and putting standards of behavior in the context of some greater good.

It's easy to conclude from the VW code that "demeanor," "actions," "behavior," "reputation," "performance," and other outward displays are paramount, while principled judgment and honesty are secondary. The greatest sin from the code's viewpoint is damaging the company; the second is deviating from rule-based norms. There's little encouragement of independent, honest, and forthright thought. The code is incompatible with the new mindset that the current CEO Müller announced in his interim report:[9]

> We don't need yes-men, but managers and engineers who make good arguments in support of their convictions and projects, who think and act like entrepreneurs. I am calling for people … who follow their instincts and are not merely guided by the possible consequences of impending failure. In short: the future at Volkswagen belongs to the bold. We need a little more Silicon Valley.

Noteworthy are the emphasis on entrepreneurs with no mention of engineers and the tone-deaf invocation of "a little more Silicon Valley" with no word about honest use of technology. The summons to "the bold" to repair the failures of Dieselgate is tenuous at best, especially considering that bold dishonesty was its cornerstone. A corporate culture consistent with

Disingenuous Denials to Regulators

When confronted by US Environmental Protection Agency (EPA) and California Air Resources Board (CARB) regulators about undisclosed defeat devices, Volkswagen (VW) launched a campaign of disingenuous denials that lasted more than a year. Here we present a chronicle of the company's cover-up and eventual disclosure.

2014

Early 2014 West Virginia University's (WVU's) Center for Alternative Fuels, Engines, and Emissions (CAFEE) completes a study on the 2012 Jetta and 2013 Passat. In lab tests, the two VW vehicles produced NOx emissions "50 and 64 percent below EPA regulations for Vehicle A (the Jetta) and Vehicle B (the Passat), respectively."[1] By contrast, in real-world driving, NOx emissions of Vehicle A (the Jetta) exceed EPA emissions limits "by a factor of 15 to 35" and those of Vehicle B (the Passat) exceed EPA emissions limits "by a factor of 5 to 20 times the Tier2-Bin5 standard."[2] In other words, emissions on the road vastly exceeded EPA limits that were inexplicably met under static test conditions.

31 March Marc Besch of the WVU test team presents the test results at the 24th Coordinating Research Council Real World Emissions Workshop in San Diego[3] and the data is "questioned by Volkswagen."[4]

15 May CAFEE publishes its final report "In-Use Emissions Testing of Light-Duty Diesel Vehicles in the United States."[2]

Mid-2014 CAFEE's findings prompt EPA and CARB to "start an investigation and discussions with Volkswagen Group of America on the reasons behind these high NOx emissions observed on their 2.0 liter diesel vehicles over real world driving conditions."[5]

May–December VW asserts to CARB and the EPA that "the increased emissions from these vehicles could be attributed to various technical issues and unexpected in-use conditions."[6] As recollected by CARB communications director Stanley Young at meetings between CARB officials and VW, engineers from VW "tried to 'discredit the findings' [by WVU] by challenging the data and methodology of the study.... '[VW's engineers] were recalcitrant. ... It was a range of issues, every time it was something different.' ... VW said that 'our calibration was off' and that the discrepancies had to do with 'the conditions under which the test was done.'"[7]

18 September EPA and CARB inform VW that they believe its vehicles far exceed emissions limits and have used a defeat device to circumvent the emissions tests.[8]

September "VW initiated testing to replicate" the CAFEE work and "identify the technical reasons for the high on-road emissions."[5]

September–December VW entities "represented to regulators that the vehicles' software could be optimized to address the excess NOx emissions issue."[9]

2 December VW meets with CARB staff, shares the results of VW's tests, and proposes a "recalibration fix for Gen1 ... and Gen2 [vehicles]" that would involve a "software recall" of approximately 500,000 vehicles. CARB agrees, but cautioned VW that if "confirmatory testing showed that the fix did not address the on-road NOx issues, they would have to conduct another recall."[10]

December VW issues a recall for the 2-liter vehicles to address the excess emissions issue.[9]

2015

March VW issues another recall for 2-liter vehicles to address the excess emissions issue.[9]

April VW America sends letters to California owners of diesel-powered VWs and Audis notifying them of "emissions service action" needed on their vehicles and telling them to bring their cars to a dealer for a software update, stating, "The vehicle's engine management software has been improved to assure your vehicle's tailpipe emissions are optimized and operating efficiently."[11]

April–May CARB "broadened the testing" of VW vehicles "to pinpoint the exact technical nature of the vehicles' poor [emissions] performance, and to investigate why the vehicles' onboard diagnostic system was not detecting the increased emissions. None of the potential technical issues suggested by VW explained the higher test results consistently confirmed during CARB's testing."[11]

May CARB tests show that the "recall calibration did reduce emissions to some degree but NOx ... emissions were still significantly higher than expected" and, in fact, allowed "uncontrolled NOx emissions."[5] A CARB officer discloses that "[VW] would say the tests weren't at the right temperature, or some other issue."[12]

9 July CARB shares its test results with EPA and VW; several discussions with VW follow, during which VW "disclosed that Gen1, Gen2 and the 2015 model-year improved ... Gen3 ... had a second calibration intended to run only during certification testing."[5]

August EPA and CARB demand an explanation from VW.[13] EPA notifies VW that it won't receive certificates for US importation of its 2016 models if it doesn't answer the EPA's allegations candidly.

VW's code would probably not prevent dysfunctional practices. The code doesn't demand that engineers and officers honor a guiding set of ethical principles. Rather, it declares that their duty is to perform as directed by their superiors, who are, in turn, responsible for subordinates' performance: "Every superior has responsibility for his or her employees. Every superior sets an example and must act in strict accordance with the Code of Conduct."[26]

A requirement to "act in strict accordance" with a code that provides no restriction on means is an invitation to make poor decisions, which is amplified by

19 August According to reports based on Lower Saxony State Chancellery records, in discussions with the CARB, VW makes "partial confessions" of irregularities in the programming of engine controls in VW vehicles.[14]

August–September CARB and EPA make clear to VW they won't approve the Certificates of Conformity (CoCs) for VW's 2016 models (and thus will bar their importation to the US) until VW adequately explains the "anomalous emissions and assures the agencies that the 2016 model year vehicles would not have similar issues."[6]

21 August At a conference on transportation and energy in Pacific Grove, California, VW representatives disclose to Chris Grundler, director of the EPA Office of Transportation and Air Quality, that VW "hacked its own cars to deceive US regulators about how much their diesel engines pollute."[7] At the same meeting, VW also told CARB officials of the deception.

August–2 September VW CEO Martin Winterkorn negotiates an extension of his contract with VW through 2018. The Executive Committee of VW's Supervisory Board agrees to submit a resolution at its 25 September 2015 meeting for a new contract as "Chairman of the Board of Management" [CEO] of VW through 31 December 2018.[15]

3 September During a meeting or conference call, VW America and VW executives in Germany admit to EPA and CARB that its Gen1, Gen2, and Gen3 diesel vehicles were "designed and manufactured with a defeat device."[5,10]

VW executives reportedly "went over written details provided to the participants explaining how software used in its diesel cars was able to manipulate emissions tests in the United States"—thus ending 15 months of denials by VW.[7]

August–September Winterkorn receives word that VW America has admitted using defeat device, but decides to postpone disclosing that to VW's Supervisory Board. In ensuing weeks, he concludes negotiation with the Board regarding his new employment contract.

18 September EPA issues a notice of violation (NoV) of the Clean Air Act (CAA) to Volkswagen AG, Audi AG, and VW Group of America, alleging that vehicles from model years 2009 to 2015 contain "defeat devices" that "bypass, defeat, or render inoperative elements of the vehicles' emission control system that exist to comply with CAA emission standards," that VW failed as required to disclose these devices on its CoC applications, and imported and sold vehicles whose "emissions of NOx increased by a factor of 10 to 40 times above the EPA compliant levels."[6]

18 September CARB determines that VW's earlier recall "did not address the high on-road NOx emissions and also resulted in the vehicle failing certification standards." In its notice to VW, CARB deems the recall "ineffective" and "unapproved."[16]

20 September Winterkorn makes a statement regarding "manipulations that violate American environmental standards" and adds "we do not and will not tolerate violations of any kind of our internal rules or of the law."[17]

22 September VW issues press release stating, "VW is working at full speed to clarify irregularities concerning a particular software used in diesel engines. ... The software in question does not affect handling, consumption or emissions. This gives clarity to customers and dealers. ... [T]he relevant engine management software is also installed in other Volkswagen Group vehicles with diesel engines. For the majority of these engines the software does not have any effect. Discrepancies relate to vehicles with Type EA189 engines, involving some eleven million vehicles worldwide."[18]

Media report VW's use of "defeat device," saying Winterkorn intends to stay on and see VW through the crisis.[19]

23 September Winterkorn resigns, stating, "Above all, I am stunned that misconduct on such a scale was possible in the Volkswagen Group. ... I am doing this in the interests of the company even though I am not aware of any wrong doing on my part."[20]

14 October VW reportedly scraps its "existing emissions technology in its diesel engines in favor of more expensive AdBlue ... technology to reduce" NOx emissions—thereby reverting to the technology it had originally licensed to use. "The switch to AdBlue ... is a major change for Volkswagen and would appear to be an acknowledgment that its existing so-called lean nitrogen trap technology can't meet strict US restrictions on tailpipe emissions."[21]

16 October KBA (German Federal Motor Transport Authority) orders VW to recall 2.4 million vehicles and contends in a press release that VW used impermissible software and must remove it.[22]

VW America CEO Michael Horn testifies before Congress, stating "it wasn't a corporate decision to cheat. It was a couple of software engineers." And that "he first learned of the existence of the defeat devices 'a couple of days before' the 3 September meeting [conference call among EPA, CARB, and VW].[23]

26 October The internal investigation of VW reportedly widens, "focusing not only on who was responsible for installing illegal software ... but also on which managers may have learned of the deception and failed to take appropriate action."[24] VW suspends "anyone who could have been involved in the scam—from high-level decision

Continued on page 26

providing senior officers broad discretion to set objectives and direct others to achieve them without fail:[26]

> By providing regular information and instruction about the relevant responsibilities and powers for each work area, supervisors promote behavior by their employees that conforms to the Code of Conduct. The superior places trust in his employees, agrees on ambitious and realistic goals. ... Superiors particularly honor top achievements.

Urging superiors to "honor top achievements" is appropriate in a performance/reward system, not a

continued from page 25

makers to ordinary engineers" ranging from "board-level executives at some Volkswagen units to low-level technicians."[25]

2 November VW discloses it had "understated emissions" of NOx by its "Cayenne sport utility vehicle."[26]

EPA issues a second NoV of the Clean Air Act to VW AG, Audi AG, VW Group of America, Porsche AG, and Porsche Cars North America, alleging VW "developed and installed a defeat device in certain VW, Audi and Porsche ... diesel vehicles equipped with 3.0 liter engineers for model years ... 2014 through 2016 that increases emissions of ... NOx ... up to nine times EPA's standard"—the NoV "covers approximately 10,000 ... cars already sold in the United States since May 2014" and an "unknown volume of 2016 vehicles."[27]

VW's Supervisory Board issues a press release to "emphasize that no software has been installed in the 3-liter V6 diesel power units to alter emissions characteristics in a forbidden manner."[28]

3 November VW discloses "irregularities" in CO_2 emissions, that is, it understated CO_2 emissions on "800,000 VW vehicles"[26] and estimated the initial economic risk at "two billion euros."[29]

20 November CARB Chair Mary Nichols confirms that VW has "conceded" it deceptively manipulated emissions on its Porsche models (reversing its earlier denial)[30]—the company whose CEO, Matthias Müller, was selected to be the new CEO for VW.[31]

23 November VW's Audi CEO admits to the EPA that the illegal software was installed in the larger diesel engines.[32]

1 December Germany's KBA discloses in an email that software VW installed in the EA189 engine "is an illegal defeat device according to the KBA's legal interpretation."[33]

10 December VW issues an interim report providing "initial results" of its internal investigations on the "origin and development" of the NOx issue: "It proves not to have been a one-time error, but rather a chain of errors that were allowed to happen. ...Initially, it proved impossible to have the EA189 engine meet by legal means the stricter nitrogen oxide requirements in the United States within the required timeframe and budget. This led to the incorporation of software that adjusted nitrogen oxide emission levels according to whether vehicles were on the road or being tested."[34]

References

1. E. Jaffe, "The Study that Brought Down Volkswagen," *Atlantic Citylab*, 24 Sept. 2015; www.citylab.com/crime/2015/09/the-study-that-brought-down-volkswagen/407149.
2. "In-Use Emissions Testing of Light-Duty Diesel Vehicles in the United States," West Virginia Univ., Center for Alternative Fuels, Engines, and Emissions, 15 May 2014; www.theicct.org/sites/default/files/publications/WVU_LDDV_in-use_ICCT_Report_Final_may2014.pdf.
3. "Preliminary Agenda, 24th CRC Real World Emissions Workshop," Coordinating Research Council, 2014; www.crcao.org/workshops/24th_RWE_Workshop/24RWE%20Draft%20Agenda%202014%202014.03.11%20complete.pdf.
4. D. Morgan, "West Virginia Engineer Proves to Be a David to VW's Goliath," *Reuters*, 23 Sept. 2014; www.reuters.com/article/2015/09/24/us-usa-volkswagen-researchers-idUSKCN0RM2D720150924#bcYK1fxiiBCwvW0V.97.
5. "California Air Resources Board Letter to VW," Air Resources Board, 18 Sept. 2015; www.arb.ca.gov/newsrel/in_use_compliance_letter.htm.
6. "Notice of Violation to Volkswagen AG, Audi AG, Volkswagen Group of America, Inc.," US Environmental Protection Agency, 18 Sept. 2015; www.eenews.net/assets/2015/09/21/document_cw_01.pdf.
7. T. Gardner, P. Lienert, and D. Morgan, "INSIGHT—After Year of Stonewalling, VW Stunned US Regulators with Confession," *Reuters*, 24 Sept. 2015; www.reuters.com/article/2015/09/24/usa-volkswagen-deception-idUSL1N11U1OB20150924#RGd1UEfbOUQEPMP4.97.
8. "The Allegations," *FuelScandal*, May 2014; www.fuelscandal.com/allegations.
9. United States of America v. Volkswagen AG et al., Complaint, 4 Jan. 2016; www.justice.gov/opa/file/809826/download.
10. D. Lardner, "After VW Recall, EPA Will Now Test All Diesel Cars to Find Cheaters," *Clark Howard*, 23 Sept. 2015; www.clarkhoward.com/the-vw-recall-and-what-we-know-so-far.
11. A. Sage, "Exclusive: VW Recall Letters in April Warned of an Emissions Glitch," *Reuters*, 24 Sept. 2015; www.reuters.com/article/2015/09/24/us-usa-volkswagen-letters-exclusive-idUSKCN0RO0BD20150924#Kes03416FsMCuYtt.97.
12. P. Whoriskey and J. Warrick, "Anatomy of Volkswagen's Deception: The Recall that Never Fixed Any Cars," *Washington Post*, 22 Sept. 2015; www.washingtonpost.com/news/wonk

code. It cements the impression of a strict corporate autocracy.

Although a top-down directive structure ensured unquestioning development of the defeat device, only strict secrecy could have sustained it for seven years. Here again, VW's code is consistent with VW's behavior. In the section on treatment of information lies a subsection entitled "Secrecy." It demands that personnel hermetically seal within the company any information that could deprive it of a competitive advantage:[26]

> Each of our employees is obligated to maintain secrecy regarding the business or trade secrets with which they are entrusted within the scope of the performance of their duties. ... Silence must be maintained regarding work and matters within the Company that

/wp/2015/09/22/anatomy-of-volkswagons-deception-the-recall-that-never-fixed-any-cars.

13. "EPA, California Notify Volkswagen of Clean Air Act Violations," US Environmental Protection Agency, 18 Sept. 2015; http://yosemite.epa.gov/opa/admpress.nsf/a883dc3da7094f97852572a00065d7d8/dfc8e33b5ab162b985257ec40057813b!OpenDocument.
14. "VW Management Knew Early of Exhaust Problems," *Frankfurter Allgemeine*, 19 Nov. 2015; www.faz.net/aktuell/wirtschaft/vw-abgasskandal/volkswagen-abgasskandal-war-fuehrungskraeften-wohl-frueher-bekannt-13920562.html (in German).
15. "Resolution of the Executive Committee of the VW AG Supervisory Board," VW AG, 2 Sept. 2015; www.volkswagenag.com/content/vwcorp/info_center/en/news/2015/09/AR_Strategie.html.
16. "CARB Letter re Admission of Defeat Device," California Environmental Protection Agency, Air Resources Board, 18 Sept. 2015; www.arb.ca.gov/newsrel/in_use_compliance_letter.pdf.
17. "News, Statement of Prof. Dr. Martin Winterkorn," VW AG, 20 Sept. 2015; www.volkswagenag.com/content/vwcorp/info_center/en/news/2015/09/statement_ceo_of_volkswagen_ag.html.
18. "News, Volkswagen AG Has Issued the Following Information," VW AG, 2 Sept. 2015; www.volkswagenag.com/content/vwcorp/info_center/en/news/2015/09/Volkswagen_AG_has_issued_the_following_information.html.
19. C. Bryant, "Directors Meet to Decide Volkswagen Chief's Fate," *Financial Times*, 22 Sept 2015; www.ft.com/intl/cms/s/0/decc3722-6112-11e5-a28b-50226830d644.html#axzz3w2m3zJ8Q.
20. "News, Statement by Prof. Dr. Winterkorn," VW AG, 23 Sept. 2015; www.volkswagenag.com/content/vwcorp/info_center/en/news/2015/09/Statement.html.
21. W. Boston and F. Geiger, "Volkswagen to Swap Emissions Systems," *Wall Street J.*, 14 Oct. 2015, p. B5.
22. "Federal Motor Vehicle Office Assigns the Recall of 2.4 Million to Volkswagen," *Kraftfahrt-Bundesant*, 16 Oct. 2015; www.kba.de/DE/Home/infotext_startseite_VW_komplett.html?nn=456892 (in German).
23. M. Odell and A. Sharman, "As It Happened: VW Emissions—Michael Horn Grilled in Congress," *Financial Times* live blog, 8 Oct. 2015; http://blogs.ft.com/the-world/liveblogs/2015-10-08.
24. J. Ewing, "VW Investigation Focus to Include Managers Who Turned a Blind Eye," *New York Times*, 26 Oct. 2015, p. B3.
25. W. Boston, "Scope of VW Suspensions Grows," *New York Times*, 26 Oct. 2015, p. B1–B2.
26. A. Sharman, "Volkswagen Scandal Spills beyond Diesel," *Financial Times*, 4 Nov. 2015; www.ft.com/intl/cms/s/0/15cb2940-8305-11e5-8095-ed1a37d1e096.html#axzz3sFsh80uY.
27. "EPA, California Notify Volkswagen of Additional Clean Air Act Violations," US Environmental Protection Agency, 2 Nov. 2015; http://yosemite.epa.gov/opa/admpress.nsf/bd4379a92ceceeac8525735900400c27/4a45a5661216e66c85257ef10061867b!OpenDocument.
28. "Statement on the Announcement by the United States Environmental Protection Agency (EPA)," VW AG Supervisory Board, 2 Nov. 2015; www.volkswagen-media-services.com/en/detailpage/-/detail/Statement-on-the-announcement-by-the-United-States-Environmental-Protection-Agency-EPA/view/2853105/7a5bbec13158edd433c6630f5ac445da?p_p_auth=1UaaqEW9.
29. "Clarification Moving Forward: Internal Investigations at Volkswagen Identify Irregularities in CO_2 Levels," VW Media Services, 3 Nov. 2015; www.volkswagen-media-services.com/detailpage/-/detail/Clarification-moving-forward-internal-investigations-at-Volkswagen-identify-irregularities-in-CO2-levels/view/2857367/7a5bbec13158edd433c6630f5ac445da?p_p_auth=jGfw2EFr.
30. "VW's Legal Tsunami," *Handelsblatt Global Ed.*, 20 Nov. 2015; https://global.handelsblatt.com/edition/311/ressort/companies-markets/article/vws-legal-tsunami.
31. K. O'Brien and G. Kreijger, "Volkswagen Taps Porsche Chief as CEO," *Handelsblatt Global Ed.*, 25 Sept. 2015; https://global.handelsblatt.com/edition/271/ressort/companies-markets/article/volkswagen-taps-porsche-chief-as-ceo.
32. "VW's New CEO under Fire," *Handelsblatt Global Ed.*, 23 Nov. 2015; https://global.handelsblatt.com/edition/312/ressort/companies-markets/article/vws-new-ceo-under-fire.
33. D. Hakim and J. Ewing, "Volkswagen's Software Was 'Illegal Defeat Device,' German Regulator Determines," *New York Times*, 2 Dec. 2015, p. B4.
34. "Volkswagen Making Good Progress with Its Investigation, Technical Solutions, and Group Realignment," VW AG, 10 Dec. 2015; www.volkswagenag.com/content/vwcorp/info_center/en/news/2015/12/VW_PK.html.

> are significant to the Volkswagen Group or its business partners and that have not been made known publicly, such as, for example, product developments, plans, and testing.

The defeat device was certainly a product development. Consequently, the code requires employees to treat it as a trade secret. Because VW adopted the code in 2010, for the five subsequent years, the code had its intended effect. VW employees fulfilled their duty of secrecy, conferring a tremendous competitive advantage on the company. Only when outside discovery rendered secrecy moot did VW face the folly of a code that insisted on secrecy at all costs.

As a window into VW's culture, it will be worthwhile to watch for changes in the code of conduct. Indeed, drastic change is needed to effect the new mindset demanded by CEO Müller and to promote to senior positions persons who might have foreseen and avoided the current trouble: persons of mettle. A barometer of VW's ability to heal itself will be the degree to which a new code adopts a changed tone and priority scheme.

The Aftermath of Disclosure

If the code of conduct is a harbinger of problems in VW's corporate culture, then VW's postdisclosure statements have only reinforced this impression. Denials of EPA and CARB findings, reversals only when forced, perfunctory apologies, and a dearth of meaningful explanations have encouraged opinions worldwide that the company has much to hide.

An additional indicator appeared in *The Wall Street Journal* as we were completing work on this article. Although VW's interim report dates Dieselgate's beginnings to 2005, its willingness to skirt emissions law was evident a year earlier.[27] In 2004, a US VW employee informed superiors in Germany that the number of Audis returned for repair of broken emissions sensors had triggered a "legal requirement to include the part in mandatory reports to regulators." The employee dutifully listed the faulty part—an exhaust-gas temperature sensor (EGT)—in a draft report to California regulators. According to the newspaper: "[A]n Audi official in Germany called for a revision. 'Delete the EGT.'"[27]

Two days later, the employee's supervisor obediently reported: "Der EGT ist raus"—"the EGT is out."[27] Indeed, it didn't appear in VW's report to California regulators.

VW's strategies with regulators have backfired. On 4 January 2016, the US Department of Justice filed a civil complaint covering VW's use of defeat devices in 580,000 vehicles, its tampering with emissions controls, and its nondisclosure of defeat devices in more than 70 CoC applications. The upshot: VW must negotiate a settlement under threat of tens of billions in fines. The fines might exceed the profits VW made on its misdeeds. The lost trust might never fully return. And resurrecting ethics might find many obstacles in VW's culture.[28]

Ethics and Mettle Fatigue

Good engineering design avoids "single points of failure"—any single component whose failure would bring down the entire system. By analogy, VW's climate of results at any cost and lack of checks on dishonest behavior set the stage for a complete organizational breakdown. The strict secrecy that VW's personnel maintained for seven years about the defeat device implies a uniform acceptance of dishonest practices, which is further evidenced by the absence of publicly stated questions, reservations, misgivings, and refusals by employees to participate in the defeat device work. Ethics were VW's single point of failure.

For people who work in situations in which no one questions ethically dubious activities, including outright subterfuge like the defeat device, there can be a corrosion of character. Long exposure can only worsen the effect, preventing those who succumb from recognizing reality, accepting facts, and responding with integrity.[29,30] We refer to this as "mettle fatigue."

When decent engineers join their colleagues and senior officers as corrupters of software in company products, there's something wrong with the company itself. Whether the corrupters work across the enterprise or in a tight-knit engineering group, it's unlikely that they were inherently evil. Rather, the company's culture probably forced them to make a no-win choice: leave the company with mettle intact or stay and embrace dishonest work, consistent with the cultural norm.

Those who stayed at VW, conforming with the enterprise's value system and pursuing its aggressive growth strategy, in fact ensured its fall. Their work producing corrupt software constituted an insider threat, regardless of their intent. The software they wrote put people at risk in a manner so stealthy that it was discovered only after seven years and nearly by accident during an emissions test study by engineering researchers at West Virginia University.[31] That discovery led to losses: billions of euros, probably thousands of jobs, and the pride of a national industry. The probable explanation for their actions? Mettle fatigue.

Trust: Another Casualty

The scope of trust broken by VW's corrupt software is hard to comprehend. It allowed the company to misrepresent the environmental impact of 11 million cars. It betrayed buyers who believed they were doing something positive with their purchase, but now know the reverse. Those buyers face burdens in VW's recalls and uncertainty as to what performance or economy their cars will retain in the aftermath, not to mention resale value.

More abstractly, we live in a time when people routinely put trust in machines and the people who create them. Software involves perhaps the greatest trust of all. It's the most malleable, most complex, and least visible of engineering artifacts. Future developments like the Internet of Things and robotics can only magnify this trend. Consider the trust implicit in riding a self-driving car or in a walking robot carrying a person with a disability. In this context, the VW story is a cautionary tale. The potential for current and future technologies to improve mankind's lot hinges on a trust the VW affair has broken at a fundamental level. The mechanism of that break—corrupt software written by insiders—is a true cyberthreat that behooves all engineers, not just VW's, to address.

Codes of the Profession

If the VW code is a window into its culture, so are the codes of the engineering profession. What does IEEE's code of ethics say about engineering professionals? More saliently, does it say enough for those who find themselves in an adverse culture, perceiving an expectation—explicit or implicit—to do wrong? IEEE's code provides some of what's needed. It commits an engineer to "accept responsibility in making decisions consistent with the safety ... of the public" and "to disclose promptly factors that might endanger the public." VW might quibble—and its spokesmen have—that their vehicles are safe to drive. Of course, this ignores the high risk to respiratory health that NOx emission standards are meant to curb. The crux is that the words of the IEEE code assume that full knowledge of the end use of the engineer's work is in hand, when gaining that knowledge might be the most difficult task of all. Missing in the IEEE code is follow-through: a call for engineers to understand and consider the broader effect of their work when making decisions and disclosing dangers.

IEEE's code of ethics also commits engineers "to be honest ... in stating claims." That's important but, again, lacking follow-through. The VW engineers who developed, tested, and installed defeat devices were probably not called upon to be dishonest in their statements. They probably reported honestly to their superiors. The VW engineers who met with the EPA and CARB probably thought that they owed their loyalty and honesty to their employer, not the regulators. The IEEE code asks too little in this respect: it omits a call to act responsibly when those around them are doing wrong. We are reminded of West Point's elegant honor code: "A cadet will not lie, cheat, steal, or tolerate those who do." IEEE should consider a "toleration clause" in its code. This ought to provoke a serious discussion of engineering ethics, with focus on the crises that engineers experience when company expectations conflict with their professional code.

Perhaps the best outcome of VW's plight would be for mettle fatigue to be taken seriously as a danger to both engineers and the organizations that employ them. Continuous vigilance and education to ward off its pernicious effects, avoiding VW-like crises in the future, are cheap insurance in a world in which trust in engineers and their work is becoming ever more fundamental. ■

Acknowledgments

We express our deep gratitude to the following individuals for reading drafts and giving thoughtful criticisms and suggestions that substantially improved this article: Shari Lawrence Pfleeger, Charles P. Pfleeger, Jeffrey A. Fillman, Gerald E. Daniels, Takaji (Ted) Hishiyama, Christine Anthony, and Winston L. Trope. Any deficiencies in the article are solely the responsibility of the authors. *The views expressed herein are the personal views of the authors and have not been reviewed or approved by, and should not be attributed to, the US Military Academy, the Department of the Army, the Department of Defense, or the US Government.*

References

1. A. Davies, "The Real Winner in the VW Diesel Scandal? Hybrid Cars," *Wired,* 24 Sept. 2015; www.wired.com/2015/09/volkswagen-diesel-cheating-scandal-is-good-for-hybrid-cars.
2. "2015 Volkswagen AG Press Conference Hans Dieter Pötsch Speech," AutoEmotionenTV, 10 Dec. 2015; www.youtube.com/watch?v=UTnBELcUXoQ.
3. "The Volkswagen Group's New Global Strategy: 1.1 Strategy 2018: Competitor Toyota as the Standard," *Bertelsmann-stiftung,* 2008; www.bertelsmann-stiftung.de/fileadmin/system/flexpaper/rsmbstpublications/download_file/3424/3424_31.pdf.
4. "A Mucky Business," *Economist,* 26 Sept. 2015, www.economist.com/news/briefing/21667918-systematic-fraud-worlds-biggest-carmaker-threatens-engulf-entire-industry-and.
5. "Strategy 2018," Volkswagen Aktiengesellschaft (VW AG), 2008; www.volkswagenag.com/content/vwcorp/content/en/investor_relations/Warum_Volkswagen/Strategy.html.
6. J. Muller, "How Volkswagen Will Rule the World," *Forbes,* 17 Apr. 2013; www.forbes.com/sites/joannmuller/2013/04/17/volkswagens-mission-to-dominate-global-auto-industry-gets-noticeably-harder.
7. J. Ewing, "Pressure Growing on Volkswagen's Chief Executive," *Boston Globe,* 22 Sept. 2015; www.bostonglobe.com/business/2015/09/21/volkswagen-denied-deception-epa-for-nearly-year/PvO8P2rQnPDdeFkBxBgI0J/story.html.
8. W. Boston and F. Geiger, "VW to Switch to a Costlier Diesel Technology," *Wall Street J.,* 13 Oct. 2015; www.wsj.com/articles/vw-to-cut-investment-by-1-billion-a-year-1444728786.
9. "Volkswagen Making Good Progress with Its Investigation, Technical Solutions, and Group Realignment," VW AG, 10 Dec. 2015; www.volkswagenag.com/content/vwcorp/info_center/en/news/2015/12/VW_PK.html.
10. U. Weidenfeld, "VW and Germany's Curse of Provincial Corporate Culture," *Financial Times,* 28 Sept. 2015, p. 11.
11. J. Ewing and J. Mouawad, "Directors Say Volkswagen Delayed Informing Them of Trickery," *New York Times,* 23 Oct. 2015; www.nytimes.com/2015/10/24/business/international/directors-say-volkswagen-delayed-informing-them-of-trickery.html?_r=0.

12. "Annual Report 2010," VW AG, 10 Mar. 2011; www.volkswagenag.com/content/vwcorp/content/en/misc/pdf-dummies.bin.html/downloadfilelist/downloadfile/downloadfile_14/file/Y_2010_e.pdf.
13. J. Puzzanghera and J. Hirsch, "VW Exec Blames 'a Couple of' Rogue Engineers for Emissions Scandal," *Los Angeles Times*, 8 Oct. 2015; www.latimes.com/business/autos/la-fi-hy-vw-hearing-20151009-story.html.
14. "Annual Report 2011," VW AG, 12 Mar. 2012; http://annualreport2011.volkswagenag.com/servicepages/downloads/files/entire_vw_ar11.pdf.
15. F. Rother and S. Theil, "The VW Files," *Handelsblatt Global Ed*, Dec. 2015, https://global.handelsblatt.com/wp-content/uploads/2015/12/global_edition_magazine_no2_2015.pdf.
16. P.A. Eisenstein, "Could Rogue Software Engineers Be Behind VW Emissions Cheating?," *NBC News*, 9 Oct. 2015; www.nbcnews.com/business/autos/could-rogue-software-engineers-be-behind-vw-emissions-cheating-n441451.
17. "Notice of Violation to Volkswagen AG, Audi AG, Volkswagen Group of America, Inc.," US Environmental Protection Agency, 18 Sept. 2015; www.eenews.net/assets/2015/09/21/document_cw_01.pdf.
18. "List of Diesel VW (and Audi) Cars Recalled; Here's What You Need to Know," *Autoweek*, 21 Sept. 2015; http://autoweek.com/article/car-news/list-diesel-vw-cars-recalled-heres-what-you-need-know.
19. E. Jaffe, "The Study that Brought Down Volkswagen," *Atlantic Citylab*, 24 Sept. 2015; www.citylab.com/crime/2015/09/the-study-that-brought-down-volkswagen/407149.
20. P.E. Ross, "How Engineers at West Virginia University Caught VW Cheating," *IEEE Spectrum*, 22 Sept. 2015; http://spectrum.ieee.org/cars-that-think/transportation/advanced-cars/how-professors-caught-vw-cheating.
21. "Bosch Warned VW about Illegal Software Use in Diesel Cars, Report Says," *Autonews*, 27 Sept. 2015; www.autonews.com/article/20150927/COPY01/309279989/bosch-warned-vw-about-illegal-software-use-in-diesel-cars-report-says.
22. "Notice of Violation to Volkswagen AG, Audi AG, Porsche AG, Volkswagen Group of America, Inc., Porsche Cars North America, Inc.," US Environmental Protection Agency, 2 Nov. 2015; www2.epa.gov/sites/production/files/2015-11/documents/vw-nov-2015-11-02.pdf.
23. "Statement on the Announcement by the United States Environmental Protection Agency (EPA)," Volkswagen, 2 Nov. 2015; www.volkswagen-media-services.com/en/detailpage/-/detail/Statement-on-the-announcement-by-the-United-States-Environmental-Protection-Agency-EPA/view/2853105/7a5bbec13158edd433c6630f5ac445da?p_p_auth=1UaaqEW9.
24. R. Milne, "VW Admits Second Illegal Device in 85,000 Audi Engines," *Financial Times*, 23 Nov. 2015; www.ft.com/intl/cms/s/0/ee578522-91ee-11e5-9e3e-eb48769cecab.html#axzz3sFsh80uY.
25. "VW's New CEO under Fire," *Handelsblatt Global Ed.*, 23 Nov. 2015; https://global.handelsblatt.com/edition/312/ressort/companies-markets/article/vws-new-ceo-under-fire.
26. "The Volkswagen Group Code of Conduct," Volkswagen, Sept. 2015; www.volkswagenag.com/content/vwcorp/info_center/en/publications/2015/09/Verhaltensgrundsaetze_des_Volkswagen_Konzerns.bin.html/binarystorageitem/file/20150930_Verhaltensgrundsätze+-+update_coc_englisch_digital.pdf.
27. J. Scheck, M. Spector, and M. Maremont, *VW Kept Earlier Emissions Issue from Regulator, Wall Street J.*, 9 Dec. 2015; www.wsj.com/articles/vw-kept-earlier-emissions-issue-from-regulator-1449612215.
28. United States of America v. Volkswagen AG et al., Complaint, 4 Jan. 2016; www.justice.gov/opa/file/809826/download.
29. R.L. Trope and G.E. Upchurch, *Checkpoints in Cyberspace*, American Bar Assoc., 2005, p. 54.
30. D.C. LaCroix, "Ethical Atrophy," LAPBC blog, 12 Dec. 2012; http://lapbc.com/articles-media/ethical-atrophy-derek-c-lacroix-qc.
31. D. Morgan, *West Virginia Engineer Proves to Be a David to VW's* Goliath, Reuters, 23 Sept. 2015; www.reuters.com/article/us-usa-volkswagen-researchers-idUSKCN0RM2D720150924.

Roland L. Trope is a partner in the New York offices of Trope and Schramm LLP and an adjunct professor at the US Military Academy at West Point. His research interests include intellectual property, cybersecurity, and ethics. Trope received a BA and MA from Oxford University and a JD from Yale Law School. Contact him at rltrope@tropelaw.com.

Eugene K. Ressler is the former head of the Electrical Engineering and Computer Science Department at the US Military Academy at West Point. He is currently working as a software engineer. Ressler received a PhD in computer science from Cornell University. Contact him at gene.ressler@gmail.com.

CHAPTER 10

VW, Part 2: Plea Bargain*

UNITED STATES DISTRICT COURT
EASTERN DISTRICT OF MICHIGAN

United States of America,	No. 16-CR-20394
Plaintiff,	HONORABLE SEAN F. COX
v.	
VOLKSWAGEN AG,	Offenses: (1) Conspiracy (2) Obstruction of Justice (3) Entry of Goods by False Statement
Defendant.	
	Violations: (1) 18 U.S.C. § 371 (2) 18 U.S.C. § 1512(c) (3) 18 U.S.C. § 542
	Statutory Maximum Period of Probation: Five years per count
	Statutory Minimum Period of Probation: None/Not Applicable
	Statutory Maximum Fine: 18 U.S.C. § 3571(d) (the greater of twice the gross gain or twice the gross loss)
	Statutory Minimum Fine: None/Not Applicable

* Rule 11 Plea Agreement, United States of America v. Volkswagen AG, United States District Court for the Eastern District of Michigan, Case No. 16-CR-20394 (January 11, 2017), available at https://www.justice.gov/usao-edmi/page/file/930026/download.

Rule 11 Plea Agreement

The United States of America, by and through the Department of Justice, Criminal Division, Fraud Section, the United States Attorney's Office for the Eastern District of Michigan, and the Department of Justice, Environment and Natural Resources Division, Environmental Crimes Section and with the approval of the Deputy Attorney General (collectively hereafter, "the Offices"), and the Defendant, Volkswagen AG (the "Defendant"), by and through its undersigned attorneys, and through its authorized representative, pursuant to authority granted by the Defendant's Management Board, with the consent of the Supervisory Board, hereby submit and enter into this plea agreement (the "Agreement"), pursuant to Rule 11(c)(1)(C) of the Federal Rules of Criminal Procedure. The terms and conditions of this Agreement are as follows:

1. Guilty Plea

A. Waiver of Indictment and Venue

Pursuant to Fed. R. Crim. P. 7, the Defendant agrees to knowingly waive its right to grand jury indictment and its right to challenge venue in the United States District Court for the Eastern District of Michigan, and to plead guilty to Counts One through Three of the Third Superseding Information.

B. Counts of Conviction

The Third Superseding Information charges three counts: (1) Count One—conspiracy in violation of 18 U.S.C. § 371, (2) Count Two—obstruction of justice in violation of 18 U.S.C. § 1512(c), and (3) Count Three—introducing imported merchandise into the United States by mean of false statements in violation of 18 U.S.C. § 542. The Defendant further agrees to persist in that plea through sentencing and, as set forth below, to cooperate fully with the Offices in their investigation into the conduct described in this Agreement and other conduct related to the introduction into the United States of diesel vehicles with defeat devices as defined under U.S. law.

C. Elements of Offenses

<u>The elements of Count One (conspiracy) are as follows</u>:

(1) The elements for conspiracy to defraud the United States by obstructing the lawful function of the federal government are as follows:

(a) That two or more persons conspired, or agreed, to defraud the United States or one of its agencies or departments, in this case, the Environmental Protection Agency (EPA), by dishonest means;

(b) That the defendant knowingly and voluntarily joined the conspiracy; and

(c) That a member of the conspiracy did one of the overt acts described in the indictment for the purpose of advancing or helping the conspiracy.

(2) The elements for conspiracy to violate the wire fraud statute and Clean Air Act are as follows:

(a) That two or more persons conspired, or agreed, to commit a crime, in this case, a violation of the wire fraud statute (18 U.S.C. § 1343) and the Clean Air Act (42 U.S.C. § 7413(c)(2)(A)) as described below;

(b) That the defendant knowingly and voluntarily joined the conspiracy; and

(c) That a member of the conspiracy did one of the overt acts described in the indictment for the purpose of advancing or helping the conspiracy.

Object of the Conspiracy—Wire Fraud—18 U.S.C. § 1343:

(a) The defendant knowingly participated in, devised, or intended to devise a scheme to defraud in order to obtain money or property;

(b) The scheme included a material misrepresentation or concealment of a material fact;

(c) The defendant had the intent to defraud; and

(d) The defendant used (or caused another to use) wire, radio or television communications in interstate or foreign commerce in furtherance of the scheme.

Object of the Conspiracy—Clean Air Act—42 U.S.C. § 7413(c)(2)(A)

(a) The defendant knowingly made (or caused to be made) a false material statement, representation, or certification, or omission of material information;

(b) The statement, representation or certification that was made (or omitted), or caused to be made or omitted, was in a notice, application, record, report, plan or other document required to be filed or maintained under the Clean Air Act; and

(c) The statement, representation, certification, or omission of information, was material.

<u>The elements of Count Two (obstruction of justice) are as follows:</u>

(1) That the defendant altered, destroyed, mutilated, or concealed a record, document or other object;

(2) That the defendant acted knowingly;

(3) That the defendant acted corruptly; and

(4) That the defendant acted with the intent to impair the record, document or object's integrity or availability for use in an official proceeding.

<u>The elements of Count Three (entry of goods by false statement) are as follows:</u>

(1) That merchandise was imported;

(2) That the defendant entered or introduced merchandise into the commerce of the United States;

(3) That the defendant did so by means of a false statement, which it knew was false; and

(4) That the false statement was material to the entry of the merchandise.

D. Statutory Maximum Penalties

. . . .

E. Factual Basis for Guilty Plea

The Defendant is pleading guilty because it is guilty of the charges contained in the Third Superseding information. The Defendant admits, agrees, and stipulates that the factual allegations set forth in Exhibit 2 (the Statement of Facts) are true and correct, that it is responsible under the laws of the United States for the acts of its employees described in Exhibit 2, and that the facts set forth in Exhibit 2 accurately reflect the Defendant's criminal conduct and provide a factual basis for the guilty plea. The Defendant agrees that it will neither contest the admissibility of, nor contradict, the Statement of Facts contained in Exhibit 2 in any proceeding.

2. Sentencing Guidelines

. . . .

c. <u>Base Fine</u>. Based upon U.S.S.G. § 8C2.4(a), the base fine is $8,543,169,187 (the pecuniary loss from the offense caused by the Defendant)

d. <u>Culpability Score</u>. Based upon U.S.S.G. § 8C2.5, the culpability score is 11, calculated as follows:

(a)	Base Culpability Score	5
(b)(1)	the unit of the organization within which the offense was committed had 5,000 or more employees and an individual within high-level personnel of the unit participated in, condoned, or was willfully ignorant of the offense	+5
(e)	obstruction of justice	+3
(g)(3)	The organization fully cooperated in the investigation and clearly demonstrated recognition and affirmative acceptance of responsibility for its criminal conduct	–2
TOTAL		**11**

Calculation of Fine Range:

Base Fine	$8,543,169,187[1]
Multipliers	2 (min)/4 (max)
Fine Range	$17,086,338,374 (min)/ $34,172,676,746 (max)

3. Sentence

Pursuant to Fed. R. Crim. P. 11(c)(1)(C), the United States and the Defendant agree that the appropriate disposition of this case is as set forth in this Section and agree to recommend jointly that the Court at a hearing to be scheduled at an agreed upon time impose it.

A. Relevant Considerations

The Offices enter into this Agreement based on the individual facts and circumstances presented by this case and the Defendant. Among the factors considered were the following:

1. the Defendant did not voluntarily disclose to the Offices the conduct described in Exhibit 2 (the Statement of Facts);

2. the Defendant cooperated with the Offices' investigation by, among other things, (i) gathering substantial amounts of evidence and performing

---

[1] The base fine amount consists of the loss amount as calculated under USSG § 2B1.1 and accompanying Application Notes, discounted to reflect a 50% reduction for the litigation risk that both parties would bear were there a contested sentencing proceeding. *See, e.g., United States v. Giovenco,* 773 F.3d 866 (7th Cir. 2014); *United States v. Prosperi,* 686 F.3d 32 (1st Cir. 2012).

forensic data collections in multiple jurisdictions; (ii) producing documents, including translations, to the Offices in ways that did not implicate foreign data privacy laws; (iii) collecting, analyzing, organizing, and producing voluminous evidence and information; (iv) interviewing hundreds of witnesses in the United States and overseas; (v) providing non-privileged facts relating to individuals and companies involved in the criminal conduct; and (vi) facilitating and encouraging cooperation and voluntary disclosure of information and documents by current and former company personnel;

3. the Defendant has already agreed to compensate members of the class in *In re Volkswagen "Clean Diesel" Marketing, Sales Practices, and Products Liability Litigation*, No. 3:15-md-2672 (N.D. Cal.), which consists of victims of the underlying criminal conduct that is the subject of this Agreement, and to pay into a NOx remediation trust, in an aggregate amount of approximately $11 billion (based on net present value);

4. despite obstruction of justice committed by certain of the Defendant's employees, principally in the form of document destruction, the Defendant, including through its outside counsel, self-disclosed this conduct to the Offices, remediated the conduct by recovering large portions of the deleted documents through a variety of forensic means, and conducted a thorough investigation of the conduct, the findings of which it reported to the Offices;

5. the Defendant engaged in remedial measures, including creation of a management board position to supervise the Defendant's legal and compliance functions, reorganization of the whistleblower system, improvements to its risk assessment systems, specific reforms to its engine-related practices, including a program to audit these reforms, termination the employment of six individuals who participated in, or failed to supervise employees who participated in, the misconduct described in the Statement of Facts, suspending an additional eight individuals who participated in the misconduct described in the Statement of Facts for varying periods, and disciplining an additional three employees who participated in the misconduct described in the Statement of Facts; however, the Defendant's remediation remains incomplete;

6. the Defendant has committed to continue to enhance its compliance program and internal controls;

7. the Defendant has agreed, as part of its continuing cooperation obligations, and to ensure that the Defendant and its wholly-owned subsidiary Volkswagen Group of America ("VW GOA") implements an effective compliance program, to the appointment of an independent monitor (the

"Monitor") for a period of up to three years, who will have authority with respect to the Defendant and VW GOA;

8. the nature and seriousness of the offenses;

9. the Defendant has no prior criminal history;

10. the Defendant has agreed to continue to cooperate with the Offices in any ongoing investigation of the conduct of the Defendant and its officers, directors, employees, agents, business partners, and consultants relating to the violations to which the Defendant is pleading guilty; and

11. the Defendant has agreed to pay an additional $1,500,000,000 to the United States to resolve claims for civil penalties arising from the underlying conduct that is the subject of this Agreement;

12. accordingly, after considering (1) through (11) above, (a) the Defendant received an aggregate discount of approximately 20% off of the bottom of the otherwise applicable U.S. Sentencing Guidelines fine range, reflecting its cooperation in the investigation, and (b) after application of the foregoing discount, the Defendant in addition received a credit of $11 billion, representing the net present value of the Defendant's settlements with consumers and payments to the NOx remediation trust in settlement of civil litigation.

B. Fine

The Defendant shall pay to the United States a criminal fine of $2,800,000,000, payable in full within ten days of the entry of judgment following the sentencing hearing in this matter. The Defendant shall not seek or accept directly or indirectly reimbursement or indemnification from any source with regard to the penalty amount that the Defendant pays pursuant to this Agreement. The Defendant further agrees that it shall not claim, assert, or apply for, either directly or indirectly, any tax deduction, tax credit, or any other offset with regard to any U.S. federal, state, or local tax or taxable income for any fine or forfeiture paid pursuant to this Agreement.

C. Probation

The parties agree that a term of organizational probation for a period of three years should be imposed on the Defendant pursuant to 18 U.S.C. §§ 3551(c)(1) and 3561(c)(1). The parties further agree, pursuant to U.S.S.G. § 8D1.4, that the term of probation shall include as conditions the obligations set forth in Paragraphs 5 and 6 below as well as the payment of the fine set forth in this Paragraph, but shall not include the obligations set forth in Paragraph 7 below.

D. Special Assessment

The Defendant shall pay to the Clerk of the Court for the United States District Court for the Eastern District of Michigan within ten days of the time of sentencing the mandatory special assessment of $1,200 ($400 per count).

E. Restitution

No order of restitution is appropriate in this case pursuant to 18 U.S.C. § 3663A(c)(3), as the number of identifiable victims is so large as to make restitution impracticable and/or determining complex issues of fact related to the cause or amount of victims' losses would complicate or prolong the sentencing process to a degree that the need to provide restitution to any victim is outweighed by the burden on the sentencing process. Moreover, as noted in Paragraph 2(A) above, the Defendant has already agreed to compensate members of the class in *In re Volkswagen "Clean Diesel" Marketing, Sales Practices, and Products Liability Litigation,* No. 3:15-md-2672 (N.D. Cal.), which consists of individuals who purchased affected vehicles described in Exhibit 2.

4. Other Charges

In exchange for the guilty plea of the Defendant and the complete fulfillment of all of its obligations under this Agreement, the Offices agree that they will not file additional criminal charges against the Defendant or any of its direct or indirect affiliates or subsidiaries related to: (1) any conduct described in the Third Superseding Information or Exhibit 2; (2) any conduct related to the emissions, or compliance with U.S. emissions standards, of the Subject Vehicles or the Porsche Vehicles as described and defined in the Third Superseding Information and Exhibit 2; and (3) any conduct disclosed by, or on behalf of, the Defendant or otherwise known to the Offices or the EPA as of the date of this Agreement. The Offices, however, may use any information related to the conduct described in the Statement of Facts against the Defendant: (a) in a prosecution for perjury or obstruction of justice apart from the charge in the Third Superseding Information and identified in the Statement of Facts; (b) in a prosecution for making a false statement; (c) in a prosecution or other proceeding relating to any crime of violence; or (d) in a prosecution or other proceeding relating to a violation of any provision of Title 26 of the United States Code. This Paragraph does not provide any protection against prosecution for any other conduct, including but not limited to crimes committed in the future by the Defendant or by any of its affiliates, subsidiaries, officers, directors, employees, agents or consultants, whether or not disclosed by the Defendant pursuant to the terms of this Agreement. In addition, this Agreement does not provide any protection against prosecution of any joint ventures of which the Defendant is a part, or any individuals, regardless of their affiliation with the Defendant. The Defendant agrees that nothing in this Agreement is intended to release the Defendant from any and all of the Defendant's excise and income tax liabilities and reporting obligations for any and all income not properly reported and/or legally or illegally obtained or derived.

5. The Defendant's Obligations

A. Except as otherwise provided in Paragraph 6 below in connection with the Defendant's cooperation obligations, the Defendant's obligations under the Agreement shall last and be effective for a period beginning on the date on which the Third Superseding Information is filed and ending three years from the later of the date on which the Third Superseding Information is filed or the date on which the Monitor is retained by the Defendant, as described in Paragraph 15 below (the "Term"). The Defendant agrees, however, that, in the event the Offices determine, in their sole discretion, that the Defendant has failed specifically to perform or to fulfill each of the Defendant's obligations under this Agreement, an extension or extensions of the Term may be imposed by the Offices, in their sole discretion, for up to a total additional time period of one year, without prejudice to the Offices' right to proceed as provided in Paragraph 9 below. Any extension of the Term extends all terms of this Agreement, including the terms of the Monitorship in Exhibit 3, for an equivalent period. Conversely, in the event the Offices find, in their sole discretion, that there exists a change in circumstances sufficient to eliminate the need for the Monitorship in Exhibit 3, and that the other provisions of this Agreement have been satisfied, the Term may be terminated early, except for the Defendant's cooperation obligations described in Paragraph 6 below.

B. The Defendant agrees to abide by all terms and obligations of this Agreement as described herein, including, but not limited to, the following:

1. to plead guilty as set forth in this Agreement;
2. to abide by all sentencing stipulations contained in this Agreement;
3. to appear, through its duly appointed representatives, as ordered for all court appearances, and obey any other ongoing court order in this matter, consistent with all applicable U.S. and foreign laws, procedures, and regulations;
4. to commit no further crimes;

5. to be truthful at all times with the Court and the Offices;

6. to pay the applicable fine and special assessments;

7. to cooperate with and report to the Offices as provided in Paragraph 6; and

8. to continue to implement a compliance and ethics program designed to prevent and detect fraudulent conduct throughout its operations.

. . . .

7. Other Obligations

A. The Defendant agrees to retain an independent compliance monitor in accordance with Exhibit 3 of this Agreement.

B. While the obligation set forth in this Paragraph is not a condition to the term of probation, any failure to comply with the obligation set forth in this Paragraph shall constitute a breach of this Agreement and be subject to the terms set forth in Paragraph 9 below.

8. Waiver of Appellate and Other Rights Under United States Law

. . . .

9. Breach of Agreement

A. If the Defendant (a) commits any felony under U.S. federal law; (b) provides in connection with this Agreement deliberately false, incomplete, or misleading information; (c) fails to cooperate as set forth in Paragraph 6 of this Agreement; (d) fails to implement a compliance program as set forth in Paragraph 3(A)(7) of this Agreement; or (e) otherwise fails specifically to perform or to fulfill each of the Defendant's obligations under the Agreement, regardless of whether the Offices become aware of such a breach after the Term of the Agreement, the Defendant shall thereafter be subject to prosecution for any federal criminal violation of which the Offices have knowledge, including, but not limited to, the charges in the Third Superseding Information described in Paragraph 1, which may be pursued by the Offices in the United States District Court for the Eastern District of Michigan or any other appropriate venue. Determination of whether the Defendant has breached the Agreement and whether to pursue prosecution of the Defendant shall be in the Offices' sole discretion. Any such prosecution may be premised on information provided by the Defendant. Any such prosecution relating to the conduct described in the attached Statement of Facts or relating to conduct known to the Offices prior to the date on which this

Agreement was signed that is not time-barred by the applicable statute of limitations on the date of the signing of this Agreement may be commenced against the Defendant, notwithstanding the expiration of the statute of limitations, between the signing of this Agreement and the expiration of the Term of the Agreement plus one year. Thus, by signing this Agreement, the Defendant agrees that the statute of limitations with respect to any such prosecution that is not time-barred on the date of the signing of this Agreement shall be tolled for the Term of the Agreement plus one year. The Defendant gives up all defenses based on the statute of limitations, any claim of pre-indictment delay, or any speedy trial claim with respect to any such prosecution or action, except to the extent that such defenses existed as of the date of the signing of this Agreement. In addition, the Defendant agrees that the statute of limitations as to any violation of federal law that occurs during the term of the cooperation obligations provided for in Paragraph 6 of the Agreement will be tolled from the date upon which the violation occurs until the earlier of the date upon which the Offices are made aware of the violation or the duration of the term plus three years, and that this period shall be excluded from any calculation of time for purposes of the application of the statute of limitations.

B. In the event the Offices determine that the Defendant has breached this Agreement, the Offices agree to provide the Defendant with written notice of such breach prior to instituting any prosecution resulting from such breach. Within thirty (30) days of receipt of such notice, the Defendant shall have the opportunity to respond to the Offices in writing to explain the nature and circumstances of such breach, as well as the actions the Defendant has taken to address and remediate the situation, which explanation the Offices shall consider in determining whether to pursue prosecution of the Defendant.

C. In the event that the Offices determine that the Defendant has breached this Agreement: (a) all statements made by or on behalf of the Defendant to the Offices or to the Court, including the attached Statement of Facts, and any testimony given by the Defendant before a grand jury, a court, or any tribunal, or at any legislative hearings, whether prior or subsequent to this Agreement, and any leads derived from such statements or testimony, shall be admissible in evidence in any and all criminal proceedings brought by the Offices against the Defendant; and (b) the Defendant shall not assert any claim under the United States Constitution, Rule 11 (f) of the Federal Rules of Criminal Procedure, Rule 410 of the Federal Rules of Evidence, or any other federal rule that any such statements or testimony made by or on behalf of the Defendant prior or subsequent to this Agreement, or any leads derived there from, should be suppressed or are otherwise inadmissible. The decision whether conduct or statements of any current director, officer or employee, or any person acting on behalf of, or at the direction of, the Defendant, will be imputed to the Defendant for the purpose of determining whether the Defendant has violated any provision of this Agreement shall be in the sole discretion of the Offices.

D. The Defendant acknowledges that the Offices have made no representations, assurances, or promises concerning what sentence may be imposed by the Court if the Defendant breaches this Agreement and this matter proceeds to judgment. The Defendant further acknowledges that any such sentence is solely within the discretion of the Court and that nothing in this Agreement binds or restricts the Court in the exercise of such discretion.

10. Parties to Plea Agreement

The Defendant understands and agrees that this Agreement is between the Offices and the Defendant. Nevertheless, the Offices will bring this Agreement and the nature and quality of the conduct, cooperation and remediation of the Defendant, its direct or indirect affiliates and subsidiaries to the attention of other prosecuting authorities or other agencies, as well as debarment authorities, if requested by the Defendant.

. . . .

The Defendant agrees that it has the full legal right, power, and authority to enter into and perform all of its obligations under this Agreement.

11. Change of Corporate Form

. . . .

12. Failure of Court to Accept Agreement

This Agreement is presented to the Court pursuant to Fed. R. Crim. P. 11(c)(1)(C). The Defendant understands that, if the Court rejects this Agreement, the Court must: (a) inform the parties that the Court rejects the Agreement; (b) advise the Defendant's counsel that the Court is not required to follow the Agreement and afford the Defendant the opportunity to withdraw its plea; and (c) advise the Defendant that if the plea is not withdrawn, the Court may dispose of the case less favorably toward the Defendant than the Agreement contemplated. The Defendant further understands that if the Court refuses to accept any provision of this Agreement, neither party shall be bound by the provisions of the Agreement.

13. Presentence Report

The Defendant and the Offices waive the preparation of a Pre-Sentence Investigation Report. . . .

14. Public Statements by the Defendant

A. The Defendant expressly agrees that it shall not, through present or future attorneys, officers, directors, employees, agents or any other person authorized to speak for the Defendant make any public statement, in litigation or otherwise, contradicting the acceptance of responsibility by the Defendant set forth above, contradicting the fact that the Defendant has pled guilty to the charges set forth in the Third Superseding Information, or contradicting the facts described in Exhibit 2. Any such contradictory statement shall, subject to cure rights of the Defendant described below, constitute a breach of this Agreement, and the Defendant thereafter shall be subject to prosecution as set forth in Paragraph 9 of this Agreement. The decision whether any such contradictory statement will be imputed to the Defendant for the purpose of determining whether it has breached this Agreement shall be at the sole discretion of the Offices. If the Offices determine that a public statement by any such person contradicts in whole or in part the fact that the Defendant pled guilty to the charges in the Third Superseding Information or a statement contained in Exhibit 2, the Offices shall so notify the Defendant, and the Defendant may avoid a breach of this Agreement by publicly repudiating such statement(s) within five business days after notification. The Defendant shall be permitted to raise defenses, to take legal positions and to assert affirmative claims in other proceedings relating to the matters set forth in the Third Superseding Information and Exhibit 2 provided that such defenses and claims do not contradict, in whole or in part, the fact that the Defendant pled guilty to the charges in the Third Superseding Information or a statement in Exhibit 2. This Paragraph does not apply to any statement made by any present or former officer, director, employee, or agent of the Defendant in the course of any criminal, regulatory, or civil case initiated against such individual, unless such individual is speaking on behalf of the Defendant.

B. The Defendant agrees that if it or any of its direct or indirect subsidiaries or affiliates issues a press release or holds any press conference in connection with this Agreement, the Defendant shall first consult the Offices to determine (a) whether the text of the release or proposed statements at the press conference are true and accurate with respect to matters between the Offices and the Defendant; and (b) whether the Offices have any objection to the release or statement.

15. Independent Compliance Monitor

A. Promptly after the Offices' selection pursuant to Paragraph 15(B) below, the Defendant agrees to retain the Monitor for the term specified in Paragraph 15(C). The Monitor's duties and authority, and the obligations of the Defendant with respect to the Monitor and the Offices, are set forth in Exhibit 3, which is incorporated by reference into this Agreement. . . .

16. Complete Agreement

This document states the full extent of the Agreement between the parties. There are no other promises or agreements, express or implied. Any modification of this Agreement shall be valid only if set forth in writing in a supplemental or revised plea agreement signed by all parties.

AGREED:

FOR VOLKSWAGEN AG:

Date: January 11, 2017 By: [signature]
Manfred Doess
General Counsel of Volkswagen AG

Date: January 11, 2017 By: [signature]
Reid Weingarten
Jason Weinstein
Christopher Niewoehner
Steptoe & Johnson LLP
Outside counsel for Volkswagen AG

Date: 11 January 2017 By: [signature]
Aaron R. Marcu
Olivia A. Radin
Linda Martin
Freshfields Bruckhaus Deringer US LLP
Outside counsel for Volkswagen AG

Date: January 11, 2017 By: [signature]
Robert J. Giuffra, Jr.
Sharon L. Nelles
Brent J. McIntosh
Sullivan & Cromwell LLP
Outside counsel for Volkswagen AG

FOR THE DEPARTMENT OF JUSTICE:

ANDREW WEISSMANN
Chief, Fraud Section
Criminal Division

Date: 1/11/17 By: __________

Benjamin D. Singer
Chief, Securities and Financial Fraud Unit
Gary A. Winters
Alison Anderson
David Fuhr
Trial Attorneys

JOHN CRUDEN
Assistant Attorney General
Environment and Natural Resources Division

Date: 1/11/17 By: __________

Jennifer L. Blackwell
Trial Attorney

BARBARA L. McQUADE
United States Attorney Eastern District of Michigan

Date: 1/11/17 By: __________

John K. Neal
Chief, White Collar Crime Unit

NOTES

Of course, we edited out the rest of the plea agreement (the exhibits). But you get the gist of what Volkswagen agreed to do.

Realize that it's Volkswagen the company, not the individuals inside VW, that is pleading guilty in this plea agreement.* But that's not the end of this story. VW executive Oliver Schmidt pleaded guilty, too, and a federal judge sentenced him to up to seven years in prison and a fine of between $40,000 and $400,000.** And that's likely not the end of the story, either.

By the way, we find it interesting that Enron executives Ken Lay and Jeff Skilling preferred to go to trial on their indictments rather than to plead guilty.

* *See* Nick Carey, *Volkswagen executive pleads guilty in U.S. emissions cheating case,* REUTERS (Aug. 4, 2017), available at https://www.reuters.com/article/us-volkwwagen-emissions/volkswagen-executive-pleads-guilty-in-u-s-emissions-cheating-case-idUSKBN1AK1OY.

** *A Volkswagen Executive Got a 7-Year Sentence in the Diesel Emissions Cheating Case,* FORTUNE, Dec. 6, 2017, available at http://fortune.com/2017/12/06/oliver-schmidt-vw-emissions-cheating/. The story goes on to observe that "Schmidt was charged with 11 felony counts and federal prosecutors said he could have faced a maximum of up to 169 years in prison. As part of his guilty plea, prosecutors agreed to drop most of the counts and Schmidt consented to be deported at the end of his prison sentence."

CHAPTER 11

Wells Fargo, Part 1: *The Vision & Values of Wells Fargo**

John G. Stumpf, Chairman, President & CEO

. . . .

Welcome

Documents such as this are rare these days in corporate America. Most companies have a mission statement and a set of core values, but few for as long as we've had *The Vision & Values of Wells Fargo*. Even fewer have resisted fads and remained faithful to their founding principles. We have stayed true to our vision for more than two decades.

In those two decades, a lot has changed. We've seen advances in technology and communications we could not have imagined only a few years ago. We've seen the U.S. population grow more diverse and the globalization of almost every aspect of our lives. We've witnessed periods of economic growth and decline and the worst economic downturn since the Great Depression. We've seen the collapse of major financial institutions and a new wave of industry regulations. Through all of this, we've seen the needs and interests of our customers and stakeholders change, and we've adapted right along with them.

Our progress has not been perfect. The expectations of others, and the even higher expectations we have of ourselves, have not always been met. When we make mistakes, we admit them, we learn from them, and we keep moving forward with even more understanding and a deeper commitment to doing what's right.

We first published a *Vision & Values* booklet in the early 1990s as Wells Fargo's predecessor, Norwest Corporation. Since then, we've grown from a small

* John G. Stumpf, *The Vision & Values of Wells Fargo*, used to be available at https://www08.wellsfargomedia.com/pdf/invest_relations/VisionandValues04.pdf, but that page doesn't exist any more. The new Vision and Values page is at https://www.wellsfargo.com/about/corporate/vision-and-values/.

regional bank into a national company with a growing global presence. Today, many of our team members trace their heritage to legacy companies that are now part of the Wells Fargo brand. Each of these companies brought with it new geographies, new capabilities, and inspiring stories. All have found a common cause in adopting our vision and values.

We believe in our vision and values just as strongly today as we did the first time we put them on paper, and staying true to them will guide us toward continued growth and success for decades to come. As you read more about our vision and values, you will learn about who we are, where we're headed, and how every Wells Fargo team member can help us get there.

We've become one of the nation's largest financial institutions, serving one in three U.S. households and employing approximately one in 600 working Americans. We have team members in 36 countries, serving 70 million customers in more than 130 countries around the world. *Forbes* magazine ranks us among the top 10 publicly traded companies in the world based on a composite of sales, assets, profits, and market value. And we are consistently ranked as one of the world's most respected banks by *Barron's* magazine and one of the world's most admired companies by *Fortune* magazine. The reason for this is simple. We've never lost sight of putting our customers first and helping them succeed financially.

Regardless of our growing size, scope, and reach, our common vision and distinct values form the fabric that holds us together wherever we are, whatever we do. As members of the same team, it doesn't matter what our respective responsibilities are, our levels or titles, what businesses we're part of, or where we live and work.

Our shared vision and values unite us as One Wells Fargo.

Our vision is:

"We want to satisfy our customers' financial needs and help them succeed financially."

It is just as relevant today as when it was written more than 20 years ago. We didn't know then that at only 84 characters, it would be succinct enough to tweet today!

Our vision of financially successful customers is based on a simple premise: We believe customers across all business segments can be better served, and save time and money, if they bring their financial services to one trusted provider that knows them well, provides reliable guidance and advice, and can serve their full range of financial needs through a wide choice of products and services.

Our journey toward this customer-centered vision has required hard work, persistence, and determination. We've made steady progress toward this goal. But we still have much to accomplish. For example, our own customers still give a significant amount of their financial business to our competitors. Our job—central to our vision—is to make it easy for them to bring more of their business to us so we can satisfy their financial needs.

Our vision has nothing to do with transactions, selling products, or getting bigger for the sake of bigness. **It's about building lifelong relationships one customer at a time.**

Each of our customers defines "financial success" differently and very personally. Some want financial security and self-sufficiency. Others want to be disciplined about spending and saving so they can afford to buy a home, start or grow a business, save for education, or prepare for retirement. And some just want to be better informed about financial matters. Knowing what financial success means to each of our customers is the starting point for serving them well.

The *reason* we wake up in the morning is to help our customers succeed financially and to satisfy their financial needs, and the *result* is that we make money. It's never the other way around. Our time-tested vision will forever be what matters to Wells Fargo. **We'll never put the stagecoach ahead of the horses.**

The *reason* we wake up in the morning is to help our customers succeed financially and to satisfy their financial needs, and the *result* is that we make money. It's never the other way around.

Our values

Our values should guide every conversation, decision, and interaction. Our values should anchor every product and service we provide and every channel we operate. If we can't link what we do to one of our values, we should ask ourselves why we're doing it. It's that simple.

All team members should know our values so well that if our policy manuals didn't exist, we would still make decisions based on our common understanding of our culture and what we stand for. Corporate America is littered with the debris of companies that crafted lofty values on paper but, when put to the test, failed to live by them. We believe in values lived, not phrases memorized. If we had to choose, we'd rather have a team member who lives by our values than one who just memorizes them.

We have five primary values that are based on our vision and pro foundation for everything we do:

- **People as a competitive advantage**
- **Ethics**
- **What's right for customers**
- **Diversity and inclusion**
- **Leadership**

People as a competitive advantage

We value and support our team members as a competitive advantage.

We strive to attract, develop, retain, and motivate the most talented, caring team members who work together as partners across businesses and functions. In hiring, we really don't care how much people know until we know how much they care. We like to say that we hire for attitude and train for aptitude. We provide the tools and training that team members need to succeed in their work, and we want them to be responsible and accountable for their businesses and functions.

We expect the best from our team members, and we thank them for their outstanding performance.

We say "team members," not "employees," because our people are resources to be invested in, not expenses to be managed—and because teamwork is essential to our success in helping customers. Our culture is about plural pronouns—we, us, and ours—instead of I, me, and mine. The star of the team is the team; we win by playing "us" ball.

We believe everyone on our team is important and deserves respect for who they are and how they can contribute to our work together. Products and technology don't fulfill the promise behind a brand, people do—people who are talented, motivated, and more energized than our competitors.

When our team members are in the right jobs, spending time on the right things, feeling good about their contributions, fully using their skills and learning new ones, leading well, and having fun, they'll do what's right for the customer. When they're properly supported, rewarded, and encouraged, they're even more satisfied with their jobs, providing even better service for our customers. This can generate happy, more loyal, and lifelong customers, which can lead to more revenue, greater profits, and a higher stock price.

We want to be an employer of choice, a company that truly cares about people, where teamwork is valued and rewarded, where how the work gets done is just as important as getting the work done. **We're a relationship company, but our relationships with our customers are only as strong as our relationships with each other.**

We want to create an environment where team members feel included, valued, and supported to do work that energizes them and where we are inspired to go further together—for one another, our customers, our communities, and our shareholders.

We survey our team members regularly to determine how well we're doing and to measure their level of engagement. Using those survey results, managers across the company work with their teams to develop specific action plans.

In a company our size, jobs are always changing, going away, or being added to satisfy customer needs. A company has a responsibility to its stockholders and its customers to eliminate duplicate jobs and operate as efficiently as possible while also providing outstanding customer service. That doesn't mean we have to lose good people and their experience, loyalty, and commitment. New jobs are being created virtually every day somewhere in Wells Fargo. We would like team members whose jobs have been eliminated to find positions elsewhere in the company.

Our team members are our most important constituents because they're the single most important influence on our customers. We want our team members to be our customers, too. Some people say loyalty to a company is a thing of the past. We don't believe that. People naturally aspire to a larger purpose beyond themselves. They want to believe in their company and the good it can do. Don't we all?

We want every team member to be able to say, "I chose the right company. I'm valued. I'm rewarded. I'm recognized. We work hard, and we have fun, too. I can improve my professional skills and reach my career goals here. I enjoy my work."

Ethics

We strive to be recognized by our stakeholders as setting the standard among the world's great companies for integrity and principled performance. This is more than just doing the right thing. We also have to do it in the right way.

Honesty, trust, and integrity are essential for meeting the highest standards of corporate governance. They're not just the responsibility of our senior leaders and our board of directors. We're all responsible.

Our ethics are the sum of all the decisions each of us makes every day. If you want to find out how strong a company's ethics are, don't listen to what its people say. Watch what they do. This is even more important in our industry because everything we do is built on trust. It doesn't happen with one transaction, in one day on the job, or in one quarter. It's earned relationship by relationship.

Our customers trust us as their financial resource. They trust our tellers to complete transactions accurately and promptly. They trust our bankers to provide them with products and services to meet their needs. They trust our financial advisors to give them sound advice. They trust our mortgage consultants to manage their application process completely, accurately, and as quickly as possible. They trust our investment bankers to build financial models to analyze business trends, shape investment ideas, raise capital, and meet their strategic objectives.

And they trust all of us to act as risk managers—to ask the right questions, protect their assets, and help them reach their goals. **We have to earn that trust every day by behaving ethically; rewarding open, honest, two-way communication; and holding ourselves accountable for the decisions we make and the actions we take.**

What's right for customers

We value what's right for our customers in everything we do.

We're proud to compete in an industry that's central to the growth of our local, national, and global economies—an industry where doing what's right for customers and communities enables us to make a reasonable profit at the same time. Our customers are our friends. We treat them as our guests. We want them to be successful. We want them to feel as if they're part of Wells Fargo—that we're their company. We want to be approachable and caring, exceed their expectations, and invest in relationships that last a lifetime.

One of our top priorities is protecting customers' confidential data and information. Customers trust us to use that information to provide them with products and services that can save them time and money. They expect us to help guide them, help grow and protect their financial assets, and help them succeed financially. Our focus on customers is unwavering. That is how we have been doing business for more than 160 years and is the key to our future.

Diversity and inclusion

. . . .

The spirit of diversity and inclusion lives in our hearts and minds and, most importantly, in our behaviors—the way we interact with each other and conduct our business. These include:

- **Diverse segment outreach.** Our team reaches out to help us better serve and earn more business from important communities including Hispanics; Asian Americans; African Americans; the lesbian, gay, bisexual, transgender community; women; members of the military and veterans; and people with disabilities. Today, our customer base reflects the general population and, in some cases, is more diverse—a trend we expect to continue in the years ahead.

. . . .

Leadership

We're all called to be leaders.

We all have the responsibility to be the link between the vision of Wells Fargo and our customers. This is not the exclusive domain of managers. We define leadership as the act of establishing, sharing, and communicating our vision, and as the art of motivating others to understand and embrace our vision.

Leaders are accountable. They share the credit and shoulder the blame. They give others the responsibility and opportunity for success. Good leaders inspire teams to have confidence in their leadership; great leaders inspire team members to have confidence in themselves.

We want all team members to be able to lead themselves, lead the team, and lead the business.

When a customer needs an answer, we have to be able to respond quickly. That's a competitive advantage. Leaders consider themselves equal partners in a team effort to achieve our vision. When the team needs help, leaders pitch in just like everyone else. Leaders are involved. They're hands-on and available. They take personal ownership for a customer's problem and don't let go until that problem is solved. No one tells them to do it; they just do it.

The best leaders are the best coaches. They don't rely on authority or force of personality. They are confident in the inherent knowledge and talent of every team member. They believe our team members have the answer to every problem and see the potential in every opportunity. Leaders empower themselves and team members to develop ideas, test them, quantify the results, and then share the good ones with our other businesses and functions.

Leaders connect to our vision. They share their passion and their discipline about how to make our vision come alive. Leaders inspire outstanding performance. How we behave as leaders is just as important as the results we get. Leaders care about their team members' success, development plans, and professional dreams.

Leaders learn from each other. That's an advantage of being a big company. We share ideas and search for the best ones. We don't resist a good idea simply because "it wasn't invented here." We're always searching for the best way to do something and adopting it wherever it applies—to improve our service, keep customers and attract new ones, support communities, increase revenue, and manage expenses. It's not the strongest or most intelligent companies that survive in our industry but those that best adapt to change and take full advantage of the knowledge and experience of the whole team.

> **Good leaders inspire teams to have confidence in their leadership; great leaders inspire team members to have confidence in themselves.**

Our culture

I have always believed that culture is the most important part of a company's success. At Wells Fargo, we have been focused for more than 160 years on a culture of working together to help our customers. **We define "culture" as understanding our vision and values so well that you instinctively know what you need to do when you come to work each day.**

Culture is the attitude we bring to work every day—the pattern of thinking and acting with the customer in mind. It's the habit of doing the right things, and doing things right. It's a thousand behaviors inherited from team members who came before us, behaviors that we model today and then pass on as our legacy for team members who will come after us. It's behaviors and attitudes that are core to who we are: respecting differences, honoring deadlines, listening to each other, keeping promises, returning phone calls and emails as promptly as we can, and being actively engaged in meetings.

If there is one job that I as CEO must do for our team members, customers, communities, and shareholders, it is to be the keeper of our company's culture. It is the role of all team members to understand our culture, internalize it, live it, teach it, and reinforce it.

Culture of Caring℠

Our success has as much to do with attitude as aptitude—what's in our hearts, not just our heads. Our success depends on how much we care for each other, our customers, our communities, and our stockholders.

Our culture is reflected in the essence of our brand: "Together we'll go far℠." We want our team members to feel proud of working for a company that truly cares about people, goes the extra mile to do what's right—in good times and bad—and believes that "better" is possible for everyone.

Central to our culture are the following mindsets:

- **Caring.** Caring is core to who we are. We always want to be warm, welcoming, and humble; to take the time to listen and genuinely understand; to have empathy during the tough times; and to make a positive difference in people's lives.
- **Can-do attitude.** If there is a better way, we'll work hard to find it. We want to go the extra mile to do what's right; find options that are simpler, easier, and better; and own each moment to make lasting, positive experiences for our customers.
- **Better together.** Working together makes the difference. We all work for the customer; we honor our promises to each other and our customers; and we know our customers and work closely with them.

Enthusiasm and caring are what allow ordinary people to do extraordinary things. As part of our culture, we want our team members to have fun—because success without fun never lasts, and fun without success isn't much fun. This means enjoying our work, enjoying the people we work with, enjoying the difference we make in the lives of our customers and communities, and celebrating our achievements together as a team.

One Wells Fargo

All team members can bring our *Culture of Caring* mindsets to life in their daily work, whether we interact directly with customers or work for them behind the scenes. We believe that operating according to our mindsets not only makes Wells Fargo a great place to work, but also helps us deliver the best experience for our customers. That's something we call "One Wells Fargo."

We have approximately 265,000 team members across more than 90 businesses. Customers expect us to work across business lines to help them meet their financial needs.

One Wells Fargo means that we show our customers we know them at every moment of the relationship by making it easy for them to do business, providing guidance to them, and ensuring they feel valued.

Every moment we have with our customers is important. There are everyday moments—the daily transactions customers need, such as depositing a check, executing a trade, or making a payment. There are moments of truth—the more complex, less frequent, and often high-emotion interactions, such as buying a home, starting a business, or resolving an issue.

And finally, there are signature moments—the times when we differentiate ourselves by helping customers succeed financially or recognizing relationships, such as working with customers to help them reach financial goals, rewarding them for giving us more of their business, or doing something as simple as wishing them "happy birthday" at the ATM.

When we communicate with customers, we should do it with C-A-R-E: Consistent. Approachable. Respectful. Empathetic. We should be consistent in our messages to customers across events, across lines of business, and across the company. We should be approachable and easy to understand. We should be respectful, polite, courteous, considerate, and empathetic. We should speak and write in language our customers can understand.

Every time we serve a customer, we should ask ourselves, "If I were the customer in this situation, how would this experience feel for me? Did the transaction feel simple and easy? Did my problem get resolved quickly? Did the team members I contacted first accept responsibility for making sure I got what I needed?" **That's what we mean by One Wells Fargo—imagining ourselves as the customer.**

Customers want to do business with companies they connect with emotionally, that speak their language, that are sensitive to their culture, that value what they value, and that help them succeed financially. To make that emotional connection, we must put our customers at the center of everything we do.

Customers expect us to be One Wells Fargo. None of us can know everything about the thousands of products and services across our businesses. Customers don't expect that. What they *do* expect are systems that work smoothly across all our businesses. They expect finding the right team members, or the right answers to their questions.

Every team member has one thing in common: **We all work for the customer.** Every day, our customers say to us, "Know me. Know who I am. Know what I need. When I come into the bank or go online or use your phone bank or ATM, have all my information there about my accounts. Don't ask me the same questions over and over about information you already have. Don't transfer me to someone else who might do the same thing." They say, "Appreciate me and all the business I bring you. Treat me like a friend. Thank me. Reward me. If I give you more of my business, then give me a better deal and keep up your great service." Everything we need to know about a customer must be available easily, accurately, and securely, as fast as the best internet search engine.

Disciplined, responsible lending

To be the best in our industry, we have to be the best in credit and risk management. This expertise provides the foundation for our reputation and industry leadership. Our time-tested discipline in lending has made it possible for us to grow and prosper through many economic cycles. It's helped us avoid many of the credit traps experienced by others.

Because of our discipline, we can be there for our creditworthy customers when they need us, in good times and bad.

The fundamental principle of sound credit is to know your customers and understand their needs. This allows us to respond quickly. We expect our credit and lending officers to be well trained and knowledgeable, and to use common sense and conservative assumptions. **We should always ask, "Does this credit decision make sense for the customer and for Wells Fargo?"** We should not sacrifice credit quality for short-term financial gain.

Lending can anchor a customer relationship, but we don't view a loan as just a transaction. It must be part of a broader, deeper relationship with a customer—whether an individual or a business—because lending is simply one facet of any customer's total financial need. Banks that do transactional lending or that compete on price alone are doomed to fail. Successful bankers build long-term relationships, providing virtually every product or service a customer requires and seeing the loan as part of the overall customer relationship.

In our consumer lending businesses, we have four principles that guide our lending practices:

1. Pricing on all loans is fully disclosed and competitive, reflecting a complete view of the customer's finances, credit history, characteristics of the transaction, and collateral.
2. Offering customers enough information to allow them to make an informed decision.
3. Ensuring every loan we provide makes sense for the customer, and the customer clearly understands how the product works.
4. Exercising due diligence to determine that customers have the ability to repay a loan before we provide it.

It's contrary to our culture to try to provide our customers any product or service that is not appropriate for them.

Risk management

For more than 160 years, Wells Fargo has been in the risk management business. It's central to what we do, and it's never been more important than it is today. We're not rewarded unless we take risk, but we must identify, understand, quantify, control, and price appropriately for that risk. Risk management is so important that we have added it as one of our strategic pillars and priorities that you will see later in this booklet.

Although we've seen a lot of change over the years, the fundamentals of our risk management remain the same. We are guided by our statement of risk appetite, which defines the nature and level of risk that Wells Fargo is willing to take while operating in a safe and sound manner. This statement provides the philosophical underpinnings that guide businesses and risk professionals as they manage risk on a day-to-day basis. It is based on seven core principles:

1. **Relationship focus.** We take only as much risk as is necessary to efficiently, effectively, and prudently serve our consumer, small business, commercial, and wealth customers. We do not offer products that are inappropriate for our customers' needs and circumstances.
2. **Understanding risk.** We are willing to take risks when we understand them, and we avoid or minimize risk where we have no competitive advantage or limited experience.
3. **Reputation.** We will not engage in activities or business practices that could cause damage to our reputation.

4. **Price for risk.** We price our business to cover risk to capital and will retain risk only if priced for a sufficient risk-adjusted return.

5. **Conservatism.** We have a significant bias for conservatism. While we want to grow the company, we will do so only in a way that supports our longterm goals and does not compromise our ability to manage risk.

6. **Operational excellence.** Our customers expect that we will be a reliable provider of services. Our team members are committed to excellence and are focused on optimizing efficiency and effectiveness while minimizing errors.

7. **Clear accountability.** Our lines of business have primary accountability for risk. They own the risk, have their own risk team members, and are the first line of defense. Our Corporate Risk group is the second line of defense and provides oversight to ensure our corporate functions and businesses soundly manage risk, comply with applicable laws and regulations, and offer products and services that help our customers meet their financial needs. Corporate Risk also provides "credible challenge" to the business lines and corporate functions, when appropriate. We believe this approach is a competitive advantage. In addition, we have a third line of defense with our internal audit team.

While we rely on risk professionals in the lines of business to take primary responsibility for managing and escalating risks, we firmly believe that risk is everyone's business. All team members have a responsibility for managing risk. Compliance and risk management are part of our culture and are an extension of our code of ethics. We expect team members to identify and escalate potential risks, and we recognize and thank them for doing so.

Corporate social responsibility

. . . .

Culture first, size second

We use acquisitions as a cost-effective way to help us set the stage to earn the business of more customers. We don't acquire another company simply to get bigger. We never put size ahead of culture. So we get bigger by getting better—we don't get better by getting bigger. By "better" we mean putting ourselves in the best position to be there for our customers when they need their next financial product.

We want to be a leader in our industry in return on equity, return on assets, and growth in revenue and profitability. Our stock should be among the best performers in any industry. But we think about achieving these goals in a very different way. If we do what's right for our team members, customers, and communities, then—and only then—we will earn sustained profits and have our shareholders see us as a great investment.

When it comes to acquisitions, we build relationships that often take years to bear fruit. We look for economies of skill, not just economies of scale. We buy companies and assets we understand. We use conservative assumptions. We acquire only what will benefit shareholders. Every acquisition must add to earnings per share no later than the third year after purchase and earn at least a 15 percent internal rate of return. We integrate the acquired company and its people quickly and smoothly into our culture.

Our priorities for newly acquired companies are the same as those of any other Wells Fargo business: first, ensure safe and sound management practices are in place; second, achieve acceptable profitability; and third, grow the business and have fun succeeding.

Who we are

As we have grown over the years, we have never lost sight of our focus on helping customers and businesses in the "real economy." From checking accounts and debit cards to savings products to treasury management services, we help customers manage their daily financial lives. We help families buy that first home or car. We provide funding to businesses, small and large, to expand and hire. We help our customers plan and save for retirement. We support our communities.

Some call this a "Main Street" focus. We believe that this community-based approach to financial services lets us serve our customers in the best way possible and differentiates us from the other large banks.

Community based

By "community based" we mean we're not just a bank that happens to be in the community; we're a community bank. We're "in and of" every community in which we do business, whether it's Columbia, South Carolina; Des Moines, Iowa; or Roseville, California. And we're in more U.S. communities than any of our competitors.

We all identify with our communities and take geographic pride in where we live and where we're from. That's my town. That's my state. As part of our work to find what's best for each of our customers, we think about what's best for our communities—the places where we live and work, pay taxes, raise families, educate children, buy groceries, and support local nonprofits.

We're local first, then national. We weren't born as a national bank that then decided to be local. We were born as a local bank in one community that does business on Main Street, and then we grew into a family of many local banks in many communities.

Every segment of the industry in which we do business—including banking, mortgage, investments, and insurance—started in a neighborhood and a town and grew to be national, not the other way around.

"Out-local the nationals and out-national the locals®"

Since we're local and national at the same time, we say that we want to *out-local the nationals and out-national the locals.*

This means we look like a national bank but behave like a smaller bank. It means customers know local tellers by name, and tellers refer customers to a global world of financial products and services. "Out-national the locals" means we must offer better products, more channels, superior technology, and a broader product line than smaller local competitors. "Out-local the nationals" means we stay closer to our customers than any national competitor in our communities; we understand our local customer needs; and we provide professional, personalized, timely service on a first-name basis.

We offer our retail customers the most extensive, convenient distribution system in our industry. We have more than 8,700 locations and more than 12,800 ATMs. Our customers call our phone banks hundreds of millions of times a year. As the first U.S. bank to offer online banking, we provide products through our online and digital channels to meet the financial needs of every one of our customers, including consumers, small businesses, middle-market companies, and large corporations. We want our digital services to be known as the best, most integrated "trusted gateway" for our customers' financial services.

We have three major customer segments: individuals, small businesses, and large businesses. We have four major business groups: Community Banking (individuals and small businesses); Wealth and Investment Management; Consumer Lending (home mortgage, home equity, credit cards, student lending, and auto lending); and Wholesale Banking (larger and medium-sized businesses).

Our corporate headquarters is in San Francisco, but we believe our real "head"quarters is where our customers are. Likewise, our talent and resources are broadly dispersed. We have significant "hubquarters" of employment and expertise in many large metro areas, including Charlotte, Boston, New York, Atlanta, Philadelphia, Miami, Chicago, Des Moines, St. Louis, Minneapolis-Saint Paul, Phoenix, Denver, Los Angeles, and Houston.

Many of our products and services are ranked No. 1, 2, or 3 in the U.S. For example, we're No. 1 in the number of retail banking locations, originating and servicing home mortgages, small business lending, commercial real estate lending, and auto lending. We're No. 2 in private student loans, debit cards, and annuity sales. And we're No. 3 among full-service retail brokerage providers. For a full list of how we rank, see the latest edition of the "Wells Fargo Today" fact sheet on wellsfargo.com.

Rankings such as these are important measures not because they indicate how big we are, but because they indicate how well we are satisfying our customers' financial needs.

Our brand

The Wells Fargo brand is consistently ranked as one of the most valuable banking brands in the world.

Our brand is what people say about Wells Fargo to their friends and family. It's how they feel about doing business with us and how they describe those feelings.

We have a brand platform that defines our brand and who we are for customers and team members. At the center of that platform is our brand purpose. It says what we believe, how we differ from our competitors, and how we care for customers. Our brand purpose is: "To help our customers succeed financially. We believe better is possible for everyone. This is why team members work together every day to help our customers reach their goals."

Our brand purpose is supported by these principles, or brand pillars, to deliver on our purpose and promise to work together to differentiate Wells Fargo from our competitors:

- **Relationships that last a lifetime.** We know our customers and care about them as individuals. In every interaction with us, they feel understood, recognized, and supported through their financial journey.
- **Expertise and guidance to help our customers make confident decisions.** We provide guidance and options so that customers can make informed choices.

- **Going the extra mile to do what's right.** We put the interests of customers and communities first in all we do. We come through for them so they know we are there in good times and bad. We work to make their lives easier.

Our customers depend on us to help them succeed on their financial journey. Our team members *are* the Wells Fargo brand and the foundation of our brand's success.

Our stagecoach symbolizes our strength and stability, and it's recognized worldwide. It says to our customers, "We've been here for more than 160 years, and we'll be here for you in the future, too." It reinforces the essence of our brand, "Together we'll go far." We're one of only about a dozen U.S. public companies of that vintage that's still in its founding business under its founding name.

Our strategy

Having a vision is not enough. You need a strategy to achieve that vision, along with a business model that can succeed in any economic cycle. You also need extraordinary execution. In fact, it's all about execution. A good strategy perfectly executed will beat a great strategy poorly executed every time.

Our unwavering focus on customers is the foundation of our strategy. While industry trends and the competitive landscape will continue to evolve, our strategy will guide us in successfully navigating these challenges and doing what is right for customers.

Our strategy drives our choices, enables us to prioritize our efforts, differentiates us from our peers, and ultimately builds lasting value for team members, customers, communities, and shareholders. Our diversified business model provides strength and stability as we assure customers and communities that we will be here to serve them and future generations.

With our vision and values as anchors, the core pillars of our strategy reflect our focus on deepening customer relationships while serving them anywhere, at any time, and earning their trust through every interaction.

Deepen relationships and attract new customers

We strive to create deep and enduring relationships with our customers by discovering their needs and delivering the most relevant products, services, and guidance. This approach, combined with our broad expertise across businesses, enables us to anticipate and profitably serve our customers' financial needs.

The relationships we have developed over the years are valuable and continue to inspire us to provide even greater value to existing customers while attracting new ones. We do not view any product in isolation but as part of a full and long-lasting relationship with a customer. **We start with what the customer needs—not with what we want to sell them.**

Every moment that our team members share with a customer is an opportunity to genuinely and proactively help our customers with their individual needs. Whether the customer is a college student applying for his first credit card, a business owner setting up her company's payroll, a large enterprise executing an acquisition, or a young family saving for the future, each moment is a chance to provide a rewarding experience that reminds our customers that, above all, we are here to support their financial successes through our guidance and services.

An outcome of offering customers the products and services they need, want, and value is that we earn more opportunities to serve customers, or what we call cross-sell. Cross-sell is the result of serving our customers extraordinarily well, understanding their financial needs and goals over their lifetimes, and ensuring we innovate our products, services, and channels so that we earn more of their business and help them succeed financially. We succeed when our customers succeed.

Seamlessly serve our customers—anywhere, any time

Technological innovations have fundamentally changed the way individuals and businesses communicate and transact. As the pace of innovation accelerates, customer experiences are being redefined. We want to engage with our customers in ways that are most convenient to them. This means all of our distribution channels—locations, phone banks, ATMs, online, and mobile banking—work together, integrated with our products, to benefit customers.

Driven by our focus on convenience and ease of use across products and services, we are expanding our capabilities and exploring new distribution formats to create seamless, integrated, and consistently exceptional customer experiences—which ultimately lead to greater customer loyalty and retention.

When we focus our technology resources on serving customers, we can achieve a true competitive advantage for Wells Fargo. But technology alone does not guarantee such an advantage. What's important is the creativity and speed with which we deploy that technology to benefit our customers.

Consistently earn customer trust through sound risk management

At the core of any meaningful relationship is trust. Establishing a deeper customer relationship is not solely about offering the most relevant products and services; it also means we must ensure and proactively protect our customers' financial security through a risk-focused culture.

Being a leader in risk management has been fundamental to the sustainability and longevity of our business. We remain as committed as ever to caring for our customers, earning their trust, and ensuring their peace of mind by protecting their assets, personal information and data, and privacy through robust controls, discipline, and proven risk management capabilities. Effective management of our capital structure will further ensure the safety and soundness of our business.

As expressed throughout this booklet, our sound risk culture is built into our vision of doing what is right for the customer, and we will continue to uphold the same rigorous management philosophy that has won the trust of our customers for generations. By understanding our customers and their financial needs, we are better able to identify and address risk at its source. This conservative approach has helped sustain our long-term profitability and growth through all economic cycles.

Our six priorities

Our priorities are how we bring our vision and values and our strategy to life in today's environment. By making progress in these areas, and being faithful to our vision and values, we can continue to earn the trust of our customers, help them succeed financially, and be known as one of the world's great companies.

Putting customers first

Our first job is to understand our customers' financial objectives, then provide products and services to help satisfy those goals so they can be financially successful. And, the best way for us to meet our customers' needs is by working together, as a team. This is why we place so much value on teamwork.

We put our customers at the center of everything we do and give them such outstanding service and guidance that they'll give us more of their business, honor us with repeat purchases, and rave about us to their family, friends, and business associates. **We want to be the first provider our customers think of when they need their next financial product.**

Simply put, our product is service. Our value added is our financial guidance. We want our customers to have financial plans that are unique to their individual needs and provide a roadmap to reach their goals and objectives.

Serving our customers starts with knowing who they are. The more we know about our customers' needs, the more we can offer them the choices, convenience, and price benefits they look for. Our customers don't do business with us just so they can be another account number. They want us to know them, respect them, appreciate them, and reward them for doing business with us. The winners in financial services will be companies that know the most about their customers, obtain that information efficiently and securely, treat it respectfully, and use it wisely.

Growing revenue

Wells Fargo is a growth company that believes the key to the bottom line is the top line. The ability to grow profits consistently is based on sustainable revenue growth.

Revenue is the measure that shows us how well we serve our customers' needs, earn their trust, and grow our market share. It's the vote our customers cast every day about our company. When they rave about our service, they'll give us more of their business, increasing revenue. They'll refer new customers to us. They'll stay with us for life.

We can't control the economy, interest rates, the markets, or world events. We focus on what we *can* control and what we can sustain long term: our core performance and our revenue growth. That's our priority, whether the road is bumpy or smooth. Whether interest rates or unemployment are high or low. Whether the yield curve is flat or steep. Whether the economy is growing or contracting. What we can influence is our ability to serve customers and make smart business decisions. That's what propels our revenue growth and creates shareholder value.

We see opportunities to continue increasing revenue across all of our businesses and serve more of our customers' financial needs. For example, we want more of our retail bank customers to consider us for their brokerage and retirement needs. And we want to continue expanding the number of customers who have a mortgage or credit card with us. We also want to be the bank of choice for our business, commercial, and global customers.

Managing expenses

. . . .

Living our vision and values

Every day when we come to work, we have the opportunity to bring our vision and values to life. That's what we do every time we help a customer or support a fellow team member. That's where our vision and values need to live—in our everyday behaviors.

There's an old saying: Actions speak louder than words. We need to show people what we believe. They need to see our vision and values come alive in everyday actions, not just in posters on the wall. Our customers need to see us doing the right thing and helping them succeed financially. Our team members need to see us respecting, honoring, caring for, and appreciating one another. Our communities need to see us taking part and investing in projects that are important to them. That's how we truly bring our vision and values to life.

We want to be known as one of the world's great companies, but we know that an outstanding reputation cannot be bought or manipulated. It has to be earned over decades by ethical, customer-centered behavior and team members who care. Our vision and our values come first, not our reputation.

Our reputation extends from our character, not the other way around. We should want to do something—or not do something—based first on whether it's right for our customers, team members, communities, and shareholders, not for how it will affect our reputation. If it's the right thing to do, it will be good for our reputation.

Connecting with communities and stakeholders

. . . .

Managing risk

We have always been strong in risk management, particularly credit risk. Our goal is to build on that strength and set the global standard for risk management excellence among all financial institutions.

We understand that to continue our success and meet the heightened expectations of our key stakeholders, we must excel in all types of risk management, including credit, market, liquidity, operational, information security, compliance, model, and reputational risk.

Strong risk management practices further enable our ability to serve customers. There is a strong correlation between risk management and the customer experience. Customers want to do business with companies they can trust and that act in their best interest. We will continue to invest in building excellence across all types of risk management to best serve and protect our customers.

Our future

I've grown up with our vision and values during my more than 33 years with our company. I've never been more confident of our vision and never more certain of our values than today. I have no doubt our company can persevere through any economic cycle and that we'll be even stronger, even more secure, and even more dependable and reliable for our customers and communities.

Never before in our company's history has our physical presence meant more for a neighborhood or a community than it does now. More than ever, our customers need a safe, trustworthy, capable financial services provider that can help them plan for and achieve their financial goals of buying a home, providing education for their children, building a business, and saving for retirement.

Never before has it been as important for us to see our customers as our friends and neighbors—to make them feel at home, show them we care, make them feel special, give them well-informed guidance, provide them value, know them, and thank them. If we continue doing all these things well, we'll earn not just their gratitude, but also their business for a lifetime.

It's up to us

We have what it takes to be great. We're united under one vision. We share values that form the basis of a well-understood, effective, and caring culture. We enjoy a time-tested, diversified business model with proven strategies and goals. We benefit from an operating philosophy that provides sustainable, competitive advantages. And, most importantly, we have great people.

Our foundation for success can be summarized in three beliefs in who we are and what we do:

- **Our product is service.**
- **Our value added is financial guidance.**
- **Our competitive advantage is our people.**

Our formula for greatness starts and ends with people: mind share + heart share = market share.

Our vision:

We want to satisfy our customers' financial needs and help them succeed financially.

NOTES

You might ask yourself why we put an excerpt of Wells Fargo's vision and values statement in this edition. We wanted you to see what Wells Fargo thought it was doing—declaring its governing principles to those both inside and outside the company—or at least what it wanted the outside world to think its values were. But remember what we told you in the introduction to this chapter: Wells Fargo's employees created millions of fake accounts for its customers. How could a company whose values include ethics and thinking about what's right for customers have created such a disconnect between what it said it valued and what, apparently, it did value (the "aggressive sales goals" to which Senators Jeffrey Merkley, Elizabeth Warren, and Robert Menendez refer in the letter that follows this note)? And even more to the point, when you're in charge of an organization, how can you make sure that the values that you say you have are actually the values that your employees use at work?

CHAPTER 12

Wells Fargo, Part 2: Senate Letter to Mary Jo White of the SEC*

United States Senate

WASHINGTON, DC 20510

September 28. 2016

The Honorable Mary Jo White
Chair
Securities and Exchange Commission
100 F Street NE
Washington, DC 20549

Dear Chair White:

We write to urge the Securities and Exchange Commission to investigate whether Wells Fargo and its senior executives—including Chairman of the Board and CEO John Stumpf—violated federal securities laws in connection with the conduct described in the Consumer Financial Protection Bureau's September 8, 2016 Consent Order.[1]

For years, Wells Fargo touted its ability to sell additional products to existing customers—a tactic it called "cross-selling." According to the CFPB consent order, Wells Fargo Bank, N.A. "set sales goals and implemented sales incentives, including an incentive-compensation program" to promote cross-selling by its

* Letter to Chair Mary Jo White, Securities and Exchange Commission, from U.S. Senators Jeffrey A. Merkley, Robert Menendez, and Elizabeth Warren (Sept. 28, 2016), available at https://www.warren.senate.gov/files/documents/2016-9-28_Letter_to_SEC_RE_Wells_Investigation.pdf.

1 CFPB Consent Order (Sept. 8, 201 6), available at http://files.consumerfinance.gov/f/documents/092016_cfpb WFBconsentorder.pdf.

employees. In response to these aggressive sales goals and incentives, thousands of Wells Fargo employees engaged in improper behavior, including opening deposit accounts and credit card accounts without customer authorization. Wells Fargo fired more than 5,300 employees between 2011 and 2016 for engaging in this kind of conduct.[2]

After regulators discovered this widespread problem, Wells Fargo conducted an analysis that revealed that employees may have opened as many as 1.5 million checking accounts and obtained as many as 565,000 credit cards without customer authorization. Those fraudulent accounts cost customers millions in fees.[3]

These facts—as well as testimony from Mr. Stumpf before the Senate Banking Committee on September 20, 2016—justify an investigation into at least three types of securities law violations.

Sarbanes-Oxley

During the Enron scandal, Enron's Chairman and CEO, Ken Lay, claimed that he did not know the extent of the fraud at his company. In response, Congress enacted the Sarbanes-Oxley Act and created a series of internal control disclosures that were meant to reduce corporate fraud and protect investors by holding senior executives more accountable.

Now CEOs are required to sign off on their company's financial reporting. Under Section 302 of Sarbanes-Oxley, CEOs and CFOs must certify in each annual or quarterly report that the signing officer has reviewed the report and that, based on the officer's knowledge, the report does not contain untrue statements of material fact, does not omit to state a material fact resulting in a misleading report, and fairly represents in all material respects the financial condition and results of operations of the company.

Further, Section 906 of Sarbanes-Oxley requires each periodic report containing financial statements filed with the SEC to include a written certification from the CEO and CFO that the information "fairly presents, in all material respects, the financial condition and results of operations" of the company. If the CEO or CFO submits a certification knowing that the statement does not meet this standard, they can be fined up to $5 million and imprisoned for up to 20 years.

Mr. Stumpf's testimony under oath before the Senate Banking Committee raises questions about whether he violated the Sarbanes-Oxley Act. According to his testimony before the Banking Committee, Mr. Stumpf became aware of the

---

2 *Id.*

3 *Id.*

widespread fraud occurring at his bank in 2013,[4] yet Mr. Stumpf and the company's CFO submitted certifications relating to SEC filings after 2013 that did not indicate any knowledge of this massive fraud.[5]

Securities Fraud

The Commission should also investigate whether Wells Fargo and its senior executives committed securities fraud by failing to promptly disclose material facts to investors and by knowingly providing investors with material false information.

As you know, Section 17(a) of the Securities Act of 1933,[6] Section 10(b) of the Securities Exchange Act of 1934,[7] and SEC Rule 10b–5[8] prohibit companies from misleading investors about facts that could affect their business and their stock price.

Mr. Stumpf admitted that he became aware of widespread fraud at the bank in 2013, yet neither he nor the company disclosed that information to investors until the CFPB Consent Order became public in September 2016. In the interim, during quarterly earnings calls, Mr. Stumpf personally touted Wells' cross-sell ratio[9]—its measure of the average number of accounts per customer—as well as

---

4 United States, Congress, Senate Banking, Housing, and Urban Affairs Committee, "An Examination of Wells Fargo's Unauthorized Accounts and the Regulatory Response," 114th Congress, 2nd Session, Accessed September 28, 2016. Available at: http://www.banking.senate.gov/public/index.cfm/hearings?ID=B80F988l-433l-4F95-91BC-718288EC9DA0.

5 See, e.g., Wells Fargo 10-K for 2014, available at https://www.sec.gov/Archives/edgar/data/72971/000007297115000449/wfc-12312014×10k.htm.

6 15 U.S.C. § 77q(a).

7 15 U.S.C. § 78j(b).

8 17C.F.R. § 240. 10b–5(b).

9 *See, e.g.,* Transcript of QI 2013 Wells Fargo Earnings Conference Call, April 12, 2013, *available at* http://www.warren.senate.gov/files/documents/2013Q1_WellsFargoEarningsCall.pdf ("Our growth reflects the benefit of our relationship model, as demonstrated by achieving record Retail Banking cross-sell of 6.1 products per household."); Transcript of Q2 2013 Wells Fargo Earnings Conference Call, July 12, 2013, *available at* http://www.warren.senate.gov/files/documents/2013Q2_WellsFargoEarningsCall.pdf ("We achieved record retail cross-sell of 6.14 products per household."); Transcript of Q3 2013 Wells Fargo Earnings Conference Call, Oct. 11, 2013, *available at* http://www.warren.senate.gov/files/documents/2013Q3_WellsFargoEamingsCall.pdf ("We deepened relationships across our Company achieving record retail banking cross-sell of 6.15 products per household."); Transcript of Q4 2013 Wells Fargo Earnings Conference Call, Jan. 14, 2014, *available at* http://www.warren.senate.gov/files/documents/2013Q4_WellsFargoEarningsCall.pdf ("By focusing on meeting our customers' financial needs, we achieved record cross-sell across the company with retail banking cross-sell growing to 6.16 products per household."); Transcript of Q1 2014 Wells Fargo Earnings Conference Call, April 11, 2014, *available* at http://www.warren.senate.gov/files/documents/2014Q1_WellsFargoEarningsCall.pdf ("We deepened relationships across our Company, achieving record retail banking cross-sell of 6.17 products per household."); Transcript of Q2 2014 Wells Fargo Earnings Conference Call, *available at* http://www.warren.senate.gov/files/documents/2014Q2_WellsFargoEamingsCall.pdf ("We deepened relationships across our company. Retail banking cross-sell was 6.17 products per household.").

Wells' success in opening new deposit accounts[10] and credit card accounts.[11] He did so apparently with knowledge that many of these retail accounts were created without customer authorization.

The SEC has previously found securities fraud when an executive makes misleading statements on earnings calls. For example, in April 2014, the SEC entered into a $20 million settlement with CVS Caremark Corp. based in part on allegations that CVS "misled investors on an earnings call."[12] Similarly, in 2010, the SEC entered into a $75 million settlement with Citigroup and two of its executives based in part on allegations that bank officials provided misleading information during investor phone calls about the bank's subprime mortgage exposure.[13]

At the recent Senate Banking Committee hearing, Mr. Stumpf claimed under oath that the firing of more than 5000 employees for creating more than two million possibly fake accounts was not "material" to investors.[14] But Mr. Stumpf personally emphasized the company's increasing number of retail accounts and growing cross-sell ratio on quarterly earnings calls with investors and analysts, and a number of analyst reports from that period recommend purchasing Wells Fargo stock in part because of those strong numbers.[15] Mr. Stumpf and Wells Fargo investors clearly believed that the cross-sell ratio and the number of retail accounts were material to investment decisions—and yet Mr. Stumpf did not disclose that those numbers had been inflated by millions of fraudulent accounts.

Whistleblower Retaliation

The Commission should also investigate whether Wells Fargo violated whistleblower protection laws when it fired employees who reported misconduct to the company.

---

10 *See, e.g.,* Transcript of Q3 2014 Wells Fargo Earnings Conference Call, Oct. 14, 2014, *available at* http://www.warren.senate.gov/files/documents/2014Q3_WellsFargoEarningsCall.pdf ("We grew primary consumer checking customers by 4.9%."); Transcript of Q4 2014 Wells Fargo Earnings Conference Call, Jan. 14, 2015, *available at* ("And we grew the number of primary consumer checking customers by 5.2%.").

11 *See, e.g.,* Transcript of Q3 2014 Wells Fargo Earnings Conference Call, Oct. 14, 2014, *available at* http://www.warren.senate.gov/files/documents/2014Q3_WellsFargoEarningsCall.pdf ("And the increases you're seeing in debit card activity and credit card, we almost have 40% of our customers now [ ] carry our credit card. That was 22% in 2009.").

12 https://www.sec.gov/News/PressRelease/Detail/PressRelease/1370541437806.

13 https://www.sec.gov/news/press/2010/2010-136.htm.

14 United States, Congress, Senate Banking, Housing, and Urban Affairs Committee, "An Examination of Wells Fargo's Unauthorized Accounts and the Regulatory Response," 114th Congress, 2nd Session, Accessed September 21, 2016. Available at: http://www.banking.senate.gov/public/index.cfm/hearings?ID=B80F9B81-4331-4F95-91BC-718288EC9DA0.

15 *See, e.g.,* analyst reports available at http://www.warren.scnate.gov/wellsfargo/.

Wells Fargo has reportedly fired several employees who had reported misconduct to their superiors or called Wells Fargo's internal ethics hotline.[16] Other former Wells Fargo employees have contacted Members of Congress to share similar stories of being fired shortly after having reported misconduct internally.

Congress enacted whistleblower protections to encourage employees to report misconduct. These protections allow whistleblowers to come forward without having to fear that they will lose their jobs or suffer other consequences at work. Both Sarbanes-Oxley and the Dodd-Frank Wall Street Reform and Consumer Protection Act have anti-retaliation provisions to protect employee whistleblowers who report certain types of fraud and violations of securities law.

For instance, Sarbanes-Oxley prohibits a publicly-traded company from terminating or discriminating against an employee who provides information about what he or she reasonably believes is a type of fraud, a violation of any SEC rule or regulation, or a violation of federal law related to fraud against shareholders.[17] The language explicitly protects employees who report information internally to "a person with supervisory authority over the employee (or such other person working for the employer who has the authority to investigate, discover, or terminate misconduct)."[18]

Dodd-Frank also has an anti-retaliation provision to protect whistleblowers "in making disclosures that are required or protected under the Sarbanes-Oxley Act of 2002."[19] The SEC has interpreted the anti-retaliation provision in Dodd-Frank to apply to an employee who reports information consistent with the way one would do so under Sarbanes-Oxley, which therefore would include employees who report misconduct internally.[20] Several courts, including the U.S. Court of Appeals for the Second Circuit, have held that whistleblowers who report internally are protected under the anti-retaliation provision in Dodd-Frank.[21]

---

16 Matt Egan, *I called the Wells Fargo ethics line and was fired,* CNN Money (Sept. 21, 2016), *available at* http://money.cnn.com/2016/09/21/investing/wells-fargo-fired-workers-retaliation-fake-accounts/; Stacy Cowley, *Wells Fargo Workers Claim Retaliation for Playing by the Rules* New York Times (Sept. 26, 2016), at http://www.nytimes.com/2016/09/27/business/dealbook/wells-fargo-workers-claim-retaliation-for-playing-by-the-rules.html?ref=business&_r=0.

17 18 U.S.C. § 1514A(a)(1).

18 18 U.S.C. § 1514A(a)(l)(C).

19 15 U.S.C. § 78u–6(h)(1)(A).

20 17 C.F.R. 240.21 F–2(b)(1). *See also* Securities Whistleblower Protections & Incentives, 76 Fed. Reg. 34300, at 34304 (June 13, 2011) *available at* https://www.sec.gov/rules/final/2011/34-64545fr.pdf ("the statutory ant retaliation protections apply Lo three different categories of whistleblowers, and the third category includes individuals who report to persons or governmental authorities other than the Commission.").

21 *See, e.g.,* Berman v. Nco@Ogilvy LLC, 80 I F.3d 145 (2d Cir. 20 15).

Published reports and court filings indicate that Wells Fargo harassed and ultimately terminated employees for raising concerns about the creation of fake deposit and credit card accounts. These claims deserve the SEC's careful investigation.

Conclusion

Wells Fargo recently disclosed to the SEC and its investors that it is under investigation by "Federal, state and local government agencies, including the United States Department of Justice, and state attorneys general and prosecutors' offices."[22] Additionally, the United States Department of Labor announced that it would conduct a "top-to-bottom" review to determine whether Wells Fargo violated labor laws.[23]

The SEC should join in these efforts to ensure that Wells Fargo and its senior executives are held accountable for a massive, years-long fraud that hurt thousands of customers and potentially cost investors billions of dollars.

We appreciate your consideration of this matter.

Sincerely,

Jeffrey A. Merkley
United States Senator

Elizabeth Warren
United States Senator

Robert Menendez
United States Senator

cc: SEC Commissioner Kara Stein

SEC Commissioner Michael Piwowar

NOTES

We included this letter in our materials to illustrate that big organizational failures will also likely draw their fair share of political pressure. As the senators pointed out, Enron begat the Sarbanes-Oxley legislation, which doubled the fines for certain types

22 Wells Fargo & Company, Form 8-K, filed Sept. 27, 2016.

23 Letter from Secretary of Labor Thomas E. Perez to Senator Elizabeth Warren, Sept. 26, 2016, available at http://www.warren.senate.gov/files/documents/2016-9-26_DOL_ltr_to_Warren.pdf.

of corporate misbehavior. Though the two of us have our doubts about whether legislation really can change behavior, having enforcement tools on the books can help with punishment, if not with deterrence.

We still think that smart people are likely to discount the risk of getting caught and that not-so-smart people won't worry about the risk of getting caught in the first place. Therefore, looking to criminal penalties to deter behavior—especially white-collar crime—is likely not the most efficient way to prevent bad behavior. What might work? Possibly, a combination of understanding how humans think and behave and creating a structure that uses that knowledge to create incentives for encouraging good behavior could work. The problem is that even logical incentives also can trigger unintended consequences. A 2014 article that one of us wrote (and the other one edited)* discussed a fairly gory example of a good incentive "gone wrong":

> Appealing to both civic duty and to the pocketbook, a one-cent bounty was paid for each rat tail brought to the authorities (it was decided that the handing in of an entire rat corpse would create too much of a burden for the already taxed municipal health authorities). Unfortunately, this scheme backfired. Despite initial apparent success, the authorities soon discovered that the best laid plans of mice and men often go awry. As soon as the municipal administrators publicized the reward program, Vietnamese residents began to bring in thousands of tails. While many desk-bound administrators delighted in the numbers of apparently eliminated rats, more alert officials in the field began to notice a disturbing development. There were frequent sightings of rats without tails going about their business in the city streets. After some perplexity, the authorities realized that less-than-honest but quite resourceful characters were catching rats, but merely cutting off the tails and letting the still-living pests go free (perhaps to breed and produce more valuable tails). Later, things became even more serious as health inspectors discovered a disturbing development in the suburbs of Hanoi. These officials found that more enterprising but equally deceptive individuals were actually raising rats to collect the bounty. One can only imagine the frustration of the municipal authorities, who realized that their best efforts at *dératisation* had actually increased the rodent population by indirectly encouraging rat-farming.**

* Nancy B. Rapoport, *"Nudging" Better Lawyer Behavior: Using Default Rules and Incentives to Change Behavior in Law Firms,* 4 ST. MARY'S J. L. ETHICS & MALP. 42 (2014).

** *Id.* at n.227 (citing Michael C. Vann, *Of Rats, Rice, and Race: The Great Hanoi Rat Massacre, an Episode in French Colonial History,* 4 FRENCH COLONIAL HIST. 191, 198 (2003)) (italization in original).

The point isn't to gross you out with images of tail-less rats running about. The point is that every new rule and regulation has consequences. Maybe Volkswagen engineers wouldn't have figured out a way to game the emissions standards had they not convinced themselves that the standards themselves were misguided.

But here's another point: there are laws on the books that say that banks aren't supposed to sign their customers up for fraudulent accounts, either, and yet, that's what the report of the independent directors of Wells Fargo's report (the next part of our book) concluded that Wells Fargo employees did. Read on.

CHAPTER 13

Wells Fargo, Part 3: Independent Directors of the Board of Wells Fargo & Company Sales Practices Investigation Report*

April 10, 2017

Overview of the Report

This is the report of the Independent Directors of the Board of Wells Fargo & Company on their investigation of sales practices at the Community Bank, conducted by a four-director Oversight Committee, assisted by independent counsel Shearman & Sterling LLP. The Independent Directors' goals in conducting the investigation were to understand the root causes of improper sales practices in the Community Bank, to identify remedial actions so these issues can never be repeated and to rebuild the trust customers place in the bank. Shearman & Sterling conducted 100 interviews and searched across more than 35 million documents.

Principal Findings

The root cause of sales practice failures was the distortion of the Community Bank's sales culture and performance management system, which, when combined with aggressive sales management, created pressure on employees to sell unwanted or unneeded products to customers and, in some cases, to open unauthorized accounts. Wells Fargo's decentralized corporate structure gave too much autonomy to the Community Bank's senior leadership, who were unwilling to change the sales model or even recognize it as the root cause of the problem.

* Independent Directors of the Board of Wells Fargo & Company Sales Practices Investigation Report (April 10, 2017), available at https://www08.wellsfargomedia.com/assets/pdf/about/investor-relations/presentations/2017/board-report.pdf.

Community Bank leadership resisted and impeded outside scrutiny or oversight and, when forced to report, minimized the scale and nature of the problem.

The former Chief Executive Officer, relying on Wells Fargo's decades of success with cross-sell and positive customer and employee survey results, was too slow to investigate or critically challenge sales practices in the Community Bank. He also failed to appreciate the seriousness of the problem and the substantial reputational risk to Wells Fargo.

Corporate control functions were constrained by the decentralized organizational structure and a culture of substantial deference to the business units. In addition, a transactional approach to problem-solving obscured their view of the broader context. As a result, they missed opportunities to analyze, size and escalate sales practice issues.

Sales practices were not identified to the Board as a noteworthy risk until 2014. By early 2015, management reported that corrective action was working. Throughout 2015 and 2016, the Board was regularly engaged on the issue; however, management reports did not accurately convey the scope of the problem. The Board only learned that approximately 5,300 employees had been terminated for sales practices violations through the September 2016 settlements with the Los Angeles City Attorney, the OCC and the CFPB.

Reform and Accountability

The Board has taken numerous actions and supported management steps to address these issues. Wells Fargo has replaced and reorganized the leadership of the Community Bank. It has also eliminated sales goals and reformed incentive compensation. Centralization of control functions is being accelerated. The Board has separated the role of the Chairman and the CEO, strengthened the charters of Board Committees and established regular reporting to the Board by the new Office of Ethics, Oversight and Integrity. As a result of the investigation, the Board has terminated for cause five senior executives of the Community Bank and has imposed forfeitures, clawbacks and compensation adjustments on senior leaders totaling more than $180 million.

. . . .

I.

Investigative Process

On September 25, 2016, the Independent Directors created the Committee, which consists of four Independent Directors, Stephen W. Sanger (current

Chairman of the Board and the Committee), Elizabeth A. Duke (Vice Chair of the Board), Donald M. James and Enrique Hernandez, Jr. The Independent Directors authorized the Committee to take all actions it deemed appropriate and necessary to examine the issues relating to improper sales practices, and to make findings and recommendations to the Independent Directors; the Independent Directors retained Shearman & Sterling LLP ("Shearman & Sterling"), which had been determined to be independent of Wells Fargo, to assist the Committee in conducting the investigation. . . .

. . . .

Shearman & Sterling also retained the services of FTI Consulting, Inc. ("FTI Consulting"), a forensic consulting and data analytics firm, which had direct and unrestricted access to relevant Wells Fargo account, investigations and human resources systems and databases.

II.

Executive Summary

When the Independent Directors of the Board authorized this investigation, the purpose was to examine the root causes of sales practice abuses and to assess how issues of corporate structure and culture as well as individual actions contributed to the injuries inflicted upon Wells Fargo's customers and the extraordinary damage to Wells Fargo's brand and reputation, not merely to determine compensation or disciplinary action. The Board did so in the spirit of lessons to be learned, to promote accountability, to strengthen the organization and to minimize the likelihood of future occurrences. This section of the Report summarizes the factual findings of the investigation, which are developed in greater detail in the subsequent sections. It also sets forth some of the key steps and corrective actions that have been and are being undertaken to address sales practice issues and the findings of this Report.

The Community Bank

Wells Fargo, with its successful Community Bank, had a long history of strong performance as a self-identified sales organization with a decentralized corporate structure guided by its Vision & Values statement. While there is nothing necessarily pernicious about sales goals, a sales-oriented culture or a decentralized corporate structure, these same cultural and structural characteristics unfortunately coalesced and failed dramatically here. There was a growing conflict over time in the Community Bank between Wells Fargo's Vision & Values and the Community Bank's emphasis on sales goals. Aided by a culture of strong deference to management of the lines of business (embodied in the oft-repeated "run it like you own it" mantra), the Community Bank's senior leaders distorted the sales model and performance management system, fostering an atmosphere that prompted low quality sales and improper and unethical behavior.

Senior management in the Community Bank had a deep-seated adherence to its sales model. The model generally called for significant annual growth in the number of products, such as checking accounts, savings accounts and credit cards, sold each year. Even when challenged by their regional leaders, the senior leadership of the Community Bank failed to appreciate or accept that their sales goals were too high and becoming increasingly untenable.

Over time, even as senior regional leaders challenged and criticized the increasingly unrealistic sales goals—arguing that they generated sales of products that customers neither needed nor used—the Community Bank's senior management tolerated low quality accounts as a necessary by-product of a sales-driven organization. In particular, the Community Bank's senior leaders were concerned that tightening up too much on quality would risk lowering sales of products that customers actively used; and, more generally, the senior leaders were reluctant to take steps that they believed might have a negative impact on the Community Bank's financial performance. They also failed to adequately consider that low quality accounts could be indicative of unauthorized accounts. It was convenient instead to blame the problem of low quality and unauthorized accounts and other employee misconduct on individual wrongdoers and poor management in the field rather than on the Community Bank's sales model.

To assist the investigation, Shearman & Sterling retained FTI Consulting. The firm analyzed various metrics to assist in determining the impact of the Community Bank's sales culture. First, it examined Wells Fargo's investigations data for allegations of sales integrity violations and associated terminations and resignations. And second, it analyzed information relating to the rate at which the Community Bank's customers were funding—that is, making initial deposits into—new checking and savings accounts. While there can be many reasons a customer might not fund an account, lower funding rates (the proportion of new accounts with more than de minimis deposits) suggest that some customers were sold accounts that they may not have wanted or needed.

Trends in the data show, perhaps not surprisingly, that as sales goals became harder to achieve, the number of allegations and terminations increased and the quality of accounts declined. Thus, the number of sales integrity-related allegations and associated terminations and resignations increased relatively steadily from the second quarter of 2007 and both peaked in the fourth quarter of 2013, when a newspaper article brought to light improper sales practices in Los Angeles. After the Community Bank and the corporate control functions started to focus more resources and attention on the problem and the growth of sales goals moderated somewhat starting in 2013, the number of sales integrity-related allegations and associated terminations and resignations steadily fell.

This was mirrored by the funding rate. It dropped steadily, from approximately 90% in 2005 to below 80% in 2012; it then rose somewhat in 2013, continued climbing thereafter, and exceeded 95% by 2016, paralleling Wells Fargo's increasing focus on sales practices after 2013.

As reflected in the reduction in plan sales goals for 2013, while the Community Bank did take steps over time to address issues associated with sales practice violations and aggressive sales goals, those steps were incremental, implemented slowly and insufficient to address the root cause of the problem. There was a disinclination among the Community Bank's senior leadership, regardless of the scope of improper behavior or the number of terminated employees, to see the problem as systemic. It was common to blame employees who violated Wells Fargo's rules without analyzing what caused or motivated them to do so. Effect was confused with cause. When Wells Fargo did identify misconduct, its solution generally was to terminate the offending employee without considering causes for the offending conduct or determining whether there were responsible individuals who, while they might not have directed the specific misconduct, contributed to the environment that increased the chances of its occurrence. Carrie Tolstedt, head of the Community Bank, and certain of her senior leaders paid insufficient regard to the substantial risk to Wells Fargo's brand and reputation from improper and unethical sales practices even as they failed to recognize the potential for financial or other harm to customers.

In addition, keeping the sales model intact and sales growing meant that the Community Bank's performance management system had to exert significant, and in some cases extreme, pressure on employees to meet or exceed their goals. Many employees felt that failing to meet sales goals could (and sometimes did) result in termination or career-hindering criticism by their supervisors. Employees who engaged in misconduct most frequently associated their behavior with sales pressure, rather than compensation incentives, although the latter contributed to problematic behavior by over-weighting sales as against customer service or other factors. Conversely, employees saw that the individuals most likely to be praised, rewarded and held out as models for success were high sales performers.

This was especially true in areas where bad practices tended to disproportionately cluster, like Los Angeles and Arizona. Senior bankers there were particularly associated with extreme pressure, in some cases calling their subordinates several times a day to check in on sales performance and chastising those who failed to meet sales objectives. Certain managers also explicitly encouraged their subordinates to sell unnecessary products to their customers in an effort to meet the Community Bank's sales goals.

The Community Bank identified itself as a sales organization, like department or retail stores, rather than a service-oriented financial institution. This provided justification for a relentless focus on sales, abbreviated training and high employee turnover. Wells Fargo's decentralized organizational structure and the deference paid to the lines of business contributed to the persistence of this environment. Tolstedt and certain of her inner circle were insular and defensive and did not like to be challenged or hear negative information. Even senior leaders within the Community Bank were frequently afraid of or discouraged from airing contrary views. Tolstedt effectively challenged and resisted scrutiny both from within and outside the Community Bank. She and her group risk officer not only failed to escalate issues outside the Community Bank, but also worked to impede such escalation, including by keeping from the Board information regarding the number of employees terminated for sales practice violations. Although they likely did so to give themselves freedom to address these issues on their own terms, rather than to encourage improper behavior,[1] the dire consequences and cost to Wells Fargo are the same.

As this investigation confirmed, the only way definitively to address the broken sales model and the root cause of sales practice abuses was to emphasize other metrics for performance and to abandon exerting pressure through sales goals and sales-driven incentive programs. With the concurrence of the Board, Wells Fargo announced on September 13, 2016, that the Community Bank would eliminate product sales goals in the retail bank. To address misaligned compensation incentives, in January 2017 Wells Fargo put in place a new incentive program that focused on customer service rather than selling products.

Also, growing out of this investigation, on February 21, 2017, the Board announced the termination for cause of four officers within the Community Bank: its Group Risk Officer, its Head of Strategic Planning and Finance, who was primarily responsible for overseeing the sales goals and incentive system, and two senior regional banking leaders who had headed Los Angeles and Arizona and

1 Tolstedt provided no explanation since she declined, on advice of counsel, to be interviewed as part of this investigation.

who encouraged and deployed especially improper and excessive sales practices. In doing so, the Board accorded credit to and treated differently other senior Community Bank leaders who made reasonable, good faith efforts to challenge and escalate concerns over sales goals and conduct.

Previously, on September 25, 2016, the Board caused to be forfeited $19 million of Carrie Tolstedt's unvested equity awards and determined that she should not receive a bonus or severance. On April 7, 2017, following consideration by the Human Resources Committee and by the Independent Directors, it was determined that the finding made by the Board on September 25, 2016, that cause existed for terminating Tolstedt's employment was appropriate, with resulting forfeiture of her outstanding stock options awards with a current intrinsic value of approximately $47.3 million.

Senior Management

John Stumpf

On September 29, 2016, in testimony before the House Financial Services Committee, John Stumpf stated that he is "fully accountable for all unethical sales practices in our retail banking business" and acknowledged his failure for "not doing more sooner to address the causes of this unacceptable activity." While responsibility most surely does not lie with John Stumpf alone, he rightfully acknowledged that he made significant mistakes and helped create the culture that resulted in sales practice abuses.

After decades of success, Stumpf was Wells Fargo's principal proponent and champion of the decentralized business model and of cross-sell and the sales culture. His commitment to them colored his response when sales practice issues became more prominent in 2013 and subsequent years and led him to stand back and rely on the Community Bank to fix the problem, even in the face of growing indications that the situation was worsening and threatened substantial reputational harm to Wells Fargo. Because it was the responsibility of Community Bank leadership to run the business "like they owned it," Stumpf did not engage in investigation and critical analysis to fully understand the problem. And, as discussed below, the corporate control functions that reported to him and upon which he relied were similarly constrained by Wells Fargo's decentralized model.

Stumpf's commitment to the sales culture also led him to minimize problems with it, even when plausibly brought to his attention. Stumpf was by nature an optimistic executive who refused to believe that the sales model was seriously impaired. His reaction invariably was that a few bad employees were causing issues, but that the overwhelming majority of employees were behaving properly.

He was too late and too slow to call for inspection of or critical challenge to the basic business model.

Stumpf's long-standing working relationship with Tolstedt influenced his judgment as well. Tolstedt reported to Stumpf until late 2015 and he admired her as a banker and for the contributions she made to the Community Bank over many years. At the same time, he was aware that many doubted that she remained the right person to lead the Community Bank in the face of sales practice revelations, including the Board's lead independent director and the head of its Risk Committee. Stumpf nonetheless moved too slowly to address the management issue.

On September 25, 2016, in recognition of his accountability for unacceptable retail banking sales practices, John Stumpf agreed with the Board to forfeit all of his unvested equity awards in the approximate amount of $41 million and to receive no annual bonus for 2016. He resigned as CEO and Chairman on October 12, 2016. On April 7, 2017, the Board additionally determined that Wells Fargo will claw back approximately $28 million of Stumpf's incentive compensation paid in March 2016 under an equity grant made in 2013.

Tim Sloan

Sloan served as Chief Financial Officer from 2011 to 2014 and then as head of the Wholesale Bank until he was promoted to President and Chief Operating Officer in November 2015. In the latter position, he became Tolstedt's immediate supervisor and assessed her performance over several months before deciding that she should not continue to lead the Community Bank.

In his two earlier positions, Sloan had little contact with sales practice matters. He heard complaints about Tolstedt, including that she was a controlling manager who was not open to criticism and did not work well with other parts of the organization. But by virtue of his positions and responsibilities prior to becoming President and COO, his direct involvement with sales practice issues was limited.[2]

Corporate Control Organizations

Sections of the Report below describe how Wells Fargo control functions, specifically Corporate Risk, the Law Department, Human Resources, Internal Investigations and Audit, dealt with sales practice issues in the Community Bank. Several common themes—again, substantially related to Wells Fargo's culture and

---

2 Sloan's 2016 bonus and 2014 performance share payouts were reduced as part of the senior leadership collective accountability actions . . . .

structure—hampered the ability of these organizations to effectively analyze, size and escalate sales practice issues.

First, Wells Fargo's decentralized organizational structure meant that centralized functions had parallel units in the Community Bank, which impeded corporate-level insight into and influence over the Community Bank. Historically, the risk function at Wells Fargo was highly decentralized. The line of business risk managers were answerable principally to the heads of their businesses and yet took the lead in assessing and addressing risk within their business units. The Risk Committee of the Board, consisting of the chairs of all the Board's standing committees, was created in 2011 to oversee risk across the enterprise. This involved a multi-year plan starting in 2013 to substantially grow Corporate Risk, to move toward centralization of more risk functions and to enhance Corporate Risk's ability to oversee the management of risk in the lines of business. Consistent with this plan, the Board supported major funding increases for Corporate Risk for 2014–2016. But, as problems with sales practices in the Community Bank became more apparent in 2013–2015, Corporate Risk was still a work in progress and the Chief Risk Officer had limited authority with respect to the Community Bank. As events were unfolding, his visibility into risk issues at the Community Bank was hampered by his dependence on its group risk officer and he was essentially confined to attempting to cajole and persuade Tolstedt and the Community Bank to be more responsive to sales practice-related risks.

Similarly, the decentralized structure of Human Resources contributed to a lack of visibility into the scope and nature of sales practice problems. . . . [T]here was no coordinated effort by HR, either within the Community Bank or in Corporate HR, to track, analyze or report on sales practice issues.

The fragmentation and decentralization of control functions needs to be and is being addressed. In 2016, Corporate Risk realigned 4,100 risk employees from the business units to the central risk organization, with an additional 1,100 to be realigned in 2017. Similarly, in 2016, Wells Fargo realigned and centralized various HR groups, including compensation and employee relations, so that they now report to Corporate HR rather than to the lines of business. As a result, the head of HR in the Community Bank now reports to Corporate HR rather than to the head of the Community Bank.

Second, and relatedly, the culture of substantial deference accorded to the lines of business carried over into the control functions. Even when senior executives came to recognize that sales practice issues within the Community Bank were a serious problem or were not being addressed timely and sufficiently, they relied on Tolstedt and her senior managers to carry out corrective actions. This culture of deference was particularly powerful in this instance since Tolstedt was respected for her historical success at the Community Bank, was perceived to have strong support from the CEO and was notoriously resistant to outside intervention and oversight.

Third, certain of the control functions often adopted a narrow "transactional" approach to issues as they arose. They focused on the specific employee complaint or individual lawsuit that was before them, missing opportunities to put them together in a way that might have revealed sales practice problems to be more significant and systemic than was appreciated. As an example, while HR had a great deal of information recorded in its systems, it had not developed the means to consolidate information on sales practice issues and to report on them.

Similarly, attorneys in the Law Department's Employment Section had visibility into the scope and causes of sales practice misconduct and in fact made commendable attempts to address it through, among other things, work on various committees. However, the Law Department, particularly at its senior levels, did not discuss or appreciate the seriousness and scale of sales practice issues within the Community Bank or fully consider whether there might be a pattern of illegal conduct involved. Rather, the Department's focus was on advising on discrete legal problems as they arose and on managing Wells Fargo's exposure to specific litigation risks.

The same holds true for Audit. Audit reviewed relevant controls and processes and largely found them to be effective; however, while it had access to information regarding sales practice concerns, it did not view its role to include analyzing more broadly the root cause of improper conduct.

Finally, until as late as 2015, even as sales practices were labeled a "high risk" in materials provided to the Risk Committee of the Board, there was a general perception within Wells Fargo's control functions that sales practice abuses were a problem of relatively modest significance, the equivalent of a tolerable number of minor infractions or victimless crimes. This underreaction to sales practice issues resulted in part from the incorrect belief, extending well into 2015, that improper practices did not cause any "customer harm"; and "customer harm" itself was narrowly construed to mean only financial harm such as fees and penalties. This flawed perspective made it easy to undervalue the risk to Wells Fargo's brand and reputation arising from the misuse of customer information and the breaches of trust occasioned by improper sales practices.

On February 28, 2017, the Board reduced compensation for eight current members of Wells Fargo's Operating Committee, including the heads of Corporate Risk, the Law Department, Human Resources and Audit, based on senior leadership's collective accountability for operational and reputational risk. Annual 2016 bonuses for these individuals were eliminated and the 2014 Performance Share Award payout was reduced by up to 50%, for an aggregate reduction in compensation for these individuals of approximately $32 million. No further adjustments to the compensation of Operating Committee members are contemplated based on the findings of this investigation.

The Board of Directors

In February 2014, following publication of newspaper articles critical of Wells Fargo's practices in Los Angeles, and continuously thereafter, management identified sales practices as a "noteworthy risk" to the Board and Risk Committee. Before that time, sales practice issues had not been identified to the Board as a noteworthy risk. The directors in 2014 received reports from the Community Bank, from Corporate Risk and from Corporate Human Resources that sales practice issues were receiving scrutiny and attention and, by early 2015, that the risks associated with them had decreased. At the same time, as referenced above, the Risk Committee and the Chief Risk Officer were continuing the program that had begun in 2013 to centralize and increase the resources of Corporate Risk.

In May 2015, the Los Angeles City Attorney filed a lawsuit alleging widespread improper sales practices at Wells Fargo branches in Los Angeles. Regulatory scrutiny intensified as well. From May 2015 until settlements were announced in September 2016, the Board's and Risk Committee's meetings addressed sales practice issues, resolving the Los Angeles litigation, responding to regulatory concerns and remediating customer harm. The Board and Risk Committee authorized the retention of third-party consultants to investigate sales practices and procedures in the Community Bank and to conduct an analysis of customer harm and remediation.

While management appropriately identified sales practice issues to the Board and Risk Committee by way of the written noteworthy risk reports, the written and oral presentations made to the Risk Committee in May 2015 and to the full Board in October 2015 were inadequate. Board members believe that they were misinformed by the presentation made to the Risk Committee in May 2015—which disclosed that 230 employees had been terminated in the Community Bank but did not provide aggregate Community Bank-wide termination figures that the Risk Committee had expressly requested and which were far higher. A subsequent report to the entire Board by Tolstedt in October 2015 was widely viewed by directors as having minimized and understated problems at the Community Bank.

. . . .

On September 8, 2016, through settlements with the Consumer Financial Protection Bureau (the "CFPB"), the Office of the Comptroller of the Currency ("OCC") and the Los Angeles City Attorney, the Board learned for the first time that approximately 5,300 Wells Fargo employees had been terminated for sales practice violations between January 1, 2011, and March 7, 2016. Discontinuation of sales goals and commencement of this investigation followed shortly thereafter.

The Committee believes that the Board's own actions could have been improved in three respects. First, even though the Risk Committee and Board initiated a comprehensive program in 2013, noted above, to increase the resources and enhance the effectiveness of Corporate Risk, Wells Fargo should have moved toward the centralization of the risk function earlier than it did. While the advisability of centralization was subject to considerable disagreement within Wells Fargo, events show that a strong centralized risk function is most suited to the effective management of risk.

Second, starting in February 2014 and continuing thereafter, the Board and Risk Committee received from management assurances that Corporate Risk, HR and the Community Bank were undertaking enhanced monitoring and otherwise were addressing sales practice abuses, which were said to be subsiding. Management's reports, however, generally lacked detail and were not accompanied by concrete action plans and metrics to track plan performance. The Risk Committee and Board should have insisted on more detailed and concrete plans, a practice initiated this year.

Third, in light of the Board's substantial doubts about and dissatisfaction with Tolstedt's leadership by the time of the October 2015 Board meeting, the Board should have been more forceful in pushing Stumpf to change leadership so that the Community Bank could move forward more quickly.

Finally, without waiting for completion of this investigation, the Board made several changes to its own corporate governance. In early 2017, Wells Fargo combined Global Ethics and Integrity, Internal Investigations and sales practices and complaint oversight into a new Office of Ethics, Oversight, and Integrity, and the Risk Committee's responsibilities have been expanded to include oversight of that office. In addition, the Office of Ethics, Oversight, and Integrity will report on its activities to the full Board at least twice a year. The Human Resources Committee's charter was modified to expand oversight of the incentive compensation risk management program, with support from Corporate HR, and to increase its oversight of terminations, culture and EthicsLine implementation. The Corporate Responsibility Committee's charter was also amended to require that the committee receive enhanced reporting from management on customer complaints and allegations from other sources, such as the EthicsLine, relating to customers. And the A&E Committee's oversight responsibilities for legal and regulatory compliance were broadened to include the company's compliance culture. These steps should help to clarify Board oversight of conduct risk, provide for greater centralization of review and oversight and augment reporting to the Board of the type of issues that contributed to the breakdown in Wells Fargo's sales culture.

III.

Key Factual Findings

The Community Bank

A. Introduction

Wells Fargo operated on a decentralized model inherited from Norwest. Since at least the time of the 1998 merger between the two banks, a commonplace phrase within the company was "run it like you own it." This guiding principle encapsulated the freedom Wells Fargo's lines of business traditionally had not only to determine their own business activities, but also to independently exercise staff and control functions, such as Risk and Human Resources.

Carrie Tolstedt, who was promoted to be the head of regional banking in the Community Bank in 2002 and the head of the Community Bank in 2007, was one of those leaders. And while Wells Fargo's decentralized model naturally afforded Tolstedt significant independence in that position, her record of success and strong financial performance enabled Tolstedt to maintain and enhance her authority.

B. The Community Bank's Aggressive Sales Culture

The Community Bank's sales model emphasized sales volume and relied heavily on consistent year-over-year sales growth. While the level of input into each year's goals by regional banking leaders—those responsible for particular retail banking regions—rose and fell over time, sales goals were ultimately the responsibility of Community Bank leadership, in particular Carrie Tolstedt and Matthew Raphaelson, the Community Bank's head of Strategic Planning and Finance. In many instances, Community Bank leadership recognized that their plans were unattainable—they were commonly referred to as 50/50 plans, meaning that there was an expectation that only half the regions would be able to meet them.

Once set, the sales goals were pushed down to the regions, and ultimately to Wells Fargo retail bank branches, and at each level in the hierarchy, employees were measured on how they performed relative to these goals. They were ranked against one another on their performance relative to goals, and their incentive compensation and promotional opportunities were determined relative to those goals. That system created intense pressure to perform and, in certain areas, local or regional managers imposed excessive pressure on their subordinates.

1. Regional Bank-Wide Rankings and Campaigns

a. Motivator Reports

Regional bank-wide sales-reporting processes included frequent rankings against individual, branch and regional sales goals, and against one another. Witnesses frequently cited daily and monthly "Motivator" reports as a source of pressure. These reports contained monthly, quarterly and year-to-date sales goals, and highlighted sales rankings down to the retail bank district level. Circulation of the reports—and their focus on sales-based rankings—ramped up pressure on managers, such that some "lived and died by" the Motivator results. Witnesses also described that in some areas there was an extremely competitive environment, driven in significant part by regular rankings. These reports were ultimately discontinued in 2014 after the Community Bank hosted "Leadership Summits" in which regional leaders recommended changing or eliminating Motivators due to the culture of shaming and sales pressure they perpetuated.

b. Retail Scorecards

Similarly, retail scorecards generated significant sales pressure within the Community Bank. The scorecards, instituted by Tolstedt when she took over the Community Bank, measured how an employee or manager was performing compared to the sales plan. Scorecards were segmented by business drivers and updated on a daily basis, and employees and managers could check their progress against the sales plan at any time and were actively encouraged to do so. Certain managers made meeting scorecard requirements their sole objective, a tactic referred to as "managing to the scorecard." As a result, employees reporting to these managers were consistently pressured to meet scorecard goals.

c. Sales Campaigns (Including Jump into January)

Regional bank-wide sales campaigns—most significantly, the Jump into January campaign—were also closely associated with increasing misconduct over time. Jump into January, created in 2003, aimed to motivate employees to "start the New Year strong by achieving and exceeding January goals." The Community Bank imposed higher daily sales targets on bankers in the month of January and emphasized and rewarded higher sales activity levels. While many witnesses suggested that the initial impetus for the campaign was appropriate, witnesses almost universally agreed that the campaign was distorted over time and became a breeding ground for bad behavior that helped cement the sales culture's negative characteristics. Witnesses recalled that bankers were encouraged to make prospect lists of friends and family members who were potential Jump into January sales targets, and often would "sandbag" (temporarily withhold) December account openings until January in order to meet sales targets and incentives. The pressure associated with the campaign manifested itself in higher rates of low quality accounts, as confirmed by the "Rolling Funding Rate," a quality metric used by the Community Bank to track the rate at which its customers "fund" (place more than a de minimis amount into) new checking or savings accounts.[3] FTI Consulting's analysis of the Rolling Funding Rate showed that the Community Bank rate of funding for January was lower than the average Community Bank monthly Rolling Funding Rate in all years starting in 2008. The January campaign also resulted in increased employee turnover and, in some areas, no paid-time-off or training during the month.

As the Jump into January program continued, many senior regional leaders expressed concerns over the high sales pressure it fostered and referenced the prevalence of lower quality accounts opened in January. But, according to one witness, the Community Bank was hesitant to end the program because Tolstedt was "scared to death" that it could hurt sales figures for the entire year. In 2013, Jump into January was replaced with Accelerate, a sales campaign that ran from January to March. The Accelerate campaign placed more emphasis on banker-customer interactions and the customer experience, but some witnesses described Accelerate as feeling like a mere "name change" from the Jump into January campaign.

2. Regional Management Practices

The negative consequences of these regional bank-wide processes were exacerbated by management in certain regions who over-emphasized the use of sales rankings and campaigns and employed other aggressive practices. California and Arizona in particular consistently ranked among the top states for sales

---

3 While many reasons may explain why a customer chooses not to fund a new account, the Rolling Funding Rate was useful in measuring the rate at which the Community Bank was making "quality" sales to its customers.

practice problems, in part based on sales pressure tactics encouraged by certain regional managers.

. . . .

c. Simulated Funding

Wells Fargo's sales practice issues first came to public attention through articles in the LOS ANGELES TIMES that spotlighted troubling practices engaged in by some employees in Los Angeles. Those practices included simulated funding, where an employee transferred funds from one customer account to another, sometimes unauthorized, account (or deposited and withdrew the employee's own funds) to make it appear that the second account had been "funded" by the customer. Employees did this because the number of accounts they opened and the rate at which those accounts were funded were important to achieve sales goals and incentive compensation targets.

In 2015, Wells Fargo retained PricewaterhouseCoopers ("PwC") to identify, among other things, checking and savings accounts across the Wells Fargo retail bank potentially subject to simulated funding;[4] PwC's analysis included accounts opened in May 2011 through July 2015.

. . . .

C. Performance Management and Incentive Plans Added Significant Additional Risk to the Sales Model

1. Performance Management

How employees were hired, promoted and incentivized added significant additional risk to the Community Bank's sales model. Community Bank leadership regularly likened the retail bank to non-bank retailers, a view that created a tolerance for high employee turnover. Community Bank-wide rolling 12-month average turnover reached at least 30% in every period from January 2011 to December 2015, and as high as 41% for the 12-month period ending in October 2012.[5] Some Community Bank leaders did not view reducing turnover as a priority because they saw high turnover as a normal aspect of a retail business. Tolstedt's view, as described by one witness, was that there were always people willing to work in Wells Fargo branches.

As a result of the retail focus, many Wells Fargo branch employees were relatively inexperienced, and many witnesses stated that together with the high-

---

[4] [footnotes have been renumbered; some have been omitted]

[5] [footnote omitted]

pressure environment this contributed to employees not doing things "the right way." In addition, witnesses said that inexperienced bankers frequently were promoted based on sales success and became inexperienced managers who understood that success was measured by sales performance. More generally, witnesses consistently stated that promotions at all levels in the Community Bank were regularly—though not exclusively or in every region—based on sales performance. To many employees, the route to success was selling more than your peers. Conversely, witnesses said that many employees feared being penalized by their managers for failing to meet sales goals; while the investigation did not establish the numbers, witnesses stated that employees were at times transferred to different roles or terminated for failing to meet sales goals.

2. Incentive Compensation

Compensation plans for branch bankers were structured such that bankers had to meet certain threshold requirements to be eligible for incentive compensation. The thresholds varied by employee position and changed over time. Typically there were minimum requirements for products sold per day, daily profit, packages sold per quarter, quarterly partner referrals and/or the number of loans made per quarter. Once employees satisfied the minimum thresholds, they could earn compensation based on "opportunities," which included rewards based on the number of products sold per day, daily profit and 11 Ways to WOW! (a customer experience metric), among other categories. There were various tiers of incentive compensation within each opportunity, including bronze, silver, gold and, for certain years, platinum; each tier included a goal bankers could meet and a corresponding financial reward. The goals graduated for each performance tier, and, as the goals went up, the payout rose. . . .

After 2010, Wells Fargo also aligned performance management and recognition with sales goals, so that incentive compensation and performance rating were both associated with sales. This effectively meant that bankers, branch managers and district managers who did not meet sales goals not only could miss out on opportunities to earn incentive compensation, but were also at risk of poor performance reviews. However, two witnesses stated that in around 2013 or 2014, Community Bank HR instructed that people should not be terminated for failure to meet sales goals, and Wells Fargo transitioned into a qualitative rating system. According to one of the witnesses, this transition was made in part because of concern that connecting sales goals to performance rating was driving unethical behavior.

Incentive compensation for all regional bankers above the branch-banker level likewise included a sales component. For district managers, sales were weighted at a third of total incentive compensation requirements (other factors included a "profit proxy" and customer experience). Beginning in 2010, sales quality became an additional component (in 2010, for instance, district managers were required to achieve a Rolling Funding Rate of 85%, or risk having their incentive compensation reduced). Sales achievement was similarly a component of incentive compensation requirements for more senior managers (for example, region presidents). For these positions, sales were generally weighted at between 20 and 25% of total incentive compensation requirements.

Many witnesses believed that incentive compensation plans overly emphasized sales performance, and many complained to Community Bank leadership that incentive plan goals were too high, too focused on sales and led to bad behavior. Because good performance was deemed in large part to mean meeting or exceeding sales goals, and poor performance in many instances led to shaming or worse, many employees believed that their future at Wells Fargo depended on how many products they sold. . . .

Ironically, in a 2004 email to Stumpf, Tolstedt acknowledged the importance of setting compensation plans such that they incentivize appropriate behaviors. Specifically, she noted: "I think you have to balance cross sell with the right incentive plan and other measures so that you ensure you have quality cross sell. Many banks . . . build products that encourage the wrong sales behavior. They encourage their sales force to sell a second account free, multiple savings accounts free, etc. Then if you incent a team of bankers on top of that around sales per day alone you are asking for trouble." Tolstedt acknowledged the need to balance cross-sell, household penetration and household profitability measures, and to have a balanced incentive plan based on units and profit. "If you look at one metric alone and don't build an integrated model, you are asking for low value, unfunded bad cross sell that will not add up to revenue growth or retention." As described herein, Tolstedt did not follow her own advice.

D. Discovery of and Growth in Sales Practice Violations

1. Overview

In 2002, the Community Bank took steps to address an increase in sales practice violations, including the creation of a sales integrity task force. The task force undertook various initiatives, including the implementation of a sales integrity training program and certification, the modification of incentive plans to reduce the promotion of undesirable behaviors and utilization of audit programs to identify suspicious activity. The Community Bank also began to track funding rates to measure the quality of sales.

In 2004, a member of Wells Fargo's Internal Investigations group drafted a memorandum addressing sales practice issues. As described in more detail at pages 89–90 below, the memorandum noted an increase in annual sales gaming cases—defined as the manipulation and/or misrepresentation of sales to receive compensation or meet sales goals—from 63 in 2000 to a projected 680 in 2004. The memorandum noted a similar increase in terminations, from 21 in 2000 to a projected 223 in 2004.

Despite the recognition by 2004 of both the increasing scope of sales practice issues and their association with sales incentives, the problem continued to grow. While some good-faith efforts were made to address the issue, witnesses consistently stated that the Community Bank's leadership was unwilling to make fundamental changes—as one witness put it, there was "no appetite to change the model"—and felt that the associated risks could be managed appropriately by increasing training, detecting wrongdoing and punishing wrongdoers.

Both within and outside the Community Bank, there was insufficient appreciation of the impact of, or harm caused by, sales practice misconduct, due in part to the failure to frame the issue appropriately. First, insufficient regard was paid to the effect of the violations on customers. When individuals were terminated for sales practice violations, absent clear theft or specific customer complaints, the potential effect on customers was not regularly assessed. Even when Wells Fargo investigated or terminated employees following publication of the LOS ANGELES TIMES articles in 2013, there was no adequate investigation to identify and address injuries that customers might have suffered. While this may have been due to an incorrect understanding of how the bank's system in certain instances collected fees charged to an unauthorized account from a linked authorized account, more should have been done sooner to determine customer harm. It was not until the Los Angeles City Attorney suit in May 2015 that it was even recognized that customer harm—in the form of fees—was possible with simulated funding. Second, and perhaps more importantly, the Community Bank did not consider non-financial harm to customers resulting from the misuse of personal information or the opening of accounts in their names without their authorization. Third, the Community Bank did not adequately consider the significant reputational risk associated with sales practice misconduct.

The failure to frame the issue properly extended to senior management's view that firing 1% of the Community Bank workforce every year for sales integrity violations was acceptable. . . .

2. ICE Data

FTI Consulting examined data extracted from Wells Fargo's Investigations Controlled Electronically ("ICE") database to determine how the volume of allegations and terminations associated with sales practice misconduct trended over time. The volume of reported allegations[6] of employee involvement in sales practice-related misconduct[7] steadily increased from 288 in the second quarter of 2007 to 1,469 in the fourth quarter of 2013 (because of significant changes in employee populations over this period, FTI Consulting also analyzed the trend on a "per-employee" basis; it nearly tripled over this same period). Reported allegations then decreased to 958 in the first quarter of 2016. FTI Consulting also looked at the subset of these allegations likely to have affected customers by backing out allegations unlikely to have had customer impact.[8] The volume of allegations rose from a low of 336 in the first quarter of 2008 to a high of 1,050 allegations in the fourth quarter of 2013 (on a "per employee" basis, the rate doubled over this same period). There were 730 such allegations in the first quarter of 2016.

FTI Consulting performed similar analyses with respect to terminations and resignations arising out of investigations triggered by the allegations referenced in the previous paragraph. The trends were the same as with allegations; in the second quarter of 2007 there were 61 terminations or resignations relating to sales practice misconduct, and the number rose to a high of 447 in the fourth quarter of 2013 (on a "per employee" basis, the rate quadrupled). The number of terminations or resignations declined to 162 in the first quarter of 2016. Focusing on those subtypes of sales practice misconduct most likely to be associated with conduct affecting customers, the trends remained the same; the volume of terminations and resignations rose from 106 in the first quarter of 2008 to a high of 339 in the fourth quarter of 2013 (on a "per employee" basis, an increase of 50%). The number then decreased to 122 in the first quarter of 2016.

. . . .

---

6 For purposes of its analysis, FTI Consulting considered each ICE record to be a unique allegation, termination or resignation. Allegations include referrals or reports of misconduct to be investigated and substantiated by Internal Investigations.

7 [footnote omitted].

8 [footnote omitted].

3. Review of Investigation Descriptions in Wells Fargo's ICE Database

Separate from FTI Consulting's quantitative analyses, Shearman & Sterling reviewed 1,341 of the individual ICE investigation records associated with employee terminations and resignations taking place from 2008 to 2016 to better understand what motivated employees to commit sales practice misconduct.

a. Types of Misconduct

Sales practice or sales integrity issues encompass an array of misconduct, ranging from behavior that affected only Wells Fargo (such as claiming an improper referral credit) to behavior that affected customers (such as opening unauthorized accounts and simulated funding). The misconduct represented in the ICE records reviewed by Shearman & Sterling included customer consent, generally employees opening unauthorized personal checking or savings accounts for existing customers;[9] falsification of bank records, generally falsifying customer identification or contact information or forging customer signatures; funding manipulation, generally employees funding an account held by a customer with their own money or money from another account held by that customer; and the creation of unnecessary accounts, generally employees opening accounts which served no customer financial need (a category added in 2015).[10]

Shearman & Sterling did not statistically sample the records, but focused on a cross-section related to investigations resulting in terminations or resignations and coded by Wells Fargo as associated with activity that likely affected customers. . . .

b. Rationales for Misconduct

A majority of terminated employees, whether branch bankers or managers, admitted to engaging in misconduct during the investigation. They frequently claimed that sales pressure drove them to do so. Branch-level managers often felt

---

9 Sales practice concerns also have been implicated with respect to the Community Bank's online insurance referral program, in which customers could purchase insurance directly from third-party carriers via a link on the Wells Fargo website and branch kiosks. . . .

10 "Off-site" applications, associated with initiatives in which Wells Fargo bankers would collect product applications at events or workplaces outside a Wells Fargo branch, featured prominently in records relating to both customer consent and record falsification. In the reviewed records, employees often processed these applications, which did not require the customer to complete paperwork or provide authorization at the branch, without first properly acquiring customer consent or relevant customer information, such as drivers' license details. For example, one branch banker cited explicit instructions from her branch manager to confirm customer consent only after opening accounts. "Friends and family" accounts were also frequently referenced in the reviewed investigation records; employees often described opening accounts for family and friends in order to meet sales goals. For example, a branch manager had a teenage daughter with 24 accounts, an adult daughter with 18 accounts, a husband with 21 accounts, a brother with 14 accounts and a father with 4 accounts.

pressure from their supervisors to make sales, but only rarely did they state that they were explicitly instructed to engage in misconduct. In addition to sales pressure, branch-level managers often cited the need to help branch employees meet individual goals or reach branch goals. For example, one branch manager investigated for creating unauthorized debit cards for existing customers stated that he often did so to help branch bankers reach their targets; but in the case under investigation, he ordered the cards because of difficulty keeping his branch staffed and his need to meet branch sales goals.

In nine of the 1,341 reviewed records, investigated employees accused district managers (one level above branch managers) of explicitly directing misconduct; for example, one district manager, according to the investigated employee, taught personal bankers to disguise unnecessary accounts for family members within the computerized system. In ten cases, the investigated employee referenced a district manager as creating pressure by sending multiple daily emails to branches. In one instance, a district manager warned an employee during onboarding that Wells Fargo provided a challenging and intense sales environment and that he should be prepared to "[d]o whatever it took to meet numbers unless it was downright unethical."

Employees below the branch manager level—lower level in-branch managers and non- managers—frequently cited branch managers as actively directing misconduct or offering inappropriate guidance to subordinates on what constituted acceptable conduct. Non-managers in particular attributed sales pressure to branch managers, and occasionally to district managers, who incessantly pushed employees to make sales. As one branch employee described, "everyone was aware of what was implied when the manager would state 'it's late in the day and we need a certain number of accounts by the end of the day.' "

Some employees who engaged in funding manipulation, including simulated funding, also cited sales quality thresholds necessary to receive sales credit as having prompted the misconduct. . . .

Of note, while sales pressure and sales goals frequently figured in the investigation descriptions, employees only infrequently referenced incentive compensation as a motivating factor in their misconduct. While that may have been to some degree self-serving, it is consistent with other evidence indicating that sales pressure and goals, rather than incentive compensation directly, were the primary motivators of improper practices.

c. How Misconduct Spread

The review of the investigation records shed light on the manner by which improper sales practices spread within branches or districts. Several investigated employees, particularly those who had received promotions, had worked in multiple branches at Wells Fargo. Inappropriate coaching techniques spread between branches as employees relocated; for example, one East Coast branch manager described learning to improperly bundle products (for example, presenting debit cards as "coming with" personal accounts) while working on the West Coast. Within branches, employees learned to manipulate customer information from former or fellow managers, resulting in a high number of violations in particular branches.

E. Community Bank Leadership Insisted on Maintaining the Sales Model Despite Growing Dissent from Regional Banking Leaders

The imposition of sales plans with significant annual growth and the regions' increasing difficulty in meeting those plans led senior Community Bank regional leadership to more actively push back against Community Bank leadership over time. Despite the concerns being expressed, senior Community Bank leaders paid insufficient attention to how increasingly unattainable goals resulted in low quality accounts and, worse, improper behavior. . . .

Regional leaders also emphasized in communications with senior Community Bank leaders that the baseline for sales goals included a large number of low quality accounts that were not fulfilling customer needs (multiple witnesses and email communications referred to these as "junk" accounts). The problem built on itself: attaining growth when the prior year's sales included a large number of low quality accounts meant that even more low quality accounts had to be opened to hit the increased target.

The Community Bank's senior leaders held a different perspective from their regional leadership colleagues. They did not recognize the regions' concerns about sales quality and sales integrity, did not sufficiently appreciate the relationship between low quality accounts and sales practice issues and generally viewed resistance from regional leaders as merely an attempt to negotiate for reduced goals. In particular, senior Community Bank leaders viewed the efforts to address goals by West Coast leadership as simply a cover-up for poor management; to them, sales quality and integrity issues had to be resolved through better management, not decreased goals. Community Bank leaders also tolerated low quality accounts—despite the fact that they cost the bank money—in part because they thought that placing too much emphasis on quality would result in the sale of fewer active accounts, which was an important driver of the sales model. . . .

Management characterized these low quality accounts, including products later canceled or never used and products that the customer did not want or need, as "slippage" and believed a certain amount of slippage was the cost of doing business in any retail environment. . . .

In the course of these discussions about "quality," "slippage" and "product/customer mismatch," senior Community Bank leadership never adequately came to terms with the fact that their sales model resulted in increasing and unacceptable levels of both low quality accounts and employee misconduct, and that some low quality accounts were likely opened without customer consent. Despite senior Community Bank leaders' reluctance to acknowledge the relationship between the goals and bad behavior, that relationship is clearly seen in the data. As sales goals became more difficult to achieve, the rate of misconduct rose, peaking in the fourth quarter of 2013 (see pages 33–34). At the same time, quality fell; the Rolling Funding Rate—the metric designed by the Community Bank to measure the quality of new accounts—steadily declined from approximately 90% in 2005 to below 80% in 2012.[11] Starting in 2013, it rose and exceeded 95% by 2016.[12]

F. Remedial Measures Taken by Community Bank to Address Sales Practice Issues

1. Measures Taken to Address Sales Practice Issues

Many witnesses acknowledged—as did John Stumpf in his Congressional testimony—that the Community Bank was far too slow in addressing sales practice issues. Indeed, the fundamental issue—the sales goal model itself—was

---

[11] As suggested by the Rolling Funding Rate, a significant number of Community Bank checking and savings accounts were never funded. PwC identified a population of unfunded accounts opened during the period May 2011 to July 2015. Based on FTI Consulting's examination of the transaction history of these accounts, this population included accounts that were (i) opened but had no transaction activity, or (ii) opened with no net positive customer-initiated transaction activity (in other words, reflected only bank-initiated activity like reversed transactions or bank fees). FTI Consulting examined those unfunded accounts to determine the extent to which customers paid fees or other charges. FTI Consulting found that no fees or charges were paid on the vast majority of these accounts. (In general, unfunded accounts were automatically closed within 60 to 90 days of opening. In addition, due to the structure of the accounts, in those instances where fees or other charges were charged to an account, they were not generally collected except in some instances where there was a linked account belonging to the customer for overdraft protection.) 1.7% of these unfunded accounts incurred fees or charges not reversed by the bank. FTI Consulting did not attempt to analyze any secondary impact relating to this population (i.e., overdraft fees on a customer account that became overdrawn in connection with covering fees on an unfunded account). FTI Consulting was unable to determine through the account data which, if any, of the unfunded accounts may have been opened without customer authorization.

[12] [footnote omitted]

not fully addressed until September 2016. Still, albeit incremental and implemented gradually, the Community Bank took steps over time to address some of the problems associated with its sales model. Community Bank HR initiated a sales quality project group in 2011–2012 resulting in some improvements in training and monitoring. A sales quality team, later known as Sales & Service Conduct Oversight Team ("SSCOT"), developed as a unit within the Community Bank responsible for monitoring and researching allegations of inappropriate sales practices. In 2012, the Quality of Sale Report Card ("QSRC"), administered by SSCOT, was introduced to measure key quality-of-sale indicators, including signature rates, activation rates, procedural issues (such as closures and duplicate products) and the Rolling Funding Rate. By the end of 2013, the QSRC was incorporated into incentive compensation plans for district managers, and the Rolling Funding Rate metric was incorporated into incentive compensation plans for line-level bankers.

As noted above, the Community Bank modestly reduced sales goals for 2013, although the goals were still not achievable. It also reduced average per-day product sales for branch banker incentive compensation eligibility. In 2013, the Community Bank also began work on an "Evolving Model" for products and service delivery, which was intended to address sales conduct as well as other business objectives.

2. Impact of the Los Angeles Times Articles on Remediation Efforts

According to many witnesses, the publication of the Los Angeles Times articles regarding the sales culture in Los Angeles acted as an accelerant to change. Goals for 2014 were reduced, as they had been in 2013, though they were still set at an unachievable level. The Community Bank also began to set sales goals not only for the regions but also for individual branches to avoid unreasonable allocation of goals, although this had the effect of further cutting senior regional leaders out of the sales planning process (multiple senior regional leaders stated that they did not feel as though they had sufficient input into their regional sales plans until 2015, for the 2016 plan year, and even then they noted pushback). Additionally, in early 2014, product packages (i.e., a checking account sold as a unit with other products) were eliminated to prevent products being bundled and sold without customer need. New employees in 2015 were given a separate and substantially lower set of sales goals for their first three to six months of employment.

The Community Bank also revised its incentive compensation plans for bankers and its performance management scheme. It modified performance management metrics to better balance quantitative factors with qualitative ones, such as good customer service. According to one witness, this was partially a result of HR's view that connecting sales goals to performance ratings was driving unethical behavior. Further, sales targets to achieve incentive compensation eligibility were reduced. The list of products included in incentive compensation gradually changed in 2014 and 2015, but it was not until 2016 that Tolstedt finally agreed to pilot a program for removing secondary checking accounts from incentive compensation plans. That program was not implemented before sales goals were eliminated in September 2016.

G. Community Bank Leadership Failed to Adequately Address Underlying Problems That Resulted in Extensive Sales Practice Violations

1. Carrie Tolstedt

Carrie Tolstedt was the head of the Community Bank's Central California region and then the head of California Community and Border Banking before becoming head of the entire regional bank in 2002 and of the Community Bank in 2007. She was credited with the Community Bank's strong financial results over the years, and was perceived as someone who ran a "tight ship" with everything "buttoned down." Community Bank employee engagement and customer satisfaction surveys reinforced the positive view of her leadership and management. Stumpf had enormous respect for Tolstedt's intellect, work ethic, acumen and discipline, and thought she was the "most brilliant" Community Banker he had ever met.

Nonetheless, Tolstedt mismanaged the Community Bank's response to the rise in sales practice issues, failing to appreciate both the negative impact on customers and the grave risk to Wells Fargo's brand and reputation. There is no evidence that Tolstedt showed serious concern about the effects of improper sales practices on Wells Fargo's customers or that she initiated efforts to evaluate or remediate customer harm.

Tolstedt resisted change to the Community Bank's sales model even when confronted with evidence that it led to low quality sales and improper sales practices. She viewed the sales model as an engine of the Community Bank's historical success and did not want to take steps that could impede its operation. Instead, she reinforced the high-pressure sales culture. . . . Despite the universal criticism of the "Jump into January" program as an incubator of low quality sales and bad sales practices, Tolstedt was "scared to death" that changing it could hurt sales figures for the entire year and opted instead for only incremental changes.

Numerous witnesses provided a consistent account of Tolstedt's management style: she was "obsessed" with control, especially of negative information about the Community Bank, and extremely reluctant to make changes. Tolstedt fostered an insular culture at the top of the Community Bank and had an "inner circle" of staff that supported her, reinforced her views and protected her. She resisted and rejected the near-unanimous view of senior regional bank leaders that the sales goals were unreasonable and led to negative outcomes and improper behavior. Under her direction, the Community Bank continued to increase its sales goals until 2013, and then lowered them only modestly.

Tolstedt reinforced a culture of tight control over information about the Community Bank, including sales practice issues. This hampered the ability of control functions outside the Community Bank and the Board to accurately assess the problem and work toward a solution. Numerous witnesses referred to, and documents confirmed, the difficulties in getting information from her senior leadership team. Tolstedt actively discouraged providing information to people outside the Community Bank. . . .

The Community Bank's reporting to the ERMC [Enterprise Risk Management Committee] and the Board demonstrated this tight control of information and lack of transparency. Tolstedt never voluntarily escalated sales practice issues, and, when called upon specifically to do so, she and the Community Bank provided reports that were generalized, incomplete and viewed by many as misleading. Senior leaders of the Community Bank came before the ERMC twice (in September 2012 and April 2014) to discuss sales pressure and sales practices; on both occasions their presentations did not provide a forthright description and assessment of the problem. Tolstedt was directly involved in preparing presentations on sales practices to the Board's Risk Committee and the entire Board.

Those presentations likewise did not present a forthright and complete depiction of sales practice issues and . . . her presentation to the Risk Committee in May 2015 was misleading. By 2015, many Board members believed that she was intentionally understating the problem which she had helped to create.

2. Matthew Raphaelson

Matthew Raphaelson was ultimately responsible for regional bank sales goals and supervising the sales incentive program, subject to Tolstedt's approval. He was described as Tolstedt's "right hand." Despite being a senior leader of the

Community Bank, Raphaelson did not view it as his job to police sales integrity violations.

Raphaelson was aware that excessive sales goals and pressures led to employee misconduct, and was often confronted with objections to his goals and numbers-driven system. Multiple witnesses stated that Raphaelson received repeated complaints that his sales goals were too high, were too focused on the number of products sold and led to bad behavior, such as the opening of unauthorized accounts and the sale of unnecessary products to customers. Raphaelson had received information demonstrating that certain locations were responsible for high numbers of unfunded accounts and accounts funded for only short periods of time—indicia of potential inappropriate behavior, including simulated funding.

Even when told that the goals he established were leading to bad behavior, Raphaelson was unwilling to adequately address sales goals or incentives to sell unnecessary products to customers because doing so might result in fewer sales of high quality accounts; he was willing to tolerate poor quality accounts rather than change the sales model. While Raphaelson authorized incremental changes over time, such as a modest reduction in goals in 2013, these changes were inadequate.

In his interview, Raphaelson disclaimed knowledge of high levels of sales integrity-related terminations, but . . . emails show that he was aware at least by November 2013 of approximately 1,000 sales integrity-related terminations per year and believed that to be a favorable number.[13]

3. Claudia Russ Anderson

Russ Anderson led the first line of defense for risk in the Community Bank, a particularly significant role in light of the decentralized nature of the risk function at Wells Fargo during her tenure as Group Risk Officer. She contributed to the development of improved systems and processes in the Community Bank's SSCOT unit to detect sales misconduct, and, particularly after the LOS ANGELES TIMES articles, participated in efforts by the Community Bank to communicate to managers that undue sales pressure and sales misconduct were not acceptable. In most other respects, however, Russ Anderson's performance fell far short of what was expected and required of the senior risk officer in the Community Bank. Russ Anderson failed to adequately assess and advocate for changes in the business

13 Raphaelson was terminated for cause in connection with the Committee's investigation on February 21, 2017.

practices that resulted in sales integrity violations. She also did not adequately address customer harm arising from improper sales practices.

Russ Anderson exhibited a lack of transparency and failed to escalate sales integrity issues and related terminations to Wells Fargo's Board of Directors and the ERMC. Multiple witnesses, including senior officers of Wells Fargo, reported that Russ Anderson was likewise not forthcoming or candid in her communications with them, a view supported by email communications. Instead, witnesses stated that Russ Anderson was "running interference" for Tolstedt and filtering communications with other Wells Fargo control officers.

Russ Anderson minimized and obscured issues in reporting on the Community Bank, including sales practices. From late 2011, Russ Anderson challenged language in the Corporate Security portions of the reports to the A&E Committee. In one email exchange in 2012, Michael Bacon, the head of Corporate Security (responsible for Internal Investigations), stated that Russ Anderson "often challenge[d] the Audit and CS A&E reporting verbiage," but that at that point, he had "gotten good with the credible challenge" in response. Bacon noted that "our data continues to highlight a concerning trend in the area of Sales Integrity—from the increase in EthicsLine reports, to the increase in executive complaint letters," and "increases in confirmed fraud, thus, we need to continue to escalate this issue with senior leadership." Russ Anderson told him that his reporting made the problem sound "so much worse than it is."

One witness called her an advocate, rather than independent and objective, when dealing with regulators on sales practice issues. When personnel in Corporate Risk expressed the view that a draft presentation to the ERMC by the Community Bank about sales practices did not provide information about the "current state," Russ Anderson wrote to another Community Bank leader, "I am worried about putting something like that into a deck. I'd rather we did that verbally because this deck is subject to the regulators [*sic*] review." . . . [S]he challenged Internal Investigations' data on the number of employee terminations related to sales integrity, with the result that the information was omitted from a report to the Risk Committee. Finally, Russ Anderson moved too slowly to address sales practice issues. The head of Corporate Security was frustrated with Russ Anderson when she took over SSCOT in 2011/2012, as he thought she would be more proactive in investigating sales integrity issues. Though she became more focused after the LOS ANGELES TIMES articles, her actions were oriented toward messaging and detection rather than reforming or addressing the sales model or underlying causes. To the extent she faced resistance from Tolstedt,

Russ Anderson should have escalated the issues to Loughlin, the Chief Risk Officer, with whom she had a dotted-line reporting relationship.[14]

H. Recent Remedial Changes

Wells Fargo has implemented a system to send an automated email to a customer shortly after the opening of a consumer or small business checking, savings or credit card account to confirm that the account was properly authorized by the customer. In addition, revised credit card application procedures require an applicant's documented consent before a credit report is pulled.

Wells Fargo has also added centralized monitoring and controls to augment its oversight of sales practices. Monitoring includes a third-party "mystery shopper" program and additional local, regional and corporate oversight; the increased quality assurance efforts will involve between 15,000 and 20,000 site visits each year and an additional 600 conduct risk reviews.

In July 2016, Wells Fargo replaced Tolstedt with Mary Mack, the former head of Wells Fargo's brokerage business. Addressing root causes, Wells Fargo eliminated product sales goals in the Community Bank effective October 1, 2016. In the fourth quarter of 2016, Wells Fargo implemented a new incentive compensation plan for retail branch employees; a larger percentage of compensation is now "base pay," and incentives are focused on customer experience, with metrics designed to emphasize customer service, retention and long-term relationship building.

Senior Management

A. John Stumpf

John Stumpf, Wells Fargo's previous Chief Executive Officer and Chairman, joined Norwest in 1982; Norwest merged with Wells Fargo in 1998. . . . Stumpf became Wells Fargo's Chief Operating Officer in 2005 and served in that role until he became CEO in June 2007. As CEO, Stumpf oversaw Wells Fargo's four main business groups: the Community Bank, Consumer Lending, Wealth & Investment Management and Wholesale Banking. Stumpf joined the Board of Directors in 2006 and became Chairman of the Board in January 2010. Stumpf resigned in October of 2016, at which point Tim Sloan was elevated to CEO.

A product of Norwest, where the head of a region was the "king" or "queen" of his or her territory, Stumpf was a supporter of decentralized management during much of his time as CEO of Wells Fargo. As did others, Stumpf believed

[14] Russ Anderson was terminated for cause in connection with the Committee's investigation on February 21, 2017.

decentralization better managed risk by spreading decision-making and produced better business decisions because they were made "closer to the customer." Over time, however, he recognized that increased cross-business collaboration was better for the customer and Wells Fargo. He later came to support increased centralization and authority for risk and control systems as well, but that only occurred after the sales practice issues had emerged.

Stumpf was ultimately responsible for enterprise risk management at Wells Fargo, but was not perceived within Wells Fargo as someone who wanted to hear bad news or deal with conflict. In accordance with the decentralized model, a deferential culture existed whereby there was limited encouragement for the management of different businesses to challenge each other or comment on significant issues in the other lines of business. Under Stumpf, weekly Operating Committee meetings generally did not serve as a forum for discussion, engagement or challenge among its members.

Much like his predecessor, Richard Kovacevich, Stumpf was also a proponent of cross-sell and product sales. Kovacevich had initiated the "GR-8" program to pursue cross-sell at Norwest and brought that focus to Wells Fargo, which had not measured cross-sell in a programmatic way before the Norwest merger. . . .

Stumpf received reports on cross-sell success and spoke frequently on its importance. Referring to efforts to cross-sell in an email to Tolstedt and another executive vice president, he stated that Wells Fargo "fight[s] like cats and dogs for those numbers!"

Stumpf was aware that Wells Fargo's focus on cross-sell, combined with aggressive sales goals and associated incentive compensation plans, could encourage employee "gaming" and sales practice issues. In June 2015, an email between Stumpf and one of his line of business heads discussed the potential of purely quantitative incentive plans based on sales numbers to influence people "to make bad decisions, i.e. cheat" and, in the summer of 2015, Stumpf challenged Tolstedt to try to manage the Community Bank without sales goals. However, Stumpf was not engaged in managing the balance between positive and negative incentives, and it was not until September 2016 that Wells Fargo decided to eliminate product sales goals for Community Bank employees. . . .

Stumpf was also aware of specific sales practice issues over the years. . . . Stumpf received numerous customer and employee complaints about sales practices and sales pressure, which he or his assistants referred to appropriate subordinates without further follow-up. According to Wells Fargo employees, concerns about sales practices and "gaming" were raised with Stumpf during the 2012–2014 timeframe.

Stumpf was informed by late 2013 that approximately 1,000 (or approximately 1% of) Community Bank employees were being terminated for sales integrity violations each year. Stumpf reacted positively to the 1% number; in his view, the fact that only 1% of Wells Fargo employees were terminated meant that 99% of employees were doing their jobs correctly. It does not appear that he initiated any follow-up investigation or inquiry into the issue in 2013 or 2014.

Even in 2015 and 2016, Stumpf did not appreciate the scope and severity of the problem. He continued to publicly support the appropriateness of Wells Fargo's sales goals and to highlight that the vast majority of Wells Fargo employees "got it right." An example is an email Stumpf wrote to Sloan on May 17, 2015, after the filing of the Los Angeles City Attorney lawsuit:

> I have worked over the weekend with Carrie on the LA issue—I really feel for Carrie and her team. We do such a good job in this area. I will fight this one to the finish. Do you know only around 1% of our people lose their jobs [for] gaming the system, and about 2/3 of those are for gaming the monitoring of the system, i.e. changing phone numbers, etc. Nothing could be further from the truth on forcing products on customers. In any case, right will win and we are right. Did some do things wrong—you bet and that is called life. This is not systemic.

In his interview, Stumpf could not recall whether in this email he was referring to 1% of employees working across the regional bank or whether the 1% figure was limited to those working in the Los Angeles area. In retrospect, he acknowledged that 1% was too high in either case.

Tolstedt reported to Stumpf, and he supported her during her time as the head of Community Bank. He was aware of Tolstedt's shortcomings as a leader but also viewed her as having significant strengths. Stumpf believed that the Community Bank's positive customer service and team member satisfaction survey results and consistently strong financial performance reflected positively on Tolstedt's leadership abilities. Stumpf understood that Tolstedt could be resistant to change and inflexible, but for a long time he considered that to be advantageous from a risk perspective; he believed her conservative decision-making was less likely to result in hasty decisions that could expose Wells Fargo to harm.

Many have noted that Stumpf was hesitant to criticize Tolstedt and, ultimately, hesitant to terminate her, even after the lead independent director and the Chair of the Risk Committee suggested that he do so in December 2015. For example, according to one director, Stumpf advised the Board of problems with Tolstedt's leadership style, including that she was controlling, but also praised her as the "best banker in America." Eventually, Tim Sloan, upon assuming the role of Chief Operating Officer, was assigned responsibility for making the decision on whether to retain Tolstedt as head of the Community Bank.

Stumpf was accepting of Tolstedt's flaws in part because of her other strengths and her ability to drive results, including cross-sell. For example, in her 2009 performance review, Stumpf wrote that Tolstedt "knows the business cold—nothing gets by her" and that a management structure she had devised was a "stroke of genius." In 2013, Stumpf attributed the Community Bank's success, including in achieving "record cross-sell," to Tolstedt's leadership. He also pushed Tolstedt to work to increase cross-sell when strong growth proved more elusive. Many observers expressed their belief that Tolstedt operated the Community Bank in the way she did because she thought Stumpf would approve. This is also supported by contemporaneous emails, particularly with respect to the setting of aspirational sales goals and focus on improving cross-sell.

B. Tim Sloan

Tim Sloan joined Wells Fargo in 1987 and has held various leadership roles over the course of his Wells Fargo career, including CAO (September 2010 to February 2011), CFO (2011 to 2014), Head of Wholesale Banking (2014 to 2015) and COO (2015 to October 2016). He was chosen to take over the CEO position upon Stumpf's retirement in October 2016.

Sloan's knowledge of sales practice issues was limited prior to 2014, but increased after the publication of the LOS ANGELES TIMES article on sales practice issues at Wells Fargo in December 2013.

While Sloan had some awareness of sales practice issues within the Community Bank prior to the publication of the LOS ANGELES TIMES articles, including from sporadic internal discussions with colleagues and anonymous complaint emails, he was not aware of the magnitude of the issues or of their potential to cause customer harm. The decentralized, "run it like you own it" structure and ethos within Wells Fargo limited the amount of negative information Sloan received regarding the Community Bank and the opportunities Sloan had to engage on Community Bank issues. Sloan was also aware of Tolstedt's management issues, including her resistance to providing or receiving negative information. He understood that Tolstedt was a controlling manager and was not always a good partner when working with other parts of the business. He knew that Tolstedt did not like to have any critical discussion of her management of the Community Bank, and could be resistant to advice to change or adapt, and was aware that this resistance also attached to discussions of sales practice issues. Sloan had observed that Tolstedt surrounded herself with supportive people who insulated her and told her what she wanted to hear.

In December 2013, Sloan told the LOS ANGELES TIMES, "I'm not aware of any overbearing sales culture." After the publication of the LOS ANGELES TIMES article, Sloan became aware of Wells Fargo's efforts to detect and address sales practice issues, including that a team had been assigned to investigate and that a larger sales practice review would then need to be done.

Sloan was also included on internal correspondence concerning the need to lower sales goals after 2013. In a May 2014 email, Tolstedt informed Sloan and other senior executives of adjustments to the sales plan and banker goals, noting that one of the purposes of lowering sales goals was that it "encourages the right behaviors." In 2015, Sloan attended Risk Committee meetings in which sales practice violations were discussed, including a meeting where Tolstedt noted the high inherent risk associated with the Community Bank. This was when he and others within Wells Fargo first began to appreciate the potential for sales practices to cause financial harm, although he understood that the level of harm was small and the matter was being addressed.

Sloan has acknowledged that Wells Fargo should have been more focused on determining which customers were harmed and remediating it. In a company-wide address in October 2016, he said that "[Wells Fargo] had product sales goals that sometimes resulted in behaviors and practices that did not serve our customers' or our team members' interests. And we were slow to see the harm they caused." He added: "[D]espite our ongoing efforts to combat these unacceptable bad practices and bad behaviors, they persisted, because we either minimized the problem, or we failed to see the problem for what it really was—something bigger than we originally imagined."

Beginning in November 2015, when Sloan became President and COO, he discussed with Tolstedt that she needed to be more open to change and to resolve the sales practice issues quickly. Sloan, Stumpf and members of the Board agreed that Tolstedt was likely not the right person to guide the Community Bank as it went forward—and members of the Board expressed more pointed and immediate concerns about Tolstedt—but Sloan felt that he needed to evaluate and work with her to help her change before reaching a final decision about her future at Wells Fargo.

In the spring of 2016, it became clear that Tolstedt was not changing her management practices sufficiently. During the April 2016 Board meeting, Sloan and the Board discussed replacing her as the head of the Community Bank. Subsequently, in the June 2016 Board meeting, Sloan reiterated his intention of replacing Tolstedt. In early July, Sloan informed Tolstedt that she would no longer serve as the head of the Community Bank. They ultimately agreed that she would retire.

Corporate Risk

. . . .

C. Evolution of the Structure of the Risk Management at Wells Fargo

. . .[T]he Board established a Risk Committee in 2011, and thereafter worked on rationalizing its scope and functions. Along with efforts to enhance oversight of risk at the Board level, the CRO made significant efforts to revamp the risk function at Wells Fargo to provide for more effective oversight and control of risks. These efforts, however, were still in process at the time the sales practice issues became prominent in 2013 and were escalated to the Board in 2014.

At Loughlin's recommendation, the Board authorized the engagement of McKinsey & Co. in early 2013 to analyze Wells Fargo's risk function and organization and to make suggestions for its improvement. Recommendations from the McKinsey report were presented to the Board and reflected in part in an October 2013 memorandum to the Board describing the corporate risk program's aspirations, strategy and three-year plan, and in Wells Fargo's Risk Management Framework adopted in July 2014. The enhancements of the risk organization required substantially increased levels of funding and staffing, which the Board approved. The McKinsey report and Wells Fargo's risk management framework did not provide for centralization of the risk function. Instead, they included measures for, among other things, more effective and comprehensive oversight by Corporate Risk (the second line of defense) of risk in the lines of business (the first line of defense).

With regard to sales practices, Corporate Risk had started to plan for more formal oversight in late 2013, but these initiatives did not start to be implemented until 2015. Loughlin's October 2013 memorandum on the corporate risk program included a plan for Corporate Risk to take a leading role in "driv[ing] a systematic and disciplined approach to operational excellence in processes across the bank, particularly those that impact customers." Because "errors previously viewed as immaterial can have significant consequences, including increased risk of financial and reputational harm" and rising customer and regulatory expectations were especially evident in areas that touched consumers such as (among others) sales practices, "Wells Fargo will address these risks at the source through improving the customer experience and preventing errors, rather than remediating issues after-the-fact." Wells Fargo's July 2014 Risk Management Framework provided that the Corporate Enterprise Risk Group (led by one of Loughlin's direct reports) was responsible for Corporate Risk's oversight of sales practice risk, which was a subtype of "cross-functional" risk. However, no one from Corporate Risk was assigned responsibility as the "owner" of that area until 2015.

D. Corporate Risk's Response to Issues Concerning Sales Pressure and Improper Sales Practices

1. 2012

Loughlin recalled that he first became aware of terminations for improper sales practices in October 2013, when he was advised by Wells Fargo's BSA Officer of terminations in the Los Angeles area. However, at least as early as 2012, Loughlin was concerned about excessive sales pressure in the Community Bank and the possibility that it could result in employee turnover and sales of products that customers did not understand or need.

Lisa Stevens raised with Loughlin issues concerning unrealistic sales goals and her frustration with Community Bank leadership. Loughlin asked the Community Bank to come to an ERMC meeting on September 11, 2012, to address those and related issues. Before the meeting, Loughlin sent Matthew Raphaelson questions that the Community Bank representatives should address at the ERMC meeting, including "whether the emphasis on cross-sell leads to increased turnover; how do we or the managers on the front line know that our cross sells (solutions) are high quality and in the customer's benefit; whether emphasizing the number of solutions runs the risk of flogging product and irritating customers; whether we should emphasize revenue over the number of solutions; and how we pay people for cross-sell and how that compares to the practice of the competition."

Raphaelson and another representative of the Community Bank made a written and oral presentation to the ERMC on September 11, 2012. Loughlin recalled he was very dissatisfied with the presentation, as were most of the other ERMC members. The presentation did not give the committee a better understanding of the controls on sales goals, and it was jargon-filled, lacking in metrics and dismissive of some of the questions posed. The written presentation did not refer to unauthorized accounts or customer consent issues, although it did list detective and preventative controls, including monitoring and others. Loughlin had also asked Russ Anderson to present at the ERMC in 2012, but in October 2012 decided that she need not appear.

On September 19, 2012, Loughlin attended Stevens' West Coast presidents' meeting and addressed the attendees. His planned outline for the discussion included topics similar to those Loughlin had raised with Raphaelson in connection with the ERMC meeting. In a discussion after the meeting, two managers spoke to Loughlin about high sales pressure. Loughlin was surprised by the allegation and suggested that the managers report those issues to Stevens, and then to Tolstedt if Stevens was not responsive.

After the West Coast meeting, Stevens got a call from Tolstedt, who told her not to talk to Loughlin any[ ]more and that she needed to "toe the line." Stevens told Loughlin about the call with Tolstedt, and Loughlin expressed to Stevens that Tolstedt's direction was "ridiculous." Loughlin had a similar conversation with Stevens in December 2015, during which Loughlin encouraged Stevens to approach Tolstedt directly, but also told her that the instruction from Tolstedt was "stupid" and that Stevens should feel free to continue to call him with problems.

In an apparent follow-up to the September 2012 ERMC meeting, Raphaelson sent Loughlin an email on October 5, 2012, on the subject of "sales goals." Raphaelson said that setting sales goals was a "balancing act," and that he "carr[ied] this Charlie Munger wisdom with me in my head," namely that " 'Low goals do cause lower performance and high goals increase the percentage of cheating.' " Loughlin responded: "I wonder if the emphasis on individual unit sales produces low quality sales (not really in customers best interests, but sold because someone has to make their goals), and higher turnover than is necessary (due to pressure to make goals). I just wonder if a revenue based approach would be better. Every store, district, etc[.] must increase revenue each year by x percent. Let them figure out how. Just thinking out loud." Loughlin raised the issue of employee turnover in the Community Bank with the Community Bank's representative on the ERMC after the October 16, 2012 ERMC meeting. He also invited the Community Bank HR head to come to a future ERMC meeting to discuss, among other things, "trends in store turnover, the drivers of those trends, how we perform compared with peers/in different geographies" and how the risk was managed. As noted above, Tolstedt objected to the request, and Loughlin deferred the presentation.

2. 2013–2014

On June 5, 2013, the Community Bank HR head, Debra Paterson, presented to the ERMC on employee turnover, noting that it was approximately 42% in 2012 among branch and call center personnel, which made up 90% of the Community Bank's employees. This rate was described as "slightly lower than turnover for similar types of roles in the retail industry." Later in June 2013, Corporate Risk personnel contacted the Community Bank to discuss the possibility of another ERMC presentation by the Community Bank to address whether "there was a linkage between the high turnover and the quality of sales, thus, if we could improve upon the former it would potentially enhance the quality of sales."

In the summer of 2013, Loughlin also encouraged Tolstedt to consult with European banks on conduct risk issues, including those related to sales practices, as U.K. banks in particular had been subject to regulatory scrutiny for sales practices. This resulted in an August 2013 trip to London and Stockholm by Tolstedt and others in the Community Bank.

Later, after the first LOS ANGELES TIMES article was published, Tolstedt criticized Loughlin when he or his team attempted to get information about sales practices in the Community Bank without directly involving Tolstedt. On October 9, 2013, Tolstedt emailed Loughlin as follows: "I would very much appreciate the team talking to me directly about any concerns on sales practices versus arriving at broad conclusions without all the information on trends, controls, and future controls. It continues to frustrate me greatly that I am left out of the conversation. I appreciate credible challenge but the team needs to be talking to people who have the facts and information." Fourteen minutes later, she followed up with an email clarifying that she "appreciated the question," but was just frustrated that she was not "involved in the discussion." Loughlin responded, "I actually don't know what you are referring to. I put in a call to Claudia [Russ Anderson] to see what I had done or my team had done. We're all on the same team."

Loughlin became more concerned about sales practices in October 2013. At that time, he was advised of the employee terminations resulting from the Los Angeles/Orange County investigation. He also read highly critical comments by Wells Fargo employees in an online petition relating to sales pressure and sales practices. This heightened concern led him to make the decision to escalate sales practices to the Board as a significant risk (which was done in early 2014, as discussed below). Also in the fall of 2013, at Stumpf's urging, Loughlin began to meet quarterly with Tolstedt and Russ Anderson to try to reduce sales pressure in the Community Bank. In his 2013 self-review submitted to Stumpf, Loughlin stated: "Sales practices: we have been pushing Carrie for some time about concerns here. She has been receptive and has implemented some very good systems to track sales practices, but the recent LA Times article makes me think that while process improvements are good, we have issues in hiring, training, and management. I should have pushed harder."

Loughlin caused sales practices to be included in the January 2014 Significant Enterprise Risks memorandum to the Board, and again in the February 2014 Noteworthy Risk Issues report. In addition, a February 18, 2014 memorandum from Loughlin and Hope Hardison (then the HR Director) was provided to the Board's Human Resources Committee ("HRC") referring to sales practices: "In addition, we also recommend monitoring in 2014 for sales integrity in Community Banking, specifically ongoing monitoring and review of store level quality processes. This issue presents potential operational and reputational risk. Action plans are in progress including: heightened monitoring processes; communication of sales quality expectations; strengthening of control function review of incentive plans, goals, and performance management programs; and continued focused attention on consistent and high-touch communication strategies."

Hernandez, Chair of the Risk Committee of the Board, had spoken to Loughlin about the sales practice issues since the December 2013 LOS ANGELES TIMES article and had instructed Loughlin to be among the people within Wells Fargo to focus on the issue. In part as a result of these discussions, Loughlin brought Community Bank representatives to speak about sales practices at the ERMC meeting on April 9, 2014. Claudia Russ Anderson and a member of Matthew Raphaelson's team provided a written presentation and spoke at the meeting. Loughlin found the Community Bank's written presentation unsatisfactory, as it did not address the current state of the problem or outline concrete steps to deal with it (as Loughlin's deputies had asked them to do). At the ERMC meeting, Loughlin asked how many people in the Community Bank were terminated for sales practice violations, and was told approximately 1,000 in 2013. Loughlin was surprised and concerned by this number, and expressed his dissatisfaction about the presentation in the meeting.

At the Board Risk Committee's request, Loughlin scheduled Tolstedt to appear at their April 2014 meeting to address sales practices, which ultimately did not happen when she was summoned for jury duty. The draft of Tolstedt's written presentation was sent to Loughlin for his review, and he wrote back to Tolstedt and her team: "The risk committee will want to hear from Carrie her view on:

does the pressure of cross sell goals cause bad behavior? That is what Rick [Hernandez] asked."

At the April 29, 2014 Board meeting, Loughlin briefly reported on sales practice issues as part of his Chief Risk Officer report. At the August 4, 2014 Risk Committee meeting, in response to a director's question on cross-sell risk issues, Loughlin and Stumpf discussed Wells Fargo's focus on ensuring its cross-sell strategies were consistent with the development of long-term customer relationships.

Over the course of 2014, Loughlin developed a more positive view regarding the efforts of the Community Bank to address the sales practice problems. On December 9, 2014, Loughlin emailed the Chair of the Risk Committee about agenda items for upcoming Risk Committee meetings and, as to sales practices, said that Tolstedt had made very good changes in the Community Bank, that there was a "good story" on the subject and that he did not think the Risk Committee wanted to hear about good stories. (The Chair responded that the Risk Committee nonetheless wanted to hear about sales practices.) In late 2014 to early 2015, Loughlin participated in reviews of risk outcomes throughout Wells Fargo in order to determine risk- related compensation impacts for 2014. In the review of the sales practice issue in the Community Bank, Loughlin concluded that the Community Bank leaders had made significant progress during 2014 to remove pressure from the system, and that they planned to take additional steps in the future. Although he considered it a "close call," he determined that no compensation impacts were warranted for 2014, and so advised the HRC in a February 16, 2015 memorandum from him and Hardison:

> As a follow up to issues identified as part of 2013 compensation process for monitoring in 2014, we reviewed the progress against Sales Integrity issue in Community Banking, specifically store level quality processes. We believe appropriate actions were taken to address the issues during the performance year and no compensation adjustment is required for the 2014 cycle.

Consistent with that determination, in February 2015, the Noteworthy Risk Issues report to the Board downgraded the risks posed by sales practices from "High" to "Medium." Tolstedt made a written and oral presentation on sales practices to the Risk Committee on April 28, 2015. Shortly after the meeting, Risk Committee Chair Hernandez called Loughlin and Stumpf to tell them that Tolstedt's presentation was highly unsatisfactory and did not address the issues that needed to be addressed. Prompted by this, Loughlin determined that

Corporate Risk needed to become more actively involved in the oversight of sales practices and had one of his direct reports put together a team in Corporate Risk for that purpose.

Following the filing of the Los Angeles City Attorney lawsuit on May 4, 2015, Loughlin understood that Hernandez believed that someone outside the Community Bank needed to take the lead on the sales practice issues. On May 8, 2015, Hernandez sent an email to the Risk Committee, Stumpf and Loughlin about his discussions with Loughlin concerning the sales practice issues and the plan for the upcoming Risk Committee meeting on May 19, 2015. Hernandez told Loughlin that he sent the email to help put Loughlin in a position to take charge of the sales practice issue.

Loughlin was on vacation during the period in which the materials for the May 19 Risk Committee meeting were prepared and the meeting took place. . . . After the meeting, Stumpf called Loughlin and told him that the meeting had not gone well and that the presentation for the meeting was not well done. At this time, Loughlin determined that it was necessary to have an outside third-party conduct a comprehensive review of the sales practice issues, which was done in 2015.

Loughlin and Corporate Risk thereafter heightened their efforts to oversee and manage the sales practice issues throughout the rest of 2015 and into 2016. Corporate Risk's efforts were hampered to some extent by the absence of a formal governance structure for exercising oversight. In late 2015, a Sales Practices Oversight ("SPO") unit was established in Corporate Risk; among other things, it provided challenge to the first line of defense in the Community Bank over key risk decisions and processes and coordinated with other second line oversight functions responsible for complaints management, corporate investigations, global ethics, human resources and employee relations. As of May 2016, the SPO unit, despite some progress, acknowledged that there was still "considerable work to do in order to build a fully functioning, integrated, and sustainable sales practices oversight program."

E. Recent Remedial Changes

The buildout of Corporate Risk is continuing and efforts to centralize the risk function have been accelerated. In 2016, 4,100 risk employees who previously reported to the lines of business were realigned and now report into Corporate Risk. In 2017, an additional 1,100 are scheduled to be similarly realigned. Thus, group risk officers in the lines of business, including the Community Bank, now report to the CRO, removing one of the key organizational impediments that limited Corporate Risk in addressing sales practice problems in the Community Bank.

The Law Department

The Law Department is divided into several divisions, each of which is headed by a deputy general counsel who reports to the General Counsel. Of these divisions, two had significant involvement with sales integrity issues—the Enterprise Services Division, primarily through its Employment Law Section, and the Litigation & Workout Division. . . .

A. Prior to the Los Angeles/Orange County Investigation in Mid-2013

Prior to mid-2013, lawyers in the Employment Law Section encountered sales integrity issues as they worked with the Community Bank's Human Resources personnel on terminations. These lawyers were involved in an advisory capacity in investigations, decisions regarding terminations and discussions regarding the application of Wells Fargo's fidelity bond's proscription against "dishonest acts."[15]

Employment Section lawyers were not brought into every internal investigation; when they were, their role primarily involved identifying and assessing litigation risk associated with the resulting terminations. Where employment-related litigation arose out of terminations, employment lawyers managed that litigation. Certain employment lawyers within the Employment Law Section also participated in cross-functional teams set up to address sales integrity issues, and, in that context, lawyers identified and conveyed concerns about "reputational risk" to the Section head.

Employment Section lawyers encountered sales misconduct and the termination of several employees at one time (discussed within the Law Department as "mass terminations"), dating back at least to 2002. In summer 2002, Internal Investigations determined that almost an entire branch in Colorado engaged in a form of "gaming" in connection with a promotional campaign in the second quarter of 2002. Although most within Wells Fargo recall this incident as involving improper teller referral credits, it also involved employees issuing debit cards without customer consent. Tellers involved in the gaming scheme reported that managers instructed them to input the referrals or supported the activity.

---

[15] A fidelity bond is a form of insurance protection that covers policyholders for losses that they incur as a result of the fraudulent activity of specified individuals, specifically, in the case of a bank, the dishonest acts of employees. If an employee is known to have previously committed certain dishonest acts, that employee becomes unbondable, such that the bank is not protected against any future losses he or she causes. Because federal law requires that national banks maintain adequate fidelity coverage for all officers and employees, an employee who is unbondable must be terminated.

Wells Fargo's normal application of its fidelity bond required termination. Several employees involved in the incident, including managers, were terminated or resigned. Rather than terminate everyone else involved, which would have eliminated most of the branch's tellers and personal bankers, Wells Fargo sought and obtained an exception to the fidelity bond from its underwriter. Employment Law Section attorneys advised in connection with the incident.

. . . .

Additional "mass terminations" for gaming of Wells Fargo's incentive compensation system continued sporadically over the next ten years (in addition to individual terminations). Employment lawyers at all levels were either made aware of or were themselves involved in addressing these terminations. During this period, Wells Fargo's employment lawyers generally focused on the litigation costs of sales integrity cases in the event of lawsuits by terminated employees. The costs of sales integrity cases, however, were generally small as a proportion of overall employment litigation costs. (In 2013, when the head of the Employment Section requested a report detailing this breakdown, all sales integrity cases over the previous year and a half had settled for less than a million dollars.)

Beginning around 2011, however, a recurrence of sales integrity events led employment lawyers to recognize sales pressure in the Community Bank environment as a root cause of gaming cases. Lawyers in the Employment Law Section and the Deputy General Counsel responsible for the Section also began to recognize the existence of significant reputational risk to Wells Fargo arising out of sales integrity issues, particularly mass gaming cases.

In 2011, Wells Fargo terminated 13 bankers and tellers in a branch in California for engaging in manipulation of teller referral credits, which brought sales integrity issues back to the fore. When questioned, the bankers and tellers charged management with being aware of, encouraging and benefitting from their conduct. The terminated employees wrote a letter to John Stumpf asserting that they had been unjustly terminated, and that the practice had not only been condoned by management in their branch, but was also happening across the Community Bank.

Following these terminations, Wells Fargo convened another task force in May 2011 to address sales integrity in the Community Bank. Three Employment Law Section attorneys participated. The group discussed issues such as "excessive terminations and the risks associated with them," "mass terminations" and "reputational risk" and the effect that pressure, incentive compensation plan structure and employees' desire to meet sales goals had on their behavior.

Again in this context, members of the Law Department recognized reputational concerns.

Notwithstanding the growing awareness of the reputational risk associated with mass terminations, and the fact that many of these incidents involved unauthorized products or accounts, the perception persisted in the Law Department that sales integrity issues involved "gaming" the Community Bank's incentive programs and not conduct affecting customers. That led them to underestimate the need to escalate and more directly manage sales integrity issues.[16]

B. From Publication of LOS ANGELES TIMES Articles in October and December 2013 to Filing of Los Angeles City Attorney Lawsuit in May 2015

From the publication in the LOS ANGELES TIMES of articles about the Los Angeles/Orange County investigation in October and December of 2013 until the filing of the Los Angeles City Attorney lawsuit in May 2015, Law Department attorneys provided legal advice in connection with two sales integrity projects. While sales practices were conveyed to the Risk Committee and the Board in 2014 as a "noteworthy risk," the information, discussion and advice that accompanied that risk did not highlight or identify the potential consequences of the misconduct that were distinctly legal in nature—e.g., a cascade of civil litigation, regulatory action from a host of federal and state agencies and the resulting serious harm to Wells Fargo's reputation.

In September 2013, SSCOT and Internal Investigations launched an investigation into the Los Angeles/Orange County regional bank as a result of sales quality reports that identified unusual funding and phone number change activity. At the time, simulated funding was considered to be a new and different form of gaming behavior.

Although some line-level employment lawyers provided advice and guidance in the course of the investigation, its significance was not escalated, and senior employment attorneys only learned details of the investigation after the media began to inquire about the terminations. At that point, in early October 2013, the then-head of the Enterprise Services Division and the head of the Employment

[16] As a member of Wells Fargo's Ethics Committee and Team Member Misconduct Executive Committee ("TMMEC"), the General Counsel received reports in April 2012, October 2012, February 2013 and August 2013 about high or increasing numbers of sales integrity complaints and cases. The August 2013 report was the first to delineate the specific types of conduct that fell under the category of "sales integrity" issues.

Law Section became concerned at this lack of escalation by the line-level attorneys.

At the end of October, the Head of Enterprise Services briefed General Counsel James Strother and later CRO Loughlin about the investigation. The Law Department did not further escalate the existence or details of the investigation to the Board or any Board Committees at that time.

Over the following 18 months, attorneys in the Law Department participated actively in two main work streams designed to address sales integrity issues: the "Evolving Model" initiative . . . and the Core Team. The Core Team was created in the wake of the Los Angeles/Orange County investigation to ensure consistency in the implementation of terminations following the first phase of that investigation.

C. Following Commencement of the Los Angeles City Attorney Lawsuit

On May 4, 2015, the Los Angeles City Attorney filed a lawsuit against Wells Fargo alleging that Wells Fargo set unrealistic sales goals, which pressured employees to resort to abusive and fraudulent tactics to meet their targets, and that Wells Fargo profited through fees levied on customers. Regulatory inquiries followed; the Law Department moved directly into litigation-management mode. Strother chose the head of the Law Department's General Litigation Section, who had joined Wells Fargo three months earlier, to manage the litigation (in conjunction with outside counsel). The Law Department and the Community Bank also received a request from the Chair of the Risk Committee to brief the committee about the lawsuit at the committee's next meeting on May 19, 2015. . . .

The lawsuit's allegations led the Law Department attorneys and others within Wells Fargo to consider whether employees' "gaming" behavior carried with it the potential of customer harm. Consequently, the Community Bank and the Law Department collectively began to work with the Community Bank's deposits team to better understand that issue. When it became clear that a full understanding of the scope of possible harm would require data analysis, the Law Department engaged PwC to assist it.

Nevertheless, there continued to be a lack of recognition within the Law Department (as in other parts of Wells Fargo) about the significance of the number of sales integrity terminations, and the potential reputational consequences associated with that number, as late as the settlement of the Los Angeles City Attorney lawsuit and regulatory consent decrees in September 2016. The Law Department's focus was principally on quantifiable monetary costs—damages, fines, penalties, restitution. Confident those costs would be relatively modest, the Law Department did not appreciate that sales integrity issues reflected a systemic breakdown in Wells Fargo's culture and values and an ongoing failure to correct the widespread breaches of trust in the misuse of customers' personal data and financial information.

Human Resources/Chief Administrative Officer

A. Decentralization of the Human Resources Function at Wells Fargo

As with Risk, the HR function at Wells Fargo was decentralized, with most HR responsibilities and functions embedded in the lines of business. The HR heads in the lines of business reported to the business heads rather than to the Corporate HR Director. As a result of Wells Fargo's historical emphasis on decentralization, and the resulting autonomy of the Community Bank in its HR-related activities, Corporate HR had limited authority and influence over, and limited visibility into, the Community Bank. The Community Bank was not accustomed to involving Corporate HR in its discussions and decisions and was generally protective and defensive in keeping control of HR-related activities within the line of business.

Almost all of the sales integrity cases and issues touched some facet of the HR function in some way, including with respect to employee terminations, hiring, training, coaching, discipline, incentive compensation, performance management, turnover, morale, work environment, claims and litigation. Despite this, while HR collectively had a great deal of information recorded in its systems, there was no coordinated effort by HR, in the Community Bank or at the enterprise level, to track or size the sales practice issues or to report on them.

B. Community Bank HR

The problem with sales practices in the Community Bank persisted over several years despite efforts by the Community Bank and its embedded HR function to improve training and detection of misconduct. While recognizing many of the serious issues posed by sales pressure and improper sales practices, the HR function in the Community Bank was either unable or unwilling to effectively challenge Community Bank leadership on the sales model that resulted in the sales practice issues, and did not effectively escalate the issues outside the Community Bank.

Starting in at least 2002, Community Bank HR participated in efforts to stem sales practice issues. At Tolstedt's direction, a task force was established in 2002 to address the increasing focus on sales integrity issues in regional banking and to develop recommendations that would minimize them, to identify processes to handle issues when they arose and to clarify roles in the process. The task force created training materials for managers and employees, including materials relating to "Rules of the Road" for everyday sales scenarios, Code of Ethics and bond requirements, appropriate and inappropriate sales activity, consequences of gaming and methods to ask questions or report issues.

Debra Paterson was the head of HR in the Community Bank from April 2009 to September 2014. While she recognized negative effects of the sales pressure and improper sales practice issues and made efforts to address them, she was either unwilling or unable to effectively challenge Tolstedt with respect to the sales model that resulted in the problems.[17]

. . . .

Tracy Kidd succeeded Paterson as head of Community Bank HR upon Paterson's retirement in September 2014. She also reported to Carrie Tolstedt, with a dotted line reporting relationship to Hardison. Kidd believed that the Community Bank was proceeding appropriately to address the sales practice issues in 2014 to 2016.

C. Corporate HR/Chief Administrative Officer

Hope Hardison joined Wells Fargo in 1993 and became the Corporate HR Director in 2010. As HR Director, Hardison reported to Patricia Callahan until spring 2014, when she became a member of the Operating Committee and began to report directly to John Stumpf. Hardison became Chief Administrative Officer ("CAO") in September 2015, after Callahan's retirement.

Hardison was aware of sales practice issues throughout her tenure as HR Director, but until the Los Angeles/Orange County investigation in late 2013 she did not understand them to be pervasive; she generally understood them to involve the "gaming" of the incentive compensation system. Hardison was a member of the Ethics Committee and the Team Member Misconduct Executive Committee ("TMMEC"), which received reports from Michael Bacon (head of Corporate Security, which included Internal Investigations) on various forms of misconduct by employees, including sales integrity violations. The Ethics Committee reports generally noted increases in sales integrity violations, which Bacon at times characterized as a matter for concern. In 2013, reports to the TMMEC included the number of sales integrity allegations and cases. From 2012 to September 2014, Bacon was Hardison's direct report, and in that capacity provided her with reports relating to sales integrity violations and other types of

---

17 Paterson, like Tolstedt, declined to be interviewed, and her interactions with Tolstedt on this subject have not been confirmed.

team member misconduct, including ad hoc reports on specific cases. In February 2013, Bacon sent Hardison a report he had provided to the Community Bank, which included a table showing, with respect to sales integrity violations, the number of allegations, cases worked, employees cleared, confirmed fraud or policy violations and related terminations and resignations (935 in 2011 and 1,142 in 2012), broken down by case subtype, including, among others, customer consent, false entries and referrals. Hardison did not recall reviewing this report in detail or having understood at that time the scope and nature of the sales integrity violations.

. . . .

In late 2013, after the first LOS ANGELES TIMES article and during the Los Angeles/Orange County investigation, Callahan and Hardison urged the involvement of enterprise-level representatives in the Community Bank's efforts to address the sales practice problems.

Callahan became involved with efforts at the corporate level (including media relations, which was within her purview as CAO) and in the Community Bank to address the sales practice issues, both from a reputational perspective and to address the underlying issue itself. In an email exchange on November 8–9, 2013, with Tim Sloan (then CFO), Callahan confirmed that she was working with Tolstedt on the sales practice review. She noted, "We are trying to limit the damage of further terms [terminations] in the short term hoping the LA Times story doesn't become national." She added that "then the larger sales practice review needs to be done, although Carrie is already trying to find ways to reduce pressure—goals, referrals, etc."

Hardison and Callahan were very concerned about the number of people being fired by the Community Bank. Hardison in particular was concerned that the Community Bank was blindly firing people and not looking for a root cause of the problem, while Callahan was also concerned about the reputational risks arising from the firings. As a result of this concern, the Community Bank "paused" its proactive monitoring for sales integrity violations in late 2013 into early 2014 to try to evaluate the root cause of the sales practice issues. Ultimately, however, Hardison believed that this effort did not get to the fundamental cause of the problem.

In late 2013, Callahan and Hardison also asked a senior Corporate HR person and a senior employment lawyer to work with the Community Bank in analyzing the causes of the sales practice issue and recommending measures to address those causes. Matthew Raphaelson led this effort, and Hardison was advised by the

Corporate HR representative that the Community Bank was reluctant to provide information and resistant to significant change. The enterprise-level representatives involved in this effort do not appear to have had a significant impact on the actions taken by the Community Bank in late 2013 to early 2014.

On April 9, 2014, Hardison attended a meeting of the ERMC where she was advised of approximately 1,000 terminations for sales integrity violations in the Community Bank in 2013. Hardison had a strong negative reaction (which she expressed at the meeting) about the number. Hardison was also vocal in expressing her dissatisfaction with the efforts made by the Community Bank to understand and fix the problems, noting that it appeared that they had not really done anything. After the ERMC meeting, Tolstedt called Hardison to chastise her for her behavior and for "bullying" Tolstedt's people at the meeting. Hardison spoke to several people after the meeting to try to push the Community Bank to address sales practices more quickly.

Callahan was involved in the process of reviewing the Community Bank's efforts and proposed actions with respect to sales practices in 2014 and early 2015. She met with Raphaelson about the Community Bank's proposed actions, and spoke with Tolstedt as well. Callahan had known Tolstedt for many years and had an informed understanding of Tolstedt's strengths and weaknesses as a manager and leader of the Community Bank. In Callahan's view, while Tolstedt was capable of managing and organizing the huge enterprise that was the Community Bank and structuring programs that could get the Community Bank to move in the direction she wanted it to move, she was also obsessed with control and extremely cautious and slow in making decisions and implementing changes. In 2014 and early 2015, Callahan's sense was that the Community Bank was not doing enough fast enough to address the sales practice issues, but she did not push the pace of its efforts.

. . . .

In late 2014 and early 2015, Corporate HR participated with Corporate Risk in risk assessments throughout Wells Fargo to determine any recommended adjustments to 2014 compensation for risk issues. In Hardison's view, these determinations were primarily the responsibility of Corporate Risk, although she also signed off on them. Although Hardison believed in early 2014 that the Community Bank was not doing enough with respect to the sales practice issues, by the end of 2014, the prevailing view at Wells Fargo, with which she agreed, was that the Community Bank had been putting in a lot of effort and was making progress.

Accordingly, . . . she and Loughlin recommended that no adjustments be made to 2014 compensation for sales integrity issues.

In late 2015 and early 2016, Hardison and Loughlin conducted another review of risk issues to determine compensation adjustments for management employees below the Operating Committee level. In February 2016, they reported to the HRC that they recommended that such adjustments be made based on sales integrity issues in the Community Bank. These compensation adjustments ranged from 1% to 3% of the total incentive compensation for the affected individuals.

D. Recent Remedial Changes

The efforts to centralize HR functions, which began in earnest in 2015, have been accelerated along with the associated authority and responsibility to manage risk and cultural change throughout the company. Since 2016, the HR leads in the lines of business have reported directly to Corporate HR. In addition to improving visibility into the lines of business and enhancing oversight generally, centralizing these reporting lines is intended to strengthen the independent oversight of the incentive compensation programs within the lines of business, as well as the management of talent development and leadership training.

In addition to these structural changes, the HR function has taken specific action in response to the sales practice issues. It organized a program to re-hire former employees who left Wells Fargo, including because of sales pressure. It is also actively reassessing and considering new methods for determining and measuring employee engagement and satisfaction, as the positive "top-line" metrics reported in employee surveys in the past contributed to Wells Fargo's failure to understand the scope and nature of the sales practice issues and their impact on employees.[18]

Internal Investigations

Internal Investigations is a group within Wells Fargo that investigated allegations of employee misconduct and made determinations if misconduct was proved. Internal Investigations also made the determinations about whether to file a suspicious activity report ("SAR") in particular cases. It made recommendations concerning terminations, but not the final decisions. Internal Investigations appears to have operated independently of the lines of business. Investigators do not appear to have felt pressure to forgo investigating sales

[18] Based on a limited review completed to date, Shearman & Sterling has not identified a pattern of retaliation against Community Bank employees who complained about sales pressure or practices. . . .

integrity violations or to have believed that their determinations could be overruled by the lines of business or other control functions within Wells Fargo.

Internal Investigations reported in to Audit until 2012, when a new Chief Auditor was appointed. From 2012 until September 2014, Internal Investigations reported in to Corporate HR, and from September 2014 forward it was part of the Corporate Risk organization. Michael Bacon led Internal Investigations until September 2014, when he left Wells Fargo following an internal reorganization that eliminated his position as head of Corporate Security.

Internal Investigations first noticed an increase in sales integrity cases in 2002. Representatives of Internal Investigations participated in the 2002 sales integrity task force led by the Community Bank. . . . In 2004, Internal Investigations was involved in the work of a sales integrity investigations task force, which also included representatives of Community Bank HR, Community Bank management and the Law Department. It addressed and implemented, among other things, additional measures for training and the screening and investigation of allegations of gaming.

In the course of the work of the task force, a manager in Internal Investigations prepared a report in August 2004 on "Gaming," regarding sales integrity violations and what Internal Investigations had learned about the subject. The report contained information about the scope of the sales practice issues at that time and observations about its causes and impacts. According to the report, "it is the conclusion by Corporate Security Internal Investigations" that "whether real or perceived, team members on the current Corporate Sales Incentive Plan feel they cannot make sales goals without gaming the system. The incentive to cheat is based on the fear of losing their jobs for not meeting performance expectations." The report warned of the reputational risks for Wells Fargo, specifically, "[i]f customers believe that Wells Fargo team members are not conducting business in an appropriate and ethical manner, it will result in loss of business and can lead to diminished reputation in the community." In that regard, the report noted that Wells Fargo had been losing unemployment insurance cases involving sales integrity terminations, in which judges "made disparaging comments" about the sales incentive system.

. . . .

Audit

A. Audits of Sales Practice-Related Issues and Incentive Compensation Plans

Between 2011 and 2016, Wells Fargo Audit Services ("Audit") conducted periodic audits that touched on sales practice issues within the Community Bank. These audits generally found that processes and controls designed to detect, investigate and remediate sales practice violations were effective at mitigating sales practice-related risks. In addition to auditing these detective functions, Audit also reviewed the Community Bank's compensation plans and found that their design did not promote unethical behavior. As a general matter, however, Audit did not attempt to determine the root causes of unethical sales practices.

In April 2011, Audit reviewed the Regional Bank's "Sales, Service & Development" ("SS&D") group, which is responsible for a variety of controls designed to monitor and mitigate potential unethical conduct, such as gaming behavior, by regional banking employees. Audit rated SS&D's processes "Effective" (giving it 4 out of 5 on Audit's then-applicable ratings scale). Audit did identify a "moderate" issue regarding controls to monitor debit card sales integrity; Audit had learned about potential sales practice issues around debit cards from Internal Investigations. As a general matter, Audit witnesses indicated that, while Audit would not regularly seek out issues like this one, it would consider those issues when they arose.

In December 2013, an audit of regional banking's sales quality/sales integrity function once again rated the processes for detection of sales integrity violations "Effective." At that time, the sales quality/sales integrity function, consisting of sales quality analyst and service polling analyst teams, researched allegations of inappropriate branch sales practices. In reviewing the sales quality/sales integrity function, Audit examined risk management, systems of controls and governance processes to determine whether the function was effectively receiving and responding to sales integrity allegations. While Audit did not review individual allegations or conduct interviews of bankers to determine the root causes of sales practice issues, Audit witnesses explained that they were comfortable with their "Effective" rating because sales integrity violations were identified, investigated and, when violations were confirmed, responsible employees were terminated. One witness also indicated that Audit was aware at the time of this December 2013 audit that proactive monitoring had prompted the simulated funding investigation in Los Angeles, which gave Audit comfort that the monitoring systems could appropriately detect problematic conduct.[19]

In lieu of conducting its own branch-level audits, Audit periodically audited the "Store Operations Control Review" group ("SOCR"), the Community Bank's internal quality assurance team. SOCR rated every Wells Fargo branch location on an annual basis after observing team member behavior, conducting branch-level employee interviews and inspecting key account- related documentation, such as customer IDs and signature capture, which were collected in a centralized image-processing center on account opening. In 2010, Audit rated SOCR "Effective" (a 4 out of 5). It again rated SOCR "Effective" in 2012 (4 out of 5), but identified a "moderate" issue encompassing several items, including that ATM cards were not being timely destroyed, that there were errors in certain wire-related documents and that quality assurance work papers were not consistently or accurately completed. The audit noted, however, that "none of these unidentified errors . . . would have impacted the overall SOCR rating." In 2013, Audit did validation work around the corrective action plan for these items, found the implementation of the plan inadequate and re-opened the issue. When Audit reviewed SOCR in 2014, it found that the 2012 items had still not been fully remediated. Audit issued a "Needs Improvement" rating; thereafter, Audit discontinued its reliance on SOCR's work and began conducting its own in-branch reviews.

In addition to auditing the above detective and operational processes, Audit also conducted incentive compensation-related audits at both the enterprise and regional bank levels. In particular, in addition to looking at processes around the compensation systems, these audits included testing to ensure that incentive compensation plans were not designed so that they incentivized employee misconduct. Most relevantly, in 2012, Audit conducted a regional bank compensation audit that reviewed, among other things, incentive compensation plans applicable to branch employees and lower level managers above the branch level. This review considered, among other things, the "mix of drivers" within the incentive plans and the plans' potential impact on team member conduct. While Audit concluded that incentive compensation plans were largely sales driven, it

---

19 In 2014, Audit reviewed the regional banking in-store customer complaint process with a focus on how written complaints were tracked and resolved. While Audit identified a concern regarding bankers on occasion failing to timely refer complaints to the "Resolution Team," Audit concluded that complaints were handled appropriately once received by the Resolution Team and issued an "Effective" rating. Also in 2014, Audit reviewed the Risk Operations and Fraud Prevention Services customer and account servicing process, which, among other things, investigated and resolved customer disputes regarding debit cards and ATM transactions. While Audit identified a "moderate" issue regarding the group's tracking system, Audit rated the group "Effective."

determined that the plans were adequately balanced by customer service and sales quality-related components.[20] Audit reached this conclusion primarily based on reviewing plan documents; it did not do field-work, such as banker interviews, to determine how the plans were in fact impacting employees. According to an Audit witness, it was felt to be the purview of the first and second lines of defense (business and Risk) to evaluate the operation of incentive compensation plan design in practice.

B. Audits of "Culture"

In connection with its annual Enterprise Risk Management Assessments ("ERMA"), Audit rated risk and ethical culture in Wells Fargo at the enterprise level, and, beginning in 2013, at the Community Bank and other lines-of-business level. Audit's methodology for testing culture was less systematic than its approach to testing processes and controls: witnesses explained that culture is a "squishy" concept, difficult to quantify and test using the tools available to Audit. Audit rated culture in the Community Bank "Strong" in 2013, based on observations regarding the stature of risk management within the organization, audit results and various "key initiatives . . . focus[ed] on the customer." In 2014, the Community Bank ERMA appears to have focused on risk culture in particular; in support of another "Strong" culture rating, Audit wrote that risk management had "appropriate stature within Community Banking" and was "actively involved in strategic planning." Moreover, Audit found "strong and effective controls implemented across the business segments which demonstrate[d] the focus on risk management," as well as evidence of a strong risk culture through Audit's "monitoring of risk council committees and through ongoing participation in business meetings" in addition to "other committee meetings such as the CB Risk Management Committee, Deposit Loss Management Leadership Committee, Large Loss Review Team, and Business Direct Risk and Control meetings."

The emerging sales practice issues were first reflected in Audit's 2015 Community Bank culture assessment, issued in March 2016. Audit rated overall risk management—a component of the culture analysis—as "Needs Improvement" in recognition of enhancements needed to become "fully effective relative to heightened regulatory expectations." One area specifically identified as needing enhancement was "Sales Practices"—particularly the need to implement

[20] Between 2011 and 2015, Audit performed several additional audits that included in their scope Community Bank compensation plans for branch employees and management. As was true with respect to the 2012 audit, Audit generally found that the Community Bank's incentive compensation plan controls were effective, that they aligned sales and performance objectives with the business's risk appetite and that they adequately mitigated risks caused by financial incentives to engage in or overlook questionable sales behavior.

actions to improve related governance and controls in order to address regulatory concerns. Audit nonetheless rated culture "Satisfactory," observing that actions were underway to strengthen sales practices by fostering a culture where "only needs-based and value-add product and service solutions [would be] delivered to customers." The 2015 culture assessment also based its "Satisfactory" rating on "observations of Tone at the Top, credible challenge, incentive compensation, performance management, and stature."

C. Additional Audit Awareness of Sales Practice Issues

In addition to its audit work, Audit had access to data from quarterly reporting and committee presentations that indicated an increasing number of Community Bank sales practice issues over time. Audit personnel participated in various internal committees in which sales integrity issues were discussed. Audit witnesses explained that these committees did not generate action items or determine governance and ethics policies; rather, they were intended to raise awareness of "macro trends" among senior management. Additionally, Audit personnel attended semi-annual regional bank leadership meetings, at which data regarding sales integrity allegations were discussed. Audit witnesses indicated that the information they received at the meetings helped the business identify emerging risks, but did not appear alarming. Audit also prepared quarterly reports to the A&E Committee that included high-level summaries of sales quality and team member fraud data.

Senior Audit personnel, among others, received a July 2012 email from Michael Bacon (the head of Corporate Security, who also presented at the regional meetings attended by Audit) referencing "a spike in egregious Sales Integrity matters" and "a concerning trend in the area of Sales Integrity—from the increase in EthicsLine reports, to the increase in executive complaint letters" and "increases in confirmed fraud." Audit did not follow up on this communication, although one of the email's Audit recipients said he assumed that Bacon was doing so, in part because the email stated that "Corporate Security Investigations continues to work on several Community Bank project teams to analyze root causes and implement additional controls that are focused on minimizing future occurrences and mitigating the risks associated with" issues around "fictitious sales referrals," "customer consent concerns" and "false entry of customer identification information."[21]

---

21 The email from Bacon to Audit personnel and others forwarded an email from Claudia Russ Anderson, which questioned whether Bacon's draft reporting to the A&E Committee made an increase in Suspicious Activity Reports "so much worse than it really is . . ." Bacon noted in his email that "Claudia is a fantastic business partner and I enjoy a great relationship with her, but she often challenges the Audit and CS

In general, Audit witnesses said that they had no reason to believe that the Community Bank's detection and remediation processes relating to sales practice misconduct were inadequate. To the contrary, witnesses stated that the information they saw suggested that the controls in place—which were detective by nature—were functioning as intended. Audit witnesses also stated that the sales practice misconduct figures they received were not so pronounced as to suggest an urgent problem requiring modification of audit coverage. They further stated that their reaction to data suggesting an increase in sales integrity allegations generally would be to examine whether the monitoring functions responded appropriately, and Audit believed those functions were effective. Audit witnesses also said that, as the third line of defense, Audit's job was to ensure that the control environment established by the first (business) and second (Risk) lines of defense was appropriate. Audit personnel indicated that their focus was on testing the operation of specific processes and the processes' effectiveness at managing the risks they were designed to control, but that they did not generally investigate root causes of risks; according to the witnesses, that task rests with the business, which they said has greater familiarity with the risk environment, better access to operational data and both proximity to and responsibility for its employees' actions.

The Board of Directors

This section provides a detailed chronology describing the escalation of sales practice concerns to Wells Fargo's Board of Directors and committees of the Board. Board materials were reviewed back to 2002, where available, with primary focus from January 1, 2009, when Wells Fargo's and Wachovia's merger became effective, through September 25, 2016. That period encompassed approximately 80 Board meetings, 80 meetings of the A&E Committee, a similar number of Human Resources Committee meetings, 31 Risk Committee meetings and three joint A&E and Risk meetings.

Reports to the Board regarding sales practice issues are framed by three time periods: prior to 2014; 2014 through May 2015; and May 2015 through September 25, 2016.

A. Prior to 2014

Prior to 2014, sales practice or sales integrity issues were not flagged as noteworthy risks either to the Board of Directors as a whole or to any Board

A&E reporting verbiage. It is often a classic case of minimizing the negative information being submitted to executive management." Audit personnel stated that they found Russ Anderson reasonable to work with, although she generally did not raise issues about emerging risks but only responded to those raised by Audit.

committee. The principal report on noteworthy risks provided to the Board of Directors, starting at least with the first quarter of 2010, was prepared by the Enterprise Risk Management Committee, which included the most senior executives in the Risk, Compliance, Legal and Finance organizations. The ERMC prepared quarterly written reports to the Board of Directors that identified the Top Enterprise Risks facing Wells Fargo, typically flagging 20–40 such risks. Prior to 2014, sales practice issues were not among the identified risks.

. . . .

Sales integrity issues were mentioned in materials prepared for the A&E Committee. The primary responsibility of a public company audit committee is to monitor and oversee the integrity of the company's financial statements and financial reporting and to oversee the external and internal auditors. The A&E Committee reviews a number of risk issues, including operational risk, legal and regulatory compliance, financial crimes risk, information and security risk and technology risk.

Materials prepared for the A&E Committee prior to 2014 did not highlight sales practices as a noteworthy risk. Going back to at least 2002, however, committee materials referenced sales conduct or "gaming" issues. . . .

. . . .

Wells Fargo Audit & Security (renamed Wells Fargo Audit Services in 2012, both "WFAS") also prepared a quarterly report of 50–150 pages covering multiple topics including issues most important to the enterprise (such as BSA/AML), emerging issues, integration activities between Wells Fargo and Wachovia, audit review and tracking, special audit projects, investigations and annual reporting requirements under federal statutes and regulations. The WFAS report referred to sales integrity in two contexts. First, Corporate Security conducted investigations of "team member misconduct involving a possible violation of law, code of ethics policy violation or information security policy violation." This could include embezzlement, loan fraud, falsification of records and sales integrity. Second, EthicsLine reports and resulting investigations from anonymous reports of "possible violations of the Code of Ethics, violations of law, and suspicious activity" involving employees could also include sales practices. The WFAS reports referenced allegations and investigations concerning sales practices in most, but not all, quarters.

In the A&E Committee's materials prior to 2014, sales integrity SARs and investigations were therefore categorized together with other internal matters, such as defalcation, embezzlement, Code of Ethics violations, falsification of records, business expense fraud and a teller's forced balancing of his or her drawer, all matters that were viewed as having minimal, if any, customer impact.

Pre-2014 A&E Committee reports did not identify sales integrity as a noteworthy risk or as requiring special attention. . . .

B. 2014 Through May 2015

Sales integrity issues received heightened Board reporting and attention in 2014 following publication of a December 21, 2013 LOS ANGELES TIMES article about improper sales-related conduct, principally in Los Angeles. Hernandez, the Risk Committee Chair, instructed Loughlin that Corporate Risk should be involved in addressing the sales practice issues and that the Risk Committee should be kept informed of the status and developments. Much of the oversight now shifted to the Risk Committee, with primary responsibility for enterprise-wide risk and comprising among its members the chairs of the other Board committees.

Sales practices and the cross-sell strategy were identified as a risk issue to the Risk Committee for the first time in February 2014.[22] The ERMC circulated a report titled "Noteworthy Risk Issues." Among 19 risks identified as noteworthy, sales practices was included as a "High" risk and a risk likely to increase over the next year. In a similar report to the Board dated January 22, 2014, and delivered to the Board at its February 2014 Board meeting, the ERMC also identified sales conduct as one of 10 significant risks, supplemented by an appendix of 11 additional risks. The report stated that management was specifically focused on "the risks associated with sales practices, our cross sell strategy, and team member conduct." In February 2014, the HR Director and the Chief Risk Officer reported to the Human Resources Committee that, while they recommended monitoring for sales integrity in the Community Bank in 2014, action plans were in progress to address the issue, including heightened monitoring, and there was no need to adjust compensation for the 2013 cycle for sales integrity matters.

In an April 17, 2014 email exchange between Loughlin and Tolstedt regarding a draft of her presentation on sales practices scheduled for the April 2014 Risk Committee meeting, Loughlin advised that the Risk Committee wanted to hear from Tolstedt whether "the pressure of cross sell goals cause bad behavior." Tolstedt's presentation was removed from the agenda when she was summoned to jury duty. At the full Board meeting in April, Loughlin reported that sales practices had now become a current "focus" for Corporate Risk.

[22] "Risks associated with sales practices, [our] cross sell strategy and team member conduct" were also first identified as a "noteworthy" operational risk to the A&E Committee at its April 2014 meeting.

Sales practices were raised by the Risk Committee with senior management at the August 4, 2014 Risk Committee meeting. At that meeting, in response to a director's question on cross-sell risk issues, Loughlin and Stumpf discussed Wells Fargo's focus on ensuring its cross-sell strategies were consistent with the development of long-term customer relationships.

Overlapping in time, a broader project was underway since early 2013 to strengthen the Corporate Risk Group overall and oversight by the Risk Committee. In February 2013, McKinsey, an independent consulting firm, was engaged to evaluate Wells Fargo's risk management practices. McKinsey prepared a 402-page report that proposed many changes to the risk organization, and identified the need to "manage comprehensively the risks associated with sales (including product design, suitability and cross-selling)" without further description of the actual problems. McKinsey's report was presented to the Risk Committee, the Board and Wells Fargo's regulators in the summer of 2013. In October 2013, Corporate Risk presented to the Board a three-year plan to implement changes proposed by McKinsey and Wells Fargo's regulators. For 2014, the Board supported $60 million of additional funding for Corporate Risk to take on additional personnel, and the Risk Committee and Loughlin discussed whether forecasted Corporate Risk staffing levels were sufficient and compared favorably to peer institutions.

Throughout 2014, the quarterly "Noteworthy Risk Issues" submitted to the Risk Committee, two of which were also provided to the Board, continued to rank sales practices as a High and increasing risk, although it was not included in the Executive Summary covering the most important enterprise risks. The Board and Risk Committee thereafter received assurances from the Corporate Risk group, the Community Bank and Human Resources that sales practice issues were the subject of heightened attention, that the control environment was operating effectively and that the situation was improving.

Because of these improvements, in February 2015, the Noteworthy Risk Issues report reduced sales conduct from High to Medium risk, stating that management was "build[ing] out additional second line of defense oversight of Sales Practices." Also in February 2015, Audit reported to the A&E Committee that in 2014 it had conducted audits of sales practices, sales conduct and cross-sell, which were rated effective with no reportable issues. And in February 2015, the Director of Human Resources and the Chief Risk Officer advised the Human Resources Committee that the Community Bank had taken appropriate actions to address sales integrity issues, and therefore, there was no need to adjust compensation for 2014 for sales integrity concerns.

In April 2015, Tolstedt presented to the Risk Committee on sales practices. She acknowledged the need to address sales integrity issues in the Community Bank but reported favorable changes to address those issues. Tolstedt discussed improvements in risk management practices by enhancing monitoring capabilities of the Sales and Service Conduct Oversight Team, strengthening ethics training in the Community Bank, modifying compensation structures and incentive plans to encourage good behavior, and bolstering controls through a Quality of Sales Report Card, which was said to provide management with "key indicators around quality of sales in the areas of customer signatures, activations, procedures and account funding." She reported that the percent of branches achieving "Acceptable" ratings using the QSRC system increased to 93% in the first quarter of 2015 and that all Regional Banking Executives "performed well above Acceptable levels." She also reported that EthicsLine sales quality allegations decreased by 10% in 2014. Tolstedt emphasized that a large organization could not be perfect, and that the sales practice problem was a result of improper action on the part of individual employees.

The Risk Committee members viewed Tolstedt's presentation as too superficial and optimistic. After the meeting, Committee Chair Hernandez called Loughlin to tell him that the presentation was unsatisfactory and that Tolstedt should be brought back to the Risk Committee again to address sales practices.

C. May 2015 Through September 2016

On May 4, 2015, the Los Angeles City Attorney filed a lawsuit challenging Wells Fargo sales practices in Los Angeles. On May 7, the Risk Committee Chair, troubled by the allegations in the complaint, instructed Loughlin to coordinate a presentation "for the Risk Committee concerning the issues alleged and the WF policies, frameworks and activities that relate to them." The May 2015 "Noteworthy Risk Issues" restored sales practices to High risk and stated: "[w]e added sales practices to the enterprise priorities as this is an area receiving significant regulatory attention and poses a reputational risk due to a recent lawsuit filed alleging inappropriate sales practices."

In a May 12, 2015 email, Stumpf reported to the senior members of the Law Department, Corporate Risk and the Community Bank, that he and the Chair of the Risk Committee "decided to review the 'L.A. issue' as the first order of business for the Risk Committee next week." Stumpf instructed Tolstedt to work with the legal team to get relevant information to the committee members before the meeting.

In discussions with Stumpf, Hernandez had stated that the May presentation should not only discuss the Los Angeles case but also provide the broader context of sales practices and resulting actions. After reviewing a draft presentation to the Risk Committee prepared by the Community Bank, Stumpf instructed the drafting team that the presentation should include additional information: "My guess [is that] the [Risk] Committee of the board will want more supporting information," including specific information about the number of employees terminated for sales practice violations in the last twelve months and since Wells Fargo began implementing changes, the percentage of employees terminated for sales practice violations, whether and how Wells Fargo made sure it remedied customer harm, and the number of inappropriate accounts opened, as well as remedial steps.

A revised draft was prepared containing some of the requested information: it disclosed that approximately 1% of employees in the regional bank had been terminated for sales integrity violations in 2013 and 2014. A lawyer questioned the basis for that 1% number, and the topic became a subject of a prescheduled call among representatives of the Community Bank and the legal team. During that call, the 1% figure was deleted from the report to the Board. Every participant on the call that was interviewed has stated that he or she does not remember that discussion or the reason for the deletion. A review of emails shows that the most likely explanation is that Russ Anderson, backed by Tolstedt on the telephone call, argued that the 1% figure was unreliable, notwithstanding that the head of Internal Investigations had defended the data and reported that there had been 1,229 sales practice terminations/resignations in the Community Bank in 2013 and 1,293 in 2014. Russ Anderson continued even after the call to question the validity of the figure.

At the May 19, 2015 meeting, the Risk Committee met with management and company counsel and heard their presentation. After Strother made an opening presentation, Tolstedt spoke. The message communicated to the Risk Committee was that: (i) as a result of an investigation commenced in Southern California and thereafter expanded across "the retail banking footprint" in 2013 and 2014, 230 employees had been terminated; (ii) 70% of the terminations were related to telephone number changes (principally to frustrate telephone quality control surveys) and 30% to simulated funding abuses; (iii) the root cause was intentional employee misconduct, not systemic issues arising from sales goals or compensation; and (iv) Wells Fargo's controls had been effective in detecting improper behavior.

The Risk Committee was highly critical of the presentation. The 230 number from the 2013–2014 investigation was the first time the directors had heard of large-scale terminations and, as noted in a contemporaneous email from a participant in the meeting, the committee felt blindsided by the disclosure. In addition, in identifying possible violators, the Community Bank had used as a threshold or filter the commission of 50 phone number change violations over a three-month time period. As several witnesses recalled, Hernandez vigorously questioned that approach. Witnesses also recalled that the Risk Committee was critical of the Community Bank for taking too long to conduct a customer harm analysis.

The actual aggregate termination numbers for 2013 and 2014 of 1,229 and 1,293, respectively, as determined by Internal Investigations, went unmentioned at the May 19 meeting. Even if the Community Bank genuinely believed that the actual termination figures were unnecessary or had shortcomings, the Risk Committee had asked for that exact information, which was readily available, and its deletion created an inaccurate picture as to the scope and extent of sales practice problems. Multiple Board members have stated that they felt misled by the presentation; they left with the understanding that sales integrity terminations were in the range of 200–300 and were largely localized in Southern California. The Board was not provided with the correct aggregated termination data until well into 2016.

After the meeting, Stumpf called Loughlin, who was on vacation, and told him that the meeting (which Stumpf had not attended) did not go well, and the presentation was not well done.

Following the Risk Committee's harsh reaction to the May presentation, management reported that it was ramping up attention to the issue. At the full Board of Directors meeting in June, Loughlin reported that Corporate Risk was now planning a comprehensive review and initiative regarding the company's sales practices, to cover Community Bank, Mortgage Banking and Wealth Brokerage and Retirement. He planned also to retain a third-party consulting firm to conduct an independent review of Wells Fargo's training, compensation and sales practices. Management committed to report to the full Board at its scheduled October 2015 meeting. On a risk awareness "Dashboard" submitted to the Board in June 2015, sales practices, including lawsuits and heightened regulatory compliance activity, were elevated to cross-functional and reputational risks.

The October 27, 2015 Board of Directors meeting was largely dedicated to a review of sales practices. The full Board received a report from Accenture, the consultant engaged by Wells Fargo to review sales practices in the Community Bank; a presentation from Tolstedt on steps being taken to effectuate the reforms called for by Accenture; and a report from Loughlin on how Risk was bolstering oversight of sales practices. The Board also had discussions with management on the retention of PwC to conduct an analysis of customer harm, with a completion date of January 31, 2016. As witnesses recalled, Hernandez again was highly critical of the presentation by Tolstedt; he believed she was minimizing the issue before the Board.

Management reported to the Board regarding its intensified efforts. At the November 17, 2015 A&E Committee meeting, the BSA Officer reported that Internal Investigations was now "working with the new Corporate Risk-led Sales Practices Initiative." He reported that sales integrity now made up roughly 25% of internal investigation cases, and that confirmed fraud or confirmed policy violations were being found in 75% of those investigations. At the same meeting, the Chief Compliance Officer reported to both the A&E and Risk Committees on discussions with regulators and compliance activities on remediation of sales practices. Sales practices remained ranked as a High risk and as an "Enterprise Priority."

In December 2015, Hernandez and the lead independent director, Stephen Sanger, met with Stumpf in Washington, D.C., over dinner. They expressed to Stumpf their view that Tolstedt could no longer effectively lead the Community Bank.

Meanwhile, with the support of the Risk Committee, the risk organization was growing rapidly. At the February 2016 Risk Committee meeting, Loughlin reported that risk professionals had grown by 16% in 2015, with over 10,000 professionals now monitoring risk. A new Head of Sales Practice Oversight for Risk was added in November 2015, and a new head for Community Banking Sales and Service Conduct Risk was hired the previous month. For 2016, the Corporate Risk budget was set to increase another 15.9%, with additional professionals to be hired in many areas including oversight of sales practices.

Throughout 2016, management kept the Board informed of ongoing discussions with the Los Angeles City Attorney and with Wells Fargo's banking regulators to resolve the litigation and to respond to regulatory concerns and implement corrective actions for sales practices. PwC summarized its findings on customer harm for the directors. Also, the Risk Committee continued to authorize Corporate Risk's rapid expansion.

On February 23, 2016, the Board's Human Resources Committee met to determine compensation for 2015 for senior executives, including Tolstedt. By now, the reaction of Board members to Tolstedt was a complicated one. The

Board, especially the Risk Committee, was concerned and critical of the sales practice issues, but, at this point, Board members still understood it to be mostly a Southern California problem with terminations in the range of 230. Hernandez was especially critical of Tolstedt, whom he believed was intentionally misleading the Board. Most other directors, while believing that she had been overly optimistic and minimized problems, were not yet that critical. Many thought, however, that because of her defensiveness, controlling management style, resistance to change and reluctance to cooperate or work with individuals outside the Community Bank, she was the wrong person to continue to lead the Community Bank. By now she was reporting directly to Sloan, who had requested six months to assess her performance and her ability to change and improve, a request viewed as reasonable by most Board members. And Stumpf still was supportive of her. He strongly advocated before the HRC that all the senior executives on his team, including Tolstedt, should be treated similarly in compensation. After several directors on the HRC challenged Stumpf, he persisted and the HRC accepted his recommendation.

Throughout the spring and summer, management advised the Board of ongoing settlement discussions with the Los Angeles City Attorney, the CFPB and the OCC. In early May 2016, after A&E directors had asked for more robust involvement by the ethics office, the A&E Committee received a written report from the Chief Global Ethics Officer. That report included information about sales integrity violations, including, for the first time, accurate termination/ resignation numbers for 2014 and 2015: 1,327 in the Community Bank for 2014, declining by 30% to 960 in 2015. The A&E Committee was shown termination data at its July meeting for the first five months of 2016.

With Sloan's assessment of Tolstedt completed, effective July 31, 2016, a Board resolution provided that she would cease serving as an executive officer of Wells Fargo. At that time, it was announced that she would retire as of December 31, 2016.

Settlements with the Los Angeles City Attorney, the OCC and the CFPB followed on September 8, 2016. From the CFPB settlement, the directors for the first time learned that approximately 5,300 Wells Fargo employees had been terminated between January 1, 2011, and March 7, 2016, for sales practice violations. Board members advocated the discontinuance of all retail product sales goals, which management announced on September 13, 2016, effective January 1, 2017. Subsequently, at the Board's urging, the effective date for discontinuing sales goals was moved up to October 1, 2016.

On approximately September 21, 2016, the independent members of the Board of Directors retained Shearman & Sterling to advise them as independent (and previously uninvolved) counsel. The Independent Directors met on September 25, 2016. They took the compensation actions with respect to John Stumpf and Carrie Tolstedt summarized in Wells Fargo's September 28, 2016 Form 8-K. Stumpf agreed to forfeit all unvested equity awards, valued approximately at $41 million, and receive no 2016 bonus. The Board caused to be forfeited all of Tolstedt's unvested equity awards, approximately $19 million, and provided that she would receive no 2016 bonus and no severance.[23] The directors that same day created the independent Sales Practice Oversight Committee with full authority to conduct a comprehensive investigation of sales practices. Instead of waiting for the completion of the investigation, Board committees made governance changes to their charters . . . expanding their monitoring and scope of review over conduct risk, including sales practices.

NOTES

1. This report said something that we consider very important: "The Community Bank identified itself as a sales organization, like department or retail stores, rather than a service-oriented financial institution. This provided justification for a relentless focus on sales, abbreviated training and high employee turnover."* That's framing in action. Employees were pressured to make sales in whatever ways would meet the bank's goals. But the demand for bank accounts is limited. At some point, a customer will believe that he or she has a sufficient number of accounts already and will not want to open any more (at least not at the same bank). When the pressure on an employee to open more and more accounts intersects with a customer's desire *not* to have any more accounts opened at that bank, someone's desires will get frustrated. Either the employee will not meet the required benchmarks, or the customer is going to open more accounts.

Think back to Judge Harner's article on enterprise risk management in the last chapter. Wells Fargo had risk management procedures in place. The board of directors had a Risk Committee. The company itself had an arm called Corporate

---

[23] At its September 25, 2016 meeting, the Board also determined that Tolstedt would be immediately separated from Wells Fargo and that cause existed to terminate her employment. The Board directed that a notice of termination for cause be delivered to Tolstedt on September 26, 2016, but that the notice would be rescinded if she agreed in writing by September 27, 2016, not to exercise any of her outstanding options until the conclusion of the Board's investigation. On September 27, 2016, Tolstedt agreed not to exercise any outstanding stock options previously awarded until the completion of the investigation and that at such time the Board of Directors would have the authority to determine the extent to which the options would be forfeited.

* Report at 7, which you can find at p. 376 of our book.

Risk, an Internal Investigations group, and an Audit group. And, of course, Wells Fargo had lawyers, who, apparently, misunderstood just what was being "gamed":

> Notwithstanding the growing awareness of the reputational risk associated with mass terminations, and the fact that many of these incidents involved unauthorized products or accounts, the perception persisted in the Law Department that sales integrity issues involved "gaming" the Community Bank's incentive programs and not conduct affecting customers. That led them to underestimate the need to escalate and more directly manage sales integrity issues.*

So, with all of these various levels of risk management in place, why do you think that so many Wells Fargo employees opened so many spurious accounts?

2. If you were on the Wells Fargo board, what metrics would you want to track to monitor whether your incentives were eliciting the behavior that you wanted employees to do, rather than behavior that rewarded fraud? How would you test those metrics?

3. What do you think is the proper relationship between a board of directors and management once it appears that management is not controlling risk adequately?

* Report at 75, which you can find at p. 414 of our book.

PART IV

Example from the Government—NASA and the Space Shuttle Disasters

Let's be clear: both of us love NASA with all of our hearts. We believe that NASA has, literally, opened up the universe for humankind. You'd be amazed by how much in your life exists because, well, we decided to go to the moon.* If you haven't heard President John F. Kennedy deliver the speech about going to the moon, then here's our favorite part:

> We choose to go to the moon. We choose to go to the moon in this decade and do the other things, not because they are easy, but because they are hard, because that goal will serve to organize and measure the best of our energies and skills, because that challenge is one that we are willing to accept, one we are unwilling to postpone, and one which we intend to win, and the others, too.**

We know many, many heroes at NASA. One of us has a best friend who works there.*** But there are two episodes in NASA's history that broke everyone's heart: the *Challenger* disaster and the *Columbia* disaster. We've edited one of the reports that details the various failures that contributed to these two accidents. And, just as we foreshadowed in the VW section of last chapter, we have a particular question for you: why did the NASA engineers fight so hard to do the right thing here, when other engineers in other organizations chose the path of engineering "around" the rules? That question plays over and over in our minds. The engineers at NASA fought hard to stop the launches until they could figure out the safety issues. The engineers at VW fought hard to engineer around

* https://er.jsc.nasa.gov/seh/ricetalk.htm. One of us is compelled to point out that he delivered this classic speech in the stadium at Rice University.

** Our second-favorite part is this one: "But why, some say, the moon? Why choose this as our goal? And they may well ask why climb the highest mountain? Why, 35 years ago, fly the Atlantic? Why does Rice play Texas?" That was back when Rice University was in the Southwest Conference.

*** And the other one of us considers him to be her friend, too, as we've mentioned earlier in this book.

environmental regulations. We know that engineers like to figure out solutions to problems, so why did the engineers at NASA frame the problem as "do we have a safety issue?," but the engineers at VW framed the problem as "these regulations are impossible, so how do we work around them?" Was there subtle (or not-so-subtle) pressure from their managers to frame the problem in a particular way?

For that matter, NASA really thought it had fixed various company culture problems that had led to the O-ring disaster described in the first part of the report. Not only do we want you to compare the various actions by NASA's and VW's engineers, but we also want you to spend some time asking yourself this question as you read through the report: what if you think you've fixed the company's culture, but you're wrong? Try to figure out how you might test your assumptions about whether you've fixed a deep-seated problem or only scratched the surface.

CHAPTER 14

Columbia Accident Investigation Board Report, Vol. I, August 2003*

*Harold W. Gehman, Jr., Chair; John L. Barry, Duane W. Deal, James H. Hallock, Kenneth W. Hess, G. Scott Hubbard, John M. Logsdon, Douglas D. Osheroff, Sally K. Ride, Roger E. Tetrault, Stephen A. Turcotte, Steven B. Wallace, and Sheila E. Widnall***

The February 1 disintegration of *Columbia* during re-entry, 17 years after *Challenger* was destroyed on ascent, is the most recent reminder that sending people into orbit and returning them safely to Earth remains a difficult and perilous endeavor.

It is the view of the Columbia Accident Investigation Board that the *Columbia* accident is not a random event, but rather a product of the Space Shuttle Program's history and current management processes. Fully understanding how it happened requires an exploration of that history and management. This chapter charts how the Shuttle emerged from a series of political compromises Nthat produced unreasonable expectations—even myths—about its performance, how the *Challenger* accident shattered those myths several years after NASA began acting upon them as fact, and how, in retrospect, the Shuttle's technically ambitious design resulted in an inherently vulnerable vehicle, the safe operation of which exceeded NASA's organizational capabilities as they existed at the time of the *Columbia* accident. The Board's investigation of what caused the *Columbia* accident thus begins in the fields of East Texas but reaches more than 30 years into the past, to a series of economically and politically driven decisions that cast the Shuttle program in a role that its nascent technology could not support. To understand the cause of the *Columbia* accident is to understand how a program

* Columbia Accident Investigation Board Report Vol. I, August 2003, available at http://s3.amazonaws.com/akamai.netstorage/anon.nasa-global/CAIB/CAIB_lowres_full.pdf.

** Editors' note: We've edited this report, so the renumbered footnotes reflect the edited version.

promising reliability and cost efficiency resulted instead in a developmental vehicle that never achieved the fully operational status NASA and the nation accorded it.[1]

. . . .

1.5 The *Challenger* Accident

The illusion that the Space Shuttle was an operational system, safe enough to carry legislators and a high-school teacher into orbit, was abruptly and tragically shattered on the morning of January 28, 1986, when *Challenger* was destroyed 73 seconds after launch during the 25th mission . . . . The seven-member crew perished. To investigate, President Reagan appointed the 13-member Presidential Commission on the Space Shuttle Challenger Accident, which soon became known as the Rogers Commission, after its chairman, former Secretary of State William P. Rogers. Early in its investigation, the Commission identified the mechanical cause of the accident to be the failure of the joint of one of the Solid Rocket Boosters. The Commission found that the design was not well understood by the engineers that operated it and that it had not been adequately tested.[2]

When the Rogers Commission discovered that, on the eve of the launch, NASA and a contractor had vigorously debated the wisdom of operating the Shuttle in the cold temperatures predicted for the next day, and that more senior NASA managers were unaware of this debate, the Commission shifted the focus of its investigation to "NASA management practices, Center-Headquarters relationships, and the chain of command for launch commit decisions." As the investigation continued, it revealed a NASA culture that had gradually begun to accept escalating risk, and a NASA safety program that was largely silent and ineffective.

The Rogers Commission report, issued on June 6, 1986, recommended a redesign and recertification of the Solid Rocket Motor joint and seal and urged that an independent body oversee its qualification and testing. The report concluded that the drive to declare the Shuttle operational had put enormous pressures on the system and stretched its resources to the limit. Faulting NASA safety practices, the Commission also called for the creation of an independent NASA Office of Safety, Reliability, and Quality Assurance, reporting directly to the NASA Administrator, as well as structural changes in program management.[3]

. . . .

---

1 Report at 21.

2 *Id.* at 24 (footnote omitted).

3 *Id.* at 25 (footnotes omitted).

[*Columbia's* Final Flight]

2.5 Debris Strike Analysis and Requests for Imagery

As is done after every launch, within two hours of the liftoff the Intercenter Photo Working Group examined video from tracking cameras. An initial review did not reveal any unusual events. The next day, when the Intercenter Photo Working Group personnel received much higher resolution film that had been processed overnight, they noticed a debris strike at 81.9 seconds after launch. A large object from the left bipod area of the External Tank struck the Orbiter, apparently impacting the underside of the left wing near RCC panels 5 through 9. The object's large size and the apparent momentum transfer concerned Intercenter Photo Working Group personnel, who were worried that *Columbia* had sustained damage not detectable in the limited number of views their tracking cameras captured. This concern led the Intercenter Photo Working Group Chair to request, in anticipation of analysts' needs, that a high-resolution image of the Orbiter on-orbit be obtained by the Department of Defense. By the Board's count, this would be the first of three distinct requests to image *Columbia* on-orbit. . . .

After discovering the strike, the Intercenter Photo Working Group prepared a report with a video clip of the impact and sent it to the Mission Management Team, the Mission Evaluation Room, and engineers at United Space Alliance and Boeing. In accordance with NASA guidelines, these contractor and NASA engineers began an assessment of potential impact damage to *Columbia's* left wing, and soon formed a Debris Assessment Team to conduct a formal review.[4]

The first formal Debris Assessment Team meeting was held on January 21, five days into the mission. It ended with the highest-ranking NASA engineer on the team agreeing to bring the team's request for imaging of the wing on-orbit, which would provide better information on which to base their analysis, to the Johnson Space Center Engineering Management Directorate, with the expectation the request would go forward to Space Shuttle Program managers. Debris Assessment Team members subsequently learned that these managers declined to image *Columbia.*

Without on-orbit pictures of *Columbia*, the Debris Assessment Team was restricted to using a mathematical modeling tool called Crater to assess damage, although it had not been designed with this type of impact in mind. Team members concluded over the next six days that some localized heating damage would most likely occur during re-entry, but they could not definitively state that

[4] Report at 39.

structural damage would result. On January 24, the Debris Assessment Team made a presentation of these results to the Mission Evaluation Room, whose manager gave a verbal summary (with no data) of that presentation to the Mission Management Team the same day. The Mission Management Team declared the debris strike a "turnaround" issue and did not pursue a request for imagery.

Even after the Debris Assessment Team's conclusion had been reported to the Mission Management Team, engineers throughout NASA and Mission Control continued to exchange e-mails and discuss possible damage. These messages and discussions were generally sent only to people within the senders' area of expertise and level of seniority.

The team worked through the de-orbit preparation checklist and re-entry checklist procedures. Weather forecasters, with the help of pilots in the Shuttle Training Aircraft, evaluated landing site weather conditions at the Kennedy Space Center. At the time of the de-orbit decision, about 20 minutes before the initiation of the de-orbit burn, all weather observations and forecasts were within guidelines set by the flight rules, and all systems were normal.

Shortly after 8:00 a.m., the Mission Control Center Entry Flight Director polled the Mission Control room for a GO/NO-GO decision for the de-orbit burn, and at 8:10 a.m., the Capsule Communicator notified the crew they were GO for de-orbit burn. . . .

. . . .

At 8:48:39 a.m. (EI+270), a sensor on the left wing leading edge spar showed strains higher than those seen on previous *Columbia* re-entries. This was recorded only on the Modular Auxiliary Data System, and was not telemetered to ground controllers or displayed to the crew . . . . At 8:49:32 a.m. (EI+323), traveling at approximately Mach 24.5, *Columbia* executed a roll to the right, beginning a preplanned banking turn to manage lift, and therefore limit the Orbiter's rate of descent and heating.[5]

Now crossing California, the Orbiter appeared to observers on the ground as a bright spot of light moving rapidly across the sky. Signs of debris being shed were sighted at 8:53:46 a.m. (EI+577), when the superheated air surrounding the Orbiter suddenly brightened, causing a noticeable streak in the Orbiter's luminescent trail. Observers witnessed another four similar events during the following 23 seconds, and a bright flash just seconds after *Columbia* crossed from California into Nevada airspace at 8:54:25 a.m. (EI+614), when the Orbiter was

---

5 *Id.* at 38.

traveling at Mach 22.5 and 227,400 feet. Witnesses observed another 18 similar events in the next four minutes as *Columbia* streaked over Utah, Arizona, New Mexico, and Texas.

In Mission Control, re-entry appeared normal until 8:54:24 a.m. (EI+613), when the Maintenance, Mechanical, and Crew Systems (MMACS) officer informed the Flight Director that four hydraulic sensors in the left wing were indicating "offscale low," a reading that falls below the minimum capability of the sensor. As the seconds passed, the Entry Team continued to discuss the four failed indicators.

. . . .

Around 8:58:00 a.m. (EI+831), wing leading edge temperatures typically decreased to 2,880 degrees Fahrenheit. At 8:58:20 a.m. (EI+851), traveling at 209,800 feet and Mach 19.5, *Columbia* crossed from New Mexico into Texas, and about this time shed a Thermal Protection System tile, which was the most westerly piece of debris that has been recovered.

Searchers found the tile in a field in Littlefield, Texas, just northwest of Lubbock. At 8:59:15 a.m. (EI+906), MMACS informed the Flight Director that pressure readings had been lost on both left main landing gear tires. The Flight Director then told the Capsule Communicator (CAPCOM) to let the crew know that Mission Control saw the messages and was evaluating the indications, and added that the Flight Control Team did not understand the crew's last transmission.

At 8:59:32 a.m. (EI+923), a broken response from the mission commander was recorded: "Roger, [cut off in midword] . . ." It was the last communication from the crew and the last telemetry signal received in Mission Control. Videos made by observers on the ground at 9:00:18 a.m. (EI+969) revealed that the Orbiter was disintegrating.[6] . . .

[Chapter 4: Other Factors Considered (In Terms of Causation)]

During its investigation, the Board evaluated every known factor that could have caused or contributed to the *Columbia* accident, such as the effects of space weather on the Orbiter during re-entry and the specters of sabotage and terrorism. In addition to the analysis/scenario investigations, the Board oversaw a NASA "fault tree" investigation, which accounts for every chain of events that could possibly cause a system to fail. Most of these factors were conclusively eliminated as having nothing to do with the accident; however, several factors have yet to be

6 *Id.* at 39.

ruled out. Although deemed by the Board as unlikely to have contributed to the accident, these are still open and are being investigated further by NASA. In a few other cases, there is insufficient evidence to completely eliminate a factor, though most evidence indicates that it did not play a role in the accident. In the course of investigating these factors, the Board identified several serious problems that were not part of the accident's causal chain but nonetheless have major implications for future missions.

In this chapter, a discussion of these potential causal and contributing factors is divided into two sections. The first introduces the primary tool used to assess potential causes of the breakup: the fault tree. The second addresses fault tree items and particularly notable factors that raised concerns for this investigation and, more broadly, for the future operation of the Space Shuttle.

4.1 Fault Tree

The NASA Accident Investigation Team investigated the accident using "fault trees," a common organizational tool in systems engineering. Fault trees are graphical representations of every conceivable sequence of events that could cause a system to fail. The fault tree's uppermost level illustrates the events that could have directly caused the loss of *Columbia* by aerodynamic breakup during re-entry. Subsequent levels comprise all individual elements or factors that could cause the failure described immediately above it. In this way, all potential chains of causation that lead ultimately to the loss of *Columbia* can be diagrammed, and the behavior of every subsystem that was not a precipitating cause can be eliminated from consideration.

NASA chartered six teams to develop fault trees, one for each of the Shuttle's major components: the Orbiter, Space Shuttle Main Engine, Reusable Solid Rocket Motor, Solid Rocket Booster, External Tank, and Payload. A seventh "systems integration" fault tree team analyzed failure scenarios involving two or more Shuttle components. These interdisciplinary teams included NASA and contractor personnel, as well as outside experts.

Some of the fault trees are very large and intricate. For instance, the Orbiter fault tree, which only considers events on the Orbiter that could have led to the accident, includes 234 elements. In contrast, the Systems Integration fault tree, which deals with interactions among parts of the Shuttle, includes 295 unique multi-element integration faults, 128 Orbiter multi-element faults, and 221 connections to the other Shuttle components. These faults fall into three categories: induced and natural environments (such as structural interface loads and electromechanical effects); integrated vehicle mass properties; and external impacts (such as debris from the External Tank). Because the Systems Integration team considered multi-element faults—that is, scenarios involving several Shuttle components—it frequently worked in tandem with the Component teams.[7]

In the case of the *Columbia* accident, there could be two plausible explanations for the aerodynamic breakup of the Orbiter: (1) the Orbiter sustained structural damage that undermined attitude control during re-entry; or (2) the Orbiter maneuvered to an attitude in which it was not designed to fly. The former explanation deals with structural damage initiated before launch, during ascent, on orbit, or during re-entry. The latter considers aerodynamic breakup caused by improper attitude or trajectory control by the Orbiter's Flight Control System. Telemetry and other data strongly suggest that improper maneuvering was not a factor. Therefore, most of the fault tree analysis concentrated on structural damage that could have impeded the Orbiter's attitude control, in spite of properly operating guidance, navigation, and flight control systems.

When investigators ruled out a potential cascade of events, as represented by a branch on the fault tree, it was deemed "closed." When evidence proved inconclusive, the item remained "open." Some elements could be dismissed at a high level in the tree, but most required delving into lower levels. . . .[8]

[Why the Accident Occurred]

Many accident investigations do not go far enough. They identify the technical cause of the accident, and then connect it to a variant of "operator error"—the line worker who forgot to insert the bolt, the engineer who miscalculated the stress, or the manager who made the wrong decision. But this is seldom the entire issue. When the determinations of the causal chain are limited to the technical flaw and individual failure, typically the actions taken to prevent a similar event in the future are also limited: fix the technical problem and replace or retrain the individual responsible. Putting these corrections in place leads to another mistake—the belief that the problem is solved. The Board did not want to make these errors.

Attempting to manage high-risk technologies while minimizing failures is an extraordinary challenge. By their nature, these complex technologies are intricate, with many interrelated parts. Standing alone, the components may be well understood and have failure modes that can be anticipated. Yet when these components are integrated into a larger system, unanticipated interactions can occur that lead to catastrophic outcomes. The risk of these complex systems is

---

7 *Id.* at 85.

8 *Id.* at 86.

increased when they are produced and operated by complex organizations that also break down in unanticipated ways.

In our view, the NASA organizational culture had as much to do with this accident as the foam. Organizational culture refers to the basic values, norms, beliefs, and practices that characterize the functioning of an institution. At the most basic level, organizational culture defines the assumptions that employees make as they carry out their work. It is a powerful force that can persist through reorganizations and the change of key personnel. It can be a positive or a negative force.

In a report dealing with nuclear wastes, the National Research Council quoted Alvin Weinberg's classic statement about the "Faustian bargain" that nuclear scientists made with society. "The price that we demand of society for this magical energy source is both a vigilance and a longevity of our social institutions that we are quite unaccustomed to." This is also true of the space program. At NASA's urging, the nation committed to building an amazing, if compromised, vehicle called the Space Shuttle. When the agency did this, it accepted the bargain to operate and maintain the vehicle in the safest possible way. The Board is not convinced that NASA has completely lived up to the bargain, or that Congress and the Administration has provided the funding and support necessary for NASA to do so. This situation needs to be addressed—if the nation intends to keep conducting human space flight, it needs to live up to its part of the bargain.

Part Two of this report examines NASA's organizational, historical, and cultural factors, as well as how these factors contributed to the accident. As in Part One, this part begins with history. Chapter 5 examines the post-*Challenger* history of NASA and its Human Space Flight Program. This includes reviewing the budget as well as organizational and management history, such as shifting management systems and locations. Chapter 6 documents management performance related to *Columbia* to establish events analyzed in later chapters. The chapter reviews the foam strikes, intense schedule pressure driven by an artificial requirement to deliver Node 2 to the International Space Station by a certain date, and NASA management's handling of concerns regarding *Columbia* during the STS-107 mission.

In Chapter 7, the Board presents its views of how high-risk activities should be managed, and lists the characteristics of institutions that emphasize high-reliability results over economic efficiency or strict adherence to a schedule. This chapter measures the Space Shuttle Program's organizational and management practices against these principles and finds them wanting. Chapter 7 defines the organizational cause and offers recommendations. Chapter 8 draws from the previous chapters on history, budgets, culture, organization, and safety practices, and analyzes how all these factors contributed to this accident. This chapter captures the Board's views of the need to adjust management to enhance safety margins in Shuttle operations, and reaffirms the Board's position that without these changes, we have no confidence that other "corrective actions" will improve the safety of Shuttle operations. The changes we recommend will be difficult to accomplish—and will be internally resisted.[9]

[Chapter 5 From *Challenger* to *Columbia*]

The Board is convinced that the factors that led to the *Columbia* accident go well beyond the physical mechanisms discussed in Chapter 3. The causal roots of the accident can also be traced, in part, to the turbulent post-Cold War policy environment in which NASA functioned during most of the years between the destruction of *Challenger* and the loss of *Columbia.* The end of the Cold War in the late 1980s meant that the most important political underpinning of NASA's Human Space Flight Program—U.S.-Soviet space competition—was lost, with no equally strong political objective to replace it. No longer able to justify its projects with the kind of urgency that the superpower struggle had provided, the agency could not obtain budget increases through the 1990s. Rather than adjust its ambitions to this new state of affairs, NASA continued to push an ambitious agenda of space science and exploration, including a costly Space Station Program.

If NASA wanted to carry out that agenda, its only recourse, given its budget allocation, was to become more efficient, accomplishing more at less cost. The search for cost reductions led top NASA leaders over the past decade to downsize the Shuttle workforce, outsource various Shuttle Program responsibilities—including safety oversight—and consider eventual privatization of the Space Shuttle Program. The program's budget was reduced by 40 percent in purchasing power over the past decade and repeatedly raided to make up for Space Station cost overruns, even as the Program maintained a launch schedule in which the Shuttle, a developmental vehicle, was used in an operational mode. In addition, the uncertainty of top policymakers in the White House, Congress, and NASA as to how long the Shuttle would fly before being replaced resulted in the delay of upgrades needed to make the Shuttle safer and to extend its service life.

The Space Shuttle Program has been transformed since the late 1980s implementation of post-*Challenger* management changes in ways that raise questions, addressed here and in later chapters of Part Two, about NASA's ability

---

[9] *Id.* at 97.

to safely operate the Space Shuttle. While it would be inaccurate to say that NASA managed the Space Shuttle Program at the time of the *Columbia* accident in the same manner it did prior to *Challenger*, there are unfortunate similarities between the agency's performance and safety practices in both periods.

5.1 The *Challenger* Accident and Its Aftermath

The inherently vulnerable design of the Space Shuttle, described in Chapter 1, was a product of policy and technological compromises made at the time of its approval in 1972. That approval process also produced unreasonable expectations, even myths, about the Shuttle's future performance that NASA tried futilely to fulfill as the Shuttle became "operational" in 1982. At first, NASA was able to maintain the image of the Shuttle as an operational vehicle. During its early years of operation, the Shuttle launched satellites, performed on-orbit research, and even took members of Congress into orbit. At the beginning of 1986, the goal of "routine access to space" established by President Ronald Reagan in 1982 was ostensibly being achieved. That appearance soon proved illusory. On the cold morning of January 28, 1986, the Shuttle *Challenger* broke apart 73 seconds into its climb towards orbit. On board were Francis R. Scobee, Michael J. Smith, Ellison S. Onizuka, Judith A. Resnick, Ronald E. McNair, Sharon Christa McAuliffe, and Gregory B. Jarvis. All perished.

Rogers Commission

On February 3, 1986, President Reagan created the Presidential Commission on the Space Shuttle Challenger Accident, which soon became known as the Rogers Commission after its chairman, former Secretary of State William Rogers. The Commission's report, issued on June 6, 1986, concluded that the loss of *Challenger* was caused by a failure of the joint and seal between the two lower segments of the right Solid Rocket Booster. Hot gases blew past a rubber O-ring in the joint, leading to a structural failure and the explosive burning[10] of the Shuttle's hydrogen fuel. While the Rogers Commission identified the failure of the Solid Rocket Booster joint and seal as the physical cause of the accident, it also noted a number of NASA management failures that contributed to the catastrophe.

The Rogers Commission concluded "the decision to launch the *Challenger* was flawed. Communication failures, incomplete and misleading information, and poor management judgments all figured in a decision-making process that permitted, in the words of the Commission, "internal flight safety problems to bypass key Shuttle managers." As a result, if those making the launch decision

[10] *Id.* at 99.

"had known all the facts, it is highly unlikely that they would have decided to launch." Far from meticulously guarding against potential problems, the Commission found that NASA had required "a contractor to prove that it was not safe to launch, rather than proving it was safe."

The Commission also found that NASA had missed warning signs of the impending accident. When the joint began behaving in unexpected ways, neither NASA nor the Solid Rocket Motor manufacturer Morton-Thiokol adequately tested the joint to determine the source of the deviations from specifications or developed a solution to them, even though the problems frequently recurred. Nor did they respond to internal warnings about the faulty seal. Instead, Morton-Thiokol and NASA management came to see the problems as an acceptable flight risk—a violation of a design requirement that could be tolerated.

During this period of increasing uncertainty about the joint's performance, the Commission found that NASA's safety system had been "silent." Of the management, organizational, and communication failures that contributed to the accident, four related to faults within the safety system, including "a lack of problem reporting requirements, inadequate trend analysis, misrepresentation of criticality, and lack of involvement in critical discussions." The checks and balances the safety system was meant to provide were not working.

Still another factor influenced the decisions that led to the accident. The Rogers Commission noted that the Shuttle's increasing flight rate in the mid-1980s created schedule pressure, including the compression of training schedules, a shortage of spare parts, and the focusing of resources on near-term problems. NASA managers "may have forgotten—partly because of past success, partly because of their own well-nurtured image of the program—that the Shuttle was still in a research and development phase."

The *Challenger* accident had profound effects on the U.S. space program. On August 15, 1986, President Reagan announced that "NASA will no longer be in the business of launching private satellites." The accident ended Air Force and intelligence community reliance on the Shuttle to launch national security payloads, prompted the decision to abandon the yet-to-be-opened Shuttle launch site at Vandenberg Air Force Base, and forced the development of improved expendable launch vehicles. A 1992 White House advisory committee concluded that the recovery from the *Challenger* disaster cost the country $12 billion, which included the cost of building the replacement Orbiter *Endeavour*.

It took NASA 32 months after the *Challenger* accident to redesign and requalify the Solid Rocket Booster and to return the Shuttle to flight. The first post-accident flight was launched on September 29, 1988. As the Shuttle returned to flight, NASA Associate Administrator for Space Flight[11] Richard Truly commented, "We will always have to treat it [the Shuttle] like an R&D test program, even many years into the future. I don't think calling it operational fooled anybody within the program . . . It was a signal to the public that shouldn't have been sent."

Selected Rogers Commission Recommendations

. . . .

- "The Shuttle Program Structure should be reviewed. The project managers for the various elements of the Shuttle program felt more accountable to their center management than to the Shuttle program organization."
- "NASA should encourage the transition of qualified astronauts into agency management positions."
- "NASA should establish an Office of Safety, Reliability and Quality Assurance to be headed by an Associate Administrator, reporting directly to the NASA Administrator. It would have direct authority for safety, reliability, and quality assurance throughout the agency. The office should be assigned the work force to ensure adequate oversight of its functions and should be independent of other NASA functional and program responsibilities."
- "NASA should establish an STS Safety Advisory Panel reporting to the STS Program Manager. The charter of this panel should include Shuttle operational issues, launch commit criteria, flight rules, flight readiness and risk management."
- "The Commission found that Marshall Space Flight Center project managers, because of a tendency at Marshall to management isolation, failed to provide full and timely information bearing on the safety of flight 51-L [the *Challenger* mission] to other vital elements of Shuttle program management . . . NASA should take energetic steps to eliminate this tendency at Marshall Space Flight Center, whether by changes of personnel, organization, indoctrination or all three."
- "The nation's reliance on the Shuttle as its principal space launch capability created a relentless pressure on NASA to increase the

---

[11] *Id.* at 100.

flight rate . . . NASA must establish a flight rate that is consistent with its resources."[12]

The Shuttle Program After Return to Flight

After the Rogers Commission report was issued, NASA made many of the organizational changes the Commission recommended. The space agency moved management of the Space Shuttle Program from the Johnson Space Center to NASA Headquarters in Washington, D.C. The intent of this change was to create a management structure "resembling that of the Apollo program, with the aim of preventing communication deficiencies that contributed to the *Challenger* accident." NASA also established an Office of Safety, Reliability, and Quality Assurance at its Headquarters, though that office was not given the "direct authority" over all of NASA's safety operations as the Rogers Commission had recommended. Rather, NASA human space flight centers each retained their own safety organization reporting to the Center Director.

. . . .

5.2 The Nasa Human Space Flight Culture

Though NASA underwent many management reforms in the wake of the *Challenger* accident and appointed new directors at the Johnson, Marshall, and Kennedy centers, the agency's powerful human space flight culture remained intact, as did many institutional practices, even if in a modified form. As a close observer of NASA's organizational culture has observed, "Cultural norms tend to be fairly resilient . . . The norms bounce back into shape after being stretched or bent. Beliefs held in common throughout the organization resist alteration." This culture, as will become clear across the chapters of Part Two of this report, acted over time to resist externally imposed change. By the eve of the *Columbia* accident, institutional practices that were in effect at the time of the *Challenger* accident—such as inadequate concern over deviations from expected performance, a silent safety program, and schedule pressure—had returned to NASA.

. . . .

The human space flight culture within NASA originated in the Cold War environment. The space agency itself was created in 1958 as a response to the Soviet launch of Sputnik, the first artificial Earth satellite. In 1961, President John F. Kennedy charged the new space agency with the task of reaching the moon

12 *Id.* at 100.

before the end of the decade,* and asked Congress and the American people to commit the immense resources for doing so, even though at the time NASA had only accumulated 15 minutes of human space flight experience. With its efforts linked to U.S.-Soviet competition for global leadership, there was a sense in the NASA workforce that the agency was engaged in a historic struggle central to the nation's agenda.

The Apollo era created at NASA an exceptional "can-do" culture marked by tenacity in the face of seemingly impossible challenges. This culture valued the interaction among[13] a dependence on the exceptional quality of . . . its workforce and leadership that provided in-house technical capability to oversee the work of contractors. The culture also accepted risk and failure as inevitable aspects of operating in space, even as it held as its highest value attention to detail in order to lower the chances of failure.

The dramatic Apollo 11 lunar landing in July 1969 fixed NASA's achievements in the national consciousness, and in history. However, the numerous accolades in the wake of the moon landing also helped reinforce the NASA staff's faith in their organizational culture. Apollo successes created the powerful image of the space agency as a "perfect place," as "the best organization that human beings could create to accomplish selected goals." During Apollo, NASA was in many respects a highly successful organization capable of achieving seemingly impossible feats. The continuing image of NASA as a "perfect place" in the years after Apollo left NASA employees unable to recognize that NASA never had been, and still was not, perfect, nor was it as symbolically important in the continuing Cold War struggle as it had been for its first decade of existence. NASA personnel maintained a vision of their agency that was rooted in the glories of an earlier time, even as the world, and thus the context within which the space agency operated, changed around them.

As a result, NASA's human space flight culture never fully adapted to the Space Shuttle Program, with its goal of routine access to space rather than further exploration beyond low-Earth orbit. The Apollo-era organizational culture came to be in tension with the more bureaucratic space agency of the 1970s, whose focus turned from designing new spacecraft at any expense to repetitively flying a reusable vehicle on an ever-tightening budget. This trend toward bureaucracy and the associated increased reliance on contracting necessitated more effective communications and more extensive safety oversight processes than had been in

* Editors' Note: You can read (and see) President Kennedy's speech at Rice University at https://er.jsc.nasa.gov/seh/ricetalk.htm.

[13] Report at 101.

place during the Apollo era, but the Rogers Commission found that such features were lacking.

In the aftermath of the *Challenger* accident, these contradictory forces prompted a resistance to externally imposed changes and an attempt to maintain the internal belief that NASA was still a "perfect place," alone in its ability to execute a program of human space flight. Within NASA centers, as Human Space Flight Program managers strove to maintain their view of the organization, they lost their ability to accept criticism, leading them to reject the recommendations of many boards and blue-ribbon panels, the Rogers Commission among them.

External criticism and doubt, rather than spurring NASA to change for the better, instead reinforced the will to "impose the party line vision on the environment, not to reconsider it," according to one authority on organizational behavior. This in turn led to "flawed decision making, self deception, introversion and a diminished curiosity about the world outside the perfect place." The NASA human space flight culture the Board found during its investigation manifested many of these characteristics, in particular a self-confidence about NASA possessing unique knowledge about how to safely launch people into space. As will be discussed later in this chapter, as well as in Chapters 6, 7, and 8, the Board views this cultural resistance as a fundamental impediment to NASA's effective organizational performance.[14]

. . . .

Space Shuttle Program Budget Patterns

For the past 30 years, the Space Shuttle Program has been NASA's single most expensive activity, and of all NASA's efforts, that program has been hardest hit by the budget constraints of the past decade. Given the high priority assigned after 1993 to completing the costly International Space Station, NASA managers have had little choice but to attempt to reduce the costs of operating the Space Shuttle. This left little funding for Shuttle improvements. The squeeze on the Shuttle budget was even more severe after the Office of Management and Budget in 1994 insisted that any cost overruns in the International Space Station budget be made up from within the budget allocation for human space flight, rather than from the agency's budget as a whole. The Shuttle was the only other large program within that budget category.[15]

. . . .

---

14 *Id.* at 102 (footnotes omitted).

15 *Id.* at 104.

5.4 Turbulence in Nasa Hits the Space Shuttle Program

In 1992 the White House replaced NASA Administrator Richard Truly with aerospace executive Daniel S. Goldin, a self-proclaimed "agent of change" who held office from April 1, 1992, to November 17, 2001 (in the process becoming the longest-serving NASA Administrator). Seeing "space exploration (manned and unmanned) as NASA's principal purpose with Mars as a destiny," as one management scholar observed, and favoring "administrative transformation" of NASA, Goldin engineered "not one or two policy changes, but a torrent of changes. This was not evolutionary change, but radical or discontinuous change." His tenure at NASA was one of continuous turmoil, to which the Space Shuttle Program was not immune.

Of course, turbulence does not necessarily degrade organizational performance. In some cases, it accompanies productive change, and that is what Goldin hoped to achieve. He believed in the management approach advocated by W. Edwards Deming, who had developed a series of widely acclaimed management principles based on his work in Japan during the "economic miracle" of the 1980s. Goldin attempted to apply some of those principles to NASA, including the notion that a corporate headquarters should not attempt to exert bureaucratic control over a complex organization, but rather set strategic directions and provide operating units with the authority and resources needed to pursue those directions. Another Deming principle was that checks and balances in an organization were unnecessary[16] and sometimes counterproductive, and those carrying out the work should bear primary responsibility for its quality. It is arguable whether these business principles can readily be applied to a government agency operating under civil service rules and in a politicized environment. Nevertheless, Goldin sought to implement them throughout his tenure.

Goldin made many positive changes in his decade at NASA. By bringing Russia into the Space Station partnership in 1993, Goldin developed a new post-Cold War rationale for the agency while managing to save a program that was politically faltering. The International Space Station became NASA's premier program, with the Shuttle serving in a supporting role. Goldin was also instrumental in gaining acceptance of the "faster, better, cheaper" approach to the planning of robotic missions and downsizing "an agency that was considered bloated and bureaucratic when he took it over."

Goldin described himself as "sharp-edged" and could often be blunt. He rejected the criticism that he was sacrificing safety in the name of efficiency. In

---

[16] *Id.* at 105.

1994 he told an audience at the Jet Propulsion Laboratory, "When I ask for the budget to be cut, I'm told it's going to impact safety on the Space Shuttle . . . I think that's a bunch of crap."

One of Goldin's high-priority objectives was to decrease involvement of the NASA engineering workforce with the Space Shuttle Program and thereby free up those skills for finishing the space station and beginning work on his preferred objective—human exploration of Mars. Such a shift would return NASA to its exploratory mission. He was often at odds with those who continued to focus on the centrality of the Shuttle to NASA's future.

Initial Shuttle Workforce Reductions

With NASA leadership choosing to maintain existing programs within a no-growth budget, Goldin's "faster, better, cheaper" motto became the agency's slogan of the 1990s. NASA leaders, however, had little maneuvering room in which to achieve efficiency gains. Attempts by NASA Headquarters to shift functions or to close one of the three human space flight centers were met with strong resistance from the Centers themselves, the aerospace firms they used as contractors, and the congressional delegations of the states in which the Centers were located. This alliance resembles the classic "iron triangle" of bureaucratic politics, a conservative coalition of bureaucrats, interest groups, and congressional subcommittees working together to promote their common interests.

With Center infrastructure off-limits, this left the Space Shuttle budget as an obvious target for cuts. Because the Shuttle required a large "standing army" of workers to[17] keep it flying, reducing the size of the Shuttle workforce became the primary means by which top leaders lowered the Shuttle's operating costs. These personnel reduction efforts started early in the decade and continued through most of the 1990s. They created substantial uncertainty and tension within the Shuttle workforce, as well as the transitional difficulties inherent in any large-scale workforce reassignment.

In early 1991, even before Goldin assumed office and less than three years after the Shuttle had returned to flight after the *Challenger* accident, NASA announced a goal of saving three to five percent per year in the Shuttle budget over five years. This move was in reaction to a perception that the agency had overreacted to the Rogers Commission recommendations—for example, the notion that the many layers of safety inspections involved in preparing a Shuttle for flight had created a bloated and costly safety program.

---

[17] *Id.* at 106 (footnotes omitted).

. . . .

Anticipating this impending need, a 1994–1995 NASA "Functional Workforce Review" concluded that removing an additional 5,900 people from the NASA and contractor Shuttle workforce—just under 13 percent of the total—could be done without compromising safety. These personnel cuts were made in Fiscal Years 1996 and 1997. By the end of 1997, the NASA Shuttle civilian workforce numbered 2,195, and the contractor workforce 17,281.

Shifting Shuttle Management Arrangements

Workforce reductions were not the only modifications to the Shuttle Program in the middle of the decade. In keeping with Goldin's philosophy that Headquarters should concern itself primarily with strategic issues, in February 1996 Johnson Space Center was designated as "lead center" for the Space Shuttle Program, a role it held prior to the *Challenger* accident. This shift was part of a general move of all program management responsibilities from NASA Headquarters to the agency's field centers. Among other things, this change meant that Johnson Space Center managers would have authority over the funding and management of Shuttle activities at the Marshall and Kennedy Centers. Johnson and Marshall had been rivals since the days of Apollo, and long-term Marshall employees and managers did not easily accept the return of Johnson to this lead role.

The shift of Space Shuttle Program management to Johnson was worrisome to some. The head of the Space Shuttle Program at NASA Headquarters, Bryan O'Connor, argued that transfer of the management function to the Johnson Space Center would return the Shuttle Program management to the flawed structure that was in place before the *Challenger* accident. "It is a safety issue," he said, "we ran it that way [with program management at Headquarters, as recommended by the Rogers Commission] for 10 years without a mishap and I didn't see any reason why we should go back to the way we operated in the pre-*Challenger* days." Goldin gave O'Connor several opportunities to present his arguments against a transfer of management responsibility, but ultimately decided to proceed. O'Connor felt he had no choice but to resign. (O'Connor returned to NASA in 2002 as Associate Administrator for Safety and Mission Assurance.)

In January 1996, Goldin appointed as Johnson's director his close advisor, George W.S. Abbey. Abbey, a space program veteran, was a firm believer in the values of the original human space flight culture, and as he assumed the directorship, he set about recreating as many of the positive features of that culture as possible. For example, he and Goldin initiated, as a way for young engineers to get hands-on experience, an in-house X-38 development program as a prototype for a space station crew rescue vehicle. Abbey was a powerful leader, who through the rest of the decade exerted substantial control over all aspects of Johnson Space Center operations, including the Space Shuttle Program.

Space Flight Operations Contract

By the middle of the decade, spurred on by Vice President Al Gore's "reinventing government" initiative, the goal of balancing the federal budget, and the views of a Republican-led House of Representatives, managers throughout the government sought new ways of making public sector programs more efficient and less costly. One method considered was transferring significant government operations and responsibilities to the private sector, or "privatization." NASA led the way toward privatization, serving as an example to other government agencies.

In keeping with his philosophy that NASA should focus on its research-and-development role, Goldin wanted to remove NASA employees from the repetitive operations of various systems, including the Space Shuttle. Giving primary responsibility for Space Shuttle operations to the private sector was therefore consistent with White House and congressional priorities and attractive to Goldin on its own terms. Beginning in 1994, NASA considered the feasibility of consolidating many of the numerous Shuttle operations contracts under a single prime contractor. At that time, the Space Shuttle Program was managing 86 separate contracts held by 56 different firms. Top NASA managers thought that consolidating these contracts could reduce the amount of redundant overhead, both for NASA and for the contractors[18] themselves. They also wanted to explore whether there were functions being carried out by NASA that could be more effectively and inexpensively carried out by the private sector.

An advisory committee headed by early space flight veteran Christopher Kraft recommended such a step in its March 1995 report, which became known as the "Kraft Report." (The report characterized the Space Shuttle in a way that the Board judges to be at odds with the realities of the Shuttle Program.)

. . . .

Although the Kraft Report stressed that the dramatic changes it recommended could be made without compromising safety, there was considerable dissent about this claim. NASA's Aerospace Safety Advisory Panel—independent, but often not very influential—was particularly critical. In May 1995, the Panel noted that "the assumption [in the Kraft Report] that the Space Shuttle

---

[18] *Id.* at 107 (footnotes omitted).

systems are now 'mature' smacks of a complacency which may lead to serious mishaps. The fact is that the Space Shuttle may never be mature enough to totally freeze the design." The Panel also noted that "the report dismisses the concerns of many credible sources by labeling honest reservations and the people who have made them as being partners in an unneeded 'safety shield' conspiracy. Since only one more accident would kill the program and destroy far more than the spacecraft, it is extremely callous" to make such an accusation.

The notion that NASA would further reduce the number of civil servants working on the Shuttle Program prompted senior Kennedy Space Center engineer José Garcia to send to President Bill Clinton on August 25, 1995, a letter that stated, "The biggest threat to the safety of the crew since the *Challenger* disaster is presently underway at NASA." Garcia's particular concern was NASA's "efforts to delete the 'checks and balances' system of processing Shuttles as a way of saving money . . . Historically NASA has employed two engineering teams at KSC, one contractor and one government, to cross check each other and prevent catastrophic errors . . . although this technique is expensive, it is effective, and it is the single most important factor that sets the Shuttle's success above that of any other launch vehicle . . . Anyone who doesn't have a hidden agenda or fear of losing his job would admit that you can't delete NASA's checks and balances system of Shuttle processing without affecting the safety of the Shuttle and crew."

NASA leaders accepted the advice of the Kraft Report and in August 1995 solicited industry bids for the assignment of Shuttle prime contractor. In response, Lockheed Martin and Rockwell, the two major Space Shuttle operations contractors, formed a limited liability corporation, with each firm a 50 percent owner, to compete for what was called the Space Flight Operations Contract. The new corporation would be known as United Space Alliance.

In November 1995, NASA awarded the operations contract to United Space Alliance on a sole source basis. (When Boeing bought Rockwell's aerospace group in December 1996, it also took over Rockwell's 50 percent ownership of United Space Alliance.) The company was responsible for 61 percent of the Shuttle operations contracts. Some in Congress were skeptical that safety could be maintained under the new arrangement, which transferred significant NASA responsibilities to the private sector. Despite these concerns, Congress ultimately accepted the reasoning behind the contract. NASA then spent much of 1996 negotiating the contract's terms and conditions with United Space Alliance.

The Space Flight Operations Contract was designed to reward United Space Alliance for performance successes and penalize its performance failures. Before being eligible for any performance fees, United Space Alliance would have to meet a series of safety "gates," which were intended to ensure that safety remained the top priority in Shuttle operations. The contract also rewarded any cost reductions that United Space Alliance was able to achieve, with NASA taking 65 percent of any savings and United Space Alliance 35 percent.

NASA and United Space Alliance formally signed the Space Flight Operations Contract on October 1, 1996. Initially, only the major Lockheed Martin and Rockwell Shuttle contracts and a smaller Allied Signal Unisys contract were transferred to United Space Alliance. The initial contractual period was six years, from October 1996 to September 2002. NASA exercised an option for a two-year extension in 2002, and another two-year option exists. The total value of the contract through the current extension is estimated at $12.8 billion. United Space Alliance currently has approximately 10,000 employees.[19]

The contract provided for additional consolidation and then privatization, when all remaining Shuttle operations would be transferred from NASA. Phase 2, scheduled for 1998–2000, called for the transfer of Johnson Space Center-managed flight software and flight crew equipment contracts and the Marshall Space Center-managed contracts for the External Tank, Space Shuttle Main Engine, Reusable Solid Rocket Motor, and Solid Rocket Booster.

However, Marshall and its contractors, with the concurrence of the Space Shuttle Program Office at Johnson Space Center, successfully resisted the transfer of its contracts. Therefore, the Space Flight Operations Contract's initial efficiency and integrated management goals have not been achieved.

The major annual savings resulting from the Space Flight Operations Contract, which in 1996 were touted to be some $500 million to $1 billion per year by the early 2000s, have not materialized. These projections assumed that by 2002, NASA would have put all Shuttle contracts under the auspices of United Space Alliance, and would be moving toward Shuttle privatization. Although the Space Flight Operations Contract has not been as successful in achieving cost efficiencies as its proponents hoped, it has reduced some Shuttle operating costs and other expenses. By one estimate, in its first six years the contract has saved NASA a total of more than $1 billion.

Privatizing the Space Shuttle

To its proponents, the Space Flight Operations Contract was only a beginning. In October 1997, United Space Alliance submitted to the Space Shuttle

---

[19] *Id.* at 108 (footnotes omitted).

Program Office a contractually required plan for privatizing the Shuttle, which the program did not accept. But the notion of Shuttle privatization lingered at NASA Headquarters and in Congress, where some members advocated a greater private sector role in the space program. Congress passed the Commercial Space Act of 1998, which directed the NASA Administrator to "plan for the eventual privatization of the Space Shuttle Program."

By August 2001, NASA Headquarters prepared for White House consideration a "Privatization White Paper" that called for transferring all Shuttle hardware, pilot and commander astronauts, and launch and operations teams to a private operator. 49 In September 2001, Space Shuttle Program Manager Ron Dittemore released his report on a "Concept of Privatization of the Space Shuttle Program," which argued that for the Space Shuttle "to remain safe and viable, it is necessary to merge the required NASA and contractor skill bases" into a single private organization that would manage human space flight. This perspective reflected Dittemore's belief that the split of responsibilities between NASA and United Space Alliance was not optimal, and that it was unlikely that NASA would ever recapture the Shuttle responsibilities that were transferred in the Space Flight Operations Contract.

Dittemore's plan recommended transferring 700 to 900 NASA employees to the private organization, including:

- Astronauts, including the flight crew members who operate the Shuttle[20] Program and project management, including Space Shuttle Main Engine, External Tank, Redesigned Solid Rocket Booster, and Extravehicular Activity
- Mission operations, including flight directors and flight controllers
- Ground operations and processing, including launch director, process engineering, and flow management
- Responsibility for safety and mission assurance

After such a shift occurred, according to the Dittemore plan, "the primary role for NASA in Space Shuttle operations . . . will be to provide an SMA [Safety and Mission Assurance] independent assessment . . . utilizing audit and surveillance techniques."

With a change in NASA Administrators at the end of 2001 and the new Bush Administration's emphasis on "competitive sourcing" of government operations, the notion of wholesale privatization of the Space Shuttle was replaced with an

[20] *Id.* at 109 (footnotes omitted).

examination of the feasibility of both public- and private-sector Program management. This competitive sourcing was under examination at the time of the *Columbia* accident.

Workforce Transformation and the End of Downsizing

Workforce reductions instituted by Administrator Goldin as he attempted to redefine the agency's mission and its overall organization also added to the turbulence of his reign. In the 1990s, the overall NASA workforce was reduced by 25 percent through normal attrition, early retirements, and buyouts—cash bonuses for leaving NASA employment. NASA operated under a hiring freeze for most of the decade, making it difficult to bring in new or younger people. . . .

NASA Headquarters was particularly affected by workforce reductions. More than half its employees left or were transferred in parallel with the 1996 transfer of program management responsibilities back to the NASA centers. The Space Shuttle Program bore more than its share of Headquarters personnel cuts. Headquarters civil service staff working on the Space Shuttle Program went from 120 in 1993 to 12 in 2003.

While the overall workforce at the NASA Centers involved in human space flight was not as radically reduced, the combination of the general workforce reduction and the introduction of the Space Flight Operations Contract significantly impacted the Centers' Space Shuttle Program civil service staff. Johnson Space Center went from 1,330 in 1993 to 738 in 2002; Marshall Space Flight Center, from 874 to 337; and Kennedy Space Center from 1,373 to 615. Kennedy Director Roy Bridges argued that personnel cuts were too deep, and threatened to resign unless the downsizing of his civil service workforce, particularly those involved with safety issues, was reversed.

By the end of the decade, NASA realized that staff reductions had gone too far. By early 2000, internal and external studies convinced NASA leaders that the workforce needed to be revitalized. These studies noted that "five years of buyouts and downsizing have led to serious skill imbalances and an overtaxed core workforce. As more employees have departed, the workload and stress [on those] remaining have increased, with a corresponding increase in the potential for impacts to operational capacity and safety." NASA announced that NASA workforce downsizing would stop short of the 17,500 target, and that its human space flight centers would immediately hire several hundred workers.[21]

. . . .

21 *Id.* at 110 (footnotes omitted).

5.6 A Change in NASA Leadership

Daniel Goldin left NASA in November 2001 after more than nine years as Administrator. The White House chose Sean O'Keefe, the Deputy Director of the White House Office of Management and Budget, as his replacement. O'Keefe stated as he took office that he was not a "rocket scientist," but rather that his expertise was in the management of large government programs. His appointment was an explicit acknowledgement by the new Bush administration that NASA's primary problems were managerial and financial.

By the time O'Keefe arrived, NASA managers had come to recognize that 1990s funding reductions for the Space Shuttle Program had resulted in an excessively fragile program, and also realized that a Space Shuttle replacement was not on the horizon. In 2002, with these issues in mind, O'Keefe made a number of changes to the Space Shuttle Program. He transferred management of both the Space Shuttle Program and the International Space Station from Johnson Space Center to NASA Headquarters. O'Keefe also began considering whether to expand the Space Flight Operations Contract to cover additional Space Shuttle elements, or to pursue "competitive sourcing," a Bush administration initiative that encouraged government agencies to compete with the private sector for management responsibilities of publicly funded activities. To research whether competitive sourcing would be a viable approach for the Space Shuttle Program, NASA chartered the Space Shuttle Competitive Sourcing Task Force through the RAND Corporation, a federally funded think tank. In its report, the Task Force recognized the many obstacles to transferring the Space Shuttle to non-NASA management, primarily NASA's reticence to relinquish control, but concluded "NASA must pursue competitive sourcing in one form or another."

NASA began a "Strategic Management of Human Capital" initiative to ensure the quality of the future NASA workforce. The goal is to address the various external and internal challenges that NASA faces as it tries to ensure an appropriate mix and depth of skills for future program requirements. A number of aspects to its Strategic Human Capital Plan require legislative approval and are currently before the Congress.[22]

. . . .

In November 2002, NASA made a fundamental change in strategy. In what was called the Integrated Space Transportation Plan . . ., NASA shifted money from the Space Launch Initiative to the Space Shuttle and International Space Station programs. The plan also introduced the Orbital Space Plane as a

---

[22] *Id.* at 115 (footnote omitted).

complement to the Shuttle for the immediate future. Under this strategy, the Shuttle is to fly through at least 2010, when a decision will be made on how long to extend Shuttle operations—possibly through 2020 or even beyond.[23]

. . . .

[The Report discusses the return of the factor of schedule pressure, a problem that had contributed to the *Challenger* disaster.[24]]

It is the Board's view that . . . [t]he Program was operating too close to too many margins. The Board also finds that recent modest increases in the Shuttle Program's budget are necessary and overdue steps toward providing the resources to sustain the program for its now-extended lifetime. Similarly, NASA has recently recognized that providing an adequately sized and appropriately trained workforce is critical to the agency's future success.

An examination of the Program's management changes also leads to the question: Did turmoil in the management structure contribute to the accident? The Board found no evidence that the transition from many Space Shuttle contractors to a partial consolidation of contracts under a single firm has by itself introduced additional technical risk into the Space Shuttle Program. The transfer of responsibilities that has accompanied the Space Flight Operations Contract has, however, complicated an already complex Program structure and created barriers to effective communication. Designating the Johnson Space Center as the "lead center" for the Space Shuttle Program did resurrect some of the Center rivalries and communication difficulties that existed before the *Challenger* accident. The specific ways in which this complexity and lack of an integrated approach to Shuttle management impinged on NASA's performance during and before the flight of STS-107 are discussed in Chapters 6 and 7.

As the 21st century began, NASA's deeply ingrained human space flight culture—one that has evolved over 30 years as the basis for a more conservative, less technically and organizationally capable organization than the Apollo-era NASA—remained strong enough to resist external pressures for adaptation and change. At the time of the launch of STS-107, NASA retained too many negative (and also many positive) aspects of its traditional culture: "flawed decision making, self deception, introversion and a diminished curiosity about the world outside the perfect place." These characteristics were reflected in NASA's less than stellar

---

23 *Id.* at 116.

24 *Id.* at 116–17.

performance before and during the STS-107 mission, which is described in the following chapters.[25]

[Chapter 6 Decision-Making at NASA]

. . . .

Conclusion

Despite original design requirements that the External Tank not shed debris, and the corresponding design requirement that the Orbiter not receive debris hits exceeding a trivial amount of force, debris has impacted the Shuttle on each flight. Over the course of 113 missions, foam-shedding and other debris impacts came to be regarded more as a turnaround or maintenance issue, and less as a hazard to the vehicle and crew.

Assessments of foam-shedding and strikes were not thoroughly substantiated by engineering analysis, and the process for closing In-Flight Anomalies is not well-documented and appears to vary. Shuttle Program managers appear to have confused the notion of foam posing an "accepted risk" with foam not being a "safety-of-flight issue." At times, the pressure to meet the flight schedule appeared to cut short engineering efforts to resolve the foam-shedding problem.

NASA's lack of understanding of foam properties and behavior must also be questioned. Although tests were conducted to develop and qualify foam for use on the External Tank, it appears there were large gaps in NASA's knowledge about this complex and variable material. . . .

While NASA properly designated key debris events as In-Flight Anomalies in the past, more recent events indicate that NASA engineers and management did not appreciate the scope, or lack of scope, of the Hazard Reports involving foam shedding. Ultimately, NASA's hazard analyses, which were based on reducing or eliminating foam-shedding, were not succeeding. Shuttle Program management made no adjustments to the analyses to recognize this fact. The acceptance of events that are not supposed to happen has been described by sociologist Diane Vaughan as the "normalization of deviance." The history of foam-problem decisions shows how NASA first began and then continued flying with foam losses, so that flying with these deviations from design specifications was viewed as normal and acceptable. Dr. Richard Feynman, a member of the Presidential Commission on the Space Shuttle Challenger Accident, discusses this phenomen[on] in the context of the *Challenger* accident. The parallels are striking:

---

[25] *Id.* at 118 (footnote omitted).

> *The phenomenon of accepting . . . flight seals that had shown erosion and blow-by in previous flights is very clear. The Challenger flight is an excellent example. There are several references to flights that had gone before. The acceptance and success of these flights is taken as evidence of safety. But erosions and blow-by are not what the design expected. They are warnings that something is wrong . . . The O-rings of the Solid Rocket Boosters were not designed to erode. Erosion was a clue that something was wrong. Erosion was not something from which safety can be inferred . . . If a reasonable launch schedule is to be maintained, engineering often cannot be done fast enough to keep up with the expectations of originally conservative certification criteria designed to guarantee a very safe vehicle. In these situations, subtly, and often with apparently logical arguments, the criteria are altered so that flights may still be certified in time. They therefore fly in a relatively unsafe condition, with a chance of failure of the order of a percent (it is difficult to be more accurate).*[26]

. . . .

6.2 Schedule Pressure

Countdown to Space Station "Core Complete:" A Workforce Under Pressure

During the course of this investigation, the Board received several unsolicited comments from NASA personnel regarding pressure to meet a schedule. These comments all concerned a date, more than a year after the launch of *Columbia,* that seemed etched in stone: February 19, 2004, the scheduled launch date of STS-120. This flight was a milestone in the minds of NASA management since it would carry a section of the International Space Station called "Node 2." This would configure the International Space Station to its "U.S. Core Complete" status.

At first glance, the Core Complete configuration date seemed noteworthy but unrelated to the *Columbia* accident. However, as the investigation continued, it became apparent that the complexity and political mandates surrounding the International Space Station Program, as well as Shuttle Program management's responses to them, resulted in pressure to meet an increasingly ambitious launch schedule.

In mid-2001, NASA adopted plans to make the over-budget and behind-schedule International Space Station credible to the White House and Congress. The Space Station Program and NASA were on probation, and had to prove they could meet schedules and budgets. The plan to regain credibility focused on the February 19, 2004, date for the launch of Node 2 and the resultant Core Complete

---

[26] *Id.* at 130 (footnotes omitted).

status. If this goal was not met, NASA would risk losing support from the White House and Congress for subsequent Space Station growth.

By the late summer of 2002, a variety of problems caused Space Station assembly work and Shuttle flights to slip beyond their target dates. With the Node 2 launch endpoint fixed, these delays caused the schedule to become ever more compressed.

Meeting U.S. Core Complete by February 19, 2004, would require preparing and launching 10 flights in less than 16 months. With the focus on retaining support for the Space Station program, little attention was paid to the effects the aggressive Node 2 launch date would have on the Shuttle Program. After years of downsizing and budget cuts (Chapter 5), this mandate and events in the months leading up to STS-107 introduced elements of risk to the Program. *Columbia* and the STS-107 crew, who had seen numerous launch slips due to missions that were deemed higher priorities, were further affected by the mandatory Core Complete date. The high-pressure environments created by NASA Headquarters unquestionably affected *Columbia,* even though it was not flying to the International Space Station.

February 19, 2004—"A Line in the Sand"

Schedules are essential tools that help large organizations effectively manage their resources. Aggressive schedules by themselves are often a sign of a healthy institution. However, other institutional goals, such as safety, sometimes compete with schedules, so the effects of schedule pressure in an organization must be carefully monitored. The Board posed the question: Was there undue pressure to nail the Node 2 launch date to the February 19, 2004, signpost?

The management and workforce of the Shuttle and Space Station programs each answered the question differently. Various members of NASA upper management gave a definite "no." In contrast, the workforce within both programs thought there was considerable management focus on Node 2 and resulting pressure to hold firm to that launch date, and individuals were becoming concerned that safety might be compromised. The weight of evidence supports the workforce view.

Employees attributed the Node 2 launch date to the new Administrator, Sean O'Keefe, who was appointed to execute a Space Station management plan he had proposed as Deputy Director of the White House Office of Management and Budget. They understood the scrutiny that NASA, the new Administrator, and the

Space Station Program were under,[27] but now it seemed to some that budget and schedule were of paramount concern.

. . . .

The importance of this date was stressed from the very top. The Space Shuttle and Space Station Program Managers briefed the new NASA Administrator monthly on the status of their programs, and a significant part of those briefings was the days of margin remaining in the schedule to the launch of Node 2—still well over a year away. The Node 2 schedule margin typically accounted for more than half of the briefing slides.

. . . .

NASA Headquarters stressed the importance of this date in other ways. A screen saver (see Figure 6.2–3) was mailed to managers in NASA's human spaceflight program that depicted a clock counting down to February 19, 2004—U.S. Core Complete.[28]

. . . .

Shuttle and Station managers worked diligently to meet the schedule. Events gradually ate away at the schedule margin. Unlike the "old days" before the Station, the Station/Shuttle partnership created problems that had a ripple effect on both programs' manifests. As one employee described it, "the serial nature" of having to fly Space Station assembly missions in a specific order made staying on schedule more challenging. Before the Space Station, if a Shuttle flight had to slip, it would; other missions that had originally followed it would be launched in the meantime. Missions could be flown in any sequence. Now the manifests were a delicate balancing act. Missions had to be flown in a certain order and were constrained by the availability of the launch site, the Russian Soyuz and Progress schedules, and a myriad of other processes. As a result, employees stated they were now experiencing a new kind of pressure. Any necessary change they made on one mission was now impacting future launch dates. They had a sense of being "under the gun."

Shuttle and Station program personnel ended up with manifests that one employee described as "changing, changing, changing" all the time. One of the biggest issues they faced entering 2002 was "up mass," the amount of cargo the Shuttle can carry to the Station. Up mass was not a new problem, but when the Shuttle flight rate was reduced to four per year, up mass became critical. Working

---

27 *Id.* at 131.

28 *Id.* at 132.

groups were actively evaluating options in the summer of 2002 and bartering to get each flight to function as expected.

Sometimes the up mass being traded was actual Space Station crew members. A crew rotation planned for STS-118 was moved to a later flight because STS-118 was needed for other cargo. This resulted in an increase of crew duration on the Space Station, which was creeping past the 180-day limit agreed to by the astronaut office, flight surgeons, and Space Station international partners. A space station worker described how this one change created many other problems, and added: ". . . we had a train wreck coming . . ." Future on-orbit crew time was being projected at 205 days or longer to maintain the assembly sequence and meet the schedule

By July 2002, the Shuttle and Space Station Programs were facing a schedule with very little margin. Two setbacks occurred when technical problems were found during routine maintenance on *Discovery*. STS-107 was four weeks away from launch at the time, but the problems grounded the entire Shuttle fleet. The longer the fleet was grounded, the more schedule margin was lost, which further compounded the complexity of the intertwined Shuttle and Station schedules. As one worker described the situation:

> *. . . a one-week hit on a particular launch can start a steam roll effect including all [the] constraints and by the time you get out of here, that one-week slip has turned into a couple of months.*

In August 2002, the Shuttle Program realized it would be unable to meet the Space Station schedule with the available Shuttles. *Columbia* had never been outfitted to make a Space Station flight, so the other three Orbiters flew the Station missions. But *Discovery* was in its Orbiter Maintenance Down Period, and would not be available for another 17 months. All Space Station flights until then would have to be made by *Atlantis* and *Endeavour.* As managers looked ahead to 2003, they saw that after STS-107, these two Orbiters would have to alternate flying five consecutive missions, STS-114 through STS-118. To alleviate this pressure, and regain schedule margin, Shuttle Program managers elected to modify *Columbia* to enable it to fly Space Station missions. Those modifications were to take place immediately after STS-107 so that *Columbia* would be ready to fly its first Space Station mission eight months later. This decision put *Columbia* directly in the path of Core Complete.

As the autumn of 2002 began, both the Space Shuttle and Space Station Programs began to use what some employees termed "tricks" to regain schedule margin. Employees expressed concern that their ability to gain schedule margin using existing measures was waning.

In September 2002, it was clear to Space Shuttle and Space Station Program managers that they were not going to meet the schedule as it was laid out. The two Programs proposed a new set of launch dates, documented in an e-mail . . . that included moving STS-120, the Node 2 flight, to mid-March 2004.

. . . .

The problems that had grounded the fleet had been handled well, but the program nevertheless lost the rest of its margin. As the pressure to keep to the Node 2 schedule continued, some were concerned that this might influence the future handling of problems. One worker expressed the concern:

> *. . . and I have to think that subconsciously that even though you don't want it to affect decision-making, it probably does.*[29]

. . . .

Columbia: Caught in the Middle

STS-112 flew in October 2002. At 33 seconds into the flight, a piece of the bipod foam from the External Tank struck one of the Solid Rocket Boosters. As described in Section 6.1, the STS-112 foam strike was discussed at the Program Requirements Control Board following the flight. Although the initial recommendation was to treat the foam loss as an In-Flight Anomaly, the Shuttle Program instead assigned it as an action, with a due date after the next launch. (This was the first instance of bipod foam loss that was not designated an In-Flight Anomaly.) The action was noted at the STS-113 Flight Readiness Review. Those Flight Readiness Review charts (see Section 6.1) provided a flawed flight rationale by concluding that the foam loss was "not a safety-of-flight" issue.[30]

Interestingly, during *Columbia's* mission, the Chair of the Mission Management Team, Linda Ham, would characterize that reasoning as "lousy"—though neither she nor Shuttle Program Manager Ron Dittemore, who were both present at the meeting, questioned it at the time. The pressing need to launch STS-113 to retrieve the International Space Station Expedition 5 crew before they surpassed the 180-day limit and to continue the countdown to Node 2 were surely in the back of managers' minds during these reviews.

---

29 *Id.* at 134.

30 *Id.* at 137.

By December 2002, every bit of padding in the schedule had disappeared. Another chart from the Shuttle and Station Program Managers' briefing to the NASA Administrator summarizes the schedule dilemma. . . . Even with work scheduled on holidays, a third shift of workers being hired and trained, future crew rotations drifting beyond 180 days, and some tests previously deemed "requirements" being skipped or deferred, Program managers estimated that Node 2 launch would be one to two months late. They were slowly accepting additional risk in trying to meet a schedule that probably could not be met.

Interviews with workers provided insight into how this situation occurred. They noted that people who work at NASA have the legendary can-do attitude, which contributes to the agency's successes. But it can also cause problems. When workers are asked to find days of margin, they work furiously to do so and are praised for each extra day they find. But those same people (and this same culture) have difficulty admitting that something "can't" or "shouldn't" be done, that the margin has been cut too much, or that resources are being stretched too thin. No one at NASA wants to be the one to stand up and say, "We can't make that date."

STS-107 was launched on January 16, 2003. Bipod foam separated from the External Tank and struck *Columbia's* left wing 81.9 seconds after liftoff. As the mission proceeded over the next 16 days, critical decisions about that event would be made.

The STS-107 Mission Management Team Chair, Linda Ham, had been present at the Program Requirements Control Board discussing the STS-112 foam loss and the STS-113 Flight Readiness Review. So had many of the other Shuttle Program managers who had roles in STS-107. Ham was also the Launch Integration Manager for the next mission, STS-114. In that capacity, she would chair many of the meetings leading up to the launch of that flight, and many of those individuals would have to confront *Columbia's* foam strike and its possible impact on the launch of STS-114. Would the *Columbia* foam strike be classified as an In-Flight Anomaly? Would the fact that foam had detached from the bipod ramp on two out of the last three flights have made this problem a constraint to flight that would need to be solved before the next launch? Could the Program develop a solid rationale to fly STS-114, or would additional analysis be required to clear the flight for launch?[31]

. . . .

In fact, most of Linda Ham's inquiries about the foam strike were not to determine what action to take during *Columbia's* mission, but to understand the

[31] *Id.* at 138.

implications for STS-114. During a Mission Management Team meeting on January 21, she asked about the rationale put forward at the STS-113 Flight Readiness Review, which she had attended. Later that morning she reviewed the charts presented at that Flight Readiness Review. Her assessment, which she e-mailed to Shuttle Program Manager Ron Dittemore on January 21, was "*Rationale was lousy then and still is . . .*"

. . . .

One of Ham's STS-114 duties was to chair a review to determine if the mission's Orbiter, *Atlantis,* should be rolled from the Orbiter Processing Facility to the Vehicle Assembly Building, per its pre-launch schedule. In the above e-mail to Ron Dittemore, Ham indicates a desire to have the same individual responsible for the "lousy" STS-113 flight rationale start working the foam shedding issue—and presumably present a new flight rationale—very soon.

As STS-107 prepared for re-entry, Shuttle Program managers prepared for STS-114 flight rationale by arranging to have post-flight photographs taken of *Columbia's* left wing rushed to Johnson Space Center for analysis.

As will become clear in the next section, most of the Shuttle Program's concern about *Columbia's* foam strike were not about the threat it might pose to the vehicle in orbit, but about the threat it might pose to the schedule.

Conclusion

The agency's commitment to hold firm to a February 19, 2004, launch date for Node 2 influenced many of decisions in the months leading up to the launch of STS-107, and may well have subtly influenced the way managers handled the STS-112 foam strike and *Columbia's* as well.

When a program agrees to spend less money or accelerate a schedule beyond what the engineers and program managers think is reasonable, a small amount of overall risk is added. These little pieces of risk add up until managers are no longer aware of the total program risk, and are, in fact, gambling. Little by little, NASA was accepting more and more risk in order to stay on schedule.[32]

. . . .

Shuttle Program Management's Low Level of Concern

While the debris strike was well outside the activities covered by normal mission flight rules, Mission Management Team members and Shuttle Program managers did not treat the debris strike as an issue that required operational action

---

32 *Id.* at 139.

by Mission Control. Program managers, from Ron Dittemore to individual Mission Management Team members, had, over the course of the Space Shuttle Program, gradually become inured to External Tank foam losses and on a fundamental[33] level did not believe foam striking the vehicle posed a critical threat to the Orbiter. In particular, Shuttle managers exhibited a belief that RCC panels are impervious to foam impacts. Even after seeing the video of *Columbia's* debris impact, learning estimates of the size and location of the strike, and noting that a foam strike with sufficient kinetic energy could cause Thermal Protection System damage, management's level of concern did not change.

The opinions of Shuttle Program managers and debris and photo analysts on the potential severity of the debris strike diverged early in the mission and continued to diverge as the mission progressed, making it increasingly difficult for the Debris Assessment Team to have their concerns heard by those in a decision-making capacity. In the face of Mission managers' low level of concern and desire to get on with the mission, Debris Assessment Team members had to prove unequivocally that a safety-of-flight issue existed before Shuttle Program management would move to obtain images of the left wing. The engineers found themselves in the unusual position of having to prove that the situation was unsafe—a reversal of the usual requirement to prove that a situation is safe.

Other factors contributed to Mission management's ability to resist the Debris Assessment Team's concerns. A tile expert told managers during frequent consultations that strike damage was only a maintenance-level concern and that on-orbit imaging of potential wing damage was not necessary. Mission management welcomed this opinion and sought no others. This constant reinforcement of managers' pre-existing beliefs added another block to the wall between decision makers and concerned engineers.

Another factor that enabled Mission management's detachment from the concerns of their own engineers is rooted in the culture of NASA itself. The Board observed an unofficial hierarchy among NASA programs and directorates that hindered the flow of communications. The effects of this unofficial hierarchy are seen in the attitude that members of the Debris Assessment Team held. Part of the reason they chose the institutional route for their imagery request was that without direction from the Mission Evaluation Room and Mission Management Team, they felt more comfortable with their own chain of command, which was outside the Shuttle Program. Further, when asked by investigators why they were not more vocal about their concerns, Debris Assessment Team members opined

---

33 *Id.* at 168.

that by raising contrary points of view about Shuttle mission safety, they would be singled out for possible ridicule by their peers and managers.

A Lack of Clear Communication

Communication did not flow effectively up to or down from Program managers. As it became clear during the mission that managers were not as concerned as others about the danger of the foam strike, the ability of engineers to challenge those beliefs greatly diminished. Managers' tendency to accept opinions that agree with their own dams the flow of effective communications.

After the accident, Program managers stated privately and publicly that if engineers had a safety concern, they were obligated to communicate their concerns to management. Managers did not seem to understand that as leaders they had a corresponding and perhaps greater obligation to create viable routes for the engineering community to express their views and receive information. This barrier to communications not only blocked the flow of information to managers, but it also prevented the downstream flow of information from managers to engineers, leaving Debris Assessment Team members no basis for understanding the reasoning behind Mission Management Team decisions.

The January 27 to January 31, phone and e-mail exchanges, primarily between NASA engineers at Langley and Johnson, illustrate another symptom of the "cultural fence" that impairs open communications between mission managers and working engineers. These exchanges and the reaction to them indicated that during the evaluation of a mission contingency, the Mission Management Team failed to disseminate information to all system and technology experts who could be consulted. Issues raised by two Langley and Johnson engineers led to the development of "what-if" landing scenarios of the potential outcome if the main landing gear door sustained damaged. This led to behind-the-scenes networking by these engineers to use NASA facilities to make simulation runs of a compromised landing configuration. These engineers—who understood their systems and related technology—saw the potential for a problem on landing and ran it down in case the unthinkable occurred. But their concerns never reached the managers on the Mission Management Team that had operational control over *Columbia*.[34]

A Lack of Effective Leadership

The Shuttle Program, the Mission Management Team, and through it the Mission Evaluation Room, were not actively directing the efforts of the Debris

---

[34] *Id.* at 169.

Assessment Team. These management teams were not engaged in scenario selection or discussions of assumptions and did not actively seek status, inputs, or even preliminary results from the individuals charged with analyzing the debris strike. They did not investigate the value of imagery, did not intervene to consult the more experienced Crater analysts at Boeing's Huntington Beach facility, did not probe the assumptions of the Debris Assessment Team's analysis, and did not consider actions to mitigate the effects of the damage on re-entry. Managers' claims that they didn't hear the engineers' concerns were due in part to their not asking or listening.

The Failure of Safety's Role

As will be discussed in Chapter 7, safety personnel were present but passive and did not serve as a channel for the voicing of concerns or dissenting views. Safety representatives attended meetings of the Debris Assessment Team, Mission Evaluation Room, and Mission Management Team, but were merely party to the analysis process and conclusions instead of an independent source of questions and challenges. Safety contractors in the Mission Evaluation Room were only marginally aware of the debris strike analysis. One contractor did question the Debris Assessment Team safety representative about the analysis and was told that it was adequate. No additional inquiries were made. The highest-ranking safety representative at NASA headquarters deferred to Program managers when asked for an opinion on imaging of *Columbia.* The safety manager he spoke to also failed to follow up.

Summary

Management decisions made during *Columbia's* final flight reflect missed opportunities, blocked or ineffective communications channels, flawed analysis, and ineffective leadership. Perhaps most striking is the fact that management—including Shuttle Program, Mission Management Team, Mission Evaluation Room, and Flight Director and Mission Control—displayed no interest in understanding a problem and its implications. Because managers failed to avail themselves of the wide range of expertise and opinion necessary to achieve the best answer to the debris strike question—"Was this a safety-of-flight concern?"—some Space Shuttle Program managers failed to fulfill the implicit contract to do whatever is possible to ensure the safety of the crew. In fact, their management techniques unknowingly imposed barriers that kept at bay both engineering concerns and dissenting views, and ultimately helped create "blind spots" that prevented them from seeing the danger the foam strike posed.

Because this chapter has focused on key personnel who participated in STS-107 bipod foam debris strike decisions, it is tempting to conclude that replacing them will solve all NASA's problems. However, solving NASA's problems is not quite so easily achieved. Peoples' actions are influenced by the organizations in which they work, shaping their choices in directions that even they may not realize. The Board explores the organizational context of decision making more fully in Chapters 7 and 8.[35]

. . . .

[Chapter 7 The Accident's Organizational Causes]

Many accident investigations make the same mistake in defining causes. They identify the widget that broke or malfunctioned, then locate the person most closely connected with the technical failure: the engineer who miscalculated an analysis, the operator who missed signals or pulled the wrong switches, the supervisor who failed to listen, or the manager who made bad decisions. When causal chains are limited to technical flaws and individual failures, the ensuing responses aimed at preventing a similar event in the future are equally limited: they aim to fix the technical problem and replace or retrain the individual responsible. Such corrections lead to a misguided and potentially disastrous belief that the underlying problem has been solved. The Board did not want to make these errors. A central piece of our expanded cause model involves NASA as an organizational whole.

Organizational Cause Statement

The organizational causes of this accident are rooted in the Space Shuttle Program's history and culture, including the original compromises that were required to gain approval for the Shuttle Program, subsequent years of resource constraints, fluctuating priorities, schedule pressures, mischaracterizations of the Shuttle as operational rather than developmental, and lack of an agreed national vision. Cultural traits and organizational practices detrimental to safety and reliability were allowed to develop, including: reliance on past success as a substitute for sound engineering practices (such as testing to understand why systems were not performing in accordance with requirements/specifications); organizational barriers which prevented effective communication of critical safety information and stifled professional differences of opinion; lack of integrated management across program elements; and the evolution of an

---

[35] *Id.* at 170.

informal chain of command and decision-making processes that operated outside the organization's rules.

Understanding Causes

In the Board's view, NASA's organizational culture and structure had as much to do with this accident as the External Tank foam. Organizational culture refers to the values, norms, beliefs, and practices that govern how an institution functions. At the most basic level, organizational culture defines the assumptions that employees make as they carry out their work. It is a powerful force that can persist through reorganizations and the reassignment of key personnel.

Given that today's risks in human space flight are as high and the safety margins as razor thin as they have ever been, there is little room for overconfidence. Yet the attitudes and decision-making of Shuttle Program managers and engineers during the events leading up to this accident were clearly overconfident and often bureaucratic in nature. They deferred to layered and cumbersome regulations rather than the fundamentals of safety. The Shuttle Program's safety culture is straining to hold together the vestiges of a once robust systems safety program.

As the Board investigated the *Columbia* accident, it expected to find a vigorous safety organization, process, and culture at NASA, bearing little resemblance to what the Rogers Commission identified as the ineffective "silent safety" system in which budget cuts resulted in a lack of resources, personnel, independence, and authority. NASA's initial briefings to the Board on its safety programs espoused a risk-averse philosophy that empowered any employee to stop an operation at the mere glimmer of a problem. Unfortunately, NASA's views of its safety culture in those briefings did not reflect reality. Shuttle Program safety personnel failed to adequately assess anomalies and frequently accepted critical risks without qualitative or quantitative support, even when the tools to provide more comprehensive assessments were available.

Similarly, the Board expected to find NASA's Safety and Mission Assurance organization deeply engaged at every[36] level of Shuttle management: the Flight Readiness Review, the Mission Management Team, the Debris Assessment Team, the Mission Evaluation Room, and so forth. This was not the case. In briefing after briefing, interview after interview, NASA remained in denial: in the agency's eyes, "there were no safety-of-flight issues," and no safety compromises in the long history of debris strikes on the Thermal Protection System. The silence of Program-level safety processes undermined oversight; when they did not speak

[36] *Id.* at 177.

up, safety personnel could not fulfill their stated mission to provide "checks and balances." A pattern of acceptance prevailed throughout the organization that tolerated foam problems without sufficient engineering justification for doing so.

This chapter presents an organizational context for understanding the *Columbia* accident. Section 7.1 outlines a short history of safety at NASA, beginning in the pre-Apollo era when the agency reputedly had the finest system safety-engineering programs in the world. Section 7.2 discusses organizational theory and its importance to the Board's investigation, and Section 7.3 examines the practices of three organizations that successfully manage high risk. Sections 7.4 and 7.5 look at NASA today and answer the question, "How could NASA have missed the foam signal?" by highlighting the blind spots that rendered the Shuttle Program's risk perspective myopic. The Board's conclusion and recommendations are presented in 7.6. (See Chapter 10 for a discussion of the differences between industrial safety and mission assurance/quality assurance.)

7.1 Organizational Causes: Insights from History

NASA's organizational culture is rooted in history and tradition. From NASA's inception in 1958 to the *Challenger* accident in 1986, the agency's Safety, Reliability, and Quality Assurance (SRQA) activities, "although distinct disciplines," were "typically treated as one function in the design, development, and operations of NASA's manned space flight programs." Contractors and NASA engineers collaborated closely to assure the safety of human space flight. Solid engineering practices emphasized defining goals and relating system performance to them; establishing and using decision criteria; developing alternatives; modeling systems for analysis; and managing operations. Although a NASA Office of Reliability and Quality Assurance existed for a short time during the early 1960s, it was funded by the human space flight program. By 1963, the office disappeared from the agency's organization charts. For the next few years, the only type of safety program that existed at NASA was a decentralized "loose federation" of risk assessment oversight run by each program's contractors and the project offices at each of the three Human Space Flight Centers.

Fallout from Apollo—1967

In January 1967, months before the scheduled launch of Apollo 1, three astronauts died when a fire erupted in a ground-test capsule. In response, Congress, seeking to establish an independent safety organization to oversee space flight, created the Aerospace Safety Advisory Panel (ASAP). The ASAP was intended to be a senior advisory committee to NASA, reviewing space flight safety studies and operations plans, and evaluating "systems procedures and management policies that contribute to risk." The panel's main priority was human space flight missions. Although four of the panel's nine members can be NASA employees, in recent years few have served as members. While the panel's support staff generally consists of fulltime NASA employees, the group technically remains an independent oversight body.

Congress simultaneously mandated that NASA create separate safety and reliability offices at the agency's headquarters and at each of its Human Space Flight Centers and Programs. Overall safety oversight became the responsibility of NASA's Chief Engineer. Although these offices were not totally independent—their funding was linked with the very programs they were supposed to oversee—their existence allowed NASA to treat safety as a unique function. Until the *Challenger* accident in 1986, NASA safety remained linked organizationally and financially to the agency's Human Space Flight Program.

Challenger—1986

In the aftermath of the *Challenger* accident, the Rogers Commission issued recommendations intended to remedy what it considered to be basic deficiencies in NASA's safety system. These recommendations centered on an underlying theme: the lack of independent safety oversight at NASA. Without independence, the Commission believed, the slate of safety failures that contributed to the *Challenger* accident—such as the undue influence of schedule pressures and the flawed Flight Readiness process—would not be corrected. "NASA should establish an Office of Safety, Reliability, and Quality Assurance to be headed by an Associate Administrator, reporting directly to the NASA Administrator," concluded the Commission. "It would have *direct authority* for safety, reliability, and quality assurance throughout the Agency. The office should be assigned the workforce to ensure adequate oversight of its functions and should be independent of other NASA functional and program responsibilities" [emphasis added].

In July 1986, NASA Administrator James Fletcher created a Headquarters Office of Safety, Reliability, and Quality Assurance, which was given responsibility for all agency-wide safety-related policy functions. In the process, the position of Chief Engineer was abolished. The new office's Associate Administrator promptly initiated studies on Shuttle in-flight anomalies, overtime levels, the lack of spare parts, and landing and crew safety systems, among other issues. Yet NASA's response to the Rogers Commission recommendation did not meet the Commission's intent: the Associate Administrator did not have direct authority, and safety, reliability, and mission assurance activities across the agency remained dependent on other programs and Centers for funding.

General Accounting Office Review—1990

A 1990 review by the U.S. General Accounting Office questioned the effectiveness of NASA's new safety organizations[37] in a report titled "Space Program Safety: Funding for NASA's Safety Organizations Should Be Centralized." The report concluded *"NASA did not have an independent and effective safety organization"* [emphasis added]. Although the safety organizational structure may have "appeared adequate," in the late 1980s the space agency had concentrated most of its efforts on creating an independent safety office at NASA Headquarters. In contrast, the safety offices at NASA's field centers "were not entirely independent because they obtained most of their funds from activities whose safety-related performance they were responsible for overseeing." The General Accounting Office worried that "the lack of centralized independent funding may also restrict the flexibility of center safety managers." It also suggested "most NASA safety managers believe that centralized SRM&QA [Safety, Reliability, Maintainability and Quality Assurance] funding would ensure independence." NASA did not institute centralized funding in response to the General Accounting Office report, nor has it since. The problems outlined in 1990 persist to this day.

Space Flight Operations Contract—1996

The Space Flight Operations Contract was intended to streamline and modernize NASA's cumbersome contracting practices, thereby freeing the agency to focus on research and development (see Chapter 5). Yet its implementation complicated issues of safety independence. A single contractor would, in principle, provide "oversight" on production, safety, and mission assurance, as well as cost management, while NASA maintained "insight" into safety and quality assurance through reviews and metrics. Indeed, the reduction to a single primary contract simplified some aspects of the NASA/contractor interface. However, as a result, experienced engineers changed jobs, NASA grew dependent on contractors for technical support, contract monitoring requirements increased, and positions were subsequently staffed by less experienced engineers who were placed in management roles.

Collectively, this eroded NASA's in-house engineering and technical capabilities and increased the agency's reliance on the United Space Alliance and its subcontractors to identify, track, and resolve problems. The contract also

---

[37] *Id.* at 178 (footnotes omitted).

involved substantial transfers of safety responsibility from the government to the private sector; rollbacks of tens of thousands of Government Mandated Inspection Points; and vast reductions in NASA's in-house safety-related technical expertise. . . . In the aggregate, these mid-1990s transformations rendered NASA's already problematic safety system simultaneously weaker and more complex.

The effects of transitioning Shuttle operations to the Space Flight Operations Contract were not immediately apparent in the years following implementation. In November 1996, as the contract was being implemented, the Aerospace Safety Advisory Panel published a comprehensive contract review, which concluded that the effort "to streamline the Space Shuttle program has not inadvertently created unacceptable flight or ground risks." The Aerospace Safety Advisory Panel's passing grades proved temporary.

Shuttle Independent Assessment Team—1999

Just three years later, after a number of close calls, NASA chartered the Shuttle Independent Assessment Team to examine Shuttle sub-systems and maintenance practices (see Chapter 5). The Shuttle Independent Assessment Team Report sounded a stern warning about the quality of NASA's Safety and Mission Assurance efforts and noted that the Space Shuttle Program had undergone a massive change in structure and was transitioning to "a slimmed down, contractor-run operation."

The team produced several pointed conclusions: the Shuttle Program was inappropriately using *previous success as a justification* for accepting increased risk; the Shuttle Program's *ability to manage risk was being eroded* "by the desire to reduce costs;" the size and complexity of the Shuttle Program and NASA/contractor relationships *demanded better communication practices*; NASA's safety and mission assurance organization was *not sufficiently independent*; and "the workforce has received a conflicting message due to the emphasis on achieving cost and staff reductions, and the *pressures placed on increasing scheduled flights* as a result of the Space Station" [emphasis added]. The Shuttle Independent Assessment Team found failures of communication to flow up from the "shop floor" and down from supervisors to workers, deficiencies in problem and waiver-tracking systems, potential conflicts of interest between Program and contractor goals, and a general failure to communicate requirements and changes across organizations. In general, the Program's organizational culture was deemed "too insular."

NASA subsequently formed an Integrated Action Team to develop a plan to address the recommendations from previous Program-specific assessments, including the Shuttle Independent Assessment Team, and to formulate improvements. In part this effort was also a response to program missteps in the drive for efficiency seen in the "faster, better, cheaper" NASA of the 1990s. The NASA Integrated Action Team observed: *"NASA should continue to remove communication barriers and foster an inclusive environment where open communication is the norm."* The intent was to establish an initiative where *"the importance of communication and a culture of trust and openness permeate all facets of the organization."* The report indicated that *"multiple processes to get the messages across the organizational structure"* would need to be explored and fostered [emphasis added].

The report recommended that NASA solicit expert advice in identifying and removing barriers, providing tools, training, and education, and facilitating communication processes. The Shuttle Independent Assessment Team and NASA Integrated Action Team findings mirror those presented by the Rogers Commission. The same communication problems persisted in the Space Shuttle Program at the time of the *Columbia* accident.

Space Shuttle Competitive Source Task Force—2002

In 2002, a 14-member Space Shuttle Competitive Task Force supported by the RAND Corporation examined competitive[38] sourcing options for the Shuttle Program. In its final report to NASA, the team highlighted several safety-related concerns, which the Board shares:

- Flight and ground hardware and software are obsolete, and safety upgrades and aging infrastructure repairs have been deferred.
- Budget constraints have impacted personnel and resources required for maintenance and upgrades.
- International Space Station schedules exert significant pressures on the Shuttle Program.
- Certain mechanisms may impede worker anonymity in reporting safety concerns.
- NASA does not have a truly independent safety function with the authority to halt the progress of a critical mission element.

Based on these findings, the task force suggested that an Independent Safety Assurance function should be created that would hold one of "three keys" in the Certification of Flight Readiness process (NASA and the operating contractor would hold the other two), effectively giving this function the ability to stop any

[38] *Id.* at 179 (footnotes omitted).

launch. Although in the Board's view the "third key" Certification of Flight Readiness process is not a perfect solution, independent safety and verification functions are vital to continued Shuttle operations. This independent function should possess the authority to shut down the flight preparation processes or intervene post-launch when an anomaly occurs.

7.2 Organizational Causes: Insights from Theory

To develop a thorough understanding of accident causes and risk, and to better interpret the chain of events that led to the *Columbia* accident, the Board turned to the contemporary social science literature on accidents and risk and sought insight from experts in High Reliability, Normal Accident, and Organizational Theory. Additionally, the Board held a forum, organized by the National Safety Council, to define the essential characteristics of a sound safety program.

High Reliability Theory argues that organizations operating high-risk technologies, if properly designed and managed, can compensate for inevitable human shortcomings, and therefore avoid mistakes that under other circumstances would lead to catastrophic failures. Normal Accident Theory, on the other hand, has a more pessimistic view of the ability of organizations and their members to manage high-risk technology. Normal Accident Theory holds that organizational and technological complexity contributes to failures. Organizations that aspire to failure-free performance are inevitably doomed to fail because of the inherent risks in the technology they operate. Normal Accident models also emphasize systems approaches and systems thinking, while the High Reliability model works from the bottom up: if each component is highly reliable, then the system will be highly reliable and safe.

Though neither High Reliability Theory nor Normal Accident Theory is entirely appropriate for understanding this accident, insights from each figured prominently in the Board's deliberation. Fundamental to each theory is the importance of strong organizational culture and commitment to building successful safety strategies.

The Board selected certain well-known traits from these models to use as a yardstick to assess the Space Shuttle Program, and found them particularly useful in shaping its views on whether NASA's current organization of its Human Space Flight Program is appropriate for the remaining years of Shuttle operation and beyond. Additionally, organizational theory, which encompasses organizational culture, structure, history, and hierarchy, is used to explain the *Columbia* accident, and, ultimately, combines with Chapters 5 and 6 to produce an expanded explanation of the accident's causes. The Board believes the following considerations are critical to understand what went wrong during STS-107. They will become the central motifs of the Board's analysis later in this chapter.

- **Commitment to a Safety Culture:** NASA's safety culture has become reactive, complacent, and dominated by unjustified optimism. Over time, slowly and unintentionally, independent checks and balances intended to increase safety have been eroded in favor of detailed processes that produce massive amounts of data and unwarranted consensus, but little effective communication. Organizations that successfully deal with high-risk technologies create and sustain a disciplined safety system capable of identifying, analyzing, and controlling hazards throughout a technology's life cycle.
- **Ability to Operate in Both a Centralized and Decentralized Manner:** The ability to operate in a centralized manner when appropriate, and to operate in a decentralized manner when appropriate, is the hallmark of a high-reliability organization. On the operational side, the Space Shuttle Program has a highly centralized structure. Launch commit criteria and flight rules govern every imaginable contingency. The Mission Control Center and the Mission Management Team have very capable decentralized processes to solve problems that are not covered by such rules. The process is so highly regarded that it is considered one of the best problem-solving organizations of its type. In these situations, mature processes anchor rules, procedures, and routines to make the Shuttle Program's matrixed workforce seamless, at least on the surface.

  Nevertheless, it is evident that the position one occupies in this structure makes a difference. When supporting organizations try to "push back" against centralized Program direction—like the Debris Assessment Team did during STS-107—independent analysis generated by a decentralized decision-making process can be stifled. The Debris Assessment Team, working in an essentially decentralized format, was well-led and had the right expertise to work the problem, but their charter was "fuzzy," and the team had little direct connection to the Mission Management Team. This lack of connection to the Mission Management Team and the Mission Evaluation Room is the single most compelling reason why communications were so poor during the debris[39] assessment. In this case, the Shuttle Program was unable to simultaneously manage both the centralized and decentralized systems.

- **Importance of Communication:** At every juncture of STS-107, the Shuttle Program's structure and processes, and therefore the managers in charge, resisted new information. Early in the mission, it became clear that the Program was not going to authorize imaging of the Orbiter because, in the Program's opinion, images were not needed. Overwhelming evidence indicates that Program leaders decided the foam strike was merely a maintenance problem long before any analysis had begun. Every manager knew the party line: "we'll wait for the analysis—no safety-of-flight issue expected." Program leaders spent at least as much time making sure hierarchical rules and processes were followed as they did trying to establish why anyone would want a picture of the Orbiter. These attitudes are incompatible with an organization that deals with high-risk technology.
- **Avoiding Oversimplification:** The *Columbia* accident is an unfortunate illustration of how NASA's strong cultural bias and its optimistic organizational thinking undermined effective decision-making. Over the course of 22 years, foam strikes were normalized to the point where they were simply a "maintenance" issue—a concern that did not threaten a mission's success. This oversimplification of the threat posed by foam debris rendered the issue a low-level concern in the minds of Shuttle managers. Ascent risk, so evident in *Challenger*, biased leaders to focus on strong signals from the Shuttle System Main Engine and the Solid Rocket Boosters. Foam strikes, by comparison, were a weak and consequently overlooked signal, although they turned out to be no less dangerous.
- **Conditioned by Success:** Even after it was clear from the launch videos that foam had struck the Orbiter in a manner never before seen, Space Shuttle Program managers were not unduly alarmed. They could not imagine why anyone would want a photo of something that could be fixed after landing. More importantly, learned attitudes about foam strikes diminished management's

[39] *Id.* at 180 (footnotes omitted).

wariness of their danger. The Shuttle Program turned "the experience of failure into the memory of success." Managers also failed to develop simple contingency plans for a re-entry emergency. They were convinced, without study, that nothing could be done about such an emergency. The intellectual curiosity and skepticism that a solid safety culture requires was almost entirely absent. Shuttle managers did not embrace safety-conscious attitudes. Instead, their attitudes were shaped and reinforced by an organization that, in this instance, was incapable of stepping back and gauging its biases. Bureaucracy and process trumped thoroughness and reason.

- **Significance of Redundancy:** The Human Space Flight Program has compromised the many redundant processes, checks, and balances that should identify and correct small errors. Redundant systems essential to every high-risk enterprise have fallen victim to bureaucratic efficiency. Years of workforce reductions and outsourcing have culled from NASA's workforce the layers of experience and hands-on systems knowledge that once provided a capacity for safety oversight. Safety and Mission Assurance personnel have been eliminated, careers in safety have lost organizational prestige, and the Program now decides on its own how much safety and engineering oversight it needs. Aiming to align its inspection regime with the International Organization for Standardization 9000/9001 protocol, commonly used in industrial environments—environments very different than the Shuttle Program—the Human Space Flight Program shifted from a comprehensive "oversight" inspection process to a more limited "insight" process, cutting mandatory inspection points by more than half and leaving even fewer workers to make "second" or "third" Shuttle systems checks. . . .

Implications for the Shuttle Program Organization

The Board's investigation into the *Columbia* accident revealed two major causes with which NASA has to contend: one technical, the other organizational. As mentioned earlier, the Board studied the two dominant theories on complex organizations and accidents involving high-risk technologies. These schools of thought were influential in shaping the Board's organizational recommendations, primarily because each takes a different approach to understanding accidents and risk.

The Board determined that high-reliability theory is extremely useful in describing the culture that should exist in the human space flight organization. NASA and the Space Shuttle Program must be committed to a strong safety culture, a view that serious accidents can be prevented, a willingness to learn from mistakes, from technology, and from others, and a realistic training program that empowers employees to know when to decentralize or centralize problem-solving. The Shuttle Program cannot afford the mindset that accidents are inevitable because it may lead to unnecessarily accepting known and preventable risks.

The Board believes normal accident theory has a key role in human spaceflight as well. Complex organizations need specific mechanisms to maintain their commitment to safety and assist their understanding of how complex interactions can make organizations accident-prone. Organizations cannot put blind faith into redundant warning systems because they inherently create more complexity, and this complexity in turn often produces unintended system interactions that can lead to failure. The Human Space Flight Program must realize that additional protective layers are not always the best choice. The Program must also remain sensitive to the fact that despite its best intentions, managers, engineers, safety professionals, and other employees, can, when confronted with extraordinary demands, act in counterproductive ways.

The challenges to failure-free performance highlighted by these two theoretical approaches will always be present in an organization that aims to send humans into space. What[40] can the Program do about these difficulties? The Board considered three alternatives. First, the Board could recommend that NASA follow traditional paths to improving safety by making changes to policy, procedures, and processes. These initiatives could improve organizational culture. The analysis provided by experts and the literature leads the Board to conclude that although reforming management practices has certain merits, it also has critical limitations. Second, the Board could recommend that the Shuttle is simply too risky and should be grounded. [But] the Board is committed to continuing human space exploration, and believes the Shuttle Program can and should continue to operate. Finally, the Board could recommend a significant change to the organizational structure that controls the Space Shuttle Program's technology. As will be discussed at length in this chapter's conclusion, the Board believes this option has the best chance to successfully manage the complexities and risks of human space flight.

---

[40] *Id.* at 181 (footnotes omitted).

[The Board then compared NASA's safety procedures to three other protocols: the U.S. Navy Submarine Flooding Prevention and Recovery (SUBSAFE), the Naval Nuclear Propulsion (Naval Reactors) programs, and the Aerospace Corporation's Launch Verification Process.]

. . . .

[In analyzing the Naval Reactors program, the Board noted some themes:]

- **Communication and Action:** Formal and informal practices ensure that relevant personnel at all levels are informed of technical decisions and actions that affect their area of responsibility. Contractor technical recommendations and government actions are documented in peer-reviewed formal written correspondence. Unlike NASA, PowerPoint briefings and papers for technical seminars are not substitutes for completed staff work. In addition, contractors strive to provide recommendations[41] based on a technical need, uninfluenced by headquarters or its representatives. Accordingly, division of responsibilities between the contractor and the Government remain clear, and a system of checks and balances is therefore inherent.
- **Recurring Training and Learning From Mistakes:** The Naval Reactor Program has yet to experience a reactor accident. This success is partially a testament to design, but also due to relentless and innovative training, grounded on lessons learned both inside and outside the program. For example, since 1996, Naval Reactors has educated more than 5,000 Naval Nuclear Propulsion Program personnel on the lessons learned from the *Challenger* accident. Senior NASA managers recently attended the 143rd presentation of the Naval Reactors seminar entitled "The *Challenger* Accident Re-examined." The Board credits NASA's interest in the Navy nuclear community, and encourages the agency to continue to learn from the mistakes of other organizations as well as from its own.
- **Encouraging Minority Opinions:** The Naval Reactor Program encourages minority opinions and "bad news." Leaders continually emphasize that when no minority opinions are present, the responsibility for a thorough and critical examination falls to management. Alternate perspectives and critical questions are always encouraged. In practice, NASA does not appear to embrace

[41] *Id.* at 182.

these attitudes. Board interviews revealed that it is difficult for minority and dissenting opinions to percolate up through the agency's hierarchy, despite processes like the anonymous NASA Safety Reporting System that supposedly encourages the airing of opinions.

- **Retaining Knowledge:** Naval Reactors uses many mechanisms to ensure knowledge is retained. The Director serves a minimum eight-year term, and the program documents the history of the rationale for every technical requirement. Key personnel in Headquarters routinely rotate into field positions to remain familiar with every aspect of operations, training, maintenance, development and the workforce. Current and past issues are discussed in open forum with the Director and immediate staff at "all-hands" informational meetings under an in-house professional development program. NASA lacks such a program.
- **Worst-Case Event Failures:** Naval Reactors hazard analyses evaluate potential damage to the reactor plant, potential impact on people, and potential environmental impact. The Board identified NASA's failure to adequately prepare for a range of worst-case scenarios as a weakness in the agency's safety and mission assurance training programs.[42]

. . . .

7.4 Organizational Causes: A Broken Safety Culture

Perhaps the most perplexing question the Board faced during its seven-month investigation into the *Columbia* accident was "How could NASA have missed the signals the foam was sending?" Answering this question was a challenge. The investigation revealed that in most cases, the Human Space Flight Program is extremely aggressive in reducing threats to safety. But we also know—in hindsight—that detection of the dangers posed by foam was impeded by "blind spots" in NASA's safety culture.

From the beginning, the Board witnessed a consistent lack of concern about the debris strike on *Columbia.* NASA managers told the Board "there was no safety-of-flight issue" and "we couldn't have done anything about it anyway." The investigation uncovered a troubling pattern in which Shuttle Program management made erroneous assumptions about the robustness of a system based

---

42 *Id.* at 183 (footnotes omitted).

on prior success rather than on dependable engineering data and rigorous testing.[43]

. . . .

Conclusions

Throughout the course of this investigation, the Board found that the Shuttle Program's complexity demands highly effective communication. Yet integrated hazard reports and risk analyses are rarely communicated effectively, nor are the many databases used by Shuttle Program engineers and managers capable of translating operational experiences into effective risk management practices. Although the Space Shuttle system has conducted a relatively small number of missions, there is more than enough data to generate performance trends. As it is currently structured, the Shuttle Program does not use data-driven safety methodologies to their fullest advantage.

7.5 Organizational Causes: Impact of a Flawed Safety Culture on STS-107

In this section, the Board examines how and why an array of processes, groups, and individuals in the Shuttle Program failed to appreciate the severity and implications of the foam strike on STS-107. The Board believes that the Shuttle Program should have been able to detect the foam trend and[44] more fully appreciate the danger it represented. Recall that "safety culture" refers to the collection of characteristics and attitudes in an organization—promoted by its leaders and internalized by its members—that makes safety an overriding priority. In the following analysis, the Board outlines shortcomings in the Space Shuttle Program, Debris Assessment Team, and Mission Management Team that resulted from a flawed safety culture.

Shuttle Program Shortcomings

The flight readiness process, which involves every organization affiliated with a Shuttle mission, missed the danger signals in the history of foam loss.

Generally, the higher information is transmitted in a hierarchy, the more it gets "rolled-up," abbreviated, and simplified. Sometimes information gets lost altogether, as weak signals drop from memos, problem identification systems, and formal presentations. The same conclusions, repeated over time, can result in problems eventually being deemed non-problems. An extraordinary example of this phenomenon is how Shuttle Program managers assumed the foam strike on STS-112 was not a warning sign (see Chapter 6). During the STS-113 Flight

---

[43] *Id.* at 184.

[44] *Id.* at 190.

Readiness Review, the bipod foam strike to STS-112 was rationalized by simply restating earlier assessments of foam loss. The question of why bipod foam would detach and strike a Solid Rocket Booster spawned no further analysis or heightened curiosity; nor did anyone challenge the weakness of External Tank Project Manager's argument that backed launching the next mission. After STS-113's successful flight, once again the STS-112 foam event was not discussed at the STS-107 Flight Readiness Review. The failure to mention an outstanding technical anomaly, even if not technically a violation of NASA's own procedures, desensitized the Shuttle Program to the dangers of foam striking the Thermal Protection System, and demonstrated just how easily the flight preparation process can be compromised. In short, the dangers of bipod foam got "rolled-up," which resulted in a missed opportunity to make Shuttle managers aware that the Shuttle required, and did not yet have a fix for the problem.

Once the *Columbia* foam strike was discovered, the Mission Management Team Chairperson asked for the rationale the STS-113 Flight Readiness Review used to launch in spite of the STS-112 foam strike. In her e-mail, she admitted that the analysis used to continue flying was, in a word, "lousy" (Chapter 6). This admission—that the rationale to fly was rubber-stamped—is, to say the least, unsettling. The Flight Readiness process is supposed to be shielded from outside influence, and is viewed as both rigorous and systematic. Yet the Shuttle Program is inevitably influenced by external factors, including, in the case of the STS-107, schedule demands. Collectively, such factors shape how the Program establishes mission schedules and sets budget priorities, which affects safety oversight, workforce levels, facility maintenance, and contractor workloads. Ultimately, external expectations and pressures impact even data collection, trend analysis, information development, and the reporting and disposition of anomalies. These realities contradict NASA's optimistic belief that pre-flight reviews provide true safeguards against unacceptable hazards. The schedule pressure to launch International Space Station Node 2 is a powerful example of this point (Section 6.2).

The premium placed on maintaining an operational schedule, combined with ever-decreasing resources, gradually led Shuttle managers and engineers to miss signals of potential danger. Foam strikes on the Orbiter's Thermal Protection System, no matter what the size of the debris, were "normalized" and accepted as not being a "safety-of-flight risk." Clearly, the risk of Thermal Protection damage due to such a strike needed to be better understood in quantifiable terms. External Tank foam loss should have been eliminated or mitigated with redundant layers of protection. If there was in fact a strong safety culture at NASA, safety experts would have had the authority to test the actual resilience of the leading edge Reinforced Carbon-Carbon panels, as the Board has done.

Debris Assessment Team Shortcomings

Chapter Six details the Debris Assessment Team's efforts to obtain additional imagery of *Columbia.* When managers in the Shuttle Program denied the team's request for imagery, the Debris Assessment Team was put in the untenable position of having to prove that a safety-of-flight issue existed without the very images that would permit such a determination. This is precisely the opposite of how an effective safety culture would act. Organizations that deal with high-risk operations must always have a healthy fear of failure—operations must be proved safe, rather than the other way around. NASA inverted this burden of proof.[45]

. . . .

Mission Management Team Shortcomings

In the Board's view, the decision to fly STS-113 without a compelling explanation for why bipod foam had separated on ascent during the preceding mission, combined with the low number of Mission Management Team meetings during STS-107, indicates that the Shuttle Program had become overconfident. Over time, the organization determined it did not need daily meetings during a mission, despite regulations that state otherwise.

Status update meetings should provide an opportunity to raise concerns and hold discussions across structural and technical boundaries. The leader of such meetings must encourage participation and guarantee that problems are assessed and resolved fully. All voices must be heard, which can be difficult when facing a hierarchy. An employee's location in the hierarchy can encourage silence. Organizations interested in safety must take steps to guarantee that all relevant information is presented to decision-makers. This did not happen in the meetings during the *Columbia* mission (see Chapter 6). For instance, e-mails from engineers at Johnson and Langley conveyed the depth of their concern about the foam strike, the questions they had about its implications, and the actions they wanted to take as a follow-up. However, these e-mails did not reach the Mission Management Team.

The failure to convey the urgency of engineering concerns was caused, at least in part, by organizational structure and spheres of authority. The Langley e-mails were circulated among co-workers at Johnson who explored the possible effects of the foam strike and its consequences for landing. Yet, like Debris

---

45 *Id.* at 190.

Assessment Team Co-Chair Rodney Rocha, they kept their concerns within local channels and did not forward them to the Mission Management Team. They were separated from the decision-making process by distance and rank.

Similarly, Mission Management Team participants felt pressured to remain quiet unless discussion turned to their particular area of technological or system expertise, and, even then, to be brief. The initial damage assessment briefing prepared for the Mission Evaluation Room was cut down considerably in order to make it "fit" the schedule. Even so, it took 40 minutes. It was cut down further to a three-minute discussion topic at the Mission Management Team. Tapes of STS-107 Mission Management Team sessions reveal a noticeable "rush" by the meeting's leader to the preconceived bottom line that there was "no safety-of-flight" issue (see Chapter 6). Program managers created huge barriers against dissenting opinions by stating preconceived conclusions based on subjective knowledge and experience, rather than on solid data. Managers demonstrated little concern for mission safety.

Organizations with strong safety cultures generally acknowledge that a leader's best response to unanimous consent is to play devil's advocate and encourage an exhaustive debate. Mission Management Team leaders failed to seek out such minority opinions. Imagine the difference if any Shuttle manager had simply asked, "Prove to me that *Columbia* has not been harmed."

Similarly, organizations committed to effective communication seek avenues through which unidentified concerns and dissenting insights can be raised, so that weak signals are not lost in background noise. Common methods of bringing minority opinions to the fore include hazard reports, suggestion programs, and empowering employees to call "time out". . . . For these methods to be effective, they must mitigate the fear of retribution, and management and technical staff must pay attention. Shuttle Program hazard reporting is seldom used, safety time outs are at times disregarded, and informal efforts to gain support are squelched. The very fact that engineers felt inclined to conduct simulated blown tire landings at Ames "after hours," indicates their reluctance to bring the concern up in established channels.

Safety Shortcomings

The Board believes that the safety organization, due to a lack of capability and resources independent of the Shuttle Program, was not an effective voice in discussing technical issues or mission operations pertaining to STS-107. The safety personnel present in the Debris Assessment Team, Mission Evaluation Room, and on the Mission Management Team were largely silent during the events leading up to the loss of *Columbia.* That silence was not merely a failure of safety, but a failure of the entire organization.

7.6 Findings and Recommendations

The evidence that supports the organizational causes also led the Board to conclude that NASA's current organization, which combines in the Shuttle Program all authority and responsibility for schedule, cost, manifest, safety, technical requirements, and waivers to technical requirements, is not an effective check and balance to achieve safety and mission assurance. Further, NASA's Office of Safety and Mission Assurance does not have the independence and authority that the Board and many outside reviews believe is necessary. Consequently, the Space Shuttle Program does not consistently demonstrate the characteristics of organizations that effectively manage high risk. . . .[46]

[Chapter 8 History as Cause: *Columbia* and *Challenger*]

. . . .

Connecting the parts of NASA's organizational system and drawing the parallels with *Challenger* demonstrate three things. First, despite all the post-*Challenger* changes at NASA and the agency's notable achievements since, the causes of the institutional failure responsible for *Challenger* have not been fixed. Second, the Board strongly believes that if these persistent, systemic flaws are not resolved, the scene is set for another accident. Therefore, the recommendations for change are not only for fixing the Shuttle's technical system, but also for fixing each part of the organizational system that produced *Columbia's* failure. Third, the Board's focus on the context in which decision making occurred does not mean that individuals are not responsible and accountable. To the contrary, individuals always must assume responsibility for their actions. What it does mean is that NASA's problems cannot be solved simply by retirements, resignations, or transferring personnel.[47]

. . . .

History became cause as the repeating pattern of anomalies was ratified as safe in Flight Readiness Reviews. The official definitions of risk assigned to each anomaly in Flight Readiness Reviews limited the actions taken and the resources spent on these problems. Two examples of the road not taken and the devastating implications for the future occurred close in time to both accidents. On the October 2002 launch of STS-112, a large piece of bipod ramp foam hit and

---

[46] *Id.* at 192 (footnotes omitted).

[47] *Id.* at 195 (footnote omitted).

damaged the External Tank Attachment ring on the Solid Rocket Booster skirt, a strong signal of danger 10 years after the last known bipod ramp foam event. Prior to *Challenger,* there was a comparable surprise. After a January 1985 launch, for which the Shuttle sat on the launch pad for three consecutive nights of unprecedented cold temperatures, engineers discovered upon the Orbiter's return that hot gases had eroded the primary and reached the secondary O-ring, blackening the putty in between—an indication that the joint nearly failed.

But accidents are not always preceded by a wake-up call. In 1985, engineers realized they needed data on the relationship between cold temperatures and O-ring erosion. However, the task of getting better temperature data stayed on the back burner because of the definition of risk: the primary erosion was within the experience base; the secondary O-ring (thought to be redundant) was not damaged and, significantly, there was a low probability that such cold Florida temperatures would recur. The scorched putty, initially a strong signal, was redefined after analysis as weak. On the eve of the *Challenger* launch, when cold temperature became a concern, engineers had no test data on the effect of cold temperatures on O-ring erosion. Before *Columbia,* engineers concluded that the damage from the STS-112 foam hit in October 2002 was not a threat to flight safety. The logic was that, yes, the foam piece was large and there was damage, but no serious consequences followed. Further, a hit this size, like cold temperature, was a low-probability event. After analysis, the biggest foam hit to date was redefined as a weak signal. Similar self-defeating actions and inactions followed. Engineers were again dealing with the poor quality of tracking camera images of strikes during ascent. Yet NASA took no steps to improve imagery and took no immediate action to reduce the risk of bipod ramp foam shedding and potential damage to the Orbiter before *Columbia.* Furthermore, NASA performed no tests on what would happen if a wing leading edge were struck by bipod foam, even though foam had repeatedly separated from the External Tank.

During the *Challenger* investigation, Rogers Commission member Dr. Richard Feynman famously compared launching Shuttles with known problems to playing Russian roulette. But that characterization is only possible in hindsight. It is not how NASA personnel perceived the risks as they were being assessed, one launch at a time. Playing Russian roulette implies that the pistol-holder realizes that death might be imminent and still takes the risk. For both foam debris and O-ring erosion, fixes were in the works at the time of the accidents, but there was no rush to complete them because neither problem was defined as a show-stopper. Each time an incident occurred, the Flight Readiness process declared it safe to continue flying. Taken one at a time, each decision seemed correct. The agency allocated attention and resources to these two problems accordingly. The consequences of living with both of these anomalies were, in its view, minor. Not all engineers agreed in the months immediately preceding *Challenger,* but the dominant view at NASA—the managerial view—was, as one manager put it, "we were just eroding rubber O-rings," which was a low-cost problem. The financial consequences of foam debris also were relatively low: replacing tiles extended the turnaround time between launches. In both cases, NASA was comfortable with its analyses. Prior to each accident, the agency saw no greater consequences on the horizon.

8.3 System Effects: The Impact of History and Politics on Risky Work

The series of engineering decisions that normalized technical deviations shows one way that history became cause in both accidents. But NASA's own history encouraged this pattern of flying with known flaws. Seventeen years separated the two accidents. NASA Administrators, Congresses, and political administrations changed. However, NASA's political and budgetary situation remained the same in principle as it had been since the inception of the Shuttle Program. NASA remained a politicized and vulnerable agency, dependent on key political players who accepted NASA's ambitious proposals and then imposed strict budget limits. Post-*Challenger* policy decisions made by the White House, Congress, and NASA leadership resulted in the agency reproducing many of the failings identified by the Rogers Commission. Policy constraints affected the Shuttle Program's organization culture, its structure, and the structure of the safety system. The three combined to keep NASA on its slippery slope toward *Challenger* and *Columbia.* NASA culture allowed flying with flaws when problems were defined as normal and routine; the structure of NASA's Shuttle Program blocked the flow of critical information up the hierarchy, so definitions of risk continued unaltered. Finally, a perennially weakened safety system, unable to critically analyze and intervene, had no choice but to ratify the existing risk assessments on these two problems. The following comparison shows that these system effects persisted through time, and affected engineering decisions in the years leading up to both accidents.[48]

. . . .

8.4 Organization, Culture, and Unintended Consequences

A number of changes to the Space Shuttle Program structure made in response to policy decisions had the unintended effect of perpetuating dangerous aspects of pre-*Challenger* culture and continued the pattern of normalizing things that were not supposed to happen. At the same time that NASA leaders were

48 *Id.* at 197 (footnotes omitted).

emphasizing the importance of safety, their personnel cutbacks sent other signals. Streamlining and downsizing, which scarcely go unnoticed by employees, convey a message that efficiency is an important goal. The Shuttle/Space Station partnership affected both programs. Working evenings and weekends just to meet the International Space Station Node 2 deadline sent a signal to employees that schedule is important. When paired with the "faster, better, cheaper" NASA motto of the 1990s and cuts that dramatically decreased safety personnel, efficiency becomes a strong signal and safety a weak one. This kind of doublespeak by top administrators affects people's decisions and actions without them even realizing it.

Changes in Space Shuttle Program structure contributed to the accident in a second important way. Despite the constraints that the agency was under, prior to both accidents NASA appeared to be immersed in a culture of invincibility, in stark contradiction to post-accident reality. The Rogers Commission found a NASA blinded by its "Can-Do" attitude, a cultural artifact of the Apollo era that was inappropriate in a Space Shuttle Program so strapped by schedule pressures and shortages that spare parts had to be cannibalized from one vehicle to launch another. This can-do attitude bolstered administrators' belief in an achievable launch rate, the belief that they had an operational system, and an unwillingness to listen to outside experts. The Aerospace Safety and Advisory Panel in a 1985 report told NASA that the vehicle was not operational and NASA should stop treating it as if it were. The Board found that even after the loss of *Challenger,* NASA was guilty of treating an experimental vehicle as if it were operational and of not listening to outside experts. In a repeat of the pre-*Challenger* warning, the 1999 Shuttle Independent Assessment Team report reiterated that "the Shuttle was not an 'operational' vehicle in the usual meaning of the term." Engineers and program planners were also affected by "Can-Do," which, when taken too far, can create a reluctance to say that something cannot be done.

How could the lessons of *Challenger* have been forgotten so quickly? Again, history was a factor. First, if success is measured by launches and landings, the machine appeared to be working successfully prior to both accidents. *Challenger* was the 25th launch. Seventeen years and 87 missions passed without major incident. Second, previous policy decisions again had an impact. NASA's Apollo-era research and development culture and its prized deference to the technical expertise of its working engineers was overridden in the Space Shuttle era by "bureaucratic accountability"—an allegiance to hierarchy, procedure, and following the chain of command. Prior to *Challenger,* the can-do culture was a result not just of years of apparently successful launches, but of the cultural belief that the Shuttle Program's many structures, rigorous procedures, and detailed system of rules were responsible for those successes. The Board noted that the pre-*Challenger* layers of processes, boards, and panels that had produced a false sense of confidence in the system and its level of safety returned in full force prior to *Columbia.* NASA made many changes to the Space Shuttle Program structure after *Challenger.* The fact that many changes had been made supported a belief in the safety of the system, the invincibility of organizational and technical systems, and ultimately, a sense that the foam problem was understood.

8.5 History as Cause: Two Accidents

Risk, uncertainty, and history came together when unprecedented circumstances arose prior to both accidents. For *Challenger,* the weather prediction for launch time the next day was for cold temperatures that were out of the engineering experience base. For *Columbia,* a large foam hit—also outside the experience base—was discovered after launch. For the first case, all the discussion was pre-launch; for the second, it was post-launch. This initial difference determined the shape these two decision sequences took, the number of people who had information about the problem, and the locations of the involved parties.

For *Challenger,* engineers at Morton-Thiokol, the Solid Rocket Motor contractor in Utah, were concerned about the effect of the unprecedented cold temperatures on the rubber O-rings. Because launch was scheduled for the next morning, the new condition required a reassessment of the engineering analysis presented at the Flight Readiness Review two weeks prior. A teleconference began at 8:45 p.m. Eastern Standard Time (EST) that included 34 people in three locations: Morton-Thiokol in Utah, Marshall, and Kennedy. Thiokol engineers were recommending a launch delay. A reconsideration of a Flight Readiness Review risk[49] assessment the night before a launch was as unprecedented as the predicted cold temperatures. With no ground rules or procedures to guide their discussion, the participants automatically reverted to the centralized, hierarchical, tightly structured, and procedure-bound model used in Flight Readiness Reviews. The entire discussion and decision to launch began and ended with this group of 34 engineers. The phone conference linking them together concluded at 11:15 p.m. EST after a decision to accept the risk and fly.

For *Columbia,* information about the foam debris hit was widely distributed the day after launch. Time allowed for videos of the strike, initial assessments of the size and speed of the foam, and the approximate location of the impact to be dispersed throughout the agency. This was the first debris impact of this

---

[49] *Id.* at 199 (footnotes omitted).

magnitude. Engineers at the Marshall, Johnson, Kennedy, and Langley centers showed initiative and jumped on the problem without direction from above. Working groups and e-mail groups formed spontaneously. The size of Johnson's Debris Assessment Team alone neared and in some instances exceeded the total number of participants in the 1986 *Challenger* teleconference. Rather than a tightly constructed exchange of information completed in a few hours, time allowed for the development of ideas and free-wheeling discussion among the engineering ranks. The early post-launch discussion among engineers and all later decision-making at management levels were decentralized, loosely organized, and with little form. While the spontaneous and decentralized exchanging of information was evidence that NASA's original technical culture was alive and well, the diffuse form and lack of structure in the rest of the proceedings would have several negative consequences.

In both situations, all new information was weighed and interpreted against past experience. Formal categories and cultural beliefs provide a consistent frame of reference in which people view and interpret information and experiences. Pre-existing definitions of risk shaped the actions taken and not taken. Worried engineers in 1986 and again in 2003 found it impossible to reverse the Flight Readiness Review risk assessments that foam and O-rings did not pose safety-of-flight concerns. These engineers could not prove that foam strikes and cold temperatures were unsafe, even though the previous analyses that declared them safe had been incomplete and were based on insufficient data and testing. Engineers' failed attempts were not just a matter of psychological frames and interpretations. The obstacles these engineers faced were political and organizational. They were rooted in NASA history and the decisions of leaders that had altered NASA culture, structure, and the structure of the safety system and affected the social context of decision-making for both accidents. In the following comparison of these critical decision scenarios for *Columbia* and *Challenger,* the systemic problems in the NASA organization are in italics, with the system effects on decision-making following.

NASA had conflicting goals of cost, schedule, and safety. Safety lost out as the mandates of an "operational system" increased the schedule pressure. Scarce resources went to problems that were defined as more serious, rather than to foam strikes or O-ring erosion.

In both situations, upper-level managers and engineering teams working the O-ring and foam strike problems held opposing definitions of risk. This was demonstrated immediately, as engineers reacted with urgency to the immediate safety implications: Thiokol engineers scrambled to put together an engineering assessment for the teleconference, Langley Research Center engineers initiated simulations of landings that were run after hours at Ames Research Center, and Boeing analysts worked through the weekend on the debris impact analysis. But key managers were responding to additional demands of cost and schedule, which competed with their safety concerns. NASA's conflicting goals put engineers at a disadvantage before these new situations even arose. In neither case did they have good data as a basis for decision-making. Because both problems had been previously normalized, resources sufficient for testing or hardware were not dedicated. The Space Shuttle Program had not produced good data on the correlation between cold temperature and O-ring resilience or good data on the potential effect of bipod ramp foam debris hits.

Cultural beliefs about the low risk O-rings and foam debris posed, backed by years of Flight Readiness Review decisions and successful missions, provided a frame of reference against which the engineering analyses were judged. When confronted with the engineering risk assessments, top Shuttle Program managers held to the previous Flight Readiness Review assessments. In the *Challenger* teleconference, where engineers were recommending that NASA delay the launch, the Marshall Solid Rocket Booster Project manager, Lawrence Mulloy, repeatedly challenged the contractor's risk assessment and restated Thiokol's engineering rationale for previous flights. STS-107 Mission Management Team Chair Linda Ham made many statements in meetings reiterating her understanding that foam was a maintenance problem and a turnaround issue, not a safety-of-flight issue.

The effects of working as a manager in a culture with a cost/efficiency/safety conflict showed in managerial responses. In both cases, managers' techniques focused on the information that tended to support the expected or desired result at that time. In both cases, believing the safety of the mission was not at risk, managers drew conclusions that minimized the risk of delay. At one point, Marshall's Mulloy, believing in the previous Flight Readiness Review assessments, unconvinced by the engineering analysis, and concerned about the schedule implications of the 53-degree temperature limit on launch the engineers proposed, said, "My God, Thiokol, when do you want me to launch, next April?" Reflecting the overall goal of keeping to the Node 2 launch schedule, Ham's priority was to avoid the delay of STS-114, the next mission after STS-107. Ham was slated as Manager of Launch Integration for STS-114—a dual role promoting a conflict of interest and a single-point failure, a situation that should be avoided in all organizational as well as technical systems.

NASA's culture of bureaucratic accountability emphasized chain of command, procedure, following the rules, and going by the book. While rules and procedures were essential for coordination, they had an unintended but negative effect. Allegiance to hierarchy and procedure had replaced deference to NASA engineers' technical expertise.[50]

In both cases, engineers initially presented concerns as well as possible solutions—a request for images, a recommendation to place temperature constraints on launch. Management did not listen to what their engineers were telling them. Instead, rules and procedures took priority. For *Columbia,* program managers turned off the Kennedy engineers' initial request for Department of Defense imagery, with apologies to Defense Department representatives for not having followed "proper channels." In addition, NASA administrators asked for and promised corrective action to prevent such a violation of protocol from recurring. Debris Assessment Team analysts at Johnson were asked by managers to demonstrate a "mandatory need" for their imagery request, but were not told how to do that. Both *Challenger* and *Columbia* engineering teams were held to the usual quantitative standard of proof. But it was a reverse of the usual circumstance: instead of having to prove it was safe to fly, they were asked to prove that it was unsafe to fly.

In the *Challenger* teleconference, a key engineering chart presented a qualitative argument about the relationship between cold temperatures and O-ring erosion that engineers were asked to prove. Thiokol's Roger Boisjoly said, "I had no data to quantify it. But I did say I knew it was away from goodness in the current data base." Similarly, the Debris Assessment Team was asked to prove that the foam hit was a threat to flight safety, a determination that only the imagery they were requesting could help them make. Ignored by management was the qualitative data that the engineering teams did have: both instances were outside the experience base. In stark contrast to the requirement that engineers adhere to protocol and hierarchy was management's failure to apply this criterion to their own activities. The Mission Management Team did not meet on a regular schedule during the mission, proceeded in a loose format that allowed informal influence and status differences to shape their decisions, and allowed unchallenged opinions and assumptions to prevail, all the while holding the engineers who were making risk assessments to higher standards. In highly uncertain circumstances, when lives were immediately at risk, management failed to defer to its engineers and failed to recognize that different data standards—qualitative, subjective, and intuitive—and different processes—democratic rather than protocol and chain of command—were more appropriate.

---

50 *Id.* at 200 (footnotes omitted).

The organizational structure and hierarchy blocked effective communication of technical problems. Signals were overlooked, people were silenced, and useful information and dissenting views on technical issues did not surface at higher levels. What was communicated to parts of the organization was that O-ring erosion and foam debris were not problems.

Structure and hierarchy represent power and status. For both *Challenger* and *Columbia,* employees' positions in the organization determined the weight given to their information, by their own judgment and in the eyes of others. As a result, many signals of danger were missed. Relevant information that could have altered the course of events was available but was not presented.

Early in the *Challenger* teleconference, some engineers who had important information did not speak up. They did not define themselves as qualified because of their position: they were not in an appropriate specialization, had not recently worked the O-ring problem, or did not have access to the "good data" that they assumed others more involved in key discussions would have. Geographic locations also resulted in missing signals. At one point, in light of Marshall's objections, Thiokol managers in Utah requested an "off-line caucus" to discuss their data. No consensus was reached, so a "management risk decision" was made. Managers voted and engineers did not. Thiokol managers came back on line, saying they had reversed their earlier NO-GO recommendation, decided to accept risk, and would send new engineering charts to back their reversal. When a Marshall administrator asked, "Does anyone have anything to add to this?," no one spoke. Engineers at Thiokol who still objected to the decision later testified that they were intimidated by management authority, were accustomed to turning their analysis over to managers and letting them decide, and did not have the quantitative data that would empower them to object further.

In the more decentralized decision process prior to *Columbia's* re-entry, structure and hierarchy again were responsible for an absence of signals. The initial request for imagery came from the "low status" Kennedy Space Center, bypassed the Mission Management Team, and went directly to the Department of Defense separate from the all-powerful Shuttle Program. By using the Engineering Directorate avenue to request imagery, the Debris Assessment Team was working at the margins of the hierarchy. But some signals were missing even when engineers traversed the appropriate channels. The Mission Management Team Chair's position in the hierarchy governed what information she would or would not receive. Information was lost as it traveled up the hierarchy. A demoralized Debris Assessment Team did not include a slide about the need for better imagery in their presentation to the Mission Evaluation Room. Their presentation included the Crater analysis, which they reported as incomplete and uncertain. However, the Mission Evaluation Room manager perceived the Boeing analysis as rigorous and quantitative. The choice of headings, arrangement of information, and size of bullets on the key chart served to highlight what management already believed. The uncertainties and assumptions that signaled danger dropped out of the information chain when the Mission Evaluation Room manager condensed the Debris Assessment Team's formal presentation to an informal verbal brief at the Mission Management Team meeting.

As what the Board calls an "informal chain of command" began to shape STS-107's outcome, location in the structure empowered some to speak and silenced others. For example, a Thermal Protection System tile expert, who was a member of the Debris Assessment Team but had an office in the more prestigious Shuttle Program, used his personal network to shape the Mission Management Team view and snuff out dissent. The informal hierarchy among and within Centers was also influential. Early identifications of problems by Marshall and Kennedy may have contributed to the Johnson-based Mission Management Team's indifference to concerns about the foam strike. The engineers and managers circulating e-mails at Langley were peripheral to the Shuttle Program, not structurally connected to the proceedings, and[51] therefore of lower status. When asked in a post-accident press conference why they didn't voice their concerns to Shuttle Program management, the Langley engineers said that people "need to stick to their expertise." Status mattered. In its absence, numbers were the great equalizer. One striking exception: the Debris Assessment Team tile expert was so influential that his word was taken as gospel, though he lacked the requisite expertise, data, or analysis to evaluate damage to RCC. For those with lesser standing, the requirement for data was stringent and inhibiting, which resulted in information that warned of danger not being passed up the chain. As in the teleconference, Debris Assessment Team engineers did not speak up when the Mission Management Team Chair asked if anyone else had anything to say. Not only did they not have the numbers, they also were intimidated by the Mission Management Team Chair's position in the hierarchy and the conclusions she had already made. Debris Assessment Team members signed off on the Crater analysis, even though they had trouble understanding it. They still wanted images of *Columbia's* left wing.

In neither impending crisis did management recognize how structure and hierarchy can silence employees and follow through by polling participants, soliciting dissenting opinions, or bringing in outsiders who might have a different perspective or useful information. In perhaps the ultimate example of engineering

[51] *Id.* at 201 (footnotes omitted).

concerns not making their way upstream, *Challenger* astronauts were told that the cold temperature was not a problem, and *Columbia* astronauts were told that the foam strike was not a problem.

NASA structure changed as roles and responsibilities were transferred to contractors, which increased the dependence on the private sector for safety functions and risk assessment while simultaneously reducing the in-house capability to spot safety issues.

A critical turning point in both decisions hung on the discussion of contractor risk assessments. Although both Thiokol and Boeing engineering assessments were replete with uncertainties, NASA ultimately accepted each. Thiokol's initial recommendation against the launch of *Challenger* was at first criticized by Marshall as flawed and unacceptable. Thiokol was recommending an unheard-of delay on the eve of a launch, with schedule ramifications and NASA-contractor relationship repercussions. In the Thiokol off-line caucus, a senior vice president who seldom participated in these engineering discussions championed the Marshall engineering rationale for flight. When he told the managers present to "Take off your engineering hat and put on your management hat," they reversed the position their own engineers had taken. Marshall engineers then accepted this assessment, deferring to the expertise of the contractor. NASA was dependent on Thiokol for the risk assessment, but the decision process was affected by the contractor's dependence on NASA. Not willing to be responsible for a delay, and swayed by the strength of Marshall's argument, the contractor did not act in the best interests of safety. Boeing's Crater analysis was performed in the context of the Debris Assessment Team, which was a collaborative effort that included Johnson, United Space Alliance, and Boeing. In this case, the decision process was also affected by NASA's dependence on the contractor. Unfamiliar with Crater, NASA engineers and managers had to rely on Boeing for interpretation and analysis, and did not have the training necessary to evaluate the results. They accepted Boeing engineers' use of Crater to model a debris impact 400 times outside validated limits.

NASA's safety system lacked the resources, independence, personnel, and authority to successfully apply alternate perspectives to developing problems. Overlapping roles and responsibilities across multiple safety offices also undermined the possibility of a reliable system of checks and balances.

NASA's "Silent Safety System" did nothing to alter the decision-making that immediately preceded both accidents. No safety representatives were present during the *Challenger* teleconference—no one even thought to call them. In the case of *Columbia,* safety representatives were present at Mission Evaluation Room,

Mission Management Team, and Debris Assessment Team meetings. However, rather than critically question or actively participate in the analysis, the safety representatives simply listened and concurred.[52]

. . . .

NOTES

1. As we've said before, cognitive errors play a large part in many organizational failures. The *Challenger* and *Columbia* accidents were no exception. Of all of the causes that the Report posits, we want to emphasize the role of framing the risk. We think that framing a problem matters a great deal. During both the *Challenger* disaster and the *Columbia* disaster, managers were asked to prove that something was definitively dangerous.* They couldn't. No one could have. But we think that some of the decisions made during both events would have changed had the question been framed as "what are the odds that this flight is safe?" Maybe that framing would have gotten NASA to think about the risk differently: if the odds of a flight being unsafe are, say, 10%, what does that mean in terms of the potential magnitude of the consequences? Might that reframing cause NASA to ask, "at 10% risk, will we lose the crew, or just the space vehicle?" *That* question isn't quite right, either, though, because no space flight is ever going to be 100% safe. (For that matter, no simple drive down the street is 100% safe, either.) So spend a bit of time thinking about the right way to frame the safety question. You'll feel a bit like Goldilocks: requiring NASA to prove that a flight is not 100% unsafe is too extreme on one end and requiring NASA to prove that a flight is 100% safe is too extreme on the other end. What's "just right"?

2. We also want to draw a parallel about silos inside organizations. In NASA, just as in the GM case, information tended to circulate only within the individual work area silos, not across them.** How would you develop a system of making sure that each silo had access to information in the other silos—and that each silo actually paid attention to the information that the other silos were using?

---

[52] *Id.* at 202 (footnotes omitted).

* *See, e.g.*, Report at 38, which is p. 441 of our book ("Team members concluded over the next six days that some localized heating damage would most likely occur during re-entry, but they could not definitively state that structural damage would result.") and *id.* at 100 ("Far from meticulously guarding against potential problems, the Commission found that NASA had required "a contractor to prove that it was not safe to launch, rather than proving it was safe.").

** *See* Report at 38, which is at p. 441 of our book ("Even after the Debris Assessment Team's conclusion had been reported to the Mission Management Team, engineers throughout NASA and Mission Control continued to exchange e-mails and discuss possible damage. These messages and discussions were generally sent only to people within the senders' area of expertise and level of seniority.").

3. At the risk of overusing a Goldilocks metaphor, sometimes an organization needs to cut its budget, but there's such a thing as counter-productive cost-cutting. Cut too little, and the organization can't thrive. Cut too much, and the organization can't function. The Report emphasizes the interaction of NASA's budget cuts and the demands of extremely precise scheduling requirements. (The flights had to be timed correctly in order to achieve the appropriate launch windows so that a launch would be successful.) One of the most poignant (to us, anyway) sections of the report illustrates the dangers of bad cost-cutting decisions:

> The notion that NASA would further reduce the number of civil servants working on the Shuttle Program prompted senior Kennedy Space Center engineer José Garcia to send to President Bill Clinton on August 25, 1995, a letter that stated, "The biggest threat to the safety of the crew since the *Challenger* disaster is presently underway at NASA." Garcia's particular concern was NASA's "efforts to delete the 'checks and balances' system of processing Shuttles as a way of saving money . . . Historically NASA has employed two engineering teams at KSC, one contractor and one government, to cross check each other and prevent catastrophic errors . . . although this technique is expensive, it is effective, and it is the single most important factor that sets the Shuttle's success above that of any other launch vehicle . . . Anyone who doesn't have a hidden agenda or fear of losing his job would admit that you can't delete NASA's checks and balances system of Shuttle processing without affecting the safety of the Shuttle and crew."*

Mr. Garcia was prescient. Now, let's fast-forward to an organization that you're running and that needs to trim some of its expenses. How might you be able to tell when your budget-cutting decisions hit the "just right" mark?

4. Finally, to draw a parallel with some of the examples in our previous chapter, we have to turn to organizational culture. Organizational culture matters. What a culture rewards is what its employees will value. Wells Fargo valued the money that it made off each new customer account more than it did the potential profits that it might have made by treating each customer honestly and fairly. In much the same way, many companies value short-term profits more than they do long-term potential

* *See* Report at 108, which is at p. 458 of our book. We actually toured a NASA contractor's site when we lived in Houston, and we watched an interesting safety procedure during glove manufacture: one person turned the screwdriver as part of the assembly process, and another person watched the first person turn the screw to affirm that the assembly was being done properly. That's a system of checks and balances right there. It's not a perfect system, because the two workers could collude, but as long as there's no collusion and both parties pay attention to the work being done, that's a pretty powerful system for something with a low risk of failure but high consequences for that failure.

gains, in part because many executives get rewarded based more on short-term performance than long-term growth.

Here, the Report emphasized that "[i]n our view, the NASA organizational culture had as much to do with this accident as the foam. Organizational culture refers to the basic values, norms, beliefs, and practices that characterize the functioning of an institution. At the most basic level, organizational culture defines the assumptions that employees make as they carry out their work. It is a powerful force that can persist through reorganizations and the change of key personnel. It can be a positive or a negative force."*

Think back to GM's culture, or Volkswagen's, or Wells Fargo's. What did those cultures reward? Did those cultures invite suggestions or criticism? We want to close with an observation that the Report made that stands out for us: the importance of eliciting important information from inside an organization.

> Organizations with strong safety cultures generally acknowledge that a leader's best response to unanimous consent is to play devil's advocate and encourage an exhaustive debate. Mission Management Team leaders failed to seek out such minority opinions. Imagine the difference if any Shuttle manager had simply asked, "Prove to me that *Columbia* has not been harmed."
>
> Similarly, organizations committed to effective communication seek avenues through which unidentified concerns and dissenting insights can be raised, so that weak signals are not lost in background noise. Common methods of bringing minority opinions to the fore include hazard reports, suggestion programs, and empowering employees to call "time out". . . . For these methods to be effective, they must mitigate the fear of retribution, and management and technical staff must pay attention. Shuttle Program hazard reporting is seldom used, safety time outs are at times disregarded, and informal efforts to gain support are squelched. The very fact that engineers felt inclined to conduct simulated blown tire landings at Ames "after hours," indicates their reluctance to bring the concern up in established channels.**

As you move from this chapter to the next one, which focuses on the business of, and the behavior in, big law firms, think about the interaction of hierarchy and the need for good information in decision-making.

---

* *See* Report at 177, which is at p. 458 of our book.

** *See* Report at 192, which is at p. 492 of our book.

PART V

Examples from the Legal World

It's not surprising, given that both of us are lawyers, that we've been fascinated by the seriously bad decisions made by some law firms. Bad law firm decisions usually end in the firm's death.*

One law firm in particular—Dewey & LeBeouf—bears discussing, because the business decisions that it made during its last merger were, in retrospect, astonishingly inappropriate. Dewey & LeBeouf filed for chapter 11 protection in 2012, and its plan of reorganization was confirmed in 2013. Normally, chapter 11 cases involve restructuring a business, but this case involved an orderly liquidation of the firm.** In between the chapter 11 filing and the plan confirmation, though, there were several juicy pleadings filed with the court. One of them opens this chapter. Normally, in chapter 11 cases, the "debtor in possession" (a fancy name for the post-filing entity that used to be the debtor and, thanks to the Bankruptcy Code, has all sorts of fancy duties) would prosecute and settle claims. In this case, though, the Official Committee of Unsecured Creditors (think of the members of that committee like a representative class in a class action) didn't trust Dewey actively to pursue its partners and former partners to recover money for distribution to creditors, so it asked the Court's permission to let it—not the debtor in possession, but the creditors' committee—do the prosecuting and settling of claims. The *Motion of the Official Committee of Unsecured Creditors For Entry Of An Order Pursuant to §§ 1103(C) and 1109(B), Granting Leave, Standing and Authority to Prosecute and, If Appropriate, Settle Certain Claims on Behalf of the Debtor's Estate* (yes, that's a long title) sets out one side's theory about what caused Dewey to founder.*** We then contrast that description of the firm's downfall with a

* For a good discussion of the untimely demise of several prominent law firms, see Edward S. Adams, *Lessons from Law Firm Bankruptcies and Proposals for Reform,* 55 SANTA CLARA L. REV. 507 (2015).

** For a good write-up of the plan confirmation hearing, see Peter Lattman, *Court Approves Dewey Bankruptcy Plan, Officially Dissolving Firm,* N.Y. TIMES (Feb. 27, 2013), available at https://dealbook.nytimes.com/2013/02/27/court-approves-dewey-bankruptcy-plan-officially-dissolving-firm/.

*** We are not going to make you read any of the attachments to this motion.

pleading filed in the same case by the former chairman of Dewey & LeBeouf, Steven Davis, who has an understandably different perspective about the causes of his firm's downfall. Just to close the loop on that case for you, the bankruptcy court, in an opinion marked "not for publication," overruled Mr. Davis's objection, in part because "the Motion meets the standard for establishing a colorable claim against the Defendants."* That court opinion doesn't mean that the Court agreed with the allegations against Mr. Davis—just that the other side had written a pleading that was legally sufficient. As you read this chapter, try to figure out what you might have done had you been in charge of running Dewey in the last few years before its bankruptcy filing became necessary.** What decisions might you have made differently?

After you've done that, double-check your ideas against those of one of our favorite people, Amee McKim, who has some very good advice for you about bringing on lateral employees in her article, *A Discussion of the Risks of Lateral Partner Hiring.* If the Dewey & LeBeouf story represents what not to do when bringing new senior people into an organization, Ms. McKim's article gives good advice about how to avoid Dewey's fate.

Our next entry into the world of how law firms operates, *Compromising One's Principles: The Lesson of Mahlon Perkins and the Berkey-Kodak Case,* concerns a different firm (Donovan, Leisure) that also no longer exists. This article draws from various transcripts and an actual criminal indictment, and it discusses a well-respected partner at the firm who lied about discovery*** in a big antitrust case. We put the article in this chapter because it uses excerpts from court documents to illustrate various cognitive errors that this particular lawyer made when he lied to the judge and when he explained his actions at the sentencing hearing.

We close this chapter with a now-classic essay by Jennifer K. Robbennolt and Jean R. Sternlight, *Behavioral Legal Ethics,* which is designed to remind you how easy it is for smart people (yes, even smart lawyers) to forget that all humans are

* Matter of Dewey & LeBeouf, *Memorandum Opinion and Order Granting Motion of Creditors['] Committee for Standing to Prosecute and Settle Certain Claims on Behalf of the Estate,* Case No. 12-12321(MG), Bankr. S.D.N.Y., Doc. 675 at 14.

** You might not know this unless you've taken a bankruptcy law course, but some decisions that the debtor made in the year or two before bankruptcy can be unraveled under certain circumstances. Understanding some bankruptcy law is useful for businesses, even those that are doing well, because some businesses become creditors in bankruptcy cases. And understanding bankruptcy law is crucial for businesses that aren't doing well financially. You might also want to explore the law of deepening insolvency: how should officers and directors behave when it appears that there won't be sufficient assets to pay creditors? What we're saying here is that, should you be in charge of an organization, it's not just what happens when you file for bankruptcy protection but the moves that you make long before that time that may have lasting repercussions.

*** "Discovery" is lawyer-speak for all of the ways in which litigators try to establish facts in a case. Discovery can involve the production of documents, sworn testimony, and answers to written questions.

prone to a variety of cognitive errors. And if you think that only lawyers are subject to these cognitive errors, we will point you back to chapters III and IV, which are chock-full of the same errors, all committed by non-lawyers.

CHAPTER 15

Motion, *In re* Dewey and Leboeuf*

Hearing Date: November 29, 2012 at 10:00 a.m.
(Prevailing Eastern Time)
Objection Date: November 22, 2012 at 4:00 p.m.
(Prevailing Eastern Time)

BROWN RUDNICK LLP
Edward S. Weisfelner
Howard S. Steel
7 Times Square
New York, New York 10036
Telephone: 212-209-4800
Facsimile: 212-209-4801

Counsel for the Official
Committee of Unsecured Creditors

UNITED STATES BANKRUPTCY COURT
FOR THE SOUTHERN DISTRICT OF NEW YORK

In re:	:	Chapter 11
DEWEY & LEBOEUF LLP,	:	Case No. 12-12321 (MG)
Debtor.	:	

* Motion of the Official Committee of Unsecured Creditors For Entry of An Order Pursuant to §§ 1103(C) and 1109(B), Granting Leave, Standing and Authority to Prosecute and, If Appropriate, Settle Certain Claims on Behalf of the Debtor's Estate, *In re* Dewey & LeBeouf LLP, United States Bankruptcy Court for the Southern District of New York, Case No. 12-12321 (MG), Docket No. 628 (Nov. 12, 2012).

MOTION OF THE OFFICIAL COMMITTEE OF UNSECURED CREDITORS FOR ENTRY OF AN ORDER PURSUANT TO §§ 1103(C) AND 1109(B), GRANTING LEAVE, STANDING AND AUTHORITY TO PROSECUTE AND, IF APPROPRIATE, SETTLECERTAINCLAIMSONBEHALFOFTHEDEBTOR'SESTATE

The Official Committee of Unsecured Creditors (the "Committee") appointed in the above-captioned chapter 11 case of Dewey & LeBoeuf LLP (the "Debtor," or the "Firm") hereby files this motion (the "Motion"), pursuant to sections 1103(c) and 1109(b) of title 11 of the United States Code (as amended, the "Bankruptcy Code"), for entry of an order granting the Committee leave, standing and authority to prosecute and, if appropriate, settle certain meritorious claims against the Debtor's former management team for, among other things, breaches of their fiduciary duties to the Firm and its creditors. The Debtor has consented to the Committee obtaining derivative standing to prosecute these claims on behalf of the Debtor's estate.[1] In support of the Motion, the Committee respectfully states as follows:

Preliminary Statement

1. In order to protect the interests of the Debtor's estate and its creditors, the Committee seeks standing to prosecute, and potentially settle, claims against the Debtor's former management team: Steven Davis ("Davis"), the Debtor's former Chairman; Steven DiCarmine ("DiCarmine"), the Debtor's former Executive Director; and Joel Sanders ("Sanders"), the Debtor's former Chief Financial Officer (collectively the "Defendants"), for, among other things, breaches of their fiduciary duties to the Firm and its creditors. The Court should grant the Committee standing to prosecute these claims because: (i) the Debtor has consented to the relief sought in the Motion; (ii) these claims are likely to benefit the Debtor's estate; and (iii) the grounds for such claims are "colorable."

Jurisdiction and Venue

2. This Court has jurisdiction to consider this matter pursuant to 28 U.S.C. §§ 157 and 1334. Venue is proper pursuant to 28 U.S.C. §§ 1408 and 1409. This is a core proceeding pursuant to 28 U.S.C. § 157(b). The statutory predicates for the relief requested herein are Bankruptcy Code Sections 105, 1103(c) and 1109(b).

---

1 The Debtor's consent to the Committee's standing is a requirement under applicable law and is not to be deemed solicitation, assistance, participation or intervention within the meaning of Section 3(g) of the Policy (defined below).

Background

3. The claims against the Defendants arise out of the collapse of Dewey & LeBoeuf LLP, a prominent law firm that was created through the merger of two old-line New York firms: Dewey Ballantine LLP and LeBoeuf, Lamb, Greene & MacRae LLP.

4. The Firm operated as a limited liability partnership with a thousand plus employees and 26 offices world-wide. Davis was responsible for day-to-day management of the Firm. See Partnership Agreement § 4.6(a). A copy of the Partnership Agreement is attached hereto as Exhibit A. Davis also was responsible for: (i) designating all of the Firm's non-legal executive and administrative positions; (ii) acting with the full authority of the Firm's Executive Committee; (iii) nominating candidates to serve as successors to members of the Executive Committee; and (iv) serving as Chairman of the Executive Committee. *Id.* at §§ 4.4(b), 4.4(f), 4.4(g). Davis also had authority to borrow funds on behalf of the Firm, without additional consent, under any of the Firm's credit lines which were previously approved by the Executive Committee. *Id.* at § 4.6(a). From 2007–2010, Davis earned close to $10.8 million in compensation from the Firm.

5. Davis appointed DiCarmine and Sanders to their executive leadership positions within the Firm. Davis granted DiCarmine broad authority and responsibility for the Firm's operations. Davis granted Sanders broad authority and responsibility for the Firm's financial affairs. Davis granted both DiCarmine and Sanders extremely generous compensation packages that included above-market compensation and incentive plans and non-market features, including six year contracts, irrevocable grantor trusts established for their benefit, and generous signing bonuses, severance and change in control payments.

6. The Defendants were responsible for the Firm's compensation and financing decisions. By virtue of their management positions within the Firm, each of the Defendants owed fiduciary duties of care, loyalty, and candor to all partners and the Firm and its creditors. Instead of properly exercising these duties, the Defendants grossly mismanaged the Firm and engaged in rampant self-dealing that caused, ultimately, the Firm's demise. Examples of the Defendants mismanagement giving rise to colorable claims include: (i) their over-distribution of the Firm's available cash to select partners; (ii) their abusive reliance on guarantee agreements that bore no economic rationality; and (iii) their concealment of the Firm's true financial condition from its partners, employees and creditors. The actions of the Defendants were neither reasonable nor economically rational.

7. The Defendants' self-serving behavior was motivated by greed. They engaged in reckless conduct with the Firm's assets in an effort to maintain their lucrative above-market compensation packages and their actions bled the Debtor dry of cash. The Defendants paid themselves over $7 million dollars on an aggregate basis within one year of the Petition Date, despite the Debtor's dire financial condition.

8. The Firm's failure cannot be equated to the legal industry's economic downturn. The Firm failed because of the Defendants' reckless management of the Firm's financial affairs. The Defendants engaged in a secret and reckless campaign of handing out guarantees atypical of industry norms. The Defendants' wanton control of the Firm extended to misrepresenting the Firm's financial performance to leading industry publications, including The American Lawyer's Am Law 100. The Defendants also deceived several lateral partners about the Firm's financial performance to obtain fresh capital infusions to continue their reign.

9. Pursuant to the Partnership Agreement, profits of the Firm should have been shared in accordance with partners' respective interests in the Firm, defined as Participation Targets, which would be established each year by the Executive Committee. See Partnership Agreement § 6.1. Beginning as early as 2008, the Firm's economic performance was insufficient to compensate partners according to their respective Participation Targets. Although actual compensation was adjusted downward to reflect available net income as provided by the Partnership Agreement, the Defendants awarded make-up bonuses to partners in most cases equal to or greater than the shortfall to be paid out of future income. This practice continued for over three years, leaving less each year to allocate for current compensation and ultimately resulting in the failure of the Firm.

10. The Defendants also embarked on a strategy of retaining existing partners and hiring new lateral partners by agreeing to fixed compensation agreements. Many of the agreements did not have performance clauses or requirements. Approximately 130 partners had some form of guarantee for 2011 and/or 2012, and the number of guarantees actually *accelerated* as the Firm's financial performance declined. The guarantees were atypical for the industry and reckless due to: (i) their sheer number (approximately 30% of partners had guarantees); (ii) the magnitude of the guarantees (a majority greater than $2 million per year); (iii) their duration (many for multiple years); and (iv) that each was without regard to future individual performance. Entering into these guarantees was a breach of the Defendants' fiduciary duties to manage the Firm with due care.

11. The damage to the Firm caused by these undisclosed guarantees ultimately proved fatal. Between 2009 and 2011, the Firm consistently paid certain partners in excess of available income. The Defendants knew or should have known that the Firm was insolvent, and yet continued to make unwarranted payments. During 2009 and 2010, the Defendants caused the Firm to distribute over $60 million in excess of net profits, depleted the Firm's capital to an amount almost equal to 50% of the minimum capital balance, and increased the Firm's debt in order to fund unwarranted distributions. In 2011 and 2012 alone, over $188 million was paid to 119 active partners with guaranteed contracts, while the remaining 214 active partners received less than $153 million. By the end of 2011, the Firm had only $34 million in cash on hand, reduced from $158 million at the start of 2008. At the same time, the Defendants were incurring even more debt on behalf of the Firm by drawing on secured bank and bond debt to finance operations.

12. After the partners finally learned the true state of the Firm's financial affairs at a January 2012 partnership meeting, they began to rapidly leave the Firm. During January and February of 2012, 20 partners transferred their practices from the Firm; and in March, 24 more departed. With further details emerging in the first quarter of 2012, including the extent to which declining profits and debt were being used to pay only a select few partners, an additional 48 partners left in April. Between May 1 and May 27, 2012, another 243 partners left.

13. On May 28, 2012, the Debtor filed a voluntary petition in this Court for relief under chapter 11 of the Bankruptcy Code.

14. On May 31, 2012, the Office of the United States Trustee appointed the Committee.

15. The Committee was duly appointed and organized under Bankruptcy Code Section 1102. The Committee represents the interest of all unsecured creditors of the Debtor. The Committee is expressly authorized by statute to investigate the assets and liabilities of the Debtor, and is empowered to perform such other services as are in the interests of unsecured creditors generally. See 11 U.S.C. § 1103(c).

16. The Debtor consents to the relief requested in the Motion. Not granting the Committee standing to prosecute the claims against the Defendants could impair the estate's ability to maximize its recovery against $50 million of aggregate insurance coverage under the Firm's Law Firm Management Liability and Company Reimbursement Insurance Policy (the "Primary Policy") and two related excess policies (collectively, the "Policies"), as a complaint brought directly

by the Debtor may be subject to the so-called "insured versus insured" exclusions set forth in the Policies. The "insured versus insured" exclusion appears in the Primary Policy as Article III.G. The excess policies are so-called "following form policies," meaning that coverage under those policies is based on the terms of the Primary Policy. A copy of the Primary Policy is attached hereto as Exhibit B. The Committee would not be subject to such a defense to coverage.

Relief Requested

17. With the consent of the Debtor, the Committee hereby respectfully requests that the Court grant leave, standing, and authority to the Committee to prosecute, and if appropriate settle claims against the Defendants.

Argument

18. The Second Circuit has recognized a qualified right for creditors' committees to initiate adversary proceedings in the name of the debtor in possession with the approval of the bankruptcy court. . . .

19. The Second Circuit has adopted a three-part test for determining when a creditors' committee may acquire standing to pursue the debtor's claims: "if (1) the committee has the consent of the debtor in possession or trustee, and (2) the court finds that suit by the committee is (a) in the best interest of the bankruptcy estate, and (b) is necessary and beneficial to the fair and efficient resolution of the bankruptcy proceedings." Commodore, 262 F.3d at 100.

20. As a threshold requirement, the Committee must show that its claims are "colorable." In re Adelphia Commc'ns Corp., 330 B.R. 364, 376 (S.D.N.Y. 2005) (noting that while Commodore does not explicitly include a requirement that claims be colorable, the "expression has been repeatedly used in articulating the appropriate standard"). If such colorable claims are "likely to benefit the reorganization estate," the Committee can obtain standing to prosecute them. See Official Comm. of Unsecured Creditors of Am.'s Hobby Ctr., Inc. (In re Am.'s Hobby Ctr., Inc.), 223 B.R. 275, 282 (Bankr. S.D.N.Y. 1998).

21. The required showing that any claims be "colorable" is a "relatively easy one to make." Adelphia, 330 B.R. at 376. This inquiry is "much the same as that undertaken when a defendant moves to dismiss a complaint for failure to state a claim." In re Am.'s Hobby Ctr., Inc., 223 B.R. at 282. It involves the "weighing of the probability of success and financial recovery, whether it is preferable to appoint a trustee to bring suit instead of the creditors' committee, and the 'terms relative to attorneys' fees on which suit might be brought.' " *Id.* (quoting In re STN Enters., 779 F.2d at 905).

22. The Committee should be granted standing to pursue the claims against the Defendants because: (i) it has the consent of the Debtor; (ii) it is in the best interest of the estate; and (iii) it is necessary and beneficial to the fair and efficient resolution of the chapter 11 case.

I. The Estate Has Colorable Claims Against the Defendants.

23. The Defendants' reckless mismanagement of the Firm and breaches of fiduciary duties directly led to the Firm's failure, causing massive loss of enterprise value to the Firm and damages to the Firm's creditors, including approximately $262 million in secured claims and upwards of $500 million in general unsecured claims.

24. The Defendants breached their fiduciary duties of care, loyalty, and candor by mismanaging the Firm through the practice of distributing vast amounts of money to certain partners without regard to ownership share. The practice of making such distributions was reckless and was only sustainable through the depletion of the Firm's capital and the assumption of unsustainable debt.

25. The Defendants also breached their fiduciary duties of care, loyalty and candor by recklessly doling out individual partner contracts that guaranteed compensation without regard to future partner performance. Once these guarantees came to light, along with the precarious financial situation of the Firm, they caused a mass exodus of partners, causing the implosion of the Firm and its resultant bankruptcy.

26. Also, in derogation of their fiduciary duties, the Defendants misrepresented and concealed the Firm's financial condition and may have operated a Ponzi scheme to lure lateral partners' capital.

27. As the Firm was insolvent in 2011 (and may have been insolvent even earlier), the Defendants caused the distribution of at least $180 million to certain partners during a time when the Firm should have been holding such funds in trust for creditors.

II. The Committee Satisfies the Commodore Test.

A. The Committee Has the Consent of the Debtor.

28. The first prong of the Commodore test requires the Committee to show that it has the consent of the Debtor to bring suit on its behalf. See Commodore, 262 F.3d at 100. The Debtor's consent to the Committee is manifest in its assent to this Motion. Thus, this requirement of Commodore is satisfied.

B. Suit by the Committee Is in the Best Interest of the Estate.

29. The Committee has satisfied the second prong of Commodore because prosecution of the claims by the Committee would be in the best interest of the estate. Bankruptcy courts in this Circuit have noted that suit is in the best interest of the estate when, if successful, it would result in a money judgment for the estate. . . .

30. The claims for breach of fiduciary duties would, if successful, result in a dollar judgment in the hundreds of millions against the Defendants (and may include the claw-back of the Defendants' ill-gotten compensation). These claims are covered under the Policies, which collectively provide $50 million in indemnity limits. It is undeniable that recovery under the Policies would maximize the value of the estate, and therefore is in the best interest of the estate.

31. The Committee does not expect that the costs to be incurred in prosecuting these claims will be significant in relation to the potential recovery. See In re Adelphia Commc'ns Corp., 330 B.R. at 386 (noting that litigation costs must be considered, but a court need only have comfort that the prosecution of claims represents a sensible expenditure of the estate's resources). Moreover, the Secured Lenders support the Committee's prosecution of the claims and the costs of such prosecution are included in the wind down budget through confirmation of a chapter 11 plan, being finalized between the Committee, the Secured Lenders and the Debtor. Access to recovery under the Policies is in the best interests of and beneficial to the estate because it maximizes estate value available to creditors and provides access to funds that may otherwise be wasted.

32. Additionally, prosecution of the claims by the Committee is in the best interest of the estate to avoid the Policies' "insured versus insured" exclusion. In the context of a Rule 9019 settlement motion, one court has recognized that granting a creditors' committee standing to bring derivative actions on behalf of the debtor is both necessary and beneficial to the fair and efficient resolution of the bankruptcy estate, precisely because of the potential issues surrounding the "insured versus insured" exclusion. See Hydrogen, 2009 WL at *2 (suit was "necessary" where debtor was "conflicted" from bringing suit itself and "beneficial" where "potentially valuable causes of action would be wasted," in light of "potential constraints on the suit pertaining to a director and officer insurance policy").

C. Suit by the Committee Is Necessary and Beneficial to the Fair and Efficient Resolution of the Bankruptcy Proceeding.

33. To establish that a suit is likely to benefit a bankruptcy estate, bankruptcy courts engage in a limited merits assessment to ensure "that there is a sufficient likelihood of success to justify the anticipated delay and expense to the bankruptcy estate that initiation and continuation of litigation will likely produce." In re Adelphia Commc'ns Corp., 330 B.R. at 374 (quoting In re STN Enters., 779 F.2d at 905). In other words, there must a "fair chance that the benefits to be obtained from the litigation will outweigh its costs." In re Am.'s Hobby Ctr., Inc., 223 B.R. at 284.

34. The prosecution of the claims against the Defendants is "necessary and beneficial" to the fair and efficient resolution of the chapter 11 case because the Debtor's estate will not be able to recover from the Defendants unless the claims are prosecuted, and recovery from the Defendants or under the Policies will help ensure fair distribution of the Debtor's assets among all of its creditors. See Glinka v. Murad (In re Housecraft Indus. USA, Inc.), 310 F.3d 64, 71 (2d Cir. 2002).

35. As with most Director and Officer liability policies, the Policies have "insured versus insured" exclusions that preclude coverage under the Policies when suit is brought by one insured against another. Certain courts have dismissed derivative claims brought by the Debtor-in-Possession by applying an "insured versus insured" exclusion. See Biltmore Assocs., LLC v. Twin City Fire Ins. Co., 572 F.3d 663, 671 (9th Cir. 2009) (dismissing complaint brought on behalf of Debtor-in-Possession against insurance company to recover proceeds under D&O policy because Debtor-in-Possession was considered to be same entity as Debtor, and therefore an "insured" under the policy). Other courts have held that the debtor-in-possession is a separate and distinct entity for purposes of application of the exclusion. See Fed. Ins. Co. v. Cont'l Cas. Co., No. 2:05-cv-305, 2006 WL 3386625, at *12–13 (Bankr. W.D. Pa. Nov. 12, 2006) (noting that the debtor-in-possession and debtor are "clearly not the same entity" and therefore the "insured versus insured" exception does not apply). Upon information and belief, New York courts have not ruled on this issue. Accordingly, if the Debtor were to bring the derivative claims directly, there is the possibility that the "insured versus insured" exclusion would apply to the coverage under the Policies.

36. Conferring standing on the Committee avoids this problem. . . .

Reservation of Rights

37. The Committee reserves its rights to seek authority to commence and prosecute other claims and causes of action against the Debtor's former management and other parties, on behalf of the Debtor's estate.

Notice

38. This Motion has been served in accordance with the *Administrative Order Establishing Case Management Procedures*, dated May 30, 2012 [Docket 30]. The Committee submits that no other notice need be provided.

Conclusion

WHEREFORE, the Committee respectfully requests that the Court enter an order substantially in the form annexed hereto as Exhibit C granting the Committee: (i) leave, standing and authority to prosecute certain claims against the Defendants on behalf of the Debtor's estate and if appropriate, propose and effectuate settlements in respect of the claims, subject to further order of this Court; and (ii) such other and further relief as the Court deems appropriate.

Dated: November 12, 2012
New York, New York

Respectfully submitted,

BROWN RUDNICK LLP

By: */s/ Edward S. Weisfelner*

Edward S. Weisfelner
Howard S. Steel
BROWN RUDNICK LLP 7
Times Square
New York, New York 10036
Telephone: (212) 209-4800
Facsimile: (212) 209-4801

Counsel for the Official Committee of Unsecured Creditors

NOTES

1. As you think about the Dewey & LeBeouf example, note that there were two paths* that ran concurrently, at least for a while: Dewey's bankruptcy case (more on that with the next part of this chapter) and the criminal indictments for some of the people in the firm. Let's talk about the criminal indictments first. The Manhattan District Attorney indicted four people: the former firm chairman, Steven Davis; the

* Well, more than two, really, but we're going to simplify things.

firm's executive director, Stephen DiCarmine; the firm's chief financial officer, Joel Sanders; and the firm's client relations manager, Zachary Warren. Davis and Warren entered into deferred prosecution agreements, with Warren eventually cleared of charges* and Davis agreeing not to practice law for five years.** The first trial for Joel Sanders ended in a hung jury, but his second trial ended in a conviction for securities fraud and conspiracy; Stephen DiCarmine's retrial, on the other hand, ended in an acquittal.*** In October 2017, Sanders was sentenced to $1 million fine and 750 hours of community service.****

2. As for the bankruptcy case, you've just read one motion in the case, and you're about to read a limited objection to that motion. There are some wonderful news articles about Dewey's downfall, including one by Victor Li, *How Dewey management's rosy picture masked an ugly truth,****** and one by James B. Stewart, *The Collapse: How a top legal firm destroyed itself,******* but we didn't get reprint permission to excerpt them.

---

* Casey Sullivan, *Junior Employee of Dewey & LeBeouf Cleared of Charges*, BLOOMBERG LAW BIG LAW BUSINESS, available at https://biglawbusiness.com/junior-employee-of-dewey-leboeuf-cleared-of-charges/.

** Matthew Goldstein, *Deal Means No Fraud Retrial for Ex-Chairman of Dewey & LeBeouf*, N.Y. TIMES (Jan. 8, 2016), available at https://www.nytimes.com/2016/01/09/business/dealbook/deal-means-no-fraud-retrial-for-ex-chairman-of-dewey-leboeuf.html.

*** Brendan Peirson, *Split verdict for Dewey & LeBeouf executives in second trial*, REUTERS, May 8, 2017, available at https://www.reuters.com/article/usa-crime-dewey/split-verdict-for-dewey-leboeuf-executives-in-second-trial-idUSL1N1IB01A.

**** Christine Simmons, N.Y. L.J. (Oct. 11, 2017), available at https://www.law.com/newyorklaw journal/sites/newyorklawjournal/2017/10/10/ex-dewey-leboeuf-cfo-avoids-jail-time/.

***** ABA J., Feb. 2015, available at http://www.abajournal.com/magazine/article/how_dewey_managements_rosy_picture_masked_an_ugly_truth.

****** NEW YORKER, October 14, 2013, available at https://www.newyorker.com/magazine/2013/10/14/the-collapse-2.

CHAPTER 16

Limited Objection to Motion, *In re* Dewey and LeBoeuf*

Paul M. Basta
KIRKLAND & ELLIS LLP
601 Lexington Avenue
New York, New York 10022
Telephone: (212) 446-4800
Facsimile: (212) 446-4900

- and -

Richard C. Godfrey, P.C.
Kevin T. Van Wart, P.C.
KIRKLAND & ELLIS LLP
300 North LaSalle
Chicago, Illinois 60654
Telephone: (312) 862-2000
Facsimile: (312) 862-2200

Counsel to Steven H. Davis

UNITED STATES BANKRUPTCY COURT
SOUTHERN DISTRICT OF NEW YORK

	)	
In re:	)	Chapter 11
	)	
DEWEY & LEBOEUF LLP,	)	Case No. 12-12321 (MG)
	)	
Debtor.	)	
	)	**Re: Docket No. 628**

---

* Limited Objection of Steven H. Davis to Motion of the Official Committee of Unsecured Creditors For Entry of An Order Pursuant to §§ 1103(C) and 1109(B), Granting Leave, Standing and Authority to Prosecute and, If Appropriate, Settle Certain Claims on Behalf of the Debtor's Estate, *In re* Dewey & LeBeouf LLP, United States Bankruptcy Court for the Southern District of New York, Case No. 12-12321 (MG), Docket No. 654 (Nov. 21, 2012).

LIMITED OBJECTION OF STEVEN H. DAVIS TO MOTION OF THE OFFICIAL COMMITTEE OF UNSECURED CREDITORS FOR ENTRY OF AN ORDER PURSUANT TO SECTION 1103(C) AND 1109(B), GRANTING LEAVE, STANDING AND AUTHORITY TO PROSECUTE AND, IF APPROPRIATE, SETTLE CERTAIN CLAIMS ON BEHALF OF THE DEBTOR'S ESTATE

Steven H. Davis ("Mr. Davis"), by and through his undersigned counsel, hereby files this limited objection ("Limited Objection") to the *Motion of The Official Committee of Unsecured Creditors For Entry of An Order Pursuant To Section 1103(C) And 1109(B), Granting Leave, Standing And Authority To Prosecute And, If Appropriate, Settle Certain Claims On Behalf of The Debtor's Estate* (the "Motion"), filed on November 12, 2012 [Docket No. 628].[1]

Limited Objection

1. Mr. Davis was formerly the Chairman of Dewey & LeBoeuf LLP and a Member of its Executive Committee. While he does not oppose the request of the Official Committee of Unsecured Creditors' (the "Committee") for standing to bring a suit against him relating to his alleged role in the Firm's failure, Mr. Davis denies that he engaged in any wrongdoing and disputes the allegations described in the Committee's Motion. As the Motion makes clear, the Committee has targeted Mr. Davis and made him its scapegoat for a very practical reason: he has up to $50 million in coverage under various management liability insurance policies. Motion at ¶30 ("These claims are covered under the Policies, which collectively provide $50 million in indemnity limits.").

2. Mr. Davis recognizes that he will have the opportunity to mount a full and vigorous defense against any complaint that the Committee actually files. The reason for this limited objection is that instead of focusing on the narrow procedural issue underlying its request, the Committee has used the Motion as a platform for launching needless and inappropriate personal attacks on Mr. Davis[2] and promoting fanciful theories of wrongdoing, some of which contradict the sworn testimony this Court heard in September relating to the motion seeking approval of the Partner Contribution Plan (the "PCP Motion"). By not opposing standing, Mr. Davis is not agreeing to any of the false and unsubstantiated allegations contained in the Committee's Motion, and he expressly reserves all of his rights in any action that the Committee eventually brings.

3. For good reason, the Committee should have shown more restraint and discipline in describing its potential suit. In connection with the approval of the

---

1 Capitalized terms not defined herein have the meanings ascribed to them in the Motion.

2 *E.g.*, Motion at ¶ 6 ("rampant self-dealing"), ¶ 7 ("motivated by greed"), ¶ 8 ("wanton control"), ¶ 26 ("Ponzi scheme"), ¶ 30 ("ill-gotten compensation").

PCP Motion, several witnesses admitted that insufficient time, funding, and resources had prevented a full investigation of the facts underlying a potential suit and the assignment of responsibility. *E.g., Declaration of David Pauker in Support of the Debtor's Motion for an Order, Pursuant to Bankruptcy Rule 9019 and 11 U.S.C. §§ 105 and 362, Approving Partner Contribution Settlement Agreements and Mutual Releases for Participating Partners* [Docket No. 401] ("Pauker Decl.") ¶ 34 (". . . there was neither time nor financial resources available to fully investigate the potential liability of individual members of the Executive Committee"); 9/21/12 Hr'g Tr. at 61:17–21 (Pauker) ("We determined that we did not have the time . . . to undertake a yearlong review of these matters in order to get to individual partners' numbers and look at this in terms of what each partner's issues might be."). The result, Mr. Mitchell explained, was "a rough justice plan." 9/21/12 Hr'g Tr. at 34:17. The Committee has pointed to no additional investigation that it or the Debtor has conducted since that time that would in any way justify the heated rhetoric of the Motion.

4. Once the Committee files its complaint against Mr. Davis, the full panoply of discovery tools will become available and investigatory corners will not similarly be cut. The Committee should understand that the more sweeping its allegations against Mr. Davis and the more pointed its personal attacks, the greater the resources Mr. Davis will have to expend defending himself. The result could be litigation that is far more costly and protracted than the Committee anticipates and proceedings that will inevitably entangle many of the former Dewey partners who participated in the management of the Firm, had knowledge of and share responsibility for the actions the Committee seeks to attribute to Mr. Davis, and demanded and received much of the compensation the Committee contends should not have been paid.

5. The evidence that Mr. Davis will eventually have the opportunity to present will show that he at all times acted in what he reasonably believed was the best interest of the Firm and its partners. In the interim, Mr. Davis comments briefly on some of the statements and allegations in the Committee's Motion.

6. Allegations Relating To Mr. Davis' Compensation. The Committee's Motion contains misleading information about Mr. Davis' compensation. For no apparent reason other than rhetorical effect, the Motion asserts that Mr. Davis (and his co-defendants) engaged in "self- serving behavior" that was "motivated by greed." Motion at ¶ 7. The only support the Motion provides for this charge is its allegation that defendants "paid themselves over $7 million on an aggregate basis within one year of the Petition Date." *Id.* Elsewhere, the Motion asserts that

"From 2007–2010, Davis earned close to $10.8 million from the Firm." *Id.* at ¶ 4. Here are the facts.

(a) Despite his position as Firm Chairman, Mr. Davis never placed himself at the front of the line when it came to compensation. To the contrary, in the years leading up to the bankruptcy, he repeatedly deferred his own compensation to future years so that others could be paid more. For example, Mr. Davis deferred all but $275,000 of his 2010 compensation—just eleven months of his annual draw. His other compensation that year was all compensation he was owed from prior years. During 2011 and 2012, Mr. Davis received just $25,000 of his deferred 2010 compensation, meaning he was compensated only $300,000 for 2010.

(b) The picture is the same if one looks at Mr. Davis' compensation in the aggregate. In the one-year period before the Petition Date, Mr. Davis received $1,290,000, but that included out-of-pocket reimbursements of $202,783.70. His compensation was a small fraction—about one half of one percent—of the roughly $234 million in total compensation that the Firm paid its partners during that same period and far below the compensation paid that year to many other Dewey partners, some of whom received as much as $6.5 million. In fact, during this one-year period, fifty-one partners received a higher distribution than Mr. Davis.

(c) And for all of 2011 and 2012—the period during which the Committee alleges the Firm was insolvent—Mr. Davis received a total of $1,670,000, far below his annual compensation target of $5 million. This includes $1,460,000 in 2011 (of which $245,000 was attributable to amounts owed from prior years) and $210,000 in 2012.

(d) There is nothing remarkable about the level of Mr. Davis' compensation. The allegation that he was "motivated by greed" is baseless. Mr. Davis was not among the Dewey partners threatening to leave the Firm if they did not receive greater compensation.

7. The "Ponzi Scheme" Allegation. As another way to spice up their Motion, the Committee asserts that Mr. Davis and his co-defendants "may have operated a Ponzi scheme to lure lateral partners' capital." Motion at ¶ 26 (emphasis added). The Committee cites no facts to substantiate this allegation, which rests on nothing more than the sensationalism of the phrase "Ponzi scheme." The Committee does not identify the lateral partners it contends should

not have been hired or who were hired only for their capital contributions, and it provides no information showing that the amount of capital contributed by lateral partners exceeded their compensation. This omission is important because the claim defies logic.

(a) Lateral partners were compensated, *i.e.*, Dewey expended money on laterals who paid a capital contribution, which was set at 36 percent of a partner's annual compensation target. There is no credible argument that lateral partners—who immediately began receiving draws and had to be compensated—were hired to obtain capital contributions that could then be used to pay existing partners, as would be required to prove a Ponzi scheme.[3] Indeed, any capital contributions the Firm would have received from lateral partners would necessarily have been a drop in the bucket compared to the revenue the Firm generated in fees ($759.3 million in 2010, for example) and the compensation the Firm paid its partners ($272.5 million in 2010).

(b) On this record, a reasonable person could conclude that the Committee's real purpose in suggesting that Mr. Davis "may" have operated a Ponzi scheme is demagoguery.

8. The "Reckless Management" and Insolvency Allegations. The Committee accuses Mr. Davis (and his co-defendants) of "reckless management of the Firm's financial affairs" and asserts that Dewey "was insolvent in 2011(and may have been insolvent even earlier)." Motion at ¶¶ 8, 27. These allegations are inconsistent with testimony presented in proceedings relating to the approval of the PCP Motion.

(a) The Dewey & LeBoeuf firm was formed shortly before a global recession that triggered one of the worst economic downturns in the country's history and decimated the demand for legal services. As a newly formed firm with partners who were still getting to know and have confidence in each other and trust in the Firm's future, Dewey was much more vulnerable compared to more established law firms. Despite the enormous challenges posed by these unforeseen conditions, the Firm held together, responsibly managed its financial affairs, and, as a result, performed reasonably well. From 2008 through 2011, the Firm, under Mr. Davis' leadership, generated more than $3 billion in revenue, paid its debts, complied with its loan agreements, and distributed more than $1 billion to its partners.

---

3 SEC, *Ponzi Schemes—Frequently Asked Questions*, http://www.sec.gov/answers/ponzi.htm.

(b) In September, Mr. Pauker, Executive Managing Director of Goldin Associates, LLC and a financial advisor to the Debtor, testified that Dewey failed not because of "reckless management," but because some key partners, after initially agreeing to reduce their compensation, unexpectedly decided to leave the Firm toward the end of the first quarter in 2012. 9/21/12 Hr'g Tr. at 84:10–12 ("[T]he proximate reason that this firm failed is that the partners, the assets Your Honor was referring to, walked out the door."). According to Mr. Pauker:

> And the members of the committee—the key committee—had all agreed that they were going to take these cuts. And there appeared to be, I understand in hindsight, momentum towards this, which would have saved the firm. But what happened unexpectedly is a handful of the partners who had committed to do this, left the firm. And when the partners who people understood were sticking by the firm, because they were the business generators, even though they were going to take less, began to leave the firm, you had a snowball.
>
> 9/21/12 Hr'g Tr. at 98:13–19.

(c) Mr. Pauker also addressed the issue of insolvency. He testified that the Firm was "balance sheet solvent" under the enterprise value method and "would likely be solvent" on an asset-by-asset basis as of December 31, 2011. 9/21/12 Hr'g Tr. at 87:9. And far from describing a Firm that was on the ropes and "grossly mismanaged," he noted that Dewey had ended 2011 on a good note, was continuing to generate substantial revenue and per partner profits, and had a business plan for 2012 (which he had helped prepare in January 2012) that he concluded was "conservative" and "reasonable." *Id.* at 84–86. As he explained:

> The business plan was conservative. It had a twelve-month projection. The first four months of it were basically calculated by rolling forward BVA—billable value added. So they had a book of WIP and AR that was in place. They rolled that forward into collections based on their average collection rate historically. And then for the next eight months, they used 2011 monthly projections for 2012. That was very conservative because the four months of collections of BVA that they were using, were significantly up ten to fifteen percent from the prior month.
>
> *Id.* at 87:3–12.

(d) Likewise, Mr. Mitchell, the Debtor's Chief Restructuring Officer, testified that experienced third-party professionals had examined Dewey's finances through 2010 and raised no concerns about the Firm's management or its financial health:

> We looked at and noted the firm's clean audit opinion at the end of 2010. We noted that the firm had been able to refinance a significant portion of its debt in 2010. And so from those two things, we concluded that third-party professionals had taken a good look at the finances of the firm and at least they had presumably concluded that they were confident in issuing a clean audit opinion, on the one hand, and confident in having their clients refinance the firm, on the other.
>
> 9/21/12 Hr'g Tr. at 28:18–29:1.

(e) While it is easy, in hindsight, to second-guess some of the management decisions the Firm made, there is no basis for the vitriol and personal attacks that the Committee has used as its instrument for calling those decisions into question.

9. The Compensation Guarantee Allegations. The Committee's Motion includes numerous assertions relating to "fixed compensation agreements" that purportedly "guaranteed" the compensation of approximately 130 partners. Motion at ¶¶ 10–11, 25. The Committee calls these agreements "reckless" and attacks them on multiple grounds, including their number, the amounts guaranteed, their duration, and the lack of performance benchmarks. *Id.* The Committee makes these sweeping allegations without ever discussing the language of any of these agreements or acknowledging that many of them differed in material ways. While Mr. Davis realizes that these agreements will receive substantial attention in any suit that the Committee files, the Committee's assertions are so broad brush as to be misleading in several important respects.

(a) First, that the Firm made these agreements was not secret. The idea that it was is nonsensical, particularly considering, as the Motion asserts, that almost 30 percent of the partners had them. In addition, numerous partners participated in the negotiation of these agreements or otherwise had knowledge of them, including office heads and practice leaders who were involved in recruiting lateral talent, as well as members of the Compensation Committee and the Executive Committee.[4]

[4] According to Mr. Pauker, no formal investigation was undertaken to assess the role of the Executive Committee or to determine the roles and knowledge of particular members: "During the several months

(b) Second, while the Committee contends that the "number of guarantees actually accelerated as the Firm's financial performance declined," Motion at ¶ 10, Mr. Pauker's testimony on September 21 was just the opposite. He explained that Dewey was taking reasonable steps to address partner compensation issues, including securing agreements from partners to restructure and reduce their compensation. 9/21/12 Hr'g Tr. at 97–98. In his words: "I think it's worth noting that by the time we were looking at solvency issues in 2011/2012, many of those guarantees either were rolling off or had rolled off. The stage of it—you know, [the firm was] in the down side of the guarantee comp cycle, if you will." 9/21/12 Hr'g Tr. at 101:4–8.

(c) Third, these agreements were not all the same. Contrary to what the Committee implies, many only set a partner's "Participation Target," but contained provisions explicitly tying the compensation to Firm performance or individual performance.[5] The Committee has not identified the agreements that it contends are true "guarantees."

(d) Fourth, regardless of how they are characterized, these so-called guarantees are not the reason Dewey collapsed. Notwithstanding these agreements, relatively few of the partners who had them were paid the full amount of their specified Participation Targets. Thus, while the Committee contends that Dewey paid its partners too much, many of the partners who controlled substantial books of business believed just the opposite—that they were paid too little. And some of them, despite their own fiduciary duties to the Firm, believing they deserved more and not willing to accept what Dewey could afford to pay them, decided to leave. While "greed" is a theme of the Committee's Motion, the litigation that eventually ensues will address the question of whose greed.

10. Although the Committee appears determined to personalize its disputes and pursue allegations that effectively ensure costly and protracted litigation, Mr.

---

available to fully develop the PCP, there was neither time nor financial resources available to fully investigate the potential liability of individual members of the Executive Committee." Pauker Decl. ¶ 34.

[5] For example, one such agreement (actual compensation omitted) states, "Your Participation Target shall be guaranteed at the annual rate of no less than $___ for 2011 and 2012, assuming that you fulfill the normal expectations of a partner by devoting your full time and attention to the practice of law and partnership activities for the Firm. Your Participation Target is divided into two components: (i) a draw paid monthly at a rate of $300,000 annually; and (ii) an excess target over draw ("Distribution(s)") payable from time to time as warranted by the Firm's cash flow." (emphases added). Another such agreement states: "Your compensation shall be linked to the Firm's net income; that is, you shall share in the profits and the losses of the Firm commencing with your first full year as a partner in the Firm in accordance with Article 6 of the Agreement."

Davis is just as committed to taking reasonable and appropriate steps to defend himself. As the evidence will show, Mr. Davis was devoted to Dewey & LeBoeuf and wanted it to succeed, and at all times he acted in what he reasonably believed was the best interest of the Firm and its partners.

Reservation of Rights

11. Mr. Davis expressly reserves, and does not waive, any of his claims, rights, or defenses in connection with the Motion, applicable law, or otherwise, in this or any action the Committee brings.

New York, New York
Dated: November 21, 2012

/s/ Kevin T. Van Wart, P.C.
Paul M. Basta
KIRKLAND & ELLIS LLP
601 Lexington Avenue
New York, New York 10022
Telephone: (212) 446-4800
Facsimile: (212) 446-4900

- and -

Richard C. Godfrey, P.C. Kevin T. Van Wart, P.C. KIRKLAND & ELLIS LLP 300 North LaSalle
Chicago, Illinois 60654
Telephone: (312) 862-2000
Facsimile: (312) 862-2200

Counsel to Steven H. Davis

NOTES

1. One of the reasons that we included this motion is that it is well-written. Non-lawyers (and some law students*) often have the notion that legal writing has to be obtuse and stuffy. It doesn't. The best writing that we've seen involves simple, declarative sentences and tells a story that captivates the reader. Whether or not you think that Steven Davis behaved well or badly at Dewey, you should be impressed by the caliber of his lawyers' rhetoric.**

2. Imagine that you worked at Dewey & LeBeouf, either as an associate or as a member of the professional staff, like a legal assistant or a legal secretary. What warning signs do you think you might have seen?

---

* And, for that matter, some law professors, too.

** The first motion (by the Creditors' Committee) is also good. See? Legal writing doesn't have to be boring.

3. Now that you have a sense of what may have caused Dewey & LeBeouf to collapse, think about what questions you might ask before your company enters into a merger. What information would you like to know? What information would you ask the company's management to give you? What would you do if management refused to give you that information? Would your answer change if you'd just started working at the firm? What about if you were close to retirement age? Would the strength of the job market in your field factor in to how hard you might press management for information? And, if you're one of the company's officers, how much information are you going to give to the non-partner employees of the firm (its associates, paralegals, and support staff)? How much information would you give to the senior employees, and how would you protect confidential information?

4. Our next article, by Amee McKim, ties into the two *Dewey* pleadings because part of the problem at Dewey had to do with merging two cultures: Dewey Ballantine and LeBeouf, Lamb, Greene & MacRae. Her article will help you think about lateral employees: those who come into your organization not as entry-level workers but with some experience. We want you to think about how to help lateral employees integrate into your culture in a healthy way, and her advice, though focused on lateral law firm partners, has broader implications that just law firm hiring.

CHAPTER 17

A Discussion of the Risks of Lateral Partner Hiring

Amee R. McKim

Lateral partner hiring is risky. Despite the hazards that firms face when adding partners with portable business, there is no end in sight to the rapid movement of lawyers. Firms approach and manage the risks associated with lateral partner hiring differently; some firms are far less risk-averse, sometimes to their peril, and other firms are highly conservative in their approach to lateral partner hiring. Firms with more risk tolerance likely have a faster and more streamlined selection process for new partners. Firms that approach lateral hiring more conservatively will spend more time on research and due diligence, thus lengthening the time to get a new lateral partner in place. Although it might be easier and faster to be picked up by a firm with more tolerance for risk, and at a higher price point, laterals with solid options would be well advised to proceed with caution, as well, as a "bad" move can be career limiting.

What Do Firms Want?

Presumably, firms are in the lateral partner hiring game to add to the firm's bottom line—they are seeking accretive hires that will be "successful" on the firm's platform (that is, the firm's geographic footprint, breadth and depth of practices, compensation structure, credit allocation, billing rate structure, etc.) at a minimum, and optimistic that the new hire will produce a synergistic effect on the firm's bottom line. In addition to the financial rewards, most firms are also seeking new partners who are good cultural matches for their firm—partners who can be integrated with ease and who contribute to (or who at least don't detract from) the culture of the firm.

Unfortunately, given the small number of lateral partners who live up to their recruitment business projections, success too often becomes defined as "break even" or "not a loss." There may be practical reasons that firms participate in such a risk-filled game and are satisfied merely by breaking even. Those possibilities include reputation, branding, internal politics, market expansion, practice expansion, growth in numbers, firm morale, and keeping up with other Am Law 100 firms. But, by accurately assessing the risks, and managing an abundance of risk by either declining to proceed with a specific candidate or through conservative compensation arrangements that share the risk with the transitioning lawyer, firms can point the needle towards a better measure of success.

Why Do Lawyers Move?

For some partners, the transition is involuntary. They have been asked (relatively nicely) to move on from their current firm, usually because they are not adding to the bottom line but sometimes because the firm has made a decision to jettison a practice that it no longer finds lucrative (i.e., labor and employment, trusts and estates, insurance work). There may be other reasons as well, such as business or actual conflicts or policy decisions. Involuntarily departing lawyers are higher risk as laterals. Identifying candidates who have been asked to leave is not easy, but careful and thorough due diligence can help. Such diligence practices include putting into place measures to assess and weigh the risk factors discussed below. And, although one firm's "trash" may be another firm's "treasure," that is not typical when it comes to lateral partners.

For other lawyers, the move is voluntary, and they are seeking greener pastures (for valid or not-so-valid reasons). Factors motivating lawyers to change firms can be well thought-out decisions or a spur-of-the-moment consideration based on a well-timed call from a recruiter—and everything in between. Reasons for considering a move run the gamut from the need for a broader platform to expand client work and client base to a better compensation package or because of disputes with firm leadership.

Understanding what is motivating a partner to move is a key initial step in risk assessment. Does the reason make sense, and is it consistent with the other aspects of the partner's practice and history? If the partner is seeking relief from high rates at a "lockstep bill rate firm,"[1] can the new firm offer alternative rate structures that work for the candidate and the firm at the compensation level that the candidate is seeking? If the partner is leaving due to a lack of collaboration and cross-selling opportunities, does the problem really lie with the current firm's culture and structure, or it the candidate who is unwilling to collaborate and cross-

[1] A lockstep bill rate is set for each lawyer solely based on his/her seniority/years out of law school (and it is increased by a set amount each year). Lockstep bill rates do not take into account individual factors, such as the lawyer's practice area, the profitability of the lawyer's work, and the tolerance of specific clients or the market sector for such rates.

sell and will that change in a new firm? If the candidate feels underpaid and is seeking higher compensation, is it because the current firm really undervalues the partner's contributions, or because the firm doesn't make its budget regularly, or because the candidate is not really worth additional compensation? Will she or he quickly become dissatisfied, even at a higher compensation level? Too often, firms overlook the vital step of testing the explanations of the motivation behind making the move.

What Are Some Other Signs of Riskier Candidates?

Besides ascertaining the true motivating factors behind a possible move, a firm should examine a variety of other possible signs in order to identify potential risky recruits. Recruiting lateral partners with books of business to a firm is a hybrid process: not only is a firm hiring a new employee, but it is also purchasing a business. As such, the firm considering the potential lateral should use best practices from both of those processes to assess the potential risk and reward of lateral candidates.

One of the biggest internal risk factors is that individual partners who interview or sponsor candidates may approach lateral hiring more like dating: if there is chemistry, they want to move forward without a careful examination of the risk. Firms should have solid practices for identifying the risk factors that are present with a candidate and determine the firm's level of tolerance in advance in order to offset the very real human likelihood that the interviewing or sponsoring partners have fallen in "love" (or "lust") with a candidate who otherwise broadcasts "high risk" like a neon sign. Firms will have different tolerance levels for each of the following risk markers, but firms that are most likely to add accretive laterals to their firms are vigilant in their hiring practices. And although having one or two risk characteristics should not necessarily end a candidate's chances, having multiple risk characteristics makes the picture far more unattractive. As with all general rules of thumb, these risk characteristics all have exceptions that mitigate the risk. The best judges of risk are those firm leaders who have a solid track record of recruiting accretive partners.

Laterals Who Frequently Jump Ship. As with any candidate for any position, firms should be on the lookout for laterals who move frequently. Although there may be credible explanations for switching firms several times, candidates who don't have any staying power and who jump every 2–3 years are unlikely to change that pattern.

Boomerang Laterals. Continuing interest in a firm is often a "plus factor" for traditional employment scenarios, but with lateral partner candidates, just the opposite can be true. Candidates who are passed over for multiple risk characteristics seldom become more attractive over time and usually have even more moves on their resume the next time around. On the other hand, one obvious exception would be a partner whose portable business level was initially smaller than the firm's threshold and who managed to increase that book of business over time.

Financial Data Provided is Incomplete. Firms need solid financial data in order to assess the lateral's likely success on the firm's platform. Candidates who are unwilling to provide the same are higher-risk whether the data are incomplete because their projections are exaggerated, or they are not business-savvy enough to understand the metrics of their practice and why it's important, or (worst case scenario) they have something to hide. In any case, avoiding this particular risk characteristic means refusing to proceed with the lateral's candidacy until sufficient data is provided.

Lateral Partner Forms/Questionnaires Are Sloppy, Inconsistent, or Inaccurate. There really is no excuse for a lateral partner candidate not putting his or her best foot forward with the forms that he or she is asked to complete in order to be considered. Firms expect a law student to produce a resume without typos and errors when applying for jobs; they should expect the same from potential lateral partners. Not following directions, leaving out data, completing the forms in a sloppy manner, or providing information that is not internally consistent (and smart firms do ask for the same data several different ways in order to assess the consistency factor) point to a lawyer who is potentially a cultural misfit at best, or a risk management threat at worst.

First-Year Projections That Far Exceed Historical Performance. Lateral partners are asked to provide projections of some sort as part of the consideration process, usually for the first 1–2 years at the new firm. In theory, laterals move and firms take them on because they anticipate increased client work on the new platform. In reality, transition issues and ramp-up time can take a toll on client work for many transitioning laterals, so a consistent performance is often a true win. Absent some compelling information (such as a verified current conflict that won't exist at the new firm) a lateral candidate who anticipates doubling or tripling the work that he or she receives from each client sounds too good to be true, and probably is.

The Attorney Does Not Have Originating/Billing Attorney Responsibility for His or Her Clients. Effective lateral hiring is based on portable client business that approximates or exceeds the amount promised by the lateral. Ethics rules mandate that it is always up to the client as to who will perform the client's legal work, so whether the client will stay at the current firm or follow a partner to his or her new firm is the client's choice, not the partner's. Whether a client is truly portable or not is never possible to ascertain with 100% certainty until after the fact. There are, however, a number of signs to observe to better calculate the odds. It is true that non-partners do originate clients, but non-partners also (and more often) service the work of partners who have originated the business, so one tally mark in the "risk" column is whether the current candidate is a non-partner and cannot document that he or she is the billing or originating attorney of record at his or her current firm. Non-partners who are not promoted to partner at their current firm sometimes try to move to a new firm to attain partner status. Unfortunately, non-partners who want to become partners at the new firm tend to overestimate the probability that a client will move its work to follow the lawyer or underestimate the lengths to which the current firm will go to keep the business.

Other factors to consider in assessing the likely portability of the business include (1) the amount of work for a particular client that is being serviced by other partners in the firm and whether the new firm has sufficient breadth and depth (and relevant geographic presence) to service all of the work; (2) the duration of the client relationship (riskier candidates have clients that were all developed recently); (3) the strength of the client relationship; (4) whether the current firm of the lateral tends to have primarily institutional clients (who thus tend stay to with the institution), and (5) the consistency or growth of the candidate's work for each client over time. Finally, the risk is high if the candidate's entire portable book lies with one or two clients, even if the business is significant. The lack of client diversification can make a new lateral, literally an all-or-nothing proposition.

Lack of a Solid Business Plan. Lateral candidates who have not taken the time to develop a thorough business plan outlining their current relationships, the untapped potential for new business with existing clients and potential new clients, and their plans for integrating to a new platform are riskier candidates who likely will perform in a similar undeveloped and haphazard fashion upon joining a new firm. Although some laterals actually are so successful that they don't need a business plan, such lawyers are few and far between.

Lack of a Staffing Plan. Another risk characteristic is a lateral who purports to have a high level of portable business (more than he or she can service on his or her own) but fails to ask about a staffing plan at the new firm. Some laterals plan to have the non-partners who are currently performing work for their clients follow them to the new firm at the appropriate time, and that issue should be discussed in advance even though the non-partners cannot be recruited in advance. Those who don't have staffing support that they want to bring to the new firm and who demonstrate a lack of curiosity about the new firm's resources tend not to be busy partners with a lot of portable business. Candidates who press hard to ensure that the appropriate talent is in place to service their clients seamlessly throughout the transition to the new firm are less risky prospects.

Few Active Matters. Candidates who provide extensive client names and relationships but who don't have active matters in progress are also riskier candidates. Although practices do ebb and flow and some practice areas are more susceptible to volatility, it's rare that busy and successful partners have few active matters. On the contrary, however, there are plenty of candidates on the market precisely because they don't have active matters, and those present a risky proposition for a new firm. A transitioning partner with purported portable business who plans a vacation or time off between firms is equally suspect. Transitioning to a new firm is a time when effective partners want to be especially attentive to their clients' needs to ensure that the clients follow the partner and that the transition goes smoothly. Planning to take a vacation at that specific time is a good indication that the lateral does not understand the nuances of transitioning, that the business won't be following the partner, and that he or she is unconcerned about transition issues.

Character and Fitness Issues. Most firms ask partner candidates a variety of "character and fitness" type questions on the forms that the partners complete during the recruiting process. Candidates may be asked about prior malpractice claims, current or past civil or criminal proceedings against them, discrimination or harassment charges, judgments and liens, and any number of similar questions. Obviously, some categories of disclosures are more concerning than others, and

process, some partners will still become productive partners at the firm, but a strong integration program can provide critical and necessary support and early intervention, when needed, to those new partners who would otherwise struggle. Firms should take all necessary measures to protect the significant investments they make in new lateral partners.

Despite Best Efforts, Mistakes Will Happen

Notwithstanding careful management of the risk, both throughout the recruitment process and with the compensation structure afforded a new partner, partner recruiting is not an exact science. There will be partners who transition in but cannot develop or maintain a substantial amount of their anticipated business, either for unexpected reasons or because risk markers (identified or otherwise) on the portability of the business during the recruitment phase became a reality. And some partners who are known investments (with little or no portable business or who are coming from in-house or government positions) fail in their attempts to develop their books of business.

Unwinding such mistakes can be challenging and painful—and public. Partner moves are tracked closely in the news on a national basis and even more meticulously within the smaller market at issue. The firm then faces a dilemma of whether to cut its loss early, double down on its investment by providing more time and resources to the partner, or find some in-between approach. In terms of sorting through options, two factors are key: the compensation level of the partner and the egregiousness of the mistake. Internal political considerations and firm morale issues will no doubt also have a role in the consideration process at most firms.

There are a variety of ways that firms can and do choose to respond to such mistakes. In the interest of providing every opportunity for the partner to succeed, a firm may elect to reduce the partner's compensation in the short term while providing ongoing support to his or her efforts to build the client base. Giving the partner a timetable for delivery over the next six or twelve months or face a compensation reduction is another option. Of course, on the other end of the spectrum, cutting its losses immediately upon non-delivery of the expected portable clients is another, more dramatic response. A less dramatic version of asking the partner to leave involves the request that the partner provide a transition plan out of the firm. The firm could also attempt to facilitate a good landing for the partner in-house at a client, thus turning the partner into a valued firm alumnus or alumna who is in a position to send work to the firm. There are, of course, any number of creative ways that firms can elect to address a lack of performance, including that of existing, non-lateral partners. Newly added partners have a higher visibility internally and externally, however, and a quick exit of a newly joined partner does, rightly or wrongly, tend to garner more attention.

Unprofitable and unproductive partners are a drain on a firm's finances, morale, and bottom line, and most firms can no longer afford to keep such partners in place over the long term. Lateral partner recruiting is not meant to grow the pool of unprofitable partners. When that happens, a firm must also assess the risks of taking a shorter-term view on partner productivity and the possibility of creating a resulting revolving door.

Conclusion

Even with a careful, impartial assessment of the risk characteristics of a lateral partner candidate, lateral partner hiring remains a dicey but necessary undertaking for most firms. Although firms have different cultures, challenges, and risk tolerance levels, they would all be well-served to have solid recruiting, onboarding, and integration programs in place to assess and mitigate the risk and to protect the firm's investment on a going-forward basis.

NOTES

1. One of the most important points that this article makes has to do with the relationship of risk to risk tolerance. Organizations with a high risk tolerance will view risk very differently from those with a lower risk tolerance. (That statement isn't exactly rocket science, is it?) But there's also human risk tolerance. We think that, on average, lawyers have a lower risk tolerance than businesspeople do, mostly because lawyers are trained to identify and manage risk and businesspeople consider risk to be part of the art of making a profit. That's one of the reasons that one of us teaches a seminar that mixes MBA students and law students: to get each cohort to understand the other's risk tolerance. (When lawyers don't understand that businesspeople like taking risks, their legal advice can fall on deaf ears; when businesspeople don't understand that lawyers live to control risk, they miss the opportunity to manage their exposure to potentially bad consequences.) Regardless of the client's risk tolerance, a lawyer is obligated to explain the various issues that exist in a case or transaction. Only then is the client able to make an informed decision.*

2. Another really important point involves what to do after you've hired someone who used to work somewhere else. It's not enough to plop the new person

* One of us was a litigator who spent a fair amount of his time at one of firms poking holes in draft transactional documents (by invitation, not because he was nosy) so that the transactional attorneys knew when certain language might cause problems if the deal later was litigated.

down in your organization and say, "have at it!" You need to provide, as the article says, "support, structure, evaluation, and feedback." Just as an organization provides guidance for its most junior members, it should provide guidance to its newest senior members as well. Frankly, support, structure, evaluation, and feedback are all important for every employee—the new and the not-so-new. Sometimes, the person failing spectacularly has been in an organization for a very long time, without any mishaps. We discuss one example (one that was first discussed in *Unethical Obedience* in Chapter 3) of a fall from grace, as it were, in the next article.

CHAPTER 18

Compromising One's Principles: The Lesson of Mahlon Perkins and the Berkey-Kodak Case

Nancy B. Rapoport[1]

One of the saddest chapters in lawyer disciplinary history ended with this bare-bones summary of the disciplinary ramifications of a contempt conviction caused by lying about discovery:

> Respondent was admitted to the practice of law in the Second Judicial Department on May 5, 1950. On or about October 17, 1978, respondent was convicted in the United States District Court for the Southern District of New York, by plea of guilty, of criminal contempt of Court in violation of 18 U.S.C. § 401(1) and (3); Federal Rules of Criminal Procedure 42(b) and sentenced thereon to imprisonment for a term of one month. . . .
>
> As to the appropriate sanction, we note the following mitigating circumstances. Respondent's record is otherwise unblemished and while his dereliction is serious, his misconduct came to light through disclosures made by him and did not result in a miscarriage of justice. Consideration is given to respondent's service to the People of the United States in O.S.S.,[2] as well as to his extensive service to the People of his local community. *Having served a term of imprisonment, suffered*

---

1 Special thanks go to Jennifer Gross, whose yeoman's work of finding the best way to get the various documents made this article possible; Carey Stumm, the Archivist at the National Archives at New York City, who sent us the complete file; Jamilah Brewington, the world's most patient assistant; my two best editors, Morris Rapoport and Jeff Van Niel; and Bernie Burk, Tigran Eldred, Randy Gordon, and Jean Sternlight, for their great comments on an earlier draft. The views expressed in this article are, of course, my own and not anyone else's at UNLV.

2 O.S.S. (the Office of Strategic Services) was a precursor to the Central Intelligence Agency. *See* https://www.cia.gov/library/publications/intelligence-history/oss/art03.htm.

resignation from partnership in a major law firm, tarnishing of his previously impeccable reputation with consequent humiliation and disgrace, we believe that the conduct is not likely to recur, and, accordingly, we consider severe censure to be condign[3] to the dereliction. Respondent should be severely censured.

Respondent severely censured.[4]

What would cause a well-respected partner in a top law firm to lie to a federal judge about a discovery issue, when the results of such a lie could (1) jeopardize the fairness of the litigation, (2) form grounds for a criminal contempt action, and (3) trigger state bar discipline? Although many people tend to assume that lawyers lie for a living (we do not), and that liars are always evil to the core (they are not), I find it more interesting to assume that some people lie because people are subject to various types of cognitive errors that can play out in odd ways.[5]

A fair amount has been written about Mahlon[6] Perkins, the lawyer who made the bad decision to lie about whether certain documents existed.[7] You can find a marvelous discussion of this case in David Luban's essay, *The Ethics of Wrongful Obedience*.[8] But here's a short, good summary from Thomas Tew:

---

[3] I had to look up that word, too. It means that a punishment was appropriate for a particular crime. *See* https://www.merriam-webster.com/dictionary/condign.

[4] Dept. Disciplinary Comm. for the First Judicial Department v. Perkins (Matter of Perkins), 69 A.D.2d 160, 160–61 (1979) (per curiam) (emphasis added).

[5] So many of us are writing in this area (loosely called behavioral legal ethics) that there's no way for me to list everybody. I will, though, point out some of my favorite authors and their work to get you started. *See, e.g.*, JENNIFER K. ROBBENNOLT & JEAN R. STERNLIGHT, PSYCHOLOGY FOR LAWYERS: UNDERSTANDING THE HUMAN FACTORS IN NEGOTIATION, LITIGATION AND DECISION MAKING (2013); MILTON C. REGAN, JR., EAT WHAT YOU KILL: THE FALL OF A WALL STREET LAWYER (2005); Tigran W. Eldred, *Insights from Psychology: Teaching Behavioral Legal Ethics as a Core Element of Professional Responsibility*, 2016 MICH. ST. L. REV. 757 (2016); Andrew M. Perlman, *A Behavioral Theory of Legal Ethics*, 90 IND. L.J. 1639 (2015); Jennifer K. Robbennolt & Jean R. Sternlight, *Behavioral Legal Ethics*, 45 ARIZ. ST. L. REV. 1107 (2013); Catherine Gage O'Grady, *Wrongful Obedience and the Professional Practice of Law*, 19 J.L. BUS. & ETH. 9 (2013); Andrew M. Perlman, *Unethical Obedience by Subordinate Attorneys: Lessons from Social Psychology*, 36 HOFSTRA L. REV. 451 (2007). And, of course, there are all of the articles in Issue 2 of 15 NEVADA L.J., *Psychology and Lawyering: Coalescing the Field* (2015), available at http://scholars.law.unlv.edu/nlj/vol15/iss2/. You can find some of my own work in this area listed in n. 34, *infra*.

[6] Yes, his first name is unusual.

[7] *See, e.g.*, Thomas C. Tew, *Electronic Discovery Misconduct in Litigation: Letting the Punishment Fit the Crime*, 61 U. MIAMI L. REV. 289 (2007); Pamela S. Karlan, *The Path of the Law Firm: A Comment on Ribstein's "Ethical Rules, Agency Costs, and Law Firm Structure,"* 84 VA. L. REV. 1761, 1767–68 (1998); Robert E. Hinerfeld, *A Broader View of Discovery Ethics: The Societal Context*, 2002 PROF. LAW. 35; Pamela S. Karlan, *The Path of the Law Firm: A Comment on Ribstein's "Ethical Rules, Agency Costs, and Law Firm Structure,"* 84 VA. L. REV. 1761, 1767–68 (1998).

[8] David J. Luban, *The Ethics of Wrongful Obedience*, in ETHICS IN PRACTICE: LAWYERS' ROLES, RESPONSIBILITIES, AND REGULATION 94, 101 (Deborah L. Rhode ed., 2000).

The sad tale of Mahlon Perkins, a former senior partner at the major Wall Street firm of Donovan Leisure, provides an example of the first category. In the 1970s, Kodak was sued by upstart Berkey Photo, a film development chain, for violation of various antitrust laws. Donovan Leisure represented Kodak. Perkins furnished documents to Kodak's economics expert, who had later returned the documents to Perkins in a suitcase. When asked by Berkey's counsel what happened to the material, Perkins said he discarded it[,] thinking the documents were duplicates of other documents already produced. However, Perkins had lied about the status of the documents. He then submitted a sworn statement affirming the lie. The suitcase remained hidden until the final days of trial, when Perkins disclosed the fact that he lied about the destruction of the contents of the suitcase. The contents of the suitcase were then produced. Ironically, the material contained nothing particularly damaging to Kodak.[9] However, the fact that Perkins had lied under oath became a "smoking gun"; as the trial judge commented in the Microsoft antitrust trial, "untrue in small things, untrue in all things." After receiving an adverse jury verdict, Kodak ultimately settled the case for a fraction of the award. One can only guess what motivated Perkins.[10]

Part of what makes Perkins's story so shocking is that he lied so baldly and waited so long to recant.[11] In this essay, I'll explore Perkins's motivations, as reflected by some of the original documents in his contempt case. Then I'll work backwards to see if what we know about human behavior from social science is reflected in the transcripts and related documents themselves.

The first record of Perkins's confession appears to be a sealed transcript dated January 14, 1978, recorded in Judge Frankel's robing room.[12] In that

---

9 Author's note: Actually, the Second Circuit wasn't too impressed with the expert witness who had kept funneling the documents to Perkins in the first place. *See* n. 33, *infra*.

10 Thomas C. Tew, *Electronic Discovery Misconduct in Litigation: Letting the Punishment Fit the Crime*, 61 U. MIAMI L. REV. 289, 298–99 (2007) (footnotes omitted). Of the many articles discussing *Berkey-Kodak*, this sentence stuck out: "Perkins'[s] deception and lying began during the discovery phase but was not revealed to opposing counsel and the court until the last defense witness had begun to testify to the jury on the 109th day of trial." Robert E. Hinerfeld, *A Broader View of Discovery Ethics: The Societal Context*, 2002 PROF. LAW. 35, 42.

11 As my friend Bernie Burk explains it, "[D]eliberate misrepresentation is, in my experience at least, surprisingly rare. We all gasp when we discover it, in part because it represents a direct threat to the 'officer of the court' status that gives us lawyers so much . . . power to operate the litigation system (initiate proceedings; comply with discovery; issue civil subpoenas with our signature; etc.)." Email from Bernard Burk to author (Sept. 11, 2017) (on file with author).

12 I question just how "sealed" the transcript is, give that it was provided to me as part of an overall search for all of Perkins's contempt records, but out of respect for the fact that the transcript says "sealed" on

transcript, one of Perkins's partners, John Doar,[13] reported to Judge Frankel that certain documents that Perkins had stated had been destroyed actually did exist. The court allowed Perkins, who was represented by counsel, to explain what had happened. According to James B. Stewart,[14] Perkins told Judge Frankel:

> Mr. Stein was asking Professor Peck [Kodak's expert witness] about documents that he said he had sent to Donovan, Leisure. He asked me where the documents were and I said they had been discarded. He asked me who destroyed them, and I said, "I did." That was not the truth, Your Honor. As I recall it now, that answer came into my head for some reason at the deposition. I had not planned to make that answer. I don't believe that I had really considered it."[15]

Ultimately, that explanation set the eventual contempt charge in motion.

The contempt charge was initiated in September 1978 by an Application for an Order to Show Cause. The Order to Show Cause issued on September 18, 1978. The Notice of Charges included the following allegations:

Specification of Contempt

> 1. On or about January 29, 1973, a complaint was filed in the United States District Court for the Southern District of New York in the case of Berkey Photo, Inc. v. Eastman Kodak Company, 73 Civ. 424 (MEF) ("the Berkey case"), and assigned for all purposes to the Honorable Marvin E. Frankel, United States District Judge.

---

the front page, I won't quote from it. The transcript is captioned Berkey Photo, Inc. v. Eastman Kodak Co., 73 Civil 424 (Jan. 14, 1978, 2:30 p.m.) (on file with author). Instead, I'll use James Stewart's account in THE PARTNERS. JAMES B. STEWART, THE PARTNERS 355–56 (1983) [hereinafter STEWART].

[13] Doar himself led a fascinating life. For an interesting take on Doar, see Tigran Eldred's blog post, *Moral Courage,* BEHAVIORAL LEGAL ETHICS BLOG (July 10, 2017). Stewart was not as enamored of Doar. *See* STEWART, *supra* n. 12, at 358–64.

[14] STEWART, *supra* n. 12, at 355–56. The particular tragedy of this case is that the timeline of events (Perkins lying about documents being destroyed → alert opposing counsel figuring out that something was fishy → Perkins drafting an affidavit perpetuating the lie → documents getting "re-discovered" in a suitcase at the firm → most documents in the suitcase found to be irrelevant) really ended up being about one particular letter written by Kodak's expert witness long before the trial. The letter wasn't produced by Perkins's firm (that decision not to produce the letter is a whole story in itself), but it wasn't part of the "suitcase documents." *See id.* at 346–48. And the most ironic thing about *that* letter? It eventually emerged in the Berkey-Kodak trial as document number 666. *See* Walter Kiechel III, *The Strange Case of Kodak's Lawyers,* FORTUNE 190–93 (May 8, 1978). For a discussion of the irrelevance of most of the suitcase documents, see STEWART, *supra* n. 12, at 357 ("Only when Perkins opened the suitcase with Doar that night did he learn that virtually all the documents it contained had already been produced to Stein. The few papers that hadn't been produced proved to be entirely inconsequential, and were never submitted as evidence by Berkey. The attempt to conceal them, in the end, did nothing to benefit Kodak.")

[15] STEWART, *supra* n. 12, at 355–56.

2. On April 20, 1977, Professor Merton Joseph Peck ("Professor Peck"), an expert in the economics of industrial organization and antitrust theory, was examined by counsel for Berkey and testified at a deposition conducted in the Berkey case.

3. On April 20, 1977, during the course of the Peck deposition, MA[H]LON[16] F. PERKINS, JR., the defendant, then a member of the firm of Donovan Leisure Newton & Irvine ("Donovan Leisure"), counsel to Eastman Kodak Company ("Kodak"), falsely stated in response to a demand for particular materials that he had destroyed documents furnished to Professor Peck for his review in connection with the pending litigation and returned by Professor Peck to counsel ("the Peck documents"). At the time MA[H]LON F. PERKINS, JR., the defendant, made the foregoing false statement, he knew that he had not destroyed any such document and that a suitcase containing documents shipped to him by Peck on or about January 31, 1977, was located in Perkins'[s] auxiliary office at 770 Broadway, New York, New York.

4. In and about the evening of April 20, 1977, MA[H]LON F. PERKINS, JR., the defendant, upon his return to the office after the conclusion of the deposition proceeding of that day, falsely stated to John Doar, a member of the firm of Donovan Leisure and chief-counsel for Kodak, that he had destroyed the Peck documents and had so stated that day to Berkey's counsel during the deposition. Thereafter, Mr. Doar and MA[H]LON F. PERKINS, JR., the defendant, agreed that the latter would locate other copies of all materials furnished to Peck by Kodak and its counsel and make such documents available to Berkey, with the exception of four notebooks relating to the case prepared by Doar and given to Peck for his review ("the Doar notebooks"). The following day, on April 21, 1977, Mr. Doar appeared at the Peck deposition proceedings and advised Berkey's counsel that the Doar notebooks were privileged and would not be produced.

5. On April 21, 1977, in connection with the reproduction of documents for discovery purposes noted in paragraph four above, a paralegal assistant, without the knowledge of MA[H]LON F. PERKINS, JR., the defendant, brought the suitcase containing Peck documents from 770 Broadway to the uptown offices of Donovan

[16] Apparently, the court reporter didn't believe that Perkins's first name was "Mahlon," not "Marlon."

Leisure, located at 30 Rockefeller Plaza. The suitcase remained in an office being used by the paralegal assistants during the evening of April 21, 1977.

6. During the evening of April 21, 1977, MA[H]LON F. PERKINS, JR., the defendant, learned that the suitcase containing documents returned by Peck had been brought to the offices of Donovan Leisure. Sometime thereafter, MA[H]LON F. PERKINS, JR., the defendant, retrieved the suitcase and placed it in a cabinet in his office, without inspecting its contents or arranging to have the documents copied and produced to counsel for Berkey.

7. On April 25, 1977, proceedings were held before the Honorable Sol Schreiber, United States Magistrate, in the United States District Court for the Southern District of New York, to consider, among other things, Berkey's motion requesting production of the Doar notebooks. John Doar and MA[H]LON F. PERKINS, JR., the defendant, appeared [o]n behalf of Kodak. During the course of oral argument, Mr. Doar, acting under the belief that copies of all of the material which had been furnished to Professor Peck in connection with the Berkey case had been, or were in the process of being, produced to Berkey's counsel, incorrectly stated that all documents had been produced with the exception of the Doar notebooks. After hearing oral argument from both Kodak and Berkey, the Magistrate ordered the Doar notebooks produced to Berkey as part of pre-trial discovery.

8. Thereafter, Kodak sought review of the Magistrate's order with respect to the Doar notebooks from the Honorable Marvin E. Frankel, United States District Judge. On May 5, 1977, after affidavits and memoranda had been filed for both sides, proceedings were held before Judge Frankel in the United States District Court for the Southern District of New York, to determine, among other things, whether the Magistrate's order compelling production by Kodak to Berkey of the Doar notebooks should be sustained.

9. Berkey's counsel, in affidavits submitted to the District Court in support of its request for the production of the Doar notebooks, argued, among other things, that production should be ordered because of the alleged destruction by MA[H]LON F. PERKINS, JR., the defendant, of relevant documents furnished to, and returned by, Professor Peck. Kodak's counsel argued that other copies of virtually all

the Peck documents had been located, reproduced and made available to Berkey and that, accordingly, no prejudice could result to Berkey from the alleged destruction of documents. In fact, there were documents in the suitcase as to which copies had not been made and which had not been made available to Berkey.

10. During the aforementioned proceedings held on May 5, 1977, before the Honorable Marvin E. Frankel, the Court addressed Kodak's counsel on the subject of the claimed destruction of documents, and the following colloquy ensued:

> THE COURT: Are you saying now that everything the expert was shown other than this work product material [the Doar notebooks] you have already given to the plaintiff?
>
> MR. DOAR: I am saying that I can't be absolutely sure of that. Because there may have been some memoranda back and forth. But underlying data, factual data, upon which the witness—which the witness took into consideration in preparing for his testimony has been produced.
>
> THE COURT: Are you saying that those things that were destroyed, whatever they are, thick or thin, were copies of things that the plaintiff had?
>
> MR. DOAR: Yes, I believe. Could Mr. Perkins speak to that inasmuch as he was at the deposition?
>
> THE COURT: Sure.
>
> MR. PERKINS: Yes, sir, those were not released [sic; unique?] copies of anything. Over a period of years a great variety of materials were prepared specifically for the information of the experts. They were distributed principally at a number of meetings in Rochester, some were mailed later. We have made available to the experts other copies of the same materials. They are well over 1000 pages of such materials that deal with all the kinds of subject matter referred to in Mr. Brett's [counsel for Berkey] memoranda there. All kinds of market share data for different kinds of product, product history, financial data, sales data, advertising data.
>
> <u>And so far as I am aware, while the particular copies seen by the witness were not retained the duplicates of that material were in</u>

existence and copies of these have been furnished during the course of the deposition to the plaintiffs.

THE COURT: And you are able to know just what it was that was destroyed, is that what you are saying?

MR. PERKINS: What I know, your Honor, is the material that was distributed to the experts, because of a number of copies of those were made. I had my own file, and in the course of the deposition when these materials were being demanded we made available everything we could identify that had been made available to our experts over a period of years.

THE COURT: I will have to look at your affidavit. I don't think I can decide that—I don't think I should without having a response in this record to what Mr. Brett has said . . . .

Thereafter, the Court noted, "I want Mr. Perkins' affidavit, and anything else that he proposes to submit, by let's say Monday morning [May 9, 1977]."

11. On May 9, 1977, in response to the Court's request for a submission relating to the circumstances and effect of the alleged destruction of documents, MA[H]LON F. PERKINS, JR., the defendant, filed and caused to be filed in the United States District Court for the Southern District of New York, a sworn affidavit in the case of Berkey Photo, Inc. v. Eastman Kodak Company, 73 Civ. 424 (MEF), which reads, in pertinent part, as follows:

MA[H]LON F. PERKINS, JR., being duly sworn, deposes and says:

. . .

3. The principal purpose of this affidavit is to state the following facts with respect to documents made available to Peck:

(a) All materials which we know or believe were made available to Peck have been made available to Brett with the exception of counsel's trial preparation materials and a report prepared by counsel on market share statistical data which we have learned since the May 5 hearing was available to Peck and as to which we also claim privilege. All of the material in this volume relating

> to any of the markets as to which Peck will testify have been produced.
>
> . . .
>
> (c) Specific pieces of paper made available to Peck—and to Brett in duplicate—were returned to me by Peck and were destroyed by me as duplicates.
>
> 12. Thereafter, the Court held the motion with respect to the Doar notebooks sub judice. On June 1, 1977, the Court rendered its decision by Memorandum and Order, entered in the United States District Court for the Southern District of New York, by the Honorable Marvin E. Frankel, United States District Judge, denying discovery of the Doar notebooks to Berkey.

13. At the time MA[H]LON F. PERKINS, JR., the defendant, made the statements noted in paragraphs Ten and Eleven of this Notice of Charges, in which he told the Court, in response to the Court's request, that he had destroyed documents sent to him by Professor Peck but had succeeded, by reproducing other copies of said documents, in making available to opposing counsel "all materials which we know or believe were made available to Peck," MA[H]LON F. PERKINS, JR., the defendant, then and there well knew that the documents to which he had referred had not been destroyed[;] that he had in his possession a suitcase containing documents relating to the Berkey case which had been shipped to him by Professor Peck; that he intentionally failed to inspect the contents of the suitcase; that, accordingly, the documents contained in the suitcase were not reproduced and made available to Berkey; that therefore his statement that "all materials which we know and believe were made available to Peck had been reproduced and made available" to counsel for Berkey was false; that his false statements with respect to these matters were in direct disobedience to the Court's direction that he furnish to the Court truthful information, orally and by affidavit, with respect to the matters involved; and that said false statements had the effect of misleading the Court and obstructing it in its effort to supervise the course of pre-trial proceedings and rule on matters of fact and law based upon full and accurate information supplied by attorneys practicing before it.

Statutory Allegations

> 14. On or about May 5, 1977, and on or about May 9, 1977, in the Southern District of New York, MA[H]LON F. PERKINS, JR., the defendant, did commit acts of misbehavior in the presence of a Court of the United States so as to mislead the court and thereby obstruct the administration of justice and act in disobedience to a lawful order and command of a Court of the United States, in that he willfully and knowingly did make, and cause to be made, false statements to a United States District Judge in the United States District Court for the Southern District of New York, as underscored in paragraphs Ten and Eleven of this Notice of Charges, in criminal contempt of Court.[17]

On October 17, 1978, Perkins pleaded guilty to "unlawfully, wil[l]fully and knowingly making, and causing to be made; false statements to a United States District Judge in the United States District Court for the Southern District of New York, in criminal contempt of Court."[18]

At the sentencing hearing,[19] which naturally followed from Perkins's guilty plea on the contempt charge, Perkins's lawyer, Harold Tyler, argued that "[n]othing has been developed to show anything other than the presentence report [,which] concludes that though Mahlon Perkins did what he has told your Honor . . . he did, there is absolutely no evidence that he intended to undermine or subvert the adversary or his office in that litigation or anyone else."[20] Tyler's "no intent" argument is a classic "no harm, no foul" presentation, buttressed by the fact that, at some point, Perkins eventually had come forward with the truth:

> So that ironically now today we know that he, and really virtually he alone, has suffered as a result of his mistake.
>
> Although it is true that he did not come forward before January 8, which, as your Honor knows, was a Sunday prior to the liability trial going to verdict, it was he who did come forward at a time when he could have remained silent, and no one would have been the wiser.

---

17 Notice of Charges, filed Sept. 18, 1978 (on file with author) at 1–7 (underscoring in original).

18 Judgment and Probation/Commitment Order, filed October 17, 1978 (on file with author).

19 The sentencing transcript, which was filed on February 2, 1979, is captioned *United States v. Mahlon Perkins, Jr.* The file stamp differs from the date on the caption. The caption, United States v. Mahlon Perkins, Jr., 78 Cr Misc. #1, p.33 (Oct. 17, 1978), is file-stamped Feb. 2, 1979, so I'm going with the latter date (hereinafter "2/2/79 transcript").

20 2/2/79 transcript at 3.

> So that we have the situation here that he finds himself out of the firm with which he spent his entire professional life and built the friendships which I think perhaps were most important to him.
>
> He has not in fact been practicing law since the afternoon of Sunday, January 8. He has been put in certainly professional isolation as a result of his own actions.
>
> It has been a situation which has been exposed to the public glare in a way which has been blown way out of proportion, as we now know.
>
> But I think that one thing is rather clear: that those in our profession who know about this, if they are honest about it, would admit that possibly but for the grace of God go I, because of the pressures which come upon men and women who practice law in big cases. There is no doubt this had its impact here, for which Mr. Perkins has already suffered perhaps more than I will ever be able to describe, or anyone else, including himself.[21]

It is hard to imagine an argument that *would* have worked well, but this combination of "hey, he finally confessed," "the deception wasn't a big deal," and "there but for the grace of God" doesn't work for me, even though Tyler didn't have any other good arguments to make. There are many big cases in the world, and lawyers are supposed to follow the discovery rules, even when they'd rather hide discoverable information.

The district court judge wasn't persuaded by the argument:

> THE COURT: I have, of course, read the presentence report and the sentencing memorandum which was submitted, together with the portion of the transcript of the proceedings on January 14, 1978,[22] where Mr. Perkins made his statement to Judge Frankel.
>
> As I have reviewed the record given to me in this case, I have been troubled, as I am sure anyone would be, about the question of why—why an experienced lawyer with almost thirty years at the bar, a partner in a leading law firm in this city, representing the large corporations which do business around the world, would at a deposition, when his adversary calls for documents, state that they were destroyed when in fact he knew that they were not. His conduct after that is much like

21 2/2/79 transcript at 3–5.

22 The court is referring to the sealed transcript.

something we saw three or four years ago on a national scale.[23] Up to that Sunday of disclosure, it was a form of cover[-]up.

I saw the material about reconstructing the file from other documents. I had concluded, and I should like some enlightenment on this, in trying to figure out why he did it in the first instance, that Professor Peck had managed to inscribe various thoughts on these documents, notes of one kind or another, possibly difficult to explain when, as, and if he took the stand, and that for the sake of keeping this away from the adversary, the initial untruth was uttered and all that we know followed came to pass.

It may be that Mr. Perkins can explain it when he gets up. It may be that you would prefer to explain it now.

I read the presentence report. I read your excellent sentencing memorandum. The answer does not come out at me, and I would very much want to know that as a matter which would permit me to better understand what happened here.[24]

Perkins's lawyer tried a second time to minimize his client's actions, reiterating that Perkins had not intended to cause harm. Again, the court didn't find the argument to be persuasive:

[MR. TYLER:] He got caught in an impulsive misstatement of fact. He froze[,] in effect. He told his partner, John Doar, and others in the firm who were working on this difficult case. I think that is a significant point. It doesn't answer the whole thing, your Honor, I quite agree, but I think it is a point worth making.

THE COURT: Of course, he told them rather a while after the event, and one thing that stood out as I read the material was the young associate in the firm urging him to make a disclosure and Mr. Perkins ignoring the urgings, which I found very difficult to understand and to comprehend. In other words, more than one person knew about it, more than one person was there aware of the facts, wanted him to disclose, and he didn't, and the matter continued on before Judge Frankel for some time before what I would call the ultimate disclosure was made. It is, if I may say so, very troublesome.[25]

---

[23] Author's note: The court is referring to the Watergate break-in and the Nixon administration's subsequent cover-up. Perkins's lawyer disagrees with that characterization, 2/2/79 transcript at 6–7.

[24] 2/2/79 transcript at 5–6.

[25] *Id.* at 8.

Valiantly trying to find some argument that would resonate with the court, Perkins's lawyer then chose to go with the "well, it could have been worse" response:

> Now, it is easy to say that he should have done this earlier. But I would suggest, your Honor, that there is a very interesting twist in this. A less candid and forthright individual could have rather cleverly, I might submit, and rather obviously cleverly, could have come forward and told a half-truth. Let us say some time in July, just when the trial is beginning, or maybe sometime in the fall, as the trial went on and on, and said, "Oh, by the way, partners and associates, oh, by the way, Judge Frankel, I made a terrible mistake, I found these documents after all." I find that somewhat revealing in his favor, that he did not resort to that stratagem, which would have been, I think, almost surely accepted, even by a cynical man, saying, "Maybe he didn't quite mean that, but how are we going to really make much of it?"
>
> I don't press the point. I leave it lie where it is.[26]

Ultimately, the court heard from Perkins himself:

> THE DEFENDANT: Well, I will say this, your Honor, that I have no wish to be judged by this Court or anyone for things I didn't do or purposes I didn't have, but neither do I want this Court or anyone to think that I condone what I did do.
>
> I have always placed the highest value on truth and truthfulness. I believe that lying is morally wrong most of the time, and that the occasions on which it may be justified are far fewer than we like to tell ourselves. And I have not pretended to myself or maintained to anyone else that this was such an occasion.
>
> I therefore owe an apology and do apologize to this Court for having lied to it and to the bar for conduct that may tend to discredit it in the public eye.
>
> The questions you ask I think are the questions that anyone would ask, and as my counsel has said, I have been asked them many times over. And I have no good explanation for my original statement that the documents were discarded. It was from that point on that I think I was drawn into what seemed to be further and further positions from which I had not had courage to extricate myself. But I think on my own behalf

26 *Id.* at 10.

I will say that it was not my intention to withhold documents from the plaintiff to which I thought they were entitled.

The question is: Why didn't I verify from the suitcase that I had indeed produced everything? I think I didn't know of everything. I had no reason to believe that there was anything of any substance or materiality that had not been produced to the plaintiff. I still believe that is true, your Honor. But I think I can say that in making that affidavit with the false statements in it I was horrified—I did it, but I was horrified at the time when I did it. I tried to block this whole thing out of my consciousness and to separate myself afterwards entirely from the whole part of the case that dealt with the economic defense. And during those succeeding months I worked very hard on what for me was a difficult and important assignment, and this thing did recur to me from time to time, but I didn't do anything about it until it was very forcibly all brought back to me on that weekend.

I think that is the best account. Maybe it isn't a very satisfactory account, your Honor, because I don't fully understand all of it myself. I will just add one footnote to that, about the notes that Professor Peck may have written. At the time I made the statement I had no idea whatever that he had included any personal notes or drafts of his own. And afterwards I think I also had in mind the ruling of Magistrate Schreiber that personal notes, minutes, drafts, that Professor Peck had made which he had not communicated to us were not producible. So I think that also was part of my thinking.

I think I only want to add to this, and maybe it isn't relevant to your sentence, but I do want to say that I have been appalled by the consequences of my conduct, their reach and their ramification. It may be that not all of those consequences were necessary or predictable or justifiable, but I know they took their origin in my conduct and they have borne very heavily on many old friends and associates, and I am heartily sorry for that.[27]

After Perkins's statement, the court asked the United States Attorney if he had anything to add. He did:

One thing Mr. Tyler said I think I might just try and clear up. He said that Mr. Perkins had spoken to Mr. Doar and his colleagues in the firm. I think your Honor responded, "But that didn't come for some

[27] *Id.* at 11–13.

time." I think what Mr. Tyler had in mind was that immediately after the false statement at the deposition, Mr. Perkins returned to the office and told his colleagues, including Mr. Doar—

THE COURT: That the documents had been destroyed.

MR. BELLER: That he had stated that the documents had been destroyed. And it was that, I gather, that was a difficulty from then on in.

THE COURT: In other words, what you are saying is that at that point not only had he not been honest with his adversary, but also had misled his partners.

MR. BELLER: That is correct, your Honor.[28]

After a recess, the court pronounced its sentence:

THE COURT: This is the sentence of the Court.

I have before me a defendant, age 60, who appears for sentencing following a plea of guilty to criminal contempt for untrue statements made to this court in connection with a case tried in this court. The untrue statements were both oral and written. The contempt arose out of the trial of a civil antitrust case, Berkey Photo v. Eastman Kodak Company. The case was tried before the Honorable Marvin E. Frankel, the former judge of this court, for a period of several months, during, if I recall correctly, both 1977 and into 1978. I could be in error as to whether it extended back that far. But just prior to when the parties thought they were going to trial, in the spring of 1977, during the course of the pretrial deposition of an expert obtained by Kodak, Mr. Perkins falsely stated to opposing counsel that he had destroyed certain documents which had been furnished to the expert for his review in connection with the pending litigation.

At the time the statement was made it would appear to the Court that Mr. Perkins was aware—if he wasn't clearly aware at that point he became aware very shortly thereafter—that a suitcase containing documents shipped to him by the expert was in fact located in his office. After telling his adversary that the material had been destroyed, he continued his deception by telling his partners, his colleagues, the same thing. It was thereafter determined that an attempt would be made to duplicate the allegedly destroyed documents. As I gather, most if not all

[28] *Id.* at 14.

of the documents were ultimately duplicated and did ultimately find their way to the adversary prior to the jury determination of the case.

Having started down this unfortunate road, there came a time when Mr. Perkins, having lied to his adversary and deceived his partners, came before the Court and made a false statement to Judge Frankel orally that he had duplicated and made available everything which had been made available to the expert over a period of years. Judge Frankel, an experienced trial judge, requested a written submission in affidavit form.

Having gone this far down the path, the defendant proceeded further and made a false affidavit that he had destroyed the documents in the normal course and had thereafter duplicated and made available to opposing counsel all unprivileged documents which had been shown to the expert.

At the time these oral and written statements were made, Mr. Perkins knew that the documents to which he referred had not been destroyed but were in his possession in a suitcase in his office.

After a period of some eight months, from April 1977, when the deposition was conducted, until January of 1978, Mr. Perkins maintained his silence.

Finally, as the trial moved to its conclusion, the matter surfaced and Mr. Perkins, having lived with his conscience, his lies, his deception for these many months, came forward, to his credit, [and] acknowledged his wrongdoing.

It is clear to the Court that the defendant is contrite. He has suffered, having resigned from a partnership in a major law firm in this city, and will undoubtedly suffer with this matter for the rest of his life. He has been punished, he will receive additional punishment from this Court, and he will have to live with himself in the future[.]

The matter before the Court is one which has caused deep concern. Here I have a man—intelligent, hard-working—who served honorably in the United States Army during World War II and was a decorated officer in the OSS. He served overseas and served with distinction. After the war he attended and graduated from Harvard Law School and has been with the same law firm from which he recently resigned for almost thirty years, having been a partner for almost twenty.

> The Court is aware of this, his personal life, his marriage, his family situation. The Court has received numerous letters from both family, colleagues, adversaries, people who came in contact with him. Up to this time he had compiled an excellent reputation as a successful, diligent, able attorney.
>
> All of this makes what happened here more inexplicable. This was not a defendant who needed money. This was not a person who was socially deprived. This was a person who in the normal course would be considered a leading citizen and member of the bar.
>
> The letters which I have reflect all of this.
>
> There is little more that one can say when a career has been destroyed and a reputation destroyed as well. Sentencing is difficult in the normal course. It is more difficult here.
>
> This is the sentence of the Court. It is adjudged that the defendant is hereby committed to the custody of the Attorney General or his authorized representative for imprisonment for a term of one month. That is the sentence of the Court.[29]

At this point in my essay, you may be wondering why Perkins only received a one-month sentence (and no disbarment). Was it because the case itself didn't turn on the issue of the hidden documents? Was it because Perkins came from a fancy law firm?[30] It's hard to say. Certainly, the fact that Perkins worked at a prestigious firm could have cut either way. The court could have punished him even more harshly as an example to all lawyers and as a way of saying, "your fancy pedigree won't protect you." But the court went the other way and used a very light touch in sentencing.

So why did Perkins do it? In a 1990 interview, he said " 'It was sort of an impromptu kind of thing and then I sort of got stuck with it[.]' "[31] But that can't possibly be the complete answer. Maybe the lawyers on the other side ticked off Perkins so much during the litigation that he subconsciously sought ways to

---

29 *Id.* at 15–19.

30 Bernie Burk has pointed out that, in part, Perkins's lies were shocking *because* he was a member of a fancy law firm, but that the consequences of Perkins's lies were so light "because (1) his fall from his elevated status [wa]s punishment enough; and (2) because of his elevated status the risk of recidivism [wa]s low (remembering that bar discipline is supposed to be about protecting the public, and thus about specific rather than general deterrence)." Email from Bernard Burk to author (Sept. 11, 2017) (on file with author).

31 David Margolick, *The Long Road Back for a Disgraced Patrician*, N.Y. TIMES (Jan. 19, 1990).

punish them.[32] Perhaps. But I want to add the framework of the myriad of cognitive errors that affect us all.

There are so many social science aspects related to Perkins's decision to conceal the documents (and, frankly, about Kodak's own expert witness's credibility)[33] to explore that it's difficult to limit them. I've written before about how social science can help us understand the bad decisions of even the smartest and best educated of humans.[34] For example, if we examine Perkins's behavior by looking at the role that cognitive dissonance played, his explanation of his behavior during his sentencing hearing makes perfect sense.

Leon Festinger's cognitive dissonance theory essentially says that, if we are faced with two competing moral views of ourselves (that we are good people but that we have done something that we recognize was morally wrong), we will come

---

32 Randy Gordon suggested this hypothesis as a possible rationale for Perkins's behavior. See email from Randy Gordon to author (Aug. 10, 2017) (on file with author). And Jean Sternlight raises a variety of possibilities (which I wish we could confirm or deny):

> [Was] Perkins under some kind of special stress that might have led him to tell that first "impulsive" lie? Perhaps (as you imply) there really was some "bad" stuff in that suitcase that would have sunk the case if not Perkins himself? (Too much coaching/too many drafts). Perkins was 60[,] but not one of the top partners. . . . Was he at some risk perhaps of being put out to pasture? Had he had previous issues with Doar, who he knew was that Watergate stickler? Or, had opposing counsel been playing games that Perkins thought justified a response? Or, Perkins says that he did not think there was anything in the suitcase that he should have legitimately had to disclose—or something like that—but maybe he thought the magistrate/judge was making bad rulings and would force him to give up stuff he shouldn't have to?? And why did he finally come clean? The whole thin[g] still seems bizarre to me.

Email from Jean Sternlight to author (Aug. 14, 2017) (on file with author).

33 *See, e.g.,* the discussion about the concealment and about the credibility of the witness (who kept funneling Perkins's firm documents even after learning that the firm was destroying some of them, rather than preserving them for discovery purposes) in Berkey Photo, Inc. v. Eastman Kodak Co., 603 F.2d 263, 305–08 (2d Cir. 1979).

34 *See, e.g.,* Nancy B. Rapoport & Charlie Douglas, *High Performance Organizational Teams,* LISI Estate Planning Newsletter #2563 (July 3, 2017), available at http://www.leimbergservices.com and at https://papers.ssrn.com/sol3/papers.cfm?abstract_id=2998424; Nancy B. Rapoport, *Ethics: Why We Must Play Well with Others (and Why We Don't),* Rocky Mountain Mineral Law Foundation, MANUAL OF THE ADVANCED PUBLIC LANDS SPECIAL INSTITUTE 587 (2017), available at https://papers.ssrn.com/sol3/papers.cfm?abstract_id=2917346; Randy D. Gordon & Nancy B. Rapoport, *Virtuous Billing,* 15 NEV. L.J. 698 (2015); Nancy B. Rapoport, *"Nudging" Better Lawyer Behavior: Using Default Rules and Incentives to Change Behavior in Law Firms,* 4 ST. MARY'S J. L. ETHICS & MALP. 42 (2014); Nancy B. Rapoport, *The Client Who Did Too Much,* 47 AKRON L. REV. 121 (2014); Nancy B. Rapoport, *Black Swans, Ostriches, and Ponzi Schemes,* 42 GOLDEN GATE L. REV. 627 (2012); Nancy B. Rapoport, *The Case for Value Billing in Chapter 11,* 7 J. BUS. L. & TECH. LAW 117 (2012); Nancy B. Rapoport, *Rethinking Fees in Chapter 11 Bankruptcy Cases,* 5 J. BUS. & TECH. LAW 263 (2010); Colin Marks & Nancy B. Rapoport, *Corporate Ethical Responsibility and the Lawyer's Role in a Contemporary Democracy,* 77 FORDHAM L. REV. 1269 (2009); Nancy B. Rapoport, *The Curious Incident of the Law Firm That Did Nothing in the Night-Time* (reviewing MILTON C. REGAN, JR., EAT WHAT YOU KILL: THE FALL OF A WALL STREET LAWYER (Univ. of Michigan Press 2004)), in 10 LEGAL ETHICS 98 (2007), available at http://papers.ssrn.com/sol3/papers.cfm?abstract_id=1017627 and at http://www.tandfonline.com/doi/abs/10.1080/1460728X.2007.11423884; Nancy B. Rapoport, *Enron, Titanic, and the Perfect Storm,* 71 FORDHAM L. REV. 1373 (2003).

up with an internal justification for the bad behavior.[35] Stanley Milgram tested Festinger's theory with experiments that are well known to social scientists (and to those who watch ENRON: THE SMARTEST GUYS IN THE ROOM[36] on late-night television), and David Luban has a wonderful explanation of Milgram's design:

> Perhaps the most famous example of the slippery slope to fatal commitment is the Milgram experiments, in which subjects are ordered to administer escalating electrical shocks to another subject in an experiment on the effects of pain on learning. The victim, of course, is a confederate of the experimenter, and the shocks are fake; the real goal of the experiment is to study subjects' responses to destructive orders. Milgram's astonishing discovery, replicated many times in several countries, is that almost two-thirds of the subjects prove willing to go all the way to the end of the sequence of shocks, despite the fact that the victim spends much of the time screaming for the experiment to stop, and eventually falls ominously silent, while the label on the shock-generator reads "Danger: Severe Shock." The literature on these famous and alarming experiments is large, and many explanations have been offered for the depressingly high rate of compliance. The one I find most satisfactory focuses on the gradually escalating character of the shocks. The shock-generator has thirty switches, beginning at 15 volts and going up in 15-volt increments to 450. The result is that Milgram's subjects never confronted the pure question "Should I administer this 330-volt shock?" Instead, the question was "Should I administer this 330-volt shock given that a minute ago I administered a 315-volt shock—and I did that after administering twenty previous shocks?" To think "That would be wrong!" virtually requires a subject to conclude that the previous shock, only insignificantly less severe, was also wrong—and cognitive dissonance makes that a very difficult conclusion to accept. It's not that Milgram's subjects became committed sadists. Rather, each shock they administered committed them to the belief that

---

35 *See, e.g.*, David Crump, *The Social Psychology of Evil: Can the Law Prevent Groups From Making Good People Go Bad?*, 2008 B.Y.U. L. REV. 1441, 1444:

> Festinger's Theory of Cognitive Dissonance is one of the more important developments in social psychology. Stated in ordinary language, it explains how people "rationalize" bad behavior. Leon Festinger theorized that there is a mental tension created by contradictory perceptions, which he called "cognitive dissonance." The theory can be summarized by saying that "behavior determines attitudes, as well as the other way around," because individuals are motivated to reduce the tension (or dissonance) by modifying their attitudes to fit their perceptions of their own behavior. The mind, in other words, rationalizes bad behavior—or justifies it—by changing the actor's cognition (the attitude that conflicts with it), to make bad behavior seem not so bad.") (footnotes omitted).

36 ENRON: THE SMARTEST GUYS IN THE ROOM (2005).

> the next shock is neither sadistic nor even wrong (because the prior shocks were not sadistic or wrong). The dissonance-induced commitment leads the subjects unconsciously to gerrymander the boundary between right and wrong. Commitment breeds commitment, and leads to overshooting the bounds of reasonableness as outside observers perceive those bounds, but as the subject clearly does not. The subject is keeping faith with his own commitments, and the shock-victim must suffer at the hands of the subject's pursuit of integrity.[37]

In essence, cognitive dissonance can build as part of a slippery slope. Take one wrong turn, ethically speaking, and it's easier to take more wrong turns.[38] One way to reduce such dissonance is by disengaging, morally speaking, from analyzing one's behavior.[39] In other words, "It's not my fault; I hardly did anything wrong; it's no big deal." That's not an ethical way to reduce the dissonance; apologizing and making reparations is far better. But humans often don't see themselves as

---

[37] David Luban, *Integrity: Its Causes and Cures,* 72 FORDHAM L. REV. 279, 286–87 (2003) (footnotes omitted).

[38] Tigran Eldred has pointed me to an interesting series of studies about slippery slopes and ethics: David T. Welsh, Lisa D. Ordóñez, Deirdre G. Snyder, & Michael S. Christian, *The Slippery Slope: How Small Ethical Transgressions Pave the Way for Larger Future Transgressions,* J. APPLIED PSYCH. 2 (May 26, 2014) ("[P]eople are prone to engage in minor indiscretions up to a certain threshold of severity in one-off experiments."). As these authors explain,

> Individuals tend to rationalize minor unethical acts so that they may derive some benefit without being forced to negatively update their self-concept. For example, a minor transgression such as taking a pen home from the office may seem permissible, whereas taking money out of the company cash drawer may more clearly be thought of as stealing. When unethical behavior becomes too egregious, the external rewards may be outweighed by the internal psychological cost of misconduct. For example, Mazar et al. found that participants paid to solve math problems within a time limit frequently overreported their performance when they were compensated $0.10 or $0.50 for each problem solved but rarely cheated when compensated $2.50 or $5.00 per problem solved. According to Mazar et al., taking an extra dime might have seemed trivial, whereas the severity of the act of pocketing an unearned $5.00 bill may have forced individuals to recognize that taking unearned money is a form of stealing.

Id. (citations omitted); *see* email from Tigran Eldred to author (Aug. 21, 2017) (on file with author).

[39]

> [M]oral disengagement is a form of moral self-deception that allows individuals to justify unethical behavior and avoid self-censure. Normally, people engage in ethical self-regulation to conform their behavior to moral standards. However, through moral disengagement, individuals rationalize questionable conduct, minimize their personal responsibility, and dehumanize potential victims. For example, people may rationalize theft from a wealthy company as having little impact, redefine lies to a competitor as "strategic misrepresentation[,]" and blame questionable decisions on teammates or superiors. Furthermore, recent research has shown that moral disengagement can facilitate motivated forgetting of ethical standards and can occur even when merely contemplating an unethical act.

David T. Welsh, Lisa D. Ordóñez, Deirdre G. Snyder, & Michael S. Christian, *The Slippery Slope: How Small Ethical Transgressions Pave the Way for Larger Future Transgressions,* J. APPLIED PSYCH. 3 (May 26, 2014).

ethical failures until they are so mired in a situation that it's difficult to extricate themselves.

Part of the reasons that we don't see ourselves as having done something unethical involves our own internal narration of what we're doing—our "framing" of the situation. Here's a good example of bad framing creating bad ethical choices:

> Decisions made by business people are often significantly affected by how they are framed. For example, as it neared its end, Enron actually tried to effect savings by encouraging employees to reduce their expenses. An Enron employee later wrote that he intentionally violated the policy. From one point of view, this appears to be wrongdoing in flagrant disregard of company policy. However, in the employee's mind, he deserved to stay in the most expensive hotels and to eat at the best restaurants because of how very hard he was working. Had he framed the issue in terms of the broader picture rather than his narrow self-serving interests, he might have chosen differently.[40]

Framing helps humans recast their own situations in ways that can cascade into good decisions or bad ones. But there's also another hard-wired cognitive error that comes into play in Perkins's case—loss aversion:

> Few frame changes affect decisions more than a change from a "gain" frame to a "loss" frame. This is because of the phenomenon of *loss aversion*, the notion that most people hate losses about twice as much as they enjoy gains. So, "[w]hen directly compared or weighted against each other, losses loom larger than gains." Because of this asymmetry, people tend to choose to take larger risks in order to avoid a loss than they would take to achieve an equal gain. Loss aversion's interaction with framing creates a volatile mix.
>
> Famed psychologist John Darley believes that it is at the cover up stage that many actors who have almost inadvertently acted unethically first cross over to conscious wrongdoing so that they do not lose the status that they currently have. There is certainly experimental evidence to support this surmise. For example, one set of experiments found that subjects were more likely to be in favor of gathering "insider

40 Robert A. Prentice, *Beyond Temporal Explanations of Corporate Crime*, 1 VA. CRIM. L.J. 397, 409–10 (2013) (footnotes omitted) [hereinafter *Temporal*].

> information" and more likely to lie in a negotiation if facing a loss rather than a potential gain.[41]

That "cover-up" moment, in Perkins's case, was the first affidavit, drafted to justify his lie about the documents during the deposition. Possibly, the shock to his system that caused him to stop the lying was Judge Frankel's request that he draft a second affidavit:

> Not long after that discussion with Doar, Perkins recalled that the judge had ordered him to draft yet another affidavit explaining the destroyed documents. "I started to revise it," Perkins recalled, referring to his affidavit, "and then it began to grow on me that I shouldn't be handing in any more affidavits to Your Honor." It had been that evening that Perkins had gone to Doar and confessed . . . "I am not going to go into my feelings on the subject of the documents which were not destroyed in the suitcase and my affidavit to you, but I understand absolutely that what I did was wrong," Perkins sadly concluded. "I injured many people as a consequence."[42]

Cognitive dissonance and its cousins are only some of the hundreds of ways that humans can fool themselves into thinking that something that is clearly wrong is, well, less wrong. Certainly, some of the pressures of practice—the stress of long hours and short deadlines; competition for promotions and financial rewards; social pressure in general[43]—can cause whole groups of people to make bad ethics choices. In my view, cognitive errors involve both the person (psychology) and the situation (sociology).

Armed with a working understanding of how some of these cognitive errors work, let's go back through Perkins's February 2, 1979 testimony:

> The questions you ask I think are the questions that anyone would ask, and as my counsel has said, I have been asked them many times over. And I have no good explanation for my original statement that the documents were discarded. It was from that point on that I think I was drawn into what seemed to be further and further positions from which I had not had courage to extricate myself. *[Loss aversion.]* But I think on my own behalf I will say that it was not my intention to withhold

---

[41] *Temporal* at 412 (footnotes omitted).

[42] STEWART, *supra* n. 12, at 357.

[43] For a discussion of Solomon Asch's social pressure experiments, see, e.g., *Temporal, supra* n. 40, at 403; Tigran W. Eldred, *Insights from Psychology: Teaching Behavioral Legal Ethics as a Core Element of Professional Responsibility*, 2016 MICH. ST. L. REV. 757, 775–78.

documents from the plaintiff to which I thought they were entitled. *[Cognitive dissonance; framing ("I didn't intend to do wrong").]*

The question is: Why didn't I verify from the suitcase that I had indeed produced everything? I think I didn't know of everything. I had no reason to believe that there was anything of any substance or materiality that had not been produced to the plaintiff. *[Framing.]* I still believe that is true, your Honor. *[Cognitive dissonance.]* But I think I can say that in making that affidavit with the false statements in it I was horrified—I did it, but I was horrified at the time when I did it. *[Just as the Milgram experiments' subjects were deeply distressed at being asked to continue the shocks, Perkins's statement that he was "horrified" still resonates as evidence of cognitive dissonance.]*[44]

The fact that all humans are subject to cognitive errors also helps us understand the first line of defense that Perkins's lawyer, Harold Tyler, tried: the "there but for the grace of God" defense. In one sense, that defense is spot-on as an explanation, in that all of us—me included—have justified seriously bad behavior through the step-by-step, incremental evil that cognitive dissonance creates. Cognitive dissonance, though, is an explanation for a behavior, though, and not a defense, and that is why Tyler's first argument fell flat. His "there but for the grace of God" defense tried to frame Perkins's false statement as caused by the pressures of practice.[45] But there are no ethics rules that have an escape hatch along the lines of "anyone could succumb to such pressures." Yes, practice in the late 1970s was stressful. It's stressful today.[46] But stress doesn't excuse lawyers from behaving competently.[47] Stress doesn't excuse lawyers from telling the truth to a tribunal.[48] Stress doesn't excuse lawyers from "playing fair" in litigation.[49] A "there but for the grace of God" defense is useless in circumstances

---

44 2/2/79 transcript at 11–13.

45 2/2/79 transcript at 3–5.

46 Some might argue that the speed of practice today has created additional stresses.

47 *See, e.g.*, MODEL RULE OF PROFESSIONAL CONDUCT 1.1 (Competence). Yes, I know that these Model Rules were enacted after Perkins's behavior and after Tyler's defense; but the old rules were essentially the same. *See, e.g.*, MODEL CODE OF PROFESSIONAL CONDUCT DR 6–101.

48 *See, e.g.*, MODEL RULE OF PROFESSIONAL CONDUCT 3.3 (Candor Toward the Tribunal); *cf.* MODEL CODE DR 1–102(A)(4) (prohibiting "dishonesty, fraud, deceit, or misrepresentation"); DR 7–102(A) (describing what is outside the bounds of zealous representation).

49 *See, e.g.*, MODEL RULE OF PROFESSIONAL CONDUCT 3.4(a) ("A lawyer shall not unlawfully obstruct another party's access to evidence or unlawfully alter, destroy or conceal a document or other material having potential evidentiary value."); *cf.* DR 7–102(B)(2) ("A lawyer who receives information clearly establishing that . . . A person other than his client has perpetrated a fraud upon a tribunal shall promptly reveal the fraud to the tribunal.").

like these—helpful to social scientists, but useless in the face of a contempt charge.

If the "anyone could have done it" argument didn't work, the "he didn't mean to do it" argument wasn't much better. Tyler had suggested to the court that the lie was an impulsive one,[50] and maybe it *had* been impulsive—at first. But the court rightly pointed out that it's hard to call the behavior an impulse with an associate tugging at Perkins's sleeve in a deposition to remind him that the documents hadn't been destroyed after all.[51] And Tyler's last-ditch argument—"hey, at least he confessed *eventually*"[52]—wasn't exactly a ringing endorsement of Perkins's behavior. I recognize that Tyler didn't have many good facts with which he could craft solid defenses, but these three arguments remind me of that old joke defining *chutzpah:* "Perhaps the classic 'legal' definition of chutzpah is the closest; a person who kills his parents and pleads for the court's mercy on the ground of being an orphan."[53] One plays with the cards that one is dealt, but when I think about Tyler's arguments and even Perkins's own explanations, I also think of this passage from the classic Robbennolt & Sternlight article:

> Given this general human tendency, it is unsurprising that lawyers who face ethical complaints or questions tend to recruit a range of justifications. Conduct that is inconsistent with one's image of oneself as an ethical person can be attributed to situational, rather than dispositional, factors. Attempts may also be made to locate blame elsewhere—on adversaries, on the circumstances, on regulators, on clients, and on judges. The omission bias described above can be invoked to minimize blame of one who did not engage in an affirmative act. Unethical conduct can also be rationalized post-hoc through appeals to different metrics of fairness or to other accepted values—for example, notions of lawyers as zealous advocates or creative interpreters

[50] 2/2/79 transcript at 8.

[51] *Id.* According to James Stewart, Perkins had confessed to Judge Frankel that an associate, Joseph Fortenberry, had actually reminded him about the existence of the suitcase of documents: "During the morning of the second day of the deposition [when Stein was pursuing the matter of the destroyed documents] . . . Mr. Fortenberry . . . whispered in my ear, something to the effect . . . 'You have forgotten about the suitcase.' " STEWART, *supra* n. 12, at 356.

[52] 2/2/79 transcript at 10 ("A less candid and forthright individual could have rather cleverly, I might submit, and rather obviously cleverly, could have come forward and told a half-truth.").

[53] Jack Achiezer Guggenheim, *The Supreme Chutzpah,* JEWISH LAW COMMENTARY, available at https://www.jlaw.com/Commentary/SupremeChutzpah.html. Of course, that definition goes on to conclude: "However, in defining chutzpah in the context of American jurisprudence it is also important to note, as a court in the federal district of New Jersey did in 1995, that 'Legal chutzpah is not always undesirable, and without it our system of jurisprudence would suffer.' " *Id., quoting* Chaffee v. Kraft Gen. Foods, Inc., 886 F. Supp. 1164, 1167–68 (D.N.J.1995).

of legal rules, rules protecting client confidences, principles of reciprocity or self-defense, or the need to fight against injustice.[54]

What are the lessons that we can draw from Perkins's own words at his sentencing hearing? I think that the biggest lesson is that the line between an ethical lawyer and an unethical one isn't thick and obvious but razor-thin and dependent in large part on circumstances. Perkins may not have been a bad person. He did some very bad things, and his behavior made the Berkey-Kodak trial less fair. He lied, he sustained the lie, and only at the nth hour did he recant his lie. But you can't put him in a box labeled "evil lawyer" and assume that you would never, under any circumstances, do something similar. Lawyers talk themselves into what they'll call "grey areas" all the time: this document is protected by attorney-client privilege, that document falls outside the scope of the discovery request, this assumption underlying a negotiation is just as discoverable by the other side as it was by us, and so on. The trick, of course, is in being aware of how grey the area is, and—more important—whether you made it grey by wishing it to be grey in the first place.

The other lesson from Perkins's own testimony is that organizations, including law firms, need to think carefully about putting safeguards in place that work against an individual's temptation to cheat (whether consciously or subconsciously).[55] Coming up with ways—incentives, nudges, cultural reinforcement[56]—to build in some safeguards against hard-wired aspects of human nature may help us avoid Mahlon Perkins's fate. Could Perkins's law firm have set up safeguards to prevent the lie and the cover-up? The firm didn't think so. It asked a senior associate to investigate whether the firm could have prevented the situation; the answer, at least from that associate's perspective, was no.[57] But

---

[54] Jennifer K. Robbennolt & Jean R. Sternlight, *Behavioral Legal Ethics*, 45 ARIZ. ST. L. REV. 1107, 1154–55 (2013) (footnotes omitted).

[55] For a great set of lessons in how *not* to prevent bad behavior at prestigious law firms, see MILTON C. REGAN, EAT WHAT YOU KILL: THE FALL OF A WALL STREET LAWYER (2005); for my take on that book, see Nancy B. Rapoport, *The Curious Incident of the Law Firm That Did Nothing in the Night-Time* (reviewing MILTON C. REGAN, JR., EAT WHAT YOU KILL: THE FALL OF A WALL STREET LAWYER (Univ. of Michigan Press 2004)), in 10 LEGAL ETHICS 98 (2007), available at http://papers.ssrn.com/sol3/papers.cfm?abstract_id=1017627 and at http://www.tandfonline.com/doi/abs/10.1080/1460728X.2007.11423884. For a discussion of whether adding a frame of loss-aversion to an organization's ethos could be one way to prevent some cognitive errors, see David T. Welsh, Lisa D. Ordóñez, Deirdre G. Snyder, & Michael S. Christian, *The Slippery Slope: How Small Ethical Transgressions Pave the Way for Larger Future Transgressions,* J. APPLIED PSYCH. 2–5 (May 26, 2014).

[56] For some ideas about how to create different cultures with small nudges, see, e.g., Randy D. Gordon & Nancy B. Rapoport, *Virtuous Billing,* 15 NEV. L.J. 698 (2015); Nancy B. Rapoport, *"Nudging" Better Lawyer Behavior: Using Default Rules and Incentives to Change Behavior in Law Firms,* 4 ST. MARY'S J. L. ETHICS & MALP. 42 (2014).

[57] STEWART, *supra* n. 12, at 358–59.

Robert Prentice thinks that law firms can do something to help avoid a Perkins-like situation:

> The main thing that firms can do in this arena is to educate employees regarding the ubiquitous use of rationalizations and to emphasize their commitment to ethical behavior by all their employees. Anand and colleagues argue that "[e]mployee education and the establishment of independent ethics ombudspersons could go a long way toward protecting against the onset of rationalization/socialization tactics." Creating a pervasive culture of ethical behavior can have a significant beneficial impact upon the ethical decision making of individual employees. The less room a situation provides for employees to rationalize their actions, the more likely they are to act ethically.
>
> Corporations must monitor the use of euphemisms by their employees and law firms must do the same regarding their attorneys, because this is a common way to rationalize wrongdoing by making it sound harmless.[58]

I'd like to think that this education could work, but I'm skeptical. Maybe it's possible to spend time on a regular basis in firmwide meetings to talk about cases involving bad ethics decisions, but frankly, I doubt that even deconstructing such cases in group meetings will overcome the human proclivity of the fundamental attribution error.[59] We think, "I am good, and those evil people did bad things because they are evil." But even good people can find themselves having done evil things.

We can't leave an examination of this case without discussing the associate, Joseph Fortenberry, who allegedly told Perkins, during a deposition, that the documents still existed and were located in a suitcase at the firm. If Fortenberry knew that Perkins was lying about the documents' existence, Perkins's then-silence on the matter would not have excused Fortenberry from having to come forward with the truth.[60] But Fortenberry has disputed Perkins's account:

---

[58] Robert A. Prentice, *Behavioral Ethics: Can It Help Lawyers (and Others) Be Their Best Selves?*, 29 NOTRE DAME J.L. ETHICS & PUB. POL'Y 35, 72–73 (2015) (footnotes omitted).

[59] "In a nutshell, the [fundamental attribution error] describes the established tendency to overestimate the predictive value of personality and disposition, while undervaluing the power of situational forces, in explaining behavior." Tigran W. Eldred, *Insights from Psychology: Teaching Behavioral Legal Ethics as a Core Element of Professional Responsibility*, 2016 MICH. ST. L. REV. 757, 774 (footnote omitted).

[60] *See* MODEL RULE 5.2 (which doesn't let subordinate attorneys off the hook for clear violations of ethics rules) & cmt. 2 ("If the question can reasonably be answered only one way, the duty of both lawyers is clear and they are equally responsible for fulfilling it."). We know that "unlawfully obstruct[ing] [or assisting another in obstructing] another party's access to evidence or unlawfully alter[ing], destroy[ing] or conceal[ing]

> It is doubtful that, despite being implicated by Perkins, Fortenberry really knew the true story about the destroyed documents. (If he did, he would have been obligated to reveal Perkins'[s] misconduct to the bar association, or at least to senior members of the firm.) Fortenberry claims that a paralegal, not he, carried the suitcase of documents from the Wanamaker building to Rockefeller Center, and says he "does not recall" whispering anything about the suitcase to Perkins at the deposition.[61]

In the end, we are left with a tragedy. A lawyer widely recognized as smart, experienced, and kind[62] blurted out a lie—for whatever reason, he blurted out a lie—and the big antitrust case was lost. Perkins's career at the firm was ruined, his firm's ethics were called into question, and he served time. The only thing that we can salvage from this story is that, by studying cases like these, we can remind ourselves how easily we, too, can slip from one bad decision into others. As Tigran Eldred has pointed out, "[t]he metaphor of the boiling frog is well known: A frog that is placed in a boiling pot of water will attempt to jump out, but when placed in water that is slowly heated, the frog does not realize that the temperature is rising until it is too late. The point is that slow, incremental changes often go unnoticed. In the realm of ethics, it is the same."[63]

NOTES

You may be wondering whatever happened to Mahlon Perkins after he served his time. According to David Margolick, a reporter for the NEW YORK TIMES, Perkins started fresh by becoming a *pro bono* public interest lawyer:

> In sentencing Mr. Perkins, Federal District Judge Robert Ward—a Harvard Law School classmate of his—mourned a career ended and a reputation destroyed.

---

a document or other material having potential evidentiary value" is a clear violation of MODEL RULE 3.4(a), but we don't know whether Perkins was recalling Fortenberry's alleged tug at his sleeve accurately.

61 STEWART, *supra* n. 12, at 363.

62

> "[Perkins] was one of the kindest, gentlest, most thoughtful men I've ever known," says one associate—who also worked directly with Doar—of Perkins. "My first thought when I heard about this incredible incident was that Perkins could not have done something like that." [Partner John] Tobin agrees, though he said nothing at the time. "Perkins was sixty years old, with forty years of professional experience. It was utterly uncharacteristic."

STEWART, *supra* n. 12, at 365.

63 Tigran W. Eldred, *Insights from Psychology: Teaching Behavioral Legal Ethics as a Core Element of Professional Responsibility*, 2016 MICH. ST. L. REV. 757, 791 (2016) (footnote omitted).

> That assessment, it turns out, was premature. In an ending that is not only happy but also quite unfor[e]seeable, Mr. Perkins has come back, reincarnated as a civil liberties lawyer.
>
> Three days each week, Mr. Perkins volunteers his services at the center, which handles primarily civil rights, First Amendment and criminal justice cases. In his former life, he represented institutions like the American Association of Advertising Agencies and the Hughes Tool Company, and earned $200,000 a year doing it. Now, his clients include Corazon Aquino, President of the Philippines; the White Earth Band of Chippewa Indians, and Harvard alumni seeking South African divestiture—and he serves them without pay, living off past earnings.*

Perkins died on March 28, 2011. We think that he rehabilitated himself with his subsequent career, but you might have a different opinion.

We tried to find information on Joseph Fortenberry, but all that we could find was a second NEW YORK TIMES article, which mentioned him as part of a larger discussion about lawyer ethics.

> Mr. Perkins is now fighting to preserve his license, but his actions created a difficult ethical problem for Joseph Fortenberry, a senior associate in the firm. For Mr. Fortenberry knew that his partner had lied. Under the A.B.A.'s code, Mr. Fortenberry was obligated to reveal that Mr. Perkins lied to the court, but he said nothing.
>
> Steven Brill, a columnist on legal affairs for ESQUIRE magazine, pointed out in Mr. Fortenberry's defense that law firms "teach young associates that they are apprentices to the partners, not whistle blowers. The partners, after all, are supposed to be the ones with the experience and standing to make decisions about right and wrong."**

Brill's comment highlights what we've emphasized about cognitive errors. Good people can make bad mistakes, not out of premeditation but because of how humans tend to think. The last article in this chapter—one of our all-time favorites—wraps up our journey through cognitive errors.

---

* David Margolick, *Law; The long road back for a disgraced politician,* N.Y.TIMES (Jan. 19, 1990), available at http://www.nytimes.com/1990/01/19/us/law-the-long-road-back-for-a-disgraced-patrician.html?page wanted=all.

** Judith Miller, *What a Lawyer Owes His Client,* N.Y. TIMES (Dec. 17, 1978), available at http://www.nytimes.com/1978/12/17/archives/what-a-lawyer-owes-his-client-aba-sec-study-change-in-corporate-law.html.

CHAPTER 19

*Behavioral Legal Ethics**

Jennifer K. Robbennolt & Jean R. Sternlight[1]

Introduction

Lawyers' ethical improprieties[2] are frequently the subject of jokes,[3] movies,[4] public opinion surveys,[5] disciplinary filings,[6] and news stories. Open a recent

---

* This piece was originally published as Jennifer K. Robbennolt & Jean R. Sternlight, *Behavioral Legal Ethics*, 45 ARIZ. ST. L.J. 1107 (2013).

1 Robbennolt is Professor of Law and Psychology, University of Illinois. Sternlight is Saltman Professor and Director Saltman Center for Conflict Resolution, University of Nevada, Las Vegas Boyd School of Law. The paper is an expanded version of a chapter in our book, PSYCHOLOGY FOR LAWYERS: UNDERSTANDING THE HUMAN FACTORS IN NEGOTIATION, LITIGATION AND DECISION MAKING (2012). We thank Michael Kagan, Kate Kruse, Jeff Meyer, Nancy Rapoport, Arden Rowell, Bill Stempel, Jeff Stempel, Nina Tarr, and participants at the ABA Dispute Resolution Section Annual Meeting, the Yale-Quinnipiac Dispute Resolution Workshop, and Vanderbilt Law School for their helpful comments. We thank Patrick Beisell, Jessica Bregant, Jhaniel James, Geordan Logan, Sarah Mead, and David Schnell-Davis for their research assistance.

2 When we discuss lawyers' "ethics" we refer not only to compliance with the formal professional rules of ethics and other relevant statutory provisions, but also to behavior that is consistent with one's own moral compass.

3 *See, e.g.,* Roger C. Cramton, *What Do Lawyer Jokes Tell Us About Lawyers and Lawyering,* 23 CORNELL L.F. 3, 3 (1996); Marc Galanter, *The Faces of Mistrust: The Image of Lawyers in Public Opinion, Jokes, and Political Discourse,* 66 U. CIN. L. REV. 805, 816 (1998); Robert C. Post, *On the Popular Image of the Lawyer: Reflections in a Dark Glass,* 75 CALIF. L. REV. 379, 379 (1987); Robert E. Scott, *The Lawyer as Public Citizen,* 31 U. TOL. L. REV. 733, 733 (2000).

4 *See, e.g.,* THE DEVIL'S ADVOCATE (Regency Enterprises 1997) (portraying an attorney who is offered a job by a high profile law firm run by the devil); LIAR LIAR (Universal Pictures 1997) (portraying a successful attorney who is forced to be truthful for twenty-four hours); RUNAWAY JURY (Regency Enterprises 2003) (portraying litigation involving an unethical jury consultant).

5 *See, e.g., Gary A. Hengstler & R. William Ide III, Vox Populi; The Public Perception of Lawyers: ABA Poll,* 79 A.B.A. J. 60 (1993); David W. Moore, *Nurses Top List in Honesty and Ethics Poll,* GALLUP NEWS SERV. (Dec. 7, 2004), http://www.gallup.com/poll/14236/nurses-top-list-honesty-ethics-poll.aspx (placing lawyers nineteenth of twenty-one professions with respect to honesty and ethical standards); Sarah Parikh, *Public Perceptions of Lawyers: Consumer Research Findings,* 2002 A.B.A. SEC. LITIG. 8, 18, available at http://www.cliffordlaw.com/abaillinoisstatedelegate/publicperceptions1.pdf.

6 *See, e.g.,* A.B.A. Ctr. For Profl Resp., 2010 Survey on Lawyer Discipline Systems (S.O.L.D.) 1–35 (2010), available at http://www.americanbar.org/content/dam/aba/administrative/professional_responsibility/2010_sold_finalreport.authcheckdam.pdf (collecting statistics relating to attorney discipline).

newspaper or check your favorite website and you may see stories about attorneys failing to investigate (let alone discipline) alleged child abusers,[7] allowing corporate employers to pay illegal bribes[8] or commit fraudulent acts,[9] hiding or destroying evidence,[10] lying in negotiations,[11] mishandling prosecutions,[12] or representing clients in the face of seemingly obvious conflicts of interest.[13] By perusing bar

---

7 *See, e.g.*, Robert K. Vischer, *Legal Advice as Moral Perspective,* 19 GEO. J. LEGAL ETHICS 225, 247–54 (2006) (discussing role of church attorneys in defending Catholic priests accused of sexual misconduct); Michael Rubinkam, *Testimony at Sandusky Trial Shows Missed Chances,* HUFFINGTON POST (June 16, 2012, 1:51 PM), http://www.huffingtonpost.com/huff-wires/20120616/us-penn-state-abuse-under-their-noses (describing district attorney's decision not to charge Jerry Sandusky over a 1998 molestation allegation).

8 *See* David Barstow, *Vast Mexico Bribery Case Hushed up by Walmart After Top-Level Struggle,* N.Y. TIMES, Apr. 22, 2012, at A1; *cf.* Upjohn Co. v. United States, 449 U.S. 383, 394–95 (1981) (discussing Upjohn Company's self-report to the Internal Revenue Service about questionable payments by a subsidiary to a foreign government).

9 *See, e.g.*, Final Report of Neal Batson, Court-Appointed Examiner at app. C, *In re* Enron Corp., No. 01-16034 (AJG), 2003 WL 25544836 (Bankr. S.D.N.Y. Nov. 4, 2003), available at http://www.concerned shareholders.com/CCS_ ENRON_Report.pdf (finding "sufficient evidence from which a fact-finder could conclude that certain of Enron's attorneys . . . aided and abetted the Enron officers' breaches of fiduciary duty"). *See generally* NANCY B. RAPOPORT ET AL., ENRON AND OTHER CORPORATE FIASCOS: THE CORPORATE SCANDAL READER (2d ed. 2009); *see also* W. Bradley Wendel, *Professionalism as Interpretation,* 99 NW. U. L. REV. 1167, 1170–71 (2005) (describing role of Enron attorneys); Sung Hui Kim, *The Banality of Fraud: Re-Situating the Inside Counsel as Gatekeeper,* 74 FORDHAM L. REV. 983, 985 (2005).

10 *See, e.g.*, Qualcomm Inc. v. Broadcom Corp., No. 05CV1958-B (BLM), 2008 WL 66932, at *12 (S.D. Cal. Jan. 7, 2008) (discussing attorneys' failure to produce 46,000 "critical" documents in a major lawsuit); Coleman (Parent) Holdings, Inc. v. Morgan Stanley, Inc., No. CA 03-5045 A1, 2005 WL 674885 (Fla. Cir. Ct. Mar. 23, 2005) (granting default judgment to plaintiff on ground that attorneys for Morgan Stanley egregiously failed to produce requested computer disk drives); Off. of Prof'l Resp., U.S. Dep't of Justice, Investigation of Allegations of Prosecutorial Misconduct in United States v. Theodore F. Stevens, Crim. No. 08-231 (D.D.C. 2009) (EGS) (2011), available at http://www.leahy.senate.gov/imo/media/doc/052412-081511Report.pdf (detailing investigation into alleged prosecutorial misconduct); Walter Kiechel III, *The Strange Case of Kodak's Lawyers,* FORTUNE, May 8, 1978, at 188 (describing failure to turn over a suitcase containing documents relied upon by expert witness).

11 *See, e.g.*, Art Hinshaw et al., *Attorneys and Negotiation Ethics: A Material Misunderstanding?,* 29 NEGOT. J. 265 (2013) (reporting that a substantial minority of practicing attorneys engaged in unethical or even fraudulent behavior in experimental settings); Art Hinshaw & Jess K. Alberts, *Doing the Right Thing: An Empirical Study of Attorney Negotiation Ethics,* 16 HARV. NEGOT. L. REV. 95, 148 (2011) (finding that attorneys are willing to violate the requirements of the Model Rules of Professional Conduct Rule 4.1 governing legal negotiations).

12 *See, e.g.*, Alafair S. Burke, *Prosecutorial Passion, Cognitive Bias, and Plea Bargaining,* 91 MARQ. L. REV. 183, 183–86 (2007); Duff Wilson, *Prosecutor in Duke Case Is Disbarred for Ethics Breaches,* N.Y. TIMES, June 16, 2007, http://www.nytimes.com/2007/06/16/us/16cnd-nifong.html; *cf.* Connick v. Thompson, 131 S. Ct. 1350, 1355 (2011) (finding that although prosecutor's office failed to disclose an exculpatory crime report, plaintiff failed to make sufficient showing of "deliberate indifference" for liability under 42 U.S.C. § 1983). *See generally* Susan A. Bandes, *The Lone Miscreant, the Self-Training Prosecutor, and Other Fictions: A Comment on Connick v. Thompson,* 80 FORDHAM L. REV. 715 (2011).

13 MILTON C. REGAN, JR., EAT WHAT YOU KILL: THE FALL OF A WALL STREET LAWYER 1–12 (Univ. of Mich. Press 2004) (discussing attorney who was sentenced to prison for making false affidavits hiding conflict of interest). In addition, one might identify more politically controversial examples. *See* Patrick Gavin, *PBS Documentary Looks at Bill Clinton's Career,* POLITICO (Jan. 1, 2012, 2:16 PM), http://www.politico.com/news/stories/0112/71382.html (reviewing documentary discussing President Clinton's sexual dalliances and his subsequent dishonesty regarding those dalliances). *See generally* David Luban, *The Torture Lawyers of Washington,* in LEGAL ETHICS AND HUMAN DIGNITY (2007); *see also* W. Bradley Wendel, *Executive Branch*

disciplinary records one would also learn about a myriad of less newsworthy but nonetheless important ethical violations—failure to communicate with clients, neglect of client matters, failure to provide competent representation, and misuse of client trust funds.[14] Whether one is most concerned with some lawyers' failure to comply with even minimal ethical rules, or whether one advocates that lawyers hold themselves to higher standards, one will likely be disturbed by such reports.[15]

A survey by the American Bar Association found that 118,054 ethics complaints were made against U.S. lawyers in 2010.[16] Of course, such complaints are both over and under inclusive as a measure of attorneys' ethical misconduct. Some complaints may make allegations that are unfounded. Conversely, much misconduct may never be discovered or reported. Still, the anecdotes, press reports, and ethical complaints suggest that there is reason for concern.

Concerns about ethics cut across all sizes and types of practice. While lawyers at smaller firms tend to be disciplined by the Bar more often than attorneys who practice at larger or more prestigious firms,[17] it is by no means clear that small firm lawyers are inherently less ethical.[18] Indeed, it is evident that attorneys at some

---

Lawyers in a Time of Terror: The 2008 F.W. Wickwire Memorial Lecture, 31 DALHOUSIE L.J. 247, 265 (2009) (urging that the arguments relied upon by Bush administration attorneys to justify harsh inquisition tactics were so far outside the range of reasonable as to be considered unethical).

14 MODEL RULES OF PROF'L CONDUCT R. 1.1 (2012) (concerning Client-Lawyer Relationship); *see* Jennifer Gerarda Brown & Liana G.T. Wolf, *The Paradox and Promise of Restorative Attorney Discipline,* 12 NEV. L.J. 253, 259–60 (2012) (reporting that the most common disciplinary complaints made against attorneys involve neglect and lack of communication); Carla Messikomer, *Ambivalence, Contradiction, and Ambiguity: The Everyday Ethics of Defense Litigators,* 67 FORDHAM L. REV. 739, 754 (1998) ("It is difficult to comprehend and define the extraordinary violations without understanding the ordinary ethical issues that practicing lawyers routinely confront and resolve in their everyday professional life. Focusing on the tail of the distribution of ethical conduct tells us little (as the use and misuse of horror stories starkly demonstrates) about the dominant value system that informs everyday conduct."). Lawyers may also act in a variety of other ways that may be considered unethical or otherwise inappropriate. For example, they may make decisions that are discriminatory, take undue credit for joint work, or treat others with disrespect.

15 In this Article, we neither take a position on what ethical standards ought to be applied to attorneys, nor on how ethical misconduct ought to be sanctioned. Instead, our goal is to educate attorneys and legal organizations on how best to fulfill their own ethical goals. *Cf.* Andrew M. Perlman, *A Behavioral Theory of Legal Ethics* (Suffolk Univ. Law Sch. Research Paper No. 13–31, Sept. 4, 2013), available at http://ssrn.com/abstract=2320605 (urging that legal ethical rules ought to be made clearer and less discretionary in light of our inability to maintain objectivity while maintaining partisan positions).

16 A.B.A. Ctr. For Prof'l Resp., *supra* note 6 (surveying lawyer disciplinary agencies across the 50 states). In 2010, there were approximately 1.4 million licensed attorneys in the U.S., 73,240 complaints against lawyers were investigated, and 5,241 lawyers were charged with an ethics violation following a probable cause determination. *Id.*

17 Leslie C. Levin, *The Ethical World of Solo and Small Law Firm Practitioners,* 41 HOUS. L. REV. 309, 312 (2004).

18 *See* Brown & Wolf, *supra* note 14, at 260 (noting that the "higher claim rate [against solo and small firm practitioners] appears to stem . . . from challenges that are specific to small scale practice: a client base composed primarily of individuals rather than institutions, lower average hourly billing rates, and a high volume of clients to balance lower rates."); Levin, *supra* note 17, at 387 (noting that many solo and small firm lawyers

of the biggest and most respected firms sometimes commit serious ethical infractions—lying in affidavits,[19] failing to produce discovery,[20] helping their client's officers breach their fiduciary duties,[21] and other ethical improprieties.[22] Ethical missteps reach all levels of prominence. Indeed, two former U.S. presidents (Richard Nixon and Bill Clinton) were disbarred or suspended from the practice of law.[23]

Ethical problems afflict criminal attorneys as well as those handling civil cases. Prosecutors have been found to have committed ethical violations such as concealing exculpatory evidence, knowingly presenting false testimony, misleading witnesses, or continuing to prosecute criminals after DNA testing seems to show they are not guilty.[24] Similarly, criminal defense attorneys, whether in public defenders' or private offices, have been found to have failed to exercise adequate diligence in representing their clients.[25]

Some have suggested that lawyers behave badly because they are inherently "bad"[26] or "stupid,"[27] because they are susceptible to undue pressure from their

---

are "overwhelmed by their financial circumstances or caseloads"). It may also be true that the Bar comes down harder on attorneys at smaller or solo firms. Levin, *supra* note 17, at 314 ("It may be easier for under-financed discipline systems to successfully prosecute cases against solo or small firm practitioners—who have fewer resources to defend against these complaints.").

19 REGAN, *supra* note 13, at 1, 3 (describing John Gellene from Milbank, Tweed, Hadley & McCloy).

20 Qualcomm Inc. v. Broadcom Corp., No. 05CV1958-B (BLM), 2008 WL 66932, at *16 (S.D. Cal. Jan. 7, 2008) (involving attorneys from Heller Ehrman LLP); Kiechel, *supra* note 10 (describing lawyers at Donovan Leisure who hid documents).

21 Final Report of Neal Batson, supra note 9, at 6–13; *see also* Robert W. Gordon, *A New Role for Lawyers? The Corporate Counselor After Enron,* 35 CONN. L. REV. 1185, 1187 (2003) (observing that Enron lawyers from Vinson & Elkins facilitated flawed transactions).

22 *See* Symposium, In the Matter of *Kaye, Scholer, Fierman, Hays & Handler: A Symposium on Government Regulation, Lawyers' Ethics, and the Rule of Law,* 66 S. CALIF. L. REV. 977, 979–84 (1993) (detailing the chronology of events leading to the Kaye, Scholer scandal). *See generally Ed Hendricks & Mary Berkheiser, Where Were the Lawyers?,* 18 LITIG. 30, 30 (1992); William H. Simon, *The Kaye Scholer Affair: The Lawyer's Duty of Candor and the Bar's Temptations of Evasion and Apology,* 23 LAW & SOC. INQUIRY 243, 243 (1998).

23 *In re* Nixon, 53 A.D.2d 178 (N.Y. App. Div. 1976); Neal v. Clinton, No. CIV 2000-5677, 2001 WL 34355768 (Ark. Cir. Jan. 19, 2001) (five-year suspension).

24 *See generally* Monroe H. Freedman, *The Use of Ethical and Unconstitutional Practices and Policies by Prosecutors' Offices,* 52 WASHBURN L.J. 1, 1 (2012).

25 Tigran W. Eldred, *Prescriptions for Ethical Blindness: Improving Advocacy for Indigent Defendants in Criminal Cases,* 65 RUTGERS L. REV. 333, 344 (noting that "public defenders, contract lawyers, or appointed counsel—fail to properly investigate in a substantial number of cases").

26 *See* Oliver Wendell Holmes, Jr., *The Path of the Law,* 110 HARV. L. REV. 991, 992 (1997) (observing that a "bad" man, who "cares nothing for an ethical rule which is believed and practised [sic] by his neighbors," nonetheless has an incentive to obey the law in order to avoid fines and stay out of jail).

27 *Robert W. Gordon, The Ethical Worlds of Large-Firm Litigators: Preliminary Observations,* 67 FORDHAM L. REV. 709, 711 (1998) (noting that lawyers often characterize ethics violations as "isolated examples of lawyers being 'stupid,' that is, failing to take adequate account of the downside risks to themselves and to their clients of rule violations").

clients,[28] because they are under-regulated,[29] or even because they are over-regulated.[30] Surely some attorneys do deliberately engage in conduct that they know to be wrong in order to benefit themselves or their client. However, psychological research suggests a more complex story: that those who commit ethical infractions are not necessarily "bad apples," but are human beings. Many ethical lapses result from a combination of situational pressures and all too human modes of thinking.[31]

The psychology we present here helps explain how ethical lapses can occur more easily and less intentionally than we might imagine, providing substantial insight into why attorneys sometimes behave unethically, why attorneys may have difficulty curbing or reporting the unethical conduct of their clients or fellow attorneys, and why it is often difficult for attorneys to learn from their own ethical missteps and the missteps of others. It also helps us see how, even as we make what could be considered to be unethical decisions, we may still believe we are ethical actors. At the same time, the psychological research also provides insight

---

[28] Levin, *supra* note 17, at 337 (discussing the ethical challenge of dealing with "a client who wished to engage in some form of fraud").

[29] Eugene R. Gaetke, *Expecting Too Much and Too Little of Lawyers,* 67 U. PITT. L. REV. 693, 750 (2006) (advocating better use of "rulemaking to restrain the current professional default principle of zealous advocacy").

[30] *See, e.g.,* Heidi Li Feldman, *Codes and Virtues: Can Good Lawyers be Good Ethical Deliberators?,* 69 S. CAL. L. REV. 885, 885–86 (1996) (arguing that typical statutory prohibitions are likely to stifle "sentimental responsiveness, a key feature of good ethical deliberation," by encouraging lawyers to take a technocratic approach rather than to engage a more virtuous approach); Reed Elizabeth Loder, *Tighter Rules of Professional Conduct: Saltwater for Thirst?,* 1 GEO. J. LEGAL ETHICS 311, 311 (1987) (arguing that "increasing ethical regulation may magnify troublesome problems of role morality and even impede lawyers' moral development"); *see also* Trina Jones, *Inadvertent Disclosure of Privileged Information and the Law of Mistake: Using Substantive Legal Principles to Guide Ethical Decision Making,* 48 EMORY L.J. 1255, 1282–83 (1999) (critiquing reliance on ethical rules on grounds that they inevitably leave too much room for discretion and discourage lawyers from thoroughly considering how to behave when rules do not apply).

[31] *See, e.g.,* Gerd Gigerenzer, *Moral Satisficing: Rethinking Moral Behavior as Bounded Rationality,* 2 TOPICS COGNITIVE SCI. 528, 540 (2010) (raising the concept of "ecological morality, that is, that moral behavior results from an interaction between mind and environment"); Jennifer J. Kish-Gephart et al., *Bad Apples, Bad Cases, and Bad Barrels: Meta-Analytic Evidence About Sources of Unethical Decisions at Work,* 95 J. APPLIED PSYCHOL. 1, 1 (2010) (finding that characteristics of the individual, the ethical issue, and the environment work together to influence ethical decision making and behavior); Benoît Monin & Alexander H. Jordan, *The Dynamic Moral Self: A Social Psychological Perspective,* in PERSONALITY, IDENTITY, AND CHARACTER: EXPLORATIONS IN MORAL PSYCHOLOGY 341 (Darcia Narvaez & Daniel K. Lapsley eds., 2009). *See generally* BUSINESS ETHICS: SHAPING AN EMERGING FIELD (David De Cremer & Ann E. Tenbrunsel eds., 2011); Yuval Feldman, *Behavioral Ethics Meets Behavioral Law and Economics,* in HANDBOOK OF BEHAVIORAL ECONOMICS AND THE LAW (Eyal Zamir & Doron Teichman eds., forthcoming); Max H. Bazerman & Francesca Gino, *Behavioral Ethics: Toward a Deeper Understanding of Moral Judgment and Dishonesty,* 8 ANN. REV. L. & SOC. SCI. 85 (2012); Michael Bommer et al., *A Behavioral Model of Ethical and Unethical Decision Making,* 6 J. BUS. ETHICS 265 (1987); Celia Moore et al., *Why Employees Do Bad Things: Moral Disengagement and Unethical Organizational Behavior,* 65 PERSONNEL PSYCHOL. 1 (2012) (developing a measure of an individual's propensity to morally disengage); Linda Klebe Trevino, *Ethical Decision Making in Organizations: A Person-Situation Interactionist Model,* 11 ACAD. MGMT. REV. 601 (1986).

into why attorneys are often able to resist substantial pressure to act unethically—pressure that comes from clients, adversaries, superiors, and their own self-interest.[32]

While we are not the first to apply certain social science insights to the ethical behavior of attorneys in particular settings or situations,[33] this Article is the first to provide a comprehensive survey of the implications of psychology for legal ethics. In addition, we provide detailed suggestions about how individuals, attorneys, and legal organizations scan improve attorneys' ethics across practice areas and settings.

In Part I of the Article we examine the ethical blind spots, slippery slopes, and "ethical fading" that may lead good people to behave badly. These insights may offer some comfort—suggesting that there are not as many inherently bad people (or lawyers) in the world as we might have believed. But this psychologically rich understanding also raises concerns, because it implies that all of us are in danger of behaving unethically should the right (or wrong) circumstances present themselves.

The nature of legal practice means that lawyers face a set of particularly difficult challenges. Part II explains that complex and ambiguous ethical rules and standards, agency relationships, the ethos of the adversarial system, the pressures of modern legal practice, positions or feelings of relative status or power, and cues or pressure from others are all characteristics of the practice of law that attorneys need to pay attention to if they want to avoid crossing ethical lines.[34]

---

[32] *See, e.g.*, Levin, *supra* note 17, at 337 (describing how attorneys report resisting pressures to act unethically).

[33] *See, e.g.*, Alafair S. Burke, *Improving Prosecutorial Decision Making: Some Lessons of Cognitive Science*, 47 WM. & MARY L. REV. 1587 (2006) (prosecutors); Burke, *supra* note 12 (prosecutors); Eldred, *supra* note 25 (criminal defense lawyers); Kath Hall & Vivien Holmes, *The Power of Rationalisation to Influence Lawyers' Decisions to Act Unethically*, 11 LEGAL ETHICS 137 (2009) (in-house counsel); Kim, *supra* note 9 (in-house counsel); Kimberly Kirkland, *Ethics in Large Law Firms: The Principle of Pragmatism*, 35 U. MEM. L. REV. 631 (2005) (attorneys in large firms); Donald C. Langevoort, *Where Were the Lawyers? A Behavioral Inquiry Into Lawyers' Responsibility for Clients' Fraud*, 46 VAND. L. REV. 75 (1993) (corporate counsel); Levin, *supra* note 17 (small and solo law firm practitioners); Gregory S. McNeal, *Organizational Culture, Professional Ethics and Guantánamo*, 42 CASE W. RES. J. Int'l L. 125 (2009) (military attorneys); Robert L. Nelson, *The Discovery Process as a Circle of Blame: Institutional, Professional, and Socio-Economic Factors that Contribute to Unreasonable, Inefficient, and Amoral Behavior in Corporate Litigation*, 67 FORDHAM L. REV. 773 (1998) (large firm litigators); Andrew M. Perlman, *Unethical Obedience by Subordinate Attorneys: Lessons from Social Psychology*, 36 HOFSTRA L. REV. 451 (2007); Cassandra Burke Robertson, *Beyond the Torture Memos: Perceptual Filters, Cultural Commitments, and Partisan Identity*, 42 CASE W. RES. J. INT'L L. 389 (2009) (government lawyers); see also Lawrence J. Fox, *I'm Just an Associate . . . At a New York Firm*, 69 FORDHAM L. REV. 939, 939–53 (2000) (recounting fictional story of an associate who is instructed by a senior partner to engage in unethical behavior).

[34] We also recognize that many ethical improprieties within the profession are related to drug or alcohol issues or mental health problems. While these issues are important, and may relate in part to the stresses we identify, they are not our focus. *See, e.g.*, Sheila Blackford, *Dealing with Impaired Attorneys*, LAW PRAC. TODAY

In Part III, we examine why it is difficult to recognize and learn from ethical lapses. Unfortunately, the same kinds of psychological phenomena that can make it hard for lawyers to notice and avoid ethical issues in the first instance also make it difficult for them to identify and learn from ethical mistakes.

Finally, in Part IV, we draw on the psychological research to make some suggestions for how individual attorneys and legal employers can enhance their ethics.[35] While in the end, we do not pretend to offer complete solutions that will ensure attorneys' ethical behavior, we do hope that our psychological lens will help equip lawyers to better resist the temptations of unethical conduct.

I. Bounded Ethicality

Ethical lapses occur more easily and less intentionally than we might imagine. While most of us desire to act ethically,[36] "psychological processes . . . [can] lead people to engage in ethically questionable behaviors that are inconsistent with their own preferred ethics."[37]

As an initial example, consider the downfall of prominent bankruptcy attorney John Gellene, as described by Milton Regan in the book EAT WHAT YOU KILL.[38] Gellene, a "bankruptcy partner at the prestigious Wall Street law firm of Milbank, Tweed, Hadley & McCloy. . . . was regarded as one of the best bankruptcy lawyers in the country, and had worked on some of the largest corporate reorganizations in the world."[39] In the mid-1990s, Gellene and Milbank represented Bucyrus-Erie, a manufacturer of mining tools, as it reorganized in bankruptcy. Following the bankruptcy proceedings, Bucyrus-Erie was healthy enough to be purchased by "a large private investment partnership."[40] But the

---

(June 2009), http://apps.americanbar.org/lpm/lpt/articles/pma06091.shtml (noting that impaired lawyers "are frequently the subject of ethics complaints for not communicating with clients and neglecting legal matters"); Michael A. Bedke & John W. Keegan, A.B.A. Young Law. Div., Comm'n on Impaired Attorneys, Report to the House of Delegates P I (1995) (reporting estimates that a substantial proportion of lawyer discipline cases are related to impairment).

35 While the psychology we review here surely has implications for the content of the rules of professional conduct as well, we do not address those implications here. Instead, we take as a given the legal and regulatory structure governing professional conduct and explore the implications of behavioral ethics for individual attorneys and their employers within the existing regulatory context.

36 *See* Nina Mazar et al., *The Dishonesty of Honest People: A Theory of Self-Concept Maintenance,* 45 J. MKTG. RES. 633, 634 (2008) (arguing that people strive to maintain a self-concept that includes honesty).

37 MAX H. BAZERMAN & DON A. MOORE, JUDGMENT IN MANAGERIAL DECISION MAKING 123 (7th ed. 2008); *see also* C. Daniel Batson et al., *Moral Hypocrisy: Appearing Moral to Oneself Without Being So,* 77 J. PERSONALITY & SOC. PSYCHOL. 525, 525 (1999) ("Moral people often fail to act morally.").

38 *See* REGAN, *supra* note 13, at 1.

39 *Id.*

40 *Id.*

Bucyrus-Erie bankruptcy would not turn out so successfully for Gellene, who ended up in jail.[41]

> [Gellene had originally] been asked by powerful Milbank partner Larry Lederman to provide his services to Bucyrus because of Gellene's experience in bankruptcy and financial restructuring. Lederman had advised Bucyrus off and on for five years. He also had provided legal guidance for several years to investment banker Mikael Salovaara. Salovaara had furnished financial advice to Bucyrus over the same five-year period. He was a former Goldman Sachs partner who had recently left the firm with a colleague to establish an investment fund known as South Street. In 1992, South Street had advanced $35 million to Bucyrus in return for a lien on all the company's manufacturing equipment. As the company's major secured creditor, South Street would be first in line to be paid if Bucyrus filed for bankruptcy. . .
>
> [In applying to be appointed as Bucyrus-Erie's counsel,] Gellene was required under Bankruptcy Rule 2014 to list his and Milbank's connections with any party in interest in the bankruptcy. At the time, Milbank also was representing Mikael Salovaara on one matter and South Street on another. Gellene himself was the lead counsel in the South Street matter, although he had done very little work on the case. The work for Salovaara and South Street created a potential conflict of interest for the law firm. As counsel for Bucyrus in its bankruptcy, Milbank would represent a debtor that had a duty to treat fairly all parties with a claim on its assets. As counsel for Salovaara and South Street, Milbank might have an incentive to provide advice to Bucyrus that favored South Street over other creditors.
>
> [But] Gellene didn't disclose these Milbank ties to Salovaara when he submitted the affidavits that accompanied his application.[42]

When Milbank's ties to Salovaara and South Street were eventually uncovered, the firm was required to return the $1.86 million in fees that it had earned in the bankruptcy case and settled a professional malpractice suit for between $27 and $50 million.[43] For his part, Gellene was charged with and convicted of violating Bankruptcy Rule 2014 for "making false declarations in the affidavits he had submitted to [the judge and] . . . for using a false affidavit under oath to claim that

---

41 *Id.* at 287.

42 *Id.* at 2–3.

43 *Id.* at 3.

Milbank was eligible to receive payment for its work on the bankruptcy."[44] He was sentenced to 15 months in prison and a $15,000 fine.[45] How did John Gellene fall so far and so hard?

It is wishful thinking to assume that only "bad apples"—people who differ from us in important ways—will make unethical decisions:

> In our conventional way of thinking about ourselves, we are confident that we would know in advance that to do some set of actions would be morally wrong, and that this realization occurring prior to the actions, would prevent us from taking them. These comforting thoughts turn out to be not true.[46]

Instead, we will see that many psychological phenomena contribute to decisions to act unethically and make it challenging to identify and appropriately respond to the ethical lapses of others—including colleagues and clients.

A. Ethical Blindspots

Unethical decisions are more likely when the decision maker does not see the decision at hand as involving ethical issues or when she believes that any potential ethical challenges can easily be overcome. Each of us tends to believe that we see the world objectively;[47] to see ourselves as more fair, unbiased, competent, and deserving than average;[48] and to be overconfident about our abilities and prospects.[49] This tendency to view the self in positive terms is heightened when

---

[44] *Id.*

[45] *Id.* at 1–3, 287; *see also* Nancy B. Rapoport, *The Curious Incident of the Law Firm That Did Nothing in the Night-Time*, 10 LEGAL ETHICS 98, 98–114 (2007) (reviewing REGAN, *supra* note 13).

[46] John M. Darley, *The Cognitive and Social Psychology of Contagious Organizational Corruption*, 70 BROOK. L. REV. 1177, 1180 (2005).

[47] Emily Pronin et al., *Objectivity in the Eye of the Beholder: Divergent Perceptions of Bias in Self Versus Others*, 111 PSYCHOL. REV. 781, 793 (2004); Lee Ross & Andrew Ward, *Naïve Realism in Everyday Life: Implications for Social Conflict and Misunderstanding*, in VALUES AND KNOWLEDGE 103, 110–11 (Edward S. Reed et al. eds., 1996).

[48] *See, e.g.*, DAVID ALAIN ARMOR, THE ILLUSION OF OBJECTIVITY: A BIAS IN THE PERCEPTION OF FREEDOM FROM BIAS (1998) (unpublished Ph.D. dissertation, University of California Los Angeles); Scott T. Allison et al., *On Being Better but Not Smarter Than Others: The Muhammad Ali Effect*, 7 SOC. COGNITION 275, 291 (1989); Nicholas Epley & David Dunning, *Feeling "Holier Than Thou": Are Self-Serving Assessments Produced by Errors in Self- or Social Prediction?*, 79 J. PERSONALITY & SOC. PSYCHOL. 861, 861 (2000); Roderick M. Kramer et al., *Self-Enhancement Biases and Negotiator Judgment: Effects of Self-Esteem and Mood*, 56 ORGANIZATIONAL BEHAV. & HUM. DECISION PROCESSES 110, 124 (1993); Wim B.G. Liebrand et al., *Why We Are Fairer Than Others: A Cross-Cultural Replication and Extension*, 22 J. EXPERIMENTAL SOC. PSYCHOL. 590 (1986); David M. Messick et al., *Why We Are Fairer Than Others*, 21 J. EXPERIMENTAL SOC. PSYCHOL. 480 (1985).

[49] *See, e.g.*, Roger Buehler et al., *The Planning Fallacy: Cognitive, Motivational, and Social Origins*, 43 Advances EXPERIMENTAL SOC. PSYCHOL. 1, 8 (2010); Jane Goodman-Delahunty et al., *Insightful or Wishful: Lawyers' Ability to Predict Case Outcomes*, 16 PSYCHOL., PUB. POL'Y, & L. 133, 144–45 (2010); Don A. Moore & Paul J. Healy, *The Trouble With Overconfidence*, 115 PSYCHOL. REV. 502, 502 (2008).

the characteristic at issue is socially desirable—as is the case with ethical behavior. Indeed, attorneys tend to believe that their own ethics and their firm's ethical standards are more stringent than those of other attorneys and other firms.[50]

These views of the self can lead to an ethical blind spot that impedes our ability to perceive and thoughtfully consider the ethical tensions we inevitably face.[51] If we are objective, fair, and unbiased, then we need not be concerned that we might take unfair advantage of another or unfairly privilege one person or position over another. If we are competent, then we need not question our ability to act or decide appropriately. If we are deserving, then any benefits we receive must be warranted. If we do not realize that our judgments of fairness are influenced by our own interests, then we do not need to be on guard against such conflicts.[52] And if we are overconfident—in our own ethical judgment, or in our ability to fix or otherwise manage ethical problems—then we are unlikely to stop and think carefully about a decision or to revisit that decision later.

In addition, people commonly make inaccurate forecasts of their own future emotions and behavior—and, thus, may predict that they will act ethically when this is not necessarily so.[53] It is clear that in the heat of the moment, we respond to a variety of incentives and practical forces.[54] We want to impress (or at least not disappoint) the client by reaching the settlement, getting the contract signed,

---

[50] Jonathan R.B. Halbesleben et al., *The Role of Pluralistic Ignorance in Perceptions of Unethical Behavior: An Investigation of Attorneys' and Students' Perceptions of Ethical Behavior,* 14 ETHICS & BEHAV. 17, 18 (2004). With regard to attorneys' views of their firms, see Gordon, *supra* note 27; Messikomer, *supra* note 14; Nelson, *supra* note 33.

[51] Dolly Chugh et al., *Bounded Ethicality as a Psychological Barrier to Recognizing Conflicts of Interest,* in CONFLICTS OF INTEREST: CHALLENGES AND SOLUTIONS IN BUSINESS, LAW, MEDICINE, AND PUBLIC POLICY 74, 80 (Don A. Moore et al. eds., 2005). *See generally* Pronin et al., *supra* note 47; Richard F. West et al., *Cognitive Sophistication Does Not Attenuate the Bias Blind Spot,* 103 J. PERSONALITY & SOC. PSYCHOL. 506 (2012).

[52] Nicholas Epley & Eugene M. Caruso, *Egocentric Ethics,* 17 SOC. JUST. RES. 171, 181–82 (2004).

[53] *See, e.g.,* Kristina A. Diekmann et al., *From Self-Prediction to Self-Defeat: Behavioral Forecasting, Self-Fulfilling Prophecies, and the Effect of Competitive Expectations,* 85 J. PERSONALITY & SOC. PSYCHOL. 672, 674 (2003) (finding that people mispredict their behavior in negotiation); Oriel Feldman Hall et al., *What We Say and What We Do: The Relationship Between Real and Hypothetical Moral Choices,* 123 COGNITION 434, 438 (2012); Janet K. Swim & Lauri L. Hyers, *Excuse Me—What Did You Just Say?! Women's Public and Private Responses to Sexist Remarks,* 35 J. EXPERIMENTAL SOC. PSYCHOL. 68, 83 (1999); Julie A. Woodzicka & Marianne LaFrance, *Real Versus Imagined Gender Harassment,* 57 J. SOC. ISSUES 15, 24 (2001) (finding that people mispredict their response to inappropriate interview questions). *See generally* Emily Balcetis & David A. Dunning, *A Mile in Moccasins: How Situational Experience Diminishes Dispositionism in Social Inference,* 34 PERSONALITY & SOC. PSYCHOL. BULL. 102 (2008); Buehler et al., *supra* note 49 (finding that people predict they will get projects done more quickly than they do).

[54] Karl Aquino et al., *Testing a Social-Cognitive Model of Moral Behavior: The Interactive Influence of Situations and Moral Identity Centrality,* 97 J. PERSONALITY & SOC. PSYCHOL. 123, 131 (2009); Ann E. Tenbrunsel, *Misrepresentation and Expectations of Misrepresentation in an Ethical Dilemma: The Role of Incentives and Temptation,* 41 ACAD. MGMT. J. 330, 334–35 (1998) (finding that incentives increase temptation and also the likelihood of acting on temptation); *see also* Uri Gneezy, *Deception: The Role of Consequences,* 95 AM. ECON. REV. 384, 391 (2005).

or winning the case. We want to be seen (and to see ourselves) as competent.[55] Members of a firm don't want to act against the culture of the firm,[56] or put their promotion or job at risk.[57] Decision makers feel pressure to make decisions quickly and efficiently. But when we are predicting our future behavior, we focus on our idealistic self—the self that "places principles and values above practical considerations and seeks to express the person's sense of true self."[58] With this ideal self in mind, abstract ethical considerations, rather than situational pressures, tend to be our focus and we anticipate that we will act ethically. When the time horizon shortens and we are in the moment, our attention shifts to our pragmatic self—the self that is "primarily guided by practical concerns" and is likely to seize opportunity, act impulsively, and focus on the pragmatics of the situation.[59]

B. Slippery Slopes and Boiling Frogs

Another factor that can contribute to our bounded ethics is that the path to unethical conduct often runs along a slippery slope. Just as it is frequently extremely difficult for people to visually detect changes in their environment,[60] so can it be quite difficult to notice when conduct degrades gradually. Psychologist Stanley Milgram famously found that people would follow the instructions of an experimenter to administer slightly increasingly severe shocks to another person, ostensibly as part of an experiment on punishment and learning.[61] The step-by-step nature of the shift may be one reason why so many people (63% of

---

55 Dennis J. Moberg, *Ethics Blind Spots in Organizations: How Systematic Errors in Person Perception Undermine Moral Agency*, 27 ORGANIZATIONAL STUD. 413, 417 (2006).

56 *See, e.g.*, Kirkland, *supra* note 33, at 705 (noting that lawyers are affected by the "logic of their firms").

57 *See, e.g.*, Garcetti v. Ceballos, 547 U.S. 410, 426 (2006) (refusing to grant First Amendment protection to deputy district attorney who alleged he was denied a promotion after criticizing the legitimacy of a warrant); *see also* Fox, *supra* note 33, at 949 (discussing fears of junior associate who knew he ought to report partner's unethical conduct).

58 Yifat Kivetz & Tom R. Tyler, *Tomorrow I'll Be Me: The Effect of Time Perspective on the Activation of Idealistic Versus Pragmatic Selves,* 102 ORGANIZATIONAL BEHAV. & HUM. DECISION PROCESSES 193, 193 (2007).

59 *Id.; see also* Hal E. Hershfield et al., *Short Horizons and Tempting Situations: Lack of Continuity to Our Future Selves Leads to Unethical Decision Making and Behavior,* 117 ORGANIZATIONAL BEHAV. & HUM. DECISION PROCESSES 298, 303 (2012) (finding that feeling continuous with and able to imagine one's future self makes future consequences more prominent and decreases unethical behavior); Daniel Read et al., *Mixing Virtue and Vice: Combining the Immediacy Effect and the Diversification Heuristic,* 12 J. BEHAV. DECISION MAKING 257, 258 (1999); Yaacov Trope & Nira Liberman, *Temporal Construal,* 110 PSYCHOL. REV. 403, 403 (2003). More generally, taking a broad perspective is less likely to result in unethical behavior than is a narrow perspective that focuses on individual decisions in isolation. Amos Schurr et al., *Is That the Answer You Had In Mind? The Effect of Perspective on Unethical Behavior,* 7 JUDGMENT & DECISION MAKING 679, 679 (2012).

60 *See, e.g.,* Daniel J. Simons et al., *Change Blindness in the Absence of a Visual Disruption,* 29 PERCEPTION 1143, 1143 (2000).

61 STANLEY MILGRAM, OBEDIENCE TO AUTHORITY 123 (1974); *see also* Jerry M. Burger, *Replicating Milgram: Would People Still Obey Today?,* 64 AM. PSYCHOL. 1, 8 (2009) (attempting to partially replicate Milgram's study and obtaining similar results).

participants) ended up being willing to administer shocks that elicited increasingly "desperate" cries of pain to the point that the other person became seemingly non-responsive.[62] It seems that the gradual intensification of the shock made it difficult for participants to determine precisely when they were being asked to cross the line. This ride down the slippery ethics slope turns out to be a bit like the apocryphal story about how to boil frogs: "Folk wisdom says that if you throw a frog in boiling water, it will jump out. But if you put a frog in nice warm water and slowly raise the temperature, by the time the frog realizes the water has become too hot, it will already be cooked."[63]

Early decisions may be made in circumstances in which the ethical course of action is not clear. Wanting to believe that the small steps we have already taken have been good ones and preferring to act in ways that are consistent with our previous behavior,[64] we find it difficult to shift course. Eventually, as a practice becomes routine, the points at which deliberation might have occurred disappear, as do the decision's ethical contours.[65] "Over time, people become more comfortable pushing the boundaries of professional propriety, and they also find themselves having to continue previous courses of action in order to avoid admitting that their earlier actions were improper."[66]

C. Ethical Fading

Ethical blindspots and the contours of the slippery slope contribute to a process of ethical fading or moral disengagement in which decision makers "do not 'see' the moral components of an ethical decision, not so much because they are morally uneducated, but because psychological processes fade the 'ethics' from an ethical dilemma."[67] A variety of additional psychological processes also play a

---

[62] Burger, *supra* note 61, at 8.

[63] Bazerman & Moore, *supra* note 37, at 48; *see also* Francesca Gino & Max H. Bazerman, *When Misconduct Goes Unnoticed: The Acceptability of Gradual Erosion in Others' Unethical Behavior,* 45 J. EXPERIMENTAL SOC. PSYCHOL. 708, 717 (2009).

[64] *See* ROBERT B. CIALDINI, INFLUENCE: SCIENCE AND PRACTICE 52 (5th ed. 2009).

[65] *See* Blake E. Ashforth & Vikas Anand, *The Normalization of Corruption in Organizations,* 25 RES. ORGANIZATIONAL BEHAV. 1, 3 (2003); Linda K. Treviño et al., *Behavioral Ethics in Organizations: A Review,* 32 J. MGMT. 951, 970 (2006). *See generally* HERBERT C. KELMAN & V. LEE HAMILTON, CRIMES OF OBEDIENCE 18 (1989).

[66] Don A. Moore & George Loewenstein, *Self-Interest, Automaticity, and the Psychology of Conflict of Interest,* 17 SOC. JUST. RES. 189, 196 (2004); *see also* Michael Guttentag, *Stumbling into Crime: Stochastic Process Models of Accounting Fraud,* in RESEARCH HANDBOOK ON THE ECONOMICS OF CRIMINAL LAW 204 (Alon Harel & Keith Hylton eds., 2011); Donald C. Langevoort, *Getting (Too) Comfortable: In-House Lawyers, Enterprise Risk, and the Financial Crisis* (Georgetown Pub. Law and Legal Theory Research Paper, No. 11-135, 2011), available at http://scholarship.law.georgetown.edu/cgi/viewcontent.cgi?article=1156&context=fwps_papers (noting that "by the time reality starts to set in, our complicity is set as well").

[67] Ann E. Tenbrunsel & David M. Messick, *Ethical Fading: The Role of Self-Deception in Unethical Behavior,* 17 SOC. JUST. RES. 223, 224 (2004); *see also* Albert Bandura, *Moral Disengagement in the Perpetration of* Inhumanities,

role in fading ethical considerations from view, making unethical decisions more likely.

For example, the scripts—knowledge structures that guide our understanding of how events typically unfold—that govern a particular situation may determine whether or not ethical considerations are taken into account.[68] One "may approach a particular [decision] with a script that has moral content, triggering moral judgment processes, or with one that is devoid of moral content, triggering non-moral judgment processes."[69] The relevant script may characterize a particular decision—such as whether a conflict is an obstacle to taking on representation of a new client—as a business decision as opposed to an ethical decision, fading the ethical implications from view.[70] Consider the Ford Pinto. The Pinto's gas tank was susceptible to rupture and burst into flames in slow-speed crashes. Observe how Ford's Field Recall Coordinator describes his reaction to early reports of fires involving the Pinto:

> My cue for labeling a case as a problem either required high frequencies of occurrence or directly-traceable causes. I had little time for speculative contemplation on potential problems that did not fit a pattern that suggested known courses of action leading to possible recall. . . . I remember no strong ethical overtones to the case

3 PERSONALITY & SOC. PSYCHOL. REV. 193, 193 (1999); James R. Detert et al., *Moral Disengagement in Ethical Decision Making: A Study of Antecedents and Outcomes,* 93 J. APPLIED PSYCHOL. 374, 374 (2008); Moore et al., *supra* note 31, at 2.

68 *See* Robert P. Abelson, *Psychological Status of the Script Concept,* 36 AM. PSYCHOLOGIST 715, 715 (1981).

69 Kenneth D. Butterfield et al., *Moral Awareness in Business Organizations: Influences of Issue-Related and Social Context Factors,* 53 HUM. REL. 981, 989 (2000).

70 *See id.;* Tenbrunsel & Messick, *supra* note 67. Aspects of a situation can evoke business or competitive norms. *See, e.g.,* Aaron C. Kay et al., *Material Priming: The Influence of Mundane Physical Objects on Situational Construal and Competitive Behavioral Choice,* 95 ORGANIZATIONAL BEHAV. & HUM. DECISION PROCESSES 83 (2004) (finding that those primed with things associated with business tend to act less cooperatively); Maryam Kouchaki et al., *Seeing Green: Mere Exposure to Money Triggers a Business Decision Frame and Unethical Outcomes,* 121 ORGANIZATIONAL BEHAV. & HUM. DECISION PROCESSES 53 (2013); Kathleen D. Vohs et al., *The Psychological Consequences of Money,* 314 SCI. 1154, 1154 (2006) (finding that when reminded of money, people tend to behave more selfishly); Francesca Gino & Lamar Pierce, *The Abundance Effect: Unethical Behavior in the Presence of Wealth,* 109 ORGANIZATIONAL BEHAV. & HUM. DECISION PROCESSES 142, 142 (2009); *see also* Qing Yang et al., *Diverging Effects of Clean Versus Dirty Money on Attitudes, Values, and Interpersonal Behavior,* 104 J. PERSONALITY & SOC. PSYCHOL. 473, 473 (2013). For evidence that clearing conflicts is often thought of as a business, rather than an ethical, decision, see Kimberly Kirkland, *Ethical Infrastructures and De Facto Ethical Norms at Work in Large US Law Firms: The Role of Ethics Counsel,* 11 LEGAL ETHICS 181, 181 (2008). More generally, legal rules or practices may cue moral intuitions in a variety of ways. *See, e.g.,* Ben Depoorter & Stephan W. Tontrup, *How Law Frames Moral Intuitions: The Expressive Effect of Specific Performance,* 54 ARIZ. L. REV. 673, 673 (2012); Uri Gneezy & Aldo Rustichini, *A Fine is a Price,* 29 J. LEGAL STUD. 1, 1 (2000); Tess Wilkinson-Ryan & Jonathan Baron, *Moral Judgment and Moral Heuristics in Breach of Contract,* 6 J. EMPIRICAL LEG. STUD. 405, 405 (2009).

> whatsoever. It was a very straightforward decision, driven by dominant scripts for the time, place, and context.[71]

The early reports of Pintos "lighting up" did not fit the Coordinator's schema for what a problem would look like—these reports "trickle[d] in" and "did not fit the pattern of recallable standards; the evidence was not overwhelming that the car was defective in some way." Accordingly, the ethical dimensions of the decision about whether to recall were not focal in his mind.[72]

This account is consistent with lawyers' frequent reactions to discussions of ethics. In interviews, lawyers' responses

> suggest[ ] that they simply did not think very much about legal ethics or that they did not consider the issues they confronted in moral or ethical terms. One lawyer explained that he did not confront ethical issues because "when you're dealing with big companies, it doesn't seem to come up." . . . In some cases lawyers appeared to be so acculturated to certain practices they did not consider the ethical issues implicated by those practices.[73]

Certain routine decisions or practices—providing competent services, maintaining sufficient support staff, or communicating with clients—may not be thought of as raising ethical issues in the same ways as more egregious behaviors, such as fraudulent misrepresentation or sleeping with a client.[74] But, these practices are covered by the formal rules of ethics[75] and tend to comprise a significant proportion of the complaints made to bar disciplinary authorities.[76]

Along these same lines, the language that we use to describe a particular act or decision can mask its ethical contours. Euphemisms—such as friendly fire, collateral damage, downsizing, strategic misrepresentation, creative time-keeping, bluffing, decedent, a case with bad facts, or Ford Pintos lighting up—can strip the decision of much of its ethical content.[77] These effects of language can even be seen in the ways that lawyers prefer to talk about ethical issues. Lawyers tend to

---

71 Dennis A. Gioia, *Pinto Fires and Personal Ethics: A Script Analysis of Missed Opportunities,* 11 J. BUS. ETHICS 379, 381–82, 388 (1992).

72 *Id.* at 380; *see also* Mark Dowie, *Pinto Madness,* MOTHER JONES, Sept./Oct. 1977, available at http://www.motherjones.com/politics/1977/09/pinto-madness.

73 Levin, *supra* note 17, at 336 (citation omitted).

74 *See, e.g., id.* at 336 (finding that attorneys were unlikely to raise such routine issues in discussions of ethics).

75 *See infra* note 91.

76 *See supra* note 14.

77 Tenbrunsel & Messick, *supra* note 67, at 226; *see also* Bandura, *supra* note 67, at 195; William Safire, *The Fine Art of Euphemism,* S.F. SUN. EXAMINER & CHRON., May 13, 1979, at 34.

shy away from labeling behavior as "misconduct," and are seemingly more comfortable discussing issues involving "gray areas" or "incivility."[78]

This minimizing of the ethical implications of an act is also seen in the ways that we compare the act to other real or hypothetical acts. One might be able to construct a tenuous justification for the unethical act.[79] And, it is usually possible to imagine instances of behavior that are worse than the act at issue and such advantageous comparisons can be used to cast a particular decision in a more positive light.[80] Indeed, this sort of comparison is common among lawyers who have been disciplined for ethical breaches, with lawyers pointing to more egregious breaches than those with which they are charged.[81]

The perceived moral intensity of a decision can also be influenced by the ease with which the nature, magnitude, probability, and timing of any potential consequences can be drawn to mind.[82] For example, decisions are seen as more unethical when they result in observable harm (the outcome bias)[83] and when they harm identifiable victims.[84] In contrast, when harm is perceived as less likely to occur or more removed in time, the decision will feel less ethically fraught.[85]

Decision makers are also more likely to engage in a range of unethical behaviors when facing a decision that is framed as a loss than when the same

---

78 Messikomer, *supra* note 14, at 742; *see also* RICHARD L. ABEL, LAWYERS IN THE DOCK: LEARNING FROM ATTORNEY DISCIPLINARY PROCEEDINGS 101 (2008) (noting disciplined lawyer's argument that he "was guilty of 'mistakes,' not 'professional misconduct.' ").

79 *See* Shaul Shalvi et al., *Justified Ethicality: Observing Desired Counterfactuals Modifies Ethical Perceptions and Behavior,* 115 ORGANIZATIONAL BEHAV. & HUM. DECISION PROCESSES 181, 181 (2011); *see also* Francesca Gino & Dan Ariely, *The Dark Side of Creativity: Original Thinkers Can Be More Dishonest,* 102 J. PERSONALITY & SOC. PSYCHOL. 445, 446 (2012); Shaul Shalvi et al., *Honesty Requires Time (and Lack of Justifications),* 23 PSYCHOL. SCI. 1264, 1264 (2012).

80 *See* Bandura, *supra* note 67, at 196.

81 Abel, *supra* note 78, at 32, 200.

82 This is an instance of the availability heuristic. When particular information is available or accessible in memory, it has a greater influence on judgments and decisions. *See, e.g.,* Amos Tversky & Daniel Kahneman, *Availability: A Heuristic for Judging Frequency and Probability,* 4 COGNITIVE PSYCHOL. 207 (1973).

83 The outcome bias occurs when people judge the quality of a decision based on its outcome—for example, decisions resulting in negative consequences are judged to have been bad decisions. *See* Jonathan Baron & John C. Hershey, *Outcome Bias in Decision Evaluation,* 54 J. PERSONALITY & SOC. PSYCHOL. 569, 569 (1988); Francesca Gino et al., *No Harm, No Foul: The Outcome Bias in Ethical Judgments* (Harv. Bus. School, Working Paper No. 08-080, 2008).

84 Francesca Gino et al., *Nameless + Harmless = Blameless: When Seemingly Irrelevant Factors Influence Judgment of (Un)ethical Behavior,* 111 ORGANIZATIONAL BEHAV. & HUM. DECISION PROCESSES 93, 94 (2010); *see also* Karen E. Jenni & George Loewenstein, *Explaining the "Identifiable Victim Effect,"* 14 J. RISK & UNCERTAINTY 235, 236 (1997).

85 Sefa Hayibor & David M Wasieleski, *Effects of the Use of the Availability Heuristic on Ethical Decision-Making in Organizations,* 84 J. BUS. ETHICS 151, 153 (2009); *see also* Kish-Gephart et al., *supra* note 31, at 5.

decision is framed as a gain.[86] For instance, professional tax preparers have been found to be more likely to approve returns containing large deductions associated with ambiguous tax rules when they are faced with the possibility of losing an existing client as compared to when they are in the position of trying to develop new clients.[87] In addition, decision makers who are falling just short of reaching their goals are more likely to act unethically (for example, to misrepresent their performance).[88]

Consider how this might apply to a young associate trying to meet the firm's billable hour requirement. Taking the billable hour requirement as the relevant reference point, the associate may fall just short and may perceive this failure as a loss.[89] Both of these features of the situation tend to increase the likelihood of unethical behavior. Similarly, a client and lawyer who are engaged in selling an unsuccessful business[90] are likely to find themselves in a loss frame and at greater risk of unethical behavior. By the same token, once one has stumbled into an unethical decision, considerations about what to do next are likely to be made in a loss frame. One can own up to one's unethical decision and face the negative consequences now, or keep quiet and face a possible and uncertain loss sometime in the future. Such a posture can make risk-seeking behavior more likely.

II. Ethics in Law Practice

The psychological tendencies that may lead people to behave unethically can be compounded by particular aspects of legal practice. The rules governing professional conduct, the agency relationship between attorney and client, the role

---

86 Jessica S. Cameron & Dale T. Miller, *Ethical Standards in Gain Versus Loss Frames*, in PSYCHOLOGICAL PERSPECTIVES ON ETHICAL BEHAVIOR AND DECISION MAKING 91 (David De Cremer ed., 2009); Mary C. Kern & Dolly Chugh, *Bounded Ethicality: The Perils of Loss Framing*, 20 PSYCHOL. SCI. 378, 378 (2009); Jeffrey J. Rachlinski, *Gains, Losses, and the Psychology of Litigation*, 70 S. CAL. L. REV. 113, 119 (1996) (Study 2); Christopher P. Reinders Folmer & David De Cremer, *Bad for Me or Bad for Us? Interpersonal Orientations and the Impact of Losses on Unethical Behavior*, 38 PERSONALITY & SOC. PSYCHOL. BULL. 760, 766–77 (2012) (exploring moderators of the effect of loss frame on ethics); *see also* Francesca Gino & Joshua D. Margolis, *Bringing Ethics Into Focus: How Regulatory Focus and Risk Preferences Influence (Un)Ethical Behavior*, 115 ORGANIZATIONAL BEHAV. & HUM. DECISION PROCESSES 145, 147 (2011); *see generally* Daniel Kahneman & Amos Tversky, *Choices, Values, & Frames*, 39 AM. PSYCHOL. 341, 343–44 (1984).

87 Kaye J. Newberry et al., *An Examination of Tax Practitioner Decisions: The Role of Preparer Sanctions and Framing Effects Associated with Client Condition*, 14 J. ECON. PSYCHOL. 439, 441 (1993); *see also* Henry S. J. Robben et al., *Decision Frame and Opportunity as Determinants of Tax Cheating: An International Experimental Study*, 11 J. ECON. PSYCHOL. 341, 344–45 (1990); Elizabeth F. Loftus, *To File, Perchance to Cheat*, PSYCHOL. TODAY, Apr. 1985, at 35, 37–38.

88 Maurice E. Schweitzer et al., *Goal Setting as a Motivator of Unethical Behavior*, 47 ACAD. MGMT. J. 422, 422 (2004).

89 Cameron & Miller, *supra* note 86, at 102–03.

90 *See* Richard W. Painter, *Lawyers' Rules, Auditors' Rules and the Psychology of Concealment*, 84 MINN. L. REV. 1399, 1417–18 (2000).

of advocate, the demands of practice, the status inherent in the legal profession, and the social environment of the firm or practice area can all influence how lawyers make decisions about issues that implicate ethics. While we recognize that other professions face ethical challenges as well, we think it is helpful to focus on those aspects of law practice that are most likely to influence attorneys.

A. Ethical Rules and Standards

The regulation of lawyers' professional conduct draws on rules and norms from a variety of sources. Attorneys are, of course, regulated by the rules of professional conduct adopted in their own jurisdiction. These rules typically cover, for example, conflicts of interest, veracity, confidentiality, advertising, billing, trust funds, and sex with clients.[91] Ethical constraints in particular contexts are also sometimes set out in statutes or regulations. For example, statutory provisions governing wiretapping,[92] corporate accountability,[93] and foreign corruption[94] require particular disclosures, proscribe certain behavior, or seek to hold lawyers accountable in other ways. Court rules regarding evidence, discovery, and other matters provide additional regulation.[95]

While abundant, the ethical rules governing attorneys leave many gaps, and can be ambiguous and even conflicting.[96] In addition, many of these rules articulate a minimum standard of conduct that must be supplemented with guidance from one's own internal moral code.[97] The frequent opacity of the Model Rules of Professional Conduct is attributable, at least in part, to the potential for

---

91 *See, e.g.*, N.Y. RULES OF PROF'L CONDUCT R. 1.7 (2009) (Conflict of Interest: Current Clients); ILL. RULES OF PROF'L CONDUCT R. 3.3 (2010) (Candor Toward the Tribunal); CAL. RULES OF PROF'L CONDUCT R. 1–400 (2012) (Advertising and Solicitation).

92 18 U.S.C. §§ 2510–22 (2006).

93 Sarbanes-Oxley Act of 2002, Pub. L. No. 107–204, 116 Stat. 745.

94 Foreign Corrupt Practices Act of 1977, 15 U.S.C. § 78dd–1 (2006).

95 Recall that John Gellene, the attorney in our opening example, was tripped up by Bankruptcy Rule 2014. *See* Fed. R. Bankr. P. 2014 (requiring "a verified statement of the person to be employed setting forth the person's connections with the debtor, creditors, any other party in interest, their respective attorneys and accountants, the United States trustee, or any person employed in the office of the United States trustee"). *See generally* Fred C. Zacharias & Bruce A. Green, *Rationalizing Judicial Regulation of Lawyers*, 70 OHIO ST. L.J. 73 (2009) (discussing different forms of lawyer regulation).

96 *See* Wendel, *supra* note 9, at 1168 (arguing that the rules can never be completely clear).

97 *See* MODEL RULES OF PROF'L CONDUCT, Preamble and Scope (2010) (noting the importance of a lawyer's "personal conscience" as a guide to professional responsibility and observing that the "Rules do not . . . exhaust the moral and ethical considerations that should inform a lawyer, for no worthwhile human activity can be completely defined by legal rules"); *see also* Suchman, *infra* note 101, at 837 ("[A]n ethical profession requires more than just professional ethics. It requires a sense of right and wrong . . . that rises above the letter of the rules . . . [and] a set of social structures for creating, preserving, and transmitting this understanding in the face of real-world challenges."); Fred C. Zacharias, *Integrity Ethics*, 22 GEO. J. LEGAL ETHICS 541, 541 (2009) (arguing that "the very structure of the codes is to provide a framework under which lawyers can and will act as ordinary moral individuals").

intense tension between the duty to diligently represent one's client and duties to opponents, to the public at large, or to the judicial system.[98] While the Prologue to the Model Rules contemplates that these various responsibilities "are usually harmonious,"[99] it also recognizes that "[v]irtually all difficult ethical problems arise from conflict between a lawyer's responsibilities to clients, to the legal system and to the lawyer's own interest in remaining an ethical person while earning a satisfactory living."[100] The Rules endeavor to resolve these conflicts when possible, but also provide that often "[s]uch issues must be resolved through the exercise of sensitive professional and moral judgment guided by the basic principles underlying the Rules."[101]

Resolving such ambiguities is particularly challenging because while laudable values can underlie good behavior, they can also motivate unethical behavior.[102] And, lawyers' expertise at parsing rules, paying attention to exceptions and loopholes, interpreting text, and making arguments on both sides of an issue, while commendable in many ways, can also be problematic in this context.[103] Indeed, psychologists have compared the process of post-hoc moral reasoning to that of lawyering: "moral reasoning is not left free to search for truth but is likely to be hired out like a lawyer by various motives, employed only to seek confirmation of preordained conclusions."[104] This lawyerly approach can

---

[98] MODEL RULES OF PROF'L CONDUCT, Prologue (2010) ("A lawyer, as a member of the legal profession, is a representative of clients, an officer of the legal system and a public citizen having special responsibility for the quality of justice.").

[99] *Id.*

[100] *Id.; see also* Keith Leavitt *et al.,* Different Hats, Different Obligations: Plural Occupational Identities and Situated Moral Judgments, 55 ACAD. MGMT. J. 1316 (2012) (exploring the effects on moral judgment of different occupational identities and roles).

[101] *Id.; see also* Mark C. Suchman, *Working Without a Net: The Sociology of Legal Ethics in Corporate Litigation,* 67 FORDHAM L. REV. 837, 837 (1998) ("[P]rofessional ethics must explicitly incorporate the existence of various competing moral obligations, in a way that purely aspirational principles . . . do not."). Attorneys who work in transnational contexts face even greater challenges as they will inevitably encounter conflicting rules and norms across jurisdictions. *See* John Flood, *Transnational Lawyering: Clients, Ethics, & Regulation,* in Lawyers in PRACTICE: ETHICAL DECISION MAKING IN CONTEXT 176, 182 (Leslie C. Levin & Lynn Mather eds., 2012).

[102] Jaime D. Crowley & Michael C. Gottlieb, *Objects in the Mirror are Closer Than They Appear: A Primary Prevention Model for Ethical Decision Making,* 43 PROF. PSYCHOL.: RES. & PRAC. 65, 68 (2012) ("Sound values can build resiliency, but they can also function as vulnerabilities."); Linda J. Skitka & G. Scott Morgan, *The Double Edged Sword of a Moral State of Mind,* in PERSONALITY, IDENTITY, AND CHARACTER: EXPLORATIONS IN MORAL PSYCHOLOGY, *supra* note 31, at 355; Alan C. Tjeltveit & Michael C. Gottlieb, *Avoiding the Road to Ethical Disaster: Overcoming Vulnerabilities and Developing Resilience,* 47 PSYCHOTHERAPY: THEORY, RES., PRAC., TRAINING 98, 98 (2010).

[103] While the ethics rules that are applicable to other professionals may share many of the features we have described, the particular analytical approach of lawyers may interact with the nature of the rules to make these characteristics more problematic. This strikes us as an interesting empirical question that would benefit from additional research.

[104] Jonathan Haidt, *The Emotional Dog and Its Rational Tail: A Social Intuitionist Approach to Moral Judgment,* 108 PSYCHOL. REV. 814, 822 (2001); *see also* JONAH LEHRER, HOW WE DECIDE 173 (2009) ("When it comes

contribute to unethical conduct when it comes to ethical rules that specify only minimum standards, that raise conflicting standards and gray areas, that involve discretionary application of underlying moral principles, and that may be supplemented by additional personal morality.

All of this is enhanced by the fact that lawyers tend to be more comfortable talking about "rules" and "norms" and less comfortable talking about "morality" or "values."[105] Indeed, law students conclude early on that what matters is not their opinion about a matter but whether they can articulate a credible argument, complicating their inclination to consult their own sense of right and wrong.[106] One study of lawyers' ethics found:

> When [attorneys] spoke of "doing the right thing," they tended to define this term as respecting some external source of authority or opinion: the civil discovery rules, ethics codes, judges' orders, clients' orders and preferences. They clearly preferred utilitarian (cost-benefit) analysis to normative reasoning, and they exhibited a positive allergy to moral language and an inclination to express even the norms of basic truth telling and fairness in compliance with the standard of some external standard or group.[107]

This discomfort echoes, and may stem in part from, debates over the role that personal morality should (or should not) play in conjunction with the lawyer's professional duties.[108] It may also encourage lawyers to take a minimalist approach to ethics, substituting rules that may only articulate minimum standards for thoughtful reflection on the ethical implications of a decision.

---

to making ethical decisions, human rationality isn't a scientist, it's a lawyer. This inner attorney gathers bits of evidence, post hoc justifications, and pithy rhetoric in order to make the automatic reaction seem reasonable.").

105 Messikomer, *supra* note 14, at 742; Lynn Mather & Leslie C. Levin, *Why Context Matters*, in LAWYERS IN PRACTICE: ETHICAL DECISION MAKING IN CONTEXT, *supra* note 101, at 11; *see also* Suchman, *supra* note 101, at 844–45. Business managers, too, resist casting decisions in moral terms. *See* Frederick B. Bird & James A. Waters, *The Moral Muteness of Managers*, 32 CAL. MGMT. REV. 73, 73 (1989); *see also* Tamar A. Kreps & Benoît Monin, *"Doing Well By Doing Good"? Ambivalent Moral Framing in Organizations*, 31 RES. ORGANIZATIONAL BEHAV. 99, 102 (2011).

106 Our thanks to a law student at the Yale-Quinnipiac Dispute Resolution Workshop for putting the problem in these terms.

107 Gordon, *supra* note 27, at 732.

108 DAVID LUBAN, LAWYERS AND JUSTICE: AN ETHICAL STUDY 394 (1988) (describing the "standard conception" of the lawyer's role as "partisanship and nonaccountability"); *see* Katherine R. Kruse, *The Jurisprudential Turn in Legal Ethics*, 53 ARIZ. L. REV. 493, 501 (2011) (describing the evolution of this debate); *see also* Gordon, *supra* note 21, at 1195 (describing conception of the adversary role and offering an alternative role for corporate lawyers).

Lawyers may also be affected by the human tendency to be less compliant with rules or authorities that they see as illegitimate.[109] Lawyers in different specialties or communities of practice may encounter different norms or find that particular rules fit the contours of that practice area more or less well.[110] Ethical guidelines that make sense for litigators may not fit transactional work as well—and vice versa.[111] Many solo and small firm attorneys see certain rules as calculated to "interfere with [their] business-getting activities" and, therefore, do not respect them.[112]

All of these factors can lead attorneys to adopt a situationist approach to ethics. In discussing discovery ethics with attorneys, for example, Robert Nelson found that "[t]he answer to almost every question was that it 'depends.' Aggressiveness generally is inappropriate, unless the war was initiated by the other side. Hardball usually is inappropriate, unless there is a specter of mischievous plaintiffs' lawyers waiting to use the information from discovery for other suits."[113]

In similar ways, ambiguity provides open space for other influences to operate as lawyers construct arguments about what is and is not appropriate.[114] In one study, the lawyers interviewed indicated that they "assumed that the 'real' meaning of ethical rules was consistent with pragmatic concerns, even when the letter of the rules was not."[115] Other lawyers talk about the need to "get comfortable" with what a client wants them to do—a process by which they convince themselves that a course of action is acceptable. This process of getting comfortable is made easier when the rules are ambiguous.[116]

---

[109] *See, e.g.*, TOM R. TYLER, WHY PEOPLE OBEY THE LAW 108 (2006); Tom R. Tyler, *Psychological Perspectives on Legitimacy and Legitimation*, 57 ANN. REV. PSYCHOL. 375, 387 (2006).

[110] Lynn Mather & Craig McEwen, *Client Grievances and Lawyer Conduct: The Challenges of Divorce Practice*, in LAWYERS IN PRACTICE: ETHICAL DECISION MAKING IN CONTEXT, *supra* note 101, at 69 (noting that the rules may "ignore the highly variable circumstances of legal practice . . . because they must be framed at a level of generality that crosses practice areas").

[111] Carrie Menkel-Meadow, *The Limits of Adversarial Ethics*, in ETHICS IN PRACTICE: LAWYERS' ROLES, RESPONSIBILITIES, AND REGULATION 123, 126 n.14 (Deborah L. Rhode ed., 2000); REGAN, *supra* note 13, at 328 (describing how conflicts of interest differ in litigation and transactional work).

[112] *See, e.g.*, Levin, *supra* note 17, at 371; *see also* Mather & Levin, *supra* note 105.

[113] Nelson, *supra* note 33, at 780 (emphasis added).

[114] *See* Wendel, *supra* note 9, at 1171 ("[N]o matter how clear a rule appears to be, it will always be ambiguous enough to be manipulated."). *See generally* Feldman, *supra* note 30, at 885 (describing how technocratic lawyering interferes with ethical decision making).

[115] Suchman, *supra* note 101, at 844 (emphasis added). *See also* Levin, *supra* note 17, at 369–71 (providing examples of small firm and individual practitioners who felt that there was a "disconnect" between the ethical rules and the "realities of practice").

[116] Langevoort, *supra* note 66, at 22.

B. The Agency Relationship

The fact that attorneys are charged with representing clients in agency relationships can complicate ethical decision making in several important ways. First, although an agent is expected to further the interests of the principal, it is clear that attorneys have their own personal interests that may or may not be directly compatible with those of their client. In addition, clients may be willing to engage in conduct through their attorneys that they would not engage in on their own. Similarly, lawyers who might not have been independently disposed to undertake or to propose a particular course of unethical conduct may be more willing to do so when it is suggested by a client.

1. The Role of the Lawyer's Interests

The interests of lawyer and client are often aligned and often favor ethical behavior. Specifically, lawyers and clients will generally share an interest in winning a case or negotiating a favorable deal.[117] Lawyers have interests in seeing themselves as ethical legal professionals, in avoiding discipline, and in maintaining a good reputation.[118] Clients, too, may have interests in behaving ethically.[119]

But, lawyers also routinely face situations in which their interests come into conflict with clients' interests and with their professional responsibilities. Lawyers' judgments can be influenced by a myriad of desires—including the desire to satisfy the client, to make partner, to generate fees, to manage their own cash flow, to win a case, to achieve or maintain a particular reputation or status, to "do justice," or to manage limited time.[120]

These interests can influence the ways in which lawyers seek out and interpret information and generate arguments.[121] There is a tendency to conflate what is fair or ethical with what serves one's own interest, especially as there are many metrics

---

117 Note that there are ethical limits on attorneys being too closely aligned with their client. *See, e.g.*, MODEL RULES OF PROF'L CONDUCT R. 1.8 (2010).

118 *See, e.g.*, Joshua E. Perry et al., *The Ethical Health Lawyer: An Empirical Assessment of Moral Decision Making*, 37 J. L. MED. & ETHICS 461, 466 (2009).

119 We recognize that clients may also have interests in behaving unethically, at least in the short run and as long as they don't get caught.

120 *See, e.g.*, Donald C. Langevoort & Robert K. Rasmussen, *Skewing the Results: The Role of Lawyers in Transmitting Legal Rules*, 5 S. CAL. INTERDISC. L.J. 375, 412 (1997) (discussing how attorney self-interest might affect advice about risk); Suchman, *supra* note 101 (describing the variety of interests that attorneys bring to ethical decision making). For a general discussion of how legal actors manage multiple, sometimes conflicting, interests, *see* Jennifer K. Robbennolt et al., *Symbolism and Incommensurability in Civil Sanctioning: Decision Makers as Goal Managers*, 68 BROOK. L. REV. 1121, 1153–54 (2003).

121 *See* Ziva Kunda, *The Case for Motivated Reasoning*, 108 PSYCHOL. BULL. 480, 480 (1990).

by which one can judge fairness.[122] And, confirmation bias can lead us to interpret new information in ways that favor our existing beliefs and to ignore dissent or other indications of ethical challenges.[123] Thus, when an unethical course of action serves our interests, it may be easy to latch on to the particular metric that validates that course of action or to interpret the facts or the law in ways that are consistent with a judgment that the desired course of action is appropriate. "The ethical failure [then,] is not in the commitment to fairness but in the biased interpretation of information."[124] But because we tend to believe that we make decisions based on objective criteria—the illusion of objectivity—it is difficult for us to recognize these effects.[125]

Such interests can affect how attorneys bill their time, the factual and legal conclusions they draw, how they behave in negotiation, and the advice they give their clients. Consider, for example, the lawyers advising Enron, who "agreed to review the propriety of Enron transactions in which [the lawyers'] own services had been used."[126] It would not be surprising if the lawyers were motivated (consciously or unconsciously) to find that those prior transactions had been appropriate.[127] Consider, too, how an attorney might feel the need to engage in puffing in order to land a particular client, how an attorney might be influenced by the desire to obtain or keep a client, or how an attorney's desire for or fear of publicity might impact his representation of a client.

Or think about how different billing arrangements might influence lawyer decision making.[128] A lawyer who is paid by the hour might be inclined to spend

---

[122] *See* Morton Deutsch, *Equity, Equality, and Need: What Determines Which Value Will be Used as the Basis of Distributive Justice?*, 31 J. SOC. ISSUES 137, 147 (1975).

[123] Scott Sonenshein, *The Role of Construction, Intuition, and Justification in Responding to Ethical Issues at Work: The Sensemaking-Intuition Model*, 32 ACAD. MGMT. REV. 1022, 1029–30 (2007). *See generally* Raymond S. Nickerson, *Confirmation Bias: A Ubiquitous Phenomenon in Many Guises*, 2 REV. GEN. PSYCHOL. 175, 175 (1998); Barbara O'Brien, *Prime Suspect: An Examination of Factors that Aggravate and Counteract Confirmation Bias in Criminal Investigations*, 15 PSYCHOL. PUB. POL'Y & L. 315, 315 (2009).

[124] Chugh et al., *supra* note 51, at 83; *see also* David M. Messick & Keith P. Sentis, *Fairness and Preference*, 15 J. EXPERIMENTAL SOC. PSYCHOL. 418, 418 (1979).

[125] Armor, *supra* note 48, at 11–12.

[126] Deborah L. Rhode, *Moral Counseling*, 75 FORDHAM L. REV. 1317, 1334 (2006).

[127] If the lawyers were to find that their own prior advice was improper, they might not only embarrass themselves but also expose themselves to possible legal liability. *See* Roger C. Cramton, *Enron and the Corporate Lawyer: A Primer on Legal and Ethical Issues*, 58 BUS. LAW. 143, 164–66 (2002).

[128] *See* SUSAN SHAPIRO, TANGLED LOYALTIES: CONFLICT OF INTEREST IN LEGAL PRACTICE 242–46 (2002); A.B.A. Commission on Billable Hours Report 2001–2002, at 5 (2002), available at http://ilta.ebiz.uapps.net/productfiles/productfiles/914311/FMPG4_ABABillableHours2002.pdf; Geoffrey P. Miller, *Some Agency Problems in Settlement*, 16 J. LEGAL STUD. 189, 193–95 (1987). *See generally* Herbert M. Kritzer, *Lawyer Fees and Lawyer Behavior in Litigation: What Does the Empirical Literature Really Say?*, 80 TEX. L. REV. 1943, 1979–80 (2002).

more (conceivably unnecessary) time on a matter, be "aggressive rather than conservative" in billing his time, and have a tendency to be slow in settling his clients' disputes.[129] In contrast, a lawyer who is paid on a flat-fee or other fixed-rate basis might be inclined to minimize the amount of time devoted to the matter.[130] And, while a lawyer working on a contingent fee may be motivated to spend time on the case in order to increase the amount of the verdict, settlement, or deal on which her fee will be based, she will only want to do so to the extent that such an increase is greater than her investment.[131] In addition, the contingent fee attorney may be more likely to focus on the financial aspects of settlement which will impact her fee, rather than non-financial aspects which could benefit the client but not directly benefit the lawyer.

Finally, consider the case of the lawyer who represented the plaintiff in a sexual harassment and discrimination suit.[132] During a break in a deposition, plaintiff found a set of privileged documents belonging to the other side on a conference room table, read them, and removed them from the room.[133] Upon learning of his client's action and unsure about how to respond, the lawyer began to interpret the facts in a favorable way (noting that the documents "were right in front of her" and were not marked "confidential"), to blame the other side ("they certainly knew how to handle documents"), and to read selectively prior case law (relying on a case involving the inadvertent delivery of privileged documents). He obtained a second opinion, but from someone who also had an interest in the outcome of the case. In all these ways, he convinced himself that the use of the documents was allowable.[134]

2. Conflicts and Disclosure

Conflicts of interest can arise not only between attorneys and their clients, but also between the interests of multiple clients, or between current and future

---

129 *See* Jean R. Sternlight, *Lawyers' Representation of Clients in Mediation: Using Economics and Psychology to Structure Advocacy in a Nonadversarial Setting,* 14 OHIO ST. J. ON DISP. RESOL. 269, 320 (1999); *see also* Ronald J. Gilson & Robert H. Mnookin, *Disputing Through Agents: Cooperation and Conflict Between Lawyers in Litigation,* 94 COLUM. L. REV. 509, 531–33 (1994) (distinguishing between interests of firm, which may desire to keep client happy, and interests of individual attorney, who may have need to bill a large numbers of hours).

130 Deborah L. Rhode, *Ethics in Practice,* in ETHICS IN PRACTICE: LAWYERS' ROLES, RESPONSIBILITIES, AND REGULATION, *supra* note 111, at 7.

131 *See* Sternlight, *supra* note 129, at 327–28.

132 Abel, *supra* note 78, at 389.

133 *Id.*

134 The disciplinary authorities disagreed with the lawyer's interpretation, ultimately finding him in violation of ethics rules. *Id.;* Leslie C. Levin, *Bad Apples, Bad Lawyers or Bad Decisionmaking: Lessons from Psychology and from Lawyers in the Dock,* 22 GEO J. LEGAL ETHICS 1549, 1570 (2009) (reviewing Abel, *supra* note 78).

or former clients.[135] While many believe that adequate disclosure of conflicts and consent thereto can help to address any potential problems,[136] and while the Model Rules seem to be based on this assumption,[137] recent research suggests that disclosure as a remedy is potentially problematic.

Ideally, the disclosure of a conflicting interest permits the affected party to discount the conflicted party's advice or opinion to account for the conflict.[138] In practice, however, the affected party may not sufficiently discount the advice.

First, although disclosure of a conflict of interest is likely to decrease trust in the advisor's recommendation,[139] the discounting that results may not be sufficient. Because we tend to underestimate the extent to which situational pressures influence the behavior of others, the client may underestimate the extent to which the conflict may have influenced the attorney's advice.[140] Further, even were the client to attempt to discount the conflicted advice, the client may have difficulty sufficiently adjusting away from the anchor provided by the advice[141] and may find it difficult to ignore the advice once it has been proffered.[142] Moreover, disclosure is also likely to generate some countervailing degree of increased trust in the conflicted advisor in some cases. In particular, to the extent

---

[135] *See generally* Shapiro, *supra* note 128, at 289.

[136] *See generally* Omri Ben Shahar & Carl E. Schneider, *The Failure of Mandated Disclosure,* 159 U. PA. L. REV. 647, 649–50 (2011) (surveying the frequency of disclosure as remedy in a range of contexts). Note also that there are practical considerations involved in disclosing conflicts and asking for a waiver. *See* Shapiro, *supra* note 128, at 376–92.

[137] *See, e.g.,* MODEL RULES OF PROF'L CONDUCT R. 1.6–1.9 (2010) (allowing representation in some instances following disclosure and informed consent).

[138] *Id.* R. 1.7 cmt. 18 (2010). A client deciding whether to retain a conflicted attorney might similarly discount the likely impact of the conflict and overestimate their ability to discount the advice given.

[139] *See, e.g.,* Daylian M. Cain et al., *The Dirt on Coming Clean: Perverse Effects of Disclosing Conflicts of Interest,* 34 J. LEGAL STUD. 1, 5–6 (2005); Sunita Sah et al., *The Burden of Disclosure: Increased Compliance with Distrusted Advice,* 104 J. PERSONALITY & SOC. PSYCHOL. 289, 289 (2013).

[140] This tendency is known as the fundamental attribution error. *See* Edward E. Jones & Victor A. Harris, *The Attribution of Attitudes,* 3 J. EXPERIMENTAL SOC. PSYCHOL. 1, 11 (1967).

[141] Anchors provide a starting point for a judgment; adjustments are then made away from the anchor, but these adjustments are often insufficient and result in judgments that are skewed toward the starting point. *See* Amos Tversky & Daniel Kahneman, *Judgment Under Uncertainty: Heuristics and Biases,* in JUDGMENT UNDER UNCERTAINTY: HEURISTICS AND BIASES 3, 14 (Daniel Kahneman et al. eds., 1982).

[142] Cain et al., *supra* note 139, at 6; *see also* Colin Camerer et al., *The Curse of Knowledge in Economic Settings: An Experimental Analysis,* 97 J. POL. ECON. 1232, 1246–47 (1989); Fritz Strack & Thomas Mussweiler, *Explaining the Enigmatic Anchoring Effect: Mechanisms of Selective Accessibility,* 73 J. PERSONALITY & SOC. PSYCHOL. 437, 437 (1997). Legal fact-finders have similar difficulties in ignoring inadmissible evidence. *See, e.g.,* Mark Kelman et al., *Context-Dependence in Legal Decision Making,* 25 J. LEGAL STUD. 287, 301–03 (1996); Stephan Landsman & Richard F. Rakos, *A Preliminary Inquiry into the Effect of Potentially Biasing Information on Judges and Jurors in Civil Litigation,* 12 BEHAV. SCI. & L. 113, 124–25 (1994); William C. Thompson et al., *Inadmissible Evidence and Juror Verdicts,* 40 J. PERSONALITY & SOC. PSYCHOL. 453, 453 (1981); Andrew J. Wistrich et al., *Can Judges Ignore Inadmissible Information? The Difficulty of Deliberately Disregarding,* 153 U. PA. L. REV. 1251, 1253–58 (2005).

that the disclosure signals to the recipient that the attorney is attentive to potential conflicts and wants to address them with integrity, disclosure may make the advisor seem particularly forthright.[143]

Even when trust in the recommendation is degraded, there may be increased pressure to act in accordance with the recommendation because the client does not want to signal her distrust of the advisor (insinuation anxiety).[144] Wanting to be consistent in her own decision making,[145] the client may also resist second-guessing her original decision to consult the attorney and may compare the certain and immediate loss of the attorney's assistance with the less certain and future consequences stemming from the conflict.[146]

Further, in addition to the failure of clients to sufficiently take account of the potentially biasing effect of a conflict, attorneys' disclosure of a conflict might actually increase the influence of the conflict on attorney judgments and actions. Research has found that behaving ethically at one point in time can result in less ethical behavior at a later point in time by establishing the moral credentials of the actor in her own mind and licensing her to behave less ethically later.[147] This is consistent with research finding that an individual who discloses a conflict may actually give more biased advice than the attorney who does not disclose—a process known as disclosure distortion.[148]

---

143 *See* Sah et al., *supra* note 139, at 290; *see also* Steven D. Pearson et al., *A Trial of Disclosing Physicians' Financial Incentives to Patients,* 166 ARCH. INTERNAL MED. 623, 626 (2006); Denise M. Rousseau et al., *Not So Different After All: A Cross-Discipline View of Trust,* 23 ACAD. MGMT. REV. 393, 399 (1998) (explaining the development of relational trust).

144 Sah et al., *supra* note 139, at 290.

145 *See* Cialdini, *supra* note 64, at 52 (describing the pressure for consistency).

146 *See* Leonard E. Gross, *Are Differences Among the Attorney Conflict of Interest Rules Consistent with the Principles of Behavioral Economics?,* 19 GEO J. LEGAL ETHICS 111, 114 (2006); Cameron & Miller, *supra* note 86, at 91–101 (discussing loss aversion).

147 Dale T. Miller & Daniel A. Effron, *Psychological License: When It Is Needed and How It Functions,* 43 ADVS. EXPERIMENTAL SOC. PSYCHOL. 115 (2010); Benoît Monin & Dale T. Miller, *Moral Credentials and the Expression of Prejudice,* 81 J. PERSONALITY & SOC. PSYCHOL. 33, 34 (2001); *see also* Anna C. Merritt et al., *The Strategic Pursuit of Moral Credentials,* 48 J. EXPERIMENTAL SOC. PSYCHOL. 774, 774 (2012). It is possible that acceptance of routine disclosure as a remedy for conflicts might license the profession as a whole to believe that they have effectively dealt with conflicts situations. *See* George Loewenstein et al., *The Unintended Consequences of Conflict of Interest Disclosures,* 307 J. AM. MED. ASS'N 669, 669 (2012) (applying this literature to conflicts of interest in the medical profession).

148 Cain et al., *supra* note 139, at 13; Daylian Cain et al., *When Sunlight Fails to Disinfect: Understanding the Perverse Effects of Disclosing Conflicts of Interest,* 37 J. CONSUMER RES. 836, 841 (2011); *see* Daylian M. Cain et al., *Coming Clean But Playing Dirtier: The Shortcomings of Disclosure as a Solution to Conflicts of Interest,* in CONFLICTS OF INTEREST: CHALLENGES AND SOLUTIONS IN BUSINESS, LAW, MEDICINE, AND PUBLIC POLICY, *supra* note 51, at 104; GEORGE LOEWENSTEIN ET AL., *THE LIMITS OF TRANSPARENCY: PITFALLS AND POTENTIAL OF DISCLOSING CONFLICTS OF INTEREST,* 101 AM. ECON. REV.: PAPERS & PROCEEDINGS 423, 424 (2011); Moore & Loewenstein, *supra* note 66, at 190–91.

3. Acting Unethically Indirectly—Through and on Behalf of Others

Another complication that flows from the agency relationship between attorney and client relates to the omission bias—the tendency to prefer options that entail inaction to options that require action.[149] Because harms caused indirectly entail less moral intensity than harms inflicted directly, people tend to be more willing to engage in unethical conduct when acting through an agent than when acting for themselves.[150] For example, in one variant of the Milgram shock experiments in which the study participant relied on another person to administer the shock[151] over 90% of participants administered the highest shock, as compared to "only" 63% of solo participants who themselves had to shock a person in the next room and 30% of participants who had to directly place the other's hand on a plate to administer the shock.[152] Clients, similarly, may be more willing to have their attorneys act unethically on their behalf than they would be to themselves engage in a particular unethical act. Indeed, some clients may hold a schema[153] or mental representation for "lawyer" that inclines them to make such proposals.[154]

At the same time, because people tend to be more willing to endorse an unfair proposal suggested by someone else than they would be to originate such a suggestion themselves,[155] lawyers may be more willing to approve a client's

---

[149] *See generally* Jonathan Baron & Ilana Ritov, *Reference Points and Omission Bias,* 59 ORGANIZATIONAL BEHAV. & HUM. DECISION PROCESSES 475, 475 (1994); Mark Spranca et al., *Omission and Commission in Judgment and Choice,* 27 J. EXPERIMENTAL SOC. PSYCHOL. 76, 78–79 (1991).

[150] Lucas C. Coffman, *Intermediation Reduces Punishment (and Reward),* 3 AM. ECON. J. MICROECON. 77, 78 (2011); Neeru Paharia et al., *Dirty Work, Clean Hands: The Moral Psychology of Indirect Agency,* 109 ORGANIZATIONAL BEHAV. & HUM. DECISION PROCESSES 134, 134 (2009). Harms caused indirectly also tend to be punished less severely. *Id.* at 141; *see also* Björn Bartling & Urs Fischbacher, *Shifting the Blame: On Delegation and Responsibility* 2 (Univ. of Zurich Institute for Empirical Research in Economics, Working Paper No. 380, 2008), available at www.iew.uzh.ch/wp/iewwp380.pdf; Edward B. Royzman & Jonathan Baron, *The Preference for Indirect Harm,* 15 SOC. JUST. RES. 165, 182 (2002). *See generally* Jason Dana et al., *Ethical Immunity: How People Violate Their Own Moral Standards Without Feeling They Are Doing So,* in BEHAVIORAL BUSINESS ETHICS: SHAPING AN EMERGING FIELD 201 (David De Cremer & Ann E. Tenbrunsel eds., 2012).

[151] *See supra* Section I.B.

[152] MILGRAM, *supra* note 61, at 119–22.

[153] *See* LEE ROSS & RICHARD E. NISBETT, THE PERSON AND THE SITUATION 76 (1991) (defining "schema").

[154] Levin, *supra* note 17, at 339 (reporting the comments of one lawyer: "There's an expectation that people have that you are going to lie for them. That you're going to make up things for them. That that's expected of them.").

[155] Don A. Moore et al., *Conflicts of Interest and the Case of Auditor Independence: Moral Seduction and Strategic Issue Cycling,* 31 ACAD. MGMT. REV. 10, 17 (2006) (describing Kristina A. Diekmann et al., *Self-Interest and Fairness in Problems of Resource Allocation: Allocators Versus Recipients,* 72 J. PERSONALITY & SOC. PSYCHOL. 1061, 1072 (1997)); Paharia et al., *supra* note 150, at 141. This willingness to endorse another's unethical suggestions is in step with norms that "assign[ ] ultimate responsibility for the moral content of a client's position to the client himself," rather than to the attorney as agent. Austin Sarat, *Ethics in Litigation: Rhetoric of Crisis, Realities of Practice,* in ETHICS IN PRACTICE: LAWYERS' ROLES, RESPONSIBILITIES, AND REGULATION, *supra* note 111, at 149.

proposed unethical course of action than they would be to initiate such a course. One recent study examined the extent to which attorneys would disclose a material but damaging piece of information that had come to their attention on the eve of reaching a favorable settlement agreement. One of the primary justifications given by lawyers who chose not to disclose was that their client did not want them to divulge the information.[156] While, legally, the fact that nondisclosure was requested by the client does not justify the attorney's action,[157]

> the principal may feel more detached, and hence less responsible, for such an action if it is delegated, while the agent may feel that he or she was "just carrying out orders" . . . . Through the use of agents, therefore, accountability for morally questionable behavior can become vertically diffused, with no individual taking responsibility.[158]

Finally, psychologists have found that people are more willing to engage in unethical conduct when they believe such conduct will benefit another person.[159] For example, questionable actions in discovery might be seen as more appropriate when done to benefit a client one sees as being "railroaded," or a conflict of interest might be ignored to spare a client added expense. Thus, lawyers may be more inclined to engage in unethical acts they believe will benefit clients than they would be to engage in the same behavior to benefit themselves alone.[160]

4. Benefits of Agency Relationship

While we have seen that agency relationships can create ethical difficulties for attorneys, attorney-client relationships can also serve as a check on ethics. First, as we have noted, attorneys will not share all of their clients' interests—and attorneys have their own interests in avoiding censure. This different perspective

---

156 Hinshaw & Alberts, *supra* note 11, at 125; *see also* Levin, *supra* note 17, at 338–40 (discussing lawyers requested to do things by "bad" clients).

157 Hinshaw & Alberts, *supra* note 11, at 123–25.

158 John R. Hamman et al., *Self-Interest Through Delegation: An Additional Rationale for the Principal-Agent Relationship,* 100 AM. ECON. REV. 1826, 1826 (2010).

159 *See, e.g.,* Francecsa Gino & Lamar Pierce, *Dishonesty in the Name of Equity,* 20 PSYCHOL. SCI. 1153, 1159 (2009); Francesca Gino & Lamar Pierce, *Lying to Level the Playing Field: Why People May Dishonestly Help or Hurt Others to Create Equity,* 95 J. BUS. ETHICS 89, 101 (2010); Francesca Gino & Lamar Pierce, *Robin Hood Under the Hood: Wealth-Based Discrimination in Illicit Customer Help,* 21 ORGANIZATIONAL SCI. 1176, 1189 (2010); Scott S. Wiltermuth, *Cheating More When the Spoils are Split,* 115 ORGANIZATIONAL BEHAV. & HUM. DECISION PROCESSES 157, 166–67 (2011).

160 *See, e.g.,* Robert K. Vischer, *Legal Advice As Moral Perspective,* 19 GEO. J. LEGAL ETHICS 225, 243 (2006) ("The lawyers bought into an understanding of Enron as a valiant corporate renegade, looking to manipulate the system in furtherance of the greater corporate good."); Michael Powell & Lois Romano, *Roman Catholic Church Shifts Legal Strategy: Aggressive Litigation Replaces Quiet Settlements,* WASH. POST, May 13, 2002, at A1 (discussing attorneys for Catholic priests accused of sexual abuse "fighting to keep documents secret and engaging in new tactics to minimize settlements," so as to defend "good priests").

on clients' decisions may allow the attorney to see the ethical contours of a decision that have faded for the client. Similarly, to the extent that an attorney has only periodic involvement with a client, the attorney may be in a position to notice shifts in practice that are not noticeable to a client who sees only the more incremental changes. That is, the attorney may be better positioned to notice the client's slide down the slippery slope. In addition, harmful behavior is less likely in the presence of a dissenter.[161] Thus, developing a relationship in which attorney and client are able to effectively express dissent can mean that each can serve as an ethical check for the other. And, finally, to the extent that searching analysis is part of our basic understanding of or schema for attorneys, a client may be more receptive to the questioning of her plans or activities that comes from her attorney than to similar critique from another source.

C. The Challenges of the Adversarial System

To advocate for a client's interests implies some level of partisanship. Both litigators and transactional attorneys often represent parties with opposed positions and lawyers representing regulated entities can also come to see regulators as their adversaries.[162]

Many ethical issues arise in this adversarial context. In the service of "zealous advocacy,"[163] attorneys may fail to ask their client important or probing questions, fail to disclose material information to an opponent, exaggerate claims, dissemble about alternative deals, coach rather than prepare witnesses, aggressively cross-examine even candid witnesses, and so on. Indeed, some lawyers view "an ability to push the ethical envelope [as] a source of pride, rather than an embarrassing confession of susceptibility to temptation."[164] In this view, "cautious punctiliousness [is] at least as ethically troubling as venturesome zeal."[165] The structure of attorneys' relationships with their clients can sometimes mean that attorneys are ethically obligated to behave in ways that would be viewed as

---

161 *See, e.g.*, MILGRAM, *supra* note 61, at 116; *see also* Solomon E. Asch, *Studies of Independence and Conformity: A Minority of One Against a Unanimous Majority*, 70 PSYCHOL. MONOGRAPHS: GEN. & APPLIED 1, 2 (1956).

162 *See, e.g.*, Langevoort, *supra* note 66, at 22 ("Where a loyalty to the corporate mission comes to color the lawyers' thinking, it becomes easy to start thinking of regulators and the courts as rivals.").

163 Although the Model Rules were revised in 2002 to make "zealous advoca[cy]" part of the preamble, rather than part of the Rules, many attorneys continue to believe and act as if "zealous advocacy" is required in all circumstances. The comment to Rule 1.3, requiring "reasonable diligence," makes clear however that "zeal" is limited by ethics and professional discretion.

164 Suchman, *supra* note 101, at 854 ("Zealous advocacy was, to them, an affirmative moral obligation, even when it came into conflict with other ethical rules."); Wendel, *supra* note 9, at 1170 (recounting how long-time Enron attorneys defended their behavior as "creative and aggressive" structuring of transactions for the benefit of their client).

165 Suchman, *supra* note 101, at 854.

unethical in other contexts.[166] But, the adversary system can also incline lawyers take this zealousness too far and to "treat[ ] behavior that would be ethically problematic in other contexts as not problematic."[167]

Consider how an adversarial mindset might have influenced John Gellene as he considered whether to disclose his ties to South Street and Salovaara in the Bucyrus bankruptcy:

> In the moral calculus that likely had emerged for Gellene during [the bankruptcy] negotiations, [disclosure] would mean that the party [(JNL)] that had behaved so unreasonably during the past year would gain the upper hand. The debtor would have to hire new counsel. That counsel would have to spend valuable time becoming familiar with Bucyrus, the other parties, and the plan. Furthermore, JNL undoubtedly would use this disruption as an opportunity to push for drastic changes in the plan. . . . Given the hostility of other parties to JNL, the result might be a bloody mess that would leave Bucyrus beyond repair.
>
> For these reasons, Gellene may have convinced himself that non-disclosure not only was not morally blameworthy, but that it was morally justified. . . . Disclosure would do little to add to the integrity of the bankruptcy process, but could seriously undermine the chance for a timely and successful reorganization.[168]

Acting in a way that would provide an advantage to an opponent may have been unthinkable.

Consider, too, that approaching a conflict or negotiation from a competitive perspective tends to increase unethical behavior.[169] Similarly, we tend to evaluate behavior as being more ethical when we believe that we are acting in response to

---

166 *See* Gordon, *supra* note 27, at 710 (noting that "much of what is characterized as aggressive or 'hardball' behavior is legitimate and functional in view of valid litigation objectives and the conventional norms of the adversary game"); *see also, e.g.,* People v. Belge, 376 N.Y.S.2d 771, 771 (N.Y. App. Div. 1975) (holding that attorney-client privilege exempted attorney from duty to report death occurring without medical attendance); Adam Liptak, *When Law Prevents Righting A Wrong,* N.Y. TIMES, May 4, 2008, at WK4; *Slayer's 2 Lawyers Kept Secret of 2 More Killings,* N.Y. TIMES, June 20, 1974, at 81.

167 Sarat, *supra* note 155, at 149; *see* KARL N. LLEWELLYN, THE BRAMBLE BUSH 156 (1930) ("Why should you expect the ethics of the game to be different from the game itself?").

168 REGAN, *supra* note 13, at 347–48 (emphasis added).

169 Deepak Malhotra, *The Desire to Win: The Effects of Competitive Arousal on Motivation and Behavior,* 111 ORGANIZATIONAL BEHAV. & HUM. DECISION PROCESSES 139, 139 (2010); Maurice E. Schweitzer et al., *Conflict Frames and the Use of Deception: Are Competitive Negotiators Less Ethical?,* 35 J. APPLIED SOC. PSYCHOL. 2123, 2140 (2005); Wolfgang Steinel & Carsten K.W. De Dreu, *Social Motives and Strategic Misrepresentation in Social Decision Making,* 86 J. PERSONALITY & SOC. PSYCHOL. 419, 431 (2004); *see also* Gillian Ku et al., *Towards a Competitive Arousal Model of Decision-Making: A Study of Auction Fever in Live and Internet Auctions,* 96 ORGANIZATIONAL BEHAV. & HUM. DECISION PROCESSES 89, 101–02 (2005).

unfair behavior by another.[170] These findings are consistent, for example, with many lawyers' views of the discovery process:

> A question I have often asked lawyers is this: If the other side does it, can you retaliate? The legal answer is no. The federal rule against discovery abuse (Rule 26) does not have a "they started it!" exception. But many lawyers think that if the other side starts playing discovery games, they would be hurting their clients to turn the other cheek.[171]

The tendency to assess the propriety of questionable negotiation tactics more positively when they are described as responses to a questionable tactic used by the other side[172] can be particularly pernicious when combined with our tendency to attribute bias or unfairness to those with whom we simply disagree.[173]

Consider how all of this might influence a prosecutor's application of Brady v. Maryland.[174] Brady requires the prosecution to disclose evidence that is favorable to the defense when it "could reasonably be taken to put the whole case in such a different light as to undermine confidence in the verdict."[175] In particular,

> Brady requires a prosecutor who is determining whether to disclose a piece of evidence to the defense to speculate first about how the remaining evidence will come together against the defendant at trial, and then about whether a reasonable probability exists that the piece of evidence at issue would affect the result of the trial. During the first step, a risk exists that prosecutors will engage in biased recall, retrieving from memory only those facts that tend to confirm the hypothesis of guilt. Moreover, because of selective information processing, the prosecutor will accept at face value the evidence she views as inculpatory, without subjecting it to the scrutiny that a defense attorney would encourage jurors to apply.

---

[170] Maurice E. Schweitzer & Donald E. Gibson, *Fairness, Feelings, and Ethical Decision-Making: Consequences of Violating Community Standards of Fairness,* 77 J. BUS. ETHICS 287, 298 (2008).

[171] David Luban, *Making Sense of Moral Meltdowns,* in MORAL LEADERSHIP: THE THEORY AND PRACTICE OF POWER, JUDGMENT, AND POLICY 60 (Deborah L. Rhode ed., 2006). Many litigated discovery disputes involve allegations by all parties about their opponents' bad behavior. *See, e.g.,* 6 MICHAEL B. KEATING, BUSINESS & COMMERCIAL LITIGATION IN FEDERAL COURTS § 66:8 (Robert L. Haig ed., 3d ed. 2012); *see also* Charles Yablon, *Stupid Lawyer Tricks: An Essay on Discovery Abuse,* 96 COLUM. L. REV. 1618, 1630 (1996).

[172] Stephen M. Garcia et al., *Morally Questionable Tactics: Negotiations Between District Attorneys and Public Defenders,* 27 PERSONALITY & SOC. PSYCHOL. BULL. 731, 739 (2001).

[173] Kathleen A. Kennedy & Emily Pronin, *When Disagreement Gets Ugly: Perceptions of Bias and the Escalation of Conflict,* 34 PERSONALITY & SOC. PSYCHOL. BULL. 833, 845 (2008).

[174] 373 U.S. 83 (1963).

[175] Kyles v. Whitley, 514 U.S. 419, 435 (1995); *see also* United States v. Bagley, 473 U.S. 667, 675 (1985).

Cognitive bias would also appear to taint the second speculative step of the Brady analysis, requiring the prosecutor to determine the value of the potentially exculpatory evidence in the context of the entire record. Because of selective information processing, the prosecutor will look for weaknesses in evidence contradicting her existing belief in the defendant's guilt. In short, compared to a neutral decision maker, the prosecutor will overestimate the strength of the government's case against the defendant and underestimate the potential exculpatory value of the evidence whose disclosure is at issue. As a consequence, the prosecutor will fail to see materiality where it might in fact exist.[176]

D. The Tolls of Law Practice

Long hours, deadlines, and workplace politics can combine to take a toll on lawyers, as can lack of sleep, frequent interruptions, travel, difficult decisions, and the struggle to balance work and family life.[177] In *Eat What You Kill,* Regan describes John Gellene as working in an "environment of constant urgency" in which getting five hours of sleep was thought to be a "luxury." Gellene did not sleep at all during the two days leading up to the filing of the bankruptcy petition and the application for appointment as Bucyrus' counsel, two days that were described as being " 'a circus,' with people running around, papers flying, and a large group of lawyers, legal assistants, and financial advisors turning the Bucyrus board room into command central. The stress on everyone was palpable."[178]

These sorts of job stresses impact ethical decision making. In a classic study on time pressures, seminary students were assigned to give a three- to five-minute impromptu talk in an adjacent building. Some students were told that they were late for their turn to talk; others were led to believe they had more time. On the way to the other building each student encountered a person in need of help—a

---

176 Burke, *supra* note 33, at 1611–12 (2006). It is also worth noting that there are circumstances in which it is good rapport, rather than an adversarial relationship, that puts one at risk of engaging in unethical behavior. In particular, one recent study demonstrated that "negotiators seeking to build or maintain rapport may be more likely to deceive their partners than to disappoint them with the truth." Sandy D. Jap et al., *The Dark Side of Rapport: Agent Misbehavior Face-to-Face and Online,* 57 MGMT. SCI. 1610, 1612 (2011).

177 *See, e.g.,* Janine Robben, *Burnout: Cautionary Tales,* 69 OR. ST. B. BULL. 16, 22–24 (2008), available at http://www.osbar.org/publications/bulletin/08oct/burnout.html; *see also* Public Defender v. Florida, 115 So. 3d 261, 285 (Fla. 2013), available at http://www.floridasupremecourt.org/decisions/2013/sc09-1181.pdf (finding that excessive workloads justified withdrawal by public defenders from an array of cases); JEAN WALLACE, JUGGLING IT ALL: A STUDY OF LAWYERS' WORK, HOME, AND FAMILY DEMANDS AND COPING STRATEGIES, REPORT OF STAGE 2 FINDINGS 12–15 (2004); Stephanie Francis Ward, *The Ultimate Time-Money Trade-Off,* 93 A.B.A. J. 24, 24–25 (2007); Mary Flood, *New Lawyers Say, 'Pay Us Less, Don't Work Us So Hard',* HOUS. CHRON., Apr. 16, 2007, at 1, available at http://www.chron.com/disp/story.mpl/business/flood/4714709.html.

178 REGAN, *supra* note 13, at 134.

person planted by the researchers: "the victim was sitting slumped in a doorway, head down, eyes closed, not moving. As the subject went by, the victim coughed twice and groaned, keeping his head down." Those participants who were in a hurry were significantly less likely to stop to help than were those who were less rushed.[179] More recent research has found that time pressure also results in a greater likelihood of lying.[180]

Studies have also found that unethical decisions are more common when the decision maker suffers from a lack of sleep or is otherwise cognitively taxed.[181] And, the process of making decisions, being deprived of food, and even resisting the desire to snack can also result in cognitive depletion.[182] When a decision maker's cognitive resources have already been challenged, the decision maker is more likely to put himself in temptation's way and then succumb to that temptation.[183] Depleted individuals are also less likely to recognize the moral dimensions of decisions[184] and experience less guilt.[185] Making matters worse, decision makers do not anticipate these effects on decision making.[186]

---

[179] John M. Darley & C. Daniel Batson, *'From Jerusalem to Jericho": A Study of Situational and Dispositional Variables in Helping Behavior,* 27 J. PERSONALITY & SOC. PSYCHOL. 100, 104 (1973). Interestingly, participants who were assigned to speak about the parable of the "Good Samaritan"—a story about helping someone in need—were no more likely to stop to help than those assigned to speak about another topic. *Id.*

[180] Shalvi et al., *Honesty Requires Time, supra* note 79, at 1265.

[181] *See, e.g.,* Christopher M. Barnes et al., *Lack of Sleep and Unethical Conduct,* 115 ORGANIZATIONAL BEHAV. & HUM. DECISION PROCESSES 169, 178 (2011); Michael S. Christian & Aleksander P.J. Ellis, *Examining the Effects of Sleep Deprivation on Workplace Deviance: A Self-Regulatory Perspective,* 54 ACAD. MGMT. J. 913, 926 (2011); Francesca Gino et al., *Unable to Resist Temptation: How Self-Control Depletion Promotes Unethical Behavior,* 115 ORGANIZATIONAL BEHAV. & HUM. DECISION PROCESSES 191, 199 (2011); Nicole L. Mead et al., *Too Tired to Tell the Truth: Self-Control Resource Depletion and Dishonesty,* 45 J. EXPERIMENTAL SOC. PSYCHOL. 594, 596 (2009); Mark Muraven et al., *Self-Control Depletion and the General Theory of Crime,* 22 J. QUANTITATIVE CRIMINOLOGY 263, 273 (2006); *see also* William D.S. Kilgore et al., *The Effects of 53 Hours of Sleep Deprivation on Moral Judgment,* 30 SLEEP 345, 350 (2007).

[182] Roy F. Baumeister et al., *Ego Depletion: Is the Active Self a Limited Resource?,* 74 J. PERSONALITY & SOC. PSYCHOL. 1252, 1263 (1998); Shai Danziger et al., *Extraneous Factors in Judicial Decisions,* 108 PROC. NAT'L ACAD. SCI. 6889, 6890 (2011) (finding more generous parole board decisions when board members were well fed); Kathleen D. Vohs et al., *Making Choices Impairs Subsequent Self-Control: A Limited-Resource Account of Decision Making, Self-Regulation, and Active Initiative,* 94 J. PERSONALITY & SOC. PSYCHOL. 883, 897 (2008). President Barack Obama has eliminated all suits that are neither gray nor blue, so that he need not expend cognitive energy making clothing choices. Obama says: "I'm trying to pare down decisions. I don't want to make decisions about what I'm eating or wearing. Because I have too many other decisions to make." Michael Lewis, *Obama's Way,* VANITY FAIR, Oct. 2012, at 216, available at http://www.vanityfair.com/politics/2012/10/michael-lewis-profile-barack-obama.

[183] Mead et al., *supra* note 181, at 596.

[184] Gino et al., *supra* note 181, at 199.

[185] Hanyi Xu et al., *Too Fatigued to Care: Ego Depletion, Guilt, and Prosocial Behavior,* 48 J. EXPERIMENTAL SOC. PSYCHOL. 1183, 1185 (2012).

[186] Mead et al., *supra* note 181, at 596.

At the same time, these unfortunate forces can be countered. There is evidence that decision makers who recognize the need for self-control, and who are motivated to exercise that control, may be able to temper the depleting effects of cognitive strain.[187] Other research has found that those who believe that their willpower is a non-limited resource are less likely to show decreased performance following a demanding task.[188]

Finally, some of the most common sorts of ethical failures—such as poor client communication, the neglect of client matters, overbilling, or abuse of client trust funds—can stem in part from the economic pressures of law practice.[189] For example, a lawyer or firm may feel economic pressure to accept cases that would be better declined. A lawyer may succumb to the planning fallacy, overconfidently believing that he can competently handle another case, and then find himself overwhelmed.[190] A lawyer may decide to engage in advertising that she otherwise finds disagreeable in order to generate scarce business.[191] Or, a lawyer who is surviving hand-to-mouth may begin her slide down the slippery slope when she is tempted to "borrow" from client accounts or to co-mingle funds—just a little bit, for just a little while—in order to deal with perceived temporary cash flow problems.[192] Even attorneys at the largest and most prestigious firms feel serious financial pressure to try to maintain or build their reputation as being highly profitable.[193]

---

187 *See* Michael Inzlicht & Brandon J. Schmeichel, *What Is Ego Depletion? Toward a Mechanistic Revision of the Resource Model of Self-Control,* 7 PERSP. ON PSYCHOL. SCI. 450, 459 (2012) (reviewing studies); Mark Muraven & Elisaveta Slessareva, *Mechanisms of Self-Control Failure: Motivation and Limited Resources,* 29 PERSONALITY & SOC. PSYCHOL. BULL. 894, 905 (2003) (finding that motivation moderates depletion effects).

188 Joshua J. Clarkson et al., *When Perception is More Than Reality: The Effects of Perceived Versus Actual Resource Depletion on Self-Regulatory Behavior,* 98 J. PERSONALITY & SOC. PSYCHOL. 29, 45 (2010); Veronika Job et al., *Ego Depletion—Is It All in Your Head?: Implicit Theories About Willpower Affect Self-Regulation,* 21 PSYCHOL. SCI. 1686, 1692 (2010).

189 For a discussion of the changing economics of legal practice, see Gordon, *supra* note 27, at 717–18; Marc Galanter & William Henderson, *The Elastic Tournament: A Second Transformation of the Big Law Firm,* 60 STAN. L. REV. 1867, 1913 (2008). As part of this transformation, the relationship between in-house and outside counsel has changed as well. *See* Robert L. Nelson, *Ideology, Practice, and Professional Autonomy: Social Values and Client Relationships in the Large Law Firm,* 37 STAN. L. REV. 503, 543–44 (1985).

190 Buehler et al., *supra* note 49, at 2.

191 *See, e.g.,* Stephen Daniels & Joanne Martin, *Plaintiffs' Lawyers and the Tension between Professional Norms and the Need to Generate Business,* in LAWYERS IN PRACTICE: ETHICAL DECISION MAKING IN CONTEXT, *supra* note 101, at 118 (highlighting one lawyer's belief that a failure to use the same tactics as others forfeits business to those that do).

192 *See, e.g.,* Levin, *supra* note 17, at 359.

193 *See* Jeffrey W. Stempel, *Embracing Descent: The Bankruptcy of a Business Paradigm for Conceptualizing and Regulating the Legal Profession,* 27 FLA. ST. U. L. REV. 25, 31 (2000).

E. Status and Power

In addition to being a demanding profession, lawyering also tends to be a relatively high status profession and lawyers may frequently perceive themselves to be more powerful than others, such as clients.[194] Attorneys may also draw power in particular situations (such as a negotiation) from their possession of private information or an attractive alternative.[195] Thus, while attorneys will not always be more powerful than others with whom they interact and will vary in the degree to which they occupy positions of status or power, they may regularly find themselves functioning from a position of perceived status, power, or strength.

All this matters for attorney ethics because social status tends to be negatively associated with ethics, with those in higher status positions tending to engage in more unethical behavior.[196] There is even evidence that simply conceiving of the self as a professional—which entails a belief in one's technical and ethical competence—is associated with unethical behavior.[197] In addition, people who feel powerful can be more likely to engage in unethical behaviors such as cheating.[198] Power tends to make people more attuned to the attraction of rewards, feel more entitled, be more goal directed, be more overconfident, and be less concerned about social censure than are those who feel more powerless.[199]

---

[194] *See, e.g.,* Keiko Nakao & Judith Treas, *Updating Occupational Prestige and Socioeconomic Scores: How the New Measures Measure Up,* 24 SOC. METHODOLOGY 1, 48 (1994); Gillian Stevens & David L. Featherman, *A Revised Socioeconomic Index of Occupational Status,* 10 SOC. SCI. RES. 364, 383 (1981); Robert M. Hauser & John Robert Warren, *Socioeconomic Indexes for Occupations: A Review, Update, and Critique* app. A at 5 (Ctr. Demography & Ecology, Working Paper No. 96-01, 1996). A recent Harris Poll reported that 81% of respondents felt lawyers have "some" to "very great prestige." *Firefighters, Scientists and Doctors Seen as Most Prestigious Occupations,* HARRIS INTERACTIVE (Aug. 4, 2009), http://www.harrisinteractive.com/vault/Harris-Interactive-Poll-Research-Pres-Occupations-2009-08.pdf.

[195] *See* Ann E. Tenbrunsel & David M. Messick, *Power Asymmetries and the Ethical Atmosphere in Negotiations,* in SOCIAL INFLUENCES ON ETHICAL BEHAVIOR IN ORGANIZATIONS 209 (John M. Darley et al. eds., 2001).

[196] Paul K. Piff et al., *Higher Social Class Predicts Increased Unethical Behavior,* 109 PROC. NAT'L ACAD. SCI. 4086, 4088 (2012); *see also* Bella L. Galperin et al., *Status Differentiation and the Protean Self: A Social-Cognitive Model of Unethical Behavior in Organizations,* 98 J. BUS. ETHICS 407, 416 (2011).

[197] Maryam Kouchaki, *Professionalism and Moral Behavior: Does a Professional Self-Conception Make One More Unethical?* 37 (Edmond J. Safra Res. Lab Working Papers, Paper No. 4, 2013), available at http://papers.ssrn.com/sol3/papers.cfm?abstract_id=2243811.

[198] Joris Lammers et al., *Power Increases Hypocrisy: Moralizing in Reasoning, Immorality in Behavior,* 21 PSYCHOL. SCI. 737, 742 (2010); *see also* Terry L. Boles et al., *Deception and Retribution in Repeated Ultimatum Bargaining,* 83 ORGANIZATIONAL BEHAV. & HUM. DECISION PROCESSES 235, 237 (2000); Helmut Crott et al., *The Effects of Information Exchange and Communication in an Asymmetrical Negotiation Situation,* 10 EUR. J. SOC. PSYCHOL. 149, 160 (1980). Ironically, powerful people tend to judge others more harshly for unethical conduct. Lammers et al., *supra.*

[199] *See, e.g.,* Nathaneal J. Fast et al., *Power and Overconfident Decision-Making,* 117 ORGANIZATIONAL BEHAV. & HUM. DECISION PROCESSES 249, 257 (2012); Ana Guinote, *Power and Goal Pursuit,* 33 PERSONALITY & SOC. PSYCHOL. BULL. 1076, 1084 (2007); Dacher Keltner et al., *Power, Approach, and Inhibition,* 110 PSYCHOL. REV. 265, 279 (2003); Lammers et al., *supra* note 198, at 738; Deepak Malhotra & Francesca Gino, *The Pursuit of Power*

In addition, more powerful people tend to be less likely to take the perspective or feel the emotions of another person. In particular, powerful people are less likely to take into account another person's visual perspective, less likely to adjust for the fact that others lack access to their private information, and are less accurate at identifying emotions in others.[200] Predictably, less empathy or understanding of the emotions of another is associated with more unethical behavior.[201] And, for lawyers, such difficulties in reading others may result in a failure to attend to the needs of clients and lead to ethical violations such as a failure to communicate.

While feeling powerful can increase unethical behavior, powerful people may be more protected than are others against at least one set of pressures. To the extent that powerful people are less concerned about social censure or other situational pressures, they may be better able to resist conforming to unethical social norms.[202] In addition, power tends to increase the focus on salient goals. To the extent that these focal goals are strongly linked to ethical or cooperative behavior, more ethical conduct may be expected.[203]

F. Lawyers as Social Actors

> No dilemma causes [students] more anxiety than the prospect of being pressured by their boss to do something unethical. Not only do they worry about losing their jobs if they defy the boss to do the right thing,

---

Corrupts: How Investing in Outside Options Motivates Opportunism in Relationships, 56 ADMIN. SCI. Q. 559, 563 (2011). People in more powerful roles may also be "buffered" from feeling the effects of unethical behavior. *See, e.g.,* Dana R. Carney et al., *How Power Corrupts: Power Buffers the Emotional, Cognitive, and Physiological Stress of Lying* 20 (Univ. of Cal. Berkeley, Haas Sch. of Bus. Research Grant, 2011–2016, 2011), http://mors.haas.berkeley.edu/papers/Carney.HowPowerCorrupts.pdf.

200 Adam D. Galinsky et al., *Power and Perspectives Not Taken,* 17 PSYCHOL. SCI. 1068, 1072 (2006).

201 *See* Taya R. Cohen, *Moral Emotions and Unethical Bargaining: The Differential Effects of Empathy and Perspective Taking in Deterring Deceitful Negotiation,* 94 J. BUS. ETHICS 569, 576 (2010).

202 *See* Adam D. Galinsky et al., *Power Reduces the Press of the Situation: Implications for Creativity, Conformity, and Dissonance,* 95 J. PERSONALITY & SOC. PSYCHOL. 1450, 1462 (2008). It also seems to be the case that power asymmetries can result in unethical behavior by either the more powerful or the weaker party. *See* Tenbrunsel & Messick, *supra* note 195, at 210.

203 *See* Jacob B. Hirsh, Adam D. Galinsky, & Chen-Bo Zhong, *Drunk, Powerful, and in the Dark: How General Processes of Disinhibition Produce Both Prosocial and Antisocial Behavior,* 6 PERSP. ON PSYCHOL. SCI. 415, 418 (2011); *see also* Stéphane Côté et al., *Social Power Facilitates the Effect of Prosocial Orientation on Empathic Accuracy,* 101 J. PERSONALITY & SOC. PSYCHOL. 217, 217 (2011). For discussion of the ways in which different dimensions of social class may influence ethical behavior in different ways, see Stefan T. Trautmann et al., *Social Class and (Un)Ethical Behavior: A Framework, With Evidence From a Large Population Sample,* 8 PERSP. ON PSYCHOL. SCI. 487 (2013).

> they also fear that the pressures of the situation might undermine their ability to know what the right thing is.[204]

These students are right to be worried.

First, recall the Milgram studies in which people followed the instructions of an authoritative experimenter to administer increasingly severe shocks to another person.[205] These studies make evident "that each of us ought to believe three things about ourselves: that we disapprove of destructive obedience, that we think we would never engage in it, and more likely than not, that we are wrong to think we would never engage in it."[206] In the context of legal practice, the influence of authority can come in the form of a more senior lawyer, a colleague, or a client.[207]

While the rules of professional responsibility do not allow a lawyer who acts "at the direction of another person" to escape responsibility for ethical misconduct, the rules do provide that a "subordinate lawyer does not violate the Rules of Professional Conduct if that lawyer acts in accordance with a supervisory lawyer's reasonable resolution of an arguable question of professional duty."[208] Given all that we know about ethical blindspots, it would not be surprising if subordinate lawyers had difficulty making objective judgments about whether a question is "arguable" and about the "reasonableness" of the superior's resolution. And, as we have discussed, lawyers are skilled at making arguments on multiple sides of an issue.[209] Thus, when a partner tells an associate to do something the associate initially finds ethically questionable, the associate may well be able to craft an argument to convince himself that the particular behavior is acceptable.

---

[204] David J. Luban, *The Ethics of Wrongful Obedience,* in *Ethics in Practice: Lawyers' Roles, Responsibilities, and Regulation, supra* note 111, at 94–95.

[205] *See* MILGRAM, *supra* note 61.

[206] Luban, *supra* note 204, at 97 (emphasis omitted); *see also* Perlman, *supra* note 33; Kim, *supra* note 9; Kelman & Hamilton, *supra* note 65. For examples from other professions, see Annamarie Krackow & Thomas Blass, *When Nurses Obey or Defy Inappropriate Physician Orders: Attributional Differences,* 10 J. SOC. BEHAV. & PERSONALITY 585, 585 (1995); Eugen Tarnow, *Self-Destructive Obedience in the Airplane Cockpit and the Concept of Obedience Optimization,* in OBEDIENCE TO AUTHORITY: CURRENT PERSPECTIVES ON THE MILGRAM PARADIGM 111 (Thomas Blass ed., 2000).

[207] *See, e.g.,* Eldred, *supra* note 25, at 354–55 (describing pressure from superiors on public defenders to handle more cases); Perlman, *supra* note 33, at 451 (describing associate told not to produce documents within scope of discovery request). Young lawyers or lawyers who lack mobility may be particularly susceptible in this regard. Psychological research has found that those who are more dependent upon an organization are more likely to engage in compliant unethical behaviors. *See, e.g.,* Judy Wahn, *Organizational Dependence and the Likelihood of Complying with Organizational Pressures to Behave Unethically,* 12 J. BUS. ETHICS 245, 248 (1993).

[208] MODEL RULES OF PROF'L CONDUCT R. 5.2 (2010).

[209] See *supra* text accompanying note 103.

Even in the absence of directions from an authority, ethical behavior can be influenced by other people. We learn how to comport ourselves, in part, by watching the actions of those around us, looking to see how others—particularly those with more experience or expertise—behave.[210] "[L]awyers are social beings; like other human beings in social and occupational groups, lawyers behave largely in accordance with group norms."[211] For attorneys this might be other lawyers within a firm or agency, lawyers who share space, or other formal or informal advice networks—their "communities of practice."[212] The more widespread an attorney believes a particular practice is, the more likely he is to indicate that he would engage in it[213] and the more tempting the unethical behavior, the more widespread he will believe it to be.[214]

> When [lawyers] begin work at law firms, they watch the more experienced lawyers to see what the real standards of conduct are. Each firm quickly communicates its institutional norms to new associates; many associates are anxious to assimilate themselves into an institution and to be successful within it. Therefore, they are not critical of the norms they are asked to adopt. They redraw their lines to fit into the value systems of their firms. If the senior lawyers are not precise in their billing practices, the junior lawyers will not be. If the senior lawyers

---

210 *See, e.g.*, ELLIOT ARONSON, THE SOCIAL ANIMAL 27 (Erik Gilg ed., 11th ed. 2012); Bibb Latané & John M. Darley, *Group Inhibition of Bystander Intervention in Emergencies,* 10 J. PERSONALITY & SOC. PSYCHOL. 215, 220 (1968); *see also* MUZAFER SHERIF, THE PSYCHOLOGY OF SOCIAL NORMS 84–85 (1936); PHILIP ZIMBARDO, THE LUCIFER EFFECT: UNDERSTANDING HOW GOOD PEOPLE TURN EVIL 221 (2007) (describing the Stanford Prison Experiment); Asch, *supra* note 161, at 70; Gregory S. Berns et al., *Neurobiological Correlates of Social Conformity and Independence During Mental Rotation,* 58 BIOLOGICAL PSYCHIATRY 245, 251 (2005) (examining the effects of conformity and independence on brain activity); Michael J. O'Fallon & Kenneth D. Butterfield, *The Influence of Unethical Peer Behavior on Observers' Unethical Behavior: A Social Cognitive Perspective,* 109 J. BUS. ETHICS 117, 126 (2012).

211 Jeffrey W. Stempel, *Embracing Descent: The Bankruptcy of a Business Paradigm for Conceptualizing and Regulating the Legal Profession,* 27 FLA. ST. U. L. REV. 25, 27 (2000).

212 LYNN M. MATHER ET AL., DIVORCE LAWYERS AT WORK: VARIETIES OF PROFESSIONALISM IN PRACTICE 41 (2001) (describing communities of practice and their effects); Lynn Mather, *How and Why Do Lawyers Misbehave? Lawyers, Discipline, and Collegial Control,* in THE PARADOX OF PROFESSIONALISM: LAWYERS AND THE POSSIBILITY OF JUSTICE 109, 116 (Scott L. Cummings ed., 2011) (reviewing empirical literature on different communities of practice); *see also* Elizabeth Chambliss, *Whose Ethics? The Benchmark Problem in Legal Ethics Research,* in LAWYERS IN PRACTICE: ETHICAL DECISION MAKING IN CONTEXT, *supra* note 101, at 47, 48 (describing the "ethical learning" that takes place as "lawyers gradually acquire specialized ethical expertise"); Leslie C. Levin, *Specialty Bars as a Site of Professionalism: The Immigration Bar Example,* 8 U. ST. THOMAS L.J. 194, 196–97 (2011) (describing communication of professional norms within specialty bars). The Model Rules of Professional Conduct point lawyers to "the approbation of professional peers" as a source of ethical guidance. MODEL RULES OF PROF'L CONDUCT, Preamble and Scope (2010).

213 *See, e.g.*, Hinshaw & Alberts, *supra* note 11, at 150.

214 Tenbrunsel, *supra* note 54, at 336.

exaggerate their credentials or expertise when talking with new clients, the junior lawyers will do the same.[215]

We are particularly influenced by others who we consider to be members of our group. Studies have found that observing an in-group peer acting unethically increases the likelihood that the observer will similarly act unethically.[216] When someone with whom one shares similarities (even the same name or birthday, let alone the same profession or firm) acts unethically, we judge their behavior as less unethical and feel greater distance from our own moral compass.[217] The Milgram studies also show the importance of social norms—when participants worked together with a (confederate) peer who administered the shocks, compliance reached over 90%. But when peers refused to comply, compliance dropped to 10%.[218]

When a lawyer is discomfited by what he sees, he may struggle to make sense of and justify that conduct. For example, David Luban describes an associate who observed a senior litigator lie to an opponent about a discovery matter and then watched the senior litigator compound that mistake by lying to a federal judge in an attempt to cover up the initial lie. The associate did not take any steps to correct the record and labored to make sense of what he was seeing—he "couldn't believe it . . . [and] kept thinking there must be a reason."[219]

Consider also the possibility of pluralistic ignorance—mistakenly believing that others do not share one's understanding or perception of the world.[220] When one looks around the firm (or to other observers such as accountants or regulators) and does not see anyone else objecting to questionable behavior, one may conclude that nothing is amiss, judging others' failure to object as evidence

---

[215] Lisa G. Lerman, *Lying to Clients,* 138 U. PA. L. REV. 659, 681 (1990); *see* JEROME E. CARLIN, LAWYERS ETHICS: A SURVEY OF THE NEW YORK CITY BAR 116–17 (1966); *see also* Kirkland, *supra* note 33, at 691; Levin, *supra* note 17, at 322; Nelson, *supra* note 189, at 527; Suchman, *supra* note 101, at 860–61.

[216] Francesca Gino et al., *Contagion and Differentiation in Unethical Behavior: The Effect of One Bad Apple on the Barrel,* 20 PSYCHOL. SCI. 393, 397 (2009). In contrast, "observing an out-group peer engaging in unethical behavior reduced participants' likelihood of acting unethically themselves." *Id.* (emphasis added); *see also* Francesca Gino et al., *Contagion or Restitution? When Bad Apples Can Motivate Good Behavior,* 45 J. EXPERIMENTAL SOC. PSYCHOL. 1299, 1301 (2009) (finding that seeing a member of one's in-group act unethically can trigger compensatory ethical behavior when an out-group member is present).

[217] Francesca Gino & Adam D. Galinsky, *Vicarious Dishonesty: When Psychological Closeness Creates Distance From One's Moral Compass,* 119 ORGANIZATIONAL BEHAV. & HUM. DECISION PROCESSES 15, 24 (2012). The study also found a similar, but smaller, effect with respect to vicarious honesty. *Id.* at 23.

[218] MILGRAM, *supra* note 61, at 119.

[219] Luban, *supra* note 204, at 95 (emphasis added).

[220] Dale T. Miller & Deborah A. Prentice, *Collective Errors and Errors About the Collective,* 20 PERSONALITY & SOC. PSYCHOL. BULL. 541, 541 (1994); Deborah A. Prentice & Dale T. Miller, *Pluralistic Ignorance and the Perpetuation of Social Norms by Unwitting Actors,* in 28 ADVANCES IN EXPERIMENTAL SOC. PSYCHOL. 161, 161 (Mark P. Zanna ed., 1996).

that the behavior is not improper. But those others may be silent because they too are attempting to assess the situation.[221]

To make matters worse, the illusion of transparency—the tendency to overestimate our ability to accurately read others' emotional states and their ability to read ours—can compound the difficulties that people have in assessing each other's reactions.[222] In one set of studies, for example, observers' ratings of the extent to which people appeared outwardly concerned about another person's unethical behavior were significantly lower than those same people's self-rated levels of actual concern. That is, people were more concerned than they looked. But people also overestimated the degree to which they manifested their concern to others. Thus, individuals may believe that their own concern is apparent to others when it is not.[223]

Finally, the presence of others can sometimes result in a diffusion of responsibility in which no one assumes responsibility for acting.

> A well-known example involves the failure of top Salomon Brothers officials to report or take prompt corrective action against a trader who submitted false auction bids to evade Treasury Department purchase limits. Four top executives knew of the misconduct and failed to act for several months: the CEO, the president, the general counsel, and the vice chairman, who was the trader's supervisor. According to findings by the Securities and Exchange Commission, each of these officials "placed responsibility for investigating [and curbing the trader's] conduct . . . on someone else." The result was a major financial crisis when the threat of a public investigation ultimately forced disclosure.[224]

Similar diffusion of responsibility can occur, for example, when an associate assumes that someone else will make a decision about how to bill her hours.[225]

---

221 In a classic study, psychologists Bibb Latané and John Darley investigated what would happen when smoke started to drift into a room in which research participants were filling out questionnaires. When participants were alone, most (75%) reported the smoke. But, when more participants were in the room, far fewer reported the smoke. Latané & Darley, *supra* note 210, at 217–18. Looking to others for social cues often provides useful information—but not always.

222 *See* Thomas Gilovich et al., *The Illusion of Transparency: Biased Assessments of Others' Ability to Read One's Emotional States,* 75 J. PERSONALITY & SOC. PSYCHOL. 332, 344 (1998).

223 *Id.* at 343 (studies 3a and 3b).

224 Deborah L. Rhode, *Introduction: Where is the Leadership in Moral Leadership?,* in MORAL LEADERSHIP: THE THEORY AND PRACTICE OF POWER, JUDGMENT, AND POLICY 1, 27–28 (Deborah L. Rhode ed., 2006).

225 *See, e.g.,* Lerman, *supra* note 215, at 716 (describing firm in which associates and paralegals were to keep complete billing records and partners would reduce if they thought the work was excessive).

G. Responding to Others' Ethicality

Lawyers often find themselves in the position of dealing with the ethicality of others—clients, colleagues, and opponents.[226] Interestingly, we tend to be much more judgmental of the ethical failings of others than we are of our own, to see ourselves as being more ethical, objective, and fair than others,[227] to doubt others' reasons for engaging in cooperative acts, and to assume that other people are motivated by self-interest.[228] We often have an interpersonal ethics blind spot in which others' unethical behaviors are more noticeable than their ethical ones.[229] Consistent with the actor-observer bias, we attribute others' moral failings to flaws in their dispositions, but attribute our own missteps to situational factors.[230] We focus more on ethics when judging others, but find competence more important than integrity when judging ourselves.[231] And we judge others based on faulty predictions about what we might have done under the same circumstances.[232]

But while we can be relatively harsh judges of others' ethics, our psychology can make it difficult to notice and respond to others' unethical behavior.[233] First, limits on our ability to pay attention can lead us to miss unethical behavior taking place right in front of us when we are focused on other things like our own cases

---

[226] MODEL RULES OF PROF'L CONDUCT R. 8.3 (2010) ("A lawyer who knows that another lawyer has committed a violation of the Rules of Professional Conduct that raises a substantial question as to that lawyer's honesty, trustworthiness or fitness as a lawyer in other respects, shall inform the appropriate professional authority.").

[227] *See* Gilovich et al, *supra* note 222.

[228] Epley & Caruso, *supra* note 52, at 172; *see also* Clayton R. Critcher & David Dunning, *No Good Deed Goes Unquestioned: Cynical Reconstruals Maintain Belief in the Power of Self-Interest,* 47 J. EXPERIMENTAL SOC. PSYCHOL. 1207, 1212 (2011); Epley & Dunning, *supra* note 48, at 873; Tal Eyal et al., *Judging Near and Distant Virtue and Vice,* 44 J. EXPERIMENTAL SOC. PSYCHOL. 1204, 1209 (2008); Dale T. Miller & Rebecca K. Ratner, *The Disparity Between the Actual and Assumed Power of Self-Interest,* 74 J. PERSONALITY & SOC. PSYCHOL. 53, 60 (1998).

[229] Moberg, *supra* note 55, at 416.

[230] EDWARD E. JONES & RICHARD E. NISBETT, THE ACTOR AND THE OBSERVER: DIVERGENT PERCEPTIONS OF THE CAUSES OF BEHAVIOR, IN ATTRIBUTION: PERCEIVING THE CAUSES OF BEHAVIOR 80 (Edward E. Jones et al. eds., 1972).

[231] *See, e.g.,* Bogdan Wojciszke, *Morality and Competence in Person- and Self-Perception,* 16 EUR. REV. SOC. PSYCHOL. 155, 181 (2005).

[232] *See* DAVID A. DUNNING, SELF-INSIGHT: ROADBLOCKS AND DETOURS ON THE PATH TO KNOWING THYSELF 131 (2005); Mark D. Alicke, *Egocentric Standards of Conduct Evaluation,* 14 BASIC & APPLIED SOC. PSYCHOL. 171, 189 (1993); Balcetis & Dunning, *supra* note 53, at 112; Kristina A. Diekmann, *"She Did What? There Is No Way I Would Do That!" The Potential Interpersonal Harm Caused by Mispredicting One's Behavior,* 80 J. BUS. ETHICS 5, 5 (2008); Woodzicka & LaFrance, *supra* note 53, at 17; *see also* Rachel Barkan et al., *The Pot Calling the Kettle Black: Distancing Response to Ethical Dissonance,* 141 J. EXPERIMENTAL PSYCHOL.: GEN. 757, 768 (2012) (finding process of "double distancing" in that acting unethically causes us to judge others more harshly and to present the self as more virtuous).

[233] Francesca Gino et al., *See No Evil: When We Overlook Other People's Unethical Behavior,* in SOCIAL DECISION MAKING: SOCIAL DILEMMAS, SOCIAL VALUES, & ETHICAL JUDGMENTS 241, 241–42 (Roderick M. Kramer et al. eds., 2010).

and deadlines.[234] Second, we have a tendency to identify with other people—colleagues or clients—whose interests are aligned with ours,[235] making it harder to notice and objectively assess their ethics. Similarly, it can be difficult to acknowledge the unethical behavior of others when doing so would harm one's own interests. This motivated blindness can cause our judgments to be biased in favor of our client or colleague and we are inclined to view their actions favorably, disinclined to believe that they have acted wrongly, and able to recruit reasons to support their actions.[236] Third, we may let others off the hook because we are aware of other instances in which they have acted ethically—a form of moral licensing.[237] Fourth, just as it can be difficult to identify the point at which one's own behavior has gradually crossed the line, detection of when others' incrementally degrading behavior becomes unethical can be challenging.[238] Fifth, the fact that outcome bias may cause our evaluations of the quality of a decision to be influenced by how the decision turns out,[239] can lead us to ignore others' unethical decisions unless and until something bad happens.[240]

Finally, people tend to think that they "will take socially risky actions, when they, in fact, do not"—the illusion of courage.[241] In the abstract we might think we would have the courage to call out the unethical behavior of a client or

---

234 *See* Christopher F. Chabris et al., *You Do Not Talk About Fight Club If You Do Not Notice Fight Club: Inattentional Blindness for a Simulated Real-World Assault,* 2 I-PERCEPTION 150, 150 (2011); Graham Davies & Sarah Hine, *Change Blindness and Eyewitness Testimony,* 141 J. PSYCHOL. 423, 431–33 (2007); Kally J. Nelson et al., *Change Blindness Can Cause Mistaken Eyewitness Identification,* 16 LEGAL & CRIMINOLOGICAL PSYCHOL. 62, 62 (2011); Daniel J. Simons & Christopher F. Chabris, *Gorillas in Our Midst: Sustained Inattentional Blindness for Dynamic Events,* 28 PERCEPTION 1059, 1059 (1999).

235 Don A. Moore et al., *Conflict of Interest and the Intrusion of Bias,* 5 JUDGMENT & DECISION MAKING 37, 45 (2010); Leigh Thompson, *"They Saw a Negotiation": Partisanship and Involvement,* 68 J. PERSONALITY & SOC. PSYCHOL. 839, 850 (1995); *see also* Leigh Thompson & George Loewenstein, *Egocentric Interpretations of Fairness and Interpersonal Conflict,* 51 ORGANIZATIONAL BEHAV. & HUM. DECISION PROCESSES 176, 194 (1992).

236 Moore et al., *supra* note 235, at 40; *see* Langevoort, *supra* note 33, at 104; *see also* Kimberly Kirkland, *Self-Deception and the Pursuit of Ethical Practice: Challenges Faced by Large Law Firm General Counsel,* 9 U. ST. THOMAS L.J. 593, 593–94 (2011) (describing the difficulty that large firm general counsel have in characterizing colleagues as unethical).

237 *See* Daniel A. Effron & Benoît Monin, *Letting People Off the Hook: When Do Good Deeds Excuse Transgressions?,* 36 PERSONALITY & SOC. PSYCHOL. BULL. 1618, 1631 (2010) (finding this to be the case when the unethical act is somewhat ambiguous and the prior ethical behavior is in the same domain).

238 Bazerman & Moore, *supra* note 37, at 48 (discussing how auditors might gradually come to accept corporation's unethical accounting practices).

239 Baron & Hershey, *supra* note 83, at 578.

240 Gino et al., *supra* note 84, at 93; *see also, e.g.,* Robert Prentice, *Contract-Based Defenses in Securities Fraud Litigation: A Behavioral Analysis,* 23 U. ILL. L. REV. 337, 404 (2003) (noting that a supervisor may rate an employee's bad conduct negatively upon learning of a poor outcome, but is less likely to do so if the outcome is unknown).

241 Dunning, *supra* note 232, at 148.

colleague,[242] but when actually deciding whether to do so the immediate negative consequences of confronting the other person—a difficult conversation, the loss of a client, the ire of a partner, the loss of a job, or the difficulty of procuring future employment—loom large. Consider also another key lesson from the Milgram obedience studies—that although most of the participants noticed that what they were being asked to do was problematic, and indeed, many clearly expressed reservations,[243] they were nonetheless unable to turn their objections into a course of behavior that effectively resisted the direction to continue. As psychologists Lee Ross and Richard Nisbett have noted: "the Milgram experiments ultimately may have less to say about 'destructive obedience' than about ineffectual, and indecisive, disobedience."[244] For example, there were lawyers who raised questions about Enron's dealings before its collapse. "In the end, [however,] the doubting lawyers never pressed the issues."[245]

In this vein, consider again the story of John Gellene and his false declarations about potential conflicts of interest in affidavits submitted to the court. At several points in the course of the representation, one of Gellene's partners, Toni Lichstein, raised questions about the potential conflict of interest. Lichstein, however, was repeatedly told by Gellene and Lederman that "it was not a problem ... [and] that Milbank had undertaken all of its disclosure obligations."[246] Although Lichstein questioned the conduct on several occasions, she was not able to push the issue hard enough to convince the firm to take action.

When faced with others' potentially unethical conduct, attorneys may make decisions with an eye toward minimizing the regret that they anticipate feeling—worrying more about making a false accusation than about failing to intervene.[247] Attorneys may overweight such anticipated losses as compared to the less certain

---

[242] Here, too, there is a blind spot: we tend to believe that we are more likely to call out bad behavior than are our peers (and that our reporting is more internally driven, while that of our peers is more driven by external rewards). Yuval Feldman & Orly Lobel, *The Incentives Matrix: The Comparative Effectiveness of Rewards, Liabilities, Duties, and Protections for Reporting Illegality*, 88 TEX. L. REV. 1151, 1190 (2010).

[243] MILGRAM, *supra* note 61, at 116.

[244] ROSS & NISBETT, *supra* note 153, at 57 (emphasis added).

[245] Gordon, *supra* note 21, at 1193 (citing Mike France, *What About the Lawyers?*, BUS. WK., Dec. 23, 2002, at 58; Ellen Joan Pollock, *Limited Partners: Lawyers for Enron Faulted Its Deals, Didn't Force Issue*, WALL ST. J., May 22, 2002, at A1).

[246] REGAN, *supra* note 13, at 250.

[247] Mark D. Rogerson et al., *Nonrational Processes in Ethical Decision Making*, 66 AM. PSYCHOL. 614, 616 (2011). This is also another example of the omission bias. *See* Baron & Hershey, *supra* note 83, at 569.

and more abstract future consequences of remaining silent. Yet, the future consequences may turn out to be severe.[248]

III. Why Don't We Recognize and Learn from Ethical Failures?

For many of the same reasons that we find it difficult to identify ethical challenges in the moment, we also find it difficult to see the ethical implications of our decisions after the fact. Indeed, in one study of lawyer discipline cases, most of the lawyers "were convinced that they had done nothing wrong."[249] And, in many notorious cases—such as the collapse of Enron—the lawyers involved maintain that they acted properly.[250] Once we have engaged in unethical behavior, we feel the need to reconcile that behavior with our otherwise positive views of ourselves, to avoid the distressing feeling known as cognitive dissonance.[251] Thus, we may engage in a post-hoc process of moral disengagement in which we re-characterize what happened so that questionable conduct becomes more permissible.[252] While many people think of ethical decision making as being the product of deliberative ethical reasoning, psychologists have found that ethical decision making tends to be based on relatively intuitive judgments, with moral reasoning occurring after the fact.[253] Once we have made a choice, we are usually able to mobilize reasons to bolster that decision.[254]

---

248 For example, some of those who heard about or witnessed Penn State coach Jerry Sandusky's transgressions, but failed to report them, are themselves now being prosecuted. Mark Scolforo, *Graham Spanier Charged: Ex-Penn State President Facing Perjury Charge in Jerry Sandusky Case,* HUFFINGTON POST, Nov. 1, 2012, http://www.huffingtonpost.com/2012/11/01/graham-spanier-charged-penn-state-sandusky_n_2057723.html.

249 Abel, *supra* note 78, at 491.

250 *See* Gordon, *supra* note 21, at 1190; *see also* The Financial Collapse of Enron—Part 4: Hearing Before the S. Comm. On Oversight and Investigations, 107th Cong. 19–22 (2002) (statement of Joseph C. Dilg, Managing Partner of Vinson & Elkins, L.L.P.), available at http://www.gpo.gov/fdsys/pkg/CHRG-107hhrg78506/html/CHRG-107hhrg78506.htm (expressing his confidence that the firm "fully met its ethical and professional responsibilities" in representing Enron).

251 *See* LEON FESTINGER, A THEORY OF COGNITIVE DISSONANCE 8 (1957); *see also* Shahar Ayal & Francesca Gino, *Honest Rationales for Dishonest Behavior,* in THE SOCIAL PSYCHOLOGY OF MORALITY: EXPLORING THE CAUSES OF GOOD AND EVIL 149, 150 (Mario Mikulincer & Phillip R. Shaver eds., 2012) (describing ethical dissonance); Luban, *supra* note 204, at 95.

252 Bandura, *supra* note 67, at 194; Lisa L. Shu et al., *Dishonest Deed, Clear Conscience: When Cheating Leads to Moral Disengagement and Motivated Forgetting,* 37 PERSONALITY & SOC. PSYCHOL. BULL. 330, 331 (2011).

253 Haidt, *supra* note 104, at 818. For a general discussion of intuitive and deliberative thinking, see DANIEL KAHNEMAN, THINKING FAST AND SLOW (2011).

254 *See, e.g.,* Christopher K. Hsee, *Elastic Justification: How Unjustifiable Factors Influence Judgments,* 66 ORGANIZATIONAL BEHAV. & HUM. DECISION PROCESSES 122, 123 (1996); Michael I. Norton, Joseph A. Vandello, & John M. Darley, *Casuistry and Social Category Bias,* 87 J. PERSONALITY & SOC. PSYCHOL. 817, 817 (2004); Samuel R. Sommers & Michael I. Norton, *Race-Based Judgments, Race Neutral Justifications: Experimental Examination of Peremptory Use and the Batson Challenge Procedure,* 31 LAW & HUM. BEHAV. 261, 264 (2007); *see also* Richard Nisbett & Timothy Wilson, *Telling More Than We Can Know: Verbal Reports on Mental Processes,* 84 PSYCHOL. REV. 231, 232 (1977). The analytic skills of lawyers seem well suited to this sort of thinking. Indeed,

Given this general human tendency, it is unsurprising that lawyers who face ethical complaints or questions tend to recruit a range of justifications.[255] Conduct that is inconsistent with one's image of oneself as an ethical person can be attributed to situational, rather than dispositional, factors.[256] Attempts may also be made to locate blame elsewhere—on adversaries,[257] on the circumstances,[258] on regulators,[259] on clients,[260] and on judges.[261] The omission bias described above can be invoked to minimize blame of one who did not engage in an affirmative act.[262] Unethical conduct can also be rationalized post-hoc through appeals to different metrics of fairness or to other accepted values—for example, notions of lawyers as zealous advocates or creative interpreters of legal rules, rules protecting client confidences, principles of reciprocity or self-defense, or the need to fight against injustice.

---

people engaging in this sort of rationalization are sometimes characterized as "intuitive lawyers." *See, e.g.,* Haidt, *supra* note 104, at 821; Roderick M. Kramer & David M. Messick, *Ethical Cognition and the Framing of Organizational Dilemmas: Decision Makers as Intuitive Lawyers,* in CODES OF CONDUCT: BEHAVIORAL RESEARCH INTO BUSINESS ETHICS 59 (David M. Messick & Ann E. Tenbrunsel eds., 1996).

[255] *See, e.g.,* Abel, *supra* note 78, at 100.

[256] *See* Jones & Harris, *supra* note 140; *see also* Austin Sarat, *Enactments of Professionalism: A Study of Judges' and Lawyers' Accounts of Ethics and Civility in Litigation,* 67 FORDHAM L. REV. 809, 828 (1998) (reporting that each group of attorneys "presents itself as a 'victim' of forces over which it has little or no control").

[257] *See, e.g.,* Sarat, *supra* note 256, at 822 (reporting attorney's view that "[r]efusal to answer (a discovery request) is not an ethical problem because plaintiffs' counsel can remedy it (through motions to compel)"); *see also* Yablon, *supra* note 171, at 1624 n.18 ("Lawyers tend to blame discovery abuse on the fact that their opponents act like jerks . . . ."); Michael Powell & Lois Romano, *Roman Catholic Church Shifts Legal Strategy: Aggressive Litigation Replaces Quiet Settlements,* WASH. POST, May 13, 2002, at Al (reporting that lawyers for the church "said some plaintiffs are delusional, while others blame every problem in their life on past abuse by priests").

[258] *See, e.g.,* Abel, *supra* note 78, at 33, 65, 100 (noting that lawyers blame circumstances such as workload, judicial backlog); Lerman, *supra* note 215, at 713–14 (describing lawyers who justified unethical billing practices by pointing to the "unreasonable" billing requirements of their firms).

[259] Langevoort, *supra* note 66; *see also* Abel, *supra* note 78, at 32 (noting disciplined lawyers' objections to "selective prosecution"); REGAN, *supra* note 13, at 328 ("Lawyers in large firms . . . tend to be skeptical that strict application of the bankruptcy conflict rule serves important ethical purposes.").

[260] *See, e.g.,* Abel, *supra* note 78, at 65 (describing a lawyer who "blamed his personal injury clients for his own failure to pursue their claims"), at 101 (describing lawyer who deceived client because "it would have been very hard for him to understand" and failed to tell another her case had been dismissed (due to his negligence) because "she never asked me specifically"). Billing disputes are often blamed on clients, with attorneys arguing that clients received regular billing statements and should have raised any questions at earlier stages, that big clients can afford to pay more, that aggressively billing big clients allows them to represent other clients who cannot afford them, and that they only billed what they were worth. *See, e.g.,* Abel, *supra* note 78, at 350–51; Lisa G. Lerman, *Blue-Chip Bilking: Regulation of Billing and Expense Fraud by Lawyers,* 12 GEO. J. LEGAL ETHICS 205, 258–62 (1999); *cf.* Lisa G. Lerman, *Scenes From A Law Firm,* 50 RUTGERS L. REV. 2153, 2187–88 (1998).

[261] *See, e.g.,* Sarat, *supra* note 256, at 832 (reporting lawyers' consensus "that judges hate to get involved in discovery disputes . . . leaving it to the lawyers to play the discovery game with relatively little supervision").

[262] For example, an attorney might tell herself or others that she would have disclosed particular information if the other side had specifically asked about it.

Confirmation bias also helps us remember aspects of the decision or situation that are consistent with an ethical self-image, rather than the details of any ethical lapse. "If mistakes were made, memory helps us remember that they were made by someone else. If we were there, we were just innocent bystanders."[263] Such memory effects can result in what ethicist Patricia Werhane has called moral amnesia or "an inability to remember or learn from one's own and other's past mistakes and to transfer that knowledge when fresh challenges arise."[264]

All of this can conspire with the pressure to act in ways that are consistent with our own prior behavior,[265] making it difficult to learn from or acknowledge any missteps. Consider again John Gellene, the bankruptcy attorney described in EAT WHAT YOU KILL. Why didn't he, at some point, recognize his mistake and correct his misstatements to the court?

> It likely would have been psychologically stressful for Gellene to do so at this point, however. He had made a prior decision not to disclose the Salovaara and South Street connections. He had publicly proclaimed Milbank's fitness for the job in the face of an attack. He likely had rationalized his conduct in a way that permitted him to deny that he had done anything unethical. It would be hard at this point to disavow those representations and to reassess that rationalization.[266]

Finally, engaging in unethical behavior can itself change one's perspective on and memory of the relevant ethical standards.[267] When our behavior and our beliefs conflict, one way to reduce the resulting discomfort is to change our beliefs to match our behavior. For example, those who cheat tend to become more lenient in their judgments of cheating, and those who resist cheating become more intolerant of cheating.[268] Also, the effects of pluralistic ignorance can mean that

---

263 CAROL TAVRIS & ELLIOT ARONSON, MISTAKES WERE MADE (BUT NOT BY ME): WHY WE JUSTIFY FOOLISH BELIEFS, BAD DECISIONS, AND HURTFUL ACTS 70 (2007).

264 PATRICIA H. WERHANE, MORAL IMAGINATION AND THE SEARCH FOR ETHICAL DECISION-MAKING IN MANAGEMENT 7 (1999). As a result of this sort of self-deception, people can fail to discount their accomplishments for the fact that such successes were gained through unethical means. This can make learning particularly difficult. *See* Zoë Chance et al., *Temporal View of the Costs and Benefits of Self-Deception,* 108 PROC. NAT'L ACAD. SCI. 15655, 15656 (2011) (finding that participants who obtained high scores by cheating predicted that they would score well on a subsequent test on which they could not cheat).

265 Cialdini, *supra* note 64, at 57.

266 REGAN, *supra* note 13, at 343; *see also* Langevoort, supra note 66, at 512 ("To blow the whistle now on any common practice or pattern of innovation would raise troubling questions about the prior months or years when the lawyer acquiesced in what was happening. The mind fights such inference.").

267 Shu et al., *supra* note 252, at 332; Lisa Shu & Francesca Gino, *Sweeping Dishonesty Under the Rug: How Unethical Actions Lead to Forgetting of Moral Rules,* 102 J. PERSONALITY & SOC. PSYCHOL. 1164, 1168 (2012).

268 *See, e.g.,* Judson Mills, *Changes in Moral Attitudes Following Temptation,* 26 J. PERSONALITY 517, 518 (1958). *See generally* Leon Festinger & James M. Carlsmith, *Cognitive Consequences of Forced Compliance,* 58 J.

as no one speaks up about particular unethical behavior, new norms of ethics begin to emerge that alter attitudes about ethics.

IV. What Can We Do?

The common prescriptions for ethical failures are to increase the severity and enforcement of applicable sanctions and to pay greater attention to educating attorneys about the relevant ethical rules.[269] But while some ethical failures are the result of deliberate moral reasoning and cost-benefit analysis that lead to an unethical decision and some ethical failures are due to a lack of knowledge of the relevant rules, a range of evidence suggests that many ethical failures occur unconsciously and unintentionally, even where the attorney has basic knowledge of the relevant ethical rules. Thus, individual attorneys and legal employers[270] should take steps that go beyond these common responses, steps that focus on dealing with ambiguities in rules and standards,[271] ethical issues arising out of the agency relationship, the challenges of the adversarial system, the tolls of law practice, the influence of status and power, issues relating to lawyers' practice in groups, and the difficulties lawyers face in responding to instances in which others fail to act ethically.

A. Improving Individual Ethics

For all the reasons discussed, even attorneys who begin their careers with the purest of motives and the highest of ethical aspirations are at risk for committing ethical infractions. Yet, attorneys can take affirmative steps to minimize the likelihood that they will behave unethically and to create the capacity for ethical courage.[272]

ABNORMAL & SOC. PSYCHOL. 203, 203–04 (1959). Even considering the behavior from the perspective of the person who has acted unethically can affect judgments of ethicality. Shirit Kronzon & John Darley, *Is This Tactic Ethical? Biased Judgments of Ethics in Negotiation,* 21 BASIC & APPLIED SOC. PSYCHOL. 49, 58 (1999).

[269] *See, e.g.,* MONROE FREEDMAN, FOREWARD, *ETHICS, TRUTH, AND JUSTICE IN CRIMINAL LITIGATION,* 68 FORDHAM L. REV. 1371, 1375 (2000).

[270] The psychology of ethical decision making and behavior that we review here also has important implications for how we teach about ethics in law schools. For one recent discussion on this subject see Art Hinshaw, *Teaching Negotiation Ethics,* 63 J. LEGAL EDUC. 82 (2013).

[271] We do not, in this Article, offer suggestions as to how ethical rules might be changed to better accommodate human psychology. While improvement in the content of the rules is likely possible and desirable, our focus here is on improvements that can be made in the context of the existing ethical rules.

[272] *See generally* THE PSYCHOLOGY OF COURAGE: MODERN RESEARCH ON AN ANCIENT VIRTUE (Cynthia L.S. Pury & Shane J. Lopez, eds., 2010); *see also* ZIMBARDO, *supra* note 210, at 21–22, 485 (discussing the "banality of heroism" and noting that just as each of us is capable of unethical behavior, so too are we each a "potential hero, waiting for the right situational moment to make the decision to . . . [do the right thing] despite personal risk and sacrifice"); *Psychology & Heroism: Defining Heroism,* HEROIC IMAGINATION PROJECT, http://www.heroicimagination.org/welcome/psychology-and-heroism (last visited Sept. 8, 2013).

1. Be Aware of the Psychology of Ethics

It is important for lawyers to recognize their susceptibility to bounded ethicality and to have an awareness of the factors that can influence ethical decision making. While many of the phenomena we discuss operate outside of conscious awareness, recognizing their existence makes it possible to take steps to address them.[273] Attorneys can better plan for how to handle ethical dilemmas if they understand that their predictions about how they will react to future ethical issues are not always accurate. Attorneys who understand that unethical decisions are more likely when losses loom can exercise particular caution in those circumstances—such as when they are at risk of losing an important client. Attorneys who understand the nature of the slippery ethics slope can seek to resist the pull of each step. Attorneys who understand that even (or especially) their core values can lead them astray, can be alert for such vulnerability. Attorneys who understand the dynamics of social norms and pluralistic ignorance will be equipped to reject the assumption that no one else is bothered.[274] Attorneys who recognize the temptation of post-hoc rationalization can question the reasons they generate for their own behavior.[275] Attorneys who know that disclosure distortion may lead them to act more unethically in a situation in which interests conflict can take steps to guard against that result. And, attorneys who are aware that the agency relationship may tempt them to overstep can watch how far they go to try to help their client.[276]

2. Make Ethics Salient

"[I]f we are reminded of morality at the moment we are tempted, then we are much more likely to be honest."[277] Thus, it can be important for attorneys to find ways to include ethical factors in the mix of considerations reviewed in making a

---

273 *See* NATE SILVER, THE SIGNAL AND THE NOISE: WHY SO MANY PREDICTIONS FAIL—BUT SOME DON'T 366 (2012) (quoting Daniel Kahneman: " 'There's no way that you can control yourself not to have [the Müller-Lyer] illusion,' Kahneman told me. 'You look at [the arrows], and one of the arrows is going to look longer than the other. But you can train yourself to recognize that this is a pattern that causes an illusion, and in that situation, I can't trust my impressions; I've got to use a ruler.' ").

274 For example, the Enron whistleblower, Sherron Watkins, spoke out even though others at Enron acted as if all were well. Nancy B. Rapoport, *Enron, Titanic, and The Perfect Storm,* 71 FORDHAM L. REV. 1373, 1379–81 (2003).

275 Tenbrunsel & Messick, *supra* note 67, at 234.

276 *See generally* Emily Pronin & Matthew B. Kugler, *Valuing Thoughts, Ignoring Behavior: The Introspection Illusion as a Source of the Bias Blind Spot,* 43 J. EXPERIMENTAL SOC. PSYCHOL. 565, 565 (2007) (finding that educating people about the limits of introspection reduced the bias blind spot).

277 DAN ARIELY, PREDICTABLY IRRATIONAL: THE HIDDEN FORCES THAT SHAPE OUR DECISIONS 289 (2008); *see also* Mazar et al., *supra* note 36, at 635 (hypothesizing that "when people attend to their own moral standards . . . any dishonest action is more likely to be reflected in their self-concept . . . which in turn will cause them to adhere to a stricter delineation of honest and dishonest behavior").

given decision,[278] even when the decision does not obviously turn on ethical considerations.

Bringing ethical considerations to the forefront can also help us encourage others to behave ethically. For example, negotiators are less likely to engage in deception when they have recently been reminded of ethical norms.[279] Similarly, negotiators who give reasons for their offers or demands that are in step with fairness norms are more likely to elicit ethical behavior from the other side.[280]

To bring ethics to the fore, individual attorneys can:

- Reflect regularly on core values. Keeping a journal or engaging in other forms of self-reflection can help keep ethics on the table and can facilitate detection of moments in which decisions challenge those values.[281]
- Keep a reminder of core values front and center. A paperweight, wall hanging, or other memento can be a visual reminder of the standards one wants to uphold.[282]
- Avoid euphemisms.[283]

---

[278] Kish-Gephart et al., *supra* note 31, at 20 (suggesting that organizations can reduce unethical behavior by "making behavioral norms . . . more prominent and clearly defined"); *see also* David F. Caldwell & Dennis Moberg, *An Exploratory Investigation of the Effect of Ethical Culture in Activating Moral Imagination,* 73 J. BUS. ETHICS 193, 201 (2007).

[279] *See, e.g.,* Karl Aquino, *The Effects of Ethical Climate and the Availability of Alternatives on the Use of Deception During Negotiation,* 9 INT'L J. CONFLICT MGMT. 195, 200 (1998).

[280] *See* Maurice E. Schweitzer & Donald E. Gibson, *Fairness, Feelings, and Ethical Decision-Making: Consequences of Violating Community Standards of Fairness,* 77 J. BUS. ETHICS 287, 287 (2008).

[281] *See, e.g.,* Crowley & Gottlieb, *supra* note 102, at 68 (recommending self-reflection activities to help practitioners consider the origin of their personal morals and how they align with the ethics code). Law professor Kate Kruse, who has her students write letters to themselves discussing their core values and ambitions and then returns the letters (unopened) to students when they graduate, reports that students have found the letter helps keep them on their intended path. Professor Jennifer Brown has commenced a journaling project with her students, designed to help them think about their internal values and recall their early goals and values once they become attorneys. Jennifer Gerarda Brown, *Beginner's Wisdom: A Guided Journal for Reflecting Upon the Professional and Personal Lessons of the 1L Year* (unpublished work in progress) (on file with author); *see also* Alison L. Antes et al., *Applying Cases to Solve Ethical Problems: The Significance of Positive and Process-Oriented Reflection,* 22 ETHICS & BEHAV. 113, 115, 123 (2012); Hugo J.E.M. Alberts et al., *Fighting Self-Control Failure: Overcoming Ego Depletion by Increasing Self-Awareness,* 47 J. EXPERIMENTAL SOC. PSYCHOL. 58, 58 (2011) (finding that self-awareness increases self-control).

[282] *See* ARIELY, *supra* note 277.

[283] *See supra* notes 77–78.

- Imagine and individualize the people on the other side or the people who will experience the consequences of a decision.[284]
- Bear in mind the long-term reputational consequences—to the individual lawyer and the organization—of unethical conduct.[285]

3. Be Self-Critical

It can be helpful for individual lawyers to develop a critical stance toward their own ethics. Given how easy it can be for attorneys to justify a desired course of action or fall into telling clients, colleagues, or supervising attorneys what they want to hear, attorneys should ask themselves whether their advice or ethical decisions would be the same if they were on the other side of the decision. Questioning one's judgments, considering the opposite,[286] and examining "the justifications that we concoct to rationalize our actions" with a critical eye can help to temper the fading of ethics from decision making.[287]

Similarly, seeking or adopting an outside perspective—ideally before one takes the first step, but also when one finds oneself elsewhere on the slope—can lead to a more nuanced consideration of a decision's potential ethical implications.[288] Consulting past experience can help one more realistically assess whether a contemplated workload is manageable or whether another case can be competently handled.[289] Considering how a "disinterested" or "disagreeable" observer might evaluate the situation, decision, or conduct, can provide a valuable

---

284 *See supra* notes 83–85; *see also* Kish-Gephart et al., *supra* note 31, at 20 (suggesting that organizations can reduce unethical behavior by teaching employees to "learn to associate potential unethical behavior with severe, well-defined harm . . . to a familiar or recognizable victim similar to the actor").

285 *See supra* note 59 and accompanying text.

286 Charles G. Lord, et al., *Considering the Opposite: A Corrective Strategy for Social Judgment*, 47 J. PERSONALITY & SOC. PSYCHOL. 1231, 1231 (1984); *see also* Laura J. Kray & Adam D. Galinsky, *The Debiasing Effect of Counterfactual Mind-sets: Increasing the Search for Disconfirmatory Information in Group Decisions*, 91 ORGANIZATIONAL BEHAV. & HUM. DECISION PROCESSES 69, 76 (2003).

287 Tenbrunsel & Messick, *supra* note 67, at 234.

288 Rhode, *supra* note 126, at 1320–21; Tenbrunsel & Messick, *supra* note 67, at 231 (recognizing also that the best one may be able to do is to "try to imagine what the other would experience from our own perspective").

289 *See* Daniel Kahneman & Dan Lovallo, *Timid Choices and Bold Forecasts: A Cognitive Perspective on Risk Taking*, 39 MGMT. SCI. 17, 24–25 (1993) (discussing the "outside view" as one that takes into account past cases that are similar to the present one).

perspective.[290] Consulting ethics counsel[291] or calling an ethics hotline[292] may contribute to this critical analysis. Attorneys may also find it helpful to consider how a trusted friend or family member might view a particular action—asking themselves, for example, whether they could look a parent in the eyes and explain a particular choice.[293] Similarly, one might be careful not to do anything one would not feel comfortable having made public.[294]

As part of this critical stance, a focus on attentively striving to behave ethically is key. Valuing ethics as part of one's identity helps to sustain ethical behavior when time and cognitive resources are in short supply. That is, one who puts great stock in having a positive moral identity is better equipped to resist the pull towards unethical conduct.[295] Attorneys might prime the importance of ethics to their identity by attending conferences or participating in other groups focused on professional responsibility[296] as well as through the other ways in which they choose to make ethics salient.

---

290 *See* Russell Korobkin, *Psychological Impediments to Mediation Success: Theory and Practice,* 21 OHIO ST. J. ON DISP. RESOL. 281, 296 (2006) (discussing the "disagreeable adjudicator"); Lord et al., *supra* note 286, at 1231–32 (finding that considering an "opposite" perspective is effective in reducing biased evaluation). Prior to 2002, the commentary to Rule 1.7 advised that lawyers consider the perspective of a "disinterested lawyer" in evaluating conflicts of interest, but that language was removed as part of the Ethics 2000 revisions to the rules. *See* MODEL RULES OF PROF'L CONDUCT R. 1.7 cmt. 5 (2001).

291 *See* Kimberly Kirkland, *Ethical Infrastructures and De Facto Ethical Norms at Work in Large US Law Firms: The Role of Ethics Counsel,* 11 LEGAL ETHICS 181, 199 (2008) (evaluating the role of ethics counsel).

292 *See, e.g.,* Ethics Hotline, St. B. of Cal., http://ethics.calbar.ca.gov/Ethics/Hotline.aspx (last visited Sept. 10, 2013).

293 In describing decisions to act ethically, many people evoke the notion that they want to be able to "look at themselves in the mirror." This idea has been attributed to a German ambassador who purportedly resigned rather than provide prostitutes to a royal party, stating "I refused to see a pimp in the mirror in the morning when I shave." HOWARD GARDNER ET AL., GOOD WORK: WHEN EXCELLENCE AND ETHICS MEET 11 (2001). Consistent with this instinct, increasing awareness of one's self and values—for example, looking at one's image in a mirror—reduces the incidence of unprincipled behavior. *See, e.g.,* Arthur L. Beaman et al., *Self-Awareness and Transgression in Children: Two Field Studies,* 37 J. PERSONALITY & SOC. PSYCHOL. 1835, 1842 (1979); Edward Diener & Mark Wallbom, *Effects of Self-Awareness on Antinormative Behavior,* 10 J. RES. PERSONALITY 107, 107 (1976); Carl A. Kallgren et al., *A Focus Theory of Normative Conduct: When Norms Do and Do Not Affect Behavior,* 26 PERSONALITY & SOC. PSYCHOL. BULL. 1002, 1008–10 (2000); Lynne C. Vincent et al., *Stretching the Moral Gray Zone: Positive Affect, Moral Disengagement, and Dishonesty,* 24 Psychol. Sci. 595, 598 (2013).

294 *See* Leslie C. Levin, *Immigration Lawyers and the Lying Client,* in LAWYERS IN PRACTICE: ETHICAL DECISION MAKING IN CONTEXT, *supra* note 101, at 101–03.

295 Francesca Gino et al., *Unable to Resist Temptation: How Self-Control Depletion Promotes Unethical Behavior,* 115 ORGANIZATIONAL BEHAV. & HUM. DECISION PROC. 191, 199 (2011); Barry R. Schlenker et al., *Moral Identity, Integrity, and Personal Responsibility,* in PERSONALITY, IDENTITY, AND CHARACTER: EXPLORATIONS IN MORAL PSYCHOLOGY, *supra* note 31, at 316; *see also Gert Cornelissen et al., Rules or Consequences? The Role of Ethical Mind-Sets in Moral Dynamics,* 24 PSYCHOL. SCI. 482, 487 (2013).

296 *See* Cassandra Burke Robertson, *Judgment, Identity, and Independence,* 42 CONN. L. REV. 1, 13 (2009) (suggesting that people often identify with groups and adopt a set of standards that guide behavior).

At the same time, it is also very important to be humble about one's likely success in this endeavor. Given the tendency to be overconfident about our own ethics,[297] attorneys should resist the "reassuring illusion of invulnerability"—the misapprehension that they will always be able to identify and resist the influences that shape behavior.[298] In particular, all else being equal, people who are primed to think of themselves as highly ethical are more likely to act unethically (as a result of moral licensing) than are those who focus on their own past unethical deeds.[299] It is better, then, to admit and remember mistakes, rather than to overestimate one's virtue.[300]

Overall then, striving for ethical success but recognizing one's ethical fallibility may be the best path toward ethical behavior.

4. Plan Ahead

Critical thought takes time and cognitive resources, and as previously discussed, a lack of time and the presence of cognitive stressors can lead to unethical decision making. But attorneys can enhance their ethical behavior by planning ahead and cultivating a set of ethical habits, so that making the right call becomes more automatic.[301]

Because it can be quite difficult to predict how we will handle ethical challenges, we should try to anticipate ethical dilemmas and to specifically plan and rehearse our responses ahead of time—creating scripts for ourselves that we can follow when necessary.[302] Engaging in an ethical planning process allows us to step away from the relevant pressures and focus instead on how to rise to one's ethical ideals.[303] Similarly, exploring one's "ethics autobiography"—reflecting on personal values, professional responsibilities, and how they relate, can help

---

[297] *See supra* Section I.A.

[298] ZIMBARDO, *supra* note 210, at 180.

[299] Jennifer Jordan et al., *Striving for the Moral Self: The Effects of Recalling Past Moral Actions on Future Moral Behavior,* 37 PERSONALITY & SOC. PSYCHOL. BULL. 701, 702 (2011); *see also* ZIMBARDO, *supra* note 210; Sonya Sachdeva et al., *Sinning Saints and Saintly Sinners: The Paradox of Moral Self-Regulation,* 20 PSYCHOL. SCI. 523, 524 (2009).

[300] Jordan et al., *supra* note 299.

[301] *See* Don A. Moore & George Loewenstein, *Self-Interest, Automaticity, and the Psychology of Conflict of Interest,* 17 SOC. JUST. RES. 189, 197 (2004). In particular, some of the effects we have described here—such as the impact of loss frames on ethical decision making—can be moderated when there is less time pressure. Mary C. Kern & Dolly Chugh, *Bounded Ethicality: The Perils of Loss Framing,* 20 PSYCHOL. SCI. 378, 378 (2009). Because busy attorneys will not always have time for extended analysis, it is important to take time to make thoughtful decisions when that is possible and to plan ahead for when it is not.

[302] Ann E. Tenbrunsel et al., *The Ethical Mirage: A Temporal Explanation as to Why We Aren't as Ethical as We Think We Are* 37 (Harvard Bus. Sch., Working Paper 08–012, 2009); *see also* Trope & Liberman, *supra* note 59, at 404.

[303] Kivetz & Tyler, *supra* note 59, at 208.

establish ethical intuitions and increase awareness of one's ethical weaknesses.[304] Identifying the resources that might be available—for example, in-house ethics counsel, an ethics hotline, or a trusted confidant—can mean that these resources will more likely spring to mind when needed. Anticipating the pressures that are likely to be dominant at the time of the decision can minimize misprediction.[305] And, establishing implementation intentions—anticipating concrete triggers and planning specific responses—can help one to act consistently with one's ideals.[306] Imagining and practicing, for example, the specifics of how one will respond when a negotiation counterpart or discovery request asks for information one would rather not disclose, how one will respond when one is asked to do something with which one is uncomfortable, how one will deal with pressures to bill inappropriately, how one will proceed when one suspects that a client has not been candid or when a client asks the attorney to lie, or how one will act when one observes a colleague behaving unethically, can make it much easier to follow through with those plans.[307]

To reduce the possibility of unwittingly sliding into problematic behavior, it can be helpful to identify concrete behaviors that can serve as warnings that a line may be crossed.

> Set yourself some telltale sign—something that you know is wrong. Write down on a piece of paper: "I will never backdate a document." Or "I will never let a co-worker get blamed for something that was my fault." Or "I will never paper a deal that I don't understand." Or "I will never do anything that I couldn't describe to my dad while looking him

[304] Crowley & Gottlieb, *supra* note 102, at 68 ("[I]ncreased insight may enable practitioners to recognize how good intentions can be assets and liabilities and help them detect the direction of this influence in complex ethical situations.").

[305] MAX H. BAZERMAN & ANN E. TENBRUNSEL, BLIND SPOTS: WHY WE FAIL TO DO WHAT'S RIGHT AND WHAT TO DO ABOUT IT 154 (2011) (citing Kristina A. Diekmann et al., *An Examination of the Relationship Between Behavioral Forecasts and Interpersonal Condemnation in Two Organizational Conflict Situations* (Univ. of Utah, Working Paper, 2010)).

[306] *See* Peter M. Gollwitzer & Paschal Sheeran, *Implementation Intentions and Goal Achievement: A Meta-Analysis of Effects of Processes,* 38 ADV. EXPERIMENTAL SOC. PSYCHOL. 69, 69 (2006).

[307] *See* G. Richard Shell, *Bargaining with the Devil Without Losing Your Soul,* in WHAT'S FAIR: ETHICS FOR NEGOTIATORS 57, 71–73 (Carrie Menkel-Meadow & Michael Wheeler eds., 2004) (discussing ways to respond to questions without lying). In similar ways, crafting a strategy in advance for how one might disobey authority might channel disobedience. Lee Ross and Richard Nisbett propose the following "thought experiment":

> Suppose that the experimenter had announced at the beginning of the session that, if at any time the teacher wished to terminate his participation in the experiment, he could indicate his desire to do so by pressing a button on the table in front of him. We trust the reader agrees with us that if this channel factor had been opened up, the obedience rate would have been a fraction of what it was. The converse of this is that the absence of such a 'disobedience channel' is precisely what condemned Milgram's subjects to their hapless behavior.

ROSS & NISBETT, *supra* note 153, at 57.

> in the eye." Pick your telltale sign carefully—and, the moment the alarm rings, evacuate the building.[308]

One immigration lawyer "recalled that his mentor in his first job taught him 'that the minute that fraud comes up, you show people the door.' "[309] Similarly, it can be helpful to identify warning signs of less egregious missteps.

Because we feel inclined to act in ways that are consistent with our previous actions, making a commitment to an ethical course of conduct—particularly an active or public commitment—can help us stay the course. Thus, one might "precommit to [an] intended ethical choice by sharing it with an unbiased individual whose opinion you respect and whom you believe to be highly ethical"[310] or one might write down a set of ethical commitments.[311]

Finally, planning ahead can sometimes help one to eliminate potential problems—such as conflicts of interest. For example, one might avoid a certain type of fee agreement in a particular case. Or, one can decline to provide counsel when one's judgment might be compromised. "No ethically sensitive (or even reasonably prudent) attorney should follow the example of Vinson & Elkins, which agreed to review the propriety of Enron transactions in which its own services had been used."[312] Similarly, if one believes an organization does not operate ethically, one may choose not to work there.[313]

5. Recognize and Confront Others' Unethical Conduct

Many of these same strategies can help attorneys notice and respond to potential ethical missteps by clients, colleagues, or supervisors. But, we have seen that it can be quite difficult to recognize others' unethical conduct and that group settings often make it even harder to recognize unethical conduct, due to the pressures of phenomena such as social conformity, pluralistic ignorance, and the illusion of transparency.[314] To fight against these phenomena, attorneys should make ethics salient, exercise critical thought, and remind themselves that others' silence is not necessarily an endorsement of particular behavior.

Of course, even once attorneys have recognized questionable ethical actions involving clients, colleagues, or supervisors, it can also be particularly difficult to

---

308 Luban, *supra* note 171, at 369.

309 Levin, *supra* note 294, at 102.

310 Bazerman & Tenbrunsel, *supra* note 305, at 156. Thus, one might plan, with colleagues, law school classmates, or others, how one will respond to specific ethical challenges.

311 *See* Crowley & Gottlieb, *supra* note 102, at 68 (discussing the benefits of journaling).

312 Rhode, *supra* note 126, at 1334.

313 *See* Mather et al., *supra* note 212, at 124–27.

314 *See supra* Section II.F.

critique or challenge that behavior. Instead, it is tempting to withhold criticism from clients, colleagues, and supervisors, particularly in a workplace where collegiality is valued. But, attorneys should remind themselves that taking a critical stance better serves the client or colleague than does letting them blithely slide down a slippery ethical slope. Moreover, raising ethical concerns need not result in nasty confrontations. Instead, it is possible that the "[c]onduct that attorneys find ethically objectionable can be more diplomatically packaged as unduly risky, as something that will not play well with jurors, government regulators, the media, or the general public. By the same token, the moral high road can also be portrayed as desirable for prudential reasons," important to the reputation of the client, lawyer, organization or profession, or as a means of forestalling regulation.[315] Admittedly, such characterizations are not always possible or sufficient, and in some instances attorneys will have to be more blunt—serving the client, organization, or colleague by providing a reality check. In extreme circumstances, the attorney may even be required to withdraw from a representation or report a client or colleague's improper act.[316] Again, planning ahead can facilitate doing the right thing in these difficult circumstances.

B. Enhance Organizational Ethical Culture

Legal organizations cannot assume that law schools have taught junior attorneys everything they need to know about legal ethics, nor about reporting any problems they may find.[317] "To assume that any 20-year-old of good general character can function ethically in professional situations is no more warranted than assuming that any logical 20-year-old can function as a lawyer without special education."[318] Similarly, legal organizations cannot assume that more senior lawyers know all that is necessary to prevent unethical behavior. Indeed, their very seniority and experience can contribute to the fading of ethics. Thus, organizations need to help all lawyers engage with ethics on an on-going basis.

The ethical culture of a firm, company, agency, or practice group is an important determinant of how ethically the attorneys within that entity will

---

[315] Rhode, *supra* note 126, at 1318–19.

[316] *See* MODEL RULES OF PROF'L CONDUCT R. 1.6 (2010).

[317] For example, Harvard grads "almost uniformly felt that their ethics training in law school had done little to prepare them for the issues they now confront as practicing attorneys." Robert Granfield & Thomas Koenig, *"It's Hard to be a Human Being and a Lawyer": Young Attorneys and the Confrontation with Ethical Ambiguity in Legal Practice,* 105 W. VA. L. REV. 495, 508 (2003).

[318] LINDA K. TREVIÑO & KATHERINE A. NELSON, MANAGING BUSINESS ETHICS: STRAIGHT TALK ABOUT HOW TO DO IT RIGHT 15–16 (2007) (quoting James Rest, *Moral Judgment: An Interesting Variable for Higher Education Research,* paper presented at the Annual Convention for the Association for the Study of Higher Education (1987)).

behave.[319] Importantly, the ethical culture of an organization depends not only on its expressed ethical codes and policies but also far more broadly on its systems and practices.[320] Just as group norms may have a negative impact, so too may group norms set the stage for attorneys to do the right thing.[321] Lawyers who observe others within the organization engaging in ethical behavior (particularly those seen as experts[322] and those with whom they work closely)[323] and who observe that the organization rewards ethical behavior are likely to make more ethical decisions themselves. Consider how two different prosecutors describe the

---

319 *See, e.g.,* Caldwell & Moberg, *supra* note 278, at 199–202; Muel Kaptein, *Developing and Testing a Measure for the Ethical Culture of Organizations: The Corporate Ethical Virtues Model,* 29 J. ORGANIZATIONAL BEHAV. 923, 923 (2008) (discussing characteristics of ethical climate: clarity of expectations, congruent signals, sufficient time/resources/systems, transparency, discussability, sanctionability); Kish-Gephart et al., *supra* note 31, at 21; James C. Wimbush & Jon M. Shepard, *Toward An Understanding of Ethical Climate: Its Relationship to Ethical Behavior and Supervisory Influence,* 13 J. BUS. ETHICS 637, 638 (1994) (defining ethical climate as a set of "stable, psychologically meaningful, shared perceptions employees hold concerning ethical procedures and policies existing in their organizations"); *see also* Milton C. Regan, Jr., *Moral Intuitions and Organizational Culture,* 51 ST. LOUIS U. L.J. 941, 942 (2007) (stating that culture "helps establish what is considered legitimate or unacceptable in an organization"). *See generally* Mather et al., *supra* note 212; EMMANUEL LAZEGA, THE COLLEGIAL PHENOMENON: THE SOCIAL MECHANISMS OF COOPERATION AMONG PEERS IN A CORPORATE LAW PARTNERSHIP 255 (2001).

320 In fact, research on the effects of codes of conduct alone has yielded mixed results. A recent meta-analysis concluded that the "existence of a code of conduct had a trivial connection with unethical choice." Gary S. Weaver & Linda K. Treviño, *Compliance and Values Oriented Ethics Programs: Influence on Employees' Attitudes and Behavior,* 9 BUS. ETHICS Q. 315, 316–18 (1999) (finding, however, a "strong negative link . . . between code enforcement and unethical choice"). Other research has found that having a code of conduct or other set of ethical strictures at the forefront of one's mind when making a decision can lead to more ethical decision making. *See, e.g.,* Mazar et al., *supra* note 36, at 635 (suggesting that dishonesty increases as attention to standards for honesty decreases); *see also* Robert C. Ford & Woodrow D. Richardson, *Ethical Decision Making: A Review of the Empirical Literature,* 13 J. BUS. ETHICS 205, 216 (1994) (reviewing studies); Terry W. Loe et al., *A Review of Empirical Studies Assessing Ethical Decision Making in Business,* 25 J. BUS. ETHICS 185, 194 (2000) (reviewing studies); O'Fallon & Butterfield, *supra* note 210, at 117–31 (reviewing studies). For exploration of the meaning of organizational culture generally, see Susan S. Silbey, *Legal Culture and Cultures of Legality,* in SOCIOLOGY OF CULTURE: A HANDBOOK 470 (John R. Hall et al. eds., 2010).

321 *See, e.g.,* Levin, *supra* note 17, at 316 (finding attorney ethics to be influenced more by communities of practice than by the rules); Linda K. Treviño et al., *Managing Ethics and Legal Compliance: What Works and What Hurts,* 41 CAL. MGMT. REV. 131, 131 (1999) ("A firm's approach to ethics and legal compliance management has an enormous impact on employees' attitudes and behaviors."). For a discussion of the influence of norms found in communities of practice, see Darryl K. Brown, *Criminal Procedure Entitlements, Professionalism, and Lawyering Norms,* 61 OHIO ST. L.J. 801, 809–13 (2000).

322 *See generally* CARL I. HOVLAND ET AL., COMMUNICATION AND PERSUASION: PSYCHOLOGICAL STUDIES OF OPINION CHANGE (1953); Carl I. Hovland & Walter Weiss, *The Influence of Source Credibility on Communication Effectiveness,* 15 PUB. OPINION Q. 635, 647 (1952).

323 Gary R. Weaver et al., *"Somebody I Look Up To:" Ethical Role Models in Organizations,* 34 ORGANIZATIONAL DYNAMICS 313, 316–17 (2005); *see also* David M. Mayer et al., *How Low Does Ethical Leadership Flow? Test of a Trickle-Down Model,* 108 ORGANIZATIONAL BEHAV. & HUM. DECISION PROCESSES 1, 8 (2009) (finding that ethical leadership at higher levels influences employee behavior through its effect on mid-level supervisors). *See generally* Melissa S. Anderson et al., *What Do Mentoring and Training in the Responsible Conduct of Research Have To Do with Scientists' Misbehavior? Findings From a National Survey of NIH-Funded Scientists,* 82 ACAD. MED. 853 (2007).

culture within their offices and the messages those cultures send about ethics. The first culture emphasizes winning:

> "The trial atmosphere is that you're there to win and have to win. That was really pushed, not a spoken rule but there was that pressure. You got it from the supervisor, his boss and those around you. It's celebrated when you win." In other words, regardless of what the chief prosecutor says to the public or within the office about the importance of procedural fairness, prosecutors get the message that winning at trial is the key to career success and that fair-process values are comparatively unimportant.[324]

In contrast, consider how another prosecutor describes the tone set by the district attorney in his office:

> As prosecutors we're not just out to win but to see that justice is done. We follow the principle that full disclosure is better in order to protect the process and the people subject to the process. Our office provides full disclosure and by adhering to the idea that we want to see justice done we protect the process and avoid wrongful convictions.[325]

Different ethical climates can push behavior in different directions. But, while it is important to promote ethical behavior, it is also important to promote ethical behavior for the right reasons. It turns out that instrumental ethical climates grounded in not getting caught, self-interest, or individual advancement tend to be associated with a greater likelihood of unethical behavior as compared to ethical climates based on benevolence or concern for clients, colleagues, or social justice.[326] Thus, whereas a culture of "eat what you kill" might be a fertile breeding ground for unethical behavior, climates based on principles or rules and standards tend to be associated with more ethical behavior.[327]

1. Discuss and Model Ethical Behavior

Whether at trainings, lunches, or by the water cooler, open discussion of ethics offers attorneys opportunities to grapple with thorny ethical issues, primes attorneys to more automatically consider ethics in their own decision making, creates an atmosphere that encourages attorneys to seek guidance from others

---

[324] Ellen Yaroshefsky & Bruce A. Green, *Prosecutors' Ethics in Context: Influences on Prosecutorial Disclosure, in Lawyers in Practice: Ethical Decision Making in Context, supra* note 101, at 286–87.

[325] *Id.* at 282.

[326] Kish-Gephart et al., *supra* note 31, at 12–13.

[327] *Id.* at 3, 6; *see also* Weaver & Treviño, *supra* note 320 (comparing values-based and compliance-based ethics programs). *See generally* Bart Victor & John V. Cullen, *The Organizational Bases of Ethical Work Climates*, 33 ADMIN. SCI. Q. 101 (1988).

when they encounter ethical dilemmas, and helps demonstrate to employees that ethics matter. Openly discussing ethics in organizations is associated with more ethical conduct[328] and tends to have positive effects on "employee commitment, the perception that it's acceptable to deliver bad news, the belief that employees would report an ethics violation, and [the belief] that decision making is better because of the ethics/compliance program."[329]

The stories that get told around the office send messages about what is valued. These messages can either reinforce or undermine the more formal ethics policies of the organization.

> [I]n one [prosecutor's] office with an open file policy, a laudatory story about a prosecutor's compliance with the policy to the office's strategic disadvantage had entered office lore: Several different prosecutors recounted it independently. . . . Prosecutors told the story in the office to convey the importance of complying with the full disclosure policy, even at the cost of a conviction, because doing so furthers the office's broader mission to do justice.[330]

Such epic stories need to be told. But so too do stories that describe ethical behavior that is less visible—stories that highlight the normalcy and value of such acts. Because others' unethical conduct is more noticeable than their ethical conduct,[331] not highlighting routine ethical behavior can reinforce the perception that unethical behavior is more normal and acceptable than it really is.[332] And we have seen that attorneys may ultimately adjust their own values and practices to be consistent with what they incorrectly believe to be the norms of their peers.[333]

---

[328] Treviño et al., *supra* note 65, at 967.

[329] Treviño et al., *supra* note 321, at 143. In contrast, when firms discourage discussion of ethical issues they may minimize any value that could otherwise have been produced by ethics training sessions or rules. "An oil company employee asked if he could bring an ethical problem to a meeting of divisional presidents. Their immediate response was, 'If he wants to talk ethics, let him talk to a priest or a psychiatrist. The office is no place for it.' Imagine what employees would think of a formal ethics/compliance program in such an environment." *Id.*

[330] Yaroshefsky & Green, *supra* note 324, at 281–82; *see also* Scott Killingsworth, *Modeling the Message: Communicating Compliance* THROUGH *Organizational Values and Culture,* 25 GEO. J. LEGAL ETHICS 961 (2012) (discussing the relationships among communication, culture, and compliance).

[331] *See generally supra* note 276 (discussing the interpersonal ethics blind spot).

[332] *See, e.g.*, Michael E. Brown et al., *Ethical Leadership: A Social Learning Perspective for Construct Development and Testing,* 97 ORGANIZATIONAL BEHAV. & HUM. DECISION PROCESSES 117, 120 (2005) ("[P]rivately or stoically carrying out ethical actions may be insufficient to focus attention on ethical conduct."); *see also* Robert B. Cialdini, *Descriptive Social Norms as Underappreciated Sources of Social Control,* 72 PSYCHOMETRIKA 263, 263 (2007).

[333] *See supra* notes 220–221 and accompanying text (discussing pluralistic ignorance). Entities may also encourage their attorneys to network with attorneys outside the firm with respect to ethics issues. While confidentiality concerns will prevent attorneys from sharing the details of a situation with others outside the

These stories and discussions should communicate why ethical rules and practices are important—for example, that ethical behavior in the prosecutors' office is important for due process reasons and to maintain the respect of the public. People seek to make decisions they can justify[334]—to themselves and to others—and are more likely to follow rules that they believe in and support, than they are to abide by those that they view as an imposition.[335]

Respected role models within the organization can demonstrate that ethics are valued and how to successfully approach practice ethically.[336] Leaders who treat others in a fair and respectful manner, hold themselves to high and consistent ethical standards and communicate those standards to others, accept responsibility for their own errors, demonstrate ethical awareness and a commitment to ethics even while being concerned about business concerns, remain open to input and feedback, and hold others accountable for their ethical decisions contribute to an overall climate that values ethics.[337] By modeling good ethical behavior, key figures in the organization will also help develop junior attorneys' schemas for what it means to be a successful attorney.[338] In this way, legal organizations can help their attorneys rid themselves of an image—shaped in part by images of lawyers in popular culture—of attorneys as unethical and replace that image with a more positive view of attorneys' ethics.

---

firm, there may be ways, particularly in a high tech world, for attorneys to network to discuss ethics with one another anonymously. Kim, *supra* note 9, at 1074–75.

[334] *See, e.g.*, Christopher K. Hsee, Jiao Zhang, Fang Yu & Yiheng Xi, *Lay Rationalism and Inconsistency Between Predicted Experience and Decision,* 16 J. BEHAV. DECISION MAKING 257, 267 (2003); Eldar Shafir et al., *Reason-Based Choice,* 49 COGNITION 11, 14 (1993). Jury researchers have also found that providing an explanation of the reasons underlying a rule can help jurors comply with the requirements of the rule. *See, e.g.*, Shari Seidman Diamond & Jonathan D. Casper, *Blindfolding the Jury to Verdict Consequences: Damages, Experts, and the Civil Jury,* 26 LAW & SOC'Y REV. 513, 557–59 (1992); Duane T. Wegener et al., *Flexible Corrections of Juror Judgments: Implications for Jury Instructions,* 6 PSYCHOL. PUB. POL'Y & L. 629, 646 (2000); Roselle L. Wissler et al., *The Impact of Jury Instructions on the Fusion of Liability and Compensatory Damages,* 25 LAW & HUM. BEHAV. 125, 134–35 (2001).

[335] *See supra* notes 109–112.

[336] *See* Linda K. Treviño & Stuart A. Youngblood, *Bad Apples in Bad Barrels: A Causal Analysis of Ethical Decision-Making Behavior,* 75 J. APPLIED PSYCHOL. 378, 382 (1990) (finding that vicarious reward influenced outcome expectancies which were associated with ethical decision making). *See generally* ALBERT BANDURA, SOCIAL LEARNING THEORY (1977).

[337] *See, e.g.*, Brown et al., *supra* note 332, at 120 (finding that ethical leadership is associated with outcomes such as a greater willingness to report unethical conduct); Mayer et al., *supra* note 323, at 3–7; Mitchell J. Neubert et al., *The Virtuous Influence of Ethical Leadership Behavior: Evidence From the Field,* 90 J. BUS. ETHICS 157, 165–67 (2009); Linda K. Treviño et al., *A Qualitative Investigation of Perceived Executive Ethical Leadership: Perceptions From Inside and Outside the Executive Suite,* 56 HUM. REL. 5, 14, 18–20 (2003); Weaver et al., *supra* note 323, at 316; Wimbush & Shepard, *supra* note 319, at 642; *see also* Kish-Gephart et al., *supra* note 31, at 21 (reporting a meta-analysis that found that a strong ethical climate, including strong ethical role models, was associated with less unethical behavior); Marshall Schminke et al., *The Effect of Leader Moral Development on Ethical Climate and Employee Attitudes,* 97 ORGANIZATIONAL BEHAV. & HUM. DECISION PROCESSES 135, 147 (2005).

[338] *See supra* note 153 and accompanying text (defining "schema").

All those who are visible and credible within the organization must model ethical behavior and take seriously their role of transmitting ethical norms.[339] They must both " 'walk the talk' and 'talk the walk' "—making sure that behavior is consistent with other messages about ethics.[340]

> In a highly competitive environment of intense focus on the bottom line, employees need to know that the executive leaders in their organization care about ethics at least as much as financial performance. An ethical leader makes it clear that strong bottom-line results are expected, but only if they can be delivered in a highly ethical manner.[341]

Ethical neutrality or silence is not sufficient. Role models need to publicly enact the organization's ethical mission through their words and their actions, including criticizing, disciplining, or even firing those who do not act consistently with the ethical mission.[342] When New York Governor Andrew Cuomo fired the director of the State Office of Emergency Management for deploying government workers to clear his personal driveway during Hurricane Sandy,[343] Cuomo sent a strong message to all state employees that unethical self-dealing would not be tolerated.

2. Educate About Ethics

On-going ethics education and self-evaluation are key elements of a culture that is open about ethics. Ethics training must make ethical standards clear and avoid sending mixed signals. Clear rules can result in more ethical behavior and more willingness to confront ethical misconduct.[344] Organizations, however, need to go beyond teaching the Rules of Professional Conduct or other ethical rules

---

339 *See* Brown et al., *supra* note 332, at 130; Michael E. Brown & Linda K. Treviño, *Ethical Leadership: A Review and Future Directions,* 17 LEADERSHIP Q. 595, 601–02 (2006) (suggesting importance of seeing "reinforcement of ethical behavior (i.e., ethical leaders get ahead, unethical leaders do not)"); *see also* Robert S. Rubin et al., *Do Ethical Leaders Get Ahead? Exploring Ethical Leadership and Promotability,* 20 BUS. ETHICS Q. 215, 223 (2010). Bar disciplinary authorities, too, have a role to play in communicating acceptable norms. *See* Fred C. Zacharias, *The Purposes of Lawyer Discipline,* 45 WM. & MARY L. REV. 675, 739 (2003) ("[W]hen rule violations that are visible or well-known go unsanctioned, such failure to prosecute undermines the professional standard as a credible threat. It encourages other lawyers to violate the particular standard or the codes as a whole.").

340 Michael E. Brown & Marie S. Mitchell, *Ethical and Unethical Leadership: Exploring New Avenues for Future Research,* 20 BUS. ETHICS Q. 583, 584 (2010) (also exploring the notion of "unethical leadership").

341 Treviño & Nelson, *supra* note 318, at 166.

342 *Id.* at 292–303.

343 Danny Hakim, *Cuomo Fires Emergency Office Chief for Misusing Workers in Hurricane,* N.Y. TIMES, Nov. 8, 2012, at A15.

344 *See, e.g.,* Kaptein, *supra* note 317, at 924–25. One commentator has opined that military attorneys who were uncomfortable with the Military Commission Act adopted in the wake of the 9/11 terrorist attacks were willing and able to speak out against it, even though they operated within the authoritative context of the military, because they had been trained so effectively to take responsibility for fair application of the law. McNeal, *supra* note 33, at 139. At the same time, clearer rules can make employees less likely to report the problem outside the organization. *See* Kaptein, *supra* note 319, at 924–25.

and standards and acknowledge that most difficult ethical dilemmas arise when important principles conflict. Thus, just as when learning to write, negotiate, engage in trial practice, or conduct legal analysis, lawyers need to learn how to think about the problems they will encounter and acquire specific skills to address them.[345]

Organizations should equip attorneys to stand firm in the face of ethical challenges by teaching them about the psychological factors that inform decision making processes and set the stage for ethical missteps. Effective training will also familiarize lawyers and their supervisors with potential indicia of ethical misconduct and should address the mechanisms for and benefits of reporting misconduct.[346] Training can be used to help attorneys develop implementation intentions[347] and to make explicit ethical commitments. To be effective, trainings need to avoid vague generalities and instead address the kinds of ethical issues that are most likely to arise in the particular settings. Focusing on actual issues that have come up in the organization in the past is one way to make the training more directly meaningful.

Role playing may help make ethical temptations more concrete and allow opportunities for thinking about specific alternative responses. In addition, such practice can strengthen attorneys' moral "muscles," focus their attention on the need to exercise self-control at times of depletion, motivate them to do so, and, thus, increase their capacity to resist temptation.[348]

One of us frequently asks law students to engage in a negotiation exercise as part of a class on negotiation ethics. Even though the students are primed to focus on ethical concerns (the very topic of the class is negotiation ethics and the relevant ethical rules and contract doctrines are assigned as reading prior to class),

---

[345] Disciplinary authorities, too, ought to consider education about the psychology of ethics as a component of discipline or as part of a set of measures aimed at prevention. Common approaches to ethical violations include disbarment, suspension, reprimand, and ethics education. *See generally* A.B.A. STANDARDS FOR LAWYER DISCIPLINE AND DISABILITY PROCEEDINGS (1979); Leslie C. Levin, *The Emperor's Clothes and Other Tales About the Standards for Imposing Lawyer Discipline Sanctions,* 48 AM. U. L. REV. 1 (1998). None of these responses adequately addresses the psychological susceptibilities that we identify here, nor are they likely to build ethical resilience.

[346] Marcia P. Miceli et al., *A Word to the Wise: How Managers and Policy-Makers Can Encourage Employees to Report Wrongdoing,* 86 J. BUS. ETHICS 379, 385 (2009).

[347] *See supra* note 306 and accompanying text.

[348] While resisting unethical behavior may deplete capacity in the short term, it can be possible to strengthen it in the long term. See generally Roy F. Baumeister et al., *The Strength Model of Self-Control,* 16 CURRENT DIRECTIONS IN PSYCHOL. SCI. 351 (2007); Mark Muraven et al., *Longitudinal Improvement of Self-Regulation Through Practice: Building Self-Control Strength Through Repeated Exercise,* 139 J. SOC. PSYCHOL. 446 (1999); Martin S. Hagger et al., *Ego Depletion and the Strength Model of Self-Control: A Meta-Analysis,* 136 PSYCHOL. BULL. 495 (2010).

many students engage in conduct that their counterparts find problematic. Students on each side often lie or fail to disclose information that the other side believes is "material." Whereas each side is often able to justify their conduct—explaining, for example, that the other side "didn't ask," or that their client did not want them to disclose the information—their opponents are typically outraged and feel they have been lied to. Exploring these reactions can help attorneys understand the consequences of their ability to justify their own conduct.[349]

Finally, the attitude organizations convey when conducting ethics training is critically important. To encourage a principled rather than an instrumental ethical culture,[350] training should communicate the value of ethics and the principles underlying the relevant ethical requirements.[351] Organizations that convey that ethics training is a required inconvenience—just a box to be checked on the CLE form or window dressing to be displayed for particular audiences—seriously diminish the value of the training.

3. Encourage Learning from Mistakes

The challenges of learning from ethical mistakes[352] affect legal organizations as well as individual lawyers. One study of how ethics were handled in law firms found that "information regarding the nature of the problems or questions, and how they are resolved was rarely, if ever, fed back into the firm. Both associates and partners seemed unaware of the extent of reported (or unreported) problems, questions, or violations of ethical standards."[353] Yet, when there is no feedback, learning will suffer,[354] and this may lead to further deterioration in the entity's ethical norms.

The mindset with which one approaches mistakes can make a tremendous difference for the ability to learn from them. Specifically, those with a fixed

---

[349] Ethics educators Linda Treviño and Katherine Nelson recommend an exercise that presents participants with ethical dilemmas related to their work that do not have clear answers. Participants discuss the problems in groups, present their course of action, are challenged by a devil's advocate, and are scored on their responses. Participants can then appeal to a board of senior colleagues with whom they can discuss the problems. In addition to providing an opportunity to engage with each other about difficult ethical dilemmas, the exercise facilitates ethical communication between people at different levels of the organization, and by including senior colleagues on the "appeals board" signals that the conversations are worth having. Treviño & Nelson, *supra* note 318, at 233–35.

[350] *See supra* notes 326–327.

[351] *See supra* notes 326–327, 334–335.

[352] *See supra* Part III.

[353] Messikomer, *supra* note 14, *at 760.*

[354] See Chip Heath et al., *Cognitive Repairs: How Organizational Practices Can Compensate for Individual Shortcomings,* 20 RES. ORGANIZATIONAL BEHAV. 1, 29 (1998).

mindset see mistakes as an indication of incompetence or stupidity, react to them with anger or depression, and therefore miss out on opportunities to learn and improve. But those with a growth mindset see mistakes as opportunities to learn how to do better.[355] Thus, part of establishing an ethical culture is to inculcate a learning or growth orientation to dealing with mistakes—providing and embracing opportunities for self-criticism.

In this vein, organizations may want to establish processes to help attorneys learn from ethical missteps. For example, consider how Penn State University hired former FBI Director Louis Freeh and his staff to conduct a report on Penn State officials' response to the reports of child abuse by Assistant Football Coach Jerry Sandusky. The resulting report found that Penn State officials had made numerous missteps and suggested that specific reforms be made to avoid such lapses in the future.[356] While not all organizations can afford—nor do all issues require—such a large-scale investigation, organizations would be well advised to appropriately explore what led an attorney to overstate her hours, borrow trust fund money, omit crucial information from a filing, or fail to consider evidence of a defendant's innocence.

4. Protect Attorneys from Cognitive, Temporal, and Financial Stresses

Cognitive and temporal overloads tend to increase the likelihood that attorneys will engage in unethical conduct.[357] Although some of these stresses seem inherent to many legal jobs, their connection to ethical problems should give firms an incentive to provide attorneys with sufficient support staff, effective software, and office systems and structures to help prevent and catch problems.[358]

---

[355] CAROL DWECK, MINDSET: THE NEW PSYCHOLOGY OF SUCCESS 6–7 (2007). *See also* Julie A. Oseid & Stephen D. Easton, *"And Bad Mistakes, I've Made Few": Sharing Mistakes to Mentor New Lawyers*, ___ ALBANY L. REV. ___ (forthcoming 2014), available at http://papers.ssrn.com/abstract=2337241.

[356] Brad Wolverton, *Penn State's Culture of Reverence Led to 'Total Disregard' for Children's Safety*, CHRON. HIGHER EDUC., July 12, 2012, http://chronicle.com/article/Penn-States-Culture-of/132853; *see also, e.g.*, Terry Frieden, *Fast and Furious Report Finds DOJ Management Failures*, CNN.COM (Sept. 19, 2012, 2:13 PM), http://news.blogs.cnn.com/2012/09/19/fast-and-furious-report-finds-doj-management-failures (describing DOJ report about a year-long investigation that uncovered widespread failures at the BATF); *cf.* David Barstow, *Vast Mexico Bribery Case Hushed Up by Wal-Mart After Top-Level Struggle*, N.Y. TIMES, Apr. 21, 2012, http://www.nytimes.com/2012/04/22/business/at-wal-mart-in-mexico-a-bribe-inquiry-silenced.html (describing how Wal-Mart executives shut down an investigation that started to "unearth[ ] evidence of widespread bribery" in Mexico).

[357] *See supra* Part II.D.

[358] For example, firms can provide systems for screening and dealing with conflicts of interest. *See, e.g.*, Shapiro, *supra* note 128, at 289–307 (describing firms without systems or using systems that rely on lawyer memory to catch conflicts). Relying on memory to flag conflicts is fraught with peril. *Id.* at 344; *see also* Kaptein, *supra* note 319, at 925 (identifying "feasibility" as a dimension of ethical culture—"unethical conduct occurred when employees lacked adequate or sufficient time, budgets, equipment, information, and authority to fulfill their responsibilities").

Firms can also strive to treat their attorneys humanely, and to schedule work in a reasonable fashion. Even providing exercise opportunities to employees[359] may pay ethical dividends. While all of these steps have costs, so too do ethical mistakes.

Even when it proves impractical to limit cognitive and temporal stresses, organizations should urge their attorneys to do those tasks that involve ethical challenges when they are most fresh, rather than most depleted.

> Whenever they face tasks that afford opportunities to cheat, managers may benefit by scheduling these tasks when they are fresh and well rested (e.g., not after a long flight). Similarly, managers may benefit from arranging tasks to reduce the likelihood that their employees will face ethical decisions when their self-regulatory resources are depleted.[360]

Firms can also take steps to relieve the economic pressures that may lead attorneys to cross ethical lines. While organizations cannot fully protect their attorneys from financial problems, they may be able to provide financial counseling, short term low interest loans,[361] or information on how to access other sources of psychological or financial assistance (such as through a local bar association).

5. Structure Rewards to Encourage Ethical Behavior

Organizations should do what they can to reward conduct that promotes ethics[362] and to judge decisions based on the quality of the underlying decision making process rather than solely on the ultimate outcomes.[363] In other words, firms need to figure out ways to reward attorneys who engage in the kinds of conduct and decision making processes that are most likely to lead to the most

---

359 *See, e.g.*, Workplace Health Promotion: Physical Activity, Ctrs. for Disease Control and Prevention, http://www.cdc.gov/workplacehealthpromotion/implementation/topics/physical-activity.html (describing benefits of providing exercise opportunities to employees) (last visited Oct. 25, 2013).

360 Gino et al., *supra* note 181, at 200. When depleted, attorneys can do their best to revive themselves by taking a rest, having a snack, going for a short walk, or meditating.

361 *See* Levin, *supra* note 17, at 387 (advising that firms should "try to limit the situations in which lawyers are overwhelmed by their financial circumstances or case loads and to provide for more outside support for handling these situations when they arise").

362 *See* Kim *supra* note 9, at 1053 (suggesting companies regulate compensation to decrease self-interest); John M. Darley, *The Dynamics of Authority Influence in Organizations and the Unintended Action Consequences*, in SOCIAL INFLUENCES ON ETHICAL BEHAVIOR IN ORGANIZATIONS, *supra* note 195, at 40 ("[I]ncentive systems have an elevated status for communicating what the organization 'really wants' and 'really values.' In a world in which talk is regarded as cheap, bonuses, promotions, and other tangible marks of valuing are what really matter."); JOHN M. DARLEY, HOW ORGANIZATIONS SOCIALIZE INDIVIDUALS INTO EVILDOING, IN CODES OF CONDUCT: BEHAVIORAL RESEARCH INTO BUSINESS ETHICS, *supra* note 254, at 25 ("Corporations that put in place a corporate ethics code and do not consider its relationship to existing corporate practices and bonus and promotion systems seem to me to be engaging in window dressing of a particularly cynical sort.").

363 Baron & Hershey, *supra* note 83, at 574.

effective and ethical strategies. While it may be more difficult to look beyond hours, wins, and fees to assess lawyering, it is important to avoid rewarding unethical attorneys. Consider the positive messages sent in the following environment:

> One CEO of a financial services firm was very serious about identifying and rewarding people who lived his organization's values. He challenged his executives to bring him stories of employees who were doing the right things in the right way, who were models of the culture. He collected these stories and sent personal, handwritten thank-you notes to those model employees. While a phone call might have sufficed, employees were so thrilled with his written recognition and praise that they displayed his notes in their offices. Those framed notes sent a rather loud message to other employees about what kind of behavior was valued at high levels. Of course, they also helped spread word of the 'heroes' and their deeds.[364]

Consider also the messages sent by a firm that provides attorneys with a pay bonus for billing 1,800 hours, and an even greater bonus for billing each additional 1,000 hours. Such an incentive scheme is likely to tempt even the most ethical of attorneys to round up her hours, double-bill a few hours to multiple clients, or perhaps "borrow" some hours from a future billing period. Or, consider a prosecutor's office that provides kudos or promotions to those prosecutors with the highest conviction rates. While these practices can be defended as encouraging "hard work," it is clear that they can also incentivize unethical conduct. Entities that take the trouble to reward attorneys based on a broader set of accomplishments will likely be repaid with more ethical work habits.[365]

6. Encourage Ethical Reporting

No matter how hard organizations try to prevent unethical conduct, lapses may occur and will need to be addressed. Understanding the thought processes that decision makers go through before reporting an ethical violation can help organizations identify the measures that they can take to ensure that employees

---

[364] Treviño & Nelson, *supra* note 318, at 181–82.

[365] *See* Kirkland, *supra* note 236, at 615 (quoting Interview with General Counsel No. 4, at 38 (2007–2008) (on file with author)) ("[describing reports of] statistics collected by malpractice insurers that show a correlation between firms' compensation systems and firm risk profiles. One general counsel explained, 'The liability insurers will tell you the closer you are to a 'lock step' compensation system, the safer your profile. The closer you are to an 'eat what you kill' system the riskier the profile—the greater the number of claims.' "); *see also* John M. Darley, *Setting Standards Seeks Control, Risks Distortion,* 32 PUB. AFF. REP. 3, 5 (1991) (describing the distorting effects of criterial-control systems).

will make reports of ethical misconduct when appropriate. A potential reporter must:

(1) recognize that a violation has occurred;

(2) decide that the infraction warrants intervention;

(3) decide that the observer is responsible for taking action on the matter;

(4) identify what responsive actions are available; and

(5) conclude that the benefits of reporting the violation outweigh the costs.[366]

Measures that take these steps into account are likely to be most effective in encouraging reporting. For example, ethical training and culture can help attorneys recognize that an ethical violation has occurred and warrants intervention.[367] In addition, organizations can make clear that ensuring organization-wide ethical compliance is part of attorneys' job responsibilities and will benefit the organization.[368] Attorneys may hesitate to "tattle" on their peers if they feel they are stepping outside their role, but will more likely report problems if such reporting is considered part of their job, and if they know that reporting is designed to benefit the organization.[369]

Organizations can also encourage attorneys to raise ethics issues by providing specific and multiple channels through which individuals can dissent and raise questions.[370] Multiple channels for reporting allow employees to choose one with which they are comfortable.[371] As one possible reporting channel, some large

---

366 *See* Marcia P. Miceli et al., *Who Blows the Whistle and Why?,* 45 INDUS. & LAB. REL. REV. 113, 115 (1991); *see also* Michael E. Roloff & Gaylen D. Paulson, *Confronting Organizational Transgressions,* in SOCIAL INFLUENCES ON ETHICAL BEHAVIOR IN ORGANIZATIONS, *supra* note 195, at 57–60 (dividing the preconfrontation process into "Sense-Making" and "Action Formation").

367 *See supra* Section IV.B.2 (discussing appropriate ethical training).

368 Employees are more likely to report perceived ethical problems internally when they view such reporting as part of their assigned role. Jessica R. Mesmer-Magnus & Chockalingam Viswesvaran, *Whistleblowing in Organizations: An Examination of Correlates of Whistleblowing Intentions, Actions, and Retaliation,* 62 J. BUS. ETHICS 277, 286 (2005); Marcia Parmerlee Miceli & Janet P. Near, *The Relationships Among Beliefs, Organizational Position, and Whistle-Blowing Status: A Discriminant Analysis,* 27 ACAD. MGMT. J. 687, 696 (1984); see also Miceli et al., *supra* note 366, at 123; Linda Klebe Treviño & Bart Victor, *Peer Reporting of Unethical Behavior: A Social Context Perspective,* 35 ACAD. MGMT. J. 38, 47 (1992); Bart Victor et al., *Peer Reporting of Unethical Behavior: The Influence of Justice Evaluations and Social Context Factors,* 12 J. BUS. ETHICS 253, 258 (1993).

369 Victor et al., *supra* note 368, at 258.

370 Kurt Lewin, *Group Decision and Social Change,* in READINGS IN SOCIAL PSYCHOLOGY 330 (Guy E. Swanson et al. eds., 1952) (focusing on shaping behavior by using channel factors—relatively minor changes in the relevant situation—that can have a significant influence on behavior by leading or "channeling" people in a particular direction).

371 Miceli et al., *supra* note 346, at 388.

firms now have outside or in-house ethics counsel, an ethics committee, or an ethics ombudsperson who can serve this role.[372] While lawyers in such a role may share some incentives with others in the firm,[373] they may be more removed from the immediate pressures of at least some ethical situations. Because such counsel will not be directly involved with the client, case, or deal at issue, she may be more objective than the attorney directly affected and thus less tempted to counsel unethical actions.[374] For example, when exploring a potential conflict of interest, ethics counsel can consider the matter as a part of the firm's interests and larger book of business rather than leaving the decision to the attorney for whom the potential conflict may represent significant new business.[375] In addition, consulting ethics counsel can be designated as an accepted part of the entity's practice and the attorney's role.[376]

Organizations must not only provide the channels for reporting, but also ensure that reporting leads to outcomes that are perceived to be appropriate. When employees believe that their ethical reports are likely to be taken seriously, they are more likely to make such reports.[377] While organizations will have to find a balance between treating reports of real wrongdoing seriously and not "rewarding the gadfly or chronic low performer seeking to distract attention, . . . [or] wasting time on frivolous complaints,"[378] it is important to investigate claims fully and fairly.

---

372 *See generally* Elizabeth Chambliss & David B. Wilkins, *The Emerging Role of Ethics Advisors, General Counsel, and Other Compliance Specialists in Large Law Firms,* 44 ARIZ. L. REV. 559 (2002); Elizabeth Chambliss, *The Professionalization of Law Firm In-House Counsel,* 84 N.C. L. REV. 1515 (2005–2006); Jonathan D. Glater, *In a Complex World, Even Lawyers Need Lawyers,* N.Y. TIMES, Feb. 3, 2004, http://www.nytimes.com/2004/02/03/business/in-a-complex-world-even-lawyers-need-lawyers.html?pagewanted=all&src=pm.

373 Kirkland, *supra* note 70, at 188, 192 (explaining that "ethics counsel see their jobs as finding ways to take on as much new work as they can without running afoul of the ethics rules" and that they "struggle to find ways to say yes even when there is a conflict"); Suchman, *supra* note 101, at 864 (describing interview with lawyer at a firm at which the "ethics committee" was called the "No Business Committee").

374 Ronald D. Rotunda, *Why Lawyers are Different and Why We are the Same: Creating Structural Incentives in Large Law Firms to Promote Ethical Behavior—In-House Ethics Counsel, Bill Padding, and In-House Ethics Training,* 44 AKRON L. REV. 679, 704 (2011).

375 *See, e.g.,* Shapiro, *supra* note 128, at 363–64. Ethics counsel who are compensated directly for their special role tend to take the position more seriously and see it as less burdensome than do those ethics counsel who are asked to do the job on top of their other duties. *See* Chambliss & Wilkins, *supra* note 372, at 572–73. Because attorneys are subject to group pressures and may become committed to positions they have taken, fresh perspectives can be helpful. Langevoort, *supra* note 33, at 113 (suggesting rotating personnel as a means to encourage more ethical behavior).

376 Rotunda, *supra* note 374, at 706.

377 Miceli et al., *supra* note 346, at 388–89 (employees are less likely to report perceived ethical problems if they don't think anything will or can be done to rectify the problem); *see also* Kaptein, *supra* note 319, at 927 (finding that "sanctionability" is positively associated with confrontation of unethical behavior and reporting to management and negatively related to external whistleblowing).

378 Miceli et al., *supra* note 346, at 388.

When the organization finds a complaint to be legitimate, it should take prompt action to address the concern and communicate that action to the reporter. This action should focus not only on any "bad apples" who have acted unethically, but also on correcting any systemic problems.[379] Sometimes it will also be appropriate to publicize instances in which reporting led to positive change, while at the same time being careful to protect confidentiality and not to spark retaliation. Providing feedback to reporting attorneys about the actions taken also encourages continued reporting.

> A client did not want to disclose a particular document; instead, he wanted to get rid of it. I told the senior associate, and he told me that the partners did not want to know about it. However, I did not like that result. I wrote a legal memorandum politely describing the problem and discussing the case law requiring us to turn over the document. I sent it to the partners who promptly overruled the senior associate and turned over the document. Later, one of the partners called me in his office and thanked me for what I had done. "We could have gotten into a problem over that," he said. The partner was promoting the right culture.[380]

When the organization ultimately finds that a report was not well founded, it is equally important to provide feedback to the attorney reporter. This feedback should include clarifying what conduct is unethical and what conduct the company believes should be reported.[381]

Finally, it is also important to assure attorneys that they will be protected rather than punished for reporting possible ethical issues.[382] Fear of retaliation reduces the likelihood of internal reporting.[383] It is not that people "expect or want a reward for doing the right thing. They just don't want to be punished for it."[384] Of course, it is critically important to ensure that the protections that organizations provide to attorneys are "real" and not just window dressing that is ignored when promotion, compensation, and retention decisions are made.[385]

---

[379] *Id.* at 389.

[380] Rotunda, *supra* note 374, at 703.

[381] Miceli et al., *supra* note 346, at 388–89.

[382] *See* Miceli et al., *supra* note 366, at 115; *see also, e.g.*, Kim, *supra* note 9, at 1064–71 (suggesting that companies offer better whistle-blower protection).

[383] David M. Mayer et al., *Encouraging Employees to Report Unethical Conduct Internally: It Takes a Village*, 121 ORGANIZATIONAL BEHAV. & HUM. DECISION PROCESSES 89, 89 (2013).

[384] Treviño & Nelson, *supra* note 318, at 281.

[385] *Id.* at 280 ("The organization's treatment of whistle-blowers is a relevant reward system concern and a frequent source of misalignment.").

Certain employees may be more likely to report perceived ethical problems than others. For example, employees are more likely to report ethical problems internally when they have greater commitment to their job, higher job satisfaction,[386] and feel they are treated fairly.[387] Thus, organizations that are interested in encouraging ethical reporting by their attorneys will also want to focus more generally on their attorneys' workplace satisfaction. Because more junior employees are generally less likely to report perceived ethical problems, organizations may want to focus on helping these more junior attorneys recognize what misconduct needs to be reported, understand the organization's commitment to ethics, know how to report,[388] and feel secure in reporting ethical issues. More junior employees are likely to feel more vulnerable and, thus, may need greater assurances.[389]

7. Monitor Ethics

Finally, organizations can and indeed are required to take steps to monitor the ethical performance of their attorney employees.[390] Given the very human ways in which people can fall prey to ethical temptations, entities should not assume that attorneys are behaving ethically, but should instead develop systems to provide checks on behavior—whether by using software to monitor billing patterns, having colleagues double-check what discovery or due diligence is produced, reviewing how attorneys conduct negotiations, or monitoring how attorneys prepare their clients for depositions or trial. It is most important to monitor situations in which attorneys, due to cognitive or temporal depletion or structural temptations, are most likely to engage in ethical misconduct.[391] As noted earlier, when ethical improprieties are found, organizations should discipline attorneys found to have behaved inappropriately, determine whether systemic changes should be made, and provide appropriate feedback to the community.

While structural systems to monitor ethical performance are perhaps necessary, research has found that intrinsic motives, identification with the rules

---

386 Mesmer-Magnus & Viswesvaran, *supra* note 368, at 286; Miceli et al., *supra* note 366, at 123.

387 Victor et al., *supra* note 368, at 259.

388 Mesmer-Magnus & Viswesvaran, *supra* note 368, at 293–94.

389 More accomplished, more competent employees are more likely to blow the whistle on perceived ethical problems. Marcia P. Miceli & Janet P. Near, *Individual and Situational Correlates of Whistle-Blowing,* 41 PERSONNEL PSYCHOL. 267, 275 (1988); Miceli et al., *supra* note 366, at 123.

390 MODEL RULES OF PROF'L CONDUCT R. 5.1 ("A partner in a law firm . . . shall make reasonable efforts to ensure that the firm has in effect measures giving reasonable assurance that all lawyers in the firm conform to the Rules of Professional Conduct."); *see also* Irwin D. Miller, *Preventing Misconduct by Promoting the Ethics of Attorneys' Supervisory Duties,* 70 NOTRE DAME L. REV. 259, 276 (1994).

391 Brown & Treviño, *supra* note 339, at 602; Gino et al., *supra* note 181, at 200; *see also* Langevoort, *supra* note 33, at 101–04 (suggesting that firms watch for red flags).

of the organization, and believing that the organization is legitimate tend to have a greater effect on rule following (and a commitment to following the rules) than do perceptions of the likelihood of detection and the nature of the likely sanctions.[392] Thus, even as they build systems to help attorneys avoid missteps, organizations should act in ways—enacting fair processes and treating attorneys fairly—that help attorneys see the entity as legitimate and as embodying values that are congruent with their own.[393] Of particular importance are providing opportunities for input into organizational policies, making decisions in a neutral fashion using transparent and objective criteria, making decisions that treat people consistently and respectfully, and providing explanations for decisions reached.[394] Developing such procedures can reap a variety of benefits:

> First, in a culture where transparent procedures are voluntarily embraced, the self-policing mechanisms that will thrive in the organization will be more likely to expose wrongdoing in its infancy. . . Second, a culture in which rule-following is the expected norm and cynicism is low will be a far less comfortable environment for those who would prefer to break the rules. And finally, in a culture in which rule-following is the accepted norm, scoundrels and cheats will be far less likely to ascend to the positions of power in which they can do significant damage.[395]

V. Conclusion

> "[T]o understand all is not to forgive all . . . [b]ut . . . to understand all may well put us on guard against doing the unforgivable."[396]

While research into the psychology of legal ethics is ongoing,[397] current knowledge can help individual attorneys and organizations employing those attorneys resist the pull of unethical behavior. Having learned that "[a]ttributing blame solely to flawed individuals or corrupt organizations rarely captures the subtleties of how ethical misconduct occurs," and instead "offers false reassurance that only moral

---

392 Tom R. Tyler & Steven L. Blader, *Can Businesses Effectively Regulate Employee Conduct? The Antecedents of Rule Following in Work Settings*, 48 ACAD. MGMT. J. 1143, 1153 (2005); *see also* Tom R. Tyler et al., *The Ethical Commitment to Compliance: Building Value-Based Cultures*, 50 CAL. MGMT. REV. 31, 32 (2008).

393 Tyler et al., *supra* note 392, at 33.

394 *Id.* at 38.

395 TOM R. TYLER, WHY PEOPLE COOPERATE: THE ROLE OF SOCIAL MOTIVATIONS 117 (2011).

396 Luban, *supra* note 204, at 116.

397 Empirical research should build on our analysis to further explore how the ethical decision making of attorneys compares to that of other actors.

deviants, not ordinary people, engage in such behavior,"[398] we are better equipped to fight against the slide into misconduct.

NOTES

1. One of the reasons that we included this article is that it has a great discussion of John Gellene, the bankruptcy lawyer whose bad decisions resulted in a 15-month federal prison term and a multi-million dollar loss to his law firm.* The article also harkens back to the Ford Pinto memo that we discussed as a note following the GM report in Chapter 8. Authors Robbennolt and Sternlight used the Ford Pinto memo to discuss one of their key concepts: ethical fading. See how all of these threads weave together into a whole cloth?

2. Another reason that we included this article involves its listing of so many different cognitive errors. There are hundreds and hundreds of such errors, and you might want to look at a book by the same two authors who wrote this article (Robbennolt and Sternlight): PSYCHOLOGY FOR LAWYERS: UNDERSTANDING THE HUMAN FACTORS IN NEGOTIATION, LITIGATION AND DECISION MAKING (2013). Their book provides both a compendium of these errors and a discussion of how understanding how those errors work might help in the practice of law.

3. Take a moment to think about all of the case studies that we've had you read. Think about GM and its silos, Volkswagen and its development of software that helped VW cheat in emissions testing, Wells Fargo and its millions of bogus customer accounts, NASA's struggle to learn from experience from the first shuttle disaster, Dewey & LeBeouf's fall into bankruptcy, and Mahlon Perkins's discovery violations. Although each of these cases is different—with different causes, different personnel, and different consequences—there are some common issues. Here are at least some of the takeaways:

- Smart humans can trick themselves into doing stupid things, even though they intended to be ethical. Not every misdeed is due to a person's character. Sometimes, bad people intend to do bad things—and succeed. But good people can also do bad things, in part because of the situations in which they find themselves, and in part because of the cognitive errors to which humans are susceptible.

---

[398] REGAN, *supra* note 13, at 294.

* Want to read more about John Gellene? Take a gander at Nancy B. Rapoport, *The Curious Incident of the Law Firm That Did Nothing in the Night-Time* (reviewing MILTON C. REGAN, JR., EAT WHAT YOU KILL: THE FALL OF A WALL STREET LAWYER (Univ. of Michigan Press 2004)), in 10 LEGAL ETHICS 98 (2007), available at http://papers.ssrn.com/sol3/papers.cfm?abstract_id=1017627 and at http://www.tandfonline.com/doi/abs/10.1080/1460728X.2007.11423884.

- Thinking about possible triggers for misbehavior in advance, and developing structures (incentives, checks and balances, and the like) that take those triggers into account, can help. But there are unintended consequences to every incentive. (Remember the rat example?) Be on the lookout for those unintended consequences and recalibrate the incentives accordingly.
- An organization's culture matters. Organizations that allow for input all along a hierarchy and that welcome the devil's advocate* who poses counterarguments to the majority's ideas are healthier than those that brook no dissent. It's important for an organization to reward the type of behavior it wants. Remember the story in the article about the CEO who wrote personal notes to certain employees?

  > One CEO of a financial services firm was very serious about identifying and rewarding people who lived his organization's values. He challenged his executives to bring him stories of employees who were doing the right things in the right way, who were models of the culture. He collected these stories and sent personal, handwritten thank-you notes to those model employees. While a phone call might have sufficed, employees were so thrilled with his written recognition and praise that they displayed his notes in their offices. Those framed notes sent a rather loud message to other employees about what kind of behavior was valued at high levels. Of course, they also helped spread word of the 'heroes' and their deeds.**

  Employees will do what their bosses value.
- Honesty is important.

You've probably found even more lessons from the cases than those in this list. As you head into our last chapter, we want you to think even more broadly about culture and about how group dynamics affect an individual's behavior.

---

* The Merriam-Webster's definition of "devil's advocate" has two meanings:

Definition of devil's advocate

1: a Roman Catholic official whose duty is to examine critically the evidence on which a demand for beatification or canonization rests

2: a person who champions the less accepted cause for the sake of argument

https://www.merriam-webster.com/dictionary/devil's%20advocate.

** *Behavioral Legal Ethics* at 1176 (citation omitted).

PART VI

Some Last Thoughts

We hope that our book has given you some new food for thought: what the likely causes of certain scandals may have been, what you can extrapolate about the likely causes of future scandals, and what role you might have in developing structures and incentives to help counteract the hard-wired way that humans tend to think. In this last chapter, we'd like to go beyond a scandal-oriented look at human behavior. We'd like you to think about how groups might solidify their views rather than opening them up for dissent and new ideas, in part because managers rely on groups, as well as on individuals, to get suggestions. We also want you to think about how your own integrity can help you work through tough decisions, and we want you to think about how you should communicate your organization's values consistently and clearly. To help you think through each of these issues, we've collected three good articles: Cass Sunstein's article, *Deliberative Trouble? Why Groups Go To Extremes*, David Luban, *Integrity: Its Causes and Cures,* and Scott Killingsworth's *Modeling the Message: Communicating Compliance Through Organizational Values and Culture.*

Here's our big point: ultimately, you're going to find yourself in many positions of power. We want to help you prepare for those moments of crisis that we know that you'll experience, and we want to help you avoid some crises entirely. That is why we're including these last few essays, and that's the real point of our book.

CHAPTER 20

Deliberative Trouble? Why Groups Go to Extremes[*]

Cass R. Sunstein[**]

> The differences of opinion, and the jarring of parties in [the legislative] department of the government . . . often promote deliberation and circumspection, and serve to check excesses in the majority.
>
> —Alexander Hamilton[1]

> In everyday life the exchange of opinion with others checks our partiality and widens our perspective; we are made to see things from their standpoint and the limits of our vision are brought home to us. . . . The benefits from discussion lie in the fact that even representative legislators are limited in knowledge and the ability to reason. No one of them knows everything the others know, or can make all the same inferences that they can draw in concert. Discussion is a way of combining information and enlarging the range of arguments.
>
> —John Rawls[2]

---

* This piece was originally published as Cass R. Sunstein, *Deliberative Trouble? Why Groups Go To Extremes,* 110 YALE L.J. 71 (2000).

** Karl N. Llewellyn Distinguished Service Professor of Jurisprudence, University of Chicago Law School and Department of Political Science. I am grateful above all to Daniel Kahneman and David Schkade for many helpful discussions. Thanks too to C. Edwin Baker, Robert Ellickson, Edward Glaeser, Robert Goodin, Christine Jolls, Dan Kahan, Timur Kuran, Lawrence Lessig, John Manning, Andrei Marmor, Wiktor Osiatynski, Eric Posner, Richard Posner, Jeffrey Rachlinski, and David Strauss for valuable comments. Participants in workshops at Cornell and the University of Chicago provided a great deal of help. I am also grateful to participants in a conference on deliberative democracy at the University of Texas at Austin, and in particular to my commentators Norman Bradburn and Robert Luskin. Brian Lehman and Brooke May provided excellent research assistance.

1 THE FEDERALIST NO. 70, at 426–27 (Alexander Hamilton) (Clinton Rossiter ed., 1961).

2 JOHN RAWLS, A THEORY OF JUSTICE 358–59 (1971).

> Each person can share what he or she knows with the others, making the whole at least equal to the sum of the parts. Unfortunately, this is often not what happens . . . .
>
> . . . As polarization gets underway, the group members become more reluctant to bring up items of information they have about the subject that might contradict the emerging group consensus. The result is a biased discussion in which the group has no opportunity to consider all the facts, because the members are not bringing them up.
>
> . . . .
>
> . . . Each item they contributed would thus reinforce the march toward group consensus rather than add complications and fuel debate.
>
> —Patricia Wallace[3]

I. Introduction

Consider the following events:

- Affirmative action is under attack in the state of Texas. A number of professors at a particular branch of the University of Texas are inclined to be supportive of affirmative action; they meet to exchange views and, if necessary, to plan further action. What are these professors likely to think, and to do, after they talk?
- After a nationally publicized shooting at a high school, a group of people in the community, most of them tentatively in favor of greater gun control, come together to discuss the possibility of imposing new gun control measures. What, if anything, will happen to individual views as a result of this discussion?
- A jury is deciding on an appropriate punitive damage award in a case of recklessly negligent behavior by a large company; the behavior resulted in a serious injury to a small child. Before deliberating as a group, individual jurors have chosen appropriate awards, leading to an average of \$1.5 million and a median of \$1 million. As a statistical generalization, how will the jury's ultimate award tend to compare to these figures?
- A group of women is concerned about what they consider to be a mounting "tyranny of feminism." They believe that women should be able to make their own choices, but they also think that men and

3 PATRICIA WALLACE, THE PSYCHOLOGY OF THE INTERNET 81–82 (1999).

> women are fundamentally different, and that their differences legitimately lead to different social roles. The group decides to meet every two weeks to focus on common concerns. Is it possible to say what its members are likely to think after a year?

Every society contains innumerable deliberating groups. Church groups, political parties, women's organizations, juries, legislative bodies, regulatory commissions, multimember courts, faculties, student organizations, those participating in talk radio programs, Internet discussion groups, and others engage in deliberation. It is a simple social fact that sometimes people enter discussions with one view and leave with another, even on moral and political questions.[4] Emphasizing this fact, many recent observers have embraced the traditional American aspiration to "deliberative democracy," an ideal that is designed to combine popular responsiveness with a high degree of reflection and exchange among people with competing views.[5] But for the most part, the resulting literature has not been empirically informed.[6] It has not dealt much with the real-world consequences of deliberation, and with what generalizations hold in actual deliberative settings, with groups of different predispositions and compositions.

The standard view of deliberation is that of Hamilton and Rawls, as quoted above. Group discussion is likely to lead to better outcomes, if only because competing views are stated and exchanged. Aristotle spoke in similar terms, suggesting that when diverse people

> all come together . . . they may surpass—collectively and as a body, although not individually—the quality of the few best . . . . [W]hen there are many [who contribute to the process of deliberation], each has his

---

4 Sometimes it may seem that moral and political arguments are unlikely to have an effect on individual judgments; the evidence discussed here shows that arguments often induce considerable movement.

5 *E.g.*, DELIBERATIVE DEMOCRACY (Jon Elster ed., 1998); AMY GUTMANN & DENNIS THOMPSON, DEMOCRACY AND DISAGREEMENT 128–64 (1996); JÜRGEN HABERMAS, BETWEEN FACTS AND NORMS 287–328 (William Rehg trans., Polity Press 1996) (1992); CASS R. SUNSTEIN, THE PARTIAL CONSTITUTION 133–45 (1993).

6 Exceptions include James D. Fearon, *Deliberation as Discussion*, in DELIBERATIVE DEMOCRACY, *supra* note 5, at 44; and Susan C. Stokes, *Pathologies of Deliberation*, in DELIBERATIVE DEMOCRACY, *supra* note 5, at 123. Of special interest are James Fishkin's continuing experiments with the "deliberative opinion poll," in which groups of diverse people are asked to deliberate on public issues. *See* James S. Fishkin & Robert C. Luskin, *Bringing Deliberation to the Democratic Dialogue*, in THE POLL WITH A HUMAN FACE 3 (Maxwell McCombs & Amy Reynolds eds., 1999). Fishkin's groups do not polarize, at least not systematically; this result is undoubtedly a product of the distinctive setting, in which materials are presented on each issue, with corresponding claims of fact and value. For a discussion of Fishkin, see *infra* text accompanying notes 193–203.

> share of goodness and practical wisdom . . . . [S]ome appreciate one part, some another, and all together appreciate all.[7]

But an important empirical question is whether and under what circumstances it is really true that "some appreciate one part, some another, and all together appreciate all."

My principal purpose in this Essay is to investigate a striking but largely neglected[8] statistical regularity—that of group polarization—and to relate this phenomenon to underlying questions about the role of deliberation in the "public sphere"[9] of a heterogeneous democracy. In brief, group polarization means that members of a deliberating group predictably move toward a more extreme point in the direction indicated by the members' predeliberation tendencies.[10] "[L]ike polarized molecules, group members become even more aligned in the direction they were already tending."[11] Thus, for example, members of the first deliberating

---

7 ARISTOTLE, THE POLITICS 108–09 (Ernest Barker trans., Oxford Univ. Press 1995).

8 Though the topic has been much studied within psychology, e.g., ROGER BROWN, SOCIAL PSYCHOLOGY: THE SECOND EDITION 200–48 (1986), I have been unable to find sustained discussions in the relevant literature in economics, sociology, philosophy, law, or political science, and there appears to be no treatment of the implications of group polarization for social behavior or the theory of democracy. Within the economics literature, an exception is Timothy Cason & Vai-Lam Mui, *A Laboratory Study of Group Polarisation in the Team Dictator Game,* 107 ECON. J. 1465 (1997), described by the authors as "the first study that attempts to incorporate this psychological literature into economics." *Id.* at 1466. For one of the rare treatments within sociology, see Noah E. Friedkin, *Choice Shift and Group Polarization,* 64 AM. SOC. REV. 856 (1999). Group polarization is also explored in Kenneth L. Bettenhausen, *Five Years of Groups Research: What We Have Learned and What Needs To Be Addressed,* 17 J. MGMT. 345, 356–59 (1991).

There have been some valuable discussions of group polarization in the context of jury deliberations. A 1976 jury simulation study, Brown, *supra,* at 226–29, tests for, and finds, group polarization, *id.* at 228; and a number of other mock jury studies, not intended to test for group polarization, collect evidence that it occurred in "every instance where the report of data makes it possible to check." *Id.* at 229; *see also* David Schkade et al., *Deliberating About Dollars: The Severity Shift,* 100 COLUM. L. REV. 1139 (2000).

9 The term is associated with Jürgen Habermas. Habermas, *supra* note 5, at 360–87; JÜRGEN HABERMAS, THE STRUCTURAL TRANSFORMATION OF THE PUBLIC SPHERE (Thomas Burger trans., Mass. Inst. of Tech. Press 1989) (1962).

10 Note that this statement has two different implications. First, a deliberating group, asked to make a group decision, will shift toward a more extreme point in the direction indicated by the median predeliberation judgment. Second, the tendency of individuals who compose a deliberating group, if polled anonymously after discussion, will be to shift toward a more extreme point in the direction indicated by the median predeliberation judgment. Frequently these two phenomena are collapsed in the empirical literature, and I will not always distinguish between them here. But for some purposes it is important to distinguish them, and hence some work refers to the movement of groups as "choice shifts" and the movement of individuals as "group polarization." *E.g.,* Johannes A. Zuber et al., *Choice Shift and Group Polarization: An Analysis of the Status of Arguments and Social Decision Schemes,* 62 J. PERSONALITY & SOC. PSYCHOL. 50, 50, 59 (1992). I discuss this distinction in more detail below. *Infra* text accompanying notes 64–65.

Note also that in the experimental work, both extremism and tendencies are measured not by reference to anything external, nor to a normative standard, but by reference to the particular scale that is brought before the individuals who compose the group. Thus, for example, people might be asked, on a scale of –5 to 5, how strongly they agree or disagree with a particular statement.

11 JOHN C. TURNER ET AL., REDISCOVERING THE SOCIAL GROUP 142 (1987).

group are likely to become more firmly committed to affirmative action; the second group will probably end up favoring gun control quite enthusiastically; the punitive damages jury will likely come up with an award higher than the median, perhaps higher than the average as well, and very possibly as high as or higher than that of the highest predeliberation award of any individual member; and the group of women concerned about feminism is likely to become very conservative indeed on gender issues. Notably, groups consisting of individuals with extremist tendencies are more likely to shift, and likely to shift more; the same is true for groups with some kind of salient shared identity (like Republicans, Democrats, and lawyers, but unlike jurors and experimental subjects).[12] When like-minded people are participating in "iterated polarization games"—when they meet regularly, without sustained exposure to competing views—extreme movements are all the more likely.

Two principal mechanisms underlie group polarization. The first points to social influences on behavior and in particular to people's desire to maintain their reputation and their self-conception. The second emphasizes the limited "argument pools" within any group, and the directions in which those limited pools lead group members. An understanding of the two mechanisms provides many insights into deliberating bodies. Such an understanding illuminates a great deal, for example, about likely processes within multimember courts, juries, political parties, and legislatures—not to mention ethnic groups, extremist organizations, criminal conspiracies, student associations, faculties, institutions engaged in feuds or "turf battles," workplaces, and families. At the same time, these mechanisms raise serious questions about deliberation from the normative point of view.[13] If deliberation predictably pushes groups toward a more extreme point in the direction of their original tendency, whatever that tendency may be, is there any reason to think that deliberation is producing improvements?

One of my largest purposes is to cast light on enclave deliberation as simultaneously a potential danger to social stability, a source of social fragmentation, and a safeguard against social injustice and unreasonableness.[14] Group polarization helps explain an old point, with clear constitutional resonances, to the effect that social homogeneity can be quite damaging to good

---

12 Dominic Abrams et al., *Knowing What To Think by Knowing Who You Are,* 29 BRIT. J. SOC. PSYCHOL. 97, 112 (1990).

13 I am speaking here of real-world deliberation, not of deliberation accompanied by preconditions of the sort that have been identified by those thinking of it in ideal terms. *See, e.g.,* Habermas, *supra* note 5, at 99–131.

14 On the last point, see the discussion of African-American newspapers in RONALD JACOBS, RACE, MEDIA, AND THE CRISIS OF CIVIL SOCIETY: FROM WATTS TO RODNEY KING 140–51 (2000).

deliberation.[15] When people are hearing echoes of their own voices, the consequence may be far more than support and reinforcement. An understanding of group polarization thus illuminates social practices designed to reduce the risks of deliberation limited to like-minded people. Consider the ban on single-party domination of independent regulatory agencies, the requirement of legislative bicameralism, and debates, within the United States and internationally, about the value of proportional or group representation. Group polarization is naturally taken as a reason for skepticism about enclave deliberation and for seeking to ensure deliberation among a wide group of diverse people.

But there is a point more supportive of enclave deliberation: Participants in heterogeneous groups tend to give least weight to the views of low-status members[16]—in some times and places, women, African Americans, less-educated people. Hence enclave deliberation might be the only way to ensure that those views are developed and eventually heard. Without a place for enclave deliberation, citizens in the broader public sphere may move in certain directions, even extreme directions, precisely because opposing voices are not heard at all. The ambivalent lesson is that deliberating enclaves can be breeding grounds both for the development of unjustly suppressed views and for unjustified extremism, indeed fanaticism.

This Essay is organized as follows. Part II discusses social influences on individual judgments, with particular reference to the phenomenon of social cascades. When a number of people have acted or spoken, observers who lack much private information are highly likely to follow their lead, a phenomenon that can drive participants in politics in unexpected and sometimes extreme directions. Part III offers a basic account of group polarization, with an elaboration of the underlying mechanisms of social influence and persuasive arguments. Parts IV, V, and VI deal with the implications of group polarization for democracy and law. Part IV is descriptive; it explores the likely consequences of group polarization for a number of issues at the intersection of law and democratic theory, including feuds, ethnic strife, juries, commissions, multimember courts, and deliberation via the Internet. Part V is normative; it draws the various strands together in an effort to show how group polarization can create deliberative trouble. It also traces the implications of the phenomenon for structuring deliberative institutions and links group polarization to central aspects of constitutional design. Part VI focuses on the role of deliberation inside and outside enclaves of like-minded people,

---

[15] For the constitutional resonances, *see infra* notes 164–165, 169–171.

[16] Caryn Christensen & Ann S. Abbott, *Team Medical Decision Making*, in DECISION MAKING IN HEALTH CARE 267, 273–76 (Gretchen Chapman & Frank Sonnenberg eds., 2000).

emphasizing the need to ensure that members of deliberating enclaves are not walled off from other points of view. Part VII is a brief conclusion.

II. Social Influences and Cascades

A. In General

A great deal of attention has recently been devoted to the topic of social influences on individual behavior.[17] Because many of these influences are analogous to what happens in group polarization, and because they have a bearing on democratic deliberation as well, it is worthwhile to offer some brief notations here.

Social influences can lead groups to go quite rapidly in identifiable directions, often as a result of "cascade" effects involving either the spread of information (whether true or false) or growing reputational pressure. Sometimes cascade effects are highly localized, and lead members of particular groups, quite rationally,[18] to believe or to do something that members of other groups, also quite rationally, find to be baseless or worse. Local cascades can ensure that different groups end up with very different, but equally entrenched, views about the same issues and events.[19]

People frequently think and do what they think and do because of what they think relevant others think and do.[20] Thus, for example, employees are more likely to file suit if members of the same work group have also done so;[21] littering and nonlittering behavior appear to be contagious;[22] a good way to increase the incidence of tax compliance is to inform people of high levels of voluntary tax

---

17 *E.g.*, Dan M. Kahan, *Social Influence, Social Meaning, and Deterrence*, 83 VA. L. REV. 349 (1997). For extended overviews, see ELLIOT ARONSON, THE SOCIAL ANIMAL (7th ed. 1995); and LEE ROSS & RICHARD E. NISBETT, THE PERSON AND THE SITUATION (1991). Group polarization is a surprising omission from both of these lengthy and highly illuminating treatments.

18 On the rationality of participation in a cascade, see *David Hirschleifer, The Blind Leading the Blind: Social Influence, Fads, and Informational Cascades*, in THE NEW ECONOMICS OF HUMAN BEHAVIOR 188, 189 (Mariano Tommasi & Kathryn Ierulli eds., 1995).

19 For an entertaining and candid discussion, see the outline of attitudes of Microsoft employees, by a Microsoft employee, in Michael Kinsley, *The View from the Cafeteria: Microsoft Employees Don't Recognize Themselves in the Government's Suit*, TIME, Apr. 10, 2000, at 152, 2000 WL 17632849; the discussion can reasonably be taken to show both cascade effects and group polarization.

20 ROSS & NISBETT, *supra* note 17, at 28–57; Dan M. Kahan, *Gentle Nudges vs. Hard Shoves: Solving the Sticky Norms Problem*, 67 U. CHI. L. REV. 607 (2000); Kahan, *supra* note 17.

21 Harold H. Gardner et al., *Workers' Compensation and Family and Medical Leave Act Claim Contagion*, 20 J. RISK & UNCERTAINTY 89, 101–10 (2000).

22 Robert B. Cialdini et al., *A Focus Theory of Normative Conduct: Recycling the Concept of Norms To Reduce Littering in Public Places*, 58 J. PERSONALITY & SOC. PSYCHOL. 1015, 1017 (1990).

compliance;[23] television networks tend to follow one another;[24] and students are less likely to engage in binge drinking if they think that most of their fellow students do not engage in binge drinking, so much so that disclosure of low numbers of binge drinkers is one of the few successful methods of reducing binge drinking on college campuses.[25]

Social influences affect behavior via two different mechanisms.[26] The first is informational. What other people do, or say, carries an informational externality;[27] if many other people support a particular candidate, or refuse to use drugs, or carry guns, observers, and particularly observers within a common group, are given a signal about what it makes sense to do. The second mechanism is reputational, as group members impose sanctions on perceived deviants, and would-be deviants anticipate the sanctions in advance.[28] Even when people do not believe that what other people do provides information about what actually should be done, they may think that the actions of others provide information about what other people think should be done. Thus each person's expressive actions come with a reputational externality. People care about their reputations and they have an incentive to do what (they think) other group members think they should do. For example, reputational considerations may lead people to obey or not to obey the law, urge a certain view in group discussions, buy certain cars,[29] drive while drunk, help others, or talk about political issues in a certain way. A concern for reputation exerts a ubiquitous influence on behavior, including that

---

[23] Stephen Coleman, Minn. Dep't of Revenue, The Minnesota Income Tax Compliance Experiment State Tax Results 1, 5–6, 18–19 (1996), http://www.state.mn.us/ebranch/mdor/reports/compliance/pdf.

[24] Robert E. Kennedy, STRATEGY FADS AND COMPETITIVE CONVERGENCE: AN EMPIRICAL TEST FOR HERD BEHAVIOR IN PRIME-TIME TELEVISION PROGRAMMING (Aug. 1999) (unpublished manuscript, on file with The Yale Law Journal).

[25] Timur Kuran & Cass R. Sunstein, *Availability Cascades and Risk Regulation,* 51 STAN. L. REV. 683, 767 (1999); H. Wesley Perkins, *College Student Misperceptions of Alcohol and Other Drug Norms Among Peers: Exploring Causes, Consequences, and Implications for Prevention Programs* 177, 194, in U.S. DEP'T OF EDUC., DESIGNING ALCOHOL AND OTHER DRUG PREVENTION PROGRAMS IN HIGHER EDUCATION: BRINGING THEORY INTO PRACTICE (1997), available at http://www.edc.org/hec/pubs/theorybook/perkins.pdf. A good outline of contagion effects can be found in Gardner et al., *supra* note 21, at 91–93.

[26] *E.g.*, Aronson, *supra* note 17, at 22; ROSS & NISBETT, *supra* note 17, at 44–45.

[27] Andrew Caplin & John Leahy, *Miracle on Sixth Avenue: Information Externalities and Search,* 108 ECON. J. 60, 61 (1998).

[28] George A. Akerlof, *A Theory of Social Custom, of Which Unemployment May Be One Consequence,* in AN ECONOMIC THEORIST'S BOOK OF TALES 69 (1984).

[29] *See* ROBERT H. FRANK, LUXURY FEVER 8–10, 122–45 (1999) (connecting luxury purchases to competition for better relative position). This is only part of Frank's account; he also emphasizes the "frame of reference" created by most people's decisions. *Id.* at 131–32.

of participants in democratic debate, who often shift their public statements in accordance with reputational incentives.[30]

B. Some Classic Experiments

In the most vivid experiments involving group influences, conducted by Solomon Asch, individuals were apparently willing to abandon the direct evidence of their own senses.[31] In the relevant experiments, a certain line was placed on a large white card. The task of the subjects was to match that line by choosing, as identical to it in length, one of three other lines that had been placed on a separate large white card. One of the lines on the second white card was in fact identical in length to the line to be matched to it; the other two were substantially different, with the differential varying from an inch and three-quarters to three-quarters of an inch. The subject in the original experiments was one of eight people asked to engage in the matching. Unbeknownst to the subject, the other people apparently being tested were actually there as Asch's confederates, serving as part of the experiments.

In the first two rounds of the experiment, everyone agreed about the right answer; this seemed to be an extremely dull experiment. But the third round introduced "an unexpected disturbance."[32] Other group members made what was obviously, to the subject and to any reasonable person, a clear error. They matched the line at issue to one that was obviously longer or shorter. In these circumstances the subject had the choice of maintaining his independent judgment or instead yielding to the crowd. A large number of people ended up yielding. In ordinary circumstances, subjects erred less than 1% of the time, but in rounds in which group pressure supported the incorrect answer, subjects erred 36.8% of the time.[33] Indeed, in a series of twelve questions, no fewer than 70% of subjects went along with the group, and defied the evidence of their own senses, at least once.

Susceptibility to group influence was hardly uniform. Some people agreed with the group almost all of the time, whereas others were entirely independent in their judgments. Significantly, a modest variation in the experimental conditions made all the difference. The existence of at least one compatriot, or voice of sanity, dramatically reduced both conformity and error. When just one other person

---

30 Kuran & Sunstein, *supra* note 25, at 691–703, 715–35 (discussing the relationship between certain cascades and democratic politics). *See generally* TIMUR KURAN, PRIVATE TRUTH, PUBLIC LIES 3–21 (1995) (discussing preference falsification because of public pressures).

31 For an overview, see Solomon E. Asch, *Opinions and Social Pressure*, in READINGS ABOUT THE SOCIAL ANIMAL 13 (Elliot Aronson ed., 1995).

32 *Id.* at 15.

33 *Id.* at 16.

made an accurate match, errors were reduced by three-quarters, even if there was a strong majority the other way.[34] By contrast, varying the size of the group unanimously making the erroneous decision mattered only up to a number of three; increases from that point had little effect. Opposition from one person did not increase subjects' errors at all; opposition from two people increased error to 13.6%; and opposition from three people increased error to 31.8%, not substantially different from the level that emerged from further increases in group size.

More recent studies have identified an important feature of social influence, directly bearing on group behavior in democracies. Much depends on the subject's perceived relationship to the experimenters' confederates and in particular on whether the subject considers himself part of the same group in which those confederates fall. Thus conformity—and error—is dramatically increased in public statements when the subject perceives himself as part of a reasonably discrete group that includes the experimenter's confederates (all psychology majors, for example).[35] By contrast, conformity is dramatically decreased, and hence error is also dramatically decreased, in public statements when the subject perceives himself as in a different group from the experimenter's confederates (all ancient history majors, for example).[36] Notably, private opinions, expressed anonymously afterwards, were about the same whether or not the subject perceived himself as a member of the same group as others in the experiment. Apparently, public statements of agreement with a majority view are particularly likely to be both inaccurate and insincere when relevant speakers identify themselves as members of the same group as the majority.[37]

Both informational and reputational considerations appear to lead people toward the relevant errors. In Asch's own studies several people said, in private interviews, that their own opinions must have been wrong.[38] On the other hand, these statements may have been an effort to avoid the dissonance that would come

---

[34] *Id.* at 18.

[35] Abrams et al., *supra* note 12, at 106–08. *See also* the discussion of the "downside" of social ties among group members in BROOKE HARRINGTON, COHESION, CONFLICT AND GROUP DEMOGRAPHY (1999) (unpublished manuscript, on file with The Yale Law Journal), which shows that when social ties are in place, dissent may be suppressed and decisions may be worse as a result.

[36] Abrams et al., *supra* note 12, at 106–08.

[37] The least conformity, and the greatest accuracy, were found when people who thought of themselves as being in a different group were speaking publicly. At the same time, the largest number of conforming, inaccurate responses came when people thought of themselves as being in the same group and were speaking publicly—even though the number of inaccurate private responses in that experimental condition was not notably higher than in other conditions. *Id.* at 108.

[38] Asch, *supra* note 31, at 17.

from confessing that the statement was false but made only for reputational reasons. Notably, experimenters find greatly reduced error when the subject is asked to give a purely private answer.[39] And in the study described in the immediately preceding paragraph, people who thought that they were members of the same group as the experimenter's confederates gave far more accurate answers, and far less conforming answers, when they were speaking privately.[40]

Asch concluded that his results raised the possibility that "the social process is polluted" by the "dominance of conformity. . . . That we have found the tendency to conformity in our society so strong that reasonably intelligent and well-meaning young people are willing to call white black is a matter of concern."[41] Asch's experiments did not involve deliberation, for people were not exchanging reasons; indeed, one might expect that reason-giving on the part of Asch's confederates would have lessened the amount of conformity and error. What reasons could have been given for incorrect matches? But the existence of substantial numbers of mistakes as a result of mere exposure to the incorrect conclusions of others raises questions about whether and when deliberation within groups will lead people in the right directions.

C. Social and Law-Related Cascades

A great deal of recent work on social influence has raised the possibility of informational and reputational "cascades";[42] this work has obvious relevance to law and politics.[43] (Consider issues involving race and sex equality, global warming, capital punishment, AIDS, the filing of lawsuits, or presidential candidates.) Indeed, Asch's work demonstrates considerable individual susceptibility to cascade effects. What is striking about such effects is their epidemic-like nature, or the quality of apparent contagion. Group polarization is

---

39 Aronson, *supra* note 17, at 23–24.

40 Abrams et al., *supra* note 12, at 108. By contrast, people who thought that they were members of a different group actually gave more accurate, nonconforming answers when speaking publicly, which creates an interesting puzzle: Why was there more accuracy in public than in private statements? The puzzle is solved by considering the likelihood that subjects could consider it an affirmative good to disagree with people from another group (even if they secretly suspected that those people might be right). In the real world, this effect may well be heightened when people are asked whether they agree with opponents or antagonists; they might well say "no" even when the answer is "yes," simply because agreement carries costs, either to reputation or to self-conception.

41 Asch, *supra* note 31, at 21.

42 E.g., Lisa R. Anderson & Charles A. Holt, *Information Cascades in the Laboratory*, 87 AM. ECON. REV. 847 (1997); Abhijit V. Banerjee, *A Simple Model of Herd Behavior,* 107 Q.J. ECON. 797 (1992); Sushil Biikhchandani et al., *Learning from the Behavior of Others: Conformity, Fads, and Informational Cascades,* 12 J. ECON. PERSP. 151 (1998); Andrew F. Daughety & Jennifer F. Reinganum, *Stampede to Judgment: Persuasive Influence and Herding Behavior by Courts,* 1 AM. L. & ECON. REV. 158, 159–65 (1999).

43 *See* Kuran & Sunstein, *supra* note 25, at 763–67.

sometimes, but not always, a product of cascade effects. It is useful to understand the former against the background of the latter.

1. Informational Cascades

When individuals lack a great deal of private information (and sometimes even when they have such information), they rely on information provided by the statements or actions of others. If A is unaware whether abandoned toxic waste dumps are in fact hazardous, he may be moved in the direction of fear if B seems to think that fear is justified. If A and B both believe that fear is justified, C may end up thinking so too, at least if she lacks reliable independent information to the contrary. If A, B, and C believe that abandoned toxic waste dumps are hazardous, D will need a good deal of confidence to reject their shared conclusion.

People typically have different thresholds for choosing to believe or do something new or different. As those with low thresholds come to a certain belief or action, people with somewhat higher thresholds join them, possibly to a point where a critical mass is reached, making groups, possibly even nations, "tip."[44] The result of this process can be to produce snowball or cascade effects, as small or even large groups of people end up believing something—even if that something is false—simply because other people seem to believe that it is true. There is a great deal of experimental evidence of informational cascades, which are easy to induce in the laboratory;[45] real-world phenomena also seem to have a great deal to do with cascade effects.[46] Consider, for example, smoking, participating in protests, striking, rioting, buying stocks,[47] choosing what to put on television,[48] even leaving bad dinner parties.[49]

Though the cascades phenomenon has been discussed largely in connection with factual judgments, the same processes should be at work for political, legal,

---

[44] Mark Granovetter, *Threshold Models of Collective Behavior,* 83 AM. J. SOC. 1420, 1441–42 (1978). For a recent popular treatment, see MALCOLM GLADWELL, THE TIPPING POINT 5–22 (2000).

[45] *See generally* Anderson & Holt, *supra* note 42.

[46] *See* Sushil Bikhchandani et al., *A Theory of Fads, Fashion, Custom, and Cultural Change as Informational Cascades,* 100 J. POL. ECON. 992 (1992); Kuran & Sunstein, *supra* note 25, at 715–35.

[47] ROBERT J. SHILLER, IRRATIONAL EXUBERANCE 151–67 (2000).

[48] Kennedy, *supra* note 24.

[49] Several of these examples are discussed in Kuran & Sunstein, *supra* note 25, at 725–35; and Granovetter, *supra* note 44, at 1422–24. With respect to AIDS, unfortunate and literally deadly cascade effects can be found in South Africa. President Mbeke's widely publicized doubts about a connection between AIDS and HIV came from learning about the views of "denialists" as a result of surfing the Internet. Thomas H. Maugh II, *AIDS Researchers Meet at Ground Zero,* L.A. TIMES, July 10, 2000, at A1, 2000 WL 2258962. In addition, many myths have spread, suggesting, for example, that there is a "miracle cure" and that organic food is a shield or a cure. *See* Donald G. McNeil, Jr., *South Africa: Aw C'mon, You Don't Really Believe Those AIDS Myths,* AFRICA NEWS, June 11, 1999, 1999 WL 19530508.

and moral questions. Suppose, for example, that A believes that affirmative action is wrong and even unconstitutional, that B is otherwise in equipoise but shifts upon hearing what A believes, and that C is unwilling to persist in his modest approval of affirmative action when A and B disapprove of it. It would be a very confident D who would reject the judgments of three (apparently) firmly committed others. Sometimes people are not entirely sure whether capital punishment should be imposed, whether the Constitution protects the right to have an abortion, whether it is wrong to litter or to smoke. Many people, lacking firm convictions of their own, end up believing what relevant others seem to believe.

Judges are also vulnerable to cascade effects.[50] The same process is sometimes at work for the choice of political candidates, as a fad develops in favor of one or another—a cascade "up" or "down," with sensational or ruinous consequences. One can easily imagine cascade effects in the direction of certain judgments about the appropriate course of government regulation, the minimum wage, or even constitutional law; indeed, such effects seem to have been at work in the legal culture in the 1960s (with mounting enthusiasm for the Warren Court) and the 1980s (with mounting skepticism about that Court). It is even possible to imagine cascade effects with respect to questions of constitutional method (for example, textualism, originalism, democracy-reinforcing judicial review). Note that a precondition for an informational cascade is a lack of much private information on the part of many or most people. If people have a good deal of private information, or are confident about their own judgments, they are unlikely to be susceptible to the signals sent by the actions of others.[51]

2. Reputational Cascades

There can be reputational pressures and reputational cascades as well,[52] in which people speak out, or remain silent, or even engage in certain expressive activity, partly in order to preserve their reputations, at the price of failing to say what they really think. Suppose, for example, that A believes that hazardous waste dumps pose a serious environmental problem; suppose too that B is skeptical. B might keep quiet, or (like some of Asch's subjects) even agree with A, simply in order to preserve A's good opinion. C might see that A believes that hazardous

50 *See* Daughety & Reinganum, *supra* note 42, at 167–82 (discussing the possibility of herd behavior by courts).

51 This point has an echo in findings on group polarization, as those with entrenched views are less likely to "move" as a result of discussion. *See infra* text accompanying notes 98–99.

52 Kuran, *supra* note 30, at 4–21.

waste dumps pose a serious problem and that B seems to agree with A; C might therefore voice agreement even though privately she is skeptical or ambivalent.

It is easy to see how this kind of thing might happen in political life—with, for example, politicians expressing their commitment to capital punishment (even if they are privately skeptical) or their belief in God (even if they are privately agnostic). People typically have different thresholds for yielding to perceived reputational pressure. Some people follow perceived pressure only when it is very severe (for example, because a large number of people impose it), whereas others will follow when it is mild (for example, simply because some relevant others impose it). Here too the consequence can be cascade effects—large social movements in one direction or another—as increasing numbers of people yield to a pressure that they simultaneously impose, eventually reaching a critical mass. At that stage, a large number of people eventually appear to support a certain course of action simply because others (appear to) do so.

As in the context of the informational cascade, what is true for factual beliefs may be true as well for moral, legal, and political judgments. People might say, for example, that affirmative action violates the Constitution simply because of perceived reputational sanctions from saying the opposite; they might support or oppose the death penalty largely in order to avoid the forms of social opprobrium that might come, in the relevant community, from taking the opposing view. A precondition for reputational cascades is that in making the decision at issue, reputational considerations loom large. If people do not care about their reputations, or if reputation is a small component of the choice involved, the perceived intrinsic merits will be crucial, and cascades are unlikely to result.

Are social cascades good or bad? No general answer would make sense. Sometimes cascades are quite fragile, precisely because people's commitments are based on little private information; sometimes cascades are rooted in (and greatly fuel) blunders. Sometimes cascade effects will eliminate group or public torpor by generating concern about serious though previously ignored problems. But sometimes cascade effects will make people far more worried than they should be, or otherwise produce large-scale distortions in private judgments, public policy, and law. It is reasonable to speculate that both the antislavery and the Nazi movements had distinctive cascade-like features, as did the environmental movement in the United States and the fall of communism.[53] The serious risk with social cascades, both informational and reputational, is that they can lead to

---

[53] *See* Susanne Lohmann, *The Dynamics of Informational Cascades: The Monday Demonstrations in Leipzig, East Germany*, 1989–91, 47 WORLD POL. 42, 76 (1994).

widespread errors, factual or otherwise. Cascades need not involve deliberation, but related problems infect processes of group deliberation, as I show below.

III. How and Why Groups Polarize

How do small groups of like-minded people differ from large groups of heterogeneous people? What is likely to happen within isolated deliberating enclaves? How does all this bear on deliberative democracy? To answer these questions, and to understand the relationship between social processes within groups[54] and democratic theory, it is necessary to have an understanding of group polarization.

A. The Basic Phenomenon

Group polarization is among the most robust patterns found in deliberating bodies, and it has been found in many diverse tasks. Polarization "is said to occur when an initial tendency of individual group members toward a given direction is enhanced following group discussion."[55] The result is that groups often make more extreme decisions than would the typical or average individual in the group (where "extreme" is defined solely internally, by reference to the group's initial dispositions). There is a clear relationship between group polarization and cascade effects: Both have a great deal to do with informational and reputational influences. An important difference is that group polarization, unlike cascade effects, involves deliberation. In addition, polarization may or may not involve a cascade-like process; polarization can result simply from simultaneous independent decisions to move toward the group extreme.

Though standard, the term "group polarization" is somewhat misleading. It is not meant to suggest that group members will shift to two poles, nor does it refer to an increase in variance among groups, though this may be the ultimate result.[56] Instead the term refers to a predictable shift within a group discussing a case or problem. As the shift occurs, groups and group members move and coalesce, not toward the middle of antecedent dispositions, but toward a more extreme position in the direction indicated by those dispositions. The effect of

---

54 I do not deal here with the general and related question whether groups amplify or eliminate various cognitive and motivational biases in individual decisions. For a general overview, finding mixed results, see Norbert L. Kerr et al., *Bias in Judgment: Comparing Individuals and Groups*, 103 PSYCHOL. REV. 687 (1996).

55 Daniel J. Isenberg, *Group Polarization: A Critical Review and Meta-Analysis*, 50 J. PERSONALITY & SOC. PSYCHOL. 1141, 1141 (1986).

56 When different deliberating groups polarize in different directions, the consequence can be greater variance among groups, notwithstanding small initial differences. A group whose members are initially but tentatively disposed to reject some proposal might start out very close to a group whose members are initially but tentatively disposed to approve of that proposal. If the two groups have a number of intragroup discussions, but no intergroup discussions, they may end up very far apart.

deliberation is both to decrease variance among group members, as individual differences diminish, and also to produce convergence on a relatively more extreme point among predeliberation judgments.

The basic phenomenon has been found in many nations.[57] Consider some examples:

- After discussion, citizens of France become more critical of the United States and its intentions with respect to economic aid.[58]
- A group of moderately profeminist women becomes more strongly profeminist after discussion.[59]
- As a result of deliberation, whites predisposed to greater racial prejudice offer more negative responses to the question of whether white racism is responsible for conditions faced by African Americans in American cities.[60]
- After discussion, whites predisposed not to show racial prejudice offer more positive responses to the same question.[61]

In all of these cases, deliberation moves people toward a more extreme point in line with their predeliberation positions.[62]

B. Risky Shifts and Cautious Shifts

Group polarization was first found in a series of experiments involving risk-taking decisions. These experiments found what has become known as the "risky shift."[63] In the original experiments, male graduate students of industrial

---

57 Brown, *supra* note 8, at 222–26. These include the United States, England, and France. *See also, e.g.*, Abrams et al., *supra* note 12, at 112 (New Zealand); Zuber et al., *supra* note 10 (Germany). Of course, it is possible that some cultures would show a greater or lesser tendency toward polarization; this would be an extremely interesting area for empirical study.

58 Brown, *supra* note 8, at 224.

59 David G. Myers, *Discussion-Induced Attitude Polarization*, 28 HUM. REL. 699, 710–12 (1975).

60 Brown, *supra* note 8, at 224 (discussing a study in David G. Myers & George D. Bishop, *The Enhancement of Dominant Attitudes in Group Discussion*, 20 J. PERSONALITY & SOC. PSYCHOL. 386 (1971)).

61 *Id.*

62 In laboratory studies, polarization occurs in terms of a specified issue and a specified scale. Thus any tendency toward extremism is scale-relative; it need not mean extremism as a normative matter, or across a full population. In the real world, political entrepreneurs, with self-interested or altruistic agendas, are in some sense aware of the importance of the scale at issue, and attempt to produce shifts along the scale that has been self-consciously made salient. The salient scales ("Do you approve of quotas?" as opposed to "Do you believe in remedial steps for traditionally disadvantaged groups?") can be extremely important.

63 Brown, *supra* note 8, at 248 (citing J.A.F. STONER, A COMPARISON OF INDIVIDUAL AND GROUP DECISIONS INCLUDING RISK (1961) (unpublished M.S. thesis, Massachusetts Institute of Technology) (on file with the Massachusetts Institute of Technology Library)); James A.F. Stoner, *Risky and Cautious Shifts in* Group

management were asked a range of questions involving risk. For twelve of the thirteen groups, the group decisions showed a repeated pattern toward greater risk-taking. After discussion, for example, the unanimous outcome assessed the acceptable probability of financial soundness as consistently lower than the median judgment of group members prior to deliberation. In addition, there was a clear shift toward greater risk-taking in private opinions. This shift—the "risky" shift—was promptly duplicated in a number of diverse studies, some involving all men and some involving all women.

It is important to distinguish at this point between two aspects of these findings[64] usually not separated in the psychological literature and both relevant to law and policy. The first involves the movement of deliberating groups, when a group decision is necessary, toward the group's extreme end; call this a choice shift. This means that if a group decision is required, the group will tend toward an extreme point, given the original distribution of individual views. Undoubtedly the group's decision rule will matter here; a requirement of unanimity, for example, may well produce a shift toward the most extreme points, at least if those with the most extreme views are least tractable and most confident. The second involves the movement of (even private) individual judgments as a result of group influence; call this simply (as is standard) group polarization. This means that to the extent that the private judgments of individuals are moved by discussion, the movement will be toward a more extreme point in the direction set by the original distribution of views. It is possible to have one kind of movement without the other, though ordinarily the two accompany one another,[65] as with risky shifts.

Studies have shown that under certain conditions, it is possible, even easy, to induce a "cautious shift" as well. Indeed, certain problems reliably produce cautious shifts.[66] The principal examples involve the decision whether to marry and the decision whether to board a plane despite severe abdominal pain possibly requiring medical attention. In these cases, deliberating groups move toward caution, as do the members who compose them. Burglars, in fact, show cautious shifts in discussions, though when they work together, the tendency is toward greater risk-taking.[67]

Decisions, 4 J. EXPERIMENTAL SOC. PSYCHOL. 442 (1968). In this and the following paragraph, I draw from Brown, supra note 8, at 200–06.

64 For an insistence on this distinction, see Zuber et al., *supra* note 10, at 50, 59.

65 *Id.* at 59 ("[I]t is necessary to differentiate between choice shift and group polarization. . . .[T]he ongoing processes at these two levels may differ.").

66 *See* Brown, *supra* note 8, at 208–10, for an overview.

67 Paul F. Cromwell et al., *Group Effects on Decision-Making by Burglars,* 69 PSYCHOL. REP. 579, 586 (1991).

In Stoner's original data, researchers noticed that the largest risky shifts could be found when group members "had a quite extreme risky initial position," in the sense that the predeliberation votes were weighted toward the risky end, whereas the items "that shifted a little or not at all started out near the middle of the scale."[68] Thus the direction of the shift seemed to turn on the location of the original disposition, and the size of the shift depended on the extremeness of that original disposition. Similar results have been found in many contexts relevant to law and democracy, involving, for example, questions about economic aid, architecture, education, political leaders, race, and judgments of guilt or innocence.[69] Polarization has been found for questions of obscure fact as well as for evaluative questions, including political and legal issues[70] and even the attractiveness of people in slides.[71]

C. Mechanisms

What explains group polarization? It is tempting to think that conformity plays a large role, and as the Asch experiments suggest, individual judgments can be greatly influenced by the desire to conform. Perhaps conformity is sometimes at work, but the data make it clear that group polarization is not a matter of conformity; people do not shift to the mean of initial positions.[72] The relevant movement goes to one or another side. Indeed, this is what defines, and what is most distinctive about, group polarization.

There have been two main explanations for group polarization. Both of these have been extensively investigated and supported.[73] The first explanation of group polarization—social comparison—begins with the claim that people want to be perceived favorably by other group members and also to perceive themselves favorably. Most people seek to take a position of a certain socially preferred sort. In the case of risk-taking, for example, they may want to be perceived (and to

---

68 Brown, *supra* note 8, at 211.

69 *Id.* at 224, 226–27.

70 A relatively recent treatment is Russell Spears et al., *De-Individuation and Group Polarization in Computer-Mediated Communication*, 29 BRIT. J. SOC. PSYCHOL. 121 (1990).

71 Turner et al., *supra* note 11, at 153.

72 Brown, *supra* note 8, at 207–08. Note, however, that one account of group polarization finds that the effect lies in conformity to the "prototypical group member," defined as such by reference to a "meta-contrast principle: the less a person differs from in-group members and the more he or she differs from out-group members, the more representative is he or she of the in-group." Craig McGarty et al., *Group Polarization as Conformity to the Prototypical Group Member*, 31 BRIT. J. SOC. PSYCHOL. 1, 3 (1992). This position raises many questions; it seems to have the strongest fit with the data in cases in which in-groups and out-groups can readily be understood as such by subjects. *See id.*

73 Brown, *supra* note 8, at 210–29, and Isenberg, *supra* note 55, review this literature; *see also* Turner et al., *supra* note 11, at 142–70, for an overview and an attempt to generate a new synthesis.

perceive themselves) as daring risk-takers, and their choice of position is partly a product of these desires.[74] No one can know what the desirable position would be until the positions of others are revealed.[75] People move their judgments in order to preserve their image to others and their image to themselves. Evidence confirms that mere exposure to the positions of others, without discussion, induces a substantial risky shift (though this shift is only about half as large as the shift produced by discussion).[76] This effect helps explain a shift toward caution (the "cautious shift") as well.[77]

The second explanation is based on the commonsense intuition that any individual's position on an issue is partly a function of which arguments presented within the group seem convincing. The choice therefore moves in the direction of the most persuasive position defended by the group, taken as a whole. Because a group whose members are already inclined in a certain direction will have a disproportionate number of arguments going in that same direction, the result of discussion will be to move people further in the direction of their initial inclinations. The key is the existence of a limited argument pool, one that is

---

74 For a quite vivid demonstration of a related process in the enactment of the Clean Air Act—one that does not, however, identify the mechanisms discussed here—see E. Donald Elliott et al., *Toward a Theory of Statutory Evolution: The Federalization of Environmental Law,* 1 J.L. ECON. & ORG. 313 (1985).

75 Brown notes:

> Once the real location of the mean was known, should it not be the case, granting that everyone wanted to see himself as reasonably audacious, that those who were really below the mean would be motivated to adopt riskier positions and so change the mean and produce the risky shift?

Brown, *supra* note 8, at 214.

76 Allan I. Teger & Dean G. Pruitt, *Components of Group Risk Taking,* 3 J. EXPERIMENTAL SOC. PSYCHOL. 189 (1967).

77 One might point here to both one-upsmanship and the removal of pluralistic ignorance, that is, ignorance of what other people think (or are willing to say they think). It is implicit in these findings that people seem to want not to conform, but to be different from others in a desirable way. While highly suggestive, however, the "mere exposure" finding does not confirm the social influence account; it is possible that the views of others simply provide an informational signal, quite apart from arguments, and hence that people move not in order to maintain reputation, but to do what is right.

skewed (speaking purely descriptively) in a particular direction.[78] Hence there will be a shift in the direction of the original tilt.[79]

There is a related possibility, not quite reducible to either of the two standard arguments, but incorporating elements of each. In their individual judgments, people are averse to extremes; they tend to seek the middle of the relevant poles.[80] It is possible that when people are making judgments individually, they err on the side of caution, expressing a view in the direction that they really hold, but stating that view cautiously, for fear of seeming extreme. Once other people express supportive views, the relevant inhibition disappears, and people feel free to say what, in a sense, they really believe. There appears to be no direct test of this hypothesis, but it is reasonable to believe that the phenomenon plays a role in group polarization and choice shifts.[81]

D. Refinements—and Depolarization

I now turn to some refinements that complicate the basic account of group polarization. First, it matters a great deal whether people consider themselves part of the same social group as the other members. A sense of shared identity heightens the shift, and a belief that identity is not shared reduces and sometimes eliminates it. Second, deliberating groups tend to depolarize if they consist of equally opposed subgroups and if members have a degree of flexibility in their

---

[78] The phenomenon of group polarization may seem to raise doubts about rational actor models in economics or law. (On those models generally, see GARY S. BECKER, ACCOUNTING FOR TASTES (1996); BEHAVIORAL LAW AND ECONOMICS (Cass R. Sunstein ed., 2000).) But individual behavior within groups, as described thus far, should create no such doubts. It is certainly rational to make assessments on the basis of arguments offered; if the most numerous and convincing arguments seem to justify a shift, individual shifts are entirely rational. More difficult questions might seem to be raised by "social influence" accounts of group polarization. But it is also rational for people to care about their reputations. If they change their assessment because of reputational considerations, then maintaining a certain reputation is simply part of what people care about (and there is nothing irrational about that). If people shift not for reputational reasons but because of a certain self-conception—if, for example, they think of themselves as people who are bold, or committed to a strong national defense, or left of center on issues of race—a change in position, after exposure to the views of others, also seems entirely rational.

[79] Brown, *supra* note 8, at 219–20. An experimental study (on willingness to sacrifice money for the sake of fairness) has found support for the social influence explanation but not for the persuasive arguments explanation. Cason & Mui, *supra* note 8, at 1476–78.

[80] *See, e.g.*, Mark Kelman et al., *Context-Dependence in Legal Decision Making*, in BEHAVIORAL LAW AND ECONOMICS, *supra* note 78, at 61, 71–76 (discussing, inter alia, findings that the same option is evaluated more favorably when it is seen as the intermediate choice within a range of options).

[81] A related possibility is that hearing other similar opinions produces greater confidence in individual positions, opening members to more extreme judgments in the same direction. This possibility has been raised by Heath and Gonzalez. Chip Heath & Rich Gonzalez, *Interaction with Others Increases Decision Confidence but Not Decision Quality: Evidence Against Information Collection Views of Interactive Decision Making*, 61 ORG. BEHAV. & HUM. DECISION PROCESSES 305, 318–19 (1995).

positions. Both of these findings have great relevance to any account of the relationship between group polarization and democratic institutions. . . .

1. Statistical Regularities

Of course, not all groups polarize. If the people defending the original tendency are particularly unpersuasive, group polarization is unlikely to occur. If the outliers are especially convincing, groups may even shift away from their original tendency and in the direction held by few or even one.[82]

Sometimes, moreover, external constraints or an external "shock" may prevent or blunt group polarization. Group members with well-defined views on a certain issue may be prone to polarization, but in order to maintain political effectiveness, even basic credibility, they will sometimes present a relatively moderate face, publicly or even privately. Groups that have started to polarize may move toward the middle in order to promote their own legitimacy or because of new revelations of one kind or another. Perhaps something like this happened with the Democratic Party in the early 1990s and the Republican Party in the late 1990s.

2. Affective Factors and the Role of Confidence

Affective factors are quite important in group decisions, and when manipulated, such factors will significantly increase or decrease polarization. If group members are linked by affective ties, dissent is significantly less frequent.[83] The existence of affective ties thus reduces the number of divergent arguments and also intensifies social influences on choice. Hence people are less likely to shift if the direction advocated is being pushed by unfriendly group members; the likelihood of a shift, and its likely size, are increased when people perceive fellow members as friendly, likeable, and similar to them.[84] In the same vein, physical

---

82 This is of course the plot of the movie TWELVE ANGRY MEN, in which the single holdout, played by Henry Fonda, shifts the judgment of the jury. *See* TWELVE ANGRY MEN (United Artists 1957); *see also* Brown, *supra* note 8, at 229–39 (discussing the movie's psychological realism).

83 Brooke Harrington, *The Pervasive Effects of Embeddedness in Organizations* 23–24 (1999) (unpublished manuscript, on file with The Yale Law Journal).

84 Hermann Brandstätter, *Social Emotions in Discussion Groups,* in DYNAMICS OF GROUP DECISIONS 93, 93–97, 106–08 (Hermann Brandstätter et al. eds., 1978). In Turner et al., *supra* note 11, at 154–59, the authors attempt to use this evidence as a basis for a new synthesis, one that they call "a self-categorization theory of group polarization." *Id.* at 154. In this account, "persuasion is dependent upon self-categorizations which create a common identity within a group" and polarization occurs "because group members adjust their opinion in line with their image of the group position (conform) and more extreme, already polarized, prototypical responses determine this image." *Id.* at 156. When a group is leaning in a certain direction, the perceived "prototype" is determined by where the group is leaning, and this is where individuals will shift. *Id.* For possible differences in predictions, and supporting evidence, *see id.* at 158–70. An especially interesting implication, perhaps in some tension with the persuasive arguments theory, is that a group of comparative extremists will show a comparatively greater shift toward extremism. *Id.* at 158.

spacing tends to reduce polarization; a sense of common fate and intragroup similarity tends to increase it, as does the introduction of a rival "outgroup."[85] Mistakes are thus likely to be increased when group members are united mostly through affective ties, and not through concentration on a particular task; it is in the former case that alternative views will less likely find expression.[86]

The confidence of particular members also plays an important role.[87] Indeed, part of the reason for group polarization appears to be that as a class, extreme positions tend to be more confidently held. This point is an important complement to the persuasive arguments theory: The persuasiveness of arguments depends not simply on the grounds given, but also on the confidence with which they are articulated. Group polarization can also be fortified through "exit," as members leave the group because they reject the direction in which things are heading. If exit is pervasive, the tendency to extremism will be aggravated.

3. Identity and Solidarity

If people think of themselves as part of a group having a degree of solidarity, group polarization is all the more likely, and it is likely to be more extreme.[88] Thus when the context emphasizes each person's membership in the social group engaging in deliberation, polarization increases.[89] This finding is in line with more general evidence that social ties among deliberating group members tend to suppress dissent and in that way to lead to inferior decisions.[90] This should not be surprising. If ordinary findings of group polarization are a product of social influences and limited argument pools, it stands to reason that when group members think of one another as similar along a salient dimension, or if some external factor (for example, politics, geography, race, or sex) unites them, group polarization is heightened.[91] Considerable evidence so suggests.[92]

---

85 *Id.* at 151.

86 Harrington, *supra* note 35, at 26.

87 Maryla Zaleska, *The Stability of Extreme and Moderate Responses in Different Situations,* in GROUP DECISION MAKING 163, 164 (Hermann Brandstätter et al. eds., 1982).

88 Wallace, *supra* note 3, at 73–76; Abrams et al., *supra* note 12, at 113–16; Spears et al., *supra* note 70, at 130–31.

89 Spears et al., *supra* note 70, at 122–24.

90 Harrington, *supra* note 83, at 26.

91 See the illuminating remarks on herd behavior, repression, and social identity in AMARTYA SEN, REASON BEFORE IDENTITY 19–22 (1999).

92 Turner et al., *supra* note 11, at 159–62; Abrams et al., *supra* note 12, at 98–99; Spears et al., *supra* note 70, at 123–24, 130–31.

4. Depolarization and Deliberation Without Shifts

Is it possible to construct either groups that will depolarize—that will tend toward the middle—or groups whose members will not shift at all? Both phenomena seem to be real in actual deliberating bodies. In fact, the persuasive arguments theory implies, and evidence demonstrates, that there is depolarization if and when new persuasive arguments are offered that are opposite to the direction initially favored by group members. Depolarization, rather than polarization, also occurs when a group consists of individuals drawn equally from two extremes.[93] If people who initially favor caution are put together with people who initially favor risk-taking, the group judgment will move toward the middle.

Group members with extreme but not fixed positions sometimes shift to a more moderate position.[94] Consider a study consisting of six-member groups specifically designed to contain two subgroups, each consisting of three people initially committed to opposed extremes.[95] The effect of discussion was to produce movement toward the center. One reason may be the existence of persuasive arguments in both directions.[96] A study of opposed subgroups found the greatest depolarization with obscure matters of fact (for example, how far below sea level is the town of Sodom)—and the least depolarization with highly visible public questions (for example, whether capital punishment is justified). Matters of personal taste depolarized a moderate amount (for example, preference for basketball or football, or for colors for painting a room).[97]

These findings fit well with the persuasive arguments account of polarization. Note too that when people have a fixed view of some highly salient public issue, they are likely to have heard a wide range of arguments in various directions, producing a full argument pool, and additional discussion is not likely to produce movement. "[F]amiliar and long-debated issues do not depolarize easily."[98] With respect to such issues, people are less likely to shift at all. And when one or more people in a group know the right answer to a factual question, the group is likely to shift in the direction of accuracy.[99]

---

93 Eugene Burnstein, *Persuasion as Argument Processing*, in GROUP DECISION MAKING, *supra* note 87, at 103, 107–11.

94 Duncan A. Ferguson & Neil Vidmar, *Effects of Group Discussion on Estimates of Culturally Appropriate Risk Levels*, 20 J. PERSONALITY & SOC. PSYCHOL. 436, 443–44 (1971).

95 Brown, *supra* note 8, at 225.

96 Amiram Vinokur & Eugene Burnstein, *Effects of Partially Shared Persuasive Arguments on Group-Induced Shifts: A Group-Problem-Solving Approach*, 29 J. PERSONALITY & SOC. PSYCHOL. 305, 314 (1974).

97 Burnstein, *supra* note 93, at 111–12.

98 Brown, *supra* note 8, at 226.

99 *See* Fishkin & Luskin, *supra* note 6, at 29–30.

5. Several Regularities

These remarks suggest some general, commonsense conclusions about how and when group discussion will move predeliberation opinions. Views based on a great deal of thought are least likely to shift; depolarization can occur with equal subgroups tending in opposite directions; groups will usually shift in the direction of an accurate factual judgment where one or more members knows the truth; where views are not firmly held, but where there is an initial predisposition, group polarization is the general rule. The effects of discussion are also likely to depend on members' perception of the group and of their relationship to it. If a group consists of "people," less polarization is likely than if it consists of "Republicans" or "defenders of the Second Amendment" or "opponents of American imperialism." Depolarization may well occur in groups with equal subgroups having opposite tendencies. But this is less likely and less pronounced if (1) subgroup members have fixed positions, and (2) subgroup members know that they are members of identifiable groups, and that their co-discussants are members of different identifiable groups.

An important general conclusion is that polarization will likely occur among heterogeneous as well as homogeneous groups, so long as there is a determinate initial predisposition among members, taken as a whole. The fact that some people oppose the dominant view will not prevent polarization from occurring. On the other hand, larger shifts are naturally to be expected within groups of like-minded people,[100] and as noted, depolarization is likely if the group is lacking a median predeliberation view in one direction or another, or if it consists of equally opposed subgroups whose members are willing to listen to one another.

A final question involves the effect of holding the median constant, but varying the "width" of the distribution of view within the deliberating group. In case A, for example, a group of six people, asked for their views on nuclear power on a scale of –5 ("strongly opposed") to +5 ("strongly in favor"), might have a predeliberation median of +2, with one at +1, one at +3, and four at +2. Here the prediction is that the group would come out at +3, and also that this would be the median of postdeliberation views, anonymously expressed. But compare case B, with a group with a predeliberation median also of +2 but with two at +4, two at +2, and two at 0. Because the median is the same, the predicted outcome is the same in case B as case A; but is this likely? I am aware of only one study that tests

---

[100] This is an oversimplication. What really matters is the predeliberation mean; the more extreme means will produce more extreme shifts, and a more extreme mean can exist within a heterogeneous group (say, a mean of +3, on a scale of –5 to +5, with a range of views) than in a group of like-minded people (say, a mean of +1, on the same scale, because every member is at +1).

this question: the punitive damage study referred to above, which also contains the largest data set on the choice shift phenomenon, involving 3000 people and 500 deliberating groups.[101] In this study, the shift depended on the median predeliberation judgment, and was not affected by wide or narrow spreads.[102]

E. Actual Deliberation Within Identifiable Groups: Iterated "Polarization Games"?

Studies of group polarization involve one-shot experiments. What are the implications for people who meet with each other not once, but on a regular basis? The basic answer is that if participants engage in repeated discussions—if, for example, they meet each month, express views, and take votes—there should be repeated shifts toward, and past, the defined pole. If a group of citizens is thinking about genetic engineering of food, or the minimum wage, or the World Trade Organization, the consequence of their discussions, over time, should be to lead in quite extreme directions. In these iterated "polarization games," deliberation over time should produce a situation in which individuals hold positions more extreme than those of any individual member before the series of deliberations began. In fact, the idea of iterated polarization games seems far more realistic than the processes studied in one-shot experiments.

There appears to be no study of such iterated polarization games. But the hypothesized outcomes are less fanciful than they might seem. In the jury study referred to above, deliberating groups frequently came up with punishment ratings, and with dollar awards, as high as or even higher than that of any individual, prior to deliberation.[103] And it is not difficult to think of real-world groups in which deliberation, over time, appears to shift both groups and individuals to positions that they could not possibly have accepted early on.[104] Iterated polarization games are an important real-world phenomenon.

But this raises two questions: Why and when do groups stop polarizing? Why and when do they terminate at a certain point, or even shift in the opposite

101 Schkade et al., *supra* note 8. There is also a question about the effects, in experiments or in the real world over time, of small differences in initial views. Is it really the case, for example, that a group with five people opposed to affirmative action, and six in favor, will end up in a very different place from a group with six people opposed, and five in favor? Probably the best answer is that because the initial median is so close in the two cases, significant shifts over time are unlikely in experimental settings and probably in the real world.

102 *Id.* at 1156.

103 *Id.* at 1140.

104 For a relevant discussion of deliberating groups in the 1960s, see JAMES MILLER, "DEMOCRACY IS IN THE STREETS": FROM PORT HURON TO THE SIEGE OF CHICAGO (1994), which traces increased radicalism and the spread of radical ideas; compare this with the discussion of "ethnification" in Eastern Europe in Timur Kuran, *Ethnic Norms and Their Transformation Through Reputational Cascades*, 27 J. LEGAL STUD. 623, 648–49 (1998). *See infra* notes 125–126 and accompanying text.

direction? Nothing in the literature on group polarization adequately answers these questions.[105] But it is possible to speculate that polarization often ends or reverses as a result of some external shock—as, for example, when new members add new arguments, when the simple self-interest of political leaders produces a shift in direction,[106] or when new changes in fact or value alter the perspectives and incentives of group members. Social cascades often change direction as a result of such external shocks, as through the release of new information;[107] the same processes seem to terminate or to reverse group polarization.

F. Rhetorical Asymmetry and the "Severity Shift": A Pervasive Phenomenon?

The previously discussed study of punitive damages awards by juries found a striking pattern for dollar awards.[108] For any dollar award above zero, the general effect of deliberation was to increase awards above those of the median voter. This was a kind of "severity shift." Dollar awards did not simply polarize; while higher awards increased dramatically, as compared to the median of predeliberation votes, lower awards increased as well. Both the original experiment and a follow-up experiment suggest that the severity shift is a product of a rhetorical asymmetry that favors, other things being equal, the person or persons urging higher awards.[109] The reason appears to be that with respect to dollar awards involving a corporate defendant, certain arguments—"we need to deter this kind of conduct," "we need to send a powerful signal," "we need to attract their attention"—tend to have comparatively greater weight.[110]

Undoubtedly there are many other contexts that give rise to rhetorical asymmetry, and undoubtedly the asymmetry can affect outcomes in democratic institutions, as it did in the jury study. Legislative judgments about criminal punishment may, for example, involve an asymmetry of exactly this kind; those favoring greater punishment for drug-related offenses appear to be at a systematic advantage over those favoring lesser punishment. In certain settings, those favoring lower taxes, or more aid for scholarship students, or greater funding for environmental protection, may have a similar rhetorical advantage. For present

---

105 *See* Turner et al., *supra* note 11, at 152 (suggesting that there is no clear answer to the question, "For what range of situations is polarization predicted?").

106 See the discussion of legislators *infra* Subsection IV.E.4. Note, as inevitably noisy real-world examples, the centrist shift of the Democratic Party from 1980 to 1992 and the apparent centrist shift of the Republican Party from 1995 to 2000.

107 Hirschleifer, *supra* note 18, at 198–200 (discussing effects of public releases of information).

108 Schkade et al., *supra* note 8.

109 *Id.* at 1161–62.

110 *Id.*

purposes, the point is that when there is an initial distribution of views in a certain direction, and when existing norms give a rhetorical advantage to a more extreme movement in that direction, quite extreme shifts can be expected.[111]

. . . .

V. Deliberative Trouble?

This Part turns to normative issues involving the relationship among group polarization, democratic theory, and legal institutions. I focus in particular on the implications of group polarization for institutional design, with special reference to the uses of heterogeneity and the complex issues presented by deliberation inside particular "enclaves."

The central problem is that widespread error and social fragmentation are likely to result when like-minded people, insulated from others, move in extreme directions simply because of limited argument pools and parochial influences. As an extreme example, consider a system of one-party domination, which stifles dissent in part because it refuses to establish space for the emergence of divergent positions; in this way, it intensifies polarization within the party while also disabling external criticism.

In terms of institutional design, the most natural response is to ensure that members of deliberating groups, whether small or large, will not isolate themselves from competing views—a point with implications for multimember courts, open primaries, freedom of association, and the architecture of the Internet. Here, then, is a plea for ensuring that deliberation occurs within a large and heterogeneous public sphere, and for guarding against a situation in which like-minded people wall themselves off from alternative perspectives.

But there is a difficulty with this response: A certain measure of isolation will, in some cases, be crucial to the development of ideas and approaches that would not otherwise emerge and that deserve a social hearing.[112] Members of low-status groups are often quiet within heterogeneous bodies, and deliberation in such bodies tends to be dominated by high-status members. Any shift—in technology,

111 Data from the study of punitive damages awards strongly support this speculation, with many deliberating juries producing dollar awards higher—and sometimes significantly higher—than the highest individual dollar award prior to deliberation. *See id.* at 1155–56. *See also* Cason & Mui, *supra* note 8, at 1476–78, which finds that, regardless of the initial distribution of views, groups systematically shift in the direction of greater willingness to sacrifice their material self-interest for the sake of fairness. Cason and Mui study choice shifts in the distinctive setting of the Dictator Game, in which a proposer is asked to divide a certain sum of money between herself and another subject, who must accept any allocation that the proposer selects. They find that for groups generally, the consequence of group discussion is to shift the proposed allocation in the direction of equality.

112 See the empirical references in Christensen & Abbott, *supra* note 16, at 273–77.

norms, or legal practice—that increases the number of deliberating enclaves will likewise increase the diversity of society's aggregate "argument pool" while also increasing the danger of extremism and instability, ultimately even violence. Shifts toward a general "public sphere," without much in the way of enclave deliberation, will decrease the likelihood of extremism and instability, but at the same time produce what may be a stifling uniformity.[113] And shifts toward more in the way of enclave deliberation will increase society's aggregate "argument pool," and hence enrich the marketplace of ideas,[114] while also increasing fragmentation, hostility, and perhaps even violence.

No algorithm is available to solve the resulting conundrums. But some general lessons do emerge. It is important to ensure social spaces for deliberation by like-minded persons, but it is equally important to ensure that members of the relevant groups are not isolated from conversation with people having quite different views. The goal of that conversation is to promote the interests of those inside and outside the relevant enclaves, by subjecting group members to competing positions, by allowing them to exchange views with others and to see things from their point of view, and by ensuring that the wider society does not marginalize, and thus insulate itself from, views that may turn out to be right or at least informative.

Ideas of this kind have a central place in the constitutional framework, with the system of checks and balances, bicameralism, and the Framers' explicit rejection of the "right to instruct" representatives.[115] They also have an important emerging place on the Internet, where there are many current proposals to create a "public sphere" involving discussions among diverse people who would otherwise be in contact largely with those who are like-minded.[116] In these ways, an understanding of group polarization helps provide a better sense of how institutions, both old and new, might be restructured in the service of democratic ideals.

A. Doubts and Questions

1. Why Deliberate?

It should be clear that the phenomenon of group polarization, placed alongside the phenomenon of social cascades, raises severe doubts about the view

---

[113] See the discussion of the shift, over time, from the "unthinkable" to the "unthought" in Kuran, *supra* note 30, at 176–95.

[114] See the discussion of African-American newspapers in Jacobs, *supra* note 14, at 31–53.

[115] *Infra* text accompanying notes 163–172.

[116] *E.g.*, Shapiro, *supra* note 127, at 205–07; Sunstein, *supra* note 131 (manuscript at 102–03, 111–14).

that deliberation is a simple or unambiguous good. Of course deliberation might be justified on many different grounds.[117] It may be that on the question at issue, there is a truth of the matter—a correct answer—and deliberation might be thought to be the best way of reaching it. Perhaps group decisions, based on an exchange of reasons, are more likely to be right than decisions made by individuals. Alternatively, society might favor deliberation on a quite different ground: Doubting whether there is a truth of the matter, a society might seek a deliberative process on the theory that this is the only reasonable and fair way to reach a decision that will be imposed on the group.[118] Or deliberation might be seen as a way to reach some sort of shared understanding or to ensure a form of mutual respect. Group polarization does not create obvious difficulties for all of these accounts. But it does raise real questions about the widespread idea that deliberation is the best way of producing right answers.

If the effect of deliberation is to move people toward a more extreme point in the direction of their original tendency, why is it anything to celebrate? The underlying mechanisms do not provide much reason for confidence. If people shift their position in order to maintain their reputation and self-conception, is there any reason to think that deliberation is making things better rather than worse? If shifts occur as a result of partial and frequently skewed argument pools, the results of deliberative judgments may be far worse than the results of simply taking the median of predeliberation judgments.

To be sure, those who emphasize the ideals associated with deliberative democracy tend to emphasize its preconditions, which include political equality, an absence of strategic behavior, full information, and the goal of "reaching understanding."[119] In real-world deliberations, behavior is often strategic, and equality is often absent in one or another form. But group polarization is likely to occur even in the face of equality and of entirely conscientious efforts at reaching both truth and understanding. The existence of a limited argument pool, strengthening the existing tendency within the group, will operate in favor of group polarization even if no individual behaves strategically. By itself, this will produce group polarization, whether or not social influence is operating.

---

117 For various perspectives, *see* DELIBERATIVE DEMOCRACY, *supra* note 5.

118 See the discussion of imperfect procedural justice and pure procedural justice in Rawls, *supra* note 2, at 83–90.

119 *E.g.*, 1 JÜRGEN HABERMAS, THE THEORY OF COMMUNICATIVE ACTION 99 (Thomas McCarthy trans., Beacon Press 1984). Thus Habermas distinguishes between strategic and communicative action and stresses "the cooperatively pursued goal of reaching understanding." *Id.* Compare Habermas's view with the treatment in Gutmann & Thompson, *supra* note 5, at 52–94, referring to the idea of reciprocity, which emphasizes the desire to justify one's position by reference to reasons.

In any case, social influences need not be inconsistent with the effort to produce truth and understanding. When people attempt to position themselves in a way that fits with their best self-conception or their preferred self-presentation, nothing has gone wrong, even from the standpoint of deliberation's most enthusiastic defenders.[120] Perhaps group polarization could be reduced or even eliminated if we emphasized that full information is a precondition for good deliberation. By hypothesis, argument pools would not be limited if all information were available. But that requirement is extremely stringent, and if there is already full information, the role of deliberation is greatly reduced.[121] In any case, the group polarization phenomenon suggests that, in real-world situations, deliberation is hardly guaranteed to increase the likelihood of arriving at truth.

2. Movements Right and Wrong

Polarization does not necessarily mean that there has been a movement in the wrong direction. Perhaps the more extreme tendency is better. Recall that group polarization is likely to have fueled the antislavery movement and many other movements that deserve widespread approval. In the context of punitive damages awards, perhaps a severity shift produces good outcomes. Extremism need hardly be a word of opprobrium; everything depends on what extremists are arguing for. But when group discussion leads people to more strongly held versions of the same view with which they began, and when social influences and limited argument pools are responsible, there is little reason for great confidence in the effects of deliberation.

If it is possible to identify a particular viewpoint as unreasonable, it is also possible to worry about group discussion among people who share that viewpoint. As noted, this is a basis for justifying the decision to make criminal conspiracy an independent crime; the act of conspiring itself raises the stakes, and by hypothesis the actions ultimately at issue are unlawful and beyond the pale.[122] An analogy can be found in discussions within hate groups, on the Internet and elsewhere. If the underlying views are unreasonable, it makes sense to fear that these discussions may fuel increasing hatred. This does not mean that the discussions can or should be regulated in a system dedicated to freedom of speech. But it does raise questions about the idea that "more speech" is necessarily an adequate remedy.

---

[120] *See* Robert E. Goodin, *Laundering Preferences,* in FOUNDATIONS OF SOCIAL CHOICE THEORY 75, 77–90 (Jon Elster & Aanund Hylland eds., 1986) (discussing self-censorship as a check on invidious views).

[121] The role of deliberation is not eliminated. There remains the question of what to do, given a certain understanding of the facts.

[122] *Supra* note 123 and accompanying text.

B. The Virtues of Heterogeneity

The simplest lesson here involves both individual susceptibility and institutional design. For many people, mere awareness of the role of limited argument pools and social influences might provide some inoculation against inadequately justified movements of opinion within groups. More importantly, institutions should be designed to ensure that when shifts are occurring, it is not because of arbitrary or illegitimate constraints on the available range of arguments. This is a central task of constitutional design. In this light, a system of checks and balances might be explained, not as an undemocratic check on the will of the people, but as an effort to protect against potentially harmful consequences of group discussion.[123]

We have seen that the system of bicameralism, often challenged on populist grounds,[124] might be defended by reference to the risk of group polarization. Indeed, James Wilson's great lectures on law spoke of bicameralism in these terms, referring to "instances, in which the people have become the miserable victims of passions, operating on their government without restraint," and seeing a "single legislature" as prone to "sudden and violent fits of despotism, injustice, and cruelty."[125] Efforts to assure a plurality of views on regulatory commissions and courts can be defended on similar grounds. As supporting evidence, consider the findings that cohesive groups of like-minded people whose members are connected by close social ties often suppress dissent and reach inferior decisions, whereas heterogeneous groups, building identification through focus on a common task rather than through other social ties, tend to produce the best outcomes.[126]

C. A Thought Experiment: Vindicating Hamilton

To explore some of the advantages of heterogeneity, imagine a deliberating body consisting of all citizens in the relevant group; this may mean all citizens in a community, a state, a nation, or the world. By hypothesis, the argument pool would be very large. It would be limited only to the extent that the set of citizen views was similarly limited. Social influences would undoubtedly remain. Hence people might shift because they want to maintain their reputation and self-conception, and to do this they must stand in a certain relation to the rest of the

---

123 FEDERALIST NO. 51 can well be read in this light. THE FEDERALIST NO. 51 (James Madison).

124 See the recent proposals in Minnesota, outlined and discussed in George Will, Editorial, *One-House Town,* WASH. POST, Nov. 4, 1999, at A35, 1999 WL 23312778.

125 James Wilson, *Lectures on Law,* in 1 THE WORKS OF JAMES WILSON 291 (Robert Green McCloskey ed., 1967).

126 Harrington, *supra* note 83, at 25–26.

group. But to the extent that deliberation revealed to people that their private position was different from what they thought it was in relation to the group, any shift would be in response to an accurate understanding of all relevant citizens, and not a product of a skewed group sample.

This thought experiment does not suggest that the hypothesized deliberating body would be ideal. Perhaps all citizens, presenting all individual views, would offer a skewed picture from the normative point of view; in a pervasively unjust society, a deliberating body consisting of everyone may produce nothing to celebrate. Perhaps weak arguments would be made and repeated and repeated again, while good arguments would be offered infrequently. As I suggest below,[127] it is often important to ensure that there are enclaves in which polarization will take place, precisely in order to ensure the emergence of views that are suppressed, by social influences or otherwise, but are reasonable or even right. But at least a deliberating body of all citizens would remove some of the distortions in the group polarization experiments, where generally like-minded people, not exposed to others, shift in large part because of that limited exposure.[128] Many studies show that organizational performance is impaired by people's failure to voice diverse views,[129] and this is a tendency against which heterogeneity might guard.

Here, in fact, is a way of vindicating the passages from Hamilton and Rawls with which I began. On this view, Hamilton and Rawls are not naive enthusiasts for deliberation, oblivious to empirical realities, but are insisting on the advantages of heterogeneity and of a wide argument pool being placed before the deliberators. Indeed, this was Hamilton's claim with respect to the "jarring of parties" within a bicameral legislature, a process that, Hamilton contended, would "check the excesses of the majority"—excesses that can be reinterpreted in terms of the phenomena I have been describing. The Framers of the Bill of Rights originally rejected a "right to instruct," by which constituents could tell their representatives how to vote; the rejection was based on the idea that one job of the representative was to "consult" with people from different states of the Union, and to make decisions only after that consultation.[130] The rejection of the right to instruct, on the theory that deliberators should be talking to people with different experiences and viewpoints, seems to show an appreciation of the risks of group polarization.

---

[127] *Infra text* accompanying notes 173–177.

[128] *See* Harrington, *supra* note 83, for supporting evidence in the context of concrete group tasks (involving investment clubs).

[129] Charlan Jeanne Nemeth, *Differential Contributions of Majority and Minority Influence*, 93 PSYCHOL. REV. 23 (1986); Harrington, *supra* note 83.

[130] Sunstein, *supra* note 5, at 22.

As I have suggested, central features of the constitutional design, including the system of checks and balances, can be understood in similar terms. Indeed, Madison defended his preference for large election districts and long terms of service as a way of counteracting polarization-type forces within particular constituencies.[131] Rawls's reference to the need to "combin[e] information and enlarg[e] the range of arguments" through discussion with a range of people strikes precisely the same note.[132]

VI. Enclave Deliberation and Suppressed Voices

There are also potential vices in heterogeneity and potentially desirable effects from deliberating "enclaves," consisting of groups of like-minded individuals. It seems obvious that such groups can be extremely important in a heterogeneous society, not least because members of some demographic groups tend to be especially quiet when participating in broader deliberative bodies. A special advantage of "enclave deliberation" is that it promotes the development of positions that would otherwise be invisible, silenced, or squelched in general debate.[133] In numerous contexts, this is a great advantage; many social movements have been made possible through this route (as possible examples, consider feminism,[134] the civil rights movement, religious conservatism, environmentalism, and the movement for gay and lesbian rights).

The efforts of marginalized groups to exclude outsiders, and even of political parties to limit their primaries to party members, can be justified in similar terms. Even if group polarization is at work—perhaps because group polarization is at work—enclaves can provide a wide range of social benefits, not least because they greatly enrich the social argument pool. In fact, the First Amendment right of expressive association should be understood in precisely these terms. According protection to collective effort on behalf of shared goals is especially important in preserving political and cultural diversity and in shielding dissident expression from suppression by the majority.

---

131 Cass R. Sunstein, *Interest Groups in American Public Law,* 38 STAN. L. REV. 29, 41–42 (1985).

132 RAWLS, *supra* note 2, at 359.

133 See, for example, the discussion of consciousness raising in CATHARINE A. MACKINNON, TOWARD A FEMINIST THEORY OF THE STATE 83–105 (1989).

134 A controversial and highly publicized case in point is the effort by the theologian Mary Daly to exclude men from her class at Boston University. *See* Carey Goldberg, *Facing Forced Retirement, Iconoclastic Professor Keeps On Fighting,* N.Y. TIMES, Aug. 15, 1999, at A13, 1999 WL 30476861; *see also* Boy Scouts of America v. Dale, 120 S. Ct. 2446 (2000) (upholding the associational interest and right of exclusion of Boy Scouts); Roberts v. U.S. Jaycees, 468 U.S. 609, 622 (1984) (rejecting the right of exclusion of the Jaycees).

A. Low Status and High Status

In deliberating bodies, high-status members tend to initiate communication more than others, and their ideas are more influential, partly because low-status members lack confidence in their own abilities, partly because they fear retribution.[135] For example, women's ideas are often less influential and sometimes are "suppressed altogether in mixed-gender groups,"[136] and in ordinary circumstances, cultural minorities have disproportionately little influence on decisions by culturally mixed groups.[137] It makes sense to promote deliberating enclaves in which members of multiple groups may speak with one another and develop their views.

But there is a serious danger in such enclaves. The danger is that through the mechanisms discussed here, members will move to positions that lack merit but are predictable consequences of the particular circumstances of enclave deliberation. In the extreme case, enclave deliberation may even put social stability at risk (for better or for worse). And it is impossible to say, in the abstract, that those who sort themselves into enclaves will generally move in a direction that is desirable for society at large or even for its own members. It is easy to think of examples to the contrary, such as the rise of Nazism, hate groups, and numerous "cults" of various sorts;[138] readers can think of their own preferred illustrations.

There is no simple solution to the dangers of enclave deliberation. Sometimes the threat to social stability is desirable. As Jefferson wrote, turbulence can be "productive of good. It prevents the degeneracy of government, and nourishes a general attention to . . . public affairs. I hold . . . that a little rebellion now and then is a good thing . . . ."[139] Any judgments about enclave deliberation are hard to make without a sense of the underlying substance—of what it is that divides the enclave from the rest of society. From the standpoint of institutional design, the problem is that any effort to promote enclave deliberation will ensure group polarization within a wide range of groups, some necessary to the pursuit of

---

[135] *See* Christensen & Abbott, *supra* note 16, at 273.

[136] *Id.* at 274.

[137] Catherine Kirchmeyer & Aaron Cohen, *Multicultural Groups: Their Performance and Reactions with Constructive Conflict,* 17 GROUP & ORG. MGMT. 153, 166 (1992). Interestingly, there is evidence that with changes in gender norms, some tasks show no gender differences in influence on groups. *See* Katherine W. Hawkins, *Effects of Gender and Communication Content on Leadership Emergence in Small Task-Oriented Groups,* 26 SMALL GROUP RES. 234, 243–44 (1995).

[138] *See, e.g.,* Aronson, *supra* note 17, at 242–43 (discussing the role of cult leaders); LEON FESTINGER ET AL., WHEN PROPHECY FAILS 3–30 (1956) (discussing conditions for continued commitment to implausible beliefs, including the need for social support).

[139] Letter from Thomas Jefferson to James Madison (Jan. 30, 1787), in THE PORTABLE THOMAS JEFFERSON 416–17 (Merrill D. Peterson ed., 1975).

justice, others likely to promote injustice, and some potentially quite dangerous. This makes clearer the sense in which Edmund Burke's conception of representation—rejecting "local purposes" and "local prejudices" in favor of "the general reason of the whole"[140]—is not contingently but instead essentially conservative (speaking purely descriptively, as a safeguard of existing practices). The reason is that the submersion of "local purposes" and "local prejudices" into a heterogeneous "deliberative assembly"[141] will inevitably tend to weaken the resolve of groups—and particularly low-status or marginalized groups—whose purely internal deliberations would produce a high degree of polarization.

Hence James Madison—with his fear of popular passions producing "a rage for paper money, for an abolition of debts, for an equal division of property, or for any other improper or wicked project"[142]—would naturally be drawn to a Burkean conception of representation, favoring large election districts and long length of service[143] to counteract the forces of polarization. By contrast, those who believe that "destabilization" is an intrinsic good,[144] or that the status quo contains sufficient injustice that it is worthwhile to incur the risks of encouraging polarization on the part of diverse groups, will, or should, be drawn to a system that enthusiastically promotes insular deliberation within enclaves.

In a nation in which most people are confused or evil, enclave deliberation may be the only way to develop a sense of clarity or justice, at least for some. But even in such a nation, enclave deliberation is unlikely to produce change unless the members of different enclaves are eventually brought into contact with others. In democratic societies, the best response is to ensure that any such enclaves are not walled off from competing views, and that at certain points, there is an exchange of views between enclave members and those who disagree with them. It is total or near-total self-insulation, rather than group deliberation as such, that carries with it the most serious dangers, often in the highly unfortunate (and sometimes deadly) combination of extremism with marginality.

---

140 Edmund Burke, *Speech to the Electors* (Nov. 3, 1774), in BURKE'S POLITICS: SELECTED WRITINGS AND SPEECHES OF EDMUND BURKE ON REFORM, REVOLUTION, AND WAR 116 (Ross J.S. Hoffman & Paul Levack eds., 1949).

141 *Id.*

142 THE FEDERALIST NO. 10, at 84 (James Madison) (Clinton Rossiter ed., 1961).

143 *See* Sunstein, *supra* note 171, at 41–42.

144 This is a possible reading of ROBERTO MANGABEIRA UNGER, THE CRITICAL LEGAL STUDIES MOVEMENT 39, 43, 53–57 (1986), which asserts the need for destabilization rights.

B. The Public Sphere and Appropriate Heterogeneity

1. The Public Sphere

For a designer or leader of any institution, it makes sense to promote ample social space both for enclave deliberation and for discussions involving a broad array of views, including views of those who have been within diverse enclaves.[145] The idea of a "public sphere," developed most prominently by Jürgen Habermas, can be understood as an effort to ensure a domain in which multiple views can be heard by people with multiple perspectives.[146] This understanding strongly supports current initiatives designed to ensure deliberation among dissimilar people on the Internet.[147] The fact of group polarization suggests that it could be desirable to take steps to reduce the likelihood that panels on federal courts of appeals consist solely of appointees of presidents of any single political party.[148]

Of course, any argument pool will be limited. No one has time to listen to every point of view. But an understanding of group polarization helps show that heterogeneous groups are often a far better source of good judgments, simply because more arguments will be made available.

2. A New Look at Group Representation

An understanding of group polarization is also relevant to the continuing debate over group representation.[149] The central issue here is whether identifiable groups should be represented as such in political institutions. Perhaps political groups should be allowed to have representation to the extent that they are able to get more than a minimal share of the vote. Perhaps steps should be taken to increase the likelihood that members of disadvantaged or marginal groups have their own representatives in the deliberating body. An understanding of group polarization is hardly sufficient to reach a definitive conclusion about these issues. But at least it can be said that group representation should help counteract the risks of polarization, and susceptibility to cascade effects, that come from deliberation among like-minded people. At the same time, group representation

---

[145] *See* IRVING L. JANIS, GROUPTHINK: PSYCHOLOGICAL STUDIES OF POLICY DECISIONS AND FIASCOS 267–71 (2d ed. 1982).

[146] *See* Habermas, *supra* note 9, at 231–50.

[147] *See* Sunstein, *supra* note 131 (manuscript at 102–03, 111–14).

[148] *See supra* Subsection IV.E.3.

[149] *See, e.g.*, IRIS MARION YOUNG, JUSTICE AND THE POLITICS OF DIFFERENCE 183–91 (1990) (urging group representation as a means of ensuring expression of plural perspectives); Cass R. Sunstein, *Beyond the Republican Revival*, 97 YALE L.J. 1539, 1585–89 (1988) (urging group representation as a means of ensuring good deliberation about the public good). For an overview of the debate, see also the essays in CHOOSING AN ELECTORAL SYSTEM: ISSUES AND ALTERNATIVES (Arend Lijphart & Bernard Grofman eds., 1984).

should help reduce the dangers that come from insulation of those in the smaller enclave, by subjecting enclave representatives to a broader debate.

Seen in this light, the point of group representation is to promote a process in which those in the enclave hear what others have to say, and in which those in other enclaves, or in no enclaves at all, are able to listen to people with very different points of view. When groups are represented as such in private and public institutions, it is to promote the airing of points of view that otherwise go unheard. And there is a further benefit to group representation: It works to prevent self-insulation on the part of group members by ensuring that they hear what others have to say as well. Here the benefits of group representation extend to both members and nonmembers of the relevant groups.

3. Appropriate Heterogeneity

For a deliberative democracy, a central question is how to ensure appropriate heterogeneity. For example, it would not make sense to say that in a deliberating group attempting to think through issues of affirmative action, it is important to allow exposure to people who think that slavery was good and should be restored. The constraints of time and attention call for limits to heterogeneity; and—a separate point—for good deliberation to take place, some views are properly placed off the table, simply because time is limited and they are so invidious, or implausible, or both. This point might seem to create a final conundrum: To know what points of view should be represented in any group deliberation, it is important to have a good sense of the substantive issues involved, indeed a sense sufficient to generate judgments about what points of view must be included and excluded. But if we already know that, does deliberation have any point at all?

The answer is that we often do know enough to see which views count as reasonable, without knowing which view counts as right, and this point is sufficient to allow people to construct deliberative processes that should correct for the most serious problems potentially created by group polarization. What is necessary is not to allow every view to be heard, but to ensure that no single view is so widely heard, and reinforced, that people are unable to engage in critical evaluation of the reasonable competitors.

Of course, the provision of diverse views does not guarantee good deliberation. Among other things, most people are subject to "confirmation bias," in accordance with which exposure to a competing position will not dislodge and may even strengthen the antecedently held position.[150] On questions of morality

---

[150] Charles G. Lord et al., *Biased Assimilation and Attitude Polarization: The Effects of Prior Theories on Subsequently Considered Evidence*, 37 J. PERSONALITY & SOC. PSYCHOL. 2098, 2102–04 (1979).

and fairness, and undoubtedly other questions as well, those who listen to diverse opinions may well emerge from the experience with an enhanced belief in the soundness of their original commitment.[151] But this is not a universal phenomenon, and at least an understanding of competing views is likely to weaken the forms of fragmentation and misunderstanding that come from deliberation among the like-minded.[152]

C. The Deliberative Opinion Poll: A Contrast

James Fishkin has pioneered the idea of "deliberative polling," in which small groups consisting of highly diverse individuals are asked to come together and to deliberate about various issues.[153] Deliberative opinion polls have now been conducted in several nations, including the United States, England, and Australia. Fishkin finds some noteworthy shifts in individual views, but he does not find a systematic tendency toward polarization. In his studies, individuals shift both toward and away from the median of predeliberation views. For present purposes, what is noteworthy about Fishkin's experiments is that they do not involve isolated enclaves; this is part of the reason for the absence of polarization effects.

. . . .

Fishkin's experiments suggest that group polarization can be heightened, diminished, or possibly even eliminated by seemingly small alterations in institutional arrangements. To the extent that limited argument pools and social influences are likely to have unfortunate effects, correctives can be introduced, perhaps above all by exposing group members, at one point or another, to arguments to which they are not antecedently inclined. Current proposals would do well to incorporate an understanding of these sometimes neglected facts.[154] But the most important lesson is the most general: It is desirable to create spaces for enclave deliberation without insulating enclave members from those with opposing views, and without insulating those outside of the enclave from the views of those within it.

---

[151] *Id.*

[152] *See* Brian Mullen et al., *Group Cohesiveness and Quality of Decision Making*, 25 SMALL GROUP RES. 189, 199–202 (1994); Brian Mullen & Carolyn Copper, *The Relation Between Group Cohesiveness and Performance: An Integration*, 115 PSYCHOL. BULL. 210, 225 (1994). For evidence to this effect, see Harrington, *supra* note 35, at 30–34.

[153] JAMES S. FISHKIN, THE VOICE OF THE PEOPLE 43, 161–81 (1997).

[154] Hence there is reason for caution about the proposal for "deliberation day" offered by Bruce Ackerman and James Fishkin. BRUCE ACKERMAN & JAMES FISHKIN, DELIBERATION DAY (forthcoming). The problem lies in the highly territorial nature of the proposal, in which people would deliberate with those in their community. This is a recipe for group polarization and social fragmentation.

VII. Conclusion

In this Essay, I have discussed the phenomenon of group polarization and explored some of its implications for deliberation generally and deliberative democracy in particular. The central empirical finding is that group discussion is likely to shift judgments toward a more extreme point in the direction indicated by the median of predeliberation judgments. This is true if a group decision is required; if individuals are polled anonymously afterwards, they are likely to shift in precisely the same way.

The underlying mechanisms are twofold. The first involves people's desire to stand in a particular relation to the group, perhaps for reputational reasons, perhaps to maintain their self-conception. Shifts occur as people find that it is necessary to alter their positions in order to maintain their self-conception or their desired relation to the group. The second mechanism involves limited "argument pools," as members of groups with a certain initial tendency typically hear a large number of arguments in support of that tendency, and few arguments in the other direction. When arguments are skewed toward a particular point of view, group members will move in the direction of that point of view. In a finding of special importance to democratic theory, group polarization is heightened if members have a sense of shared identity. And in an equally important finding, group polarization is diminished, and depolarization may result, if members have a degree of flexibility in their views and groups consist of an equal number of people with opposing views.

In the abstract, and without knowing anything about the underlying substance, it is impossible to say whether group polarization is good or bad. But the mechanisms that underlie group polarization raise serious questions about the view that deliberation is likely to yield correct answers to social questions. Like-minded people engaged in discussion with one another may lead each other in the direction of error and falsehood, simply because of the limited argument pool and the operation of social influences. This point very much bears on deliberation within insulated groups and hence on emerging communications technologies, which allow a high degree of individual filtering;[155] insulation and filtering can compound error. The point also bears on the design of deliberating courts, legislatures, and regulatory agencies. Above all, an understanding of group polarization helps explain why like-minded people, engaged in deliberation with

155 *See* LAWRENCE LESSIG, CODE AND OTHER LAWS OF CYBERSPACE 186 (2000); Shapiro, *supra* note 127, at 105–23.

one another, sometimes go to astonishing extremes and commit criminal or even violent acts.[156]

This is the dark side of "enclave deliberation." But I have also emphasized that deliberation within protected enclaves can be highly desirable. Partly as a result of group polarization, enclave deliberation can produce positions that would otherwise fail to emerge and that emphatically deserve a public hearing. The case for enclave deliberation is strengthened by evidence that members of low-status groups are likely to be silent in, or silenced by, broader deliberating bodies. Group polarization within enclaves might even operate as a counterweight to this problem.

In the abstract, it is not possible to specify the appropriate mix of enclave deliberation and deliberation within larger publics. But an appreciation of group polarization helps show why a free society takes steps to protect deliberation within enclaves, to ensure that those inside enclaves hear alternative views, and to ensure as well that those outside of particular enclaves are exposed to what enclave members have to say. Above all, it is important to avoid a situation in which people are exposed to softer and louder echoes of their own voices.

In a heterogeneous society, this form of self-insulation can create serious deliberative trouble, in the form of mutual incomprehension or much worse. Legal arrangements will increase or reduce that trouble. I have outlined some approaches that might ensure that heterogeneity, far from being a source of social fragmentation, will operate as a creative force, helping to identify problems and even solutions that might otherwise escape notice.

NOTES

1. We included this essay for two reasons: first, because we're living in a time of great polarization, and we ourselves crave a return to a world that is less polarized; and second, because part of managing risk involves getting input both from groups and from individuals. If a group's deliberations are affected by polarization, then those who receive recommendations from that group are not getting the best advice. Figuring out how to disrupt polarization in order to get input from a variety of perspectives should be on your managerial "to-do" list.

2. Knowing what you do now about group polarization and social cascades, how would you organize teams of colleagues within your organization to get the best

[156] The case of like-minded deliberators is the simplest one, but note that as long as there is a defined median, group polarization can occur in heterogeneous groups as well.

use from discussions within the team? Might you be able to apply what you now know to student organizations of which you're currently a member?

3. One of the passages in this article that caused us to pause is how easily it might be to manipulate a group with one's "affect." In psychology lingo, "affect" is the "expression of emotion or feelings displayed to others through facial expressions, hand gestures, voice tone, and other emotional signs such as laughter or tears."* Sunstein links affect and group decision-making:

> Affective factors are quite important in group decisions, and when manipulated, such factors will significantly increase or decrease polarization. If group members are linked by affective ties, dissent is significantly less frequent. The existence of affective ties thus reduces the number of divergent arguments and also intensifies social influences on choice. Hence people are less likely to shift if the direction advocated is being pushed by unfriendly group members; the likelihood of a shift, and its likely size, are increased when people perceive fellow members as friendly, likeable, and similar to them. In the same vein, physical spacing tends to reduce polarization; a sense of common fate and intragroup similarity tends to increase it, as does the introduction of a rival "outgroup." Mistakes are thus likely to be increased when group members are united mostly through affective ties, and not through concentration on a particular task; it is in the former case that alternative views will less likely find expression.**

Let's assume that you're an ethical person who wants to influence a group's decisions, and let's assume that you've learned how to use your own affect to appear friendly and part of the team. You start using words like "we" and "us" to convey your solidarity with the rest of the group. At what point does your acting ability stop being persuasive and start being overtly manipulative? Should it matter to you that you're manipulating the group's decision, say, by acting friendlier than you might actually feel toward the group? At what point does politeness cross over into something nefarious?

---

* Encyclopedia of Mental Disorders, "Affect," http://www.minddisorders.com/A-Br/Affect.html.

** *Deliberative Trouble* at 91–92 (footnotes omitted).

CHAPTER 21

*Integrity: Its Causes and Cures**

*David Luban***

Integrity is a good thing, isn't it? In ordinary parlance, we sometimes use it as a near synonym for honesty, but the word means much more than honesty alone. It means wholeness or unity of person, an inner consistency between deed and principle. "Integrity" shares etymology with other unity-words—integer, integral, integrate, integration. All derive from the Latin integrare, to make whole. And the person of integrity is the person whose conduct and principles operate in happy harmony.

Our psyches always seek that happy harmony. When our conduct and principles clash with each other, the result, social psychology teaches us, is cognitive dissonance. And dissonance theory hypothesizes that one of our fundamental psychic mechanisms is the drive to reduce dissonance.

You can reduce dissonance between conduct and principles in two ways. The high road, if you choose to take it, requires you to conform your conduct to your principles. That occasionally demands agonizing, sacrificial choices: to resign your job, for example, when continuing to do what your client asks requires you to cheat and shred and cover up. Think of the Enron lawyers. This is a lot to ask of people, particularly when those around you send the message that the actions you object to are nothing more than what grown-ups do to keep a competitive edge in a dog-eat-dog world.[1] In the business world, gaining a competitive edge is

---

* This piece was originally published as David Luban, *Integrity: Its Causes and Cures*, 72 FORDHAM L. REV. 279 (2003).

** Frederick Haas Professor of Law and Philosophy, Georgetown University Law Center. For comments on an earlier draft, I would like to thank Sam Fraidin, Neal Katyal, Deborah Rhode, Mike Seidman, and Dan Tarullo.

1 Robert Jackall, in his superb study of moral line-drawing in corporate settings, tells the story of an accountant who got himself fired from a big company for making waves about an internal slush fund. The accountant told Jackall that he was "frightened of losing. . . my self-respect. . . a fear of falling down in a place where you have stuck a flag in the ground and said: 'This is where I stand.' " ROBERT JACKALL, MORAL

universally recognized as good rather than bad, and if it conflicts with Sunday-school morality, those around you will send mixed signals about which you're supposed to obey. They will say both, deny the conflict, and leave you to draw your own conclusions about what their denial is supposed to mean. It's hard to maintain the courage of your convictions when your convictions are at war with each other, and those around you say they back one side, but behave as though they back the other.

Taking the high road to integrity may prove unappealing as an intellectual matter as well, because we recognize that hanging on to principles regardless of situations often bespeaks a kind of rigid inflexibility rather than a virtuous soul. Training in the common law teaches lawyers that the meaning of principles gets determined only in their application to specific cases, so that someone who insists on taking general principles literally can be fairly accused of misunderstanding the basic realist insight that rules have no existence apart from cases. For this reason, some leading legal ethicists argue for contextualism, the view that ethical judgment must be sensitive to situational differences that cannot be captured in abstract principles.[2] Contextualists will not necessarily endorse rigid moralism—and the high road to integrity seems nothing if not rigidly moralistic.

The low road is so much simpler—that, of course, is what makes it the low road. If your conduct conflicts with your principles, modify your principles. This is the path of least resistance; so much so that apparently we follow it unconsciously all the time. That, at any rate, is what fifty years of research in social psychology teaches us. In situation after situation, literally hundreds of experiments reveal that when our conduct clashes with our prior beliefs—when, in the jargon of social science, we act "counterattitudinally"—our beliefs swing into conformity with our conduct, without our ever noticing.[3]

MAZES: THE WORLD OF CORPORATE MANAGERS 109 (1988). But his colleagues had no pity for him. In their opinion, he broke the rules of corporate life and ignored good excuses for not acting. To them, the slush fund was simply business as usual, and the accountant's moralism was abstract and maybe even hypocritical, because nobody rises as high in a corporation as the accountant had without having dirtied his hands. Worst of all, the accountant's moral code made everyone else uncomfortable. "The guy's an evangelist." *Id.* at 109–11.

[2] *E.g.*, WILLIAM H. SIMON, THE PRACTICE OF JUSTICE: A THEORY OF LAWYERS' ETHICS 9–10, 69–74, 138–39 (1998) (defining and defending a "Contextual View" of legal ethics, which rejects categorical norms in favor of context-sensitive norms); David B. Wilkins, *Making Context Count: Regulating Lawyers After Kaye, Scholer*, 66 S. CAL. L. REV. 1147 (1993) (arguing that different contexts of legal practice demand different norms of professional conduct); Geoffrey C. Hazard, Jr., *Context in Ethics*, 2 APA NEWSLETTERS No. 2, Spring 2003, at 163 (arguing that philosophers' overreliance on categorical norms wrongly neglects the context-sensitive aspects of moral judgment).

[3] Both here and in the remainder of this article, my discussion of the impact of social-psychological forces on lawyer behavior draws instruction and inspiration from work of my colleague Donald Langevoort. *See* Donald C. Langevoort, *Behavioral Theories of Judgment and Decision Making in Legal Scholarship: A Literature Review*, 51 VAND. L. REV. 1499 (1998); Donald C. Langevoort, *Ego, Human Behavior, and Law*, 51 VA. L. REV.

I. Integrity as Dissonance Reduction

A. Counterattitudinal Advocacy

In one classic dissonance experiment, subjects were asked to perform a boring, repetitive task—rotating screws in holes of a pegboard—and afterwards were paid to tell the next student waiting to perform the same task that it was really very interesting. This is "counterattitudinal advocacy," known more colloquially as "lawyering." The reigning behaviorist paradigm in social psychology of the day hypothesized that higher rewards would reinforce the task more strongly, and therefore predicted that the higher the pay, the more likely the subjects were to evince belief in what they were advocating. But dissonance theory yields the opposite prediction. Deceiving one's fellows for little or no benefit to oneself creates dissonance, and so the "pro bono" advocates should be more likely to internalize the belief they were advocating. And so the experiments proved, to the dismay of behaviorists and the delight of dissonance theorists. Apparently, when my behavior makes me, as Saint Augustine says, "a great riddle to myself,"[4] I solve the riddle in the simplest way: if I said it, I must believe it, at least a bit; if I did it, I must think it's right.[5] All this, I emphasize, goes on unconsciously. But the net effect is a happy harmony between what I do and what I believe—the textbook definition of integrity. It is, however, a kind of integrity in which my beliefs always rationalize my actions after the fact, and in which I therefore automatically inhabit the best of all possible moral worlds: the world of my own inevitable righteousness.

Subsequent research has refined the dissonance idea. Experiments reveal that we don't always resolve dissonance between cognitions by changing our beliefs. Rather, we do so when the dissonant cognitions threaten to undermine our own self-concept—paradigmatically, when it occurs to us that we may have done

853 (1995); Donald C. Langevoort, *The Epistemology of Corporate-Securities Lawyering: Beliefs, Biases and Organizational Behavior,* 63 BROOK. L. REV. 629 (1997); Donald C. Langevoort, *Where Were the Lawyers? A Behavioral Inquiry into Lawyers' Responsibility for Clients' Fraud,* 46 VAND. L. REV. 75 (1993) [hereinafter Langevoort, *Where Were the Lawyers?*]. I am in overall agreement with Langevoort; and the principal addition to his work in the present article lies in two observations at the heart of my argument: first, that as a matter of psychological theory, cognitive dissonance theory has a kind of primacy, because it organizes a great deal of the subsequent research into disparate topics; and secondly, that dissonance reduction bears an uncomfortable resemblance to the quest for integrity.

4 ST. AUGUSTINE, CONFESSIONS, BK. 4, available at http://www.sacred-texts.com/chr/augconf/aug04.htm (last visited Oct. 18, 2003).

5 *See* Leon Festinger & James M. Carlsmith, *Cognitive Consequences of Forced Compliance,* 58 J. ABNORMAL & SOC. PSYCH. 203 (1959). See also the discussion in LEE ROSS & RICHARD E. NISBETT, THE PERSON AND THE SITUATION: PERSPECTIVES OF SOCIAL PSYCHOLOGY 66 (1991), and additional sources cited therein.

something wrong.[6] Apparently, we are all highly resistant to the thought of our own wrongdoing, and the result is that we will bend our moral beliefs and even our perceptions to fight off the harsh judgment of our own behavior. As some psychologists say, we are intuitive lawyers.[7] As usual, Nietzsche put it best. " 'I have done that,' says my memory. 'I cannot have done that,' says my pride, and remains inexorable. Eventually—memory yields."[8]

Of course, a little niggling voice might call this self-deception. Some might find it less than entirely admirable. If so, lawyers for pay can perhaps take comfort from the counterattitudinal advocacy experiment: it suggests that the higher they bill, the less likely they are to deceive themselves into believing what they say on behalf of clients. But they shouldn't take too much comfort, because the difference between them and their pro bono peers is only a matter of degree. Other experiments have shown that counterattitudinal advocacy, whether it be cheap or dear, typically nudges beliefs in the direction of the advocacy. Furthermore, bystanders aren't immune to the same effect. Observers hearing someone give a speech supporting or opposing Fidel Castro will believe that the speaker's own attitude is either pro- or anti-Castro even if they know that someone else has picked which side the speaker should argue.[9] Indeed, observers will draw conclusions about the speaker's belief even knowing that the speaker is merely reading out loud an essay written by someone else.[10] More bizarrely, subjects told that a person being described to them had been assigned to write a pro- or anti-abortion essay will believe that the person favors the conclusion supported in the essay, without reading the essay.[11] Our tendency to infer attitudes from advocacy-behavior apparently leads us to discount almost entirely information about external constraints on what others are advocating.[12] Add to this finding the fact—

---

6 *See* ELLIOT ARONSON, THE SOCIAL ANIMAL 230–33 (7th ed. 1995), on this refinement of the dissonance idea.

7 *See* Roderick M. Kramer & David M. Messick, *Ethical Cognition and the Framing of Organizational Dilemmas: Decision Makers as Intuitive Lawyers*, in CODES OF CONDUCT: BEHAVIORAL RESEARCH INTO BUSINESS ETHICS 59 (David M. Messick & Ann E. Tenbrunsel eds. 1996); see generally Aronson, supra note 6, at 175–245.

8 FRIEDERICH NIETZSCHE, BEYOND GOOD AND EVIL § 68 (Walter Kaufmann trans., 1966).

9 Edward E. Jones & Victor A. Harris, *The Attribution of Attitudes*, 3 J. EXPERIMENTAL SOC. PSYCH. 1 (1967).

10 Arthur G. Miller, *Constraint and Target Effects in the Attribution of Attitudes*, 12 J. EXPERIMENTAL SOC. PSYCH. 325, 330–33 (1976).

11 Icek Ajzen et al., *Consistency and Bias in the Attribution of Attitudes*, 37 J. PERSONALITY AND SOC. PSYCH. 1871, 1874 (1979).

12 *See generally* EDWARD E. JONES, INTERPERSONAL PERCEPTION 138–66 (1990); Edward E. Jones, *The Rocky Road from Acts to Dispositions*, 34 AM. PSYCHOLOGIST 107 (1979).

about which more later[13]—that what those around us believe influences what we believe, and it should scarcely be surprising that the very process of advocacy tends to swing our beliefs into line with the positions we advocate.

More importantly, well-paid lawyers have people around them, called clients, who may believe strongly in what they tell their lawyer to say—and our beliefs have a tendency to fall in line with those of the people around us. In the famous experiments of Solomon Asch, many people identified a short line-segment as longer than a long line-segment, after having heard other people (who in reality were confederates of the experimenter) say that the shorter line was longer. Asch's results have been duplicated in numerous settings, both in and out of the laboratory, and the startling conclusion that bare-bones sense perception can be influenced by the company we keep is robustly supported by the evidence.[14]

Lon Fuller noticed the phenomenon in the work-lives of lawyers. He puts the observation in the form of a hypothetical story about a young lawyer, five or six years out of law school,

> working in an office with at least, let us say, six other lawyers—perhaps with as many as a hundred or more . . . . When he was in law school he used to worry that he might be called upon by his office to advocate causes in which he did not personally believe. He finds that this is not a real problem . . . . In those instances where he had some doubts about the client's case at the beginning, these doubts evaporate after he has worked on the case for a few days; his client's cause then comes to seem at once logical and just. He worries a little that he might have experienced the same conversion had he been working on the other side, but this slight concern does not detract from his zeal or his desire to advance his client's interests.[15]

In Fuller's shrewdly perceptive fable, we see dissonance-reduction in the direction of advocacy and the socially-induced perception of the justness of the client's cause as two sides of a single phenomenon.

---

13 *See infra* Part I.B.

14 *See, e.g.*, Solomon E. Asch, *Effects of Group Pressures upon the Modification and Distortion of Judgments*, in GROUPS, LEADERSHIP, AND MEN 177 (Harold Guetzkow ed., 1951). *See* ROSS & NISBETT, *supra* note 5, at 30–35.

15 Lon L. Fuller, *Philosophy for the Practicing Lawyer*, in PRINCIPLES OF SOCIAL ORDER 287–88 (Kenneth I. Winston ed., 1981).

B. Diffusion of Responsibility and Social Cognition

The socially-influenced character of perception also helps to explain so-called "diffusion of responsibility," the well-known fact that groups of people are often less likely to respond helpfully in emergency situations than are individuals. (The relevance of diffusion of responsibility to the behavior of organizational lawyers who do nothing about client wrongdoing should be clear.[16]) When a college student has an apparent epileptic seizure in the company of five bystanders, he receives help only a third of the time.[17] Does this show heartless indifference? Not necessarily: when the student has a seizure in front of a single bystander, he receives help 85 percent of the time.[18] In a classic set of experiments by Darley and Latané, subjects either heard a crash of glass and a woman screaming from the next room, or witnessed smoke coming through the vent into their own room. When the subjects were alone, most responded to the apparent emergency; but when another person sat next to them and failed to respond, most subjects mimicked the other person and did not respond themselves.[19] Evidently, we respond to situations by checking to see how other people respond, and their response in large measure determines how we perceive the situation and therefore how we ourselves will respond. And of course the phenomenon is reciprocal: as we watch the other, the other watches us. We reinforce each other, in wrong beliefs as well as accurate ones (a phenomenon psychologists call pluralistic ignorance). The shaping and reciprocal reinforcement of perception by seeing how others perceive the same thing constitutes the basic phenomenon of socially influenced cognition, or, for short, social cognition. Pedestrians stepping around the body of a homeless man collapsed in the street may simply be taking their cues from each other; the evidence suggests that they would stop to help if they were alone. Our moral compass may point true north when we are by ourselves, but place us next to a few dozen other compasses pointing East, and our needle will fall into alignment with theirs—and, in doing so, influence the needles of others' compasses.

It may appear that social cognition theory and cognitive dissonance theory represent two distinct ideas: one, that we conform our beliefs to the perceived beliefs of the people around us, and the other, that we conform our beliefs to our

---

16 *See* Langevoort, *Where Were the Lawyers?*, *supra* note 3.

17 John M. Darley & Bibb Latané, *Bystander Intervention in Emergencies: Diffusion of Responsibility*, 8 J. PERSONALITY & SOC. PSYCH. 377 (1968).

18 *Id.*

19 *See generally* BIBB LATANÉ & JOHN M. DARLEY, THE UNRESPONSIVE BYSTANDER: WHY DOESN'T HE HELP? (1970); for a literature review, see Bibb Latané & Steve Nida, *Ten Years of Research on Group Size and Helping*, 89 PSYCH. BULL. 308 (1981).

own prior actions. In fact, however, psychological theorists regard them as two aspects of the same theory. Here, the significant idea came from a 1967 paper by Daryl Bem.[20] Recall that dissonance theory and behaviorism originally seemed to be rival theories. Bem provided a behaviorist reinterpretation of dissonance. The Achilles' heel of classical dissonance theory consisted of its need to postulate a felt inner tension—the irritating psychological experience of dissonance—that we need to resolve. The problem was that subjects did not report an inner experience of tension, and the theory therefore had to stipulate that the felt tension was unconscious. The unconscious experience of tension thus turned out to be a postulate founded not on observed data, but on the needs of the theory, always an embarrassment in a supposedly experimental science.[21]

Bem suggested a simpler mechanism than unconscious experiences (unexperienced experiences) to explain the alteration of belief after counterattitudinal action. According to Bem, we have no direct introspective access to our own beliefs. Man, remember, is a great riddle to himself. Instead, we infer our own beliefs in exactly the same way we infer other people's beliefs: by observing our behavior and its context, and reasoning from outward manifestation to inner belief.

In effect, Bem invites us to regard our own self as a sequence of different selves, each one a time-slice of the four-dimensional space-time worm called "me." Inferring my own beliefs from the observed behavior of the society of my own past selves seems, on this interpretation, no different from inferring my own beliefs about the length of a line-segment or the urgency of a scream in the next room from the observed behavior of those around me. Dissonance reduction turns out to be a special case of social cognition.

C. Recursively Reinforcing Commitment and the Road to Perdition

One consequence of dissonance theory is that once I act, my beliefs will rationalize the action and therefore impel me to further action of the same sort—which, in turn, calls for renewed rationalization, and further action. Action, we might say, breeds commitment, and commitment breeds further action in an ever-steeper slippery slope. The pattern

---

20 Daryl J. Bem, *Self-Perception: An Alternative Interpretation of Cognitive Dissonance Phenomena,* 74 PSYCH. REV. 183 (1967).

21 *But cf.* Aronson, *supra* note 6, at 235–37 (arguing that dissonance does cause actual psychological arousal). However, the experiments Aronson cites infer the existence of psychological arousal rather than measuring it directly. I suspect that this issue can only be settled by experiments in which subjects are tested for physiological indicators of arousal.

> action→ rationalization→ commitment→ further action has a recursive character. Psychologists call this the foot-in-the-door effect. In 1966, Freedman and Frazer dramatically demonstrated that persuading someone to place a one-inch-square pro-driving-safety sticker in their window quadruples their willingness to consent two weeks later to having a ferociously ugly, large pro-driving-safety sign in their yard.[22]

To moralists, the step-by-step road to perdition forms a familiar trope. "Let me tell you how you will start acting unethically," Patrick Schiltz writes in a well-known article on life in large law firms.[23] It starts with the time sheets, Schiltz tells us—with the moment when you first pad a time sheet just a little bit, intending to pay back the "loan" from the client with a little unbilled time next month. Soon the loans become more frequent, and after a while you lose the desire to pay them back. Then come the lies—first, the white lie about why you missed a deadline, then the darker lie that you carefully proofread the prospectus that you didn't, then the misleading answer to a deposition that you prep your client to give, then the smoking gun document that you don't turn over in discovery. In every case, you will have a rationalization. Speaking, he tells us, from personal experience, Schiltz ruefully observes that "[a]fter a couple years of this, you won't even notice that you are lying and cheating and stealing every day that you practice law."[24]

C. S. Lewis concurs. According to Lewis, "To nine out of ten of you the choice which could lead to scoundrelism will come, when it does come, in no very dramatic colours. Obviously bad men, obviously threatening or bribing, will almost certainly not appear."[25] According to Lewis, the fatal first step on the road to perdition comes simply because you want oh so much to belong to the Inner Ring, or, as we Americans say, the inner circle or in-crowd. A member of the in-crowd offers you a hint of friendship and a glimpse of life on the inside, and tempts you to do something that "we always do"—"and at the word "we" you try not to blush for mere pleasure"[26]—that isn't quite kosher. Once you have been tempted,

> next week it will be something a little further from the rules, and next year something further still, but all in the jolliest, friendliest spirit. It may

---

[22] Jonathan L. Freedman & Scott C. Fraser, *Compliance Without Pressure: The Foot-in-the-Door Technique,* 4 J. PERSONALITY & SOC. PSYCH. 195 (1966).

[23] Patrick J. Schiltz, *On Being a Happy, Healthy, and Ethical Member of an Unhappy, Unhealthy, and Unethical Profession,* 52 VAND. L. REV. 871, 917 (1999).

[24] *Id.* at 918.

[25] C.S. Lewis, *The Inner Ring,* in THEY ASKED FOR A PAPER: PAPERS AND ADDRESSES 139, 146 (1962).

[26] *Id.* at 146–47.

> end in a crash, a scandal, and penal servitude: it may end in millions, a peerage and giving the prizes at your old school. But you will be a scoundrel.[27]

The trope, I have said, is familiar—but what strikes me as less familiar is that this pattern, the very picture of lost integrity, exemplifies to social psychologists something close to the opposite—the self's incessant pursuit of integrity, of harmony between belief and action. That first small departure from the straight and narrow is like the one-inch-square sticker in Freedman and Fraser's experiments.[28] Agreeing to place it in our window leads us to reformulate our self-concept in a way that rationalizes the action, and the new self-concept impels us toward further action of the same sort as its own vindication. What Lewis implies, and Schiltz says outright, is that all the while that you're giving the Devil his due, a little bit more each day, you're also persuading yourself that the Devil is a misunderstood fellow whose hidden virtues are only now becoming transparent to you.

Perhaps the most famous example of the slippery slope to fatal commitment is the Milgram experiments, in which subjects are ordered to administer escalating electrical shocks to another subject in an experiment on the effects of pain on learning. The victim, of course, is a confederate of the experimenter, and the shocks are fake; the real goal of the experiment is to study subjects' responses to destructive orders. Milgram's astonishing discovery, replicated many times in several countries, is that almost two-thirds of the subjects prove willing to go all the way to the end of the sequence of shocks, despite the fact that the victim spends much of the time screaming for the experiment to stop, and eventually falls ominously silent, while the label on the shock-generator reads "Danger: Severe Shock."[29] The literature on these famous and alarming experiments is large, and many explanations have been offered for the depressingly high rate of compliance. The one I find most satisfactory focuses on the gradually escalating character of the shocks. The shock-generator has thirty switches, beginning at 15 volts and going up in 15-volt increments to 450. The result is that Milgram's subjects never confronted the pure question "Should I administer this 330-volt shock?" Instead, the question was "Should I administer this 330-volt shock given that a minute ago I administered a 315-volt shock—and I did that after

---

27 *Id.* at 147.

28 Freedman & Fraser, *supra* note 22.

29 *See generally* STANLEY MILGRAM, OBEDIENCE TO AUTHORITY: AN EXPERIMENTAL VIEW (1974); ARTHUR A. MILLER, THE OBEDIENCE EXPERIMENTS: A CASE STUDY OF CONTROVERSY IN SOCIAL SCIENCE (1986).

administering twenty previous shocks?" To think "That would be wrong!" virtually requires a subject to conclude that the previous shock, only insignificantly less severe, was also wrong—and cognitive dissonance makes that a very difficult conclusion to accept. It's not that Milgram's subjects became committed sadists. Rather, each shock they administered committed them to the belief that the next shock is neither sadistic nor even wrong (because the prior shocks were not sadistic or wrong). The dissonance-induced commitment leads the subjects unconsciously to gerrymander the boundary between right and wrong.[30] Commitment breeds commitment, and leads to overshooting the bounds of reasonableness as outside observers perceive those bounds, but as the subject clearly does not. The subject is keeping faith with his own commitments, and the shock-victim must suffer at the hands of the subject's pursuit of integrity.

D. Advocacy to Excess

These reflections on the self-reinforcing character of commitment may help us explain puzzling cases in which lawyers whom one would have expected to dislike a particular cause or client, and to do the bare minimum that competent advocacy requires, instead go the extra mile on behalf of a cause they presumably detest. A celebrated example is Francis Bacon, who at one point in his career found himself prosecuting his own friend and patron, the Earl of Essex. As Macaulay reports, Bacon

> did not confine himself to what would have been amply sufficient to procure a verdict. He employed all his wit, his rhetoric, and his learning, not to ensure a conviction,—for the circumstances were such that a conviction was inevitable—but to deprive the unhappy prisoner of all those excuses which, though legally of no value, yet tended to diminish the moral guilt of the crime, and which, therefore, though they could not justify the peers in pronouncing an acquittal, might incline the Queen to grant a pardon.[31]

Then, after the execution of Essex, Bacon published a pamphlet to traduce his memory.[32] It was this miserable last straw that led Macaulay to his often-quoted rhetorical question about lawyers, "whether it be right that a man should, with a wig on his head, and a band round his neck, do for a guinea what, without those

---

[30] That, at any rate, is the analysis of the Milgram experiments I develop (following Milgram's own suggestion) in David J. Luban, *The Ethics of Wrongful Obedience,* in ETHICS IN PRACTICE: LAWYERS' ROLES, RESPONSIBILITIES, AND REGULATION 94 (Deborah L. Rhode ed., 2000).

[31] Thomas Babington Macaulay, *Francis Bacon,* in 2 CRITICAL AND HISTORICAL ESSAYS 290, 314 (1926).

[32] "The faithless friend who had assisted in taking the Earl's life was now employed to murder the Earl's fame." *Id.* at 315.

appendages, he would think it wicked and infamous to do for an empire."[33] But those who quote this celebrated epigram sometimes forget that Macaulay did not criticize Bacon for following the role-morality of lawyers—the separation of the personal and the professional. Macaulay had no wish to question the prevailing professional rules. "If . . . Bacon did no more than these rules required of him, we shall readily admit that he was blameless, or, at least, excusable."[34] The problem was that Bacon went so much further than the rules required, as Macaulay goes to great and entertaining rhetorical lengths to emphasize.[35] Bacon did everything in his power to ensure that no mercy would or could be shown to Essex. Why? Macaulay thinks he knows the reason. "The real explanation of all this is perfectly obvious . . . . The moral qualities of Bacon were not of a high order."[36] According to Macaulay's diagnosis, Bacon's "desires were set on things below."[37] Bacon was simply too enamored of "[w]ealth, precedence, titles, patronage, the mace, the seals, the coronet, large houses, fair gardens, rich manors, massy services of plate, gay hangings, curious cabinets."[38]

Perhaps so; Bacon would hardly be the first or last lawyer to succumb to such temptations. But before accepting this diagnosis, let us consider a more contemporary example. In 1993, a black lawyer named Anthony Griffin made headlines by representing the grand dragon of the Texas Knights of the Ku Klux Klan as an ACLU volunteer. The KKK had engaged in a campaign to terrorize black residents who wished to move into an all-white housing project, and the State of Texas attempted to obtain the Klan's membership lists in an effort to prosecute them. The ACLU agreed to represent the Klan's grand dragon, and steered him to Griffin—who, as it happens, not only worked with the ACLU, but was also General Counsel for the Port Arthur Branch of the NAACP, which soon fired Griffin because he was representing the Klan.[39]

No great mystery exists about why the ACLU—or even a black ACLU lawyer—might wish to defend the Klan's right to keep its membership lists secret. During the civil rights movement, the state of Alabama harassed the NAACP by demanding membership lists, and the Supreme Court's decision in *NAACP v. Alabama* that the lists need not be given to the state stands as a landmark First

33 *Id.* at 317.

34 *Id.*

35 *See id.* at 318–19.

36 *Id.* at 319–20.

37 *Id.* at 320.

38 *Id.*

39 David B. Wilkins, *Race, Ethics, and the First Amendment: Should a Black Lawyer Represent the Ku Klux Klan?*, 63 GEO. WASH. L. REV. 1030, 1030 (1995).

Amendment protection of political association.[40] The puzzle is that Griffin went much further than defending *NAACP v. Alabama* by representing the Klan. Apparently, Griffin couldn't stop. He went on to represent the Klan in its attempt to "adopt-a-highway" next to the housing project, a transparent effort to evade a restraining order to keep away from the project.[41] The integrity of the First Amendment hardly required this further representation, any more than Bacon's persecution and assassination of the Earl of Essex had anything to do with the requirements of the prosecutor's role. Yet no one would suggest that Griffin had fallen under the sway of curious cabinets or massy services of plate.

David Wilkins, who has analyzed the ethics of Griffin's representation of the Klan in great detail, gets closer to the truth than Macaulay in explaining the puzzle of counterattitudinal advocacy that goes above and beyond the call of duty in its zeal:

> [I]t is virtually impossible for someone in an adversarial role to keep their clients, and more importantly their client's view of the world, at arms' length. It is a familiar truth in social science that those who are called upon to support positions that they initially find morally abhorrent will search for ways to reduce the distance between their beliefs and their practices.[42]

In short, cognitive dissonance strikes again. If Wilkins is right, Griffin—and, I am speculating, Bacon—went the extra mile in their advocacy to keep faith with their initial decision to undertake the advocacy in the first place. Apparently, their integrity called for nothing less.

E. Group Polarization in Adversary Systems

I have suggested, in the spirit of Bem's version of dissonance theory, a structural similarity between social cognition (the way our beliefs adapt to the beliefs of others) and individual belief-modification (the way our beliefs adapt to our own prior actions).[43] The similarity runs in both directions. Not only do we become committed to our own courses of action—out of solidarity, one might say, with the company of our prior selves—but we become equally committed to other members of our own "team" in social competitions. Here, too, the relevance of the research to lawyer behavior should be obvious: the adversary system sets up a social competition in litigation, and the free enterprise system sets up a social

---

40 NAACP v. Alabama, 357 U.S. 449 (1958).

41 Wilkins, *supra* note 39, at 1051–53.

42 *Id.* at 1055–56.

43 *See supra* notes 21–22 and accompanying text.

competition in transactional practice. Henry Tajfel told subjects that a test of their aesthetic tastes showed that they prefer Klee to Kandinsky—and that bit of misinformation proved sufficient for them to discriminate in favor of others who supposedly prefer Klee, and against those who supposedly prefer Kandinsky.[44] Similarly, thirty-two young boys were told, after an experiment in visual perception, that they belong to a group that systematically overestimates (or underestimates) the number of dots flashed on a screen. They were then given the task of dividing money among the group. They systematically discriminated in favor of those supposedly in the same perceptual group and against those in the other group—the phenomenon of in-group favoritism resulting from group polarization, intimately familiar to participants in adversarial proceedings.[45] Remember that advocacy makes others think that we believe what we are advocating, even when they ought to know better—and, through a combination of commitment and taking cues from those others, we are likely to believe it ourselves. Group polarization and belief-change in the direction of one's group reinforce one another.

F. Blaming the Victim

In a 1973 experiment, subjects were assigned tasks in pairs, in which a "worker" would carry out the task for pay while the "supervisor" would give instructions. They then watched an event in which a supervisor bungled the task, ruining a highly successful effort by the worker. Knowing the results of the other group polarization experiments, it should not surprise us that those who expected to be workers themselves blamed the supervisor, while those who expected to be supervisors blamed the equipment or circumstances, but did not blame the supervisor. More surprisingly, however, when it became clear that the mishap would cost the worker the money he had earned, the other "supervisors" went one step further, and severely disparaged the personal qualities of the worker.[46]

This last phenomenon—blaming the victim—occurs even in settings where us-and-them polarization is not the issue. In an ingenious series of experiments, Melvin Lerner confirmed repeatedly that the worse someone is treated, the more likely observers are to regard the victim as an unattractive, flawed person.[47] Lerner explains this phenomenon as an unconscious attempt to ward off the scary

---

44 *See* Henri Tajfel et al., *Social Categorization and Intergroup Behaviour,* 1 EUR. J. SOC. PSYCH. 149 (1971); *see also* SOCIAL IDENTITY AND INTERGROUP RELATIONS (Henri Tajfel ed., 1982).

45 Harvey A. Hornstein, *Out of the Wilderness?,* 29 CONTEMP. PSYCH. 11, 11 (1984).

46 Alan L. Chaikin & John M. Darley, *Victim or Perpetrator?: Defensive Attribution of Responsibility and the Need for Order and Justice,* 25 J. PERSONALITY & SOC. PSYCH. 268 (1973).

47 MELVIN J. LERNER, THE BELIEF IN A JUST WORLD: A FUNDAMENTAL DELUSION 89–103 (1980).

thought that if unfair treatment can happen to the victim, it can happen to me. We disparage the victim in order to find a distinction, some distinction, between her and us in order to reassure ourselves that we won't be victimized next.[48]

Lerner's explanation of blaming the victim has the ring of truth, but I think that it may work in tandem with another phenomenon, more akin to the dissonance-based effects discussed above. Strikingly, out of over a thousand subjects in Lerner's experiments, not a single one tried to help the victim or walked out of the experiment in protest.[49] Why not? One explanation, in the spirit of Darley and Latané's diffusion-of-responsibility research, is that the subjects witnessed the scene of victimization in groups—and groups don't act as readily as individuals do.[50] Whether or not that explanation is right, the fact that no subject protested the injustice done to the victim suggests, according to dissonance theory, that these subjects will justify their own inaction to themselves by minimizing the injustice—and the simplest way to minimize the injustice is to denigrate the victim. This, too, is familiar common sense about lawyers: even if lawyers dislike the side they are representing, they often wind up disliking the other side even more, and they relieve their own discomfort at what representing their client requires them to do by the consoling thought that at least the party they are harming is a bad person who has it coming.

G. The Scripted Self: Playing Roles

Another important feature of the worker-supervisor experiment is that the subjects conformed their own pro- and con-attitudes to the role they themselves anticipated playing. When placed in the role of worker before witnessing a scene in which a supervisor's mistake costs the worker his pay, one faults the supervisor. When placed in the role of supervisor, one blames the equipment or circumstances and denigrates the worker. Along with the other dissonance-based phenomena discussed above—belief modification,[51] social cognition,[52] diffusion

---

48 *Id.* at 21.

49 *Id.* at 51–52.

50 The diffusion-of-responsibility phenomenon should not be confused with the well-known economic result, based in the free-rider problem, that groups typically underprovide collective goods. *See generally* MANCUR OLSON, JR., THE LOGIC OF COLLECTIVE ACTION (1965). What Darley and Latané discovered was not the logic of collective action, but the illogic of collective action—that is, they discovered not the rational decision to free ride on others, leading to mutual inactivity, but an irrational overreliance on our perception of what others think, leading to mutual inactivity because nobody wants to make the first move.

51 *See supra* text accompanying notes 44–46.

52 *See supra* text accompanying notes 16–22.

of responsibility,[53] commitment-escalation,[54] the foot-in-the-door effect,[55] group polarization,[56] and blaming the victim[57]—conformity to social role plays a prominent part in our psychic makeup.

Undoubtedly the most famous of all experiments in the power of roles to shape cognitions is the Stanford Prison Experiment ("SPE"), conducted by Philip Zimbardo, Craig Haney, and their associates. Volunteer undergraduate subjects were divided randomly into "guards" and "inmates" in a mock prison. In less than a day, guards began bullying and brutalizing the inmates, while the inmates began to exhibit the pathologies of real-life prisoners, so much so that five had to be released very soon because of "extreme emotional depression, crying, rage and acute anxiety."[58] By the second day, the prisoners revolted and the guards put down the rebellion by blasting them with fire extinguishers.[59]

The transformation of the subjects almost defies belief. One guard wrote in his diary before the experiment, "[a]s I am a pacifist and nonaggressive individual, I cannot see a time when I might maltreat other living things."[60] By day five of the experiment, this same student wrote the following in his diary:

> This new prisoner, 416, refuses to eat. That is a violation of Rule Two: "Prisoners must eat at mealtimes," and we are not going to have any of that kind of shit . . . . Obviously we have a troublemaker on our hands. If that's the way he wants it, that's the way he gets it. We throw him into the Hole ordering him to hold greasy sausages in each hand. After an hour, he still refuses . . . . I decide to force feed him, but he won't eat. I let the food slide down his face. I don't believe it is me doing it. I just hate him more for not eating.[61]

Partway through the experiment, some of the inmates' parents came to visit them, and were horrified by the degraded state their sons had been reduced to. But after

---

53 *See supra* text accompanying notes 16–22.

54 *See supra* text accompanying notes 23–31.

55 *See supra* text accompanying notes 23–31.

56 *See supra* text accompanying notes 44–46.

57 *See supra* text accompanying notes 47–51.

58 Craig Haney et al., *Interpersonal Dynamics of a Simulated Prison,* 1 INT'L. J. CRIMINOLOGY & PENOLOGY 69, 81 (1973).

59 Philip Zimbardo et al., *The Mind Is a Formidable Jailer: A Pirandellian Prison,* N.Y. TIMES, Apr. 8 1973, § 6 (Magazine), at 41.

60 Craig Haney & Philip Zimbardo, *The Socialization into Criminality: On Becoming a Prisoner and a Guard,* in LAW, JUSTICE, AND THE INDIVIDUAL IN SOCIETY: PSYCHOLOGICAL AND LEGAL ISSUES 198, 207 (Tapp & Levine eds., 1977).

61 *Id.* at 209.

a little tough talk from Warden Zimbardo, the parents simply backed down.[62] Later, the inmates were visited by a prison priest and a lawyer. Like the parents, neither of these professionals had been instructed to act in a role, or had agreed to do so—but both of them did. For example, it simply never occurred to the lawyer (or parents, or priests) to tell the students that they were not inmates, but rather volunteers in an experiment that they could leave at any time. Astoundingly, the prison script seemed to induce everyone to act in role.

II. Taking Stock of Situationism

The Stanford Prison Experiment seems to portray a world in which the very idea of personal integrity seems absent—a Goffmanesque world where there are no selves, only selves-in-roles, selves who slide frictionlessly from role to role, in each case conforming to the expectations of the role and whatever principles of right behavior come attached to its script. Behind the mask, another mask; behind all the masks, a vacuum; beneath the vacuum, a mask once again. Indeed, some theorists have drawn conclusions very close to the claim that when it comes to character, there's no there there. John Doris, in his recent book LACK OF CHARACTER, concludes from a careful examination of the experimental literature that human character, defined as a fixed set of dispositions toward certain behavior, is largely a myth.[63] Gilbert Harman, drawing on the same experimental literature, agrees.[64] Both draw on an interpretation of the experiments I have been reviewing called situationism, defended most cogently by Lee Ross and Richard Nisbett.[65] At this point, I want to detour briefly to discuss the merits of situationism, in order to distinguish the argument I am offering from a version of situationism that I think is wrong.

The thesis of situationism is, quite simply, that differences in situations account for much more of the observed variation in human behavior than do differences in personality. Our tendency to believe otherwise, that is, to ascribe

---

[62] PHILIP G. ZIMBARDO, STANFORD PRISON EXPERIMENT: A SIMULATION STUDY OF THE PSYCHOLOGY OF IMPRISONMENT CONDUCTED AT STANFORD UNIVERSITY (1999), at http://www.prison exp.org/slide-24.htm. Some of the parents got upset when they saw how fatigued and distressed their son was. But their reaction was to work within the system to appeal privately to the Superintendent to make conditions better for their boy. When one mother told me she had never seen her son looking so bad, I responded by shifting the blame from the situation to her son. "What's the matter with your boy? Doesn't he sleep well?" Then I asked the father, "Don't you think your boy can handle this?" He bristled, "Of course he can—he's a real tough kid, a leader." Turning to the mother, he said, "Come on Honey, we've wasted enough time already." And to me, "See you again at the next visiting time." *Id.*

[63] *See generally* JOHN M. DORIS, LACK OF CHARACTER: PERSONALITY AND MORAL BEHAVIOR (2002).

[64] Gilbert Harman, *Moral Philosophy Meets Social Psychology: Virtue Ethics and the Fundamental Attribution Error*, 99 PROC. ARISTOTELIAN SOC'Y 315 (1999).

[65] *See generally* ROSS & NISBETT, *supra* note 5.

people's behavior to their personality or character—or, for that matter, their voluntary choices—rather than the situation they are in, is what situationists criticize as the "fundamental attribution error."[66] Situationists point, for example, to some of Milgram's findings.[67] In one variant of his shock experiment, Milgram placed the subject on a team with another subject—actually, of course, a confederate of Milgram. When the confederate uncomplainingly obeyed orders to continue the shocks, 90% of the subjects went along; but when the confederate refused to administer high level shocks and walked away from the experiment, compliance by subjects plummeted to 10%. Clearly, it would be implausible to assume that the subject population in one variant differs radically in propensity to comply from the subject population in the other. Instead, the conclusion must be that situational differences generate this dramatic swing from near-universal compliance to near-universal rebellion. Similarly, Doris points to experiments by Isen and Levin that showed that people who find a dime in the coin return of a pay telephone were vastly more likely to help a stranger pick up papers she has dropped than people who find no dime.[68] Again, the power of the situation appears to dominate or even dwarf the power of personality and character in determining behavior. The lesson of situationism, drawn by Harman and Doris, seems to be that we have no character that disposes us to behave consistently across situations.[69] The disconcerting picture seems to be a near-determinism of

---

66 *Id.* at 29–89.

67 Doris, *supra* note 63, at 46; MILGRAM, *supra* note 29 at 116–22.

68 Doris, *supra* note 63, at 30–31 (discussing A. M. Isen & P. F. Levin, *Effect of Feeling Good on Helping: Cookies and Kindness*, 21 J. PERSONALITY & SOC. PSYCHOL. 384 (1972)). Fourteen of sixteen subjects who found the dime helped pick up the stranger's fallen papers, while only one out of twenty-five subjects who found no dime stopped to help. *Id.* at 387.

69 Doris puts the idea nicely in a chapter entitled "The Fragmentation of Character":

> [I]t's not crazy to think that someone could be courageous in physical but not moral extremity, or be moderate with food but not sex, or be honest with spouses but not with taxes. If we take such thoughts seriously, we'll qualify our attributions: "physical courage" or "moral courage," instead of "courage," and so on. Would things were so simple. With a bit of effort, we can imagine someone showing physical courage on the battlefield, but cowering in the face of storms, heights, or wild animals. Here we go again: "battlefield physical courage," "storms physical courage," "heights physical courage," and "wild animals physical courage." Things can get still trickier: Someone might exhibit battlefield courage in the face of rifle fire but not in the face of artillery fire. If we didn't grow sick of it, we could play this little game all day.

Doris, *supra* note 63, at 62 (internal citation omitted). Doris's point is that the quest to explain experiments by reference to personality traits should simply be abandoned.

The salience to legal ethics of this critique of character should be clear, but nowhere clearer than in the bar admissions process, with its requirement of screening applicants on the basis of character. In the leading article on the subject, Deborah Rhode points to the lack of empirical support for belief in character traits that are consistent across situations, and the lack of predictive power of behavior in one situation for behavior in another. She argues, in a fashion similar to Doris, that the experimental findings undermine the entire enterprise of character-assessment, which she believes that the bar should abandon. Deborah L. Rhode, *Moral Character as a Professional Credential*, 94 YALE L.J. 491, 555–62 (1985).

situations, in which minuscule differences in the situation—a dime or no dime, the presence or absence of other people in the room—turn into major differences in behavior, and individual idiosyncrasy explains very little of the differences. (It is a near-determinism, not a strict determinism, because individual idiosyncrasy still plays some explanatory role.[70])

I believe that caution is in order about what conclusions to draw from these observations, however. There's no denying the situationists' point that minute changes in situation can dramatically affect the proportion of people exhibiting a given behavior. But the situationists have a hard time explaining why different people behave differently in the same situation. In Milgram's basic experiment, two-thirds of the subjects complied, but one-third did not. The point is more general. Throughout the experimental literature of social psychology we find striking and statistically significant correlations between experimental variables and subjects' responses—but, significant as they may be, the correlation coefficients seldom exceed 0.5, which by the standards of physics is a low correlation, signifying that the manipulated variable accounts for only one-fourth of the variance in behavior. People differ, and the question for situationism is how these differences should be explained.

The answer, Ross and Nisbett tell us, lies in the fact that people construe situations differently, that "it is the situation as construed by the subject that is the true stimulus."[71] Thus, the differences in response arise not from differences in human character, but rather from differences in perception and construal.

Perhaps. Yet I find this explanation, according to which the one-third noncompliance rate in the Milgram experiment is explained by arguing that the noncompliant third perceived the situation differently from the two-thirds of compliers, to be both too convenient and too ad hoc, given that we don't actually know anything about how Milgram's subjects construed the situation. In Ross and

[70] One must be careful about this question, however. Psychologists sometimes write as though what I am calling "individual idiosyncracy" is itself a set of deterministic factors—personality traits, perhaps biological in origin, that cause whatever component of behavior the situations do not cause. *See, e.g.*, Lerner, *supra* note 47, at 120 ("[A]s any reasonable psychologist will tell you, all behavior is 'caused' by a combination of antecedent events and the genetic endowment of the individual."). We leave the framework of determinism only when we insist that "individual idiosyncracy" includes a component of individual choice. Thinking in this way of course lands one squarely in the midst of the problem of free will; but when were we ever out of that problem? Here I agree with John Doris, who argues that situationism pretty much leaves the problem of free will, with its unsettled and unsettling debates between hard and soft determinism, compatibilism and incompatibilism, untouched. Doris, *supra* note 63, at 132–33. *But cf. id.* at 133–46 (Doris'sensuing arguments about ways in which situationism complicates some approaches to the free-will problem). In an earlier paper, I tried to lay out the assumptions necessary for a compatibilist analysis of the Milgram experiments. Luban, *supra* note 30, at 112–16.

[71] ROSS & NISBETT, *supra* note 5, at 11; *see generally id.* at Chapter 3.

Nisbett's view, what I have called a near-determinism of situations becomes more like a true determinism. Ross and Nisbett localize individual idiosyncrasy in the capacity for perception and construal, while accepting a version of stimulus-response determinism according to which the stimulus (the situation-as-construed) leads subjects to uniform responses. But why? Why parse the individual this way, into a perception/construal capacity that exhibits idiosyncrasy and a responsive capacity that exhibits little or none? To do so seems arbitrary, and borders on downright inconsistency. After all, construing a situation is itself a kind of action, and one would suppose that a consistent situationist should posit that situations account for most of the variation in construals as well as responses. In that case, however, the situationist is left with no explanation for variation among individuals placed in the same situation. Moreover, even if the situationist is right about individual variability in construing situations, one can reply that personality lies in large part in our habits of perception and construal, so at least some form of personality theory survives the situationist objection.

I prefer to think of situations—the independent variables that experimenters manipulate—as sources of pressure or temptation. Quite simply, the experiments demonstrate how difficult—but not impossible—acting against the situational tide is. It's so difficult that in the basic Milgram experiment only a third of the subjects are able to bring it off. Adding a compliant teammate makes it more difficult still, so that only one subject out of ten was able to resist; while adding a noncompliant team-mate makes resistance easy enough that nine out of ten subjects were able to succeed at resisting the orders to continue administering shocks. In the terms of our initial metaphor, situational changes alter the relative gradient of both the high road and the low road. What the experiments do show, quite graphically, is that seemingly-minor manipulations of the environment can cause astonishingly large changes in the ease or difficulty of action, the angle of incidence between the two roads.

Putting the situationists' point in these terms—that is, that situations transform the ease or difficulty of certain courses of action—avoids the implication of determinism. The situation sets conditions under which we choose, but the numbers strongly imply that these conditions do not render choice impossible. Notice that if every subject complied with Milgram's experiment, it would provide evidence that the experiment had uncovered a mechanism akin to a physical reflex, over which we have no choice or control. And if only a few subjects out of the thousand complied, we might regard them as pathological cases, and excuse them from blame on the grounds that they have a screw loose somewhere. The actual two-thirds/one-third split precludes us from drawing either of these deterministic conclusions about the compliers.

Because I resist situational determinism, I resist as well the radical suggestion that our deep-seated propensity to fall into predetermined roles (as in the SPE) means that we have no core self whose integrity matters, only a collection of selves-in-roles, each seeking its own harmony between behavior and principle, but without any larger unity of self. The experiments do show that we lack robust consistency across situations. This should not surprise us, however. After all, if some of my roles impose inconsistent moral demands—if, for example, with a wig on my head and a band round my neck I will be asked to do for a guinea what I would otherwise think it wicked and infamous to do for an empire[72]—and my daily life leads me to occupy all these roles; and if, further, the actions I take in each role lead me to adopt beliefs that vindicate those actions, then dissonance theory predicts that I will preserve my conception of myself as a morally upright individual in the only way left: by abandoning the belief that my other beliefs should be consistent.[73] We purchase integrity, what Gerald Postema calls the "unity of practical consciousness," at the price of logic, the unity of theoretical consciousness.[74] The experimental demonstration that we lack robust consistency across situations shows that integrity consists of a complex unity, stitched together with a great deal of self-deception that allows us to deny inconsistencies and the dissonance they induce. Integrity remains something that we seek. The problem, then, remains the one we began with: that the quest for integrity, manifested in all the psychological phenomena we have been reviewing, can drive us to behavior as disconcerting and morally repellent as that shown in the Stanford Prison Experiment or in Milgram's demonstration.

III. The Difference Between Integrity and Dissonance Reduction

I do not suppose that I am reporting anything novel or recondite. All of these experiments are widely known, and the Milgram and Stanford experiments are famous, almost legendary. My argument, which is perhaps less familiar, is that these are not simply an array of discrete, unrelated psychological curiosities. Rather, they are aspects of cognitive dissonance, in its social and individual guises. They emerge, therefore, from our drive toward inner harmony—our drive toward integrity. The quest for integrity kills, and in killing it leaves the survivors with

---

72 *See* Macaulay, *supra* note 31, at 217.

73 The philosopher Sidney Morgenbesser, asked if he believes in the law of non-contradiction, replied, "Yes and no."

74 Gerald J. Postema, *Self-Image, Integrity, and Professional Responsibility*, in THE GOOD LAWYER: LAWYERS' ROLES AND LAWYERS' ETHICS 286, 296 (David Luban ed., 1983).

their own sense of rectitude intact, like a tattered flag flapping in the wind over the fallen.

To all this there is a simple reply: You are not talking about genuine integrity. Integrity does not consist of molding and adapting one's principles to whatever behaviors we and those around us find convenient. Integrity consists of taking the high road, the road of conforming our behavior to our principles. I mentioned earlier that the word "integrity", like "integer", "integral", and "integrate", comes from the Latin integrare, to make whole. That word, in turn, derives from in-, "not", plus tangere, "touch." An entity is whole if it is untouched, unsullied; the Latin integer vitae meant innocent, pure, blameless in life.[75] And thus the person of integrity is not merely the person whose principles and behavior harmonize, regardless of how that harmony gets achieved, but rather the person who has kept her principles intact ("intact" is another word whose Latin root means "untouched"). We think of the person of integrity in the terms C.S. Lewis uses in Perelandra to describe Ransom, his protagonist: "even if the whole universe were crazy and hostile, Ransom was sane and wholesome and honest."[76] His moral compass never turns from true north, no matter how many other compasses point elsewhere.

Of course, as an analysis of the concept of integrity this must be right. When we are done in by situational forces that distort our moral judgment, we are hardly "untouched." Just the opposite: we are all too touched. The low road to integrity is simply not the same as the high road, and bending your principles to rationalize your actions is not the same as bringing your actions into conformity with your principles.

The problem, however, lies in telling them apart from the inside. As I noted above, merely asserting categorical principles and refusing to deviate from them regardless of the situation we find ourselves in may be Ransom-like integrity, but it may also be an inability to learn from experience, a kind of fatal priggishness and narrow-minded inflexibility. Every normal life contains episodes of learning from experience, during which principles are reinterpreted, contexts are distinguished, and precommitments modified, along with episodes of sticking to your guns, drawing lines in the sand that you will not cross, and keeping faith with your ideals. This implies that a life of integrity—the high-road, genuine kind of integrity, not the low-road, ersatz kind—will normally contain episodes in which pre-existing moral judgments get discarded in the face of experience. Ransom may

---

[75] *See* HORACE, ODES AND CARMEN SAECULARE, I:22.

[76] C.S. LEWIS, PERELANDRA 6 (1944).

always have been sane and wholesome and honest, but his judgment of what particular behaviors are sane, wholesome, and honest may well have changed between the ages of fifteen and fifty. One supposes and hopes that they did. His fifteen-year-old self might view some of the fifty-year-old's beliefs as sold-out ideals, where the fifty-year-old Ransom sees a story of growing wiser (and maybe sadder). From the agent's point of view—from the inside—how do you tell which is which?

One plausible answer is that genuine integrity consists not simply of adherence to principles, but adherence to the right principles, or at any rate to reasonable principles. As Deborah Rhode puts it in her contribution to this symposium,

> At a minimum, persons of integrity are individuals whose practices are consistent with their principles, even in the face of strong countervailing pressures. Yet the term also implies something more than steadfastness. Fanatics may be loyal to their values, but we do not praise them for integrity. What earns our praise is a willingness to adhere to values that reflect some reasoned deliberation, based on logical assessment of relevant evidence and competing views. Some theorists would add a requirement that the values themselves must satisfy certain minimum demands of consistency, generalizability, and respect for others.[77]

That may be true in a formal sense, but from the agent's point of view the formula won't help. For one thing, many of the psychological forces discussed here leave our principles untouched, instead affecting our judgment of whether or not a case falls under a principle. It seems likely, for example, that Milgram's compliant subjects believed before, during, and after the experiment that it is wrong to inflict undeserved suffering on the innocent. What changed was their perception of whether the 330 volt shock they were administering was an instance of inflicting undeserved suffering on the innocent. Even when cognitive dissonance reduction causes a change in values, it will not help the agent to be told that integrity consists in adherence to values that are right and reasonable, because the agent knows only what is right and reasonable to her, and what seems right and reasonable to her may have been corrupted by the psychological forces we have been examining.

---

[77] Deborah L. Rhode, *If Integrity Is the Answer, What Is the Question?*, 72 FORDHAM L. REV. 333, 335–36 (2003). In support of this point, Rhode cites Sharon Dolovich, *Ethical Lawyering and the Possibility of Integrity*, 70 FORDHAM L. REV. 1629, 1654–56 (2002), who in turn refers to MARK S. HALFON, INTEGRITY: A PHILOSOPHICAL INQUIRY 32–33, 133–37 (1989) and Jody L. Graham, *Does Integrity Require Moral Goodness?*, 14 RATIO 234, 244 (2001).

But perhaps matters are not as hopeless as they appear. Many of the phenomena revealed by experimentalists are short-lived aberrations, recognized as such even by the subjects once the spell wears off. As Doris puts it, the motives induced by the experiments "are not readily enmeshed in . . . biographies; they look like psychological tics or glitches."[78] Asch's subjects did not continue to perceive shorter lines as longer after they left the experiment. Nor did most of Milgram's compliant subjects continue to believe that compliance was the right thing to do once the experiment ended and they talked it over with the experimenter and the man they had supposedly been shocking. In fact, they probably never believed that compliance was the right thing to do. When Milgram described his experimental set-up to audiences and asked them to guess the rate of total compliance, and whether they themselves would comply, most guessed around one percent (as compared with the sixty-five percent compliance rate in the actual experiment); and no one believed that they themselves would comply—an unmistakable sign that normal people believe compliance would be wrong. We have no reason to suppose that Milgram's compliant subjects would have responded any differently to the question. Instead, as I suggested earlier, the experiment seemed to corrupt their judgment temporarily, disabling their capacity to apply their principles correctly to the situation they found themselves in.

Perhaps the most dramatic evidence that dissonance-induced belief change is an ephemeral thing comes from Zimbardo's personal recollections of the SPE. At one point, Prisoner #819 became ill and broke down emotionally. Zimbardo found him "sobbing uncontrollably while in the background his fellow prisoners were yelling that he was a bad prisoner" because the guards had ordered them to do so.[79] Remarkably, when Zimbardo tried to lead him away he refused, because he had to show his fellow-inmates that he was not a bad prisoner. Zimbardo said to him, " 'Listen, you are not #819. You are [his name], and my name is Dr. Zimbardo. I am a psychologist, not a prison superintendent, and this is not a real prison. This is just an experiment, and those are students, not prisoners, just like you. Let's go.' He stopped crying suddenly, looked up at me like a small child awakened from a nightmare, and replied, 'Okay, let's go.' "[80]

The suggestion, then, is that dissonance-induced belief change does not resemble genuine integrity, even from within, because outside the experimental situation it fades and vanishes, unlike our genuine long-term moral and personal commitments.

---

[78] Doris, *supra* note 63, at 143 (internal citation omitted).

[79] ZIMBARDO, *supra* note 62, at http://www.prisonexp.org/slide-31.htm.

[80] *Id.*

Unfortunately, there is one crucial state of affairs in which this will not be true: the state of affairs in which the agent returns again and again to the situation that caused the belief-change. Recall the earlier argument that the pattern

> action→ rationalization→ commitment→ further action has a recursive character. Put the same subject in the belief-altering situation day after day—or, better yet, have the subject put herself in the situation day after day—and it seems overwhelmingly likely that the transitory will become permanent.

For example, suppose that the belief-altering situation is your job, and that each day you voluntarily go to the office and put yourself back in the situation—for, let us say, 2,400 billable hours a year, year in and year out. And each night you take yourself out of the situation. By day, with a wig on your head and a band round your neck, you occasionally have to do things for a guinea that at night you would think it wicked and infamous to do for an empire. It seems very likely that before too long you will find yourself believing that a special professional morality, distinct from the morality of your extra-professional life, justifies what you do—and this belief will be no transitory thing, but rather a fixed part of your moral personality. Nor will this dualistic view of morality bother you. You will effortlessly negotiate the transition from one form of life to the other, with no sense of tension or contradiction.

Let me give two literary examples. One comes from LAWYERLAND, Lawrence Joseph's fictionalized account of a dozen or so Southern Manhattan lawyers.[81] In a chapter entitled "Something Split," a corporate dealmaker named Wylie relates a story about his partner, Jack, who is in psychoanalysis.

> So what does the mind doctor say? He tells Jack that, as a lawyer, he has to be capable of deep moral compromise . . . . Well, you can't argue with that. We all know there are times when you're working on some deal that, if you were to think it through, you'd realize that it was going to ruin the lives of thousands of people and their families. We all do it—in one size, shape, form, or other.[82]

But Wylie and Jack think the psychoanalyst is a fool—and Wylie finds Jack's reply to the soul doctor hilarious: "Well, yes, doctor, that is what I do . . . . Yes, I am a lawyer. That is how I make my living, doctor. I make my living by committing acts

---

[81] LAWRENCE JOSEPH, LAWYERLAND (1997). Joseph states that the book is "a work of nonfiction." *See id.* at *A Note to the Reader.* It is unclear, however, what exactly that means, for Joseph also indicates that many details are changed, and the book is "truthful rather than factual, but solidly based on facts." *Id.* On the fictional nature of Joseph's portrayals, see David Luban, *The Art of Honesty,* 101 COLUM. L. REV. 1763, 1763–65 (2001).

[82] Joseph, *supra* note 81, at 41.

of violence against myself and acts of violence against others."[83] Jack baits the psychoanalyst until he flees his own office—and Wylie and Jack laugh about it later.

My guess is that most lawyers would respond to the psychoanalyst the same way, and I must admit that it is hard not to sympathize with Jack. But Wylie agrees with the gravamen of the shrink's accusation ("We all do it," that is, "ruin the lives of thousands"), and the point of the story seems to be that lawyers like Wylie and Jack have no difficulty living with that diagnosis—that where one would expect to find "something split," eerily enough the protagonists experience no split at all.

The second example comes from a very different quarter, Montaigne's essay "Of Husbanding Your Will."[84] The essay praises those who remain aloof and emotionally detached from causes and enterprises, and in part it is a reflection on Montaigne's own tenure as mayor of Bordeaux. At one point he writes,

> The mayor and Montaigne have always been two, with a very clear separation. For all of being a lawyer or a financier, we must not ignore the knavery there is in such callings. An honest man is not accountable for the vice or stupidity of his trade, and should not therefore refuse to practice it: it is the custom of his country, and there is profit in it.[85] A few paragraphs earlier, Montaigne wrote, "I have been able to take part in public office without departing one nail's breadth from myself, and to give myself to others without taking myself from myself."[86]

These boasts bear the telltale signs of dissonance-reduction at work, especially striking in a self-observer and psychologist as acute as Montaigne. As Gerald Postema points out, Montaigne seemed to be making two different claims: first, that "the mayor and Montaigne have always been two people, clearly separated," suggesting that the professional self and the personal self are two distinct selves; and second, perhaps inconsistently, that because Montaigne served as mayor "without moving the length of my nail from myself," there is only one true self, and Montaigne (but not the mayor) is the true self.[87] In Postema's terminology, the first claim is a "schizophrenic" strategy for proving that an honest man "is not accountable for the vices or stupidity of his calling"; the second is a "restricted

---

[83] *Id.* at 43.

[84] Michel de Montaigne, *Of Husbanding Your Will,* in THE COMPLETE WORKS OF MONTAIGNE 766 (Donald M. Frame trans. 1943).

[85] *Id.* at 774.

[86] *Id.* at 770.

[87] Postema, *supra* note 74, at 292 (quoting Charles P. Curtis, *The Ethics of Advocacy,* 4 STAN. L. REV. 3, 20 (1951–52)).

identification" strategy.[88] Both strategies seem like self-deception, convenient ruses for denying that a person should be held responsible for the "knavery" of his calling. On the schizophrenic strategy, Montaigne is not responsible because the other fellow—"the mayor"—should bear the blame. On the restricted identification strategy, no one bears the blame, because Montaigne's true self is not invested in the mayoralty. Apparently, the mayoralty itself bears the blame—a rhetorical strategy similar to lawyers' frequent recourse to the excuse that "the adversary system did it."[89] Both arguments neglect the fact that Montaigne is the mayor, and regardless of whether Montaigne is invested in the mayoralty, it is he who performs the mayor's duties.

Strikingly, Montaigne resorts to these psychological fictions of schizophrenia and restricted identification in order to argue that one need not abandon professions that are customary and profitable, regardless of their knavery. If I am right that schizophrenia and restricted identification are fictions, and that Montaigne's arguments for non-accountability therefore fail, we are left with the situation of someone whose practice of a customary, profitable profession drives him to stable, self-justifying belief changes whose only drawback is that they happen to be lies. Montaigne claims that he has kept his integrity—he has not departed one nail's breadth from himself. But he has kept it, it appears, by fooling himself. This is a significant point for legal ethics, because one of the first modern articles on the subject quotes these sentences from Montaigne and takes them as a model of Stoic morality to justify the ethics of advocacy.[90] As Trollope, another astute literary psychologist, observed, "Men will not be talked out of the convictions of their lives. No living orator would convince a grocer that coffee should be sold without chicory; and no amount of eloquence will make an English lawyer think that loyalty to truth should come before loyalty to his client."[91]

The problem, in the end, comes to this: the ethical value of integrity is experienced from the inside as a kind of harmony or equilibrium between values and actions, whereby one does what one does without departing a nail's breadth from oneself. But the experiments show that integrity has a kind of evil twin,

---

88 *Id.*

89 To cite one example, Charles Fried distinguishes between a lawyer's personal wrongs and institutional wrongs in which the lawyer is merely the occasion, the person who pulls the legal levers enabling the system to operate. Charles Fried, *The Lawyer as Friend: The Moral Foundations of the Lawyer-Client Relation,* 85 YALE L.J. 1060, 1084–85 (1976). For criticism of the idea that the adversary system provides robust moral excuses for otherwise-objectionable acts performed by lawyers and for criticism of Fried's views, see David Luban, *The Adversary System Excuse,* in THE GOOD LAWYER: LAWYERS' ROLES AND LAWYERS' ETHICS 107–08 (David Luban ed., 1983).

90 *See* Charles P. Curtis, *The Ethics of Advocacy*, 4 STAN. L. REV. 3, 20 (1951–52).

91 ANTHONY TROLLOPE, ORLEY FARM 130 (1951).

induced by our need to see ourselves as ethically righteous people regardless of the knavery of our calling. From the inside, the quest for integrity and the process of rationalizing our actions prove nearly impossible to distinguish. We would like our moral compass to point true north, but our only instrument for detecting true north is our moral compass. And so, even though integrity and its evil twin may differ, the quest for integrity can drive us to the high road or the low road, without any landmarks to alert us about which path we have taken.

IV. Is There a Cure for Integrity?

A. The Truth Cure

I fear that no cure for integrity exists. The problem is, quite simply, that the dissonance-based phenomena we have been examining, our urgent desire as intuitive lawyers to arrange our world so that we remain upstanding citizens in it regardless of what we do, all operate unconsciously.

One comforting idea is that the truth will set us free—or, more precisely, that understanding the dynamics of self-corruption (integrity's sturdy twin) can help us fend it off. Robert Cialdini has written an admirable textbook on the power of social-psychological forces to influence us in directions we don't want.[92] At the end of each chapter, Cialdini offers a section entitled "Defense," which distills from the experimental literature recommendations about how not to be taken in by the fundamental forces of reciprocation, commitment and consistency, social proof, liking, authority, and scarcity—the "weapons of influence."[93] Cialdini's basic defensive recommendation is enhanced awareness.[94] Yet he understands that enhanced awareness of unconscious forces may be impossible precisely because the forces are unconscious.[95] His recommendations may well be the best we can do, but I have doubts that the best we can do will often be good enough.[96]

---

92 ROBERT B. CIALDINI, INFLUENCE: SCIENCE AND PRACTICE (4th ed. 2000).

93 *Id.*

94 For example: "The only effective defense I know against the weapons of influence embodied in the combined principles of commitment and consistency is an awareness that, although consistency is generally good, even vital, there is a foolish, rigid variety to be shunned." *Id.* at 90. "If we can become sensitive to situations where the social proof automatic pilot is working with inaccurate information, we can disengage the mechanism and grasp the controls when we need to." *Id.* at 134. "A better understanding of the workings of authority influence should help us resist it." *Id.* at 196.

95 "Here's our predicament, then: Knowing the causes and workings of scarcity pressures may not be sufficient to protect us from them because knowing is a cognitive act, and cognitive processes are suppressed by our emotional reaction. . . ." *Id.* at 228.

96 In saying this, I take issue not only with Cialdini, but also with Doris, *supra* note 63, at 153 (expressing cautious optimism that knowing situationist results can help us lead better lives)—and also with myself, for in Luban, *supra* note 30, at 116, I argued that "[p]erhaps the best protection is understanding the illusions themselves, their pervasiveness, the insidious way they work on us. Understanding these illusions warns us against them, and forewarned truly is forearmed, at least to some extent."

A personal recollection: Two years ago, I was walking across a park in Dublin with my wife and in-laws. It was a nice summer day, and I noticed a man napping on the grass. As we drew nearer, I noticed that he was lying on his stomach, not his back. Then, as we walked by, I saw that his head was not turned to one side like someone asleep. His face was pressed directly into the ground. His limbs were splayed at awkward angles, and he was completely motionless. I had what I can only describe as a moment of listless recognition that he seemed to be dead—listless, because although I recall the thought that he was dead passing through my mind, I kept walking. The listlessness was not too surprising, as we had taken a red-eye from America and spent the whole day touring: all four of us had been awake more than twenty-four hours. It just seemed so natural to keep walking.

At that time, I had been a consumer of experimental social psychology for more than five years, and had discussed the Darley-Latané experiments on bystander passivity in my classes at least three times. It wasn't until we were past the motionless man that I suddenly recognized why none of us were doing anything. It had nothing to do with the red-eye. It had everything to do with diffusion of responsibility. I said, "That guy looks dead! We should do something." We all turned back to look at him, and saw a good Samaritan with a cell-phone standing next to the fallen man, excitedly phoning for help. Just as the experiments predicted, the Good Samaritan was all by himself. Score one for Darley and Latané.

Of course, one explanation for my passivity is that Luban is a weak vessel, who talks the talk of morality and compassion but won't walk the walk—or rather, who walks the walk right past collapsed strangers in a park. Perhaps that's it. But another example might persuade you that the case is not simply one of man's fecklessness and hypocrisy. The example comes from Philip Zimbardo's recollections of his Stanford Prison Experiment. Zimbardo recalls a critical moment several days into the experiment:

> One of the guards overheard the prisoners talking about an escape that would take place immediately after visiting hours. The rumor went as follows: Prisoner #8612, whom we had released the night before, was going to round up a bunch of his friends and break in to free the prisoners.
>
> How do you think we reacted to this rumor? Do you think we recorded the pattern of rumor transmission and prepared to observe the impending escape? That was what we should have done, of course, if we were acting like experimental social psychologists. Instead, we reacted

> with concern over the security of our prison. What we did was to hold a strategy session with the Warden, the Superintendent, and one of the chief lieutenants, Craig Haney, to plan how to foil the escape.[97] Haney was one of the psychologists conducting the experiment. Zimbardo continues:
>
> After our meeting, . . . I went back to the Palo Alto Police Department and asked the sergeant if we could have our prisoners transferred to their old jail. My request was turned down . . . . I left angry and disgusted at this lack of cooperation between our correctional facilities (I was now totally into my role).[98]

It only got worse:

> I was sitting there all alone, waiting anxiously for the intruders to break in, when who should happen along but a colleague and former Yale graduate student roommate, Gordon Bower. Gordon had heard we were doing an experiment, and he came to see what was going on. I briefly described what we were up to, and Gordon asked me a very simple question: "Say, what's the independent variable in this study?"
>
> To my surprise, I got really angry at him. Here I had a prison break on my hands. The security of my men and the stability of my prison was at stake, and now, I had to deal with this bleeding-heart, liberal, academic, effete dingdong who was concerned about the independent variable! It wasn't until much later that I realized how far into my prison role I was at that point—that I was thinking like a prison superintendent rather than a research psychologist.[99]

When I first described the Stanford Prison Experiment, I noted that the "prisoners" and "guards" were not the only ones to become captives of their roles. Their parents, the priest who visited them, and even the lawyer who came in to consult with them about their "parole hearings" all did as well. Why not? None of these people were trained to recognize psychological mechanisms of influence at work. But Haney and Zimbardo were. If anyone should have recognized the "Pirandellian prison" of the mind, it is psychologists who devote their careers to mapping its gates and cell-blocks. Apparently, it isn't so. Nor should that surprise us: If cognitive dissonance and social cognition truly represent universal psychological forces, it is a little much to expect that scientific expertise can free

---

97 ZIMBARDO, *supra* note 62, at www.prisonexp.org/slide-25.htm.

98 *Id.* at www.prisonexp.org/slide-26.htm.

99 *Id.* at www.prisonexp.org/slide-27.htm.

us of them. Understanding how Snell's Law explains the bent-stick effect does not make the partially-submerged stick look any less bent to the physicist.

B. The Canary in the Mineshaft

I have said that there is no real cure for integrity—the low-road kind of integrity, that is, the unconscious gerrymandering of principles to rationalize commitments and actions that are too inconvenient to forego. I do have a few suggestions, however. If you really fear the gradual unconscious corruption that performing in role induces, you must decide in advance what line you won't cross—and then, when you find yourself standing at that line, or, worse, when you find yourself having just crossed it, you will know that it's time to quit. The inspiration for this suggestion comes from David Heilbroner, a former New York City prosecutor who wrote a fascinating memoir of his time in the D.A.'s office—a story of inexperience and naiveté gradually replaced by competence and cynicism. Heilbroner underwent a deep immersion in the seamy side of life where the good guys and the bad guys all lie sometimes, and where even doing good often leaves a bad taste. Heilbroner writes:

> Before joining the DA's office I had promised myself that above all, I would never take a case to trial if I had any doubt about the defendant's guilt. At the time it seemed an easy enough standard to abide by. But during the past few weeks I realized that the Quintana case would probably force me to put my personal ethics to the test.[100]

Heilbroner was prosecuting Quintana for theft, and had just learned that his star witness, the clean-cut, appealing, young victim was really a drug dealer, bail jumper, and liar. Heilbroner's supervisor was unimpressed by the revelations about the witness, and insisted that Heilbroner take the case to trial. He did so, and Quintana was acquitted. Soon after, Heilbroner quit his job. "To stay on much longer meant maintaining a blindered belief in the rectitude of our work, wanting to punish defendants, believing that our policies were all to the good: becoming the very sort of prosecutor I had always disliked and distrusted. It was time to leave."[101] Heilbroner admits that he was temperamentally unsuited to the prosecutor's job,[102] and that some Assistant District Attorneys "loved prosecuting in an unquestioning way that I never could."[103] Perhaps, then, Heilbroner's resignation was inevitable and overdetermined. Nevertheless, I like the way he set

---

[100] DAVID HIELBRONER, ROUGH JUSTICE: DAYS AND NIGHTS OF A YOUNG D.A. 261–62 (1990).

[101] *Id.* at 279.

[102] *Id.* at 283.

[103] *Id.* at 284.

himself a mental tripwire, or, switching metaphors, a single action that would serve as his canary in the mineshaft. The moment the canary died, he knew that it was time to evacuate. Heilbroner's canary was taking a case to trial when he wasn't convinced that the defendant was guilty. Other lawyers, in other practices, must choose their own canaries. The formula is simple: "Whatever else I do, and however else my views change, I will never, ever . . . ." You name it. Cover up someone else's crime. Lie about money. Falsify a document. Let a colleague suffer the consequences for my own screw-up. Do something where I couldn't look my father in the eye if I told him about it.

My advice is to choose your canary carefully, understanding that before you enter a role your ideas about what ethical demands it entails may well be naive. But, once you've selected the canary, never ignore it. If necessary, write down the "I will never, ever" formula. Put it in an envelope, keep it in a drawer, and pull it out sometimes to remind yourself what it says. And, the moment the canary dies, get out of the mineshaft.

C. Noticing When You Are Deflecting Blame to Someone Else

A second recommendation takes its inspiration from Milgram's research. When he debriefed subjects after the electric-shock experiment, Milgram asked them to apportion responsibility for shocking the victim among the three protagonists—the subject himself, the "scientist" giving him orders to proceed, and the victim repeatedly earning electric shocks by giving wrong answers. As one might expect, compliant subjects seldom attributed the horrible outcome of the experiment to themselves. Characteristically, they blamed it on the scientist, and often on the victim. Taking a cue from this, my recommendation is the following: whenever you find yourself doing things but denying (to yourself or to others) that you are responsible for doing them, treat it as a sign that you have succumbed to the unconscious psychological drive toward intuitive lawyering.

This recommendation may sound peculiar, given the situationists' warning that assigning responsibility for behavior to personality, not situational pressures, amounts to a "fundamental attribution error." Am I now suggesting that you must not blame the situation for what you have done, that you must take personal responsibility—in short, that you must commit the fundamental attribution error? Well, yes, in a way. Recall my earlier critique of situational determinism, where I argued that situations do not determine behavior, but merely alter the difficulty gradient, making it easier or harder to behave in certain ways. This, I suggested, is wholly compatible with a view that emphasizes the responsibility of agents in dealing with situations. To blame others—one's boss, one's co-workers, one's situation—amounts (to borrow Sartre's term) to a kind of bad faith.[104] Regardless of whether or not it is bad faith, however, my suggestion at the moment is simply that whenever you find yourself blaming others for your actions, treat that as an alarm-bell, signaling that you may well be in the grips of the psychological forces of rationalization.

D. Socratic Skepticism

My third and final suggestion is less specific, but perhaps more important. Throughout this discussion I have been emphasizing the dangers of our innate tendency to falsify facts and abandon principles in order to avoid the belief that we are doing wrong. Apparently, the need to believe in our own righteousness runs deep. One possible antidote to the drive toward self-righteousness is a stance toward the world that might be labeled "Socratic skepticism."

In Plato's APOLOGY, Socrates tells the Athenian jury at his trial that throughout his life he has listened to an inner voice, a daimon. The voice tells him when he is in danger of doing wrong. It never speaks when he is doing right—only when he is doing wrong.[105] To give an example, Socrates mentions a period in which Athens was ruled by the Thirty Tyrants. These rulers wished to implicate as many Athenians as possible in their crimes. At one point, they called Socrates and some others in and ordered them to arrest Leon the Salaminian so that he might be executed. The others went off to fulfill the command, but (Socrates tells his hearers), his daimon spoke up, and, at risk of forfeiting his own life, he simply went home. Socrates adds that his own life was spared only because the Tyrants were overthrown very soon after.[106]

Socrates goes on to explain that throughout his life he has made it his mission to seek out those who claim to know, and test them with probing questions, hoping (in vain, he informs us) to find someone whose high opinion of his own wisdom stood the test. He insists that he himself knows only that he does not know.[107] Although Socrates does not draw the connection between his daimon and his skeptical stance toward his own knowledge and that of others, it seems straightforward enough: the daimon tells him when his action has no justification, and his skepticism leads him to test every justification that he hears.

---

[104] *See* JEAN-PAUL SARTRE, BEING AND NOTHINGNESS 71–79 (Hazel E. Barnes trans. 1956). I would make an exception in genuine cases of duress—for example, the situation of soldiers who are told that unless they execute prisoners they will themselves be shot. In such cases, it does not seem like bad faith to blame their commander.

[105] PLATO, APOLOGY *31d.

[106] *Id.* at *32c–d.

[107] *Id.* at *23a–b.

This stance toward the world—a stance of perpetual doubt toward one's own pretensions as well as the pretensions of others—is what I am calling Socratic skepticism. It aims to combat our basic drive to believe in our own righteousness in the most straightforward way possible: by trying to make a habit of doubting one's own righteousness, of questioning one's own moral beliefs, of scrutinizing one's own behavior—"know thyself!"—with a certain ruthless irony.

This advice will no doubt seem strange and disagreeable to many. Americans admire confident, can-do leaders who never second-guess their own decisions, and who avoid skepticism and self-doubt, the telltale signs of neurotics and losers. In the world of business and government, feelings of guilt or regret are career destroyers, best cabined to ceremonial occasions like Bible breakfasts and sentencing hearings. Nevertheless, I suggest chronic skepticism and discomfort with oneself as a possible antidote for integrity—if, that is, any antidote for integrity can be found.

NOTES

1. In our notes after the last article, we raised the spectre of you perhaps using your knowledge "not for good, but for evil (manipulation)."* Taking that point one step further, we figured that a good discussion of integrity would be in order; hence, the inclusion of this article. We love Luban's adage that "genuine integrity consists not simply of adherence to principles, but adherence to the right principles, or at any rate to reasonable principles."** And, as he points out, our principles will shift over time due to what we've learned through various experiences (both good and bad). Do you have core principles that you now hold and that you believe that you will still hold even when you're an octogenarian? What are they? Can you imagine a situation that might cause you to adjust any of those core principles?

2. Just as Luban suggests, you need your own version of a canary in a coal mine—a way to say to yourself, "hey, this situation has gone on far enough, so I need to stop." You need a line in the sand (to mix our metaphors) that you refuse to cross, and you need to remind yourself where that line is. We're rooting for you to succeed in your chosen career, so go ahead and write down your own line in the sand somewhere for safekeeping. (We know that, if you change careers, you'll have to create a new line in the sand for your new career.) We have ours, and you should have yours.

* *See* Note 3 of the Notes section after *Deliberative Trouble, supra* p. 687.

** *Integrity* at 299.

Here's an example. One of us is an expert witness in various types of cases. Her line in the sand is that she won't shape her opinion based on who's paying her fee, and that principle means that, sometimes, she has to tell the person who hired her that he won't like her opinion and might want to consider settling the case. Divorcing her opinion from her fees lets her sleep pretty well at night.

3. The last article in the book takes you from an understanding of group deliberations and your own sense of integrity to how you can communicate your values (and your organization's values) to your colleagues. It's a fitting way to end this book, because this book is all about helping you avoid future corporate scandals.

CHAPTER 22

Modeling the Message: Communicating Compliance Through Organizational Values and Culture*

*Scott Killingsworth***

"Culture, more than rule books, determines how an organization behaves."

Warren Buffett[1]

Introduction

Compliance professionals do a lot of communicating. We publish codes, policies and procedures, newsletters, training materials, posters, and tips-of-the-month. We write, meet, blog, and tweet. Most of these communications are content-rich and operationally focused on objective requirements for legal and policy compliance. They play the essential role of defining clear boundaries of acceptable behavior so that employees have the basic knowledge they need in order to avoid trouble.

But how can we most effectively motivate people to stay within these carefully-defined boundaries? What kinds of communications—what channels, themes, and content—actually exert a measurable positive effect on employee behavior? In short, once the essentials of a compliance program are in place, what does the evidence tell us about how we should deploy scarce company resources to promote compliance? The answers would surprise many corporate executives and probably most lawyers as well.

* This piece was originally published as Scott Killingsworth, *Modeling the Message: Communicating Compliance Through Organizational Values and Culture,* 25 GEO. J.L. ETHICS 961 (2012).

** Partner, Bryan Cave LLP, Atlanta, Georgia. © 2012, Scott Killingsworth.

1 Memorandum from Warren Buffet to Berkshire Hathaway Managers (July 26, 2010).

Over the past decade and a half behavioral scientists—cognitive, organizational, and social psychologists and behavioral economists—have devoted considerable attention to compliance issues, and the state of the art has advanced dramatically. One lesson from the research is clear: it's not enough to educate employees about their responsibilities, provide them with written guidance, and warn them of the consequences if they stray. We need to expand the scope of the "communications" discussion in at least two ways. First, our explicit compliance messaging must appeal broadly to workers' best values and aspirations, engaging and activating those values so that they are expressed in workplace compliance decisions. Second, we should acknowledge, and harness, powerful drivers of ethical behavior that, while not usually thought of as communications channels, nevertheless send unmistakable messages which employees internalize and act upon. Along the way, our conception of what constitutes a compliance communication, and of who the key communicators are, should expand.

This article focuses on the benefits of values-based communications and on the communicative effects of compliance program orientation, corporate cultural attributes and management behaviors, all three of which have been proven to dramatically affect both employee compliance and internal reporting of misconduct. We will lean quite strongly on the behavioral science evidence of these effects, with the aim of showing not only what works, but why.

This essay is organized as follows. We set the stage with two examples from the experimental literature that show how ambient ethical messages in one's immediate environment can profoundly influence behavior. After a brief excursion into the relationship between communication and culture, we critique the "command and control" messaging that is at the heart of most corporate compliance programs (and dominant in first-generation programs), exposing flaws in its underlying assumptions, and showing how messages implicit in a strong command-and-control regime can sometimes undermine program goals.

We then review two key psychological mechanisms—decision framing and group membership dynamics—and their relationship to organizational culture, values, intrinsic motivation, and ultimately to compliance. This leads us to the behavioral-science findings on how these mechanisms can be harnessed—via a positive ethical culture, a values-based compliance regime, and management practices informed by notions of integrity, fairness, respect, and dignity—to drive measurable improvement in employee compliance and reporting of misconduct. Finally, we offer suggestions as to how these teachings can be applied in practice, using communication in the broadest sense to create the effective "culture of compliance" that the Federal Sentencing Guidelines demand.

I. Environmental Messages and Activation of Values

A person's behavior in a given situation is not influenced solely by communications that explicitly address that situation, such as workplace rules, policies, and procedures. Our decisions are also influenced by values and beliefs that we bring to work, by a broad range of incentives, disincentives, and internal and social motivations, and by cues in the work environment that "nudge" our behavior in one direction or another.[2] Some of those nudges[3] come from messages about topics other than the situation at hand.

Consider Dan Ariely's investigation of the circumstances under which people either cheat or don't cheat.[4] He gave college students a 20-question timed math test and promised to reward them based on the number of correct answers. Baselines were established for the difficulty of the test and the propensity for cheating by manipulating whether cheating could be detected. When it was impossible to cheat, the students averaged four correct answers; but when conditions were changed so that it was not just possible to cheat, but obviously impossible to *get caught* cheating, the students reported getting an average of seven answers right.

Next, the version of the experiment that permitted risk-free cheating was repeated, but with an added warm-up task. Half the students were instructed to try to list up to ten books they had read in high school. As expected, this group averaged seven right answers. The other students were asked to try to list the Ten Commandments before taking the test. That group averaged four answers right: statistically, at least, cheating had been completely eliminated.

Ariely believes that thinking about the Ten Commandments served as a powerful, just-in-time reminder to the students of their own internal values. In

---

2 For a highly accessible review of some of the factors that affect our decision-making, many of them hidden or irrational, see JONAH LEHRER, HOW WE DECIDE (2009).

3 This apt term is borrowed from RICHARD THALER & CASS SUNSTEIN, NUDGE: IMPROVING DECISIONS ABOUT HEALTH, WEALTH AND HAPPINESS (2008), which proposes that as a society we should seek to compensate for the inherent limitations and quirks of individuals' cognitive and decision-making faculties by designing "choice architectures" that can improve the quality of decisions on important but complex issues.

4 Several variations of this experimental paradigm are discussed in Nina Mazar, On Amir, & Dan Ariely, *The Dishonesty of Honest People: A Theory of Self-Concept Maintenance*, 45 J. MARKETING RES. 633–644 (2008); DAN ARIELY, PREDICTABLY IRRATIONAL 195–216 (2008); Dan Ariely, TED talk, *Why We Think It's OK to Cheat and Steal (Sometimes)* (Mar. 18, 2009), *available at* http://www.youtube.com/watch?v=nUdsTizSxSI.

psychological terms it increased the salience[5] of ethics in the context of the test. And that small ethical prompt "primed" the students to adhere to their values even in the presence of financial temptation and in the absence of any form of monitoring. The Ten Commandments task was presented as a memory exercise, not as a communication, and certainly not a communication *about* the math test—but nevertheless the students received and acted upon a powerful message.[6]

Admittedly, this experiment involved low stakes, and it took place in a laboratory setting with no authority figures, performance pressure, group ties, or continuing relationships. Still, it is natural to ask whether a compliance and ethics program and an ethical corporate culture can operate in the same way as the Ten Commandments in the experiment, surrounding employees with messages and cues that bring their values to the fore and influence them to behave ethically even when there is no risk of detection. It is fair, too, to ask what other messages transmitted in the workplace may *lower* the salience of ethical values and thereby undermine compliance efforts.

This latter danger is illustrated by another experiment[7] in which business students played the part of corporate managers and performed a prescribed series of office tasks such as reassigning sales personnel, ordering supplies, etc. The two tasks relevant to the experiment were reading a memo from the CEO that praised the company culture and, later, filing a property insurance claim. Students randomly received one of two versions of the CEO memo: the first described the company culture as one "that emphasizes success—we do what it takes to be competitive!" while the other version described it as a culture "that emphasizes values—we will always do what is right!"

On the insurance matter, all of the subjects received a collection of data from various legitimate and dubious sources that could be selected and marshaled in ways that would support either an honest or an inflated claim. Separately, the

---

5 Salience can be thought of as the percentage of a person's cognitive windshield space occupied by an idea. Everyone has an idea of chocolate lurking in their mind, but if you want to increase its salience you might, in order of increasing effectiveness, ask them whether they like chocolate; show them a box of chocolates; or give them a sample to taste.

6 To determine whether these results were specifically driven by religious beliefs, in another variation of the experiment, instead of the Ten Commandments task the students were asked to acknowledge that their school's honor code applied to the test. In that instance cheating was also eliminated, *whether or not the school actually had an honor code.* In contrast to the use of the Ten Commandments as discussed above, though, the "honor code" condition was explicitly expressed not as an apparently unrelated quiz, but as a communication to the students, and one directly applicable to the test and to cheating.

7 Scott J. Reynolds et al., *Automatic Ethics: the Effects of Implicit Assumptions and Contextual Cues on Moral Behavior*, 95 J. APPLIED PSYCHOL. 752–760 (2010).

students were tested to find out their underlying beliefs as to whether "business" was, in general, inherently moral or immoral.

The hypothesis was that people who have a strong implicit faith in the notion that business is inherently moral might be less inclined to examine the ethical implications of their actions at work: essentially, that if an action felt like business, they would tend to assume it must be acceptable. Moreover, these same people might be more vulnerable to environmental cues—like the "do what it takes" CEO memo—that could be interpreted as encouraging or implicitly accepting questionable business behavior.

The results were stunning. Subjects who considered business to be inherently on the low end of the morality scale filed very few inflated insurance claims regardless of which memo they received. But those who believed strongly that business is inherently moral and also received the "we do what it takes" memo were *33 times* more likely to file an inflated insurance claim than the average study participant.[8] The memo was not "about" filing insurance claims, but the participants got the message[9] . . . and acted on it.

II. Culture Simplified: Communication That Sticks

Organizational culture can be easy to identify—we know it when we see it—but hard to define in a way that actually helps us change or reinforce a given culture. One good "soft" definition tells us that culture is "the set of enduring and underlying assumptions and norms that determine how things are actually done in the organization."[10] A coherent culture is based on shared values and beliefs, and the proof that they are shared is that they shape behavior across the organization. But how do we instill or modify those "enduring assumptions and norms"?

Up close, culture is about communication in the broadest sense. In his book EXPLAINING CULTURE,[11] Dan Sperber proposes that culture is the summed effect of communications within a group over history, the stable "precipitate of cognition and communication in a human population."[12] All cultural transmission

---

8 This result was statistically significant at the .01 level of probability.

9 The potency of the contextual cue furnished by the CEO memo was likely amplified by the "authority bias," the tendency of people to defer to authority rather than exercising independent judgment that was memorably demonstrated in the famous Milgram electric shock-administration experiment. *See* Stanley Milgram, *Behavioral Study of Obedience*, 67 J. ABNORMAL AND SOCIAL PSYCHOL. 371–378 (Oct. 1963). The implications of this bias for corporate messaging should not be overlooked.

10 John C. Lenzi & Timothy T. Lupfer, *Measuring Corporate Culture: Enhancing the Board's Understanding*, Deloitte Corporate Governance presentation (Aug. 8, 2007).

11 DAN SPERBER, EXPLAINING CULTURE: A NATURALISTIC APPROACH (1996).

12 *Id.* at 97.

is effected by someone either making public (communicating) an idea or other mental representation, or, conversely, taking an external experience, message, or communication, and internalizing it.[13]

Sperber's work bridges the gap between psychologists, who are concerned with the internal world of individual mental representations and processes, and social scientists, who study representations that are in some sense collective or shared. Communication via countless individual interactions and messages is the means by which groups instantiate ideas, norms, and beliefs in individuals ("equal justice under law"), as well as the means by which individuals can perpetuate or influence culture ("I have a dream"). To the extent that a group of people internalize the same messages—beliefs, values, ideologies, aesthetics, symbols and stories—they share a culture. Thus, communication is the fundamental means by which we can build, transmit, or change an organizational culture.

Most communications, of course, are transitory and culturally insignificant—they do not contribute to the inculcation of beliefs or values that are shared by large numbers of people and that remain stable over time. Messages have a better chance at cultural impact if they hang together as a coherent story; if they draw on already-established ideas, themes, or symbols; if they are consistent and frequently repeated through multiple channels; if they come from admired or authoritative sources; if they are relevant to our status in a group we consider important; if they resonate with experience (or constitute experience!); if they are broadly useful; and if they carry a strong emotional charge.

The more consistent and pervasive the messaging is within an organization—explicit messaging and, crucially, messaging through behavior—the more likely that employees will internalize the corresponding values and principles, will frame decisions in terms of those values, and will put them into action.

Let's look at some of the workplace messages that are relevant to compliance, and at the evidence of their effects on compliance and reporting.

III. Command-and-Control Messaging

Contrast the indirect messaging in the cheating and insurance fraud experiments with the direct, rules-based, results-focused, and absolutely necessary communications at the heart of most compliance programs: codes, policies, training materials, and procedures. Like the laws they emulate, these documents explain the applicable rules, lay out specific processes for compliance, and prescribe consequences for failure to comply. They educate and instruct workers

[13] In Sperber's model, the study of cultural change and transmission is likened to an epidemiology of communicable ideas.

about compliance requirements and, often, include built-in monitoring or auditing processes.

Compliance programs that place primary or exclusive emphasis on communications of this type are often described as "command-and-control" oriented programs. These programs, and their associated communications, aim to govern employee behavior largely through concrete incentives, principally deterring misconduct via monitoring and detection mechanisms and the threat of punishment. The explicit message is the same as the message from law enforcement: follow the rules or pay the penalty.

It's an important message, but when we unpack it, we find other messages inside. The command-and-control approach is based on the assumption that workers will behave like the "rational actors" of economic theory:[14] they will weigh the costs and benefits of compliance versus rule-breaking and make a rational, self-interested decision to avoid the risk of punishment.[15] The greater the emphasis on monitoring, detection, and punishment, the more this assumption rises to the surface.

The implicit message, then, is one of pursuing self-interest (avoiding punishment) rather than one of doing the right thing: the employee is encouraged to frame the question in terms of personal risks and rewards. And if you frame compliance as an essentially economic proposition, you invite misconduct whenever its reward is significant and either the risk of detection, or the

---

14 Gary Becker's Nobel Prize was awarded in part for his work on the rational-actor theory of criminal decisionmaking. One day in the 1960s he realized that for a relatively short stop it made economic sense to park illegally in New York City, given the cost of private parking, versus the cost of a parking ticket multiplied by the likelihood of being ticketed within that time span. Being a future Nobel Prize-winning economist, he immediately thought, in effect, "I'll bet all the other lawbreakers think just the way I do!" and a theory was born. Gary S. Becker, *The Economic Way of Looking at Life,* Nobel Lecture (Dec. 9, 1992).

15 Roughly, the rational-actor formula is: compare the expected reward for rule-breaking to the risk of punishment. That risk is equal to the severity of the punishment, multiplied by the likelihood of getting caught. Though this model is intuitively persuasive and often right, behavioral economists and cognitive psychologists have made mincemeat of the "rational" assumption, exposing a large number of variables that distort our perception of risks and rewards, or influence whether proposed behavior is even perceived as noncompliant or punishable in the first place. Examples of these variables include motivated reasoning, rationalization, over-valuing present rewards while under-valuing remote consequences such as the risk of getting caught, the self-serving bias, the authority bias, in-group norms and conformity pressures, and the ever-amusing Dunning/Kruger effect. *See generally*, David M. Messick & Max H. Bazerman, *Ethical Leadership and the Psychology of Decisionmaking*, SLOAN MGMT. REV. (Winter 1996); Sung Hui Kim, *The Banality of Fraud: Re-situating the Inside Counsel as Gatekeeper*, 74 FORDHAM L. REV. 983 (2005); Joyce Ehrlinger, Kerri Johnson, Matthew Banner, David Dunning, & Justin Kruger, *Why the Unskilled are Unaware: Further Explorations of (absent) Self-Insight among the Incompetent*, 105 ORGANIZATIONAL BEHAVIOR AND HUMAN DECISION PROCESSES 98–121 (2008).

punishment if caught, is perceived as acceptably low.[16,17] Instead of conveying the message that compliance is non-negotiable, risk/reward framing implies that it may be negotiable if the price is right. A tragicomic instance of this phenomenon occurred when experimenters persuaded several day care centers to impose small fines on parents who were late picking up their children, on the theory that an economic incentive would reduce lateness. But unwittingly, the day care centers were giving parents a cue to re-frame the situation, not as a non-negotiable social obligation, but as an economic transaction at a bargain "price." Rather than diminishing, the incidence of lateness nearly doubled.[18]

By no means should we conclude that incentives are irrelevant to compliance or uniformly counterproductive: people do respond to incentives, positive and negative, particularly if the punishments or rewards are large. The point is that incentives send messages too. In some cases, the message may have more impact than the incentive itself: an affordable fine signals that lateness, which the fine was intended to prevent, is actually acceptable. In other cases the incentive's message may be so loud that it drowns out other messages of equal or greater importance: the prospect of a large[19] bonus for achieving a certain goal may signal that reaching the goal is all that matters, regardless of the method used to get there. In both cases, the incentive's message has displaced, or "crowded out," a competing social expectation or ethical norm.[20]

---

16 As one commentator put it, "*homo economicus* is—not to put too fine a point on it—a psychopath." LYNN STOUT, CULTIVATING CONSCIENCE: HOW GOOD LAWS MAKE GOOD PEOPLE 45 (2011).

17 *See* Ann E. Tenbrunsel & David M. Messick, *Sanctioning Systems, Decision Frames, and Cooperation*, 44 ADMIN. SCI. Q. 684 (1999). As suggested in note 15, *supra*, a number of cognitive and social influences may cause people to underestimate the risks, or expected costs, of misconduct, but attempting to compensate for this by raising the stakes for violators has its own drawbacks for employers: monitoring is expensive, and if the punishment for a given offense is felt to be unfairly harsh, reporting of misconduct will suffer.

18 *See* ARIELY, PREDICTABLY IRRATIONAL, *supra* note 4, at 67–88; Uri Gneezy and Aldo Rustichini, *A Fine is a Price*, 29 J. LEGAL STUDIES 1 (2000).

19 "Large" is in the eye of the beholder and incentives can misfire at any pay grade: when Green Giant sought to improve quality by offering incentives to employees who found and removed insect parts from its food products, some employees apparently responded by bringing insects from home, "finding" them, and claiming the bounty. Adam Grant & Jitendra Singh, *The Problem with Financial Incentives—and What to Do About It*, KNOWLEDGE@WHARTON (Mar. 30, 2011) http://knowledge.wharton.upenn.edu/article.cfm?articleid=2741.

20 There is a substantial literature on the "crowding out" of internally driven, or intrinsic, motivation by external incentives, particularly in the area of altruistic behavior, which can actually be suppressed by the offering of financial incentives. You may experience a strong feeling of reward for performing an altruistic act, one that is rooted in your values and makes you feel good about yourself, but if someone pays you to do it, you are robbed of this altruistic reward. Once the act is re-framed as an economic transaction, you will be less likely to perform the act unless the pay is high enough to create a motivation as strong as the altruistic motivation that it displaced. *See generally, e.g.*, Bruno Frey & Reto Jegen, *Motivation Crowding Theory*, 15 J. ECON. SURV. 589 (2011); Bruno Frey & Felix Oberholzer-Gee, *The Cost of Price Incentives: An Empirical Analysis of*

Another implicit message in a strong command-and-control communications focus is that management does not trust employees.[21] Potential side effects of this message range from resentment, to an "us-versus-them" attitude towards management, to a reverse-Pygmalion effect[22] in which employees may tend to "live down" to the low expectations that are projected upon them.

Without being overly alarmist about these side effects, we must recognize that they are real and can be triggered in ways that may be subtle in individual cases, but are measurable across employee populations. At a minimum, we should ask how other, more values-based, messages can counteract these effects, priming employees to frame compliance decisions in terms that are both more absolute and more compelling.

IV. Values, Framing, and Group Dynamics

The three experiments described earlier are best understood as instances where external messages, or cues, affected the *frames of reference* that guided the subjects' decisions. Framing is how we answer the question, "What kind of situation is this?"[23] That is, is it social, economic, romantic, legal, ethical, competitive, cooperative, political? Which set of rules applies? We know that in ambiguous situations, cues that seem to resolve this question in one direction or another can be enormously potent. For example, in Prisoner's Dilemma games,[24] which involve a decision by each of two players to either cooperate or go it alone without knowing what the other player will do, cooperation rates can be roughly doubled simply by changing the name of the game from The Wall Street Game to The Community Game.[25] The first cue signals that the appropriate response to the situation is the competitive pursuit of self-interest; the second suggests that the game is about achieving the best total outcome for the participants.

Motivation Crowding-Out, 87 AM. ECON REV.746 (1997). *See* Uri Gneezy and Aldo Rustichini, *Pay Enough or Don't Pay at All*, 115 Q. J. OF ECON. 791 (2000).

21 *See generally* Michael E. Enzle & Sharon C. Anderson, *Surveillant Intentions and Intrinsic Motivation*, 64 J. PERS. SOC. PSYCH. 257 (February 1993) (finding that surveillance that is perceived as having the purpose of control, such as evaluating performance or detecting rule violations, has a significant negative impact on intrinsic motivation to perform a task, and also finding that absent a benign explanation for task surveillance, subjects are likely to infer both evaluative and distrusting intent).

22 *See* J. Sterling Livingston, *Pygmalion in Management*, HARV. BUS. REV., Aug. 1969, at 81.

23 This elegant explanation of framing is from JAMES G. MARSH, PRIMER ON DECISION MAKING: HOW DECISIONS HAPPEN 58 (1994).

24 Prisoner's Dilemma and similar social dilemma games are basically the white lab rats of the social psychology and game theory set.

25 Varda Liberman et al., *The Name Of The Game: Predictive Power Of Reputations Versus Situational Labels In Determining Prisoner's Dilemma Game Moves*, 30 PERS. & SOC. PSYCHOL. BULL. 1175, 1177 (2004).

As we've seen, issues that are framed as purely economic decisions—"it's just business"—are always negotiable. Ethical issues may sometimes be difficult and subtle, but any clear-cut choice between right and wrong, between compliance and misconduct, should be non-negotiable.

We know that framing decisions about conduct in terms of values, or in terms of positive group norms, can promote compliance more effectively than framing in terms of external risk and reward. In two large-scale studies of compliance in the workplace, Tom Tyler and his colleagues found that over eighty percent of compliance choices were motivated by internal perceptions of the legitimacy of the employer's authority and by a sense of right and wrong, while less than twenty percent were driven by fear of punishment or expectation of reward.[26]

When motivation derives from internalized ethical values, it follows that making the right choice is less dependent on external factors such as monitoring and the possibility of detection, rewards, and punishments. In short, a person's values work even when no one is looking. And most of the time, at work, no one is looking.

This distinction between internally-driven, or intrinsic, motivation and externally-driven motivation has important implications. Intrinsic motivation relates to activities that you do for their own sake—because they are inherently enjoyable or satisfying in some way. This includes doing something because it fulfills a duty that you believe in, advances a goal you want to achieve, or promotes a value that is important to you.[27] Hence one goal of a values-based compliance program is to instill or reinforce the employee's ethical values and thus generate intrinsic motivation. Another goal is to keep those values near the top of mind so that they will be readily available when events call for their use in framing the situation and choosing what to do.

An important advantage of values-based decision framing is that it is empowering when most needed. People who are encouraged to act in accordance with their values have a source of internal guidance in novel situations[28] and those

---

26 Tom R. Tyler et al, *The Ethical Commitment to Compliance: Building Value-Based Cultures*, 50 CALIF. MGMT. REV. 31, 35 (2008); Tom R. Tyler & Steven L. Blader, *Can Businesses Effectively Regulate Employee Conduct? The Antecedents of Rule Following in Work Settings*, 48 ACADEMY MGMT. J. 1143, 1153 (2005). For a similar study in the criminal context finding that only about five percent of the variance in controlled-substance violations is attributable to the risk of punishment, see Robert J. MacCoun, *Drugs and the Law: A Psychological Analysis of Drug Prohibition*, 113 PSYCHOL. BULL. 497, 501 (1993).

27 *See* Frey & Jegen, *supra* note 20 with respect to the risk of "crowding out" of intrinsic motivations by external incentives.

28 For a dramatic example see Alex Spiegel, *Heroes of the Taj Hotel: Why They Risked Their Lives*, NPR (Dec. 23, 2011) *available at* http://www.npr.org/2011/12/23/144184623/mumbai-terror-attacks-the-heroes-of-the-taj-hotel (describing the corporate-culture roots of the heroism of Taj Mahal Hotel employees, remaining

in which authoritative guidance like policies, procedures, or an FCPA specialist are otherwise unavailable. By contrast, a strong command-and-control environment sends the message that employees should look externally for guidance—and in the absence of on-the-spot authoritative direction from the company, external guidance may sometimes appear in the unlovely form of a high payoff for misconduct, a low likelihood of detection, or a toxic and persuasive co-worker.

Framing compliance issues in ethical or values-laden terms may also affect internal reporting of violations—the most desirable brand of whistleblowing. In one study, researchers examining the effect of incentives on the reporting of compliance violations encountered dramatically different effects depending on whether the subjects considered a particular infraction morally repugnant or not. For violations that did not provoke a sense of moral outrage, external incentives made a substantial difference in reporting; but where the violations offended the person's values, reporting was *much higher across the board*, and incentives to report made very little difference.[29] The motivation to report morally offensive behavior is intrinsic. The lesson I draw from this is that we should try to ensure that employees connect compliance mandates to basic values like honesty, integrity, respect, teamwork, loyalty,[30] citizenship, and accountability, thus triggering their intrinsic motivation to report and reducing the need for extrinsic incentives.

Those last four values—teamwork, loyalty, citizenship, and accountability—lead us to the connection between group membership and compliance.

One of the strongest human needs is to feel good about ourselves,[31] and as social animals we use groups to support and nourish our identities and cultivate

---

behind to see to their guests' safety in the wake of the 2008 terrorist attack. The Taj explicitly hired for compassion, respect and empathy, trained for kindness, promptly rewarded workers for every compliment expressed to management by a guest, and had a culture based on exceptional customer service. The workers needed no further guidance when the unprecedented attack occurred).

29 *See* Yuval Feldman & Orly Lobel, *The Incentives Matrix: The Comparative Effectiveness of Rewards, Liabilities, Duties and Protections for Reporting Illegality*, 87 TEX. L. REV. 1151 (2010).

30 Consider for example a pure "regulatory" offense that has little inherent moral force, such as a reporting requirement designed to support the compilation of government statistics. To the extent the company is vulnerable to punishment for failing to adhere to the requirement, a sense of loyalty to the company could imbue the issue with a values dimension: a loyal employee's motivation to report an infraction in order to "keep the company [or her workgroup] out of trouble" might be much stronger than the motivation to report it for its own sake.

31 This powerful motivation to maintain a positive self-concept played a major part in the analysis of the Ten Commandment experiments by Ariely's team. First, it helps explain why people cheated "just a little" when they had an unlimited cheating opportunity: the notion is that, via rationalization or self-deception, people are able to cheat, but only to a plausible degree, without affecting their positive self-concept. Imagine thinking "I *could* have gotten seven answers right (but not 15 or 20)." Second, in the follow-up experiment the

positive self-concepts.[32] Groups can be unforgiving of behavior that deviates from group social and behavioral expectations, and so the desire to be regarded as a member in good standing of an important group is a powerful motivator of behavior. We place a high value on membership in groups that treat us as if we are important, because they reinforce our own feelings of importance. We also prize membership in groups that we admire, because we can "borrow" some of their virtues or status for ourselves. And we admire groups that share our values, both in word and in deed.[33]

When membership in a group is important to us, we identify positively with the group, forming an emotional commitment to it; we internalize the group's values, expectations and norms (or, in a larger group, its culture), we become intrinsically motivated to adhere to the values and expectations that we have internalized, and we govern our behavior within the group by those norms. Even where group norms may not be internalized, if we consider a group important, we frame decisions in terms of their impact on group relationships.[34] We pay our civic association dues, attend interminable meetings, and participate in Neighborhood Watch because we are serving worthy community values and because it's what good neighbors do.

Researchers have looked specifically at cultural factors that contribute to employee commitment to the organization, and at the effects of the resulting commitment on workplace compliance. For example, a Deloitte study showed strong links between employees' organizational commitment and their perceptions that management's actions show character and integrity and that management is receptive to those seeking advice about reporting policy violations. Training on acceptable behavior is also strongly associated with increased commitment.[35] Another research team examined the effects of nine different

---

Ten Commandments ethical prompt may have counteracted this fudge factor, such that a positive self-concept could be maintained only by much stricter adherence to ethical values.

[32] *See* Steven L. Blader & Tom R. Tyler, *Testing and Extending the Group Engagement Model: Linkages between Social Identity, Procedural Justice, Economic Outcomes, and Extrarole Behavior*, 94 J. APPLIED PSYCHOL. 445, 457 (2009) (noting that ". . . the basis of employees' relationship to their organizations is primarily linked to the role the organization plays in determining how employees think and feel about themselves").

[33] Tom R. Tyler & Steven L. Blader, *The Group Engagement Model: Procedural Justice, Social Identity and Cooperative Behavior*, 7 PERS. & SOC. PSYCHOL. REV. 349 (2003).

[34] We should be mindful of the implications of this principle with respect to toxic leaders who create noncompliant subgroups within a company: the group dynamic is a two-edged sword.

[35] Tiffany McDowell, *The Hidden Bonus in "Doing the Right Thing,"* DIRECTORS' MONTHLY, Sept. 2006, at 13.

indicia of a positive ethical culture and discovered that all nine measurably amplified employee commitment.[36]

Commitment, in turn, has been shown to promote voluntary adherence to rules, reporting of violations, and going above and beyond job requirements to benefit the organization, as well as to reduce the need for external monitoring.[37]

When group norms and ethical values coincide and reinforce one another, the effect is doubly powerful. Have you ever participated in a blood drive? Frame the issue economically and ask how much a for-profit blood bank would have to pay you to buy a pint of your blood for resale. Your answer would probably be, "a lot," or perhaps, "it's not for sale." But blood drives are not usually presented as economic transactions: you give your blood away for free because it saves people's lives, it's the right thing to do, and it makes you feel good about yourself—and maybe also because all your co-workers down the hall are giving blood too, and it's expected of you. Values, plus group norms and commitment, equals voluntary compliance.[38]

Attentive readers will have noted that a company's values-based messaging can operate simultaneously and beneficially in two directions: on the one hand, influencing employees by instilling and articulating values that the company wishes its people to internalize and follow; on the other, explicitly aligning the company with admirable values that most employees already accept, making it more evident that the company is a group worthy of commitment. Both effects, if achieved, should foster convergence between employee values and employee perceptions of the company's values. When large numbers of employees perceive alignment between their own values and those of the company, the cultural build-out is complete: those employees have become the carriers of the organizational culture.

In sum, values-based messaging and a positive corporate culture can promote employee identification with and commitment to the company, harness the employee's ethical values, and bring those values to the surface in the work setting

---

36 Linda K. Treviño et al., *Managing Ethics and Legal Compliance: What Works and What Hurts*, 41 Cal. Mgmt. Rev. 131–151 (1999). For a listing of some of the cultural factors evaluated, see the further discussion of this study in the next section.

37 Tyler et al., *supra* note 26 at 33; Ethics Resource Center, National Business Ethics Survey, 4 (2009), http://www.ethics.org/files/u5/NBESResearchBrief2.pdf.

38 In another context, the power of group norms of this type—and the shortcomings of "rational actor" self-interest theory—are vividly illustrated by the sustained success of the open-source software movement and of Wikipedia.

to produce voluntary compliance.[39] It is time to drill down and explore how, exactly, we should go about achieving this.

A values-based communication paradigm recognizes that people—and they are mostly good people—show up at work every day with a full set of values, mostly good values. It seeks to engage those existing values so that workers identify positively with the company, accept the legitimacy of the company's authority and leadership, and voluntarily follow the rules. Effectively engaging these positive values requires a communications plan whose dominant message is about integrity, honesty, and ethical behavior, as opposed to one that frames compliance primarily in terms of external incentives or mandates.

Most importantly, an effective values-based communications program is one whose message is consistently reinforced by the actions of the company and its management at all levels.

V. Compliance Program Orientation and Corporate Culture: What Works

What is the evidence about the efficacy and impact of this approach? In a landmark large-scale survey, "What Works and What Hurts,"[40] Linda Trevino and others compared compliance programs that emphasized traditional command-and-control elements to programs that expressed a more values-oriented message. They wanted to learn whether program orientation—the overall thrust or message or dominant theme of the program—made a difference in the achievement of key compliance goals such as reducing unethical conduct, promoting the reporting of misconduct, better ethical decision-making, increasing awareness of ethical issues and comfort delivering bad news to management.

The study showed that a values-based approach produces significant[41] benefits across the entire spectrum of compliance goals, and works better than the command-and-control approach.

Separately, the researchers assessed the effect of a set of cultural factors on these compliance goals. These factors were not compliance program elements or explicit management messages, but measures of how the *employees* perceived the *company*, on such issues as:

---

39 Much of the research on the benefits of a values-based compliance regime owes its inspiration to a groundbreaking essay by Lynn Sharp Paine. *See* Lynn Sharp Paine, *Managing for Organizational Integrity*, HARV. BUS. REV., Mar.-Apr. 1994, at 106.

40 Trevino et al., *supra* note 36.

41 "Significant" in both senses: substantial and statistically significant.

- commitment to ethics on the part of executive leadership and direct supervisors,
- fair treatment of employees,
- rewarding ethical and punishing unethical behavior,
- open discussion of ethical issues, and
- consideration of ethical issues in decision-making.

In other words, they studied the implicit messages about the company's values that employees absorbed through their own experience and believed, as opposed to only the explicit messages that the companies sought to convey.

It turned out that the presence of these positive cultural factors had an even greater effect on achievement of compliance goals than which type of compliance program was in use. In fact, every one of the nine positive cultural factors they studied had a significant positive effect on every one of the seven compliance goals. Evidently, compliance program orientation sends a certain kind of beneficial message, but how the company behaves sends a much more powerful one: actions speak louder than codes.

The cultural message, of course, can be positive or negative: one study distilled forty-five potential predictors of misconduct down to five "vital factors" that strongly predict the frequency of misconduct within an organization.[42] At the top of this final five[43] was "fear of retaliation and discomfort with speaking up," the polar opposite of Trevino's "open discussion of ethical issues" and "rewarding ethical behavior."

One way a company can send a demonstrably beneficial values message is simply to conspicuously implement a compliance program. Recently, KPMG measured employee attitudes about their employers, comparing companies that had a comprehensive compliance program (meeting nine distinct requirements) with those that had anything less than a comprehensive program (meeting

---

42 *See* Michael Griffin & Tracy Davis, Corporate Executive Board Research Alert, Sourcing Competitive Advantage from Organizational Integrity: the Hidden Cost of Misconduct, *available at* https://www.celc.executiveboard.com/public/CELC_ResearchAlert.html. Interestingly, this summary of a proprietary 2007 study by the Corporate Executive Board's Compliance and Ethics Leadership Council also indicated that variations in an organization's compliance control environment "do not appear to meaningfully influence the frequency of observed misconduct."

43 According to Lenzi & Lupfer, *supra* note 10, the Corporate Executive Board study found that fear of retaliation was almost twice as important a predictor of misconduct as all the other factors in the study combined. This seems to suggest that fear of retaliation may not only be significant in and of itself, but may be a proxy indicating the existence of a variety of other toxic cultural factors, such as distrust of management generally, that could lead to fear of retaliation.

between zero and eight).[44] Companies with comprehensive programs scored more than twice as high as the other group on employee perceptions of "tone at the top," the belief that appropriate action would be taken if misconduct were discovered, the belief that a whistleblower would be protected from retaliation, and comfort with reporting violations to the legal department. They also scored substantially higher on employee comfort in reporting violations to their immediate supervisor, and actual observed misconduct was lower. This is powerful evidence that a compliance program can directly affect not only objective compliance outcomes, but also employee attitudes and beliefs about the company's culture.

VI. Culture, Legitimacy, and Voluntary Obedience to Workplace Rules

We move now to the messages implicit in key company behaviors, which can either reinforce, undermine, or obliterate explicit compliance messages. All the values-based training, admonishments, and exhortations in the world will be of little use if employees do not believe management means what it says. Employees measure the credibility of management's words about ethics and compliance, and thus the legitimacy of the company's compliance rules, by observing management's deeds in a handful of critical arenas.

Tom Tyler, who early in his career was known for his work on why people obey the law in general,[45] later applied and tested his findings in the specific context of corporate compliance. He tried to sort out exactly what factors have the greatest impact on voluntary compliance in the workplace, also known as individual self-regulation.[46]

The short answer is that we will voluntarily obey authority if we believe it is "legitimate," that is, that the company is entitled to have its rules followed. A company's authority is considered legitimate only to the extent that the organization is perceived as being ethical and fair in its interactions with employees and third parties. In essence, when managers say "ethics," employees hear "fairness."[47]

---

[44] KPMG LLP, KPMG Integrity Survey 2008–2009, (2009) available at http://www.kpmg.com/global/en/issuesandinsights/articlespublications/pages/integrity-survey-2008SH0l09.aspx.

[45] *See generally* TOM R. TYLER, WHY PEOPLE OBEY THE LAW (1990).

[46] The following discussion draws principally on Tyler et al. and Tyler & Blader, *supra* note 26.

[47] This epigram is attributed to Kent Druyman, former ethics officer at General Dynamics, in Trevino et al., *supra* note 36.

Treviño's team reached the same conclusion, both in the "What Works and What Hurts" study[48] and in another aimed specifically at exploring the role that workplace fairness perceptions play in compliance.[49] They found that employee perceptions of overall fairness in the workplace are very strongly correlated with the incidence of misconduct—the more fairness, the less misconduct—and the link between fairness and voluntary internal reporting of misconduct was even stronger.[50]

Tyler also found that a person is more likely to follow rules if he believes that the company's values agree with his own. This is the command-and-control paradigm turned upside-down. Command-and-control is about coercing the "bad" employees to follow the law and the company's rules, but here the roles are reversed: the employee observes the company's conduct and judges whether the company's values live up to his expectations, and thus whether the company's ethical leadership is credible.[51]

Both perspectives have merit. Around three or four percent of any sizable group operate largely without a conscience,[52] and command-and-control is the only way to govern these amoral actors. But compliance is a numbers game, and compliance officers must focus on factors that can influence the behavior of the great middle of the bell curve—people who are neither amoral nor saintly, whose behavior is subject to change depending on the circumstances. These people have a conscience and most of them embrace accepted ethical values. Living up to employees' values should not be a difficult threshold for a company to meet in

---

48 *See* the discussion in the previous section of the influence of cultural factors, including fair treatment of employees, on compliance outcomes as measured in the What Works and What Hurts study.

49 LINDA K. TREVIÑO & GARY R. WEAVER, MANAGING ETHICS IN BUSINESS ORGANIZATIONS: SOCIAL SCIENTIFIC PERSPECTIVE 267–92 (2003).

50 *Id.* The correlation coefficient between workplace fairness and incidence of misconduct was a negative 0.49 and that between fairness and willingness to report internally was a positive 0.71; both results were statistically significant.

51 As suggested earlier, this result may be related not only to legitimacy, but also to the attractiveness of committed membership in the group.

52 TIMOTHY T. LUPFER & AJIT KAMBIL, MANAGING THE BAD APPLES AND PROTECTING THE BARREL (2009) (noting that antisocial personality disorder is *diagnosed* in approximately three percent of males and two percent of the general population, and estimating the likely percentage of persons in the general population who manifest "antisocial personality disorder," (the condition formerly known as psychopathy or sociopathy) or other conditions characterized by absence of conscience as falling somewhere between three and ten percent). Similarly, the 2001–2002 National Epidemiologic Survey on Alcohol and Related Conditions found that 3.6 percent of a large random sample of the noninstitutionalized U.S. adult population met the diagnostic criteria for antisocial personality disorder specified in the DIAGNOSTIC AND STATISTICAL MANUAL OF MENTAL DISORDERS-FOURTH EDITION. NATIONAL EPIDEMIOLOGIC SURVEY ON ALCOHOL AND RELATED CONDITIONS, NATIONAL INSTITUTE ON ALCOHOL ABUSE AND ALCOHOLISM OF THE NATIONAL INSTITUTES OF HEALTH (2004).

general, but a given employee's experience at work is highly specific and heavily dependent on the behavior of immediate supervisors and peers.

Surprisingly to adherents of the rational-actor model, Tyler's research indicated that these two overarching factors, legitimacy and value congruence, were actually more influential on compliance than either rewards for good behavior or fear of punishment for transgressions.

Drilling deeper into the relationship between legitimacy and fairness, Tyler uncovered two critical components that drive compliance:

- Does the company observe *procedural fairness* in decisions affecting employees, such as hiring, promotions, compensation, transfers, and discipline?
- In its interactions with employees, does the company treat them with respect, dignity, courtesy, and trust?

The elements of procedural fairness are familiar to lawyers under the rubric of due process: an opportunity to be heard; clear, understandable rules and decision processes; consistency of management decisions over time and across cases; articulated reasons for decisions; and application of the same rules to everyone regardless of position or status.[53] Unless these foundations of basic workplace justice are in place, the company's claim to moral high ground will ring hollow. What is startling about Tyler's findings is that the presence of these structural attributes actually turned out to be more influential on employee compliance than whether employees thought the company's actual decisions were substantively fair, or whether the company's policies were considered favorable to the employees.[54]

Quality interpersonal treatment in the workplace is also a key barometer of a company's values, as far as employees are concerned. Respecting the employee's legal rights is necessary but not sufficient; what resonates here is when people feel respected, listened to, trusted,[55] and valued as members of the team. Recall that people identify with and feel committed to groups that treat them as important,

---

53 One of the most common and effective ways to sabotage employees' perceptions of workplace fairness is, of course, giving top performers a pass on expectations that apply to everyone else.

54 *See* Tyler et al., *supra* note 26, at 36 (stating that as between procedural fairness, distributive fairness (outcomes), and policy favorability (when employees believe that a policy benefits them), procedural fairness accounted for seventy-four percent of the variance in voluntary rule-following in the workplace. Again, a "rational actor" model based on self-interest alone would not predict this result).

55 The observation that whether employees feel trusted affects the likelihood of compliance is consistent with the notion expressed earlier that overly intrusive command-and-control and monitoring systems may undermine compliance, at least for some employees.

as well as groups that are admirable: how a company treats employees in everyday interactions strikes both of these chords. As Trevino and Weaver have noted, the fact that more than half the calls to corporate ethics hotlines relate to human resources issues such as hiring, promotion, performance appraisal, fairness, and appropriate treatment tells us something about how employees link company ethics, personnel decision-making, and interpersonal treatment.[56]

These findings about the importance of positive relationships with management have been replicated on the dark side as well: among the five leading indicators of employee misconduct identified by the Corporate Executive Board's Compliance and Ethics Leadership Council was "direct manager lacks trust in and respect for employees."[57] On the other side of the trust ledger, the 2007 National Business Ethics Survey showed a strong relationship between a lack of employee trust in direct supervisors or in top management and the incidence of workplace misconduct.[58]

As these two studies suggest, relationships are two-way streets: it is not easy to respect someone who belittles you or to place your trust in someone who is distrustful of you. Whatever may be the compliance-related effects of feeling mistrusted or disrespected, the fallout when employees hold the converse opinions about supervisors is intuitively clear: you probably would cede no more authority than absolutely necessary to someone you do not respect, and it is hard to imagine reporting misconduct to, or openly questioning a compliance choice made by, a superior that you do not trust. Not surprisingly, Tyler and others have pointed to trust in management as another element that supports organizational legitimacy.[59] Employees gather an abundance of data points on this, every day and across multiple contexts, including management's dealings with fellow employees, customers, and other third parties.[60] And negative experiences are much more

---

56 *See* TREVIÑO & WEAVER, *supra* note 49, at 287.

57 *See* CORPORATE EXECUTIVE BOARD RESEARCH ALERT, *supra* note 42.

58 Ethics Resource Center, National Business Ethics Survey, 2 (2007), http://www.ethics.org/resource/2007national-business-ethics-survey. This survey of over 3450 employed adults examined the relationship of six indicia of a "negative work environment" to observed misconduct at work. Two of the six were lack of trust that top management and direct supervisors, respectively, would keep promises and commitments. At companies where none of the six negative factors were present, an average of thirty-seven percent of employees had witnessed misconduct within the previous year. With any two of the six negative factors present, the observed-misconduct number jumped to seventy-four percent, and with any three, it rose to eighty-eight percent.

59 Tyler et al., *supra* note 26, at 40. In addition, recall that in the "What Works and What Hurts" study, leaders' perceived commitment to ethics was one of the most influential cultural factors affecting compliance outcomes (along with fair treatment of employees). Trevino et al., *supra* note 36, at 136–137, 141–142.

60 For example, it is fair to wonder about the impact of large-company procurement departments on company culture. What values messages do line employees take from the required insistence on form procurement contracts that make no pretense at logical allocation of risks to the party that can best control

salient, memorable and influential than positive ones.[61] If we consider all the management interactions that workers are exposed to, at all levels of management, and imagine the impact of a single betrayal of trust when an employee is directly involved,[62] it's easy to see how a few treacherous, deceitful, or hypocritical leaders can rapidly dismantle employee trust in the organization. A little sleaze goes a long way.[63]

Against this background, we might think of trust in management as the glue that holds all the data together, so much so that causation seems to go in circles (virtuous or vicious as the case may be). We trust leaders whom we believe to be ethical, while at the same time one of the main ways we judge a leader's ethics is by observing whether their actions justify our trust. We also attribute leaders' ethical character to the organization, trusting our company to the extent we trust its leadership. And if we trust the company, we tend to admire it, identify with its goals and interests, grant legitimacy to its rules, and behave accordingly. Yet, in the other direction, fair rules and policies, fairly applied, show an ethical commitment at the corporate level that may confer a corresponding halo effect on company leadership. The causation may be intricate and recursive, but what we know is that compliance rises and falls with our trust in the ethical values of our leaders and our organization.

Have we wandered completely away from our theme of communications and compliance? Not at all. First, we can use explicit communications to improve management transparency, which supports both procedural fairness and quality interpersonal treatment—and also has been linked independently to compliance

---

them, but rather exploit the buyer's bargaining leverage to achieve across-the-board risk transfer as a goal that trumps everything else?

61 *See* Roy F. Baumeister et al., *Bad Is Stronger Than Good*, 5 REV. GEN. PSYCH. 323, 323–70 (2001), for a classic review of the disproportionate effects of negative experiences across a large number of psychological contexts, including trust and other evaluations of character.

62 *See* Dwight R. Riskey & Michael H. Birnbaum, *Compensatory Effects in Moral Judgment: Two Rights Don't Make Up for a Wrong*, 103 J. EXPERIMENTAL PSYCHOL. 1, 171–73 (1974) (concluding that judgments of the overall goodness of a person are determined mostly by his worst bad deed: "Given a person has done evil, an infinite number of good deeds may not produce a favorable overall impression").

63 These results dovetail with another of Trevino and Weaver's findings: that less management follow-up on reports of misconduct, including disciplining violators, leads to diminished reporting of violations. *See supra* note 49. Whether management deals appropriately with reported violations touches on both fairness (to the company and to the whistleblower) and the trustworthiness of management: if I report, and you do nothing, you have broken faith, and I will not bother to report again—at least not internally. Externally there are always people willing to listen. *See, e.g.*, Dodd-Frank Wall Street Reform and Consumer Protection Act, 15 U.S.C. §§ 78u–6, 78u–7 (2011) (creating whistleblower awards and protection).

outcomes.[64] In terms of procedural fairness, it is much easier for an employee to make reliable judgments about ethical commitment and trust if the company communicates in advance what its principles, rules, and decision processes are, and is willing to be held accountable for its own adherence to them. Likewise, at the interpersonal level, employees feel respected and valued if their input is sought and their interests explicitly considered on matters that affect them and if decisions are explained.[65]

Second, all the management practices we have outlined send powerful, incessant, and inescapable implicit messages about the company's values, the sincerity of its ethical leadership, and the legitimacy of its claim to authority. These messages affect allegiance to the company, and they can either reinforce our explicit compliance communications or cancel them out.

Explicit compliance communications are not enough. Compliance officers must reach across functional boundaries to executive management and the human resources group and, if necessary, educate them about the principles of employee engagement and the value of consistent explicit and behavioral messaging that activates the employees' values and brings out their better natures.[66] Compliance officers must secure the active cooperation of these groups not only in transmitting the right words, but also in modeling ethical behavior, trustworthiness, fairness, and quality interpersonal treatment of employees. Equally, their cooperation is critical to ensure that this modeling is replicated and enforced all the way down the management chain via careful hiring of managers, leadership and soft-skills training at all levels of management, reinforcement of respectful treatment, and judicious firing of those who refuse to get on board. In short, hire your values, value your hires, and tolerate no jerks.

---

64 The six "negative work environment" factors linked to elevated misconduct included two transparency measures: lack of satisfaction with information from top management and lack of satisfaction with information from supervisors. *See* National Business Ethics Survey, *supra* note 58.

65 Tyler et al., *supra* note 26, at 39–40. For examples of company communications that explain decisions in the compliance arena. *See infra* the text accompanying note 69.

66 A certain number of executives (legal counsel often among them) can be expected to glaze over at the mention of "soft" concepts like culture, and an even greater number may be skeptical of the effectiveness of values-based messaging, or the notion that there may be a causal connection between compliance outcomes and personnel practices. The *homo economicus* rational-actor model has been endemic in business schools and economics courses for generations, and command-and-control is, frankly, how law is done. The thinking goes, there ought to be no more to compliance than this: people should learn the rules and having learned them, should follow them; and if they don't they should be caught and punished, which will deter the rest. Fortunately, many of these skeptics are also very smart and can change their minds if confronted with convincing evidence. This paper was written for them.

VII. Putting It All Together

If this essay so far seems long on science and short on specific suggestions for implementation, I have my reasons. First, unless you are convinced by the science, any suggestions for implementation would be futile. I hope we have crossed that hurdle. Second, how a company can best implement these teachings will vary according to a host of factors such as the organization's size, budget, number and location of employees, history, management structure, line of business, regulatory concerns, and, of course, its incumbent culture.

I would like to conclude, though, with a few strategy suggestions and a few examples of values-based messaging that I've found particularly effective.

A. Get a Checkup

Companies seeking to improve their culture and implement a more comprehensive, values-based communications plan would do well to begin by finding out where they stand with their employees. There are a number of available culture-assessment tools, and no shortage of qualified consultants who can help create a custom version.

Learning how your employees perceive the company's values can be an eye-opener, particularly if you can stratify the results by position, functional area, geography, or operating unit without compromising anonymity. Never assume that culture is uniform across departments or locations, or that line employees will have the same opinion of the company's values as the executives, the law department, or the human resources group. Even if a simple, one-size-fits-all anonymous survey is used, it may be useful to get the C-suite on the record in advance as to what they think employees will identify as the company's key values and cultural drivers. Later, they can compare and contrast these predictions with actual results.

By identifying both cultural strengths and areas needing improvement, a cultural assessment can guide the creation of a communications plan and culture-building initiatives that are tailored to the company's needs. In many cases, an effective strategy may be to target weak spots while simultaneously anchoring the overall message to positive values already strongly shared across the organization.

B. Proselytize the C-Suite and Enlist Their Help Throughout the Chain of Command

There is no more powerful driver of positive culture change than the committed participation of top management. By this I mean participation that is rooted in belief not only in the appropriateness but also the behavioral effectiveness of a positive ethical culture.[67] CEO cover memos to the Code of Conduct, introductory videos for new hires, and ghost-written inspirational stories in the company newsletter are nothing new, and initiatives like this should figure in any communications plan—but the real bonus of committed leadership comes from the impact of unscripted moments. Let me share a couple of examples.

Not long ago I was getting to know a new public-company client, and was listening to its first quarterly earnings call after they retained us. During the question-and-answer period, while addressing a question about new regulatory developments, the CEO happened to mention, with no hint of artifice, that adapting to the change was a company-wide priority within its overall efforts to maintain a firm wide culture of compliance. Here was the CEO of the largest company in its industry, to whom the phrase "culture of compliance" came as naturally as "debt covenants" or "EBITDA." If this tumbled out in an earnings call, I could only imagine the other contexts in which compliance and ethics would be salient to him, and the impact of his attitude on the company's employees and culture.

At another client, one with hundreds of locations and 80,000 employees, the Human Resources Vice President sent out a mass e-mail about California's new requirements for sexual harassment training for managers and supervisors. The e-mail stated that the company was required by law to provide this training and so it would be rolled out shortly to the California locations. Within minutes, a terse Reply All arrived from the CEO stating that "we are not going to do this because it's required, we are going to do it because it's the right thing to do, and we are going to do it nationwide." The message was lost on no one. No scripted video or Code cover letter could have begun to convey the conviction, the genuine tone at the top, that the CEO got across with his e-mail.

The company's executive leadership also has the ability to put in place any number of culture-related initiatives that are beyond the authority of any Chief Compliance Officer, such as adding ethics and compliance as a component of evaluations for compensation and promotion, leveraging the assets of other functional groups such as Human Resources, Corporate Communications and Training, Risk Management, Law, and yes, even Marketing and Sales, in service of the compliance and ethics mission, and, of course, requiring cooperation with Compliance Department initiatives.

67 For senior executives who are not already convinced, an evidence-based approach may be useful. *See id.*

Among the most important of those initiatives would be propagating the "tone at the top" until it becomes the "mood in the middle"—soft skills and ethics training for managers and supervisors, adding "ethical moments" to management meetings, and, most crucial of all, enforcing management behavioral standards, especially for high performers. It is one thing for a manager to get a call from Human Resources about an unpleasant encounter with an employee; it's quite another to get the same call from the division COO who controls your salary, bonus, assignments, and tenure.

The promotion of a positive, values-driven company culture is not just about compliance; creating an environment where people are proud to work has been shown to produce many other, equally practical advantages.[68] Executives should be encouraged to think of the cultural initiative in terms of its potential to achieve broader, universally desirable business goals such as employee engagement, job satisfaction, reduced turnover, better attendance, and enhanced performance, not to mention a reduction in employment litigation. As we've seen, the kind of culture that achieves these goals produces compliance as a byproduct, and vice-versa.

C. Make a List

No state requires that Articles of Incorporation list a company's core values. If your company wasn't born with a silver values statement in its mouth, you have to find out what they are or determine what they should be. By its nature, a core values list must be short, and cannot be exclusively concerned with ethics and compliance. With or without the benefit of a cultural assessment, the compliance group should work with executive management to develop a focused values list that resonates with the company's particular mission, objectives and structure, sets expectations, guides behavior in key areas, and can inspire employees and earn the board's endorsement.

The values statement is an opportunity to distill the most important elements of a positive culture while at the same time defining in broader terms "how things are done around here." For example, the biopharmaceutical company Amgen begins with a three-word mission statement ("To serve patients"), proceeds to an aspirational statement of goals, lists eight core values, and concludes with four leadership attributes. Every one of these statements can function as an independent guide to behavior, all are consistent with an overall vision, and many

---

68 *See generally* James K. Harter et al., *Well-Being in the Workplace and its Relationship to Business Outcomes: A Review of the Gallup Studies*, FLOURISHING: THE POSITIVE PERSON AND THE GOOD LIFE 205–224 (Corey L.M. Keyes & Jonathan Haidt, eds., 2002) (analyzing the connection between positive workplace affect and variables such as turnover, customer satisfaction, productivity, and profit).

are business values, as opposed to distinctly ethical ones. The lead value, "Be Science-Based," speaks clearly about the industry and about what it takes to succeed with integrity in that industry.

Hewitt-Packard pairs its "Shared Values" list with "Our Corporate Objectives," implicitly inviting the reader, and the employee, to map one list onto the other. Along with distinctly ethical values such as "Uncompromising Integrity" and "Trust and Respect for Individuals," we see in "Speed and Agility" and "Meaningful Innovation" the formula for success in the fast-changing technology sector.

Discover what specific core values work for *your* company, and do not take the task lightly.

D. Tell Stories

Stories have a special appeal. People are natural storytellers; we like to make sense of things, to weave our experiences into a coherent narrative (whether the experience is actually coherent or not). Stories are easy to remember and pass along, and with this durability and reach, it's not surprising that every culture replicates and renews itself through stories. In the context of ethics and values, stories help make abstract issues concrete and accessible, especially when we can sympathize or identify with one of the characters.

There are several kinds of stories we can tell. First, we should tell stories that illustrate compliance or ethical issues in the workplace, how they are encountered, approaches for dealing with them, and especially successful outcomes. The best ones are true and come from the particular workplace—these stories have a chance of being spontaneously repeated and could even become self-sustaining vectors of culture transmission. In a large company it is not at all hard to come by a substantial collection of exemplary stories. The best example I know of is on the website of Best Buy's Chief Ethics Officer, Kathleen Edmond.[69] Edmond collects stories of ethical or compliance issues that come up at her company, discusses how individual (anonymous) employees have grappled with these issues, sought advice, or stumbled, and how things turned out for the company and for the employee. Woven in with all these object lessons are short, accessible commentaries on recent research in the behavioral science of ethics, and brief lessons on recurring ethical issues such as conflicts of interest, the "everyone does it" defense, and the "slippery slope" problem.

---

69 *See generally* KATHLEEN EDMOND, BEST BUY'S CHIEF ETHICS OFFICER, www.kathleenedmond.com (last visited June 3, 2012).

A second kind of story is the type we usually use in training: stories that could plausibly happen at the company, that illustrate problems one is likely to encounter in the specific context of that company's business, and that represent areas of significant risk to the company. Compared to those harvested from real life, these stories usually have a more carefully structured narrative designed to provoke discussion and to make specific points efficiently. Like Edmond's blog, values-based training stories illustrate recurring ethical or compliance issues, with the primary goal of enabling workers to spot issues and the secondary goal of teaching them how to navigate these issues successfully, including seeking help where appropriate.

One well-known curriculum, the Giving Voice to Values program,[70] uses hypothetical situations to achieve several training goals such as showing employees that it is often possible to talk through ethical issues with co-workers successfully and that occasional ethical conflicts are a normal part of life; training employees in useful ways of thinking about and talking through ethical issues; familiarizing them with the common "reasons and rationalizations" used to justify ethical breaches ("everyone does it"; "it was only that one time"); and providing counter-arguments for the latter. Although this curriculum was designed for business school courses and in its original form is too extensive for practical use in employee training, its principles have been distilled by some companies for training use.

Stories are even better if we can be a part of them, and Parsons Corporation has taken advantage of the flexibility of web-based communications to that end. Parsons publishes "Ethics Challenges" on its intranet, describing ethical scenarios and inviting employees to involve themselves in the story by voting on how the person in the story should deal with the situation. Employees can also post narrative comments. The votes are then counted and the results published on the intranet, along with a sample of the comments received and an analysis of the problem by the company's ethics committee.[71]

The final group of stories I want to mention are those dealing with the company's response to ethics and compliance violations. Recall that whether a company is perceived as following up on ethics violations and dealing appropriately with the culprits strongly affects the rate of internal reporting of misconduct. Yet in most cases, the outcomes of disciplinary actions are kept

---

[70] This curriculum, commonly known as GVV, was developed by the Aspen Institute and the Yale School of Management and is curated by Professor Mary Gentile at Babson College.

[71] *See* Charles L. Harrington, *Ethics and Organizational Culture*, Ethisphere (Mar. 26, 2010), http://ethisphere.com/ethics-and-organizational-culture/.

confidential, mainly for fear of privacy or defamation claims by disciplined employees. This invisible discipline can lead others to assume that the company is not following up on misconduct, which in turn could suppress reporting. Certainly the privacy of the disciplined employee is a consideration, but it is not always an issue. In notorious cases where there has been a "public hanging"[72] and, say, law enforcement involvement, there may be no privacy to breach; and in larger companies, there are usually many opportunities to tell true stories of crime and punishment in a way that ensures anonymity. In such cases the multiple benefits of providing employees with feedback about the company's disciplinary actions—demonstrating management's commitment to compliance, encouraging internal whistleblowers, and deterring wrongdoers—can far outweigh the risks.

E. Repeat Yourself

Remember that in the Ten Commandments and insurance-fraud experiments, the cues that successfully influenced behavior (for better or worse) occurred very close in time to the target behavior. Both memory and salience have short half-lives, especially the latter. As with any communications or marketing campaign, the goal is to be both persuasive and pervasive, to flood the environment with positive cues so that the desirable mental associations surface readily when needed. This means communicating consistent messages as often as possible and through as many channels as possible. Returning to where we started, we can write, meet, blog and tweet, and use screensavers, posters, awards and recognition, e-mails, web pages, and videos.

We sometimes overlook the fact that you can say something once and deliver the message many times, if the medium is durable and prominent and people are repeatedly exposed to it. I recall clearly the day in 1996 when I walked into a Johnson & Johnson subsidiary's building, and it was necessary to go right or left to get around a large print of the famous Credo that Robert Wood Johnson himself composed for the company in 1943. Of course there may be a habituation effect, but given its prominent placement facing the building's entrance, I find it hard to imagine that this particular copy of the Credo has ever quite sunk to the status of mere wallpaper.

Similarly, as a Fortune 500 Chief Compliance Officer once said to me, "Never underestimate the value of tchotchkes." Plenty of these mementos and promotional gifts do get promptly discarded, and others have inherently limited lives, but a really good tchotchke can be a daily messenger. There is one on my desk, a coffee coaster with my firm's Core Values on it. I see it every day, and it's

---

72 A "public hanging" is, of course, a potent message all by itself.

meaningful to me. Judging by the number of my colleagues who also use them, more than three years after they were delivered in connection with a merger, I'm not alone.

F. Recognize and Reward

Recognition is a powerful motivator[73] and sends a beneficial message. Even if given privately, it tells the recipient that the organization values both the relevant behavior and, by extension, the recipient, and will tend to reinforce the employee's commitment to the organization and her acceptance of its authority.[74] If public, the benefit is multiplied as others in the organization witness this affirmation of the company's commitment to ethics and compliance: the gift reflects well on the giver.

As we have seen,[75] material incentives, both positive and negative, can be tricky, and we must be wary of the law of unintended consequences. As suggested earlier, a reward program for turning in violators of the company's policies could be valid in theory and positive in direction, but disastrous in practice. It could appeal to the best instincts in some workers and the worst in others, such that any positive results in uncovering noncompliance would be more than offset by the undertow of false accusations,[76] reports of petty or borderline issues, breakdown of workplace trust and destruction of team cohesion and, of course, re-framing of reporting from an ethical to an economic proposition.[77]

But many recognition, reward, and incentive programs can convey positive cultural messages with little, if any, risk.[78] Examples of low-hanging fruit in this area include consideration of ethical leadership and compliance in performance

---

73 Recall Napoleon's message to the captain of HMS Bellerophon in 1815 that "A soldier will fight long and hard for a bit of colored ribbon." ROBERT DEBS HEINL, DICTIONARY OF MILITARY AND NAVAL QUOTATIONS 22 (Naval Institute Press 1966).

74 *See supra* the discussion of group commitment accompanying note 33.

75 *See supra* the discussion accompanying notes 18 and 19.

76 If manufactured or exaggerated reports of misconduct in response to a reward program seem implausible, *see* Grant & Singh, *supra* note 19, and contemplate the impact of even a small number of "bugs in the beans."

77 An apt admonition for those designing financial incentive programs might be "scrutiny on the bounty."

78 Moreover, the use of incentives is encouraged by the Federal Sentencing Guidelines' standards for what constitutes an "effective compliance and ethics program." Standard 6 requires that the company promote its program through "appropriate incentives" for employee compliance. As Murphy observed, the context of this standard makes it clear that the intent is to encourage positive incentives for ethical behavior, not just "incentives" in the form of punishment for violations. *See infra* note 80; *see* U.S SENTENCING GUIDELINES MANUAL § 8B2.1(b)(6) (2011).

reviews, compensation and promotion decisions, especially for managers;[79] recognition of employees who have conspicuously done "the right thing" in difficult situations; and time off or a pizza party for the work group that finishes compliance training first.[80]

G. Keep It Simple

One of the great virtues of basic ethical values is that they are simple. Take advantage of this and create simple, memorable messages. Make the core values statement a mantra. Train mainly for ethical awareness and issue-spotting, and on the procedures for seeking advice and reporting problems. Not everybody needs to understand the complexity of the Sherman Act and all the cases interpreting it: they need to understand that collusion with competitors might be a red flag, and they need to know where to find someone who can expertly deal with the issue. The goal is not to create an amateur legal corps, it is to help people recognize when something malodorous may be afoot and to give them options for dealing with the situation.

Conclusion

We now have ample evidence of how communication of positive values and the projection of an honorable, respectful, and fair ethical culture can dramatically affect compliance and reporting. If command and control is at the heart of every serious compliance program, culture is its soul, and culture is built through communication in both word and deed. The tools for achieving this are available to everyone and do not require great financial investment.

Culture change is seldom easy and never fast; but with knowledge of the critical factors and use of the right messaging strategy, it is achievable. And it is worth the effort.

NOTES

1. The higher up you go in an organization, the more that compliance with laws, rules, guidelines, and social norms will matter to you, whether you have direct responsibility for compliance or not. The point of this last article is to show you how

---

[79] Of course, at the level of actual and potential "substantial authority personnel," the federal organizational sentencing guidelines require consideration of a person's prior illegal behavior or "conduct inconsistent with an effective compliance and ethics program" in connection with employment and promotion decisions. *See id.*, at § 8B1.2 (b) and § 8B1.2 (b) cmt., n.4(B).

[80] *See generally* JOSEPH E. MURPHY, SOCIETY OF CORPORATE COMPLIANCE AND ETHICS, USING INCENTIVES IN YOUR COMPLIANCE AND ETHICS PROGRAM (2011) (providing a thoughtful and thorough discussion of incentive, recognition, and reward systems in the corporate compliance arena, to which the author is indebted for much of the above analysis of incentives.).

to help your colleagues think about their behavior and their choices, not because someone at the top of a hierarchy is telling them to "comply with our rules, darn it, because we say so," but because compliance meshes with their own values. As Killingsworth points out, "we should try to ensure that employees connect compliance mandates to basic values like honesty, integrity, respect, teamwork, loyalty, citizenship, and accountability, thus triggering their intrinsic motivation to report and reducing the need for extrinsic incentives."* He makes a second, equally important point: values-based communication only works if management's actions are consistent with their espoused values. It's not too early to think about how you would build and reinforce a culture of compliance as you become a senior manager.

2. To go full circle to the beginning of this book, Enron did a horrible job of matching its values with its internal reward systems. It had a code of ethics (which you can read at http://bobsutton.typepad.com/files/enron-ethics.pdf), which included four very specific values:

Values

> *Respect*
>
> We treat others as we would like to be treated ourselves. We do not tolerate abusive or disrespectful treatment. Ruthlessness, callousness and arrogance don't belong here.
>
> *Integrity*
>
> We work with customers and prospects openly, honestly and sincerely. When we say we will do something, we will do it; when we say we cannot or will not do something, then we won't do it.
>
> *Communication*
>
> We have an obligation to communicate. Here, we take the time to talk with one another . . . and to listen. We believe that information is meant to move and that information moves people.
>
> *Excellence*
>
> We are satisfied with nothing less than the very best in everything we do. We will continue to raise the bar for everyone. The great fun here will be for all of us to discover just how good we can really be.**

---

* *Modeling the Message* at 970 (footnote omitted).

** Enron Code of Ethics (July 2000) at 4.

Nice language, right?* The Code of Ethics even had a foreword from then-Chairman and CEO Ken Lay, just as Scott Killingsworth had suggested would help to reinforce an organization's values. That foreword said in part,

> To be sure that we understand what is expected of us, Enron has adopted certain policies, with the approval of the Board of Directors, which are set forth in this booklet. I ask that you read them carefully and completely and that, as you do, you reflect on your past actions to make certain that you have complied with the policies. It is absolutely essential that you fully comply with these policies in the future. If you have any questions, talk them over with your supervisor, manager, or Enron legal counsel.
>
> We want to be proud of Enron and to know that it enjoys a reputation for fairness and honesty and that it is respected. Gaining such respect is one aim of our advertising and public relations activities, but no matter how effective they may be, Enron's reputation finally depends on its people, on you and me. Let's keep that reputation high.**

My, my. Virtuous words; execrable deeds. Let's contrast Enron's failures to match its values to its deeds with a company that followed its values during an emergency: Tylenol. Here's a short description of what happened:

> During the fall of 1982, for reasons not known, a malevolent person or persons, presumably unknown, replaced Tylenol Extra-Strength capsules with cyanide-laced capsules, resealed the packages, and deposited them on the shelves of at least a half-dozen or so pharmacies, and food stores in the Chicago area. The poison capsules were purchased, and seven unsuspecting people died a horrible death. Johnson & Johnson, parent company of McNeil Consumer Products Company which makes Tylenol, suddenly, and with no warning, had to explain to the world why its trusted product was suddenly killing people (Berge, 1998).
>
> *Primary Evidence.* Robert Andrews, assistant director for public relations at Johnson & Johnson recalls how the company reacted in the first days of the crisis: "We got a call from a Chicago news reporter. He told us that the medical examiner there had just given a press conference-people were dying from poisoned Tylenol. He wanted our comment. As it was the first knowledge we had here in this department, we told him we knew nothing about it. In that first call we learned more from the reporter than he did from us." Andrew's dilemma points out something that has become more prevalent with the expansion of 24[-]hour electronic media. The media will

* One of us is still irked, all these years later, that the values spell out the word "RICE."

** *Id.* at 2.

often be the first on the scene, thus have information about the crisis before the organization does (Berge, 1990).

Johnson & Johnson chairman [] James Burke [] reacted to the negative media coverage by forming a seven-member strategy team. The team's strategy guidance from Burke was first, "How do we protect the people?" and second, "How do we save this product?" The company's first actions were to immediately alert consumers across the nation, via the media, not to consume any type of Tylenol product. They told consumers not to resume using the product until the extent of the tampering could be determined. Johnson & Johnson, along with stopping the production and advertising of Tylenol, withdraw all Tylenol capsules from the store shelves in Chicago and the surrounding area. After finding 2 more contaminated bottles Tylenol realized the vulnerability of the product and ordered a national withdraw of every capsule (Broom, 1994).

By withdrawing all Tylenol, even though there was little chance of discovering more cyanide[-]laced tablets; Johnson & Johnson showed that they were not willing to take a risk with the public's safety, even if it cost the company millions of dollars. The end result was the public viewing Tylenol as the unfortunate victim of a malicious crime (Broom, 1994).*

Remember the Johnson & Johnson credo to which Killingsworth referred?** Here it is, straight from Johnson & Johnson's web page:

Our Credo

We believe our first responsibility is to the doctors, nurses and patients, to mothers and fathers and all others who use our products and services. In meeting their needs[,] everything we do must be of high quality. We must constantly strive to reduce our costs in order to maintain reasonable prices. Customers' orders must be serviced promptly and accurately. Our suppliers and distributors must have an opportunity to make a fair profit.

We are responsible to our employees, the men and women who work with us throughout the world. Everyone must be considered as an individual. We must respect their dignity and recognize their merit. They must have a sense of security in their jobs. Compensation must be fair and adequate, and working conditions clean, orderly and safe. We must be mindful of ways to help our employees fulfill their family responsibilities. Employees must feel free to make suggestions and complaints. There must be equal

---

* Crisis Communication Strategies, Analysis, *Case Study: The Johnson & Johnson Tylenol Crisis,* available at http://www.ou.edu/deptcomm/dodjcc/groups/02C2/Johnson%20&%20Johnson.htm.

** *Modeling the Message* at 985.

> opportunity for employment, development and advancement for those qualified. We must provide competent management, and their actions must be just and ethical.
>
> We are responsible to the communities in which we live and work and to the world community as well. We must be good citizens—support good works and charities and bear our fair share of taxes. We must encourage civic improvements and better health and education. We must maintain in good order the property we are privileged to use, protecting the environment and natural resources.
>
> Our final responsibility is to our stockholders. Business must make a sound profit. We must experiment with new ideas. Research must be carried on, innovative programs developed and mistakes paid for. New equipment must be purchased, new facilities provided and new products launched. Reserves must be created to provide for adverse times. When we operate according to these principles, the stockholders should realize a fair return.*

Johnson & Johnson lived its credo, and its credo guided its response to the poisoning. Enron didn't live its values. In fact, its internal incentives encouraged just the opposite of its values. We're not saying that every company that lives its values survives and every company that ignores its values dies. That's not how the world works. But we're pretty sure that Johnson & Johnson's employees, to this day, understand how the company's credo shapes its behavior, and we'll bet that each employee thinks of that credo when faced with a difficult problem. Matching words to deeds is the most important thing that a company can do if it wants to reinforce its values.

3. One of the ways that you can match your organization's words to its deeds is by monitoring how well each leader of a department treats his or her employees. We've both been in situations in which one of our colleagues was a bully. (More than once, actually, for each of us.) You can often measure how bad a bully someone is by the turnover of the high performers within that person's department. Those who can escape a bully's clutches will; those who can't will be miserable, and you won't get their best work. But how do you deal with a bully? Most bullies aren't 100% bad people. They might perform well in certain areas—high billers, for example, who attract more clients to a firm or whose divisions make better-than-average profits—but the question that you'll have to ask yourself is whether the bully's benefits outweigh the costs. Both of us think that the answer is "never," because few managers ever include the costs of employee morale in their cost/benefit analysis. It's not just the bully's employees who suffer. It's those in other departments who see how management lets the bully get away with bad behavior. That which management

* https://www.jnj.com/about-jnj/jnj-credo.

doesn't correct (such as the bullying behavior), it values. That's why we both think that, if a bully can't change his or her behavior, no amount of profit is worth the cost of keeping that person inside the organization.

4. Killingsworth suggests several ways that an organization can keep its values front and center as a way of encouraging its employees to do the right thing. Could a university use some of those same suggestions in instilling its values?

Now that you've finished our book, here are some final takeaways:

- Corporate scandals will always happen. No matter how much social science tells us about how people behave, people will always be subject to cognitive errors.* You can reduce your risk of being front-and-center in a corporate scandal by using what you know about human behavior to build in some checks and balances, but you can't eliminate your risk.
- Theories about human behavior are useful, but nothing replaces actually knowing your colleagues well enough to predict how they will behave in certain situations. Understanding your colleagues gives you specific information about their values. (Of course, if some of those colleagues end up doing things that are bad enough to get them fired, knowing them well—and liking them as people—might make a decision to fire them more difficult.) The theories that we covered in this book will help you to understand more about human behavior, but your own powers of observation and intuition will help you as well.
- You're going to make mistakes in your own career. We all do. Some of those mistakes will be public (and, thanks to the Internet, probably searchable throughout the end of time). You'll have two options: curl up into a ball and let your mistake(s) affect your self-image forever, or learn from them and move forward. We hope that you'll pick option #2.

* And there will always be sociopaths and psychopaths out there. Sometimes, bad things *are* caused by bad people.

Index